Food for All

Food for All

*International Organizations and the
Transformation of Agriculture*

UMA LELE,
MANMOHAN AGARWAL,
BRIAN C. BALDWIN,
and
SAMBUDDHA GOSWAMI

OXFORD
UNIVERSITY PRESS

OXFORD
UNIVERSITY PRESS

Great Clarendon Street, Oxford, OX2 6DP,
United Kingdom

Oxford University Press is a department of the University of Oxford.
It furthers the University's objective of excellence in research, scholarship,
and education by publishing worldwide. Oxford is a registered trade mark of
Oxford University Press in the UK and in certain other countries

First Edition published in 2021

Impression: 2

Published in the United States of America by Oxford University Press
198 Madison Avenue, New York, NY 10016, United States of America

British Library Cataloguing in Publication Data
Data available

Library of Congress Control Number: 2021938236

ISBN 978–0–19–875517–3

DOI: 10.1093/oso/9780198755173.001.0001

Printed and bound in the UK by
TJ Books Limited

Acknowledgments

The preparation of our manuscript benefited from inputs from many colleagues; our consultations included extensive discussions over the years in person, by emails, Skype, and telephone calls.

Prabhu Pingali's effort to stimulate work on international organizations instigated this long journey. Some were willing to read draft chapters and felt free to offer criticism on earlier drafts of this and related work, including: Awudu Abdulai, Ammad Bahalim, David Blandford, Mark Cackler, Richard Carey, Ruben Echeverría, Javier Ekboir, Shenggen Fan, Marco Ferroni, Hafez Ghanem, Elwyn Grainger-Jones, Arif Hussain, Friederike Greb, Gregory Ingram, Leslie Lipper, Ramón Lohmar, Thomas Lumpkin, Alex McCalla, Constantine Michalopoulos, Gerald Nelson, Anna Ong, Mumukshu Patel, Elise Perset, Carlisle Runge, Ad Spijkers, Jitendra Srivastava, Kostas Stamoulis, Heiner Thofern, C. Peter Timmer, Greg Traxler, Laurian Unnevehr, Jonathan Wadsworth, Brian Wright, and Usha Zehr.

Others answered specific queries and often referred us to the related literature. Some were particularly knowledgeable on international aid issues, and others on the nitty gritty of numerous development issues; some participated and commented on the individual draft chapters at the American and International Association of Agricultural Economics in 2014 and 2015. We are grateful for the support and advice of so many when writing this book, including: Mohamed Ait Kadi, Harold Alderman, Anupam Anand, Jock Anderson, Kym Anderson, Cristina Ascone, Suresh Babu, Sham Banerji, Christopher Barrett, Raju Barwale, Nienke Beintema, Karmen Bennett, Alan Berg, Robert Bertram, Shakeel Bhatti, Malcolm Blackie, Jan Ties Boerma, Howarth Bouis, Francesco Branca, Edward W. Bresnyan, Karen Brooks, Lynn Brown, Balu Bumb, Derek Byerlee, Paul Cadario, Carlo Cafiero, Gero Carletto, Kenneth Cassman, Carlos Perez Castillo, Nadareh Chamlou, Ramesh Chand, Luc Christiansen, Piero Conforti, Julia Crompton, Máximo Torero Cullen, Partha Dasgupta, David Dawe, Dennis de Tray, Klaus Deininger, Ramesh Deshpande, Warren Evans, Gershon Feder, Fabrizio Felloni, Gustavo Alberto Fonseca, Keith Fuglie, Sushma Ganguly, Alessandro Garbero, Oscar Garcia, Subhash Chandra Garg, Madhur Gautam, Pietro Gennari, Kristalina Georgieva, Chris Gerrard, Michael Gilmont, J. N. von Glahn, Madhav Godbole, Ian Goldman, Arthur Goldsmith, Douglas Gollin, Aparajita Goyal, Ashok Gulati, Daniel Gustafson, Lawrence Haddad, Michael Haws, Peter Hazell, Jonathan Hepburn, Thomas Hertel, Norman Hicks, John Hoddinott, Alexis Hoskins, Jikun Huang, Liz Humphreys, William B. Hurlbut, Sirkka Immonen, Suresh Jadhav, Ajay Vir Jakhar, Thomas S. Jayne, Emmanuel Jimenez, Kundhavi Kadiresan, Nanak Kakwani, Ravi Kanbur, Amir Kassam, Timothy Kelley, Madhu Khanna, Homi Kharas, Nadim Khouri, Pierre-Joseph Kingbo, Nalin Kishor, Jochen Kraske, Nalini Kumar, Shalander Kumar, Rattan Lal, Julian Lampietti, Manny Lantin, Punji Leagnavar, Roberto Lenton, Leslie Lipper, Michael Lipton, Ramón Lohmar, Ed Luce, Johannes Lynn, Richard Manning, Ajay Markanday, Will Martin, William Masters, Shantanu Mathur, Peter Matlon, John McArthur, John McIntire, J. V. Meenakshi, Ruth Meinzen-Dick, Bart Minten, Mohinder S. Mudahar, Ashwani Muthoo, Ryo Nakamura, Ridley Nelson, David J. Nielson, Alejandro Nin Pratt, Rob Nooter, Chandra Sekhara Rao Nuthalapati, Stephen O'Brien, Selcuk Özgediz, Sushil Pandey, Rajul Pandya-Lorch, Aneesh Paranjape, Philip Pardey, Miguel Székely Pardo, Chris

Parel, Raj Paroda, Chris Perry, Per Pinstrup-Andersen, Herve Plusquellec, Barry Popkin, Jyotsna Puri, Matin Qaim, Nicholas Rada, T. Ramasami, Bharat Ramaswami, Elizabeth Ramborger, Chandrashekhar Ranade, Thomas Reardon, Richard Reidinger, Elil Renganathan, Dani Rodrik, Mark Rosegrant, Patricia Rosenfield, Scott Rozelle, Claudia Sadoff, Yashpal Singh Saharawat, T. V. Sampath, N. C. Saxena, Sara Savastano, Pasquale Lucio Scandizzo, Josef Schmidhuber, Stephen Schonberger, Tushaar Shah, Animesh Shrivastava, Benjamin Singer, Jakob Skoet, Jacqueline Souza, David Spielman, Jitendra Srivastava, Pasquale Steduto, Gretchen Stevens, Johan Swinnen, Prabhakar Tamboli, Dina Umali-Deininger, Alberto Valdés, Rob D. van den Berg, Anna Birgitta Viggh, Nick Vink, Juergen Voegele, Joachim von Braun, Huan Wang, Ren Wang, Sudhir Wanmali, Brittaney Warren, Neil Watkins, Howard White, Kendra White, Louise Whiting, Vicki Wilde, Klaus Winkel, Paul Winters, Adrian Wood, Wusheng Yu, Zhou Yuan, André Zandstra, Aaron Zazueta, and Charles Ziegler.

Two of our valued colleagues passed away before we completed this manuscript, and we want to acknowledge here their contribution to the subject matter contained in this book: Hans Binswanger-Mkhize, a longtime colleague who always brought new ideas to rural development and chaired the International Association of Agricultural Economists (IAAE) meeting in Foz do Iguaçu, Brazil, in 2012, and D. John Shaw, a scholar and prolific writer on international cooperation in food security, who urged Uma Lele to write a book on international organizations. We have missed them.

Patricia Mason, our editor, has made singular contributions. She has steadfastly provided editing, reviewing, and continually perceptive comments and queries to guide the finalization of the chapters, diagrams, and references through a plethora of ever-changing documents. Her patience, support, and enthusiasm has been central to bringing this work to conclusion.

At Oxford University Press, we want especially to express thanks for their guidance in the preparation of this manuscript: Adam Swallow, Lowri Ribbons, Katie Bishop, and Henry Clarke. Adam Swallow has been a terrific editor/publisher, with very many useful comments/suggestions at critical stages of the manuscript.

All weaknesses that remain are our own.

Contents

List of Figures

List of Tables

List of Boxes

List of Abbreviations

3IE	International Initiative for Impact Evaluation
A&P	Asia and the Pacific
A4NH	Agriculture for Nutrition and Health (CGIAR Research Program)
AAEA	Agricultural and Applied Economics Association
AAS	Aquatic Agricultural Systems (CGIAR Research Program)
AATF	African Agricultural Technology Foundation
ABC/MRE	Brazilian Cooperation Agency of the Ministry of Foreign Relations of Brazil
ACA	Advance commitment authority
ACC/SCN	UN Administrative Coordination Committee's Subcommittee on Nutrition
ACCI	African Center for Crop Improvement
ACET	African Center for Economic Transition
ACIAR	Australian Centre for International Agricultural Research
ACTN	African Conservation Tillage Network
ADB	Asian Development Bank
ADG	Assistant Director-General (FAO)
ADM	Accountability and Decision Making framework (World Bank)
ADMARK	Agricultural Development Marketing Corporation
AECID	Spanish Agency for International Development Cooperation
AF	Alkire–Foster Method
AfCFTA	African Continental Free Trade Area
AFD	Agence Française de Développement
AfDB	African Development Bank
AFF	Agriculture, Forestry and Fishing sector
AFS	Agri-Food Systems Programs (CGIAR)
AFSI	L'Aquila Food Security Initiative
Ag2Nut CoP	Agriculture–Nutrition Community of Practice
AGI	Adolescent Girls Initiative
AGR	Agricultural and Natural Resources Department (World Bank)
AgR&D	Agricultural research and development
AGRA	Alliance for a Green Revolution in Africa
AGRISurvey	Agricultural Integrated Surveys (FAO)
AGRODEP	African Growth and Development Policy Modeling Consortium
AGSECAL	Agriculture Sector Adjustment Loan
AI	Artificial intelligence
AICR	American Institute for Cancer Research
AIDS	Acquired immunodeficiency syndrome
AIFS	ASEAN Integrated Food Security Framework
AIIB	Asian Infrastructure Investment Bank
AIR	Agriculture Investment Ratio
AISCO	Agricultural Input Supplies Corporation (Ethiopia)
AKIS	Agricultural Knowledge and Innovation Systems
AMA	Australian Multilateral Assessment
AMIS	Agricultural Market Information System

AMR   Antimicrobial resistance
AMS   Aggregate Measure of Support
AOI   Agriculture Orientation Index
APEC   Asia–Pacific Economic Cooperation
APL   Adaptive Project Loan
APLU   Association of Public and Land-Grant Universities
APMA   Agricultural Produce Marketing Act (India)
ARD   Agriculture and Rural Development sector (World Bank)
ARENA-II   Advancing Research on Nutrition and Agriculture Phase II (IFPRI)
ARRI   Annual Report on the Results and Impact of Operations (IFAD)
ARTF   Afghanistan Reconstruction Trust Fund
ASA   Advisory services and analytics
ASAL   Agriculture sector adjustment loan
ASAP   Adaptation for Smallholder Agriculture Programme (IFAD)
ASEAN   Association of Southeast Asian Nations
ASMC   After-service Medical Coverage
ASPIRE   Atlas of Social Protection: Indicators of Resilience and Equity (World Bank)
ASTI   Agricultural Science and Technology Indicators
ATA   Agricultural Transformation Agency (Ethiopia)
ATI   Aid Transparency Index
AU   African Union
AusAID   Australian Agency for International Development
AVRDC   World Vegetable Center, formerly the Asian Vegetable Research and Development
                Center
AWARD   African Women in Agricultural Research and Development
BCR   Benefit–cost ratio
BETF   Bank-executed trust fund
BHN   Basic Human Needs
BMCU   Bulk milk chilling unit
BMGF   Bill and Melinda Gates Foundation
BMI   Body mass index
BMZ   Ministry for Economic Cooperation and Development (Germany)
BNDS   Brazilian National Development Bank
BRAC   Building Resources Across Communities
BRICS   Brazil, Russia, India, China, and South Africa (BRICS Development Bank)
C2A   Credit to Agriculture
C2Cs   Communes de Convergence
CA   Conservation agriculture
CAADP   Comprehensive Africa Agriculture Development Programme
CAC   Codex Alimentarius Commission (FAO)
CAFTA   Central America Free Trade Association
CAFTA-DR   Dominican Republic—Central America Free Trade Association
CAS   Country Assistance Strategy
CB   Consortium Board (CGIAR)
CBD   Community-based development
CBT   Cash-based transfer
CCAFS   Climate Change, Agriculture and Food Security (GGIAR Research Program)
CCS   Country capacity strengthening (WFP)
CCSD   World Centre on Conflict, Security and Development
CDB   China Development Bank

CDC	Centers for Disease Control and Prevention
CDCF	Community Development Carbon Fund
CDD	Community-driven development
CDF	Comprehensive Development Framework
CDP	Committee for Development Policy (UN)
CEO	Chief Executive Officer
CEPR	Center for Economic Policy Research (Washington, DC)
CERF	Central Emergency Response Fund (UN)
CFC	Consumption of fixed capital
CFS	Committee on World Food Security
CFSAM	Crop and Food Security Missions (WFP)
CFS-FFA	Framework for Action for Food Security and Nutrition in Protracted Crises
CFSG	Climate Finance Study Group (of the G20)
CFSVA	Comprehensive Food Security and Vulnerability Analysis (WFP)
CGAP	Consultative Group to Assist the Poor
CGD	Center for Global Development
CGFPI	Consultative Group on Food Production and Investment in Developing Countries
CGIAR	Formerly, the Consultative Group for International Agricultural Research
CIAT	International Center for Tropical Agriculture
CIDA	Canadian International Development Agency
CIFF	Children's Investment Fund Foundation
CIFOR	Center for International Forestry Research (CGIAR)
CIGI	Centre for International Governance Innovation
CIMMYT	International Maize and Wheat Improvement Center
CIP	Center for Innovation and Partnership
CIP	International Potato Center
CMUs	Country Management Units (World Bank)
CNSTAT	Committee on National Statistics of the National Academies of Science
CO	Consortium Office (CGIAR)
CO	Country office (WFP)
COAG	Committee on Agriculture (FAO)
COMPAS	Common Performance Assessment System
COP	Conferences of the Parties
COP21	United Nations Climate Change Conference/Paris Climate Conference
COP22	UN Framework Convention on Climate Change
COSOP	Country Strategic Opportunities Programme (IFAD)
CP	Challenge Program (CGIAR)
CPA	Corporate political activity
CPA	Country programmable aid
CPB	Country Portfolio Budget (WFP)
CPE	Country programme evaluation
CPF	Country Program Framework (FAO)
CPI	Climate Policy Initiative
CPIA	Country Policy and Institutional Assessment (World Bank)
CPM	Country Programme Manager (IFAD)
CPS	Corporate Partnership Strategy (WFP)
CPWF	Challenge Program on Water and Food (CGIAR)
CRF	Corporate Results Framework
CRPs	CGIAR Research Programs
CRS	Creditor Reporting System

CSA	Climate-Smart Agriculture
CSD	Commission on Sustainable Development (UN)
CSD–16	Sixteenth Session of the Commission on Sustainable Development, New York, May 15–16, 2008
CSD–17	Seventeenth Session of the Commission on Sustainable Development, New York, May 4–15, 2009
CSISA	Cereal Systems Initiative for South Asia
CSM	Civil Society Mechanism
CSO	Civil society organization
CSP	Country Strategic Plans (WFP)
CTA	Chief Technical Officer
CTF	Clean Technology Fund
DAC	Development Assistance Committee (OECD)
DANIDA	Danish International Development Agency
DDA	Doha Development Agenda
DDG	Deputy Director-General (FAO)
DDGS	Distiller's dried grains with solubles
DESA	Department of Economic and Social Affairs (UN)
DEV	Development projects (WFP)
DFA	Development flows to agriculture
DFCs	Development Finance Corporations
DFID	Department for International Development (UK)
DG	Director-General
DLIS	Desert Locust Information Service
DPI	Investment Centre Division (FAO)
DRCs	Domestic resource costs
DSF	Debt Sustainability Framework (IFAD)
DSSI	Debt Service Suspension Initiative
DTCs	Developing and Transition Countries
EAP	East Asia and the Pacific
EBRD	European Bank for Reconstruction and Development
EC	European Commission
ECA	Economic Commission for Africa
ECA	Essential Commodities Act (India)
ECA	Europe and Central Asia
ECG	Evaluation Cooperation Group (IFAD)
ECHO	European Commission Civil Protection and Humanitarian Aid Operations
ECOSOC	Economic and Social Council (UN)
ECTAD	Emergency Centre for Transboundary Animal Diseases (FAO)
EDI	Economic Development Institute (later, World Bank Institute)
EFSA	Emergency Food Security Assessment (WFP)
EHNRI	Ethiopian Health and Nutrition Research Center
EIB	European Investment Bank
EMBRAPA	Brazilian Agricultural Research Program
EMOP	Emergency operations (WFP)
EMPEA	Emerging Market Private Equity Association
EMPRES	Emergency Prevention System
EMT	Executive Management Team (CGIAR)
ENV	Environment Department
EPZ	Export processing zone

ESN	Nutrition and Food Systems Division (FAO)
ESSP	Earth System Science Partnership
ESSP	Ethiopia Strategy Support Program
ET	Evapotranspiration
EU	European Union
EUFF	European Union Food Facility
EVI	Economic Vulnerability Index
FAA	Food Assistance for Assets (WFP)
FAC	Food Assistance Convention
FACCE–JPI	Joint Programming Initiative on Agriculture, Food Security and Climate Change (EU)
FAIS	Food Aid Information System
FAO	Food and Agriculture Organization of the United Nations
FAO–CP	FAO Cooperative Program (with World Bank)
FAOSTAT	FAO Statistics Division
FARA	Forum for Agricultural Research in Africa
FARMD	Forum for Agricultural Risk Management in Development
FATF	Financial Action Task Force (World Bank)
FAW	Fall armyworm
FBD	Foodborne disease
FBDGs	Food-based dietary guidelines
FBS	Food Balance Sheets
FBT	Food, Beverages and Tobacco
FC	Fund Council (CGIAR)
FCDO	Foreign, Commonwealth and Development Office (UK)
FCI	Food Corporation of India
FCS	Fragile and conflict-affected states
FCTC	Framework Convention on Tobacco Control (WHO)
FCV	Fragile, Conflict, and Violence group
FDI	Foreign direct investment
FEWS NET	Famine Early Warning Systems Network
FFA	Food Assistance for Assets
FFR	Financial Framework Review
FFS	Farmers' field school
FHIT	Funds held in trust
FIES	Food Insecurity Experience Scale
FIF	Financial intermediary funds
FIVIMS	Food Insecurity and Vulnerability Information and Mapping Systems
FLEGT	Forest Law Enforcement, Governance and Trade (EU–FAO)
FLFP	Female labor force participation
FMM	Multipartner Programme Support Mechanism (FAO)
FNSARD	Food and Nutrition Security/Agriculture and Rural Development
FNS-REPRO	Food and Nutrition Security Resilience Programme
FO	Fund Office (CGIAR)
FSC	Food Security Cluster
FSF	Fast-Start Finance
FSIN	Food Security Information Network
FSMS	Food safety management systems
FSN	Food security and nutrition
FSS	Food Systems Summit (UN, 2021)

FTA	Forests, Trees, and Agroforestry (CGIAR Research Program)
FTA	Free trade agreement
FTE	Full-time equivalent
FTF	Feed the Future (US initiative)
FTF–ITT	Feed the Future–India Triangular Training Program
G7	Group of 7 (Canada, France, Germany, Italy, Japan, the United Kingdom, and the United States)
G20	Group of 20 (Argentina, Australia, Brazil, Canada, China, France, Germany, India, Indonesia, Italy, Japan, South Korea, Mexico, Russia, Saudi Arabia, South Africa, Turkey, the United Kingdom and the United States—along with the European Union [EU])
G77	Group of 77 (OECD countries)
GAAP2	Gender, Agriculture, and Assets Project
GACSA	Global Alliance for Climate-Smart Agriculture
GAFSP	Global Agriculture and Food Security Program
GAIN	Global Alliance for Improved Nutrition
GAO	Gross agricultural output
GATT	General Agreement on Tariffs and Trade (replaced by the WTO)
GAVI	Global Alliance for Vaccines and Immunizations
GBD	Global burden of disease
GCARD	Global Conference on Agricultural Research for Development
GCC	Gulf Cooperation Council
GCCS	Gulf Cooperation Council States
GCF	Green Climate Fund
GCF	Gross capital formation
GCFF	Global Concessional Financing Facility
GCS	Gross capital stock
GDI	Gender Development Index (UNDP)
GDP	Gross domestic product
GDPRD	Global Donor Platform for Rural Development
GEA	Government Expenditure on Agriculture (FAO)
GEF	Global Environment Facility
GEI	Green Economy Initiative (UNEP)
GenCap	Gender Capacity Project
GENNOVATE	Enabling Gender Equality in Agricultural and Environmental Innovation project
GFAR	Global Forum on Agricultural Research and Innovation
GFATM	Global Fund to Fight AIDS, Tuberculosis and Malaria
GFCF	Gross fixed capital formation
GFDRR	Global Facility for Disaster Reduction and Recovery
GFF	Global Financing Facility
GFRP	Global Food Crisis Response Program (World Bank)
GFSP	Global Food Safety Partnership
GHA	Global Humanitarian Assistance
GHGs	Greenhouse gases
GHI	Global Harvest Initiative
GHO	Global Health Observatory (WHO data)
GIEWS	Global Information and Early Warning System (FAO)
GIFT	Global Individual Food Consumption Data Tool
GII	Gender Inequality Index (UNDP)
GIP	Global Integrating Program (CGIAR)

GIS	Geographic Information Systems
GLDC	Grain Legumes and Dryland Cereals (CGIAR Research Program)
GLOPAN	Global Panel on Agriculture and Food Systems for Nutrition
GM	Genetically modified (crops)
GMG	Global Migration Group
GMOs	Genetically modified organisms
GNI	Gross national income
GNP	Gross national product
GNR	*Global Nutrition Report*
GNSS	Global Navigation Satellite System
GPAI	Global Program on Avian Influenza
GPEDC	Global Partnership for Effective Development Co-operation
GPF	Global Policy Forum
GPGs	Global public goods
GPPi	Global Public Policy Institute
GPS	Global Positioning System
GPs	Global Practice units (World Bank)
GREAN	Global Research on the Environmental and Agricultural Nexus
GRFC	Global Report on Food Crises (FSIN)
GRiSP	Global Rice Science Partnership (CGIAR Research Program)
GTA	Gender transformative approach
GVCs	Global value chains
HAI	Human Asset Index
HDI	Human Development Index
HFLAC	Hunger-Free Latin America and the Caribbean
HIPC	Heavily Indebted Poor Country
HIPC–DI	Heavily Indebted Poor Countries Debt Initiative
HIV/AIDS	Human immunodeficiency virus/acquired immune deficiency syndrome
HLF	High Level Forum
HLPE	High Level Panel of Experts (on Food Security and Nutrition)
HLTF	High Level Task Force
HNP	Health, Nutrition and Population department (World Bank)
HPAI	Highly Pathogenic Avian Influenza
HQ	Headquarters
HR	Human Resources
HYV	High-yielding variety
IAAE	International Association of Agricultural Economists
IAASTD	International Assessment of Agricultural Knowledge, Science and Technology for Development
IAEA	International Atomic Energy Agency
IAGFS	International Advisory Group on FAO Statistics
IAI	International Assessment Initiative (IFAD9)
IASC	Inter-Agency Standing Committee
IATI	International Aid Transparency Initiative
IBRD	International Bank for Reconstruction and Development
ICABR	International Consortium on Applied Bioeconomy Research
ICAR	Indian Council of Agricultural Research
ICARDA	International Center for Agricultural Research in the Dry Areas
ICCIDD	International Coordinating Committee on Iodine Deficiency Disorders
ICE	US Immigration and Customs Enforcement

ICMR–NIN	Indian Council of Medical Research–National Institute of Nutrition
ICN	International Conference on Nutrition
ICN2	Second International Conference on Nutrition
ICO	IFAD Country Office
ICOR	Incremental capital–output ratio
ICR	Implementation Completion and Results report (IEG, World Bank)
ICRAF	International Center for Research in Agroforestry (CGIAR)
ICRIER	Indian Council for Research on International Economic Relations
ICRISAT	International Crops Research Institute for the Semi-Arid Tropics
ICSID	International Centre for Settlement of Investment Disputes
ICT	Information and communications technology
ICTSD	International Centre for Trade and Sustainable Development
IDA	International Development Association (of the World Bank)
IDB	Inter-American Development Bank
IDC	International Development Committee (Great Britain)
IDDs	Iodine deficiency disorders
IDO	Intermediate Development Outcome (CGIAR)
IDPs	Internally displaced persons
IDRC	International Development Research Centre (Canada)
IDS	Institute of Development Studies (University of Sussex)
IE	Implementing entities
IEA	Independent Evaluation Arrangement (CGIAR)
IEA	International Energy Agency
IEE	Independent internal evaluation
IEG	Independent Evaluation Group (World Bank)
IETA	International Emissions Trading Association
IFAD	International Fund for Agricultural Development
IFC	International Finance Corporation
IFI	International financial institution
IFPRI	International Food Policy Research Institute
IGAD	Intergovernmental Authority for Development
IGIDR	Indira Gandhi Institute of Development Research
IGO	Intergovernmental organization
IHD	Institute for Human Development
IHME	Institute for Health Metrics and Evaluation (Seattle, WA)
IIAG	Ibrahim Index of African Governance
IICA	Inter-American Institute for Cooperation on Agriculture
IIF	Integrated Implementation Framework
IIRR	International Institute of Rural Reconstruction
IISD	International Institute for Sustainable Development
IITA	International Institute of Tropical Agriculture
ILO	International Labour Organization
ILO–GET	ILO–Global Employment Trend
ILRI	International Livestock Research Institute
IMF	International Monetary Fund
INGO	International nongovernmental organization
IO	International organization
IOD PARC	International Organisation Development Ltd
IOE	Independent Office of Evaluation
IoT	Internet of Things

IP	Intellectual property
IPBES	Intergovernmental Science–Policy Platform on Biodiversity and Ecosystem Service
IPC	Integrated Food Security Phase Classification (UN)
IPCC	Intergovernmental Panel on Climate Change
IPL	International poverty line
IPM	Integrated Pest Management
IPNS	Integrated Plant Nutrient Systems
IPPC	International Plant Protection Commission
IR	Inverse relationship
IRA	Immediate Response Account (WFP)
IRAI	IDA Resource Allocation Index (World Bank)
IRDP	Integrated Rural Development Programs (World Bank)
IRM	Integrated Road Map
IRR	Internal rate of return
IRRI	International Rice Research Institute
ISDC	Independent Science for Development Council (CGIAR)
ISFS	Information Systems for Food Security
ISIC	International Standard Industrial Classification
ISIS	Islamic State of Iraq and Syria
ISNAR	International Service for National Agricultural Research
ISPC	Independent Science and Partnership Council (CGIAR)
IT	Information technology
ITA	In-Trust Agreement
ITC	International Trade Centre
IUCN	International Union for Conservation of Nature
IWMI	International Water Management Institute
JAI	Joint Africa Institute
JAM	Joint Assessment Missions (WFP)
JICA	Japan International Cooperation Agency
JNSP	Joint Nutrition Support Programme (UNICEF/WHO)
KFF	Kaiser Family Foundation
KfW	KfW Bankengruppe
KIT	Royal Tropical Institute
KNOMAD	Global Knowledge Partnership on Migration and Development
LAC	Latin America and the Caribbean
LDCs	Least developed countries
LIBOR	London Interbank Offered Rate
LIC	Low-income country
LICUS	Low-income countries under stress
LIFDC	Low-income, food-deficit country
LMIC	Lower-middle-income country
LOSAN	National Law on Food and Nutrition Security (Brazil)
LRP	Local and Regional Purchase
LSMS	Living Standards Measurement Study (World Bank)
LSMS–ISA	Living Standards Measurement Study's Integrated Surveys on Agriculture
M&A	Mergers and acquisitions
M&E	Monitoring and evaluation
MADIA	Managing Agricultural Development in Africa (World Bank)
MAR	Multilateral aid review
M-BoSs	Building Successes of the Marketplace (MKTPlace)

MC9	WTO Ministerial Conference in Bali, 2013
MCC	Millennium Challenge Corporation
MCHN	Maternal-and-child health nutrition
MDB	Multilateral development bank
MDER	Minimum Daily Energy Requirement
MDGs	Millennium Development Goals
MDP	Multidimensional poverty
MDR	Multilateral Development Review
MDs	Managing Directors (CGIAR)
MDTF	Multi-donor trust fund
MEL	Monitoring, evaluation, and learning
MENA	Middle East and North Africa
MFA	Ministry of Foreign Affairs
MFA-Sida	Sweden's Ministry for Foreign Affairs—International Development Cooperation Agency
MfDR	Management for Development Results (Multilateral Development Bank working group)
MGNREGA	Mahatma Gandhi National Rural Employment Guarantee Act
MIC	Middle-income country
MIF	Mo Ibrahim Foundation
MIGA	Multilateral Investment Guarantee Agency
MIRAGE	Modelling International Relations under Applied General Equilibrium
MIRAGRODEP	Modelling International Relationships under Applied General Equilibrium for AgRODEP
MIT	Massachusetts Institute of Technology
MIYCN	Maternal, infant, and young child nutrition
MKTPlace	Africa–Brazil Innovation Marketplace
ML	Machine learning
MNE	Multinational enterprise
MOPAN	Multilateral Organisation Performance Assessment Network
MoU	Memorandum of Understanding
MPI	Multidimensional Poverty Index
MSP	Minimum support price
MT	Metric tons
MTPs	Medium Term Plans
MUV	Manufactures unit value
N4G	Nutrition for Growth Summit
NAFTA	North American Free Trade Agreement
NAHEP	National Agricultural Higher Education Project (India)
NARS	National agricultural research systems
NASEM	National Academies of Sciences, Engineering, and Medicine
NATO	North Atlantic Treaty Organization
NCD	Noncommunicable disease
NCS	Net capital stock
NDB	New Development Bank
NDDB	National Dairy Development Board (India)
NDP	National Dairy Plan
NELGA	Network of Excellence on Land Governance in Africa
NEN	Near East and North Africa
NEPAD	New Partnership for Africa's Development

NFSA	National Food Security Act (India)
NGLS	Non-Governmental Liaison Service (UN)
NGO	Nongovernmental organization
NIPN	National Information Platforms for Nutrition
NORAD	Norwegian Agency for Development Cooperation
NRC	National Research Council (of the US National Academies of Science, Engineering, and Medicine)
NRM	Natural resource management
NSSO	National Sample Survey Office (India)
NT	No-till agriculture
NVA	New Vision for Agriculture (World Economic Forum)
OAU	Organization of African Unity
OCHA	Office for the Coordination of Humanitarian Affairs (UN)
OCHA FTS	OCHA Financial Tracking Service
ODA	Official development assistance
ODI	Overseas Development Institute
OECD	Organisation for Economic Co-operation and Development
OED	Operations Evaluation Department (World Bank, now the IEG)
OIE	World Organisation for Animal Health
OOF	Other Official Flows
OP	Operational policy
OPEC	Organization of the Petroleum Exporting Countries
OPHI	Oxford Poverty and Human Development Initiative
OPV	Open pollinated varieties
OSAA	Office of the Special Advisor on Africa
P4P	Purchase for Progress (WFP assistance program)
P4R	Program-for-Results financing (World Bank)
PATH	Program for the Appropriate Technology in Health
PBAS	Performance-based allocation system
PDS	Public Distribution System (India)
PEM	Protein–energy malnutrition
PES	Payment for environmental services
PHL	Postharvest losses
PHN	Population, Health and Nutrition department (World Bank), now HNP
PIC	Public Information Center (World Bank)
PIM	Perpetual inventory method
PIM	Policies, Institutions, and Markets (CGIAR Research Program)
PMI	Industrial Modernization Programme (Tunisia)
PNAE	School meal program (Brazil)
PNSAN	National Food and Nutritional Security Policy (Brazil)
PNSP	Productive Safety Net Program (Ethiopia)
PoLG	Programme of Loans and Grants (IFAD)
POR	Policy-oriented R&D
PoU	Prevalence of Undernourishment
PoW	Programme of work (IFAD)
POWB	Plan of Work and Budget (CGIAR)
PPP	Purchasing power parity
PRAI	Principles for Responsible Agricultural Investment
PRC	People's Republic of China
PREM	Poverty Reduction and Economic Management (World Bank)

PRGA	Participatory Research and Gender Analysis (CGIAR Program)
PRISMA	President's Report on the Implementation Status of Evaluation Recommendations and Management Actions (IFAD)
ProCap	Protection Standby Capacity Project
PRRO	Protracted Relief and Recovery Programs (WFP)
PRS	Poverty Reduction Strategy
PRSP	Poverty Reduction Strategy Paper (World Bank)
PSA	Program Support and Administrative (budget) (WFP)
PSC	Project steering committee
PSE	Producer Support Estimate
PSH	Public stockholding
PSM	Private Sector Mechanism
PSNP	Productive Safety Net Program (Ethiopia)
PSSC	Professional Staff and Selection Committees (FAO)
QR	Quantitative restrictions
R&D	Research and development
RB	Regional bureau (WFP)
RBAs	Rome-based agencies
RB–COSOP	Results-Based Country Strategic Opportunities Programs
RBP	Ration Balancing Program
RCEP	Regional Comprehensive Economic Partnership
RCT	Randomized control trial
REACH	Renewed Efforts against Child Hunger and Undernutrition
REDD	Reducing Emissions from Deforestation and Forest Degradation
REDD+	Reducing Emissions from Deforestation and Forest Degradation in Developing Countries (UN)
REN21	Renewable Energy Policy Network for the 21st Century
ReSAKSS	Regional Strategic Analysis and Knowledge Support System
RETF	Recipient-executed trust fund
RFID	Radio-frequency identification
RIDE	Report on Development Effectiveness (IFAD)
RIMS	Results and Impact Management System (IFAD)
RMC	Regional Member Countries
RMF	Results Management Framework
RP	Regular Programme (FAO)
RTB	Roots, Tubers, and Bananas (CGIAR Research Program)
SA	South Asia
SAA	Sasakawa Africa Association
SADEV	Swedish Agency for Development Evaluation
SAFANSI	South Asia Food and Nutrition Security Initiative
SAL	Structural adjustment lending
SAP	Structural Adjustment Program
SARS	Severe acute respiratory syndrome
SAU	State agricultural university
SC	System Council (CGIAR)
SCF	Standing Committee on Finance (UNFCCC)
SCI	Selective capital increase
SCP	System cost percentage (CGIAR)
SD	Standard deviation
SDA	Social Dimensions of Adjustment initiative (World Bank)

SDGs	Sustainable Development Goals
SDR	Special Drawing Rights (IFAD)
SDTFs	Single-donor trust funds
SEATO	Southeast Asia Treaty Organization
SECAL	Sectoral Adjustment Lending
SECAP	Social, Environmental and Climate Assessment Procedures (IFAD)
SEWA	Self Employed Women's Association (India)
SF	Strategic Framework
SIAC	Strengthening Impact Assessment in CGIAR
SIDA	Swedish International Development Agency
SIMEC	System Integrated Monitoring and Evaluation Committee (CGIAR)
SIPA	Swedish Institute of Public Administration
SIPRI	Stockholm International Peace Research Institute
SISAN	National System for Food and Nutrition Security (Brazil)
SITC	Standard International Trade Classification
SLO	System Level Outcome (CGIAR)
SMART	Specific, measurable, achievable, relevant, timebound
SMB	System Management Board (CGIAR)
SMEs	Small- and medium-sized enterprises
SMO	System Management Office (CGIAR)
SNAP	Supplemental Nutrition Assistance Program
SO	Strategic objective
SO	System Organization (CGIAR)
SOFA	*State of Food and Agriculture* (FAO report)
SOFI	*State of Food Insecurity and Nutrition* (FAO report)
SP	Strategic Programme (FAO)
SPAAR	Special Program for African Agricultural Research
SPA–FS	Strategic Plan of Action for Food Security (ASEAN)
SPEED	Statistics on Public Expenditures for Economic Development (IFPRI)
SPIA	Standing Panel on Impact Assessment (CGIAR)
SPS	Sanitary and Phytosanitary Measures
SRF	Strategic Results Framework
SSA	Sub-Saharan Africa
SSB	Sustainable and balanced growth
SSN	Social safety net
ST	Structural transformation
Sub-IDO	Sub-Intermediate Intermediate Development Outcome (CGIAR)
SUN	Scaling Up Nutrition
SWOT	Strengths, weaknesses, opportunities, and threats
T&V	Train and Visit (extension)
TAAT	Technologies for African Agricultural Transformation
TAC	Technical Advisory Committee (CGIAR)
TB	Tuberculosis
TBT	Technical Barriers to Trade
TCI	Investment Centre (FAO)
TCP	Technical Cooperation Programme (FAO)
TCPF	Technical Cooperation Program Facility (FAO)
TF	Trade facilitation
TFA	Trade facilitation agreement
TFP	Total factor productivity

TNC	Transnational corporation
TOC	Theory of change
TPP	Trans-Pacific Partnership
TTCSP	Think Tanks and Civil Societies Program (University of Pennsylvania)
TTL	Task Team Leader (World Bank)
TWG	Technical working group
UHC	Universal health care
ULYSSES	Understanding and Coping with Food Markets Volatility towards More Stable World and EU Food Systems (project)
UMIC	Upper-middle-income country
UN HTLF	United Nations High Level Task Force on Global Food and Nutrition Security
UN	United Nations
UNAIDS	Joint United Nations Programme on HIV/AIDS
UNCCD	UN Convention to Combat Desertification
UNCED	United Nations Conference on the Environment and Development
UNCTAD	United Nations Conference on Trade and Development
UNDAF	United Nations Development Assistance Framework
UNDP	United Nations Development Programme
UNDS	United Nations Development System
UNEP	United Nations Environment Programme
UNESCO	United Nations Educational, Scientific and Cultural Organization
UNFCCC	United Nations Framework Convention on Climate Change
UNFPA	United Nations Population Fund
UN-Habitat	United Nations Human Settlements Programme
UNHCR	United Nations High Commissioner for Refugees (the UN Refugee Agency)
UNICEF	United Nations Children's Fund
UNIDO	United Nations Industrial Development Organization
UNISDR	United Nations Office for Disaster Risk Reduction
UN–OAD	United Nations Operational Activities for Development
UN–OHCHR	United Nations Office of the High Commissioner for Human Rights
UNOPS	United Nations Office for Project Services
UNRWA	United Nations Relief and Works Agency for Palestinian Refugees
UNSCN	United Nations Standing Committee on Nutrition
UNSD OCD	United Nations Statistics Division Official Country Data
UNSDCF	UN Sustainable Development Cooperation Framework
UNTT	United Nations System Task Team
US EIA	US Energy Information Administration
USAID	United States Agency for International Development
USDA	United States Department of Agriculture
USMCA	United States–Mexico–Canada Agreement (replacement for NAFTA)
UTF	Unilateral Trust Fund (FAO)
VAM	Vulnerability Analysis and Mapping
VAT	Value-added tax
VC	Value chain
VR	Virtual reality
W1	Window 1 (CGIAR funding window)
W2	Window 2 (CGIAR funding window)
W3	Window 3 (CGIAR funding window)
WACCI	West African Center for Crop Improvement
WASH	Water, sanitation, and hygiene

WBG	World Bank Group
WBI	World Bank Institute
WCED	World Commission on Environment and Development
WDI	World Development Indicators
WDR	*World Development Report* (World Bank)
WEAI	Women's Empowerment in Agriculture Index
WEF	World Economic Forum
WEO	Women's Economic Opportunity Index (*The Economist* Intelligence Unit)
WEO	World Economic Outlook (IMF)
WEOF	Women Entrepreneurs Opportunity Facility
WFP	World Food Programme
WGI	Worldwide Governance Index
WHA	World Health Assembly
WHO	World Health Organization
WLE	Water, Land, and Ecosystems (CGIAR Research Program)
WMO	World Meteorological Organization
WTO	World Trade Organization

Notes on the Authors

Uma Lele, an independent scholar and development economist, has a PhD from Cornell University and five decades of experience in research, operations, policy analysis, and evaluation in the World Bank, universities, and international organizations. Among her notable works are *Food Grain Marketing in India: Private Performance and Public Policy* (1973); *The Design of Rural Development: Lessons from Africa* (1976); *Managing Agricultural Development in Africa* (1991); *Transitions in Development: From Aid to Capital Flows* (1991), with Ijaz Nabi; *Intellectual Property Rights in Agriculture: The World Bank's Role in Assisting Borrower and Member Countries* (1999), with William Lesser and Gesa Horstkotte-Wesseler; *Managing a Global Resource: Challenges of Forest Conservation and Development* (2002); and *Patterns of Structural Transformation and Agricultural Productivity Growth* (2018), with Manmohan Agarwal and Sambuddha Goswami. She has also written papers on agricultural productivity growth and structural transformation, and on the changing roles of forests and water in the course of economic development. As Senior Advisor in the World Bank's Operations Evaluation Department (now called the Independent Evaluation Group), she led evaluations of the World Bank's Forest Strategy (2002), the Consultative Group on International Agricultural Research (CGIAR) (2003), and the World Bank's approach to global programs (2005). She co-chaired an International Taskforce of the China Council on Environment and Development on Forests and Grasslands (2000–2002), served on the panel for the independent external evaluation of the Food and Agriculture Organization (2007), and co-authored a theme paper for the first Global Conference on Agricultural Research for Development. She has served on numerous advisory, expert, and award panels in international organizations, including on the Sasakawa 2000 Program (1992–1994), the World Food Prize (1987–1994), and the MacArthur Foundation (1991–1995). She was a Graduate Research Professor (1991–1995), and Director of International Studies (1992–1993) at the University of Florida, co-chaired an international taskforce on Global Research on the Environmental and Agricultural Nexus (GREAN) (1992–1995), and established and directed the Global Development Initiative of the Carter Center and the Carnegie Corporation (1992–1993). She was on the founding board of CGIAR's Centre for International Policy Research (1993) and a member of CGIAR's Technical Advisory Committee (1994–1995). She is a winner of a number of recognitions, including the M. S. Swaminathan Award, the B. P. Pal Award, and the Clifton Wharton Award. She is a Fellow of the American Agricultural and Applied Economic Association and of India's National Academy of Agricultural Sciences and of the International Association of Agricultural Economists (IAAE). She was elected President Elect of IAAE in 2018. In 2011, she established an award for Best Research on Gender in Agriculture at the International Agricultural Economic Association, and in 2013, she established the Uma Lele Mentorship Program for students from developing countries at the American Agricultural Economic Association. In 2020, she was invited to be a member of the Scientific Group for the UN Secretary-General's 2021 Food Systems Summit.

Prof. Manmohan Agarwal is an independent researcher, an adjunct Senior Fellow at Research and Information Systems for Developing Countries, New Delhi, and an adjunct senior fellow with the Institute of Chinese Studies. He retired as the Reserve Bank of India Chair Professor at the Centre for Development Studies at Thiruvananthapuram, Kerala, India. Earlier, he retired as a professor from Jawaharlal Nehru University, New Delhi, India, where he had taught for almost 30 years. Subsequently, he was a senior fellow at the Centre for International Governance Innovation (CIGI) at Waterloo, Ontario, Canada, where he worked on issues of the world economy, including the G20 and

South–South cooperation. He worked for a number of years at the World Bank and at the International Monetary Fund. His research has been mainly in the area of international economics and development economics. More recently, he has been working on the role of the G20, South–South cooperation, and the international monetary system. He is currently editing books on the G20 and has a number of working papers on the international monetary system written prior to integrating them into a book. Along with his colleagues, John Whalley and Jing Wang, he has edited three volumes on the Chinese and Indian economies: *The Economies of China and India: Cooperation and Conflict.* This was a follow-up on an earlier two-volume set on China and India, edited with John Whalley, as part of a series on Asia and the World Economy. A volume titled *Did the Millennium Development Goals Work? Meeting Future Challenges with Past Lessons,* which was edited with Leah Polonenko and Hany Besada, was published in September 2017. More recently, he has edited, with John Whalley, two volumes on the G20: *Economics of G20, Vol. 1: Developing Countries* and *The Need for G20, Vol. 2: How Developing Countries can Achieve Sustainable Development Goals.*

Brian C. Baldwin, geographer and agricultural economist, held field posts with the UK's Overseas Development Administration (the precursor of the Department for International Development [DFID]) in Sri Lanka and Zambia in design and evaluation of agricultural and rural development programs. These long-term, in-country positions within the civil service structure gave him an important perspective on the needs and priorities of emerging countries, their constraints and opportunities. Subsequently, he worked as an independent economist with the United States Agency for International Development (USAID), the United Nations Industrialization Development Organization (UNIDO), the Food and Agriculture Organization of the United Nations (FAO), the International Fund for Agricultural Development (IFAD), the European Union (EU), and the private sector in the Caribbean, Thailand, Philippines, Tanzania, Malawi, Botswana, and Zambia. He began working with IFAD in 1988, as a country program manager in the Asia Region (Pakistan, Philippines, Sri Lanka, Cambodia, and Myanmar). With a focus on project preparation and implementation, his tasks included stakeholder workshops, appraisal, loan negotiation, and management of loan administration and supervision. Partnerships were developed with co-financiers (World Bank, Asian Development Bank, Islamic Development Bank) and bilateral donors, such as Sweden, the Australian Agency for International Development (AusAID), Germany, UNDP, FAO, and the World Food Programme (WFP). From 2004, he was IFAD's Senior Operations Management Adviser in the office of the Asst. President for Programme Management. He led IFAD's involvement in the Heavily Indebted Poor Countries Debt Initiative (HIPC–DI) and Debt Management to provide debt relief to selected IFAD member countries, the implementation of IFAD's financial allocation system, and the Multilateral Organisation Performance Assessment Network (MOPAN) exercise. He managed IFAD's harmonization and alignment initiatives under the Paris Declaration and Accra accords. He co-chaired the Global Donor Platform for Rural Development, chaired the Multilateral Development Bank working group on Management for Development Results, and was the IFAD representative on the Organisation for Economic Co-operation and Development (OECD) Development Assistance Committee (DAC) working party on Aid Effectiveness, which evolved into the Global Partnership for Effective Development, and the Steering Committee of the International Aid Transparency Initiative (IATI). Since leaving IFAD, he continues to work as a development and policy adviser with both the public and private sector, including work in Thailand, Ghana, Sri Lanka, and Tanzania.

Sambuddha Goswami has been working with Dr. Uma Lele as a researcher since 2009, on a variety of papers. After completing his master's degree in Economics from Delhi School of Economics, his work has included data analysis, research support, and co-authoring of papers, presentations, and publications. This has involved performing statistical and econometric analysis of meta data sets (including assembling, analyzing, interpreting, and disseminating large sets of global-, regional-, and country-level micro and macro data), and reviews of diverse bodies of literature in the areas of structural transformation, productivity growth, food, agriculture, nutrition, water and forest management, poverty, health, gender, energy and the environment, global public goods, external assistance, and partnerships. The focus has been on the overall global challenges and the sources of global-, regional-, and country-level growth in demand for and supply of food and agriculture, and the related changes in the environment. He served as consultant (November 2014–April 2016) at the Agricultural Development Economics Division of the FAO Statistics Division to support the Technical Working Group on Measuring Food and Nutrition Security of the Food Security Information Network (FSIN) of FAO, WFP, and the International Food Policy Research Institute (IFPRI); and at the World Bank (December 2015–June 2016) on the National Agricultural Higher Education Project (NAHEP) in India.

Introduction

Uma Lele

The world has produced enough food since the Second World War to feed itself despite rapid population growth, owing to extraordinary technological and institutional change. The rise in world food production, however, has been accompanied by unequal access to that abundance, as well as soil degradation, loss of biodiversity, and growing water scarcities. There have also been dramatic changes in the world economic order and several other transformations. They include successive food and energy crises, and debt and financial crises, followed by the embrace of the Sustainable Development Goals (SDGs) and the Paris Accord on Climate Change to deal with these challenges. Then, the COVID-19 pandemic presented a tragic external shock for which the world was not prepared. The narrative on food and nutrition has changed, too, from a single-minded focus on productivity growth of cereals to sustainable and diversified food production and healthy food systems. A signature event among these changing processes has been the rise of China and other emerging countries, changing the global balance of power from the Organisation of Economic Co-operation and Development (OECD) countries in the (broadly defined) North to the East and the South. A single, most important event was the US presidential election in 2020, with the hope for a return of multilateralism. However, the Biden–Harris victory is complicated in changing to a more benign foreign policy due to the 72 million votes Trump received. While Trump has departed, Trumpism may yet be alive and well and that will determine the wiggle room the Biden–Harris administration will have in restoring US leadership. The recent US election also presents an opportunity for a new dynamic of how the United States, among other countries, including the European Union (EU), will work with allies to pursue multilateralism on such matters as delivering on the Paris Accord, Agenda 2030 and the SDGs, on the Middle East peace plan that is at the root of the refugee crisis, and for more predictable trade and aid policies.

The first part of this book addresses how several developing countries, particularly in Asia, have transformed and industrialized successfully through smallholder agricultural development, becoming global players, while others in the same region and in sub-Saharan Africa have lagged behind. Political instability, weak governance, weak internal capacity, limited accountability, and a lack of understanding of what it takes to develop smallholder agriculture, as a means to industrialize over a long haul, explain some countries' slow transformation, in contrast to the countries that have transformed successfully. China and emerging economies play increasingly important roles in international commerce, finance, and technology generation and transfer. Chapters 1–4 and 7 of this book explore structural transformation of developing countries in a period of rapid change from such a perspective. They show how complexity of development has increased, leading to the need for increased international cooperation among a growing number of actors in addition to sovereign governments. Yet, skepticism about multilateralism has also increased, especially in the

Food for All: International Organizations and the Transformation of Agriculture. Uma Lele, Manmohan Agarwal, Brian C. Baldwin, and Sambuddha Goswami, Oxford University Press. © Uma Lele, Manmohan Agarwal, Brian C. Baldwin, and Sambuddha Goswami 2021. DOI: 10.1093/oso/9780198755173.003.0001

very country—the United States—that was the key architect of international cooperation, with increasing calls for transformative changes in our food and health systems.

The US leadership played a key role in the establishment of several international organizations in the post-Second World War period. These organizations have played key roles in this transformation process, including in the near universal embrace of SDGs and the Climate Change Agreement by member countries, but their work is often seen as "black boxes." Alternatively, they face stereotyping by the general public and lack the broad public support they need to play critical roles in an ever more complex world, which is calling for transformative changes in our food and health systems.

The "Big Five" organizations of our focus are the **Food and Agriculture Organization of the United Nations (FAO)**, established in 1944; the **World Bank**, one of two Bretton Woods institutions established in 1945, and the International Development Association (IDA), the World Bank's concessional window, established in 1961; the **World Food Programme (WFP)**, established in 1960; **CGIAR** (formerly, the Consultative Group for International Agricultural Research), established in 1971; and the **International Fund for Agricultural Development (IFAD)**, established in 1974.

- FAO is the only global platform for agreements on international norms and standards, and for global data and information on all aspects of food, agriculture, and related natural resources, but norms of cooperation and agreements have changed radically since FAO's inception.
- The World Bank and IDA have been the largest public funders of policy advice and investment projects for well over 75 years, but their role as suppliers of assistance has declined in relative terms as investment needs of developing countries run into the trillions.
- WFP is the largest provider of emergency food and cash assistance for people in extreme need, and demands for its services have skyrocketed.
- CGIAR has been the largest provider of international agricultural research in the public sector for well over 50 years.
- IFAD was founded initially with the thought of using recycled petrodollars, matched by OECD donors, in the aftermath of the first world food crisis in 1972. It became the focus for investment support to small-scale and marginal farmers, many of whom are women.

Together, these organizations have seen the world economy through oil price shocks and responded to a variety of changes in subsequent decades, including the latest migration crisis associated with the largest displacement of human population since the Second World War. Chapters 5, 6, and 8–12 start with the rapidly changed global governance of food and agriculture, followed by the discussion of the five international organizations as operating arms of global governance.

Before the COVID-19 pandemic struck in 2020, much progress was achieved on poverty reduction and food security. Nearly a billion people have moved out of poverty since 1990, although only about a quarter of those are reportedly free of hunger, and the numbers of food-insecure people are increasing yet again. Global under-five infant and child mortality rates have declined, too. Irrigated agriculture was the driving force in food production growth in Asia, also, as a resilience strategy, but now resilience has a new meaning— maintaining production while conserving natural resources, an agenda which needs to move more rapidly to contain climate change and other natural calamities. Whereas international organizations contributed to past transformations, huge challenges remain in the 21st century.

As of 2015, 10 percent of the world's people (736 million) lived on less than US\$1.90 a day.[1] More than 820 million, or 1 in 9 people in the world, are undernourished,[2] with more than 2 billion suffering from one or more micronutrient deficiencies,[3] and importantly, nearly 2 billion are overweight or obese and their numbers are growing,[4] while 5.4 million children died in 2017 before reaching their fifth birthdays, mostly from preventable diseases.[5] Despite economic growth, more poor live in South Asia than in sub-Saharan Africa, and 70.8 million people were displaced at the time of sending this book to the publisher.[6]

Going forward, the challenges for the transformation of agriculture include:

1. Rebuilding and recognizing the role of strong, more participatory, multilateral processes to reflect the changing balance and dynamics of power, as the US reengages, Asia continues its emergence, Latin America reasserts itself, Africa further coalesces, and Europe finds a common voice, all contributing to a multipolar world.
2. Population will reach 9.7 billion by 2050, with evident consequences for availability of healthy food (SDG2). Most of the population growth is projected to occur in sub-Saharan Africa, where the population will double by 2050, while some growth will occur in South Asia. India is expected to overtake China by 2027, as the world's most populous country.[7]
3. Increased income inequality within and across countries can lead to further poverty, unless political will is harnessed to meet the SDGs—in particular, SDG1 (no poverty), SDG5 (gender equality), and SDG10 (reduce inequalities).[8] COVID-19 has brought this reality home starkly.
4. Climate change is an existential threat, especially to a billion poor people, bringing planetary changes, with melting glaciers, rising oceans, and extreme events.
5. Increasing pressure on natural resources (land, water, and energy) is already leading to calls for harnessing new knowledge to manage food and agricultural systems sustainably without harming human health.

Will farmers, particularly small farmers in rural areas, be able to take advantage of the dramatic technological changes taking place, known as the fourth industrial revolution, or will they continue to leave agriculture to establish ever larger urban slums, in the absence of productive, remunerative employment? FAO projects that, globally, there is little scope for expansion of lands equipped for irrigation, with only a small increase possible in irrigated

---

[1] World Bank, "Poverty": https://www.worldbank.org/en/topic/poverty/overview

[2] FAO et al., *The State of Food Security and Nutrition in the World 2019. Safeguarding against Economic Slowdowns and Downturns*: http://www.fao.org/3/ca5162en/ca5162en.pdf

[3] HarvestPlus, "Nutrition": https://www.harvestplus.org/what-we-do/nutrition

[4] EatForum.org, "More Than Two Billion People Overweight or Obese": https://eatforum.org/learn-and-discover/more-than-two-billion-people-overweight-or-obese/

[5] United Nations Children's Fund (UNICEF), "Under-five Mortality": https://data.unicef.org/topic/child-survival/under-five-mortality/

[6] United Nations High Commissioner for Refugees (UNHCR), "Figures at a Glance, June 18, 2020": https://www.unhcr.org/en-us/figures-at-a-glance.html

[7] United Nations, Department of Economic and Social Affairs, "World Population Prospects 2019": https://population.un.org/wpp/Publications/Files/WPP2019_DataBooklet.pdf

[8] United Nations, Department of Economic and Social Affairs, "Sustainable Development: The 17 Goals": https://sdgs.un.org/goals

hectares, mostly in sub-Saharan Africa and South America, albeit a low base. Deforestation is on the rise, and widespread soil degradation continues, often but not only as a result of intensive agriculture, with both leading to biodiversity loss. Challenges of agriculture have been made worse by extreme weather events and increasing risk and uncertainty, including in the global trading environment. The interconnectivity of these changes and events, however, is increasingly being realized. The consequence is the pressing need for better understanding, evidence, and analysis of these relationships and systems.

International organizations have depended on the United States and OECD countries for financing. The organizations are underfunded with fragmented funding support. Increasing roles of emerging countries offer new opportunities for global governance of food and agriculture, South–South international cooperation, and harnessing private and public capital. However, international cooperation among traditional partners has changed slowly, incrementally, and organically, and at times, moved in the wrong direction, often missing the opportunities for new modalities of cooperation.

The basic foundations of the international architecture, starting with the founding of the United Nations, the Bretton Woods institutions, FAO, and many others, were built with the leadership of the United States. The US disengagement by the Trump administration from the Paris Accord on Climate Change, withdrawal from the Trans-Pacific Partnership, reduction of funding of IFAD, withdrawal of support for the United Nations Educational, Scientific and Cultural Organization (UNESCO) and the Court of Human Rights, and reduction of support for some other UN operations raised questions about the existing "rules-based," old liberal order on which international cooperation was based for decades. The US election in 2020 would presume a reset and reengagement. Nevertheless, a renewed EU, philanthropic foundations, emerging countries, think tanks, private capital flows, and civil society have become increasingly important players in global governance. It is timely, given that the 17th SDG calls for multi-stakeholder partnerships to support the means of implementation to achieving the SDGs. In addition, the fourth industrial revolution has brought extraordinary technological changes in connectivity, computing, genomics, and many other fields, not the least of which are the giant information technology (IT) companies and social media.

As global governance dynamics shift, this book critically examines the roles played by developing countries in partnership with major multilateral agencies and their bilateral counterparts, in addressing agricultural and rural development, as a way to achieve economic transformation. With most of the poverty now in low-middle-income and middle-income countries, future challenges are multisectoral, multidimensional, and multilevel. Developing countries need trillions of dollars of investment in infrastructure, health, education, and agriculture. There is immense need for public goods: for example, agricultural R&D, mitigation and adaptation to climate change, building of resilience by communities to address growing risks, and control of communicable diseases, among others. The UN Secretary General's Food Summit in 2021 is intended to address some of these issues.[9]

In several individual chapters, the book explores what member nations of the United Nations, working with international organizations, have been able to achieve thus far in food and agriculture and in economic transformation. How have they responded to the rapidly changing external and internal factors, and how well equipped are they to address future challenges of poverty, food security and nutrition, inequality, climate change, and

---

[9] United Nations, "UN Food Systems Summit 2021": https://www.un.org/en/food-systems-summit

conflict, in the face of rapidly deteriorating natural resources? Discovering the answers to these questions make this discussion all the more urgent. Most importantly, we explore the roles of the international organizations vis-à-vis new actors, philanthropists, and the private sector.

The book was written before the global COVID-19 pandemic. The pandemic was predicted for several years by experts, including Bill Gates, but ignored by policymakers at the time. The International Monetary Fund estimates the pandemic has led to a global gross domestic product (GDP) loss of US$9 trillion in nearly 200 countries.[10] Timely investments in preparing for the pandemic would have had high rates of return. The pandemic has laid bare structural weaknesses among the mightiest economies of income inequalities, lack of universal access to health, and lack of trust in government. Smaller Asian Tigers—Taiwan, Singapore, and South Korea—and China, where it originated, had smarter responses, demonstrating their superiority in state capacity.

As historian Ramachandra Guha has noted, COVID-19 is at least a sixfold crisis— medical, economic, humanitarian, social, psychological, and of governance—and the worst hit are poor people throughout the world, including in the poorest countries.[11] An astute response to it of testing, isolating, and treating the infected calls for scientific, political, economic, medical, social, and psychological resources and international cooper- ation, which most countries have lacked. They are also the kind of characteristic responses that other global crises confronting the world—climate change, financial crises, and civil strife—will require.

That is why this book is both relevant and timely. It is an account of international cooperation over 70 years on food security and nutrition security and the implications for addressing the remaining challenges of hunger and food insecurity, which have been compounded by the COVID-19 pandemic.

Such responses, as the book outlines, come from a spectrum of multilateral institutions, only some of which are reviewed here. Those institutions have addressed, and continue to address, their own challenges of roles, accountability, membership, financing, and actions. Several of these changes are ongoing, driven both by current geopolitical and natural (climatic) events and by initiatives such as the forthcoming Food Systems Summit 2021. The UN Scientific Group for the Summit, an independent and diverse group of leading researchers and scientists from around the world, including Uma Lele, is responsible for ensuring the robustness and independence of the science underpinning the Summit, and will inform the Summit's content and recommended outcomes, as well as clarify the commitments emerging from the Summit.[12] The successful adaption and change of the institutions remains a critical prerequisite for the necessary agricultural transformation.

---

[10] See Gita Gopinath, "The Great Lockdown: Worst Economic Downturn Since the Great Depression," April 14, 2020, https://blogs.imf.org/2020/04/14/the-great-lockdown-worst-economic-downturn-since-the-great-depression/

[11] See Ramachandra Guha, "The Darkest Hour. Politics and Play: A Six-Fold Crisis Confronts India," May 22, 2020, https://www.telegraphindia.com/opinion/coronavirus-a-six-fold-crisis-confronts-india/cid/1775032

[12] See the membership roster for the Summit's Scientific Group: https://sc-fss2021.org/about-us/membership/

PART I
THE OVERARCHING ENVIRONMENT

1

Food for All: Setting the Scene

Uma Lele and Sambuddha Goswami

It is not the strongest of the species that survives, nor the most intelligent, but the one most responsive to change.

Leon C. Megginson[1]

The Transforming Dynamics of Poverty, Food Security, and Nutrition

In 2015, member states of the United Nations (UN) embraced two global agreements of historic proportions—one on sustainable development and the other on climate change. Will it be possible, however, to generate the political will, set the rules, and undertake the reforms in global and national governance that will be needed to achieve the promised outcomes for humanity? How, in particular, will the world produce and consume food and manage agriculture sustainably, to deliver healthy food for all, in a rapidly changing world? And how will multilateral organizations support the opportunities and face the challenges of "the fourth industrial revolution" (Schwab 2016) to achieve adequate, nutritious food for all, for all time, in all places? The fourth industrial revolution, following on from the third electronic and information revolution, is characterized by its extraordinary speed, disruptive technological change, and breadth and depth of scientific, technological, and sociopolitical changes. We do not yet understand the full significance or likely impacts of these still unfolding changes, but the revolution is occurring, with some long-term trends already underway.

Among these trends are climate change, first accelerating and then slowing globalization, expanding trade in food and agriculture, and yet, growing trade uncertainties, demographic transition, rapid urbanization, dietary transition, and growing horizontal (cross-sectoral) and vertical (from farm-to-fork) integration. Meanwhile, conflict has caused the largest displacement of human population since the Second World War. Forced migration from humanitarian disasters is making unprecedented demands on food and financial assistance, not to mention the suffering of those displaced, including women and children, with no end in sight.

Economists traditionally have viewed structural transformation from agriculture to manufacturing as a pivotal ambition of developing countries. This transformation has become increasingly difficult for lagging countries. Yet, other transformations are also reshaping the global economy, including financial transformation (a shift from the

---

[1] This quote is frequently misattributed to Charles Darwin, even placed in the stone floor of the California Academy of Sciences, only to have the original attribution removed. The quote actually comes from Megginson, a professor of management and marketing at Louisiana State University. See https://www.darwinproject.ac.uk/people/about-darwin/six-things-darwin-never-said/evolution-misquotation

Food for All: International Organizations and the Transformation of Agriculture. Uma Lele, Manmohan Agarwal, Brian C. Baldwin, and Sambuddha Goswami, Oxford University Press. © Uma Lele, Manmohan Agarwal, Brian C. Baldwin, and Sambuddha Goswami 2021. DOI: 10.1093/oso/9780198755173.003.0002

traditional North–South global savings and investment pattern to South–North: that is, developing countries, and particularly China, being the source of global savings and investments), and energy transformation (shift from fossil fuels to renewables, which could be faster with different energy policies).

Concurrently, the food and agricultural sectors are confronting new paradigms, such as environmentally sustainable food production and shifting focus in agriculture from individual energy (calorie) supply to nutritious foods with links to health, leading to a life-cycle approach to diets. These new paradigms are influencing how structural transformation and the role of agriculture are being viewed by the international development community, particularly for countries with a large proportion of poverty and hunger in rural areas. This chapter sets the stage for an inquiry into food, transformations, international organizations and their interactions, and implications for a better outcome: nutritious food for all that is environmentally sustainable.

Curious readers want to know, where does the food supply of a country come from? The Food and Agriculture Organization of the United Nations (FAO) measures food support in terms of Food Balance Sheets and defines it as:

> Domestic supply quantity: Production + imports − exports + changes in stocks (decrease or increase) = Supply for domestic utilization

There are various ways of defining supply and, in fact, many concepts are in use. The elements involved are production, imports, exports, and changes in stocks (increase or decrease). There is no doubt that production, imports, and stock changes (either decrease or increase in stocks) are genuine supply elements.[2] The concept is not without its critics. Estimates of production, utilization, and stocks are routinely criticized. Nevertheless, food balance sheets in recent years suggest that nearly 90 percent of the food supply in the United States and China in net terms (after allowing for imports and exports) comes from domestic production, and as much as 97 percent in India, 85 percent in SSA, and only 70 percent in Europe and Canada.

In the rest of this book, we discuss changes in the various components of the food balance sheets over time and across countries, and how domestic policies and international trade affect these food balance sheets.

Global Compacts: Sustainable Development Goals and Climate Change

In 2015, the 193 member countries of the UN and nearly 200 member-parties of the UN Framework Convention on Climate Change (UNFCCC) made two historic agreements. The first, in September at the UN in New York, set forth, through the 2030 Agenda for Action, 17 Sustainable Development Goals (SDGs) with 169 targets (see UN [2020] for a description of all SDGs and their targets). The SDGs take forward to 2030 the unfulfilled Millennium Development Goals (MDGs), adopted in 2000. The second agreement came, after a prolonged stalemate, at the conclusion of COP21 (the Paris Climate Conference) in

---

[2] See Food Balance Sheets (http://www.fao.org/economic/ess/fbs/en/); New Food Balances: Description of utilization variables (http://fenixservices.fao.org/faostat/static/documents/FBS/New%20FBS%20methodology.pdf); and Food Balance Sheet Methodology (http://www.fao.org/economic/ess/fbs/ess-fbs02/en/).

December 2015, when the world community reached the Paris Agreement on Climate Change (UNFCCC 2015). At the time of the signing ceremony on April 22, 2016, 175 countries had already signed the agreement, showing their strong interest in pursuing its objectives. However, at the UN Climate Change Conference (COP25) in Madrid in December 2019, UN Secretary-General António Guterres noted his disappointment with the results of COP25 on Twitter: "The international community lost an important opportunity to show increased ambition on mitigation, adaptation & finance to tackle the climate crisis."

The Paris Agreement's central aim is to strengthen the global response to climate change by keeping the rise in the global average temperatures in this century to well below 2 °C above preindustrial levels, pursuing efforts to limit the temperature increase further to 1.5 °C. Additionally, the agreement aims to strengthen the ability of countries to adapt and build resilience to impacts of climate change and to make finance flows consistent with a pathway toward low greenhouse gas (GHG) emissions and climate-resilient development. Scaling up countries' efforts to strengthen their response to climate change and making the most of co-benefits and synergistic action is vital to the aim of achieving the temperature goal of the agreement, while at the same time building countries' resilience to the adverse effects of climate change.

According to the Intergovernmental Panel on Climate Change (IPCC) special report on the impacts of global warming of 1.5 °C, the goal is possible, but requires urgent and unprecedented transitions across all aspects of society, over the next 10 to 20 years, including our energy, agricultural, urban, and industrial systems, the engagement of non-state actors, and integration of climate action into the broader public policy framework, which also addresses jobs, security, and technology (IPCC 2014). The World Meteorological Organization (WMO) reported that as 2019 ended, it was likely to be the second or third warmest year on record, with melting ice, rising sea levels, coastal flooding, powerful hurricanes, and wildfires. "Average temperatures for the five-year (2015–2019) and ten-year (2010–2019) periods are almost certain to be the highest on record" (WMO 2019). Climate change activism, particularly among the young who will face the brunt of warming, gathered new momentum, with calls for changing the way we produce and eat food and urging faster emission reductions.

Regrettably, the Trump administration announced it would withdraw from the Paris Agreement, as it did from other international agreements, as outlined in this chapter. The Biden administration has already reversed some of these policies and is reassessing others.

The Sustainable Development Goals: Resetting the Agenda

The SDGs are far more expansive and ambitious than the MDGs, which consisted of eight goals and 21 associated targets (UN 2016), developed out of several commitments set forth in the Millennium Declaration, signed in September 2000. The MDGs focused on developing countries, and SDGs have expanded the scope to acknowledge the interconnectedness of global development by including *all* developing and developed countries. Thus, SDGs are universal in scope. They have also shifted focus from inputs of aid and investment capital to development outcomes and their measurement, cross-country monitoring of performance, and accountability for results. The MDGs focused on outcomes in the low-income, developing countries of Asia and sub-Saharan Africa (SSA). They were simple in scope and easy to communicate to policymakers and citizens. They were developed by the initiative of international organizations, with input from academics and stakeholders, largely from donor countries. Progress toward the global targets of the MDGs was measured over 25 years (to 2015), applying a 1990 baseline and a uniform standard by which each developing country, irrespective of local content, was expected to achieve every goal. Based on more recent data and more consultative processes, the SDGs are applicable to all developed and developing countries, and progress toward these goals is being measured over a shorter period (to 2030). So, to reach these goals, all parties need to do their part individually and collectively—governments, the private sector, civil society, and private citizens.

The new post-2015 international development agenda, described in "Transforming Our World: The 2030 Agenda for Sustainable Development" (UN 2015b), builds on the MDGs and on the Rio +20 Summit principles, articulated in "The Future We Want" (UN 2013). Based on the deliberations of the Secretary-General's proposed framework in their synthesis report (UN 2014b), the Sustainable Development Summit outcome document, "Transforming Our World: The 2030 Agenda for Sustainable Development," captures the broad scope of the agenda in its preamble, which identifies the "five Ps"—people, planet, prosperity, peace, and partnership. These are the key topics for policy dialogue and policy action (UN 2015b, 1–2). Table A.1.1 in the Appendix describes the five Ps in the outcome document and the six clusters of the Secretary-General's proposal, along with the related SDGs and relevant MDGs.

Most of the 17 SDGs are interrelated, reflecting the growing complexity of the development process in which many players are adapting to change and to each other. With growing risks and uncertainty, the emerging future is hard to predict, and adaptive management has become the central theme (Axelrod and Cohen 1999). SDG1 and SDG10 address poverty and inequality, and they are integrally related to the rest of the SDGs. SDGs 2, 6, and 7 are concerned with hunger, food security, improved nutrition and sustainable agriculture, water and sanitation, and energy. The relationship between monetary income/poverty in SDG1 and food security (SDGs 2, 6, and 7) is more complex than appears on the surface. Increased income does not necessarily result in increased food security, unless other SDGs have been achieved. SDGs 3, 4, and 5 focus on health, education, and gender equality. They reflect the multidimensionality of poverty and affect food security and nutrition in complex ways. SDG8 and SDG9 address economic growth, productive employment, infrastructure, industrialization, and innovation. They are integrally related to the extent of formality or informality of employment in agriculture and other sectors, and influence the rate of structural transformation of economies from agriculture to other sectors. SDGs 11 and 12 are concerned with human settlements and sustainable consumption and production, including the quality and quantity of food. SDGs 13, 14, and 15 address climate change, oceans, and conservation of natural resources. Climate change is an existential threat to agriculture and other sectors. SDGs 16 and 17 pertain to peaceful societies and fragility, crime and violence, corruption, access to justice, capable and accountable entities, and global partnerships (UN 2020).

SDG Target 8.3 aims to promote policies that support productive activities and job creation, and to encourage the formalization and growth of micro-, small- and medium-sized enterprises (SMEs), including through access to financial services. The International Labour Conference in 2015 adopted the Transition from the Informal to the Formal Economy Recommendation (No. 204), the first international labor standard that focuses on the informal economy in its entirety (ILO 2015).

The SDGs have galvanized the global community, but they also have critics. William Easterly, in a *Foreign Policy* article, called them "utopian," "unmeasurable," "unactionable," and "unattainable," as well as being unfinanced, having "both too many items and too little content for each one" (Easterly 2015). With fiscal woes and the pressure of refugees entering Europe, progress on the financing of SDGs was slow at the Addis Ababa meeting in July 2015, and even the staunchest supporters of SDGs, including Jeffrey Sachs, have taken a wait-and-see attitude (ADB 2015; Sachs 2015). A 2019 report on financing of SDGs notes that the total revenue of the UN System in 2017 was a mere US$53.2 billion, coming from a combination of assessed contributions, voluntary contributions, negotiated pledges, and a small amount of fees. Governments still provided 74 percent of the direct funding to the UN Development System (UNDS) in 2017, and as much as 57 percent came from Organisation for Economic Co-operation and Development–Development Assistance Committee (OECD–DAC) countries. The majority of government contributions actually came from a small group of UN member states, with 12 member states providing 65 percent of the total contributions in 2017 (the United States, Germany, the United Kingdom, European Union (EU) institutions, Sweden, Japan, Norway, Canada, the Netherlands, Switzerland, Denmark, and Italy, in descending order of contribution) (Jenks and Topping 2019, 14–15). The report contains arguments, such as that of John W. McArthur, Senior Fellow with the Brookings Institution's Global Economic and Development Program, that the headline "From Billions to Trillions" after the Addis Ababa conference on financing was misleading (Development Committee 2015; Jenks and Topping 2019, 89–92). More country-by-country and regional approaches are needed to develop an understanding of the extent of the financing gap.

The Sustainable Development Goals: The Need for Measurement

Beyond the ability of the MDGs and SDGs to focus attention on large development challenges, their potential value critically depends on mobilizing international and domestic efforts and monitoring progress. The biggest declines in poverty, hunger, and other social indicators over the past 25 years have occurred in China and Southeast Asia, largely as a result of domestic effort, but with critical access to international markets and finance made possible by their memberships in Bretton Woods institutions. With few exceptions, attributing achievements to external assistance is difficult in most circumstances, because unlike the case of CGIAR, and more recently, that of the International Fund for Agricultural Development (IFAD), there are no impact studies. Nevertheless, external assistance did contribute in some cases to a strong domestic commitment that has continued, with predictability of policies, investments, institutional capacity, and political will, is necessary for the creation of an enabling environment with some direct assistance at the margin. Much of the remaining poverty and hunger and other low social indicators that the SDGs aspire to eradicate are in South Asia (SA) and SSA.

In part, the lagging indicators are a result of the absence of preconditions, misdirected domestic policies, and external assistance, as we discuss in the chapters that follow. They are also explained by rapid population growth. According to UN population projections, Africa's population will continue to grow well into the end of the 21st century, reaching 4.4 billion (UN 2015c). SA's population is projected to peak at 2.5 billion in 2069, and its total rural population will peak at 1.2 billion in 2028. By 2041, urban populations in SA and Africa, 1.06 billion each, will exceed East Asia's urban population. In Africa, however, rural population will also continue to grow and will exceed SA's rural population just after 2050, putting immense pressure on natural resources (UN 2014c).

By 2030, the World Bank projects that most of the world's poverty will be eradicated, and the remaining poverty will be concentrated in SSA. These projections were moderated in 2019–2020 to suggest poverty levels of 500 million by 2030. FAO, however, projects that hunger will decline less rapidly in SA than the World Bank's scenario, so that both SA and SSA will experience the remaining incidence of global hunger. The real divergence among regions will continue after 2030. Structural transformation of countries, discussed in Chapter 2 in all its dimensions, which was taken for granted in the past, is proving to be difficult for some countries to achieve, particularly, the ability to industrialize. For the regions lagging behind in transformation, a greater burden will fall on agriculture, which will support most of the population, and hence the achievement of SDGs—the future ability to feed people and reduce hunger—will also be constrained by land availability and productivity. Generally, Asia and SA, in particular, have already reached the limit of the extensive margin of cultivable land, and pressures on natural resources have increased considerably. Parts of SSA are rapidly shifting from having surplus land to being land-constrained subregions. Agricultural productivity is low, productivity growth has been slow, and sustainable intensification is the way for the two continents to feed their growing urban and more prosperous populations.

The Paris Agreement: Progress to Date

The Climate Change Agreement sets out a global action plan to put the world on track to limit global warming to well below 2°C. The agreement will enter into force in 2020. The Kyoto Protocol's principle of binding (industrial) countries to commitments, however, already had to be abandoned for softer, "intended" commitments in the Paris Agreement, which committed all (developed, as well as developing) countries to their declared intended targets in order to reach agreement. Without the United States and China agreeing to emission reductions through bilateral talks in advance of the Paris Agreement, reaching even the diluted accord would not have been possible, given the lack of acknowledgment of climate change in some key US constituencies. The good news is that, with the Biden–Harris government in power, the United States has rejoined the Paris Agreement with great energy and appointed former Secretary of State John Kerry as the US Special Presidential Envoy for Climate with authority over energy policy and climate policy within the executive branch. How disastrous the policy of Trump administration was, however, is worth recounting. On June 1, 2017, under an "America First" policy, the US President Donald Trump announced that the United States would not implement the Paris Agreement, citing a series of arguably debatable and ill-informed reasons (WhiteHouse.gov 2017).

In December 2018, at a meeting of the parties, the US intention to withdraw was reiterated in the statement, "absent the identification of terms that are more favorable to the American people." The US State Department notified the Secretary-General that it would provide formal notification "as soon as it is eligible to do so." Under Article 28 of the Paris Agreement, the earliest possible date for the withdrawal to take effect was November 4, 2020. Until then, the US delegation continued to participate, which included reporting its GHG emissions to the United Nations (CRS 2019), and the November 2020 US election has provided an opportunity for reengagement, considering there is a significant body of US public opinion in favor of climate action, much as the Democrats in Congress demonstrated earlier (Holden 2019).

International reactions to the US withdrawal from the Paris Agreement were overwhelmingly negative. World leaders rejected Trump's claim that the Agreement could be renegotiated, expressing disapproval of his decision. France's leader, Emmanuel Macron, stated that Trump had "committed an error for the interests of his country, his people and a mistake for the future of our planet" (Watts and Connally 2017). Nevertheless, the parties have "agreed on most of the 'rulebook' for implementing the PA's provisions" (CRS 2019). China's Special Representative on Climate Change suggested the concerns about the US withdrawal had been lessened, in part, because of China's pledge to meet its commitments fully, asserting that China "sent out a strong political signal" by helping "stabilize" international climate change efforts (CRS 2019). Together, the Agreement partners pledged to push onward without the "world's second-largest emitter." Bilateral and multilateral agreements have arisen "to circumvent" traditional leadership in the US. Some of the participant countries, including China, have strengthened their Paris pledges (Chemnick 2019). Still, Chemnick noted in a 2018 essay reprinted by *Scientific American* that without the United States' involvement, other countries may be less motivated to cut their own emissions, referencing a former Cabinet member of the Indian government, Montek Singh Ahluwalia, who was concerned that in the United States' absence, there would be less pressure on other states to comply with the Agreement (Chemnick 2019). Without action on climate, food security and nutrition will be severely set back for the poorest countries and people.

In the Paris Agreement, governments decided to work to define a clear roadmap for ratcheting up climate finance to US$100 billion by 2020, while also agreeing to set a new goal on the provision of finance from the US$100 billion floor before 2025. The Obama administration and 19 other countries had promised to work toward doubling their spending over five years to support clean energy research (Goldenberg 2016). At the same time, 28 private investors, including Microsoft's Bill Gates, Facebook's Mark Zuckerberg, and Amazon's Jeff Bezos, pledged their own money to help build private businesses based on the public research. The 20 governments and investors are calling their joint effort "Mission Innovation," because incentives for individual private investment are less clear. As Bill Gates indicated, returns to clean energy in the short term are less likely than in the technology field, given the 20-year limit on patents, which are less applicable in the longer maturation of energy investments (Bennet 2015, 58).

Following Trump's rejection of the international agreement, 24 US governors joined together to form a bipartisan coalition, representing 55 percent of the population. The coalition, the United States Climate Alliance, with its Secretariat housed at the United Nations Foundation, committed to aggressive climate action, including implementing policies to advance the goals of the Paris Agreement and tracking and reporting progress to the global community (US Climate Alliance 2019).

The Governance of Transition

The processes leading to these and other global agreements offer important insights into the way the world community is governing itself without a global government—without a mandate to tax global citizens, very limited ability to enforce rules, and unequal voice and power in the "institutions" of global governance. The term "institutions" in this book is used in the sense that Nobel Laureate Douglass North conceived the term: namely, formal and informal rules by which players play the game (North 1990). By "players," we mean member governments, international organizations, philanthropists, the private sector, civil society, and professional organizations, among others (Box 1.1).

The global organizations that we review in this book form a subset of global institutions of governance, as defined in this chapter. They are unable to address many of the current challenges, or to deal with challenges of the fourth industrial revolution, consisting of extraordinary changes in technology and the associated growing importance of social media. Three important characteristics of these changes are their speed, disruptive nature, and breadth and depth, and the changes have profound implications for the future (Buytaert and Raj 2016). We do not fully understand the implications of this revolution, but there seems to be consensus that there is a heightening of risk and uncertainty, already incorporated in strategy formulations since the 2007–8 triple food, energy, and financial crises, and now in addressing the scale, speed, and complexity of the COVID-19 pandemic.

Given the rapidity with which changes are occurring, management of the transition to the fourth industrial revolution is urgently needed. Who should manage this transition? Are current fora effective, with Davos increasingly seen as a white male preserve and thereby missing a broader, more credible pool of talent and knowledge (Barry 2016)? Since then, Davos has been diversifying. Addressing the World Economic Forum's Annual Meeting at Davos, on January 17, 2017, China's President Xi Jinping stressed the importance of globalization, trade, and climate change (CGTN America 2017). At the next World Economic Summit in Davos the following year, in January 2018, Prime Minister Modi also stressed many of the same issues: the importance of globalization and climate change, and the need for taking forward the Doha Development Agenda on trade (*Financial Express* 2018).

Box 1.1 Institutions

Douglass North's analytical framework explains the ways in which institutions and institutional change affect the performance of economies, both at a given time and over time. According to North, institutions are a system of rules, which explain the link with the changes that they have undergone in terms of routines, transaction costs, political practices, and other behavioral features. The nature of institutions explains the role of transaction and production costs in their development. North's framework helps us to understand growth and development in the course of structural transformation. Institutions exist due to the uncertainties involved in human interactions; they are the constraints devised to structure the interactions. Yet, institutions vary widely in their consequences for economic performance; some economies develop institutions that produce growth and development, while other economies develop institutions that produce stagnation. Institutions create the incentive structure in an economy, and organizations will be created to take advantage of the opportunities provided within a given institutional framework. North argued that the kinds of skills and knowledge fostered by the structure of the economy shape the direction of change and gradually alter the institutional framework. He then explained how institutional development could lead to a path-dependent pattern of development.

Source: North (1990).

There is a broad scientific consensus that achieving sufficient mitigation requires an unprecedented transition to a low-carbon economy. Limiting global warming to 1.5° requires reductions of 45 percent in CO_2 emissions by 2030, and to reach net zero by 2050. Despite the 2015 Paris Agreement, GHG emissions are high and rising, fossil fuels continue to dominate the global energy mix, and the price of carbon remains low, reinforcing the need for a variety of complementary policies (UN 2019).

With the increasing number of actors, where will the leadership come from? International organizations, with their long experience, remain important players in helping to develop consensus, mobilize resources, and bring together diverse, knowledgeable, international stakeholders. Their strong legitimacy, however, has eroded since the global financial crisis in 2008, and their roles have diminished relatively, in financial terms, with the growing roles of other flows of finance, including from philanthropists, the private sector, and remittances, as well as with the growing role of emerging countries. The same is true in terms of ideas and policy prescriptions from a wider array of international stakeholders, such as nongovernmental organizations (NGOs) and think tanks. We discuss the emergence and the role of the G20 vis-à-vis international organizations in later chapters on global governance.

The State of Climate and Sustainable Development Goals Financing

The UNFCCC provides no official definition of climate finance, but its Standing Committee on Finance (SCF) proposed to view it broadly as all efforts aimed at reduction in the emissions of GHG (mitigation) or reduction of vulnerability (and increased resilience) to climate change impacts (adaptation) (UNFCCC 2014). More specifically, climate finance usually refers to finance flows from developed to developing countries in order to help them to mitigate and adapt to climate changes (Fankhauser 2013). At the UN Copenhagen Climate Change Conference in 2009, developed countries pledged to reach US$100 billion in annual funding by 2020 to help developing countries adapt to climate change and invest in low-carbon technologies. Leaders of developed economies also pledged to mobilize Fast-Start Finance (FSF) of US$30 billion between 2010 and 2012. The report by the SCF (UNFCCC 2014) indicated that the developed countries fulfilled this pledge, exceeding it by US$33 billion, but the problem of how to build a mechanism for steady flows to reach the US$100 billion annual goal is far from solved. Again, estimates vary, and it is likely that most of the finance and efforts will have to come from developing countries.[3]

The current level of funding falls far short of these needs. As of November 2017, the Green Climate Fund (GCF 2020) had raised US$10.3 billion equivalent in pledges from 43 state governments, of the estimated US$100 billion sought. According to the UNFCCC (2016) Biennial Assessment, global total climate finance had increased by almost 15 percent

---

[3] A World Bank report (2010) estimated annual funding needs of US$28 to US$100 for adaptation by 2030 and US$139–$175 billion for mitigation (in 2005 prices) to limit climate warming to 2°C. The World Economic Forum (WEF 2013) estimated that the total cost of additional, incremental infrastructure investments required by 2020 to secure the 2°C emissions path as US$700 billion annually. The International Energy Agency (IEA 2014) predicted that achieving the UNFCCC climate target requires US$5 trillion more than in the core scenario for global energy supplies. Flows of funds will have to be designed differently—less money should be spent on extraction and transportation of fossil fuels and much more on energy efficiency, particularly in the field of transport or the building industry.

since 2011–12 (US$650 billion), to US$741 billion for 2014;[4] with total finance at US$687 billion in 2013, the annual average was US$714 billion over 2013–14. Private investment in renewable energy and energy efficiency represents the largest share of the global total. Including the partial data on domestic public finance expenditures of US$192 billion per year, the upper end of the range is raised to US$880 billion in 2013 and US$930 billion in 2014.

Climate Policy Initiative (CPI) takes a different approach to accounting, estimating annual global climate finance to be US$342 billion and US$392 billion, for 2013 and 2014, respectively,[5] an annual average of US$67 billion over 2013–14, only about 51 percent of the UNFCCC estimate. The numbers differ significantly because the UNFCCC takes a more generous approach to spending on energy efficiency. According to the CPI report, total global climate finance was 9 percent higher in 2014 than in 2012, due to a steady increase in public finance and record levels of private investment in renewable energy, the dominant sector, with more than 70 percent of climate finance every year from 2012 to 2014 (Mazza, Falzon, and Buchner 2016).

The data on South–South climate finance are limited; it was estimated in the range of US $5.9–9.1 billion for 2013 and US$7.2–11.7 billion for 2014, of which about half was channeled through multilateral institutions (UNFCCC 2016). In December 2017, China announced the largest carbon trading fund, several times the European fund and the California fund, securing its position as a leader in climate finance.

China's entry into climate finance is of considerable significance because most of the investments are made in the country of origin. Flows from developed to developing countries were much lower: public entities contributed from US$35 billion to US$50 billion, and private agents contributed from US$5 billion to US$125 billion per year (UNFCCC 2014) (see, also, UNTT [2013]; Wąsiński [2015]). Most went to mitigation and relatively little to adaptation.

International Monetary Fund (IMF) staff take an altogether different approach to financing by championing a carbon tax to address climate change, along with fiscal policies to discourage carbon emissions from coal and other polluting fossil fuels, including increasing the price of carbon emissions to give people and firms incentives to reduce energy use and shift to clean energy sources (Gaspar et al. 2019).

The financing needs of the SDGs are similarly considerable, estimated to be US$4.5 trillion annually, exceeding 2014 levels of official development assistance (ODA) by 30 times (UNCTAD 2014). These are only ballpark figures, and estimates vary widely by source and are not comparable—there is a range of estimates by different entities, covering different issues—but the basic point remains.

In 2020, official development assistance (ODA) by member countries of the Development Assistance Committee (DAC) amounted to USD161.2 billion, representing 0.32% of their combined GNI [gross national income]. This total included USD158.0 billion in the form of grants, loans, to sovereign entities, debt relief, and contributions to multilateral institutions (calculated on a grant-equivalent basis); USD1.3 billion to development-oriented

---

[4] Calculated as the upper range of CPI estimates (US$346 billion in 2013 and US$397 billion in 2014) plus the investment in energy efficiency (US$334 billion in 2013 and US$337 billion in 2014), plus sustainable transport (not available), land use (US$5 billion), and adaptation (US$1.5 billion), the same for both 2013 and 2014. This estimate includes both public and private monies, from development banks, money spent domestically, and money flowing between countries.

[5] The CPI ranges for overall climate finance were US$346 billion (high boundary) and US$339 billion (low boundary) in 2013 and US$397 billion (high boundary) and US$387 billion (low boundary) in 2014.

private sector instrument (PSI) vehicles and USD1.9 billion in the form of net loans and equities to private companies operating in ODA-eligible countries.

Total ODA in 2020 rose by 3.5% in real terms compared to 2019, reaching its highest level ever recorded. (OECD 2021, 1)

The investment needs of developing countries are large, and ODA will not be a significant source of future funding,[6] as tax revenues and private investments provide much of the resources for development of developing countries (Renwick 2015). "Given the global economic impacts of the pandemic, it is uncertain if ODA volumes can continue to grow or remain stable in the coming years" (OECD 2021, 1).

Whether these projections on aid and capital flows will materialize remains to be seen, particularly in the context of slowed global economic growth.

The SDGs and the climate agreement have shifted the global dialogue from aid levels to global financial flows, including domestic resource mobilization (World Bank and IMF 2015). With fiscal woes, aid weariness, and an influx of refugees into OECD countries, the prospects for increasing aid are not bright. With rapid growth in emerging countries, however, since the beginning of the millennium, the balance of economic power has shifted from the Global North to a multipolar world, including, particularly, the Global South and East. Combined with growing inequality and the rise of philanthropy from the billionaire class, the nature of international cooperation and assistance has changed significantly, with important implications for global and national governance.

The Pace and Direction of Transformation

In this inquiry, we focus on poverty, food security, and nutrition, addressed by SDGs 1 and 2 and drawing on several other related SDGs. Furthermore, we view the SDGs through the lens of structural transformation of countries and the role of multilateral organizations. The process of structural transformation has been of intense interest to economists and frequently described as having several distinct characteristics: (1) declining share of agriculture in the gross domestic product (GDP) and in employment; (2) rural–urban migration; (3) growth of the service and the manufacturing sectors; and (4) a demographic transition with a reduction in the population growth rates. The final outcome of transformation is a state in which differences in labor productivity between the agricultural and nonagricultural sectors narrow considerably, compared to early stages of development when there is often a huge and even a widening gap in labor productivities between agriculture and nonagricultural sectors. A turning point is reached when the difference between the share of agriculture in employment and income begins to narrow.

Agricultural productivity growth is crucial to the transformation process, and analysts of structural transformation have traditionally focused on changing labor productivities among sectors over time. Analysts have noted that today's developing countries in Asia are taking longer to reach the turning point than was the historical experience of industrial

---

[6] The International Committee of Experts on Sustainable Development Financing (UN 2014a) estimated investment requirement in infrastructure (water, agriculture, telecoms, power, transport, buildings, industrial, and forestry sectors) amounting to US$5 trillion to US$7 trillion globally, and the cost of a global safety net to eliminate extreme poverty at about US$66 billion annually. The Addis Ababa Action Agenda described the global infrastructure gap as including "the $1 trillion to $1.5 trillion annual gap in developing countries" (UN 2015a).

countries. Does the period of rapid economic growth in the post-2000 period offer a more promising picture? Do these observations apply only to Asia? How do they differ among countries within Asia and across regions, such as in Africa and Latin America?

Yet, agriculture is also critical to poverty alleviation, food security, and nutrition. Agriculture is expected to perform multiple ecosystem functions from carbon sequestration to saving biodiversity, forests, marine life, and water flows. Eliminating hunger, not just to the level of the SDGs, but getting to a near zero share of the population in agriculture, as part of the growth and development process, has been the ambition and challenge for developing countries, particularly those with large shares of population, poverty, and hunger in the agricultural sector. To achieve this transformation calls for massive transformation in other areas. For example, macroeconomists expect external financing for the transformation to come largely from the East, mostly from China, and energy experts are expecting a transformation from fossil fuels to renewable energy to be largely funded by public–private partnerships. Each will be critical for structural transformation, increased agricultural productivity, and a declining share of agriculture.

Productivity Growth, Structural Transformation, and Employment

Two narratives have prevailed in the development literature on transformation, on the one hand by Kuznets (1955; 1966) and others (Lewis 1954; Johnston and Mellor 1961; Chenery and Syrquin 1975; Timmer and Akkus 2008; Binswanger-Mkhize, McCalla, and Patel 2010; Binswanger-Mkhize 2012; 2013), and on the other by those who question whether agriculture has (and should have) a primacy, or whether other sectors play (or should play) key roles, and within agriculture, whether smallholder agriculture—which has dominated in Asia—is the route to industrialization, particularly in SSA. Adrian Wood (Owens and Wood 1997; Wood 2003); Paul Collier and Stefan Dercon (Collier and Dercon 2014), Douglas Gollin (Dercon and Gollin 2014); and John Page (Page 2015a, 2015b; Newman et al. 2016; Page and Dews 2016) have questioned the role of agriculture and, in particular, the role of smallholder agriculture relative to medium-sized and large farms and relative to the industrial sector. With few exceptions, however, most recent developers in Asia and Africa have found it difficult to create productive employment in manufacturing significant enough to achieve transformation (Rodrik 2014, 2016; Page 2015a, 2015b; de Melo 2017). Service sector growth has been rapid, and most of it is of low productivity (Hallward-Driemeier and Nayyar 2018).

What does the experience of developed countries offer? Gardner (2006) in his landmark study of American agriculture (in no way typical of all industrial countries, except in the share of population in agriculture, which now involves less than 2 percent in the United States), described how factor productivities between agriculture and nonagriculture were equalized in the United States, a key feature of structural transformation, and reported the good news and bad: tremendous productivity growth and land consolidation, combined with misery, bankruptcies, and poverty. Schumpeter (1943) described this process as creative destruction, and Willard Cochrane (1958) described it as a treadmill. Technological change has been a major driving force in agriculture for all transformed countries, greatly affecting farm structure and rural economies and societies. Cochrane (1958) argued that this did not look like it was about to change. The treadmill has been part of agricultural industrialization, with winners and losers. In explaining the treadmill, Cochrane (1958) noted that, with technological breakthroughs, agricultural output per acre of land and farmer increased.

Farmers, determined to increase their production, adopted new technologies, such as fertilizers and pesticides. Except for the early adopters, however, the transition would not increase farmers' profits, but rather place them on Cochrane's treadmill, a self-perpetuating cycle of technology, debt, exhausted soils, more technology, and more debt. The concept of the treadmill is used to explain trends in modern agriculture toward bigger industrial farms and agricultural practices that rely upon chemical inputs, either aggressively pursuing new technologies, or staying small and using off-farm income to survive. Both responses rely on government payments (Mitchell 2016). A question going forward is how technological change in agriculture will affect farms of different sizes in developing countries, with quite different initial structures, in a dynamic context with new paradigms of sustainable intensification and healthy nutritious food? What will it do to farm incomes?

In Chapter 2, on structural transformation, we take up the question of the structure of farm production in today's dynamic context, and particularly the highly skewed pattern of farm sizes throughout the world—divided between the dominance of very large farms in high-income and upper-middle-income countries (UMICs), and in countries where extensive livestock grazing is a dominant part of the agricultural system, mostly in North and South America, and the vast majority of small or very small farms. According to FAO, of the more than 570 million farms in the world that produce food and agricultural products, manage agroforestry, or husband animals on range lands, the vast majority are small or very small farms (Lowder, Skoet, and Raney 2016). Asia has 87 percent of the world's 500 million farms that are less than 2 hectares in size.

Advanced countries have shown a strong tendency toward land consolidation. Among the recently emerging countries in Asia, and particularly, in China, land consolidation is advancing rapidly (Zhang 2010). Contrary to a CGIAR study, which claimed a growing tendency toward land consolidation in Asia (Masters et al. 2013), this is not a universal phenomenon in Asia, where farms are becoming smaller and the incidence of landlessness or near landlessness is growing in India (Chand, Prasanna, and Singh 2011), and it has stabilized in Bangladesh (Gautam and Faruqee 2016). Indeed, 72 percent of all farms are less than 1 hectare and control only 8 percent of all agricultural land. A similar share, 70 percent of the small or very small farms, are in Asia (FAO 2014). Only 12 percent of all farms consist of 1 and 2 hectares, and they control 4 percent of the land. Farms in the range of 2 to 5 hectares account for 10 percent of all farms and control 7 percent of the land. In Chapter 2, we further address the relationships between farm size and farm productivity.

Tenure is how people gain access to land, fisheries, forests, and other natural resources. Having secure and equitable access to natural resources can allow people to produce food for their consumption and to increase income. Inadequate and insecure tenure rights to natural resources, combined with climate change and resource degradation, often result in extreme poverty and hunger. The dynamics of the tenurial structure of land and the roles of labor and commodity and financial markets are, therefore, important to structural transformation, particularly with growing demographic pressure on the land, rapid urbanization, and concurrent growth in the vertical integration of agriculture.

These issues are the kinds that W. Arthur Lewis (1954) addressed in recognizing the presence of dualism between agriculture and nonagriculture. Land registration records are poor in many developing countries. Information technology now makes it possible to achieve universal land registration faster and more easily. Experts note that greater clarity in land rights will likely accelerate land markets and land consolidation, and poor farmers who cannot compete financially will lose access to the land, perhaps at a faster rate than they are now under communal land tenure, as is the case in much of Africa. Others suspect that even under communal ownership, it is possible to influence village chiefs and acquire large tracks of land. FAO, working closely with the Committee on World Food Security, supported an unprecedented international agreement on the governance of tenure intended to promote secure tenure rights and equitable access to land, fisheries, and forests, as a means of eradicating hunger and poverty, supporting sustainable development, and enhancing the environment. The "Voluntary Guidelines on the Responsible Governance of Tenure of Land, Fisheries and Forests" were officially endorsed by the Committee on World Food Security on May 11, 2012 (FAO 2012). Since the endorsement, implementation has been encouraged by the G20, Rio+ 20, the United Nations General Assembly, and the Francophone Assembly of Parliamentarians (CFS 2012). How this plays out is discussed in Chapter 2.

Transformation has traditionally been viewed in terms of shifting labor from agriculture to manufacturing, and developing countries typically aspire to create more employment in manufacturing than in the service sector. Service sector growth, however, has dominated all regions, particularly in Africa, where growth of manufacturing has been very limited. Much of the gain from structural change in Africa stems from movements out of agriculture and into services; the positive contributions of structural transformation have largely bypassed manufacturing. Although this raises concerns about the feasibility of expanding manufacturing in the region, it is also encouraging that the service sector is playing a positive role (Diao, McMillan, and Rodrik 2017).

The shares of the manufacturing sector in GDP and employment show great range, and there is a growing debate among economists as to whether the distinct characteristics of manufacturing—which make it an "escalator" of growth, as Rodrik (2016), and Kaldor (1966) before him, described—can be realized, and if some of these advantages also apply to the modern service sector, in modern economies with complex supply chains that span multiple continents. Failing to create productive employment outside agriculture will put more than normal pressure on the agricultural sector to create productive employment, as we discuss in Chapter 2 (Krugman 1994; Stiglitz 1996; Rodrik 2014; Page 2015b).

Evidence from China, Vietnam, Indonesia, India, and Bangladesh on productivity growth shows that smallholder agriculture is the most cost-effective way to reduce poverty (World Bank 2007; de Janvry and Sadoulet 2010; Loayza and Raddatz 2010). The relationship, however, between farm size and employment, poverty reduction, and food and nutrition security is complex and has led to much debate, as we discuss in Chapter 2.

Paradigm Shift to Sustainability

Developed countries have achieved productivity growth, often using high levels of modern inputs, and only later considering the issues of sustainability. Other more advanced developing countries, such as China and parts of India, have followed this same route, but late developers are increasingly having to address sustainability issues simultaneously with productivity growth, with a focus on the increased role of knowledge. This is far more challenging. Gardner (2006), for example, acknowledged but did not discuss the alternative model of US agriculture, which advocates eco-friendly, "small is beautiful," green agriculture, with parallels in the rest of the world (IAASTD 2009). Nevertheless, he has highlighted the need to recognize the skepticism of those criticizing technology, together with the concerns about environmental and human health threats from chemicals and biotechnology and the need to better measure and assess cost, benefits, and both positive and negative externalities from economic progress (Gardner 2006, 352). Although Gardner considered US industrial agriculture, on balance, a great "success story" (Gardner 2006, 343), he agreed with the criticism of the greens about the traditionalists. The pro-growth group is "too dismissive of criticism, pays little attention to the costs of and losers from economic progress, and is too ready to spend billions of taxpayer dollars on the promotion of commercial agriculture" (Gardner 2006, 352).

Interest in sustainable agriculture, or the so-called sustainable intensification paradigm, has increased throughout the world, and it has many dimensions. It concerns the management of numerous dimensions of agriculture, including crop choices, soil, water, forests, climate, and their complex interactions. Evaluators of the 2009 multi-stakeholder International Assessment of Agricultural Knowledge, Science and Technology for Development (IAASTD 2009) report, *Agriculture at a Crossroads*, credited the report with starting a long overdue conversation about different development paradigms (Elliott et al. 2009). The following year, a report of the Committee on Twenty-First Century Systems Agriculture of the National Research Council of the National Academies (NRC 2010) acknowledged that research on sustainability was not getting the attention it needs, noting that while a number of environmentally sensitive improvements had been made at the margin in US agriculture, no transformative changes had been made, and more research was needed on sustainable agriculture. It is too early to say if the radical shifts proposed by IAASTD have changed agriculture at scale, although concerns about sustainability are now reflected in a variety of international reports, knowledge networks, government policies, and farmer-driven innovations. They are reflected in a wide variety of paradigms and nomenclatures under the broad rubric of sustainable agriculture, including "save and grow" agriculture, conservation agriculture (CA), reduced-till or no-till (NT) farming—by far the most broadly disseminated technology—climate-smart agriculture, landscape agriculture, eco-agriculture, evergreen agriculture, and sustainable intensification.

Sustainable agriculture also includes a plethora of individual practices, such as Integrated Pest Management (IPM), Integrated Plant Nutrient Systems (IPNS), soil organic matter management (which is acquiring popularity with new sensors to measure soil moisture), integration of crops and livestock for small farmers, water harvesting, stress-resistant crop varieties, drip irrigation, as well as instruments such as certification and branding of food produced using particular farming practices (for example, organically produced fruit and vegetables). As the NRC report noted, however, adoption of these new models, with a few exceptions, has not yet made a transformative difference at scale.

Advances in Biotechnology and Other Approaches

Genetically modified organisms (GMOs) and the subsequent gene editing technologies are an exception—the biological revolution's potential remains underutilized. Biotechnology ranges from tissue culture, GMOs, fermentation technology, induced mutations, genomics, biopesticides, and biofertilizers, to marker-assisted breeding, assisted reproductive technologies in farm animals, diagnostics, and gene editing. GMOs have been adopted extensively in North and South America, but have become a lightning rod and will, perhaps, become unnecessary with the rapid advances in genomics (Fedoroff 2020). The nature of the gene editing debate is changing, as new methods to modify genomes that fall outside current regulatory systems are being developed. In the scientific community, the debate seems to be moving toward regulating what a new plant (or gene) can do and not how it was obtained (NASEM 2016; Servick 2016).

Some advocates of sustainable agriculture include supporters of organic farming who find GMOs unacceptable, even though genetically modified (GM) cotton has been adopted extensively and has been shown to reduce the use of pesticides and their harmful effects on human health (Gilbert 2013; Qaim and Kouser 2013; Hsiao 2015). In 2014, 95 percent of cotton farmers, including 7.7 million small farmers in India, the second largest producer of cotton in the world, grew cotton on 12.25 million hectares in 10 cotton-growing states (Choudhary and Gaur 2015). Similar issues are imminent on edible GM crops in India, such as eggplant (brinjal), developed in India and adopted in Bangladesh. Prospects were brighter for GM mustard at the time of writing this chapter (Bagla 2016). India is one of the world's biggest producers of mustard (*Brassica juncea*), which is cultivated for its edible leaves and oil. The GM variety is engineered with genes from a soil microbe that manipulate pollen development, such that the variety produces hybrids more easily than in the usually self-pollinating crop. The GM-derived hybrids produce about 25 percent more seeds—and thus more oil, which is pressed from the seeds—than traditional varieties now in cultivation. The safety review raises one cautionary note: it calls for more studies on whether GM mustard could harm honeybees and honey production in mustard-growing areas. It stresses the need for continued monitoring of insects and other organisms that live in or near mustard fields.

These technologies have been on hold in India due to the resistance of environmental lobbies and civil society, but their resistance efforts have strengthened the review process and made it more transparent. GM crops have not, however, made headway. In SSA, excluding South Africa, GMOs provide an excellent example of the role of institutions of governance in setting the formal and informal rules, based on the voices of stakeholders. Organizations, as players, try both to influence rules and also to implement them (Box 1.2). Nigeria is adopting GMO technologies, including its first food crop, the GM cowpea (Falck-Zepeda, Gruère, and Sithole-Niang 2013; Isaac and Conrow 2019).

IAASTD's position against biotechnology has continued to provoke debate, particularly by some member governments, whereas Qaim and others have documented the benefits of genetically modified crops for the poor in food-insecure countries (Qaim 2010; Qaim and Kouser 2013).

The report of the US National Academies of Sciences, Engineering and Medicine provided a broader perspective that noted that enduring and widespread gains will depend on institutional support and access to profitable local and global markets, especially for resource-poor farmers (NASEM 2016). In addressing the unresolved institutional issues, the increasing concentration of new technology in the hands of a few multinationals with control of the intellectual property cannot be ignored. This situation, too, is changing rapidly. In early 2016, China's government-owned agrochemical firm China National Chemical announced an all-cash proposal to buy Swiss-owned Syngenta for US$43 billion. The deal underwent a regulatory review in the United States, where Syngenta does a significant portion of its business, when a powerful US senator expressed alarm about the purchase (Bunge, Spegele, and Mauldin 2016). The regulatory hurdles were cleared, and

Syngenta was acquired by ChemChina in 2017 (Spegele and Wu 2017). The world of global and national governance of food and agriculture, including the harnessing of agricultural technology, is certainly changing with the increased roles for emerging countries, including China, India, and the countries in the Middle East and North Africa (MENA). Two additional resource management challenges are worth highlighting going forward.

Synthetic fertilizers have been critical to increasing agricultural productivity. Since they were discovered and replaced organic material well over a century ago, while saving farm labor, their use has led to the decline in soil carbon and the loss of knowledge of soil biology. To improve soil fertility and increase its carbon content, steps are needed to ward off "deleterious climate impacts." Estimates of soils' potential to sequester carbon vary, and more location-specific research is needed to promote appropriate soil management practices. "Putting the carbon back in soil is not only mitigating climate change, but also improving human health, productivity, food security, nutrition security, water quality, air quality—everything," said Rattan Lal, the director of the Carbon Management and Sequestration Center at Ohio State. "It's a win-win-win option," he said (Leslie 2017; see, also, Lal and Stewart 2015). Fertilizer's use, its pricing and subsidies, and the role of the public sector have been matters of intense international debate since the generation of the Green Revolution. We explore the implications of these debates for structural transformation.

Similarly, unsustainable water use (overdrafted aquifers, seasonally dry rivers, disappearing lakes and wetlands) has become a problem across the developing world. Particularly in regions with water shortages, human interventions have regulated water for food security, domestic, and other uses (Molden 2007). The proliferation of large-scale, storage-based systems and the development of deep tube well technology have resulted in dramatic increases in water withdrawals and created interdependence and competition across new, mostly unregulated, boundaries—often based on exploitation of nonrenewable resources. The governance of these new relationships goes much beyond the scope of traditional institutions. Many of the new improved engineering technologies to deal with problems of unsustainable water use are supposed to save water, release it for other uses, and achieve higher crop yields per unit of water. Perry and Steduto (2017) argued, however, that if yield per unit area increases, then it is likely that water consumption also increases. "Hi-tech" irrigation (which often ensures more controlled and better timed irrigation supplies) is one of the various factors that encourage farmers to invest in higher return crops. What do these changes mean for the future of food and agriculture?

From Sustainable Production Systems to Sustainable Consumption

With urbanization and income growth, there is often rapid dietary transition as consumers shift to more diversified, higher-value diets with an increasing share of processed foods related to dairy, poultry, meat, fruits, and vegetables, and an important demand pull on production and processing. Barrett et al. (2019) noted that the agri-food value chain revolution, which has been underway throughout the developing world since the early 2000s, has played a critical role in the story of structural transformation of developing economies. In much of the literature on transformation, however, it has often been overlooked, including, particularly, in terms of its development implications. From his large body of work on value chains, Reardon noted that 80 percent of the food consumed in developing regions (which he measures in value terms) goes through supply chains to consumers: 60 percent of food consumption in developing countries is in cities, where nearly all food is purchased, and rural consumption is 40 percent of the total, with rural consumers buying as much as 50 percent of their food. Governments distribute about 1 percent of food consumed (again, presumably in value terms) in developing regions, so those channels are not a substitute for the market (supply chains). Markets must continue to feed the poor, and e-commerce and delivery have been a key lifeline for poor consumers. We need to see the effect of COVID-19 on e-commerce, as part of a continuum of rapid change in the retail sector of developing regions (Thomas Reardon, personal communication, June 13–14, 2020).

Barrett, Reardon, Swinnen, and Zilberman explained, in their paper, that "by the time countries reach middle-income status, post-farmgate value addition already accounts for roughly half of total consumer food expenditures and increases rapidly as economic growth proceeds" (Barrett et al. 2019, 3). The changes tend to be influenced by the nature of technological change, farm structure, foreign direct investment (FDI), and infrastructure investments.

Farmers in SSA and Asia, where value chains have traditionally been relatively short, had a closer relationship between production and consumption. "Agrifood value chains (VCs) have shifted from being mainly local to being much longer, stretching from rural areas to urban consumers," and slightly, to export markets (Reardon et al. 2016, 2). They are beginning to face challenges similar to farmers in the United States, whereas their share in the prices that consumers pay is typically no more than 7 to 10 percent, with the rest of the transaction cost consisting of transportation, processing, and as appropriate, canning, freezing, and packaging. The implication is that development of supply chains has increased return to farmers (Reardon et al. 2016). In later work, Reardon emphasizes that value chains have evolved from the growth of supermarkets to the service sector, of restaurants and fast food enterprises, and increasingly, to e-commerce and service delivery, a phenomenon accelerated by the COVID-19 pandemic (Lu and Reardon 2018).

The Challenge of Diversifying Production to Support Diversified Dietary Choice

The gap of up to 90 percent that exists between producers and consumers needs to be addressed to improve the nutritional content of foods that consumers eat in high-income countries and are beginning to consume in developing countries. With growing evidence of the use of energy-rich additives of sugars and fats leading to obesity and noncommunicable diseases, this dietary trend is seen, particularly, in South American countries that have adopted North American food habits, which Kenneth Rogoff attributed, in part, to the effects of North American Free Trade Agreement (Rogoff 2017). Some patterns of production and consumption during structural transformation are already emerging rapidly enough across countries to necessitate developing and implementing strategies, including getting the food and beverage industries to be part of the solution rather than the problem, and independently assessing their impacts.

The current concern about healthy production, healthy consumption, and a healthy planet goes back to the Brundtland Commission, formerly known as the World

Commission on Environment and Development (WCED), which identified the need to make sustainable development "ensure that it meets the needs of the present without compromising the ability of future generations to meet their own needs" (WCED 1987, 8). Since then, there has been a proliferation of literature on sustainability, but progress on actually realizing sustainability has been slow, as noted in the growing GHG emissions, loss of biodiversity, soil degradation, and decline in water quality. We explore these issues in the book.

African farmers tend to have diversified farming systems, but most farms are rainfed, and many soils have been severely depleted of nutrients. A lack of infrastructure often inhibits access to outside resources and markets, leading to at least three classes of small farmers—those with little or no market access, those with good market access, and those in between. These and other developing countries are facing tension in making a transition from the competing production paradigms: that is, of increasing the supply of cereals—a paradigm well entrenched and in place—to production diversity consisting of livestock and poultry, pulses, vegetables and fruit, and occasionally fish, to facilitate dietary diversity. Concurrently, whereas some development advocates promote organic, on-farm diversity and mistrust markets, especially global markets, even "traditional" Green Revolution veterans, such as M. S. Swaminathan (2015) and Gordon Conway (2012), advocate an evergreen or a doubly green revolution: that is, better natural resource management and production of more with less, a result of the first Green Revolution experience and the current global promotion of global food systems.

The production sustainability paradigm is complex and challenging, hard to define operationally or measure (including trade-offs), with diversity in production systems that defies generalizations—for instance, whether farming is rainfed or irrigated; temperate or tropical; humid, sub-humid, arid, or semi-arid. It calls for long-term, interdisciplinary approaches *in situ*, closer to the farmers' fields, to address systematic, short- and long-run costs and benefits, and trade-offs among competing objectives. It often tends to be location-specific and hard to scale up. Whereas the simple technical fixes are unlikely to address all four sustainability goals that the NRC has defined for the United States (Box 1.2), the definition illustrates the complexity of the concept, which depends on where it is applied and from whose perspective it is viewed.

US biofuel policies, promoted on the grounds of sustainability, were criticized during the 2008 crisis for having contributed to the global food crisis by reducing by up to 30–40 percent the corn/maize supplied on the global market for human consumption, contributing to the price increase (Wright 2014). Furthermore, with a sharp decline in energy prices,

---

Box 1.2 National Research Council's Definition of Sustainability

- Satisfy human food, feed, and fiber needs, and contribute to biofuel needs.
- Enhance environmental quality and the resource base.
- Sustain the economic viability of agriculture.
- Enhance the quality of life for farmers, farm workers, and society as a whole.

Source: NRC (2010).

the economics of biofuels has changed, while the subsidies and mandates continue due to the stickiness of policy reforms.

Integrated systems approaches are more likely to be successful when adapted to local conditions. Scherr (2015) reported more than 450 such initiatives in Africa, Latin America, South and Southeast Asia, and Europe, jointly pursuing sustainable agriculture, healthy ecosystems, and improved livelihoods; and involving 5 or 6 sectors and 9–11 stakeholder groups, including private sector companies, linking to value chains. There is little concrete evidence yet about the impacts of their "sustainability" features.

The literature shows that governance of these multisectoral programs tends to be the biggest challenge (Sayer et al. 2013). Even in the United States, conflicts among interest groups in conservation programs can be daunting (Coppess 2017; Khanna and Shortie 2017). Additionally, research programs need to actively seek input and collaboration from farmers to ensure that technologies are developed to meet their needs (IIRR and ACTN 2005). Women farmers, who play a pivotal role in African agriculture, need to be actively engaged, provided with education and training opportunities, and involved in the development of research agendas. FAO estimated that productivity can increase by up to 30 percent with women's inclusion and with farming systems that use locally available resources and natural biophysical processes (FAO 2011). Skeptics have argued that collective efforts to manage resources are doomed to fail because of "shirking" on the part of a few key stakeholders who seek to reap the benefits without accepting the costs of collective action. Elinor Ostrom, winner of the Nobel Prize in Economics, challenged the logic behind this conclusion (Ostrom 1990). We explore the extent to which the conditions laid out by Ostrom prevail in the case of resource management or can be created in areas such as climate change, water, and land management.

Conservation Agriculture and the Need for Measurement

Farmer-led transformation of agricultural production systems based on CA provides another example.[7] Now accounting for 157 million hectares, or 11 percent of the global cropped area in 2013, CA systems include no or minimum tillage, organic mulch soil cover, and crop species diversification, in conjunction with other good practices of crop and production management (Kassam et al. 2015). The largest areas of CA are on large farms in the United States, Brazil, Argentina, Canada, Australia, and China, ranging from 35 million in the United States to 6.6 million in China. Much of the CA in the Americas uses GM crops, which makes the practice easier. The spread of CA on small farms in Asia and Africa has so far been quite limited (Mazvimavi 2011; Arslan et al. 2014; Rehman et al. 2015). In an analysis of CA adoption in SSA, Giller et al. (2009) suggested that, given present circumstances including institutional and livelihood contexts, CA may be further constraining for most resource-constrained smallholder farmers.

Concerns about performance of CA for smallholder farmers in SSA include impacts on yields and returns to labor, with the latter largely dependent on the former. Uncertainty in

---

[7] See "Conservation Agriculture" at the FAO website: http://www.fao.org/ag/ca/index.html.

CA efficacy, with respect to increasing yields, can be traced to the complexity of interacting biophysical factors and process pathways and drivers that are influenced by CA technologies (Brouder and Gomez-Macpherson 2014). Cultural and economic entrenchment of tillage agriculture, weeds, insect, pests, and disease management, as well as limited availability of seeding and planting equipment call for location-specific research and active participatory extension (Stevenson, Serraj, and Cassman 2014). Additionally, the benefits of CA (including better soils, carbon sinks, better yields, and reduced costs) tend to be medium to long term, which large farmers are better able to afford, whereas many of the costs, including the lack of silage for animals, for example, tend to be immediate and small farmers may not be able to afford them.

Therefore, economic evaluations of new technologies, based on concrete, location-specific data, are urgently needed for small farmers. Our working hypothesis is that there is often too much advocacy and not enough concrete empirical evidence to know where things work and why: that is, how technologies are deployed and institutions evolve in response to challenges. For example, is miniaturizing of technology for small farmers the answer? Or is land consolidation to take advantage of large machinery a better strategy? How do rental markets or contracts evolve? Lu, Reardon, and Zilberman (2016) addressed these issues in their article, "Supply Chain Design and Adoption of Indivisible Technology." Large farmers in the United States and Latin America are using advanced computers to fine-tune application of sustainable practices and zero tillage, which means that machinery, computers, and these modern technologies are increasingly being miniaturized, with new organizations offering machinery-for-hire services, giving tremendous scope to accelerate the spread of sustainable agriculture to smaller farmers in developing countries. Increasingly, FAO and CGIAR have been adapting and researching CA on smaller farms, through their respective workplans.

Issues in Improving Nutrition

Production and consumption of nutritious food for and by all in a globalized world pose another set of challenges and concerns for the attainment of the SDGs. Undernourishment, micronutrient deficiencies, and obesity now coexist in the same households and the same countries. The numbers are staggering: an estimated 820 million are still hungry, with 2 billion people experiencing moderate or severe food insecurity (FAO et al. 2019, vii). At least half of children worldwide, aged 6 months to 5 years, suffer from one or more micronutrient deficiencies, and globally more than 2 billion people are affected (CDC 2020). In 2016, more than 1.9 billion adults were overweight, of whom over 650 million were obese; 41 million children under the age of 5 were overweight or obese, and over 340 million children and adolescents aged 5–19 were overweight or obese (WHO 2020b). Micronutrient deficiency may be declining, albeit slowly, whereas obesity has been growing throughout the world, including in low- and low-middle-income countries (LMICs).

Malnutrition in LICs and middle-income countries (MICs) is being described increasingly by the world's nutrition experts as a deepening crisis, and nutrition is at the center stage of global policy among advocates (GLOPAN 2017). The key policy prescription from the global panels of experts, which now abound, is to ensure that everyone has access to healthy diets. The myriad recommendations on nutrition improvement blanketing the development community should be seen in the context of the experience since the 1970s and its lessons. What is different now, compared to the past?

Our analysis, based on the historical experience, is outlined in Chapter 4. First, to improve nutrition, consumers need to be educated and informed, and their knowledge needs to influence household decisions and consumer demand. That information and knowledge is currently lacking among most consumers, particularly in developing countries, and particularly among poor people. Second, high-quality diets tend to be more costly than low-quality diets. Most consumers, particularly low-income consumers, lack the income to be able to purchase high-quality diets. Evidence on the effect of increased income on improved diets, too, is mixed. Finally, the relatively cheap price of junk food and its easy accessibility made possible by the food and beverage industry has contributed to the changed consumption patterns of foods high in sugar, salt, and fats and will need to be called to account, with a focus on corporate social responsibility. We will explore the politics of "do not harm" food, including preventing access of children to bad foods and the role of global and national governance.

Recent shifts in production models raise issues of specialization versus production diversity on farms, as a way to improve environmental and household consumption, and directly health, by drawing on home production. The growth of value chains in a rapidly globalized world provides a new set of challenges in influencing dietary diversity and nutritional quality. Additionally, there are the issues of the scope for and the speed of land consolidation, scale economies, and possibilities of nonfarm employment. Food safety standards, trade policy, and dietary guidelines—vis-à-vis the regulation of the food processing industry—is a way to expand consumer choice while increasing consumer protection. These have become particularly pressing issues with the rapid rise in obesity in developed and developing countries alike. Therefore, in addition to the focus on poverty and hunger, the problem of obesity has come to the forefront.

These issues call for economy-wide and ecology-wide approaches involving critical choices, not only within agriculture, but across other sectors, in consideration of the human and environmental health implications for the food we eat, with rapidly changing lifestyles and their life-cycle impacts on food and agriculture. Developing countries face complex choices in the face of rapid urbanization, climate change, growing pressure on land and water resources, and the burgeoning demand for food and fiber from a growing and prospering population. They are also striving for the goals of zero hunger and near zero population in agriculture through structural transformation and creating productive employment for the burgeoning youth population.

Demographic transition (or its lack) is also an important issue in Africa, to which agricultural economists have paid little attention. Groth and May noted the four Asian Tigers—South Korea, Singapore, Malaysia and Hong Kong—experienced their demographic transition very rapidly, as "mortality rates in Asia decreased at a fast and steady rate ... followed by a decrease in fertility rates" and "when comparing South Korea to the sub-Saharan African regions, it clearly appears that the [economic] surplus generated by the demographic transition is going to be much lower in Africa than it has been in South Korea" (Groth and May 2017, 189).

Gordon Conway, advocate of the concept of the "Doubly Green Revolution" in his book *One Billion Hungry: Can We Feed the World?* (Conway 2012), outlined these and other challenges and concluded with 24 requirements to be able to feed the world. Kofi Annan, Raj Shah, and others have described the challenges as a bold and doable agenda, and Bill and Melinda Gates have termed the agenda a reason to be optimistic (Weber 2014; Gates and

Gates 2015; Shah 2017). Capable global and national institutions will be needed to address the complex and interacting challenges.

Healthy Diets, Nutrition, and Health: Undernutrition, Overnutrition, and Micronutrient Deficiencies—The Triple Burden of Malnutrition

Concern is growing about the triple burden of malnutrition, with an estimated 821 million undernourished in 2018, including more than 2 billion with micronutrient deficiencies and 2 billion overweight, a third of whom are obese (CDC 2020; FAO et al. 2019). The three phenomena can coexist in countries and, often, even in the same households, regardless of income levels. The number of obese has been growing rapidly; the prevalence of under-nourished had been shrinking until 2015, but was largely unchanged over the next three years. The life-cycle nature of nutritional challenges, starting from conception of life to death, is now taken as given, although health and economic impacts have become more evident and have been articulated in a variety of prestigious publications, most notably in the *Lancet* (2008, 2011, 2013, 2015), and in reports of various international organizations (Development Initiatives 2017; FAO 2015; FAO et al. 2019; IFPRI 2014, 2015, 2016; UNICEF 2016; UNICEF, WHO, and World Bank 2016; WHO 2013, 2014a, 2014b, 2014c, 2014d, 2020a). The adverse economic impacts of poor nutrition have become focused on learning disabilities of undernourished children, the long-term educational achievements and earning capacities, and the rapid growth of noncommunicable diseases—including diabetes, cancer, and heart-related ailments with life-threatening consequences.

Nutrition, nutrition-sensitive agriculture, and food consumption have been hotly de-bated for the past decade. Margaret Mead famously noted issues of the cultural legacy of gender bias, in 1976, with respect to agricultural production and consumption. In addition, Mead thought a new approach was needed: "departments or schools in which *all the skills related to* food—including plant genetics, animal husbandry, veterinary skills, nutrition, child development, food management, etc.—are taught without discrimination to both men and women. Only in this way can there be any hope of including women at every level of the decision-making process and of restoring the concept that the primary function of food is to feed people, and to feed them well," not to serve as a form of national aggrandizement (Mead 1976, 11, emphasis added). These days, the equality of men and women in agricul-tural production is yet to come (see, also, Quisumbing et al. 2014).

Lately, there is also recognition and acceptance of social safety nets: that is, public transfers in cash or kind, to augment incomes of the poor. Typically, in the 1980s and 1990s, they were frowned upon in Bretton Woods institutions, as being fiscally onerous and of limited impact. The US Supplemental Nutrition Assistance Program (SNAP) spent US$78 billion in 2014—US$125 per beneficiary, to about 45 million people.[8] Sporadic and underfunded as it is, today's welfare state in developed countries backstopped many economies during the Great Recession and is believed to be capable of providing broad security for poor people (World Bank 1981; Lancaster 1997). As with sustainable

---

[8] According to Tim Josling, Professor Emeritus at the Freeman Spogli Institute for International Studies, at Stanford University, "The 1964 Food Stamp Act put the program on a more permanent footing and established a powerful coalition between urban and rural Congressmen that has endured...The Food Stamp program supporters have allowed the farm programs to continue in exchange for the agricultural lobby backing the food stamp legislation" (Josling 2011, 6). The US Food Stamp program does not appear to address nutritional concerns typically advocated in developing countries.

intensification of production, the approach to consumption has been changing in other respects as well. Dietary shifts, with increased income and urbanization, is leading to the greater exploration of the relationship between the structure of production and patterns of dietary consumption, and increased treatment in the development literature. Popkin (2001) brought attention to the concept he termed "dietary transition." He noted, "In country after country we have documented a marked shift in the structure of the diet" (Popkin 2001, 871S), which has been taking place with related disease patterns over the last few decades (Monteiro et al. 1995; Popkin 1994, 1998; Kim, Moon, and Popkin 2000; World Cancer Research Fund and AICR 2007). Major dietary changes include large increases in the consumption of fat and added sugar, often a marked increase in animal food products, contrasted with a fall in total intake of cereals and fiber. In many ways, this seems to be an inexorable shift to the higher fat Western diet, reflected in a large proportion of the population consuming over 30 percent of energy from fat, with huge changes in disease burden (Popkin 2001). Japan, South Korea, and Singapore are a few outliers among rich countries in containing obesity, but their rates are also beginning to inch upward.

Finance for Development

Net ODA disbursement by Development Assistance Committee (DAC) member countries, as a percentage of gross national income (GNI) in 2015, was 0.3 percent OECD GNI.[9] It increased to 0.32 percent of combined GNI in 2020, up from 0.30 percent in 2019 (OECD 2021, 1). Even with this increase, ODA is a small share of public expenditures in large LMICs such as India; most ODA is now devoted to LICs. Together, these countries represent 73 and 76 percent of global poverty and hunger (FAO 2017, 2020; World Bank 2016). As the report of the multilateral institutions led by the IMF and the World Bank, in preparation for the Addis Ababa financing meeting, made clear, ODA from OECD is not expected to increase much (Development Committee 2015; UN 2015a). Greater financing would need to come from domestic finance of developing countries, from international finance from emerging countries (China and others), and from private sources (particularly, philanthropic organizations and private investments). To effectively mobilize private capital, developing countries need to put into place enabling policy and institutional environments that address risk, transaction costs, and governance at national and regional levels.

Whether the SDGs will have adequate financing from all potential sources is increasingly unclear. What is clear is that most of the funding will have to come from sources other than ODA, included, as noted, from the private sector and domestically raised resources. Secondly, while the agendas of international organizations have expanded, resources at their disposal have not increased commensurately. Core budgets of several key international organizations have stagnated in nominal terms and declined in real terms. More importantly, aid has become so fractionated as to greatly reduce its effectiveness (Birdsall and Kharas 2010). Donors have made promises that they were unable to keep. At the UN's International Conference for Financing Development in Monterrey in 2002, donors promised to support the MDGs.

---

[9] See "Final Official Development Assistance Figures in 2015": https://www.oecd.org/dac/financing-sustainable-development/development-finance-data/final-oda-2015.htm

Net ODA more than doubled in real terms since 2000 (increasing by 110%). It rose by 69% in real terms between 2000 and 2010, after the Millennium Development Goals were agreed [upon] in 2000 and other commitments were made by donors to increase their ODA, (at the Monterrey Conference on Financing for Development in 2002 and the G8 Gleneagles Summit in 2005). ODA budgets fell afterwards, by 1% in real terms in 2011 and a further 4% in 2012, due to the continuing financial crisis and euro zone turmoil, which led several governments to tighten their budgets and had a direct impact on development aid. ODA rebounded again in 2013 and continued to rise until 2016 when it reached a first peak due especially to the influx in Europe of refugees and associated in-donor refugee costs. It fell in 2017 and 2018 due to the tapering off of in-donor refugee costs and remained stable in 2019. In 2020, ODA reached its highest level ever due in part to support for the COVID-19 crisis. (OECD 2021, 5)

As a result, achieving the MDGs depended heavily on the policies, priorities, institutions, and investments of developing countries. In the case of SDGs, as country priorities may not coincide with the goals, the allocated domestic resources may turn out to be inadequate or may be spent inefficiently, and donor and private sector funding may not materialize. Development financing, therefore, will need more attention, as the clientele for aid is changing, along with the supply of and demand for finance and knowledge. For that reason, the purposes, tools, and role of the international aid system are critically important.

Role of International Organizations

There is plenty of accumulated evidence about what works and what does not, and it is mixed on whether, where, and when aid works, but there is substantial evidence that multilateral aid has been more effective than bilateral aid (Kharas et al. 2015; Morris and Gleave 2015). The UK Department for International Development (DFID)—now the Foreign, Commonwealth and Development Office (FCDO)—which routinely reviews its contributions to international organizations, has described the role of multilateral organizations as "an essential part of the international system for development and humanitarian aid [with] a global presence and the legitimacy to work even in politically sensitive contexts where national governments are not welcome" (DFID and UK Aid 2011, 2).

While the multilateral system is, as DFID noted, "complex and fragmented" (DFID and UK Aid 2011, v), a positive feature of multilateral aid (to be, arguably, noted under the new governance arrangements) is that its activities are driven less directly by the domestic political or commercial interests of its principal shareholders and more by concern for humanitarian and development outcomes.

Ravallion (2016), Clemens and Kremer (2016), and Birdsall (MacDonald 2012; Birdsall 2000; 2015; Ahluwalia et al. 2016), among other economists, have asserted that the World Bank has an important role to play in poverty reduction—that it does more than just transfer money. There are critics, too, such as Devesh Kapur, who have highlighted the need for agility and responsibility in their actions and programs (Kapur 2015).

Donors have repeatedly recognized the need for greater effectiveness, in Rome in 2003 (OECD 2019b), in Paris in 2005 (OECD 2019c), in Accra in 2008 (OECD 2019d), in Busan in 2011 (OECD 2019a), and in Mexico in 2014 (GPEDC 2014). (See Burall and Maxwell 2006.) A Brookings Institution study confirmed what recipients of aid have always known, that the quality and "effectiveness" of aid programs, and their targeting, need to be improved to have "significant global impact" (Kharas et al. 2015, 12).

A later Center for Global Development (CGD) study lent additional support to concerns about the transparency of ownership and the extent of real capital transfers or institutional capacity development of US assistance, among the "15 Feed the Future" recipients (Dunning and McGillem 2016; Rose 2016). There are many areas in which both developed and developing countries need to undertake reforms to create stronger international cooperation, based on innovative approaches, shared objectives, agreed upon processes and agendas, and as partners of equals, rather than the old-style, postcolonial, donor-recipient ODA.

Changing Global Governance—A Crowded and Fragmented Aid Architecture with Evolving Needs

With the increased number of new actors, including, in particular, China and the G20 countries, philanthropists like the Bill and Melinda Gates Foundation and the 100 billionaires whom Bill Gates has persuaded to contribute a significant share of their wealth, aid giving has become a crowded but fragmented field with huge transaction costs. Moreover, bilateral donors have increased their role in multi-bilateral aid through the use of trust funds, many of them vertical trust funds. It has been easier to raise funds for defined objectives, but vertical programs have fundamentally altered the character of international assistance and made it more difficult for developing governments to coordinate aid. The role of multilateral organizations needs to be considered in the context of growth in MICs: with a large incidence of poverty, their different funding needs, and the evolving and more diversified sources of finance, including the increased reliance on the markets and bilateral commercial credit.

Questions Addressed by This Inquiry

This book examines the challenges of global food, agriculture, and nutrition historically in the context of the structural transformation of countries, while exploring the role of the five largest international organizations concerned with food and agriculture going forward, based on their record of performance since their establishment: the World Bank, FAO, the World Food Programme (WFP), CGIAR, and IFAD, established in 1944, 1945, 1961, 1971, and 1977, respectively.

"The Big Five," as we have dubbed them, were established over the years from around the end of the Second World War until about the middle of the 1970s. Their evolution to adapt to today's radically changed world is a useful window through which to observe and understand the changes at the global, national, and subnational levels, including the implications of the explosion of new actors. By examining how the Big Five have responded, we argue, incrementally, that we can gain insights about the changing rules of the game in global and national governance. Those rules include the growing need for financing of global and national public goods, the challenges of assisting conflict-affected and fragile countries where 1.5 billion people live, and the projected graduation of 40 LICs into MICs and their growing capital needs.

The discourse that gave rise to the establishment of the Big Five has since evolved in response to the entry of new players, the growth of information and knowledge, the breakneck speed of communication, the upside and downside of social media, and rapidly advancing science and technology, among other changes. The 2007–8 food crises brought together the Big Five to deal with the crisis, and yet, global changes have put considerable stress on the old modes of conducting business at all levels. So, the big organizations search for new ways to operate and cooperate with the growing number of players on the global scene.

The five organizations form part of the larger architecture of international cooperation and global governance of food and agriculture. That architecture consists of the United Nations family with its member countries and their various groupings—G7, G20 (which includes emerging economies), and G77 (which, in reality, is a group of 150 countries and various regional groupings, the private sector, international nongovernmental organizations [INGOs], civil society, philanthropists, celebrities, indigenous organizations, and scientific communities).

While sovereign governments determine the global rules, increasingly and to varying degrees, the new global actors and their new and kaleidoscopic coalitions influence the formal and informal rules, standards, and norms of global governance and finance. In context, where the SDGs have led, in principle, to collective ownership, there are signs that the new actors, such as the emerging countries and philanthropic organizations, are already beginning to exert considerable influence—although learning curves of new entrants on the scene have been steep and the architecture is still evolving.

Each organization has a specific mandate, governance structure, and funding base defined by its stakeholders. Each has undertaken structural reforms, but despite attempts to adjust, the reforms fall short of the magnitude of the challenges in the external environment. Some consider the Big Five irrelevant. Increasingly, the Big Five are part of new alliances that include philanthropists, emerging countries, and new banks—the Asian Infrastructure Investment Bank (AIIB) established by China, and the BRICS Development Bank, established in 2014 by Brazil, Russia, India, China, and South Africa. It is imperative that they continue to find ways to work together and truly complement their individual strengths by partnering with the new sources of international financing.

The Establishment of the Big Five International Organizations Concerned with Food and Agriculture

The United States was key in the establishment of the modern system of international cooperation and remains critical as part of a larger coalition. At the end of the Second World War, President Franklin D. Roosevelt was committed to avoiding the mistakes that had led to the failure of the League of Nations in 1920, following the First World War. The concept for an international organization for food and agriculture emerged in the late 19th and early 20th centuries, primarily advanced by US agriculturalist and activist David Lubin. In May–June 1905, an international conference in Rome had led to the establishment of the International Institute of Agriculture. In 1943, President Roosevelt called a United Nations Conference on Food and Agriculture. Representatives from 44 governments gathered at the Homestead Resort in Hot Springs, Virginia, from May 18 to June 3, and decided to establish an Interim Commission to formulate a plan for the permanent organization. The First Session of the FAO Conference was held in Quebec, Canada, from October 16 to November

1, 1945, tasked with bringing FAO formally into existence. The Second World War effectively ended the International Agricultural Institute. It was officially dissolved by resolution of its Permanent Committee on February 27, 1948, and its functions were transferred to FAO (Phillips 1981).[10] Since its founding, FAO has been the only international organization with a complement of technical expertise in a range of areas related to food and agriculture under one roof. The agency's mandate is to improve nutrition, reduce hunger, increase productivity in primary industries, raise the standard of living in rural populations, and contribute to global economic growth through support of food and agriculture. FAO collects, analyzes, and disseminates data; it assists member states by providing guidance and promoting capacity development; preparing conventions, norms, and guidelines; providing expert advice in development programs; and helping to rebuild food production in disaster and conflict areas.

The term "United Nations," too, was coined by President Roosevelt and was first used in the Declaration by the United Nations of January 1, 1942, when representatives of 26 nations pledged their governments to continue fighting together against the Axis Powers. In 1945, representatives of 50 countries met in San Francisco at the United Nations Conference on International Organization to draw up the United Nations Charter. The delegates deliberated on the proposals worked out by the representatives of China, the Soviet Union, the United Kingdom, and the United States at Dumbarton Oaks in Washington, DC, in August–October 1944. The Charter was signed on June 26, 1945, by representatives of 50 countries.

A Bretton Woods Conference in July 1944, with leadership from the United States and the victors of the Second World War, with the United Kingdom playing an important role, resulted in the creation of IMF and the International Bank for Reconstruction and Development (IBRD). IMF was established to provide monetary stability on an international scale. In 2005, it adopted a poverty reduction mission.

IBRD was established in 1945 to make up for market failures in capital transfers, first for reconstruction of the war-torn economies and later for assistance to developing countries. It provides advisory services, loans, and technical assistance to governments in MICs and creditworthy LICs. It has since evolved into a part of the World Bank Group of five organizations. In 1956, the International Finance Corporation (IFC) was established as the World Bank's private sector arm. It offers loans and investment products, as well as advisory services, to private enterprises and government authorities in developing countries. The International Development Association (IDA), established in 1960, issues interest-free, long-term credits, and grants to the world's poorest countries. The credits and grants are provided out of funds provided by donor countries. In 1966, the International Centre for Settlement of Investment Disputes (ICSID) was established to provide international facilities for conciliation and arbitration of investment disputes. And the last component of the World Bank Group, the Multilateral Investment Guarantee Agency (MIGA), established in 1988, provides guarantees associated with political risk for foreign investments.

WFP was established within FAO in 1961, with the leadership of US Senator George McGovern during the administration of President John F. Kennedy, to multilateralize surplus US food aid. WFP is the world's largest humanitarian organization. Its significance

---

[10] The description draws heavily on the external reviews of the Norwegian, British, and Multilateral Organisation Performance Assessment Network (MOPAN) reviews and organizational responses. See Table A.1.2 for summary highlights of these organizations' profiles and strategic frameworks.

was emphasized during 2014 and 2015, when it handled six simultaneous severe emergencies in response to humanitarian crises unfolding in Syria and the Middle East. WFP uses food aid to meet refugee and other emergency food needs, and provides the associated logistics support. It also supports economic and social development and promotes world food security, consistent with the recommendations of the United Nations and FAO.

CGIAR (originally known as the Consultative Group of International Agricultural Research) was established in 1971 to deliver international public goods and develop high-yielding varieties of food crops. It helped to advance the Green Revolution, which was underway in India and other Asian countries, with the help of its first two Centers, the International Maize and Wheat Improvement Center (CIMYYT) and the International Rice Research Institute (IRRI), an approach CGIAR continued and has gained considerable credit for. Built on the advantage of the latest agricultural science and the increasing availability of low-cost nitrogenous fertilizer and irrigation, it has continued to conduct research with wide spillover effects, given that many developing countries would not have been able to mobilize the scientific talent, the gene pool, and the financial and scientific resources necessary to generate them. Its focus has expanded substantially beyond cereals to root crops, policy, water, livestock, forestry, and fisheries and to sustainability issues. In short, its mission has expanded, and it has moved downstream to focus on participatory research on natural resource management to achieve immediate impacts on poverty and hunger.

IFAD was established in 1977 to channel surplus petrodollars to the poorest countries in the form of concessional financing for food production. Created after the 1972–3 food crises and in the wake of a rise in energy prices, IFAD was established as a specialized agency of the United Nations. IFAD provides loans on concessional terms to poor countries, as well as to MICs with rural poverty. IFAD's distinct mission has been to reach the poorest of the poor by empowering them, such as poor rural women and men of socially and regionally marginal areas, to achieve higher incomes and improved food security and to strengthen their resilience.

Table A.1.2 presents strategic frameworks of the Big Five organizations. See Table A.6.1 in Chapter 6 for a summary of the governance of the Big Five.

Outline of the Chapters

The scope of this book expanded considerably in response to the consultations undertaken in the course of its preparation. Collectively, Chapters 2–7 outline key challenges, accumulated knowledge, and the evolving ideas and many unresolved issues in the context of which international organizations and national governments operate today. The increasingly cross-sectoral nature of agricultural transformation and the multidimensional nature of poverty, hunger, and the environment call for seeing the work of international organizations and national and global governance in the context of finance, resource allocation, and rule-setting, with an integrative view of food and agriculture with health, education, infrastructure, and power.

Chapter 2 examines the two overarching debates in development economics, the first that questions the leading role of agriculture in structural transformation, and the second that questions the role of small farmers in agriculture as a route to structural transformation, in different regions. The old conventional wisdom that small farms are more productive than large farms seems to have been replaced by a U-shaped curve on farm productivity by farm size. Farm productivity initially declines as farm size increases but then increases again. It explores how regions and countries have performed in structural transformation. Taking a deeper and wider look at the processes of structural transformation from agriculture to other sectors, the chapter draws on cross-country data and evidence on developments in 127 countries over a 33-year period, using two sectors, and from 1990 to 2014, using three sectors to explore the considerable differences across countries and regions in performance, against the overall context of premature deindustrialization. A striking conclusion is the near absence of an overarching strategy for the farm sector in most transforming countries, including, particularly, for land and capital markets and for access to technology, infrastructure, and education to facilitate transition of massive labor forces from agriculture to other sectors.

Chapter 3 discusses the food and financial crises of 2007–8 and the growing uncertainty in the interconnected world. It addresses three questions: What caused the crises? Do we have systems in place that will be able to diagnose the sources of crises relatively quickly, and minimize, or avert altogether, these kinds of crises? Will we be able to address a crisis better in the COVID-19 and post-COVID-19 future than we did in 2007–8? The chapter reviews evidence on the causes and consequences of the crises and the subsequent price rise and volatility until about 2013, and the steps taken and not taken by the international community. The international environment in 2020 has changed with abundant supplies and a larger role of trade, low energy prices, low international shipping costs, and more competition in the world market. Disruptions in supply chains in individual countries during 2020 did not seem to make a big difference in global supply chains because of widening sources of supply and low international prices.

Chapter 4 discusses the transition from food security to nutrition security, the extent and nature of the current food insecurity and nutrition challenge, and the recent reversal of the declining trend of food insecurity. The chapter shows the key role that international organizations have played in defining and influencing the agenda and the analytical issues: that is, the extent to which SDG2 and, indeed, all SDGs enable us to address the multidimensional challenge of food security and nutrition and implications. An intriguing question is the disconnect between trends in poverty and trends in food insecurity. The world has enough surplus food to eliminate undernutrition, provided access to surplus food by the poor is assured on a consistent basis. Under a business-as-usual scenario, however, the prospects of eliminating malnutrition and obesity are near zero. Transformational approaches are needed to reduce both, and there are no signs that they are forthcoming.

Chapter 5 addresses the changing nature of global governance—the shift from the primary role of governments in global governance to the role of emerging stakeholders, their different agendas and challenges in managing global governance, particularly in the context of the abrogation by the United States of its leadership role.

Chapter 6 discusses global governance at the operational level by outlining the governance of the five international organizations that are the focus of this book. The chapter examines the close relationship between governance, finance, and leadership of the organizations. Humanitarian and emergency assistance at US$7+ billion in 2018 is larger than the combined annual expenditures/commitments of FAO, CGIAR, and IFAD.[11]

---

[11] See "Contributions to WFP in 2018": https://www.wfp.org/funding/2018

Chapter 7 discusses financing. The financing needs of developing countries for agriculture and rural development run into the trillions if, in addition to investments in agriculture, complementary investments outside of agriculture in infrastructure, education, and health are considered. With few exceptions, most notably China, developing countries have not been investing enough of their own resources in the food and agricultural sector. Indeed, the most recent evidence suggests a decline in investment in agriculture and rural development as a share of GDP. Foreign flows to developing countries have increased and diversified, so that the role of ODA has shrunk relative both to the needs of developing countries and to alternative sources of funding. These flows have all declined in recent years, even before the COVID-19 pandemic, and now do not nearly meet the needs.

In Chapters 8 through 12, we discuss the work of the five organizations on the ground through their historical evolution, their most recent reforms in the context of the changes in the external and internal environment discussed in the preceding seven chapters, and the various criteria by which their performance has been assessed over the years.

In the case of the World Bank, IBRD borrowing for agriculture and rural development in MICs is relatively small, and there is resistance in the United States and elsewhere to continue lending to them. Their overall capital needs are considerable, however, and the Bank is in a position to exercise positive influence on their financial management. Thus, the World Bank's capital increase of US$13 billion was approved by governors in October 2018. The agreement includes a capital increase of US$7.5 billion paid-in capital, US$52.6 billion of callable capital for IBRD, and a US$5.5 billion paid-in capital increase for the IFC. "These increases represent a substantial and much-needed strengthening of the WBG's [World Bank Group's] financial capacity and an expression of confidence by the membership in the World Bank. . . . [T]he annual WBG financing can grow from about US$60 billion now to about US$100 billion in 2030" (Linn 2018). With the graduation of many previously LICs, fragile and conflict-affected states (FCS) now dominate IDA-eligible countries, in which absorptive capacity and aid effectiveness have been limited. The chapter documents this disjuncture between needs and absorptive capacity of most LICs.

Chapter 9 on FAO discusses how it evolved into an organization which fully embraced and, indeed, even shaped SDG2. Its organizational framework logically explains the link between SDG indicators and FAO's program of work and budget. In addition to SDG monitoring, FAO's traditional mandate has been to promote global public goods, such as norms and standards, with a focus on information and knowledge related to food security, agriculture, forestry, fisheries, and numerous other issues concerned with land, water, and climate. Its operational function of translating SDGs to match country priorities remains debated among some OECD countries. FAO's traditional strengths have been its cross-cutting, multidisciplinary knowledge in all normative aspects of food and agriculture, its convening power, and its reputation as a neutral broker with a potentially perfect arrangement to promote and conclude difficult policy agreements in food and agriculture, making it a trusted technical organization and a credible policy advisory forum. FAO's mission has expanded, but its assessed contributions have declined in real terms. It is unclear if its growing reliance on trust funds and voluntary contributions as an instrument is sufficient. FAO's agenda is much too large, relative to its resources.

Chapter 10 examines CGIAR's evolution. CGIAR was established in 1971 to deliver international public goods, developing high-yielding varieties of food crops and other regional public goods. It was built on a model of international research, complemented by strong capacity to be created at the national and regional levels, to work in partnership with CGIAR.

CGIAR has gone through a series of reforms over nearly a quarter-century to meet donor expectations, but increased funding has not been commensurate with the expectations. It has become increasingly complex, and from 2016 to 2019, CGIAR underwent yet one more organizational change, combining its finance and consortium offices, closing the World Bank office, and changing into a single governance structure in place of the two-pillar structure it had put in place only in 2010–11. CGIAR's impacts have been extraordinary— but the greatest challenges for CGIAR are in addressing the new issues of climate change and sustainability, areas in which it is still searching for both research solutions and organizational reforms attuned to those solutions. The Systems Council November 2019 approval of the One CGIAR approach and endorsement of an Executive Management Team may provide the needed platform for further governance reforms, consolidation of its fragmented financing, and agreement among CGIAR's supporters on future directions.

IFAD, explored in Chapter 11, provides loans and grants to agricultural and rural development projects with the perspective that smallholder agriculture can act as both a crucial source of rural income and nutrition and a vector for rural economic growth. Many of its projects seek to incorporate smallholders into value-chain development. The recent withdrawal of several previous donors from IFAD's latest Replenishment (IFAD11) meant that IFAD's lending program remained relatively static, unless the proposed sovereign borrowing increases and discussions on market borrowing (under IFAD12) move forward. Demand for IFAD resources and implementing approaches remains strong, but reduced funding will curtail access, particularly, from UMICs, whose access to replenishment-sourced resources is being severely reduced.

Chapter 12 explores how current demand for WFP's assistance greatly exceeds supply or WFP's capacity to meet the needs of the largest displaced population in the world. WFP's focus has been on food assistance for the poorest and most vulnerable. Its unique role in emergencies in preventing acute hunger and in disaster response and management is supported by voluntary contributions. WFP's logistical and emergency relief expertise is often crucial for other actors, particularly through its leadership role in humanitarian efforts. It also plays a role in crisis prevention and reconstruction in the wake of conflict and disasters. It is well placed to play a major role in the continuum from emergency relief to development. WFP gives priority to supporting disaster prevention, preparedness, and mitigation, and to post-disaster rehabilitation activities, as part of its development programs, while using emergency assistance to serve both relief and development purposes.

In Chapter 13, we outline the world's considerable, albeit lopsided, achievements on food and nutrition before the COVID-19 pandemic, and the failure of the global community to heed the warnings of pandemics from which we hope lessons are being learned. We argue that international organizations are needed more than ever in a context of a weakened international architecture, following Trump's withdrawals from the global stage, even as the Biden administration works to reestablish leadership. International organizations have considerable achievements to their credit, but some real failures, particularly in Africa. The chapter sets out both a set of organization-specific messages, as well as the broader implications for national and global governance of food and agriculture. The hopeful sign is the response of a number of nations to the Biden–Harris victory in the 2020 US presidential election and their eagerness to work together to strengthen global cooperation.

Appendix: Frameworks for Sustainable Development Goals/Millennium Development Goals and for the Big Five Organizations

Table A.1.1 Thematic framework of the Sustainable Development Goals and relevant Millennium Development Goals

2015 Sustainable Development Summit outcome document: "Transforming Our World: The 2030 Agenda for Sustainable Development"	2014 SG Synthesis Report "The Road to Dignity by 2030: Ending Poverty, Transforming All Lives and Protecting the Planet"	SDGs	MDGs
People: to end poverty and hunger, in all their forms and dimensions, and to ensure that all human beings can fulfill their potential in dignity and equality and in a healthy environment	**People:** to ensure healthy lives, knowledge, and inclusion of women and children **Dignity:** to end poverty and fight inequalities	Goals 2, 3, and 4 Goals 1 and 5	Goals 1, 2, 4, 5, and 6 Goals 1 and 3
Planet: to protect the planet from degradation, including through sustainable consumption and production, sustainably managing its natural resources, and taking urgent action on climate change, so that it can support the needs of present and future generations	**Planet:** to protect our ecosystems for all societies and our children	Goals 6, 12, 13, 14, and 15	Goal 7
Prosperity: to ensure that all human beings can enjoy prosperous and fulfilling lives and that economic, social, and technological progress occurs in harmony with nature	**Prosperity:** to grow a strong, inclusive, and transformative economy	Goals 7, 8, 9, 10, and 11	
Peace: to foster peaceful, just, and inclusive societies, which are free from fear and violence. There can be no sustainable development without peace and no peace without sustainable development	**Justice:** to promote safe and peaceful societies and strong institutions	Goal 16	
Partnership: to mobilize the means required to implement this Agenda through a revitalized Global Partnership for Sustainable Development, based on a spirit of strengthened global solidarity, focused in particular on the needs of the poorest and most vulnerable, and with the participation of all countries, all stakeholders, and all people	**Partnership:** to catalyze global solidarity for sustainable development	Goal 17	Goal 8

Note: For a detailed list of all SDGs and MDGs and their targets, see https://sustainabledevelopment.un.org/sdgs and http://www.un.org/millenniumgoals/
Source: UN (2016); UN (2020).

Table A.1.2 Strategic framework of the big five organizations

	Organization				
	World Bank Group	Food and Agriculture Organization of the United Nations	World Food Programme	CGIAR	International Fund for Agricultural Development
Strategic objectives	Two goals: to measure success in promoting sustainable economic development, and to monitor its own effectiveness in delivering results. 1. End extreme poverty **Target:** Reduce the percentage of people living on less than $1.25 a day to 3 percent by 2030. 2. Promote shared prosperity **Target:** Foster income growth for the bottom 40 percent of the population in every developing country. **Sustainability:** The goals of ending extreme poverty and promoting shared prosperity must be achieved in an *environmentally, socially, and fiscally sustainable manner* to ensure that progress is sustained over time and across generations. A sustainable path of	Five strategic objectives and what they are accomplishing— **1. Contribute to the eradication of hunger, food insecurity, and malnutrition—1.** Strengthening political will; 2. Enhancing governance and coordination; 3. Improving implementation, monitoring, and evaluation. **2. Increase and improve provision of goods and services from agriculture, forestry, and fisheries in a sustainable manner—**1. Supporting practices that increase sustainable agricultural productivity; 2. Providing information to support the transition to sustainable agriculture; 3. Promoting the transition to sustainable agriculture. 4. Advocating the adoption of international policies and	Four objectives: to achieve a world with zero hunger focusing on food assistance for the poorest and most vulnerable women, men, boys, and girls **1. Save lives and protect livelihoods in emergencies Targets:** 1. Meet urgent food and nutrition needs of vulnerable people and communities and reduce undernutrition to below emergency levels; 2. Protect lives and livelihoods while enabling safe access to food and nutrition for women and men; 3. Strengthen the capacity of governments and regional organizations and enable the international community to prepare for, assess, and respond to shocks. **2. Support food security and nutrition and (re)build livelihoods in fragile settings and following**	Three goals (System Level Outcomes or SLOs), and their Intermediate Development Outcomes (IDOs) **1. Reduce poverty—**1. Increased resilience of the poor to climate change and other shocks; 2. Enhanced smallholder market access; 3. Increased incomes and employment; 4. Increased productivity. **Target:** 100 million fewer poor people, of which percent are women, by 2030. **2. Improve food security and nutrition for health—**1. Increased productivity; 2. Improved diets for poor and vulnerable people; 3. Improved food safety; 4. Improved human and animal health through better agricultural practice. **Target:** 150 million fewer poor people, of which 50 percent are women by 2030.	Five strategic objectives for enabling poor rural people to improve their food security and nutrition, raise their incomes, and strengthen their resilience 1. A natural resource and economic asset base for poor rural women and men that is **more resilient to climate change, environmental degradation, and market transformation;** 2. Access for poor rural women and men to services **to reduce poverty, improve nutrition, raise incomes, and build resilience in a changing environment;** 3. Poor rural women and men and their organizations able to manage profitable, sustainable, and resilient farm and non-farm enterprises or take advantage of decent work opportunities; 4. Poor rural women and

development and poverty reduction:

(i) Manages the resources of our planet for future generations

(ii) Ensures social inclusion and

(iii) Adopts fiscally responsible policies that limit the debt burden on future generations. **Sustainability is an overarching theme** that frames the goals of reducing extreme poverty and improving shared prosperity.

14 Global Practices –

1. Agriculture
2. Education
3. Energy and Extractives
4. Environment and Natural Resources
5. Finance and Markets
6. Governance
7. Health, Nutrition, and Population
8. Macroeconomics and Fiscal Management
9. Poverty
10. Social, Urban, Rural, and Resilience
11. Social Protection and Labor

guidelines for highly productive and sustainable agriculture.

3. Reduce rural poverty— 1. Improving opportunities for the rural poor to access decent farm and nonfarm employment; 2. Improving social protection systems; 3. Empowering the rural poor in gaining sustainable access to resources and services.

4. Enable more inclusive and efficient agricultural and food systems—1. Improving the inclusiveness and efficiency of food systems; 2. Helping to strengthen public– private collaboration to improve smallholder agriculture; 3. Improving the inclusiveness and efficiency of markets.

5. Increase the resilience of livelihoods to threats and crises—1. Helping countries to govern risks and crises; 2. Helping countries watch to safeguard; 3. Helping countries to prevent and mitigate risks; 4. Supporting countries' preparation and response.

emergencies

Targets: 1. Support or restore food security and nutrition of people and communities and contribute to stability, resilience, and selfreliance; **2.** Assist governments and communities to establish or rebuild livelihoods, connect to markets, and manage food systems; **3.** Through food and nutrition assistance, support the safe, voluntary return, reintegration or resettlement of refugees, and internally displaced persons; **4.** Ensure equitable access to and control over food and nutrition assistance for women and men.

3. Reduce risk and enable people, communities and countries to meet their own food and nutrition needs

Targets: 1. Support people, communities, and countries to strengthen resilience to shocks, reduce disaster risks, and adapt to climate change through food and nutrition assistance; **2.** Leverage purchasing power to

3. Improve natural resource system and ecosystem services—1. Natural capital enhanced and protected, especially from climate change; 2. Enhanced benefits from ecosystem goods and services; 3. More sustainably managed agroecosystem. **Target:** 190 million hectares of degraded land restored by 2030

men and their organizations **able to influence policies and institutions that affect their livelihoods.**

5. Enabling institutional and policy environments to **support agricultural production and the full range of related non-farm activities.**

Areas of thematic focus:

1. Natural resources—land, water, energy, and biodiversity

2. Climate change adaptation and mitigation

3. Improved agricultural technologies and effective production services

4. A broad range of inclusive financial services

5. Integration of poor rural people within value chains

6. Rural enterprise development and non-farm employment opportunities

7. Technical and vocational skills development

8. Support to rural producers' organizations

Continued

Table A.1.2 *Continued*

Organization			
World Bank Group	Food and Agriculture Organization of the United Nations	World Food Programme	CGIAR	International Fund for Agricultural Development
12. Trade and Competitiveness 13. Transport and ICT 14. Water	**Additional Objective** 6. Technical quality, knowledge, and services	connect smallholder farmers to markets, reduce postharvest losses, support economic empowerment of women and men, and transform food assistance into a productive investment in local communities; 3. Strengthen the capacity of governments and communities to establish, manage, and scale up sustainable, effective, and equitable food security and nutrition institutions, infrastructure, and safety-net systems, including systems linked to local agricultural supply chains; **4. Reduce undernutrition and break the intergenerational cycle of hunger** **Targets:** 1. Prevent stunting and wasting, treat moderate acute malnutrition, and address micronutrient deficiencies, particularly,		

among young children, pregnant and lactating women, and people infected with HIV, tuberculosis, and malaria, by providing access to appropriate food and nutrition assistance; 2. Increase access to education and health services, contribute to learning, and improve nutrition and health for children, adolescent girls, and their families; 3. Strengthen the capacity of governments and communities to design, manage, and scale-up nutrition programs and create an enabling environment that promotes gender equality.

- Governance—Strengthening the rules and processes that affect the interactions of state and non-state actors in a variety of sectors
- Gender—Ensuring all work emphasizes gender equality, participation, and the empowerment of women
- Nutrition (new for 2016–17)

- Gender equality
- Climate risk analysis and response
- Building capacities for good governance
- Human rights-based standards
- Emergency preparedness and response
- Protection
- HIV/AIDS prevention and treatment

- Climate change—Mitigating and adapting to climate change risks and shocks
- Gender and youth—Ensuring gender and youth equity and inclusion
- Policies and institutions—Strengthening the policy and institution enabling environment
- Capacity development—Developing the capacity of

- Environment/cli mate
- Gender
- Social inclusion
- Indigenous People
- Young people
- HIV/AIDS

Crosscutting themes

- Climate change
- Fragility, conflict, and violence
- Gender
- Jobs
- Public–private partnerships

Continued

Table A.1.2 *Continued*

	Organization				
	World Bank Group	Food and Agriculture Organization of the United Nations	World Food Programme	CGIAR	International Fund for Agricultural Development
Core functions/ research priorities	Five specific principles to frame the strategy: **1. Serve poor and vulnerable people everywhere in a sustainable manner** **2. Recognize the diversity of** clients **3. Work as one World Bank Group** **4. Focus on development solutions** **5. Exercise dynamic selectivity** The strategy sets out the vision for a repositioned WBG that helps clients to address the most difficult challenges to reducing poverty and building shared prosperity. The repositioned WBG: 1. Aligned all WBG activities and resources to the two goals: maximize development impact, and	**Seven core functions to achieve concrete results:** **1. Facilitate and support countries in the** development and implementation of normative and standard-setting instruments, such as international agreements, codes of conduct, technical standards, and others **2. Assemble, analyze, monitor, and improve** access to data and information in areas related to their mandate **3. Facilitate, promote, and support policy dialogue at** global, regional, and country levels **4. Advise and support capacity development at** country and regional levels to prepare, implement, monitor, and evaluate evidence-based policies,	Four strategic objectives according to their contribution to three overlapping priorities – **1. Prepare for and respond to shocks** **2. Restore and rebuild lives** and livelihoods **3. Reduce vulnerability and** build lasting resilience Two principles to achieve their strategic objectives – **1. Deploy the right tool in** the right place at the right time **2. Enable effective and** efficient implementation	national partners and beneficiaries Eight research priorities to achieve targets: **1. Genetic improvement of** crops, livestock, fish, and trees, to increase productivity, resilience to stress, nutritional value, and efficiency of resource use **2. Agricultural systems—** adopt a systems approach to optimize economic, social, and environmental co-benefits in areas with high concentrations of poor people **3. Gender and inclusive growth—**creating opportunities for women, young people, and marginalized groups **4. Enabling policies and** institutions, to improve the performance of markets, enhance delivery of critical public goods and services, and increase the agency and	Eight principles of engagement – **1. A differentiated** approach based on country context **2. Targeting** **3. Supporting the** empowerment of poor rural people **4. Promoting gender equality and women's empowerment** **5. Creating viable opportunities for rural** youth **6. Innovation, learning, and** scaling up **7. Effective partnerships and resource mobilization** **8. Sustainability Outcomes:** 1. Increased incomes and enhanced food security and nutrition for rural people served by IFADsupported projects in a given locality or region

emphasize their comparative advantage.
2. Operationalized the goals through the new country engagement model to help country clients identify and tackle the toughest development challenges.
3. Recognized as a "Solutions WBG," offering world-class knowledge services and customized development solutions grounded in evidence and focused on results.
4. Sought transformational engagements and took smart risks.
5. Promoted scaled-up partnerships, which are strategically aligned with the goals, and crowd in public and private resources, expertise, and ideas.
6. Worked as one WBG committed to achieving the goals.

investments, and programs
5. **Advise and support activities** that assemble, disseminate, and improve the uptake of **knowledge, technologies and good practices** in the areas of their mandate
6. **Facilitate partnerships** for food security and nutrition, agriculture, and rural development, between governments, development partners, civil society, and the private sector
7. **Advocate and communicate** at national, regional, and global levels, in areas of their mandate

resilience of poor people
5. **Natural resources and ecosystem services**—focusing on productive ecosystems and landscapes that offer significant opportunities to reverse environmental degradation and enhance productivity
6. **Nutrition and health**—emphasizing dietary diversity, nutritional content, safety of foods, and development of value chains of particular importance for the nutrition of poor consumers
7. **Climate-smart agriculture**—focusing on urgently needed adaptation and mitigation options for farmers and other resource users
8. **Nurturing diversity**—ensuring in-trust plant genetic resources collections are safely maintained, and genetically and phenotypically characterized to maximize the exploitation of these critical resources for food security, productivity, nutrient-rich crops, and resilient farming systems

2. **Improved policy and regulatory frameworks** at local, national, and international levels
3. Strengthened and more inclusive **rural producers' organizations**
4. **Strengthened in country institutional capacities** for pro-poor agricultural and rural development
Outputs:
1. **Results-based country programmes and projects** (loans and grants)
2. Policy dialogue and advocacy initiatives
3. Policies and strategies
4. Knowledge products and learning tools

Source: Authors' construction.

References

ADB (Asian Development Bank). 2015. "Jeffrey Sachs on the New Sustainable Development Goals: Changing Asia." August 10 (video). https://www.adb.org/news/videos/sustainable-development-humanitys-future

Ahluwalia, Montek Singh, Lawrence Summers, Andrés Velasco (co-chairs); Nancy Birdsall, and Scott Morris (co-directors). 2016. "Multilateral Development Banking for this Century's Development Challenges: Five Recommendations to Shareholders of the Old and New Multilateral Development Banks." Center for Global Development, Washington, DC.

Arslan, Aslihan, Nancy McCarthy, Leslie Lipper, Solomon Asfaw, and Andrea Cattaneo. 2014. "Adoption and Intensity of Adoption of Conservation Farming Practices in Zambia." *Agriculture, Ecosystems & Environment* 187: 72–86.

Axelrod, R. M., and M. D. Cohen. 1999. *Harnessing Complexity: Organization Implications of a Scientific Frontier.* New York: Free Press.

Bagla, Pallava. 2016. "India's First Transgenic Food Crop Edges toward Approval." *Science,* Asia/Pacific Biology, Plants & Animals, September 7. http://www.sciencemag.org/news/2016/09/india-s-first-transgenic-food-crop-edges-toward-approval

Barrett, Christopher B., Thomas Reardon, Johan Swinnen, and David Zilberman. 2019. "Structural Transformation and Economic Development: Insights from the Agri-food Value Chain Revolution." Dyson Working Paper, Cornell University, Ithaca, NY. http://barrett.dyson.cornell.edu/files/papers/BRSZ%2013 percent20Aug%202019.pdf

Barry, Mike. 2016. "Ten Takeaways from Davos 2016." World Economic Forum. Global Agenda. Fourth Industrial Revolution. https://www.weforum.org/agenda/2016/01/10-takeaways-from-davos-2016

Bennet, James. 2015. "'We Need an Energy Miracle.'" *Atlantic Monthly* 316 (4): 56–64.

Binswanger-Mkhize, Hans P. 2012. "India 1960–2010: Structural Change, the Rural Non-farm Sector, and the Prospects for Agriculture." Symposium Series on Global Food Policy and Food Security in the 21st Century, Center on Food Security and the Environment (FSE), Stanford University, Stanford, May 10.

Binswanger-Mkhize, Hans P. 2013. "The Stunted Structural Transformation of the Indian Economy: Agriculture, Manufacturing and the Rural Non-Farm Sector." Review of Rural Affairs. *Economic & Political Weekly* XLVIII (26 & 27), June 29.

Binswanger-Mkhize, Hans P., Alex F. McCalla, and Praful Patel. 2010. "Structural Transformation and African Agriculture." *Global Journal of Emerging Market Economies* 2 (2): 113–52.

Birdsall, Nancy. 2000. "The World Bank of the Future: Victim, Villain, Global Credit Union?" *Brown Journal of World Affairs* 7 (2): 119–27.

Birdsall, Nancy. 2015. "What Is the Future Role of the World Bank?" Global Agenda, World Economic Forum, October 7. https://www.weforum.org/agenda/2015/10/what-is-the-future-role-of-the-world-bank/

Birdsall, Nancy, and Homi Kharas, with Ayad Mahgoub and Rita Perakis. 2010. "Quality of Official Development Assistance Assessment." QuODA Report, Brookings Institution and Center for Global Development (CGD), Washington, DC.

Brouder, Sylvie M., and Helena Gomez-Macpherson. 2014. "The Impact of Conservation Agriculture on Smallholder Agricultural Yields: A Scoping Review of the Evidence." *Agriculture, Ecosystems & Environment* 187: 11–32.

Bunge, Jacob, Brian Spegele, and William Mauldin. 2016. "Power U.S. Panel Clears Chinese Takeover of Syngenta." *Wall Street Journal*, August 23. http://www.wsj.com/articles/powerful-u-s-panel-clears-chinese-takeover-of-syngenta-1471914278

Burall, Simon, and Simon Maxwell, with Alina Rocha Menocal. 2006. "Reforming the International Aid Architecture: Options and Ways Forward." Working Paper 278, Overseas Development Institute, London.

Buytaert, Dries, and Devesh, Raj 2016. "Could the Fourth Industrial Revolution Help Us Reach the Global Goals?" World Economic Forum, February 12. https://www.weforum.org/agenda/2016/02/davos-2016-and-the-fourth-industrial-revolution.

CDC (Centers for Disease Control and Prevention). 2020. "Micronutrient Facts." https://www.cdc.gov/nutrition/micronutrient-malnutrition/micronutrients/index.html

CFS (Committee on World Food Security). 2012. "Voluntary Guidelines on the Responsible Governance of Tenure of Land, Fisheries and Forests in the Context of National Food Security." http://www.fao.org/cfs/home/activities/vggt/en/

CGTN America. 2017. "Full Text of Xi Jinping Keynote at the World Economic Forum." January 17. https://america.cgtn.com/2017/01/17/full-text-of-xi-jinping-keynote-at-the-world-economic-forum

Chand, Ramesh, P. A. Lakshmi Prasanna, and Aruna Singh. 2011. "Farm Size and Productivity: Understanding the Strengths of Smallholders and Improving Their Livelihoods." *Economic & Political Weekly* Supplement 46 (26 & 27): 5–11.

Chemnick, Jean. 2019. "How the World Is Coping 1 Year after Trump Abandoned Paris Climate Pact." Reprinted from Climatewire, E & E News, May 31, 2018, by *Scientific American*. https://www.scientificamerican.com/article/how-the-world-is-coping-1-year-after-trump-abandoned-climate-pact/

Chenery, Hollis B., and Moises Syrquin. 1975. *Patterns of Development: 1950–1970*. Oxford: Oxford University Press.

Choudhary, Bhagirath, and Kadambini Gaur. 2015. "Biotech Cotton in India, 2002 to 2014: Adoption, Impact, Progress & Future." ISAAA Series of Biotech Crop Profiles, International Service for the Acquisition of Agri-Biotech Applications, Ithaca, NY. https://www.isaaa.org/resources/publications/biotech_crop_profiles/bt_cotton_in_india-a_country_profile/download/Bt_Cotton_in_India-2002-2014.pdf.

Clemens, Michael A., and Michael Kremer. 2016. "The New Role for the World Bank." *Journal of Economic Perspectives* 30 (1): 53–76.

Cochrane, Willard W. 1958. *Farm Prices: Myth and Reality*. St. Paul: University of Minnesota Press.

Collier, Paul, and Stefan Dercon. 2014. "African Agriculture in 50 Years: Smallholders in a Rapidly Changing World." *World Development* 63: 92–101.

Conway, Gordon. 2012. *One Billion Hungry: Can We Feed the World?* Ithaca, NY: Cornell University Press.

Coppess, Jonathan. 2017. "CBO Baseline and the Potential for Conflicts by Expanding CRP." Agricultural & Applied Economics Association (AAEA) *Choices* 32 (4), 4th Quarter.

CRS (Congressional Research Service). 2019. "Potential Implications of U.S. Withdrawal from the Paris Agreement on Climate Change." In Focus, IF10668, updated April 5, 2019. https://fas.org/sgp/crs/misc/IF10668.pdf

de Janvry, Alain, and Elisabeth Sadoulet. 2010. "Agricultural Growth and Poverty Reduction: Additional Evidence." *World Bank Research Observer* 25 (1): 1–20.

de Melo, Jaime. 2017. "Pathways to Structural Transformation in Africa." Africa in Focus blog, October 30, The Brookings Institution, Washington, DC. https://www.brookings.edu/blog/africa-in-focus/2017/10/30/pathways-to-structural-transformation-in-africa/

Dercon, Stefan, and Douglas Gollin. 2014. "Agriculture in African Development: A Review of Theories and Strategies." CSAE Working Paper WPS/2014–22, Centre for the Study of African Economies, Oxford.

Development Committee (Joint Ministerial Committee of the Boards of Governors of the Bank and the Fund on the Transfer of Real Resources to Developing Countries). 2015. "From Billions to Trillions: Transforming Development Finance Post-2015 Financing for Development: Multilateral Development Finance." Development Committee Discussion Note. Prepared jointly by African Development Bank, Asian Development Bank, European Bank for Reconstruction and Development, European Investment Bank, Inter-American Development Bank, International Monetary Fund, and World Bank Group, April 18.

Development Initiatives. 2017. *Global Nutrition Report 2017: Nourishing the SDGs*. Bristol, UK: Development Initiatives.

DFID (Department for International Development) and UK Aid. 2011. *Multilateral Aid Review: Ensuring Maximum Value for Money for UK Aid through Multilateral Organisations*. London: DFID. http://www.who.int/country-cooperation/what-who-does/DFID_multilateral_aid_review.pdf?ua=1

Diao, Xinshen, Margaret McMillan, and Dani Rodrik. 2017. "The Recent Growth Boom in Developing Economics: A Structural Change Perspective." NBER Working Paper No. 23132, National Bureau of Economic Research, Cambridge, MA.

Dunning, Casey, and Claire McGillem. 2016. "Country Ownership: Rhetoric or Reality? Let's Find Out," Center for Global Development, March 11, 2016. http://www.cgdev.org/blog/country-ownership-rhetoric-or-reality-lets-find-out

Easterly, William. 2015. "The SDGs Should Stand for Senseless, Dreamy, Garbled." Foreign Policy, September 28. http://foreignpolicy.com/2015/09/28/the-sdgs-are-utopian-and-worthless-mdgs-development-rise-of-the-rest/

Elliott, Howard, Eduardo Trigo, Ed Rege, Krishna Alluri, and Ayman Abou-Hadid. 2009. "Independent Evaluation of IAASTD." Report to Agricultural Sector Board, World Bank, Washington, DC.

Falck-Zepeda, José, Guillaume Gruère, and Idah Sithole-Niang, eds. 2013. *Genetically Modified Crops in Africa: Economic and Policy Lessons from Countries South of the Sahara*. Washington, DC: International Food Policy Research Institute (IFPRI).

Fankhauser, Samuel. 2013. "What Is Climate Finance and Where Will It Come From?" *The Guardian*, in collaboration with the Grantham Research Institute on Climate Change and the Environment, London School of Economics and Political Science, April 4.

FAO (Food and Agriculture Organization of the United Nations). 2011. "The State of Food and Agriculture 2010–11: Women in Agriculture—Closing the Gender Gap for Development." FAO, Rome.

FAO (Food and Agriculture Organization of the United Nations). 2012. "Voluntary Guidelines on the Responsible Governance of Tenure of Land, Fisheries and Forests in the Context of National Food Security," FAO, Rome. http://www.fao.org/docrep/016/i2801e/i2801e.pdf

FAO (Food and Agriculture Organization of the United Nations). 2014. "Innovation in Family Farming." *The State of Food and Agriculture 2014* In Brief, FAO, Rome. http://www.fao.org/3/a-i4036e.pdf

FAO (Food and Agriculture Organization of the United Nations). 2015. *The State of Food Insecurity in the World 2015.* Rome: FAO.

FAO (Food and Agriculture Organization of the United Nations). 2017. "The Future of Food and Agriculture. Trends and Challenges." FAO, Rome. http://www.fao.org/3/a-i6583e.pdf

FAO (Food and Agriculture Organization of the United Nations). 2020. Statistics. Food Security Indicators (database). http://www.fao.org/economic/ess/ess-fs/ess-fadata/en/#.Wdp9KUyZNE5

FAO (Food and Agriculture Organization of the United Nations), IFAD (International Fund for Agricultural Development), UNICEF (United Nations Children's Fund), WFP (World Food Programme), and WHO (World Health Organization). 2019. "The State of Food Security and Nutrition in the World 2019. Safeguarding against Economic Slowdowns and Downturns." FAO, Rome. http://www.fao.org/state-of-food-security-nutrition

Fedoroff, Nina V. 2020. "The GM Crop Forecast: Cloudy—with a Chance of Clearing." Genetic Literacy Project, April 14–17 (essay published in 4 parts). https://geneticliteracyproject.org/glp-library/?_search_bar=Fedoroff

Financial Express. 2018. "Narendra Modi Speech in Davos: Full Text of PM's Address at WEF 2018." January 23. https://www.financialexpress.com/india-news/narendra-modi-in-davos-full-speech-at-wef-2018-from-twitter-amazon-and-more-pm-highlights-how-tech-transformed-world/1026963/

Gardner, Bruce L. 2006. *American Agriculture in the Twentieth Century: How It Flourished and What It Cost.* Cambridge, MA: Harvard University Press.

Gaspar, Vitor, Paolo Mauro, Ian Parry, and Catherine Pattillo. 2019. "Fiscal Policies to Curb Climate Change." IMFBlog, International Monetary Fund, Washington, DC. https://blogs.imf.org/2019/10/10/fiscal-policies-to-curb-climate-change

Gates, Bill, and Melinda Gates. 2015. "A Big Bet for the Future." 2015 Gates Annual Letter. https://www.gatesnotes.com/2015-annual-letter?page=0&lang=en

Gautam, Madhur, and Rashidur R. Faruqee. 2016. *Dynamics of Rural Growth in Bangladesh: Sustaining Poverty Reduction.* Washington, DC: World Bank Group.

GCF (Green Climate Fund). 2020. "How We Work: Resource Mobilization." https://www.greenclimate.fund/how-we-work/resource-mobilization

Gilbert, Natasha. 2013. "Case Studies: A Hard Look at GM Crops." *Nature* 497: 24–6. doi:10.1038/497024a

Giller, Ken E., Ernst Witter, Marc Corbeels, and Pablo Tittonell. 2009. "Conservation Agriculture and Smallholder Farming in Africa: The Heretic's View." *Field Crops Research* 114 (1): 23–34.

GLOPAN (Global Panel on Agriculture and Food Systems for Nutrition). 2017. "Urban Diets and Nutrition: Trends, Challenges and Opportunities for Policy Action." Policy Brief No. 9, GLOPAN, London. https://www.glopan.org/sites/default/files/Downloads/GlobalPanelUrbanizationPolicyBrief.pdf

Goldenberg, Suzanne. 2016. "Obama Using Final Budget Request to Push for Action against Climate Change." *The Guardian*, February 6. https://www.theguardian.com/us-news/2016/feb/06/barack-obama-final-budget-request-congress-climate-change-action-congress

GPEDC (Global Partnership for Effective Development Co-operation). 2014. "First High-Level Meeting of the Global Partnership for Effective Development Co-operation: Building Towards an Inclusive Post–2015 Development Agenda." Mexico High-Level Meeting Communiqué, April 16, GPEDC.

Groth, Hans, and John F. May, eds. 2017. *Africa's Population: In Search of a Demographic Dividend.* Cham: Springer International Publishing.

Hallward-Driemeier, Mary and Gaurav Nayyar. 2018. *Trouble in the Making? The Future of Manufacture-Led Development.* Washington, DC: World Bank Group.

Holden, Emily. 2019. "House Democrats Pass Bill Directing Trump to Stay in Paris Climate Deal." *The Guardian*, May 2, 2019. https://www.theguardian.com/us-news/2019/may/02/house-democrats-paris-climate-change-agreement-bill

Hsaio, Jennifer. 2015. "GMOs and Pesticides: Helpful or Harmful?" Science in the News, Harvard University, August 10. http://sitn.hms.harvard.edu/flash/2015/gmos-and-pesticides/

IAASTD (International Assessment of Agricultural Knowledge, Science and Technology for Development). 2009. "Agriculture at a Crossroads." A Synthesis of the Global and Sub-Global IAASTD Reports. Washington, DC: Island Press.

IEA (International Energy Agency). 2014. *World Energy Outlook 2014.* Paris: Organisation for Economic and Co-operative Development (OECD)/IEA.

IFPRI (International Food Policy Research Institute). 2014. *Global Nutrition Report 2014: Actions and Accountability to Accelerate the World's Progress on Nutrition.* Washington, DC: IFPRI.

IFPRI (International Food Policy Research Institute). 2015. *Global Nutrition Report 2015: Actions and Accountability to Advance Nutrition and Sustainable Development.* Washington, DC: IFPRI.

IFPRI (International Food Policy Research Institute). 2016. *2016 Global Nutrition Report. From Promise to Impact: Ending Malnutrition by 2030.* Washington, DC: IFPRI.

IIRR (International Institute of Rural Reconstruction) and ACTN (African Conservation Tillage Network). 2005. *Conservation Agriculture: A Manual for Farmers and Extension Workers in Africa.* Nairobi: International Institute of Rural Reconstruction and Harare: African Conservation Tillage Network.

ILO (International Labour Organization). 2015. International Labour Conference. Recommendation 204: Recommendation Concerning the Transition from the Informal to the Formal Economy. 104th Session, Geneva, June 12. https://www.ilo.org/wcmsp5/groups/public/—ed_norm/—relconf/documents/meetingdocument/wcms_377774.pdf

IPCC (Intergovernmental Panel on Climate Change). 2014. *Climate Change 2014: Impacts, Adaptation, and Vulnerability. Part A: Global and Sectoral Aspects.* Contribution of Working Group II to the Fifth Assessment Report of the Intergovernmental Panel on Climate Change. New York: Cambridge University Press.

Isaac, Nkechi, and Joan Conrow. 2019. "Nigeria Approves Its First GMO Food Crop." Cornell Alliance for Science, January 28. https://allianceforscience.cornell.edu/blog/2019/01/nigeria-approves-first-gmo-food-crop/

Jenks, Bruce, and Jennifer Topping. 2019. "Financing the UN Development System 2019: Time for Hard Choices." Dag Hammarskjöld Foundation, the United Nations (including the United Nations Development Programme), the Multi-Partner Trust Fund Office, Uppsala, Sweden. https://www.daghammarskjold.se/wp-content/uploads/2019/08/financial-instr-report-2019-interactive-1.pdf

Johnston, Bruce F., and John W. Mellor. 1961. "The Role of Agriculture in Economic Development." *American Economic Review* 51 (4): 566–93.

Josling, Tim. 2011. "Global Food Stamps: An Idea Worth Considering?" Issue Paper No. 36, International Centre for Trade and Sustainable Development (ICTSD), Geneva. http://www.ictsd.org/downloads/2011/12/global-food-stamps-an-idea-worth-considering.pdf

Kaldor, Nicholas. 1966. *Causes of the Slow Rate of Economic Growth of the United Kingdom: An Inaugural Lecture*. London: Cambridge University Press.

Kapur, Devesh. 2015. "Escape from the World Bank." Project Syndicate, October 16. https://www.project-syndicate.org/commentary/emerging-economies-development-banks-by-devesh-kapur-2015-10?barrier=true

Kassam, A., T. Friedrich, R. Derpas, and J. Kienzele. 2015. "Overview of the Worldwide Spread of Conservation Agriculture." *Field Actions Science Reports* 8. https://factsreports.revues.org/3966

Khanna, Madhu, and James Shortie. 2017. "(Theme Overview) Preserving Water Quality: Challenges and Opportunities for Technological and Policy Innovations." Agricultural & Applied Economics Association (AAEA). *Choices* Quarter 4.

Kharas, Homi, John McArthur, Geoffrey Gertz, Sinead Mowlds, and Lorenz Noe. 2015. "Ending Rural Hunger: Mapping Needs and Actions for Food and Nutrition Security." Global Economy and Development Report, Brookings Institution, Washington, DC.

Kim, Soowon, Soojae Moon, and Barry M. Popkin. 2000 "The Nutrition Transition in South Korea." *American Journal of Clinical Nutrition* 71 (1): 44–53.

Krugman, Paul R. 1994. "The Myth of Asia's Miracle." *Foreign Affairs* 73 (6): 62–78.

Kuznets, Simon. 1955. "Economic Growth and Income Inequality." *American Economic Review* 45 (1): 1–28.

Kuznets, Simon. 1966. *Modern Economic Growth: A Rate, Structure, and Spread*. New Haven, CT: Yale University Press.

Lal, Rattan, and B. A. Stewart, eds. 2015. *Soil Management of Smallholder Agriculture*. Boca Raton, FL: CRC Press.

Lancaster, Carole. 1997. "The World Bank in Africa since 1980: The Politics of Structural Adjustment Lending." In *The World Bank: Its First Half Century, Vol. 2 Perspectives*, edited by Devesh Kapur, John P. Lewis, and Richard Webb, 161–94. Washington, DC: Brookings Institution Press. http://documents.worldbank.org/curated/en/405561468331913038/pdf/578750PUB0v20W10Box353775B01PUBLIC1.pdf

Lancet. 2008. Lancet Series: Maternal and Child Undernutrition. 371 (9608). http://www.thelancet.com/series/maternal-and-child-undernutrition.

Lancet. 2011. Lancet Series: Obesity. 378 (9793). http://www.thelancet.com/series/obesity.

Lancet. 2013. Lancet Series: Maternal and Child Nutrition. 382 (9890). http://www.thelancet.com/series/maternal-and-child-nutrition.

Lancet. 2015. Lancet Series: Obesity 2015. 385 (9986). http://www.thelancet.com/series/obesity-2015.

Leslie, Jacques. 2017. "Soil Power! The Dirty Way to a Green Planet." *New York Times*, Sunday Review section, December 2.

Lewis, W. Arthur. 1954. "Economic Development with Unlimited Supplies of Labour." *The Manchester School* 22 (2): 139–91.

Linn, Johannes F. 2018. "Will a Capital Increase Mean a Greater Global Role for the World Bank?" Future Development, Brookings Institution, Washington, DC. https://www.brookings.edu/blog/future-development/2018/05/14/will-a-capital-increase-mean-a-greater-global-role-for-the-world-bank/

Loayza, Norman V., and Claudio Raddatz. 2010. "The Composition of Growth Matters for Poverty Alleviation." *Journal of Development Economics* 93 (1): 137–51.

Lowder, Sarah K., Jacob Skoet, and Terri Raney. 2016. "The Number, Size, and Distribution of Farms, Smallholder Farms, and Family Farms Worldwide." *World Development* 87: 16–29.

Lu, Liang, and Thomas Reardon. 2018. "An Economic Model of the Evolution of Food Retail and Supply Chains from Traditional Shops to Supermarkets to E-Commerce." *American Journal of Agricultural Economics* 100 (5): 1320–35.

Lu, Liang, Thomas Reardon, and David Zilberman. 2016. "Supply Chain Design and Adoption of Indivisible Technology." *American Journal of Agricultural Economics* 98 (5): 1419–31.

MacDonald, Lawrence. 2012. "The Future of the World Bank—Nancy Birdsall." Center for Global Development Podcast, CGD, Washington, DC. https://www.cgdev.org/blog/future-world-bank---nancy-birdsall

Masters, William A., Agnes Andersson Djurfeldt, Cornelis De Haan, Peter Hazell, Thomas Jayne, Magnus Jirström, and Thomas Reardon. 2013. "Urbanization and Farm Size in Asia and Africa: Implications for Food Security and Agricultural Research." *Global Food Security* 2 (3): 156–65.

Mazvimavi, Kizito. 2011. "Socio-Economic Analysis of Conservation Agriculture in Southern Africa." Network Paper 02, January, Regional Emergency Office for Southern Africa (REOSA), Food and Agricultural Organization of the United Nations (FAO), Rome.

Mazza, Federico, James Falzon, and Barbara Buchner. 2016. "Global Climate Finance: An Updated View on 2013 & 2014 Flows." Climate Policy Initiative.

Mead, Margaret. 1976. "A Comment on the Role of Women in Agriculture." In *Women and World Development*, 9–11. Edited by Irene Tinker, Michèle Bo Bramsen, and Mayra Buvinić. New York: Praeger.

Mitchell, Paul D. 2016. "Technological Change in Agricultural Production: Dealing with Cochrane's Treadmill." Powerpoint presentation, AAE 320, Farming Systems Management, University of Wisconsin-Madison.

Molden, David, ed. 2007. *Water for Food, Water for Life: A Comprehensive Assessment of Water Management in Agriculture*. International Water Management Institute. London: Earthscan.

Monteiro, C. A., L. Mondini, A. L. Medeiros de Souza, and Barry M. Popkin. 1995. "The Nutrition Transition in Brazil." *European Journal of Clinical Nutrition* 49 (2): 105–13.

Morris, Scott, and Madeleine Gleave. 2015. "The World Bank at 75." CGD Policy Paper 058, Center for Global Development, Washington, DC.

NASEM (National of Academies of Sciences, Engineering and Medicine). 2016. *Genetically Engineered Crops: Experiences and Prospects*. Washington, DC: National Academies Press.

Newman, Carol, John Page, John Rand, Abebe Shimeles, Måns Söderbom, and Finn Tarp. 2016. *Made in Africa: Learning to Compete in Industry*. Washington, DC: Brookings Institution Press.

North, Douglass C. 1990. *Institutions, Institutional Change and Economic Performance*. Cambridge, UK: Cambridge University Press.

NRC (National Research Council). 2010. *Toward Sustainable Agricultural Systems in the 21st Century. Committee on Twenty-First Century Systems Agriculture*, Board on Agriculture and Natural Resources, Division on Earth and Life Sciences. Washington, DC: National Academies Press.

OECD (Organisation for Economic Co-operation and Development). 2019a. Fourth High Level Forum on Aid Effectiveness. http://www.oecd.org/dac/effectiveness/fourthhighlevel forumonaideffectiveness.htm

OECD (Organisation for Economic Co-operation and Development). 2019b. HLF1: The First High Level Forum on Aid Effectiveness, Rome. http://www.oecd.org/dac/effectiveness/hlf-1thefirsthighlevelforumonaideffectivenessrome.htm

OECD (Organisation for Economic Co-operation and Development). 2019c. Second High Level Forum on Aid Effectiveness (HLF-2), 28 February to 2 March 2005, Paris, France. http://www.oecd.org/dac/effectiveness/secondhighlevelforumonjointprogresstowardenhancedaid-effectivenessharmonisationalignmentandresults.htm

OECD (Organisation for Economic Co-operation and Development). 2019d. Third High Level Forum on Aid Effectiveness. http://www.oecd.org/dac/effectiveness/theaccrahighlevelforumhlf3andtheaccraagendaforaction.htm

OECD (Organisation for Economic Co-operation and Development). 2021. "COVID-19 Spending Helped to Lift Foreign Aid to an All-Time High in 2020." Detailed Note, Paris, OECD, April 13. https://www.oecd.org/dac/financing-sustainable-development/development-finance-data/ODA-2020-detailed-summary.pdf

Ostrom, Elinor. 1990. *Governing the Commons: The Evolution of Institutions for Collective Action*. New York: Cambridge University Press.

Owens, Trudy, and Adrian Wood. 1997. "Export-Oriented Industrialization through Primary Processing?" *World Development* 25 (9): 1453–70.

Page, John. 2015a. "Made in Africa: Some New Thinking for Africa Industrialization Day." Africa in Focus blog, November 19, The Brookings Institution, Washington, DC. https://www.brookings.edu/blog/africa-in-focus/2015/11/19/made-in-africa-some-new-thinking-for-africa-industrialization-day/

Page, John. 2015b. "Structural Change and Africa's Poverty Puzzle." In *The Last Mile in Ending Extreme Poverty*, edited by Laurence Chandy, Hiroshi Kato, and Homi Kharas, 219–48. Washington, DC: Brookings Institution.

Page, John, and Fred Dews. 2016. "Made in Africa: Manufacturing and Economic Growth on the Continent." Brookings Cafeteria Podcast, January 22, The Brookings Institution, Washington, DC.

Perry, Chris, and Pasquale Steduto, with the contribution of Fawzi Karajeh. 2017. "Does Improved Irrigation Technology Save Water? A Review of the Evidence." Discussion Paper on Irrigation and Sustainable Water Resources Management in the Near East and North Africa, Food and Agriculture Organization of the United Nations, Cairo.

Phillips, Ralph W. 1981. *FAO: Its Origins, Formation and Evolution 1945–1981*. Rome: Food and Agriculture Organization of the United Nations (FAO).

Popkin, Barry M. 1994. "The Nutrition Transition in Low-income Countries: An Emerging Crisis." *Nutrition Reviews* 52 (9): 285–98.

Popkin, Barry M. 1998. "The Nutrition Transition and Its Health Implications in Lower Income Countries." *Public Health Nutrition* 1 (1): 5–21.

Popkin, Barry M. 2001. "The Nutrition Transition and Obesity in the Developing World." *Journal of Nutrition* 131 (3): 871S–3.

Qaim, Matin. 2010. "Benefits of Genetically Modified Crops for the Poor: Household Income, Nutrition, and Health." *New Biotechnology* 27 (5): 552–7.

Qaim, Matin, and Shahzad Kouser. 2013. "Genetically Modified Crops and Food Security." *PLoS ONE* 8 (6): e64879. doi:10.1371/journal.pone.0064879

Quisumbing, Agnes R., Ruth Meinzen-Dick, Terri L. Raney, André Croppenstedt, Julia A. Behrman, and Amber Peterman, eds. 2014. *Gender in Agriculture: Closing the Knowledge Gap.* Dordrecht: Springer.

Ravallion, Martin. 2016. "The World Bank: Why It Is Still Needed and Why It Still Disappoints." *Journal of Economic Perspectives* 30 (1): 77–94.

Reardon, Thomas, Kevin Chen, Feng Song, Bart Minten, Sunipa Das Gupta, Jianying Wang, and The Anh Dao. 2016. "Energy Costs in the Transforming Agrifood Value Chains in Asia." Staff Paper 2016–3, March, Department of Agricultural, Food and Resource Economics, Michigan State University, East Lansing.

Rehman, Hafeez-ur, Ahmad Nawaz, Abdul Wakeel, Yashpal Singh Saharawat, Muhammad Farooq. 2015. "Conservation Agriculture in South Asia." In *Conservation Agriculture*, edited by Muhammad Farooq and Kadambot H. M. Siddique, 249–83. Cham, Switzerland: Springer International Publishing.

Renwick, Danielle. 2015. "Sustainable Development Goals," Council on Foreign Relations, Global Governance, September 28. http://www.cfr.org/global-governance/sustainable-development-goals/p37051

Rodrik, Dani. 2014. "An African Miracle? Implications of Recent Research on Growth Economics," Ninth Annual Richard H. Sabot Lecture, Center for Global Development, Washington, DC. http://www.cgdev.org/event/ninth-annual-richard-h-sabot-lecture-african-miracle-implications-recent-research-growth.

Rodrik, Dani. 2016. "Premature Deindustrialization." *Journal of Economic Growth* 21 (1): 1–33.

Rogoff, Kenneth. 2017. "The US Is Exporting Obesity." Project Syndicate, December 1. https://www.project-syndicate.org/commentary/america-exports-obesity-epidemic-by-kenneth-rogoff-2017–12?barrier=accessreg

Rose, Sarah. 2016. "Shining the Light on US Foreign Assistance Transparency—An Interview with Dennis Vega." Center for Global Development, March 15. http://www.cgdev.org/blog/shining-light-us-foreign-assistance-transparency-interview-dennis-vega

Sachs, Jeffrey. 2015. "Why the Sustainable Development Goals Matter." Project Syndicate, March 30. https://www.project-syndicate.org/commentary/sustainable-development-goals-shift-by-jeffrey-d-sachs-2015–03

Sayer, Jeffrey, Terry Sunderland, Jaboury Ghazoul, Jean-Laurent Pfund, Douglas Sheil, Erik Meijaard, Michelle Venter, Agni Klintuni Boedhihartono, Michael Day, Claude Garcia, Cora van Oosten, and Louise E. Buck. 2013. "Ten Principles for a Landscape Approach to Reconciling Agriculture, Conservation, and Other Competing Land Uses." *PNAS* 110 (21): 8349–56.

Scherr, Sara J. 2015. "Changing the Role of Agriculture: Moving Beyond Production in the 21st Century." Keynote address, 2nd International Conference on Global Security, Ithaca, NY, October 11–14.

Schumpeter, Joseph A. 1943. *Capitalism, Socialism and Democracy*. London: Unwin.

Schwab, Klaus. 2016. *The Fourth Industrial Revolution*. Geneva: World Economic Forum.

Servick, Kelly. 2016. "U.S. Looking to Expert Panel to Predict Future GM Products." *Science*. Biology, Science and Policy, April 19. http://www.sciencemag.org/news/2016/04/us-looking-expert-panel-predict-future-gm-products

Shah, Rajiv J. 2017. "Remarks by Rockefeller Foundation President Dr. Rajiv Shah at World Food Prize Borlaug Dialogue International Symposium." Rockefeller Foundation News & Media, October 20. https://www.rockefellerfoundation.org/about-us/news-media/2017-world-food-prize-remarks-dr-rajiv-shah/

Spegele, Brian, and Kane Wu. 2017. "China Sews Up Record $43 Billion Foreign Takeover Deal but Work Remains." *Wall Street Journal*, May 5, 2017. https://www.wsj.com/arti cles/syngenta-shareholders-accept-chemchinas-43-billion-takeover-offer-1493963063

Stevenson, James R., Rachid Serraj, and Kenneth G. Cassman, eds. 2014. Special Issue: Evaluating Conservation Agriculture for Small-Scale Farmers in Sub-Saharan Africa and South Asia. *Agriculture, Ecosystems, & Environment* 187: 1–182.

Stiglitz, Joseph E. 1996. "Some Lessons from the East Asian Miracle." *World Bank Research Observer* 11 (2): 151–77.

Swaminathan, M. S. 2015. *Combating Hunger and Achieving Food Security*. Cambridge: Cambridge University Press.

Timmer, C. Peter, and Selvin Akkus. 2008. "The Structural Transformation as a Pathway out of Poverty: Analytics, Empirics and Politics." Working Paper No. 150, Center for Global Development, Washington, DC.

UN (United Nations). 2013. "The Future We Want." A/RES/66/288. UN General Assembly, Resolution adopted by the General Assembly on 27 July 2012. Reissued for technical reasons on January 17, 2013. http://www.un.org/ga/search/view_doc.asp?symbol=A/RES/66/288&Lang=E

UN (United Nations). 2014a. "Report of the Intergovernmental Committee of Experts on Sustainable Development Financing." A/69/315, UN General Assembly, New York. http://www.un.org/ga/search/view_doc.asp?symbol=A/69/315&Lang=E

UN (United Nations). 2014b. "The Road to Dignity by 2030: Ending Poverty, Transforming All Lives and Protecting the Planet." Synthesis Report of the Secretary-General On the Post–2015 Agenda, UN, New York.

UN (United Nations). 2014c. "World Urbanization Prospects." 2014 Revision. ST/ESA/SER.A/366, Department of Economic and Social Affairs, Population Division, UN, New York. https://esa.un.org/unpd/wup/Publications/Files/WUP2014-Report.pdf

UN (United Nations). 2015a. "Addis Ababa Action Agenda of the Third International Conference on Financing for Development." Department of Economic and Social Affairs, Financing for Development Office, New York. http://www.un.org/esa/ffd/wp-content/uploads/2015/08/AAAA_Outcome.pdf

UN (United Nations). 2015b. "Transforming Our World: the 2030 Agenda for Sustainable Development." A/RES/70/1. UN General Assembly, Resolution adopted by the General Assembly on 25 September. http://www.un.org/ga/search/view_doc.asp?symbol=A/RES/70/1&Lang=E

UN (United Nations). 2015c. "World Population Prospects: Key Findings and Advance Tables." 2015 Revision. Working Paper No. ESA/P/WP.241, Department of Economic and Social Affairs, UN, New York.

UN (United Nations). 2016. "We Can End Poverty. Millennium Development Goals and Beyond 2015." http://www.un.org/millenniumgoals/

UN (United Nations). 2019. "UN Climate Action Summit 2019." https://www.un.org/en/climatechange/un-climate-summit-2019.shtml

UN (United Nations). 2020. "Sustainable Development Goals." https://sustainabledevelopment.un.org/sdgs

UNCTAD (United Nations Conference on Trade and Development). 2014. "World Investment Report 2014: Investing in the SDGs: An Action Plan." United Nations, New York and Geneva. https://unctad.org/system/files/official-document/wir2014_en.pdf

UNFCCC (United Nations Framework Convention on Climate Change). 2014. "2014 Biennial Assessment and Overview of Climate Finance Flows Report." Standing Committee on Finance, UNFCCC, Bonn.

UNFCCC (United Nations Framework Convention on Climate Change). 2015. "Adoption of the Paris Agreement." FCCC/CP/2015/L.9/Rev.1, December 12. http://unfccc.int/resource/docs/2015/cop21/eng/l09r01.pdf

UNFCCC (United Nations Framework Convention on Climate Change). 2016. "The Second Biennial Assessment and Overview of Climate Finance Flows." UNFCCC, Bonn.

UNICEF (United Nations Children's Fund). 2016. *From the First Hours of Life: Making the Case for Improved Infant and Young Child Feeding Everywhere.* New York: UNICEF.

UNICEF (United Nations Children's Fund), WHO (World Health Organization), and World Bank. 2016. "Levels and Trends in Child Malnutrition." UNICEF, WHO, and World Bank, New York, Geneva, and Washington, DC.

UNTT (UN System Task Team). 2013. "Financing for Sustainable Development: Review of Global Investment Requirement Estimates," background paper for the Intergovernmental Expert Committee on Sustainable Development Financing, Chapter 1. UNTT Working Group on Sustainable Development Financing. https://sustainabledevelopment.un.org/content/documents/2096Chapter%201-global%20investment%20requirement%20estimates.pdf.

US Climate Alliance. 2019. United States Climate Alliance State Fact Sheet. https://www.usclimatealliance.org

Wąsiński, Marek. 2015. "Financing Climate Actions: Key to a Paris Agreement?" PISM Policy Paper No. 18 (120), June, Polish Institute of International Affairs, Warsaw. https://www.pism.pl/files/?id_plik=19962

Watts, Jonathan, and Kate Connally. 2017. "World Leaders React After Trump Rejects Paris Climate Deal." *The Guardian*, June 1. https://www.theguardian.com/environment/2017/jun/01/trump-withdraw-paris-climate-deal-world-leaders-react

WCED (World Commission on Environment and Development). 1987. *Our Common Future. Brundtland Committee.* Oxford and New York: Oxford University Press.

Weber, Rebecca L. 2014. "Fighting for African Food Security." Future Food 2050. https://futurefood2050.com/fighting-for-african-food-security/

WEF (World Economic Forum). 2013. "The Green Investment Report: The Ways and Means to Unlock Private Investment for Green Growth." A Report of the Green Growth Action Alliance, World Economic Forum, Geneva.

WhiteHouse.gov. 2017. "Statement by President Trump on the Paris Climate Accord." June 1. https://www.whitehouse.gov/briefings-statements/statement-president-trump-paris-climate-accord/

WHO (World Health Organization). 2013. "Global Nutrition Policy Review: What Does It Take to Scale Up Nutrition Action?" WHO, Geneva.

WHO (World Health Organization). 2014a. "Global Nutrition Targets 2025: Anaemia Policy Brief." WHO, Geneva. http://www.who.int/nutrition/publications/globaltargets2025_poli cybrief_anaemia/en/

WHO (World Health Organization). 2014b. "Global Nutrition Targets 2025: Child Overweight Policy Brief." WHO, Geneva. http://www.who.int/nutrition/publications/globaltargets2025_ policybrief_overweight/en/

WHO (World Health Organization). 2014c. "Global Nutrition Targets 2025: Stunting Policy Brief." WHO, Geneva. http://www.who.int/nutrition/publications/globaltargets2025_poli cybrief_stunting/en/

WHO (World Health Organization). 2014d. *Global Status Report on Noncommunicable Diseases 2014.* Geneva: WHO. http://apps.who.int/iris/bitstream/10665/148114/1/9789241564854_eng. pdf?ua=1

WHO (World Health Organization). 2020a. "Healthy Diet." Fact Sheet, April 29. http://www. who.int/news-room/fact-sheets/detail/healthy-diet

WHO (World Health Organization). 2020b. Obesity and Overweight. Fact Sheet, April 1, 2020. https://www.who.int/news-room/fact-sheets/detail/obesity-and-overweight

WMO (World Meteorological Organization). 2019. "2019 Set To Be 2nd or 3rd Warmest Year on Record." December 20. https://public.wmo.int/en/media/news/2019-set-be-2nd-or-3rd-warmest-year-record

Wood, Adrian. 2003. "Could Africa Be Like America?" In *Annual World Bank Conference on Development Economics 2003: The New Reform Agenda,* edited by Boris Pleskovic and Nicholas Stern, 163–200. Washington, DC, and New York: World Bank and Oxford University Press.

World Bank. 1981. *Accelerated Development in Sub-Saharan Africa: An Agenda for Action.* African Strategy Review Group coordinated by Elliot Berg. Washington, DC: World Bank.

World Bank. 2007. *World Development Report 2008: Agriculture for Development.* Washington, DC: World Bank. https://openknowledge.worldbank.org/handle/10986/5990

World Bank. 2010. *World Development Report 2010: Development and Climate Change.* Washington, DC: World Bank.

World Bank. 2016. "Global Community Makes Record $75 Billion Commitment to End Extreme Poverty." Press Release, December 15, World Bank, Washington, DC. http://www. worldbank.org/en/news/press-release/2016/12/15/global-community-commitment-end-poverty-ida18

World Bank and IMF (International Monetary Fund). 2015. World Bank/IMF Spring Meetings 2015: Development Committee Communiqué, Washington, DC, April 18. http://www.wor ldbank.org/en/news/press-release/2015/04/18/world-bank-imf-spring-meetings-2015-devel opment-committee-communique

World Cancer Research Fund and AICR (American Institute for Cancer Research). 2007. *Food, Nutrition, Physical Activity, and the Prevention of Cancer: A Global Perspective.* Washington, DC: AICR. https://discovery.ucl.ac.uk/id/eprint/4841/1/4841.pdf

Wright, Brian D. 2014. "Causes and Types of Food Price Volatility." Presentation at the Conference on Food Price Volatility, Food Security and Trade Policy, Washington, DC, September 18–19. http://www.worldbank.org/content/dam/Worldbank/Event/DEC/DECAR-food-conference-sep-2014/DECAR-food-conference-sep18-19-presentation-Brian-Wright-140917.pdf

Zhang, Jialin. 2010. "China's Slow-motion Land Reform." *Policy Review* 159: 59–70. Hoover Institution, Stanford University. http://www.hoover.org/research/chinas-slow-motion-land-reform

2

Transformation: From Sustainably Productive Agriculture to Industry?

Uma Lele, Manmohan Agarwal, and Sambuddha Goswami

Summary

The concept of structural transformation has evolved radically. Industrialization has progressed rapidly in some countries, like China, Indonesia, and Vietnam, following the East Asian model (World Bank 1993). However, countries in South Asia (SA) and sub-Saharan Africa (SSA) are lagging in transformation, as visualized by W. Arthur Lewis (1954) and Simon Kuznets (1955, 1966). Some explain the slow progress of countries lagging in structural transformation in terms of the very success of East Asian countries, and the growing global competition for industries in SA and SSA. Countries that have fallen behind have not created enough productive jobs in the industrial/manufacturing sector and have often relied on the low-productivity service sector to keep up with the growth in the labor force. Slow growth has been accompanied by low productivity, overcrowded agriculture, and declining farm size, with fewer people having left agriculture than would have if industrialization had proceeded rapidly.

In the meantime, international organizations have steadfastly adhered to small farm support, and their advice on industrialization through structural adjustment strategies has invited criticism. Yet, in recent years, development economists have substantially added to the complexity of the debate on structural transformation in a variety of ways. Central among these has been the relative productivity growth between agriculture and industry, and the appropriate roles of small, medium, and large farms in agriculture and of government in steering manufacturing policies. Some have questioned the role of smallholder farms, suggesting development policy, particularly in SSA, needs to consider fostering medium and large farms, with a focus on reallocation of factors of production in their favor, as the only way to achieve an increase in overall levels of productivity. Other research has, however, shown that while differences in productivity across farm sizes are real, a large share (as much as 70 percent) of that difference may be explained by measurement error and stochastic factors, so that the potential for efficiency gains through reallocation of land across farms and farmers may be relatively modest.

Recent research also suggests that there is no optimal farm size; both small and large farms can be efficient. *Growth* in productivity in developing countries has been observed in both very small and very large farms. In some cases, most notably in China among developing countries, institutional reforms toward land governance in the last decade have gone well beyond the household responsibility system. The small farm size resulting from "village collective land ownership" is increasingly accompanied by "individual household land contracts" and "operational land" (Huang 2020). These steps have led to a substantial growth in tenancy and an increase in operational farm size, which, when

Food for All: International Organizations and the Transformation of Agriculture. Uma Lele, Manmohan Agarwal, Brian C. Baldwin, and Sambuddha Goswami, Oxford University Press. © Uma Lele, Manmohan Agarwal, Brian C. Baldwin, and Sambuddha Goswami 2021. DOI: 10.1093/oso/9780198755173.003.0003

accompanied by mechanization and other technology, are contributing to productivity growth by giving rise to scale economies, a phenomenon explained later in this chapter.

However, unlike small farms, middle-sized farms in some countries typically benefit neither from sufficient household labor nor from economies of scale in the use of capital, explaining the U-shaped curve of productivity. That is, productivity is high on small farms; it declines as farm size increases, but then increases again, when larger farms are able to mobilize information, capital, and other ingredients to increase productivity. Implicit in the farm size debate is the reallocation of factors of production to more efficient use, either in agriculture or in the nonagriculture sector, but new literature argues that pay-offs from reallocation of factors of production may be smaller than economists have previously argued. Moreover, even though some argue that there are too many small farms, politically, it has not been easy to take land away from small farmers. This is why China's reforms, which secure land rights, are particularly interesting. Also, socially, it may create more welfare losses, if unlike in China, there are no productive jobs in the manufacturing sector in developing countries.

Returns to institutional reforms and investment in productivity growth are substantial; total factor productivity (TFP) is a better measure of productivity to understand differences across situations than partial measures, such as land and labor productivity. Most of the recent growth in TFP is due to technological change rather than increased input use. Therefore, policies and investments should be focused on productivity growth in agriculture, which is fundamental to achieving the transformation of agriculture. Furthermore, these new technologies, and associated institutional arrangements, such as emerging digital technologies, precision agriculture, and equipment leasing, call for reassessment of size-based advantages/disadvantages well suited to small farms (Fuglie et al. 2019, xxiv).

The outbreak of the COVID-19 pandemic in early 2020 has accelerated digital transformation that was already underway, with many governments making use of new technology to improve their service delivery. Lele and Goswami (2017) outlined this digital transformation in the case of India. The Government of India adopted the largest digital identification program, opened millions of bank accounts for poor people who did not previously have such accounts, and started transferring various kinds of subsidies and rural employment benefits directly into people's bank accounts. Kenya has been at the forefront of using its innovation of MPaisa to make rapid payments. Similarly, children with Internet access at home have started attending classes remotely; many employees have started working from home; and numerous firms have adopted digital business models to maintain operations and preserve some revenue flows. Meanwhile, mobile applications were developed to help "track and trace" the development of the pandemic; and researchers employed artificial intelligence to learn more about the virus and accelerate the search for a vaccine. Internet traffic in some countries increased by up to 60 percent shortly after the outbreak, underscoring the digital acceleration that the pandemic sparked (OECD 2020). New technologies include:

- cloud computing/big data analysis tools
- artificial intelligence (AI)
- machine learning (ML)
- distributed ledger technologies, including blockchain and smart contracts
- the Internet of Things (IoT)
- digital communications technologies, such as mobile phones

- digital platforms, such as e-commerce platforms, agro-advisory apps, and e-extension websites
- Global Positioning System (GPS)
- Global Navigation Satellite System (GNSS)
- radio-frequency identification (RFID)
- precision agriculture technologies, including:
  - sensors, including food sensors and soil sensors
  - guidance and tracking systems (often enabled by GPS, GNSS, RFID, IoT)
  - variable-rate input technologies
  - automatic section control
  - advanced imaging technologies, including satellite and drone imagery, to look at temperature gradients, fertility gradients, moisture gradients, and anomalies in a field
  - automated machinery and agricultural robots, leading to machine hire services
  - digital extension, which has similarly achieved a revolutionary change in the case of those farmers who have access to smartphones, but not all farmers can afford smartphones or have access to reliable Internet connections.

Permutations and combinations of these new technologies and their adoption rates vary across countries, and currently, there is limited research on how new technologies are affecting agricultural transformation.

This is good news so far, but recent evidence also suggests that the digital divide has increased, so that achieving total productivity growth requires investment, particularly in lagging countries, in a variety of sectors to increase productivity of all factors of production, rather than simply a seed–fertilizer revolution (OECD 2020). To advance the debate, in this chapter, we focus on measures of inputs and outputs, particularly gross capital formation (GCF) in the TFP estimates.

There also continues to be a debate on the role of agriculture versus industry, the latter traditionally having been viewed as the escalator of growth rather than agriculture. A study by Martin and Mitra (2001) challenged the conventional wisdom of the traditional Lewis (1954) model, also elaborated by Kaldor (1966) and later by Rodrik (2016), that agricultural productivity grows less rapidly than industrial productivity. Using panel data for 50 countries over the period 1967–92, Martin and Mitra (2001) showed more rapid technical progress in agriculture than in industry, and a tendency for relatively rapid convergence in agricultural productivity across countries, implying efficient transmission of knowledge across countries in modern agriculture. This occurred mainly through public sector technology. These results also suggest that a large agriculture sector may not be a disadvantage. On the contrary, it could be an advantage in terms of growth performance. The results also "weaken the case for . . . discrimination against agriculture on the ground that it is a stagnant sector" (Martin and Mitra 2001, 418). Their results potentially provide an explanation for growth convergence at the macroeconomic level across countries. In this chapter, we show a lack of convergence, however, between Africa and the rest of the developing world, and the reasons why this is so in agriculture and manufacturing.

The recent narrative of global supply chains stresses close complementarity of industry and service sectors under globalization, with less clear distinction of the "desirability" of manufacturing as the escalator of growth. The future of globalization itself is uncertain, however, with a combination of the 2008 financial crisis, the Sino-American trade war, and the Trump administration's withdrawal from major international agreements now followed by the greatest recession since 1929, and the depressive effect of the pandemic on trade, travel, and global growth.[1] While the new US administration will rejoin the multilateral system, it will need to reestablish both credibility and reliability and accept a rules-based system, which is not necessarily a US rules-based system as in the past. For example, the United States is not a member of China's new trade agreement involving 14 other countries in East and Southeast Asia, following the US withdrawal from the Trans-Pacific Partnership (TPP).

This chapter examines the concepts, the state of data and analysis, and the evidence in these debates. It demonstrates differences in agricultural TFP growth across countries, in agriculture of different farm sizes. Importantly, contrary to the usual Lewis assumption, it provides some evidence of higher TFP growth in agriculture relative to industry and confirms the hypothesis of premature deindustrialization in many low-income and low-middle-income developing countries, a concept popularized by Rodrik (2016), but explored earlier in the literature by Kaldor (1966) and his followers. Using panel data for well over 100 countries, the chapter documents the difficulty that currently lagging developing countries have faced, not just in generating productive employment in the manufacturing sector but in increasing agricultural productivity. The chapter also identifies some of the causes, including, in particular, differences across regions in investment rates overall, and especially, in the agriculture and rural sector.

Introduction

The world's population is expected to increase by 2 billion persons in the next 30 years, from 7.7 billion currently to 9.7 billion in 2050, and 11 billion by the end of the century, according to a new United Nations report (UN 2019). It will increase to 8.6 billion by 2030, the end of the SDG period. The population of SSA is projected to double by 2050 (99 percent increase). Nine countries will make up more than half the projected growth of the global population between now and 2050, including some outside of the African continent: India, Nigeria, Pakistan, the Democratic Republic of the Congo, Ethiopia, the United Republic of Tanzania, Indonesia, Egypt, and the United States (in descending order of expected increase). Around 2027, India is projected to overtake China as the world's most populous country. Regions that may experience lower rates of population growth between 2019 and 2050 include Oceania, excluding Australia/New Zealand (56 percent), Northern Africa and Western Asia (46 percent), Australia/New Zealand (28 percent), Central and Southern Asia (25 percent), Latin America and the Caribbean (18 percent), Eastern and Southeastern Asia (3 percent), and Europe and Northern America (2 percent) (UN 2019).

The proportion of urban population is expected to increase from 55 percent in 2018 to 68 percent by 2050. Projections show that urbanization, the gradual shift in residence of the human population from rural to urban areas, combined with the overall growth of the world's population could add another 2.5 billion people to urban areas by 2050, with close to 90 percent of this increase taking place in Asia and Africa, according to a new United Nations data set.

Growing urban demand has been at the center of attention. Will new technologies allow leapfrogging, which is less demanding of natural resources and more mindful of nutritious

---

[1] In 2020, the US tariff rate on imports was back to its highest level since 1993, and both the United States and China had begun to decouple their technology industries.

food for all? Will new technologies create enough productive employment to soak up the increase in the burgeoning youth population?

Projected population growth and urbanization are expected to result in a demand-led growth in agricultural production and productivity, including greater diversification of agriculture away from carbohydrates such as rice, wheat, and maize to higher value, nutritious foods like milk, fruits, vegetables, nuts, pulses, fish, poultry, and meat. And urbanization is often seen as the means to achieve such a demand-led growth, but the latter will depend on the nature of economic growth and food demand. Today, according to UN data, SSA and SA have the highest shares of slums in the urban population of any region (UN 2020). Essentially, rural poverty is being shifted to urban areas, not exactly a route to healthy food systems. And yet, there is much about structural transformation that we still do not fully understand.

Reardon and his colleagues have explored the phenomenon of supermarket revolution throughout Latin America, Asia, and Africa. Specifically, they explored the triangle of (1) rapid urbanization and urban food markets propelled by urbanization; (2) dietary changes in Asian urban and rural areas, giving rise to the consumption of horticultural products, meat, and fish, as well as lightly and more highly processed foods; and (3) an agrifood system change, which highlighted the extent and composition of value chains (Reardon et al. 2014). These enterprises constitute what Reardon et al. (2014) called a "Quiet Revolution." The triangle of changes has important implications for food sector innovations, including the need for physical infrastructure—cold storages and roads; financing for trucks and vehicles, processing, packaging, and milling facilities; and the financial infrastructure including banking systems.

Urbanization rates and levels have varied throughout Asia, along with variations in the rate of economic growth. Furthermore, urbanization has varied in terms of the extent to which populations have migrated to megacities, as distinct from smaller cities and towns, of different population sizes. These different patterns of urbanization influence the nature of midstream linkages of value chains (Reardon et al. 2014).

China and East Asia are more urbanized than Southeast Asia, and SA is the least urbanized, but in SA, too, rapid urbanization in the new millennium has been accompanied by accelerated economic growth. About 50 to 70 percent of the value of consumption in Asia is now in urban areas. Areas that have received less attention but form 40 to 70 percent of the value-added and costs (and therefore, prices) are in processing, wholesale, logistics, retail, restaurants, and take-outs (Reardon et al. 2014). Whereas cereal consumption has received the most attention, two-thirds to three-quarters of food expenditures are in non-grain foods (Reardon et al. 2014). Whether urbanization causes agricultural productivity growth or whether productivity growth leads to rapid urbanization remains a debated issue.

In the process of structural transformation (ST) envisaged by W. Arthur Lewis (1954) and Simon Kuznets (1955, 1966), they assumed productivity in the agriculture sector tends to be lower than in the nonagriculture sector, and therefore, the reallocation of labor from agriculture to the nonagriculture sector is necessary to transform economies and increase income. As outlined in Chapter 1 and discussed later in this chapter, Barrett et al. (2019, 2) have argued in a recent paper that the dualistic models of Lewis and Kuznets abstracted from the phenomenon of value chain development (an "analytically convenient simplification") in the details of transformation from agriculture to industry or the service sector. Furthermore, we reported earlier that some evidence (see, for example, Martin and Mitra 2001) has suggested that TFP *growth* in agriculture has been more rapid than in manufacturing, challenging the assumptions behind the theories of Lewis. And yet, in countries lagging behind in transformation, rapid population growth and slow industrialization are leaving larger populations in rural areas than would occur with rapid industrialization, leading to fragmentation of landholdings. However, there is also some evidence in the literature, particularly in Africa, that small- or middle-sized farms are the major drivers of growth.

At the same time, new technologies, including digitalization, are spreading rapidly in developing countries. In principle, advances in crop science, for example, will help farmers deal with changing weather patterns, and the spread of solar and wind energy, already underway, will enable the use of more power without adding more greenhouse gases to the atmosphere. Small farmers have increased access to wind and solar energy, which are already cost competitive with carbon-based generation. The additional advantage of wind and solar energy, with the possibility of decentralized generation distributed spatially, can lower the cost of rural electrification and increase access by the poor. Small farmers will also be helped by crop improvements involving developing varieties that increase yield and that are pest and disease resistant, and drought and flood tolerant. Remote sensing is helping to respond to climate change, soil analysis, and increased water use efficiency (FAO 2016). For these technologies to benefit rural populations, there must be substantial investment in research and development, physical and institutional infrastructure, skilled human capital, and incentives, and most importantly, an appropriate mindset (World Bank 2015). The solar revolution already underway is limited in scaling up by the lack of these prerequisites: for example, in South Africa (Arndt et al. 2019).[2]

Extraordinary progress in the life sciences, combined with the rapid advancements in digital and other technologies, widely referred to as the fourth industrial revolution, are providing the world with new tools, products, and processes unimagined only a few decades ago (Schwab 2016; Lele and Goswami 2017). The advances offer a cornucopia of innovations very different from what Griliches (1957) described in the adoption of hybrid corn. These developments offer scope for the incorporation of biophysical relationships into growth models and complex interactions among them. Will these models translate onto the actual fields of millions of small farmers, achieving agricultural growth and transformation under growing ecological constraints of land and water scarcity, loss of biodiversity, and climate change? Or will large and medium-sized farms feed the world?[3]

Although sustainability means different things to different people, the Brundtland Report's definition of sustainable development has an enduring quality, as "development that meets the needs of the present without compromising the ability of future generations to meet their own needs" (WCED 1987, 8). A new literature reminiscent of the 1970s, such as the "The EAT-*Lancet* Commission on Healthy Diets from Sustainable Systems" (Willett et al. 2019), stresses the planetary limits to growth posed by climate change, loss of biodiversity, and increasing pressure on natural resources. The progress on containing rising temperatures to 1.5°C is slower than needed, despite the Paris Accord (UNFCCC 2020). A UN report on biodiversity notes that human survival depends on biodiversity, but species are vanishing faster than ever.[4]

---

[2] Based on the International Food Policy Research Institute (IFPRI) policy seminar, "Faster than You Think: Renewable Energy and Developing Countries," in Washington, DC, June 13, 2019. See also http://www.ifpri.org/event/faster-you-think-renewable-energy-and-developing-countries.

[3] Zilberman (2014, 385) predicts "the pursuit of sustainable development will lead to the expansion of a bioeconomy that will be part of a larger transition from nonrenewable to renewable resource dependence."

[4] Human activity has now driven up to 1 million animal and plant species to the brink of extinction (IPBES 2019).

The focus on the sustainability discussion has been further developed with a definition of a sustainable food system as:

> ... one that delivers food security and nutrition for all in such a way that the economic, social and environmental bases to generate food security and nutrition for future generations are not compromised. This means that it is *profitable* throughout, **ensuring economic sustainability**, it has broad-based *benefits for society*, **securing social sustainability**, and that it has a *positive or* neutral impact on the natural resource environment, **safeguarding the sustainability of the environment** [emphasis added]. (FAO 2020a)

With few exceptions, these environmental costs and benefits are typically not reflected in the measurements of agricultural factor productivity, which we discuss in this chapter. There is a plethora of literature on sustainability. We cite two examples here.[5] Whereas John Landers' study of zero tillage in Brazil clearly shows the profitability of the innovation, explaining its widespread usage, examples of such *scaled-up*, environmentally sound innovations tend to be few and far between.

In short, taking the East Asian miracle as an example, much more investment in physical and human capital, institutional change, and export orientation would be needed than currently exists to pull the remaining households out of poverty and hunger, and to move faster on the transformation growth path. The transitions entail new applications, poor people's access to relevant information and data, the spread of knowledge and skills to apply new technologies, and access to finance and equip households and institutions to generate and spread innovations. While the United States has adopted a protectionist stance, Africa has taken a bold step in the opposite direction, creating the world's largest free trade area since the establishment of the World Trade Organization in 1995. The African Continental Free Trade Area (AfCFTA), which came into force on May 30, 2019, includes nearly every country on the continent (see https://au.int/en/cfta). Implementation of the free trade agreement, originally scheduled for July 1, 2020, has been delayed due to the disruptions caused by the COVID-19 pandemic. The Secretary General of AfCFTA, Wamkele Mene, asserts that intra-African trade can help lift the economies post-COVID 19 (Ighobor 2020). Intracontinental trade could boost agricultural and manufacturing production, and its future effects on the African continent could be quite positive, provided there is more investment in physical infrastructure and cross-border trade barriers come down quickly.

In any case, the transitions, while creating new jobs, will also result in the elimination of many old jobs, with profound implications for employment prospects in the coming years. Recent evidence from China, a global leader in digitization, offers a hopeful story. Although robots have eliminated millions of jobs in the industry sector in China, during the five-year period through 2016, the 14 million jobs created in e-commerce have meant a net positive effect on employment and on productivity growth (Zhang and Chen 2019). China's job growth through e-commerce in five years is equivalent to what India needs every year, nearly 7 million new jobs. Africa needs to find jobs for the 362 million young people between the ages of 15 and 24 years old by 2050, based on population estimates (Page 2019). Where will the region find so many jobs?

The African Transformation Report 2017, produced by the African Center for Economic Transition (ACET 2017), notes the collapse of commodity prices (particularly, oil and

---

[5] See, generally, Campanhola and Pandey (2019): *Sustainable Food and Agriculture: An Integrated Approach.* Also, see Landers (2001); de Freitas and Landers (2014) on zero tillage in Brazil.

minerals) since mid-2014, and the consequent slowdown in economic growth in many parts of Africa. It further notes that the "average age of farmers in Africa is estimated by some sources to be as high as 60, and few in the large and growing African youth population are...interested in agriculture as it is now practiced in Africa," with primitive farming technology and back-breaking manual work (ACET 2017, 3). "An increasing number of youth are educated, and education systems do not prepare them for farming (and even orient them away from it)" (ACET 2017, 3). And, most farming does not provide an income sufficient to maintain their modern lifestyle.

Data Challenges

Apart from slow growth in productive employment in lagging countries, reliable data on various dimensions of transformation are not yet in place, and new debates have emerged globally on the estimates of production, productivity, employment, and the emerging field of value chains, which illustrate that gross trade flows data tell little about the nature and composition of employment. As an example, an editorial in AMIS *Market Monitor*, titled "The China Conundrum," described the challenge of accommodating recent large official reported increases in China's annual cereal production data following the outcome of the first agricultural census in 10 years.[6] AMIS describes the challenge of distributing the 10-year accumulative increase in cereal supplies of 312 million tons over the various forms of utilization (AMIS 2019). In addition to China's reported total 10-year incremental production, maize production alone increased by 210 million tons. The reported increment is larger than India's total annual (bumper) grain production of 287 million tons in the year 2018–19. This would mean a higher TFP growth rate for China than those reported later in this chapter, based on past data from the Food and Agricultural Organization of the United Nations (FAO) and data provided by Keith O. Fuglie, based on the International Agricultural Productivity data of the United States Department of Agriculture.[7]

A different data challenge occurred in India in 2018. Government withheld publication of a well-reputed national survey that showed slower employment growth than policymakers would have desired, just prior to the national election, leading to the resignation of two members of the government-appointed Statistical Commission (Basu 2019; Desai 2019). Subsequently, Arvind Subramaniam, former Chief Economic Advisor to the Government of India, has argued that India's gross domestic product (GDP) may be smaller than reported, and others including Rakesh Mohan, former Deputy Chairman of the Reserve Bank of India, and India's former executive director at the International Monetary Fund (IMF), suggested the issue needs to be looked into (Mohan 2019). The new chief economic advisor concluded there was not a major problem. There is a concern that India is interfering with the respected institution of National Sample Surveys.

New trade-related data issues arise from the nature of value chains. The value-added in traded goods may be very different than the gross value of traded goods as conventionally reported in traditional trade data. In addition, value chain growth in the early years of the new millennium has slowed since the global financial crisis, with the result that trade

---

[6] AMIS (Agricultural Market Information System), a multi-stakeholder program established after the 2007 food crisis to obtain better information on world food stocks, is discussed in Chapter 3.

[7] See https://www.ers.usda.gov/data-products/international-agricultural-productivity/.

intensity, the share of output that is traded, has declined, and the share of service trade has increased, relative to trade in goods (Lund et al. 2019).

Among key findings of the 2019 McKinsey Global Institute report on the future of trade and value chains were the following:

- Goods-producing value chains have become less trade-intensive.
- Cross-border services are growing more than 60 percent faster than trade in goods.
- Less than 20 percent of goods trade is based on labor-cost arbitrage, and global value chains are becoming more knowledge-intensive and reliant on high-skill labor.
- Goods-producing value chains (particularly, automotive as well as computers and electronics) are becoming more regionally concentrated, especially within Asia and Europe (Lund et al. 2019, vi).

Structural Transformation and Poverty and Hunger Reduction

Will transformative changes to food and agricultural systems, needed urgently, occur to feed the world sustainably? Prevalence of hunger increased to 821 million in 2017, compared to the low of 784 million previously (2014–15), due to a combination of climate change and the growing incidence of internal conflicts (FAO et al. 2018). FAO has since adjusted these numbers downward from 821 million in 2019, to 690 million in 2020, prior to the pandemic (FAO et al. 2020, viii). The decline is mainly because undernourishment estimates for China have been adjusted by over 100 million people, based on using a newly available series of household data going back to 2000.

A 2019 FAO and the World Food Programme (WFP) update on conflict situations in eight places throughout the world noted that Afghanistan, the Central African Republic, the Democratic Republic of the Congo, South Sudan, and Yemen had worsened in the latter part of 2018, largely because of conflict, while Somalia, Syria, and the Lake Chad Basin had seen some improvements in line with improved security. Conflict has led to the highest number of people (56 million) in need of emergency food support (FAO and WFP 2019).

International Focus on Small Farmers

International organizations, such as FAO, the World Bank, CGIAR, and the International Fund for Agricultural Development (IFAD) have supported small farm development for well over half a century, as the only way to address issues of food security and nutrition, and to facilitate structural transformation from agriculture to manufacturing. And this support has stood on the foundation of literature produced by economists and agricultural economists favoring a small-holder strategy. However, in recent years, there are growing questions about the effectiveness of that strategy, and some economists have argued that governments, particularly in Africa, should support medium-sized and large farms as the way to achieve food security and accelerate structural transformation. Urbanization provides additional strength to the arguments of those in favor of large- and medium-scale agriculture to meet the rapidly growing urban demand but raises a question: Who is feeding the growing population, particularly in rural areas? FAO data suggest the future of small farmers is unclear, as outlined in Box 2.1.

There are more than 475 million small farms of less than 2 hectares (ha), mostly in Asia and Africa (Lowder, Skoet, and Raney 2016, 24). While land consolidation, together with a

Box 2.1 Distinguishing between Small and Family Farms: The Future of Smallholders vs. Medium- and Large-Scale Agriculture

Data on farm structure are limited, particularly well-documented data. Among the various estimates of farm structure, FAO estimates are, by far, the most comprehensive and documented. They are based on national agricultural censuses carried out in more than 100 countries, using standard concepts, albeit conducted at different times. Other estimates are based on household surveys, which are typically not well documented or representative. According to FAO, more than 570 million farms in the world produce food and agricultural products and manage agroforestry and animals on rangelands. Of these, more than 500 million are "family farms," defined as using mostly family labor. Although they range widely in size, they are sometimes confused with small farms (see, for example, HLPE [2013]; IFAD and UNEP [2013]). In 2014, FAO noted that family farms occupy nearly 70–80 percent of farmland, producing more than 80 percent of the world's food (including in the developing world), in value terms (FAO 2014a, 2014b), but noted the methodology requires a more rigorous review.

Further research by FAO (2016) noted small farms (below 2 ha) operate on only about 12 percent of the world's land. Family farms are likely responsible for the majority of the world's food and agricultural production. However, a message that often gets lost is that it is implausible that, with only 12 percent of the world's land, small farms, operating on less than 2 ha, are able to produce a large share of the world's food (Graeub et al. 2016; Lowder, Skoet, and Raney 2016).

Importantly, further analysis by FAO has underscored "the importance of not referring to family farms and small farms (i.e., those of less than 2 hectares) interchangeably: the latter account for 84 percent of all farms worldwide, but operate only around 12 percent of all agricultural land, and produce roughly 36 percent of the world's food" (Lowder, Sánchez, and Bertini 2019)

[a] From *The State of Food and Agriculture 2014: Innovation in Family Farming*:

This estimate is based on the share of land held by individuals or households (farming families) in each of the 30 countries. In each country, it is assumed that the share of food produced by family farms corresponds to their share of land. This allows estimation of the value (in international dollars) of food produced by family farms in each country based on the total value of food produced in the country. Adding the values of food produced by family farms in each of the countries and dividing by the total value of food produced in all 30 countries results in a share of 79 percent. However, family farms tend to be smaller than non-family farms, and . . . small farms in individual countries tend to have higher yields per hectare than larger farms. The share of food produced by family farms is therefore likely to be larger than 80 percent, although the exact share cannot be quantified. (FAO (2014b, 9, Footnote #13)

slight increase in average farm sizes for a small sample of low- and middle-income countries, indicates that average farm size has begun to increase, "for many low- and low-middle-income, however, average farm sizes are likely to continue to diminish for some time still" (Lowder, Skoet, and Raney 2016, 27).

Recent evidence suggests that farm size in Africa may be rising. In countries at lower levels of income, according to FAO, smaller farms operate a far greater share of farmland than do smaller farms in the higher income countries, but this, too, may be changing in Africa, if recent evidence on the growth of medium-scale farms, for a few African countries, is valid for the continent as a whole. As we discuss later in this chapter, in addition to a foreign land grab, African investors have also acquired land since 2000, creating a major rise in the number of farms between 5 and 200 ha (Jayne and Muyanga 2018). Other evidence on Africa suggests overall farm size may still be declining, perhaps implying a growing dualism.

Two additional nuances need to be added to this discussion, one related to land quality and another related to measurement. While much research has shown that small farmers in developing regions are often more efficient than those with larger farms, measured in terms of output per hectare, some have challenged the validity of that evidence, citing potential problems that come with farmers' self-reporting of land size. Doubts about the validity based on underreporting of farm size by smallholders, however, has not been supported by measurements using GPS devices, which show that farmers overreport their size. Carletto, Savastano, and Zezza (2013) showed that farmers systematically overreport the size of their farms.

A second issue relates to land quality. Are small farms of higher land quality than larger farms, and does it explain the inverse relationship? Bevis and Barrett (2020) show that "characteristics such as soil quality cannot explain the relationship."

Agriculture vs. Industry

The vast literature on structural transformation can be seen in two parts—that related to the importance of agriculture and the role of small, medium, and large farms in transformation, and that related to industrialization. We ask some key questions of this literature and evidence.

Key Questions

1. How has agriculture performed relative to manufacturing and service sectors among a number of developed and developing countries?
2. What has been the role of large, medium, and small farms in agricultural growth?
3. What are the lessons of experience, for future strategies for developing agriculture as a way to contribute to transformation?

Structural Transformation, Farm Size, and Productivity Growth

Since the 1950s, literature on structural transformation, with respect to the roles that agricultural growth and manufacturing growth have played in transformation, has grown and evolved with less consensus and more debates on the roles and impacts of smallholder strategies on outcomes. This debate is more intense in SSA than in Asia, for at least two reasons. First, the preponderance of smallholders in Asia leaves very little scope for questioning that approach as the way to develop agriculture. Second, there is considerable history of success of the smallholder strategy in Asia in achieving productivity growth, food security, and employment generation. Nevertheless, our list of literature on the subject here is illustrative rather than exhaustive, and our treatment of the issues is selective, too. See, for example, W. Arthur Lewis (1954); Simon Kuznets (1955, 1966); Johnston and Mellor (1961); Ranis and Fei (1961); Fei and Ranis (1964); Todaro (1969); Harris and Todaro (1970); Chenery and Syrquin (1975); Lele and Mellor (1981); Datt and Ravallion (1992, 1998, 2011); World Bank (2007); Timmer and Akkus (2008); Timmer (2009); Binswanger-Mkhize, McCalla, and Patel (2010); Christiaensen, Demery, and Kuhl (2011); Binswanger-Mkhize (2012, 2013); Delgado, Porter, and Stern (2014); Jayne et al. (2014); Datt, Ravallion, and Murgai (2016); Newman et al. (2016b); Mellor (2017); Lele, Agarwal, and Goswami (2018); Monga and Lin (2019).

Economists have viewed transformation as the process of change in the structure of production from low-productivity agriculture to manufacturing, and as the way to achieve economic prosperity and reduce poverty. Andersson and Axelsson (2016), in writing on relative backwardness, raise several important issues that are worth highlighting at the outset. First, transformation is about optimism and catching up, and yet, is the relative backwardness too great an obstacle to permit catching up? Their conclusion is that it is not too late. According to Gerschenkron (1962), backwardness means that the earlier path cannot be followed as initial conditions are different. Thus, different paths need to be followed to deal with these different initial conditions. We are inclined to add to this the important role of access to the right knowledge, as in the examples of East Asia and African industrialization, which our subsequent discussion here illustrates.

The authors also assert the importance of agricultural change to achieve sustained economic growth, a view that is not shared by all authors reviewed here. The *Oxford Handbook on Structural Transformation*, for example, contains a number of unconventional topics, such as Joseph Stiglitz's piece, which argues that government policy has a major role in deep downturns to ensure transformation remains on course, as witnessed in the case of Vietnam after the Asian crisis (Monga and Lin 2019; Stiglitz 2019). There are also deeper national governance issues that extend beyond periods of external shocks, discussed in this chapter in the case of Malawi, and later in Chapter 5. Not all of these important insights are covered here, but the reader is encouraged to review this literature.

Box 2.2 describes the five processes of structural transformation, which Timmer (2009) articulated.

With Asian realities in mind, and mindful of differences among developing regions, W. Arthur Lewis explained the existence of surplus labor in agriculture, the resulting poverty due to low productivity of agriculture, and the need for smallholder agricultural productivity growth to be the engine of economic transformation, as a way of stimulating the movement of populations out of low-productivity agriculture to higher productivity manufacturing. He considered increasing agricultural productivity as a *sine qua non* for industrial development, declaring, "This is also why industrial and agrarian revolutions always go together, and why economies in which agriculture is stagnant do not show industrial development" (Lewis 1954, 173). Without growth in agricultural production to keep up with the growing urban demand for food associated with industrialization, he argued, wages rise and terms of trade move against the nonagriculture sector, thereby reducing entrepreneurial profits and arresting savings and investment and the pace of

---

Box 2.2 Structural Transformation

Structural transformation (ST) consists of:

1. Declining share of agriculture in the gross domestic product (GDP);
2. Declining share of agriculture in employment;
3. Rural-to-urban migration;
4. Growth of the service and manufacturing sectors; and
5. A demographic transition from high birth and mortality rates to low birth and mortality rates, bringing about a reduction in the population growth rates.

The turning point is reached when the share of employment in agriculture has declined at a faster rate than the share of agriculture in GDP. Differences in labor productivity between the agricultural and nonagriculture sectors disappear in the final stages of structural transformation. Before labor productivities among sectors converge, a huge, and often even widening, gap occurs between labor productivities in the agricultural and nonagriculture sectors. It explains intersectoral income inequalities and concentrations of poverty in the agriculture sector (Timmer 2009).

---

economic growth and development. In an open economy, failure of agriculture to meet growing food demand results in increased imports, taking resources away from domestic investment (Lewis 1954).

Sen (1962) concluded that productivity is higher on small farms due to labor market failure: family farm laborers lack employment opportunities outside their own farms and, thus, work at levels at which marginal productivity of labor is low. Similar failures in factor markets have been identified by others: for example, Feder (1985) in credit markets; and Deininger and Feder (2001) in land markets. As a recent World Bank publication, *Accelerating Poverty Reduction in Africa*, noted, some failures have been in the relatively neglected areas in policymaking (population growth, gender inequality, risk management, and fragility) or have only come to the forefront more recently (growing natural resource dependence, a tightening fiscal environment, and the growing concentration of the world's poor in Africa). Recent technological developments provide new leapfrogging opportunities, especially to overcome infrastructure gaps (Beegle and Christiaensen 2019).

When improvements occur in technology and inputs, then labor, credit, and output markets begin to work, and growth in agriculture and in the rest of the economy follows. In this view, agricultural transformation refers to systematic changes in farm production and food markets observed in the course of economic development, as part of the larger processes of structural transformation and industrialization. The term focuses, particularly, on the rising role of markets, land consolidation, specialization, and input use within agriculture, as well as changes in labor use and farm size, the rise of nonfarm employment, and increased consumption of nonfood goods and services. Such transformation was observed in the 20th century, but it was also accompanied by degradation of natural resources, among other effects, due to poorly developed property rights (Hayami and Ruttan 1971).

Among the aspects of transformation shown in Box 2.2, changes in economic structures and labor productivity across sectors have received the most attention in the ST analysis. Developing economies that successfully make the transition from low-income to high-income status, typically experience significant changes in their economic structure (Clark 1940; Kuznets 1955; 1966; Chenery and Taylor 1968; Chenery et al. 1974; Chenery and Syrquin 1975). As factors of production move from lower-productivity uses to higher-productivity uses, there is a substantial growth payoff (Mellor 1976, 2017; Timmer and Akkus 2008; Duarte and Restuccia 2010; McMillan and Rodrik 2011).

The *World Development Report 2008* concluded that a dollar invested in agriculture results in more poverty reduction than in other sectors (World Bank 2007). Since then, in recent years, the assertion of the importance of smallholder agriculture has been questioned, particularly in the African context, based on several key areas of potential economies of scale: (1) skills and technology; (2) finance and access to capital; and (3) the organization and logistics of trading, marketing, and storage. (See, for example, Collier and Dercon [2014]; Dercon and Gollin [2014].) Related reasons for questioning traditional thinking include: (1) questions about the historical, theoretical, and empirical validity of the body of literature on the leading role of agriculture in transformation; and (2) changing comparative advantage of small and large farms under globalization and its consequences, particularly the growing injection of external capital into agriculture or foreign direct investment, also often known as "land grab" in SSA; (3) investments by the African urban elite in farming (Jayne et al. 2014); (4) inability of small farmers to compete in responding to the new opportunities provided by the growth of value chains and supermarkets; and (5) returns to investment in agriculture, relative to other sectors.

In an attempt to develop a new conceptual framework, Barrett, Reardon, Swinnen, and Zilberman, in their paper, "Structural Transformation and Economic Development: Insights from the Agri-food Value Chain Revolution," noted that W. Arthur Lewis and others overlooked the central role of "revolution in the agri-food value chain that intermediates between the shrinking [share] of... agricultural producers and the rising population of urban food consumers with evolving demand for food products... [T]he crucial intermediation role played by aggregators, food processors, wholesalers, retailers, third party logistics firms, and restaurants and other food service providers," they argue, is almost always abstracted from dual economy models with simplifications of complex development processes (Barrett et al. 2019, 2). Their analysis was simpler, as these institutional changes were not prevalent at the time, but rather were in the future. The result is economists' focus on technological change in farm-level production and neglect of markets. They note three major trends: (1) the supermarket revolution; (2) foreign direct investment (FDI) in agri-food value chains; and (3) the food services revolution. These trends are associated with urbanization, which results in increased income and, in turn, increased demand for diversified and higher quality foods (Barrett et al. 2019).

Increased profitability of value chain-related businesses raises product quality and standards, and food safety, and even explains the increased share of foods purchased for consumption by rural populations while the farm share of total consumer expenditure declines rapidly. Some of these issues are debatable, and we discuss them later in Chapter 4.

The innovations in the supply chain could be mechanical or biological, and often enter new markets. The speed of change of the "supermarket revolution," including large-scale retailers, has been astonishing and has been accompanied by the speed of agri-food value chain transformation in today's low- and middle-income countries (LMICs). Barrett et al. (2019, 20) noted: "Agri-food sector participation in GVCs [global value chains] share has increased as a share of agricultural output" (Greenville, Kawasaki, and Jouanjean 2019). "That growth has been strongest in sub-sectors where product standards are most important, i.e., in higher value sectors such as fruits, vegetables, seafood, fish, meat and dairy products" (Maertens and Swinnen 2015).

The food services revolution in LMICs has proceeded much faster than it did in today's high-income countries. Product and process innovations, initially developed for high-income markets, diffused relatively easily as multinational firms undertook FDI in search of profitable new markets. Fast-food restaurants began appearing in secondary cities at a far earlier stage of urbanization in LMICs than they did in high-income areas of the world. This includes not just modern fast-food chains diffusing from North America and Europe, but also South–South FDI from markets in earlier waves of food services transformation. The paper by Barrett et al. (2019) largely presents a positive picture of value chains. It ignores the often behind-the-scenes roles of multinationals in the establishment of World Health Organization (WHO) standards, legislation on food standards, and food safety in developing countries, as well as impacts of fatty and sugary foods on obesity and health. We discuss these issues in Chapter 4.

Also, does food quality and efficiency always increase with standardization, when much produce is rejected by supermarkets, on the basis of appearance or size? These studies consistently find that technology (and management) transfer through value chains generates significant productivity increases both for the product itself and for other production activities at the farm level. For example, Minten, Randrianarison, and Swinnen (2009) also found better technology and management practices related to contract-farming spillovers to other crops, generating large productivity increases in rice production, and further improving the food security situation of rural households. However, Barrett et al. (2019, 42) concluded: "The bulk of the welfare effects of revolutions within the agri-food system likely accrue to consumers through reduced quality-adjusted food costs, and a steadily rising share of consumer food expenditures go to value addition beyond the farmgate."

The lack of consensus on the role of agriculture, and particularly of smallholder agriculture, is evident in the writings of Collier, Dercon, and Gollin. Collier and Dercon (2014) questioned how agricultural production and labor productivity in agriculture can be increased massively in Africa, while requiring a vast reduction in the proportion of the population engaged in agriculture and a large move out of rural areas, all with a continuing commitment to smallholder agriculture, as the main route for growth in African agriculture and for poverty reduction. The lack of productive employment elsewhere in the economies, which we have documented elsewhere in the chapter, makes one wonder about the alternatives to agriculturally led growth. Collier, Dercon, and Gollin also questioned the evidence base for an exclusive focus on smallholders: for example, a long-standing assertion in the literature that small farms are more productive than large farms in terms of output per unit of land, which, they argued, overlooks diseconomies of scale in marketing and processing of agriculture and the high cost of transportation incurred in transferring produce from remote rural areas to feed coastal populations. Further, they questioned the cost effectiveness of developing agriculture, compared to other sectors: for example, greater reliance on mineral resources and other strategies, such as trade, to achieve those same objectives, in view of the diversity of countries' resource endowments (Dercon and Gollin 2014). Indeed, much of the focus on smallholders, argued Collier and Dercon (2014), may actually hinder large-scale poverty reduction: "Fast labor productivity growth is what is needed for large scale productivity reduction but smallholders and the institutions to support and sustain them are weak agents for labor productivity growth in Africa. The current policy focus ignores one key necessity for labor productivity growth: the kind of growth that will trigger successful migration out of agriculture and rural areas" (Collier and Dercon 2014, 93).

In the rest of this section, we review the accumulated literature on productivity growth by farm size, including, particularly, the inverse relationship (IR) in Asia, Latin America, and Africa, to derive implications for agricultural policy. This literature reflects considerable advancement in data and methodology to address issues of productivity and farm size, with important implications for policy.

Productivity and efficiency of farm size by scale has been a long-standing issue in Africa, and evidence of higher yields per hectare on large farms is not new. In a study of smallholder and estate or large-scale production (given that definitions have been context-specific in different circumstances) of tea and coffee in Kenya and tobacco in Malawi, spanning a period from the mid-1960s to mid-1980s, Lele and Agarwal (1989) showed that large-scale/estate production was indeed more productive, with higher yields of production per unit of land than smallholders. (The difference in yields was threefold.) However, this higher productivity occurred on estate farms in Malawi because estates sold their produce in open auctions, whereas small farmers sold their produce to ADMARK (Agricultural Development Marketing Corporation) at much lower prices. Estates used higher quantities of all factors of production per unit of land, including purchased inputs and labor, than did small farmers. The reasons for the higher input use are many, and context-specific, but can generally be described as owing to their increased and easier access to credit and markets, including labor markets. And yet, careful analysis of the domestic resource costs (DRCs) of these two types of farming organizations showed clearly that large farmers were not necessarily more efficient than small farmers.[8] Their DRCs were similar per unit of production. The study outlined how public policy and delivery of information, inputs, and markets were critical to improving access of small farmers to services and overcoming diseconomies of scale.

In one of the few recent studies on farm size and productivity relationship in Africa, Muyanga and Jayne (2019) conducted an analysis in Kenya. They examined the relationship:

> ... over a much wider range of farm sizes than most studies, which is particularly relevant in Africa given the recent rise of medium- and large-scale farms. Second, [they] test[ed] the inverse relationship hypothesis using three different measures of productivity including profits per hectare and total factor productivity ... [instead of] yield or gross output per hectare. [They found] a U-shaped relationship between farm size and all three measures of farm productivity. The inverse relationship hypothesis [IR hypothesis] holds on farms between zero and 3 hectares. The relationship between farm size and productivity is relatively flat between 3 and 5 hectares. A strong positive relationship between farm size and productivity emerges within the 5 to 70 hectare range of farm sizes. Across virtually all measures of productivity, farms between 20 and 70 hectares are found to be substantially more productive than farms under 5 hectares ... [T]he productivity advantage of relatively large farms stems at least partially from differences in technical

---

[8] The domestic resource cost for a given sector (DRC) is "the ratio of the incremental increase in primary inputs valued at their shadow prices to the incremental increase in net output valued at its shadow price in [the sectoral] industry. Thus, it is a social cost/benefit ratio although it is not the best ratio. To calculate it, one must know the shadow prices of primary factors" (Tower 1984, 21).

choice related to mechanization, which substantially reduces labor input per hectare, and from input use intensity. (Muyanga and Jayne 2019, 1140)

Based on evidence from four countries, Ghana, Kenya, Tanzania and Zambia, Jayne et al. (2016) noted, "Medium-scale farmers [with farms between 5 to 100 hectares] may be altering the strength and location of agricultural growth and employment multipliers between rural and urban areas...[M]edium-scale farms are likely to soon become the dominant scale of farming in many African countries" (Jayne et al. 2016, 203).

Using farm-level panel data from Tanzania and Uganda and a theoretical framework, however, Gollin and Udry (2019) came to a different conclusion. Unlike in developed countries, crop yields and input intensities vary greatly on African farms with enormous differences in productivity across farms. This, then, leads to a conclusion that there is considerable scope to increase overall productivity by improving resource allocation across farms. Gollin and Udry (2019) used a model that distinguished among various sources of productivity differences, such as measurement error, unobserved heterogeneity, and potential misallocation of resources. The stochastic nature of agricultural production and large shocks to production related to weather, pests, crop diseases, and so on are not well observed in the data. A second source of variation in productivity is measurement error, in spite of the high quality of the data, leading to imperfect and imprecise measurement. Finally, the third source of variation in productivity is heterogeneity in unobserved land quality. The authors found that measurement error and heterogeneity together account for as much as 70 percent of the dispersion in measured productivity. They concluded that the potential for efficiency gains through reallocation of land across farms and farmers may be relatively modest (Gollin and Udry 2019).

Medium-scale farms control more land than foreign and domestic investors in the countries they examined. In contrast, the share of land accounted for by small-scale (0–5 hectares) holdings, at least in these four countries, is declining, while the number of farms between 10 and 100 hectares is growing rapidly. They speculated that under de facto land policies, medium-scale farms will soon account for the majority of operated farmland in many African countries. Many medium-scale farms are owned by influential rural and urban people, who purchase land in customary areas and convert it to leasehold or freehold titled land. What influence they will have on agricultural policies is an important question. The authors emphasized the need to revive the study of agrarian structure to improve our understanding of the implications of rapidly changing land distribution patterns. They also noted that existing population-based surveys are poorly suited to understanding changes in the distribution of farm size holdings. Correcting this informational blind spot is critical for assessing what is happening in many African countries' agriculture sectors (Jayne et al. 2016).

Earlier, Mburu, Ackello-Ogutu, and Mulwa (2014, 1), in a study of the effect of farm size on economic efficiency among wheat producers in Kenya, estimated "the levels of technical, allocative, and economic efficiencies among the sampled 130 large and small scale wheat producers in Nakuru District." The researchers showed that the technical, allocative, and economic efficiency indices of small-scale wheat farmers, at 85 percent, 96 percent, and 84 percent, respectively, were only slightly lower than the 91 percent, 94 percent, and 88 percent, respectively, of large-scale farmers. From a strategic point of view, their observation, that the number of years of formal education that a farmer receives, the distance the farmer must travel to obtain extension advice, and the size of the farm strongly influence the efficiency levels, has important implications (Simpson et al. 2015). "The relatively high levels of technical efficiency among the small scale farmers defy the notion that wheat can only be efficiently produced by the large scale farmers" (Mburu, Ackello-Ogutu, and Mulwa 2014, 1).

Methodologically and empirically, new studies have estimated the IR hypothesis, using survey data over time, to understand the dynamics of change. A study by Deininger et al. (2015), based on three rounds of survey data in India, spanning three decades, explored the relationship between farm size and productivity. The authors noted, "While present throughout, the inverse relationship weakened significantly over time; the estimated elasticity of productivity with respect to farm size increased from 0.73 to 0.95 from 1982 to 2007. Key drivers are better functioning labor markets and a narrowing of efficiency differences between own and hired labor, possibly due to greater use of machinery. Structural transformation and a transition towards larger farms thus did not hurt productivity and economic efficiency" (Deininger et al. 2015, 1).

Otsuka, Liu, and Yamauchi (2016) reviewed evidence of different scales of production from a number of Asian countries. They noted that an increase in wage rate is typically associated with an increase in farm size, and that:

> In order to reduce labor cost, farm size expansion and mechanisation must take place, as land and machinery are complements... Also essential for farm size expansion is the migration of rural labour to urban and industrialised areas.
>
> High income countries in Asia (for example, Japan, Taiwan, and South Korea) have retained small farms and lost their comparative advantage in agriculture, thereby massively importing grains... If China and India, as well as other high-performing and populous Asian countries such as Vietnam and Indonesia, become major importers of grains in the future, world grain prices will rise and poverty will likely deepen. (Otsuka, Liu, and Yamauchi 2016, 457–8)

The authors noted that the evidence reviewed in their study offered a warning against maintaining small farms in Asia, with a risk to global food security, and argued for new policy measures to enlarge the farm size in Asia, with a need for strengthening land ownership rights and promoting land rental transactions, as well as land consolidation of parcels and the promotion of mechanization to reach scale economies (Otsuka, Liu, and Yamauchi 2016, 457–8).

A large body of conceptual and empirical evidence, including particularly the earlier failed attempts at industrialization in developing countries, demonstrated that if agricultural productivity growth does not precede, or at least accompany, labor transfers to urban areas, wage price inflation ensues in the face of rural–urban migration and stalls industrialization (Lele and Mellor 1981; Lele and Bumb 1995). This was the case in India during the 1964–6 balance of payments crises, and subsequently in 1990–1, leading policymakers to finally focus on the development of agriculture as essential for overall development; this explained the strong political support that the Green Revolution engendered (Lele and Goldsmith 1989; Lele and Bumb 1994). Notably, there was also much opposition to the Green Revolution strategy from influential economists such as T. N. Srinivasan (1991).

Peter Hazell, a longtime champion of small farm development, also questioned the relevance of small farms in Africa and Asia. The small farms are challenged by rapid urbanization, reverse farm size transition (smaller farms growing smaller), and emerging corporate farming. Hazell posits that some small farmers, with "resource endowments, good location, or sheer entrepreneurial skill" have been able to succeed as commercial farms, but face challenges of access to value chains and market opportunities. Hazell argues that "if more smallholder farms are to become commercially successful, policymakers will need to do more to support them" in terms of improving markets, rural infrastructure, and financial services, among other supports (Hazell 2015, 204–5).

Dercon and Gollin (2014) went further in asserting, "there is little evidence that would support (or oppose) the claim that public investments in agriculture will generate greater improvements in social welfare than investments in other sectors" (Dercon and Gollin 2014, 6). Others question CGIAR's rates of return studies and other studies (Ravallion and Datt 2002); or see flaws in the methodologies of studies (Fan, Hazell, and Thorat 2000; Fan, Zhang, and Zhang 2002).

Given that it was "hard to disagree" with Collier and Dercon (2014), Hazell further stated:

> We need to move beyond the small vs. big farm debate, and think more about appropriate portfolios of small, medium, and large farms that are relevant to the resource endowments and stage of development of a country ... [L]arge numbers of small farms are not going to make it as commercial businesses, especially asset-poor farmers in backward regions. Many of these kinds of farms are already diversifying their livelihoods out of farming, but there are many instances where this is not yet possible on the scale required, or where the returns to non-farm activities remain too low for them to escape poverty. (Hazell 2015, 200)

And yet, the demographic reality and the history of agriculture in most Asian and African countries are such that, under a business-as-usual scenario, small farms and small farmers will continue to dominate the development of food and agriculture, unless there is a drastic change in policies toward agricultural and industrial development. Hazell (2015) is right in stressing that small farmers are getting smaller, whereas Masters et al. (2013), in a paper prepared for CGIAR and published in *Global Food Security*, observed that the process of land consolidation has begun in Asia, but China may be unique in having achieved improved land governance, as compared to other Asian countries. Huang confirms the rapid rate of land consolidation in China, despite the small farm size.

China has also undertaken reforms in extension, mechanization, water management, and finance among other measures. In north and northeastern China, the average farm size has doubled over the past decade. Huang and Ding (2016) noted the strikingly rapid emergence of medium- and large-size farms in many regions. Bangladesh has had a stable farm size, and other Asian countries, including India, have faced declining farm sizes. According to Masters et al. (2013), rural population has peaked in Asia, partly "due to demographic [factors] ... but the average Asian farm size already has or will soon begin to rise, as some rural households cultivate land released by neighbors whose workers have stopped farming" (Masters et al. 2013, 157).

Upwards of 40 percent of all small farms in the world are in India, according to FAO (2014b), but reforms have been slow in coming. The number of operational holdings in India increased from 71.01 million in 1970–1 to 128.89 million in 2005–6, and the area of operational holdings declined from 162.18 million ha to 156.62 million ha, resulting in reduction of the average farm size from 2.28 ha to 1.21 ha. In the same period, the share of small and marginal holdings in the operated area doubled. Smallholders now cultivate 42 percent of operated land and constitute 83 percent of total landholdings. Making the market for farmland leasing more efficient would be a major step forward, with a lower political cost than full ownership (Chand, Lakshmi Prasanna, and Singh 2011).

Panagariya noted that, although many land laws were passed soon after independence, they were not implemented due to resistance from the landowning classes; ownership rights were conferred on only 4 percent of the land; and tenancy was abolished as seemingly exploitative, with the policy having the unintended consequence of providing no protection to tenants.[9] Reform of tenure, a top priority of the government, has stalled because of the opposition of the political parties to changing the Compensation and Transparency in Land Acquisition, Rehabilitation and Resettlement Act of 2013, which the Modi Government of India considers heavy on transaction costs. Panagariya urged states to pass land bills if the national government cannot get it done. He noted that the direct benefits of fertilizer subsidies to farmers cannot be achieved without tenure reform, and access to bank credit is difficult without tenure security.

There has been little progress on clarity of land rights in India. Constitutionally, the 28 states are responsible for land, water, and forests, and they have not acted on land rights.

In a personal communication with Uma Lele, Ramesh Chand noted:

> Both ownership and operational size of holdings are declining over time. This is shown both by Census data, which is based on revenue records and National Sample Survey Office (NSSO) data based on sample households. The Census did not capture tenancy, but NSSO data is expected to capture and reveal tenancy. According to NSSO data, tenancy in India is rising and is widespread in some states. In the state of Andhra Pradesh [before it was split in two], 37 percent of households reported land was leased in and 4.6 percent reported lease out. Obviously, marginal farmers and the landless are leasing in land on a large scale. There are also many cases of large farmers leasing in from small and marginal farmers . . . [I]ncrease in lease in and lease out is not resulting in an increase in operational area of farm size over time so far. Though government statistics do not reveal lease in and lease out data, it does not mean that the size of farms is rising due to under reporting of leasing. Farm size may be larger due to underreporting, but it is not rising over time. (Ramesh Chand, personal communication, January 8, 2018)

See also Chand, Srivastava, and Singh (2017).

In June 2020, the Government of India adopted three long overdue reforms relating to agricultural marketing that represented a fundamental reorientation of the existing regulatory framework. Although agriculture is a state subject, the central government took the opportunity and initiative to use the COVID-19 crisis to push through reforms, without the explicit involvement of the state governments. One bill relaxes restrictions governing the purchase and sale of farm produce; the second bill relaxes restrictions under the Essential Commodities Act (ECA), 1955, a vestige of colonial heritage; and the third introduces dedicated legislation to enable contract farming on written agreements. Despite the consensus among economists, the three bills are controversial. It is too early to know the impact of these three reforms, but they offer substantial potential to liberalize markets; contract farming could provide some security of tenure and increase overall productivity and income. For details, see Narayanan (2020).

---

[9] Arvind Panagariya, Professor of Economics and the Jagdish Bhagwati Professor of Indian Political Economy at Columbia University, served as Vice Chairman of NITI Aayog, Government of India, in the rank of Cabinet Minister, between January 2015 and August 2017.

Land ownership would not change the lot of poor households much, unless they were located in peri-urban areas where the land could be developed (and would then be priced as urban land) (Hazell 2015). A part of the challenge is that the nonagriculture sectors (service and manufacturing) have not been able to generate enough productive employment in developing countries, as we demonstrate later in this chapter. Furthermore, land serves as insurance. When industrial jobs are lost, workers go back to farming, as they did in Indonesia in 1997, and in China after the 2007 financial crisis.

Africa faces a different structural problem altogether. As noted, African agriculture faces an aging and illiterate farming community and youth uninterested in agriculture; lack of formal land rights keeps land rental low; only 5.6 percent of land is irrigated; and governments are fiscally strapped (ACET 2017). In addition, some countries are afflicted by acute governance challenges. A World Bank report documents the phenomenon of elite capture and elite competition for power in the case of Malawi (WBG 2018). A multi-stakeholder approach is needed, involving women, youth, the private sector, foundations, and involvement of farmers of all sizes, in addition to the need for leadership.

Role of Medium- and Large-Scale Farms

Those questioning the ability of small farmers to feed the world increasingly look to medium- and large-scale farms to meet that demand. Only 1 percent of all farms in the world, those larger than 50 hectares, control 65 percent of the world's agricultural land. These large farms deploy state-of-the-art biological, mechanical, and information technologies in the form of precision agriculture and enjoy economies of scale and scope. Many are becoming corporate farms (FAO 2014a).

Brazil contains farms of all sizes; it has an active agricultural policy toward agribusinesses through the Ministry of Agriculture, and toward small- and medium-scale farms though the Ministry of Agrarian Development. It has ample data, and it has attracted strong analysts. So what role has farm size played in Brazil? Helfand, Magalhães, and Rada (2015) concluded that the small and large farms are becoming more efficient more quickly than medium-sized farms. Their first hypothesis is that:

> Large and small farms, each through a separate and unique path, have advantageously adapted or developed size-dependent technologies or processes that have accelerated growth. The second is that Brazilian agricultural policy, through the Ministry of Agriculture and the Ministry of Agrarian Development, has respectively focused on the large and small producers and has, to a certain extent, ignored the needs of middling farm sizes. (Helfand, Magalhães, and Rada 2015, iii, 1)

This situation may occur because the Ministry of Agriculture provides services to small farmers, while large farms have access to technology from the market; middle-sized farmers are underserved by both. We will show evidence later that large farms increase productivity but do not generate much employment. Farm size can increase only if enough farm workers leave farming for nonfarm jobs.

Foster and Rosenzweig (2017), in their paper, the title of which asks, "Are There Too Many Farms in the World?" showed that "the existence of labor-market transaction costs can explain why the smallest farms are most efficient, slightly larger farms least efficient and larger farms as efficient as the smallest farms." They explained further that "the rising upper tail of the U characteristic of high-income countries requires there be economies of scale in the ability of machines to accomplish tasks at lower costs at greater operational scales." Data from India's village-level panel surveys conducted by the International Crops Research Institute for the Semi-Arid Tropics (ICRISAT) are consistent with these conditions. The authors also noted, "that there are too many farms, at scales insufficient to exploit locally available equipment-capacity scale-economies."

Much of the debate on farm size and productivity has been focused on land or labor productivity, generally showing respective productivity advantages to smaller or larger farms. Rada and Fuglie (2019) brought together evidence from a set of rich and poor countries, using panels of farm micro data and measures of TFP to compare performance (see Figure 2.1). Their case studies in (1) Malawi, Tanzania, and Uganda; (2) Bangladesh; (3) Brazil; (4) Australia; and (5) the United States suggest:

> There is no single economically optimal agrarian structure; rather, it appears to evolve with the stage of economic development. Certain farm sizes face relative productivity advantages, such as small farms in Africa. But with economic and market growth, that smallholder advantage will likely attenuate, moving toward constant and eventually increasing returns to size. Yet, importantly, small farms may be quite dynamic, and need not be a drag on agricultural growth [for example, in Bangladesh; see Gautam and Ahmed (2018)] until perhaps well into the development process. (Rada and Fuglie 2019, 147)

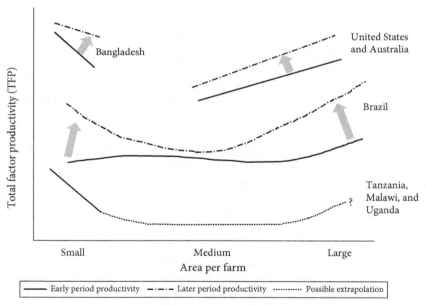

Figure 2.1 Total factor productivity over farm size varies widely by income class. (There is no optimal farm size: both large and small farms can be equally efficient.)

Note: The lines compare productivity among farms of different sizes and how those productivity differences have evolved over time, within a country. The lines should not be interpreted as comparing total factor productivity (TFP) across countries (they do not compare agricultural TFP between Bangladesh and Brazil, for example).

Source: Fuglie et al. (2019); Rada and Fuglie (2019).

Rada and Fuglie (2019) suggested flattened U-shaped curves on farm-level efficiency. Their findings suggest that policymakers need not favor medium and large farmers, at the cost of small farmers. By the same token, without attention to small farmers' productivity, differences in productivity growth between large and small farmers will continue to grow.

It is important to acknowledge some countervailing factors that may offset the negative impacts of increasingly concentrated farm structure. Lele and Stone (1989) explored the Boserupian intensification expected to occur, as a consequence of increasing relative land scarcity. However, empirical evidence for such intensification in Africa is decidedly mixed, suggesting constraints to land intensification, a conclusion that Headey and Jayne (2014) also reached a quarter-century later. Researchers, based on new evidence, challenged the inverse farm size–productivity hypothesis, with the incorporation of data on larger farm sizes than are typically observed in farm household surveys (Nkonde et al. 2015; Muyanga and Jayne 2019). The upshot of this work is that returns to scale may be an important source of intrasectoral growth. The researchers have joined in questioning the cost-effectiveness of promoting small-scale agriculture in Africa (see, for example, Collier and Dercon 2014; Dercon and Gollin 2014). Their argument would have greater validity if the literature suggested strong success in industrialization and ability of countries to absorb labor there. Unfortunately, evidence presents a dismal picture on growth in manufacturing.

Environmental Costs and Benefits of Productivity Growth

Much of the traditional economic literature did not address the environmental costs and benefits of technological change, but this is beginning to change. Modeling efforts are underway to quantify environmental impacts and implications for policy. The examples presented here are only illustrative. Taheripour, Hertel, and Ramankutty (2019, 19193) estimated the impact of rapid output expansion of palm oil output in response to rising global demand and concluded that:

> Limiting palm oil production or consumption is unlikely to halt deforestation in M&I [Malaysia and Indonesia] in the absence of active forest conservation incentives. Policies aimed at restricting palm oil production in M&I also have broader consequences for the economy, including significant impacts on consumer prices, real wages, and welfare. (Taheripour, Hertel, and Ramankutty 2019, 19193)

Quite another kind of modeling is underway in the area of climate change. Parry, Mylonas, and Vernon (2018), in their paper, "Mitigation Policies for the Paris Agreement: An Assessment for G20 Countries," provide an illustration of emissions pricing and that "results underscore the generally strong case for (comprehensive) pricing over other instruments" (Parry, Mylonas, and Vernon 2018, 2)

Jeuland and Whittington (2014) explored water resources planning with respect to climate change under alternative scenarios, assessing the robustness of real options for the Blue Nile. They concluded that "new, improved planning methods" are needed to address deep uncertainties related to climate change and its impacts on water resource development (Jeuland and Whittington 2014, 2086).

There are other important issues related to the process of small farm intensification and productivity growth, which we do not address here. One such issue is agricultural intensification and human health. For example, "pesticide use is strongly correlated with increased value of harvest, but is also correlated with higher costs associated with human illness, including increased health expenditures and time lost from work due to sickness in the recent past" (Sheahan, Barrett, and Goldvale 2017, 27). At the same time, with improvements in household incomes, "the content of the food basket is changing with a gradual shift toward high-value foods such as animal products, fruits and vegetables and processed foods. Overall, this dietary transition has important implications for the food security debate and for agricultural and food policy" (Worku et al. 2017, 73), as discussed in Chapter 4. Also, there are important trade-offs between nonfarm employment and income and farm productivity growth under smallholder agriculture. In certain circumstances, agricultural productivity declines as nonfarm income increases. This is because nonfarm employment and income can increase farm hired labor and improve input intensity; but can have "a negative effect on on-farm family labor use . . . [T]argeted policies are required to reduce these potential trade-offs between nonfarm employment and agricultural intensification and productivity change" (Amare and Shiferaw 2017, 59).

Industrialization and Structural Transformation

While Will Martin and Devashish Mitra (2001) presented evidence suggesting that there has been convergence in growth between developed countries and Asia, this has not been the case in SSA, with its special ecological challenges, diseconomies of scale, and high transportation costs. Industrialization has been much harder to achieve in many lagging countries.

Works on industrialization include: Owens and Wood (1997); Dasgupta and Singh (2006); Wood and Mayer (2011); Rodrik (2014, 2016); de Vries, Timmer, and de Vries (2015); Page (2015a, 2015b); Newman et al. (2016a); Page and Dews (2016); Tarp (2016); de Melo (2017); Diao, McMillan, and Rodrik (2017); and Wood (2017).

John Page (2015b) stressed the importance of industrialization but noted Africa's striking failure to industrialize. The average share of manufacturing in GDP in SSA in 2013 was about 10 percent, half of what would be expected from the region's level of development. Africa's share of global manufacturing fell from about 3 percent in 1970 to less than 2 percent in 2013. Manufacturing output per person is about one-third of the average for all developing countries. Manufactured exports per person, a key measure of success in global markets, are about 10 percent of the global average for low-income countries.

By comparing the examples of Vietnam and Cambodia with eight African countries (Ethiopia, Ghana, Kenya, Mozambique, Nigeria, Senegal, Tanzania, and Uganda), the country studies carried out by Newman et al. (2016b) provided further support to Page on the role that public policy and Bretton Woods institutions have played in Africa's slow industrialization, compared to East Asia's rapid progress. We draw extensively on their analysis, and at the end of the chapter, provide cross-country, econometric evidence to document patterns of transformation for well over 100 countries in different regions.

The selected countries that they studied were, according to the authors:

> . . . some of the stars of Africa's growth turnaround. Six of the eight had been among its fastest growing economies since 2000. Together they represent 54 per cent of the region's GDP and 56 per cent of its population . . . Their manufacturing sectors made about one-fifth of SSA's manufacturing value-added (excluding South Africa) . . . but they are not emerging industrial economies. Senegal has the highest share of manufacturing in GDP at

about 18 per cent. Nigeria has the lowest at less than two per cent. On average they are quite similar to Africa as a whole. Their share of manufacturing in GDP is 9.5 per cent, and the policies all eight countries adopted for industrial development closely parallel those of the region more broadly. (Newman et al. 2016b, 2)

Their industrialization policies fall into three phases: state-led, import-substituting industrialization in the early post-independence period; the "Washington Consensus"[10] and structural adjustment; and reform of the "investment climate," the physical, institutional, and regulatory environment for firms. Industrial performance has largely followed three phases as well: an early boom until about the early to mid-1970s. Newman et al. (2016b, 9–10) noted:

By the 1980s, the state-led industrialization effort had reached its limits in most countries. Between 1980 and 1985 manufacturing output began to decline in Ghana, Nigeria, and Tanzania. Contrary to the intent of the import substitution strategy, dependence on imports actually increased due to the heavy reliance of industry on imported capital and intermediate goods. Public investment exceeded the fiscal capacity of the state, and the state's capacity to manage the enterprises. The efficiency of production, measured in terms of international prices, was low, and in some cases, goods were produced at negative value-added in international prices. There was substantial excess capacity in public manufacturing enterprises, many of which were heavily constrained by lack of imported intermediates and working capital...

Between 1985 and 2000 more than thirty African countries, including all those in the country studies, adopted structural adjustment programmes (World Bank 2000).

The initial focus of public policy advice and conditionality by the IFIs [international financial institutions:] World Bank and IMF in Africa were focused on macroeconomic stabilization (World Bank 1992). Policy changes designed to improve resource allocation—liberalization of trade and finance and regulatory reform—followed closely thereafter. Across the continent governments liberalized trade and engaged in some deregulation of the domestic market. Privatization became a major objective and was often pushed, even in weak regulatory environments (Megginson and Netter 2001). Divestiture of state-owned enterprises was viewed as important both because it reduced the drain on the budget imposed by poor investment choices and because the state had proved to be a poor entrepreneur (Nellis 1986).

The reform programmes eventually restored macroeconomic balance. Fiscal deficits in the thirty-one countries covered by the Special Programme of Assistance for Africa had

---

[10] The "Washington Consensus" was used to describe a set of 10 economic reforms, which the economist John Williamson, who coined the term in 1989, argued were universally agreed upon in Washington as the "standard" reform package promoted for developing countries facing crises by Washington, DC-based institutions, such as the International Monetary Fund, World Bank, and United States Department of the Treasury. The ten policy prescriptions included: reduction of budget deficits; public expenditure for primary education and health and infrastructure to improve income distribution; tax reform to broaden the tax base and cut marginal taxes; financial liberalization; unified exchange rate; trade restrictions to be replaced by tariffs; removal of barriers for FDI; privatization of state-owned enterprises; deregulation to permit more competitive business and entry of new firms; and secure property rights. Through the years, the term acquired various meanings as a broader summary of policies directed toward client countries, by Washington-based international financial institutions. Criticism suggested the policy reforms were not actually based on consensus, and were prescribed without regard to local context. Williamson argued for the soundness of the macroeconomic policies, to assist national policymakers (Williamson 2004).

dropped to an average of 5.3 per cent of GDP in 1997 (World Bank 2000). The currency in the median African country was at PPP parity or undervalued in the early 1990s, and the black-market premium for foreign exchange had virtually disappeared (Easterly 2009). Quantitative trade restrictions were replaced by tariffs, and trade weighted average tariff rates fell from 30–40 per cent in 1980 to 15 per cent or less by 2000 (World Bank 2000). Privatization was more controversial and less widely embraced. In many countries the principal motivation to privatize was to placate the IFIs (Nellis 2003).

The authors also noted:

> The comparator Asian countries took quite different policy approaches to industrializa-
> tion and had very different industrial development outcomes. [For example,] Tunisia in
> North Africa...[has achieved] manufacturing growth exceed[ing] that for SSA for
> three decades. Cambodia and Vietnam had per capita income levels and structural
> characteristics similar to African economies as recently as 2005 in Cambodia and 2001
> in Vietnam...After an early period of state-led industrialization, both countries followed
> industrial development strategies very similar to those of other emerging East Asian
> countries with considerable success. Since 1990 manufacturing growth has averaged
> more than 10 per cent per year in both countries. (Newman et al. 2016b, 2–3)

Newman et al. (2016b, vii) argued that "Africa will not succeed in industrializing if the conventional wisdom offered by the international aid community to African governments continues to define their public policies to spur industrial development." The authors identified initiatives to address the challenge:

- Breaking into export markets will need an "export push" of the type undertaken by Cambodia, Vietnam, and Tunisia: a concerted set of public investments, policy, and institutional reforms focused on increasing the share of industrial exports in GDP. Because governments have limited scope for public investment and public action, the export push needs a government-wide commitment to focus investments and policy actions first on boosting non-traditional exports.
- In Cambodia and Vietnam the export push was accompanied by policies designed to promote the formation of industrial clusters. Spatial industrial policies are comple-mentary to both the export push and capability building. African governments can foster export-oriented industrial agglomerations by concentrating investment in high-quality institutions, social services, and infrastructure in a limited physical area such as an export processing zone (EPZ)—an industrial agglomeration designed to serve the global market—but African governments have not yet succeeded in doing so. (New-man et al. 2016b, vii)

A separate study of *Growth, Structural Transformation and Rural Change in Vietnam*, by Finn Tarp (2016), based on longitudinal household survey data, since Vietnam's adoption of the Doi Moi reforms in 1986, shows similar substantial improvement in rural income over time, including of women-headed households. The improvements are due, in addition to a proactive industrial policy, to investment in infrastructure and water, education, migrant income, and agricultural diversification to higher value crops, but also considerable continued regional income disparity between the relatively more prospering south and the north, much as China's industrialization policies show substantial regional income disparities among the three Chinese regions—the coastal industrial areas, the agricultural plateaus, and the forested, mountainous southwest.

Newman et al. noted further:

A short-lived industrial recovery

Perhaps no episode in Africa's contemporary economic history has raised as much debate as structural adjustment. The dramatic about-face in economic policies and more than a decade of very poor development outcomes sparked considerable academic and popular criticism. The early policy adjustments in combination with increased inflows of foreign aid provided a stimulus to industrial production in some countries, as firms used capacity that had been heavily constrained by lack of imported intermediates. Between 1980 and 1985 and 1985 and 1990 manufacturing growth shifted from negative to positive in Ghana, Nigeria, and Tanzania, and accelerated in Kenya, Senegal, and Uganda while it fell in Ethiopia and Tunisia.

The partial recovery of manufacturing was short-lived, however. Increased competition from imports and rising production costs due to reforms in the foreign exchange and financial markets put considerable pressure on manufacturing enterprises. Import competition, lack of technical expertise, and the shortage of working capital resulted in most government-owned firms operating at as little as 10 per cent of capacity. By 1990–5 manufacturing output was falling in Ghana, Mozambique, Nigeria, and Tanzania, and growth of manufacturing had declined in every other country except Uganda. The textile and clothing sector was especially hard hit. In Tanzania twenty-two out of twenty-four textile factories had closed by 1990, and in Nigeria employment in the textile and garments sector fell from 700,000 in 1980 to 40,000 in 1995. Tunisia in contrast maintained manufacturing growth rates of more than 5.5 per cent per year throughout the 1990s, despite embarking on its own structural adjustment programme.

Investment climate reform and new directions, 2000–

Africa entered the twenty-first century in substantially better macroeconomic shape than it had been in the last decades of the twentieth. The region began to experience positive per capita income growth around 1995, a trend that would accelerate through the 2000s. Improved economic performance led to a retreat from structural adjustment lending, and the Millennium Development Goals set a new agenda for aid to Africa, one mainly centred on human development.

Investment climate reforms

In the area of industrial development, the World Bank and many bilateral donors shifted their focus after 2000 to the "investment climate." As defined by the World Bank, the investment climate included: (1) macroeconomic stability; (2) openness; (3) good governance and strong institutions; (4) the quality of the labour force and infrastructure (Stern 2001, 2002). Led by the donors, investment climate reforms became widespread, often becoming key components of budget support programmes. Around one-quarter of official development assistance (some US$21 billion per year) currently supports investment climate reforms (OECD 2014).

The sub-Saharan case-study countries have all undertaken investment climate reform programmes in the last decade. Ghana has focused on trade policy and regulatory reforms. In Kenya reforms were undertaken to liberalize the regulatory regime. Mozambique adopted a new Industrial Policy and Strategy in which a significant role was assigned to promoting private investment. Nigeria's 2004 National Economic Empowerment and Development Strategy was explicitly targeted at making the industry sector internationally competitive. The 2005 Senegal Accelerated Growth Strategy set as its main objective establishing a "business environment consistent with international good practice." In 2010 Tanzania introduced an Integrated Industrial Development Strategy aimed at creating a "competitive business environment."

New directions

In addition to implementing the investment climate reform agenda, a number of countries have adopted more activist approaches to industrial development. In 1998 the Ethiopian government launched a strategy aimed at promoting labour-intensive manufactured exports. Kenya's Vision 2030 also emphasizes manufactured export growth. Most of the region's strategy and planning documents list a range of instruments intended to encourage private investment in targeted sectors. Ethiopia has attempted to coordinate private investment in textiles and garments, meat, leather and leather products, and agro-processing industries. Ghana's national industrial policy includes a number of highly sector-specific objectives. A prominent feature of Mozambique's industrialization strategy has been the promotion of large mining, manufacturing, and energy projects, known as "mega-projects."

Tunisia was the only African country studied in which the government undertook initiatives aimed at improving the competitiveness of individual industries and enterprises. An industrial upgrading programme, Programme de mise à niveau, was launched in 1996 followed by the Industrial Modernization Programme (PMI). These programmes were intended to provide technical assistance, training, financial subsidies, and infrastructure upgrades for firms to help them face international competition arising from the preferential trade agreement with the European Union under the Euro-Med initiative.

Not yet a turning point

For Africa as a whole neither the widespread adoption of investment climate reforms nor the new directions taken by some governments have reversed the four decade decline in industry. Manufacturing growth has remained below the growth rate of GDP. Since 2000 industrial performance among the SSAn countries covered in the country studies has been uneven. There has been some acceleration in the growth of manufacturing in Ethiopia, Kenya, Tanzania, and Uganda....Manufacturing growth in Ghana and Senegal has remained low and has lagged behind the overall growth of the economy. Nigeria was an exception; manufacturing grew at about 8 per cent per year between 2000 and 2010. (Newman et al. 2016b, 10–12)

De Vries (2015) similarly noted that manufacturing expanded during the early post-independence period, and expansion led to a growth-enhancing reallocation of resources. This process of structural change stalled in the mid-1970s and 1980s. Growth rebounded in the 1990s, but workers mainly relocated to service industries. Although service activities had above average productivity levels, productivity growth was low, and increasingly fell behind the world frontier. They also found that this pattern of static gains but with dynamic losses of reallocation, present since 1990 in many African countries, is comparable to patterns observed in Latin America, but different from those in Asia.

Rodrik (2016) has been, by far, the strongest modern advocate of the importance of the manufacturing sector as the escalator to industrial growth, as was Kaldor (1970, 1975) in the

1970s. Not only is factor productivity higher in the manufacturing sector, but there tends to be convergence in productivity across countries in the industry sectors, due to global competitiveness and the presence of exports. Rodrik noted, "It was the industrial revolution that enabled sustained productivity growth in Europe and the United States for the first time.... It was industrialization again that permitted catch-up and convergence with the West by a relatively smaller number of non-Western nations—Japan..., South Korea, [and] Taiwan..." (Rodrik 2016, 1).

Rodrik's assessment is also more pessimistic. Most developing countries are facing what Rodrik (2016, 2) terms "premature deindustrialization," or the increasing difficulty of industrialization. In response to the relentless advances of technology, it will no longer be easy to follow the path to wealth pursued by Asian countries, which used low-skilled workers to build successful export industries.

Earlier, Dasgupta and Singh (2006) explained the triple phenomenon of premature deindustrialization, jobless growth of manufacturing in the formal sector, and faster growth of services than of manufacturing. They used the Kaldorian framework and generalizations derived by Kaldor about the relationship between the growth of output and employment in different sectors of the economy. "Kaldor's laws," as the generalizations were known, explained the importance of industrialization. Like Rodrik, Kaldor had been an avid advocate of a strong role for industrialization. He justified it by focusing on demand, noting that elasticity of demand for industrial products tends to be higher than for the agriculture or service sectors until the economy matures. In addition, technological change is faster, and the scope for productivity growth in the industry sector is more rapid than in other sectors. Therefore, he argued, the faster the growth of manufacturing, the faster the growth of overall GDP. Indeed, today's industrialized countries experienced more rapid growth of manufacturing than GDP growth from the 1950s until 1973, after which their manufacturing growth decelerated and even became negative, and the service sector came into ascendancy, which was explained largely in terms of higher income elasticity of demand for services than manufacturing in mature economies.

Dasgupta and Singh also explained the reasons for the challenges to the Kaldor framework in the face of recent changes in the global environment: for example, the introduction of revolutionary new technologies such as information and communications technology (ICT). The service sector, consisting of ICT, telecommunications, business services, and finance, is replacing or complementing manufacturing as a new or an additional engine of economic growth in emerging countries, in much the same way that we documented in the case of the changing structure of trade in goods and services in the introduction.

Dasgupta and Singh (2006, 16) noted "pathological deindustrialization," in several Latin American and African countries in the 1980s and 1990s. They explained:

> As a result of Washington Consensus policies of international financial institutions (IFIs), which Latin American as well as many African countries were obliged to follow in response to the debt crisis, there has indeed been considerable structural change in these countries. But Ocampo [2004, 2005] and Shafaeddin (2005) have persuasively argued that this change has been of the wrong kind. Countries have begun to specialize according to their current comparative advantage instead of their long-term dynamic comparative advantage. (Dasgupta and Singh 2006, 16)

China is reshaping the global economy in a variety of ways. There is extensive discussion in Jenkins (2010) of the adverse impact of Chinese imports on domestic industry in the most industrialized Latin American countries—Brazil and Argentina—and also in South Africa, compared to the rest of SSA, which is not so industrialized. These countries have attempted to thwart competition through the World Trade Organization (WTO).

In both SSA and Latin America and the Caribbean (LAC), Chinese loans have played an important role in expanding the market for Chinese products. Both regions have also been a testing ground for China's Go Global policy, encouraging the international expansion of Chinese companies. Chinese construction and engineering firms have been particularly active in SSA.

In the joint report of the World Bank Group, the Organisation for Economic Co-operation and Development (OECD), WTO, and others on global value chains, Nobel laureate Michael Pence noted "a growing body of research on the impacts of globalization and digital technology on individual economies," suggesting that there has been "a huge and productive effort to reconfigure and refine trade data so as to expose the complex value-added structure of trade in goods and services" (WBG et al. 2017, iii).

The study of global value chains noted: "The patterns of specialization across countries are much more visible and clearly defined when viewed through the lens of complex value-added chains... [They explain] where employment is created, what drives productivity growth, and what factors are affecting income distribution in a wide range of developed and developing countries" (WBG et al. 2017, iii).

China has been a leader in driving growth of global value chains. As its incomes rise, it is moving away from labor-intensive manufacturing and assembly, and GVCs are moving to lower income countries, "creating growth and development opportunities and momentum... But there are impediments... low wages are not enough. Connectivity and... efficient processes for logistics and for meeting standards and regulatory require-ments are critical. And lots of countries [including India] currently lose out on this front" (WBG et al. 2017, iv).

What the World Bank Group (WBG) report probably means is that India is not connecting its service sector to manufacturing within the region, as is China, serving as a hub for Southeast Asian countries. India is exporting services to the West, albeit without being a hub that serves manufacturing in SA. The report distinguishes between wages and unit labor costs and the factors that drive a wedge between them. Low wages may help, but are not necessary. For competitiveness, unit labor costs are critical, and they depend on labor quality. The analysis explains "the divergent distributional impacts of globalization across developed and developing countries" (WBG et al. 2017, iv) and between the tradable and nontradable:

> The tradables set is expanding with the support of enabling technology. For example, small and medium-size businesses can access global markets in a way that was simply impossible before because the transaction costs of doing so were prohibitively high. But the nontradables part of any economy remains very large. The linkages between the tradables and nontradables parts of an economy on both the supply and demand sides are crucial in understanding the growth patterns... These linkages are complex. On the supply side they come through labor market shifts, and on the demand side through spillover effects of rapid income growth arising from specialization and growth on the tradables side... [where your neighborhood matters]. (WBG et al. 2017, iv)

The report compares differences in the high degree of regional integration in East Asia to South Asia, with vast differences in the extent of innovation and efficiency across countries.

Savings, Investment, and Structural Transformation

Structural transformation is related to transformation in the behavior of savings and investment, which Lewis (1954) articulated well. What comes first? Savings or investment? There seems to be no agreement among economists on this issue. Savings and investment rates have grown substantially in developing regions, and economic growth has also resulted in declines in poverty and hunger. The lowest savings rates are in LAC, followed by the African region, slightly exceeding 18 percent. They are as high as 30 percent in SA and well over 45 percent in East Asia and the Pacific (EAP) (Figure 2.2) for net capital inflows (see Chapter 7 on financing). To reignite growth, some economists, including Arvind Subramanian, former Chief Economic Advisor in the Economic Survey of India, 2017–18 (Government of India 2018a, chapter 3), have argued that raising investment is more important than raising savings. Based on cross-country experience, he argues growth slowdowns are preceded by investment slowdowns but not necessarily by savings slowdowns. This is, perhaps, because of the growing importance of international capital.

Economic performance in Asia, and especially of China and India, has been propelled by investment growth and backed by increased savings. Without that, resulting current account deficits are usually unsustainable. Only Australia and Malaysia were able to sustain

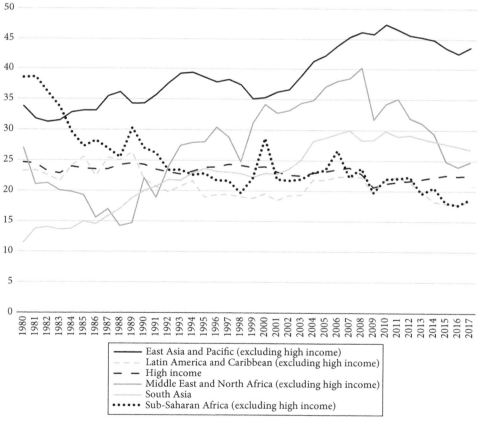

Figure 2.2 Gross domestic savings by region, 1980–2017 (% of GDP)
Source: WDI, World Bank.

large current account deficits for a sustained period. As Figure 2.3 shows, investment ratios in East Asia are almost twice those in Africa and Latin America. Investment rates in SA have been increasing, and though still considerably lower than in EAP, China invests even more than other countries in its region, almost half its GDP. In recent years, India has invested about one-third of its GDP, slightly more than other countries in its region. Also, the investment ratio is more similar between China and India than it is between either country and the ratio in LAC or SSA.

Again, differences among regions are striking. Not only are investment levels in Asia higher than in other developing country regions, but there is greater efficiency in the use of capital, as measured by the incremental capital–output ratio (ICOR). After the oil price rise of 1973, the capital–output ratio doubled in the rest of the world, and it has remained high since (Agarwal and Whalley 2013). It increased considerably less in East Asia, and it actually declined in SA. So, since the early 1980s, it has been the same in East and South Asia. The incremental capital–output ratio was considerably lower in China than in India until 1998. Since then, the ICOR in the two countries has been roughly the same, about 4 (Agarwal and Whalley 2013).[11]

According to Virmani (2018), China's ICOR[12] was slightly less than 2 in 1984, reaching 6.4 in 2016. China's ICOR has increased significantly over time, as China has moved to

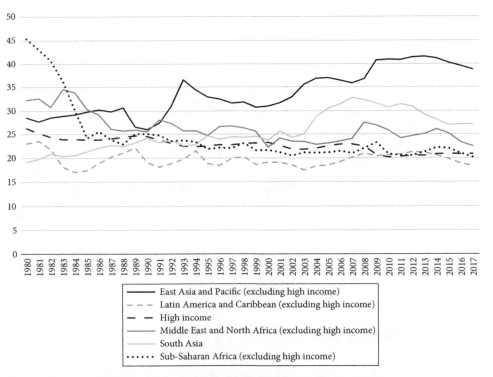

Figure 2.3 Gross fixed capital formation by region, 1980–2017 (% of GDP)
Source: WDI, World Bank.

[11] ICOR is calculated as the moving average of the sum of investment over five years, divided by the increase in income during this period, with a one-year lag: that is, $\sum_{i=1}^{5} I_i / (Y_6 - Y_1)$ (Agarwal and Whalley 2013).
[12] ICOR is calculated as investment rate/GDP growth rate.

more capital-intensive, sophisticated manufacturing, moving out of more labor-intensive commodities as wage rates increased. India's ICOR was about 4 in 2016, but much more unstable from year to year (Arvind Virmani, personal communication, February 16, 2019).

According to FAO (2020b), over the decade 2005–14, global annual physical investment flows in agriculture, as measured by gross fixed capital formation (GFCF) in agriculture, rose by almost 50 percent from US$259 to US$378 billion in constant 2005 US dollars.[13]

However, this rise is again not uniform across all regions: while the annual flow of physical investment in the agriculture sector doubled in Asia and Pacific over the last decade, it remained stagnant in Europe and in the other developed regions. For the remaining regions, agricultural physical investment flows increased by around 34 percent in Africa, 54 percent in Latin America and the Caribbean, and 62 percent in North America.

GFCF was a key driver of GDP growth, as it rose from US$3.6 trillion (2005 US dollars) to US$13.8 trillion between 1970 and 2014. The investment ratio—GFCF as a proportion of GDP—remained relatively stable at around 22 percent throughout the period. At the regional level, the investment ratios for Africa, Europe, and Latin America and Caribbean present downward trends, while North America, in contrast, saw its investment ratio increasing from 0.18 in the 1970s to 0.20 at the beginning of the 21st century.

Dubey and Donckt (2016) showed that both groups (low-income countries and middle- and high-income countries):

> ...present a similar average overall investment ratio [calculated for the total economy, total GFCF to GDP), but]...the average AIR [Agriculture Investment Ratio: that is, agriculture GFCF to agriculture value-added] is much lower in low-income countries, indicating that in those countries—where agriculture often remains an important contributor to GDP—the primary sector is behind in terms of investment in physical capital with respect to the other sectors of the economy. On the other hand, industrialized countries tend to have [a] much more mechanized agriculture sector. (Dubey and Donckt 2016)

This means China, being a middle-income country, invests more than low-income countries. These differences are seen later when TFP estimates are discussed in Figure 2.7.

The differences in FAO reported gross capital formation, specifically in the Agriculture, Forestry and Fisheries sector (AFF), and FDI in China and the rest of the world are even

---

[13] Gross fixed capital formation (GFCF) captures the net additions (acquisitions less disposals) to the stock of fixed capital assets such as machinery, transport equipment, infrastructure, and buildings within an economy.

Data on agricultural GFCF are available for over 200 countries. For some 100 countries, data on agriculture GFCF were completely missing and are imputed based on a panel regression approach (with an adjustment on the series level to ensure coherence with the agriculture consumption of fixed capital series whenever available from the United Nations Statistics Division Official Country Data [UNSD OCD] database). For many of the other countries, data are available only for a limited number of years in which case data for the missing years have been imputed using the available data as the base for investment ratio using ARMAX modeling. Data on net capital stock (NCS), gross capital stock (GCS), and consumption of fixed capital (CFC) are available for just over 200 countries. It should be noted that most of the country data have been calculated by FAO following the perpetual inventory method (PIM) approach as presented in the OECD (2009) *Manual on Capital Stock*.

The time coverage for the agricultural capital stock database is 1990–2014, as far as data availability permits. For some countries, data on GFCF are available only from 1995. Therefore, regional aggregation regarding the GFCF variable should not be performed for the period 1990–4. For many countries, NCS and GCS data start in the mid-2000s. Therefore, the greatest care should be attached to the effective country coverage when compiling regional aggregates.

For more information on the methodology regarding the agriculture capital stock database, please refer to the metadata available through FAOSTAT.

more striking. The extraordinary level of investment in Chinese agriculture is in contrast to the next best performers: namely, the United States and India. Investments in Africa are abysmally low, in both gross capital formation and FDI.

Convergence of Performance?

There is considerable debate in the literature on whether there is convergence in the growth performance of developed and developing countries.

For a long time, developing countries were stuck in low-growth scenarios, whereas developed countries were growing rapidly, thus increasing the gap between developed and developing countries (Pritchett 1997). Will Martin (2018) showed this growing gap in the rates of growth between developed and developing countries from 1820 until 1990, in Figure 2.4.

Then, Martin (2018) emphasized convergence. Subramanian in the 2017–18 Economic Survey of India also noted, "'convergence with a vengeance' (Subramanian 2011)" (Government of India 2018b, 68). The percentage of countries growing faster than the United States (a "frontier country") increased from 43.7 percent between 1960 and 1980 to 68.6 percent between 1980 and 2017, and the average growth rate accelerated from 1.4 percent to 1.7 percent (Government of India 2018b, 68–9). The record on convergence, however, is mixed. Per capita income growth has occurred mainly in Asian countries, China with 8 percent annually and India with 5 percent annually, but income growth in some of the Middle East and Latin America is barely equal to the population growth, and growth in SSA and the other parts of the Middle East has been less than the population growth (Figure 2.5). China's growth has started decelerating since 2017, and with the spread of coronavirus in 2020, it is expected to be close to 1 percent in 2020. Although India's growth increased temporarily, concern that Indian growth rates may have been overstated has been followed by an outright slowdown in its growth in 2019 (Government of India 2018b).

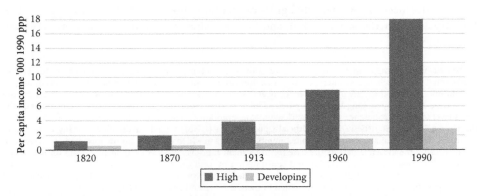

Figure 2.4 Levels and growth in per capita income by high-income and developing countries: divergence "big time," 1820–1990

Note: Average growth: High income: 1.6% per annum; Developing: 0.9% per annum.

Source: Martin (2018). Based on data from Angus Maddison, "Statistics on World Population, GDP and Per Capita GDP 1–2008 AD." Downloaded from http://www.ggdc.net/maddison/Maddison.htm, July 13, 2018.

IMF's projected economic growth rates in 2018 for 2017–23 were substantially higher for Asia and Europe, but they are significantly lower for Latin America and even lower for SSA (IMF 2018) (Figure 2.6).

Indeed, SSA's projected per capita income growth remains well below the population growth rate in Figures 2.5 and 2.6. Fuglie et al. (2019, xxii) noted in their book, *Harvesting Prosperity: Technology and Productivity Growth in Agriculture*: "Agricultural productivity is lower and is growing more slowly in poor countries, impeding their convergence to the advanced economies. Over four decades, crop yields in sub-Saharan Africa have barely doubled, even as they tripled in South Asia and increased about six-fold in East Asia."

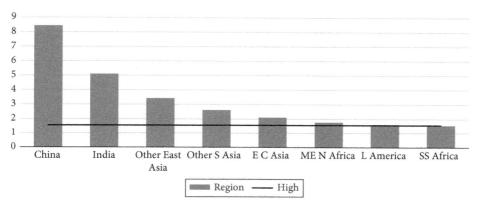

Figure 2.5 Annual GDP per capita growth rates by region and key country: Rapid per capita income growth in Asia, 1991–2017

Source: Based on WDI, World Bank data; Martin (2018).

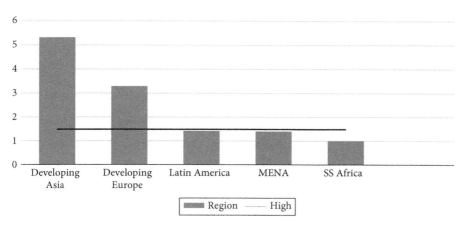

Figure 2.6 Projected economic growth rates, 2017–2023 (% per annum)

Note: MENA = Middle East and North Africa; SS Africa = sub-Saharan Africa.

Source: Based on *World Economic Outlook,* IMF (2018); Martin (2018).

Divergence in Agricultural Productivity Growth and Poverty Reduction

East and Southeast Asian countries have experienced a sharp decline in poverty, as shown in Chapter 4, Figure 4.2, but their elasticities of poverty reduction, with respect to change in per capita income, are the lowest in Asia (Agarwal 2017), moving significant populations out of agriculture to higher productivity activities and changing the structure of production. The performance of SA has been slower than that of East Asia, and the performance of SSA, after a promising start in the 1960s and 1970s, has been slowest. East and Southeast Asia managed to reduce extreme poverty dramatically over the last two decades; in SA, both the share of poverty and absolute numbers have declined, whereas SSA has failed to keep pace. The poverty rate has declined very little, and the absolute number of poor has increased, partly due to a rapid population growth and because GDP per capita did not grow for almost 25 years from 1982 onward, as documented in Agarwal and Whalley (2013), and discussed by the United Nations Conference on Trade and Development (UNCTAD) (Osakwe and Poretti 2015). UNCTAD blames it on terms of trade losses, which according to UNCTAD were larger than the aid the region received. The relationship between poverty reduction and food security has been more complex than generally assumed in the literature and is explored in the chapters that follow, particularly Chapters 3 and 4.

According to Virginia Tech's "Global Agricultural Productivity Report":

> Globally, TFP is rising by an average annual rate of 1.63 percent, less than the estimated 1.73 percent needed to sustainably double agricultural output (2010–2050) through productivity growth. TFP growth is strongest in China and South Asia, but it is slowing in the agricultural powerhouses of North America, Europe, and Latin America. TFP growth in low-income countries [including SSA, other than South Africa] is alarmingly low. (Steensland 2019)

Figure 2.7 shows sources and rates of growth in agricultural production during the period 2001–16 through a growth accounting exercise. Not only did Northeast Asia (which includes China) have the highest growth rate, but also most of the growth has come from productivity growth with very little resource input (land, labor, machinery power, livestock capital, synthetic NPK fertilizers, and animal feed) growth.[14] During the period 1961–2016,

---

[14] TFP growth is measured as the ratio of output growth to input growth, where output growth is FAO's gross agricultural output (GAO) growth, and input growth is the weighted-average growth in quality-adjusted land, labor, machinery power, livestock capital, synthetic NPK fertilizers, and animal feed, where weights are input (factor) cost shares.

Fundamentally, TFP is a ratio that measure changes in how efficiently agricultural inputs (land, labor, fertilizer, feed, machinery, and livestock) are transformed into outputs (crops and livestock). If total output is growing faster than total inputs, then the total productivity of the factors of production (that is, total factor productivity, or TFP) is increasing.

Input growth in this estimation includes:

1. Area growth = Growth of (Agricultural land area extension − Area equipped for irrigation extension), where "Agricultural land" is total agricultural land in hectares of "rainfed cropland equivalents." This is the sum of rainfed cropland (weight equals 1.00), irrigated cropland (weight varies from 1.00 to 3.00 depending on region), and permanent pasture (weight varies from 0.02 to 0.09 depending on region).

2. Irrigation extension: Growth of area equipped for irrigation extension.

3. Input intensification: (Input growth − growth of agricultural land area extension), principally inputs per land (that is, gross amount of fertilizer, machinery, feed, and labor per hectare of agricultural land). Input/resource-led growth.

4. Productivity-led growth: TFP.

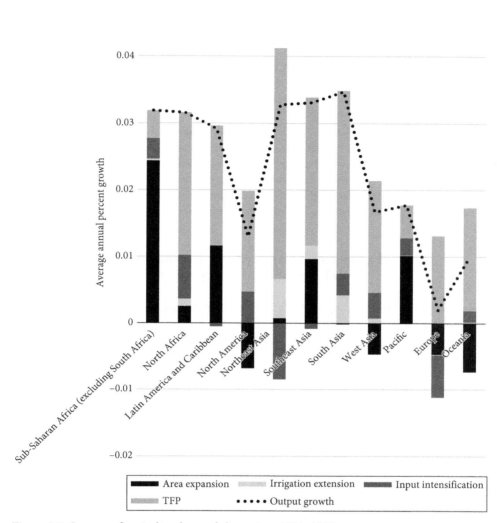

Figure 2.7 Sources of agricultural growth by region, 2001–2016

Source: Based on data from https://www.ers.usda.gov/data-products/international-agricultural-productivity/ and data provided by Keith O. Fuglie.

agricultural output increased by 60 percent, while global cropland increased by just 5 percent (OECD and FAO 2019).

Differences in agricultural growth and its sources are also noticeable for the period 2001–16 by region. Area expansion (that is, rainfed cropland and permanent pasture) was minimal in Northeast Asia, which includes China, and in SA, which includes India, was negative. Extension of irrigated cropland (area equipped for irrigation) was greater in both regions, and growth of input intensification (that is, labor, machinery power, livestock capital, synthetic NPK fertilizers, and animal feed) was negative in Northeast Asia and minimal in SA during that period. SA follows the Northeast Asia region in productivity growth among all the regions. In the case of SSA (which excludes South Africa), overall growth in production was slower, and most of it has come from land area expansion, with very little from productivity-led growth. In the case of LAC, which includes Brazil, and Southeast Asia, which includes Indonesia, a significant share of the overall growth has come from area expansion, explaining land conversation and deforestation in the Amazon and in the outer islands of Indonesia.

Separate figures (not shown here) for China, India, Brazil, and Africa show these differences more strikingly. What is unclear is the extent to which the extraordinary differences in GFCF in agriculture are reflected in these estimates as the flows of capital. Either the Chinese GFC estimates and FDIs are overstated (as Fuglie suggested in the case of GFC in a personal exchange on February 19, 2020), or we are understating the importance of capital investment in agriculture (particularly in research and development) and related services (infrastructure, communication, education, and health). Those investments are reflected in the quality of inputs and incentives (for example, through enhanced market access and reduced market costs), and these "quality" aspects of inputs are not reflected in the growth accounting estimates in Figure 2.7 on agricultural output growth but are reflected in the national-level investments.

Complexity of Agricultural Development and Demands of Policymakers

It is evident from the preceding discussion that developing agriculture is a complex business. It requires a sophisticated understanding of the different elements of the country-specific strategies that have to be put in place. In addition to political commitment, policymakers need an understanding of their roles and those of other stakeholders in addressing the multiple dimensions in a changing, highly dynamic context, such that different elements of the strategy need to respond to those external and internal circumstances. The list presented in Table 2.1 is based on Uma Lele's experience of well over four decades, combined with the analytical and operational work of the World Bank, including the *World Development Reports* and the Agriculture and Rural Development Series, and FAO's *State of Food and Agriculture* (*SOFAs*) series and *State of Food Insecurity* series, and other specialized publications. All elements of the agricultural strategy listed in Table 2.1 cannot be realistically in place at once, or indeed in many countries over time, and specific subsectors, such as livestock, forestry, and fisheries, need their own strategies. The table does provide a useful checklist that countries need to have in place over time. Rodrik (2006) argued, in the case of the 10 original points of the Washington Consensus, that it is impossible to address all these issues at once. He suggested picking the most important issue, addressing it, and then continuing with the next one (either sequentially or simultaneously, depending on the issues and resources). Table 2.1 contains a similar idea of addressing several of these elements of agricultural policy either sequentially or simultaneously, depending on the country's capacity to put into place a policy framework. It will also help throw light on the country performances that follow in the remainder of this chapter and the rest of the book.

Box 2.3 presents these and other multiple changes that are taking place globally with which countries must cope.

The stages approach, proposed by de Janvry and Sadoulet (2018), suggests the need for a regional, spatially oriented strategy, rather than focusing attention simply on urban metropoles. Several advocates, most notably Adrian Wood (Owens and Wood 1997; Wood 2003), Paul Collier and Stefan Dercon (2014), and Douglas Gollin (Dercon and Gollin 2014), have suggested the need to go beyond the "agriculturally led" strategy narrative to search for the

Table 2.1 What transformation of agriculture needs and the frequent political economy challenges

What transformation of agriculture needs	Frequent political economy challenges

• *Enabling public policies and institutions* to manage complex, diverse systems to foster innovation, including a coherent science and technology policy
• *Bottom-up,* disaggregated approaches that foster community participation supported by *overarching* macroeconomic and sectoral policies
• *Clarity and security of property rights and transparent rules of governance toward:*
  ○ Tariff and nontariff barriers
  ○ Pricing and subsidies
  ○ Commodity markets and policies
  ○ Financial markets and policies
  ○ Acquisition of national assets, particularly land
  ○ Food and other regulatory and safety standards
  ○ Accountability mechanisms
• *Investments in public goods:*
  ○ Rail, roads, power, transport, communications
  ○ Information and knowledge
  ○ Research
  ○ Extension
• *Effective management of common pool resources*
  ○ Proactive management and conservation of land, water, forests, and biodiversity
  ○ Irrigation and drainage
  ○ *Technology*—Access to biological, mechanical, and information technologies (quality seed, fertilizers, water)
  ○ *Education*—Human and organizational capacity education
  ○ *Markets*—Existence of labor, financial, and commodity markets
• An active role for the private sector
• An active role for civil society
• Farmers and community organizations
• An independent media
• An independent and fair legal system and effective dispute settlement mechanisms
	• Weak political support to agriculture
	• Elite capture or civil society capture
	• Resistance of landowning classes to tenure reforms
	• Lack of capacity to establish
	• Harder to reform than investment in R&D (World Bank 2007)
	• Easy to legislate but difficult to enforce
	• IT is not a silver bullet but is making an increasing contribution (World Bank 2015).
	• Content matters (for example, Digital Green https://www.digitalgreen.org). See Chapter 9 on FAO.
	• Informal and overlapping rights of poor and marginal people to natural resources. One of the hardest to manage. See Chapter 8 on World Bank.
	• Biodiversity loss faster than replaced, easier to mitigate in protected areas but challenging outside (GEF IEO 2016)
	• Huge investment requirements, need land access
	• Increasingly resorting to social safety nets
	  ○ According to WDR 2008 (World Bank 2007) easier than others, but, in reality, not so
	• Needs an integrated package approach; donors supplying them one by one
	• Needs infrastructure, information; IT helpful here
	• Trade-offs between the short and the long run
	• Subsidies reduce incentives to private sector
	• Weak civil society in many countries
	• Viable cooperative and farmers' organizations have proven difficult in practice
	• Lacking in many countries
	• Clogged system, does not work for the poor

most appropriate strategies for lagging countries. They have argued for a more eclectic approach, including, in particular, attention to value-added of the natural resource base of primary commodity producers (Owens and Wood 1997). Like de Vries, Timmer, and de Vries (2015), Owens and Wood (1997) noted poorer performance of SSA in resource-based industry, relative to Latin America. Some also advocate or note the inevitability of a strong role for large- and medium-sized farms (Muyanga et al. 2013; Collier and Dercon 2014; Dercon and Gollin 2014; Headey and Jayne 2014; Jayne et al. 2014; Sitko and Jayne 2014).

Box 2.3 Stages of Transformation Processes: The AB-GR-AT-RT-ST Sequence

- *Asset building (AB)*: Access to land and human capital for the landless and subfamily farmers.
- *Green Revolution (GR)*: Adoption/diffusion of high-yielding variety seeds and fertilizers for staple crops.
- *Agricultural transformation (AT)*:
  - Access to water for irrigation
  - Agricultural diversification toward high-value crops
  - Development of value chains and contracting
- *Rural transformation (RT)*:
  - Mechanization and land concentration
  - Development of land and labor markets
  - Growth of a rural nonfarm economy
- *Structural transformation (ST)*: Rural–urban migration

Source: de Janvry and Sadoulet (2018).

Urbanization provides additional strength to those in favor of large- and medium-scale agriculture in Africa to meet the rapidly growing urban demand but raises a question: Who is feeding the growing population? There is a huge opportunity for small farmers to meet the growing market demand, particularly with respect to high-value crops, which typically tend to be labor-intensive.

Structural Transformation: Data and Analysis

Our analysis of structural transformation has evolved from a two-sector to a three-sector analysis providing new insights. It started with a transformation of the economies from agriculture to the nonagriculture sector and formed an input into the World Bank's study of "Accelerating Agricultural Productivity Growth" in India (World Bank 2014). Our work essentially followed Timmer's approach to structural transformation, using more recent data on 127 countries, covering a 34-year period (1980–2013) (Lele, Agarwal, and Goswami 2013, 2014, 2018). The data generated by FAO provided estimates of economically active populations in the agricultural and nonagriculture sectors. The World Bank data were used on per capita GDP and sectoral value-added, respectively. Timmer's analysis (Timmer and Akkus 2008; Timmer 2009) covered the period 1965–2000, for 86 countries. In extending his analysis to 109 countries (88 developing + 21 developed), covering a 30-year period (1980–2009), our purpose was to explore whether there were changes in results, using more recent data, and how individual countries were progressing on structural transformation, such as the progress of India relative to its Asian neighbors, particularly China and Indonesia, and other large countries such as Brazil (Lele, Agarwal, and Goswami 2018).[15]

---

[15] The data we used were the same FAO data that Timmer used in his analysis, and the estimates of TFP used by Fuglie (2010). The Timmer analysis was for the period 1965–2000. FAO stopped publishing data before 1980,

In 2013, we had performed a similar analysis on the countries of the East African Community, comparing them to other countries, including South Africa and Egypt (Lele, Agarwal, and Goswami 2013). We then extended this analysis to 127 countries (96 developing + 31 developed), covering a 34-year period (1980–2013) (Lele, Agarwal, and Goswami 2014).[16] Some key findings of our analysis were as follows:

1. India had fallen behind in structural transformation relative to China and Indonesia, by several different criteria—that is, decline in the share of population in agriculture at the beginning and the end of the period, share of manufacturing sector in the economy over time, and demographic transition—even though the three countries started with similar initial conditions in the early 1960s of a small farm-dominated agriculture. Indonesia had developed a thriving plantation sector, producing rubber, palm oil, and other cash crops, albeit at the cost of rapid deforestation, typically not measured either in the work on transformation, or on Fuglie's TFP estimates. Labor productivity, measured as value-added per worker, increased in all three countries in both the agriculture and the nonagriculture sector, a unique achievement compared to other developing regions.
2. Productivity in the nonagriculture sector grew faster than in agriculture in all three countries, more so in China than in India. Indonesia's growth stumbled during the 1997 financial crisis and resumed after a lag.
3. Internal terms of trade between agriculture and nonagriculture moved in favor of the nonagriculture sector in all three countries: that is, relative prices moved against agriculture.

In contrast, Brazil, with a more dualistic agriculture, achieved fast agricultural TFP growth, while shedding labor in agriculture. Additionally, unlike in the three Asian countries (China, India, Indonesia) which we studied in Lele, Agarwal, and Goswami (2018), Brazil's value-added per worker in the nonagriculture sector did not keep pace with productivity growth in agriculture and declined relative to that in the agriculture sector. In Lele, Agarwal, and Goswami (2013), we documented that South Africa's bimodal pattern of development, similar to Brazil's, had behaved similarly. In South Africa, agricultural productivity growth surpassed that of East African countries, but like Brazil, South Africa was shedding labor in agriculture.

There has been a growing interest in the emergence of middle-sized farms. As we discussed earlier, middle-sized farms in Brazil, as a group, are less productive than either small or large farms. Rada and Fuglie (2019) have argued that small farmers show high productivity, productivity declines as farm size increases, and then it rises again in the case of large farmers: in short, there is a flattened U-shaped curve by farm size.

The next stage of our analysis (Lele, Goswami, and Nico 2017) used panel data on a three-way sectoral breakdown of employment in agriculture, manufacturing, and service sectors for 139 (104 developing + 35 developed) countries over the period 1991–2014, from ILO–GET. ILO's breakdown of employment in the agriculture, manufacturing, and service

---

when we started our analysis. Fuglie did backward estimation for his TFP calculation, using FAO's methodology to get values prior to 1980 (Keith Fuglie, personal communication, September 11, 2017).

[16] FAO stopped publishing data in this form, as of 2014 (that is, economically active populations in agriculture), and instead, publishes data on employment in agriculture, as part of the International Labour Organization (ILO)–Global Employment Trend (ILO–GET) data, which contain data on three sectors—agriculture, service, and manufacturing—based on surveys. Therefore, such analysis can only be conducted up to 2013.

sectors is based on household labor force surveys and employment surveys, and therefore likely measures labor input in sectors, including in agriculture, more accurately than FAO's earlier estimates of the economically active population in agriculture without the actual input. It is an important breakthrough in understanding the process of structural transformation. Where does labor move when it leaves agriculture, to manufacturing or the service sector, and what are the labor productivity differences in these sectors? A difference between ILO and FAO data used earlier, apart from the intersectoral breakdown of employment, is in the estimation of labor input.[17] With a few notable exceptions, ILO estimates of labor in agriculture, which measure labor input more directly than FAO, as the population dependent on agriculture, are lower than FAO estimates of labor in agriculture: for example, in Brazil. There are also some differences in trends in the labor inputs in agriculture between the FAO and ILO data. This data set helped us to explore differences in employment generated and changes in productivity of labor in the agriculture, industry, and service sectors over time. The analysis covered the period of rapid economic growth in developing countries—that is, from the 1990s—and the slowdown since the 2007–8 crisis. These differences are outlined in Appendix A.

Differences in Behavior among Developed and Developing Regions Using Data from the International Labour Organization

We examine and compare structural changes that occur within countries when per capita income rises. Structural change is measured in terms of the behavior of the three sectors: agriculture, industry, and services (see Appendix A on data and methodology). Structural changes in developing countries are compared to developed countries, and then among the different developing regions.

The agriculture sector share in developing countries is larger in both GDP and employment. The difference in shares between agricultural GDP and agricultural employment, however, is much larger in developing countries: that is, a larger share of the population is employed in agriculture than is agriculture's share in GDP, and agricultural GDP share decreases much faster as well. The behavior of the agriculture share of GDP is not significantly different between developing countries and developed countries, but the behavior of the employment share in agriculture is very different (Figures 2.8 and 2.9). Employment share falls much more rapidly in developing countries than developed countries.

As per capita income increases, the share of agricultural value-added in total GDP decreases at an increasing rate (the coefficient of the quadratic term of per capita, as per capita income increases, is positive) in both developing and developed regions, but after a threshold, at the very advanced stage in which per capita GDP of \$31,814 (in constant 2005 US dollars) is reached, the share of agricultural value-added starts to increase at a very slow

[17] FAO's data on economically active population refer to the number of all employed and unemployed persons, including those seeking work for the first time. The data cover employers; self-employed workers; salaried employees; wage earners; unpaid workers assisting in a family, farm, or business operation; members of producers' cooperatives; and members of the armed forces. The economically active population is also called the labor force. ILO's data on employment refer to all persons above a specified age, who were, during a specified brief period— either one week or one day—in the following categories: paid employment (whether at work or with a job but not at work) and self-employment (whether at work or with an enterprise but not at work). For the purposes of the aggregate sectors (agriculture, industry, and services), definitions of the International Standard Industrial Classification (ISIC) System are used.

pace (Figure 2.8). The reason for this increase in agriculture's share of GDP is not entirely clear. It could be that there is more rapid diversification to higher value products in developed countries. Changes in per capita income are associated with decreasing share of employment (with increasing rate) in the agriculture sector (Figure 2.9).

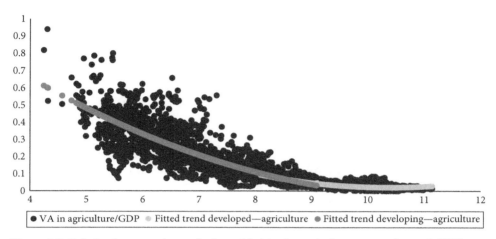

Figure 2.8 Relation between share of value-added in the agriculture sector (in total GDP) with respect to per capita income in 139 countries by developed (38 countries) and developing (101 countries) regions, 1991–2014

Source: Author's construction based on data from WDI, World Bank.

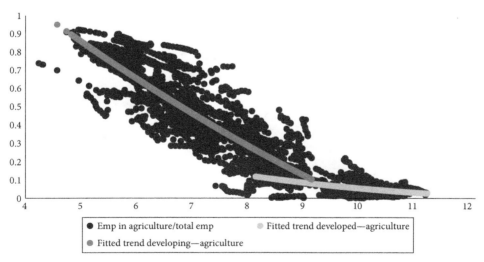

Figure 2.9 Relation between share of employment in the agriculture sector (in total employment) with respect to per capita income in 139 countries by developed (38 countries) and developing (101 countries) regions, 1991–2014

Source: Author's construction based on data from WDI, World Bank, and International Labour Organization (ILO)–Global Employment Trend (ILO–GET) data.

Per worker productivity (value-added per worker) in agriculture is lower in developing countries than developed countries. Initially, productivity per worker rises faster in developing countries as income grows, but then this growth in productivity tapers off, whereas in developed countries agricultural worker productivity growth accelerates (Figure 2.10). This is, perhaps, because FAO data on the Agriculture Orientation Index of government expenditures, which measure the central government contribution to the agriculture sector compared to the sector's contribution to GDP, continue to increase in industrial countries—that is, the governments continue to invest in agriculture—whereas developing countries, other than China, have failed to do so. (See Chapter 7 on agricultural financing for further discussion.) Figure 2.10 shows agricultural value-added per worker with respect to per capita GDP in 101 developing and 38 developed countries. In developed countries, agricultural value-added per worker increases at an increasing rate, unlike in developing countries, perhaps because of continued higher investment in agriculture.

Difference in the shares in GDP and employment is at the heart of structural transformation, and the difference is much larger in developing countries at early stages of development, reflecting the large backlog of labor in the traditional sector. This difference narrows (approaches to near zero) rapidly, as per capita income increases and labor moves out of agriculture into other sectors. In developed countries the shares of value-added and employment are very close and reach near zero as income increases (Figure 2.11).

The share of value-added in the industry sector in total GDP increases with the increase in per capita income, first in both developing and developed countries, but then the share of value-added in the industry sector starts to decline, exhibiting the phenomenon of premature deindustrialization (Rodrik 2016). Further premature deindustrialization occurs at earlier income levels in developing countries: that is, after GDP per capita of about US $4,192, compared to US$8,099 for developed countries, is reached (in constant 2005 US dollars). The inverted U-shaped curve trend in the share of industrial value-added with changes in per capita income means that as countries mature in their economic growth process, industry's share in GDP declines (Figure 2.12).

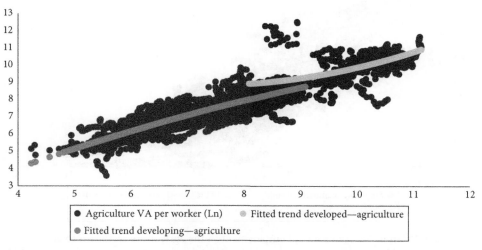

Figure 2.10 Relation between value-added per worker in the agriculture sector with respect to per capita income in 139 countries by developed (38 countries) and developing (101 countries) regions, 1991–2014

Source: Author's construction based on data from WDI, World Bank, and International Labour Organization (ILO)–Global Employment Trend (ILO–GET) data.

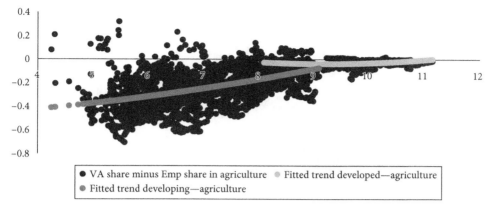

Figure 2.11 Relation between value-added share minus employment share in the agriculture sector with respect to per capita income in 139 countries by developed (38 countries) and developing (101 countries) regions, 1991–2014

Source: Author's construction based on data from WDI, World Bank, and International Labour Organization (ILO)–Global Employment Trend (ILO–GET) data.

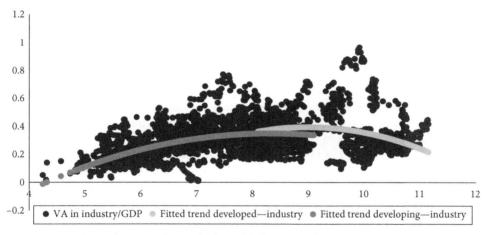

Figure 2.12 Relation between share of value-added in the industry sector (in total GDP) with respect to per capita income in 139 countries by developed (38 countries) and developing (101 countries) regions, 1991–2014

Source: Author's construction based on data from WDI, World Bank, and International Labour Organization (ILO)–Global Employment Trend (ILO–GET) data.

Where Does Labor Move When Its Share in Agriculture Declines?

Labor moves mostly to the service sector. The share of employment in the industry sector in developing countries increases (at a decreasing rate) (Figure 2.13), but in developed countries, changes in per capita GDP tend to be associated with an increase in the share of employment in the industry sector, albeit at a decreasing rate. As in value-added share, the

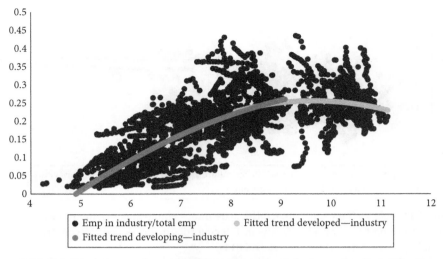

Figure 2.13 Relation between share of employment in the industry sector (in total employment) with respect to per capita income in 139 countries by developed (38 countries) and developing (101 countries) regions, 1991–2014

Source: Author's construction based on data from WDI, World Bank, and International Labour Organization (ILO)–Global Employment Trend (ILO–GET) data.

employment share in the industry sector in developed countries also peaks at a per capita GDP of \$15,582 (in constant 2005 US dollars), reflecting the deindustrialization process thereafter. The regression results show the gap between the service and industry sectors. Employment share increases as the development process advances and the change in employment share in the service sector is 1.2 times higher than the change in employment share in the industry sector in the developing countries.

Value-added per worker in industry rises faster in developed countries than developing countries. Initially, the gap in productivity is higher in developing countries. Developing countries are able to close this gap, as per capita income rises. Then, the speed at which the gap is growing tapers off. This tendency is the mirror image and a contrast to the faster growth in the service sector GDP share (Figure 2.14).

Finally, the service sector has a larger share in GDP, but a lower share in employment in developing countries than in developed countries. The greater share is proportionate, so that the value-added per worker and the difference between the value-added and employment shares are very similar in the two sets of countries. Regarding the variation with respect to per capita income, the share of services in GDP initially rises faster in developed countries than in developing countries, but then slows down so that they are increasing at the same rate (Figure 2.15).

The share in developed countries is higher in employment, but the share rises faster in developed countries, and the rate is constant in developing countries, whereas the rate of increase begins to accelerate in the developed countries (Figure 2.16).

Also, value-added per worker increases at the same rate in the two groups of countries as per capita income grows (Figure 2.17). The changes in the share in GDP and in employment as income rises, which reflect shifting relative productivities, show that the gap first increases more slowly in developing countries, but then becomes faster.

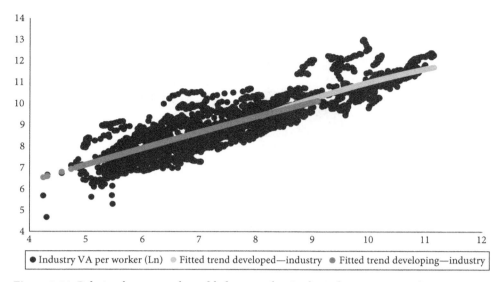

Figure 2.14 Relation between value-added per worker in the industry sector with respect to per capita income in income in 139 countries by developed (38 countries) and developing (101 countries) regions, 1991–2014

Source: Author's construction based on data from WDI, World Bank, and International Labour Organization (ILO)–Global Employment Trend (ILO–GET) data.

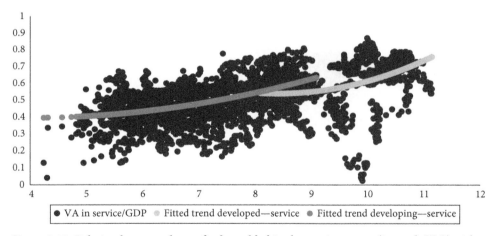

Figure 2.15 Relation between share of value-added in the service sector (in total GDP) with respect to per capita income in 139 countries by developed (38 countries) and developing (101 countries) regions, 1991–2014

Source: Author's construction based on data from WDI, World Bank.

The gap between the value-added in agriculture and the share of employment in agriculture reflects the differences between per worker productivity in the agriculture and nonagriculture (industry and service) sectors and is important for the process of convergence in incomes between the two sectors. The turning point is reached when labor

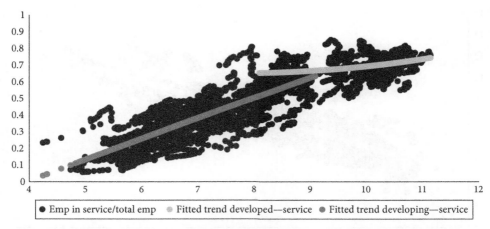

Figure 2.16 Relation between share of employment in the service sector (in total employment) with respect to per capita income in 139 countries by developed (38 countries) and developing (101 countries) regions, 1991–2014

Source: Author's construction based on data from WDI, World Bank, and International Labour Organization (ILO)–Global Employment Trend (ILO–GET) data.

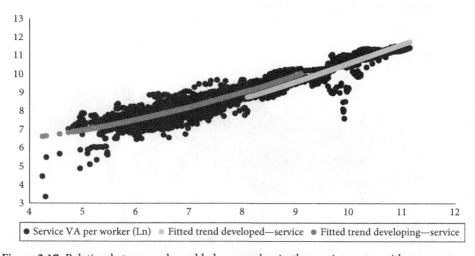

Figure 2.17 Relation between value-added per worker in the service sector with respect to per capita income in 139 countries by developed (38 countries) and developing (101 countries) regions, 1991–2014

Source: Author's construction based on data from WDI, World Bank.

productivities in the two sectors begin to converge. For this to occur, agricultural productivity needs to increase rapidly. At very low levels of per capita income, labor productivity in agriculture starts at levels far below levels for the nonagriculture (industry and service) sectors in the developing countries. It then increases at a decreasing rate and gradually runs parallel to the labor productivity in the industry sector. Labor productivity in the industry sector also increases with a decreasing rate as *per capita income increases*, but the labor productivity in agriculture increases almost 1.6 times as fast as the labor productivity in the industry sector, although the gap in productivity between those two sectors still remains substantial. Labor productivity in the service sector starts more or less at the same level, with the industry sector labor productivity at very low levels of per capita income. Up to about a per capita GDP level of US$1,201 (in constant 2005 US dollars), the labor productivity gap between those two sectors increases, but then the gap starts to narrow between the developing region and advanced economies, until at about a per capita GDP level of US$66,117 (in constant 2005 US dollars), labor productivity in the service sector crosses labor productivity in the industry sector.

The results for all 139 countries suggest that the elasticity of labor productivity, with respect to changes in per capita income, is highest in agriculture, followed by the industry and service sectors in developing economies. In developed economies, however, the elasticity of labor productivity is highest in industry, followed by the service and agriculture sectors. This outcome in the developing economies could be a result of increased investment in agriculture, but it could also be explained by the rapid movement of labor from agriculture into the industrial or service sector. Indeed, both phenomena are necessary for transformation to occur. In developing economies, the elasticity of the agriculture sector is 1.5, whereas in the industry and service sectors the elasticities are lower, 0.91 and –0.12, respectively, and the elasticity in the service sector is not statistically significant.

In short, the above described scenario reflects the stylized facts behind the process of development of the world economy (that is, 139 [38 developed and 101 developing] countries).

Differences in Behavior among the Developing Regions

We first examine the differences in the behavior of the three sectors among developing countries of different regions. We compare their performance with that of countries in EAP. The pattern of change in the countries of LAC is very similar to those of EAP. There is no significant difference in the behavior of shares in GDP or in employment as per capita GDP varies. The only difference is that value-added per worker is lower in both agriculture and services. It tends to rise faster in LAC than in EAP countries, as GDP per capita increases. Comparing SA with EAP, there is no significant difference in the share of agriculture in GDP (Figure 2.18). EAP and LAC seem to be approaching a constant level. EAP started with a much higher share of agriculture in GDP but reduced it much faster than any other developing regions. Share of agriculture in GDP in SA, SSA, and MENA is falling at constant rates, whereas in EAP and LAC, the declining rate becomes slower as per capita GDP increases (Figure 2.18). In the developing region in Europe (Armenia, Bulgaria, Romania, and Turkey), the agriculture value-added share starts to increase at higher per capita GDP, as in the developed region. In post-Soviet states, it decreases with decreasing rate.

The share of GDP is less in services (but more in industry) in SA than EAP (Figures 2.19 and 2.20). The actual shares are much lower in SA, but their incomes are also much lower, and so, for low-income countries, the share of industry is more. However, reflecting the slower rate of structural transformation in SA, the share of industry grows at a slower rate than in EAP, and the share of services grows faster.

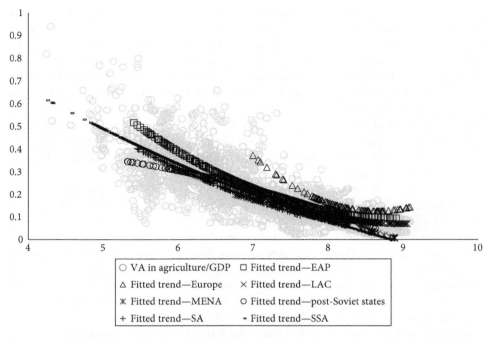

Figure 2.18 Relation between share of value-added in the agriculture sector (in total GDP) with respect to per capita income in 101 developing countries by developing regions, 1991–2014
Source: Author's construction based on data from WDI, World Bank.

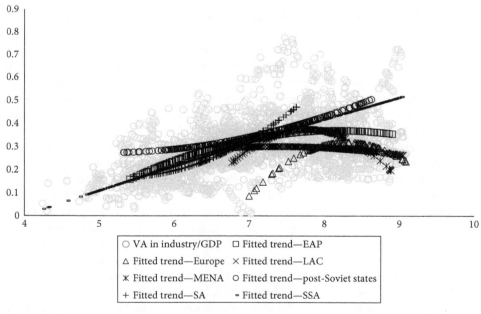

Figure 2.19 Relation between share of value-added in the industry sector (in total GDP) with respect to per capita income in 101 developing countries by developing regions, 1991–2014
Source: Author's construction based on data from WDI, World Bank.

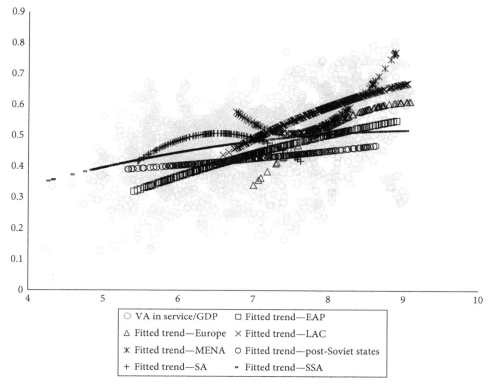

Figure 2.20 Relation between share of value-added in the service sector (in total GDP) with respect to per capita income in 101 developing countries by developing regions, 1991–2014
Source: Author's construction based on data from WDI, World Bank.

In our regression analysis of 101 developing countries, we found that EAP, LAC, MENA, and the developing region in Europe are experiencing premature deindustrialization, as seen in an inverted U-shaped trend for the value-added share in the industry sector.

The share of value-added in the industry sector in total GDP increases with the increase in per capita income first in those four regions, but after GDP per capita of about US$3,568 (for EAP), US$1,630 (for LAC), US$2,376 (for MENA), and US$4,043 (for the developing region in Europe) is reached (in constant 2005 US dollars), the share of value-added in the industry sector starts to decline. This explains the inverted U-curve trend in the share of industrial value-added with changes in per capita income (Figure 2.19).

SA, SSA, and post-Soviet states show increasing trends. There are significant differences between SSA countries, which we discuss below in our regression analysis only for the SSA region, classifying the countries based on their export orientation.

SA deviates the most from patterns shown by other regions. Bhutan and Sri Lanka are responsible for this anomalous behavior. Bhutan's industry share in GDP increases at a much faster rate and is much higher than other SA countries, so SA's trend (Figure 2.19) is upward sloping, and the service sector share is declining and much lower than other SA countries. Thus, SA (Figure 2.20) shows an inverted U-shaped trend. Significantly, Sri Lanka's agriculture share in GDP shows an upward trend, as per capita income increases, whereas all the other SA countries are downward sloping, and similarly for the agriculture employment share. Service sector employment share in Sri Lanka shows a declining trend, whereas all the other countries in the SA region show an opposite trend. In contrast, the value-added share of the industry sector in Sri Lanka shows a declining trend.

MENA deviates the most in the relationship of per capita income in the service sector with respect to change in per capita income, as shown in Figure 2.20.

As far as employment shares are concerned, in SA, the employment share in agriculture is more than that in EAP (Figure 2.21). There is no significant difference between EAP and SA in the employment share of industry (Figure 2.22) and in services are less (Figure 2.23).

Employment share in the agriculture sector is falling in all developing regions except SA and the developing region in Europe. At higher per capita GDP, the trend is upward sloping in those two regions. Sri Lanka is responsible for this anomalous behavior in SA (explained above). EAP, SSA, and MENA are shedding labor in agriculture faster than other developing regions. Post-Soviet states' and LAC's decline are taking place at slower rates.

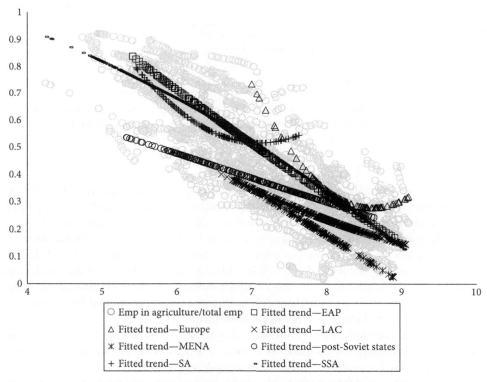

Figure 2.21 Relation between share of employment in the agriculture sector (in total employment) with respect to per capita income in 101 developing countries by developing regions, 1991–2014

Source: Author's construction based on data from WDI, World Bank, and International Labour Organization (ILO)–Global Employment Trend (ILO–GET) data.

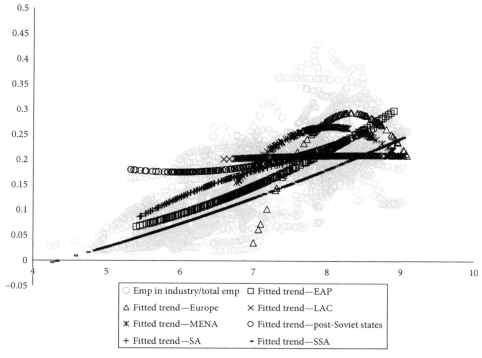

Figure 2.22 Relation between share of employment in the industry sector (in total employment) with respect to per capita income in 101 developing countries by developing regions, 1991–2014

Source: Author's construction based on data from WDI, World Bank, and International Labour Organization (ILO)–Global Employment Trend (ILO–GET) data.

In Latin America, the share of employment in the industry sector has been flat. In all developing regions, the share of employment in industry is growing, except in MENA and the developing region in Europe, where it shows an inverted U-shaped arc (Figure 2.22).

Employment share in the service sector is increasing in all developing regions, as per capita GDP grows, except in SA, which is showing an inverted U-shaped arc. Again, Sri Lanka is responsible for this anomalous behavior, as explained previously. Service sector employment share is rising fastest in SSA (Figure 2.23).

Valued added per worker is lower in SA than in EAP in all three sectors (Figures 2.24, 2.25, and 2.26); while there is a tendency for value-added per worker to catch up in agriculture (Figure 2.24) and services (Figure 2.26), this is not the case in industry (Figure 2.25). The share of employment in services is commensurate with the share in GDP. In agriculture, however, it is lower, showing that productivity in agriculture is less than in services.

Valued-added per worker in agriculture is increasing in all developing regions, except SA. Again, Bhutan and Sri Lanka are responsible for this anomalous behavior. In EAP, value-added per worker in agriculture is accelerating, and SSA, LAC, MENA, and the post-Soviet states are decelerating, as per capita GDP increases (Figure 2.24).

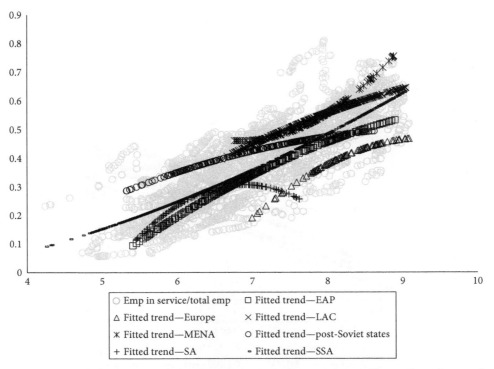

Figure 2.23 Relation between share of employment in the service sector (in total employment) with respect to per capita income in 101 developing countries by developing regions, 1991–2014

Source: Author's construction based on data from WDI, World Bank, and International Labour Organization (ILO)–Global Employment Trend (ILO–GET) data.

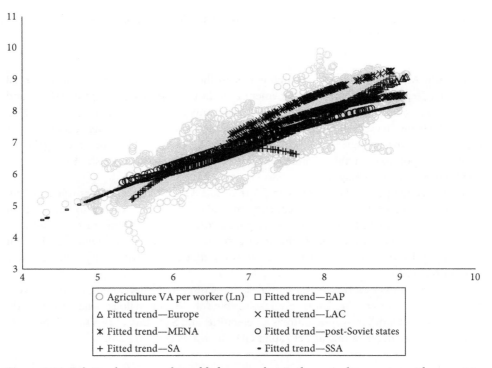

Figure 2.24 Relation between value-added per worker in the agriculture sector with respect to per capita income in 101 developing countries by developing regions, 1991–2014

Source: Author's construction based on data from WDI, World Bank, and International Labour Organization (ILO)–Global Employment Trend (ILO–GET) data.

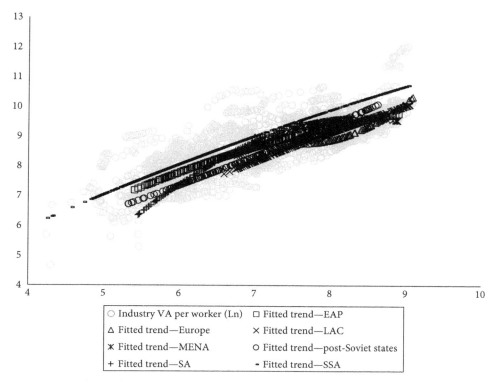

Figure 2.25 Relation between value-added per worker in the industry sector with respect to per capita income in 101 developing countries by developing regions, 1991–2014

Source: Author's construction based on data from WDI, World Bank and International Labour Organization (ILO)–Global Employment Trend (ILO–GET) data.

Value-added per worker in the industry sector shows an increasing trend with per capita GDP in all developing regions, except in MENA. In MENA, value-added per worker starts to decline at a higher per capita GDP level (Figure 2.25).

Value-added per worker in the service sector shows a very similar pattern among the developing regions, increasing in all regions and rising fastest in LAC. In EAP and post-Soviet states, valued added per worker in the service sector is accelerating, and in SSA, it is decelerating, as per capita GDP increases (Figure 2.26).

Comparing SSA with EAP, SSA has a lower share of agriculture in GDP (Figure 2.18), but a larger share of industry (Figure 2.19), and a similar share of services (Figure 2.20). The value-added share in agriculture declines faster as income rises (Figure 2.18), while that in industry rises slower, bringing about convergence (Figure 2.19). The employment share is less in agriculture in SSA (Figure 2.21) and more in services (Figure 2.23), but it is similar in industry (Figure 2.22) to EAP. The employment share is rising faster in agriculture (Figure 2.21) and slower in services (Figure 2.23), so again, there is a tendency toward convergence toward levels in EAP. Though the employment share in SSA is lower in agriculture, the share in GDP is lower still, so that value-added per worker in the agriculture sector is lower than in EAP (Figure 2.24). Value-added per worker in the service sector is lower in SSA, and there is again a tendency toward convergence

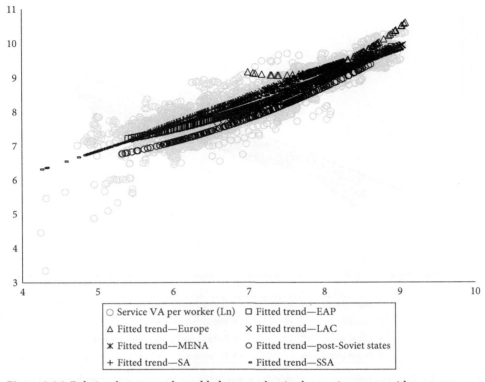

Figure 2.26 Relation between value-added per worker in the service sector with respect to per capita income in 101 developing countries by developing regions, 1991–2014

Source: Author's construction based on data from WDI, World Bank, and International Labour Organization (ILO)–Global Employment Trend (ILO–GET) data.

(Figure 2.26). There is no significant difference in value-added per worker in industry, or in the way it changes as income rises (Figure 2.25). There is no significant difference between the share in GDP and in employment between the two regions. However, the share in GDP is larger in employment than in the industry sector but lower in the service sector in SSA.

The gap share (value-added share minus employment share) in the agriculture sector approaches zero as per capita GDP increases in all developing regions, except SA and the post-Soviet states (Figure 2.27). Again, Sri Lanka is responsible for this anomalous behavior in the SA region. The gap narrows fastest in EAP, and SSA is faster than LAC, as per capita income increases (Figure 2.27).

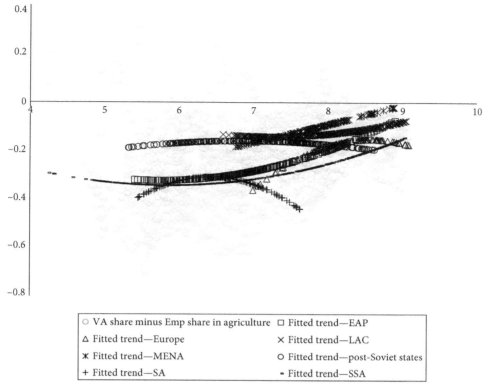

Figure 2.27 Relation between value-added share minus employment share in the agriculture sector with respect to per capita income in 101 developing countries by developing regions, 1991–2014

Source: Author's construction based on data from WDI, World Bank, and International Labour Organization (ILO)–Global Employment Trend (ILO–GET) data.

The gap share in the industry sector is almost flat in LAC, falling rapidly in EAP and MENA, as per capita income increases (Figure 2.28). In SSA, it increases with a decreasing rate, and it increases with an increasing rate (Figure 2.28). Bhutan is again responsible for this anomalous behavior in the SA region.

The gap share in the service sector is decreasing in all developing regions, except in LAC (where it has not changed), as per capita GDP increases. In SSA, the gap share has become negative with increasingly higher levels of per capita GDP (Figure 2.29).

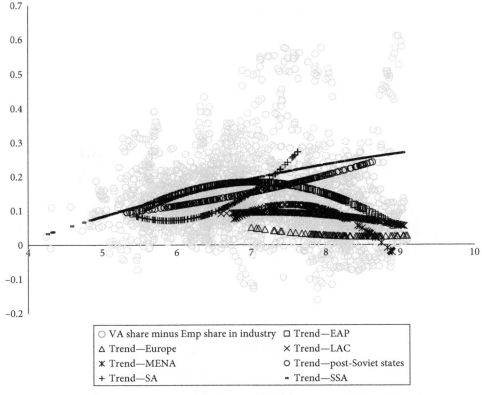

Figure 2.28 Relation between value-added share minus employment share in the industry sector with respect to per capita income in 101 developing countries by developing regions, 1991–2014

Source: Author's construction based on data from WDI, World Bank, and International Labour Organization (ILO)–Global Employment Trend (ILO–GET) data.

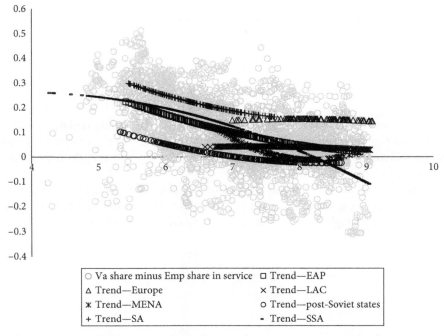

Figure 2.29 Relation between value-added share minus employment share in the service sector with respect to per capita income in 101 developing countries by developing regions, 1991–2014

Source: Author's construction based on data from WDI, World Bank, and International Labour Organization (ILO)–Global Employment Trend (ILO–GET) data.

Differences in Behavior among Sub-Saharan African Countries

In the preceding section, we have shown the structural transformation of the SSA region as a whole, compared to other regions, with changes in per capita GDP. There is considerable heterogeneity, however, among African countries. To examine the differences in structural transformation among SSA countries, we classified them into five subgroups (see Table 2.2), based on their export orientation: exporters of food (19 countries), exporters of fuels (6 countries), exporters of manufactures (8 countries), exporters of ores and metals (4 countries), and exporters of agricultural raw materials (4 countries), to compare performances of the other subgroups with the food-exporting countries.

Table 2.2 Sub-Saharan African countries (41) classified by their export orientation

Exporters of food[a] (19)	Exporters of manufactures[b] (8)	Exporters of fuels[c] (6)	Exporters of ores and metals[d] (4)	Exporters of agricultural raw materials[e] (4)
Burundi	Botswana	Angola	Congo, Dem. Rep.	Benin
Comoros	Central African Republic	Cameroon	Guinea	Burkina Faso
Côte d'Ivoire	Lesotho	Congo, Rep.	Liberia	Chad
Ethiopia	Mauritius	Gabon	Zambia	Mali
Eritrea	Namibia	Nigeria		
Gambia, The	South Africa	Sudan		
Ghana	Swaziland			
Guinea-Bissau	Togo			
Kenya				
Malawi				
Mauritania				
Mozambique				
Niger				
Rwanda				
Senegal				
Sierra Leone				
Tanzania				
Uganda				
Zimbabwe				

Notes: Classification based on the countries' export percentage as a share in total merchandise exports.

[a] Food comprises the commodities in Standard International Trade Classification (SITC) sections 0 (food and live animals), 1 (beverages and tobacco), 4 (animal and vegetable oils and fats), and SITC division 22 (oil seeds, oil nuts, and oil kernels).

[b] Manufactures comprise commodities in SITC sections 5 (chemicals), 6 (basic manufactures), 7 (machinery and transport equipment), and 8 (miscellaneous manufactured goods), excluding division 68 (non-ferrous metals).

[c] Fuels comprise the commodities in SITC section 3 (mineral fuels, lubricants, and related materials).

[d] Ores and metals comprise the commodities in SITC sections 27 (crude fertilizers, minerals), 28 (metalliferous ores, scrap), and 68 (non-ferrous metals).

[e] Agricultural raw materials comprise SITC section 2 (crude materials except fuels), excluding divisions 22, 27 (crude fertilizers and minerals, excluding coal, petroleum, and precious stones), and 28 (metalliferous ores and scrap).

Source: Authors' calculation based on the WDI, World Bank data.

Transformation literature suggests that, as per capita income increases, the difference between the share of value-added in agriculture and the share of employment in agriculture approaches zero (as labor moves out of agriculture), as poverty in agriculture declines and productivity differences between agriculture and nonagriculture close. Countries exporting food, agricultural raw material, and manufacturing show these tendencies, but the rest of the African subgroups do not.

To summarize, the share of value-added in the agriculture sector declines as per capita income increases, but in countries exporting agricultural raw materials and in countries exporting manufactures, that decline bottoms out at a threshold of US$373 (in constant 2005 US dollars) and US$2,246 (in constant 2005 US dollars), respectively, with the share taking an upward turn. Value-added in the service sector increases with an increase in GDP per capita, with the exception of these same two sets of countries. All countries, except food-exporting countries, show signs of premature deindustrialization, as identified by Rodrik (2016), at different per capita GDP thresholds (manufactures-exporting countries at US $1,161; fuels-exporting countries at US$6,064; countries exporting ores and metals at US$426; and countries exporting agricultural raw materials at US$515 (all in constant 2005 US dollars).

Appendix A: Data and Methodology

Data Source

This analysis is based on the sectoral (agriculture, industry, and service) breakdown of employment data for 139 (101 developing + 38 developed) countries over the period 1991–2014, from the ILO–GET. The value-added data by sector have been sourced from the World Bank's WDI. The same applies to per capita GDP and total population data. The remaining dependent variables (that is, the share of value-added in total GDP by sector, the share of employment in total employment by sector, value-added per worker by sector, and the difference between the share of value-added and employment by sector) and terms of trade have been constructed from the aforementioned variables.

Methodology

The baseline regression equation of our structural transformation analysis has been formulated as follows:

$$Y_{i,t} = a + \beta_1 \log(GDPpc)_{i,t} + \beta_2 \log(GDPpc)_{i,t}^2 + \beta_3 \log(Pop)_{i,t} + \beta_4 \log(Pop)_{i,t}^2$$

$$+ \beta_5(TOT1)_{i,t} + \beta_6(TOT2)_{i,t} + \mu_1(\text{Dummy\_1999})_t + \mu_2(\text{Dummy\_food\_crisis})_t + \epsilon_{i,t}, \quad (1)$$

where index i denotes countries, and index t denotes time; $GDPpc$ is per capita GDP. Pop is the population in the $i - th$ country during the $t - th$ year. The inclusion of squared terms for both per capita GDP and total population in Equation (1) allows for a nonlinear functional form of the equation. Such nonlinear functional form also allows for the estimation of the point at which $Y_{i,t}$ starts to decrease or increase, depending on the sign of the estimated coefficients. Both terms have been log-transformed. TOT is terms of trade, the ratio between the deflator of value-added of two sectors. We used A_def_S (the ratio between the deflator of value-added in agriculture and the deflator of value-added in services) as $TOT1$ and A_def_I (the ratio between the deflator of value-added in agriculture and the deflator of value-added in industry) as $TOT2$, when we looked at the agriculture sector (our dependent variables are on agriculture). We used S_def_I (the ratio between the deflator of value-added in services and the deflator of value-added in industry) as TOT1 and S_def_A (the ratio between the deflator of value-added in services and the deflator of value-added in agriculture), when we looked at the service sector (our dependent variables are on services); and I_def_S (the ratio between the deflator of value-added in industry and the deflator of value-added in services) as TOT1 and I_def_A (the ratio between the deflator of value-added in services and the deflator of value-added in agriculture), when we looked at the industry sector (our dependent variables are on industry).

Dummy_1999 is a dummy variable, taking on value 1 in the period from 1999 to 2006 and 0 in the period before 1999 and after 2006. Dummy_food_crisis is a dummy variable equal to 1 after the 2007 food crisis and 0 from 1991 to 2007. Coefficient α captures the intercept in the model, whereas $\beta_1 \ldots \beta_6$ are the coefficients associated with the six independent variables. The coefficients μ_1 and μ_2 measure the average difference in the dependent variables, with respect to the period, excluding the period 1999–2006 and the period preceding the 2007 food crisis. Finally, $\varepsilon_{i,t}$ is a noise term. Five dependent variables ($Y_{i,t}$) are taken into account for each sector; for the agriculture sector, they measure (1) the share of agriculture value-added in total GDP; (2) the share of employment in agriculture in total employment; (3) the log-transformed agriculture value-added, expressed in constant 2005 US dollars; (4) the log-transformed agriculture value-added per worker, expressed in constant 2005 US dollars; and (5) the difference between the share of agriculture value-added in total GDP and the share of employment in agriculture in total employment. For the service sector, the dependent variables measure: (1) the share of services value-added in total GDP; (2) the share of employment in services in total employment; (3) the log-transformed services value-added, expressed in constant 2005 US dollars; (4) the log-transformed services value-added per worker, expressed in constant 2005 US dollars; and (5) the difference between the share of services value-added in total GDP and the share of employment in services in total employment. For the industry sector, the dependent variables measure: (1) the share of industry value-added in total GDP; (2) the share of employment in industry in total employment; (3) the log-transformed industry value-added, expressed in constant 2005 US dollars; (4) the log-transformed industry value-added per worker, expressed in constant 2005 US dollars; and (5) the difference between the share of industry value-added in total GDP and the share of employment in industry in total employment.

The set of estimated equations is as follows:

i) As Applied to the Agriculture Sector

$$\frac{VAagr_{i,t}}{GDP_{i,t}} = a + \beta_1 log(GDPpc)_{i,t} + \beta_2 log(GDPpc)^2_{i,t} + \beta_3 log(Pop)_{i,t} + \beta_4 log(Pop)^2_{i,t}$$

$$+\beta_5(A\_def\_I)_{i,t} + \beta_6(A\_def\_S)_{i,t} + \mu_1(\text{Dummy\_1999})_t + \mu_2(\text{Dummy\_food\_crisis})_t + \epsilon_{i,t} \quad (1.1)$$

$$\frac{E_{MPagr}}{totEMP_{i,t}}_{i,t} = a + \beta_1 log(GDPpc)_{i,t} + \beta_2 log(GDPpc)^2_{i,t} + \beta_3 log(Pop)_{i,t} + \beta_4 log(Pop)^2_{i,t}$$

$$+\beta_5(A\_def\_I)_{i,t} + \beta_6(A\_def\_S)_{i,t} + \mu_1(\text{Dummy\_1999})_t + \mu_2(\text{Dummy\_food\_crisis})_t + \epsilon_{i,t} \quad (1.2)$$

$$Log(VA\_agr\_US\$) = a + \beta_1 log(GDPpc)_{i,t} + \beta_2 log(GDPpc)^2_{i,t} + \beta_3 log(Pop)_{i,t} + \beta_4 log(Pop)^2_{i,t}$$

$$+\beta_5(A\_def\_I)_{i,t} + \beta_6(A\_def\_S)_{i,t} + \mu_1(\text{Dummy\_1999})_t + \mu_2(\text{Dummy\_food\_crisis})_t + \epsilon_{i,t} \quad (1.3)$$

$$Log(VA\_agr\_per\_worker\_US\$) = a + \beta_1 log(GDPpc)_{i,t} + \beta_2 log(GDPpc)^2_{i,t} + \beta_3 log(Pop)_{i,t}$$

$$+\beta_4 \log(Pop)_{i,t}^2 + \beta_6(A\_def\_I)_{i,t} + \beta_5(A\_def\_S)_{i,t} + \mu_1(\text{Dummy\_1999})_t$$

$$+\mu_2(\text{Dummy\_food\_crisis})_t + \epsilon_{i,t} \tag{1.4}$$

$$\frac{VAagr_{i,t}}{GDP_{i,t}} - \frac{EMPagr_{i,t}}{totEMP_{i,t}} = \alpha + \beta_1 \log(GDPpc)_{i,t} + \beta_2 \log(GDPpc)_{i,t}^2 + \beta_3 \log(Pop)_{i,t}$$

$$+\beta_4 \log(Pop)_{i,t}^2 + \beta_5(A\_def\_I)_{i,t} + \beta_6(A\_def\_S)_{i,t} + \mu_1(\text{Dummy\_1999})_t$$

$$+\mu_2(\text{Dummy\_food\_crisis})_t + \epsilon_{i,t} \tag{1.5}$$

ii) As Applied to the Service Sector

$$\frac{VAser_{i,t}}{GDP_{i,t}} = \alpha + \beta_1 \log(GDPpc)_{i,t} + \beta_2 \log(GDPpc)_{i,t}^2 + \beta_3 \log(Pop)_{i,t} + \beta_4 \log(Pop)_{i,t}^2$$

$$+\beta_5(S\_def\_I)_{i,t} + \beta_6(S\_def\_A)_{i,t} + \mu_1(\text{Dummy\_1999})_t + \mu_2(\text{Dummy\_food\_crisis})_t + \epsilon_{i,t} \tag{2.1}$$

$$\frac{EMPser_{i,t}}{totEMP_{i,t}} = \alpha + \beta_1 \log(GDPpc)_{i,t} + \beta_2 \log(GDPpc)_{i,t}^2 + \beta_3 \log(Pop)_{i,t} + \beta_4 \log(Pop)_{i,t}^2$$

$$+\beta_5(S\_def\_I)_{i,t} + \beta_6(S\_def\_A)_{i,t} + \mu_1(\text{Dummy\_1999})_t + \mu_2(\text{Dummy\_food\_crisis})_t + \epsilon_{i,t} \tag{2.2}$$

$$Log(VA\_ser\_US\$) = \alpha + \beta_1 \log(GDPpc)_{i,t} + \beta_2 \log(GDPpc)_{i,t}^2 + \beta_3 \log(Pop)_{i,t} + \beta_4 \log(Pop)_{i,t}^2$$

$$+\beta_5(S\_def\_I)_{i,t} + \beta_6(S\_def\_A)_{i,t} + \mu_1(\text{Dummy\_1999})_t + \mu_2(\text{Dummy\_food\_crisis})_t + \epsilon_{i,t} \tag{2.3}$$

$$Log(VA\_ser\_per\_worker\_US\$) = \alpha + \beta_1 \log(GDPpc)_{i,t} + \beta_2 \log(GDPpc)_{i,t}^2 + \beta_3 \log(Pop)_{i,t}$$

$$+\beta_4 \log(Pop)_{i,t}^2 + \beta_5(S\_def\_I)_{i,t} + \beta_6(S\_def\_A)_{i,t} + \mu_1(\text{Dummy\_1999})_t$$

$$+\mu_2(\text{Dummy\_food\_crisis})_t + \epsilon_{i,t} \tag{2.4}$$

$$\frac{VAser_{i,t}}{GDP_{i,t}} - \frac{EMPser_{i,t}}{totEMP_{i,t}} = \alpha + \beta_1 \log(GDPpc)_{i,t} + \beta_2 \log(GDPpc)_{i,t}^2 + \beta_3 \log(Pop)_{i,t} + \beta_4 \log(Pop)_{i,t}^2$$

$$+\beta_5(S\_def\_I)_{i,t} + \beta_6(S\_def\_A)_{i,t} + \mu_1(\text{Dummy\_1999})_t + \mu_2(\text{Dummy\_food\_crisis})_t + \epsilon_{i,t} \tag{2.5}$$

iii) As Applied to the Industry Sector

$$\frac{VAind_{i,t}}{GDP_{i,t}} = \alpha + \beta_1 \log(GDPpc)_{i,t} + \beta_2 \log(GDPpc)_{i,t}^2 + \beta_3 \log(Pop)_{i,t} + \beta_4 \log(Pop)_{i,t}^2$$

$$+\beta_5(I\_def\_S)_{i,t} + \beta_6(I\_def\_A)_{i,t} + \mu_1(\text{Dummy\_1999})_t + \mu_2(\text{Dummy\_food\_crisis})_t + \epsilon_{i,t} \tag{3.1}$$

$$\frac{EMPind_{i,t}}{totEMP_{i,t}} = \alpha + \beta_1 \log(GDPpc)_{i,t} + \beta_2 \log(GDPpc)_{i,t}^2 + \beta_3 \log(Pop)_{i,t} + \beta_4 \log(Pop)_{i,t}^2$$

$$+\beta_5(I\_def\_S)_{i,t} + \beta_6(I\_def\_A)_{i,t} + \mu_1(\text{Dummy\_1999})_t + \mu_2(\text{Dummy\_food\_crisis})_t + \epsilon_{i,t} \quad (3.2)$$

$$Log(VA\_ind\_US\$) = a + \beta_1\log(GDPpc)_{i,t} + \beta_2\log(GDPpc)_{i,t}^2 + \beta_3\log(Pop)_{i,t} + \beta_4\log(Pop)_{i,t}^2$$

$$+\beta_5(I\_def\_S)_{i,t} + \beta_6(I\_def\_A)_{i,t} + \mu_1(\text{Dummy\_1999})_t + \mu_2(\text{Dummy\_food\_crisis})_t + \epsilon_{i,t} \quad (3.3)$$

$$Log(VA\_ind\_per\_worker\_US\$) = a + \beta_1\log(GDPpc)_{i,t} + \beta_2\log(GDPpc)_{i,t}^2 + \beta_3\log(Pop)_{i,t}$$

$$+\beta_4\log(Pop)_{i,t}^2 + \beta_5(I\_def\_S)_{i,t} + \beta_6(I\_def\_A)_{i,t} + \mu_1(\text{Dummy\_1999})_t$$

$$+\mu_2(\text{Dummy\_food\_crisis})_t + \epsilon_{i,t} \quad (3.4)$$

$$\frac{VAind_{i,t}}{GDP_{i,t}} - \frac{EMPind_{i,t}}{totEMP_{i,t}} = a + \beta_1\log(GDPpc)_{i,t} + \beta_2\log(GDPpc)_{i,t}^2 + \beta_3\log(Pop)_{i,t}$$

$$+\beta_4\log(Pop)_{i,t}^2 + \beta_5(I\_def\_S)_{i,t} + \beta_6(I\_def\_A)_{i,t} + \mu_1(\text{Dummy\_1999})_t$$

$$+\mu_2(\text{Dummy\_food\_crisis})_t + \epsilon_{i,t} \quad (3.5)$$

The log-transformation approach for variables, capturing the sectoral value-added and value-added per worker in Equations (1.3, 2.3, and 3.3) and (1.4, 2.4, 3.4), allows for interpreting the estimated coefficients as elasticity.

Estimates of equations are based on the following approach:

1. Equation (1) is first estimated for all 139 (101 developing and 38 developed) countries. In this specification, we introduced developed country dummy variables (both additive and multiplicative dummies), taking on value 1, to examine the differences in the behavior of the dependent variables in our model among two subgroups (developed and developing regions) of the sample in our study.

2. Second, Equation (1) is estimated only for all 101 developing countries. In this specification, we introduced regional dummies (both additive and multiplicative dummies) in order to capture the differences in the behavior of the dependent variables in our model among the developing regions of the sample in our study. These developing regions are: EAP, 12 developing countries; Europe, 4 developing countries; LAC, 19 developing countries; MENA, 7 developing countries; post-Soviet countries, 10 developing countries; SA, 6 developing countries; and SSA, 43 developing countries. We used the EAP region as a base and 6 dummy variables (both additive and multiplicative) for each region (Europe, LAC, MENA, post-Soviet countries, SA, and SSA) taking the value of 1.

3. Next, to examine the differences in the behavior of the dependent variables in our model among the SSA group of countries. we classified them into five subgroups based on their export orientation: food-exporting countries (19 countries); fuels-exporting countries (6 countries); manufactures-exporting countries (8 countries); ores and metals-exporting countries (4 countries); and raw agricultural materials-exporting countries (4 countries). In this specification, Equation (1) is estimated only for the 41 SSA developing countries, introducing both additive and multiplicative dummies for the aforementioned subgroups by taking food-exporting countries as the base.

4. Equation (1) is then estimated only for the 6 South Asian countries. In this specification, we introduced both additive and multiplicative dummies for Bhutan and Sri Lanka, to capture the differences in the behavior of the dependent variables in our model between those two countries and with the other four South Asian countries (India, Bangladesh, Pakistan, and Nepal).

5. Equation (1) is finally estimated for all 139 countries. In this specification, we introduced both additive and multiplicative dummy variables (taking the value of 1) for the 20 largest IBRD + IDA borrowers[18] to the Agriculture and Rural Development (ARD) sector in order to capture the differences in the behavior of the dependent variables in our model of the 20 largest borrowers, with respect to the rest of the world (that is, the remaining 119 countries in our sample).

Data Description

On average, for all 139 countries, the service sector enjoys the largest share of employment (47 percent), larger than agriculture's average 35 percent share of the total employed population. The greatest variation tends to be in the shares of agriculture across countries, rather than in other sectors, ranging from 0.2 percent in Singapore to 92 percent in Burundi (Table A.2.1). On average, the share

Table A.2.1 Key characteristics of 139 countries

Variable	Obs.	Mean	Std. Dev.	Min.	Max.
$\dfrac{VAagr_{i,t}}{GDP_{i,t}}$	3,336	0.17	0.15	0.00	0.94
$\dfrac{VAser_{i,t}}{GDP_{i,t}}$	3,336	0.53	0.14	0.02	0.87
$\dfrac{VAind_{i,t}}{GDP_{i,t}}$	3,336	0.30	0.13	0.01	0.97
$\dfrac{EMPagr_{i,t}}{totEMP_{i,t}}$	3,336	0.35	0.26	0.002	0.92
$\dfrac{EMPser_{i,t}}{totEMP_{i,t}}$	3,336	0.47	0.20	0.06	0.85
$\dfrac{EMPind_{i,t}}{totEMP_{i,t}}$	3,336	0.18	0.09	0.02	0.43
VA_agr_US$_constant2005_million	3,336	9,929	28,616	31	386,794
VA_ser_US$_constant2005_million	3,336	190,613	805,411	5	10,600,000
VA_ind_US$_constant2005_million	3,336	80,975	270,734	2	2,826,341
VA_agr_per_worker_US$_constant2005	3,336	9,493	18,598	37	276,990
VA_ser_per_worker_US$_constant2005	3,336	17,594	24,407	28	101,377
VA_ind_per_worker_US$_constant2005	3336	27723	44643	107	458,602
$\dfrac{VAagr_{i,t}}{GDP_{i,t}} - \dfrac{EMPagr_{i,t}}{totEMP_{i,t}}$	3,336	−0.18	0.16	−0.71	0.32
$\dfrac{VAser_{i,t}}{GDP_{i,t}} - \dfrac{EMPser_{i,t}}{totEMP_{i,t}}$	3,336	0.06	0.17	−0.82	0.51
$\dfrac{VAind_{i,t}}{GDP_{i,t}} - \dfrac{EMPind_{i,t}}{totEMP_{i,t}}$	3,336	0.12	0.13	−0.16	0.83
GDPpc_US$_constant2005	3,336	8,632.09	13,431.94	69.58	69,094.74
Pop_million	3,336	43.03	145.65	0.19	1,364.27
A_def_S	3,336	1.15	0.42	0.22	5.53
A_def_I	3,336	1.15	0.47	0.19	6.39
S_def_I	3,336	1.03	0.35	0.16	5.50
S_def_A	3,336	0.95	0.29	0.18	4.46
I_def_S	3,336	1.07	0.39	0.18	6.33
I_def_A	3,336	0.97	0.36	0.16	5.31

[18] India, China, Brazil, Indonesia, Mexico, Vietnam, Pakistan, Nigeria, Ethiopia, Bangladesh, Morocco, Turkey, Philippines, Uganda, Kenya, Argentina, Egypt, Tanzania, Colombia, and Ghana.

of value-added is the lowest in agriculture at only 17 percent of total GDP, followed by industry (30 percent), and the service sector (53 percent) with the highest share. Again, on average for 139 countries, labor productivity, defined as value-added per worker employed, tends to be higher in industry and services than in agriculture (Table A.2.1). On average, workers in the industry sector tend to produce three times more value, and those in the service sector, twice the value produced by workers in the agriculture sector. Large variation is noticeable in labor productivity across countries. Industry has the highest standard deviation, followed by the service and agriculture sectors. Table A.2.1 provides the descriptive statistics of each variable.

Appendix B: Differences between Our Two Studies

ILO uses data from both household labor force surveys and employment surveys, providing a breakdown of employment in the agriculture, manufacturing, and service sectors. A difference in the ILO and FAO data, apart from the intersectoral breakdown of employment, is in the estimation of labor input (see Table B.2.1).[19] In most cases, ILO estimates of labor in agriculture, with a few notable exceptions, such as Brazil, are lower than FAO estimates. There are also some differences in trends in the labor inputs in agriculture between the FAO and ILO data. This new data set helped us to explore differences in employment generated and productivity of labor in the agriculture, industry, and service sectors in the period of rapid growth in developing countries from the 1990s and during the slowdown, since the 2007–8 crisis.

Table B.2.1 Differences in two analyses

Difference	Structural transformation analysis based on FAO Economically Active Population data	Structural transformation analysis based on ILO Global Employment Trend data
Data and variable	Used FAOSTAT data "Economically Active Population in Agriculture," defined as "*part of the economically active population engaged in or seeking work in agriculture, hunting, fishing or forestry*" and "Total Economically Active Population," defined as "*the number of all employed and unemployed persons (including those seeking work for the first time). It covers employers; self-employed workers; salaried employees; wage earners; unpaid workers assisting in a family, farm, or business operation; members of producers' cooperatives; and members of the armed forces.*"[a] To get	Used "ILO-Global Employment trend (ILO-GET)"[b] data by sector (agriculture, industry, and service), as defined by the International Standard Industrial Classification of all Economic Activities (ISIC), where "*the 'employed' comprise all persons of working age who during a specified brief period, such as one week or one day, were in the following categories: a) paid employment (whether at work or with a job but not at work); or b) self-employment (whether at work or with an enterprise but not at work)*"[c]

Continued

[19] FAO's data on "Economically Active Population" refer to the number of all employed and unemployed persons (including those seeking work for the first time). It covers employers; self-employed workers; salaried employees; wage earners; unpaid workers assisting in a family, farm, or business operation; members of producers' cooperatives; and members of the armed forces. The economically active population is also called the labor force. ILO's data on "Employment" refer to all persons above a specified age, who during a specified brief period, either one week or one day, were in the following categories: paid employment (whether at work or with a job, but not at work) and self-employment (whether at work or with an enterprise, but not at work). For the purposes of the aggregate, sectors (agriculture, industry, and services) are defined by the International Standard Industrial Classification (ISIC) System.

Table B.2.1 *Continued*

Difference	Structural transformation analysis based on FAO Economically Active Population data	Structural transformation analysis based on ILO Global Employment Trend data
	data on the "Economically Active Population in Nonagriculture," as a nonagricultural labor force variable, subtracting the "Economically Active Population in Agriculture" value from the Total.	
Data period	1980–2013	1991–2014
Data coverage (geographical) Number of countries used in the analysis	127 countries (96 developing + 31 developed)*Our initial analysis was based on 109 countries (88 developing countries + 21 developed countries) over the period 1980–2009, using constant 2000 US dollars. Later, we used constant 2005 US dollars for the extended analysis.	139 countries (104 developing + 35 developed)Used constant 2005 US dollars.
Model specification	Used ordinary least squares (OLS) regression technique Used only one terms of trade variable (agriculture over nonagriculture)	Used fixed-effects (FE) regression technique Used two terms of trade variables (agriculture over industry and agriculture over service)
	Used regional dummies and annual dummies for ST analysis, and country dummies and decadal dummies [dum1 (1980–9) and dum2 (1990–9)] for turning point analysis	Used country dummies and the dummy variable taking the value of 1 in the period after the shock in the dependent variables was found (year 1999), and 0 in the period before the shockDummy = 0 if year < 1999; 1 if year ≥ 1999andDummy food crisis, as a dummy variable, equals 1 after the 2007 food crisis and 0 until 2007.Dummy = 0 if year < 2007; 1 if year ≥ 2007
Overall analysis	Based on only agriculture and nonagriculture sectors	Based on three sectors: agriculture, industry, and service

Notes:

[a] http://faostat.fao.org/site/379/DesktopDefault.aspx?PageID=379.

[b] The ILO–GET model provides estimates of main labor market indicators, such as unemployment and employment by sector.

[c] http://www.ilo.org/ilostat/faces/home/statisticaldata/conceptsdefinitions.

References

ACET (African Center for Economic Transformation). 2017. "Agriculture Powering Africa's Economic Transformation." African Transformation Report 2017, ACET, Accra. http://acetforafrica.org/acet/wp-content/uploads/publications/2017/10/ATR17-full-report.pdf

Agarwal, Manmohan. 2017. "India and the MDGs in the Context of Developing Countries Particularly in South Asia." In *The Economies of China and India: Cooperation and Conflict*, Vol. 3: *Economic Growth, Employment and Inclusivity: The International Environment,* edited by Manmohan Agarwal, Jing Wang, and John Whalley, 55–73. Singapore: World Scientific Publishing.

Agarwal, Manmohan, and John Whalley. 2013. "China and India: Reforms and the Response: How Differently the Economies Have Behaved." NBER Working Paper 19006, National Bureau of Economic Research, Cambridge, MA. http://www.nber.org/papers/w19006.pdf

Amare, Mulubrhan, and Bekele Shiferaw. 2017. "Nonfarm Employment, Agricultural Intensification, and Productivity Change: Empirical Findings from Uganda." *Agricultural Economics* 48 (S1): 59–72.

AMIS (Agricultural Market Information System). 2019. "The China Conundrum." *Market Monitor*, No. 65 (February), 1. http://www.amis-outlook.org/fileadmin/user_upload/amis/docs/Market_monitor/AMIS_Market_Monitor_Issue_65.pdf

Andersson, Martin, and Tobias Axelsson, eds. 2016. *Diverse Development Paths and Structural Transformation in the Escape from Poverty*. Oxford: Oxford University Press.

Arndt, Channing, Doug Arent, Faaiqa Hartley, Bruno Merven, and Alam Hossain Mondal. 2019. "Faster Than You Think: Renewable Energy and Developing Countries." *Annual Review of Resource Economics* 11 (1): 149–68.

Barrett, Christopher B., Thomas Reardon, Johan Swinnen, and David Zilberman. 2019. "Structural Transformation and Economic Development: Insights from the Agri-food Value Chain Revolution." Dyson Working Paper, Cornell University, Ithaca, NY. http://barrett.dyson.cornell.edu/files/papers/BRSZ%2013%20Aug%202019.pdf

Basu, Kaushik. 2019. "India Can Hide Unemployment Data, but Not the Truth." *New York Times*, February 1. https://www.nytimes.com/2019/02/01/opinion/india-unemployment-jobs-blackout.html

Beegle, Kathleen, and Luc Christiaensen, eds. 2019. *Accelerating Poverty Reduction in Africa*. Washington, DC: World Bank Group. https://openknowledge.worldbank.org/handle/10986/32354

Bevis, Leah E. M., and Christopher B. Barrett. 2020. "Close to the Edge: High Productivity at Plot Peripheries and the Inverse Size-Productivity Relationship." *Journal of Development Economics* 143: 102377 (March).

Binswanger-Mkhize, Hans P. 2012. "India 1960–2010: Structural Change, the Rural Non-farm Sector, and the Prospects for Agriculture." Symposium Series on Global Food Policy and Food Security in the 21st Century, Center on Food Security and the Environment (FSE), Stanford University, Stanford, May 10.

Binswanger-Mkhize, Hans P. 2013. "The Stunted Structural Transformation of the Indian Economy: Agriculture, Manufacturing and the Rural Non-Farm Sector." Review of Rural Affairs. *Economic & Political Weekly* XLVIII (26 & 27), June 29.

Binswanger-Mkhize, Hans P., Alex F. McCalla, and Praful Patel. 2010. "Structural Transformation and African Agriculture." *Global Journal of Emerging Market Economies* 2 (2): 113–52.

Campanhola, Clayton, and Shivaji Pandey, eds. 2019. *Sustainable Food and Agriculture: An Integrated Approach*. Rome: Food and Agriculture Organization of the United Nations and London: Academic Press. https://www.sciencedirect.com/book/9780128121344/sustainable-food-and-agriculture#book-info

Carletto, Calogero, Sara Savastano, and Alberto Zezza. 2013. "Fact or Artifact: The Impact of Measurement Errors on the Farm Size–Productivity Relationship." *Journal of Development Economics* 103: 254–61.

Chand, Ramesh, P. A. Lakshmi Prasanna, and Aruna Singh. 2011. "Farm Size and Productivity: Understanding the Strengths of Smallholders and Improving Their Livelihoods." *Economic & Political Weekly* Supplement 46 (26 & 27): 5–11.

Chand, Ramesh, S. K. Srivastava, and Jaspal Singh. 2017. "Lessons for Job-led Growth: Changes in Rural Economy of India, 1971 to 2012." *Economic & Political Weekly* 52, December 30.

Chenery, Hollis B., Montek S. Ahluwalia, C. L. G. Bell, John H. Duloy, and Richard Jolly. 1974. *Redistribution with Growth.* A Joint Study by the World Bank's Development Research Center and the Institute of Development Studies at the University of Sussex. Oxford: Oxford University Press.

Chenery, Hollis B., and Moises Syrquin. 1975. *Patterns of Development: 1950–1970.* Oxford: Oxford University Press.

Chenery, Hollis B., and Lance Taylor. 1968. "Development Patterns among Countries and over Time." *Review of Economics and Statistics* 50 (3): 391–416.

Christiaensen, Luc, Lionel Demery, and Jesper Kuhl. 2011. "The (Evolving) Role of Agriculture in Poverty Reduction: An Empirical Perspective." *Journal of Development Economics* 96 (2): 239–54.

Clark, Colin. 1940. *The Conditions of Economic Progress.* London: Macmillan.

Collier, Paul, and Stefan Dercon. 2014. "African Agriculture in 50 Years: Smallholders in a Rapidly Changing World." *World Development* 63: 92–101.

Dasgupta, Sukti, and Ajit Singh. 2006. "Manufacturing, Services and Premature Deindustrialization in Developing Countries: A Kaldorian Analysis." United Nations University–World Institute for Development (UNU–WIDER) Working Paper 49, WIDER, Helsinki.

Datt, Gaurav, and Martin Ravallion. 1992. "Growth and Redistribution Components of Changes in Poverty Measures: A Decomposition with Applications to Brazil and India in the 1980s." *Journal of Development Economics* 38 (2): 275–95.

Datt, Gaurav, and Martin Ravallion. 1998. "Farm Productivity and Rural Poverty in India." *Journal of Development Studies* 34 (4): 62–85.

Datt, Gaurav, and Martin Ravallion. 2011. "Has India's Economic Growth Become More Pro-Poor in the Wake of Economic Reforms?" *World Bank Economic Review* 25 (2): 157–89.

Datt, Gaurav, Martin Ravallion, and Rinku Murgai. 2016. "Growth, Urbanization, and Poverty Reduction in India." Policy Research Working Paper No. 7568, February, Poverty and Equity Global Practice Group, World Bank, Washington, DC.

de Freitas, P. L., and J. N. Landers. 2014. "The Transformation of Agriculture in Brazil through Development and Adoption of Zero Tillage Conservation Agriculture." *International Soil and Water Conservation Research* 2 (1): 35–46.

de Janvry, Alain, and Elisabeth Sadoulet. 2018. "The Puzzle of Neglecting Agriculture for Development." Presentation at "Disruptive Innovations, Value Chains, and Rural Development," International Consortium of Applied Bioeconomy Research (ICABR)–World Bank conference, Washington, DC, June 12–15. http://www.ferdi.fr/sites/www.ferdi.fr/files/icabr_conference_presentation_alain.pdf

de Melo, Jaime. 2017. "Pathways to Structural Transformation in Africa." Africa in Focus blog, October 30, The Brookings Institution, Washington, DC. https://www.brookings.edu/blog/africa-in-focus/2017/10/30/pathways-to-structural-transformation-in-africa/

de Vries, Gaaitzen, Marcel Timmer, and Klaas de Vries. 2015. "Structural Transformation in Africa: Static Gains, Dynamic Losses." *Journal of Development Studies* 51 (6): 674–88.

Deininger, Klaus, and Gershon Feder. 2001. "Land Institutions and Land Markets." In *Handbook of Agricultural Economics*, Vol. 1, edited by B. L. Gardner and G. C. Rausser, Chapter 6, 288–331. Amsterdam: Elsevier.

Deininger, Klaus, Songqing Jin, Yanyan Liu, and Sudhir Singh. 2015. "Labor Market Performance and the Farm Size-Productivity Relationship in Rural India." Presentation, International Association of Agricultural Economists (IAAE): "Agriculture in an Interconnected World," Milan, August 9–14. https://ageconsearch.umn.edu/record/212720/

Delgado, Mercedes, Michael E. Porter, and Scott Stern. 2014. "Clusters, Convergence and Economic Performance." *Research Policy* 43 (10): 1785–99.

Dercon, Stefan, and Douglas Gollin. 2014. "Agriculture in African Development: A Review of Theories and Strategies." CSAE Working Paper WPS/2014–22, Centre for the Study of African Economies, Oxford. http://www.csae.ox.ac.uk/materials/papers/csae-wps-2014-22.pdf

Desai, Sonalde. 2019. "Everyone Is Afraid of Data." *The Hindu*, February 12. https://www.thehindu.com/opinion/lead/everyone-is-afraid-of-data/article26241011.ece

Diao, Xinshen, Margaret McMillan, and Dani Rodrik. 2017. "The Recent Growth Boom in Developing Economics: A Structural Change Perspective." NBER Working Paper No. 23132, National Bureau of Economic Research, Cambridge, MA.

Duarte, Margarida, and Diego Restuccia. 2010. "The Role of the Structural Transformation in Aggregate Productivity." *Quarterly Journal of Economics* 125(1): 129–73.

Dubey, Sangita, and Marie Vander Donckt. 2016. "FAO's New Macro-Economic Statistics: Agriculture Capital Stock and Agro-Industry Measurement." United Nations Economic and Social Commission for Asia and the Pacific, Asia-Pacific Economic Statistics Week, May 2–4, Bangkok. http://communities.unescap.org/system/files/faos_new_macro-economic_statistics_escap_economicstatisticsweek_april2016_dubey.pdf

Easterly, William. 2009. "Can the West Save Africa?" *Journal of Economic Literature* 47 (2): 373–447.

Fan, Shenggen, Peter Hazell, and Sukhadeo Thorat. 2000. "Government Spending, Agricultural Growth and Poverty in Rural India." *American Journal of Agricultural Economics* 82 (4): 1038–51.

Fan, Shenggen, Linxiu Zhang, and Xiaobo Zhang. 2002. "Growth, Inequality and Poverty in Rural China: The Role of Public Investments." IFPRI Research Report 125, International Food Policy Research Institute, Washington, DC.

FAO (Food and Agriculture Organization of the United Nations). 2014a. "Innovation in Family Farming." *The State of Food and Agriculture 2014* In Brief, FAO, Rome. http://www.fao.org/3/a-i4036e.pdf

FAO (Food and Agriculture Organization of the United Nations). 2014b. *The State of Food and Agriculture 2014: Innovation in Family Farming*. Rome: FAO.

FAO (Food and Agriculture Organization of the United Nations). 2016. *The State of Food and Agriculture (SOFA) 2016: Climate Change, Agriculture, and Food Security*. Rome: FAO. http://www.fao.org/3/a-i6030e.pdf

FAO (Food and Agriculture Organization of the United Nations). 2020a. Food Systems. http://www.fao.org/food-systems/en/

FAO (Food and Agriculture Organization of the United Nations). 2020b. Statistics. Capital Stock and Investment in Agriculture. http://www.fao.org/economic/ess/ess-economic/capitalstock/en/

FAO (Food and Agriculture Organization of the United Nations), IFAD (International Fund for Agricultural Development), UNICEF (United Nations Children's Fund), WFP (World Food Programme), and WHO (World Health Organization). 2018. "The State of Food Security and Nutrition in the World 2018. Building Climate Resilience for Food Security and Nutrition." FAO, Rome. https://www1.wfp.org/publications/2018-state-food-security-and-nutrition-world-sofi-report

FAO (Food and Agriculture Organization of the United Nations), IFAD (International Fund for Agricultural Development), UNICEF (United Nations Children's Fund), WFP (World Food Programme), and WHO (World Health Organization). 2020. *The State of Food Security and Nutrition in the World 2020: Transforming Food Systems for Affordable Healthy Diets.* Rome: FAO. http://www.fao.org/3/ca9692en/online/ca9692en.html

FAO (Food and Agriculture Organization of the United Nations) and WFP (World Food Programme). 2019. "Monitoring Food Security in Countries with Conflict Situations." A joint FAO/WFP update for the United Nations Security Council, Issue no. 5. http://www.fao.org/3/CA3113EN/ca3113en.pdf

Feder, Gershon. 1985. "The Relation between Farm Size and Farm Productivity: The Role of Family Labor, Supervision and Credit Constraints." *Journal of Development Economics* 18 (2–3): 297–313.

Fei, John C. H., and Gustav Ranis. 1964. *Development of the Labor Surplus Economy: Theory and Policy.* Homewood, IL: R.D. Irwin.

Foster, Andrew D., and Mark R. Rosenzweig. 2017. "Are There Too Many Farms in the World? Labor-Market Transaction Costs, Machine Capacities and Optimal Farm Size." NBER Working Paper No. 23909, National Bureau of Economic Research, Cambridge, MA. https://www.nber.org/papers/w23909.pdf

Fuglie, Keith O. 2010. "Total Factor Productivity in the Global Agricultural Economy: Evidence from FAO Data." In *The Shifting Patterns of Agricultural Production and Productivity Worldwide*, edited by Julian Alston, Bruce A. Babcock, and Philip G. Pardey, 63–95. Ames, IA: The Midwest Agribusiness Trade Research and Information Center, Iowa State University.

Fuglie, Keith O., Madhur Gautam, Aparajita Goyal, and William F. Maloney. 2019. *Harvesting Prosperity: Technology and Productivity Growth in Agriculture.* Conference Edition. Washington, DC, World Bank. https://openknowledge.worldbank.org/bitstream/handle/10986/32350/9781464813931.pdf

Gautam, Madhur, and Mansur Ahmed. 2018. "Too Small to Be Beautiful? The Farm Size and Productivity Relationship in Bangladesh." Policy Research Working Paper 8387, Agriculture Global Practice, World Bank Group, Washington, DC.

GEF IEO (Global Environmental Facility Independent Evaluation Office). 2016. *Impact Evaluation of GEF Support to Protected Areas and Protected Area Systems.* Evaluation Report No. 104. Washington, DC: GEF IEO. https://www.gefieo.org/evaluations/impact-evaluation-gef-support-protected-areas-and-protected-area-systems-pas-2016

Gerschenkron, Alexander. 1962. *Economic Backwardness in Historical Perspective.* Cambridge, MA: The Belknap Press of Harvard University Press.

Gollin, Douglas, and Christopher Udry. 2019. "Heterogeneity, Measurement Error, and Misallocation: Evidence from African Agriculture." Global Poverty Research Lab Working Paper No. 18-108, December. Global Poverty Research Lab, Northwestern University, Evanston, IL.

Government of India. 2018a. *Economic Survey 2017–18*. Ministry of Finance, Department of Economic Affairs, Economic Division, January. http://mofapp.nic.in:8080/economicsurvey/

Government of India. 2018b. "Is there a 'Late Converger Stall' in Economic Development? Can India Escape?" In *Economic Survey 2017–18*, 68–81. Ministry of Finance, Department of Economic Affairs, Economic Division, January. http://mofapp.nic.in:8080/economicsurvey/pdf/068-081_Chapter_05_ENGLISH_Vol_01_2017-18.pdf

Graeub, Benjamin E., M. Jahi Chappell, Hannah Wittman, Samuel Ledermann, Rachel Bezner Kerr, and Barbara Gemmill-Herren. 2016. "The State of Family Farms in the World." *World Development* 87: 1–15.

Greenville, Jared, Kentaro Kawasaki, and Marie-Agnes Jouanjean. 2019. "Dynamic Changes and Effects of Agro-Food GVCs." OECD Food, Agriculture and Fisheries Papers No. 119, OECD Publishing, Paris.

Griliches, Zvi. 1957. "Hybrid Corn: An Exploration in the Economics of Technological Change." *Econometrica* 25 (4): 501–22.

Harris, John R., and Michael P. Todaro. 1970. "Migration, Unemployment and Development: A Two-Sector Analysis." *American Economic Review* 60 (1): 126–42.

Hayami, Yujiro, and Vernon W. Ruttan. 1971. *Agricultural Development: An International Perspective*. Baltimore: Johns Hopkins University Press.

Hazell, Peter B. R. 2015. "Is Small Farm-Led Development Still a Relevant Strategy for Africa and Asia?" In *The Fight against Hunger and Malnutrition: The Role of Food, Agriculture, and Targeted Policies*, edited by David E. Sahn, 192–207. Oxford: Oxford University Press.

Headey, Derek D., and T. S. Jayne. 2014. "Adaptation to Land Constraints: Is Africa Different?" *Food Policy* 48: 18–33.

Helfand, Steven M., Marcelo M. Magalhães, and Nicholas E. Rada. 2015. "Brazil's Agricultural Total Factor Productivity Growth by Farm Size." IDB Working Paper No. 609, Environment, Rural Development and Disaster Risk Management Division, Inter-American Development Bank, Washington, DC. https://economics.ucr.edu/people/faculty/helfand/Brazils_Agricultural_Total_Factor_Productivity_Growth_by_Farm_Size%20IDB%20WP%202015.pdf

HLPE (High Level Panel of Experts on Food Security and Nutrition). 2013. "Investing in Smallholder Agriculture for Food Security." HLPE Report 6, Committee on World Food Security, Rome, FAO.

Huang, Jikun. 2020. "Institutional Innovations in Accessing Land, Water, Machinery and Extension Services in China's Agriculture." CCAP Working Paper, Center for Chinese Agricultural Policy (CCAP), Chinese Academy of Sciences, Beijing.

Huang, Jikun, and Jiping Ding. 2016. "Institutional Innovation and Policy Support to Facilitate Small-scale Farming Transformation in China." *Agricultural Economics* 47 (S1): 227–37.

IFAD (International Fund for Agriculture) and UNEP (United Nations Environment Programme). 2013. "Smallholders, Food Security, and the Environment." IFAD, Rome. https://www.ifad.org/documents/38714170/39135645/smallholders_report.pdf/133e8903-0204-4e7d-a780-bca847933f2e

Ighobor, Kingsley. 2020. "AfCFTA: Implementing Free Trade Pact the Best Stimulus for Post-COVID-19 Economies." —Wamkele Mene, Secretary General, African Continental Free Trade Area (AfCFTA) Secretariat, *African Renewal*, May. https://www.un.org/africarenewal/magazine/may-2020/coronavirus/implementing-africa's-free-trade-pact-best-stimulus-post-covid-19-economies

IMF (International Monetary Fund). 2018. "World Economic Outlook (WEO): Cyclical Upswing, Structural Change." April, IMF, Washington, DC. https://www.imf.org/en/Publications/WEO/Issues/2018/03/20/world-economic-outlook-april-2018

IPBES (Intergovernmental Science–Policy Platform on Biodiversity and Ecosystem Services). 2019. *IPBES Global Assessment Report on Biodiversity and Ecosystem Services*. https://www.ipbes.net/global-assessment-report-biodiversity-ecosystem-services

Jayne, Thomas S., Jordan Chamberlin, Lulama Traub, Nicholas Sitko, Milu Muyanga, Felix K. Yeboah, Ward Anseeuw, Antony Chapoto, Ayala Wineman, Chewe Nkonde, and Richard Kachule. 2016. "Africa's Changing Farm Size Distribution Patterns: The Rise of Medium-Scale Farms." *Agricultural Economics* 47 (S1): 197–214.

Jayne, Thomas S., Antony Chapoto, Nicholas Sitko, Chewe Nkonde, Milu Muyanga, and Jordan Chamberlin. 2014. "Is the Scramble for Land in Africa Foreclosing a Smallholder Agricultural Expansion Strategy?" *Journal of International Affairs* 67 (2): 35–53.

Jayne, Thomas, and Milu Muyanga. 2018. "Are Medium-Scale Farms Driving Agricultural Transformation in Africa?" Agrilinks blog, June 21, Feed the Future. https://www.agrilinks.org/post/are-medium-scale-farms-driving-agricultural-transformation-africa

Jenkins, Rhys. 2010. "China's Global Expansion and Latin America." *Journal of Latin American Studies* 42 (4): 809–37.

Jeuland, Marc, and Dale Whittington. 2014. "Water Resources Planning Under Climate Change: Assessing the Robustness of Real Options for the Blue Nile." *Water Resources Research* 50 (3): 2086–107. doi:10.1002/2013WR013705

Johnston, Bruce F., and John W. Mellor. 1961. "The Role of Agriculture in Economic Development." *American Economic Review* 51 (4): 566–93.

Kaldor, Nicholas. 1966. *Causes of the Slow Rate of Economic Growth of the United Kingdom: An Inaugural Lecture*. London: Cambridge University Press.

Kaldor, Nicholas. 1970. "The Case for Regional Policies." *Scottish Journal of Political Economy* 17 (3): 337–48.

Kaldor, Nicholas. 1975. "Economic Growth and the Verdoorn Law: A Comment on Mr. Rowthorn's Article." *Economic Journal* 85 (340): 891–6.

Kuznets, Simon. 1955. "Economic Growth and Income Inequality." *American Economic Review* 45 (1): 1–28.

Kuznets, Simon. 1966. *Modern Economic Growth: A Rate, Structure, and Spread*. New Haven, CT: Yale University Press.

Landers, John N. 2001. "Zero Tillage Development in Tropical Brazil: The Story of a Successful NGO Activity." FAO Agricultural Services Bulletin 147, Food and Agriculture Organization of the United Nations, Rome. http://www.fao.org/3/Y2638E/y2638e00.htm

Lele, Uma, and Manmohan Agarwal. 1989. "Smallholder and Large-Scale Agriculture in Africa. Are There Tradeoffs between Growth and Equity? Managing Agricultural Development in Africa (MADIA) Discussion Paper No. 6, World Bank, Washington, DC.

Lele, Uma, Manmohan Agarwal, and Sambuddha Goswami. 2013. "Lessons of the Global Structural Transformation Experience for the East African Community." International Symposium and Exhibition on Agriculture, organized by Kilimo Trust, Kampala, Uganda, November.

Lele, Uma, with Manmohan Agarwal, and Sambuddha Goswami. 2014. Presentation at the Conference on "Innovation in Indian Agriculture: Ways Forward," Institute of Economic Growth and International Food Policy Research Institute, New Delhi, December 4–5.

Lele, Uma, Manmohan Agarwal, and Sambuddha Goswami. 2018. *Patterns of Structural Transformation and Agricultural Productivity Growth (with Special Focus on Brazil, China, Indonesia and India)*. Pune, India: Gokhale Institute of Politics and Economics.

Lele, Uma, and Balu Bumb. 1994. *South Asia's Food Crisis: The Case of India*. Washington, DC: Banco Mundial.

Lele, Uma, and Balu Bumb. 1995. "The Food Crisis in South Asia: The Case of India." In *The Evolving Role of the World Bank: Helping Meet the Challenge of Development*, edited by K. Sarwar Lateef, 69–96. Washington, DC: World Bank.

Lele, Uma, and Arthur A. Goldsmith. 1989. "The Development of National Agricultural Research Capacity: India's Experience with the Rockefeller Foundation and Its Significance for Africa." *Economic Development and Cultural Change* 37 (2): 305–43.

Lele, Uma, and Sambuddha Goswami. 2017. "The Fourth Industrial Revolution, Agricultural and Rural Innovation, and Implications for Public Policy and Investments: A Case of India." *Agricultural Economics* 48 (S1): 87–100.

Lele, Uma, Sambuddha Goswami, and Gianluigi Nico. 2017. "Structural Transformation and the Transition from Concessional Assistance to Commercial Flows: The Past and Possible Future Contributions of the World Bank." In *Agriculture and Rural Development in a Globalizing World: Challenges and Opportunities*, edited by Prabhu Pingali and Gershon Feder, 325–52. London and New York: Routledge.

Lele, Uma, and John W. Mellor. 1981. "Technological Change, Distribution Bias and Labour Transfer in a Two Sector Economy." *Oxford Economic Papers* 33 (3): 426–41.

Lele, Uma, and Steven W. Stone. 1989. "Population Pressure, the Environment and Agricultural Intensification: Variations on the Boserup Hypothesis." MADIA Discussion Paper 4, Managing Agricultural Development in Africa, World Bank, Washington, DC.

Lewis, W. Arthur. 1954. "Economic Development with Unlimited Supplies of Labour." *The Manchester School* 22 (2): 139–91.

Lowder, Sarah K., Marco V. Sánchez, and Raffaele Bertini. 2019. "Farms, Family Farms, Farmland Distribution and Farm Labour: What Do We Know Today?" FAO Agricultural Development Economics Working Paper 19-08, Food and Agriculture Organization of the United Nations, Rome.

Lowder, Sarah K., Jacob Skoet, and Terri Raney. 2016. "The Number, Size, and Distribution of Farms, Smallholder Farms, and Family Farms Worldwide." *World Development* 87: 16–29.

Lund, Susan, James Manyika, Jonathan Woetzel, Jacques Bughin, Mekala Krishnan, Jeongmin Seong, and Mac Muir. 2019. "Globalization in Transition: The Future of Trade and Value Chains." McKinsey Global Institute, McKinsey & Company Report, January. https://www.mckinsey.com/featured-insights/innovation-and-growth/globalization-in-transition-the-future-of-trade-and-value-chains

Maertens, Miet, and Johan Swinnen. 2015. "Agricultural Trade and Development: A Value Chain Perspective." WTO Staff Working Paper No. ERSD-2015-04, Economic Research and Statistics Division, World Trade Organization, Geneva.

Martin, Will. 2018. Economic Growth, Convergence, and Agricultural Economics." Presidential Address for the 30th International Conference of Agricultural Economists, Vancouver, BC, 29 July 2018.

Martin, Will, and Devashish Mitra. 2001. "Productivity Growth and Convergence in Agriculture versus Manufacturing." *Economic Development and Cultural Change* 49 (20): 403–22.

Masters, William A., Agnes Andersson Djurfeldt, Cornelis De Haan, Peter Hazell, Thomas Jayne, Magnus Jirström, and Thomas Reardon. 2013. "Urbanization and Farm Size in Asia and Africa: Implications for Food Security and Agricultural Research." *Global Food Security* 2 (3): 156–65.

Mburu, Samuel, Chris Ackello-Ogutu, and Richard Mulwa. 2014. "Analysis of Economic Efficiency and Farm Size: A Case Study of Wheat Farmers in Nakuru District, Kenya." *Economics Research International* Article ID 802706. http://dx.doi.org/10.1155/2014/802706

McMillan, Margaret S., and Dani Rodrik. 2011. "Globalization, Structural Change and Productivity Growth." NBER Working Paper No. 17143, National Bureau of Economic Research, Cambridge, MA.

Megginson, William L., and Jeffry M. Netter. 2001. "From State to Market: A Survey of Empirical Studies on Privatization." *Journal of Economic Literature* 39 (2): 321–89.

Mellor, John W. 1976. *The New Economics of Growth: A Strategy for India and the Developing World*. Ithaca, NY: Cornell University Press.

Mellor, John W. 2017. *Agricultural Development and Economic Transformation: Promoting Growth with Poverty Reduction*. Cham, Switzerland: Palgrave Macmillan.

Minten, Bart, Lalaina Randrianarison, and Johan F. M. Swinnen. 2009. "Global Retail Chains and Poor Farmers: Evidence from Madagascar." *World Development* 37 (11): 1728–41.

Mohan, Rakesh. 2019. "Moving India to a New Growth Trajectory: Need for a Comprehensive Big Push." Brookings India, June 28. https://www.brookings.edu/research/moving-india-to-a-new-growth-trajectory-need-for-a-comprehensive-big-push/

Monga, Célestin, and Justin Yifu Lin, eds. 2019. *The Oxford Handbook of Structural Transformation*. Oxford: Oxford University Press.

Muyanga, Milu, and Thomas S. Jayne. 2019. "Revisiting the Farm Size–Productivity Relationship Based on a Relatively Wide Range of Farm Sizes: Evidence from Kenya." *American Journal of Agricultural Economics* 101 (4): 1140–63.

Muyanga, Milu, Nicholas Sitko, T. S. Jayne, and Munguzwe Hichaambwa. 2013. "Medium-Scale Farmer Growth Trajectories in Africa: Implications for Broad-Based Growth and Poverty Reduction." Paper presented at the Future Agricultures Conference on Political Economy of Agricultural Policy in Africa, Pretoria, South Africa, March 18–20.

Narayanan, Sudha. 2020. "The Three Farm Bills: Is This the Market Reform Indian Agriculture Needs?" *The India Forum*, November 27. https://www.theindiaforum.in/article/three-farm-bills

Nellis, John. 1986. *Public Enterprises in Sub-Saharan Africa*. Washington, DC: World Bank.

Nellis, John. 2003. "Privatization in Africa: What Has Happened? What Is to Be Done?" Working Paper No. 25, Center for Global Development, Washington, DC.

Newman, Carol, John Page, John Rand, Abebe Shimeles, Måns Söderbom, and Finn Tarp, eds. 2016a. *Made in Africa: Learning to Compete in Industry*. Washington, DC: Brookings Institution Press.

Newman, Carol, John Page, John Rand, Abebe Shimeles, Måns Söderbom, and Finn Tarp. 2016b. *Manufacturing Transformation: Comparative Studies of Industrial Development in Africa and Emerging Asia*. United Nations University–World Institute for Development Economics Research (UNU–WIDER) Studies in Development Economics, Helsinki, Finland. Oxford: Oxford University Press.

Nkonde, Chewe, Thomas S. Jayne, Robert B. Richardson, and Frank Place. 2015. "Testing the Farm Size–Productivity Relationship over a Wide Range of Farm Sizes: Should the

Relationship be a Decisive Factor in Guiding Agricultural Development and Land Policies in Zambia?" World Bank Conference on Land and Poverty, Washington, DC, March 23–7.

Ocampo, José. 2004. "Latin America's Growth and Equity Frustrations during Structural Reforms." *Journal of Economic Perspectives* 18 (2): 67–88.

Ocampo, José, ed. 2005. *Beyond Reforms.* Palo Alto, CA: Stanford University Press.

OECD (Organization for Economic Co-operation and Development). 2009. "Measuring Capital." *OECD Manual,* 2nd ed. Paris: OECD.

OECD (Organisation for Economic Co-operation and Development). 2014. DAC CRS International Development Statistics (IDS) online databases. https://www.oecd.org/development/financing-sustainable-development/development-finance-data/idsonline.htm

OECD (Organisation for Economic Co-operation and Development). 2020. "Digital Transformation in the Age of COVID-19: Building Resilience and Bridging Divides." Digital Economy Outlook 2020 Supplement, OECD, Paris, https://imgcdn.larepublica.co/cms/2020/11/27173400/digital-economy-outlook-covid.pdf

OECD (Organisation for Economic Co-operation and Development) and FAO (Food and Agriculture Organization of the United Nations). 2019. *OECD–FAO Agricultural Outlook 2019–2028.* Paris: OECD Publishing. http://www.fao.org/3/ca4076en/ca4076en.pdf

Osakwe, Patrick N., and Miriam Poretti. 2015. "Trade and Poverty Alleviation in Africa: The Role of Inclusive Structural Transformation." Trade and Poverty Branch, United Nations Conference on Trade and Development (UNCTAD), October. https://unctad.org/en/PublicationsLibrary/webaldc2015d2_en.pdf

Otsuka, Keijiro, Yanyan Liu, and Futoshi Yamauchi. 2016. "The Future of Small Farms in Asia." *Development Policy Review* 34 (3): 441–61.

Owens, Trudy, and Adrian Wood. 1997. "Export-Oriented Industrialization through Primary Processing?" *World Development* 25 (9): 1453–70.

Page, John. 2015a. "Made in Africa: Some New Thinking for Africa Industrialization Day." Africa in Focus blog, November 19, The Brookings Institution, Washington, DC. https://www.brookings.edu/blog/africa-in-focus/2015/11/19/made-in-africa-some-new-thinking-for-africa-industrialization-day/

Page, John. 2015b. "Structural Change and Africa's Poverty Puzzle." In *The Last Mile in Ending Extreme Poverty,* edited by Laurence Chandy, Hiroshi Kato, and Homi Kharas, 219–48. Washington, DC: Brookings Institution.

Page, John. 2019. "How Industries without Smokestacks Can Address Africa's Youth Unemployment Crisis." In *Foresight Africa: Top Priorities for the Continent in 2019,* edited by Brahima S. Coulibaly, 45–58. Washington, DC: Africa Growth Institute at Brookings.

Page, John, and Fred Dews. 2016. "Made in Africa: Manufacturing and Economic Growth on the Continent." Brookings Cafeteria Podcast, January 22, The Brookings Institution, Washington, DC.

Parry, Ian, Victor Mylonas, and Nate Vernon. 2018. "Mitigation Policies for the Paris Agreement: An Assessment for G20 Countries." IMF Working Paper WP/18/193, International Monetary Fund, Washington, DC.

Pritchett, Lance. 1997. "Divergence, Big Time." *Journal of Economic Perspectives* 11 (3): 3–17.

Rada, Nicholas E., and Keith O. Fuglie. 2019. "New Perspectives on Farm Size and Productivity." *Food Policy* 84: 147–52.

Ranis, Gustav, and John C. H. Fei. 1961. "A Theory of Economic Development." *American Economic Review* 51 (4): 533–65.

Ravallion, Martin, and Gaurav Datt. 2002. "Why Has Economic Growth Been More Pro-Poor in Some States of India than Others?" *Journal of Development Economics* 68: 381–400.

Reardon, Thomas, David Tschirley, Michael Dolislager, Jason Snyder, Chaoran Hu, and Stephanie White. 2014. "Urbanization, Diet Change, and Transformation of Food Value Chains in Asia." Global Center for Food Systems Innovation, Michigan State University, East Lansing, MI. http://www.fao.org/fileadmin/templates/ags/docs/MUFN/DOCUMENTS/MUS_Reardon_2014.pdf

Rodrik, Dani. 2006. "Goodbye Washington Consensus. Hello Washington Confusion? A Review of the World Bank's 'Economic Growth in the 1990s: Learning from a Decade of Reform.'" *Journal of Economic Literature* 44 (4): 973–87.

Rodrik, Dani. 2014. "An African Miracle? Implications of Recent Research on Growth Economics," Ninth Annual Richard H. Sabot Lecture, Center for Global Development, Washington, DC. http://www.cgdev.org/event/ninth-annual-richard-h-sabot-lecture-african-miracle-implications-recent-research-growth

Rodrik, Dani. 2016. "Premature Deindustrialization." *Journal of Economic Growth* 21 (1): 1–33.

Schwab, Klaus. 2016. *The Fourth Industrial Revolution*. Geneva: World Economic Forum.

Sen, Amartya. 1962. "An Aspect of Indian Agriculture." *Economic Weekly*. 4-5-6, January 27.

Shafaeddin, S. M. 2005. "Trade Liberalization and Economic Reform in Developing Countries: Structural Change or Deindustrialization?" UNCTAD Discussion Paper No. 179, United Nations Conference on Trade and Development, Geneva.

Sheahan, Megan, Christopher B. Barrett, and Casey Goldvale. 2017. "Human Health and Pesticide Use in Sub-Saharan Africa." *Agricultural Economics* 48 (S1): 27–41.

Simpson, Brent M., Steven Franzel, Ann Dearande, Godfrey Kundhlande, and Sygnola Tsafack. 2015. "Farmer-to-Farmer Extension: Issues in Planning and Implementation." MEAS Technical Note, May, Modernizing Extension and Advisory Systems, US Agency for International Development, Washington, DC. https://meas.illinois.edu/wp-content/uploads/2017/02/MEAS-TN-Farmer-to-Farmer-Simpson-et-al-May-2015.pdf

Sitko, Nicholas J., and T. S. Jayne. 2014. "Structural Transformation or Elite Land Capture? The Growth of 'Emergent' Farmers In Zambia." *Food Policy* 48: 194–202.

Srinivasan, T. N. 1991. "Food Aid: A Cause or Symptom of Development Failure or an Instrument for Success." In *Transitions in Development: The Role of Aid and Commercial Flows*, edited by Uma Lele and Ijaz Nabi, 373–99. San Francisco: ICS Press.

Steensland, Ann. 2019. "2019 Global Agricultural Productivity (GAP) Report: Productivity Growth for Sustainable Diets, and More." (Thompson, T., ed.), Virginia Tech College of Agriculture and Life Sciences, Blacksburg, VA. https://globalagriculturalproductivity.org/wp-content/uploads/2019/01/2019-GAP-Report-FINAL.pdf

Stern, Nicholas. 2001. *A Strategy for Development*. Beijing: People's University.

Stern, Nicholas. 2002. *The Investment Climate, Governance, and Inclusion in Bangladesh*. World Bank Office of the Senior Vice President, Development Economics, Washington, DC: World Bank.

Stiglitz, Joseph. 2019. "Structural Transformation, Deep Downturns, and Government Policy." In *The Oxford Handbook of Structural Transformation*, edited by Célestin Monga and Justin Yifu Lin, 35–44. Oxford: Oxford University Press.

Subramanian, Arvind. 2011. *Eclipse: Living in the Shadow of China's Economic Dominance*. Washington, DC: Peterson Institute for International Economics.

Taheripour, Farzad, Thomas W. Hertel, and Navin Ramankutty. 2019. "Market-mediated Responses Confound Policies to Limit Deforestation from Oil Palm Expansion in Malaysia and Indonesia." *PNAS* 116 (38): 19193–9.

Tarp, Finn, ed. 2016. *Growth, Structural Transformation and Rural Change in Viet Nam: A Rising Dragon on the Move.* United Nations University–World Institute for Development Economic Research (UNU–WIDER). Oxford: Oxford University Press.

Timmer, C. Peter. 2009. *A World without Agriculture: The Structural Transformation in Historical Perspective.* Washington, DC: American Enterprise Institute Press.

Timmer, C. Peter, and Selvin Akkus. 2008. "The Structural Transformation as a Pathway out of Poverty: Analytics, Empirics and Politics." Working Paper No. 150, Center for Global Development, Washington, DC.

Todaro, Michael P. 1969. "A Model of Labor Migration and Urban Unemployment in Less Developed Countries." *American Economic Review* 59 (1): 138–48.

Tower, Edward. 1984. "Effective Protection, Domestic Resource Costs, and Shadow Prices: A General Equilibrium Perspective." World Bank Staff Working Paper No. 664, World Bank, Washington, DC. http://documents.worldbank.org/curated/en/154791468766192336/pdf/multi0page.pdf

UN (United Nations). 2019. "World Population Prospects 2019: Highlights." June 17, Department of Economic and Social Affairs, UN, New York. https://www.un.org/development/desa/publications/world-population-prospects-2019-highlights.html#:~:text=The%20world's%20population%20is%20expected,United%20Nations%20report%20launched%20today

UN (United Nations). 2020. "High-Level Political Forum Goals in Focus: Goal 11—Make Cities and Human Settlements Inclusive, Safe, Resilient and Sustainable." Department of Economic and Social Affairs, Statistics Division. https://unstats.un.org/sdgs/report/2018/goal-11/

UNFCCC (United Framework Convention on Climate Change). 2020. The Paris Agreement. https://unfccc.int/process-and-meetings/the-paris-agreement/the-paris-agreement

Virmani, Arvind. 2018. "Global Imbalances Post Global Financial Crisis (GFC 2008): China Macro-Adjustments and Growth." Presentation at G20 Seminar on Global Imbalances, Amsterdam, September 10.

WBG (World Bank Group). 2018. "Malawi Systematic Country Diagnostic: Breaking the Cycle of Low Growth and Slow Poverty Reduction." Report No. 132785, December, Malawi Country Team, Africa Region, World Bank, Washington, DC. https://openknowledge.worldbank.org/bitstream/handle/10986/31131/malawi-scd-final-board-12-7-2018-12122018-636804216425880639.pdf

WBG (World Bank Group), IDE–JETRO (Institute of Developing Economies–Japan External Trade Organization), OECD (Organisation for Economic Co-operation and Development), UIBE (University of International Business and Economics), and WTO (World Trade Organization). 2017. *Global Value Chain Development Report 2017: Measuring and Analyzing the Impact of GVCs on Economic Development.* Washington, DC: World Bank. http://documents.worldbank.org/curated/en/440081499424129960/pdf/117290-WP-P157880-PUBLIC.pdf

WCED (World Commission on Environment and Development). 1987. *Our Common Future.* Brundtland Committee. Oxford and New York: Oxford University Press.

Willett, Walter, Johan Rockström, Brent Loken, Marco Springmann, Tim Lang, Sonja Vermeulen, Tara Garnett, David Tilman, Fabrice DeClerck, Amanda Wood, Malin Jonell, Michael Clark, Line J Gordon, Jessica Fanzo, Corinna Hawkes, Rami Zurayk, Juan A Rivera, Wim De

Vries, Lindiwe Majele Sibanda, Ashkan Afshin, Abhishek Chaudhary, Mario Herrero, Rina Agustina, Francesco Branca, Anna Lartey, Shenggen Fan, Beatrice Crona, Elizabeth Fox, Victoria Bignet, Max Troell, Therese Lindahl, Sudhvir Singh, Sarah E Cornell, K Srinath Reddy, Sunita Narain, Sania Nishtar, Christopher J. L. Murray; The *Lancet* Commission. 2019. "Food in the Anthropocene: The EAT-*Lancet* Commission on Healthy Diets from Sustainable Systems." *Lancet* 393 (10170): 447–92. https://www.thelancet.com/pdfs/journals/lancet/PIIS0140-6736(18)31788-4.pdf

Williamson, John. 2004. "The Strange History of the Washington Consensus." *Journal of Post Keynesian Economics* 27 (2): 195–206.

Wood, Adrian. 2003. "Could Africa Be Like America?" In *Annual World Bank Conference on Development Economics 2003: The New Reform Agenda*, edited by Boris Pleskovic and Nicholas Stern, 163–200. Washington, DC, and New York: World Bank and Oxford University Press.

Wood, Adrian. 2017. "Variation in Structural Change around the World, 1985–2015: Patterns, Causes and Implications." WIDER Working Paper 2017/34, February, United Nations University–World Institute for Development Economic Research (UNU–WIDER), Helsinki.

Wood, Adrian, and Jörg Mayer. 2011. "Has China De-industrialised Other Developing Countries?" *Review of World Economics/Weltwirtschaftliches Archiv* 147 (2): 325–50.

Worku, Ibrahim Hassen, Mekdim Dereje, Bart Minten, and Kalle Hirvonen. 2017. "Diet Transformation in Africa: The Case of Ethiopia." *Agricultural Economics* 48 (S1): 73–86.

World Bank. 1992. "World Bank Structural and Sectoral Adjustment Operations: The Second OED Overview." World Bank, Washington, DC.

World Bank. 1993. *The East Asian Miracle: Economic Growth and Public Policy*. A World Bank Policy Research Report. New York: Oxford University Press for the World Bank. http://documents.worldbank.org/curated/en/975081468244550798/Main-report

World Bank. 2000. *Can Africa Claim the Twenty-first Century?* Washington, DC: World Bank.

World Bank. 2007. *World Development Report 2008: Agriculture for Development*. Washington, DC: World Bank. https://openknowledge.worldbank.org/handle/10986/5990

World Bank. 2014. "Republic of India: Accelerating Agricultural Productivity Growth." May 21, World Bank Group, Washington, DC. http://documents.worldbank.org/curated/en/587471468035437545/pdf/880930REVISED00ivity0Growth00PUBLIC.pdf

World Bank. 2015. *World Development Report 2015: Mind, Society, and Behavior*. Washington, DC: World Bank. http://documents.worldbank.org/curated/en/645741468339541646/pdf/928630WDR0978100Box385358B00PUBLIC0.pdf

Zhang, Longmei, and Sally Chen. 2019. "China's Digital Economy: Opportunities and Risks." IMF Working Paper WP/19/16, International Monetary Fund, Washington, DC.

Zilberman, David. 2014. "The Economics of Sustainable Development." *American Journal of Agricultural Economics* 96 (2): 385–96.

3

2007–2012 Food Price Spikes and Crisis— A Decade and a Half Later

Uma Lele, Manmohan Agarwal, and Sambuddha Goswami

Introduction

Nearly a decade and a half after the food crisis of 2007–8, this is an opportune time to look back at its causes and consequences and to ask:

1. What was the genesis of the food crisis, and the price rise and volatility that ensued for several years following the crisis?
2. What were the responses of international organizations and developed and developing countries to the crisis?
3. What lessons and implications were drawn for action, which are relevant for Sustainable Development Goal 2 (SDG2) going forward?
4. Have the responses of developed and developing countries and the donor community been commensurate with the challenges?

These questions need responses. What if similar conditions of successive droughts in major exporting countries, combined with national policies such as support for biofuels, are repeated in the future? And what are the lessons of the current COVID-19 crisis? The first two questions are addressed in this chapter. Lessons for SDG2 are explored in Chapter 4, and financing responses of developing and developed countries are considered in Chapter 7, as well as in Chapters 8 through 12 on the international organizations. Lessons of COVID-19, which were still unfolding as this book was being finalized, are discussed in Chapter 13.

Australia experienced drought conditions throughout the first decade of the new millennium, and as recently as the 2019–20 Australian bushfire season, starting with several serious uncontrolled fires in January 2019, an estimated 18.6 million hectares (46 million acres) had burned as of February 2020, with the largest loss of wildlife known to humankind in modern history, an estimated 1 billion Australian animals (Give2Asia 2020). Strong drought conditions during 2001–5 were due to El Niño, with extreme droughts in 2006 and 2007. Regional droughts and heat waves in the Ukraine and Russia occurred in 2007, then again in 2009, damaging wheat crops and causing global wheat price spikes (Janetos 2017). The record-setting drought in 2011–12 was the worst in the central regions of the United States since the 1930s, and California has had an extraordinary and ongoing drought during 2012–15 (Swain 2015). Since 2015, Australia, California, Brazil, and Indonesia have had some of the worst forest fires, arising out of and contributing to climate change. Figure 3.1 shows the fluctuating export volumes. Is the world prepared for similar circumstances?

Food for All: International Organizations and the Transformation of Agriculture. Uma Lele, Manmohan Agarwal, Brian C. Baldwin, and Sambuddha Goswami, Oxford University Press. © Uma Lele, Manmohan Agarwal, Brian C. Baldwin, and Sambuddha Goswami 2021. DOI: 10.1093/oso/9780198755173.003.0004

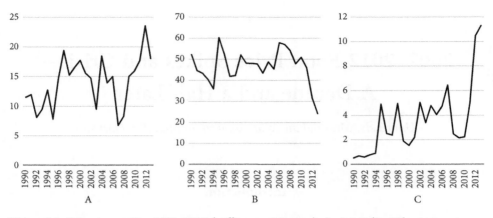

Figure 3.1 Export quantity, 1990–2013 (million metric tons): A. Australia: Wheat export quantity; B. United States: Maize export quantity; C. India: Rice (milled equivalent) export quantity

Source: http://www.fao.org/faostat/en/#data

The chapter is organized in three parts around these questions. In the first part, "A Perfect Storm," the first section presents some background, and the second section explores the different causes of the genesis of the crisis. The second part of the chapter, "Global Responses to the Crisis" addresses the proximate responses of international organizations and developed and developing countries to the crisis. The third part of the chapter, "Lessons Learned and Challenges of Implementation" summarizes lessons and implications drawn and challenges among countries. A wide variety of more organized responses of international organizations to the crisis are discussed in Chapters 5 and 8–12, after exploration of food security and nutrition issues in Chapter 4.

I. A PERFECT STORM

Background

Memories are short. Most of our (nonfood expert) interlocutors, while very familiar with the global financial crisis, could not recall the global food (and energy) crisis preceding the financial crisis in 2008. Yet, the food crisis was one of the most dissected events among agricultural economists during and following the crisis. Several factors were identified as villains of the piece, with different weights attached to each of their contributions. Some were completely off the mark. With the benefit of 20–20 hindsight and a telescopic view, new insights, perhaps, can be gained from this review conducted a decade later. We present the facts, as well as the way in which awareness of the causes of the crisis unfolded. The revised understanding, in turn, has affected responses of stakeholders. An important question is whether, with the information revolution, the quality of the information base and the speed with which information is made available to all concerned stakeholders have improved over time? The answer is partially yes.

The onset of the crisis was unanticipated by the development community at large, including by the World Bank Group (WBG) and the International Monetary Fund

(IMF), although agricultural prices had been rising since 2000 (Figures 3.2 and 3.3). The in-house independent evaluation of WBG's response to the food crisis noted this unexpectedness:

> The WBG mobilized itself quickly, compared with past crisis episodes. The additional funding it provided [to deal with the impact of higher oil and food prices] was sizable yet modest, compared to the fall in private capital flows to emerging and developing economies and to the assistance provided by some other sources (for example, the IMF and the European Union). (IEG 2009, v)

The World Bank had been concerned with the neglect of agriculture starting in the 1980s, a phenomenon discussed in detail in Chapter 8 on the World Bank (World Bank 2007; IEG 2013). The 1990s were frequently described as the "lost decade," and with good reason, as can be seen from the share of official development assistance (ODA) going to the Agriculture, Forestry and Fishing (AFF) sector, which plummeted from the peaks reached in 1983 (Figure 3.4). It is noteworthy, however, that the share of lending to the AFF sector in 2016 was about 5 percent of the total, compared to the 3.7 percent rock bottom reached in

Figure 3.2 Long-term Agricultural Commodity Price Index, 1900–2016 (1977–9 = 100)

Note: Based on the Grilli–Yang Commodity Price Index, combining food and nonfood agricultural commodities and deflated by World Bank MUV Price Index and US GDP Price Index.

Source: Pfaffenzeller, Newbold, and Rayner (2007), extended by Keith Fuglie, Economic Research Service, US Department of Agriculture.

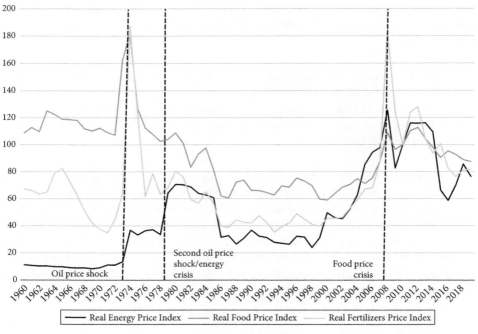

Figure 3.3 Real Energy, Food, and Fertilizers Price Index, 1960–2019 (2010 US dollars, using Deflator MUV Index 2010 = 100)

Source: Based on World Bank Commodity Price Data (The Pink Sheet), updated on August 4, 2020.

2005–6, but has never reached the peak, 20.4 percent of total lending, which occurred in 1983. Chapter 7 on the financing of structural transformation discusses these domestic and aid investment issues in more detail.

The *World Development Report 2008: Agriculture for Development* (World Bank 2007), drafted to highlight the importance of agriculture in development strategy, did not anticipate the crisis. The first-ever Independent External Evaluation (IEE) of the Food and Agriculture Organization of the United Nations (FAO), carried out in 2007, fared no better in predicting a crisis at the doorstep. The IEE was prompted by long-term concern among FAO's donor stakeholders that FAO itself was in crisis (FAO 2007). The IEE zeroed in on the reforms needed within FAO, as discussed in Chapters 6 and 9, but did not anticipate the impending world food crisis. In 2007, FAO's IEE panel, consisting of Uma Lele and Thelma Awori, visited some countries that were later seen as "crisis" countries. In 2007, these countries were engulfed in different internal political problems of their own, which also affected their agriculture.[1] This is not unusual. Like the attack on Pearl Harbor in the United

---

[1] In Bangladesh, with the fall of an elected government and threat of violence, a caretaker government was in charge, working towards restoration of democracy, which occurred in early 2009. In Thailand, the democratically elected Prime Minister Thaksin Shinawatra was ousted by a military junta, and the existing political institutions were dissolved. In Ethiopia, a low-grade conflict with the Somalian Ogaden region was underway. Food policy was a second-order issue in the context of these larger national political crises. Of the countries visited, only Tanzania was peaceful, and with its continuing liberalization, it was enjoying increased donor support and thriving foreign investment.

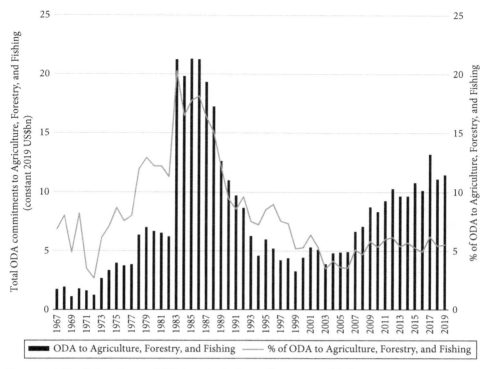

Figure 3.4 Declining share of ODA to Agriculture, Forestry and Fishing, 1967–2016
Source: Based on data from OECD.stat, http://stats.oecd.org/

States in 1941 and the Tet Offensive in Vietnam in 1968, which were not anticipated despite considerable intelligence, the COVID-19 pandemic at the end of 2019 was also not anticipated, notwithstanding repeated predictions by health experts.

Most analysts conclude that, in the short term, the higher food prices that ensued raised the poverty headcount in most developing countries, because poor farming households tend to be net purchasers of food and, generally, do not benefit from higher sales prices of their own production to offset the negative impact of higher food prices that they pay as net consumers. As a result, large numbers of rural households are pushed into poverty (Ivanic and Martin 2008; de Hoyos and Medvedev 2011; Ivanic, Martin, and Zaman 2012).

Estimating the number of poor people affected by the crisis was difficult, as "just-in-time" survey data on countries potentially affected by the crisis were not readily available. The FAO's iconic Prevalence of Undernourishment (PoU) was not meant to provide just-in-time estimates of the actual number of hungry, even under the best of circumstances, because of its method of estimation (Wanner et al. 2014; Lele et al. 2016) (see Boxes 3.1 and 3.2). FAO's Global Information and Early Warning System (GIEWS) keeps the world food supply/demand situation under continuous review, reports on the world food situation, and provides early warnings of impending food crises in *individual countries* (FAO 2020a), but it does not provide global estimates, as some authors have claimed (Headey and Fan 2008, 2010). The World Food Programme (WFP) has its own estimates, but its focus has been on countries in need of food aid, and the estimates were not suited to address a

---

Box 3.1 The Poor, Ultra-Poor, and Treatment of the Crisis by International Organizations

---

Michael Lipton coined the term "ultra-poor" to describe the plight of people who live in extreme poverty, earning less than $1.90 (originally $1 per day), and consuming less than 80 percent of their energy requirements, despite spending at least 80 percent of their income on food (Lipton 1986). In South Asia and sub-Saharan Africa (SSA), which are the global hot spots for hunger, the majority of the ultra-poor tend to be landless, marginalized populations, including rural women. An additional 2.1 billion people live on less than $3.10 per day in 2011 purchasing power parity (PPP), which is equivalent to the $2-a-day poverty line in 2005 PPP (World Bank 2012). Together, the poor and ultra-poor comprise nearly half of the world's population of 7.3 billion. Impacts of food prices on them are complex, depending on whether they are producers, consumers, or both, as we will see later. Food prices affect the poor disproportionately, however, with high impacts on their food consumption and health.

---

global food crisis (issues discussed in Chapters 4, 5, and 6 on "From Food Security to Nutrition Security for All," "Changing Global Governance Context for Food Security and Nutrition," and "Governance of the 'Big Five'," respectively).

FAO has since introduced a new measure called the Food Insecurity Experience Scale (FIES), which is a more direct measure of voices of the hungry. It is discussed in Box 3.2 in this chapter and in Chapter 4. The Independent Evaluation Group's (IEG's) evaluation of the World Bank's response to the crisis quoted the Bank's analysis, "The global crisis is expected to push more than 73 million people into poverty in 2009 alone" (IEG 2009, vi). A subsequent report, based on the work of Ivanic, Martin, and Zaman (2012) noted, "Simulation models suggested that poverty rose by 100–200 million people and the undernourished increased by 63 million in 2008," with figures later adjusted to 100 million in 2008, and 48 million in 2011 (IEG 2013, x). The work was tremendously influential, with impact on the World Bank strategy of emergency assistance, as discussed later in this chapter and in Chapter 8.

Developing countries initially reacted less to the food crisis than did international organizations. Accustomed to food shortages and confronted with important domestic political developments, our own field visits to Bangladesh, Thailand, and Ethiopia, as detailed in note 1, indicated that developing countries initially reacted to the food crisis in 2007, much as they had in the past, using an array of tools they had at their disposal. Case studies carried out by Pinstrup-Andersen (2015) and colleagues provide details. Hazell, Shields, and Shields (2005) showed that, in general, domestic shocks were a greater source of price variability than border prices.[2] Freer trade reduced price instability in small African countries, as we discuss later in this chapter. Circumstances of developing countries varied greatly, in terms of population sizes, prevailing per capita food availabilities, food policy histories, and degrees of external orientation, as described here.

---

[2] Pinstrup-Andersen (2015) showed the relative importance of domestic production variability versus international price variability.

Box 3.2   Estimates of the Number of Hungry: The Food and Agriculture Organization under Greater Fire than Other International Organizations

FAO came under greater criticism than the World Bank for allegedly exaggerating its estimates of the number of hungry, as a result of the crisis, and worse, was alleged to have used the crisis for its own purpose of bringing more business to the organization (Shelton 2013; Pinstrup-Andersen 2015). Our own research did not support such design. The reasons had parallels to those of the World Bank's varied estimates of the numbers of poor that were pushed below the poverty line—namely, the lack of timely availability of representative data on a scale that would enable regional and national estimates, and the time it would take to collect and process the data obtained from individual countries. FAO typically provides technical assistance and receives production estimates from governments, on the basis of which it prepares food balance sheets (FAO 2001; FAOSTAT 2019a, 2019b). FAO publishes food supply data as averages of three years, since harvest times vary around the world and, typically, governments issue first preliminary and then final estimates. Under pressure from the FAO's director-general at the time (who was, in turn, expected by Bretton Woods institutions to produce numbers for the IMF–World Bank Spring Meetings to highlight the issue to the policy-makers),[a] FAO staff drew on the IMF's projections (of decline) of the gross domestic product (GDP) and the United States Department of Agriculture (USDA) model predictions to prorate its Prevalence of Undernourished (PoU) estimates (King 2011; FAO et al. 2019, 148). The IMF later acknowledged that its projections of the likely decline in GDP in emerging countries turned out, in retrospect, to be too pessimistic (IMF 2015), and the USDA data covered only 70 countries, instead of FAO's global coverage, all of which led to a greater projected increase in the number of hungry (King 2011).

The need for better data, information, surveillance, and reporting is widely recognized by IMF, the World Bank, FAO, and the G20. Indeed, with the data revolution, satellites, and crowd sourcing, this state of affairs will likely change dramatically, provided FAO and other international organizations are funded adequately on a long-term, consistent basis to deliver results, with each playing to its comparative advantage and working cooperatively. FAO's inadequate funding to help developing countries generate high-quality, "just-in-time" agricultural statistics is discussed in Chapters 6 and 9.

A Lesson that Emerged: Need for Different Data for Different Purposes

Since the crisis, the "Voices of the Hungry" project has developed a new global standard for estimating the prevalence of food insecurity through the use of a tool popularly termed the Voices of the Hungry and technically known as the Food Insecurity Experience Scale (FIES) (FAO 2020b). An experience-based measure, the FIES is similar to measures used in the United States and in some Latin American countries to provide direct and timely food security metrics. The FIES has been adopted as a global indicator in the SDG process and will accompany the PoU in assessing progress toward SDG target 2.1. We should expect the FIES to provide timelier and more actionable estimates (FAO 2017).

[a]The numbers were displayed on a board outside the IMF and World Bank headquarters at 1818 H and Pennsylvania Avenue, in Washington, DC.

The Proximate Cause of the Crisis

The World Food Summit was held in Rome in 2008, with 180 countries participating. The subsequent publication of FAO's *State of Food and Agriculture 2008* (FAO 2008b) concluded that rapidly growing demand for biofuel feedstock, combined with heavy subsidies to biofuel production among the world's major food exporters, particularly in the United States and Europe, had diverted food production (corn, palm oil) to biofuel production and "contributed to higher food prices, which pose an immediate threat to the food security of poor net food buyers (in value terms) in both urban and rural areas" (FAO 2008b, 8).

Trade-distorting biofuel policies in developed countries may also have created the conditions for unfair competition for developing country producers of biofuels, perhaps also preventing a smooth transition to a lower carbon economy. As oil prices fell, market dynamics for biofuels also changed. Shale gas exploitation in the United States and slower economic growth in China also may have affected energy prices and, ultimately, prices for other commodities including biofuels and farm goods. Differences of opinion among members of the Organization of the Petroleum Exporting Countries (OPEC) on oil price policy, too, may have played a role at the time, as well as other geopolitical considerations (see Babcock [2011]; Meyer, Schmidhuber, and Barreiro-Hurlé [2013]; de Gorter [2014]; Schmidhuber and Meyer [2014]).

The *Agricultural Outlook 2010*, a joint publication of the Organisation for Economic Co-operation and Development (OECD) and FAO, contained projections of higher and more volatile food prices into the future, but food prices had started to decline after 2012 (Figure 3.2) (OECD and FAO 2010). With the low and declining food prices prevailing in 2016, the OECD–FAO *Agricultural Outlook 2016–2025* expected no significant changes in real terms until 2025 (OECD and FAO 2016). So much for predictions. As Yogi Berra supposedly said, "It's tough to make predictions, especially about the future."[3]

FAO was not alone. The World Bank and the International Food Policy Research Institute (IFPRI) had also suggested that prices would remain high and more volatile until at least the end of the next decade (World Bank 2013; Kalkuhl, von Braun, and Torrero 2016), and that the prices have resulted from a complex set of interactive factors, including rising energy prices, the depreciation of the US dollar, low interest rates, and investment portfolio adjustments in favor of commodities—all in turn related to a range of underlying global macroeconomic phenomena that have affected both food and nonfood commodities (Headey and Fan 2010).

Notwithstanding the difficulty of making predictions, there are real reasons for concern going forward. FAO's *State of Food and Agriculture 2016* warned of the impacts of climate change on agriculture (FAO 2016).

Since then, the latest reports by Rome-based agencies, as they began to be jointly issued, have stressed the increased incidence of hunger due to climate change and conflict. Such impacts could lead to a similar crisis, and it could well occur much earlier than might be predicted based on the existence of the 30–5-year food price cycle that Timmer suggested, following Bruce Gardner (Gardner 1979; Timmer 2009, 2010). FAO also highlighted the risk of trade policies of large, emerging countries—citing the case of China in destabilizing world markets by unloading their stocks (FAO 2016). India's export bans following the crisis had already been at the center of controversy (Sharma 2011).

---

[3] Neils Bohr, the respected physicist, is credited with saying something similar, as are others (see https://quoteinvestigator.com/2013/10/20/no-predict/).

In short, the crisis provided a real challenge to the world food system, shown in Figure 3.5. The diagram depicts the interacting paths that food travels from the farmer's field to consumers' plates, involving growing, harvesting, processing, packaging, transporting, and marketing through a combination of production, trade and aid, consumption, and disposal of food. Dynamic changes in the food system have occurred in how inputs such as energy are produced using agricultural lands and agricultural production. These energy inputs compete for cropland for food, influencing composition of output generated and highlighting the competing demands, between food and fuel, on what were previously seen largely as agricultural resources.[4] Food systems increasingly also highlight the fact that subsidies to biofuels and mandates created to mix ethanol with gasoline, as in the United States, once provided are difficult to withdraw. They also highlight interconnectedness of commodity and financial markets on a global scale. They serve domestic interests, such as for biofuels, which compete with global interests for an assumed global food supply that can meet the needs of consumers in import-dependent countries. As discussed in Chapter 4, the use of food systems as a basis for analysis identifies the inputs needed to undertake the activities that relate to the production, processing, distribution, preparation, and consumption of food, to generate the outputs at each step of the food system, and recognizes that food systems operate within and are influenced by social, political, economic, and natural environments.

Defining the Crisis

It is evident from the preceding discussion that prices were seen as the key barometer of the crisis. Concern about affordable access of the poor to food next ensued. The poor spend 50–80 percent of their income on food. In contrast, an average family in the United States spends 10 percent on food, and a European family, 15 percent (Bread for the World Institute 2013; Swinnen, Knops, and van Herck 2015). There was much confusion in the international discourse between price levels, rises, volatility, and spikes—vocabulary that quickly gained currency as part of the international discourse (Box 3.3) (see, also, Díaz-Bonilla and Ron [2010]; Tangermann [2010]).

Price transmission of producer-to-consumer prices was another issue of interest. Consumers in Europe and the Americas obtain most of their food in processed forms, in which the share of the cost of actual food ingredients at the retail level is relatively small, compared to transport, storage, processing, and packaging costs. Thus, international and domestic farm-gate food prices are not easily transmitted into consumer prices to the same extent as in developing countries, where most of the food sold at the retail level is without much value added.

The degree of transmission is also determined by the extent to which markets operate and the extent of transportation and storage costs, import and export taxes, and physical bans. Food prices play a significant role in domestic inflation in low- and middle-income

---

[4] Jonathan Hepburn, Senior Programme Manager, Agriculture, at the International Centre for Trade and Sustainable Development in Geneva, noted that agricultural resources have long been used for food, fiber, feed, and fuel (including vineyards involved in alcohol production for human consumption, and other nonfood industrial production such as rubber and cotton). "This comes back to the question of whether inadequate supply (availability) is the issue or whether the real concern is inadequate access to food due to low levels of purchasing power among poor people (i.e., problems associated with the persistence of poverty and inequality)" (personal communication, Jonathan Hepburn, February 19, 2018).

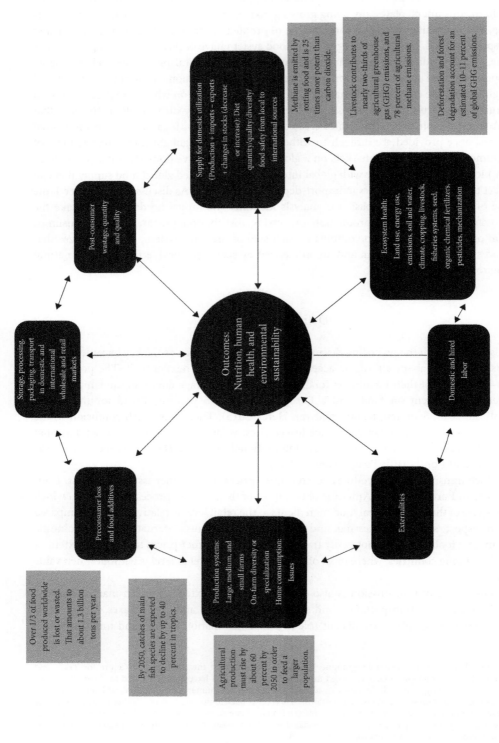

Figure 3.5 A food systems perspective on the food crisis
Source: Authors.

Box 3.3 Terminology that Acquired Currency in the Crisis

Analysis and debates focused on three interrelated price variables: volatility, spikes, and trends and related concepts[a]—for example, real prices measured after allowing for inflation rates, and prices quoted in dollars, based on changes in nominal and real effective exchange rates—the latter based on relative inflation rates in trading countries, as they explain impacts on consumers and producers.

Spikes and volatility are important in the short to medium term, and trends important for the long term. Furthermore, higher prices may ultimately reduce poverty while spikes do not (Ivanic and Martin 2014). Volatility is measured by variance within a period. Volatility is different from variance in terms of the amount of change that can occur at a point in time. Price spikes usually are sharp increases in prices from the trend lines: that is, large deviations from the trend line typically last for a short time and, therefore, are transient. There are hardly any examples of downward price spikes. This could be because large price drops lead to additional stockholding, while there are limits to the extent to which stocks (if they exist) can be released to moderate price increases (Deaton and Laroque 1996; Gilbert and Morgan 2010; Wright 2011a).

[a] Most analysts consider more than one of these issues, particularly in the post-2008 period.

---

developing countries because of the high share of consumer expenditures on food, and because both the level of inflation and the rate of change of prices influence consumer satisfaction with the government in power. Hence, food prices affect political stability—consequences range from city riots, as occurred in more than 30 countries during 2007–9, to voting at the ballot boxes. The proverbial onion prices in local markets decide election outcomes in India (Jadhav and Bhardwaj 2018).

There was relatively little mention of nutrition during the crisis—that is, of food quality and composition—even in international discussions, which described food security mainly as the poor's access to food and in terms of cereal prices and supplies. Nutrition burst onto the international agenda around the time of the crisis in 2007–8 (see Chapter 4). FAO's "State of Food Insecurity 2011" report briefly discussed impacts on nutrition. It was more the result, however, of the (parallel) advocacy underway by the nutritional community to bring nutrition back onto the global development agenda. Its timing happened to coincide with the crisis (FAO 2011).[5]

Figure 3.2 presents the Long-term Agricultural Commodity Price Index, from 1900 to 2016, and Figure 3.3 shows the Real Energy, Food, and Fertilizers Price Index from 1960 to 2017. After decades of decline, world food prices had begun to rise from about 2000. The food price rise and volatility reached the first peak in 2008, and following a short lull during 2009, surpassed its 2008 peaks. In early 2011, the World Bank's Food Price Index, which

---

[5] Lawrence Haddad differs with us on this issue and provided some samples of the mention of nutrition, some in his own writings. He, too, had complained in his blogs, however, that the SDGs were largely focused on hunger and not malnutrition (Haddad 2015). This situation, however, has changed over time. The 44th session of the Committee on World Food Security convened in Rome, October 9–13, 2017, with the theme of "Making a Difference in Food Security and Nutrition," and a particular focus on the Committee on Food Security (CFS) and the SDGs and nutrition (CFS 2017).

had declined by 30 percent from mid–2008 to mid–2010, rose sharply, reaching a peak again in February 2011. Then, in mid-2012, food prices escalated again, with the Food Price Index rising by 14 percent from January to August 2012, as world maize prices soared to an all-time high in July 2012 (surpassing their 2008 and 2011 peaks)—rising 45 percent within a month. Hepburn noted that different commodities exhibited different market dynamics, particularly rice and wheat (personal communication, Jonathan Hepburn, February 19, 2018). Nevertheless, price peaks in the recent period have not reached the high levels they did in 1974. Yet, the phenomenon came to be known as the "world food crisis," with much debate about the extent and causes of price rises, volatility, and spikes, and impacts on the poor (see World Bank [2017b]).

According to the analysis of de Gorter, Drabik, and Just (2013, 82), "the price increase in the corn market had a spillover effect on the wheat market and caused policy responses and speculation, including hoarding, which caused rice prices to spike." This situation led the researchers to conclude that "because of the sudden increase in commodity prices, the developing countries were unable to benefit from the higher prices, even though they have comparative advantage in biofuels production" (de Gorter, Drabik and Just, 2013, 82). The authors note that their conclusion was true of only a few developing countries.

The striking difference is the sharp rise in fertilizer prices in 2008, compared to the past, moving closely with food prices and steeply increasing the cost of production for fertilizer import-dependent countries.

Prices and Poverty

Impressive strides had been made in poverty eradication in developing countries since the 1980s, with a decline from 1.85 billion people living in poverty in 1990 to 767 million in 2013, and the share of poor people falling by three-quarters. The poor are defined as those earning incomes of less than US$1.90 a day in 2011 PPP (World Bank 2020). (For details on how poverty thresholds and levels have changed over time, with multiple poverty lines introduced in 2017, see Chapter 4.) Real food prices have seen a secular decline since 1900, with occasional price increases (Figure 3.2). The COVID-19 pandemic has at least tempo-rarily changed this direction (Laborde, Martin, and Vos 2020). The real food price decline explains a huge progress in food security, with food production growth outstripping population growth. However, most of this improvement in food security has occurred in East Asia and Southeast Asia, particularly in China, and more slowly in South Asia (SA), as we noted in Chapter 2. Thirty-four percent of the remaining global poverty and 34 percent of the hungry are in SA, compared to 51 percent of global poverty and 26 percent of the hungry in sub-Saharan Africa (SSA) (FAO 2020a). Such "just-in-time" estimations are hampered by lack of data in least developed countries (LDCs).[6]

Lipton stresses that subsistence and semi-subsistence farmers should be helped to increase their domestic production, even production that does not leave the farms, rather than focusing only on markets and trade (Lipton 2017). This should be done by increasing productivity. It is the most cost-effective way to increase their food security and nutrition.

---

[6] Seventy percent of the IDA countries in SSA have had no statistical survey in 15 years. According to the World Bank, over 70 countries do not meet the criteria of two surveys in a 10-year period at 5-year intervals (personal communication, Gero Carletto, July 2016). Many of these countries are in SSA. The data gap is much larger for food/calorie consumption and for gender.

There is clear evidence of progress on several other dimensions of SDGs, beyond the decline in poverty and hunger, which are discussed in Chapter 4.

Beyond the effects of food price increases on real incomes, many other factors intervene to affect poverty: family illnesses; unexpected epidemics of human, animal, and plant diseases; droughts, floods, variable and unpredictable rainfalls, rising temperatures, and loss of coastal areas; and conflict and terrorism (Krishna 2010). Those at the margin of subsistence fall into poverty as frequently as they get out of poverty, and these movements are not measured in the World Bank's type of poverty measurement. These transitory shocks are increasing with: (1) population pressure (UN 2015); (2) climate change; (3) soil degradation and loss of organic matter by erosion, salinization, nutrient depletion, and elemental imbalance; (4) decreased availability of water; (5) competition for land by biofuel and nonagricultural uses, including urbanization and brick-making; and (6) increased preferences toward more diversified diets, including fruits, vegetables, dairy, and animal-based diets, prices of which are rising far more rapidly than cereal prices (Sen 1987a, b; Lal 2013; Ganguly and Gulati 2015).

Again, at least two competing narratives about movement out of poverty exist, both relating to trends in farm sizes in developing countries. A CGIAR study presented a narrative of land consolidation in Asia (Masters et al. 2013), which also holds for China. The other concurrent narrative argues that farm sizes in major parts of the developing world have been declining, particularly in Asia and SSA; some farms amount to the size of "postage stamps" (Vyas 2016). Chand also provided evidence of declining and highly fragmented farm holdings in India (Chand 2016). Headey (2016) documented this global evolution of farming land, based largely on FAO data: "The spatial distribution of global farming land has changed dramatically, with developed countries substantially reducing their share of global agricultural land, and land-abundant developing countries [in North and South America] substantially increasing their share. In per capita terms, we see… average farm sizes increasing in rich and more commercialized agricultural systems, and generally declining or staying constant in poorer and less commercialized systems" (Headey 2016, 185).

In their volume entitled *Rising Global Interest in Farmland*, Deininger and Byerlee (2011) noted that data on land tenure and operational holdings are very poor. They indicated, "Data from country inventories highlight serious weaknesses in institutional capacity and management of land information…. Official records on land acquisitions are often incomplete, and neglect of social and environmental norms is widespread" (Deininger and Byerlee 2011, xxxii). With unclear boundary demarcations, tenure security is necessarily reduced and potential for conflict increased.

John Gibson noted that many studies have sought to measure the impacts of higher food prices on the welfare of consumers. He noted the lack of reliable data:

Real welfare levels in poor countries are rare since surveys prioritize collecting nominal living standards data over price data. Narrower questions about the impacts of prices on food quantity consumed and on the availability of nutrients are poorly answered. Most studies ignore coping responses that involved downgrading food quality to maintain quantity and therefore overstate nutritionally harmful effects of rising prices. A full accounting for the impacts of food prices on food security requires spatially detailed food price data and household survey data on both the quantity and the quality of foods. Surprisingly few developing countries have these required data. (Gibson 2013, 97)

Although the bulk of the poor still live in rural areas, a growing number are making their livings from diversified, nonfarm income. They depend on the market for food and are moving to urban areas to improve their livelihood prospects—or, with growing population densities, rural areas are being transformed into densely populated townships. With vast regional differences in endowments, stages of development, and histories of public policies, it is not surprising that the responses of developing countries have differed greatly. This raises major policy issues, which we take up in later chapters.

What Caused the Crisis?

Analysts from FAO, IFPRI, and the World Bank, as well as scholars like C. Peter Timmer (2010), Brian Wright (2011b, 2012, 2013, 2014a), Will Martin (Lin and Martin 2010), Per Pinstrup-Andersen (2015), and many others contributed actively to the understanding of the crisis and its impacts. The list of factors that analysts believed to have contributed to the crisis is long. It includes high energy prices, conversion of corn to biofuels, poor harvests in major exporting countries, low public sector stocks, export bans by a number of countries, poor information, an outsized financial bubble caused by the greatest recession since the Great Depression of 1929, the ensuing commodity speculation, and macro policies in a more integrated world, but also some misdiagnosed factors such as rising demand from China and India. FAO's *SOFA 2009* noted, "Each one of those causes commonly cited cannot of itself explain the pattern and extent of recent price movements. It is their coincidence and combination that accounts for the dramatic changes. While disentangling their separate effects is problematic, the evidence does point to biofuel demand and oil prices as the principal drivers" (FAO 2009, 22).

Asia as Culprit #1 Soon Dismissed

The initial tendency in developed countries was to attribute the food price rise of 2007–8 to the growing demand from China and India. It showed confusion between long-term demand growth and spikes caused by short- and medium-term factors. Asian policymakers were aggrieved at the G8 meeting in Japan in 2008, after US President George W. Bush and US Secretary of State Condoleezza Rice attributed the crisis to the rapidly growing Asian demand (Huang et al. 2008).[7] In particular, increase in meat consumption in China was believed to have created a derived demand for animal feed, contributing to the price increase. FAO and several others, in thorough analyses, pointed to the broadly stable shares of China and India in agricultural food commodity consumption, stressing that the two countries are largely food self-sufficient, with a declared policy of self-sufficiency, and are expected to remain so (Alexandratos 2008; FAO 2008a; Lustig 2008; FAO 2009; Baffes and Haniotis 2010; Headey and Fan 2010; Sarris 2010; Alexandratos and Bruinsma 2012). Furthermore, they did not change their net trade (Wright 2014b; Fukase and Martin 2020). Analysts from China and India also countered these observations early, noting the confusion between the long-term growth trends of Asian food demand and the

---

[7] They were not alone. A 2015 World Bank report noted that influential economists (Paul Krugman [2008]; Martin Wolf [2008]; Joel Bourne [2009]) had argued that rapid income growth in emerging economies, including China and India, was a key factor behind increases in food commodity prices after 2007 (World Bank 2015a).

consequences of the policies of biofuel subsidies and mandates in developed countries (Huang et al. 2008). The World Bank similarly noted that secular growth in China and India was not responsible for the sudden price increases (Mitchell 2008). Later, China and India each contributed to rising prices by imposing export bans, as described later. Subsequently, China also modified its biofuel policy (Huang et al. 2008).

Energy Prices, Biofuel Mandates, OECD Subsidies, and Global Food Security

By 2008, and continuing well into 2012, a strong consensus had emerged that biofuels were the game changer during 2005–15. FAO's *SOFA 2008: Biofuels: Prospects, Risks and Opportunities* emphasized:

> The rapid recent growth in production of biofuels was based on agricultural commodities, [and] the boom in liquid biofuels has been largely induced by [varied] policies in developed countries, based on their expected positive contributions to climate-change mitigation, energy security and agricultural development. The growing demand for agricultural commodities for the production of biofuels is having significant repercussions on agricultural markets, and concerns were mounting over their negative impact on the food security of millions of people across the world.... [T]he environmental impacts of biofuels are also coming under closer scrutiny. (FAO 2008b, back cover)

The United States, one of the largest world food exporters, diverted more than 40 percent of its corn in 2007 to biofuel production (US EIA 2012; Wise 2012). Babcock (2011) showed that US corn ethanol was mostly market driven, but government policies did play a role; Elliott (2015) found US governmental policies of subsidies and mandates were key to the rapid expansion of corn ethanol. High oil prices made ethanol a competitive substitute for gasoline. While the US Congress declined to extend the tax credit and tariff at the end of 2011, the Renewable Fuel Standard and blending mandate remained, keeping a floor beneath ethanol demand, though corn ethanol expansion slowed in the following years (Wisner 2014).

Other countries also contributed to this diversion of cropland to production for biofuels. US import quotas and internal, insulated sugar price supports initially depressed world sugar production and prices, leading Brazil to reallocate sugarcane production from sugar to ethanol markets. Brazilian sugar ethanol production also responded to increases in crude oil prices that have occurred since the mid-1970s. Wisner (2014) similarly showed the relationship between ethanol, gasoline, crude oil, and corn prices, including the role of US mandates to use ethanol in the crisis.

Maltsoglou, Koizumi, and Felix (2013, 104) in their paper, "The Status of Bioenergy Development in Developing Countries," noted that, with the exception of the United States, some European countries, and Brazil, bioenergy production "and more specifically, liquid biofuels... is still limited, especially in the case of Africa where the sector is still in its infancy." The authors provided a "detailed overview of production in the African, Asian and Latin American regions, illustrating how the three regions of the developing world are working toward bioenergy development, the strategies and policies, and the main hurdles being encountered" (Maltsoglou, Koizumi, and Felix 2013, 104).

As Hertel (2015) and others have noted, and Wright (2011a) concluded in his presentation to the annual Forum for Agricultural Risk Management in Development in Zurich in June 2011: "Food competing with biofuels can do more harm to the welfare of the poor and landless, globally, than the greatest conceivable aid efforts or productivity increases could compensate."[8] Other consequences of the US biofuel policy, even after the end of the crisis, include increasing the cost of livestock feed to farmers, inadequate supply of ethanol to meet the mandated requirements for mixing with gasoline in automobiles, and unanticipated delays in the second generation of cellulose biofuels (Elliott 2015).

In an earlier paper, "Market-mediated Environmental Impacts of Biofuels," Hertel and Tyner (2013, 131) noted, "despite all the research that has been done and all the advances made, there remains considerable quantitative uncertainty surrounding biofuels induced land use change. Obtaining precise estimates of these impacts is likely beyond the reach of current models and data."

Indonesia is critical in the biofuels debate. It is the largest producer of palm oil and contains some of the most carbon-rich peatlands and forests in the world. It also has the highest rate of tropical deforestation globally, caused largely by the drive for palm oil. This mix has contributed to Indonesia becoming one of the world's top 10 greenhouse gas emitters and the highest among them in terms of emission intensity: that is, emissions in relation to gross domestic product (GDP) (Ge, Friedrich, and Damassa 2014). According to some sources, the use of palm oil for European biofuels has increased sixfold since 2006 (Gerasimchuk and Koh 2013; Khairnur 2015). With decline in energy prices in 2019–20, others have dismissed the role of Indonesia in biofuels.

Higher fuel prices, as noted previously, encourage the switch to biofuels, and thus, reduction of crop production. Since biofuel policies in the United States and other OECD countries interact with fossil fuel energy markets, the level and variability of crop prices are highly susceptible to changes in oil prices, especially those that cause major shifts in transportation fuel demand. US fiscal and monetary policies magnified the crisis (Rausser and de Gorter 2015); beyond contributing to the 2007–8 food price volatility, the macro policies increased aggregate demand for food, fertilizers, and transportation services.

The net effect of these new causal mechanisms is that US biofuel policies ultimately increased, rather than lowered, world prices (without reducing volatility). High oil prices elevated crop prices in 2006–8; lower oil prices in 2008–9 spurred crop prices to plummet. Crop prices rose again to nearly the levels of the 2008 peak, and some studies have even argued that oil prices have led to increased food grain commodity prices (see, for example, Baffes and Haniotis [2010]). Rausser and de Gorter (2015) further noted that US agricultural and biofuel policies have not been the sole influences on commodities' prices, especially corn, soybean, and wheat prices.

Food prices spiked in 2008, and then again in 2013; and in 2020, they were at their lowest. Energy prices have had two important effects, by increasing (or decreasing) the price of fertilizers and by diverting corn to the production of ethanol, in addition to direct effects on farm sector costs of transport, heating, refrigeration, storage, and use of farm equipment. Although incentives for corn ethanol have weakened considerably, the mandates have remained in place. The US ethanol exports have increased by nearly 10 times in volume since 2006, and in 2013 they were slightly more in volume than those of Brazil (Roberts and Schlenker 2010; WTO 2016). With low gasoline prices, new stricter emission standards for

---

[8] Brazil's ethanol production comes mainly from sugarcane and, therefore, does not adversely affect Brazil's food-related exports, including soybeans in particular, but world sugar prices have been increasing.

automobiles, and the prospect of electric cars, the justification for investment in biofuels is weaker today than it was in the early 2000s, when the policies were introduced.

Biofuels may have less impact on food prices in the future, as alternative sources of energy become more attractive. By 2015, investment in biofuels fell by 35 percent to US$3.1 billion, whereas solar energy became the leading sector by far, in terms of money committed, accounting for US$161 billion (up 12 percent over 2014), or more than 56 percent of the total new investment in renewable power and fuels.

Derek Headey and Shenggen Fan, in *Reflections on the Global Food Crisis*, concluded:

> A major effect of rising energy prices was the consequent surge in demand for biofuels. Demand for biofuels had a stronger effect on maize than on other biofuel crops (such as oilseeds), although knock-on effects for other food items may have been substantial (especially for soybeans). Interestingly, ... the surge in U.S. maize production for biofuels was of an order-of-magnitude equivalent to the primary explanation of the 1972–74 crisis—the surge in U.S. wheat exports to the Soviet bloc. (Headey and Fan 2010, xiii)

Consequently, food prices have become intertwined with oil prices and are affected by policies that affect the demand for oil.

Since the crisis, there have been proposals for the United States to end biofuel subsidies or mandates (Elliott 2015), or to make them more flexible (FAO 2008a; G20 2011), so that in periods of crisis, more food supplies could be released to the world markets; or for the establishment of a global food safety net program, along the lines of the US food stamp program to protect the poor (Josling 2011; Díaz-Bonilla 2014).

Several policy changes concerning biofuel markets were finalized in Europe in 2015. In the European Union (EU), these included revisions to the Renewable Energy Directive and to the Fuel Quality Directive, with a 7 percent cap on renewable energy to come from food and feed crops in the transport sector by 2020. The United States, after a long delay, issued mandates in November 2015, higher than those that had been proposed earlier in the year, but considerably lower than the initial levels proposed in 2007 (OECD and FAO 2016).

Indonesia, previously one of the top biodiesel producers worldwide, saw production decline by roughly 60 percent. China's biodiesel production increased, almost overtaking Indonesia's 2015 levels (REN21 2016). According to the OECD–FAO *Agricultural Outlook 2016–2025*:

> Indonesian exports of biodiesel are expected to remain marginal ...
>
> The future evolution of energy markets, as well as possible policy changes are key uncertainties attached to the *Outlook* for biofuel markets over the next decade. However, given recent policy decisions, uncertainties concerning the future of biofuel markets should ease somewhat, at least over the short term. (OECD and FAO 2016, 117)

Payment for environmental services (PES) could arrest some of this land conversion. There is not yet a significant alternate market for environmental services. What exists is small and fragmented, based on aid resources (for example, Norway's funding for Brazil and Indonesia of US$1 billion each) and on domestic financing by middle-income countries—most notably, by China, which has brought nearly 35 million hectares of land under forests through PES (Uchida, Rozelle, and Xu 2009; Xu, White, and Lele 2010). More financing for environmental services and cost-effective alternative sources of energy, such as solar and wind energy, will reduce the economic attraction of biofuels. Expansion of wind and solar energy resources has occurred more rapidly than that of biofuels in recent years (REN21 2016).

The greater global market integration in 2007–8, relative to the 1970s, was an underlying factor in linking US markets with EU markets, and EU markets with those in Asia. Although the growth in agricultural trade has not been as rapid as trade in manufacturing, agricultural trade has grown considerably since the 1970s (Aksoy 2004; Xu 2015; Bouët and Laborde 2017). Developing countries have been important players as agricultural exporters and importers (Bouët and Laborde 2017). The policy responses of developing countries to the crisis were closely intertwined with their development concerns, no matter how poorly they were designed, implemented, and criticized by analysts, as we show here.

Whereas the food price rise (in 1972) preceded an oil price increase in 1973, as shown in Figure 3.3, and was accompanied by the huge monetary expansion to finance the Vietnam War and the largest US grain exports to the Soviet Union in history (Graefe 2013), the increasing price of oil also had another effect on food production. From 2000, the steady rise in fertilizer prices, caused by the rise in energy prices (Figure 3.3), has adversely affected the cost of food production. Currently, this is not the situation, as oil prices are very low. This situation was well documented in the case studies of developing countries in *Food Price Policy in an Era of Market Instability: A Political Economy Analysis*, edited by Pinstrup-Andersen (2015).

Declining and Low Grain Stocks and Stocks-to-Use Ratios

A major area of debate about food price increases in 2007–8 concerns the grain stocks-to-use ratios. Cereal stocks-to-use ratio reached an all-time low (20.7 percent) in 2007–8. Stocks and stock-to-use ratios were higher in 2017–18 (see Figure 3.6) (Lyddon 2017; FAO 2018). Equally important, information on stocks was not as readily and broadly available (Ghanem 2011).

In his article, "The Economics of Grain Price Volatility," Brian D. Wright argued:

> In 2007/08 the aggregate stocks of major grains carried over from the previous year were at minimal levels, much less than they would have been without mandated diversions of grain and oilseeds for biofuels which were so substantial that they could not be made up by a few years of yield increases, even if yields had not suffered due to years of global underfunding of research and diversion of resources from production-increasing research. Lack of stocks rendered the markets vulnerable to unpredictable disturbances such as regional weather problems, the further boost to biofuel demand from the oil price spike in 2007/08, and the unprecedented extension of the long Australian drought which would not, absent the mandates, have caused any great concern. (Wright 2011b, 56)

When stocks decline to a minimum feasible level, however, a modest supply reduction creates price volatility simply because it must reduce consumption demand, which requires a large increase in prices because consumption demand is inelastic. The resulting volatility may be exacerbated by hoarding and price insulation. Timmer (2010) contended that the export restrictions imposed by some of the major exporting economies induced panic buying by importers, such as in the Philippines, and hoarding by governments and other

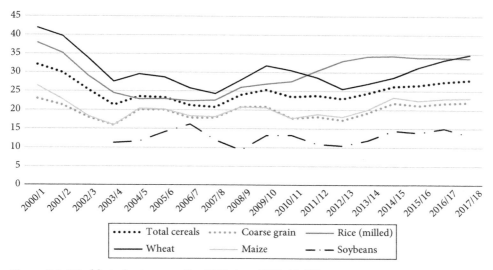

Figure 3.6 World stocks-to-use ratio, 2000–1 to 2017–18 (%)

Note: Data on soybeans are available from 2003–4.

Stocks-to-use ratio = (closing stocks/all forms of utilization); closing (or ending or carryover)

Stocks: Quantity of stocks at the end of the marketing year (before the following year's harvest), held at all levels within the food system, both by governments and by the private sector (including farm holdings and households). Closing stocks of a given marketing year are always identical to the opening stocks of the following year.

Domestic utilization includes food use, feed use, and other uses. Food use refers to direct human consumption.

Feed use refers to the quantities fed to livestock.

Other uses include seed, industrial use, and postharvest losses.

Seed: Quantity used for the planting of the following production cycle.

Industrial use refers to products intended neither for direct human consumption nor for feed. It includes the manufacture of secondary food products, such as starch, sweeteners, and alcohol.

Postharvest losses include losses incurred after harvest, from sorting, waste, storage, transport, packing, etc. For soybeans, the breakdown differs from that used for cereals; to reflect this, the relevant balance sheets are currently under modification.

See Agricultural Market Information System (AMIS) Database, http://statistics.amis-outlook.org/data/index.html#STATISTICALNOTES.

Source: Based on AMIS—Community Balance Sheet (AMIS 2011).

agents—and this caused the rice price spike. The sentiment has been echoed by others (Gilbert and Morgan 2010; Dawe and Slayton 2011; Wright 2011b).

The export bans, taxes, and hoarding raised prices more than they would have otherwise. The bans and taxes cut off importers from their usual suppliers. Timmer (2010) noted the same phenomenon with regard to rice in Asia, discussed later in this chapter in terms of the responses of developing countries. Timmer (2010) and Wright (2011b) argued, independently of each other, that hoarding keeps stocks from the needy in times of global stress on supplies, such as the period of excessive support of biofuels production.

The Role of Financial Speculation

The role of speculation has been controversial. Increased financialization of commodity markets meant that stockholdings and operations in future markets had to yield returns similar to other financial instruments. Among other causes, Headey and Fan (2010) attributed the crisis to exchange rates and speculation.[9] Modeling by Torero (2012) and others attributed increased stocks to significant financial flows into commodity markets. Cooke and Robles (2009); Robles, Torero, and von Braun (2009); and Gilbert (2010) showed that futures positions have huge effects on commodity markets (for details, see Kalkuhl, von Braun, and Torero [2016]). Similarly, Frankel (2008) noted, "A monetary expansion temporarily lowers the real interest rate (whether via a fall in the nominal interest rate, a rise in expected inflation, or both—as now)." Although the precise channels of transmission have remained in dispute, the latest evidence suggests that changes since 1995, in the intensity of financial speculation in grain and livestock futures and the world business cycle, taken together, have been an important driver of co-movements between food and financial markets, especially after 2005 (Bruno, Büyükşahin, and Robe 2017). Others have argued that the focus on the futures market is misplaced (Irwin, Sanders, and Merrin 2009).

Wright (2011b) argued, however, that speculation was not as important. He posited that if speculation were the cause of the price increases, then one should observe increased stocks, but the precise opposite had occurred.

II. GLOBAL RESPONSES TO THE CRISIS

Asian Countries' Responses to the Crisis

Countries in East and Southeast Asia and South Asia have used food price stabilization as an important part of their development strategy. And stabilization has remained a highly debated strategy, as we can see in the discussion here. Dawe and Timmer (2012) noted that most academic economists have objected to this strategy on at least four grounds:

> First, ... that trade restrictions reduce economic efficiency. Second, ... trade restrictions are not targeted to the poor and thus waste scarce resources. Third, ... [with] persistence of shocks to world prices, it is not possible to stabilize domestic prices without substantial fiscal costs. Fourth, ... trade based domestic stabilization policies destabilize the world market, thus making it worse for consumers in other countries relative to the counterfactual of no trade restrictions (see Anderson [2012]). [Dawe and Timmer argued that] while all of these objections have merit, they are all overstated. (Dawe and Timmer 2012, 128)

The sharp spikes in food grain prices in 2007–8, 2010–11, and 2012 provided motivation for the argument put forward by Dawe and Timmer. They argued that food price stability is crucial for macroeconomic stability and growth, because it protects the incomes of the poor who spend a large share of their income on food, particularly rice in the diets of most Asians (Dawe and Timmer 2012). They further suggest that:

> ... in poor countries, consumer and producer welfare should not serve as the shock absorber ...

---

[9]   Indeed, some of our interlocutors complained that IFPRI had not taken as firm a stand on the biofuel policies of the United States and the EU, or as frontally as it should have, stressing the need for independent policy analysis.

Probably the most serious objection to price stabilization programs is the practical difficulty that many governments have in implementing them in a cost-effective manner without destabilizing expectations ([G20 2011]; HLPE 2011 .... Price stabilization, which should ideally lead to domestic prices being equal to world prices on average over the medium-run, can also lead to domestic prices being consistently above world prices for extended periods of time, which hurts the poor because most of the poor are net buyers of food (FAO 2011). In the Philippines, price stabilization has turned into price support for farmers, even though it worsens poverty. (Balisacan, Sombilla, and Dikitanan 2010)

The countries most successful at this task are in East and Southeast Asia, although the experience in South Asia discussed in this chapter also has been instructive.

In a personal exchange with Madhur Gautam, however, he commented, "in a more general equilibrium sense, in the long run stabilization erodes farmer incentives to improve productivity and production, and a slow rate of growth persists. This was observed in other places, too (for example, in Tanzania), where governments imposed ad hoc export restrictions to keep the price from rising, and hence, the domestic production levels never reached [the] 110 percent (or whatever) self-sufficiency levels the policymakers wanted. Clearly, with closed borders, any increase in production leads to a lower domestic price" (Madhur Gautam, personal communication, June 17, 2020).

On the other hand, several countries experienced the fastest poverty reduction between 2005 and 2012—and many people complained that this was not "real," but driven by higher food prices. What happened? After the initial shock (bad for consumers but good for farmers), the supply response kicks in and, in turn, higher food prices translate into higher wages, resulting in more widespread poverty reduction. Seemingly counterintuitive, it actually makes a lot of economic sense. This is also what happened in India. While the prices were kept stable, over time there was a translation of global price increases to the Indian market as well. An excellent study by Hanan Jacoby (2016) showed how the rise in rural wages in India outpaced urban wages during this period, with wages rising faster where output price increases were higher. In other words, the empirical evidence, at least in this case—as well as for Bangladesh and Nepal—bears out the theory that dynamic general equilibrium results.

Of the 81 developing countries surveyed by FAO to assess their responses to the crisis, 43 reduced import taxes, and 25 (mostly in Asia) either banned exports or increased taxes on them (Demeke, Pangrazio, and Maetz 2009). Forty-five developing countries implemented measures to provide relief or partial relief from high prices to consumers. Having failed in curbing exports by imposing an export tax (that is, a minimum export price higher than the world price), India announced a complete ban on exports of non-basmati rice in April 2008—a policy that the government could enforce (Saini and Gulati 2015). Other rice-exporting countries followed suit with their own controls, and rice prices started to spike. For imposing a complete ban, India became a whipping boy of donors, in 2005–6, when its wheat stocks reached an all-time low due to bad weather and excessive exports, and when India's milder approach of discouraging exports by imposing export taxes, which it tried first, did not work (Figure 3.7) (Hindu Business Line 2017; MoneyControl.com 2017a, 2017b, 2017c; Mukherjee 2017).

Indonesia similarly tripled its domestic stocks from 1 to 3 million. Timmer (2010), an ardent supporter of price stability, argued after the crisis that China, India, and Indonesia, collectively, protected 2 billion people in a second-best world, and that Indonesia and India, both democratic governments, were richly rewarded in the 2009 elections for having imposed export bans and maintained price stability. Anderson, Ivanic, and Martin (2014)

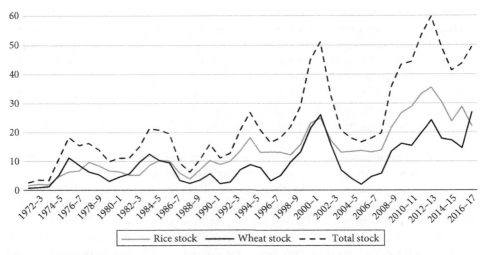

Figure 3.7 Total food grains stock in India, 1972–3 to 2016–17 (million metric tonnes)

Note: Stock at end of March, and total stocks include rice, wheat, and coarse grains.

Source: Food Corporation of India; and Ministry of Consumer Affairs, Food and Public Distribution, Government of India.

estimated that their price insulation contributed about 60 percent of the upward pressure on world rice prices.

Indonesia's overall trade regime has been relatively open, with low tariffs. Yet, in the case of rice, the country established a complete ban on rice imports in April 2006, leading to a 30 percent increase in rice prices over the April 2005 level. The World Bank argued that the import ban led to a significant upturn in poverty during 2006 (World Bank 2008). Timmer, in his previous writings, had explained China's agricultural policies of keeping producer prices high as a way to contain rural unrest. Jikun Huang, founder and director of the Center for Chinese Agricultural Policy of the Chinese Academy of Sciences, confirmed this in a personal communication (July 2015). Given China's history of political movements beginning in rural areas, the avoidance of restlessness in rural populations is an understandable concern for a country that does not tolerate political instability. The defeat of the Bharatiya Janata Party government in India, in the 14th Lok Sabha (general) election of 2004, was often explained by the hollowness of the campaign slogan "India Shining."

Beyond the role of agriculture in macroeconomic impacts, there is extensive debate about the effectiveness of the price stabilization programs in achieving anti-poverty objectives, and considerable experimentation is underway in Asia, as discussed later in this chapter. The general conclusion in the case of Asian countries is that price stabilization policies have been effective and important for political stability as well, albeit at huge fiscal costs.[10] The latter concern is leading to reforms in making stabilization more cost-effective.

A political consensus has emerged in large Asian countries, such as India, Indonesia, and China, that stable consumer and producer prices are essential for political stability and that a combination of trade and stabilization policies is essential to achieve price stability. Asian countries have largely attempted to smooth out fluctuations in international prices, rather

[10] The costs of alternate scenarios are never calculated. Not controlling prices may lead to political turmoil, resulting in large growth and fiscal costs, and importing food would have costs in terms of, perhaps, a balance of payments crisis.

than be out of line with them. Dawe and Timmer (2012) provided a thoughtful case for this argument. Saini and Gulati (2016) argued that this alignment is truer with respect to India than to China. (See, also, an analysis of public stockholding programs for food security [Montemayor 2014].) Free traders agree that Asian countries have often succeeded in stabilizing domestic prices but claim that, with better policies for stabilization, costs could have been lower (Gouel, Gautam, and Martin 2016). We return to these arguments at the end of the chapter. Furthermore, Will Martin notes that whereas this argument applies to countries individually, if advising the minister of a small country, he would agree that price insulation is an effective, low-cost way of stabilizing domestic prices relative to world prices. The problem occurs when almost everyone does it, so it does not actually stabilize prices much, or at all, unless a country stabilizes more than the average. And everyone cannot stabilize more than the average (Will Martin, personal communication, May 17, 2020). Critics of public intervention have also argued that trade insulation increased prices and volatility in international markets (FAO, IFAD, and WFP 2011).

Public Intervention in Africa

In the case of SSA, import dependence for rice and wheat has steadily increased, but the imports are still small in the context of world markets. Jayne and Minot (2014) and others (including case studies from Pinstrup-Andersen [2015]) have argued that domestic price stabilization policies in Eastern and Southern Africa have had the contrary effect of destabilizing prices. "By accepting a moderate level of price fluctuation within established bounds under a rules-based approach to intervention, African governments will reduce their chances of facing severe food crises" (Jayne 2012, 143).

OECD policies of protection, on the other hand, first caused a decline in international agricultural prices, thus providing disincentive to production of commodities such as sugar and cotton in developing countries, and later, by diverting production to biofuels, caused a rise in prices for which developing countries were not prepared.[11]

Use of export quantitative restrictions (QR) is a continuing problem in Africa. Governments continue to look at food availability, rather than access, and use QR policies that create volatility both at home and abroad. While this is similar to India's QRs during the 2008 food crisis, African countries do not have the ability to stabilize their markets via costly storage, so they end up with increased price volatility at home and abroad (Will Martin, personal communication, May 17, 2020). For an example of a ban on exports from Zambia, see Koo, Mamun, and Martin (2020).

Small, import-dependent countries in Africa were thus deeply affected by the food and economic crises. The countries most exposed to price swings on international markets were typically poor and food importers, and most were in Africa (FAO, IFAD, and WFP 2011; Konandreas 2012; Valdés and Foster 2012). The countries had few reserves and inadequate budgetary means to procure food at high prices; generally, they also lacked the option of restricting exports, although some, such as Malawi, Ethiopia, Kenya, and Zambia, did so

[11] The Uruguay Round disciplined the policies of OECD, which was initially reluctant to engage in trade negotiations, and particularly the EU. It was the eighth round of multilateral trade negotiations conducted under the General Agreement on Tariffs and Trade (GATT), from 1986 to 1993, involving 123 countries as "contracting parties." Effectively, it was a round of negotiations by and for developed countries, but with little voice or attention to the concerns of developing countries.

(Chirwa and Chinsinga 2015). They had to bear the brunt of the crisis, and domestic staple food prices rose substantially in these countries. For example, rice prices increased considerably in Senegal, following the export bans on rice imposed by several Asian countries. Some researchers on Africa have shown, however, that unlike in Asia, public intervention has not stabilized African food prices (Jayne 2012; Jayne and Minot 2014). On the contrary, it has contributed to instability by untimely and unpredictable behavior of marketing parastatals.

Structural adjustment led to the elimination of government interventions in food markets, with the expectation that the private sector would take its place. After liberalization in the 1980s, however, the private sector did not effectively take the place of marketing boards as fast and as effectively as external reformers had expected in Africa (Lele 1991a, 1991b). This was due in part to the very limited infrastructure, high internal transportation costs, poor market information, and landlocked nature of some countries: for example, Malawi and Zambia. Markets work when (1) there is competition in trading; (2) farmers have free and unfettered market access; (3) transportation costs are low; and (4) information flows effectively (Lele 1990). Far too often these conditions have not prevailed in Africa. Ethiopia's large investment in physical infrastructure is paying off in improving market access (Bachewe et al. 2015).

In addition to promoting a privatized market setting (Byerlee, Jayne, and Myers 2005), the World Bank promoted new market-based institutions and private risk management institutions, including futures markets, crop insurance, and forward pricing, arguing that trade liberalization was an important component of the strategy. These have been implemented in many countries with somewhat mixed success. A key problem is that they find it difficult to manage shocks arising from unpredictable government policies, such as export bans.

The need for some seasonal storage by the public sector is recognized (see, for example, Basu 2015). Storage by farmers, using warehouse receipts to get credit, is also recognized and increasingly encouraged: for example, in Ethiopia (Minot and Mekonnen 2012). International trade can help mitigate production shocks through intra-annual response, reducing commodity inventories and storage costs, improving efficiency, and reducing the variance of crop prices. The dynamic, long-run implications of these effects on global food markets could be considerable (Lybbert, Smith, and Sumner 2014).

African market development needs a consistent, predictable, gradual approach, including substantial investment in physical infrastructure, information, storage, and access to credit, among other requirements. Because markets do not work, traders lobby to keep control of markets. Critics have argued that government intervention can exaggerate price instability, unlike in Asia where it has stabilized prices. Since it is unlikely that public intervention in markets will disappear completely anytime soon, public policy needs to focus on cost-effective public interventions, transition to public and private partnerships, economic analysis, transparent rules, and routine improved management of public sector interventions (Lele 1971). There have been analytical/advisory efforts to this effect in Asia, as we discuss later in the chapter.

Responses of Governments in Latin America

Even though many countries in Latin America are major exporters, Krivonos and Dawe, editors of *Policy Responses to High Food Prices in Latin America and the Caribbean*, concluded:

> Governments in Latin America applied an array of policy measures in reaction to skyrocketing food prices, attempting either to contain the pass-through of world prices

to consumers or to mitigate the negative consequences of high food prices through transfers and food distribution. Market interventions to influence domestic prices ranged from border measures to direct state purchasing and distributing of staple foods, primarily cereals. At the same time, the vast majority of the countries in the region reinforced programmes to stimulate production, typically by providing farmers with inputs, access to credit and technical assistance. Some countries [most notably, Brazil and Mexico] counteracted the negative implications of the price spikes by expanding safety nets to compensate for the loss of consumers' purchasing power... Other mitigation strategies included the development of local markets and rural infrastructure to improve the flow of food products from farms to cities, encouraging the diversification of consumption to include traditional and locally produced products...

Policy makers... focused on the reduction or elimination of import tariffs and the imposition of export restrictions on some key products. (Krivonos and Dawe 2014, 189)

Most importantly, with disorderly international markets and a lack of timely market information, developing countries lost confidence in the reliability of the international food markets, leading to increased support for the rhetoric of food self-sufficiency, some of which has since receded into the background. Indeed, even donors were beginning to change their stance. For example, the US State Department and the US Agency for International Development (USAID) were advising policymakers in countries like Morocco to focus more on food self-sufficiency and less on export orientation, quickly reversing their own earlier advice and astonishing aid recipients (interviews with national policymakers in Morocco and Bangladesh). This experience brought home the need to establish market information. The Agricultural Market Information System has been one of the few significant responses to the crisis, among the many recommended by the two interagency reports addressed to G20 after the crisis (G20 2011; Bioversity et al. 2012) (Box 3.4).

Box 3.4 The Agricultural Market Information System

The Agricultural Market Information System, established at the request of the Agriculture Ministers of the G20 in 2011, has improved trade information on stocks and prices.[a] AMIS is one of the most successful post-crisis initiatives (others are discussed in Chapter 4).

Yet, there is scope for further improvement. The Doha Round of talks of the World Trade Organization and recommendations by international agencies have seen little progress. The huge tasks of investment in transport, communications, ports, and storage facilities with big investment implications remain to be addressed.

The Agricultural Market Information System (AMIS) is an inter-agency platform to enhance food market transparency and policy response for food security. It was launched in 2011 by the G20 Ministers of Agriculture... Bringing together the principal trading countries of agricultural commodities, AMIS assesses global food supplies (focusing on wheat, maize, rice and soybeans) and provides a platform to coordinate policy action in times of market uncertainty. (AMIS 2015)

[a] According to the AMIS website (http://www.amis-outlook.org/amis-about/en/).

Issues between Developed and Developing Countries Highlighted by the 2007–8 Food Crisis

OECD's Support to Agriculture

The high level of OECD support (Producer Support Estimates) has been a disincentive to production in developing countries, and it is good that the support has been declining (OECD 2016). The IMF's independent evaluations have noted its unequal treatment of developing countries with regard to agricultural subsidies in the course of loan negotiations. In comparison to the light or nonexistent treatment of agricultural policies in developed countries—where historically, the IMF only conducted surveillance—in developing countries, it provided loans for stabilization programs (IMF 2009). Having reduced their protection in the 1990s, however, emerging countries in recent years have begun to provide significant levels of support, particularly for import-competing commodities, which are converging with the levels of support provided by OECD countries (Figure 3.8) (Anderson

A   B

Figure 3.8 Evolution of Producer Support Estimates, 1995–2016 (% of gross farm receipts) compared to Chinese and OECD agricultural producer subsidies, 1990–2016 (US$bn)

A. Evolution of Producer Support Estimates, 1995–2016 (% of gross farm receipts)

Notes: The OECD total does not include the non-OECD EU member states. The Czech Republic, Estonia, Hungary, Poland, the Slovak Republic, and Slovenia are included in the OECD total for all years and in the EU from 2004. Latvia is included in the OECD and in the EU only from 2004.

The emerging economies are Brazil, China, Colombia, Costa Rica, Indonesia, Kazakhstan, the Philippines, Russia, South Africa, Ukraine, and Vietnam. Vietnam and the Philippines are included from 2000 onward. The 2016 data for Indonesia were not available and proxies were used instead.

Source: Adapted from OECD (2017, Figure 1.6, 41); OECD (2019) and OECD Stat: http://dx.doi.org/10.1787/888933506493

B. Chinese agricultural producer subsidies now equal those of all OECD countries combined: Producer Support Estimate (PSE), 1990–2016 (US$bn)

Source: OECD (2019), 2017 Producer and Consumer Support Estimates, OECD Agriculture statistics (database); http://stats.oecd.org/viewhtml.aspx?QueryId=77838&vh=0000&vf=0&l&il=&lang=en

2010b; OECD 2017). Norway, Switzerland, Iceland, Korea, and Japan still have high levels of protection, and among emerging countries, China, Indonesia, Turkey, the Philippines, and Colombia have protection levels about half the size of the former group of countries.

In the case of China, prices are higher, compared to the world market prices. Furthermore, whereas the EU has largely moved to non-production-distorting income support, the United States has moved in the opposite direction, to a form that distorts commodity production (OECD 2017). Anderson (2010b) supported the argument that protection of import-competing commodities leads to higher food prices, and its overall impact on poverty is generally adverse. Martin argues that, in the longer term, exogenously higher prices tend to lower poverty (Ivanic and Martin 2014).

Citing Ivanic and Martin (2008), Anderson (2010a, 3244) elaborated, "A new proposal for agricultural protectionism in developing countries...is based on the notion that agricultural protection is helpful and needed for food security, livelihood security, and rural development. This view has succeeded in bringing 'Special Products' and a 'Special Safeguard Mechanism' into the multilateral trading system's agricultural negotiations, despite the fact that such policies, which would raise domestic food prices in developing countries, could worsen poverty and the food security of the poor." Hertel has argued that special products are a disastrous idea. A key problem is that they are a quantitative restriction that would destabilize markets (Hertel, Martin, and Leister 2010).

Agricultural Policies of Large Developing Countries in Asia: The World Trade Organization and Emerging Food Policy Issues

Among emerging countries, Brazil and South Africa have had relatively open agricultural trade policies. Protection of small farmers through input subsidies and minimum prices has been an important feature of agricultural policies in China and India, each with high levels of grain stocks (see Box 3.5). India and China, joined by the "G–33" countries (actually

---

Box 3.5 Food Self-Sufficiency and Price Stabilization Policies of China and India

China

China is trying to increase domestic production (Ni 2013), but balancing supply and demand has not been easy (Yu 2017). It is proposing to involve the private sector in domestic purchases and storage. In 2016, China had accumulated substantial surpluses, with maize stocks rising from an estimated 45 million tons in 2005, to over 100 million tons in 2015. By 2013–15, stock-to-use ratios had reached 40 percent for wheat, 45 percent for maize, and above 60 percent for rice. The change in the internal terms of trade seems to have been a result of the food crisis, which led China to double down on the pursuit of food self-sufficiency (Huang, Yang, and Rozelle 2015). At the beginning of the crisis, China released the government's grain reserves, entered into long-term future/

Continued

Box 3.5 Continued

forward contracts with trading firms in exporting countries, canceled support for storage and transport of export grains, increased subsidies on grain production and input, and enhanced social protection for urban consumers. China is exceptional in the extent to which it learned lessons and improved its long-term strategy—for example, in addition to revising its internal biofuels strategy, it has increased investment in research and development (R&D).

China put into place a variety of policies to achieve national self-sufficiency. They included: minimum prices for rice and wheat, ad hoc interventions for maize, direct payments to support grain production, transfer payments to major grain-producing counties, and comprehensive subsidization of agricultural inputs (see Figure 3.8), as well as buffer stock norms and a few planting directives. Although price support also exists for cotton and oilseeds, persistently higher returns for grains have led to land being allocated to grain production, especially maize. With stocks rising and increasing food demand, China decided to align domestic maize prices more closely with world prices, with maize farmers receiving a deficiency payment equal to the difference between the market price and a target price since 2016. The abolition of minimum prices and the unavoidable release of stocks was expected to lower domestic prices. If the stocks-to-use ratio were to fall to a more sustainable 30 percent (implying a total of 66 MT), then about 35 MT would need to be released. The release of stocks tends to lower domestic prices, but some of the effect would be offset by increased domestic quantities demanded at lower prices. If stocks were released gradually (say, at 5 MT per year), it could add 4 percent to annual trade in 2016 (or 130 MT) and 0.5 percent to world supplies (which run at 1,000 MT). The substitution of maize for barley, sorghum, and distiller's dried grains with solubles (DDGS) would potentially result in much bigger effects on these markets. China's self-sufficiency policy has raised domestic prices and production, leading to huge stocks—100 million tons of maize—but China can hardly be described as reluctant to trade. In 2014–15, China imported 84.5 million tons of soybeans and 10 million tons of wheat, and maize imports reached 8.9 million tons in 2015. With mounting surpluses, the USDA expects its storage losses could amount to US$10 billion (see Gan 2017). China has set its minimum support price (MSP) for wheat produced in 2018 at Yuan 2,300/MT ($345.94/MT), down Yuan 60/MT from the current level (has been unchanged since 2014, at Yuan 2,360/MT for major wheat producing areas); for the first time since 2006, a downward revision was made when China introduced the MSP for wheat (S&P Global/Platts 2017).

India

India spent an estimated US$18.5 billion on subsidies annually and will spend US$4 billion annually under its right to food law, which will provide affordable food to 800 million people. Basu (2015) and others (Gulati and Saini 2015; Chand 2016; Gouel, Gautam, and Martin 2016) have noted that price stabilization has been successful in India, but it has been abominably unsuccessful as an anti-poverty program. India's food policy is highly contested within India, even among Indian intellectuals. India's stabilization policies entail a combination of MSPs, food procurement and distribution, and trade policies. The World Bank and FAO estimated the storage costs of the Food Corporation of India (FCI) to be four times higher than long-run costs estimated for other countries (World Bank and FAO 2012; Gouel, Gautam, and Martin 2016). Such high costs make it difficult to justify public storage on economic grounds, as it would be much less costly to rely on domestic private storage or on world trade and storage abroad. Gouel, Gautam, and Martin (2016) demonstrated that, in India in the current circumstances, significant cost savings could be made through a combination of storage and trade costs, without any significant net loss in pure welfare (defined as the sum of producers' or consumers' surplus), through a more open trade policy together with storage rules that are similar to, but above competitive storage levels. Some within India, however, argue that as the country is a large buyer, world market prices rise when it goes on the world market to make purchases (see discussion in Hoda and Gulati [2013]).

47 World Trade Organization [WTO] member countries) have been involved in an extended dispute with the United States and the EU, described subsequently in the chapter. Separately, the United States launched a complaint against China in September 2016, for providing domestic support to wheat, rice, and corn (Mehra 2018). The complaint was joined by the EU and a number of Asian and Latin American countries, including India.

Critics of the Indian food policy have argued that, instead of supporting agriculture by distortionary input subsidies, India should invest more in agricultural support of the Green Box variety,[12] particularly in public goods, in support of smallholder agriculture (Meijerink and Achterbosch 2009)—a criticism with which we concur and that we discuss further in Chapter 7 on the financing of agriculture.

OECD's monitoring of price behavior included 49 countries that contributed 88 percent of value-added to world agriculture, but it did not include India, the world's second largest producer of rice, wheat, and other cereals. A major global trader, India was at the center of the export ban controversy during the crisis in 2007–8, and in the negotiation of the Bali Package at the 9th WTO Ministerial Conference (FAO 2014). Countries like India sought to achieve a "permanent solution" on public food stockholdings at Buenos Aires but talks ended with no conclusive agreement (see Box 3.6 on the WTO and the controversy). India joined in the OECD monitoring of price behavior in 2017.[13]

---

[12] The Green Box is a term used by the WTO in generally describing subsidies. The colors of boxes correspond to those of traffic lights: green (permitted), amber (slow down—that is, needs to be reduced), and red (stop or forbidden). The WTO explains, "In agriculture, things are, as usual, more complicated. The Agriculture Agreement has no Red Box, although domestic support exceeding the reduction commitment levels in the Amber Box is prohibited; and there is a Blue Box for subsidies that are tied to programmes that limit production. There are also exemptions for developing countries (sometimes called an 'S&D Box')" (WTO 2020). For a further discussion, see Chapter 7 on financing in this volume.

[13] See the OECD document, "Review of Agricultural Policies in India" (TAD/CA(2018)4/FINAL), http://www.oecd.org/officialdocuments/publicdisplaydocumentpdf/?cote=TAD/CA(2018)4/FINAL&docLanguage=En

Box 3.6 The World Trade Organization

The world trading system is under stress from a variety of sources: climate change, environmental degradation, unpredictable energy prices, biofuel policies, price volatility, the changing nature of global and national food stocks, policies of major exporters that jeopardize free and fair trade, changing long-term supply and demand patterns, incomplete information, and unequal bargaining power among trading partners. Global trade agreements, on the other hand, have almost single-mindedly focused on freeing up international trade and have not been able to address many of the issues that hinder free and fair trade. The World Trade Organization (WTO), an intergovernmental organization that regulates international trade, was officially established on January 1, 1995, under the Marrakesh Agreement signed by 123 nations on April 15, 1994, replacing the General Agreement on Tariffs and Trade (GATT), which was established in 1948. When the Agriculture Agreement of the Uruguay Round was signed by ministers of agriculture in Marrakesh in 1994 to establish the WTO, the global environment for trade was very different. The Uruguay Round, negotiated with a large voice for developed countries, was a significant first step towards fairer competition, and a less distorted sector. WTO member governments agreed to improve market access and reduce trade-distorting subsidies in agriculture, which had been in place since the 1930s in response to food shortages during the pre- and post-Second World War periods. The commitments to reduce trade-distorting subsidies were to be phased in over six years from 1995 for developed countries, and over 10 years for developing countries. Meanwhile, members also agreed to continue the reform.

Further talks, which were separate from the committee's regular work, began in 2000. They were included in the broader negotiating agenda set at the 2001 Ministerial Conference in Doha, Qatar. The so-called Doha Development Round, or Doha Development Agenda (DDA), is the latest trade negotiation round of WTO, commenced in 2001. Its objective has been to lower trade barriers around the world and facilitate global trade, but by 2016, Doha had stalled, owing to disagreements among members on the terms of the next agreement—a period in which world agricultural trade, including, in particular, the role of developing countries, had increased substantially. However, developing countries were divided in their interests among exporters and importers, middle- and low-income countries, and import-dependent countries.

Thus, at the WTO Ministerial Conference in Bali (MC9) in December 2013, several proposals were presented to resolve the predicament of developing countries that were at risk of violating WTO rules on domestic support because of their public stockholding programs, which provide market price support to domestic producers. The problem is that the same price is used for Public Distribution System (PDS) targets and price stabilization. The two could be separated, the strategic stockpile at the MSP, to be counted against the domestic support limit, and for PDS, purchases made at market prices.

In Bali, WTO ministers decided to temporarily shield such programs from challenges until a "permanent" solution could be worked out. Under the WTO Agreement on Agriculture, the distortive effect of market price support programs can be quantified into a product-specific Aggregate Measurement of Support (AMS). This is equal to the difference between a fixed external reference price and an applied administered price, multiplied by the quantity of the product that is eligible to receive the administered price. The resultant AMS figure must not exceed the de minimis value for such product, which is a prescribed percentage of the value of annual production of the said product. Unfortunately, the external reference prices based on import prices during 1986–8 are hopelessly out of date. Consequently, their variance from current administered or buying prices has increased significantly over time and now risks placing some countries in breach of their de minimis caps. Montemayor (2014) presented several soft and hard options to arrive at a permanent solution, including the use of dollar prices instead of local currency prices, shifting to subsidies on inputs provided they are directed to poor deserving farmers, and equating "eligible" production only to the proportion of local output that is actually marketed by producers. A possible area of compromise would be to exempt developing countries from de minimis caps if their actual procurement does not exceed a given percentage of local production. None of these options have materialized. The mess of using 1986–8 prices as a base was introduced and should be fixed, but this will not happen without a leader for WTO, and without developed and developing countries' willingness to make compromises.

Trade facilitation (TF) emerged as a key deal maker/breaker. Major objectives of the TF agreement were developed, and major exporting developing countries were to accelerate customs procedures; reduce costs; and bring clarity, efficiency, and transparency into customs dealing, as well as to reduce bureaucracy and corruption, and promote the use of modern tools and technology at customs clearance points. The deal was estimated to generate about US$1 trillion worth of gains globally. The MC9 decision stipulated that least developed countries (LDCs) would be required to undertake commitments commensurate with their capacities. Both developed and developing country members were asked to provide capacity-building support to the LDCs.

Despite the opposition to the agreement mounted by India and joined by China, with the support of 33 other developing countries, the agreement was finally reached, marking the first baby step in trade negotiations with a stalled Doha agreement, when developing countries would have preferred a more comprehensive agreement to be reached. Proponents say the TF accord is a "good governance agreement" for customs procedures, which industrialized countries want the developing and poorest countries to implement in the coming days and years on a binding basis—failing which, the latter can be brought before the WTO's dispute settlement body. In return, the developing countries managed to secure only "best endeavor agreements" on some issues of their concern in agriculture, such as an interim mechanism for public stockholding for food security, transparency-related improvements in what are called tariff rate quota administration provisions, and most trade-distorting farm export subsidies and credits, which they argue give undue advantage to developed countries in trade.

The poorest countries, as part of the "development" dossier, secured another set of best-endeavor improvements concerning preferential rules of origin for exporting to industrialized countries, preferential treatment for services and service suppliers in LDCs, duty-free and quota-free market access for LDCs, and finally, a monitoring mechanism for special and differential treatment flexibilities.

Developed countries, on the other hand, are interested in the issues of foreign direct investment, intellectual property, food safety standards, and environmental management. In the meantime, the US presidential election of 2016 demonstrated graphically that globalization has turned sour in the United States, with a significant portion of the

Continued

Box 3.6 Continued

American population believing they have lost in terms of employment and incomes, with the consequent erosion of the middle class, when, in fact, they have benefited because of lower costs of imported goods.

At the WTO's Nairobi Ministerial Conference in December 2015, even though it had been agreed that it was important to advance negotiations on remaining Doha issues (including agricultural market access, domestic support, and export competition), members acknowledged that there was no consensus on whether to reaffirm the Doha mandate. The Nairobi agreement can be seen as "disciplining," but not "eliminating" those other "export measures with equivalent effect" (see Díaz-Bonilla and Hepburn [2016] for further analysis of the Nairobi agricultural export competition outcome).

International cooperation on trade is in considerable disarray, since the arrival of the Trump administration. Others have argued that major developed economies, whatever they may say in public, have by now lost interest in continuing to pursue the Doha Round in its present form. Separately, the Trump administration withdrew from the Trans-Pacific Partnership (TPP), in which the Obama administration had invested considerable capital and secured a bipartisan agreement in the US Congress (Granville 2017). It is, perhaps, less clear with developing countries where they stand on the DDA. Certainly, a very large number of developed countries at least say that they are committed to it and still want it to proceed. Is that serious or tactical? Meanwhile, the major developed economies have moved on. Bilateral or regional free trade agreements and plurilateral agreements are in vogue. The two mega-regional agreements (TPP and the Transatlantic Trade and Investment Partnership), as well as the Japan–EU Free Trade Agreement (FTA), represent a qualitative and a quantitative shift in that regard. Meléndez-Ortiz (2016) suggested that policymakers and negotiators could usefully consider a far broader development agenda fit for the new century—for example, whether food security could be improved by adopting a value-chain approach to markets for food and agriculture. What matters much more are issues such as foreign direct investment, services, state-owned enterprises, intellectual property protection, and transparency, not to mention such areas as the environment and labor. The rest of the world is convinced of the need to tackle these issues collectively—whether globally or regionally is unclear. Martin and Mattoo (2011) outlined the need for a more up-to-date agenda in a comprehensive study of the Doha proposals in 2011, which has not yet been followed up.

III. LESSONS LEARNED AND CHALLENGES OF IMPLEMENTATION

With substantial accumulated experience in price stabilization and trade, many lessons have emerged.

Price Stabilization: Trade vs. Storage

Many developing countries have stabilized their domestic prices through stabilization policies. Hence, domestic prices in low- and middle-income countries have typically increased less than world prices (Dawe et al. 2015), and have been less volatile than world prices, while broadly following world price movements, as many developing countries, particularly those in Asia, now tend to do.

Movements in domestic prices are influenced by many factors, including public investment in R&D, policies that promote private investment, domestic and international trade policies, and year-over-year changes in weather, as well as by stabilization policies. Finally, domestic price changes have varied widely across countries. Thus, not all price changes in domestic policies are necessarily caused by increases in world market prices.

International organizations have advocated government purchases at MSPs to promote and accelerate adoption of new technologies. India provides a good case study, because it was the largest recipient of World Bank loans and credits and US food and financial aid, the latter in the 1960s and 1970s, with considerable interaction between external advice and domestic policy. Some of India's experience is generalizable to other developing countries. Purchases of wheat and rice at guaranteed prices were meant to reduce the risks of adoption of the new Green Revolution technologies. Indeed, the World Bank and the United States (Orville Freeman, the US Secretary of Agriculture, at the direction of President Johnson) helped to institute the organizational infrastructure of the Food Corporation of India (FCI) and made other public sector interventions: for example, directing credit to farmers in the Punjab and Haryana and MSPs for rice and wheat, conditional on lending to India during the 1960s. During the 1970s, the World Bank supported parastatal marketing in Africa, inherited from the British and French colonial period. Since the era of structural adjustment, international organizations have promoted trade as the first-best solution.

In his book, *An Economist in the Real World: The Art of Policymaking*, Basu (2015), who served as the Chief Economic Advisor to the Government of India and later as the Chief Economist of the World Bank (2012–16), explained why producer and consumer price stabilization is necessary in countries such as India, where agriculture contributes 14 percent of GDP, and yet, 59 percent of the population live in poverty. Most of the poverty is found in rural areas and limits poor people's abilities to take risk. A large proportion of the poor depend on the market for food. Basu argued that the government needs to pay a higher-than-market price to command supplies, and it needs to offer food to the poor at lower-than-market prices. The nonpoor would pay a price higher than the market without government intervention. The difference and the extent of subsidy would depend on the amount the government undertakes to provide to the poor, both in quantity per person and in coverage of the population, and how efficient the government is in its task—a relatively simple piece of arithmetic that is affected by the political economy of a country.

Minimum support prices (MSPs) are a very rigid device that can easily cause programs to collapse. Australia had one of these for wool, and it collapsed, as did all the international agreements that used this approach. India combines stockholding with trade policy, which makes it more sustainable than the US loan rates or Australian wool prices. An important question, however, is whether it is cost-effective. A similar degree of stabilization without the rigid floor would cost much less and avoid the risk of collapse. See Gouel, Gautam, and Martin (2016).

Safety Nets to Deal with Chronic and Transitory Poverty in India

India's price stabilization policy has been closely related to its safety nets, discussed later in the chapter. Basu (2015) and others considered the problem of mounting stocks that India, like China, has faced to be one of timing and the extent of release of the procured grain, which requires cabinet approval and lacks transparent rules for the timing and amount of releases, rather than problems with procurement or physical or financial losses. Evidence seems to suggest otherwise.

Basu (2015) made a useful distinction between price stabilization programs and anti-poverty programs, although historically they are closely linked. In addition to the US$18.5 billion annual spending, India will spend US$4 billion annually under the right to food law, in theory providing affordable food to 800 million people. Basu (2015) and others have noted that price stabilization has been successful in India (Gouel, Gautam, and Martin 2016), but as an anti-poverty program, it is deeply flawed, making only a small dent in poverty (Basu 2015). Others argue the Public Distribution System (PDS) was only relevant for urban areas. The poor accessed PDS food either directly or indirectly through the families they worked for. This situation distorts figures that are used to argue that the middle class benefits, but the poor do not (FCI 2015).

Stabilization policies entail a combination of MSPs, food procurement and distribution, and trade policies. If FCI's storage costs are four times higher than long-run costs estimated for other countries, then it raises questions about justification of public storage (Box 3.5) (World Bank and FAO 2012; Gouel, Gautam, and Martin 2016). Critics in India have disputed these storage and transaction costs (Drèze and Khera 2013).

Empirical Research on Prices, Consumers, and Producers

Academic research has begun to catch up with policy concerns, but some recent studies have addressed only high or rising prices, and others, volatility. Some look at impacts on consumers and others, on small subsistence producers. Holistic studies by economists with policy experience, which we review later, provide a different perspective. Based on the analysis of food prices and riots in cities of developing countries, including the toppling of governments in Tunisia and Madagascar, Barrett and Bellemare (2011a, 2011b) acknowledged that high price levels did indeed adversely affect poor consumers and even explained social unrest. Anderson, Martin, and Ivanic (2017), on the other hand, argued that temporary high price spikes matter more to consumers than price volatility—that volatility has positive welfare effects on high-income consumers.

There seems to be a consensus emerging among economists that small producers and net buyers of food are adversely affected by increased price volatility, since it increases risks in their production decisions. Whether to stabilize prices or incomes is a matter of debate. In India, where the average farm size is less than 1 acre and declining, and where less than 50 percent of farm income and food supply comes from own production, Chand, Saxena, and Rana (2015, 143) attributed "farmers' distress" and even farmer suicides to the decline in farmer incomes and heightened income volatility. Bellemare (2015) confirmed that *high* food prices and political instability tend to be particularly high in low-income countries, as also addressed by Arezki and Brückner (2011), but Bellemare did not address volatility. Barrett and Bellemare (2011a) argued the need for different policy responses, depending on whether the objective is to protect consumers from high (not volatile) food prices or to protect producers (from low and volatile) prices. They, like others, have noted that policies such as export bans, price controls, and price stabilization schemes, aimed at curbing food price volatility, are misguided if the policymakers' goal is to increase the welfare of the poor or to avert political unrest in the country. Such policies have a poor record in achieving those objectives. Instead, policymakers should consider policies that prevent sharp rises in food prices, such as removing barriers to international agricultural trade—although open trade may not help when the crisis is a result of supply shortages (such as in 2007–8, when shortages were due to diversion of production to biofuels) or of decreasing investment in scientific research on crop productivity improvement, on soil and water conservation, on reducing postharvest losses (some studies have argued these losses run to nearly 50 percent in many low-income countries) (HLPE 2014), or on renewable energy sources that do not compete with food for land and harvests (Barrett and Bellemare 2011a, 2011b).

Minten et al. (2016) also demonstrated that African countries with more open trade regimes experienced less volatility than those without. They further noted that these measures are the best long- and short-run policy responses, not only to high price levels but also to high price volatility. This is generally true for countries with small imports. When large countries go on the world market, it typically leads to increased prices. While it is true that food price volatility today encourages farmers to reduce inputs, as a hedge against price risk, thereby helping drive higher price levels tomorrow, it is equally true that expanded production—or reduced harvest loss to spoilage, waste, and diversion to biofuels production—drives down prices and encourages stockbuilding, which stabilizes prices. Stocks depend, however, on expectations. Stocks will go up if expected prices, corrected for storage costs and interest rates, rise and vice versa.

Most economists in donor organizations support the positions of Barrett and Bellemare (2011a, 2011b) and have considered public storage and stabilization to be wasteful and a bad idea (Larson 2014). Plenty of evidence supports their concerns, including India's officially produced report on FCI (FCI 2015) and the Policy Research Working Paper of the Agriculture Global Practice Group of the World Bank, prepared by Gouel, Gautam, and Martin (2016).

Not all economists share the view that stabilization should be avoided at all costs, particularly for large countries. As noted earlier, Timmer (2010) argued that price stabilization in Asia has served an important purpose of protecting 2 billion people, most of them poor consumers, and maintaining political stability, even if that meant exporting instability abroad. "In terms of *aggregate global welfare*, stabilizing domestic rice prices in these large countries using border interventions might be an effective way to cope with food crises, even after considering the spillover effects on increased price volatility in the residual world market" (Timmer 2010, 6). Timmer did not explore, however, the high fiscal cost of these policies and their limited impact on intended beneficiaries, and their contributions to global market price volatility, as described here.

Wright (2013) and others have argued also that if large countries like China had not had stabilization policies, and if they had relied completely on the international market, the food price crisis of 2007–8 would have been much worse. Apart from stabilizing urban prices, high rural prices are also set by governments out of concern about rural unrest.

In food-importing countries, pressure on the balance of payments increased due to (1) the higher cost of imports; (2) the added fiscal pressures from increasing input subsidies and price supports to compensate for price increases; (3) the hardship on import-dependent consumers (for example, in the Philippines and Bangladesh) from export bans imposed by neighboring exporting countries (for example, China and India); (4) the cushioning of domestic prices from international price rises, leading to a muted supply response; and (5) the exaggeration of international price rises by countries pursuing policies to protect domestic consumers (for example, the Philippines entered into long-term rice import contracts). Indonesia (rice) and Egypt (wheat) maintained their domestic prices by sub-sidizing imports, and had to use export bans to stop this wheat flowing out.

Why Has It Been Hard to Convince Developing Countries' Policymakers to Abandon Price Stabilization Policies?

Most industrialized countries have promoted stable food supplies and prices through extensive public interventions. In Europe, the Common Agricultural Policy (CAP) was set up explicitly for this purpose and succeeded in meeting this objective, though at a high cost until it was reformed following the Uruguay Round. Agriculture also has been heavily subsidized in Japan and in the United States, the latter as "a national security issue" (Bush 2001, 920).

Import dependence also has a political dimension. Basu (2015) noted that the United States denied rice exports to Bangladesh in 1974, in a critical time of its need, because Bangladesh was trading with Cuba. President Johnson's "short tether" policy in India—food aid shipments were conditional on India keeping silent about the Vietnam War—and known in India as the "ship-to-mouth existence" of the 1960s, instilled a strong resolve in India to never again put itself in the situation of being at a disadvantage (Lele and Goldsmith 1989). The United States similarly restricted food aid flows to Bangladesh for political reasons.

Critics of the free trade policy argue that liberalized trade leads to import surges of a food staple, displacing the domestic market and, thereby, decreasing domestic production and employment by startling percentages. Anuradha Mittal argued that Indonesia's import liberalization, prompted by multilateral organizations following its economic crisis in 1998, resulted in a huge increase in imports, leading to farmer distress and to the government reimposing import controls in 2002 (Mittal 2009). Others have a different take on the impact of the import surge: a big surge in imports occurred before import controls were loosened and was due to a massive El Niño that led in turn to a massive decline in production. Throughout these years, domestic rice prices were higher than during the period 1969–96, so it is hard to say that farmers were in distress because of additional imports. Perhaps they were in distress because of bad weather and political instability (personal communication, David Dawe, February 2019).

Crisis Response and Long-term Development: The Right to Food and Social Safety Nets

Internationally, social safety nets were clear targets for cuts in the 1980s, during the decade of structural adjustment. Yet, a broad consensus has emerged, particularly in the Bretton Woods institutions, of the importance of safety nets in protecting the poor. Concurrently with increased recognition that growth is necessary but not sufficient to reduce poverty, institutionalization of safety nets has been increasingly advocated. The domestic dynamics of safety nets, however, tends to be quite different.

India's Right to Food and Domestic Support

India's right to food law, the National Food Security Act (NFSA) of 2013, is an example of the political economy of policymaking (Government of India 2016a, 2016b). Supported and promoted by UN resolutions and covering two-thirds of the population—nearly 800 million people—NFSA is the largest such safety net program. In reality, it typically distributes only a third of the production. NFSA has had strong support in the United Nations and FAO, influenced in part by Amartya Sen's ideas of capabilities of the poor (Sen 1985), and is supported by Indian nongovernmental organizations (NGOs) and economists on the left (Drèze and Sen 2013). Passed by Parliament in September 2013, on the verge of the departure of the long-standing Centre-Left United Front Parties, the Act aims to provide coverage far larger than existed previously.[14]

The right to food law has been questioned by economists on the right who advise the Modi government currently in power (Bhagwati and Panagariya 2013). There is an active debate on the merits of cash transfers versus food distribution, particularly with the passage of the "Aadhaar" (the unique electronic identity card) bill in the Indian Parliament in March 2016[15] and universal bank accounts, which enable transfer of funds directly into the bank accounts of women, reducing intermediaries and greatly increasing savings.

Drèze and Khera (2013) noted that the public distribution of food has reduced the poverty gap index, and rural poverty has declined by a fifth nationally and by considerably more in better functioning Indian states. They acknowledged, however, that the PDS still has very little impact on rural poverty in a number of large states such as Bihar, Jharkhand, Uttar Pradesh, and West Bengal, where PDS reforms are long overdue. PDS suffers from exclusion error, as well as inclusion error (Parikh 2013). Identifying the target group and scaling up are the real challenges. Drèze and Khera (2013) also favored in-kind food distribution, rather than cash transfers, since cash transfers can be spent on things other than food. Gulati, on the other hand, has often forcefully argued that in India, there is huge scope to improve the efficiency of public distribution, ensuring that benefits reach the neediest, targeting direct payments more sharply to beneficiaries, and shifting to cash transfers (see Saini and Gulati [2015]).

Indian states are beginning to experiment with cash transfers and to use information technology to monitor distribution of publicly distributed grain, to minimize "leakages" (inclusion and exclusion errors, meaning those not intended as beneficiaries benefit from the program and those intended to be beneficiaries tend to be excluded): for example, in Kerala and Bihar. Under "competitive federalism," the Government of India sets MSPs for 23 commodities but leaves to the states the responsibility of setting examples of good practice, which others may emulate. States have had a mixed record on the implementation of MSPs (Chand 2018).

The role of public procurement and distribution of food relative to cash transfers and the role of much needed investment expenditures in agriculture and related sectors to increase farm productivity, relative to the amount of resources spent on safety net programs, will continue to be debated in a country in which the majority of farmers are smallholders and experience food deficit.

---

[14] In their article, "The Political Economy of Government Responsiveness Theory and Evidence from India," Besley and Burgess (2002) found that:
Having a more informed and politically active electorate strengthens incentives for governments to be responsive. This suggests that there is a role both for democratic institutions and the mass media in ensuring that the preferences of citizens are reflected in policy. The ideas behind the model are tested on panel data from India,... [showing] that state governments are more responsive to falls in food production and crop flood damage via public food distribution and calamity relief expenditure where newspaper circulation is higher and electoral accountability greater. (Besley and Burgess 2002, 1415)

[15] See "The Aadhaar (Targeted Delivery of Financial and Other Subsidies, Benefits and Services) Bill, 2016" (http://www.prsindia.org/billtrack/the-aadhaar-targeted-delivery-of-financial-and-other-subsidies-benefits-and-services-bill-2016–4202/).

Minimum Support Prices, Diversification of Agriculture, and a Lack of Consensus

The level of food distribution commitment in India has led to a de facto nationalization of purchases of rice and wheat in surplus states, including Punjab, Haryana, Western Uttar Pradesh, and Andhra Pradesh. Recognizing the carbohydrate-centric diet of the Indian population and the decline in pulse consumption, India has adopted a new pulse mission to diversify agriculture beyond cereals, accompanied by price support and trade policies toward pulses (Aditya et al. 2017). Basu (2015) did not question the objective of price stabilization, across seasons or across poor years, nor the objective of providing food to the poor at lower than market prices. He faulted the policy for not recognizing its full implications. The policy has not been so clearly devised. Furthermore, the problems are more in the release of stocks than in procurement, and in the way the policy is executed. There is a need for clear rules and transparency, not for more cabinet meetings.

Cash transfers are more cost effective than in-kind transfers, but NGOs working on the ground do not accept this. The use of identity cards in India is the largest such experiment in the world, but the debate will likely continue on the merit of alternative approaches. There are still problems with identity cards, which need to be resolved.

Drèze and Khera (2013) argued that aid in-kind is more likely to lead to improved food consumption. Others have argued that cash transfers—even when made directly to women—are captured by the men of the household, and worse, often used for alcohol. A recent survey of Indian women indicated they prefer food distribution to cash transfers. Clearly, the precise forms of social safety nets are context specific. The efficiency of transfer programs will certainly be better informed by independent impact evaluations of different types of safety nets—payments in-kind or in cash—with results widely disseminated to influence policy.

Gouel, Gautam, and Martin (2016, 3) argued that the current stock and hold policy is costly, and furthermore, high costs "make it difficult to justify any level of public storage in the country without significant overall loss in welfare" (Gouel, Gautam, and Martin 2016, 4). It is well worth exploring whether the private sector would be willing to store across crop years, without engaging in excessively speculative behavior, and what policies would be needed to achieve it.

In India, past governments have passed food security laws to supply subsidized grain at Rs.1, 2, and 3 per kg to two-thirds of the population. To run PDS, food procurement is required. The three pillars of food security in India were globally applauded: namely, food procurement for MSPs, buffer stock-for-price stability, and the PDS.[16] A Senate committee found that if losses of FCI are included and one compares economic costs with market prices charged by private traders in deficit states, the two are at par. So, the question becomes whether to bear the so-called inefficiency of FCI or the exploitation by India's smart petty traders and middlemen. If market reforms are accomplished and prices are competitive, the need for MSP procurement will decline or even become unnecessary. Then, cash transfers rather than physical distribution of food would be preferable. China is also wrestling with issues of public–private partnerships in its policy reforms, so it could be beneficial for China and India to exchange experiences.

---

[16] As defined by the World Health Organization, the three pillars of food security are food access, food availability, and food use. See "India's Water & Food Security/Three Pillars of Food Security," https://sites.google.com/site/indiaswaterfoodsecruity/home/three-pillars-of-food-security.

Conclusion

The crisis highlighted the vulnerability of developing countries to a combination of factors: policies of large countries with global reach in trade, such as the US biofuel policies; and successive crop failures and responses of large individual countries, such as China, India, and Indonesia, to protect their domestic consumers and producers from external shocks. Import-dependent countries became particularly vulnerable. Trade is important to reduce this vulnerability, but it has its limits. The recent debacle of medical supply chains, in the context of the COVID-19 pandemic, shows that excessive focus on efficiency and cost-effectiveness needs to be balanced with resilience.

The crisis also made more acceptable the concept of "food self-sufficiency" and protection of the domestic food sector, which China and India have practiced over decades, as they emerged as important agricultural producers and traders. WTO discussions in Argentina continued to show the limitations of the Doha Development Agenda (DDA). The United States—traditionally, the strongest champion of free trade—moved toward protectionism, questioning the North American Free Trade Agreement (NAFTA) and exiting from the TPP (*Strait Times* 2018). Global trade rules were already in trouble, as biofuel policies had demonstrated. The new US–Mexico–Canada Agreement was supposed to fix some of the problems the Trump administration perceived in the old NAFTA, but it is too new to know how well it will work (Mauldin and Salama 2019).

The most important challenge is to invest much more in R&D than many developing countries are currently doing. As economies grow and diets diversify, relying on imports is much less of a concern. Singapore produces no food but is very food secure, as is Hong Kong. Japan has reduced its agricultural protection without loss of food security—although its farmers still use food security as an argument for support.

Two key issues that the crisis highlighted, on which there has been relatively little progress, are:

1. The conflict between the interest of individual nation states and global trading rules, which place limits on national behavior that harms trading partners; and
2. The need to invest in agriculture for countries to achieve a certain degree of national self-reliance in food and nutrition (Fukase and Martin 2016).

The Uruguay Round is credited with cleaning up the previously abysmal CAP price insulation that pushed world price volatility onto much more vulnerable producers in poor countries. The one area in which there has been considerable progress but could be more, with greater financial investment in data, is information on production, food systems, and trade (via AMIS), ranging from household to global levels, given the increased risk of climate change and trade uncertainty.

The combination of factors, however, which ensued over time—the "perfect storm"—compounded the impacts of the actions that developing countries took, including, in particular, the export bans that several Asian countries imposed. Both the genesis of the crisis and the bans highlighted how the solutions to the crisis seemed very different from various national perspectives, particularly of major exporting countries like the United States, India, and other developing countries trading in grain, and of other countries impacted by their actions. In the end, all policymakers were responding to consumers and producers in their individual countries, and there was little concern about spillover effects of their actions beyond their national borders and little progress on agreements such as export bans, in the interest of all.

To maintain the political legitimacy of their domestic stakeholders, policymakers of OECD continue to respond to their lobbies in support of biofuel policies, for which there is little justification. Preoccupied with concerns about food prices and domestic inflation, developing countries have pursued import and export strategies, and safety nets have acquired increasing importance (World Bank 2015b, 2017a). The crisis highlighted many of the long-standing issues between OECD countries and developing countries with respect to free trade and development concerns, which stalled the DDA, notwithstanding the economic logic of free trade. These issues were more significant in 2007 than they had been in 1972, at the time of the first global food crisis, because food and energy markets were more integrated in the new millennium than they had been in the 1970s, and developing countries were more significant economic players on the world stage in 2007–8.

A number of useful steps have been taken since the latest crisis. At the WTO meeting in Argentina, China reaffirmed economic globalization as an irreversible historic trend, and its staunch support for economic globalization and the multilateral trading system as critical safeguards for prosperity and development. More than 100 countries backed a joint proposal by China and India for eliminating the trade-distorting farm subsidies of US$160 billion in the United States, EU, Japan, Canada, Norway, and Switzerland, among other nations at WTO's 11th trade ministerial summit in Buenos Aires (ICTSD 2017c, 2017d). Another mandated issue concerned the permanent solution for public stockholding (PSH) programs in developing countries, which had been agreed to four years previously in Bali, Indonesia. India and China have pushed on the issue jointly with other developing countries (see more at ICTSD [2017a]). Reflecting differences between exporting and importing countries, Argentina, hosting the summit, warned that the China–India proposal was a recipe for the breakdown of the Buenos Aires meeting (ICTSD 2017b). India could easily solve this invented "problem" simply by changing its procedures, which would allow India to focus on real problems, in contrast to trying to break these rules to avoid making slight changes in its stockholding and PDS procedures. Interest groups at the FCI are not interested in a solution, but India at large would be much better off with such a solution.

India also took the position that new issues such as e-commerce and trade in services should not be considered until the old ones, such as OECD subsidies and permanent stockholding, had been addressed. The Trump administration refused to pursue the PSH issue, while pushing ahead with talks on e-commerce and trade in services (ICTSD 2017e; Kanth 2017). We have reviewed these developments in this chapter and in the rest of the book, and it is unclear what the future holds for the global governance of food and agriculture, including, particularly, agricultural trade rules, following the growing protectionist tendency in the United States and WTO discussions in Argentina in 2017 (WTO 2017). The future of WTO is unclear. Much will depend on whether Trump is reelected. If he is, many fear for WTO's future. Will the crisis of 2006 repeat itself in 2020?

Effect of the COVID-19 Pandemic on Poverty

IFPRI projected that for any one percentage point slowdown of the global economy, the number of poor—and with it the number of food-insecure people—would increase by 1.6 to 3 percent. Due to the paralysis of economies caused by COVID-19 containment measures, global poverty may increase by 14 million people based on a 1.9 percent increase in total factor productivity (TFP) (and possibly much more depending on the nature of the economic trade disruptions) (Vos, Martin, and Laborde 2020). This was a conservative estimate. In April 2021, IMF estimated an additional 95 million people had entered the ranks of the extreme poor in 2020, as compared to the pre-pandemic projections, and found considerable divergence in the rates of economic recovery—that is, in 2020, growth of 6.4 percent in the United States and 8.4 percent in China, but losses of 5.4 percent in LICs and 4.4 percent in emerging countries (IMF 2021).

Kharas and Hamel noted 12 countries that are likely to see an increase in poverty of over 1 million people in 2020, as a result of COVID-19. These vulnerable countries— Afghanistan, Bangladesh, Brazil, Democratic Republic of the Congo (Kinshasa), Ethiopia, India, Indonesia, Nigeria, Pakistan, the Philippines, Sudan, and Zimbabwe—are mainly located in Asia and Africa. Brazil is the exception in the Latin American region. India and Nigeria are likely to add 10 million and 8 million, respectively, to the poverty rolls in 2020. "In all these countries, COVID-19 has demonstrated the vulnerability of people who have only recently been able to escape poverty" (Kharas and Hamel 2020). (See, also, Lele, Bansal, and Meenakshi [2020].)

Schmidhuber, Pound, and Qiao (2020) of FAO note that with most countries more dependent on food imports today than they were 20 years ago, disruptions caused by COVID-19 could trigger a repeat of the food crisis of 2007–8, when a sharp rise in prices led to panicking governments, which imposed trade restrictions (Schmidhuber and Qiao 2020).

However, there are some major differences between 2007 and 2020. Both agricultural and energy prices in 2020 are low, and agricultural trade is much larger than in 2007, with the numbers of both importers and exporters higher than in 2007, and with considerable competition among exporters and importers. "Today cereal stocks are twice as high as they were then. Bulk shipping is 20 times cheaper and crude oil is just $30 a barrel. That makes all manner of inputs cheaper and pushes the price of fuel feedstocks like corn and sugar lower still…" (*Economist* 2020b).

Another important difference is that due to scale economies, and economies of agglomeration, a few multinational suppliers supply most of the volume of processed grains, livestock, and poultry; due to well-developed global value chains, they are able to purchase unprocessed agricultural materials from sources of cheapest supply and then ship, process, and package them elsewhere. Due to uncertainty, consumers have been stocking up more supplies than usual. However, due to a loss of demand from restaurants and the absence of scale purchases, there also has been huge wastage of food in the short run—this could result in farmers planting less and food prices rising. Another difference between 2007–8 and 2020 is the fewer trade barriers in 2020. *The Economist* briefing further notes:

> In 2007–2008, 33 countries declared export controls. Those bans caused most of the 116% rise in rice prices seen then. This time 19 states have so far limited exports and the impact is much less. 2007–08's control affected 19% of the world's traded calories; this year's so far affect just 5 percent. (*Economist* 2020b)

Fortunately, the COVID-19 crisis has led to a variety of innovations in the areas of food supply, delivery, small business enterprises, use of digital tools, food-related safety nets, cash and food transfers, among others, to deal with the drop in consumer demand, detailed in IFPRI's *COVID-19 and Global Food Security* (Swinnen and McDermott 2020).

The crisis has also reinforced the G20 support for AMIS, keeping market information flows accessible to all and at center stage. It will also further spur the development of the nexus between food systems and health systems, and the broader discussion on food systems that will emanate from such a connection.

References

Aditya, K. S., S. P. Subash, K. V. Praveen, M. L. Nithyashree, N. Bhuvana, and Akriti Sharma. 2017. "Awareness about Minimum Support Price and Its Impact on Diversification Decision of Farmers in India." *Asia & The Pacific Policy Studies* 4 (3): 514–26.

Aksoy, M. Ataman. 2004. "The Evolution of Agricultural Trade Flows." In *Global Agricultural Trade and Developing Countries*, edited by M. Ataman Aksoy and John C. Beghin, 17–35. Washington, DC: World Bank.

Alexandratos, Nikos. 2008. "Food Price Surges: Possible Causes, Past Experience, and Long-term Relevance." *Population and Development Review* 34 (4): 599–629.

Alexandratos, Nikos, and Jelle Bruinsma. 2012. "World Agriculture Towards 2030/2050: The 2012 Revision." ESAWorking Paper No. 12–03, Agricultural Development Economics Division, Food and Agriculture Organization of the United Nations (FAO), Rome. http://www.fao.org/docrep/016/ap106e/ap106e.pdf

AMIS. 2011. Agricultural Market Information System. http://statistics.amis-outlook.org/data/index.html

AMIS. 2015. Agricultural Market Information System. "About AMIS." http://www.amis-outlook.org/amis-about/en/

Anderson, Kym. 2010a. "International Trade Policies Affecting Agricultural Incentives in Developing Countries." In *Handbook of Agricultural Economics*, Vol. 4, edited by Prabhu L. Pingali and Robert E. Evenson, 3215–52. Amsterdam: North Holland Elsevier.

Anderson, Kym. 2010b. "Krueger/Schiff/Valdés Revisited: Agriculture Price and Trade Policy Reform in Developing Countries since 1960." Policy Research Working Paper No. 5165, January, World Bank, Washington, DC. https://openknowledge.worldbank.org/handle/10986/19952

Anderson, Kym. 2012. "Government Trade Restrictions and International Price Volatility." *Global Food Security* 1 (2): 157–66.

Anderson, Kym, Maros Ivanic, and William J. Martin. 2014. "Food Price Spikes, Price Insulation, and Poverty." In *The Economics of Food Price Volatility*, edited by Jean-Paul Chavas, David Hummels, and Brian D. Wright, 311–39. Chicago: University of Chicago Press.

Anderson, Kym, William J. Martin, and Maros Ivanic. 2017. "Food Price Changes, Domestic Price Insulation, and Poverty (When All Policymakers Want to be Above Average)." In *Agriculture and Rural Development in a Globalizing World: Challenges and Opportunities*, edited by Prabhu Pingali and Gershon Feder, 181–92. London: Routledge.

Arezki, Rabah, and Markus Brückner (authorized for distribution by Marc Quintyn). 2011. "Food Prices and Political Instability." IMF Working Paper WP/11/62, International Monetary Fund, Washington, DC.

Babcock, Bruce A. 2011. "The Impact of US Biofuel Policy on Agricultural Price Levels and Volatility." Issue Paper No. 35, International Centre for Trade and Sustainable Development (ICTSD), Geneva.

Bachewe, Fantu Nisrane, Guush Berhane, Bart Minten, and Alemayehu Seyoum Taffesse. 2015. "Agricultural Growth in Ethiopia (2004–2014): Evidence and Drivers." Working Paper 81, October, Ethiopia Strategy Support Program, Ethiopian Development Research Institute and International Food Policy Research Institute, Washington, DC.

Baffes, John, and Tassos Haniotis. 2010. "Placing the Recent Commodity Boom into Perspective." In *Food Prices and Rural Poverty*, edited by M. Ataman Aksoy and Bernard Hoekman, 41–70. Washington, DC: Center for Economic Policy Research (CEPR) and the World Bank.

Balisacan, Arsenio M., Mercedita A. Sombilla, and Rowell C. Dikitanan. 2010. "Rice Crisis in the Philippines: Why Did It Occur and What Are Its Policy Implications?" In *The Rice Crisis: Markets, Policies and Food Security*, edited by David Dawe, 123–42. London and Washington, DC: Food and Agriculture Organization of the United Nations (FAO) and Earthscan.

Barrett, Christopher B., and Marc F. Bellemare. 2011a. "The G-20's Error: Food Price Volatility Is Not the Problem." Cornell University, Ithaca, NY.

Barrett, Christopher B., and Marc F. Bellemare. 2011b. "Why Food Price Volatility Doesn't Matter: Policymakers Should Focus on Bringing Costs Down." *Foreign Affairs*, Snapshot, July 12 online, https://www.foreignaffairs.com/articles/2011-07-12/why-food-price-volatility-doesnt-matter

Basu, Kaushik. 2015. *An Economist in the Real World: The Art of Policymaking in India.* Cambridge, MA: MIT Press.

Bellemare, Marc F. 2015. "Rising Food Prices, Food Price Volatility, and Social Unrest." *American Journal of Agricultural Economics* 97 (1): 1–21.

Besley, Timothy, and Robin Burgess. 2002. "The Political Economy of Government Responsiveness: Theory and Evidence from India." *Quarterly Journal of Economics* 117 (4): 1415–51.

Bhagwati, Jagdish, and Arvind Panagariya. 2013. *Why Growth Matters: How Economic Growth in India Reduced Poverty and the Lessons for Other Developing Countries.* New York: Public Affairs.

Bioversity, CGIAR, FAO (Food and Agriculture Organization of the United Nations), IFAD (International Fund for Agricultural Development), IFPRI (International Food Policy Research Institute), IICA (Inter-American Institute for Cooperation on Agriculture), OECD (Organisation for Economic Co-operation and Development), UNCTAD (United Nations Conference on Trade and Development), Coordination team of UN High Level Task Force on the Food Security Crisis, WFP (World Food Programme), World Bank, and WTO (World Trade Organization). 2012. "Sustainable Agricultural Productivity Growth and Bridging the Gap for Small-Family Farms." Interagency Report to the Mexican G20 Presidency.

Bouët, Antoine, and David Laborde, eds. 2017. *Agriculture, Development, and the Global Trading System: 2000–2015.* Washington, DC: International Food Policy Research Institute.

Bourne, Joel K., Jr. 2009. "The Global Food Crisis: The End of Plenty." Special Report, *National Geographic*, June. http://ngm.nationalgeographic.com/2009/06/cheap-food/bourne-text

Bread for the World Institute. 2013. "Partnering to End Hunger and Poverty." In *2013 Hunger Report—Within Reach: Global Development Goals*, Chapter 2, 57–83. Washington, DC: Bread for the World Institute. http://www.hungerreport.org/2013/wp-content/uploads/2013/03/HR13-ch2.pdf

Bruno, Valentina G., Bahattin Büyükşahin, and Michel A. Robe. 2017. "The Financialization of Food?" *American Journal of Agricultural Economics* 99 (1): 243–64.

Bush, George W. 2001. *Public Papers of the Presidents of the United States*, George W. Bush. Book 02, Presidential Documents, July 1 to December 31, 2001. Washington, DC: Office of the Federal Register, National Archives and Records Administration.

Byerlee, Derek, Thomas S. Jayne, and Robert Myers. 2005. "Managing Food Price Risks and Instability in an Environment of Market Liberalization." Report No. 32727-GLB, Agriculture and Rural Development Department, World Bank, Washington, DC.

CFS (Committee on World Food Security). 2017. "Making a Difference in Food Security and Nutrition." CFS 44, FAO, Rome, October 9–13. http://www.fao.org/cfs/home/plenary/cfs44/en/

Chand, Ramesh. 2016. "Doubling Farmer's Income: Strategy and Prospects." Presidential Address, The Indian Society of Agricultural Economics, 76th Annual Conference, Assam Agricultural University, Jorhat, Assam, November 21–3.

Chand, Ramesh. 2018. "Here's How India Can Protect Its Farmers against Low Prices for Their Crops." *Business Standard*, January 17.

Chand, Ramesh, Raka Saxena, and Simmi Rana. 2015. "Estimates and Analysis of Farm Income in India, 1983–84 to 2011–12." *Economic and Political Weekly* 50 (22): 139–45.

Chirwa, Ephraim W., and Blessings Chinsinga. 2015. "The Political Economy of Food Price Policy in Malawi." In *Food Price Policy in an Era of Market Instability: A Political Economy Analysis*, edited by Per Pinstrup-Andersen, 153–73. Oxford: Oxford University Press.

Cooke, Bryce, and Miguel Robles. 2009. "Recent Food Price Movements. Time Series Analysis." IFPRI Discussion Paper No. 00942, International Food Policy Research Institute, Washington, DC.

Dawe, David, Cristian Morales Opazo, Jean Balie, Guillaume Pierre. 2015. "How Much Have Domestic Food Prices Increased in the New Era of Higher Food Prices?" *Global Food Security* 5: 1–10.

Dawe, David, and Tom Slayton. 2011. "The World Rice Market Crisis of 2007–2008." In *Safeguarding Food Security in Volatile Global Markets*, edited by Adam Prakash, 164–74. Rome: Food and Agriculture Organization of the United Nations.

Dawe, David, and C. Peter Timmer. 2012. "Why Stable Food Prices Are a Good Thing: Lessons from Stabilizing Rice Prices in Asia." *Global Food Security* 1: 127–33.

de Gorter, Harry. 2014. "Energy Markets: The Impact on Trade in Biofuels and Farm Goods." In *Tackling Agriculture in the Post-Bali Context: A Collection of Short Essays*, edited by Ricardo Meléndez-Ortiz, Christophe Bellman, and Jonathan Hepburn, 47–54. Geneva: International Centre for Trade and Sustainable Development.

de Gorter, Harry, Dusan Drabik, and David R. Just. 2013. "How Biofuels Policies Affect the Level of Grains and Oilseed Prices: Theory, Models and Evidence." *Global Food Security* 2 (2): 82–8.

de Hoyos, Rafael E., and Denis Medvedev. 2011. "Poverty Effects of Higher Food Prices: A Global Perspective." *Review of Development Economics* 15 (3): 387–402.

Deaton, Angus, and Guy Laroque. 1996. "Competitive Storage and Commodity Price Dynamics." *Journal of Political Economy* 104 (5): 896–923. http://www.princeton.edu/~deaton/downloads/Competitive_Storage_and_Commodity_Price_Dynamics.pdf

Deininger, Klaus, and Derek Byerlee, with Jonathan Lindsay, Andrew Norton, Harris Selod, and Mercedes Stickler. 2011. *Rising Global Interest in Farmland: Can It Yield Sustainable and Equitable Benefits?* Agriculture and Rural Development (ARD), Washington, DC: World Bank.

Demeke, Mulat, Guendalina Pangrazio, and Materne Maetz. 2009. "Country Responses to the Food Security Crisis: Nature and Preliminary Implications of the Policies Pursued." Agricultural Policy Support Service, Food and Agriculture Organization of the United Nations (FAO), Rome. http://www.fao.org/fileadmin/user_upload/ISFP/pdf_for_site_Coun try_Response_to_the_Food_Security.pdf

Díaz-Bonilla, Eugenio. 2014. "Food Price Volatility, Food Security and Trade Policy: The Future Ain't What It Used To Be." Presentation at the World Bank Conference on Food Price Volatility, Food Security and Trade, September 18–19, Washington, DC.

Díaz-Bonilla, Eugenio, and Jonathan Hepburn. 2016. "Export Competition Issues after Nairobi." In *Evaluating Nairobi: What Does the Outcome Mean for Trade in Food and Farm Goods?* edited by J. Hepburn and C. Bellmann, 19–36, ICTSD Programme on Agricultural Trade and Sustainable Development. Geneva: International Centre for Trade and Sustainable Development.

Díaz-Bonilla, Eugenio, and Juan Francisco Ron. 2010. "Food Security, Price Volatility and Trade: Some Reflections for Developing Countries." Issue Paper No. 28, International Centre for Trade and Sustainable Development, Geneva.

Drèze, Jean, and Reetika Khera. 2013. "Rural Poverty and the Public Distribution System." *Economic & Political Weekly* 47 (45–6): 55–60.

Drèze, Jean, and Amartya Sen. 2013. *An Uncertain Glory: India and its Contradictions.* London: Allen Lane.

Economist, The. 2020a. "COVID-19 Is Undoing Years of Progress in Curbing Global Poverty." International, May 23. https://www.economist.com/international/2020/05/23/covid-19-is-undoing-years-of-progress-in-curbing-global-poverty

Economist, The. 2020b. "Keeping Things Cornucopious: The World's Food System Has So Far Weathered the Challenge of COVID-19. But Things Could Still Go Awry." Briefing, May 9, 2020. https://www.economist.com/briefing/2020/05/09/the-worlds-food-system-has-so-far-weathered-the-challenge-of-covid-19

Elliott, Kimberly Ann. 2015. "The Time to Reform US Biofuels Policy Is Now." CGD Brief, May, Center for Global Development, Washington, DC. http://www.cgdev.org/sites/default/files/Biofuels-Final.pdf

FAO (Food and Agriculture Organization of the United Nations). 2001. *Food Balance Sheets: A Handbook.* Rome: FAO. http://www.fao.org/docrep/003/x9892e/x9892e00.htm

FAO (Food and Agriculture Organization of the United Nations). 2007. "The Challenge of Renewal." Report of the Independent External Evaluation of the Food and Agriculture Organization of the United Nations (FAO), submitted to the Council Committee for the Independent External Evaluation of FAO (CC–IEE), September 2007. http://www.oecd.org/derec/finland/40800533.pdf (Summary) and http://www.fao.org/unfao/bodies/IEE-Working-Draft-Report/K0489E.pdf

FAO (Food and Agriculture Organization of the United Nations). 2008a. "Soaring Food Prices: Facts, Perspectives, Impacts, and Actions Required." Technical report presented at the Conference on World Food Security: The Challenges of Climate Change and Bioenergy, June 3–5. Rome: FAO.

FAO (Food and Agriculture Organization of the United Nations). 2008b. *The State of Food and Agriculture 2008. Biofuels: Prospects, Risks, and Opportunities.* Rome: FAO. http://www.fao.org/3/a-i0100e.pdf

FAO (Food and Agriculture Organization of the United Nations). 2009. "The State of Agricultural Commodity Markets 2009: High Food Prices and the Food Crisis—Experiences and Lessons Learned." FAO, Rome. http://www.fao.org/3/a-i0854e.pdf

FAO (Food and Agriculture Organization of the United Nations). 2011. "The State of Food Insecurity in the World: How Does International Price Volatility Affect Domestic Economies and Food Security?" FAO, Rome. http://www.fao.org/docrep/014/i2330e/i2330e.pdf

FAO (Food and Agriculture Organization of the United Nations). 2014. "The Bali Package—Implications for Trade and Food Security," FAO Trade Policy Briefs on Issues related to the WTO Negotiations on Agriculture, No. 16, February, FAO, Rome.

FAO (Food and Agriculture Organization of the United Nations). 2016. *The State of Food and Agriculture (SOFA) 2016—Climate Change, Agriculture, and Food Security.* Rome: FAO. http://www.fao.org/3/a-i6030e.pdf

FAO (Food and Agriculture Organization of the United Nations). 2017. "Voices of the Hungry: Re-shaping the Way Food Insecurity Is Measured. Measuring Food Insecurity through People's Experiences." http://www.fao.org/in-action/voices-of-the-hungry/en/#.WCgP3BTfTl4

FAO (Food and Agriculture Organization of the United Nations). 2018. "Bumper Crops Boost Global Cereal Supplies in 2017/18." World Food Situation. FAO Cereal Supply and Demand Brief.

FAO (Food and Agriculture Organization of the United Nations). 2020a. Statistics, Food Security Indicators (database). http://www.fao.org/economic/ess/ess-fs/ess-fadata/en/#.Wdp9KUyZNE5

FAO (Food and Agriculture Organization of the United Nations). 2020b. "Voices of the Hungry: The Food Insecurity Experience Scale." http://www.fao.org/in-action/voices-of-the-hungry/fies/en/

FAO (Food and Agriculture Organization of the United Nations), IFAD (International Fund for Agricultural Development), UNICEF (United Nations Children's Fund), WFP (World Food Programme), and WHO (World Health Organization). 2019. "The State of Food Security and Nutrition in the World 2019: Safeguarding against Economic Slowdowns and Downturns." FAO, Rome. http://www.fao.org/publications/sofi/en/

FAO (Food and Agriculture Organization of the United Nations), IFAD (International Fund for Agricultural Development), and WFP (World Food Programme). 2011. *The State of Food Insecurity in the World: How Does International Price Volatility Affect Domestic Economies and Food Security?* Rome: FAO.

FAOSTAT. 2019a. Food and Agriculture Organization of the United Nations. Statistics Division. Data. http://www.fao.org/faostat/en/#data

FAOSTAT. 2019b. Food and Agriculture Organization of the United Nations. Statistics Division. Definitions and Standards Used in FAOSTAT. http://www.fao.org/faostat/en/#definitions

FCI (Food Corporation of India). 2015. "Report of the High Level Committee on Reorienting the Role and Restructuring of Food Corporation of India," Food Corporation of India, New Delhi, http://fci.gov.in/news.php?view=217

Frankel, Jeffrey. 2008. "Comment: Real Rates Key to Commodities Prices," Reuters, March 19. http://www.reuters.com/article/columns-comment-frankel-commodities-dc-idUSDIS96078820080319

Fukase, Emiko, and Will Martin. 2016. "Who Will Feed China in the 21st Century? Income Growth and Food Demand and Supply in China." *Journal of Agricultural Economics* 67 (1): 3–23. https://onlinelibrary.wiley.com/doi/epdf/10.1111/1477–9552.12117

Fukase, Emiko, and Will Martin. 2020. "Economic Growth, Convergence, and World Food Demand and Supply." *World Development* 132: 104954. https://www.sciencedirect.com/science/article/pii/S0305750X20300802

G20 (Group of 20). 2011. "Price Volatility in Food and Agricultural Markets: Policy Responses." G20 Interagency report with contributions from FAO (Food and Agriculture Organization of the United Nations), IFAD (International Fund for Agricultural Development), IMF (International Monetary Fund), OECD (Organisation of for Economic Co-operation and Development), UNCTAD (United Nations Conference on Trade and Development), WFP (World Food Programme), the World Bank, the WTO (World Trade Organization), IFPRI (International Food Policy Research Institute), and the UN HLTF (High Level Task Force on Global Food and Nutrition Security), June 2. http://www.foodsecurityportal.org/sites/default/files/g20_interagency_report_food_price_volatility.pdf

Gan, Alexis. 2017. "China Cuts Wheat Minimum Support Price by Yuan 60/Mt for 2018, First In Over A Decade." S&P Global, Platts.com, Singapore, October 27. https://www.platts.com/latest-news/agriculture/singapore/china-cuts-wheat-minimum-support-price-by-yuan-26829430

Ganguly, Kavery, and Ashok Gulati. 2015. "The Political Economy of Food Price Policy in India." In *Food Price Policy in an Era of Market Instability: A Political Economy Analysis*, edited by Per Pinstrup-Andersen, 339–61. Oxford: Oxford University Press.

Gardner, Bruce. L. 1979. *Optimal Stockpiling of Grain*. Lexington, MA: Lexington Books.

Ge, Mengpin, Johannes Friedrich, and Thomas Damassa. 2014. "6 Graphs Explain the World's Top 10 Emitters," November 25, World Resources Institute, Washington, DC. http://www.wri.org/blog/2014/11/6-graphs-explain-world's-top-10-emitters

Gerasimchuk, Ivetta, and Peng Yam Koh. 2013. "The EU Biofuel Policy and Palm Oil: Cutting Subsidies or Cutting Rainforest?" Research Report, September, Global Studies Initiative, International Institute for Sustainable Development (IISD), Geneva.

Ghanem, Hafez. 2011. "Food and Nutrition Security: Key Policy Challenges and the Role of Global Governance," Global Policy, London School of Economics, London.

Gibson, John. 2013. "The Crisis in Food Price Data." *Global Food Security* 2: 97–103.

Gilbert, Christopher L. 2010. "How to Understand High Food Prices." *Journal of Agricultural Economics* 61 (2): 398–425.

Gilbert, Christopher L., and C. Wyn Morgan. 2010. "Food Price Volatility." *Philosophical Transactions of the Royal Society B* 365 (1554): 3023–34.

Give2Asia. 2020. "Australian Bushfire Crisis." Give2Asia, Oakland, CA. https://give2asia.org/australian-bushfire-crisis-2019–2020/

Gouel, Christophe, Madhur Gautam, and Will Martin. 2016. "Managing Food Price Volatility in a Large Open Country: The Case of Wheat in India." *Oxford Economic Papers* 68 (3): 811–35. (Also available as Policy Research Working Paper No. 7551, Agriculture Global Practice Group, Work Bank, Washington, DC.)

Government of India. 2016a. Launching of "Feed the Future–India Triangular Training Program (FTF–ITT)" on July 25, 2016. Press Information Bureau, Ministry of Agriculture, Government of India, New Delhi, July 24. http://pib.nic.in/newsite/PrintRelease.aspx?relid=147597

Government of India. 2016b. National Food Security Act (NFSA), 2013. Department of Food & Public Distribution, Ministry of Consumer Affairs, Food & Public Distribution, Government of India, New Delhi. http://dfpd.nic.in/nfsa-act.htm

Graefe, Laurel. 2013. "Oil Shock of 1978–79." Federal Reserve History. http://www.federal reservehistory.org/Events/DetailView/40

Granville, Kevin. 2017. "What is TPP? Behind the Trade Deal That Died." *New York Times*, January 23. https://www.nytimes.com/interactive/2016/business/tpp-explained-what-is-trans-pacific-partnership.html

Gulati, Ashok, and Shweta Saini. 2015. "India's Political Economy Responses to the Global Food Price Shock of 2007–08: Learning Some Lessons." WIDER Working Paper 2015/120, United Nations University World Institute for Development Economics Research (UNU–WIDER), Helsinki.

Haddad, Lawrence. 2015. "Letter to the *New York Times*, Unpublished, Please Use." Development Horizons blog, January 5. http://www.developmenthorizons.com/2015/01/letter-to-new-york-times-unpublished.html

Hazell, Peter, Ghada Shields, and D. Shields. 2005. "The Nature and Extent of Domestic Sources of Food Price Instability and Risk." Paper presented at the international workshop on "Managing Food Price Instability in Low-Income Countries." Washington, DC, February 28–March 1.

Headey, Derek D. 2016. "The Evolution of Global Farming Land: Facts and Interpretations." *Agricultural Economics* 47 (S1): 185–96.

Headey, Derek, and Shenggen Fan. 2008. "Anatomy of a Crisis: The Causes and Consequences of Surging Food Prices." *Agricultural Economics* 39 (s1): 375–91.

Headey, Derek, and Shenggen Fan. 2010. "Reflections on the Global Food Crisis: How Did It Happen? How Has It Hurt? And How Can We Prevent the Next One?" Research Monograph 165, International Food Policy Research Institute (IFPRI), Washington, DC.

Hertel, Thomas W. 2015. "The Challenges of Sustainably Feeding a Growing Planet." *Food Security* 7 (2): 185–98. Also, with Uris L. C. Baldos, Plenary address to the 59th Australian Agricultural and Resource Economics Society (AARES) Annual Conference, Rotorua, New Zealand, February 10–13.

Hertel, Thomas W., Will J. Martin, and Amanda M. Leister. 2010. "Potential Implications of a Special Safeguard Mechanism in the WTO: The Case of Wheat." Policy Research Working Paper No. 5334, World Bank, Washington, DC.

Hertel, Thomas W., and Wallace E. Tyner. 2013. "Market-mediated Environmental Impacts of Biofuels." *Global Food Security* 2: 131–7.

Hindu Business Line. 2017. "FCI Foodgrain Stock at 46 MT, 53% Higher than Buffer Norm." October 9. http://www.thehindubusinessline.com/economy/agri-business/fci-foodgrain-stock/article9894576.ece

HLPE (High Level Panel of Experts on Food Security and Nutrition). 2011. "Price Volatility and Food Security: A Report by the High Level Panel of Experts on Food Security and Nutrition." HLPE Report 1, July, Committee on World Food Security, Rome. http://www.fao.org/3/a-mb737e.pdf

HLPE (High Level Panel of Experts on Food Security and Nutrition). 2014. "Food Losses and Waste in the Context Of Sustainable Food Systems." A report by HLPE of the Committee on World Food Security, Rome. http://www.fao.org/fileadmin/user_upload/hlpe/hlpe_documents/HLPE_Reports/HLPE-Report-8_EN.pdf

Hoda, Anwarul, and Ashok Gulati. 2013. "India's Agricultural Trade Policy and Sustainable Development." Issue Paper No. 49, International Centre for Trade and Sustainable Development, Geneva.

Huang, Jikun, Scott Rozelle, Bharat Ramaswami, and Ume Lele. 2008. "The Real Cost of Surviving." Live Mint, July 21. http://www.livemint.com/Opinion/9vfjNyML1KeugBjUi9ZOBN/The-real-cost-of-surviving.html

Huang, Jikun, Jun Yang, and Scott Rozelle. 2015. "The Political Economy of Food Price Policy in China." In *Food Price Policy in an Era of Market Instability: A Political Economy Analysis*, edited by Per Pinstrup-Andersen, 362–83. Oxford: Oxford University Press.

ICTSD (International Centre for Trade and Sustainable Development). 2017a. "China Signals Cautious Farm Policy Reforms Will Continue." ICTSD Bridges, February 23.

ICTSD (International Centre for Trade and Sustainable Development). 2017b. "Harvesting Outcomes or Planting Seeds for the Future?" ICTSD Bridges, WTO MC11 (Buenos Aires 2017) 21 (40), November 30.

ICTSD (International Centre for Trade and Sustainable Development). 2017c. "Negotiating Global Rules on Agricultural Domestic Support: Options for the World Trade Organization's Buenos Aires Ministerial Conference." Issue Paper, ICTSD, Geneva.

ICTSD (International Centre for Trade and Sustainable Development). 2017d. "Options for WTO Negotiations on Agriculture Domestic Support." Information Note, May 17, ICTSD, Geneva.

ICTSD (International Centre for Trade and Sustainable Development). 2017e. "WTO Ministerial: In Landmark Move, Country Coalitions Set Plans to Advance on New Issues." ICTSD Bridges, December 14.

IEG (Independent Evaluation Group). 2009. "The World Bank Group's Response to the Global Crisis. Update on an Ongoing IEG Evaluation." Evaluation Brief 8, November, World Bank, Washington, DC. http://siteresources.worldbank.org/INTOED/Resources/EB8-web.pdf

IEG (Independent Evaluation Group). 2013. "The World Bank Group and the Global Food Crisis: An Evaluation of the World Bank Group Response." IEG, World Bank Group, Washington, DC. http://ieg.worldbankgroup.org/Data/Evaluation/files/food_crisis_eval.pdf

IMF (International Monetary Fund). 2009. "IMF Involvement in International Trade Policy Issues." Evaluation Report, Independent Evaluation Office (IEO), IMF, Washington, DC.

IMF (International Monetary Fund). 2015. *World Economic Outlook (WEO) 2015—Uneven Growth: Short- and Long-Term Factors*. Washington, DC: IMF. https://www.imf.org/external/pubs/ft/weo/2015/01/pdf/text.pdf

IMF (International Monetary Fund). 2021. *World Economic Outlook (WEO) 2021—Managing Divergent Economies*, April. Washington, DC: IMF. https://www.imf.org/en/Publications/WEO/Issues/2021/03/23/world-economic-outlook-april-2021

Irwin, Scott H., Dwight R. Sanders, and Robert P. Merrin. 2009. "Devil or Angel? The Role of Speculation in the Recent Commodity Price Boom (and Bust)." *Journal of Agricultural and Applied Economics* 41 (2): 377–91. https://pdfs.semanticscholar.org/0d2f/1c2f07ebf31a854094fa2f2f3506027be275.pdf

Ivanic, Maros, and Will Martin. 2008. "Implications of Higher Global Food Prices for Poverty in Low-Income Countries." *Agricultural Economics* 39 (s1): 405–16.

Ivanic, Maros, and Will Martin. 2014. "Short- and Long-Run Impacts of Food Price Changes on Poverty." Policy Research Working Paper No. 7011, August, Development Research Group, Agriculture and Rural Development Team, World Bank Group, Washington, DC. https://openknowledge.worldbank.org/bitstream/handle/10986/20350/WPS7011.pdf

Ivanic, Maros, Will Martin, and Hassan Zaman. 2012. "Estimating the Short-Run Poverty Impacts of the 2010–11 Surge in Food Prices." *World Development* 40 (11): 2302–17.

Jacoby, Hanan. 2016. "Food Prices, Wages, and Welfare in Rural India." *Economic Inquiry* 54 (1): 159–76.

Jadhav, Rajendra, and Mayank Bhardwaj. 2018. "Insight: Collapse in India's Onion Prices Could Leave Modi Smarting in Election." Reuters, December 27. https://www.reuters.com/article/us-india-election-onions-insight-idUSKCN1OR045

Janetos, Anthony. 2017. "What If Several of the World's Biggest Food Crops Failed at the Same Time?" *The Conversation US*, June 4. https://theconversation.com/what-if-several-of-the-worlds-biggest-food-crops-failed-at-the-same-time-74017

Jayne, Thomas S. 2012. "Managing Food Price Instability in East and Southern Africa." *Global Food Security* 1: 143–9.

Jayne, T. S. and Nicholas Minot. 2014. "Managing Food Price Volatility: A Review of Experience in Sub-Saharan Africa." Conference on Food Price Volatility, Food Security, and Trade Policy, World Bank, Washington, DC, September 19.

Josling, Tim. 2011. "Global Food Stamps: An Idea Worth Considering?" Issue Paper No. 36, International Centre for Trade and Sustainable Development (ICTSD), Geneva. http://www.ictsd.org/downloads/2011/12/global-food-stamps-an-idea-worth-considering.pdf

Kalkuhl, Matthias, Joachim von Braun, and Maximo Torero, eds. 2016. *Food Price Volatility and Its Implications for Food Security and Policy*. Cham, Switzerland: Springer International Publishing.

Kanth, D. Ravi. 2017. "Over 100 Nations Back India–China Plan on Farm Subsidies before WTO Meet." Live Mint, September 21. http://www.livemint.com/Politics/rw3CgevdnrSbzGOtbJ3mVP/Over-100-nations-back-IndiaChina-plan-on-farm-subsidies-bef.html

Khairnur, Laili. 2015. "Today Is a Defining Moment for Europe's Flawed Biofuels Policy." *The Guardian*, February 24. https://www.theguardian.com/sustainable-business/2015/feb/24/today-is-a-defining-moment-for-europes-flawed-biofuels-policy

Kharas, Homi, and Kristofer Hamel. 2020. "Turning Back the Poverty Clock: How Will COVID-19 Impact the World's Poorest People?" Future Development blog, May 6. Brookings Institution, Washington, DC. https://www.brookings.edu/blog/future-development/2020/05/06/turning-back-the-poverty-clock-how-will-covid-19-impact-the-worlds-poorest-people

King, Richard. 2011. "So How Many of the World's People Are Hungry? Dunno. Work in Progress…" Post on "From Poverty to Power" blog, a conversational blog written and maintained by Duncan Green, strategic adviser for Oxfam GB. https://oxfamblogs.org/fp2p/so-how-many-of-the-worlds-people-are-hungry-dunno-work-in-progress/

Konandreas, Panos. 2012. "Trade Policy Responses to Food Price Volatility in Poor Net Food-Importing Countries." Issue Paper No. 42, International Centre for Trade and Sustainable Development, Geneva.

Koo, Jawoo, Abdullah Mamun, and Will Martin. 2020. "From Bad to Worse: Poverty Impacts of Food Availability Responses to Weather Shocks in Zambia." IFPRI Discussion Paper 01923, April, International Food Policy Research Institute, Washington, DC. https://www.ifpri.org/publication/bad-worse-poverty-impacts-food-availability-responses-weather-shocks-zambia

Krishna, Anirudh. 2010. *One Illness Away: Why People Become Poor and How They Escape Poverty*. Oxford: Oxford University Press.

Krivonos, Ekaterina, and David Dawe, eds. 2014. *Policy Responses to High Food Prices in Latin America and the Caribbean.* Country Case Studies. Rome: Food and Agriculture Organization of the United Nations (FAO), Trade and Markets Division.

Krugman, Paul R. 2008. "Grains Gone Wild." *New York Times*, April 7. http://www.nytimes.com/2008/04/07/opinion/07krugman.html

Laborde, David, Will Martin, and Rob Vos. 2020. "Poverty and Food Security Could Grow Dramatically as COVID-19 Spreads." IFPRI Blog Research Post, April 16, International Food Policy Research Institute, Washington, DC. https://www.ifpri.org/blog/poverty-and-food-insecurity-could-grow-dramatically-covid-19-spreads

Lal, Rattan. 2013. "Food Security in a Changing Climate." *Ecohydrology & Hydrobiology* 13 (1): 8–21.

Larson, Donald F. 2014. Comments on "Optimal Trade and Storage Policies." Food Price Volatility, Food Security and Trade Policy Conference, Washington, DC, September 18.

Lele, Uma. 1971. *Food Grain Marketing in India: Private Performance and Public Policy.* Ithaca, NY: Cornell University Press.

Lele, Uma. 1990. "Structural Adjustment, Agricultural Development and the Poor: Some Lessons from the Malawian Experience." *World Development* 18 (9): 1207–19.

Lele, Uma. 1991a. "The Gendered Impacts of Structural Adjustment Programs in Africa: Discussion." *American Journal of Agricultural Economics* 73 (5): 1452–55.

Lele, Uma. 1991b. "Women, Structural Adjustment and Transformation: Some Lessons and Questions from the African Experience." In *Structural Adjustment and African Women Farmers*, edited by C. H. Gladwin, 46–80. Gainesville, Florida: University of Florida, Center for African Studies.

Lele, Uma, Sangeeta Bansal, and J. V. Meenakshi. 2020. "Health and Nutrition of India's Labour Force and COVID-19 Challenges." *Economic & Political Weekly* 55 (21), May 23.

Lele, Uma, and Arthur A. Goldsmith. 1989. "The Development of National Agricultural Research Capacity: India's Experience with the Rockefeller Foundation and Its Significance for Africa." *Economic Development and Cultural Change* 37 (2): 305–43.

Lele, Uma, William A. Masters, Joyce Kinabo, J. V. Meenakshi, Bharat Ramaswami, and Julia Tagwireyi, with Winnie F. L. Bell, and Sambuddha Goswami. 2016. "Measuring Food and Nutrition Security: An Independent Technical Assessment and User's Guide for Existing Indicators." Technical Working Group on Measuring Food and Nutrition Security. Food Security Information Network (FSIN), Rome.

Lin, Justin Yifu, and Will Martin. 2010. "The Financial Crisis and Its Impacts on Global Agriculture." *Agricultural Economics* 41 (s1): 133–44.

Lipton, Michael. 1986. "Seasonality and Ultrapoverty." IDS Bulletin 17.3, Institute of Development Studies (IDS), University of Sussex, Brighton.

Lipton, Michael. 2017. "Staples Production: Efficient 'Subsistence' Smallholders Are Key to Poverty Reduction." In *Agriculture and Rural Development in a Globalizing World: Challenges and Opportunities*, edited by Prabhu Pingali and Gershon Feder, 82–102. London: Routledge.

Lustig, Nora. 2008. "Thought for Food: The Challenges of Coping with Soaring Food Prices." Working Paper No. 155, Center for Global Development, Washington, DC.

Lybbert, Travis J., Aaron Smith, and Daniel Sumner. 2014. "Weather Shocks and Inter-Hemispheric Supply Responses: Implications for Climate Change Effects on Global Food Markets." *Climate Change Economics* 5 (4): 1450010-1–11.

Lyddon, Chris. 2017. "Grain Market to Break More Records in 2017–18." World-Grain.com. http://www.world-grain.com/articles/news_home/World_Grain_News/2017/11/Grain_market_to_break_more_rec.aspx?ID=%7BA43AD697-319F-47AB-A9C9-AB9F76A8010F%7D&cck=1

Maltsoglou, Irini, Tatsuji Koizumi, and Erika Felix. 2013. "The Status of Bioenergy Development in Developing Countries." *Global Food Security* 2: 104–9.

Martin, Will, and Aaditya Mattoo, eds. 2011. *Unfinished Business? The WTO's Doha Agenda.* Washington, DC, and London: World Bank and Centre for Economic Policy Research, London School of Economics. https://voxeu.org/sites/default/files/file/unfinished_business_web.pdf

Masters, William A., Agnes Andersson Djurfeldt, Cornelis De Haan, Peter Hazell, Thomas Jayne, Magnus Jirström, and Thomas Reardon. 2013. "Urbanization and Farm Size in Asia and Africa: Implications for Food Security and Agricultural Research." *Global Food Security* 2 (3): 156–65.

Mauldin, William, and Vivian Salama. 2019. "New Nafta Is Threatened by Partisan Split over Enforcement: Democrats, White House Are Clashing over Enforcement of Provisions on the Environment, Workers' Right to Form Unions." *Wall Street Journal*, February 13.

Mehra, Puja. 2018. "Agriculture Needs a Reform Package." *The Hindu*, January 10.

Meijerink, G. W., and T. J. Achterbosch. 2009. "India's Position in Agricultural Trade Liberalization: The Puzzle of Protection." Strategy & Policy Brief #14, December, Wageningen University and Research Centre, The Netherlands.

Meléndez-Ortiz, Ricardo. 2016. "Food Security and Nutrition in the 2016 Globalized Economy." IFPRI blog, April 22. International Food Policy Research Institute, Washington, DC. http://www.ifpri.org/blog/food-security-and-nutrition-2016-globalized-economy

Meyer, Seth, Josef Schmidhuber, and Jesús Barreiro-Hurlé. 2013. "Global Biofuel Trade: How Uncoordinated Biofuel Policy Fuels Resource Use and GHG Emissions." Issue Paper No. 48, International Centre for Trade and Sustainable Development, Geneva.

Minot, Nicholas, and Daniel Ayalew Mekonnen. 2012. "Role of Agricultural Cooperatives and Storage in Rural Ethiopia: Results of Two Surveys." Research for Ethiopia's Agriculture Policy (REAP) and International Food Policy Research Institute (IFPRI), Washington, DC. https://reap.ifpri.info/files/2013/11/ATA-report-on-coops-and-storage_final.pdf

Minten, Bart, Thomas Reardon, Sunipa Das Gupta, Dinghuan Hu, and K. A. S. Murshid. 2016. "Wastage in Food Value Chains in Developing Countries: Evidence from the Potato Sector in Asia." In *Food Security in a Food Abundant World: An Individual Country Perspective*, Frontiers of Economics and Globalization Series, Book 16, edited by Andrew Schmitz, P. Lynn Kennedy, and Troy G. Schmitz, 225–38. Bingley, UK: Emerald Group Publishing Limited.

Mitchell, Donald. 2008. "A Note on Rising Food Prices." Policy Research Working Paper 4682, World Bank, Washington, DC.

Mittal, Anuradha. 2009. "The 2008 Food Price Crisis: Rethinking Food Security Policies." G-24 Discussion Paper Series, No. 56, United Nations Conference on Trade and Development (UNCTAD), New York and Geneva. http://unctad.org/en/Docs/gdsmdpg2420093_en.pdf

MoneyControl.com. 2017a. "Farm Growth May Slip to Over 3% in FY'18: Niti Member." October 13. http://www.moneycontrol.com/news/business/economy/farm-growth-may-slip-to-over-3-in-fy18-niti-member-2412399.html

MoneyControl.com. 2017b. "Foodgrain Output Likely to Touch New Record Next Crop Year: Radha Mohan Singh." May 22. http://www.moneycontrol.com/news/business/

economy/foodgrain-output-likely-to-touch-new-record-next-crop-year-radha-mohan-singh-2285415.html

MoneyControl.com. 2017c. "Govt Revises Up 2016–17 Grain Output to Record 275.68 Mn Ton." August 17. http://www.moneycontrol.com/news/business/economy/govt-revises-up-2016-17-grain-output-to-record-275-68-mn-ton-2362157.html

Montemayor, Raul. 2014. "Public Stockholding for Food Security Purposes: Scenarios and Options for a Permanent Solution." Issue Paper No. 51, International Centre for Trade and Sustainable Development, Geneva.

Mukherjee, Sanjeeb. 2017. "India Set for Record Foodgrain Output." *Business Standard*, May 10. http://www.business-standard.com/article/economy-policy/india-set-for-record-foodgrain-output-117051000083_1.html

Ni, Hongxing. 2013. "Agricultural Domestic Support and Sustainable Development in China." Issue Paper No. 47, International Centre for Trade and Sustainable Development, Geneva.

OECD (Organisation for Economic Co-operation and Development). 2016. "Agricultural Policy Monitoring and Evaluation 2016." OECD, Paris. http://www.oecd-ilibrary.org/content/book/agr_pol-2016-en

OECD (Organisation for Economic Co-operation and Development). 2017. "OECD Agriculture Policy Monitoring and Evaluation 2017." OECD Publishing, Paris. https://read.oecd-ilibrary.org/agriculture-and-food/agricultural-policy-monitoring-and-evaluation-2017_agr_pol-2017-en#page1

OECD (Organization for Economic Co-operation and Development). 2019. Producer and Consumer Support Estimates database. http://www.oecd.org/tad/agricultural-policies/producerandconsumersupportestimatesdatabase.htm

OECD (Organisation for Economic Co-operation and Development) and FAO (Food and Agriculture Organization of the United Nations). 2010. *OECD–FAO Agricultural Outlook 2010*. Paris: OECD Publishing. DOI: http://dx.doi.org/10.1787/agr_outlook-2010-en

OECD (Organisation for Economic Co-operation and Development) and FAO (Food and Agriculture Organization of the United Nations). 2016. *OECD–FAO Agricultural Outlook 2016–2025*. Paris: OECD Publishing. DOI: http://dx.doi.org/10.1787/agr_outlook-2016-en

Parikh, Kirit S. 2013. "Right to Food and Foodgrain Policy." *Economic & Political Weekly* 48 (11): 23–7.

Pfaffenzeller, Stephan, Paul Newbold, and Anthony Rayner. 2007. "A Short Note on Updating the Grilli and Yang Commodity Price Index." *World Bank Economic Review* 21 (1): 151–63.

Pinstrup-Andersen, Per, ed. 2015. *Food Price Policy in an Era of Market Instability: A Political Economy Analysis*. Oxford: Oxford University Press.

Rausser, Gordon C., and Harry de Gorter. 2015. "US Policy Contributions to Agricultural Commodity Price Fluctuations, 2006–2012." In *Food Price Policy in an Era of Market Instability: A Political Economy Analysis*, edited by Pinstrup-Andersen, 433–56. New York: Oxford University Press.

REN21 (Renewable Energy Policy Network for the 21st Century). 2016. *Renewables 2016. Global Status Report*. http://www.ren21.net/wp-content/uploads/2016/10/REN21_GSR2016_FullReport_en_11.pdf

Roberts, Michael J., and Wolfram Schlenker. 2010. "Identifying Supply and Demand Elasticities of Agricultural Commodities: Implications for the US Ethanol Mandate." NBER Working Paper No. 15921, National Bureau of Economic Research, Cambridge, MA. https://www.nber.org/papers/w15921.pdf

Robles, Miguel, Maximo Torero, and Joachim von Braun. 2009. "When Speculation Matters." IFPRI Issue Brief 57, International Food Policy Research Institute (IFPRI), Washington, DC.

S & P Global/Platts. 2017. "China Cuts Wheat Minimum Support Price by Yuan 60/Mt for 2018, First in over a Decade." Platts, Singapore, October 27.

Saini, Shweta, and Ashok Gulati. 2015. "The National Food Security Act (NFSA) 2013—Challenges, Buffer Stocking and the Way Forward." Working Paper No. 297, Indian Council for Research on International Economic Relations (ICRIER), New Delhi.

Saini, Shweta, and Ashok Gulati. 2016. "India's Food Security Policies in the Wake of Global Food Price Volatility." In *Food Price Volatility and Its Implications for Food Security and Policy*, edited by Matthias Kalkuhl, Joachim von Braun, and Maximo Torero, 331–52. Cham, Switzerland: Springer International Publishing.

Sarris, Alexander. 2010. "Trade-related Policies to Ensure Food (Rice) Security in Asia." In *The Rice Crisis: Markets, Policies and Food Security*, ed. by David Dawe, 61–87. London: Food and Agriculture Organization of the United Nations (FAO) and Earthscan.

Schmidhuber, Josef, and Seth Meyer. 2014. "Has the Treadmill Changed Direction? WTO Negotiations in the Light of a Potential New Global Agricultural Market Environment." In *Tackling Agriculture in the Post-Bali Context: A Collection of Short Essays*, edited by Ricardo Meléndez-Ortiz, Christophe Bellman, and Jonathan Hepburn, 33–46. Geneva: International Centre for Trade and Sustainable Development (ICTSD).

Schmidhuber, Josef, Jonathan Pound, Bing Qiao. 2020. "COVID-19: Channels of Transmission to Food and Agriculture." Trade and Market Division Economic and Social Development Department, FAO, Rome. https://doi.org/10.4060/ca8430en

Schmidhuber, Josef, and Bing Qiao. 2020. "Comparing Crises: 'Great Lockdown' vs 'Great Recession.'" Trade and Market Division Economic and Social Development Department, FAO, Rome. https://doi.org/10.4060/ca8833en

Sen, Amartya K. 1985. *Commodities and Capabilities*. Amsterdam: North-Holland.

Sen, Amartya K. 1987a. "The Standard of Living Lecture I, Concepts and Critiques." In *The Standard of Living*, edited by Geoffrey Hawthorn, 1–19. Cambridge: Cambridge University Press.

Sen, Amartya K. 1987b. "The Standard of Living Lecture II, Lives and Capabilities." In *The Standard of Living*, edited by Geoffrey Hawthorn, 20–38. Cambridge: Cambridge University Press.

Sharma, Ramesh. 2011. "Food Export Restrictions: Review of the 2007–2010 Experience and Considerations for Disciplining Restrictive Measures." FAO Commodity and Trade Policy Research Working Paper No. 32, Trade and Markets Division, Food and Agriculture Organization of the United Nations, Rome.

Shelton, Peter. 2013. "Cornell's Per Pinstrup-Andersen: Don't Believe the Hype (and Data) Surrounding Food Price Crises. Cites Food Price Volatility as Greater Danger than High Food Prices." IFPRI Blog, May 9, International Food Policy Research Institute, Washington, DC. http://www.ifpri.org/blog/cornell's-pinstrup-andersen-don't-believe-hype-and-data-surrounding-food-price-crises

Strait Times. 2018. "Trans-Pacific Partnership." *The Strait Times*, Singapore Press Holdings. http://www.straitstimes.com/tags/trans-pacific-partnership

Swain, Daniel L. 2015. "A Tale of Two California Droughts: Lessons amidst Record Warmth and Dryness in a Region of Complex Physical and Human Geography." *Geophysical Research Letters* 42, 9999–10,003, doi:10.1002/2015GL066628.

Swinnen, Johan, Louise Knops, and Kristine van Herck. 2015. "Food Price Volatility and EU Policies." In *Food Price Policy in an Era of Market Instability: A Political Economy Analysis*, edited by Per Pinstrup-Andersen, 457–76. Oxford: Oxford University Press.

Swinnen, Johan, and John McDermott, eds. 2020. *COVID-19 and Global Food Security*. Washington, DC: International Food Policy Research Institute (IFPRI). https://www.ifpri. org/publication/covid-19-and-global-food-security

Tangermann, Stefan. 2010. "Policy Solutions to Agricultural Market Volatility: A Synthesis." Issue Paper No. 33, International Centre for Trade and Sustainable Development, Geneva.

Timmer, C. Peter. 2009. "Did Speculation Affect World Rice Prices?" ESA Working Paper 09–07. Agricultural Development Economics Division, Food and Agriculture Organization of the United Nations, Rome.

Timmer, C. Peter. 2010. "Reflections on Food Crises Past." *Food Policy* 35 (1): 1–11.

Torero, Maximo. 2012. "Food Prices: Riding the Rollercoaster." In 2011 *Global Food Policy Report*, 15–23. Washington, DC: International Food Policy Research Institute (IFPRI).

Uchida, Emi, Scott Rozelle, and Jintao Xu. 2009. "Conservation Payments, Liquidity Constraints and Off-farm Labor: Impacts of the Grain for Green Program on Rural Households in China." In *An Integrated Assessment of China's Ecological Restoration*, edited by Runsheng Yin, 131–57. Dordrecht, The Netherlands: Springer.

UN (United Nations). 2015. "World Population Prospects: Key Findings and Advance Tables," 2015 Revision. Working Paper No. ESA/P/WP.241, Department of Economic and Social Affairs, UN, New York.

US EIA (Energy Information Administration). 2012. "Biofuels Issues and Trends," October, US Department of Energy, Washington, DC.

Valdés, Alberto, and William Foster. 2012. "Net Food-Importing Developing Countries: Who They Are, and Policy Options for Global Price Volatility." Issue Paper No. 43, International Centre for Trade and Sustainable Development, Geneva.

Vos, Rob, Will Martin, and David Laborde. 2020. "How Much Will Global Poverty Increase Because of COVID-19?" IFPRI Blog, March 20, International Food Policy Research Institute, Washington, DC. https://www.ifpri.org/blog/how-much-will-global-poverty-increase-because-covid-19

Vyas, Vijay Shankar. 2016. "The Changing Role of Government in Indian Agriculture." Professor L. S. Venkataramanan Memorial Lecture 14. Institute for Social and Economic Change (ISEC), Bengaluru, India, September 26.

Wanner, Nathan, Carlo Cafiero, Nathalie Troubat, and Piero Conforti. 2014. "Refinements to the FAO Methodology for Estimating the Prevalence of Nourishment Indicator." ESS Working Paper No. 14–05, FAO Statistics Division, Food and Agriculture Organization of the United Nations, Rome. http://www.fao.org/3/a-i4046e.pdf

Wise, Timothy A. 2012. "The Cost Of U.S. Corn Ethanol Expansion." Global Development and Environment Institute Working Paper No. 12–01, Tufts University, Medford, MA.

Wisner, Robert. 2014. "Ethanol, Gasoline, Crude Oil and Corn Prices: Are the Relationships Changing?" Agricultural Marketing Resource Center, AgMRC Renewable Energy & Climate Change Newsletter, March/April. http://www.agmrc.org/renewable-energy/ethanol/ethanol-gasoline-crude-oil-and-corn-prices-are-the-relationships-changing/

Wolf, Martin. 2008. "Food Crisis Is a Chance to Reform Global Agriculture." *Financial Times*, April 29. https://www.ft.com/content/2e5b2f36-1608-11dd-880a-0000779fd2ac

World Bank. 2007. *World Development Report 2008: Agriculture for Development.* Washington, DC: World Bank.

World Bank. 2008. *Indonesia—The World Bank in Indonesia 1999–2006: Country Assistance Evaluation.* Washington, DC: World Bank.

World Bank. 2012. "Food Prices, Nutrition, and the Millennium Development Goals." Global Monitoring Report 2012. Washington, DC: World Bank. http://www.imf.org/external/pubs/ ft/gmr/2012/eng/gmr.pdf

World Bank. 2013. "Implementing Agriculture for Development: World Bank Group Agriculture Action Plan (2013–2015)." World Bank, Washington, DC.

World Bank. 2015a. "Commodity Markets Outlook. Special Focus: How Important Are China and India in Global Commodity Markets." A World Bank Quarterly Report, Washington, DC. http://siteresources.worldbank.org/INTPROSPECTS/Resources/334934–1304428586133/ GEP2015c_commodity_Jul2015.pdf

World Bank. 2015b. "The State of Social Safety Nets 2015." World Bank, Washington, DC. http:// documents.worldbank.org/curated/en/415491467994645020/pdf/97882-PUB-REVISED-Box393232B-PUBLIC-DOCDATE-6-29-2015-DOI-10-1596978-1-4648-0543-1-EPI-1464805431.pdf

World Bank. 2017a. "Closing the Gap: The State of Social Safety Nets 2017." World Bank, Washington, DC. http://documents.worldbank.org/curated/en/811281494500586712/pdf/ 114866-WP-PUBLIC-10-5-2017-10-41-8-ClosingtheGapBrochure.pdf

World Bank. 2017b. "Commodity Prices Likely to Rise Further in 2018." Who We Are/News/ Press Release, October 26. http://www.worldbank.org/en/news/press-release/2017/10/ 26/commodity-prices-likely-to-rise-further-in-2018-world-bank

World Bank. 2020. "Povcalnet: An Online Analysis Tool for Global Poverty Monitoring." http:// iresearch.worldbank.org/PovcalNet/home.aspx

World Bank and FAO (Food and Agriculture Organization of the United Nations). 2012. "The Grain Chain: Food Security and Managing Wheat Imports in Arab Countries." World Bank, Washington, DC. http://www.fao.org/3/a-bp079e.pdf

Wright, Brian D. 2011a. "Price Volatility in Agricultural Commodities: Market Fundamentals." Presentation at the FARMD (Forum for Agricultural Risk Management in Development) Annual Conference: Price Volatility and Climate Change, Implications for the Ag-Risk Management Agenda, Zurich, June 9–10. http://www.agriskmanagementforum.org/con tent/price-volatility-agricultural-commodities-market-fundamentals

Wright, Brian D. 2011b. "The Economics of Grain Price Volatility." *Applied Economic Perspectives and Policies* 33 (1): 32–58.

Wright, Brian D. 2012. "International Grain Reserves and Other Instruments to Address Volatility in Grain Markets." *World Bank Research Observer* 27 (2): 222–60.

Wright, Brian D. 2013. "Price Volatility, Reserves, and Public Policy." Presentation at the 17th International Consortium on Applied Bioeconomy Research (ICABR) Conference on "Innovation and Policy for the Bioeconomy," Ravello, June 19. http://slideplayer.com/slide/ 1635556/

Wright, Brian D. 2014a. "Causes and Types of Food Price Volatility." Presentation at the Conference on Food Price Volatility, Food Security and Trade Policy, Washington, DC, September 18–19. http://www.worldbank.org/content/dam/Worldbank/Event/DEC/ DECAR-food-conference-sep-2014/DECAR-food-conference-sep18-19-presentation-Brian-Wright-140917.pdf

Wright, Brian D. 2014b. "Global Biofuels: Key to the Puzzle of Grain Market Behavior." *Journal of Economic Perspectives* 28 (1): 73–98.

WTO (World Trade Organization). 2016. "Members' Participation in the Normal Growth of World Trade in Agricultural Products," Article 18.5 of the Agreement on Agriculture. Note by the Secretariat. G/AG/W/32/Rev.15, WTO, Geneva.

WTO (World Trade Organization). 2017. Eleventh WTO Ministerial Conference. https://www.wto.org/english/thewto_e/minist_e/mc11_e/mc11_e.htm

WTO (World Trade Organization). 2020. "Domestic Support: Amber, Blue and Green Boxes. Agriculture Negotiations: Backgrounder." https://www.wto.org/english/tratop_e/agric_e/negs_bkgrnd13_boxes_e.htm

Xu, Jintao, Andy White, and Uma Lele. 2010. "China's Forest Land Tenure Reform: Impacts and Implications for Choice, Conservation and Climate Change." Rights and Resources Initiative, Washington, DC.

Xu, Kai. 2015. "Why Are Agricultural Goods Not Traded More Intensively: High Trade Costs or Low Productivity Variations?" *World Economy* 38 (11): 1722–43.

Yu, Wusheng. 2017. "How China's Farm Policy Reforms Could Affect Trade and Markets: A Focus on Grains and Cotton." Issue Paper, International Centre for Trade and Sustainable Trade, Geneva.

4

From Food Security to Nutrition Security for All

Uma Lele and Sambuddha Goswami

Summary

The World Health Organization (WHO) declares malnutrition, in all its forms, to be a critical global public health problem. Increasingly, undernutrition and overweight, obesity, and diet-related noncommunicable diseases (NCDs) coexist in nations, communities, and households—and even within the same individual across the life course. Undernutrition continues to cause nearly half the deaths in children under 5 years and impedes achievement in surviving children, diminishing their economic, social, educational, and occupational potentials. Similarly, overweight, obesity, and diet-related NCDs, increasing in children and adults, result in early onset of debilitating diseases, such as diabetes and heart disease, leading to premature mortality.

In this chapter, we review the evolution of the international food security and nutrition (FSN) discourse since the end of the Second World War. Nutrition was part of the founding principles of the Food and Agriculture Organization of the United Nations (FAO), but as we show in this chapter, the focus shifted to proteins and then to calories, before shifting again in recent years to food security, defined and measured largely as calorie deficits to nutrition. Attention to FSN, broadly defined, has accelerated in recent years, after its near neglect starting in the 1980s, until about 2007. Then, a major series of empirical analyses and advocacy brought nutrition to the forefront. Since, then, the food systems discourse has intensified and become more complex with both the report of the Global Panel on Agriculture and Food Systems for Nutrition (GLOPAN 2016), "Food Systems and Diets" and the report of the Committee on World Food Security (CFS)–High Level Panel of Experts on Food Security and Nutrition (HLPE), "Nutrition and Food Systems" (HLPE 2017), providing a broader and encompassing analysis of these systems, followed by the much debated the EAT–*Lancet* Commission report (Willett et al. 2019), and then, the planned United Nations (UN) Food Summit in 2021 (UN 2020b). With the increasing role of value chains and purchased foods in consumption, the nature of the debate on food systems has changed. Historically, policy focus and actions on food security have been cyclical, with attention to food policies growing in periods of food shortages and waning with surpluses. Now, climate change and resource degradation are long-term threats. They have reduced the resilience of food systems and robbed food of its nutrient content. These various factors have increased our understanding of the complexity of food and nutrition security (WHO 2018b, 2020). The situation calls for transformative change in research, information and outreach, political commitment, and financial and institutional capacity to achieve sustainable and equitable food systems. Change, to date, has been incremental, not transformative, however, to significantly improve outcomes, an issue to which will be a central theme of the Food Systems Summit 2021 and the intensive discussions leading up to it (UN 2020b).

Food for All: International Organizations and the Transformation of Agriculture. Uma Lele, Manmohan Agarwal, Brian C. Baldwin, and Sambuddha Goswami, Oxford University Press. © Uma Lele, Manmohan Agarwal, Brian C. Baldwin, and Sambuddha Goswami 2021. DOI: 10.1093/oso/9780198755173.003.0005

The Sustainable Development Goals (SDGs) have powered the recent FSN discourse. SDG2 reflects progress in conceptualizing FSN but also illustrates its complexity. It is broader in scope than Millennium Development Goal 1 (to halve the number of hungry by 2015). SDG2 aims to "end hunger and malnutrition in all its forms, double agricultural productivity and income, ensure sustainability and practice resilient agriculture, maintain genetic biodiversity, correct and prevent trade restrictions and distortions, promote markets and increase investments including through international cooperation" (UN 2020a). And, yet, SDG2 is not broad enough; it does not pay enough attention to the growing incidence of obesity, as do the World Health Assembly (WHA) targets for 2025 (FAO et al. 2019). Furthermore, the interrelationship of the subtargets of SDG2 is anything but straightforward.[1] Growth in agricultural productivity does not necessarily increase incomes of small farmers, and productivity growth does not always assure improved nutrition. Increased income does not necessarily lead to improved nutrition. This also applies to the relationship of SDG2 to several other of the 16 SDGs. The scope of this chapter is necessarily broad, therefore, extending well beyond SDG2, in considering the relationship between FSN and multiple dimensions of poverty and deprivation.

Traditionally, the World Bank and international organizations (IOs) have focused on income poverty, but increasingly the concept of multidimensional poverty (MDP) has rightly received attention in explaining FSN. MDP is substantially higher than income poverty, particularly among children. It explains better the different aspects of nutritional status than does income poverty. International aid is disproportionately skewed away from countries with high incidence of MDP. This means that national policy and its implementation is more important in countries with the highest incidence of MDP. We provide evidence in this chapter to support these observations. In addition, we examine the relationship of gender inequality and nutrition, and gender and obesity, and the roles of changing lifestyles, food systems, and modern food supply systems and value chains. We conclude with the lessons of this body of knowledge for future research and action, particularly in focusing on the multidimensional nature of poverty, the food systems approach, critical role of gender, and the need for public policy to examine the critical choices it faces in dealing with the private sector, ensuring the latter plays a more constructive role in containing the scourge of obesity and food-related diseases, including diabetes, cancer, and heart-related diseases, among others.

Introduction

In this chapter, we first outline some of the commonly used concepts of chronic and transitory undernutrition, micronutrient deficiencies, and obesity, and then define the concepts of FSN and implications of concepts for measurement. We then present some of the recent trends in hunger including, in particular, the recent rise in the incidence of hunger. We show the disconnect between trends in global and regional poverty and trends in global and regional hunger. Reported incidence of poverty have declined very rapidly, whereas reported undernourishment has declined far more slowly, and even that slow decline has been reversed in recent years, whereas poverty trends had slowed but not

---

[1] See https://sustainabledevelopment.un.org/sdg2 and "Targets & Indicators" for a list of all targets and indicators for SDG2.

declined until the onset of COVID-19. Given the focus of this book on food for all at all times, we then look at the alternative approaches to exploring the relationship between poverty and different concepts of food security: for example, calorie gap and nutrient gap, as each relates to the issues of "sustainable" food systems, an idea increasingly in vogue. We also consider an entitlement approach and the multidimensional nature of poverty. Each provides a different way out of food insecurity. Half the multidimensionally poor are children, a phenomenon that often gets overlooked in the discussion of income poverty, including the distressing conditions of destitution. Having established the conditions of poverty, we explore the relationship between MDP and different indicators of food security: for example, traditionally measured undernutrition using FAO's measures of Prevalence of Undernourishment (PoU) and the more recent Food Insecurity Experience Scale (FIES), and distinct from dietary diversity and the extent of its nutritional content, stunting, and wasting. Equally important, we look at various indicators of gender equality, as constructed by different IOs, across countries, and indicators of food security, again showing significant correlation between reducing MDP and income poverty with stunting.

This discussion is followed by how the concept of nutrition itself has evolved: for example, from protein malnutrition to calorie deficit to micronutrient deficiency, concepts that were in ascendancy in different decades. Advocacy in food and nutrition by different organizations—FAO starting in the 1970s, the United Nations Children's Fund (UNICEF) from the early 1990s, and WHO, as reflected in its WHA targets to 2025—has in each case played a role in emphasizing different aspects of food security: for example, FAO's halving the number of undernourished by 2015, UNICEF on the issues of child care and women's health indicators, and WHO on nutrition and health-related indicators. We discuss the rise, fall, and subsequent rebound of prioritizing nutrition by decade, a combination of changing expert opinion in ascendancy and the decline of attention to nutrition in the 1980s and 1990s, as a result of the external environment. Also, we describe how nutrition advocacy by the development community brought nutrition to the center stage. After a lost decade, the focus on food security from 2007 to 2012, coinciding with the period of the food and financial crises, was based almost entirely on food prices, but then changed from food to nutrition. Yet, there are some key aspects of nutrition that were overlooked in the Millennium Development Goals (MDGs) and later in SDGs, most notably the growing incidence of obesity, associated with nutrition transition and changing lifestyles with life-cycle effects on health. It is a phenomenon that has also been overlooked by economists, including multinationals' influence on the political economy and the US government's influencing of international food standards, the role of regulation and taxation in containing unhealthy foods, and the role of information, consumer education and, more generally, the public sector in the role of reining in obesity. Using empirical data from East and Southern African countries in a recent paper, Khonje, Ecker, and Qaim (2020) showed that "modern retailers contribute to higher consumption of ultra-processed foods and calories. But they also increase protein and micronutrient intakes among adults and children, mainly through higher consumption of meat and dairy." The authors noted that "the findings underline that modern retailers can influence diets and nutrition in positive and negative ways." They concluded: "Differentiated regulatory policies are needed to shape food environments for healthy food choices and nutrition." Such literature on both the positive and negative impacts of rapidly changing value chains on nutrition is relatively recent, and it has not yet led to a full examination of what healthy food systems or "sustainable" food systems mean, although both of these terms are used. Nor is there yet a systematic exploration of implications for public policy at the local, national, and international levels to contribute to better outcomes (see Béné et al. 2019).

Nevertheless, there has been an upsurge in literature on food and nutrition since 2006–7, including reports from IOs and international public policy journals such as *The Lancet*. They echo some common themes—the triple burden of food insecurity (undernourishment, malnourishment, and obesity), urbanization, population, income growth, and the profound changes in the food environment and consumption patterns, arising from the growth of the food industry and the changing economics of purchased foods, and the need to move away from business as usual (Willett et al. 2019).

The EAT–*Lancet* commission report (Willett et al. 2019), issued by *The Lancet* in January 2019, has become a subject of much debate and discussion and needs attention. It brought together 37 experts from 16 countries to develop scientific targets for healthy diets from sustainable food production. The report was supported by Wellcome Trust and had no corporate interests promoting it. The Commission calls for "widespread multi-sector, multi-level action including: a substantial global shift toward healthy dietary patterns; large reductions in food loss and waste; and major improvements in food production practices. The data are both sufficient and strong enough to warrant immediate action" (Willett et al. 2019, 26).

Diane Hatz (2019), in a review of the report, further highlighted its findings:

- Our diets should include less meat and more plants. It's healthier for us and the planet.
- By adopting a planetary healthy diet, we would help avoid severe environmental degradation and prevent approximately 11 million human deaths annually.
- Food production is responsible for 30% of global greenhouse gas [GHG] emissions and 70% of freshwater use.
- Globally, over 2 billion adults are overweight or obese, and diet-related diseases such as diabetes, cancer and heart disease are among the leading causes of global deaths.
- Currently, we waste 30–50% of our food, from the farm to your fridge. We must substantially reduce food loss at both levels.
- We must stop creating new farmland, restore and reforest degraded land, and protect 50 percent of the Earth as intact ecosystems.
- We must improve how oceans are managed so that there remain fish to eat. Fish must be harvested sustainably.
- "Sustainably intensify food production to increase high quality output"—or, in other words, we must farm regeneratively and sustainably produce more food on the land we have. Included in this is restoring the health of soil.
- Focus on producing healthy food, not large quantities of unhealthy food.

In summary, the EAT–*Lancet* commission report recommendations are:

- Adopt healthy diets: increase consumption of plant-based foods, substantially limiting animal-sourced foods;
- Reorient agricultural priorities from producing high quantities to producing healthy food;
- Sustainably intensify food production to increase high quality output;
- Feed humanity on existing cropland, adopt "Half Earth" strategy, improve ocean management;
- Halve food loss and waste, move toward circular food economy (Willett et al. 2019).

The opposition to the report comes in part from the livestock industry, with factory farms producing intensive livestock with high GHG emissions and from people consuming substantially larger quantities of meat than the report recommends. At the other end of the spectrum, objection also comes from countries where livestock is range-fed, is not intensive, and is an important source of livelihood for poor people: for example, when Ethiopia's livestock minister expressed concern about the report. There are also other issues on which the report can be challenged. Estimates of food losses are highly debated, as is the definition of a healthy diet, the relationship between diet and disease, and most importantly, the knowledge in the populations at large about healthy diets.

Notwithstanding these reservations, the report does not say anything that was not already known in general terms previously. An important question is whether it can make a material difference to diets to change planetary outcomes. And the changes have to be both in upgrading consumption, as in India, and in downsizing and improving the balance of diets in countries in North and South America, where obesity is growing at alarming rates. In India, a recent study shows a substantial gap in food consumption relative to the EAT standards, in all but the highest income level category, also a fact that was well known well before the EAT commission report was issued:

> The average daily calorie consumption in India is below the recommended 2503 kcal/capita/day across all groups compared, except for the richest 5% of the population. Calorie share of whole grains is significantly higher than the EAT-*Lancet* recommendations while those of fruits, vegetables, legumes, meat, fish and eggs are significantly lower. The share of calories from protein sources is only 6–8% in India compared to 29% in the reference diet. The imbalance is highest for the households in the lowest decile of consumption expenditure, but even the richest households in India do not consume adequate amounts of fruits, vegetables and non-cereal proteins in their diets. An average Indian household consumes more calories from processed foods than fruits. (Sharma et al. 2020)

Important questions at the national, institutional, and personal levels are of political will and need for incentives to consume healthy diets and avoid harm—personal and planetary. Those ingredients are often missing. Let us hope the UN Food System Summit creates global resolve to do better.

A discussion paper, "Shift to Healthy and Sustainable Consumption Patterns," produced by the UN Food Systems Summit 2021 Scientific Group notes:

> Food-based dietary guidelines (FBDGs) are intended to translate these common principles into nationally or regionally relevant recommendations that consider these differences, as well as context-specific diet-related health challenges. Most FBDGs recommend consuming a wide variety of foods, plentiful fruits and vegetables, inclusion of starchy staples, animal-source foods and legumes, and to limit excessive fat, salt, and sugars (Herforth et al. 2019; Springmann et al. 2020). However, there can be wide variation in inclusion of and recommendations for other foods. Only 17% of FBDGs make specific recommendations about quantities of meat/egg/poultry/animal source food to consume (20% make specific recommendations about fish), and only three countries (Finland, Sweden and Greece) make specific quantitative recommendations to limit red meat (Herforth et al. 2019). Only around a quarter of FBDGs recommend limiting consumption of ultra-processed foods, yet this is emerging as one of the most significant dietary challenges around the world.

Adherence with national FBDGs and recommendations around the world is shockingly low. The average diet [based on adjusted food availability as a proxy for consumption] in 28% of countries with national FBDGs did not meet a single dietary recommendation, and the vast majority of countries (88%) met no more than 2 out of 12 dietary recommendations (Springmann et al. 2020). Consumption surveys show vast regional and national differences in consumption of the major food groups (Afshin et al. 2019). No regions globally have an average intake of fruits, whole grains, or nuts and seeds in line with recommendations and only central Asia meets the recommendations for vegetables. In contrast, the global (and several regional) average intake of red meat, processed meat and sugar-sweetened beverages exceeds recommended limits....

The EAT–*Lancet* study demonstrated that rebalancing consumption will require different consumer behaviour shifts in different locations and contexts. For example, in low-income countries achieving the healthy diet from sustainable food systems would require increasing the consumption of most nutrient-rich food groups, including animal sourced foods, vegetables, pulses and fruits, while reducing some starches, oils and discretionary foods (Willet et al. 2019). In contrast, in many-high income countries achieving the same balance would require reducing the consumption of animal-sourced foods, sugars and discretionary/processed foods, while still increasing the consumption of healthy plant-based ingredients...Many countries experiencing the double-burden of malnutrition, would require these actions to play simultaneously to achieve the desired benefits (Willett et al. 2019; Development Initiatives 2020; HLPE 2020), while a smaller number of countries (e.g., Japan) have smaller adjustments to make....

Low- and lower-middle-income countries, where populations still suffer undernutrition and nutrient deficiencies, may need to increase the consumption of nutritious foods even when they might result in higher national carbon footprints in order to meet recommended dietary needs and nutrition goals, particularly to prevent undernutrition. Other countries, especially upper-middle-income and high-income countries, where diet patterns exceed optimal energy requirements and people consume more animal source foods than required, require major changes in dietary practices and system-wide changes in food production, food environments and trade. (Herrero et al. 2020)

Large transformations in food systems at the producer, consumer, political economy, and food environments levels will be required, and countries will need to rebalance agricultural policies with a view to how they impact health and sustainability.

Food safety is positioned at the intersection of agri-food systems and health. Food safety management systems (FSMS) are designed to prevent, reduce, or eliminate hazards along the food chain (Herrero et al. 2020). According to a World Bank report, "The Safe Food Imperative":

No representative and comprehensive benchmarking program exists for food safety management capacities in LMICs [lower middle-income countries]. This contrasts with the situation in Organisation for Economic Co-operation and Development countries, where several detailed comparative assessments of food safety performance have been completed...

The widest gaps between needed and actual food safety management capacity are found in lower-middle-income countries. Especially the larger of these countries are important food safety "hot spots," where the exposure of populations to food hazards is increasing, consumer food safety confidence is waning, and neither decentralized food safety regulatory capacity nor the governance arrangements of the formal private sector food industry are able to match the emerging challenges. These countries need comprehensive measures to curb what is likely to be a substantially higher health and economic burden of FBD [foodborne diseases] in the coming years. (Jaffee et al. 2019, xxv, xxvii)

Undernutrition, Micronutrient Deficiencies, and Obesity

Globally, the incidence of poverty and hunger (that is, people facing calorie gaps using FAO's measure of PoU) had declined steadily since 1990. Nearly a billion people had come out of poverty by 2015. The number of undernourished was 785 million, and the number of severely food insecure was nearly 80 million in 2015 (FSIN 2017; FAO et al. 2019). Reversing the downward trend by 2018, 822 million (corresponding to about 1 in every 9 people in the world) were undernourished (FAO et al. 2019). The *State of Food Security and Nutrition in the World* (*SOFI*) reported: "According to the latest estimates, 9.2 percent of the world population (or slightly more than 700 million people) were exposed to severe levels of food insecurity in 2018, implying reductions in the quantity of food consumed to the extent that they have possibly experienced hunger" (FAO et al. 2019, 15).

The *SOFI 2019* report stated further:

A broader look at the extent of food insecurity beyond severe levels and hunger reveals that an additional 17.2 percent of the world population, or 1.3 billion people, have experienced food insecurity at moderate levels. This implies that these additional 1.3 billion people did not have regular access to nutritious and sufficient food...

The combination of moderate and severe levels of food insecurity brings the estimated... [total] to 26.4 percent of the world population, amounting to... about 2 billion people." (FAO et al. 2019, 19)

SOFI 2020 has revised these numbers again, and we comment further on analysis and methodology in this chapter.

Some 113 million were facing crisis-level food insecurity or worse (Integrated Food Security Phase Classification [IPC], or Cadre Harmonisé [CH] Phase 3 and above), according to the "Global Report on Food Crises" (GRFC) of the Food Security Information Network (FSIN 2019). In discussing differing food security assessments for different objectives, the *SOFI 2019* report noted:

... while chronic food insecurity as captured by PoU [described later in this chapter] or FI$_{sev}$ [severe food insecurity] is a long-term or persistent inability to meet food consumption requirements, acute or transitory food insecurity as captured in GRFC numbers is a short-term, possibly temporary, inability to meet food consumption requirements related to sporadic crises, conditions that can be highly susceptible to change and can manifest in a population within a short time frame, as a result of sudden changes or shocks. (FAO et al. 2019)

According to the *SOFI* 2019:

One in seven newborns, or 20.5 million babies globally, suffered from low birthweight in 2015; no progress has been made in reducing low birthweight since 2012. The number of children under five years in the world affected by stunting, by contrast, has decreased by 10 percent in the past six years....

Overweight and obesity continue to increase in all regions, particularly among school-age children and adults. In 2018, an estimated 40 million children under five were overweight. (FAO et al. 2019, xiv–xv)

FAO's aggregate estimate of PoU has declined from 821 million in 2019, to 690 million in 2020, prior to the pandemic (FAO et al. 2020, viii). The decline is mainly because undernourishment estimates for China have been adjusted by over 100 million people, based on using a newly available series of household data going back to 2000, which resulted in a substantial downward shift of the number of undernourished in the world. China's undernourished decreased from 10 percent of its population to 2 percent. The new PoU estimates of 690 million hungry amount to 8.9 percent of the world population, but it is still up by 10 million people in one year and by nearly 60 million over five years from 2014 to 2019, confirming the trend reported in past editions, even as the number has changed from that published in recent reports (FAO et al. 2020, 4–5). For more details on reasons why the estimated number of undernourished changes, see Lele, Goswami, and Mekonnen (2020).

Depending on the concept of food insecurity and goals set for its eradication, the cost varies considerably as Table 4.1, presenting four different concepts, indicates.

Food Security and Nutrition: Terms and Measurement

Hunger means different things to different people. FAO often uses the term "hunger," a popular term, interchangeably with "undernourishment," a more technical term. The United States Department of Agriculture (USDA), on the other hand, states it has no measures of hunger. USDA sought the guidance of the Committee on National Statistics (CNSTAT) of the National Academies on the use of the word "hunger" in connection with food insecurity. The Committee "concluded that in official statistics, resource-constrained hunger (that is, physiological hunger resulting from food insecurity) '...should refer to a potential consequence of food insecurity that, because of prolonged, involuntary lack of food, results in discomfort, illness, weakness, or pain that goes beyond the usual uneasy sensation'" (USDA 2019a).

PoU is an estimate of the proportion of the population that has been in a condition of undernourishment over a reference period (usually one year) (FAO et al. 2017, 95). For the PoU, country-level estimates of food production, trade, and changes in stocks are used annually to infer a food balance sheet for each country, using a distribution of income, providing an estimate *of total energy consumption*. PoU, a national-level proxy measure of undernourishment, is essentially a measure of *calorie deficit* from some prescribed minimum bodily requirement. The World Food Programme (WFP) measures degrees of severity of undernourishment in populations requiring emergency operations, as we discuss later in the chapter.

Until recently, there was not an individual-level measure that could be used to make valid comparisons of food insecurity across countries. In 2013, FAO introduced a new measure of food insecurity at the individual level, called Voices of the Hungry, developed, tested, and used by the United States and some Latin American countries since 1995 (FAO 2020a). FIES is a more direct measure of people's access to food and represents the percentage of

Table 4.1 Ending hunger: Overview of four costing exercises

Model/framework and institution(s)	Question asked and time frame	Investments included	Hunger target and key modeling factors included	Annual cost (US$)
Achieving Zero Hunger (FAO, IFAD, WFP)	What are the additional transfers and investments needed to end poverty and hunger in all countries by 2030?	Poverty gap transfers and pro-poor public investment in irrigation, genetic resources, mechanization, agroprocessing, infrastructure, institutions, and agricultural R&D	Zero hunger target	265 billion
IMPACT (International Model for Policy Analysis of Agricultural Commodities and Trade, IFPRI)	How much would hunger decrease given investments to achieve target yield increases by 2030?	Agricultural R&D irrigation expansion, water use efficiency, soil management, and infrastructure	5% hunger target; effects of climate change included	52 billion
MIRAGRODEP (MIRAGE model developed by AGRODEP (IFPRI–IISD)	What is the minimum cost to end hunger for vulnerable households in all countries by 2030?	Social safety nets, farm support, and rural development	5% hunger target; bottom up approach with household-level targeted inventions	11 billion
Investment Framework for Nutrition (World Bank)	What is the minimum cost to meet the World Health Assembly (WHA) goals on reducing undernutrition by 2025?	Targeted nutrition interventions (micronutrient and protein supplementation, promoting good health and hygiene, complementary foods) and select nutrition-sensitive interventions (staple fortification and pro-breastfeeding policies)	40% reduction in child stunting; 50% reduction in anemia in women; 50% increase in exclusive breastfeeding rates; 5% child wasting	7 billion

Notes: IFAD = International Fund for Agricultural Development; IFPRI = International Food Policy Research Institute; IISD = International Institute for Sustainable Development; WFP = World Food Programme; MIRAGE = Modelling International Relations under Applied General Equilibrium; AGRODEP = African Growth and Development Policy Modeling Consortium.

Source: Fan et al. (2018, table 1, 3). [Adapted from Mason-D'Croz et al. 2016. "IMPACT Projections of Investments in Agriculture and Implications for Reducing Hunger in Africa by 2030: Results from the IMPACT Model, Version 3.3." IFPRI Project report, International Food Policy Research Institute, Washington, DC.]

individuals in the national adult population (15 or more years of age) that have experienced moderate or severe levels of food insecurity during the previous year. Relying on people's direct responses to eight questions, in the case of FAO (and 15 questions in the United States), regarding their access to adequate food, the FAO survey module has been applied to nationally representative samples of adult populations in 140 countries, since 2014, to cover 90 percent of the world's population (FAO 2017b, 2020a, 2020b).

SDGs, unlike MDGs, include addressing all 17 goals in developed as well as developing countries. Furthermore, some of FAO's approaches—for example, FIES discussed later— have been influenced by USDA. For both reasons, it is relevant to see how the United States treats food insecurity analytically and the extent of the incidence of food insecurity. Neither PoU, nor FIES tells us the actual number of poor. In the case of PoU, we do not know if the hungry are men or women, or where they are located. We discuss data issues further in the sections that follow. The relationship between poverty and food insecurity is of particular relevance, whether in developed or developing countries.

The World Bank began to include poverty estimates for developed countries in 2013. Of the 769 million people who lived on less at US$1.90 a day in 2013, the world's very poorest, 3.2 million lived in the United States, and 3.3 million in other high-income countries (most in Italy, Japan, and Spain) (Deaton 2018).The World Bank adjusts its poverty estimates for differences in prices across countries, but it ignores differences in needs. Noting that Oxford economist Robert Allen estimated needs-based absolute poverty lines for rich countries, which matched more accurately the US$1.90 line for poor countries, with US$4 per day around the middle of his estimates, Deaton uses this estimate to report "5.3 million Americans who are absolutely poor by global standards." This number is about the same as in all the poor in the rest of the Organisation for Economic Co-operation and Development (OECD) countries. For further discussion, see UN–OHCHR (2017).

Upturn in the Incidence of Hunger

The *SOFI 2018* notes: "The number of extreme [climate-related] events, including extreme heat, droughts, floods and storms, has doubled since the early 1990s, with an average of 213 of these events occurring every year during the period of 1990–2016" (FAO et al. 2018, 39).

Although there was a decline in the numbers of undernourished in developing countries, FAO estimated that until 2015, this decline was smaller in number than the decline in the number of poor that the World Bank estimated, and we explore the relationship between changes in poverty and changes in hunger later.[2] "After decades of steady decline, the trend in world hunger—as measured by the PoU—reverted in 2015, remaining virtually unchanged in the past three years at a level slightly below 11 percent. The 822 million hungry in 2018, following a steady rise from 785 million people in 2015, underscored "the immense challenge of achieving the Zero Hunger target by 2030" (FAO et al. 2019, xvi). FAO attributes the rise to the increasing incidence of conflict- affected countries (often a leading cause of famine), compounded by climate-related factors, such as the El Niño phenomenon, inflicting both drought and flood conditions (FAO et al. 2018).

---

[2] *SOFI* 2017 defines *undernourishment* "as the condition in which an individual's habitual food consumption is insufficient to provide the amount of dietary energy required to maintain a normal, active, healthy life" (FAO et al. 2017, 95).

The global PoU[3] in 2018 increased to 10.8 percent of the global population, up from 10.6 percent in 2015, representing a return to the level reached in 2014, and suggesting a reversal of the downward trend that was sustained over recent decades (FAO et al. 2018). *SOFI* 2019 reported:

> Hunger is on the rise in almost all African subregions, making Africa the region with the highest prevalence of undernourishment, at almost 20 percent. Hunger is also slowly rising in Latin America and the Caribbean, although its prevalence is still below 7 percent. In Asia, Western Asia shows a continuous increase since 2010, with more than 12 percent of its population undernourished today. (FAO et al. 2019, xiv)

SOFI 2019 also reported an alarming situation in Africa, primarily a result of increased conflict and compounded by droughts. In contrast:

> In Asia, the PoU has been steadily decreasing in most regions, reaching 11.4 percent in 2017. The exception is Western Asia, where the PoU has increased since 2010 to reach more than 12 percent of the population. This level in the region is second only to Southern Asia, which, despite great progress in the last five years, is still the subregion where undernourishment is highest, at almost 15 percent.
>
> [Again,] within the Western Asian subregion, the difference is striking between countries that have been affected by popular uprisings in Arab states and other conflicts, and those that have not been affected. For those affected countries,...an increase in the PoU from the already higher value of 17.8 percent, to 27.0 percent [is noted], almost doubling the number of undernourished between 2010 and 2018. The PoU did not change during the same period in the other countries in the region.
>
> In Latin America and the Caribbean (LAC), [too,] rates of undernourishment have increased in recent years, largely as a consequence of the situation in South America, where the PoU increased from 4.6 percent in 2013 to 5.5 percent in 2017. In fact, South America hosts the majority (68 percent) of the undernourished in Latin America....
>
> By contrast, prevalence rates of undernourishment in Central America and the Caribbean, despite being higher than those in South America, have been decreasing in recent years. This is consistent with the economic growth pattern observed in these subregions, where real GDP [gross domestic product] grew at a rate of about 4 percent between 2014 and 2018, with moderate rates of inflation consistently below 3 percent in the same period.
>
> Analysis of the distribution of the undernourished population across regions in the world shows that the majority (more than 500 million) live in Asia. The number has been increasing steadily in Africa, where it reached almost 260 million people in 2018, with more than 90 percent living in sub-Saharan Africa. (FAO et al. 2019, 6–9, 11)

GRFC "focuses specifically on the most severe manifestations of acute food insecurity in the world's most pressing food crises" (FSIN 2019, 3), the majority of which are conflict: Yemen, the Democratic Republic of the Congo, Afghanistan, Ethiopia, the Syrian

---

[3] The PoU is an estimate of the proportion of the population that has been in a condition of undernourishment over a reference period (usually one year) (FAO et al. 2017, 95). For the PoU, country-level estimates of food production, trade, and changes in stocks are used annually to infer a food balance sheet for each country, providing an estimate of total energy consumption.

Arab Republic, the Sudan, South Sudan, and north Nigeria, nearly 72 million people (FSIN 2019, 2).

Other forms of malnutrition include nearly 2 billion people with micronutrient deficiencies and 600 million obese or overweight, data monitored by WHO. The significant negative impacts of the emerging food systems and lifestyle changes on health are associated with the changing food consumption habits. A recent *Lancet* study of the global burden of disease (GBD) suggests that dietary risks were responsible for 11 million deaths, 22 percent of all deaths in 2017, demonstrating how healthy diets must be at the core of the Zero Hunger challenge (GBD 2017 Diet Collaborators 2019). As obesity and overweight increasingly become uncontrollable epidemics, easy access to cheap, energy-dense foods and sugary drinks are a key part of the challenge. Rapid globalization of the food industry and concurrent technological transformation has made prepared foods affordable. Technological change has also significantly reduced physical activity and led to sedentary lifestyles. With the abundance of foods, and the increased physical and economic access to food, frequency of snacking has replaced three square meals. Together, all these factors are leading to an epidemic growth in obesity and NCDs through a phenomenon called "nutrition transition" (Popkin 1994; Ng and Popkin 2012).

Reversal of Undernutrition Trends and Disconnect between Trends in Poverty and Hunger: A Cause for Concern about Achieving the Sustainable Development Goals

FAO's (2017a) projections of trends in undernourishment (Figure 4.1) offer a more pessimistic picture than previous projections (FAO, IFAD, and WFP 2015). The numbers of undernourished in 2030, based on a "business-as-usual" scenario, are estimated at 637 million people in low-income countries (LICs) and middle-income countries (MICs). This figure exceeds by 95 million people, or 17.5 percent, previous projections to 2030. Those LICs and MICs mostly overlap the set of developing countries in projections made earlier by Alexandratos and Bruinsma (2012). Projections of undernourishment in 2030 in Alexandratos and Bruinsma (2012) were relatively more optimistic. The number of undernourished, projected with respect to achieving zero hunger, definitely falls short of the SDG target of eradicating hunger by 2030. The sub-Saharan Africa (SSA) region shows an increasing trend in terms of the number of undernourished people up to 2030. That is also why FAO, IFAD and WFP (2015) called for a twin-track approach, merging investment in social protection to immediately raise the food consumption levels of the extremely poor with pro-poor investments in productive activities to sustainably increase the income-earning opportunities of poor people (FAO 2017a). Kharas, McArthur, and Rasmussen (2018) confirmed this observation, noting that some 30+ LICs, most located in SSA, will likely not achieve SDG2 by 2030. Therefore, the importance of social safety nets (SSNs), or social assistance, has increased. According to the World Bank Group's *The State of Social Safety Nets 2018*:

> Of 142 countries in the [World Bank's Atlas of Social Protection: Indicators of Resilience and Equity] ASPIRE administrative database, 70 percent have unconditional cash transfers, and 43 percent have conditional cash transfers. More than 80 percent of countries provide school feeding programs. Also, 67 percent of countries have public works, and

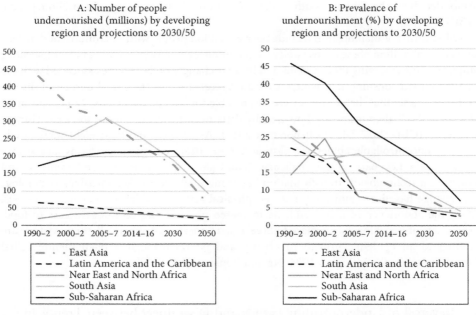

A: Number of people undernourished (millions) by developing region and projections to 2030/50

B: Prevalence of undernourishment (%) by developing region and projections to 2030/50

Figure 4.1 FAO estimates of hunger and projections show slower decline in hunger than World Bank estimates and projections of poverty: Performance and projections by region, 1990–2050

Note: 2050 data from Alexandratos and Bruinsma (2012).

Source: Authors' construction. Based on data from FAO (2017a).

56 percent have various fee waivers. The number of countries with old-age social pensions has also grown rapidly in the past two decades. (WBG 2018, 1)

Yet, the coverage of SSNs in LICs is more limited, entailing fiscal costs of 1.5 percent of the GDP. Most SSNs in LICs are funded by donors (WBG 2018). The growing emphasis on SSNs is an important departure from international approaches in the 1980s, which shunned safety nets. And yet, there is much about the relationship between reduction in poverty and food security that we do not understand.

In the *SOFI 2020*, FAO has revised the hunger estimates again, both retroactively and prospectively, so that the overall hunger level in 2019 is 690 million, compared to the earlier estimate of 822 million in 2018, and yet, incidence of hunger has been increasing by about 60 million people since 2014, with a substantially higher incidence of hunger in Africa by 2030 (FAO et al. 2020, viii). Virtually all the increase in hunger by 2030 is projected to take place in Africa, with the number of undernourished (in millions) increasing from 234 in 2019 (PoU: 17.4 percent) to 411.8 (PoU: 29.4 percent) in 2030. South Asia's (SA's) numbers of undernourished (in millions) declined, ever so slightly from 257.3 to 203.6 (FAO et al. 2020, 11, table 2). (The comparative picture is presented in Figures 13.1A, 13.1B, and 13.2). The report concludes the world is not on track to achieve Zero Hunger by 2030. If recent trends continue, the number of people affected by hunger will surpass 840 million by 2030, but that number is very close to the level that FAO announced for last year—821 million (FAO et al. 2020, 3).

Disconnect between Poverty and Food Security Estimates

The World Bank is responsible for monitoring poverty levels and changes in the context of SDGs. Its macro level estimates suggest that there has been faster progress on reducing poverty over recent decades than in reducing hunger (Figure 4.2), a puzzle that we explore later in this chapter.

From 1990 until 2015, global extreme poverty declined on average by a percentage point. Poverty declined by only by 0.6 percentage point per year, however, from 2013 to 2015, and early estimates for 2018 show extreme poverty dropped merely 1.4 percentage points between 2015 and 2018. Uneven progress across regions as well as in countries is significant In 1990, East Asia and Pacific (EAP) and SA were the two regions with the most poor people, accounting for 80 percent of the world's extreme poor (Sánchez-Páramo 2020).

The World Bank projects poverty will decline more rapidly, with most of the remaining 416 million poor, out of total projected poor of 479 million, expected to be in SSA.[4] In

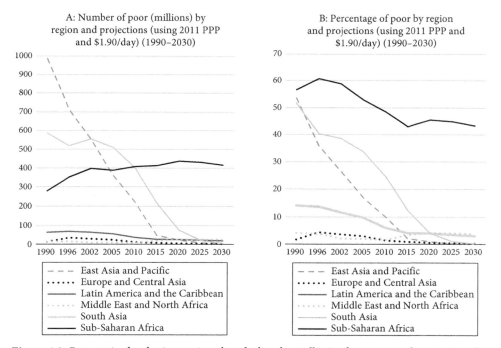

Figure 4.2 Poverty in developing regions has declined rapidly: Performance and projections by region, 1990–2030

Note: Poverty estimates are based on a poverty line of US$1.90 per capita income per day and 2011 purchasing power parity (PPP) prices. All numbers for 2015 and 2030 are statistical projections based on a growth scenario, which assumes each country grows at the country-specific average growth rate observed over 2005–15, and using distributional assumptions, should be treated with considerable circumspection. See, also, Ferreira et al. (2015).

Source: Authors' construction. Based on data from World Bank (2018).

---

[4] This projection answers the question of what would happen to extreme poverty trends if the economic growth of the past decade (2005–15) continued until 2030. The World Bank made one projection that assumes the continuation of the growth rate of each country and another projection that assumes the continuation of the growth rate specific to the world region. The difference between these two alternatives is very small (World Bank 2018).

SA, the projected 5 million poor would be only 1.04 percent of the global poor by 2030 (Figure 4.2). The world attained the first of the twin MDG targets—to cut the 1990 poverty rate in half by 2015—in 2010, five years ahead of schedule. Nearly 1.1 billion people are estimated to have moved out of extreme poverty since 1990. In 2015, 736 million people lived in extreme poverty; this number was reduced to about 650 million in 2018, "defined by the international poverty line (IPL) as consumption (or income) less than US$1.90 per day in 2011 purchasing power parity (PPP)"—down from nearly 2 billion in 1990 (World Bank 2018, 1).[5] The poverty rate in areas suffering from fragility, conflict, and violence climbed to 36 percent in 2015, up from a low of 34.4 percent in 2011, and that rate will likely increase (Barne and Wadhwa 2018). Twenty-nine percent of Africa's poor live in fragile states in 2015 and a share projected to increase to 50–80 percent by 2030 (Beegle and Christiaensen 2019).

Despite progress, the number of people living in extreme poverty globally remains high. And given global growth forecasts, poverty reduction may not be fast enough to reach the target of ending extreme poverty by 2030 (World Bank 2018). In SSA, the poverty rate remained high at 41.4 percent, and 413 million people lived on less than US$1.90 a day in 2015, 136 million more than in 1990 (World Bank 2020c). If the trend continues, by 2030, nearly 9 out of 10 extreme poor will be in SSA (Wadhwa 2018). SSA now accounts for half the world's extreme poor, and a Brookings study concluded that 30 countries, most of which are in SSA, may not reach the SDG targets (Chandy 2017). A vast majority of the global poor live in rural areas, are poorly educated, are mostly employed in the agricultural and related sectors, and over half are under 18 years of age (World Bank 2020c). Hence, gainful employment of youth is a big challenge. Extreme poverty disproportionately affects children—387 million, or 19.5 percent, of the world's children live in extreme poverty, compared to just 9.2 percent of adults. Children represent half of the poor, yet are just one-third of the underlying population.

With higher poverty thresholds, for instance, US$3.10 per person per day, children are still the largest impoverished group—47 percent of children are poor compared to 27 percent of adults (UNICEF 2016). Higher income countries, which are members of OECD and use a relative poverty line, based on one-half of median income, show children to be the most impoverished in almost all high-income OECD countries (UNICEF 2019). Only 53 percent of the world's population, about 3.9 billion of the 7.3 billion, earned at least an income of US$5.5 per day (2011 PPP) in 2015, enough to afford a nutritious diet and nearly three-quarters earned at least US$3.2 per day (2011 PPP). (See Figures 4.2A and 4.2B.) The total affected by moderate or severe food insecurity, which appears to be an estimated 2 billion people in the world, did not have regular access to safe, nutritious, and sufficient food in 2019 (FAO et al. 2020, 22). Different dimensions of nutritional maladies are high in SA and SSA. Vitamin A, iron, and iodine are the most important in global public health terms; the deficiencies represent major threats to the health and development of populations worldwide, particularly for children and pregnant women in LICs. Anemia and vitamin A deficiencies, including among pregnant women, is highest in Asia and SSA.

In an earlier blog post, Lele (2015) showed that at the global and regional levels, there was little relationship between the decline in poverty and the decline in hunger. The World Bank announced that the poverty target was met by 2010 (Figure 4.3A and 4.3B), but hunger had declined extraordinarily little by 2015 (Figure 4.1A and 4.1B). In particular, this was true in

---

[5] World Bank estimated that the share of people in extreme poverty declined to 8.6 percent of the world population in 2018 (World Bank 2018).

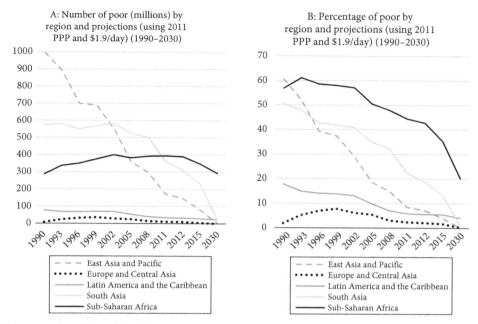

Figure 4.3 World Bank's old poverty estimates: Poverty in developing regions has declined rapidly—Performance and projections by region, 1990–2030

Note: Poverty estimates are based on a poverty line of US$1.90 per capita income per day and 2011 purchasing power parity (PPP) prices. All numbers for 2015 and 2030 are statistical projections based on a growth scenario, which assumes each country grows at the country-specific average growth rate observed over 2004–13; and using distributional assumptions, it should be treated with considerable circumspection. See, also, Ferreira et al. (2015).

Source: Authors' construction. Based on data from Cruz et al. (2015).

the case of SSA. With the World Bank's latest revised estimates of poverty (Figure 4.2A and 4.2B), and FAO's revised estimates on hunger (Figure 13.1A and 13.1B), there is even less relationship between changes in poverty and changes in hunger. In addition, the reasons for this drastic acceleration of food insecurity to 2030 in *SOFI 2020*, compared to the projections of the previous year's *SOFI* appear to be mainly due to revisions in population estimates. Indeed, the report asks readers, who tend to be consummate readers of FAO's food insecurity estimates, not to compare the old and new estimates. Furthermore, the changes appeared to be based on adjustments in just in a few countries.

We argued in Chapter 3 that the growing interest in nutrition had less to do with the food crisis in 2006–7 than with unprecedented advocacy by the nutrition community, through a series of journal articles in the influential public health journal, *The Lancet* (2008, 2011, 2013a, 2015); the Scaling Up Nutrition (SUN) Movement (SUN 2010), and four *Global Nutrition Reports* (*GNRs*) (IFPRI 2014, 2015, 2016b, 2017). Collectively, these efforts brought nutrition back onto the international agenda after nearly three decades of hiatus.

All People, at All Times

An important aspect of the 1996 definition was the phrase "*all people, at all times*" (FAO 2009, 1). The concept of universality has grown in importance since the adoption of SDGs, with the inclusion of developed countries in various roles, not just in the eradication of poverty and hunger in low-income developing countries, as was the approach under the MDGs. This means indicators are needed, which can be disaggregated to specific groups and can identify even very brief episodes of deprivation. The degree of granularity is important not only for equity and social inclusion, but also for accurately measuring changes in population averages over the long run. The conceptual framework that reflects this flexibility in the food security concept and measurement was adopted in the work of the FSIN measurement task force, chaired by Lele and Masters (Lele et al. 2016). It allows for classification of data into one of four nested categories of national, market-level, household-level, and individual-level data, based on the social scale of analysis. Data was defined at the country level, typically from national accounts and trade data, such as Food Balance Sheets (FBS). In other cases, users want data about market conditions, in which transactions may involve unknown people from various locations. Users seek data about households, typically indicators of food consumption based on the definition of a household as a group. And very often, users seek data about individuals, including anthropometric measurements of body size, such as the measurement of a child's height, or other measures such as weight, mid-upper arm or waist circumference, biomarkers, and other clinical data.

The socioecological model and each type of data shown here can be used to classify observations in any setting, from extreme undernutrition to obesity and diet-related disease. Data from each of the four categories can be used to construct indicators at that particular scale, or aggregated to a higher scale, such as the national prevalence of individual-level malnutrition. The socioecological approach to FSN measurement encompasses a diverse set of relationships that operate as a system within and across scales. For example, a country-level trade policy can cause changes that, in turn, alter the status of markets, households, and individuals, whereas individual-level vaccinations or feeding can alter decisions and outcomes at household, market, and country levels. Policies and programs can intervene at any scale, such as improvements in community-level marketing arrangements, and then drive changes at both larger and smaller scales over time.

Disconnect between Changes in Poverty and Changes in Hunger: Is the Disconnect Real?

We noted in the introduction to this chapter that estimated reductions in hunger (PoU) have been very small relative to reductions in poverty. According to the World Bank, an estimated 1.9 billion lived below US$1.90 a day (using 2011 PPP) in 1990, declined by more than 1 billion to 783 million in 2015. Meanwhile, FAO estimated that about 991 million suffered from hunger in 1990, declining to 775 million in 2015, a reduction of only 216 million in the same period, and only about one-fifth of the estimated decline in the numbers of extreme poor. Again, the biggest decline occurred in China and Southeast Asia (Cruz et al. 2015). It is clear we need more reliable measures of incidence of hunger and poverty, and changes in each. Furthermore, incidence of hunger has increased since 2015, as discussed previously.

The limited availability of empirical evidence provides a mixed picture of improvement in income and nutrition. Based on the latest household surveys in India, Meenakshi (2016) noted that the "Indian enigma," identified by Deaton and Drèze (2009), continues; income increase does not necessarily result in increased food consumption, creating the apparent paradox of the considerable income growth in India not leading to a commensurate decrease in the PoU. Also, increased food production does not necessarily result in improved nutrition—the so-called agriculture–nutrition disconnect (Gillespie, Harris, and Kadiyala 2012). And, it does not translate into commensurate reductions in anthropometric measures of undernutrition (Deaton and Drèze 2009). Other literature, including a series of articles in the *New York Times* (2017, 2018) from Mexico, Brazil, Chile, Malaysia, India, China, and Ghana (the "Planet Fat" series, discussed later) have shown that, all else being equal, diet quality worsens with increase in income, accompanied by consumption of energy-dense foods and increased amounts of salt, sugars, and fats, contributing to obesity and NCDs—the so-called dietary transition (Popkin 2001, 2009; Webb et al. 2006; Popkin, Adair, and Ng 2012; Webb 2013; Masters 2015; Masters et al. 2016). Meenakshi (2016) noted that more than food intake, the quality of diet appears to be strongly correlated with the anthropometric indicators of malnutrition, yet improvements in diet quality have not been very high. Food price inflation, driven increasingly by non-cereals, has likely hindered larger improvements in diet quality, especially for the poor. It has become increasingly difficult for them to have a diet rich in vegetables, legumes, dairy, and meat, as their prices (per unit kcal) relative to cereals have risen faster than for the rich. Meenakshi also noted that low elasticity appears to characterize the relationship between nutritional outcomes and food intake, and yet, there is an emerging sharp increase in outcomes associated with over-nutrition and obesity as a public health problem, widespread not only in urban but also in rural areas, even as magnitudes of undernutrition and micronutrient malnutrition remain large: the "triple burden of malnutrition" (Popkin 2001; Popkin, Adair, and Ng 2012; "Planet Fat" series, the *New York Times* 2017–18).

On a more positive note, some studies show positive evidence of increased household agricultural production, even of nonfood crops such as Bt cotton, with increased income leading to increased dietary diversity and diet quantity (Qaim 2003; Qaim and Janvry 2003; Qaim and Zilberman 2003). Still other literature simply shows greater consumption of milk, meat, fruits, and vegetables (Chand, Raju, and Pandey 2007; Kotwal, Ramaswami, and Wadhwa 2011; Ramaswami, Pray, and Lalitha 2012).

A recent study in Bangladesh found a positive association between diversification of farm production and the dietary diversity of the farmers, but the researchers also found that market access, commercialization of farms, income diversification that included off-farm sources of income, and women's empowerment all showed positive and significant effects on dietary diversity of households (Islam et al. 2018).

Increased dietary diversity, however, does not necessarily assure a nutritious diet, nor does diversified production assure sustainable production unless, first, we have details on farm production and individual consumption, issues well outlined in Béné et al. 2019: "When Food Systems Meet Sustainability—Current Narratives and Implications for Actions," and, second, unless public action is undertaken to improve diets.

Child dietary diversity is poor in much of rural Africa and developing Asia, prompting significant efforts to leverage agriculture to improve diets. A recent household survey-based study (Headey et al. 2019) found that children living in proximity to markets that sell more nonstaple food groups have more diverse diets, but the association between market access and child diet diversity is small and similar in magnitude to associations describing the relationship between dietary diversity and household production diversity. Moreover, for dairy, household and community production of that food is especially important. These modest associations may reflect several specific features of the data and survey design, with the study situated in very poor, food-insecure localities where even the relatively better off are poor in absolute terms and where, by international standards, relative prices for nonstaple foods are very high.

At the same time, undernutrition and micronutrient malnourishment remain large. While evidence on nutrition linkage between agricultural production income and consumption is improving, there is still remarkably little location-specific evidence that stresses the importance of information and knowledge, including the role of value chains. Therefore, it has become clear that the earlier idea of dealing with hunger first, before worrying about nutritious diets, may lead to improvements in only one form of malnutrition, while neglecting (or perhaps worsening) the others (World Bank 2014).

A later World Bank report (2017) noted what Popkin and Reardon (2018) have also recently concluded, that the rapid expansion of ultra-processed foods, more than any other subsystem within the agriculture and food system, is the major factor in the obesity epidemic. Late developers, however, do not have to follow the path of the advanced countries. To chart a different course, such as the one Japan, South Korea, or Singapore did, where obesity rates remain low despite growth in incomes, countries need to maintain their traditional plant-based diets, even in the wake of rapid economic growth. The situation, however, is now changing for the worst in South Korea after its entry into the World Trade Organization (WTO) (personal communication, Barry Popkin, June 9, 2018; Kim, Moon, and Popkin 2000; Lee, Popkin, and Kim 2002; Lee, Duffey, and Popkin 2012), as we discuss later in the chapter.

Proactive public policies are called for, which can overcome powerful influences of value chains that adversely affect diets. Currently, weak state capacity, inefficient redistribution, and the inability to effectively regulate the private sector food industry take their toll. Later in the chapter, we discuss how countries are handling these challenges. Stronger governance is needed—an efficient and trustworthy government; an effective civil society; a private sector that goes beyond corporate social responsibility rhetoric; a responsible media; and a judicial system that holds stakeholders accountable. There is much work to do to achieve SDG2 and the rest of the SDGs. As an illustration, Marion Nestle (2015), in her book, *Soda Politics* outlines how food and beverage companies use their considerable economic and political power to use marketing, lobbying, advertising budgets to influence policies toward products they produce and sell, regardless of how harmful they may be to consumers. Marcela Reyes et al. (2020) reported on changes in laws and possible impacts on consumption in Chile in their paper titled, "Changes in the Amount of Nutrient of Packaged Foods and Beverages after the Initial Implementation of the Chilean Law of Food Labelling and Advertising: A Nonexperimental Prospective Study." Sacks, Crosbie, and Mialon (2020) identified the corporate political activity (CPA) of food industry actors in South Africa, by mapping of food industry strategies to influence public health policy, using information on ten different food industry actors, with information in the public domain. They showed that food industry actors in South Africa established multiple relationships with various parties in and outside the South African government, influencing science and involving themselves in policymaking, thereby helping to frame the debate on diet and public health in South Africa. They urged need for increased transparency, disclosure, and awareness of industry strategies, and mechanisms to address and manage industry influence. Barry Popkin (2009), in his book, *The World Is Fat: The Fads, Trends, Policies, and Products That Are Fattening the Human Race*, presents evidence of the US food industry's influence on WHO via the US government. Stuckler, Ruskin, and McKee (2018) showed the influence of Coca-Cola, on research on child obesity. More recently, the state of Oaxaca in Mexico has banned the sale to children of sugary drinks and high-calorie snack foods. Lawmakers had more incentive to limit sales, as obesity crisis was associated with a higher death toll during the COVID-19 pandemic. "Coronavirus tsar Hugo López-Gatell has branded soft drinks 'bottled poison' and blamed their consumption for causing 40,000 deaths, along with high incidence of diabetes, obesity and hypertension—all COVID-19 comorbidities" (Agren 2020).

An Alternative Approach to Exploring the Relationship between Poverty and Food Security

Kakwani and Son (2016) took up the challenge of understanding the reasons behind the gap between the poverty and undernourishment estimates of the World Bank and FAO, respectively, that Uma Lele had identified in her Brookings blog post (Lele 2016). They propose a methodology of measuring food insecurity, which explains and helps bridge this huge gap.

Their approach is also consistent with the emerging literature on FSN, as well as with Sen's (1981) entitlement approach. Kakwani and Son (2016) provided an alternative definition of food security: food security exists when all people, at all times, have *entitlement* to sufficient and nutritious food that meets their dietary needs: that is, households or individuals suffer from food insecurity if they do not command enough resources to buy food sufficient to meet their nutritional needs. In short, food insecurity (or hunger) is an extreme form of poverty. Concepts of poverty and food insecurity are closely related. Policymakers can only ensure that people have the necessary resources to consume sufficient and nutritious food. Individuals make their own choices on what food they want to consume. Sen's entitlement approach is more realistic than the access approach to measuring food deprivation in the population. According to Sen (1981), every individual is endowed with a bundle of resources, which can be exchanged for food and any other commodities. A person's entitlements depend on what is owned initially and what can be acquired through exchange. If the entitlement does not include a commodity bundle with an adequate amount of food, the person would go hungry and become food insecure, an entitlement failure. Food security is influenced by factors such as poverty, food prices, social protection, unemployment, and earnings, among others, and the entitlement approach is directly linked to income or employment generation, food production, food prices, and social security, all of which have an important impact on food security.

A household suffering from food insecurity is one with its entitlement, as measured by per capita expenditure, of less than the cost of the food basket (that is, per capita monetary cost of a food basket that satisfies the caloric and nutrient needs of 2,100 kcal per person per day, meeting the recommended requirements for carbohydrates, protein, and fat to maintain a healthy body), estimated to be equal to US$1.59 in 2011 PPP (US$1.03 per day in 2005 PPP), using the data from the World Bank's PovcalNet program for 124 countries, which account for 5.7 billion people (for detailed methodology, see Kakwani and Son [2016]). The paper's approach reveals notable gains in reducing food insecurity worldwide between 2002 and 2012, in contrast to FAO's estimates.

According to the estimate of Kakwani and Son (2016), in just one decade, the percentage of the global population struggling with food insecurity significantly *decreased* from 23 percent in 2002 to 10 percent in 2012; the number of food insecure people declined by more than 576 million, from 1,133.7 million in 2002 to 557.3 million in 2012, in contrast to FAO's estimate of a reduction of 155 million (from 934 million in 2002 to 779 million in 2012) over the same period.

FAO measures hunger by comparing calorie intake with a fixed value of caloric require-ment; calorie consumption increases sluggishly, or may even remain the same, given increased growth. With a fixed calorie requirement, progress in reducing hunger is expected to be very slow. In contrast, poverty, which is measured through income or expenditure, is reduced with growth, as people's incomes increase (Kakwani and Son 2016).

Furthermore, FAO's measure of food security (undernourishment) is unable to say whether people are becoming nutritionally better or worse, since it is based on caloric "needs," and does not take undernutrition (or malnutrition) into consideration. Kakwani and Son (2016) made a clear distinction between undernourishment and malnutrition by taking into consideration the intake of the basic nutrients—carbohydrates, protein, and fat—which are required to maintain good health. They, therefore, also suggested a need for modification of FAO's food security definition from access to entitlement.

There is another reason why the approach of Kakwani and Son (2016) was consistent with today's literature on FSN. It challenged Sukhatme's (1961) earlier hypothesis that intra-individual variation is the more important source of variation by far than inter-individual variation. FAO's (1996) cutoff for undernourishment at 1,800 kcal per person per day is about 300 kcal less than the average calorie requirements of 2,100 kcal of a healthy person, as defined by WFP in their *Emergency Food Assessment Handbook*.[6] The Handbook did make note of research by the International Food Policy Research Institute (IFPRI) that questioned the validity of the 2,100-kcal benchmark (WFP 2009). In "Validation of the World Food Programme's Food Consumption Score and Alternative Indicators of House-hold Food Security," Wiesmann et al. (2009) found that WFP offered no justification of the 2,100-kcal estimation of the basic dietary energy requirement. They reported that FAO uses a *minimum* energy requirement. Based on survey data from Burundi, Haiti, and Sri Lanka, the IFPRI study concluded that the WFP cutoff point of 2,100 kcal can lead to "serious underestimation of food insecurity" (Wiesmann et al. 2009, 47).

Kakwani and Son (2016, 271) noted, "FAO's lower cutoff point is justified on the ground that the human body can adapt to a lower calorie intake without any adverse effect on health," as Sukhatme (1961) had argued. Nutritionists are deeply divided on this issue, however, and many hold the opposite view that intra-individual variation is of a minor order of magnitude (Gopalan 1992; Osmani 1992; Payne 1992; Srinivasan 1992).

Furthermore, FAO's estimates are based on a log-normal distribution of calorie intake. This model is convenient from an analytical point of view but not flexible enough to capture the variation at the bottom of the distribution. It gives a reasonable fit in the middle range of the distribution, covering about 60 percent of the population. Since undernourishment primarily occurs at the lower end of the distribution, the log-normal distribution will

---

[6] In the case of India, Chand and Jumrani (2013) and Srivastava and Chand (2017) argued that the PoU was much higher when using the Indian Council of Medical Research–National Institute of Nutrition (ICMR–NIN) recommended norms (2,400 kcal per capita per day for rural areas and 2,100 kcal per capita per day for urban areas) than FAO's uniform norm (the "minimum" amount necessary for maintaining good health is reflected in FAO's minimum dietary energy requirement [MDER] for sedentary activity) of 1,800 kcal per capita per day for both rural and urban areas for reporting undernutrition at global level and across countries. In total population (rural and urban), prevalence of undernourishment was 34.2 percent based on the FAO norm and 65 percent based on the ICMR–NIN norm (Chand and Jumrani 2013). Chand also challenges FAO's use of a standard deduction of 12.5 percent of food grains for feed, seed, industry, and waste, first assumed in 1951, but still being used in the most recent calculations. In India, about 30 percent of food grains go to nonfood uses, and thus, FAO overestimates food availability by 18 percent. Other methodological issues concerning the FAO's measurement of PoU are discussed in FAO's *SOFI 2013* and *SOFI 2015* (FAO 2013, 2015); Chand and Jumrani (2013); Wanner et al. (2014); and the FSIN Technical Working Group on Measuring Food and Nutrition Security report (Lele et al. 2016).

underestimate the percentage of population suffering from undernourishment because of its limited flexibility (Kakwani and Son 2016).

Finally, Kakwani and Son (2015) noted:

> Even if humans can adapt, households may still feel food-deprived if they purchase food with no more than about 1,800 kilo/calories per person. To address food insecurity, households and individuals must not only meet dietary energy needs, but also have adequate amount of protein, fat, carbohydrates, and other micronutrients. If households limit their consumption to only 1,800 kilo/calories per person, they may not meet other nutritional needs. (Kakwani and Son 2015, 271)

Implications of Differing Poverty Definitions

Our primary interest in the debates on the merits of income poverty vs. MDP has been to better understand determinants of food insecurity, including, particularly, their relationship with multiple deprivations (Box 4.1). We show in this section that the incidence of MDP is greater than income poverty. Low middle-income Asia has a larger incidence of MDP, although the depth of MDP is greater in SSA. MDP better explains food insecurity than income poverty, and donor aid is largely skewed against countries with the largest incidence of MDP: that is, low middle-income Asian countries. The level and the quality of domestic expenditures thus will be critical in reducing food insecurity going forward. Although this analysis started with developing countries as the focus, it is now being applied in developed countries, such as in the United States and in European countries (Alkire and Apablaza 2016; GWU 2020).

The Oxford Poverty and Human Development Initiative (OPHI) uses 10 indicators to measure MDP.[7] The indicators and their weights are shown in Table 4.2. According to OPHI, a total of 1.45 billion people from 103 countries (covering 5.4 billion people) are multidimensionally poor, which is 26.5 percent of the total population in those countries. About half of the multidimensionally poor (48 percent) live in SA, and 36 percent in SSA (Alkire and Robles 2017).

India accounts for the highest absolute numbers and a staggering number of multidimensionally poor people, more than 528 million Indians and more people than all the poor people living in SSA (OPHI 2017a). The global Multidimensional Poverty Index (MPI) has national estimates for 39 SSA countries and 866 million people, or 96 percent of the population of SSA. Of these, a total of 521 million are MPI poor—over half a billion people. Of the regions covered by the Global MPI, SSA has the highest percentage of MPI poor, although not the greatest number of MPI poor people (SA has the most). Ninety percent or more of the population are poor in 49 African regions found in 15 countries—Chad, South Sudan, Burkina Faso, Uganda, Sierra Leone, Liberia, Niger, Madagascar, Ethiopia, Benin, Central African Republic, Guinea, Gambia, Nigeria, and Mali (OPHI 2017b).

---

[7] OPHI's Alkire–Foster (AF) Method identifies multiple deprivations at the household level across the same three dimensions as the Human Development Index (health, education, and living standards), including 10 indicators (that is, child mortality and nutrition under the health dimension; years of schooling and child school attendance under the education dimension; and electricity, sanitation, drinking water, floor, cooking fuel, and asset ownership under the living standards dimension). People are considered "multidimensional poor," if they are deprived in at least one-third of the weighted indicators. The first four of these indicators carry a weight of one-sixth each (that is, 0.166), and the other six have a weight of one-eighteenth each (that is, 0.055).

Box 4.1 Income Poverty, Multidimensional Poverty, and Implications for Food Security and Nutrition

There is broad consensus that poverty is multidimensional. What then is the best measure of poverty, how does it affect food insecurity and related policy and investment decisions, and how much does the measure tell us about achievements on scores of deprivations beyond income, such as FSN and, relatedly, the frequent lack of access of households to clean water or sanitation, to primary schools and health, and to individual capabilities beyond measurable outcomes, which Sen articulated (Sen 1981, 1983). In short, what does the "poverty" measure signify about our view of development itself, about poverty monitoring and the needed country-specific (and, indeed, location-specific) investment strategies, given diversity within countries, to improve development outcomes?

In the 1990 *World Development Report*, the World Bank opted for US$1 a day as the measure of income poverty, and later revised it in 2008 to US$1.25 and in 2015 to US $1.90 (Ravallion, Chen, and Sangraula 2009; Chen and Ravallion. 2010; World Bank 2020b, "Methodology"). Multidimensional measures develop an index of several different dimensions and indicators of poverty, determine when a person is deprived of that dimension, and arrive at the relative importance of the different deprivations and a poverty cutoff to determine when a person's deprivations are sufficient to be identified as poor (Alkire and Foster 2011a, 2011b; Alkire and Seth 2015). The debate between the champions of the income measure (Ravallion 2011) and the multidimensional measure (Alkire and Foster 2011a, 2011b; Alkire et al. 2015) has rested on whether it is credible to contend that any single index could capture all that matters in all settings. The debate on the index has parallels with those on the construction of IFPRI's Global Hunger Index (Lele et al. 2016). In the case of the latter, it is often argued that it is a good tool for advocacy but not for developing an investment strategy.

Ravallion (2011) has argued that a single index cannot be a sufficient statistic for poverty assessments; Ravallion asks "whether one aggregates in the space of 'attainments,' using prices when appropriate, or 'deprivations,' using weights set by the analyst." He argues that the goal for future poverty monitoring efforts should be to develop a "credible set of multiple indices," spanning the dimensions of poverty most relevant to a specific setting, "rather than a single multidimensional index." When weights are needed, they should not be set solely by an analyst measuring poverty. Rather, they should be, as much as possible, "consistent with well-informed choices by poor people" (Ravallion 2011, 235).

Advocates of the multidimensional index (for example, Alkire, Foster, and Santos [2011]) contend that: "multidimensional measures provide an alternative lens through which poverty may be viewed and understood," and a single measure, although not always defensible, can have the same powerful effect as the measure of the gross national product (GNP)—a position argued powerfully by the likes of Drèze and Sen (2011, 2013) and Stiglitz, Sen, and Fitoussi (2009) in their Report by the Commission on the Measurement of Economic Performance and Social Progress. Sen, Drèze, and others have shown that, while India's per capita income has been higher than its neighbors, progress in social indicators has been slower. And, Alkire and others provide much more recent evidence, reported here, to show how multidimensional measures of poverty provide deeper insights into progress on poverty reduction. The debates have had three dimensions: methodologies, data, and evidence, and implications for policies and investments.

The genesis of the debate can be traced to the Basic Human Needs (BHN) approach of the 1970s. The BHN approach arose out of a reaction to the pro-growth approach, a concern about growing inequalities, and the need to generate employment, much like in 2015 (ODI 1978). The BHN approach differed from an income approach that the World Bank adopted in the early 1990s to begin monitoring poverty. The reasons were well articulated by the principal champion of the BHN approach, Paul Streeten in the late 1970s.[a] Streeten (1979) argued that, from the perspectives of the basic needs approach, the income-orientation of earlier approaches was inefficient, or partial, or both for several reasons. Many of these reasons are germane to FSN goals, advocacy, and measurement in the context of SDGs going forward. These reasons include:

(1) ... consumers [may] not always [be] efficient optimizers, especially concerning nutrition and health, or when changing from subsistence farmers to cash earners. Additional cash income is sometimes spent on food of lower nutritional value than that consumed at lower levels, or on items other than food. [This is very much today's concern as suggested by the work of Deaton and Drèze on India (2009)].
(2) The manner in which additional income is earned may affect nutrition adversely. Female employment, for example, may reduce breast feeding... [UNICEF has made similar arguments, and we discuss their position in this chapter].
(3) There is maldistribution within households, as well as between households; women and children tend to be neglected in favor of adult males....
(4) Perhaps twenty percent of the destitute are sick, disabled, aged, or orphaned children; ...
(5) Some basic needs can be satisfied effectively only through public services, sub-sidized goods and services, or transfer payments....
(6) The income approach has paid a good deal of attention to the choice of technique, but has neglected the need to provide for appropriate products. In many developing societies, the import or domestic production of over-sophisticated products, transferred from relatively high-income, high-saving economies, has frustrated the pursuit of a basic needs approach by catering to the demands of a small section of the population, or by preempting an excessive slice of the low incomes of the poor.... [These issues of consumption patterns of the poor and their local, urban, and international linkages are even more germane in the age of globalization, for the creation of employ-ment, as we demonstrate in Chapter 2 on Structural Transformation.]
(7) Finally, ... the income approach neglects the importance of "nonmaterial" needs, [such as water and sanitation, housing, and fuelwood], both in their own right and as instruments of meeting some of the material needs more effectively and at lower costs. (Streeten 1979, 137–8)

See, also Haq (1976); Hicks and Streeten (1979); Stewart (1985); Streeten et al. (1981); and UNDP (1990).
The BHN approach morphed into the multidimensional nature of poverty, the United Nations Development Programme's (UNDP's) Human Development Index, and Oxford University's focus on the multidimensional nature of poverty. In McNamara's 1973 Nairobi speech, Mahbub ul Haq contributed many of the ideas of MDP. Haq later moved to UNDP and was instrumental in establishing UNDP's Human Development Index, involving Sen and Streeten.

[a] Poverty & Equity (World Bank 2020a); and "Povcalnet: An Online Analysis Tool for Global Poverty Monitoring" (World Bank 2020b).

Table 4.2 The dimensions, indicators, deprivation cutoffs, and weights of the Global Multidimensional Poverty Index and related Sustainable Development Goals

Dimensions of poverty	Indicator	Deprived if...	Weight	Related SDG
Health	Child mortality	Any child has died in the family in the five-year period preceding the survey	1/6	SDG3 (Health and well-being)
	Nutrition	Any adult under 70 years of age or any child for whom there is nutritional information is undernourished in terms of weight-for-age*	1/6	SDG2 (Zero Hunger)
Education	Years of schooling	No household member aged 10 years or older has completed five years of schooling	1/6	SDG4 (Quality education)
	Child school attendance	Any school-aged child+ is not attending school up to the age at which he/she would complete class 8	1/6	SDG4 (Quality education)
	Assets ownership	The household does not own more than one of these assets: radio, TV, telephone, bicycle, motorbike, or refrigerator, and does not own a car or truck	1/18	SDG1 (No poverty)
Living Standard	Electricity	The household has no electricity	1/18	SDG7 (Affordable and clean energy)
	Improved sanitation	The household's sanitation facility is not improved (according to MDG guidelines) or it is improved but shared with other households**	1/18	SDG6 (Clean water and sanitation)
	Improved drinking water	The household does not have access to improved drinking water (according to MDG guidelines) or safe drinking water is at 30-minute walk or more (round trip) from home***	1/18	SDG6 (Clean water and sanitation)
	Flooring	The household has a dirt, sand, dung, or "other" (unspecified) type of floor	1/18	SDG11 (Sustainable cities and communities)
	Cooking fuel	The household cooks with dung, wood, or charcoal.	1/18	SDG7 (Affordable and clean energy)
	Assets ownership	The household does not own more than one of these assets: radio, TV, telephone, bicycle, motorbike, or refrigerator, and does not own a car or truck.	1/18	SDG1 (No poverty)

Note: *Adults are considered malnourished if their body mass index (BMI) is below 18.5 m/kg². Children are considered malnourished if their z-score of weight-for-age is below –2 standard deviations from the median of the reference population.

**Unless the survey report definitions change, a household is considered to have access to improved sanitation if it has some type of flush toilet or latrine, ventilated improved pit, or composting toilet, provided that they are not shared.

***A household has access to clean drinking water if the water source is any of the following types: piped water, public tap, borehole or pump, protected well, protected spring, or rain water, and it is less than 30 minutes' walk (round trip).

+Data source for age children start school: United Nations Educational, Scientific and Cultural Organization (UNESCO), Institute for Statistics database, Table 1. Education systems (UIS.Stat, http://stats.uis.unesco.org/unesco/TableViewer/tableView.aspx?ReportId=163).

Source: Adapted from Alkire and Robles (2017, 7, table 2); and Alkire and Kanagaratnam (2018, 5, table 1).

Over one billion people, almost three-quarters of all multidimensionally poor people (72 percent), live in MICs. Further details of distribution can be found in Alkire and Robles (2017).

Half of Multidimensionally Poor People are Children

Nearly half of all multidimensionally poor people (48 percent) are children, defined as aged 0–17. Nearly two out of every five children (37 percent) are multidimensionally poor. This means 689 million children are living in MDP. Poverty rates are also higher among children, with 37 percent of children poor, whereas 23 percent of adults aged 18 and older are poor. Most multidimensionally poor children live in SA (44 percent of all poor children) and in SSA. Across all 39 countries in SSA, with an average of 66 percent poor children, the highest rate of poverty for any age group is in SSA. In 3 countries—South Sudan, Niger, and Ethiopia—more than 90 percent of children are MPI poor (Alkire and Robles 2017).

Two-thirds of poor children live in MICs. Poor children are found to be deprived, on average, in 52 percent of weighted indicators. In SSA, poor children are deprived in 58 percent of weighted indicators (OPHI 2017b). On average, India's multidimensionally poor face 47 percent of the 10 deprivations (OPHI 2017a). The largest proportion of poor and deprived among children are in cooking fuel (35 percent), followed by sanitation (30 percent), flooring (26 percent), nutrition and electricity (22 percent); among adults, deprivations are in cooking fuel (19 percent), followed by sanitation (16 percent), flooring (14 percent), nutrition (13 percent), and electricity (10 percent). Significantly, children are poorer and more deprived than adults in each of the 10 indicators (Alkire and Robles 2017).

Results of the rank correlation analysis among MDP and its 10 indicators suggest all are significant at the 0.01 level, and the coefficient of the nutrition indicator (adults are considered malnourished if their body mass index (BMI) is below 18.5m/kg^2, and children are malnourished if their z-score of weight-for-age is below –2 standard deviations from the median of the reference population) against MDP is 0.92, which is lower than cooking fuel (0.983), improved sanitation (0.977), electricity (0.968), flooring (0.946), improved drinking water (0.944), child school attendance (0.94), and years of schooling (0.928); and higher than assets ownership (0.908) and child mortality (0.851).

The Distressing Condition of Destitution

Nearly half of all MPI poor people (706 million) are destitute[8] and experience extreme deprivations such as severe malnutrition in at least one-third of the dimensions. Most of the highest levels of destitution are found in SSA, but most of the destitute people—362 million of the 706 million—live in SA. India has more destitute people (295 million) than SSA (282 million), and Pakistan has more destitute people (37 million) than EAP (26 million) or the Arab States (26 million) (Figure 4.4) (Alkire and Robles 2017).

Appropriate action is urgently needed because of the staggering numbers of poor in SA and SSA. How well do income poverty and MDP explain the various food and nutrition security indicators?

---

[8] Destitute people are deprived in one-third or more weighted indicators, but the destitution indicators are more extreme; since 2014, OPHI has reported a measure of destitution that identifies a subset of the MPI poor—the poorest of the poor.

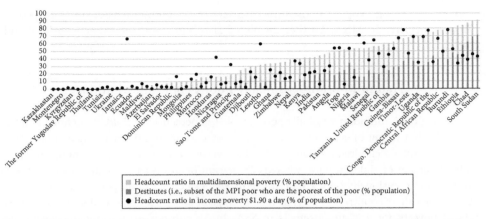

Figure 4.4 Comparison of the headcount ratios of multidimensionally poor, destitute, and US$1.90/day poor (87 countries)

Note: People are considered multidimensionally poor if they are deprived in at least one-third of the weighted indicators. The 10 indicators relate to: years of schooling, child school attendance, child mortality, nutrition, electricity, sanitation, drinking water, floor, cooking fuel, and asset ownership. The first four of these indicators carries a weight of one-sixth each (0.166). The other six have a weight of one-eighteenth each (0.055).

Destitute people are deprived in one-third or more weighted indicators, but the destitution indicators are more extreme; since 2014, OPHI has reported a measure of destitution that identifies a subset of the MPI poor, the poorest of the poor.

Poverty headcount ratio at US$1.90 a day is the percentage of the population living on less than $1.90 a day at 2011 international prices. As a result of revisions in PPP exchange rates, poverty rates for individual countries cannot be compared with poverty rates reported in earlier editions.

Source: Adapted from Global MPI Winter 2017/2018 (OPHI 2018); and PovcalNet (World Bank 2020b).

Multidimensional Poverty and Income Poverty as Determinants of Various Indicators of Food Insecurity

We measure relationship between food insecurity using two different measures of poverty (MDP and income poverty) and including indicators of child deprivation, which the preceding Kakwani and Son approach could not do: namely, stunting, wasting, overweight, underweight, and PoU across developing countries. Association, of course, does not mean causality. It is worth mentioning that one of the indicators (out of the 10 indicators) of the MDP is nutrition (that is, any adult under 70 years of age or any child for whom there is nutritional information is undernourished in terms of weight-for-age or underweight).

The regressions for the prevalence of stunting, wasting, overweight, and underweight are based on 86 developing countries, and PoU is based on 75 developing countries for the latest years' available data.

Findings of the Analysis

MDP explains more variation (R^2 value) than income poverty in the case of each child's food security indicator, and income poverty explains slightly more variation (R^2 value) than MDP in the case of PoU. Also, change in predicted values (that is, the coefficient value) of the prevalence of wasting, underweight, and overweight are larger with the changes in MDP than income poverty. The exception is prevalence of stunting (the same with income poverty) and PoU (lesser than income poverty).

Table 4.3 Regression results: Summary table comparing multidimensional poverty and income poverty versus food security indicators (prevalence of undernourishment, prevalence of stunting, prevalence of wasting, prevalence of underweight, and prevalence of overweight)

Indicators	Headcount Ratio in Multidimensional Poverty (% of population)		Headcount Ratio in Income Poverty US $1.90 a day (% of population)	
	Coefficient value	*R² value*	*Coefficient value*	*R² value*
Prevalence of undernourishment (% of population) (75 countries)	(+)0.26*	0.31	(+)0.31*	0.34
Prevalence of stunting, height-for-age (% of children under 5) (86 countries)	(+)0.32*	0.55	(+)0.32*	0.39
Prevalence of wasting, weight-for-height (% of children under 5) (86 countries)	(+)0.09*	0.26	(+)0.05**	0.06
Prevalence of underweight, weight-for-age (% of children under 5) (86 countries)	(+)0.26*	0.52	(+)0.19*	0.21
Prevalence of overweight, weight-for-height (% of children under 5) (86 countries)	(−)0.10*	0.35	(−)0.09*	0.18

Note: * Significant at 0.01 level; ** significant at 0.05 level.

Source: Authors' calculations.

The analysis suggests that income poverty and MDP are statistically significant in the case of all the five food security indicators (PoU, prevalence of stunting, prevalence of wasting, prevalence of overweight and prevalence of underweight). Both income poverty and MDP have positive impacts on PoU, stunting, wasting, and underweight and, as would be expected, negative impacts on the prevalence of overweight.

Table 4.3 summarizes the regression results.

Results suggest the regression coefficient and R² values for the prevalence of stunting are the highest among all the food security indicators for both MDP and income poverty (see Figures 4.5 and 4.6).

Role of Gender Equality in Food and Nutrition Security

Despite major strides, gender inequality remains a major barrier to development, particularly in food and nutrition security in countries lagging in development. All too often, women and girls are discriminated against in health, education, political representation, labor markets, etc.—with negative consequences for development of their capabilities and their freedom of choice.

In the section that follows, we review different international efforts to measure gender inequality and the extent to which they explain outcomes with regard to food and nutrition security. As countries' human development improves, women's choices and opportunities must be equal to those of men, so that everyone benefits from advances in human development (see Box 4.2 on how the SDGs addressed gender equality).

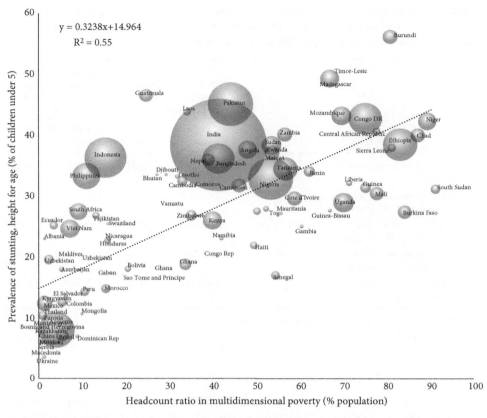

Figure 4.5 Multidimensional poverty versus prevalence of stunting (86 countries)

Note: Bubble size shows number of stunted children under five.

Source: OPHI (2018); UNICEF (2020).

A more profound issue, the undernutrition of adolescent girls, which is particularly acute in India, leading to a cycle of low birthweight and stunting of Indian children and subsequent increased risks of NCDs. This is an entire intergenerational cycle of both undernutrition and NCDs—the developmental origins, which is extremely important in SA.

FAO's *State of Food and Agriculture* (2010–11) on "Women in Agriculture—Closing the Gender Gap for Development" noted that gender matters because 43 percent of the agricultural labor force, on average, in developing countries is female. The agriculture sector is underperforming in many developing countries, in part, because across countries and contexts, women have consistently less access than men to agricultural assets, inputs, and services and to rural employment opportunities. Increasing women's access to land, livestock, education, financial services, extension, technology, and rural employment could increase yields on their farms by 20–30 percent and raise total agricultural output in developing countries by 2.5–4 percent, which alone could lift 100–150 million people out of hunger and generate gains in food security, economic growth, and social welfare (FAO 2011). UNICEF's framework also places a strong emphasis on women's roles in care and

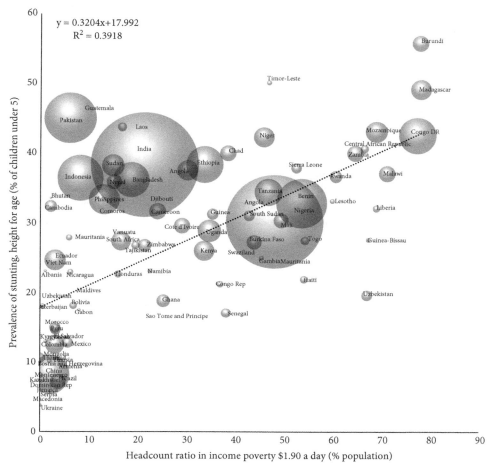

Figure 4.6 Income poverty versus prevalence of stunting (86 countries)

Note: Bubble size shows number of stunted children under five.

Source: World Bank (2020b); UNICEF (2020).

feeding of children (UNICEF 2015). Therefore, one would have expected a strong treatment of gender in food and nutrition.

International agencies have developed a variety of indices on gender: for example, *The Economist* Intelligence Unit's Women's Economic Opportunity (WEO) Index, World Economic Forum's (WEF's) Global Gender Gap Index, UNDP's Gender Inequality Index (GII), and the Gender Development Index (GDI).

By working disproportionately in unpaid labor, particularly in developing countries, women traditionally have had less access than men to income and resources. Expanding opportunities for the 1.5 billion women not employed in the formal sector takes on even greater importance. As the WEO Index shows, simply increasing the numbers of working women will not be enough. The poorest regions of the world have some of the highest levels of female labor force participation, and poverty in those regions persists. Rather, to realize greater returns from female economic activity, the legal,

Box 4.2 Gender Equality in the Sustainable Development Goals

SDGs have placed considerable emphasis on gender, and if even a fraction of those goals are realized, they should help FSN. SDG5, to *"achieve gender equality and empower all women and girls,"* calls for ending all forms of discrimination against all women and girls everywhere with various sub-SDGs (Target 5.1); for eliminating all forms of violence (Target 5.2); for eliminating all harmful practices, such as child, early, and forced marriages and female genital mutilation (Target 5.3); for recognizing and giving value to unpaid care and domestic work (Target 5.4); for ensuring women's full and effective participation and equal opportunities for leadership at all levels of decision-making in political, economic, and public life (Target 5.5), for ensuring universal access to sexual and reproductive health and reproductive rights (Target 5.6); for giving women equal rights to economic resources, as well as access to ownership and control over land and other forms of property, financial services, inheritance, and natural resources, in accordance with national laws (Target 5a); for enhancing the use of enabling technology, particularly information and communications technology, to promote the empowerment of women (Target 5.b); and for adopting and strengthening sound policies and enforceable legislation for the promotion of gender equality and the empowerment of all women and girls at all levels (Target 5c) to track and make public allocations for gender equality and women's empowerment.

SDG4 to *"ensure inclusive and equitable quality education and promote lifelong learning opportunities for all"* also includes a number of targets related to gender: to ensure all girls and boys complete free, equitable, and quality primary and secondary education (Target 4.1); to ensure all girls and boys have access to quality early childhood development, care, and pre-primary education (Target 4.2); to ensure equal access for all women and men to affordable and quality technical, vocational, and tertiary education, including university education (Target 4.3); to eliminate gender disparities in education and ensure equal access to all levels of education and vocational training for the vulnerable, including persons with disabilities, indigenous peoples, and children in vulnerable situations (Target 4.5); to ensure all youth and a substantial proportion of adults, both men and women, achieve literacy and numeracy (Target 4.6); to ensure all learners acquire the knowledge and skills needed to promote sustainable development, including, among others, through education for sustainable development and sustainable lifestyles, human rights, gender equality, promotion of a culture of peace and nonviolence, global citizenship, and appreciation of cultural diversity and of culture's contribution to sustainable development (Target 4.7); and to build and upgrade education facilities that are child-, disability- and gender-sensitive and provide safe, nonviolent, inclusive, and effective learning environments for all (Target 4a).

SDG3 to *"ensure healthy lives and promote well-being for all at all ages"* includes Target 3.1 to reduce the global maternal mortality ratio to less than 70 per 100,000 live births by 2030.

Source: UN (2020a).

social, financial, and educational barriers hindering women's productivity need to be removed. Women who are better educated, healthier, and have greater control over household financial resources are also more likely to invest time in their children's health and education—an investment in the workforce of tomorrow. The global gender gap has been widening for the first time since the WEF's Global Gender Gap Report was first published in 2006 (WEF 2017).

The GII is defined on the UNDP's *Human Development Reports* website. The GII ranges between 0 and 1, and the higher the GII value the more disparities between females and males and the more loss to human development (for details, see Seth [2009]; UNDP [2019b]). The GII is assessed in 160 countries.

First introduced by UNDP in 1995, the GDI: "…measures gender gaps in human development achievements by accounting for disparities between women and men in three basic dimensions of human development—health, knowledge and living standards using the same component indicators as in the HDI [Human Development Index].…It is a direct measure of gender gap showing the female HDI as a percentage of the male HDI" (UNDP 2019a).

The closer the ratio is to 1, the smaller the gap between women *and* men. (For details, see Technical Notes on the calculation of the indices [UNDP 2016b].)

In the case of all these indices, countries in Northern Europe, Sweden, and Norway rank at the top of the index, explained by robust, gender-sensitive legislation, and progressive cultural norms. The world average score on the GII was 0.443 in 2015. It reflects a percentage loss of 44.3 percent in achievement, across the three dimensions due to gender inequality. Regional averages range from 27.9 percent in Europe and Central Asia (ECA), followed by EAP (31.5 percent), LAC (39 percent), SA (52 percent), the Arab States (53.5 percent), to nearly 57.2 percent in SSA in 2015. At the country level, losses due to gender inequality range from 4.03 percent in Switzerland to 76.8 percent in Yemen. Other countries at the bottom of the ranking, with over 60 percent in losses due to gender inequality, were Niger, Chad, Mali, Côte d'Ivoire, Afghanistan, the Democratic Republic of Congo, Tonga, Sierra Leone, Liberia, Central African Republic, Gambia, Mauritania, Burkina Faso, Malawi, and Benin. SSA, the Arab States, and SA suffer the largest losses due to gender inequality. India has performed poorly in removing gender-based disparities, ranked 125 of 159 countries in the GII in 2015. In India, 52.9 percent losses were due to gender inequality. Neighboring countries, such as Bhutan, Bangladesh, Nepal, and Myanmar, which ranked lower than India on the overall HDI, have performed much better when it comes to achieving gender equality. In fact, across SA, only Pakistan (ranked 130) and Afghanistan (ranked 154) ranked lower than India in terms of GII. China was ranked 37, Myanmar 80, Sri Lanka 87, Bhutan 110, Nepal 115, and Bangladesh 119. Brazil, Russia, and South Africa had higher rankings of 92, 52, and 90, respectively (UNDP 2019c).

According to a recent report by Nair (2015): "In India, merely 12.2 percent of the seats are held by women as against 27.6 percent in Afghanistan with a record of violations against women's rights."

In contrast, women's representation was 13 percent in Myanmar, 20 percent each in Bangladesh and Pakistan, 23.6 percent in China, and 29.6 percent in Nepal (Bahri 2018). The top six countries for female representation in parliament were Rwanda, Bolivia, Cuba, Seychelles, Sweden, and Senegal.

The GDI assessed 160 countries in the 2016 *HDI* report, which states that women, in all regions of the world, have consistently lower HDI values than men. According to the *HDI*

2016 Report, the largest differences captured by the GDI are in SA, where the HDI value for women is 17.8 percent lower than the HDI value for men, followed by the Arab States with a 14.4 percent difference, and SSA with 12.3 percent (UNDP 2016a). The *Human Development Report 2016* further notes:

> Much of the variation in HDI between women and men is due to lower income among women relative to men and to lower educational attainment among women relative to men. Part of the variation in the HDI between men and women is generated by barriers to women working outside the home, to accessing education, to voicing their concerns in political arenas, to shaping policies and to receiving the benefits of high-quality and accessible health care. (UNDP 2016a, 54)

The world average score on the GDI was 0.938 in 2015. Regional averages ranged from 0.822 in SA, followed by Arab States (0.856), SSA (0.877), ECA (0.951), EAP (0.956), to 0.981 in LAC (UNDP 2016a).

India, which performed very poorly on the GDI, was 0.819 in 2015, compared to the developing country average of 0.913, and just above 12 countries from the bottom of the index. Afghanistan ranked lowest followed by Niger, Yemen, Pakistan, Chad, Central African Republic, Guinea, Mali, Iraq, Côte d'Ivoire, Comoros, and Mauritania. Throughout SA, only Pakistan and Afghanistan ranked lower than India in terms of GDI. On India's GDI, the *HDI 2016 Report* said the 2015 female HDI value for India was 0.549 in contrast to 0.671 for males, resulting in a GDI value of 0.624, ranked 131 among 188 countries in the year 2015. Among its neighbors, Sri Lanka and China are at the top with the rankings of 73 and 90, in terms of HDI, respectively. Other neighbors ranked below India were Bhutan (132), Bangladesh (140), Nepal (144), Myanmar (146), and Pakistan (147). India was, however, ranked the lowest among Brazil, Russia, China, and South Africa (the other countries of BRICS), with Brazil, Russia, and South Africa ranked 79, 49 and 119, respectively (UNDP 2016a). India's maternal mortality ratio remained high at 174 per 10,000 live births in 2015; its reduction goal to reach 140 was also an MDG. Women's empowerment in terms of mean number of years of schooling is only 4.8 years, compared to 8.2 years for males. Income per capita for females per year was US$2,184 (in terms of 2011 PPP) and US $8,897 for males. See Sengupta (2017).

According to UNDP's *Africa Human Development Report 2016: Accelerating Gender Equality and Women's Empowerment in Africa*:

> Gender gaps in income per capita contribute to lower achievement of human development by females. On average, African women living in countries with lower levels of gender inequality in income tend to achieve higher levels of human development than African men (30 countries). For countries with low gender inequality in income and lower female-to-male HDI ratios, the implication is that there is higher inequality in education and health outcomes, which cancels the benefit of more equal distribution [of] income. Countries in this category include: Democratic Republic of the Congo, Sierra Leone, Togo, Central African Republic, Guinea, Liberia and Chad. . . .

> In terms of Africa's sub-regions, women in East and Southern Africa show the highest achievements in terms of human development relative to men, followed by North and Central Africa and least in West Africa. . . .

North Africa has the most income inequality. The low female labour force participation rate in North Africa, especially among youth, at 19.7 per cent in 2014 compared to 52.1 per cent for sub-Saharan Africa (ILO 2015), accounts for high gender income inequality in this region. (UNDP 2016a, 27–8, 30)

Gender Indexes and Food Security Indicators

How is food insecurity related to gender? We explore the association of two different measures of gender indexes (that is, WEF's Global Gender Gap Index and UNDP's GII and GDI), with food security using four child food security indicators (stunting, wasting, overweight, and underweight) and PoU across the world based on the latest year available data (WEF's Global Gender Gap index data are for 2017 and UNDP's GII and GDI data are for the year 2015). We exclude *The Economist* Intelligence Unit's WEO Index from our analysis, because it was published only once, in 2012.

Findings of the Analysis

UNDP's GII explains more variation (R^2 value) than the other UNDP index (UNDP's GDI) in the case of each food security indicator, except prevalence of wasting, for which UNDP's GDI is able to explain more variation (R^2 value) than the other gender indexes. WEF's Global Gender Gap Index explains less variation (R^2 value) in all cases, among the three gender indexes.

The analysis suggests that both UNDP gender indexes are statistically significant for all five food security indicators (PoU, prevalence of stunting, prevalence of wasting, prevalence of overweight, and prevalence of underweight). In all cases, both UNDP gender indexes are statistically significant at 0.01 level, except in the case of UNDP's GDI on PoU, which is statistically significant at 0.05 level. UNDP's GII, which is scaled from 0 (low inequality) to 1 (high inequality), is associated positively with PoU, stunting, wasting, and underweight, as would be expected, and negatively associated with the prevalence of overweight. UNDP's GDI, which is the ratio of female to male HDI values (that is, the smaller the ratio, the larger the gap between women and men) is associated negatively with PoU, stunting, wasting, and underweight, as would be expected, and is positively associated with the prevalence of overweight. These results confirmed that the incidence of PoU, stunting, wasting, and underweight are substantial when gender inequality, the gap between women and men, is high.

Our analysis does not find any statistical significance on PoU, stunting, and overweight, except for prevalence of wasting and underweight for WEF's Global Gender Gap Index. Both prevalence of wasting and underweight are statistically significant at the 0.01 level and negatively associated with WEF's Global Gender Gap Index, which is scaled from 0 (imparity) to 1 (parity): that is, the prevalence of wasting and underweight of children under 5 is high when gender disparity is prominent.

Table 4.4 summarizes all the regression results.

Results suggest the R^2 value for prevalence of stunting is highest among all the food security indicators for UNDP's GII, and the R^2 value for prevalence of underweight is highest among all the food security indicators for UNDP's GDI.

Table 4.4 Regression results: Summary table comparing World Economic Forum's Global Gender Gap Index, UNDP's Gender Inequality Index and Gender Development Index versus food security indicators (prevalence of undernourishment, prevalence of stunting, prevalence of wasting, prevalence of underweight, and prevalence of overweight)

Indicators	WEF's Global Gender Gap index		UNDP's Gender Inequality Index		UNDP's Gender Development Index	
	Coefficient value	*R^2 value*	*Coefficient value*	*R^2 value*	*Coefficient value*	*R^2 value*
Prevalence of undernourishment (% of population)	(+)18.6	0.01	(+)34.7*	0.21	(−)32.1**	0.05
Prevalence of stunting, height-for-age (% of children under 5)	(−)44.5	0.04	(+)57.8*	0.48	(−)106.5*	0.34
Prevalence of wasting, weight-for-height (% of children under 5)	(−)32.9*	0.17	(+)12.1*	0.21	(−)32.3*	0.31
Prevalence of underweight, weight-for-age (% of children under 5)	(−)41.7*	0.06	(+)35.3*	0.39	(−)78.2*	0.37
Prevalence of overweight, weight-for-height (% of children under 5)	(+)8.1	0.008	(−)11.2*	0.12	(+)19.7*	0.08

Note: * Significant at 0.01 level; and ** significant at 0.05 level.

Source: Authors' calculations.

Rise, Fall, and Rise Again of Nutrition in a Holistic Conceptual Framework

Historically, nutrition has gone through many cycles, which explains the confusing foundation of policy (Fanzo and Byerlee 2019). The League of Nations, following the Great Depression, was concerned about the principles of an adequate diet, dietary standards, implications for country policies, and cross-country comparisons of the physical standards and the clinical and physiological methods best calculated to detect states of malnutrition.[9] Nutritional thinking was dominated by research on vitamins, even wrestling with questions of peripheral edema, wasting, diarrhea, and the role of breast milk (Semba 2008). A recent Food Security Information Network (FSIN) study demonstrated how new cell phone and geographic information systems (GIS) technology are improving the speed, accuracy, and coverage of data (FSIN 2017).

Nutrition was in FAO's mission statement when the organization was established in 1945. FAO's first director-general, John Boyd Orr, a scientist, was awarded the Nobel Prize for having employed science *"to promote cooperation between nations that they become a valuable factor in the cause of peace"* (Jahn 1999, 408). Orr was guided by President Roosevelt's frequently articulated strong belief that freedom from hunger was the foundation of peace, a concern relevant for the contemporary world.

[9] See the archive from The League of Nations, *The Problem of Nutrition*: https://archive.org/stream/pro blemofnutriti02leaguoft/problemofnutriti02leaguoft_djvu.txt

As Alan Berg (1973) and later, Gillespie et al. (2016) noted, the 1950s and 1960s were dominated by concerns among nutritionists about famine, hunger, calorie requirements, and the primacy of protein, leading to the work of numerous meetings of the Joint FAO/ WHO Expert Committee on Nutrition, set up in 1948, including work on childhood malnutrition. The FAO, WHO, and UNICEF Committee on Protein Malnutrition had a worldwide research program on high protein foods, leading to the concept of "protein-calorie malnutrition," with focus on nutrition education in proteins and calories (Burgess and Dean 1962; Ruxin 2000, 152).

Although UNICEF received the Nobel Peace Prize in December 1965, "to produce food rich in protein for children in the developing countries" (Lionaes 1999), and IOs rang the alarm that the protein "gap" or "crisis" was a global emergency in need of immediate attention—the "International Action to Avert the Impending Protein Crisis" (UN 1968)— the scientific community began to question the role of proteins in isolation and to recognize and stress the close complementarity between energy and protein (Sukhatme 1970). Adequate protein intake in a low-calorie diet was not acceptable, and attention shifted to increasing energy consumption. Thus, the term "protein–energy malnutrition" entered the literature while efforts to strengthen protein content of foods continued. The 1981 Joint FAO/WHO/United Nations University (UNU) expert consultation on Human Energy Requirements reported that, except for children, sufficient information was available to use energy expenditure to determine energy requirements (FAO, WHO, and UNU 1985).

1970s: Nutrition Enters the Development Agenda

In September 1971, at the Massachusetts Institute of Technology (MIT), the first International Conference on Nutrition, National Development, and Planning brought nutrition science to the center stage as a development agenda (Berg, Scrimshaw, and Call 1973). The level of interest in nutrition was reflected in the creation of the United Nations Standing Committee on Nutrition (UNSCN) in 1977 (Longhurst 2013), and as part of the FAO report on Nutrition Planning (Call and Levinson 1973). The political efforts through FAO's meetings on food security provided nutrition advocacy. With the strong collaboration that then existed between the World Bank and the Rome-based agencies, the World Bank joined FAO, WHO, and UNICEF on the UN coordinating agency of the day, the Protein Advisory Group. The World Food Conference, following in 1974, kept hunger and nutrition at the center of the international agenda. Nutrition began to be thought of as an essential driver of economic growth, with nutrition programs treated as investments, rather than simply for consumption and needed for specific actions, in the then famous *The Nutrition Factor: Its Role in National Development*, which became required reading on college campuses for every student of food and nutrition (Berg 1973). Robert McNamara, the fifth president of the World Bank (1968–81), became a strong advocate for nutrition as part of a multisectoral strategy, articulated in McNamara's celebrated Nairobi speech that also outlined the World Bank's MDP reduction strategy in the Agriculture and Rural Development (ARD) and Population, Health, and Nutrition (PHN) sectors (McNamara 1973). Separate departments were created for each. The World Bank's lending to both ARD and PHN sectors increased considerably in the 1970s. In July 1974, Donald S. McLaren's "The Great Protein Fiasco," published in *The Lancet*, criticized the "the protein era" for producing little that was worthwhile and noted that the experts had unwittingly closed the "protein gap" by lowering the dietary requirements for protein (McLaren 1974).

Food security concerns shifted to developing countries in the 1960s and 1970s, with the rise of food prices. "Food security" came to be defined relatively narrowly around *availability* and *stability* of food supplies on global and national markets. When FAO hosted the 1974 World Food Summit, food security was defined as: "availability at all times of adequate world food supplies of basic foodstuffs to sustain a steady expansion of food consumption and to offset fluctuations in production and prices" with a focus on *stability* (FAO 2003, 27, quoting UN [1975]). The governments attending the World Food Conference also placed emphasis on the right to food in their Universal Declaration on the Eradication of Hunger and Malnutrition, adopted on November 16, 1974: "The Conference solemnly proclaims: 1. Every man, woman and child has the inalienable right to be free from hunger and malnutrition in order to develop fully and maintain their physical and mental faculties." (UN–OHCHR 2019). Indeed, the rights-based approach to food— with its roots in the UN's Universal Declaration of Human Rights, which Eleanor Roosevelt, as the chair of the United Nations Commission on Human Rights, helped craft—has grown into a huge agenda (see, for example, McClain-Nhlapo 2004; Duger and Davis 2012; Raja 2014).

A decade of macro analysis first placed nutrition planning and then nutritional surveillance among the dominant strategies for the countries most affected. Economists began to take over from nutritionists and pediatricians, argued Gillespie et al. (2016), as the architects of new policies, with much talk about national food security. The World Bank stressed the importance of income generation. In a study by Reutlinger and Selowsky (1976), "Malnutrition and Poverty: Magnitude and Policy Options," the authors pointed out the importance of increasing the poor's access to income to purchase food. The UN Protein Advisory Group evolved into the UN Administrative Coordination Committee's Subcommittee on Nutrition (ACC/SCN, or simply, SCN) in 1977, with its attention now focused on improving breastfeeding, maternal and child nutrition, and complementary feeding. Hugh Geach's work (1973), "The Baby Food Tragedy," was a pivotal event in nutrition. Multinational companies (Nestlé, in particular) were alleged to have contributed to infant mortality in developing countries through the practices they adopted to market infant formula foods (Nestle 2013). The replacement of breast milk unknowingly risked malnutrition and death for the babies, leading to the WHA's passage of the International Code of Marketing of Breast-milk Substitutes in 1981 (WHO 1981).

1980s: "The Lost Decade"—Cross Currents of Increasing Access and Retrenching Services

As global food prices declined in the 1980s, and as the concern about debt increased, there was a strong external push on developing countries to recover costs and retrench health and educational services during the structural adjustment era of that decade. At the same time, in the *Director-General's Report on World Food Security: A Reappraisal of the Concepts and Approaches*, FAO (1983) expanded the concept of food security to include the third aspect— access—in part influenced by Sen's work on famines (1980, 1981): "Ensuring that all people at all times have both *physical and economic access* to the basic food that they need," with a better balance between the demand and supply side of the food security equation. An important World Bank report, "Poverty and Hunger," further elaborated on the terms of: "access by all people at all times to *enough food* for an *active and healthy life*" (World Bank 1986, v, emphasis added), focusing on the temporal dynamics of food insecurity. The report introduced the now widely accepted distinction between chronic food insecurity, associated with problems of continuing or structural poverty and low incomes, and transitory food insecurity, which occurs in periods of intensified pressure caused by natural disasters, economic collapse, or conflict (World Bank 1986).

Controlling iodine deficiency got a boost when the UNSCN developed a 10-year plan (in 1985) for the International Coordinating Committee on Iodine Deficiency Disorders (ICCIDD), which was formed in 1986 and brought iodine deficiency disorders (IDDs) to international attention, developing support for wide-scale salt iodization and promoting laws to enforce the participation of salt manufacturers. In the early 1990s, the subject of micronutrients pushed protein–energy malnutrition (PEM) to the background, as nutritionists, international agencies, and universities attempted quick fixes to control vitamin A deficiency, anemia, and IDD (Latham 1997).

1990s: From General Populations to Maternal and Child Malnutrition— Role of the United Nations Children's Fund

Much like the FAO framework, UNICEF's work (1990) on the causes of malnutrition has made a pivotal contribution to the understanding of food insecurity issues, and since 1990, has been an important foundation and voice in today's food security framework, albeit with some major differences from FAO. At the end of the 1980s and early 1990s, UNICEF landmark framework, described in *Adjustment with a Human Face* (Cornia, Jolly, and Stewart 1987), was based on evidence from the ground in Tanzania, as part of the Joint World Health Organization/UNICEF Iringa Nutrition Programme that was launched in 1986. UNICEF's focus is on the issues of women and children, a focus that FAO's general and largely macroeconomic work had lacked since the 1970s. UNICEF also has had greater focus on the establishment of the enabling environment and the causal chain that could lead to exploration of inputs, processes, and outcomes. UNICEF's framework (Figure 4.7), in an alternative approach, distinguishes between the immediate or proximate causes of malnutrition, and more remote, ultimate, or underlying, and basic causes. UNICEF's work has spawned a large number of variations on that framework, as well as its extension that combines FAO's macroeconomic framework with UNICEF's micro framework (Gillespie, Harris, and Kadiyala 2012). A UNICEF/WHO Joint Nutrition Support Programme (JNSP) and the WHO/UNICEF Strategy for Improved Nutrition of Mothers and Children in the Developing World were both endorsed by the UNICEF/WHO Joint Committee on Health Policy at its 27th session in Geneva in January 1989, with the recommendation that it be further elaborated. The importance of nutrition for women was recognized not just in terms of their role as mothers, or even as economic producers, but in their own right. This framework was the basis for the *Lancet* (2013a) Maternal and Child Nutrition Series and *The Lancet* Nutrition Series, in its "Framework for actions to achieve optimum fetal and child nutrition and development" (*Lancet* 2013b, 2, figure 1). An adaptation of the UNICEF framework is shown here (Figure 4.7).

In 1991, the first joint WHO–UNICEF conference "Ending Hidden Hunger" helped to strengthen micronutrient programming, and in 1993, the Micronutrient Initiative was formed. Overall, micronutrient control programs achieved considerable success during the 1990s. FAO and WHO co-convened the International Conference on Nutrition (ICN) in Rome in 1992 (FAO and WHO 1992a, 1992b).

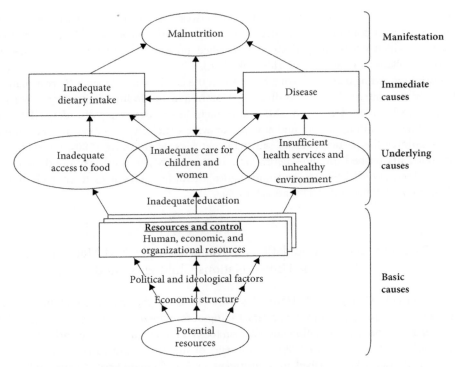

Figure 4.7 The UNICEF framework of causality in malnutrition
Source: Adapted from UNICEF (1990).

The meeting at the World Bank on "Actions to Reduce Hunger Worldwide" in 1993 made a further distinction between direct nutrition interventions to address micronutrient deficiencies and nutrition-sensitive agriculture to address issues of nutritious supply of food, announcing a major commitment by the World Bank to the eradication of hunger (Serageldin and Landell-Mills 1994; Binswanger and Landell-Mills 1995). Notwithstanding the rhetorical commitment, there was relatively little lending to nutrition in the 1990s, as we discuss in Chapter 8 on the World Bank.

Food Security and Nutrition Were on a Parallel Track from the Mid-1990s

The concept of food security adopted by 186 countries at the 1996 World Food Summit was modified only slightly in 2009 by adding the phrase "social" to the 1996 definition:

> Food security exists when all people, at all times, have physical, social and economic access to sufficient, safe and nutritious food to meet their dietary needs and food preferences for an active and healthy life. The four pillars of food security are availability, access, utilization and stability. The nutritional dimension is integral to the concept of food security. (FAO 2009, 1)

The definition and pillars of food security approved by member governments in FAO's 1996 World Food Conference, and refined in 2009, reflect the ongoing historical evolution of policymakers' concerns. FAO's World Food Summits in 1996, 2002, and 2009 reinforced the 1974 importance of food supply, while modifying the food security definition adopted in 1996 over time. In 1996, the United States argued that too many such meetings and resolutions of FAO had led to little progress, but then contributed to the definition by stressing the importance of access (Shaw 2007). In the 2002 World Food Summit, member nations adopted the "Declaration of the World Food Summit: Five Years Later," calling for the establishment of an intergovernmental working group to prepare Right to Food Guidelines (FAO 2002). In 2009, at the World Summit in Rome, 60 heads of states and governments unanimously adopted a declaration that pledged renewed commitment to eradicate global hunger at the earliest possible date (FAO 2009).

Increasingly, the rapidly growing, massive body of literature on food security recognizes the physiological, social, psychological, biological, and cultural aspects of food security. Some note that it is a concept inherently unobservable and difficult to define (Maxwell 1996; Gross et al. 2000; Clay 2002; Barrett and Lentz 2010; Simon 2012). Macro and micro concerns diverged in the 1960s and 1970s, when developing countries came into focus and food shortages were a major concern. FAO took the lead on availability and stability of the food supply with a series of World Food Summits starting in 1974, and nutritionists moved to push nutritional planning as a way to influence development policy.

The macro and micro frameworks have been coming together analytically over the years. However, policy advocacy and financing do not always offer a balanced comprehensive picture. Advocacy goes through cycles between macro and micro concerns, depending on the external environment, as we outline in this chapter. These analytical issues have been articulated over the years by Maxwell and Frankenberger (1992); Maxwell (1996); Barrett (2010); and Barrett and Lentz (2010); and influenced in recent years by various reports in *The Lancet* journal (2008, 2011, 2013a)—for example, Kadiyala et al. (2014); Gillespie et al. (2016); and policy advocacy on nutrition through *The Lancet* series (2008, 2011, 2013a, 2015); formation of SUN (SUN 2010); Second International Conference on Nutrition (ICN2) in 2014 (FAO 2019a); the various *Global Nutrition Reports* (IFPRI 2014, 2015, 2016b; Development Initiatives 2017, 2018); and other publications, such as WBG (2014); GLOPAN (2016); World Bank (2017); *Global Food Policy Reports* (IFPRI 2016a, 2017, 2018, 2019b); and Shekar et al. (2017). FAO, WFP and IFAD, increasingly joining hands with UNICEF and WHO, have continued to highlight issues of food and nutrition in *The State of Food Security and Nutrition in the World* (FAO et al. 2017, 2018, 2019, 2020). These publications build on that large body of work.

The various dimensions of the magnitude of the FSN challenge are in the center of the diagram of our framework (Figure 4.8): 1. Triple burden of malnutrition (see, also, Table 4.3), 1.1. Undernutrition—energy and protein inadequacy, undernourishment, stunting (low height-for-age), wasting (low weight-for-height), low birthweight, and underweight; 1.2. Micronutrient deficiencies—vitamin A, iron (anemia), iodine, zinc, and folic acid below healthy thresholds; 1.3. Overnutrition—overweight and obesity, and associated diet-related NCDs (diabetes, high cholesterol, high blood pressure, heart disease, and some cancers); 2. Unsafe drinking water, poor sanitation, and hygiene related diseases; and 3. Child mortality, maternal mortality, disability, and premature death because of unhealthy diet. The global scenario for the numerical magnitudes of the challenges in these major areas are described here briefly.

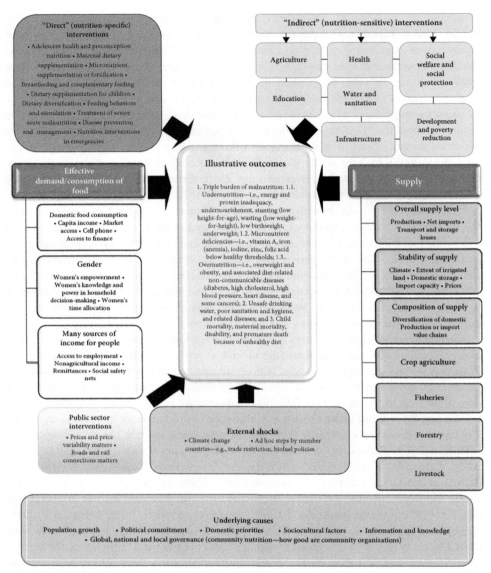

Figure 4.8 Toward a consolidated theory of change for food and nutrition security
Source: Authors' construction.

Further Conceptual Development of Food Security and Nutrition

Various authors have recognized the hierarchical nature of FSN (see, for example, Webb et al. [2006]). For example, availability is necessary to determine access, and access is necessary to determine utilization. Stability undergirds all three other dimensions. The different initiatives have led to hundreds of definitions of food security. The four pillars approach reflects a sequence of historical concerns from the 1970s (availability and stability), 1980s (access), and 1990s (utilization), as we have shown here.

Over time, however, analysts have also begun to focus on synergies among the four pillars and, particularly, on the issues of causality (Burchi, Fanzo, and Frison 2011). This has been further developed by the discussion and analysis of the Global Panel on Agriculture and Food Systems for Nutrition (GLOPAN 2016), "Food Systems and Diets" and the report of the Committee on World Food Security (CFS)–High Level Panel of Experts on Food Security and Nutrition (HLPE), "Nutrition and Food Systems" (HLPE 2017), and will be yet further elaborated in both the preparations for, and during, the 2021 Food Systems Summit (UN 2020b).

Treatment of "Nutrition Security" in Food Security

The element of nutrition in food security has become increasingly important since the mid-1990s. Both undernutrition and diet-related diseases, including obesity, have attracted increased attention. The number of indicators to measure FSN status, which had already proliferated prior to the adoption of the SDGs in 2015, has expanded beyond nutrition, to include nonfood influences on food and nutrition security, such as sanitation and disease.

Many have thought that nutrition was marginalized in the FAO's various definitions, even though the term "nutritious" was included. The CFS Reform Document adopted by the FAO Conference in 2009 added an explicit reference to nutrition in the interpretation of the official definition of food security: "The four pillars of food security are availability, access, utilization and stability. The nutritional dimension is integral to the concept of food security and to the work of CFS" (CFS 2009, 1). What comes first? Does nutrition include food security or vice versa? This has depended on the disciplinary perspective of the definers.

The World Bank's report "Repositioning Nutrition as Central to Development" offered an even broader definition of nutrition security: "Nutrition security is achieved for a household when secure access to food is coupled with a sanitary environment, adequate health services, and knowledgeable care to ensure a healthy life for all household members" (World Bank 2006, 66). This same definition of nutrition security is also used by WHO in its review of global nutrition policy (WHO 2013b).

Dietary intake has been changing remarkably rapidly since the Second World War, first in the Western world, following the growth of the agro-processing industry, particularly canning and freezing, and more recently, in developing countries. In the decades since the Second World War, the US food industry has successfully advertised the convenient labor-saving quality of its processed food for women increasingly entering the labor market. Women in developing countries, where the food industry and value chains are less developed, spend very long hours carrying out household responsibilities. As labor markets are changing rapidly, including women's increasing roles outside the households, reliance on purchased, ready-made foods, too, is increasing with profound impacts on public health, as well as implications for public policy around the emerging consumption patterns and the roles value chains play.

The growing interest among development professionals in nutrition has been strengthened by the strong advocacy of the nutrition community and articles in *The Lancet*, the launching of the Scaling Up Nutrition (SUN) Movement, merged with the UNSCN in 2020 (UNSCN 2020), and IFPRI's four *GNRs*, together with other initiatives.

2010 to 2016: Reinforcing Nutrition Advocacy

The SUN Movement, founded on the principle that all people have a right to food and good nutrition, was launched in 2010. It had a membership of 57 countries worldwide (SUN 2010). *The Lancet*'s first series on "Obesity" was published in 2011, and the second series was published in 2015 (*Lancet* 2011, 2015). The UN released a political declaration on NCDs as the outcome of a High Level Meeting on the Prevention and Control of NCDs in 2011 (UN 2011). In 2014, the UN held a follow-up meeting to the 2011 High Level Meeting to review progress. By 2015, countries made clear commitments to set national NCD targets for 2025 and established process indicators, taking into consideration nine NCD targets (IFPRI 2016b).

The WHA, consisting of 193 member countries, unanimously agreed to a set of six global nutrition targets to achieve by 2025, as part of the Comprehensive Implementation Plan on Maternal, Infant, and Young Child Nutrition (Table 4.5) in 2012.[10] In 2015, LICs and LMICs were off course by a substantial margin for meeting the six WHA global nutrition targets on maternal and child health by 2025 (WHO 2012, 2020c). In 2011, the member countries also agreed on global mechanisms to reduce the avoidable NCD burden, including a Global Action Plan for the Prevention and Control of NCDs 2013–20 (WHO 2013a). The plan aims to reduce the number of premature deaths from NCDs by 25 percent by 2025 through nine voluntary global targets, one of which is "Halt the rise in diabetes and obesity" (see Box 4.3). The biggest challenges for child and material nutrition are in SA and SSA.

In 2013, the second *Lancet* Maternal and Child Nutrition Series built on the 2008 series to review evidence and experience with "nutrition-sensitive" interventions from a range of sectors, including agriculture, social protection, education, and early childhood development (Gillespie et al. 2016). The same year, the governments of the United Kingdom and Brazil, together with the Children's Investment Fund Foundation (CIFF), co-hosted the Nutrition for Growth (N4G) Summit in London, endorsed by 90 stakeholders to beat hunger and improve nutrition and designed to raise commitments to action to achieve the global targets on Maternal, Infant, and Young Child Nutrition (WFP 2013; see nutritionforgrowth.org). Donors pledged US$4.15 billion for nutrition-specific and US$19 billion for nutrition-sensitive programs. Governments came together at the ICN2 in 2014 and agreed on a set of 10 commitments in the "Rome Declaration on Nutrition," with plans to launch an annual series of *Global Nutrition Reports* (FAO 2019a; globalnutritionreport.org).

The *GNRs* have reinforced the need for attention to nutrition as well as to establish an accountability mechanism. *GNRs* report progress toward meeting nutrition goals and

---

[10] As noted in *SOFI* 2018:

> Subsequently, in 2015, the Sustainable Development Goals established a global agenda for substantial improvement in nutrition by the year 2030, setting a specific objective of ending all forms of malnutrition by 2030, including achieving the 2025 targets and addressing the nutritional needs of adolescent girls, pregnant and lactating women, and older persons.
>
> The 2030 nutrition targets have been calculated based on a similar approach to that used for the 2025 targets. . . . For two of the indicators (low birthweight and anaemia in women of reproductive age), the past rate of improvement has been too slow to achieve the WHA target, even by 2030. Thus, for these indicators, the revised 2030 target is the same as the 2025 target, since the level of ambition for 2030 should not be less than that agreed upon for 2025.
>
> For the other indicators, more ambitious targets for 2030 are proposed. (FAO et al. 2018, 15)

Table 4.5 Global World Health Assembly nutrition targets

WHA Target for 2025	Baseline year(s)	Baseline status	Target for 2030
1. Stunting:[a] 40% reduction in the number of children under 5 who are stunted	2012	165.2 million	50% reduction in the number of children under five who are stunted. [150.8 million in 2017]
2. Anemia:[b] 50% reduction of anemia in women of reproductive age	2012	30.3%	50% reduction in anemia in women of reproductive age. [32.8% in 2016]
3. Low birthweight:[c] 30% reduction in low birthweight	2012	15%	30% reduction in low birthweight.*
4. Overweight:[d] No increase in childhood overweight for children under 5	2012	5.4%	Reduce and maintain childhood overweight to less than 3%.(5.6% in 2017)
5. Exclusive breastfeeding:[e] Increase the rate of exclusive breastfeeding in the first 6 months to at least 50%	2012	38%	Increase the rate of exclusive breastfeeding in the first six months up to at least 70%. (40% in 2016)
6. Wasting:[f] Reduce and maintain childhood wasting to less than 5%	2012	8%	Reduce and maintain childhood wasting to less than 3%. (7.5% in 2017)

Note: Collaboration between UNICEF, WHO, London School of Hygiene and Tropical Medicine, and Johns Hopkins University is working on developing country estimates based on survey and routine data. These estimates were undergoing the country consultation process when this draft was being finalized. Based on these preliminary estimates for 148 countries with data, 69 had low birthweight rates higher or equal to 10 percent in 2000. Among those, countries with the 20 percent highest rate of progress had an Annual Average Rate of Reduction of 0.935 or higher between 2000 and 2015. This rate applied over 18 years between 2012 and 2030 results in a 15 percent reduction, much lower than the 2025 target of 30 percent reduction for 2025.

[a] Children aged 0–59 months who are more than 2 standard deviations (SD) below the median height-for-age of the WHO Child Growth Standards.

[b] Prevalence of anemia is (1) percentage of pregnant women whose hemoglobin level is less than 110 g/l at sea level or (2) percentage of non-pregnant women whose hemoglobin

level is less than 120g/l at sea level.

[c] Infants born in each population and over a given period who weigh less than 2,500 g.

[d] Children aged 0–59 months who are more than 2 SD above the median weight-for-height of the WHO Child Growth Standards.

[e] Infants 0–5 months of age who are fed exclusively with breast milk.

[f] Children aged 0–59 months who are more than 2 SD below the median weight-for-height of the WHO Child Growth Standards.

Source: http://www.who.int/nutrition/indicator_progress.pdf; https://www.who.int/nutrition/global-target-2025/discussion-paper-extension-targets-2030.pdf; IFPRI (2016b; FAO et al. 2018).

describe innovative approaches to addressing malnutrition and country experiences, as well as track the follow-up to the many pledges made at the 2013 N4G summit. Some *GNR* stories are discussed later in this chapter. A new fund, the "Power of Nutrition," launched in 2015, aims to unlock US$1 billion to help millions of children get proper nutrition and reach their full potential.

The United Nations named 2016–25 the "Decade of Action on Nutrition." In 2015, the UN member countries adopted the SDGs to end all forms of malnutrition by 2030, and in 2016 the UN General Assembly's "Decade of Action on Nutrition from 2016 to 2025" led to

---

Box 4.3 Nine Voluntary Global Targets: Global Action Plan for the Prevention and Control of Noncommunicable Diseases, 2013–2020

Target 1: A 25 percent relative reduction in premature mortality from cardiovascular diseases, cancer, diabetes, or chronic respiratory diseases.

Target 2: At least 10 percent relative reduction in the harmful use of alcohol, as appropriate, within the national context.

Target 3: A 10 percent relative reduction in the prevalence of insufficient physical activity.

Target 4: A 30 percent relative reduction in the mean population intake of salt/sodium.

Target 5: A 30 percent relative reduction in the prevalence of current tobacco use in persons aged 15+ years.

Target 6: A 25 percent relative reduction in the prevalence of elevated blood pressure, or contain the prevalence of raised blood pressure, according to national circumstances.

Target 7: Halt the rise in diabetes and obesity.

Target 8: At least 50 percent of eligible people receive drug therapy and counseling (including glycemic control) to prevent heart attacks and strokes.

Target 9: An 80 percent availability of the affordable basic technologies and essential medicines, including generics, required to treat major NCDs in both public and private facilities.

Source: (WHO 2013a, 5).

---

translation of the ICN2 commitments into coherent and coordinated actions and initiatives by all national governments, both low- and high-income countries. With these initiatives, more and more people have begun to recognize the importance of addressing malnutrition in all its forms (IFPRI 2016b). These worthy efforts do not nearly address the challenges faced in achieving improved nutrition. The N4G event, hosted by the governments of Brazil, the United Kingdom, and Japan in 2016, called for world leaders to increase financial investments in nutrition and scale up successful strategies. Japan's leadership on nutrition increased in advance of the 2016 G7 meeting and the lead-up to the 2020 Tokyo Olympics and Paralympics (IFPRI 2016b).

The nutrition community has justifiably expressed a concern, in *GNRs* 2014, 2015, 2016, 2017, and 2018 (IFPRI 2014, 2015, 2016b; Development Initiatives 2017, 2018), that the nutrition agenda should not be a flash in the pan. After increasing for a few years, international aid to nutrition peaked in 2015–16, which could lead to a dilution of national commitment. If food and nutrition are to reach the ambitious 2030 targets, clear steps are needed to sustain interest and commitment to the nutrition agenda and its implementation. History has important lessons in this regard on several fronts and on two parallel tracks—conceptually and empirically, on how nutrition was viewed in food and nutritional policy by IOs, and operationally, in lending for nutrition interventions. Here, we discuss operational issues: (1) leadership, (2) impacts of external shocks on development agendas, and (3) management of complex multisectoral issues. All are relevant to contemporary challenges that the nutrition agenda faces.

Nutritionists' and Economists' Views

Nutritionists have viewed the problem in terms of direct nutrition-specific and nutrition-sensitive interventions (Figure 4.9). Nutrition-specific interventions are delivered to reduce individual micronutrient deficiencies, such as vitamin A or iron deficiencies, and to address women's anemia. The latest crop map from HarvestPlus shows their efforts to end the deficiencies or "hidden hunger" by enhancing nutrition content of crops. A part of the CGIAR Research Program on Agriculture for Nutrition and Health, HarvestPlus reports that, to date, 290 biofortified varieties of 12 staple crops have been released or are being tested in 60 countries, with more than 30 million people worldwide growing and eating at least one of the 12 crops that have been biofortified with Vitamin A, iron, or zinc (Meyer 2018). Alan Berg has been a strong champion of fortified salt as the best way to alleviate micronutrient deficiencies among the poor (*A Full Bowl* 2020).

Nutrition-sensitive interventions include treatment of all the relevant issues in all sectors of the economy, which potentially influence FSN outcomes, including agriculture, education, health, and infrastructure. SSNs have been on the increase and come in many forms, such as food and cash transfers and employment guarantee schemes (WBG 2018).

Economists, on the other hand, have viewed FSN issues in terms of supply and demand, relative prices, and access (see Figure 4.8). FAO's definition addresses many issues of supply, such as food availability, stability, and access, and those related to demand, including income, effective demand, and the factors that influence them—women's empowerment, decision-making abilities, market access, and factors that determine household decision-making. The supply side is influenced by production, net imports, transport, and storage losses; stability of supply by climate, extent of irrigated land, domestic storage, import capacity, and prices; composition of supply by diversification of domestic production or import value chains; and is comprised of crop agriculture, fisheries, forestry, and livestock sectors (FAO 2019b).

Literature has shown high rates of return to investments in food and nutrition (Hoddinott et al. 2013; Copenhagen Consensus Center 2015; Alderman, Behrman, and Puett 2017; Shekar et al. 2017). Nutrition improvement is argued to lead to poverty reduction and considerable health and educational benefits over a person's life cycle, particularly from boosting the nutritional status of pregnant mothers and infants in the first 1,000 days. These benefits are realized, in terms of better development of fetuses, development of brains and resistance to infections among infants, improved learning abilities of infants and children, educational achievements, labor productivity, and lifetime earnings (Bhutta et al. 2013; Hoddinott et al. 2013). An unintended consequence of the economic approach to food security has been the focus on low food prices as a success of food policy. The declining share of food in the consumer expenditures has had welfare benefits, allowing consumers to enjoy a higher standard of living by being able to incorporate other items in their household budget, such as education and consumer durables. However, this growth is at the cost of environment—since environmental degradation is not included in production costs—and impacts on human health, since low food prices are often accompanied by consumption of poor quality food.

Public sector interventions—prices and price variability, and roads and rail connections—all matter. Storage and handling losses received relatively little attention until recently, but now literature on this issue is growing. There are, however, inherent difficulties in measuring the losses (Chand and Jumrani 2013). Sheahan and Barrett (2017) reviewed the literature in

Food Policy concerning postharvest losses (PHL) in SSA and confirmed the difficulties in defining and measuring the losses, and new papers have been commissioned.

Demand, in turn, is influenced by income, access to employment and safety nets, food prices and, most importantly, knowledge and access to healthy food. Many sources of income for people are determined by access to employment (for example, India's Mahatma Gandhi National Rural Employment Guarantee Act [MGNREGA] and Ethiopia's large public works program), nonagricultural income that often constitutes half the rural income, remittances, and SSNs.

Also shown previously in Figure 4.8, external shocks, such as climate change and ad hoc steps by member countries (for example, trade restrictions, biofuel policies, and conflicts) also matter. Underlying causes underpinning the whole set of intervening variables and outcomes include population growth, political commitment, domestic priorities, sociocultural factors, information and knowledge, and global, national, and local governance. Figure 4.8 outlines our "consolidated theory of change" in outcomes of FSN, based on the literature. We adopted such a framework, because we found the myriad existing frameworks to be piecemeal. Our framework will also evolve, as the many knowledge gaps identified in this chapter are filled: for example, about the role of gender or climate change.

The Impact of the Food Industry

Diets are determined by a combination of factors: resource endowments determine production possibilities. Increasingly, trade and foreign direct investment (FDI) in the food industry have been shifting consumption patterns in developing countries from traditional diets toward a Western style of diet (Fiedler and Iafrate 2016). Foods are closely related to culture, history, social mores, and increasingly, with science and technical change in agriculture and agro-processing, with transport and refrigeration, incomes, and the cost of time. Not the least important, the cost of new processed and purchased food is influenced by the growth of the modern food industry, particularly in the context of globalization.

The Nutritional Basis for a Food Systems Approach

As Lawrence Haddad observed, the EAT–*Lancet* Report (Willett et al. 2019) addressed two questions simultaneously:

> First, how do we have to eat differently to significantly reduce malnutrition? Second, what food production systems do we have to put in place to use natural resources sustainably and live within climate change targets?...In other words, this diet satisfies two key objectives: were it consumed it would prevent approximately 20% of all premature adult deaths and it would operate within safe planetary boundaries for climate change, biodiversity loss, land system change, freshwater use and Nitrogen and Phosphorous cycling. (Haddad 2019)

This is a necessary initiative to look at diets holistically. We show in this chapter that in some regions of the world, individuals are consuming well above the minimum required nutrients required for healthy active lives, and in other parts of the world, a lot less. This provides the contextual basis for some of the analysis underpinning the ongoing food systems discussion.

Even before the EAT report (Willett et al. 2019), it was widely recognized that poor nutrition has widespread life-cycle health effects, including in its contribution to the growth of NCDs, such as diabetes, cancer, and heart disease. The skyrocketing fiscal costs of NCDs in OECD countries, are also increasingly noted in developing countries, as the incidence of obesity increases. Advocates of good nutrition argue that the cost can be contained by addressing nutrition improvements in the entire population and, in particular, by addressing hunger and hidden hunger: that is, energy and nutrient deficiencies among young women, pregnant women, and children. The Bill and Melinda Gates Foundation funded research on GBD, leading to a much greater understanding of the role of diet and nutrition in all forms of malnutrition. In fact, a recent study showed the two leading causes of GBD are maternal and child malnutrition, followed by poor diets (GBD 2016 Risk Factor Collaborators 2017).

The economic consequences represent losses of 11 percent of GDP each year in Africa and Asia, whereas preventing malnutrition delivers US$16 in returns on investment for every US$1 spent (IFPRI 2016b). Similarly, the neglect of nutrition is often reflected in high rates of stunting, wasting, underweight, and infant and child mortality, as we cited earlier. The correlation between reduction of the incidence of stunting and earnings later in life has been shown to have high development benefits (Bhutta et al. 2013; Hoddinott et al. 2013). Turning causality on its head—that is, viewing nutritional indicators as the cause rather than the consequence of economic development and asserting that economic development, even when it is inclusive, does not always result in improved nutrition—the evidence calls for a special emphasis on nutrition to improve development outcomes.

With increases in food supply in recent decades, the world produces more than enough food to satisfy the dietary needs of the entire global population. The average intake per person per day in LICs and MICs is around 2,750 kcal, and in high-income countries, it is around 3,350 kcal. Both of these figures exceed the minimum requirement of around 1,950 kcal per person per day (FAO, IFAD and WFP 2015, 6, Table 1; see, also, FAO 2008). A similar situation exists with respect to protein requirements.[11]

Adequate food availability does not necessarily imply adequate food intake by all, because (1) inequality in incomes and other means of subsistence influence access; (2) impediments to adequate utilization of food are related to lack of access to facilities, such as food storage, cooking equipment, and clean water, and to services such as health care and basic nutrition education; and (3) there exists an imbalance exists in the dietary transition, discussed later in this chapter, in terms of in improved access to more nutritious foods. Trends seen in the FAO FBSs suggest accelerated growth in consumption of meat and slower growth in consumption of fruits and vegetables (Del Gobbo et al. 2015).[12] With rapidly growing consumption of processed foods, often with excessive quantities of salt, sugar, and preservatives, concerns have increased over the shift toward less healthy diets and the increasing prevalence of micronutrient deficiencies and overweight individuals in the population.

---

[11] Mean protein requirements, in kg per day per kg of body weight, range between 0.66 for adults to 1.12 for infants. An average adult weighing 70 kg would therefore require around 46 g of protein per day. See the Report of a Joint FAO/WHO/UNU Expert Consultation, "Protein and Amino Acid Requirements in Human Nutrition" (FAO, WHO, and UNU 2007, 88, table 4).

[12] The comparison between results from FBSs and household-level data requires some caution. FBSs may tend to overestimate actual availability of food (Del Gobbo et al. 2015). FBSs do not consider food losses and waste at retail and household levels. However, to reconcile results, based on the two data sources, dramatic corrections of the overconsumption patterns resulting from FBSs are required (see Grünberger [2014]).

Although food production must keep the pace with increasing demand, equitable food access and adequate food utilization have to be ensured. In addition, consumer education is needed to promote healthier food consumption patterns and to ensure that the experience of developed countries is not repeated: namely, food abundance is not accompanied by poor nutritional outcomes, as we show. To achieve this, there is a need for reforms in the food industry, with a focus on the quality of processed food, to be produced with less sugar, salt, and fats, and to keep to a minimum the marketing of harmful foods to children. We need more drastic reforms, which return our diets to more legumes, fruits and vegetables, and healthy fats and oils, to address the burden of malnutrition, as well as critical climate and water constraints that the world faces. And progress on influencing food systems has only now begun, with recent shift in focus to food systems.

Dietary patterns not only have impacts on health, but also on the environment, particularly via their link to climate change. Diets rich in meat, especially that from ruminants such as cattle, are associated with higher environmental costs and higher emissions of GHGs: methane, resulting from enteric fermentation; carbon dioxide, released from the clearing of forests for pasture; and nitrous oxide, which is generated in feed production (Gerber et al. 2013; FAO 2016, Willett et al. 2019). The rapidly growing changes in food systems offer standardized food for urban areas and formal employment opportunities (FAO 2017a). The producers of the meats, along with added processed foods, are major users of water with enormous impacts on global water use (see, for example, Ercin, Aldaya, and Hoekstra [2011]). These changes have by no means led to healthy food consumption, as we show in this chapter. At the same time, the conundrum of poverty and the poverty–food security nexus continues.

Evolution from the Unfinished Millennium Development Goals to Sustainable Development Goals

The scope of FSN has expanded considerably with the adoption of SDGs (Box 4.4).

As Box 4.4 indicates, the number of nutrition-related indicators has increased, too, and the focus has incorporated—beyond lack of calorie intake—infant, young child, and maternal nutrition; overweight and obesity; and NCDs. The MDG Target 1.C was to halve the *proportion* of people who suffer from hunger (PoU) between 1990 and 2015, and is included in SDG2 as Target 2.1 and includes one more additional indicator, the prevalence of moderate or severe food insecurity in the population, based on the FIES. Malnutrition in all its forms includes: (1) undernutrition (deficiencies in energy, protein, and/or micronutrients deficiencies known as hidden hunger); (2) overweight and obesity; and (3) NCDs. Undernutrition in infant, young children, and women of reproductive age was added in the WHA, establishing six targets on maternal, infant, and young child nutrition in 2012 to achieve by 2025 (see Table 4.5 on Global World Health Assembly Nutrition Targets). Only the prevalence of child stunting and wasting are included from MDGs in SDGs as Target 2.2. Those goals are also part of the WHA targets. Adult overweight and obesity are not included in SDGs, although child overweight is reported (UN 2020a). As noted in Box 4.4, for SG2, Target 2.2, Indicator 2.2.2 is aimed at the prevalence of malnutrition (weight-for-height >+2 or <-2 SD from the median of the WHO Child Growth Standards) among children under 5 years of age, by type (wasting and overweight).

The member countries under the leadership of WHO also agreed in 2011 on global mechanisms to reduce the avoidable NCD burden, including a *Global Action Plan for the Prevention and Control of NCDs 2013–2020*. NCDs were not addressed in the MDGs,

---

Box 4.4 Sustainable Development Goal 2: Targets and Indicators

SDG Goal 2. End hunger, achieve food security and improved nutrition, and promote sustainable agriculture.

Target 2.1. By 2030, end hunger and ensure access by all people, in particular, the poor and people in vulnerable situations including infants, to safe, nutritious, and sufficient food all year round.

Indicator 2.1.1. Prevalence of undernourishment.

Indicator 2.1.2. Prevalence of moderate or severe food insecurity in the population, based on the Food Insecurity Experience Scale (FIES).

Target 2.2. By 2030, end all forms of malnutrition, including achieving by 2025, the internationally agreed targets on stunting and wasting in children under 5 years of age, and address the nutritional needs of adolescent girls, pregnant and lactating women, and older persons.

Indicator 2.2.1. Prevalence of stunting (height-for-age <–2 standard deviations from the median of the WHO Child Growth Standards) among children under 5 years of age.

Indicator 2.2.2. Prevalence of malnutrition (weight-for-height >+2 or <–2 standard deviations from the median of the WHO Child Growth Standards) among children under 5 years of age, by type (overweight and wasting).

Target 2.3. By 2030, double the agricultural productivity and incomes of small-scale food producers, in particular women, indigenous peoples, family farmers, pastoralists, and fishers, including through secure and equal access to land, other productive resources and inputs, knowledge, financial services, markets and opportunities for value addition, and nonfarm employment.

Indicator 2.3.1. Volume of production per labor unit by classes of farming/pastoral/forestry enterprise size (no data for this indicator is currently available, and its methodology is still under development; see https://unstats.un.org/sdgs/tierIII-indicators).

Indicator 2.3.2. Average income of small-scale food producers, by sex and indigenous status (no data for this indicator is currently available, and its methodology is still under development; see https://unstats.un.org/sdgs/tierIII-indicators).

Target 2.4. By 2030, ensure sustainable food production systems and implement resilient agricultural practices that increase productivity and production; that help maintain ecosystems; that strengthen capacity for adaptation to climate change, extreme weather, drought, flooding, and other disasters; and that progressively improve land and soil quality.

Indicator 2.4.1. Proportion of agricultural area under productive and sustainable agriculture (no data for this indicator is currently available and its methodology is still under development; see https://unstats.un.org/sdgs/tierIII-indicators).

Target 2.5. By 2020, maintain the genetic diversity of seeds, cultivated plants, and farmed and domesticated animals and their related wild species, including through soundly managed and diversified seed and plant banks at the national, regional, and international levels, and promote access to and fair and equitable sharing of benefits arising from the utilization of genetic resources and associated traditional knowledge, as internationally agreed.

Indicator 2.5.1. Number of plant and animal genetic resources for food and agriculture secured in either medium- or long-term conservation facilities.

Continued

Box 4.4 Continued

Indicator 2.5.2. Proportion of local breeds classified as being at risk, not-at-risk, or at unknown level of risk of extinction.

Target 2.a. Increase investment, including through enhanced international cooperation in rural infrastructure, agricultural research, extension services, technology development, and plant and livestock gene banks, in order to enhance agricultural productive capacity in developing countries, in particular, least developed countries.

Indicator 2.a.1. The agriculture orientation index for government expenditures.

Indicator 2.a.2. Total official flows (official development assistance plus other official flows) to the agriculture sector.

Target 2.b. Correct and prevent trade restrictions and distortions in world agricultural markets, including through the parallel elimination of all forms of agricultural export subsidies and all export measures with equivalent effect, in accordance with the mandate of the Doha Development Round.

Indicator 2.b.1 Agricultural export subsidies.

Target 2.c. Adopt measures to ensure the proper functioning of food commodity markets and their derivatives and facilitate timely access to market information, including on food reserves, in order to help limit extreme food price volatility.

Indicator 2.c.1. Indicator of food price anomalies.

Source: https://unstats.un.org/sdgs/metadata/

---

whereas SDGs recognized NCDs as a major challenge for sustainable development (Box 4.4). SDG Goal 3 includes the following targets related to NCDs: (1) reducing by one-third, premature mortality from NCDs (Target 3.4); (2) strengthening responses to reduce the harmful use of alcohol (Target 3.5); (3) achieving universal health coverage (UHC) (Target 3.7); (4) strengthening the implementation of the WHO Framework Convention on Tobacco Control (FCTC) (Target 3.a); and (5) supporting the research and development of vaccines and medicines for NCDs that primarily affect developing countries and providing access to affordable essential medicines and vaccines for NCDs (Target 3.b) (UN 2020a).

On safe drinking water, improved sanitation and safely managed hygiene, SDGs include Target 6.1 and Target 6.2 shifting from MDG Target 7.C (Halve the proportion of the population without sustainable access to safe drinking water and basic sanitation by 2015) (UN 2016, 2020a). According to an IFPRI study by Suman Chakrabarti, reduction of open defecation in villages, increased age at pregnancy, and education are three key sociodemographic factors in reducing anemia among pregnant women in India (Chakrabarti et al. 2018).

Global Nutrition Report 2015 (IFPRI 2015) and others have argued that nutrition has been shortchanged in the SDGs. The architectural changes in nutrition announced and underway in Rome, with the UNSCN having moved from Geneva to Rome in January 2016, are a response to increasing focus and coordination among often myriad uncoordinated and competing organizations, with the UNSCN providing a coordinating role in achieving coherence across UN agencies[13] As Haddad (2015) noted about the *Global Nutrition Report*

---

[13] The UNSCN reports: "Since 1 January 2016, the UN System Standing Committee on Nutrition (UNSCN) has [been hosted] in the FAO premises in Rome [to implement the] strategic plan (2016–2020) and a new focus for UNSCN in light of the … developments in the global nutrition architecture" (www.unscn.org/en/news-events/recent-news?idnews=1227).

2015 (IFPRI 2015): "Unfortunately, nutrition is scarcely mentioned in the Sustainable Development Goals (SDGs)."

SDG2 is specifically about FSN, but the targets specified under the other 16 SDGs are also indispensable for the success of SDG2, as we illustrate in this chapter, in the cases of income poverty, MDP, and gender-related SDGs, which profoundly affect SDG2 outcomes.

Missing are indicators on food availability and quality; political commitment; and capacity, such as the existence of the "right to food" movement, share of public budget spent on nutrition and allied programs, early warning systems, food and nutritional impact indicators (except for prevalence of stunting and wasting among children included in the targets), direct micronutrient interventions indicators, and diagnostic indicators of inadequate food and nutritional outcomes. These indicators were assessed by Technical Working Group (TWG) in the FSIN 2016 report (for detail, see Lele et al. 2016). There are many more significant ways in which the international community has attempted to increase food security and the nutritional status of populations. Foremost among those is advocacy, using a variety of means, but its impact is often difficult to assess or attribute to the interventions.

What Is Missing in the Sustainable Development Goals? Obesity

The growing epidemic of obesity is not part of SDGs, although the number of obese adults is already larger than the number of undernourished, and the number is growing rapidly.[14] More than 1.9 billion adults were overweight, of which over 650 million were obese; 39 percent (39 percent of men and 40 percent of women) of adults aged 18 years and over were overweight in 2016, and 13 percent (11 percent of men and 15 percent of women) were obese. The worldwide prevalence of obesity nearly tripled between 1975 and 2016. Both adult obesity (18+ years) and obesity among children and adolescents (aged 5–19 years) is highest in North America, and the rate of increase is also high there (Figures 4.9A and 4.9B). While Africa and Asia continue to have the lowest rates of obesity, an increasing trend can also be observed. More than 1 in 8 adults in the world is obese. Forty-one million children under the age of 5 were overweight or obese, and over 340 million children and adolescents, aged 5–19, were overweight or obese in 2016. Once considered a problem of high-income countries, overweight and obesity are now on the rise in LICs and MICs, particularly in urban settings. In Africa, the number of overweight children under 5 has increased by nearly 50 percent since 2000. Almost half of all overweight children under 5 lived in Asia and one-quarter lived in Africa. Globally, the prevalence of overweight and obesity among children and adolescents, aged 5–19, has risen dramatically from just 4 percent in 1975 to just over 18 percent in 2016. The rise has occurred similarly among both boys and girls: in 2016, 18 percent of girls and 19 percent of boys were overweight. Although just under 1 percent of children and adolescents, aged 5–19, were obese in 1975, more 124 million children and adolescents (6 percent of girls and 8 percent of boys) were obese in 2016 (WHO 2018a).

The incidence of obesity has increased with economic growth throughout the world, but more than half of the world's obese people live in just 10 countries: the United States, China,

---

[14] WHO defines overweight and obesity as follows:

For adults: Overweight is a BMI $\geq$ 25 and obesity is a BMI $\geq$ 30.

For children under 5 years: Overweight is weight-for-height $\geq$ 2 SD above the WHO Child Growth Standards median, and obesity is weight-for-height $\geq$ 3 SD above the WHO Child Growth Standards median.

For children between 15–19 years: Overweight is BMI for age $\geq$ 1 standard deviation above the WHO Growth Reference median, and obesity is BMI for age $\geq$ 2 standard deviations above the WHO Growth Reference median.

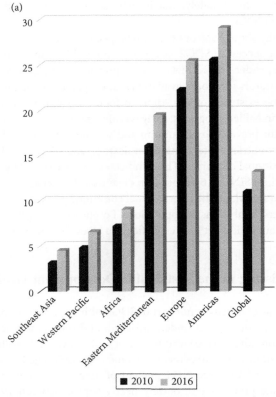

Figure 4.9A Prevalence of obesity among adults (18+ years), BMI $\geq$ 30 kg/m², crude estimates by World Health Organization region, 2010–2016 (%)

India, Russia, Brazil, Mexico, Egypt, Germany, Pakistan, and Indonesia. The highest percent of the world's obese people (13 percent) live in the United States. The United Kingdom and Australia are among the high-income countries with large gains in obesity among men and women (Ng et al. 2014). An international panel described the growing obesity as "a deepening nutrition crisis" (GLOPAN 2017, 3). An Indian nutritionist characterized it as a country "sitting on a volcano" (Anand 2017). While these observations reflect a recent phenomenon, there is also a concern that growing obesity and the associated NCDs, which are accompanying income growth and new food consumption patterns, are not being addressed through established international mechanisms such as the SDGs.

The Growing Epidemic of Obesity

Across the world, more people are now obese than underweight. At the same time, scientists say, the growing availability of high-calorie, nutrient-poor food is generating a new type of malnutrition, one in which a growing number of people are both overweight and under-nourished, with rising fiscal costs associated with malnutrition. "Obesity is "conventionally associated with food excess, but it is also associated with micronutrient deficiencies [zinc, iron, and vitamins A, C, D, and E] and even with daily hunger" (Webb et al. 2018, 3).

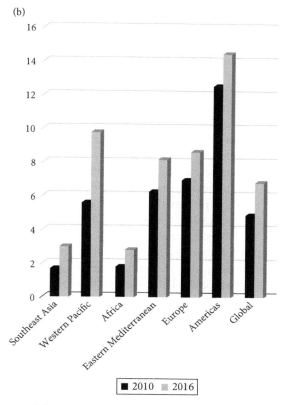

Figure 4.9B Prevalence of obesity among children and adolescents (aged 5–19 years), BMI > +2 SD, crude estimates by World Health Organization region, 2010–2016 (%)

Source: Based on Global Health Observatory Data Repository, WHO, http://apps.who.int/gho/data/view.main. REGION2480A?lang=en

IOs acknowledge (privately, if not publicly) that they have been timid and unclear in dealing with the private sector. The *New York Times* ran a series of well-researched stories on Brazil, Chile, India, Malaysia, and Ghana, among others, in 2017, on how processed food, soda, and the fast food industries' increasing focus on markets in the developing world—and the accompanying rise in obesity rates and weight-related illnesses—is playing out around the globe (personal communication, Celia Dugger and Barry Popkin, June 10, 2018; *New York Times* 2017–18). Popkin designed the series. Matt Richtel was the key *New York Times* contact. They spent over a year organizing and implementing the publications. Richtel recruited six senior reporters to help with the articles from various countries. The series was much more focused on the marketing by the companies, their politics, their ways of buying off academics [Malaysia], and fighting industry and losing [Chile, Mexico]. The series was six months in the design before they obtained all approvals and then went to the various countries.

The *Times* was able to draw on the expertise of multidisciplinary teams to research and consult a wide variety of stakeholders for each case, citing evidence from respected institutions, such as the Institute for Health Metrics and Evaluation in Washington, academics, national policymakers, activists, and consumers as stakeholders. The writers were careful to stress "that a story of this scale, driven largely by an economic and cultural transformation of the global food system, couldn't be understood solely through a scientific lens" (Bennet

2017). The stories document the extraordinary power of the food and beverage industries and the political economy of stakeholders with very different power and access to information. Only a handful of economists, particularly Popkin, Nestle (a nutritionist), and Hawkes, have told these stories, and recent international reports, referred to earlier in the chapter, have described the obesity challenges, but journalists, aided by academics, international and domestic research institutions, activists, and private companies, have brought more of the flavor of the reality in each country on the ground. That reality consists of the growth of food processing, wholesale and retail industry, restaurants, and particularly fast food chains in a globalized world. It illustrates how formidable the governance challenge is to regulate this industry, given the powerful and growing role of multinationals in developing countries and their impacts on health. According to the *New England Journal of Medicine* (Afshin et al. 2017), the prevalence of obesity has doubled in 73 countries since 1980, contributing to 4 million premature deaths, A study published in 2015 found that Mexicans bought, on average, 1,928 calories of packaged food and beverages a day, 380 more calories than in the United States and more than people in any other country, as tracked by Euromonitor International, a market research firm (Euromonitor International 2015). It is clearly not possible, nor realistic, to turn back the clock on the extent of purchased foods. Their growth could be slowed in countries that are behind Mexico on the transformation of value chains, however. Can the quality of calories be improved throughout the world by more public debate—outside of academic journals, more consumer awareness, and greater action by governments, IOs, and civil society?

Food systems are going through extraordinary changes with trade liberalization, growth in food imports, and FDI, which is accelerating the role of processed, ready-to-eat foods. Often, they are combining forces with the domestic food industry in resisting government pressure for regulation, as noted in Mexico, Chile, Colombia, Brazil, Malaysia, and India. Mexico began lifting tariffs and allowing more foreign investment in the 1980s, a transition to free trade in 1994, when Mexico, the United States, and Canada enacted the North American Free Trade Agreement (NAFTA). Opponents in Mexico warned that the country would lose its cultural and economic independence (Jacobs and Richtel 2017b).

NAFTA led to billions of dollars in FDI flowing into Mexico, fueling the growth of American fast food restaurants and convenience stores, and opening the floodgates to cheap corn, meat, high-fructose corn syrup, and processed foods. Mexicans, on the other hand, have exported fruit and vegetables to contribute to healthier diets in the United States (Jacobs and Richtel 2017b). These developments have been associated with more changes.

The first change is consumers' increased access to soft drinks and processed foods (as Corinna Hawkes' study "Exporting Obesity" found, resulting from increased investments by the US manufacturers of soft drinks and processed foods (Clark et al. 2012). Observers note that NAFTA's impact has been pervasive. Direct investment by the United States in Mexico's food and beverage companies soared to US$10.2 billion in 2012, from US$2.3 billion before NAFTA, and the link to the trade agreement is undisputed. USDA states: "Many of these investments were initiated following implementation of NAFTA in 1994" (USDA 2019b). A related piece by Popkin and Hawkes (2015) documents the rapid growth in LICs and MICs of the consumption of sugar-sweetened beverages at a time when sales are stagnant or declining in higher-income countries.

The second change is the aggressive tactics of the food industry, including the deep penetration of sales forces in rural areas, such as by Nestlé in the Brazilian Amazon (Taylor and Jacobson 2016; Jacobs and Richtel 2017a). In Mexico, convenience store chains, with hundreds of millions of dollars in foreign investment, have grown to 16,000 stores, from 400 in 1990 (Jacobs and Richtel 2017b; Searcey 2017; Searcey and Richtel 2017).

The third change is a brutal battle among academics for and against receiving funding from food companies, as noted in Malaysia (Fuller, O'Connor, and Richtel 2017), and likewise, the strong intimidation, often threatening violence, as in Colombia, or the use of malware, as in Mexico (Jacobs and Richter 2017b, 2017c; Perlroth 2017).

The fourth change is a new front—the food industry trying to use trade policies in NAFTA (also the Central America Free Trade Agreement [CAFTA]) to block the types of programs that Chile has instituted (Ahmed, Richtel, and Jacobs 2018).

Finally, not the least is important contributions of the food industry to elections in support of political parties, which can help soften the regulations that governments put in place, as has been demonstrated in the case of Brazil (Jacobs and Richtel 2017a). A more extreme example is the almost complete control of a political party in Colombia, as the major beverage company Postobón owns the major newspaper and TV station in the country (Jacobs and Richtel 2017c).

We must understand that this surge in ultra-processed food and beverages is not only reaching children and adults but also infants, as a number of Gates Foundation-funded studies have shown 25–40 percent of infants are fed sugary beverages or junk food daily in many countries (Huffman et al. 2014; Pries et al. 2016a, 2016b, 2016c; Vitta et al. 2016).

Also, these changes occur after a period when rapid introduction of modern technology into the market production, home production, transport, and leisure sectors have shifted the physical activity in lower MICs to much lower levels among the bulk of the population, making them ever more susceptible to modest increases in energy intake. Then, the shift toward increased intake of the ultra-processed foods means even greater caloric intakes (Ng and Popkin 2012). A sizeable array of studies from Asia and Latin America have documented these shifts in activity and their impact on large increases in the risk of obesity and many NCDs. However, we cannot go backward and remove these technologies, so it is within the food system that countries are focused on how to address obesity and most of the nutrition-related NCDs.

Soaring obesity rates are forcing governments around the world to confront one of the more serious threats to public health in a generation. New regulations, which corporate interests delayed for almost a decade, require explicit labeling and limit the marketing of sugary foods to children have been implemented in both Chile and Mexico, setting important precedents for food labeling (Jacobs 2018).

Nutrition experts say such measures are the world's most ambitious attempt to remake a country's food culture and could be a model for how to turn the tide on a global obesity epidemic, which researchers say contributes to four million premature deaths a year (Jacobs 2018).

Geeta Anand, in "One Man's Stand Against Junk Food as Diabetes Climbs Across India," notes:

Since 1990, the percent of children and adults in India who are overweight or obese has almost tripled to 18.8 percent from 6.4 percent, according to data from the Institute for Health Metrics and Evaluation at the University of Washington.

The International Diabetes Federation projects that the number of Indians with diabetes will soar to 123 million by 2040 as diets rich in carbohydrates and fat spread to less affluent rural areas. (Anand 2017)

India should put into place stricter regulations before it is too late. However, "ferocious opposition from the All India Food Processors Association, which counts Coca-Cola India, PepsiCo India and Nestlé India as members, as well as hundreds of other companies" has stalled such regulatory efforts (Anand 2017). Chile imposed a 12 percent value-added tax (VAT) on all packaged processed foods and beverages and 28 percent extra levy on aerated beverages. Evaluations are underway in Chile and India to assess the impacts of taxes on prices and consumption (personal communication, Barry M. Popkin, June 10, 2018). According to Anand, India has "...partially implemented a tax on sugar sweetened beverages, instituting a 40 percent tax on such drinks that are carbonated, though not on juices made with added sugars that many children drink. But so far, the regulations to ban sales near schools sought by the court...have led to naught" (Anand 2017).

India is also proposing a Chilean-style warning label on foods high in sugar, saturated fat, and sodium.

In addition to improved public policy, civil society needs to foster women's organizations, such as the Self Employed Women's Association (SEWA) in India, that both promote both healthier foods and their production and delivery (see www.sewa.org). This will lead to a triple win, more income and employment for women, better environmental management, and healthier populations.

Nutrition Transition and Food Systems

Barry M. Popkin, who first identified the phenomenon of the "nutrition transition" in the early 1990s and has written extensively on this subject, notes that IOs were slow to take the impending obesity trends and their policy implications on board (Popkin 1993, 1994, 1998, 2001, 2009; Popkin, Adair, and Ng 2012). (See Box 4.5.) Popkin teamed up with Thomas Reardon, a leading advocate of value chains, to produce a paper that explored dietary changes:

> The shifts in diet are profound: major shifts in intake of less-healthful low-nutrient-density foods and sugary beverages, changes in away-from-home eating and snacking and rapid shifts towards very high levels of overweight and obesity among all ages along with, in some countries, high burdens of stunting. Diet changes have occurred in parallel to, and in two-way causality with, changes in the broad food system—the set of supply chains from farms, through midstream segments of processing, wholesale and logistics, to downstream segments of retail and food service (restaurants and fast food chains). (Popkin and Reardon 2018, 1028)

The conventional view of transformation has not materialized for many late developing countries, as we showed in Chapter 2 on structural transformation. Their demographic transition, agricultural productivity growth, and industrialization have each been slower than that of their predecessors, particularly the Asian Tigers (Hong Kong, Singapore, Taiwan, and South Korea, and more recently, China), and the late developers contain a large share of the world's undernourished and malnourished populations concurrently with growing numbers of obese. This suggests a tremendous need and an opportunity to create employment in sustainable food systems for women and youth in the food service industry, in work environments that are more youth-oriented and gender friendly. Later in this chapter, we discuss the implications of this opportunity for policy, institutional development, and information and knowledge sharing among citizens through education going forward.

Box 4.5 What Is Nutrition and Nutrition Transition?

WHO defines nutrition at an individual level as: "the intake of food, considered in relation to the body's dietary needs. Good nutrition—an adequate, well balanced diet combined with regular physical activity—is a cornerstone of good health. Poor nutrition can lead to reduced immunity, increased susceptibility to disease, impaired physical and mental development, and reduced productivity" (WHO 2018b).

As the World Bank Group noted in their report, "Learning from World Bank History: Agriculture and Food-Based Approaches for Addressing Malnutrition":

> The nutrients in food include carbohydrates, proteins, and fats (the "macronutrients"—which contain dietary energy), and vitamins and minerals (the "micronutrients"—which do not contain dietary energy). Other components of food that are not technically "nutrients" also contribute to nutrition and health, such as fiber, probiotic bacteria, and phytonutrients....

> ...[T]he focus of the international nutrition community regarding dietary intake has shifted from proteins (in the 1960s) to dietary energy (1970s–80s) to micronutrients (primarily provided via nutrient supplements) (1990s–2000s). Now (2010s), the focus is moving toward dietary diversity and dietary quality more broadly. (WBG 2014, 3)

To protect against malnutrition in all of its forms, as well as NCDs, including diabetes, heart disease, stroke, and cancer, WHO advocates healthy dietary practices starting early in life with breastfeeding (WHO 2018b). For a healthy diet, energy intake (kcal) needs to be balanced with energy expenditure. A healthy diet includes fruits, vegetables, legumes (for example, lentils and beans), nuts, and whole grains (such as unprocessed maize, millet, oats, wheat, and brown rice).

The overall dietary shift linked with extremely rapid reduction in activity in all domains of movement—market and home production, transportation and leisure— have combined to create new challenges. Further recommendations by WHO for healthy diets include a shift in fat consumption away from saturated to unsaturated fats and toward the elimination of industrial trans fats. Healthy unsaturated or monosaturated fats (from fish, avocado, nuts, and sunflower, canola, and olive oils) are preferable to saturated fats, particularly from unhealthy sources (palm and coconut oil, lard, fatty meats, cream, cheese, ghee, and butter). Saturated fats should not exceed 10 percent of total energy intake to avoid much greater risk of NCDs. WHO recommends limiting the intake of free sugars to less than 10 percent of total energy intake for a healthy diet. A further reduction to less than 5 percent of total energy intake is suggested for additional health benefits. Keeping salt intake to less than 5 g per day (approximately one teaspoon) may help prevent hypertension and reduce the risk of heart disease and stroke in the adult population (WHO 2018b).

During the long history of food and nutrition in modern times, there has been the rise, fall, and rise again of nutrition and its advocacy. How sustained the focus on nutrition remains is not known, and we need to understand the history of dietary changes in industrial countries. We now realize that to address malnutrition in all its forms a healthy diet is essential and the agriculture sector will have to make profound changes up and down the entire food supply chain.

Overall, the share of agricultural production going through supermarkets is low in LICs but in some large cities (for example, in Africa), it is now already more than 30 percent (Figure 4.10). Supermarkets also differ from traditional retailers in terms of the food varieties offered, the prices charged, and the shopping atmosphere (Hawkes 2008). Nutritional implications of the rapid rise of supermarkets are not yet sufficiently understood. A few studies have shown that supermarkets contribute to the consumption of more calories and higher levels of processed foods, even after controlling for household income, education, and other confounding factors (Asfaw 2008; Rischke et al. 2015; Khonje and Qaim 2019). Studies also suggest that buying food in supermarkets is associated with higher BMI, a higher likelihood of overweight and obesity, and a higher risk of suffering from chronic diseases (Kimenju et al. 2015; Demmler et al. 2017; Demmler, Ecker, and Qaim 2018). Ultra-processed foods with high fat, sugar, and salt contents are known to contribute to overweight and obesity (Asfaw 2011; Popkin 2017; Law et al. 2019). The effects on children are less studied, however, and recent research in Kenya suggests that supermarkets are associated with larger effects on height than the effects on weight, which, if

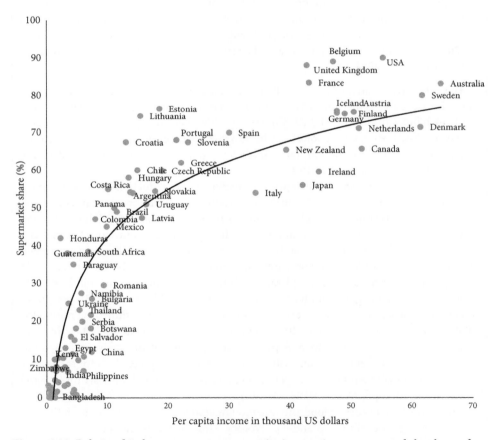

Figure 4.10 Relationship between average per capita income in a country and the share of supermarkets in food retailing

Source: Data provided by Martin Qaim, 2019, compiled from Planet Retail Country Reports at EDGE Retail Insight (https://rnetailinsight.ascentialedge.com/login) and World Development Indicators (World Bank 2020d); see, also, Qaim (2017).

generalizable, is good news, "because child stunting (low height-for-age) remains a major nutritional problem that is declining more slowly than child underweight. Supermarkets do not seem to be a driver of childhood obesity in this setting. The positive effects of super-markets on child nutrition are channeled through improvements in food variety and dietary diversity" (Debela et al. 2020).

According to William Masters et al. (2016, 97): "The nutrition transition, a term coined in the early 1990s by Popkin (1993, 1994) refers to systematic changes in nutritional intake, body size, and health associated with economic development." It relates very directly to how we eat, drink, and move, and how shifts in these patterns over time have profoundly affected our health (see Figure 4.11). Masters et al. explain further:

> The term focuses particularly on the rising rates of obesity and diet-related diseases that were increasingly observed since the 1980s, alongside the improvements in height and mortality that had occurred slowly over many decades in now-industrialized countries and then spread rapidly to lower income countries as documented by Fogel (2004), Deaton (2007), and others. (Masters et al. 2016, 97)

Increased consumption of calorically dense diets, full of salt, fats, and sugary beverages associated with poor diet quality, is an integral part of Popkin's more recent patterns of the

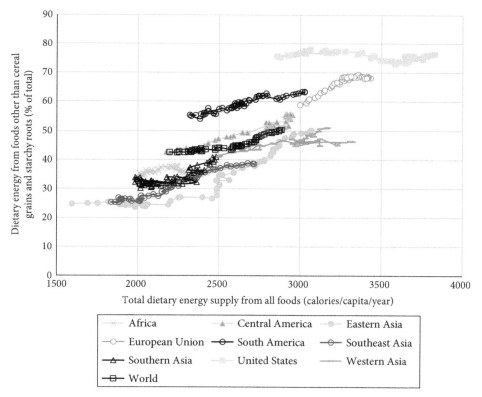

Figure 4.11 Percentage of energy from nonstaple foods and total dietary energy per capita by region, 1961–2013

Source: Based on the data from FAO Food Balance Sheet, http://www.fao.org/faostat/en/#data/FBS

nutrition transition. Now those consumption patterns have spread widely to countries that are experiencing rapid economic growth, as well as to others in which income growth has not occurred to the same extent but where purchased food and drinks have become available and led to alarming rates of growth in obesity and NCDs (Gortmaker et al. 2011; Popkin, Adair, and Ng 2012; Ng et al. 2014; Hawkes et al. 2015; Huang, Yang, and Rozelle 2015; Jaacks, Slining, and Popkin 2015; Lele 2015; Swinburn et al. 2015). An old adage among agricultural experts for well over 40 years was that Coca-Cola was more easily available in distant places than fertilizers, so agricultural service providers needed to learn lessons on how to get their services to farmers. In recent years, there is a frequent comparison in the literature of the behavior of the food industry to that of the tobacco industry, with the food industry being to diabetes what tobacco has been to cancer (Taylor and Jacobson 2016). Debate has also been renewed on individual response versus corporate response, going beyond the normal expectations for corporate social responsibility (Runge et al. 2012). By and large, IOs have been timid about dealing with the corporate sector, and they acknowledge it. This shift in dietary patterns from diets low in calories and nutrients to diets high in calories still entails inadequate intake of beneficial foods and nutrients, associated with consumption of more processed foods and more meals away from home, leading to changes in dietary composition, as well as food quantities that Paarlberg (2012) and Smith and Haddad (2015) identified. The food industry has argued that personal responsibility is more important than the food environment. We argue public policy needs to address both through far more active consumer education and through regulation of the food industry. The latter is an uphill battle, however, given the unequal power of multinationals relative to consumer advocates, and the governance issues in developing countries. Later in the chapter, we discuss the challenges that Brazil and Colombia have faced in pursuing progressive nutrition policies. In the interim, it is useful to see contemporary nutrition policies in a historical context.

Müller and Sukhdev (2018, 10), in their argument for a systems perspective to achieving food security, present as an example the complexity of the obesity epidemic, in terms of the evolution of food systems, in that obesity is not merely the result of consumption of foods of high sugar/carbohydrate content. The authors point also to the consumption of refined wheat and sugars in ultra-processed foods can trigger glycemic peaks, and to "'obesogens' released in the environment by certain endocrine-disrupting chemicals" that may also be contributing to weight gain, following exposures during early development.[15] Swinburn et al. (2015) asserted in their article in *Lancet*, that for the prevention of NCDS, the achievement of WHO targets will not occur: "without improvements in food environments at local, national, and transnational levels because obesogenic food environments are the underlying drivers of the obesity epidemic. Food environments encompass the collective physical, economic, policy, and sociocultural surroundings, opportunities, and conditions that affect people's food and beverage choices and nutritional status" (Swinburn et al. 2015, 2534).

Evidence amassed by IFPRI in its Advancing Research on Nutrition and Agriculture Phase II (ARENA-II) project suggests that the cost of nutritious food, such as fish, meat, eggs, and milk, is more expensive in rural areas relative to the cost of carbohydrates and varies greatly across commodities and locations, depending on the physical and economic

---

[15] The National Institute of Environmental Health Sciences identifies possible obesogens as cigarette smoke, air pollution, some pesticides, flame retardants, and other chemicals (see https://www.niehs.nih.gov/health/topics/conditions/obesity/obesogens/index.cfm).

access of households to those commodities. Africa's import dependence has increased, and that, too, keeps the costs of imported foods high (IFPRI 2019a).

Differential Distribution of International Aid to Multidimensionally Poor Poverty

Twenty-eight percent of poor people (identified by using the MPI, hereafter referred to as "MPI poor") live in LICs. These LICs received 42 percent of donor flows to priority social sectors. However, 66 percent of MPI poor people live in lower MICs. Aid flows to these countries amount to 49 percent of the flows. With very low allocations to India, each poor person is allocated US$1.35 of aid. A small percentage of the MPI poor live in upper middle-income countries (UMICs) (6 percent). These poor receive 9 percent of aid flows. The distribution of multilateral flows from IOs, compared to the OECD's Development Assistance Committee (DAC) bilateral flows, better reflect the distribution of MPI poor (Alkire and Robles 2017).

OPHI, in their Briefing Note on the "Global Multidimensional Poverty Index 2017," describe aid flows with respect to MPI:

> Analysis of aid flows to individual countries is also important. If we consider ODA from DAC donors, which is thought to represent the bulk of development aid, the countries that receive very low aid flows in priority social sectors may not be those who need it least. ... [E]ight lower middle income countries, including the most populous in terms of MPI poor such as Pakistan ($2.30), Nigeria ($1.40) and India ($0.64), receive very low allocations in priority social sector aid from DAC countries. ...

> To understand whether and when aid is catalyzing action and further public expenditure to fight poverty in multiple dimensions requires in-depth analysis. What is clear is that the distribution of ODA flows differs significantly from the distribution of multidimensionally poor people. (Alkire and Robles 2017, 6–7)

Aid and Domestic Budgetary Expenditures in Support of Nutrition

Aid has not been commensurate with needs, but countries are spending more. How much in relation to the need is unclear. *GNR 2017* reviewed various forms of commitments, such as policy, financial, and capacity building, which should be assessed relative to the needs of the sector. According to the World Bank (Shekar et al. 2017), "US$70 billion is needed over the next 10 years to maximise the contribution nutrition-specific interventions make towards achieving the four MIYCN [maternal, infant and young child nutrition] targets for 2025 for stunting, wasting, anaemia and exclusive breastfeeding, with a 'priority package' of interventions costing US$23 billion" (Development Initiatives 2017, 70). This does not include the cost of nutrition-sensitive interventions. In 2015, global ODA was US$867 million, which was an increase of 2 percent over 2014, when US$851 million was spent. However, the 2015 spending was less than the US$870 million spent in 2013.

GNR 2017 also reported increased budgetary allocations in several sectors, but huge differences were found among countries in their national spending on nutrition. Chad, Comoros, El Salvador, Guatemala, Guinea Bissau, and Nepal have allocated over 10 percent of their government spending for nutrition-specific and nutrition-sensitive interventions. The amounts of the allocations varied according to context and in terms of types of investments, depending on underlying causes of malnutrition. Despite the lack of "a common pattern across all countries, the highest share of nutrition-sensitive allocations is found in the social protection sector (34%) followed by health (22%), agriculture (17%), WASH (15%) and education (11%)" (Development Initiatives 2017, 68).

The World Bank report, "Investment Framework for Nutrition," provided the estimate that an additional US$7 billion is needed annually to invest in nutrition-specific interventions to reach MIYCN targets for 2025. According to Shekar et al. (2017):

> The investment can yield tremendous returns: 3.7 million child lives saved, at least 65 million fewer stunted children, 265 million fewer women suffering from anemia in 2025, 105 million more infants exclusively breastfed up to six months of age as compared to the 2015 baseline, and 91 million children treated for wasting, in addition to other health and poverty reduction efforts. (Shekar et al. 2017, 139)

What Do Success Stories in the *Global Nutrition Reports* Tell Us?

The *GNRs* listed successful cases of nutritional improvements that have one factor in common. Collectively, they suggest that there is no single factor that explains improvement in nutritional outcomes in any one country, but even the poorest countries such as Bangladesh have shown improvement, by acting on multiple fronts. Hence, they illustrate the importance of both a multisectoral approach and the recognition of country context.

There are also vast differences in nutritional status and changes among different regions within each country. That is the key message of 17 case studies, including 12 Caribbean countries contained in the *GNRs* from 2014 to 2017—from SA (2), East Asia (1), Southeast Asia (1); SSA (7); and Latin America (6). They contain rich material from well-informed authors. They use very diverse criteria of nutritional improvement, only some of which are explicit. Some are stories of changes in public policy, whereas others describe changes in outcomes. For example, some contain references to changes in the stunting of children less than five years of age. Statistical evidence is not provided in the case studies, which does not mean it does not exist. Where available, the cases indicate they relied on household surveys and other evidence. The coverage of the issues is not comparable across studies (IFPRI 2014, 2015, 2016b, 2017).

Maharashtra, India: One of the richest Indian states, Maharashtra experienced a decline in stunting of children under 5 over a decade, from 36.5 percent to 24 percent from 2004–5 to 2012. This was due to a variety of factors, including a generally more favorable underlying environment—rapid economic growth, relatively more progressive tradition of women's roles in decision-making, reasonably well-working Public Distribution System (PDS) of food with fewer leakages than elsewhere, increased spending on nutrition, fewer vacancies in the Integrated Child Development Service, higher age of mothers at first birth, improved birthweight, growth in maternal literacy, and assistance to birthing mothers at birth (Lawrence Haddad, panel 2.3 [IFPRI 2014, 13]).

Bangladesh: Bangladesh's decline in child stunting was almost twice as fast as India's over the same period. ("For India between 1999 and 2006 the decline in under-five stunting prevalence was 5 percentage points, from 51 percent to 46 percent or 0.85 percentage points a year." (India, Ministry of Health and Family Welfare 2009, quoted in IFPRI 2014, 93). For

Bangladesh between 1997 and 2007, the decline was from 59 percent to 43 percent, or 1.6 percentage points a year and is explained by improvement in household assets, parental education, and sanitation coverage (Derek Headey, panel 6.2 [IFPRI 2014, 43]).

Webb et al. (2018, 2) describe Bangladesh as "a modern nutrition superstar," in which successive governments, acting with nongovernmental organizations, have conducted targeted interventions, with nutritional measures, to address economic growth policies to reduce poverty, improve sanitation and girls' education. The "turnaround" of the agricultural sector has resulted in Bangladesh changing from being a net importer to an exporter of food. The success of efforts is reflected in the decrease in child stunting from nearly 57 percent in 1997 to 36 percent in 2014.

Colombia: Colombia's impressive nutritional performance was due to decline in conflict and a peace accord with Revolutionary Armed Forces of Colombia, also known as FARC, as well as rapid, broad-based growth, decline in poverty, and improved social protection. Intersectoral coordination and monitoring and evaluation are weak, however, as is the approach to obesity (Diana Parra and Lawrence Haddad, panel 4.2 [IFPRI 2015, 44]).

Ethiopia: In Ethiopia, Africa's largest public works program, the Productive Safety Net Program (PSNP), which reaches well over 8 million people, was made more nutrition-sensitive by working in tandem with the country's National Nutrition Program. It is building strong accountability, monitoring and evaluation, and capacity supported by donors (Andrea Warren, panel 4.3 [IFPRI 2015, 46]). Working with the private sector, Ethiopia also has an initiative to promote iodized salt. In 2014, 83 percent of children were iodine-deficient, and 40 percent had goiter (EHNRI, FMoH, and UNICEF 2005). The government provided incentives to cooperatives to produce salt, and when salt glut led to collapse of prices, it helped to form producer cooperative organizations, established cost recovery and quality assurance mechanisms with a tripartite partnership among government, private sector, and cooperatives working together to improve iodine intake in the population (Corey L. Luthringer, Alem Abay, and Greg S. Garrett, panel 5.4 [IFPRI 2016b, 56]).

Burkina Faso: In Burkina Faso, major advances have included industrial fortification of cooking oil with vitamin A and wheat flour with folic acid, supported by the Helen Keller Institute and Government of Taiwan. This support is combined with the promotion of homestead production and nutrition awareness, with positive impacts on maternal and child health (Deanna K. Olney, Andrew Dillon, Abdoulaye Pedehombga, Marcellin Ouédraogo, and Marie Ruel, panel 6.3 [IFPRI 2014, 45] and Victoria Quinn, panel 5.5 [IFPRI 2016b, 57]).

Ghana: Ghana's substantial improvement in stunting indicators is attributed to a transition to democracy, steady growth, improved attendance of girls' education, improved coverage of cash transfers to 80,000 families, and SSNs. What is needed is more budgetary support for nutrition and attention to agriculture (Richmond Aryeetey, Esi Colecraft, and Anna Lartey, panel 6.1 [IFPRI 2016b, 63]).

Guatemala and Peru: Guatemala's Integrated Government Accounting System is expenditure tracking that helps to monitor attention to FSN to achieve Zero Hunger goals. Guatemala's actual expenditures are lower than allocated. Peru, with a similar system, has exceeded its allocated budgets. Transparent and regular release of budgetary information at all levels allows various stakeholders to track use of resources and relate them to outcomes (Paola Victoria, Ariela Luna, José Velásquez, Rommy Ríos, Germán González, William Knechtel, Vagn Mikkelsen, and Patrizia Fracassi, panel 7.1 [IFPRI 2016b, 83]).

Cambodia: The government of Cambodia has undertaken integrated multisectoral planning, including water and sanitation, agriculture, and rural development, involving a variety of organizations, including UNICEF, WHO, Helen Keller International, and the World Bank, and has appointed focal people promoting cross-sectoral approaches (Dan Jones and Megan Wilson-Jones, spotlight 3.1 [Development Initiatives 2017, 56]).

Victoria, Australia: In Victoria, Australia, the Healthy Together program, which reaches 1.3 million of its 6 million population, is attempting to provide a systems approach with a complete package of policies and promotion of healthy foods in easily accessible areas, such as vending machines, schools with supportive networks, and training and guidelines to reduce obesity. It has mobilized a large number of actors from the public, private, and community sectors. Trying to promote healthy food as a social norm and not as an exception is a good approach. One would like to know how successful this has been in actually reducing obesity, or its growth. Information was not contained in the story (Shelley Bowen, panel 4.5 [IFPRI 2015, 56] and Anna Peeters, Kirstan Corben, and Tara Boelsen-Robinson, spotlight 3.2 [Development Initiatives 2017, 59]).

Kenya: In Kenya, the government is beginning to tackle the problem of the growing incidence of obesity in women, young girls, and children in urban and rural areas, resulting in a growing incidence of NCDs. The Ministry of Health and Sanitation has announced a number of specific steps to address the problem, including increased awareness and training of public health workers, but a lack of data and too few resources constrain the program (Lindsay Jaacks, Justine Kavle, Albertha Nyaku, and Abigail Perry, panel 3.2 [IFPRI 2016b, 28]).

Caribbean: Twelve of the 20 Caribbean countries have formed "whole government, whole society" nutrition and national NCD commissions to contain the problem of obesity and undernourishment following multisectoral approaches and have made useful contributions to greater awareness of NCDs and pursuit of multisectoral approaches. The efforts still need a truly multisectoral approach, however, to increase the role of non-health ministries, more funding, and more coordination (Maisha Hutton and Sir Trevor Hassell, panel 5.1 [IFPRI 2016b, 46]).

Tanzania: Poverty halved during a decade from 85 to 43 percent, but changes in undernourishment were more modest. Thinness in women of reproductive age and stunting declined. *GNR 2015* attributes this to a strong commitment by governments and donors, leading to increased funding. Even then, funding was only a quarter of the estimated needed budget. *GNR 2015* suggests ring fencing of the budget for nutrition and the need for better targeting, more data, and better capacity (Lawrence Haddad, Panel 4.4 and 5.1 [IFPRI 2015, 55, 59]).

South Korea: It is a remarkable story. Obesity rates are low despite a dramatic increase in per capita incomes, with South Korea joining the ranks of developed countries. *GNR 2015* attributes the success to Korea adhering to the traditional plant-based diet, with some increase in consumption in animal products, which helped reduce anemia. This was partly linked with a systematic push to retain a traditional diet, along with actual training of women prior to marriage in preparation of traditional South Korean vegetable dishes (Lee, Duffey, and Popkin 2012). That is an important message for modernizing countries, and a message that needs greater emphasis (Hee Young Paik, panel 7.2 [IFPRI 2015, 88]). Many of these programs in South Korea ended with its entry into the WTO and a marked shift in younger cohorts toward greater overweight status, linked with an increasingly Westernized diet and lifestyle (Lee, Duffey, and Popkin 2012).

Argentina: Argentina's dietary salt reduction campaign, "Less salt, more life," to 5g per person is SMART (Specific, measurable, achievable, relevant, and time bound). The average daily salt intake declined from 11.2g to 9.2g from 2011 to 2015, so that 2,000 annual deaths from cardiovascular disease could be avoided per gram of salt intake reduction (Chessa Lutter, panel 5.2 [IFPRI 2016b, 51]).

Chile: The Chilean government has passed a series of measures to reduce obesity and NCDs, including introduction of an 8 percent tax on sugary drinks in 2014, restrictions on display of food and labeling of food rich in salt, sugars and fats in 2016, and requirement to prohibit advertising of harmful foods to children—the most comprehensive legislation, with appeals to stakeholders to help implement the legislation. Implementation is still at an early stage, and an evaluation is underway (Camila Corvalan and Marcela Reyes, panel 5.3 [IFPRI 2016b, 53]).

Brazil: In *GNR 2016*, Brazil's example includes the most comprehensive list of steps taken to improve nutrition. Brazil's case dramatically shows the important role of leadership, as well as the larger case of governance failure. President Luiz Inácio Lula da Silva and his party came to power in 2002 (Cecilia Rocha, Patricia Constante Jaime, Marina Ferreira Rea, panel 1.5 [IFPRI 2016b, 11] and Daniel Balaban and Mariana Rocha, panel 6.2 [IFPRI 2016b, 68]). The *GNR* case for Brazil lists the following initiatives, but does not mention that Brazil has become a powerhouse in agricultural growth, leading to a decline in real domestic prices of food, and now is one of the world's largest food exporters (Lele, Agarwal, and Goswami 2018).

In Brazil, the National Breastfeeding Programme was approved in 1981. The National Code of Marketing of Breast-milk Substitutes was approved in 1988; maternity leave increased to 4 months. The National Food Strategy had already been passed in 1999, but the Zero Hunger strategy and food acquisition program was distinctly the Lula Government strategy and was approved in 2003. The government introduced the program *Bolsa Familia* for conditional cash transfers in 2004, based on strong evidence and rigorous monitoring and evaluation. The National Food Security Law was passed in 2005. The National Law on Food and Nutrition Security (LOSAN), establishing the National System for Food and Nutrition Security (SISAN), was passed in 2006. In 2009 the school meal program (PNAE) was revised. In 2010, the human right to adequate and healthy food was incorporated into the Brazilian constitution, which also passed National Food and Nutritional Security Policy (PNSAN). In 2014, the Brazilian Food Guide was published, including an Intersectoral Strategy for the Prevention and Control of Obesity. In 2015, the Decree to enable implementation of the National Code of Marketing of Breast-milk Substitutes was issued (Cecilia Rocha, Patricia Constante Jaime, and Marina Ferreira Rea, panel 1.5 [IFPRI 2016b, 11]).

How did it affect outcomes? In the early 1990s, 21 percent of the population earned less than US$2 a day, and only 2 percent of the national income went to the lowest 20 percent of the population. Open defecation was practiced by17 percent; stunting was 19 percent. With the introduction of the social protection program by 2006–8, the share of population with US$2 a day had already declined from 19 percent to 7 percent, although 30 percent of the population was food insecure. By 2011–15, income distribution had improved. The share of income accruing to the lowest 20 percent had increased from 2.2 to 3.4 percent; the share of population with less than US$2 a day had declined to 5 percent. Civil society had played a very active role, working with government (Cecilia Rocha, Patricia Constante Jaime, and Marina Ferreira Rea, Panel 1.5, [IFPRI 2016b, 11]).

Where the government failed was in making any progress is in the area of obesity. Adult obesity was 43 percent and overweight was 12 percent by 2006–8, and by 2011–15, overweight was 54 percent and obesity was 20 percent (Cecilia Rocha, Patricia Constante Jaime, and Marina Ferreira Rea, panel 1.5 [IFPRI 2016b, 11]). The baby food industry had fought hard to resist the regulation against breast-milk substitutes, and even when the legislation was passed, it failed to be ratified and was never implemented. The precise institutional and legal details are in *GNR 2016*. Immensely popular, President Luiz Inácio

Lula da Silva has since been convicted and imprisoned for corruption. His successor Dilma Rousseff was also impeached.

From Food Security to Nutrition: Conclusions and Implications for the Future

There has been a clear shift in international discourse from food security to improved nutrition. Obesity is now a larger and growing problem in the world relative to undernourishment and micronutrient deficiencies, and it is not being adequately addressed by SDGs. Indeed, IOs have been slow to catch up to the challenge (including the costs imposed on national health care systems), and even today, their efforts, carried out mostly through WHO in the context of impacts on NCDs, are weaker than they should be. History tells us this trend will likely continue, unless there is another major global food crisis prompted by a combination of bad crops in major exporting countries, or an energy or financial crisis—factors that plunge developing countries into balance of payments and debt crises and reduce their access to international food supplies, wiping away gains being made in nutrition and reported in this chapter. This happened at the end of the 1970s, followed by the food crisis in 2006–7. Each had different effects on access of importing countries to food supplies. In the latter period, developing countries were better prepared for a macroeconomic crisis, but their agricultural sectors had been neglected for nearly two decades, and food aid had dried up, creating different stresses on food and nutrition.

In many Latin America countries and others around the globe, there are pushes for fiscal policies, such as sugar-sweetened beverage taxes and many other policies, including Chile's front-of-the-package warning logos against ultra-processed foods high in sugar, fat, and sodium, as well as marketing bans. The high health and economic costs of treating diabetes, hypertension, and all the related disabilities are pushing many countries to adopt such policies, but the resistance from the food industry, often subtle, is considerable.

Complexity of the Nutrition Challenge

Nutrition is a life-cycle phenomenon and calls for attention to an individual's nutrition from cradle to the grave, or more correctly from the conception of a fetus in a mother's womb. A highly complex, multisectoral, and multilevel subject, an individual's nutritional status and health are affected by a combination of factors, operating at several levels and over several time periods across many sectors, including agriculture, water, gender, energy (cooking fuel), sanitation, value chains, international trade, and FDI. This holistic view of nutrition has profound implications for how nutrition policies and strategies are formed, implemented, and assessed.

Policymakers' Limited Understanding and Commitment

How many policymakers truly understand the full significance of the complexity of nutrition for policymaking? Despite the strong international advocacy that nutrition has enjoyed in the last decade, the exploding recent literature on nutrition suggests that experts have been more effective in communicating with their peers than with policymakers. Their job of effectively communicating with policymakers outside the nutrition community is cut out for them, particularly for getting messages across to finance ministries that determine budgetary allocations and can form policies with respect to taxes, subsidies, and regulation of the food industry to promote healthy production and consumption systems; to the food and beverage industry leaders to play to their better angels; and to consumers who, when better armed with information, can demand better quality food. This is where international approaches will have to be strengthened holistically from their current nutrition-centric focus.

It was easy to turn back the gains made in nutrition by the end of the 1970s, however small, in the wake of a global economic crisis, because there was no strong constituency for nutrition among either finance ministries or consumers. Indeed, even IOs turned away from their focus on food and nutrition, which they had championed in the previous decade, with the impending debt crisis at the end of the 1970s. The ongoing work at CFS to develop Voluntary Guidelines on Food Systems and Nutrition, following the HLPE report on "Nutrition and Food Systems," offers an example of the way forward (HLPE 2017).

Nutrition Strategies

Well over 50 countries have taken steps to establish nutrition strategies and allocate resources to nutrition programs. Some of these efforts are beginning to show results, but evidence on cause and effect is still weak, and evaluation of nutrition programs is complex and challenging. In terms of regulatory regimes, taxes, and subsidies to change incentives to curtail the supply of harmful foods, reforms are relatively new and still weak, in part because of the power of the food and beverage industry. Critical data are often missing in countries with the highest incidence of malnutrition, and a consumer information strategy is often lacking in most countries.

The implementation of the Africa Nutritional Strategy 2015–25 is aimed at improving nutrition across the African continent. With "six clear and achievable targets to be attained by 2025," the strategy seeks to (1) reduce stunting among children under 5 years by 40 percent; (2) reduce incidence of anemia among women of reproductive age by 50 percent; (3) reduce the incidence of low birthweight by 30 percent; (4) maintain weights so that there is no increase of overweight in women and in children under five; (5) promote exclusive breastfeeding for infants in the first six months of life, with a goal to increase the practice by 50 percent; and (6) reduce, or maintain at less than 5 percent, the incidence wasting among children under five. The Strategy recognizes that "the risk factors of malnutrition in Africa are multidimensional and can only be addressed in a comprehensive way with active contributions from all sectors, both government and non-government, including the private sector" (African Union 2015, iv). The challenge is to translate these intentions into action.

Relationship between Poverty, Gender Inequality, and Food Security

We explored the relationship between poverty and food security in several ways. The analysis of Kakwani and Son (2016) suggests that the gap between poverty reduction and undernourishment reduction may not be as large as the World Bank and FAO numbers suggest. These issues need further analysis. This is also true of gender inequality. Our analysis suggests that it is strongly associated with child food insecurity indicators, but issues of gender remain one of the neglected areas of public policy, particularly in countries lagging in good nutrition. A full range of steps needed to achieve nutritional outcomes are lacking in most countries, as the case studies we have presented showed. Lower cost of energy-dense food and its widespread availability has meant poor people are more adversely affected by the "junk food revolution."

Improved Governance and Increasing Accountability of Stakeholders

Accountability for results is still a nebulous area. *GNRs* do a good job of identifying the performance of various stakeholders in delivering on commitments. Journalists do an even better job in documenting how the enormous power of the food and beverage industry has been deployed over the years to stymie reforms attempting to contain the availability of foods rich in fats, sugars, and salts, and to improve food quality. By and large, OECD donors have delivered on their financial commitments, but those appear to have peaked in 2016, with a slight decline in 2017. Also, most donor resources go to LICs, but LMICs and MICs contain most of the malnutrition problems that result from the rapidly changing food environment. Governments of countries where most of the malnutrition exists must finance their own programs. Only a third of governments who have made commitments have delivered on them.

Limited Private Sector Engagement by Public Bodies

Multinational food and beverage industries have moved to global markets with, in some instances, active corporate resistance to their regulation or to efforts to limit their implementation at both the national and international levels. However, although *GNR 2017* reports confirm that the large-scale private sector has been lukewarm in its support of nutrition and has followed through with only a few of the commitments it has made (Development Initiatives 2017), there is no evidence of serious engagement with small and medium-sized enterprises (SMEs) at the local and national level. Political will to both engage with and regulate the private sector and enforce rules has been weak, despite mounting evidence of the relationship between diets and obesity.

Role of Regulation and Development of National Programs

Several MICs, including Chile and Mexico in Latin America, have imposed taxes and enacted regulations against sugary drinks and the sale of harmful food to children (Nakhimovsky et al. 2016). Brazil's example shows, however, that resistance of the private sector against regulation has been strong. It is too early to know the impact of regulation on food consumption. Nutritionists note that there is a dichotomy between the fast food industry and traditional consumption patterns. Countries, such as India, have lagged behind in FDI and development of domestic value chains, supermarkets, and restaurants.

These countries have much to learn about regulating the private sector and promoting the domestic food industry, which in turn promotes indigenous, plant-based diets that are low in fats, salts, and sugar, as South Korea did successfully.

FSN is a multisectoral issue. A narrow focus on calorie consumption misses the point about what is needed to improve the state of the world's FSN. Neither PoU nor FIES give us actual food consumption. With rapid dietary transition, advances in data collection and its reduced cost, it is time that the global community begins to collect data on actual food consumption. Currently, there are only a few cases where such data are available:

1. Global Dietary Database at Tufts University (Boston): They collect and connect consumption surveys from around the world, but because these data sets are not interoperable, they must do a lot of extrapolation. Tufts University has substantially expanded its work on the cost of food.
2. Global Burden of Disease at the Institute for Health Metrics and Evaluation (IHME) in Seattle. Here, too, they use different methods and data sets.
3. Global Individual Food Consumption Data Tool (GIFT)—World Health Organization (WHO)/FAO website—data available and in detail but for fewer countries.

(See SDG2 Advocacy Hub, http://sdg2advocacyhub.org/index.php/)

References

Agren, David. 2020. "Mexico State Bans Sale of Sugary Drinks and Junk Food to Children." *The Guardian*, August 6. https://www.theguardian.com/food/2020/aug/06/mexico-oaxaca-sugary-drinks-junk-food-ban-children

African Union. 2015. "Africa Regional Nutrition Strategy 2015–2025." African Union, Addis Ababa. https://au.int/sites/default/files/pages/32895-file-arns_english.pdf

Afshin, Ashkan, Mohammad H. Forouzanfar, Marissa B. Reitsma, Patrick Sur, Kara Estep, Alex Lee, Laurie Marczak, Ali H. Mokdad, Maziar Moradi-Lakeh, Mohsen Naghavi et al.; GBD 2015 Obesity Collaborators. 2017. "Health Effects of Overweight and Obesity in 195 Countries over 25 Years." *New England Journal of Medicine* 377: 13–27.

Afshin, Ashkan, Patrick John Sur, Kairsten A. Fay, Leslie Cornaby, Giannina Ferrara, Joseph S. Salama, Erin C. Mullany, Kalkidan Hassen Abate, Cristiana Abbafati, Zegeye Abebe et al; GBD 2017 Diet Collaborators. 2019. "Health Effects of Dietary Risks in 195 countries, 1990–2017: A Systematic Analysis for the Global Burden of Disease Study 2017." *Lancet* 393 (10184): 1958–72. https://doi.org/10.1016/S0140-6736(19)30041-8

Ahmed, Azam, Matt Richtel, and Andrew Jacobs. 2018. "In Nafta Talks, U.S. Tries to Limit Junk Food Warning Labels." *New York Times*, March 20.

Alderman, Harold, Jere. R. Behrman, and Chloe Puett. 2017. "Big Numbers about Small Children: Estimating the Economic Benefits of Addressing Undernutrition." *World Bank Research Observer* 32 (1): 107–25.

Alexandratos, Nikos, and Jelle Bruinsma. 2012. "World Agriculture Towards 2030/2050: The 2012 Revision." ESA Working Paper No. 12-03, Agricultural Development Economics Division, Food and Agriculture Organization of the United Nations (FAO), Rome. http://www.fao.org/docrep/016/ap106e/ap106e.pdf

Alkire, Sabina, and Mauricio Apablaza. 2016. "Multidimensional Poverty in Europe 2006–2012: Illustrating a Methodology." OPHI Working Paper No. 74, April, Oxford Poverty & Human Development Initiative, Oxford Department of International Development, University of Oxford. https://www.ophi.org.uk/wp-content/uploads/OPHIWP074_1.pdf

Alkire, Sabina, and James Foster. 2011a. "Counting and Multidimensional Poverty Measurement." *Journal of Public Economics* 95 (7–8): 476–87.

Alkire, Sabina, and James Foster. 2011b. "Understandings and Misunderstandings of Multidimensional Poverty Measurement." OPHI Working Paper No. 43, Oxford Poverty & Human Development Initiative, Oxford.

Alkire, Sabina, James Foster, and Maria Emma Santos. 2011. "Where Did Identification Go?" OPHI Working Paper No. 43b, Oxford Poverty & Human Development Initiative, Oxford.

Alkire, Sabina, James Foster, Suman Seth, Maria Emma Santos, José Manuel Roche, and Paola Ballon. 2015. *Multidimensional Poverty Measurement and Analysis.* Oxford: Oxford University Press.

Alkire, Sabina, and Usha Kanagaratnam. 2018. "Multidimensional Poverty Index – Winter 2017–18: Brief Methodological Note." MPI Methodological Notes 45. Oxford Poverty & Human Development Initiative, Oxford.

Alkire, Sabina, and Gisela Robles. 2017. "Global Multidimensional Poverty Index 2017." OPHI Briefing 47, Oxford Poverty & Human Development Initiative, Oxford. http://www.ophi.org.uk/wp-content/uploads/B47_Global_MPI_2017.pdf

Alkire, Sabina, and Suman Seth. 2015. "Multidimensional Poverty Reduction in India between 1999 and 2006: Where and How?" *World Development* 72: 93–108.

Anand, Geeta. 2017. "One Man's Stand Against Junk Food as Diabetes Climbs Across India." *New York Times*, December 26. https://www.nytimes.com/2017/12/26/health/india-diabetes-junk-food.html

Asfaw, Abay. 2008. "Does Supermarket Purchases Affect the Dietary Practices of Households? Some Empirical Evidence from Guatemala." *Development Policy Review* 26 (2): 227–43.

Asfaw, Abay. 2011. "Does Consumption of Processed Foods Explain Disparities in the Body Weight of Individuals? The Case of Guatemala." *Health Economics* 20 (2): 184–95.

Bahri, Charu. 2018. "Over 15 Years, India Slides on Key Marker of Gender Parity." *Bloomberg*, March 3. https://www.bloombergquint.com/global-economics/2018/03/03/over-15-years-india-slides-on-key-marker-of-gender-parity

Barne, Donna, and Divyanshi Wadhwa. 2018. "Year in Review: 2018 in 14 Charts." Feature Story, World Bank, December 21. https://www.worldbank.org/en/news/feature/2018/12/21/year-in-review-2018-in-14-charts

Barrett, Christopher B. 2010. "Measuring Food Insecurity." *Science* 327 (5967): 825–8.

Barrett, Christopher B., and Erin C. Lentz. 2010. "Food Insecurity." In *The International Studies Encyclopedia*, edited by Robert A. Denemark and Renée Marlin-Bennett, 2291–311. Malden, MA: Wiley-Blackwell.

Beegle, Kathleen, and Luc Christiaensen, eds. 2019. *Accelerating Poverty Reduction in Africa.* Washington, DC: World Bank Group. https://openknowledge.worldbank.org/handle/10986/32354

Béné, Christophe, Peter Oosterveer, Lea Lamotte, Inge D. Brouwer, Stef de Haan, and Steve D. Prager. 2019. "When Food Systems Meet Sustainability—Current Narratives and Implications for Actions." *World Development* 113: 116–30.

Bennet, Molly. 2017. "As Global Obesity Rises, Teasing Apart Its Causes Grows Harder." *New York Times*, September 17. https://www.nytimes.com/2017/09/17/insider/as-global-obesity-rises-teasing-apart-its-causes-grows-harder.html

Berg, Alan. 1973. *The Nutrition Factor: Its Role in National Development*. Washington, DC: Brookings Institution.

Berg, Alan, Nevin S. Scrimshaw, and David L. Call, eds. 1973. *Nutrition, National Development, and Planning: Proceedings of an International Conference*. Cambridge, MA: MIT Press.

Bhutta, Zulfiqar A., Jai K. Das, Arjumand Rizvi, Michelle F. Gaffey, Neff Walker, Susan Horton, Patrick Webb, Anna Lartey, Robert E. Black, *The Lancet* Nutrition Interventions Review Group, and the Maternal and Child Nutrition Study Group. 2013. "Evidence-based Interventions for Improvement of Maternal and Child Nutrition: What Can Be Done and At What Cost?" *Lancet* 382 (9890): 452–77.

Binswanger, Hans P., and Pierre Landell-Mills, P. 1995. "The World Bank's Strategy for Reducing Poverty and Hunger. A Report to the Development Community." Environmentally Sustainable Development Studies and Monographs Series No. 4, World Bank, Washington, DC.

Burchi, Francesco, Jessica Fanzo, and Emilie Frison. 2011. "The Role of Food and Nutrition System Approaches in Tackling Hidden Hunger." *International Journal of Environmental Research and Public Health* 8 (2): 358–73.

Burgess, Anne, and Reginald F. A. Dean, eds. 1962. *Malnutrition and Food Habits: Report of an International and Interprofessional Conference*. London: Tavistock Publications.

Call, David L., and Levinson, F. James. 1973. "A Systematic Approach to Nutrition Intervention Programs." In *Nutrition, National Development, and Planning*, edited by Berg, Alan, Nevin S. Scrimshaw, and David L. Call, 165–97. Cambridge, MA: MIT Press.

CFS (Committee on World Food Security). 2009. "Reform of the Committee on World Food Security." CFS:2009/2 Rev.2 , 35th Session, Food and Agricultural Organization of the UN (FAO), Rome, October 14–17. http://www.fao.org/fileadmin/templates/cfs/Docs0910/Re formDoc/CFS_2009_2_Rev_2_E_K7197.pdf

Chakrabarti, Suman, Nitya George, Moutushi Majumder, and Neha Raykar. 2018. "Identifying Sociodemographic, Programmatic and Dietary Drivers of Anaemia Reduction in Pregnant Indian Women over 10 Years." *Public Health Nutrition*, forthcoming. https://www.ifpri.org/publication/identifying-sociodemographic-programmatic-and-dietary-drivers-anaemia-reduction-pregnant

Chand, Ramesh, and Jaya Jumani. 2013. "Food Security and Undernourishment in India: Assessment of Alternative Norms and the Income Effect." *Indian Journal of Agricultural Economics* 68 (1): 39–53. http://ageconsearch.umn.edu/bitstream/206319/2/Chand_Ju mrani68_1.pdf

Chand, Ramesh, S. S. Raju, and L. M. Pandey. 2007. "Growth Crisis in Agriculture: Severity and Options at National and State Levels." *Economic and Political Weekly* 42 (26): 2528–33.

Chandy, Laurence. 2017. "No Country Left Behind: The Case for Focusing Greater Attention on the World's Poorest Countries." Global Economy and Development, Brookings Institution, Washington, DC.

Chen, Shaohua, and Martin Ravallion. 2010. "The Developing World Is Poorer Than We Thought, But No Less Successful in the Fight Against Poverty." *Quarterly Journal of Economics* 125 (4): 1577–625.

Clark, Sarah E., Corinna Hawkes, Sophia M. E. Murphy, Karen A. Hansen-Kuhn, and David Wallinga. 2012. "Exporting Obesity: US Farm and Trade Policy and the Transformation of the Mexican Consumer Food Environment." *International Journal of Occupational and Environmental Health* 18 (1): 53–64.

Clay, Edward. 2002. "Food Security: Concepts and Measurement." Paper for FAO Expert Consultation on Trade and Food Security: "Conceptualizing the Linkage," Rome, July 11–12. [Published in 2003 in FAO's *Trade Reforms and Food Security: Conceptualizing the Linkages*, 25–34. Rome: FAO.]

Copenhagen Consensus Center. 2015. "Post-Consensus 2015—Smartest Targets for the World: 2016–2030." Report on Outreach Activities, January–October. http://www.copenhagencons ensus.com/post-2015-consensus

Cornia, Giovanni Andrea, Richard Jolly, and Frances Stewart, eds. 1987. *Adjustment with a Human Face: Protecting the Vulnerable and Promoting Growth.* A Study by UNICEF. Oxford: Oxford University Press.

Cruz, Marcio, James Foster, Bryce Quillin, and Philip Schellekens. 2015. "Ending Extreme Poverty and Sharing Prosperity: Progress and Policies." Policy Research Note, World Bank, Washington, DC. http://pubdocs.worldbank.org/en/109701443800596288/PRN03Oct2015T winGoals.pdf

Deaton, Angus. 2007. "Height, Health, and Development." *Proceedings of the National Academy of Sciences* 104 (33): 13232–7.

Deaton, Angus. 2018. "The U.S. Can No Longer Hide From Its Deep Poverty Problem." Opinion, *New York Times*, January 24. https://www.nytimes.com/2018/01/24/opinion/ pov erty-united-states.html

Deaton, Angus, and Jean Drèze. 2009. "Food and Nutrition in India: Facts and Interpretations." *Economic and Political Weekly* 44 (7): 42–65.

Debela, Bethelhem Legesse, Kathrin M. Demmler, Stephan Klasen, and Matin Qaim. 2020. "Supermarket Food Purchases and Child Nutrition in Kenya." *Global Food Security* 25: 100341.

Del Gobbo, Liana C., Shahab Khatibzadeh, Fumiaki Imamura, Renata Micha, Peilin Shi, Matthew Smith, Samuel S Myers, and Dariush Mozaffarian. 2015. "Assessing Global Dietary Habits: A Comparison of National Estimates from the FAO and the Global Dietary Database." *American Journal of Clinical Nutrition* 101 (5): 1038–46.

Demmler, Kathrin M., Olivier Ecker, and Matin Qaim. 2018. "Supermarket Shopping and Nutritional Outcomes: A Panel Data Analysis for Urban Kenya." *World Development* 102: 292–303.

Demmler, Kathrin M., Stephan Klasen, Jonathan M. Nzuma, and Matin Qaim. 2017. "Supermarket Purchase Contributes to Nutrition-related Non-communicable Diseases in Urban Kenya." *PLoS One* 12 (9), Article e0185148. https://doi.org/10.1371/journal.pone.0185148

Development Initiatives. 2017. *Global Nutrition Report 2017: Nourishing the SDGs.* Bristol, UK: Development Initiatives.

Development Initiatives. 2018. *Global Nutrition Report 2018: Shining a Light to Spur Action on Nutrition.* Bristol, UK: Development Initiatives.

Development Initiatives. 2020. *2020 Global Nutrition Report: Action on Equity to End Malnutrition.* Bristol, UK: Development Initiatives.

Drèze, Jean, and Amartya Sen. 2011. "Putting Growth in Its Place." *Outlook India*, November 14. https://www.outlookindia.com/magazine/story/putting-growth-in-its-place/278843

Drèze, Jean, and Amartya Sen. 2013. *An Uncertain Glory: India and its Contradictions.* London: Allen Lane.

Duger, Angela, and Martha F. Davis. 2012. "A Human Rights-Based Approach to Food Security." *Clearinghouse Review: Journal of Poverty Law and Policy* 46 (5–6): 202–7. http://povertylaw.org/clearinghouse/articles/human-rights-based-approach-food-security

EHNRI (Ethiopian Health and Nutrition Research Center), FMoH (Federal Ministry of Health), and UNICEF (United Nations Children's Fund). 2005. *Iodine Deficiency Disorders (IDD) National Survey in Ethiopia.* Addis Ababa.

Ercin, A. Ertug, Maite Martinez Aldaya, and Arjen Y. Hoekstra. 2011. "Corporate Water Footprint Accounting and Impact Assessment: The Case of the Water Footprint of a Sugar-containing Carbonated Beverage." *Water Resources Management* 25 (2): 721–41.

Euromonitor International. 2015. "Where Are Our Calories Coming From? Actions Being Taken to Improve Nutrition." Strategy Briefing, February, Euromonitor International, London.

Fan, Shenggan, Derek D. Headey, David Laborde Debucquet, Daniel Mason-D'Croz, Christopher Rue, Timothy B. Sulser, Keith D. Wiebe. 2018. "Quantifying the Cost and Benefits of Ending Hunger And Undernutrition: Examining the Differences among Alternative Approaches." IFPRI Issue Brief, February, International Food Policy Research Institute, Washington, DC. http://www.ifpri.org/publication/quantifying-cost-and-benefits-ending-hunger-and-undernutrition-examining-differences

Fanzo, Jessica, and Derek Byerlee. 2019. "After 75 Years, Agriculture and Nutrition Meet Again: A History of Shifting Global Priorities in the Fight against Hunger." IFPRI Blog, July 31. http://www.ifpri.org/blog/after-75-years-agriculture-and-nutrition-meet-again

FAO (Food and Agriculture Organization of the United Nations). 1983. *Director-General's Report on World Food Security: A Reappraisal of the Concepts and Approaches.* Rome: FAO.

FAO (Food and Agriculture Organization of the United Nations). 2002. "World Food Summit: Five Years Later." June 10–13, Rome. http://www.fao.org/worldfoodsummit/english/index.html

FAO (Food and Agriculture Organization of the United Nations). 2003. *Trade Reforms and Food Security: Conceptualizing the Linkages.* Rome: FAO. http://www.fao.org/3/a-y4671e.pdf

FAO (Food and Agriculture Organization of the United Nations). 2008. *FAO Methodology for the Measurement of Food Deprivation: Updating the Minimum Dietary Energy Requirements.* Rome: FAO.

FAO (Food and Agriculture Organization of the United Nations). 2009. "Declaration of the World Summit on Food Security." WSFS 2009/2, Rome, November 16–18. http://www.fao.org/fileadmin/templates/wsfs/Summit/Docs/Final_Declaration/WSFS09_Declaration.pdf

FAO (Food and Agriculture Organization of the United Nations). 2011. "The State of Food and Agriculture 2010–11: Women in Agriculture—Closing the Gender Gap for Development." FAO, Rome.

FAO (Food and Agriculture Organization of the United Nations). 2013. *The State of Food and Agriculture: Food Systems for Better Nutrition.* Rome: FAO.

FAO (Food and Agriculture Organization of the United Nations). 2015. *The State of Food Insecurity in the World 2015.* Rome: FAO.

FAO (Food and Agriculture Organization of the United Nations). 2016. *The State of Food and Agriculture (SOFA) 2016—Climate Change, Agriculture, and Food Security.* Rome: FAO. http://www.fao.org/3/a-i6030e.pdf

FAO (Food and Agriculture Organization of the United Nations). 2017a. "The Future of Food and Agriculture. Trends and Challenges." FAO, Rome. http://www.fao.org/3/a-i6583e.pdf

FAO (Food and Agriculture Organization of the United Nations). 2017b. "Voices of the Hungry. Measuring Food Insecurity through People's Experiences." I7835EN/1/09.17 http://www.fao.org/3/a-i7835e.pdf

FAO (Food and Agriculture Organization of the United Nations). 2019a. "ICN2: Second International Conference on Nutrition—Better Nutrition, Better Lives, November 19–21, Rome. http://www.fao.org/about/meetings/icn2/en/

FAO (Food and Agriculture Organization of the United Nations). 2019b. *The State of Food and Agriculture 2019. Moving Forward on Food Loss and Waste Reduction*. Rome: FAO. http://www.fao.org/3/ca6030en/ca6030en.pdf

FAO (Food and Agriculture Organization of the United Nations). 2020a. "Voices of the Hungry." http://www.fao.org/in-action/voices-of-the-hungry/faq/en/

FAO (Food and Agriculture Organization of the United Nations). 2020b. "Voices of the Hungry. The Food Insecurity Experience Scale." http://www.fao.org/in-action/voices-of-the-hungry/fies/en/

FAO (Food and Agriculture Organization of the United Nations), IFAD (International Fund for Agricultural Development), UNICEF (United Nations Children's Fund), WFP (World Food Programme), and WHO (World Health Organization). 2017. "The State of Food Security and Nutrition in the World 2017. Building Resilience for Peace and Food Security." FAO, Rome.

FAO (Food and Agriculture Organization of the United Nations), IFAD (International Fund for Agricultural Development), UNICEF (United Nations Children's Fund), WFP (World Food Programme), and WHO (World Health Organization). 2018. "The State of Food Security and Nutrition in the World 2019. Building Climate Resilience for Food Security and Nutrition." FAO, Rome. http://www.fao.org/3/I9553EN/i9553en.pdf

FAO (Food and Agriculture Organization of the United Nations), IFAD (International Fund for Agricultural Development), UNICEF (United Nations Children's Fund), WFP (World Food Programme), and WHO (World Health Organization). 2019. "The State of Food Security and Nutrition in the World 2019. Safeguarding against Economic Slowdowns and Downturns." FAO, Rome.

FAO (Food and Agriculture Organization of the United Nations), IFAD (International Fund for Agricultural Development), UNICEF (United Nations Children's Fund), WFP (World Food Programme), and WHO (World Health Organization). 2020. "The State of Food Security and Nutrition in the World 2020: Transforming Food Systems for Affordable Healthy Diets." Rome: FAO. http://www.fao.org/3/ca9692en/online/ca9692en.html

FAO (Food and Agriculture Organization of the United Nations), IFAD (International Fund for Agricultural Development), and WFP (World Food Programme). 2015. *Achieving Zero Hunger: The Critical Role of Investments in Social Protection and Agriculture*. Rome: FAO. http://www.fao.org/3/a-i4951e.pdf

FAO (Food and Agriculture Organization of the United Nations) and WHO (World Health Organization). 1992a. *International Conference on Nutrition: Nutrition and Development—A Global Assessment*. Rev. edition, Rome: FAO and WHO. http://www.fao.org/docrep/017/z9550e/z9550e.pdf

FAO (Food and Agriculture Organization of the United Nations) and WHO (World Health Organization). 1992b. *International Conference on Nutrition: World Declaration on Nutrition and Plan of Action for Nutrition*. http://www.fao.org/ag/agn/nutrition/ICN/ICNCONTS.HTM

FAO (Food and Agriculture Organization of the United Nations), WHO (World Health Organization), and UNU (United Nations University). 1985. "Energy and Protein Requirements." Report of a Joint FAO/WHO/UNU Expert Consultation, World Health Organization Technical Report Series 724, WHO, Geneva.

FAO (Food and Agriculture Organization of the United Nations), WHO (World Health Organization), and UNU (United Nations University). 2007. "Protein and Amino Acid Requirements in Human Nutrition." Report of a Joint FAO/WHO/UNU Expert Consultation. WHO, Geneva. http://www.who.int/iris/handle/10665/43411

Ferreira, Francisco H. G., Shaohua Chen, Andrew L. Dabalen, Yuri M. Dikhanov, Nada Hamadeh, Dean Mitchell Jolliffe, Ambar Narayan, Espen Beer Prydz, Ana L. Revenga, Prem Sangraula, Umar Serajuddin, and Nobuo Yoshida. 2015. "A Global Count of the Extreme Poor in 2012: Data Issues, Methodology and Initial Results." Policy Research Working Paper No. WPS 7432, World Bank Group, Washington, DC. http://documents.worldbank.org/curated/en/360021468187787070/A-global-count-of-the-extreme-poor-in-2012-data-issues-methodology-and-initial-results

Fiedler, Yannick, and Massimo Iafrate. 2016. "Trends in Foreign Direct Investment in Food, Beverages, and Tobacco." FAO Commodity and Trade Policy Research Working Paper No. 51, Food and Agriculture Organization of the United Nations, Rome.

Fogel, Robert W. 2004. *The Escape from Hunger and Premature Death, 1700–2100: Europe, America, and the Third World.* Cambridge: Cambridge University Press.

FSIN (Food Security Information Network). 2017. "Global Report on Food Crises 2017." March. https://documents.wfp.org/stellent/groups/public/documents/ena/wfp291271.pdf

FSIN (Food Security Information Network). 2019. "Global Report on Food Crises 2019: Joint Analysis for Better Decisions." April. https://www.fsinplatform.org/sites/default/files/resources/files/GRFC_2019-Full_Report.pdf

A Full Bowl: The Story of Alan Berg. Directed by Theo Schear, 2020, film. https://www.youtube.com/watch?v=DFPMx6QZelo&t=90s

Fuller, Thomas, Anahad O'Connor, and Matt Richtel. 2017. "In Asia's Fattest Country, Nutritionists Take Money from Food Giants." *New York Times*, December 23.

GBD 2016 Risk Factor Collaborators (640). 2017. "Global, Regional, and National Comparative Risk Assessment of 84 Behavioural, Environmental and Occupational, and Metabolic Risks or Clusters of Risks, 1990–2016: A Systematic Analysis for the Global Burden of Disease Study 2016." *Lancet* 390 (10100): 1345–1422.

GBD 2017 Diet Collaborators. 2019. "Health Effects of Dietary Risks in 195 Countries, 1990–2017: A Systematic Analysis for the Global Burden of Disease Study 2017." *Lancet* 393 (10184): 1958–1972. https://www.thelancet.com/journals/lancet/article/PIIS0140-6736(19)30041-8/fulltext

Geach, Hugh. 1973. "The Baby Food Tragedy." *New Internationalist* August, No. 006.

Gerber, Pierre J., Henning Steinfeld, Benjamin Henderson, Anne Mottet, Carolyn Opio, Jeroen Dijkman, Alessandra Falcucci, and Guiseppe Tempio. 2013. "Tackling Climate Change through Livestock: A Global Assessment of Emissions and Mitigation Opportunities." Food and Agriculture Organization of the United Nations (FAO), Rome.

Gillespie, Stuart, Jody Harris, and Suneetha Kadiyala. 2012. "The Agriculture-Nutrition Disconnect in India, What Do We Know?" IFPRI Discussion Paper 01187, International Food Policy Research Institute, Washington, DC.

Gillespie, Stuart, Judith Hodge, Sivan Yosef, and Rajul Pandya-Lorch, eds. 2016. *Nourishing Millions: Stories of Change in Nutrition*. Washington, DC: International Food Policy Research Institute.

GLOPAN (Global Panel on Agriculture and Food Systems for Nutrition). 2016. "Food Systems and Diets: Facing the Challenges of the 21st Century." GLOPAN, London.

GLOPAN (Global Panel on Agriculture and Food Systems for Nutrition). 2017. "Healthy Diets for All: A Key to Meeting the SDGs." Policy Brief No. 10, GLOPAN, London.

Gopalan, C. 1992. "Undernutrition: Measurement and Implications." In *Nutrition and Poverty*, edited by Siddiqur Rahman Osmani, 17–47. World Institute for Development Economics Research (WIDER). Oxford: Clarendon Press.

Gortmaker, Steven L., Boyd A Swinburn, David Levy, Rob Carter, Patricia L. Mabry, Diane T. Finegood, Terry Huang, Tim Marsh, and Marjory L. Moodie. 2011. "Changing the Future of Obesity: Science, Policy, and Action." *Lancet* 378 (9793): 838–47.

Gross, Rainier, Hans Schoeneberger, Hans Pfeifer, and Hans-Joachim A. Preuss. 2000. "The Four Dimensions of Food and Nutrition Security: Definitions and Concepts." *SCN News* 20: 20–5.

Grünberger, Klaus. 2014. "Estimating Food Consumption Patterns by Reconciling Food Balance Sheets and Household Budget Surveys." FAO Statistics Division, Working Paper ESS/14-08, Food and Agriculture Organization of the United Nations, Rome.

GWU (George Washington University). 2020. "Beyond Income Poverty: Multiple Deprivations in the US and Beyond." Web seminar, November 23, Institute for International Economic Policy, Elliott School of International Affairs, GWU, Washington, DC.

Haddad, Lawrence. 2015. "50 Numbers to Help End Malnutrition by 2030." Development Horizons blog, October 16. http://www.developmenthorizons.com/2015/10/50-numbers-to-help-end-malnutrition-by.html

Haddad, Lawrence. 2019. "The EAT Lancet Report: Landmarks, Signposts and Omissions." Global Alliance for Improved Nutrition (GAIN), February 18, 2019. https://www.gainhealth.org/media/news/eat-lancet-report-landmarks-signposts-and-omissions

Haq, Mahbub ul. 1976. *The Poverty Curtain: Choices for the Third World*. New York: Columbia University Press.

Hatz, Diane. 2019. "EAT–Lancet Report—A Review." Change Food. https://www.changefood.org/2019/02/11/eat-lancet-report-a-review/

Hawkes, Corinna. 2008. "Dietary Implications of Supermarket Development: A Global Perspective." *Development Policy Review* 26 (6): 657–92.

Hawkes, Corinna, Trenton G. Smith, Jo Jewell, Jane Wardle, Ross A. Hammond, Sharon Friel, Anne Marie Thow, and Juliana Kain. 2015. "Smart Food Policies for Obesity Prevention." *Lancet* 385 (9985): 2410–21.

Headey, Derek, Kalle Hirvonen, John Hoddinott, and David Stifel. 2019. "Rural Food Markets and Child Nutrition." *American Journal of Agricultural Economics* 101 (5): 1311–27.

Herforth, Anna, Mary Arimond, Cristina Álvarez-Sánchez, Jennifer Coates, Karin Christianson, and Ellen Muehlhoff. 2019. "A Global Review of Food-Based Dietary Guidelines." *Advances in Nutrition* 10 (4): 590–605.

Herrero, Mario, Marta Hugas, Uma Lele, Aman Wira, and Maximo Torero. 2020. "Shift to Healthy and Sustainable Consumption Patterns." Discussion Paper, October 26, United Nations Food Systems Summit 2021 Scientific Group.

Hicks, Norman, and Paul P. Streeten. 1979. "Indicators of Development: The Search for a Basic Needs Yardstick." *World Development* 7 (6): 567–80.

HLPE (High Level Panel of Experts on Food Security and Nutrition). 2017. "Nutrition and Food Systems." A Report by the High Level Panel of Experts on Food Security and Nutrition of the Committee on World Food Security, Rome. http://www.fao.org/3/a-i7846e.pdf

HLPE (High Level Panel of Experts on Food Security and Nutrition). 2020. "Food Security and Nutrition: Building a Global Narrative towards 2030. Research Guides." A Report by the High Level Panel of Experts on Food Security and Nutrition of the Committee on World Food Security, Rome. http://www.fao.org/fsnforum/cfs-hlpe/discussions/global_FSN_narrative-v0

Hoddinott, John, Harold Alderman, Jere R. Behrman, Lawrence Haddad, and Susan Horton. 2013. "The Economic Rationale for Investing in Stunting Reduction." *Maternal and Child Nutrition* 9 (Suppl. 2): 69–82.

Huang, Jikun, Jun Yang, and Scott Rozelle. 2015. The Political Economy of Food Price Policy in China." In *Food Price Policy in an Era of Market Instability: A Political Economy Analysis*, edited by Per Pinstrup-Andersen, 362–83. Oxford: Oxford University Press.

Huffman, Sandra L., Ellen G. Piwoz, Stephen A. Vosti, and Kathryn G. Dewey. 2014. "Babies, Soft Drinks and Snacks: A Concern in Low- and Middle-Income Countries?" *Maternal & Child Nutrition* 10 (4): 562–74.

IFPRI (International Food Policy Research Institute). 2014. *Global Nutrition Report 2014: Actions and Accountability to Accelerate the World's Progress on Nutrition*. Washington, DC: IFPRI.

IFPRI (International Food Policy Research Institute). 2015. *Global Nutrition Report 2015: Actions and Accountability to Advance Nutrition and Sustainable Development*. Washington, DC: IFPRI.

IFPRI (International Food Policy Research Institute). 2016a. *2016 Global Food Policy Report*. Washington, DC: IFPRI.

IFPRI (International Food Policy Research Institute). 2016b. *Global Nutrition Report 2016: From Promise to Impact: Ending Malnutrition by 2030*. Washington, DC: IFPRI.

IFPRI (International Food Policy Research Institute). 2017. *2017 Global Food Policy Report*. Washington, DC: IFPRI.

IFPRI (International Food Policy Research Institute). 2018. *2018 Global Food Policy Report*. Washington, DC: IFPRI.

IFPRI (International Food Policy Research Institute). 2019a. Policy Seminar: Food Markets and Nutrition in the Developing World: Results from ARENA II, March 18, Washington, DC.

IFPRI (International Food Policy Research Institute). 2019b. *2019 Global Food Policy Report*. Washington, DC: IFPRI.

ILO (International Labour Organization). 2015. *World Employment Social Outlook: The Changing Nature of Jobs*. ILO, Geneva.

India, Ministry of Health and FamilyWelfare. 2009. *Nutrition in India: National Family Health Survey (NFHS-3) India, 2005–2006*. Mumbai: International Institute for Population Sciences.

Islam, Abu H. M. S., Joachim von Braun, Andrew L. Thorne-Lyman, and Akhter U. Ahmed. 2018. "Farm Diversification and Food and Nutrition Security in Bangladesh: Empirical Evidence from Nationally Representative Household Panel Data." *Food Security* 10 (3): 701–20.

Jaacks, Lindsay M., Meghan M. Slining, and Barry M. Popkin. 2015. "Recent Underweight and Overweight Trends by Rural–Urban Residence among Women in Low- and Middle-Income Countries." *Journal of Nutrition* 145 (2): 352–7.

Jacobs, Andrew. 2018. "In Sweeping War on Obesity, Chile Slays Tony the Tiger." *New York Times*, February 7.

Jacobs, Andrew, and Matt Richtel. 2017a. "How Big Business Got Brazil Hooked on Junk Food." *New York Times*, September 16.

Jacobs, Andrew, and Matt Richtel. 2017b. "A Nasty, NAFTA-Related Surprise: Mexico's Soaring Obesity." *New York Times*, December 11. https://www.nytimes.com/2017/12/11/health/obesity-mexico-nafta.html

Jacobs, Andrew, and Matt Richtel. 2017c. "She Took on Colombia's Soda Industry. Then She Was Silenced." *New York Times*, November 13.

Jaffee, Steven, Spencer Henson, Laurian Unnevehr, Delia Grace, and Emilie Cassou. 2019. "The Safe Food Imperative: Accelerating Progress in Low- and Middle-Income Countries." World Bank Group, Washington, DC. https://openknowledge.worldbank.org/bitstream/handle/10986/30568/9781464813450.pdf

Jahn, Gunnar. 1999. "Presentation: To Lord Boyd Orr of Brechin, 1949." In *Nobel Lectures in Peace, 1926–1950*, edited by Frederick William Haberman, 405–14. Singapore: World Scientific Publishing.

Kadiyala, Suneetha, Jody Harris, Derek Headey, Sivan Yosef, and Stuart Gillespie. 2014. "Agriculture and Nutrition in India: Mapping Evidence to Pathways." *Annals of the New York Academy of Sciences* 1331 (1): 43–56.

Kakwani, Nanak, and Hyun Hwa Son. 2015. "Measuring Food Insecurity: Global Estimates." Working Paper 370, ECINEQ, Society for the Study of Economic Inequality, Verona, Italy. http://www.ecineq.org/milano/WP/ECINEQ2015-370.pdf

Kakwani, Nanak, and Hyun Hwa Son. 2016. *Social Welfare Functions and Development: Measurement and Policy Applications*. London: Palgrave Macmillan.

Kharas, Homi, John McArthur, and Krista Rasmussen. 2018. "How Many People Will the World Leave Behind?" Report, September 14, Brookings Institution, Washington, DC. https://www.brookings.edu/research/how-many-people-will-the-world-leave-behind/

Khonje, Makaiko, Olivier Ecker, and Matin Qaim. 2020. "Effects of Modern Food Retailers on Adult and Child Diets and Nutrition." *Nutrients* 12 (6): 1714, https://doi.org/10.3390/nu12061714

Khonje, Makaiko G., and Matin Qaim. 2019. "Modernization of African Food Retailing and (Un)healthy Food Consumption." *Sustainability* 11 (16): 4306. doi:10.3390/su11164306

Kim, Soowon, Soojae Moon, and Barry M. Popkin. 2000 "The Nutrition Transition in South Korea." *American Journal of Clinical Nutrition* 71 (1): 44–53.

Kimenju, Simon C., Ramona Rischke, Stephan Klasen, and Matin Qaim. 2015. "Do Supermarkets Contribute to the Obesity Pandemic in Developing Countries?" *Public Health Nutrition* 18 (17): 3224 –33.

Kotwal, Ashok, Bharat Ramaswami, and Wilima Wadhwa. 2011. "Economic Liberalization and Indian Economic Growth: What's the Evidence?" *Journal of Economic Literature* 49 (4): 1152–99.

Lancet. 2008. Lancet Series: Maternal and Child Undernutrition. 371 (9608). http://www.thelancet.com/series/maternal-and-child-undernutrition.

Lancet. 2011. Lancet Series: Obesity. 378 (9793). http://www.thelancet.com/series/obesity.

Lancet. 2013a. Lancet Series: Maternal and Child Nutrition. 382 (9890). http://www.thelancet.com/series/maternal-and-child-nutrition

Lancet. 2013b. Maternal and Child Nutrition. Executive Summary of *The Lancet* Maternal and Child Nutrition Series. https://www.thelancet.com/pb/assets/raw/Lancet/stories/series/nutrition-eng.pdf

Lancet. 2015. Lancet Series: Obesity 2015. 385 (9986). http://www.thelancet.com/series/obesity-2015.

Latham, Michael. 1997. *Human Nutrition in the Developing World*. Food and Nutrition Series No. 29, Food and Agriculture Organization of the United Nations, Rome.

Law, Cherry, Rosemary Green, Suneetha Kadiyala, Bhavani Shankar, Cécile Knai, Kerry A. Brown, Alan D. Dangour, and Laura Cornelsen. 2019. "Purchase Trends of Processed Foods and Beverages in Urban India." *Global Food Security* 23: 191–204.

Lee, Haeng-Shin, Kiyah J. Duffey, and Barry M. Popkin. 2012. "South Korea's Entry to the Global Food Economy: Shifts in Consumption of Food between1998 and 2009." *Asian Pacific Journal of Clinical Nutrition* 21 (4): 618–29.

Lee, Min-June, Barry M. Popkin, and Soowon Kim. 2002. "The Unique Aspects of the Nutrition Transition in South Korea: The Retention of Healthful Elements in their Traditional Diet." *Public Health Nutrition* 5 (1A): 197–203.

Lele, Uma. 2015. "The Growing Obesity Epidemic Needs as Much Attention as Undernutrition in Sustainable Development Goals." July 3, Global Nutrition Report blog.

Lele, Uma. 2016. "Exit, Voice, and Loyalty: Lessons from Brexit for Global Governance." Future Development: Economics to End Poverty blog, The Brookings Institution, Washington, DC, July 7. http://www.brookings.edu/blogs/future-development/posts/2016/07/07-brexit-global-governance-lele

Lele, Uma, Manmohan Agarwal, and Sambuddha Goswami. 2018. *Patterns of Structural Transformation and Agricultural Productivity Growth (with Special Focus on Brazil, China, Indonesia and India)*. Pune, India: Gokhale Institute of Politics and Economics.

Lele, Uma, Sambuddha Goswami, and Mesfin Mekonnen. 2020. "Measuring Food Insecurity and Its Consequences." *Economic & Political Weekly*, forthcoming.

Lele, Uma, William A. Masters, Joyce Kinabo, J.V. Meenakshi, Bharat Ramaswami, and Julia Tagwireyi, with Winnie F. L. Bell, and Sambuddha Goswami. 2016. "Measuring Food and Nutrition Security: An Independent Technical Assessment and User's Guide for Existing Indicators." Technical Working Group on Measuring Food and Nutrition Security. Food Security Information Network (FSIN), Rome. http://www.fao.org/fileadmin/user_upload/fsin/docs/1_FSIN-TWG_UsersGuide_12June2016.compressed.pdf

Lionaes, Aase. 1999. Award Presentation Speech: The Nobel Peace Prize 1965 to United Nations Children's Fund. In *Nobel Lectures in Peace, 1951–1970*, edited by Frederick William Haberman, 405–14. Singapore: World Scientific Publishing. https://www.nobelprize.org/nobel_prizes/peace/laureates/1965/press.html

Longhurst, R. 2013. "Nutrition in Agriculture: A Short History of the Role of the UNSCN in Advocacy, Research and Convening Power." *SCN News* 40: 77–81.

Mason-D'Croz, Daniel, Timothy B. Sulser, Keith Wiebe, Mark W. Rosegrant, Sarah K. Lowder, Alejandro Nin-Pratt, Tingju Zhu, and Nicola Cenacchi. 2016. "IMPACT Projections of Investments in Agriculture and Implications for Reducing Hunger in Africa by 2030: Results from the IMPACT Model, Version 3.3." IFPRI Project Report, International Food Policy Research Institute, Washington, DC.

Masters, William A. 2015. "New Metrics for Evaluation under SDG2: Insights from the FSIN Technical Working Group on Measuring Food and Nutrition Security." Presentation at the CGIAR-FAO-IFAD-WFP Technical Seminar on Evaluability of SDG2, November 17–18, 2015. http://www.ifad.org/evaluation/events/2015/sdg2/presentations.htm

Masters, William A., Anaya Hall, Elena M. Martinez, Peilin Shi, Gitanjali Singh, Patrick Webb, and Dariush Mozaffarian. 2016. "The Nutrition Transition and Agricultural Transformation: A Preston Curve Approach." *Agricultural Economics* 47 (51): 97–114.

Maxwell, Simon. 1996. "Food Security: A Post-Modern Perspective." *Food Policy* 21 (2): 155–70.

Maxwell, Simon, and Timothy R. Frankenberger. 1992. "Household Food Security: Concepts, Indicators, and Measurements: A Technical Review." United Nations Children's Fund (UNICEF) and International Fund for Agricultural Development (IFAD), New York and Rome.

McClain-Nhlapo, Charlotte. 2004. "Implementing a Human Rights Approach to Food Security." IFPRI 2020 Vision Conference Brief for "Assuring Food and Nutrition Security in Africa by 2020: Prioritizing Actions, Strengthening Actors, and Facilitating Partnerships," Kampala, Uganda, April 1–3. http://ebrary.ifpri.org/utils/getfile/collection/p15738coll2/id/64619/filename/64620.pdf

McLaren, Donald S. 1974. "The Great Protein Fiasco." *Lancet* 304 (7872): 93–6.

McNamara, Robert S. 1973. "The Nairobi Speech: Address to the Board of Governors," World Bank Group, Nairobi, September 24. http://www.juerg-buergi.ch/Archiv/EntwicklungspolitikA/EntwicklungspolitikA/assets/McNamara_Nairobi_speech.pdf

Meenakshi, J. V. 2016. "Trends and Patterns in the Triple Burden of Malnutrition in India." *Agricultural Economics* 47 (S1): 115–134.

Meyer, Courtney. 2018. "Biofortification's Growing Global Reach." May 25. http://www.harvestplus.org/knowledge-market/in-the-news/biofortification's-growing-global-reach

Müller, Alexander, and Pavan Sukhdev. 2018. "Measuring What Matters in Agriculture and Food Systems." A Synthesis of the Results and Recommendations of TEEB for Agriculture and Food's Scientific and Economic Foundations Report. The Economics of Ecosystems and Biodiversity (TEEB), UN Environment, Geneva.

Nair, Shalini. 2015. "Gender Inequality Index: In South Asia, India Leads in Poor Condition of Women." *Indian Express*, December 17. http://indianexpress.com/article/explained/gender-inequality-index-in-south-asia-india-leads-in-poor-condition-of-women/

Nakhimovsky, Sharon S., Andrea B. Feigl, Carlos Avila, Gael O'Sullivan, Elizabeth Macgregor-Skinner, and Mark Spranca. 2016. "Taxes on Sugar-Sweetened Beverages to Reduce Overweight and Obesity in Middle-Income Countries: A Systematic Review." *PLoS ONE* 11 (9): e0163358.

Nestle, Marion. 2013. *Food Politics: How the Food Industry Influences Nutrition and Health.* Expanded and revised 10th anniversary edition. Berkeley: University of California Press.

Nestle, Marion. 2015. *Soda Politics: Taking on Big Soda (and Winning).* Oxford: Oxford University Press.

New York Times. 2017–18. "Planet Fat" series. https://www.nytimes.com/series/obesity-epidemic

Ng, Marie, Tom Fleming, Margaret Robinson, Blake Thomson, Nicholas Graetz, Christopher Margono, Erin C. Mullany, Stan Biryukov, Cristiana Abbafati, Semaw Ferede Abera, et al. 2014. "Global, Regional, and National Prevalence of Overweight and Obesity in Children and Adults during 1980–2013: A Systematic Analysis for the Global Burden of Disease Study 2013." *Lancet* 384 (9945): 766–81.

Ng, Shu Wen, and Barry M. Popkin. 2012. "Time Use and Physical Activity: A Shift Away from Movement across the Globe." *Obesity Reviews* 13 (8): 659–80.

ODI (Overseas Development Institute). 1978. "Basic Needs." Briefing Paper No. 5, December, ODI, London. https://www.odi.org/sites/odi.org.uk/files/odi-assets/publications-opinion-files/6616.pdf

OPHI (Oxford Poverty & Human Development Initiative). 2017a. "Multidimensional Poverty Index 2017. Highlights—South Asia." Briefing paper, OPHI, Oxford.

OPHI (Oxford Poverty & Human Development Initiative). 2017b. "Multidimensional Poverty Index 2017. Highlights—Sub-Saharan Africa." Briefing Paper, OPHI, Oxford.

OPHI (Oxford Poverty & Human Development Initiative). 2018. Global MPI Winter 2017/2018. https://ophi.org.uk/multidimensional-poverty-index/global-mpi-2017/

Osmani, Siddiqur R. 1992. "On Some Controversies in the Measurement of Undernutrition." In *Nutrition and Poverty*, edited by S. R. Osmani, 121–61. World Institute for Development Economics Research (WIDER). Oxford: Clarendon Press.

Paarlberg, Robert L. 2012. "Governing the Dietary Transition: Linking Agriculture, Nutrition, and Health." In *Reshaping Agriculture for Nutrition and Health*, edited by Shenggen Fan and Rajul Pandya-Lorch, 191–200. Washington, DC: International Food Policy Research Institute.

Payne, P. 1992. "Assessing Undernutrition: The Need for Reconceptualization." In *Nutrition and Poverty*, edited by Siddiqur Rahman Osmani, 42–96. World Institute for Development Economics Research (WIDER). Oxford: Clarendon Press.

Perlroth, Nicole. 2017. "Spyware's Odd Targets: Backers of Mexico's Soda Tax." *New York Times*, February 11.

Popkin, Barry. M. 1993. "Nutritional Patterns and Transitions." *Population and Development Review* 19 (1): 138–57.

Popkin, Barry M. 1994. "The Nutrition Transition in Low-income Countries: An Emerging Crisis." *Nutrition Reviews* 52 (9): 285–98.

Popkin, Barry M. 1998. "The Nutrition Transition and Its Health Implications in Lower Income Countries." *Public Health Nutrition* 1 (1): 5–21.

Popkin, Barry M. 2001. "The Nutrition Transition and Obesity in the Developing World." *Journal of Nutrition* 131 (3): 871S–3S.

Popkin, Barry M. 2009. *The World Is Fat: The Fads, Trends, Policies, and Products That Are Fattening the Human Race.* New York: Avery.

Popkin, Barry M. 2017. "Relationship between Shifts in Food System Dynamics and Acceleration of the Global Nutrition Transition." *Nutrition Reviews* 75 (2): 73–82.

Popkin, Barry M., Linda S. Adair, and Shu Wen Ng. 2012. "Global Nutrition and the Pandemic of Obesity in Developing Countries." *Nutrition Reviews* 70 (1): 3–21.

Popkin, B. M., and C. Hawkes. 2015. "Sweetening of the Global Diet, Particularly Beverages: Patterns, Trends, and Policy Responses." *Lancet Diabetes & Endocrinology* 4 (2): 174–86.

Popkin, Barry M., and Thomas Reardon. 2018. "Obesity and the Food System Transformation in Latin America." *Obesity Reviews.* https://doi.org/10.1111/obr.12694

Pries, Alissa M., Sandra L. Huffman, Indu Adhikary, Senendra Raj Upreti, Shrid Dhungel, Mary Champeny, and Elizabeth Zehner. 2016a. "High Consumption of Commercial Food Products among Children less than 24-Months of Age and Product Promotion in Kathmandu Valley, Nepal." *Maternal & Child Nutrition* 12 (S2): 22–37.

Pries, Alissa M., Sandra L. Huffman, Khin Mengkheang, Hou Kroeun, Mary Champeny, Margarette Roberts, and Elizabeth Zehner. 2016b. "High Use of Commercial Food Products among Infants and Young Children and Promotions for These Products in Cambodia." *Maternal & Child Nutrition* 12 (S2): 52–63.

Pries, Alissa M., Sandra L. Huffman, Khin Mengkheang, Hou Kroeun, Mary Champeny, Margarette Roberts, and Elizabeth Zehner. 2016c. "Pervasive Promotion of Breastmilk Substitutes in Phnom Penh, Cambodia, and High Usage by Mothers for Infant and Young Child Feeding." *Maternal & Child Nutrition* 12 (S2): 38–51.

Qaim, Matin. 2003. "Bt Cotton in India: Field Trial Results and Economic Projections." *World Development* 31 (12): 2115–27.

Qaim, Matin. 2017. "Globalisation of Agrifood Systems and Sustainable Nutrition." *Proceedings of the Nutrition Society* 76 (1): 12–21.

Qaim, Matin, and Alain de Janvry. 2003. "Genetically Modified Crops, Corporate Pricing Strategies, and Farmers' Adoption: The Case of Bt Cotton in Argentina." *American Journal of Agricultural Economics* 85 (4): 814–28.

Qaim, Matin, and David Zilberman. 2003. "Yield Effects of Genetically Modified Crops in Developing Countries." *Science* 299 (5608): 900–2.

Raja, Kanaga. 2014. "United Nations: Need for Rights-Based Approach to Food Security." Social Watch blog, October 29. http://www.socialwatch.org/node/16696

Ramaswami, Bharat, Carl E. Pray, and N. Lalitha. 2012. "The Spread of Illegal Transgenic Cotton Varieties in India: Biosafety Regulation, Monopoly, and Enforcement." *World Development* 40 (1): 177–88.

Ravallion, Martin. 2011. "On Multidimensional Indices of Poverty." *Journal of Economic Inequality* 9 (2): 235–48.

Ravallion, Martin, Shaohua Chen, and Prem Sangraula. 2009. "Dollar a Day Revisited." *World Bank Economic Review* 23 (2): 163–84.

Reutlinger, Shlomo, and Marcelo Selowsky. 1976. "Malnutrition and Poverty: Magnitude and Policy Options." Occasional Paper No. 23. Published for the World Bank by Johns Hopkins University, Baltimore.

Reyes, Marcela, Lindsey Smith Taillie, Barry Popkin, Rebecca Kanter, Stefanie Vandevijvere, and Camila Corvalán. 2020. "Changes in the Amount of Nutrient of Packaged Foods and Beverages after the Initial Implementation of the Chilean Law of Food Labelling and Advertising: A Nonexperimental Prospective Study." *PLOS Medicine*. https://doi.org/10.1371/journal.pmed.1003220

Rischke, Ramona, Simon C. Kimenju, Stephan Kasen, and Matin Qaim. 2015. "Supermarkets and Food Consumption Patterns: The Case of Small Towns in Kenya." *Food Policy* 52 (April): 9–21.

Runge, Carlisle Ford, Erik J. Nelson, Carlisle Piehl Runge, and James Levine. 2012. "Obesity Overtaken by Leanness as a Repeated Game: Social Networks and Indirect Reciprocity." *Environmental Economics* 3 (1). https://businessperspectives.org/journals/environmental-economics/issue-214/obesity-overtaken-by-leanness-as-a-repeated-game-social-networks-and-indirect-reciprocity

Ruxin, Josh. 2000. "The United Nations Protein Advisory Group." In *Food, Science, Policy and Regulation in the Twentieth Century: International and Comparative Perspectives*, edited by David F. Smith and Jim Phillips, 151-166. London and New York: Routledge.

Sacks, Gary, Eric Crosbie, and Melissa Mialon. 2020. "How South African Food Companies Go about Shaping Public Health Policy in Their Favour." BizCommunity.com, July 30. https://www.bizcommunity.com/Article/196/162/206805.html

Sánchez-Páramo, Carolina. 2020. "Countdown to 2030: A Race against Time to End Extreme Poverty." Voices: Perspectives on Development, World Bank blog, January 7. https://blogs.worldbank.org/voices/countdown-2030-race-against-time-end-extreme-poverty

Searcey, Dionne. 2017. "The Global Siren of Fast Food." *New York Times*, October 2.

Searcey, Dionne, and Matt Richtel. 2017. "Obesity Was Rising as Ghana Embraced Fast Food. Then Came KFC." *New York Times*, October 2.

Semba, Richard D. 2008. "Nutrition and Development: A Historical Perspective." In *Nutrition and Health in Developing Countries,* 2nd ed., edited by Richard D., and Martin W. Bloem, 1–31. Second. Totowa, NJ: Humana Press.

Sen, Amartya K. 1980. "Famines." *World Development* 8 (9): 613–21.

Sen, Amartya. 1981. *Poverty and Famines: An Essay on Entitlement and Deprivation.* Oxford: Clarendon Press.

Sen, Amartya. 1983. "Poor, Relatively Speaking." *Oxford Economic Papers* (New Series) 35 (2): 153–69.

Sengupta, Jayshree. 2017. "Indian Slips in Human Development Index despite GDP Growth." April 3, Observer Research Foundation, New Delhi. https://www.orfonline.org/expert-speak/india-slips-in-human-development-index-despite-gdp-growth/

Serageldin, Ismail, and Pierre Landell-Mills, eds. 1994. *Overcoming Global Hunger.* Washington, DC: World Bank.

Seth, Suman. 2009. "Inequality, Interactions, and Human Development. *Journal of Human Development and Capabilities* 10 (3): 375–96.

Sharma, Manika, Avinash Kishore, Devesh Roy, and Kuhu Joshi. 2020. "A Comparison of the Indian Diet with the EAT–Lancet Reference Diet." *BMC Public Health* 20, 812. https://doi.org/10.1186/s12889-020-08951-8

Shaw, D. John. 2007. *World Food Security: A History since 1945.* New York: Palgrave Macmillan.

Sheahan, Megan, and Christopher B. Barrett. 2017. "Review: Food Loss and Waste in Sub-Saharan Africa." *Food Policy* 70: 1–12. https://www.sciencedirect.com/science/article/pii/S0306919217302440

Shekar, Meera, Jakub Kakietek, Julia Dayton Eberwein, and Dylan Walters, eds. 2017. *An Investment Framework for Nutrition: Reaching the Global Targets for Stunting, Anemia, Breastfeeding, and Wasting.* Washington, DC: World Bank.

Simon, George-André. 2012. "Food Security: Definitions, Four Dimensions, History." Basic readings as introduction to Food Security for students from the IPAD Master, SupAgro, Montpellier, attending a joint training programme in Rome from March 19–24. http://www.fao.org/fileadmin/templates/ERP/uni/F4D.pdf

Smith, Lisa C., and Lawrence Haddad. 2015. "Reducing Child Undernutrition: Past Drivers and Priorities for the Post-MDG Era." *World Development* 68: 180–204.

Springmann, Marco, Luke Spajic, Michael A. Clark, Joseph Poore, Anna Herforth, Patrick Webb, Mike Rayner, and Peter Scarborough. 2020. "The Healthiness and Sustainability of National and Global Food Based Dietary Guidelines: Modelling Study." *BMJ* 370 (m2322). https://www.bmj.com/content/370/bmj.m2322

Srinivasan, T. N. 1992. "Undernutrition: Concepts, Measurements, and Policy Implications." In *Nutrition and Poverty*, edited by Siddiqur Rahman Osmani, 97–120. World Institute for Development Economics Research (WIDER). Oxford: Clarendon Press.

Srivastava, S. K. and Ramesh Chand. 2017. "Tracking Transition in Calorie-Intake among Indian Households: Insights and Policy Implications." *Agricultural Economics Research Review* 30 (1): 23–35.

Stewart, Frances. 1985. *Planning to Meet Basic Needs*. London: Palgrave Macmillan.

Stiglitz, Joseph E., Amartya Sen, and Jean-Paul Fitoussi. 2009. "Report by the Commission on the Measurement of Economic Performance and Social Progress." Commissioned by President of the French Republic, Nicholas Sarkozy, Paris.

Streeten, Paul P. 1979. "Basic Needs: Premises and Promises." *Journal of Policy Modeling* 1 (1): 136–46.

Streeten, Paul P., Shahid Javed Burki, Mahbub ul Haq, Norman Hicks, and Frances Stewart. 1981. *First Things First. Meeting Basic Human Needs in the Developing Countries*. New York: Oxford University Press, for the World Bank.

Stuckler, David, Gary Ruskin, and Martin McKee. 2018 "Complexity and Conflicts of Interest Statements: A Case-Study of Emails Exchanged between Coca-Cola and the Principal Investigators of the International Study of Childhood Obesity, Lifestyle and the Environment (ISCOLE)." *Journal of Public Health Policy* 39 (1): 49–56.

Sukhatme, P. V. 1961. "The World's Hunger and Future Needs in Food Supplies." *Journal of the Royal Statistical Society. Series A (General)* 124 (4): 463–525.

Sukhatme, P. V. 1970. "Size and Nature of the Protein Gap." *Nutrition Reviews* 28 (9): 223–6.

SUN (Scaling Up Nutrition). 2010. *A Road Map for Scaling-Up Nutrition*. 1st ed. http://scalingupnutrition.org/wp-content/uploads/pdf/SUN_Road_Map.pdf

Swinburn, Boyd, Vivica Kraak, Harry Rutter, Stefanie Vandevijvere, Tim Lobstein, Gary Sacks, Fabio Gomes, Tim Marsh, and Roger Magnusson. 2015. "Strengthening of Accountability Systems to Create Healthy Food Environments and Reduce Global Obesity." *Lancet* 385 (9986): 2534–45.

Taylor, Allyn L., and Michael F. Jacobson. 2016. "Carbonating the World: The Marketing and Health Impact of Sugar Drinks in Low- and Middle-income Countries." Technical Report, Center for Science in the Public Interest, Washington, DC.

UN (United Nations). 1968. *International Action to Avert the Impending Protein Crisis: Report to the Economic and Social Council of the Advisory Committee on the Application of Science and Technology to Development*. New York: UN.

UN (United Nations). 1975. "Report of the World Food Conference, Rome, November 5–16, 1974." UN, New York.

UN (United Nations). 2011. "2011 High Level Meeting on Prevention and Control of Non-communicable Diseases." General Assembly, United Nations, New York, September 19–20. http://www.un.org/en/ga/ncdmeeting2011/

UN (United Nations). 2016. "We Can End Poverty: Millennium Development Goals and Beyond 2015." http://www.un.org/millenniumgoals/

UN (United Nations). 2020a. "Sustainable Development Goals." https://unstats.un.org/sdgs/

UN (United Nations). 2020b. "United Nations Food Systems Summit 2020." https://www.un.org/sustainabledevelopment/food-systems-summit-2021/

UN–OHCHR (United Nations Office of the High Commissioner for Human Rights). 2017. "Statement on Visit to the USA, by Professor Philip Alston, United Nations Special Rapporteur on Extreme Poverty and Human Rights." December 15, 2017, Washington, DC. https://www.ohchr.org/EN/NewsEvents/Pages/DisplayNews.aspx?NewsID=22533

UN–OHCHR (United Nations Office of the High Commissioner for Human Rights). 2019. "Universal Declaration on the Eradication of Hunger and Malnutrition." Adopted November 16, 1974 by the World Food Conference. https://www.ohchr.org/EN/ProfessionalInterest/Pages/EradicationOfHungerAndMalnutrition.aspx

UNDP (United Nations Development Programme). 1990. *Human Development Report 1990*. New York: Oxford University Press.

UNDP (United Nations Development Programme). 2016a. "Africa Human Development Report 2015: Accelerating Gender Equality and Women's Empowerment in Africa." UNDP, Regional Bureau for Africa, New York.

UNDP (United Nations Development Programme). 2016b. "Technical Notes: Calculating the Human Development Indices—Graphical Presentation." http://hdr.undp.org/sites/default/files/hdr2016_technical_notes_0.pdf

UNDP (United Nations Development Programme). 2019a. "Gender Development Index (GDI)." http://hdr.undp.org/en/content/gender-development-index-gdi

UNDP (United Nations Development Programme). 2019b. "Gender Inequality Index (GII)." http://hdr.undp.org/en/content/gender-inequality-index-gii

UNDP (United Nations Development Programme). 2019c. *Human Development Report 2016: Human Development for Everyone*. New York: UNDP.

UNICEF (United Nations Children's Fund). 1990. "Strategy for Improved Nutrition of Children and Women in Developing Countries." *Indian Journal of Pediatrics* 58 (1): 13–24. This title also available as a UNICEF Policy Review, UNICEF, New York, at http://www.ceecis.org/iodine/01_global/01_pl/01_01_other_1992_unicef.pdf

UNICEF (United Nations Children's Fund). 2015. "Achieving Women's Economic Empowerment and Early Childhood Care and Development as Mutually Reinforcing Objectives." Technical Note, UNICEF, New York.

UNICEF (United Nations Children's Fund). 2016. "Ending Extreme Poverty: A Focus on Children." Briefing Note, October, UNICEF, New York.

UNICEF (United Nations Children's Fund). 2019. "Child Poverty: Statistics by Topic." https://data.unicef.org/topic/overview/child-poverty/#

UNICEF (United Nations Children's Fund). 2020. "Data by Topic and Country." https://data.unicef.org

UNSCN (United Nations Standing Committee on Nutrition). 2020. "Merger of the UN System Standing Committee on Nutrition (UNSCN) and the UN Network for Scaling-Up Nutrition (SUN)." Letter from Amir Abdulla, Rome, July 16. https://www.unscn.org/uploads/web/file/UN-Nutrition-Communication-for-partners-FINAL.pdf

USDA (United States Department of Agriculture). 2019a. "Food Security in the U.S.: Measurement." https://www.ers.usda.gov/topics/food-nutrition-assistance/food-security-in-the-us/measurement.aspx

USDA (United States Department of Agriculture). 2019b. "Mexico Trade & FDI." Economic Research Service, Washington, DC. https://www.ers.usda.gov/topics/international-markets-us-trade/countries-regions/nafta-canada-mexico/mexico-trade-fdi/

Vitta, Bineti S., Margaret Benjamin, Alissa M. Pries, Mary Champeny, Elizabeth Zehner, and Sandra L. Huffman. 2016. "Infant and Young Child Feeding Practices among Children under 2 Years of Age and Maternal Exposure to Infant and Young Child Feeding Messages and Promotions in Dar es Salaam, Tanzania." *Maternal & Child Nutrition* 12 (S2): 77–90.

Wadhwa, Divyanshi. 2018. "The Number of Extremely Poor People Continues to Rise in Sub-Saharan Africa." Data blog, September 19. World Bank. https://blogs.worldbank.org/opendata/number-extremely-poor-people-continues-rise-sub-saharan-africa

Wanner, Nathan, Carlo Cafiero, Nathalie Troubat, and Piero Conforti. 2014. "Refinements to the FAO Methodology for Estimating the Prevalence of Nourishment Indicator." ESS Working Paper No. 14-05, FAO Statisics Division, Food and Agriculture Organization of the United Nations, Rome. http://www.fao.org/3/a-i4046e.pdf

WBG (World Bank Group). 2014. "Learning from World Bank History: Agriculture and Food-Based Approaches for Addressing Malnutrition." Agriculture and Environmental Services Discussion Paper 10, WBG, Washington, DC.

WBG (World Bank Group). 2018. *The State of Social Safety Nets 2018*. World Bank, Washington, DC. http://documents.worldbank.org/curated/en/427871521040513398/pdf/124300-PUB-PUBLIC.pdf

Webb, Patrick. 2013. "Impact Pathways from Agricultural Research to Improved Nutrition and Health: Literature Analysis and Research Priorities." Presentation at Second International Conference on Nutrition, Food and Agriculture Organization of the United Nations (FAO) and the World Health Organization (WHO), Rome, November 19–24, 2014. http://www.fao.org/fileadmin/user_upload/agn/pdf/Webb_FAO_paper__Webb_June_26_2013_.pdf

Webb, Patrick, Jennifer Coates, Edward A. Frongillo, Beatrice Lorge Rogers, Anne Swindale, and Paula Bilinsky. 2006. "Measuring Household Food Insecurity: Why It's So Important and Yet So Difficult to Do." *Journal of Nutrition* 136 (5): 1404S–8S.

Webb, Patrick, Gunhild Anker Stordalen, Sudhvir Singh, Ramani Wijesinha-Bettoni, Prakash Shetty, Anna Lartey. 2018. "Hunger and Malnutrition in the 21st Century." *BMJ* 361. doi:10.1136/bmj.k2238

WEF (World Economic Forum). 2017. "The Global Gender Gap Report." WEF, Geneva. http://www3.weforum.org/docs/WEF_GGGR_2017.pdf

WFP (World Food Programme). 2009. *Emergency Food Security Assessment Handbook*. 2nd ed. Rome: WFP, Food Security Analysis Service.

WFP (World Food Programme). 2013. "Remarks by Ertharin Cousin at the Nutrition for Growth High Level Event, London." http://www.wfp.org/eds-centre/speeches/remarks-ertharin-cousin-nutrition-growth-high-level-event-london

WHO (World Health Organization). 1981. "International Code of Marketing of Breast-milk Substitutes." WHO, Geneva. http://www.who.int/nutrition/publications/code_english.pdf

WHO (World Health Organization). 2012. "Resolution 65.6. Comprehensive Implementation Plan on Maternal, Infant, and Young Child Nutrition." WHA65/2012/REC1, Sixty-Fifth World Health Assembly, WHO, Geneva, May 21–26. http://www.who.int/nutrition/topics/WHA65.6_resolution_en.pdf

WHO (World Health Organization). 2013a. "Global Action Plan for the Prevention an Control of Noncommunicable Diseases 2013-2020." WHO, Geneva. http://apps.who.int/iris/bitstream/handle/10665/94384/9789241506236_eng.pdf

WHO (World Health Organization). 2013b. "Global Nutrition Policy Review: What Does It Take to Scale Up Nutrition Action?" WHO, Geneva.

WHO (World Health Organization). 2018a. "Obesity and Overweight." Fact Sheet, February 16, 2018. http://www.who.int/mediacentre/factsheets/fs311/en/

WHO (World Health Organization). 2018b. "Healthy Diet." Fact Sheet, October 23. http://www.who.int/news-room/fact-sheets/detail/healthy-diet

WHO (World Health Organization). 2020. "Nutrition. Global Targets 2025." http://www.who.int/nutrition/global-target-2025/en/

Wiesmann, Doris, Lucy Bassett, Todd Benson, and John Hoddinott. 2009. "Validation of the World Food Programme's Food Consumption Score and Alternative Indicators of Household Food Security." IFPRI Discussion Paper 00870, Poverty, Health, and Nutrition Division, International Food Policy Research Institute, Washington, DC.

Willett, Walter, Johan Rockström, Brent Loken, Marco Springmann, Tim Lang, Sonja Vermeulen, Tara Garnett, David Tilman, Fabrice DeClerck, Amanda Wood, Malin Jonell, Michael Clark, Line J Gordon, Jessica Fanzo, Corinna Hawkes, Rami Zurayk, Juan A Rivera, Wim De Vries, Lindiwe Majele Sibanda, Ashkan Afshin, Abhishek Chaudhary, Mario Herrero, Rina Agustina, Francesco Branca, Anna Lartey, Shenggen Fan, Beatrice Crona, Elizabeth Fox, Victoria Bignet, Max Troell, Therese Lindahl, Sudhvir Singh, Sarah E Cornell, K Srinath Reddy, Sunita Narain, Sania Nishtar, Christopher J L Murray; The Lancet Commission. 2019. "Food in the Anthropocene: The EAT-Lancet Commission on Healthy Diets from Sustainable Systems." *Lancet* 393 (10170): 447–92. https://www.thelancet.com/pdfs/journals/lancet/PIIS0140-6736(18)31788-4.pdf

World Bank. 1986. "Poverty and Hunger: Issues and Options for Food Security in Developing Countries." A World Bank Policy Study, World Bank, Washington, DC.

World Bank. 2006. "Repositioning Nutrition as Central to Development: A Strategy for Large-Scale Action." Directions in Development, World Bank, Washington, DC. https://openknowledge.worldbank.org/bitstream/handle/10986/7409/347750PAPER0Re101OFFICIAL0USE0ONLY1.pdf

World Bank. 2014. *Republic of India: Accelerating Agricultural Productivity Growth.* May 21, World Bank Group, Washington, DC. http://documents.worldbank.org/curated/en/587471468035437545/pdf/880930REVISED00ivity0Growth00PUBLIC.pdf

World Bank. 2017. "An Overview of Links between Obesity and Food Systems: Implications for the Food and Agricultural Global Practice." June, Food and Agriculture Global Practice, World Bank, Washington, DC.

World Bank. 2018. *Poverty and Shared Prosperity 2018: Piecing Together the Poverty Puzzle.* Washington, DC: World Bank. https://openknowledge.worldbank.org/bitstream/handle/10986/30418/9781464813306.pdf

World Bank. 2020a. Poverty & Equity Data Portal. http://povertydata.worldbank.org/poverty/home/

World Bank. 2020b. "Povcalnet: An Online Analysis Tool for Global Poverty Monitoring." http://iresearch.worldbank.org/PovcalNet/povDuplicateWB.aspx

World Bank. 2020c. "Understanding Poverty: Overview." http://www.worldbank.org/en/topic/poverty/overview

World Bank. 2020d. World Development Indicators (database). http://data.worldbank.org/data-catalog/world-development-indicators

5

Changing Global Governance Context for Food Security and Nutrition

Uma Lele, Brian C. Baldwin, and Sambuddha Goswami

Summary

Why do we need global governance? Through collective action, global governance helps identify, understand, and address problems that spill over national boundaries. Those problems include maintaining peace and security; developing and implementing rules with regard to trade in commodities and services, capital flows, and migration; containing transboundary pests and diseases; containing global warming; and providing aid for needy countries and peoples. Global governance complements regional, national, and local governance in an important way and is the sum total of the informal and formal ideas, values, rules, norms, procedures, practices, policies, and institutions that govern all actors—states, intergovernmental organizations (IGOs), civil society, nongovernmental organizations (NGOs), transnational corporations (TNCs), and the general public. The number of actors on the global governance scene has proliferated, as have the sheer number of international initiatives in support of food security and nutrition (FSN) since the 2007 food crisis. Many of these are reviewed in this chapter. These efforts have lacked coherence, and the resources in support of food and agriculture at the disposal of countries lagging in reaching the Sustainable Development Goals (SDGs) are not nearly enough to tackle the ambition. Often the dynamics of climate change, population growth, and rural–urban migration compound the already stretched financial, human capital, and institutional challenges that the countries lagging in SDGs are facing.

We show in this chapter that, despite flurry of activity after the 2007 food crisis, few financial flows resulted beyond the traditional sources, such as the support for CGIAR by the International Development Association (IDA) of the World Bank, the Agricultural Market Information System (AMIS), and Global Agriculture and Food Security Program (GAFSP). This situation appears to have changed slightly for the better since the COVID-19 pandemic. According to a 2021 OECD report:

> In April 2020, DAC [Development Assistance Committee] members issued a statement that recognised ODA [official development assistance] as "an important means of supporting national responses to the COVID-19 crisis," and that they would "strive to protect ODA budgets." ODA has long been a stable source of development financing and has cushioned the immediate impact of previous financial crises (e.g. after the Mexican debt crisis in the early 1980s, the recession of the early 1990s and the financial crisis in 2008) [although we argue in this chapter that the financial assistance from OECD countries in the aftermath of the 2008 crisis was not as significant as seemed to be the case initially]. In 2020, ODA rose in a year that saw all other major external resource flows for developing

Food for All: International Organizations and the Transformation of Agriculture. Uma Lele, Manmohan Agarwal, Brian C. Baldwin, and Sambuddha Goswami, Oxford University Press. © Uma Lele, Manmohan Agarwal, Brian C. Baldwin, and Sambuddha Goswami 2021. DOI: 10.1093/oso/9780198755173.003.0006

countries—trade, foreign direct investment, tax and remittances—decline due to the pandemic. Total external private finance to developing countries fell by 13% in 2020 and trade declined by 8.5%. (OECD 2021, 5)

The emerging narrative over the last decade has been one of the important roles that private sector flows need to play. However, without good national governance, there can be little possible sustained active, often collective action, through multilateral institutions, to reduce risks and assure returns. The private sector will not fill the gap in global financing on a scale needed to meet the gap between the combined national and ODA resources to make a dent on reducing poverty and hunger where progress has been slow, the very *raison d'être* for establishing the international organizations (IOs) reviewed in this book.

Issues of governance at the national and subnational level, therefore, are immensely important, but they are relatively under-researched, particularly in a comparative context and over time.

We used what data are available and explored relationships between per capita income and control of corruption, rule of law, regulatory quality, and government effectiveness. All show stronger relationships with per capita income than do voice and accountability, political stability, and absence of violence/terrorism. The relationship between local participation and elite capture is similarly complex, and we need to understand it better if we are concerned about reaching the poor.

Scope and Outline of This Chapter and the Next Chapter

We address issues of governance, at multiple levels in these two chapters, with a particular focus on FSN from four separate, but interacting, vantage points:

1. *The concept of global governance,* and how the governance of FSN can be seen as a subsystem that fits into the larger global governance system, while also distinguishing the concept of governance from the more limited concepts of international financial or international aid architecture, although these concepts are intertwined (IDA 2007; Lele 2009);

2. *The numerous international, regional, and national initiatives related to FSN,* undertaken since the 2007–8 food and financial crises, to achieve global consensus on a complex agenda, among a growing number of actors, operating in a fractured environment;

3. *Governance of the five IOs, which provide examples of the "operating arms" of global governance*: namely, the Food and Agricultural Organization of the United Nations (FAO), the World Bank, the World Food Programme (WFP), the International Fund for Agricultural Development (IFAD), and CGIAR, and how they are responding to the changing global environment. We refer to them as the "Big Five" and as "traditional" IOs, because they were some of the earliest ones to be established. Their roles, still large in the public goods sphere, have shrunk *and become more complex*, as the world around them has grown faster than their ability to keep pace. Their governance is discussed in Chapter 6;

4. *Governance at the national and subnational levels*: This is where the conceptual becomes the practical. Effectiveness of governance within national borders helps explain the extent to which countries can formulate and implement national policies

and investments, effectively supply public goods and safety nets, carry out regulatory functions, and maintain law and order.

The four-way breakdown enables us to analyze governance questions at each level of the system empirically and separately from—but interacting with—the other levels, as a dynamic coordination mechanism, with horizontal and vertical interrelationships at multiple levels. Understanding the sprawling concept of global governance is necessary to appreciate its ever-expanding scope, in the context of the huge opportunities presented by the entry of numerous new actors on the global scene and in the context of the fourth industrial revolution (see Schwab [2016]; and Lele and Goswami [2017] for its application in India).

This chapter first describes the changed context for global governance in a historical context. The historical perspective helps in understanding the various concepts of global governance to be discussed next. This section is followed by the discussion of the variety of international initiatives, which have proliferated since the 2007–8 financial crisis. We argue that the lack of coherence of these initiatives has limited their contribution to reducing poverty and hunger.

Governance of the Big Five IOs concerned with food and agriculture is discussed separately in Chapter 6. Issues of national governance are discussed at the end of this chapter.

What Is Governance and How Is It Defined?

There are countless definitions and ways of looking at the developments in global governance discussed here (Bovaird and Löffler 2003). Thomas Weiss defines global governance as: "... the sum of the informal and formal ideas, values, rules, norms, procedures, practices, policies, and institutions that help all actors—states, IGOs, civil society, and NGOs, TNCs, and individuals—identify, understand, and address transboundary challenges that go beyond the problem-solving capacities of individual states." (Weiss 2014, 4).

Weiss (2013) and others (see, also, Birdsall, Meyer, and Sowa [2013]) identified some of the key weaknesses in global governance and argued that the world is undergoverned, a theme echoed in a great deal of the literature.

Weiss's view of global governance, in turn, has a great deal in common with Nobel Laureate economist Douglass North's concept of institutions (North 1990). North defined institutions as formal and informal rules of the game, which evolve in response to changing norms, standards, and values. He considered institutions to be umpires, "the humanly devised constraints that shape the human interaction," in which organizations and individuals operate as players. "Institutions reduce uncertainty by providing a structure to everyday life" (North 1990, 3). This distinction between institutions as formal and informal rules, and organizations and individuals as players that follow those rules, has been frequently applied in recent years in social science literature (Levy 2014; Birner and Anderson 2015; von Braun and Birner 2017). In North's conception, institutions are shaped by factors that include culture, power, and events; for example, he notes slavery was an institution whose end fundamentally transformed economic and social relations in the United States (North 1990). Women's empowerment changes the structure of family, economy, society, and polity, while also changing women's access to resources and their role in decision-making. This view of governance extends beyond the rights-based approach that has proliferated in the United Nations (UN),[1] and explains how values and norms affect governance. They change faster in some cultural milieux than in others. For example, the fall of the Berlin Wall had a profound impact on IOs and global governance. European donors pushed bilateral and multilateral organizations in the 1990s to support democracy, following the dissolution of the Soviet Union (Boughton 2012). And similarly, Brexit and the US presidential election of 2016 led to a reassessment of rules with regard to immigration, trade, and investment among all trading partners in Europe and globally (Bartels 2016a, 2016b).

North (1990) argued that the behavior of actors is critical as to who sets the rules and what rules are set. Rules typically evolve through well-established, transparent processes among groups of actors, particularly those with power and voice in rule setting. We describe what power and voice mean in different contexts and the ways in which they interact. When orderly processes fail, rules are shaped through disruptive action, including exit, a phenomenon which Hirschman articulated in his book, *Exit, Voice, and Loyalty* (Hirschman 1970). Small groups of actors, at times, take actions, through momentous changes. The establishment of the Global Fund to Fight AIDS, Tuberculosis and Malaria (GFATM) in 2002, the Asian Infrastructure Investment Bank (AIIB) in 2015, the New Development Bank (NDB, formerly referred to as the BRICS Development Bank) in 2014, the realignment of the G19 in Hamburg (2017), and indeed, even the emergence of the Islamic State of Iraq and Syria (ISIS), as well as the international migration crisis and the backlash in rich countries to these events, can all be explained by Hirschman's rich analysis in *Exit, Voice, and Loyalty*, as we discuss later in this chapter.

A Changed Context for Global Governance

These are tumultuous times for global governance. Emerging from the 2007–8 global food and financial crises, the world's nearly 200 countries, in 2015, unanimously arrived at two clear goals for the planet at the UN: the SDGs and the Paris Agreement on Climate Change (UN 2020a, 2020b). By August 2017, reflecting the sense of urgency, 160 of the 195 parties to the convention had ratified the Paris Agreement (member countries and regional organizations, such as the European Union [EU]), in record time for any major UN agreement to become effective, whereas it had already entered into force on November 4, 2016 (UN 2020b; UNFCCC 2014): that is, "the date on which at least 55 Parties to the Convention accounting in total for at least an estimated 55 percent of the total global greenhouse gas emissions had deposited their instruments of ratification, acceptance, approval or accession" (UN 2020b).

Growth has been unequal across and within countries, and despite the huge potential of the fourth industrial revolution to benefit those not reached by development, political will has often been missing (Schwab 2016; Lele and Goswami 2017). Western democracies have been, to date, the leaders of the global architecture, but they and their alliances have been weakening, and the general faith in their own institutions of governance has been declining (Luce 2018), accentuated by a lack of US leadership during the Trump era. The big challenge

---

[1] The UN is founded on the principles of peace, justice, freedom, and human rights. The Universal Declaration of Human Rights recognizes human rights as the foundation of freedom, justice, and peace. The unanimously adopted Vienna Declaration and Programme of Action states that democracy, development, and respect for human rights and fundamental freedoms are interdependent and mutually reinforcing (UN 2003).

after the 2020 US elections is how to make governance more effective *at all levels and for all stakeholders,* since governing institutions have been adjusting to the new reality at all levels, and the world is not the same as it was before Trump's 2016 election. For example, the Trump administration's withdrawal from the Trans-Pacific Partnership (TPP), which was intended to isolate China, has now had the opposite effect. After eight years of talks, China and 14 other nations, from Japan to New Zealand to Myanmar, formally signed one of the world's largest regional free trade agreements (FTAs) on November 15, 2020, a pact shaped by Beijing, partly as a counterweight to American influence in the region. The agreement, the Regional Comprehensive Economic Partnership (RCEP) is limited in scope relative to the TPP. Still, it carries considerable heft. The pact covers 2.2 billion people, more than any previous regional free trade agreement and could help further cement China's image as the dominant economic power in its neighborhood. It is widely seen as China's growing sway in the Asia–Pacific region. US President Biden has been noncommittal on whether the United States would join the successor to TPP. India did not join the RCEP—it wanted more flexibility on trade restrictions on Chinese imports into India, which already had a US$60 billion balance of trade surplus increase. China was reluctant to make the concession.

Governance challenges are also increasing and often interact across borders, as in the case of water (see, for example, Lele, Klousia-Marquis, and Goswami [2013]; Lele, Plusquellec, and Reidinger [2015]). Political will and political capacity interact with governance in a complex way, and they pose a "chicken-and-egg" problem. Which comes first, governance or political will? IOs have tended to deal with governance issues at the national and subnational levels as technocratic issues, when, in reality, governance at all levels—international, regional, national, and local—is an outcome of how power and voice are exercised, how they change and how they interact at different levels and over time. We demonstrate this phenomenon in Chapter 6 on the governance of the "Big Five." Power and voice and their exercise are contextual and dynamic, as we show in this chapter. Devising interventions and delivering results on SDGs and climate change by 2030 calls for a systematic analysis of governance, with its many moving parts in the real world. Improving governance at multiple levels is, thus, no mean feat.

A high-level side-event launched the Global Hub on the Governance for the SDGs at the UN General Assembly on September 25, 2019, bringing together about 200 participants, including the Secretary General of the Organisation for Economic Co-operation and Development (OECD), the United Nations Development Programme (UNDP) Adminis-trator, several prime ministers and cabinet ministers, and other high-level representatives from governments and IOs. Participants discussed how to advance the 2030 Agenda for Sustainable Development by fostering collaboration internationally, strengthening political leadership, and reinforcing key governance mechanisms. The group declared:

> Reaching our collective international commitments under the 2030 Agenda for Sustain-able Development will require political leadership and scalable multistakeholder action. Governments will need to coordinate, consult and work across policy areas in an unprec-edented way to dramatically accelerate progress. Achieving the 2030 Agenda will also demand the effective use of planning, budget, procurement, monitoring and evaluation processes, to better align priorities and to enhance transparency and accountability. (OECD 2019a)

UN Secretary-General António Guterres will also convene a Food Systems Summit (FSS) in 2021, "to raise global awareness and land global commitments and actions that transform food systems to resolve not only hunger, but to reduce diet-related disease and heal the planet. The Secretary-General is calling for collective action of all citizens to radically change the way we produce, process, and consume food" (UN 2020c).

The Summit comes against the background of Brexit and the 2020 US presidential election. The 2016 US election led to change in the existing liberal, rules-based world order, with the United States' withdrawal from several international initiatives and organizations, Similarly, Trump encouraged British withdrawal from the EU, unlike his predecessor Obama, who encouraged the British to remain in the EU. It is too early to know how Brexit could change the EU, and if, whether and how, even with a Biden victory, Trumpism will continue to exert influence on protectionism and erosion of democratization, and the United States' ability to deliver on a variety of fronts, such as climate change and trade. The rise of the Right is not confined to the United States. Chancellor Merkel's admission of over a million refugees has also contributed to the rise of right-wing ideology in Germany, but it has not affected Germany's foreign policy in the way it did in the United States, where the US leadership subscribed to it. In reality, these developments were reinforcing the already shifting global balance of power from the North and West to the East and South, including, particularly, the growing role of China, while the BRICS alliance (Brazil, Russia, India, China, and South Africa) has been in disarray in 2020, with the COVID-19 pandemic slowing global growth, problems of governance in Brazil and Russia, and the China–India border dispute.

The shake-up of the traditional liberal world order downplays the pivotal role that the United States has played in global governance since the Second World War and, indeed, since the First World War, if the strong US support of the establishment of the unsuccessful League of Nations by President Woodrow Wilson is considered (see Box 5.1).

The EU, too, is facing challenges beyond Brexit, including high youth unemployment, the influx of refugees and migrants, and the rise of the Right—even in Germany, the pillar of stability. Both the United States and Europe have been important in leading democratic liberalism, and while the vacuum created by the United States has given Europe an opportunity to reassess its own global role, it is unclear what will take its place. No one knows what the future will hold for global governance against this background, but multilateral interaction, mutual respect, and leadership remain key, even as bilateralism and regionalism are growing. Countries, such as China and Germany, are now filling the void left by the United States in their respective neighborhoods and globally. China has become an avid champion of climate action and a multilateral trading system, emerging as the largest donor in Africa, funding nearly 2,650 development projects worth a total of approximately US$95 billion in 51 African countries (Parks 2015). The G20, hosted by Germany in 2017, and the G19 (the G20 minus the United States) resolved to proceed with trade agreements, climate change accord, and an active aid policy to stem the tide of refugees (G20 2017).

The Global South has taken a different approach to international cooperation than the Global North. Western aid, at least in principle, is provided conditionally on progress on liberal values, such as support for democracy, good governance, respect for human rights, and poverty reduction. In reality, this support is often hard to find. Perhaps, because of their different histories of colonialism and different views about colonialism, emerging countries, in principle, do not impose their political views, ideals, or principles onto countries with which they engage in South–South cooperation, in what has come to be known as a "non-interference policy" (Agarwal 2015; Whalley, Agarwal, and Pan 2015). Skeptics of this argument, however, are quick to point out that China's expansionary external assistance is driven by its geopolitical ambitions and interest in access to resources, much as were the old colonial masters and, in addition, unlike in the case of the US Marshall Plan, which was

Box 5.1 The United States and the Evolving Global Governance

Using its near total hegemonic power and building on the lessons of the interwar years, the United States, in the aftermath of the Second World War, designed a world order to benefit the United States and its allies, and slowly but surely paved the way for a rules-based, multipolar world. It remains the largest contributor to the global governance system, despite the diminishing share of these contributions with respect to the US gross national product (GNP), compared to other rich countries' contributions. The UN, Bretton Woods institutions, and FAO were all established in 1945, with the United States taking the lead in the establishment of the rules of cooperation and financing.[a] With the help of the Marshall Plan (officially, the European Recovery Program, 1948–52), and other economic and military alliances, such as the North Atlantic Treaty Organization (NATO, 1949); the Southeast Asia Treaty Organization (SEATO, 1954); the General Agreement on Tariffs and Trade (GATT, 1949); and through financial aid, the United States helped war-ravaged Europe and Japan to regain their economic strength. The establishment of the International Development Association (IDA, 1960) as the concessional arm of the World Bank; the World Food Programme (WFP, 1961) to internationalize bilateral food aid; and CGIAR (1971, formerly the Consultative Group for International Agricultural Research) to promote international public goods research were followed by many other international cooperative arrangements and organizations. While US bilateral food and financial assistance to developing countries and contributions to IOs continued, Germany and France were able to establish the European Commission (EC) in 1958. After the fall of the Berlin Wall in 1989, the EC, as the politically independent executive arm of the EU, expanded its economic influence regionally and globally, by formally including the countries of the former Soviet Union in the EU, and economically, through trade and aid. In 1972, President Nixon's visit to China paved the way for China's integration in the global economy, and with its admission into the Bretton Woods institutions in 1979–80, its integration contributed to China's extraordinary economic growth. The emergence of the Asian Tigers in the 1980s, a phenomenon supported by Western aid and trade, also paved the way for the rise of China and other Asian countries. Singapore, an Asian Tiger (one of four Asian high-growth economies, also including Hong Kong, South Korea, and Taiwan), provided a model for China's reforms (Lee 1998). Asian growth brought large populations into the global growth process, leading to the emergence of BRICS (the association of the emerging economies of Brazil, Russia, India, China, and South Africa, with the establishment of its multilateral bank—the BRICS Development Bank, now the NDB) and the Group of Twenty (G20). The 11 emerging developing members of the G20 contribute 40 percent of the global GDP (gross domestic product) in purchasing power parity (PPP) terms, contain half the world's population, and have supplanted the G7, acquiring significant roles during and after the 2007–8 global financial crises.

[a] Unknown to historians, a transcript existed of the meeting of Allied nations during the heat of the Second World War, and three versions were in Washington-area libraries and archives. See Lowrey (2012).

based on grant money, China's aid is loans that are adding to the indebtedness. Western countries argue that they cannot agree to debt forgiveness unless China and other countries also agree to forgo their debts. With divided voters, expectations from global governance also differ within individual countries.

In a recent survey, the US public considered containment of terrorism and climate change to be among its top priorities for engagement abroad (KFF 2016). While each objective can be pursued nationally, without concerted regional and global collective action, neither can be addressed sustainably. The same is true for tackling the problem of the estimated 65.3 million displaced people—the largest number displaced since the Second World War—but global collective action is weak, with a proliferation of uncoordinated initiatives. The resources needed to fulfill the Paris Agreement, particularly for adaptation to climate change, and to achieve the SDGs are not yet there; both have been criticized as being too ambitious, without clear priorities (*Economist* 2015).

Experts from military and humanitarian sectors see the need for an agreed upon framework of commitments and responsibilities for UN member states and concerned IOs to invest in limiting the international spread of famine, hunger, epidemics, and other public health emergencies, which will ensue in ungoverned states, while minimizing disruption to travel, trade, and economies (WHO 2007). Against this background, the goals of global governance could be conceived as achieving the SDGs; focusing on outcomes in the regions lagging in SDGs; and addressing issues of peace and security, environmental sustainability, human nutrition, health, and impending climate-related and other crises, such as conflict, human displacement, and pandemics (Furusawa 2017).

Old and New Actors in Global Governance

The numerous actors in global governance bring to bear a different set of assets with which to "play," ranging from the financial wealth of the world's richest individuals to emerging countries, legitimacy, goodwill, trust, convening power, and access to knowledge and information. This broad definition enables us to accommodate the evolving nature of global governance. For example, after the 2008 financial crisis, the United States lost some of its luster, among the Bretton Woods member countries, for its good economic and financial housekeeping, as it faced growing demands for financial regulation via Basel III—a global, voluntary regulatory framework on bank capital adequacy, stress testing, and market liquidity risk. The Dodd–Frank Wall Street Reform and the Consumer Protection Act (Amadeo 2019) was signed into law in the United States in 2010. A law that regulates the US financial markets and protects consumers, it was a critical piece of the international regulation to help prevent a repetition of the 2008 financial crisis (Amadeo 2020c). It provided the most comprehensive financial reform since the Glass–Steagall Act, which regulated US banks after the 1929 stock market crash (Amadeo 2020a, 2020b). Hundreds of Dodd–Frank rules became part of international banking agreements. The Trump administration weakened the Dodd–Frank Wall Street Reform Act (Klein 2018; Onaran 2018).

The previous example and others noted in the preceding section illustrate that actors and their behavior within national boundaries constitute part of the formal and informal global governance at the global level. Those actors include UN organizations, international financial institutions, civil society organizations, philanthropic organizations, the G7 and G20, the private sector, trade associations, producers, and consumers, among others. In addition, new actors and partnerships continue to emerge. Much of the growth of civil society occurred in the 1980 and 1990s. The growth of private actors as major players ensued in the 1990s, following liberalization of commodity and capital markets. The private sector role, in particular, increased rapidly in the new millennium (see Chapter 7 on financing, Figure 7.1).

With the larger evolutionary view, we can see the roles of old entities being reformed and re-energized and new organizations entering the arena. We call our "Big Five" the traditional intergovernmental IOs concerned with food and agriculture. They were established well before the growth of organizations in the 1990s and the new millennium, which increasingly has accommodated non-state actors in governance, albeit informally. The Big Five all focus on poverty reduction and food security. Their missions and goals, shown in Table A.1.2 in Chapter 1, are quite complementary, and their very different governance structures, shown in Table A.6.1 in Chapter 6, provide us with a window on global governance from the viewpoint of the "operating arms" of the system. Their evolution and reforms are discussed in Chapter 6. In the meantime, new, emerging, and old retrofitted actors have resurfaced. The United Nations High Level Task Force on Global Food Security and Nutrition (UN HLTF) was established in 2008 to deal with the food crisis. The Committee on World Food Security (CFS), established in 1974, was reformed in 2009, as a multi-stakeholder platform to reach consensus on global food issues, giving CFS a new set of functions of global policy coordination. Around the same time, a dizzying number of other initiatives were launched and will be discussed here.

The Bill and Melinda Gates Foundation

The new actors on the scene include philanthropic organizations; among them, the Bill and Melinda Gates Foundation (BMGF), established in 2000, is the most preeminent of the private actors. Although only sovereign governments are members of the governing bodies of UN organizations and the Bretton Woods institutions, BMGF's outlays are larger than the gross national products (GNPs) of several small countries, and its influence has increased with its tremendous proactive role during the COVID-19 pandemic. Much as the Rockefeller Foundation had an extraordinary influence on generating the Green Revolution and in the health sector in an earlier era, BMGF has considerable influence on international policies and technologies, such as new vaccines and vaccine prices (particularly in the context of the pandemic), genetically modified (GM) crops, the role of the private sector, and the allocation of public sector resources. With an endowment of US$40.3 billion, BMGF's total 2016 direct grantee support amounted to US$4.6 billion, and, since its inception until the end of 2016, grant payments totaled US$41.3 billion (BMGF 2020).

While many bilateral donors, such as the United States Agency for International Development (USAID) and multilateral donors like the EU are large, too, they are traditional donors. BMGF's operations, the so-called philanthrocapitalism it practices and promotes, has come under scrutiny (see, for example, McGoey [2015]). The belief that doing good through being good is sometimes viewed with skepticism in terms of its unintended consequences. As a new actor, BMGF has made larger commitments than FAO's biannual assessed contributions of US$1 billion in 2018–19 (FAO 2020), IFAD's annual commitments to developing countries of US$823 million in 2016 (IFAD 2017), and CGIAR's annual research outlays of US$919 million in 2016 (CGIAR 2017). Unlike BMGF, activities of other philanthropists are not reported in OECD data (OECD 2019b).

As a thought leader with substantial financial power, BMGF has been influential in the mobilization of the IDA resources and to their sectoral allocations by persuading governments of rich countries and developing countries. BMGF has also supported GAFSP and, in terms of its governance, is a member of the Steering Committee. Most notable is BMGF's influence on health expenditures, including the treatment and prevention of communicable diseases, such as polio, HIV/AIDS, tuberculosis, and malaria, as well as vaccine development and delivery (Lele, Ridker, and Upadhyay 2005); and increasingly, on smallholder agriculture (McGoey 2015). BMGF increased its allocations to communicable diseases around the same time that the bilateral donors did, including, in particular, the United States and the United Kingdom, changing the balance of health spending to communicable diseases (Lele, Ridker, and Upadhyay 2005). Communicable disease investment was more attractive than NCDs in the first decade of the new millennium, perhaps because of the obvious spillovers across national borders; but these increased investments were not sufficient to anticipate the pandemic national priorities in the context of COVID-19. This balance began to change slightly in the face of the growing evidence of NCDs, but COVID-19 has highlighted the strong interactions between communicable and noncommunicable diseases. Vulnerability to COVID-19 is greater among those with adverse preexisting conditions.

In sub-Saharan Africa (SSA) and South Asia (SA), BMGF is promoting private entrepreneurship, improved seed and fertilizer use, and market access. Unlike public donors, a private foundation like BMGF, much like the Rockefeller or the Ford Foundations earlier, is accountable only to a small set of individuals. In the case of BMGF, trustees Bill Gates, Melinda Gates, Bill Gates, Sr., and Warren Buffett guide the annual investment of more than US$4 billion. While the Foundation performs a number of good, and indeed, admirable deeds, it also can have an undue impact on public policy and public resource allocation, given the sheer size of its resources. One interesting difference between BMGF and the Ford and Rockefeller Foundations is that BMGF has a declared process to conclude its operations within 20 years after Bill's and Melinda's deaths (BMGF 2020).

With increased evidence of inequality in income and wealth (Piketty 2014), and with little prospect of progressive tax reforms—the US Senate passed the largest tax cuts for corporations on December 2, 2017—wealth in the hands of billionaires has continued to grow, and wealthy private individuals continue to influence global agendas in the way that BMGF has done since the Foundation started its philanthropy, albeit possibly less transparently. Unlike BMGF, few of these wealthy philanthropists report their international expenditures in OECD databases.

Following its own good practice, BMGF supports more independent evaluations of its funded programs and makes them available to the public, as it demands also of IOs. BMGF is different from some other foundations who have governing boards. Given the size of its resource allocation, BMGF has a very large, and some would argue an undue, impact on policy and public resources. Their website describes what they believe is the right approach of focusing the work of BMGF in the 21st century, declaring, "We will spend all of our resources within 20 years after Bill's and Melinda's deaths. In addition, Warren has stipulated that the proceeds from the Berkshire Hathaway shares he still owns upon his death are to be used for philanthropic purposes within 10 years after his estate has been settled."[2] Interestingly, amortizing Warren's almost US$82 billion net worth over 10 years would require a payout nearly twice what the Foundation is currently spending.

---

[2] See https://www.gatesfoundation.org/Who-We-Are/General-Information/Financials/Foundation-Trust

Global governance could also demand more public accountability of the activities of philanthropists. Oxfam noted, in 2017, that eight men own as much wealth as the poorest half (3.6 billion people) of the world, and most of them are US nationals, including Bill Gates and Warren Buffett. Well over 100 billionaires are active in international development work to varying degrees. Oxfam (2017a, 2017b) is critical of this trend. Income inequality raises important policy issues. Is income, in the hands of private individuals, even when spent on aid, better spent than ODA?

Other Private Sector Interventions

Some private financiers are interested in the provision of global public goods. Examples include Facebook's interest in financing satellites for increasing their coverage in SSA, and Bill Gates' and a consortium of donors' interest in financing energy research. The larger-than-life influence of the Big Five private corporations in the information technology (IT) industry (Facebook, Amazon, Google, Microsoft, and Apple) through social media, use of personal data and information, and political discourse has become clearer in recent years. Their influence in collecting, using, and disseminating information, including "fake news," has come under increasing scrutiny and skepticism (King and Gabriel 2019). There is more appetite in Europe to regulate tech companies than in the United States. So, the future of governments, multinational corporations, and their interactions is less clear than in the past.

The food and beverage industry plays a growing role in a world that is facing an obesity epidemic. Some have noted that Google, Coke, and Pepsi hire academics with the potential to influence policies favorable to them (Popkin 2009; Haddad 2017). Popkin has compared the behavior of beverage companies to the early years of tobacco companies, in muting opposition to their practices. These are important questions of global public policy, which deserve more attention.

The role of big corporations poses numerous issues in global governance. The formerly "Big Six" agricultural input corporations are now five—BASF, Bayer, DowDuPont (a merger of the two corporate giants was finalized on August 31, 2017), Monsanto, and Syngenta—and are undergoing changes of their own (DowDuPont 2017). China's purchase of Syngenta added a new dimension to the story of a Northern-controlled agribusiness acquired by a Southern country. The growth of private sector agrochemical and seed industries has increased their role in research and development. How their role may be harnessed for poverty reduction through public–private partnerships is explored further in Chapter 10 on CGIAR.

It is clear that private sector and multinational corporations have acquired increased importance. Gabaix (2016) explained why, in all likelihood, economies of scale and scope lead to continued concentration of economic activity. The lack of coordination to correct the imbalance is an example of global governance failure. Bill Gates and Melinda Gates and Warren Buffett created the Giving Pledge in 2010, to invite the world's billionaires to commit more than half their wealth to philanthropy.[3] The multilateral development bank report for the Addis Ababa meeting on "Financing for Development" stressed the need to shift thinking on financing needs of developing countries from billions to trillions, and

---

[3] See "About the Giving Pledge," https://givingpledge.org/About.aspx

argued that a better environment for private sector flows will meet the gap (Development Committee 2015). The report did not address the need to mobilize resources to meet the global public goods gap, as a recent Center for Global Development (CGD) report did (Ahluwalia et al. 2016).

A difference among countries in terms of the size of their economies and contributions to global governance also explains differences in power structure. Despite contributing a far smaller share of the GDP to global institutions, relative to its GNP or relative to the shares contributed by other countries, the US contributions tend to be the largest in absolute amounts and, hence, the largest shares in the budgets of the UN and most IOs. As we detail later in Chapter 6 on the governance of the Big Five of the Bretton Woods institutions, *voice* in the running of an organization—one of the many examples of the way voice is exercised—is formally related to the size of a country's shareholdings. Emerging countries traditionally have had a small share of the subscribed capital and, hence, a small voice in the governance of Bretton Woods institutions. Big borrower countries, such as China, India, and Brazil, however, have wielded more influence on lending policies and practices of the multilateral banks: for example, in policies concerning safeguards. In *doing business*, of course, developing countries have little influence on the activities of philanthropies like BMGF, except for the operations in their own countries.

BMGF often works in collaboration with the United States and other OECD countries. The rule of "one country, one vote," which prevails in some UN organizations, is controversial. On the other hand, in the Security Council, with the exception of China, none of the world's populous developing countries—India, Brazil, or Nigeria—are represented, except on a short-term, rotating basis. In reality, the actual decision-making is more complex.[4] As the share of emerging countries in global GDP has increased, so has their financial influence and political power. They have not been able to exercise it in the formal governance arrangement of the Bretton Woods institutions, which has evolved slowly to reflect these realities, as discussed in Chapter 6. The response of the emerging countries to this disjuncture in formal voice and effective clout led to the establishment of new financial institutions, such as the AIIB and NDB. The US government opposed this move, despite the importance of capital for the capital-hungry developing countries, and despite the fact that most OECD countries joined the new banks quickly.

South–South cooperation and bilateral capital transfers from emerging countries have increased and will remain an important source of soft power. Private capital flows to developing countries have similarly exploded relative to ODA, much of it going to infrastructure, but still not nearly enough to meet all of the infrastructure needs (see Chapter 7, Figure 7.1). More importantly, South–South flows of private capital have increased, particularly Chinese investments in infrastructure throughout much of Asia and SSA, but South–North flows have also increased, with emerging countries investing their savings in the stock and bond markets in New York and London and financing of their budget deficits. A World Bank (2013) report, *Capital for the Future* predicted, in the coming decades, that the Global South will become the largest supplier of capital to the rest of the world. China has both high

---

[4] IFAD and WFP are parts of the UN and choose differently. In all three cases, their boards attempt to follow consensus decisions, rather than votes on most issues. For FAO, outside of the director-general election (and independent chair of the Council and Committee chairs), the only time decisions are voted on are budget resolutions. This consensus style of decision-making is more characteristic, perhaps, and important than the various ways that different parts of the UN System select leaders. In the case of the Secretary-General, even the Security Council decides and expects the General Assembly to endorse. It is true, of course, that for FAO, WHO, and others, the spirit of "one country, one vote" is central to their institutional personalities and ways of working.

savings and high GDP growth rates, but in other countries, such capital transfers from the South to the North can be seen as perverse—since with large incidences of poverty, they should be investing resources in their own countries. Because of the failure of Bretton Woods institutions to "recycle" savings of emerging countries through capital increases, or to check tax evasion and capital flight from developing countries to the developed, orders of magnitude of these "untapped flows" for productive investments in developing countries are large and far greater than the aid flows.

Notwithstanding these trends, with slower growth in some big emerging countries, such as Brazil, South Africa, and Turkey, and India, and with their deteriorating governance, the initial shine about alternatives to Bretton Woods institutions, such as the NDB, may have faded in the short run. The presidents of Brazil and South Korea, Dilma Rousseff and Park Geun-hye, were impeached in 2016 and 2017, respectively; another Brazilian ex-president (Lula) was convicted on charges of corruption in 2017, and Russia and South Africa each have had their own experiences of deteriorating governance. A positive view of these developments is that some governments are becoming more accountable to their constituencies, following these failures in governance.

The numbers of think tanks, public policy research and policy analysis institutions, and consulting firms have also increased, with an estimated 7,000 think tanks located not just in the West, but also in emerging countries. Their rise coincides with the end of national governments' monopolies on information, the increasing complexity and technical nature of policy problems, increasing size of governments, crisis of confidence in governments and elected officials, globalization, the growth of state and non-state actors, the need for timely information and analysis, and the growth of information and communication technology. Nearly 1,800 of the think tanks are US-based, and 400 of them are in Washington, DC, illustrating the considerable imbalance yet in their growth around the world (McGann 2007, 2016). The ability of think tanks to mobilize resources from domestic and international sources and their lobbying efforts in the US Congress have raised questions about their independence. Their growth has slowed with increased competition from consulting firms and civil society organizations.

Finally, the financial role of remittances and the intellectual and entrepreneurial capital of migrants cannot be underrated. Personal remittances amounted to US$537 billion in 2016, of which US$407 billion went to developing countries (World Bank 2020b), as compared to ODA of US$177 billion (OECD.Stat 2020) (see Chapter 7 on financing for more about remittances). The remittances are a significant share of the macroeconomic story, using a variety of indicators. For example, remittances are three times the size of ODA, several times the earnings of developing countries from agricultural exports, and they have been growing rapidly.

Governance as Cosmology: Challenges in Drawing Boundaries in a Universe

In an earlier publication, Lele (2009) described global governance as cosmology—the scientific study of the origin, evolution, and structure of the universe of actors, including the phenomenon of rising and declining stars—how they are organized or organize themselves, and perform the function of governance: that is, the provision of strategic guidance and an ability to steer the global system toward rational decision-making. Economists typically argue for clarity of objectives, appropriate choice of instruments, evaluation of results, and adaptation on the basis of experience gained. Such a system is probably una-chievable, but it would be very useful to have some clear criteria on which we could base a judgment as to how to improve the current situation. This task becomes more complex with a broadened agenda and the larger number of relevant organizations and actors in the universe of global governance (IDA 2007). Further, governance in many individual organizations has become more inclusive, both in terms of the scope of the subject matter—that is, in addressing the issues of climate change, the environment, and nutrition and health consequences of food insecurity—as well as in terms of the number and types of stakeholders, from sovereign entities to civil society and the private sector, if not formally, then as observers and partici-pants whose voice is heard, for example, in the CFS and FAO meetings.

Yet, questions of representation and voice remain vexing. Whereas civil society organiza-tions question the extent to which governments represent the voices of all of their people, particularly the marginalized populations, the governments of developing countries ask whose voice the NGOs, and particularly international NGOs, represent in the discussion of public policy issues such as safeguards.[5]

Not surprisingly, governance of IOs has become far more complex, with stakeholders, within individual countries and internationally, exercising competing interests: for example, in the forest sector between indigenous people and agricultural expansionists. Broad stakeholder participation certainly has increased the breadth of perspectives and legitimacy of IOs, but it has also increased the cost of doing business—an issue debated frequently, for example, in the context of the World Bank's safeguards, at the meetings of the board of directors who represent sovereign governments. There have also been long-standing differ-ences in the areas of safeguards between developed and developing countries, as the 2016 revision of safeguards illustrates (World Bank 2017). In the discussion of the governance of the Big Five in Chapter 6, we show how the increasing complexity of governance has been accompanied by mission creep, multiplicity of objectives, overlapping mandates, and a lack of clarity in their pursuit. Even if the objectives are well defined, the overlapping objectives of multiple organizations (see Table A.1.2 in Chapter 1) increase competition, spreading a few limited resources thinly and confusing clients.

Drawing boundaries around the concept of global governance of FSN within the global governance system, thus, has become increasingly difficult. Boundaries vary depending on the problem at hand. Climate-smart agriculture requires the inclusion of different skill sets and stakeholders than does health and nutrition, which increasingly have been main-streamed into the food security agenda. In an earlier publication, we provided an approach to looking at global environmental governance (Lele, Zazueta, and Singer 2010); and in Figure 5.1, we offer a stylized example of the 20 UN agencies and IOs that the UN Secretary General mobilized in 2008, following the world food crisis, to address the food security challenge, the High Level Task Force (HLTF). The task force did not formally include bilateral donors and philanthropic organizations, whose financing makes the work of IOs possible, nor did it formally include civil society, which provides legitimacy to such efforts—perhaps, to contain the challenge of collective action. Nevertheless, the HLTF supported these global processes with particular emphasis on the options for linkages between civil society, NGOs, private sector, donor agencies, regional bodies, development banks, and the

---

[5] The World Bank considers safeguards to be "a cornerstone of our work on investment projects" to ensure protections for people and for the environment. "Policies—often called 'safeguards'—serve to identify, avoid, and minimize harm to people and the environment. These policies require borrowing governments to address certain environmental and social risks in order to receive Bank support for investment projects" (World Bank 2016).

UN System at both national and regional levels.[6] It has important lessons for the 2021 UN Summit.

Figure 5.1 includes the many other actors that interact and partner with the 20 IOs included in the UN Secretary General's Task Force.

The HLTF, and the need to broaden and formalize the broad range of stakeholders involved addressing the food crisis, led to the reform of the Committee of World Food Security in 2009. The CFS Reform defined its functions in the first phase as coordination at the global level, policy coherence, support and advice at the country and regional levels; and in the second phase, coordination at the regional and country levels, promotion of account-ability and sharing of best practices at all levels, and development of a global strategic framework for food security. An important appeal of CFS for donors is that it included "Mechanisms" for civil society and private sector stakeholders. The CFS, as it name suggests, does not have a mandate itself or resources for implementation but operates through the member states, the "operating arms" of the three Rome-based institutions (FAO, WFP, and IFAD), which have had an active presence in developing countries since

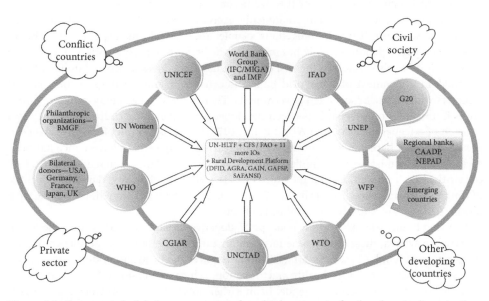

Figure 5.1 Fragmented global governance and multiple actors in food and agriculture in the immediate aftermath of the crisis: UN High Level Task Force on Global Food Security and Nutrition in 2008

Notes: AGRA = Alliance for a Green Revolution in Africa; DFID = Department for International Development (UK); GAFSP = Global Agriculture and Food Security Program; GAIN = Global Alliance for Improved Nutrition; IFC = International Finance Corporation; MIGA = Multilateral Investment Guarantee Agency; NEPAD = New Partnership for Africa's Development; SAFANSI = South Asia Food and Nutrition Security Initiative; UNCTAD = United Nations Conference on Trade and Development; UNEP = United Nations Environment Programme; UNICEF = United Nations Children's Fund; WHO = World Health Organization; WTO = World Trade Organization.

Source: Authors' construction (Lele and Goswami).

[6] The HLTF worked with the EC to establish a €1 billion European Union Food Facility (EUFF) to support urgent action by countries in need in response to consequences of the food security crisis. HLTF entities also worked together in contributing to the L'Aquila Initiative on Food Security, launched at the G8 L'Aquila Summit (July 2009), where US$20 billion were pledged for food security, leading to the creation of GAFSP.

their establishment; the Civil Society Mechanism (CSM); and the Private Sector Mechanism (PSM). The CFS's think tank, the High Level Panel of Experts (HLPE), produces annual reports on topics selected by the CFS members as a basis for policy convergence and specific sets of recommendations or guidelines. Most of the resources of CFS come from the Rome-based agencies and 4–5 individual bilateral donors, which are already strapped for resources. The EU-led evaluation of CFS (CFS 2017) highlighted the need for regular funding but also the need for more efficiency in operating modalities and the output of products. With strong support from several European donors, the CFS is finalizing the Voluntary Guidelines on Food Systems on Nutrition, which should be approved in 2021. Such guidelines would be an important input to the forthcoming FSS; the CFS Chair is part of the FSS Advisory Group and both the CSM and PSM have been invited to be part of the work of the FSS Action Tracks.[7]

How can governance be managed in this new, rapidly evolving situation, and how do we know when we are succeeding? Is coherence possible in the age of the Internet and social media, which offer immense, albeit unmanaged competition: that is, without sufficient public accountability? For example, in the past, G77 countries had shared interests, but differentiation among upper-income and low-income developing countries has increased. Sometimes, middle-income countries (MICs) share interests with some developed countries, joining them at times, but at other times, engaging in fierce competition, particularly when advancing national interests in the pursuit of spheres of influence. Developed and emerging countries share interest in access to Africa's natural resources and compete with each other. IOs are relatively less political, although there are examples when superpowers have interfered with their policies and operations. Nevertheless, they are better able to pursue collective interests, provided their resources are not tied by donors through trust funds to issues and countries or regions of political interest to donors, and objective transparent criteria are established by which resources are allocated—this is one reason why the World Bank gets higher marks than others (see Chapter 6 on the governance of the Big Five).

Collective Action among Large and Small Groups of State and Non-State Actors

Olson (1965) stated in *The Logic of Collective Action: Public Goods and the Theory of Groups* that large groups are less likely to organize themselves effectively, compared to small groups, because the cost of organizing is greater than the expected benefits. Large groups are also less likely to be as homogeneous, with a diversity of interests. Economic and political power, as well as information and knowledge within the large groups, are also likely to be asymmetric. Yet, notwithstanding the cost and the complexity of collective action, a powerful motivation for establishing effective global governance is to take advantage of the economies of scale and scope in developing solutions to common challenges—on such issues as trade, climate change, and control of communicable diseases—to maximize the positive spillovers of transboundary phenomena and to minimize negative spillovers. Following Brexit, in 2016, a strong defense for countries remaining in the EU was provided by the outgoing president of the European Parliament, Martin Schulz, noting the small size and poor bargaining power of many individual EU member countries acting alone in negotiations (European Parliament 2016).

---

[7] See "Action Tracks," https://www.un.org/en/food-systems-summit/action-tracks

On the other hand, without the bilateral agreement between the United States and China in advance of the Paris Accord, the climate change agreement would not have materialized. Previous Conferences of the Parties (COPs) illustrate the point. The expected benefits of the agreement finally reached are smaller than the 57 small island developing countries had originally hoped for. The United States, the second largest emitter of greenhouse gases, had agreed to reduce its emissions by 2025 to 26–8 percent of 2005 levels, or about 1.6 billion tonnes. There are concerns that the failure of the world's second biggest polluter to honor its commitments will make it harder for the world to curb temperature rises. The US withdrawal also sets a precedent and raises fears that other countries may renege on their commitments.

On August 4, 2017, the United States announced it would still take part in international climate change negotiations in order to protect its interests, despite its planned withdrawal from the Paris Accord on global warming (Friedman 2017). The remaining parties to the agreement have resolved, however, to proceed, even if the United States does not play its role. Similarly, following the US withdrawal from the TPP, others have resolved to proceed as "12 minus 1" (ICTSD 2017a). The Biden administration is already reversing many of these policies, but their sustainability will depend on future US administrations.

Notwithstanding these difficulties, a number of global outcomes, including control of communicable diseases and increased food production that has outpaced population growth, can be attributed to globalization and international cooperation in science, technology, and medicine. Yet, some of the achievements are fragile. For example, in the case of polio eradication, there have been small recurrences in Nigeria, Pakistan, and India—a result of waning political will, the high marginal cost of reaching those not yet treated, competing priorities for scarce resources, worker fatigue among those providing last-mile support, and a lack of trust among communities about Western governments (Rasmussen 2017; WHO 2019). For instance, suspicion exists among Muslim communities that view immunization as a conspiracy of the West, reinforced by the use of health workers as informants in the raid on Bin Laden, or of a belief in parts of India that the Hindu majority seeks to sterilize Muslim children in Northern Indian States. These issues are viewed as sensitive and have often been ignored in largely reporting of "success." Far too often, glossing over the complex sociocultural phenomena that determine outcomes have led to "surprising" outcomes, as outlined in Box 5.2.

COVID-19 provides by far the most dramatic example of the consequences of noncooperation of populations in following "rules" of wearing masks, maintaining distance, testing, and tracing based on medical advice, and its politicization, of all the places in a most scientifically advanced country, namely, the United States. It is clear that multidisciplinary research on human behavior is needed.

The proliferation of small group collective action in trade through bilateral or regional FTAs has occurred, in part, as a consequence of the failure of multilateral action through the World Trade Organization (WTO). There is an active debate about whether the outcome of bilateral and regional trade agreements, such as the North American Free Trade Agreement (NAFTA), now being replaced by the United States–Mexico–Canada Agreement (USMCA), or the US abandonment of TPP, are constructive for those not included in the agreements (ICTSD 2017a). Some have argued that they have contributed to standard setting (Valdés and McCann 2014). Yet, the support for club governance arrangements as a complementary approach to international cooperation has grown in recent years, not the least due to the difficulty of reaching agreements in large groups, but also with the recognition that climate clubs, for instance, may help bring about faster and deeper progress than the full UN membership (Hawkins 2016). Indeed, working together, the United States

---

Box 5.2 Who Sets Global Priorities and How?

Rich countries set global priorities. In health, they were driven, in the late 1990s and the first half of the new decade, by the donors' desires, reinforced by humanitarian appeals by celebrities like Bono, to control the spread of communicable diseases, particularly in SSA and were largely funded by OECD donors (see Figure 9.3 on the World Health Organization's budget in Chapter 9). Within the World Bank, which is less amenable to external lobbying, a debate raged in the late 1990s and early 2000s over the Bank's responsibility to strengthen health system capacities of developing countries as a preventive measure to control the spread of communicable diseases, as distinct from its role in drug delivery. Given the significant spillover effects of communicable diseases, such as AIDS (Acquired Immunodeficiency Syndrome), tuberculosis, and malaria—and that of other emerging pandemics, like Severe Acute Respiratory Syndrome (SARS), avian flu, Ebola, and Zika viral infections—they have attracted greater support from Western donors for their control, much more than the endemic NCDs, such as diarrhea or diabetes. The donor interest favoring the financing of climate change mitigation, rather than adaptation, could similarly be explained by the spillover benefits or costs of inaction.

The more recent interest among the donor community in financing treatment and prevention of noncommunicable diseases has arisen after a clear link between malnourishment (both undernutrition and overnutrition) and NCDs was established scientifically, followed by intense advocacy by a well-organized group of committed international nutrition advocates, with a critical mass of evidence published in *Lancet* (2008, 2011, 2013). These choices and priorities, in turn, are a result of the nature of collective action at the global level, this time with the role of the scientific community. To understand it, we need to understand the role of the principal actors. These issues are discussed further in Chapter 9.

---

and China did accelerate the Paris Agreement, which has provided a multilateral hook for the formation of climate clubs, including in the area of carbon markets. In 2017, China announced the formation of the largest carbon market, which will be effective in a few years. Such cooperation can help increase the ambition and impact of carbon markets in the global mitigation effort by addressing the constraints that result from concerns about competitiveness and carbon leakage under unilateral efforts. The clubs can provide a model for deeper carbon market cooperation (Hawkins 2016). Others have explored the role of "club goods," to help incentivize participation, ensure compliance, deter free riding, and scale up ambition (Victor 2015); still others have explored the potential of carbon markets as "club goods" (Petsonk and Keohane 2015).

Issues of Global Governance

Global governance, unlike national governance, is challenged by the absence of a global government and the inability to form and enforce rules, tax global citizens to finance global public goods, or to mitigate transboundary externalities, such as those associated with climate change. There is an important distinction to be made between public goods and externalities, particularly in terms of how these should be addressed and who should bear the costs of addressing them (Box 5.3). The issues have frequently been overlooked in

Box 5.3 Public Goods and Externalities

Public goods are goods that are non-rivalrous and non-excludable. Their benefits and/or costs potentially extend to multiple actors, depending on their scope. Traffic lights are examples of local public goods that benefit all drivers and pedestrians. Defense and financial stability are examples of national public goods. Global public goods are, in a dual sense, public—they are public as opposed to private—and global, as opposed to international or national. Rules that generate international norms and standards (for example, with regard to food or cross-border control of pests or diseases) are global public goods. They can be formal or informal rules, and member countries are expected to adhere to them.

An externality is the cost or the benefit that affects those parties who did not choose to incur the cost (for example, farmers in tropical countries suffering from extreme events prompted by climate change) or benefits of warming temperatures in temperate countries (Buchanan and Stubblebine 1962). Economists often urge governments to adopt policies that "internalize" an externality (for example, tax emissions) and compensate losers, so that costs and benefits will affect mainly parties who choose to incur them. Such issues need to be addressed at multiple levels, but are underprovided and underfunded.

Hence, the key to global governance has been the willingness of sovereign governments and their citizens to cooperate and to voluntarily contribute financial and institutional resources to conduct activities in support of global governance. According to Article 17 of the UN charter, the UN General Assembly determines assessments of the 193 members, every three years, based on per capita income, external debt, and some other minor adjustments. Assessments are hopelessly out of line with needs. The total regular UN budget for the year 2016–17 is a mere US$5.6 billion (Dubbudu 2016; UN 2016). The UN approved a US$286 million cut in its annual budget for the next biennium 2018–19, "a 5 percent 'historic reduction in spending' that the US said it had negotiated" (Live Mint 2017). As a result of the low levels of assessed contributions, late transfer of funds, and constant pressure to reduce budgets, the UN relies heavily on non-assessed voluntary contributions (UN 2017a). There's no doubt that the needs of all UN agencies go beyond the level of "assessed contribution," but the concept of assessments is a good one, although the method may require assessment—a subject beyond the scope of this inquiry. The method has stood the test of time. Should there be a greater increase built into the formula? The answer would seem to be positive or those who believe in global governance. UN member states will likely not agree, without exceptional leadership—hence, the growth and influence on program strategy and design, and of parallel voluntary contributions.

The United States contributes the largest amount, with a share of 22 percent of the UN assessed contributions. Its GNP is 27 percent of the global GNP of all UN member countries, thus its highest share of contribution is justified. The US Congress passed a measure to freeze some UN contributions.

Other major contributors include: China, Japan, Germany, the United Kingdom, France, Italy, Brazil, Russian Federation, and Canada, with the scale of assessment expected to be 10.808 percent, 8.718 percent, 6.157 percent, 4.564 percent, 4.538 percent,

3.4 percent, 3.234 percent, 2.884 percent, and 2.815 percent, respectively, in the period from 2019 to 2021, according to the *Report of the Committee on Contributions: Seventy-seventh Session* in June 2017 (UN 2017b) (Figure 5.2).[a] China is expected to overtake Japan as the second largest contributor to the general UN budget, beginning in 2019. For the period from 2016 to 2018, the scale of assessments adopted for China was 7.921 percent, while Japan is paying almost 2 percentage points more at 9.680 percent. The report also estimated that China had nearly a 14 percent share of the world's gross national income (GNI), roughly double Japan's share during the three-year period beginning in 2016 (*Strait Times* 2017).

Another seven countries contribute more than 1 percent each to the UN regular budget, and 135 countries contribute less than 0.1 percent each (see Figure 5.2) (UN 2017b). The nature of burden sharing is clear. Of the 193 member countries of the UN, the top 25 countries contribute 87.681 percent, while the other 168 countries contribute 12.319 percent (Figure 5.2). The top 10 countries account for 69.118 percent of the total UN contributions. The pattern of financing varies among the Big Five international organizations, along similar lines, and the relationship to the governance of these five organizations is discussed in the next chapter.

Notes: [a] The Committee made new recommendations so that the scale of assessments is "based on the most current, comprehensive, and comparable data available for gross national income" (UN 2017b, 3). This "2017 update" refers to the update of the 2016–18 scale, using data available in December 2016 for the period 2010–15. Each country's share of the UN general budget is reviewed every three years, based on factors such as GNI, economic strength, and the ability to contribute. The breakdown for the UN budget over the 2019–21 period was adopted December 2018 (UN 2019).

discussions of how to mitigate transboundary externalities, such as the control of climate change, communicable diseases, or transboundary financial instability. The resultant under-provision of global public goods prevails, both in terms of their quantity and quality, while trying to maintain global peace and security, to facilitate and regulate international trade and commerce, and to minimize "public bads"—activities which damage the environmental commons, cause conflict, contribute to climate change, turn the Earth's natural resources into club goods for the benefit of the few, or lead to the tragedy of the commons: for example, with the erosion of fisheries and loss of other marine resources.

Over the years, with few exceptions, the world's richest governments have made, but not met, repeated pledges to commit 0.7 percent of their GNP to ODA (Figure 5.3). The club of countries has grown, with emerging countries joining their ranks, although in terms of per capita income in China and India, these commitments are not high. Nevertheless, from the viewpoint of rebalancing global governance and financing, it is important to consider the relationship between them in the global system, such that increased contributions of member countries, through regular and predictable, multiyear commitments, would be the best option. Some rich governments, such as the United States, however, have been reluctant to provide national public goods, such as universal health care and, therefore, are understandably reluctant to finance IGOs. It will be interesting to see if COVID-19 is likely to change those views and increase financial support for public health. Other ideas for financing global governance include a carbon tax, financial transactions tax, and airlines tax—some of these have been piloted but, again, a lack of political support in key rich member countries, particularly in the United States and the United Kingdom, have prevented their being scaled up. It is unclear if philanthropists can and will provide resources

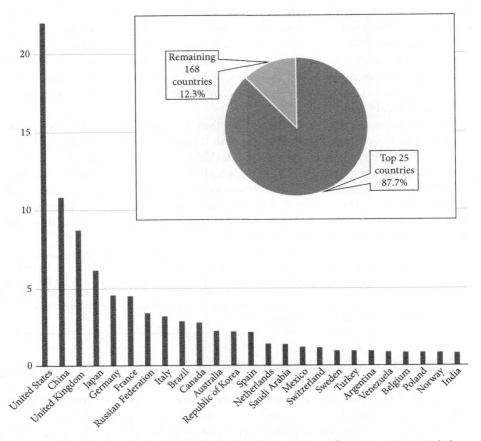

Figure 5.2 Contribution to the UN regular budget by top 25 member states, 2019–21 (%)
Source: Based on data from UN (2017b).

on a scale needed for the provision of global public goods, and if their priorities would be the same as those of IGOs, based on some transparent objective criteria.

The 0.7 percent target was first pledged in a 1970 General Assembly Resolution and has been affirmed in many subsequent international agreements, including in the March 18–22, 2002 International Conference on Financing for Development in Monterrey, Mexico, and at the World Summit on Sustainable Development in Johannesburg (August 26–September 4, 2002). The 0.7 percent target has been recognized as a vital step toward promoting international and national security and stability. The Report of the UN Secretary-General's High-Level Panel on Threats, Challenges, and Change (UN 2004) recommended that countries aspiring to global leadership, through permanent membership on the UN Security Council, be required to fulfill international commitments to ODA, including the 0.7 percent target: "The many donor countries which currently fall short of the United Nations 0.7 percent gross national product (GNP) for ODA should establish a timetable for reaching it" (UN 2004, 29). Many are skeptical that this sentiment can materialize.

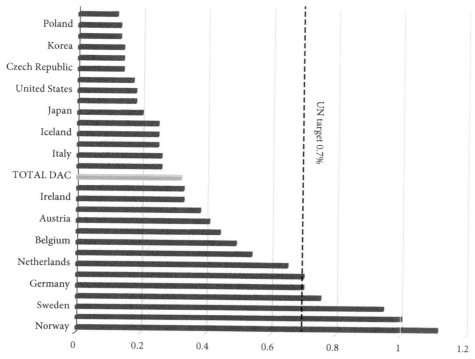

Figure 5.3 Ethics, fairness, and participation: ODA shares in GNI by DAC countries, 2016 (%)

Note: Preliminary data for 2016. The computer program used to produce the figure selectively labeled some of the countries' data. From the top, the complete list is Slovak Republic, Hungary, Poland, Greece, Korea, Czech Republic, Portugal, United States, Slovenia, Japan, Iceland, New Zealand, Australia, Italy, Canada, Ireland, Spain, France, Austria, Finland, Belgium, Switzerland, the Netherlands, United Kingdom, Germany, Denmark, Sweden, Luxembourg, and Norway.

Source: Adapted from OECD (2017).

Governance Issues at the National Level

SDG2, and indeed any other SDGs or climate change goals, cannot be achieved without national political will, strategy, policy, and capacity to plan and implement and achieve results on the ground. Private sector funding cannot be attracted without good governance. Thus, governance is at the center of achievements and has been receiving increasing attention since the 1990s. In the early 1990s, the emphasis was on service delivery (World Bank 2003, 2004), with a reduced role of government and increased role of the private sector. Then, these piecemeal approaches gave way to a more systemic approach to addressing issues of governance. The World Bank's emphasis on community-driven development (CDD) also engendered evaluations of CDDs and social funds (World Bank 2005), and development research on local participation grew (most notably, within the World Bank, by Mansuri and Rao 2013). The World Bank has committed substantial resources to governance reforms and to CDDs. Both have had mixed results. In the area of governance, the Bank's focus was on narrow project-level governance rather than on the overarching enabling environment (IEG 2007a, 2007b, 2008, 2009a, 2009b, 2009c, 2011). Interest in measuring governance at all levels has increased. On CDDs, too, the results have been mixed, but many new insights were obtained from the World Bank's analytical and evaluation work.

Measuring Quality of National Governance: Using Global Data Sets

Kaufmann, Kraay, and Mastruzzi (2011) have been at the forefront of measuring governance. Their work has also invited criticism and work by others. They considered Douglass North's definition (1990) as insightful but too broad, whereas others, such as Blandford have considered it too narrow, and defined country-level governance as the traditions and institutions by which authority in a country is exercised (David Blandford, personal communication August 12, 2017). This includes political, economic, and institutional dimensions of governance: that is, how governments are selected, monitored, and replaced; the governments' capacity to effectively formulate and implement sound policies and provide public services; and the respect of citizens and the state for the institutions that govern economic and social interactions among them. Kaufmann, Kraay, and Mastruzzi (2011) have put into place one the largest efforts at measurement, although it is by no means free of controversy. Their six dimensions, which we use to construct the Worldwide Governance Index (WGI), include: (1) Voice and Accountability; (2) Political Stability and Absence of Violence/Terrorism; (3) Government Effectiveness; (4) Regulatory Quality; (5) Rule of Law; and (6) Control of Corruption (see World Bank 2020a). Other scholars have addressed some of the elements contained in the index of Kaufmann, Kraay, and Mastruzzi (2011) in their theoretical, empirical, and historical research, which we turn to, as necessary for our overview of governance at the national level. These scholars include Olson (1965); Hirschman (1970); Sen (1984, 1985, 1999); Ostrom (1990); Dasgupta and Mäler (1997); Bardhan and Mookherjee (2007); Acemoglu and Robinson (2012); and Mansuri and Rao (2013) on the issues of decentralization, participation, and capability, including the issues of interest groups and elite capture.

An Asian Development Bank report (ADB 2013) used the work of Kaufmann, Kray, and Mastruzzi (2011) carefully, discussing each of the six components of the index, in the light of the criticisms and comparing the WGI indicators with other efforts at measurement.[8] It pointed out the pros and cons of each indicator and the disparities in results obtained, depending on the indicator used.[9]

The ADB report (2013) noted that the correlation between governance and development is weaker in lower income economies than in higher income economies. In addition,

---

[8] Criticisms of the Worldwide Governance Indicators (WGI) include: (1) the usefulness of comparisons of governance over time and across countries; (2) potential biases in the individual indicators underlying aggregate governance indicators, in terms of who is surveyed; (3) independence of the assessments of governance provided by different data sources; and (4) the consequences for the aggregate governance indicators. Some critiques have said that the WGI are an "elaborate untested hypothesis," because they fail to provide evidence of "construct validity" (Kaufmann, Kraay, and Mastruzzi 2007, 2). There has been criticism of the limited access to the data used in the WGI and for the causality between governance and growth, using data from the WGI. The reader is directed to these criticisms from Arndt and Oman (2006); Knack (2006); Thomas (2010); and Kurtz and Schrank (2007), in the responses to Kaufmann, Kray, and Mastruzzi (2007). One of the important ones, among others, has been the extent to which perceptions of governance compare with the reality of governance and comparability across time and countries.

[9] For example, the International Country Risk Guide, collected since 1980 (PRS Group 2016) and "Enterprise Surveys" (https://www.enterprisesurveys.org).

progress on governance has not matched economic progress in Asia. Government effectiveness, the rule of law, regulatory quality, and control of corruption are more closely and positively related to development performance than is voice and accountability or political stability (ADB 2013). Data are far more widely scattered along the fitted line for voice and political stability than for other indicators.

We used WGI indicators for six dimensions of governance using data over a 16-year period, covering 205 countries.[10] First, constructing a single index using the methodology suggested by Nagar and Basu (2002), we ranked countries from the top to the bottom. The usual suspects—Norway, Finland, Sweden, Denmark, the Netherlands, and other OECD countries—rank at the top, MICs typically stand in the middle, and low-income and African countries typically rank at the bottom, with some notable exceptions. For example, in Africa, Mauritius and Botswana rate higher on governance than many other nations; they are also highlighted by Acemoglu and Robinson for their good governance (2012). The results presented in Figure 5.4 provide several insights.

Our results are consistent with the ADB Report's (2013) result. Cross-country, time-series regressions show positive relationships between the six indicators and per capita income. Control of Corruption, Rule of Law, Regulatory Quality, and Government Effectiveness all show stronger relationships with per capita income than do Voice and Accountability, Political Stability, and Absence of Violence/Terrorism. The strong relationships with the four variables, noted here, suggest the important role of these four factors, perhaps, in improving economic performance. Voice and accountability, political stability, and absence of violence/terrorism show a weaker relationship to economic performance, but the direction of causality is much less clear. We believe the strong correlation between these mechanisms and GDP per capita does not tell us enough about the direction of causality. Does increased income and the growth of middle class lead to demand for better governance or vice versa?

In a similar vein, Sen has argued that a free press prevents famines (Sen 1980, 1981). Research by Besley et al. (2004, 2005) has also supported this hypothesis. Yet, the free press in India has not helped eradicate chronic hunger among its 250+ million people. Furthermore, even with increased income, food consumption does not always increase, even among households with low initial levels of food consumption, leading to the so-called Indian–South Asian enigma (Deaton and Drèze 2009). And there are important debates about how much nutrition has improved in recent years, as shown by recent UNICEF data, and what explains the improvement. We return to more micro-level, case study-based evidence on voice and accountability later.

Quality of Governance in Africa

Africa has much larger governance challenges than countries in Latin America and Asia, and this is evident from the Kaufmann, Kraay, and Mastruzzi (2011) data. Governance is of critical importance in the African continent, because it has the lowest agricultural productivity growth among regions, high incidence of food insecurity, and highest population growth rate, with a youth bulge.

---

[10] The data were from 1996 to 2014; data are not available for the years 1997, 1999, and 2001.

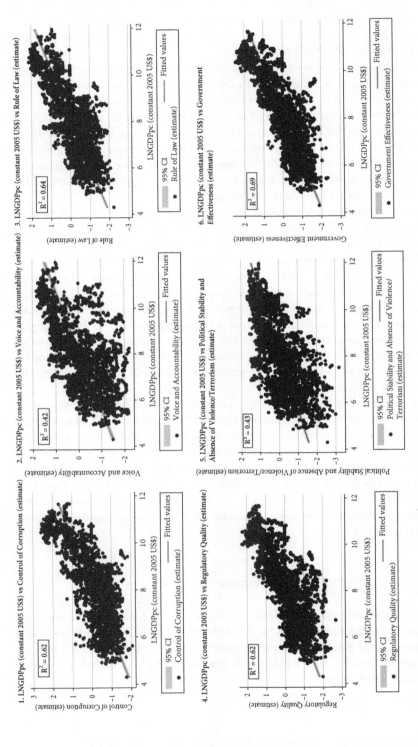

Figure 5.4 Per capita GDP and Governance Indicators

Note: Estimate of governance (ranges from approximately –2.5 (weak) to 2.5 (strong) governance performance)

Source: Lele and Goswami, based on data from https://info.worldbank.org/governance/wgi/

The Ibrahim Index of African Governance (IIAG) (MIF 2020) provides the most comprehensive collection of data on African governance. Viewing governance differently than Kaufmann, Kraay, and Mastruzzi (2011), IIAG defines it as the provision of political, social, and economic goods that citizens have the right to expect from their state, and that a state has the responsibility to deliver to its citizens. Its annual assessment of the quality of governance in 54 African countries consists of more than 90 indicators built into 14 subcategories, four categories, and one overall measurement of governance performance. Adding more indicators create difficulties on weights, if not evenly available.

Governance across Africa saw minimal improvement over 2006–15, due to widespread deterioration in Safety and Rule of Law (MIF 2016). Since 2006, 37 out of 54 African nations—home to 70 percent of African citizens—saw an overall improvement of just 1 point, measured against four categories (1) Safety and Rule of Law, (2) Participation and Human Rights, (3) Sustainable Economic Opportunity, and (4) Human Development. The index identified a worrying downward trend in the Safety and Rule of Law category: 33 out of the 54 nations experienced a decline over the decade, almost half of them (15 countries) experienced substantial decline. Two-thirds of the countries on the continent, representing 67 percent of the African population, showed deterioration in Freedom of Expression in the past 10 years.

According to the Mo Ibrahim Foundation report, "A Decade of African Governance, 2006–2015," among the top 10 overall rated countries, 6 had deteriorated in the Freedom of Expression category, with South Africa rated the worst. South Africa had been on the edge of a recession, with chronic power shortages and high unemployment. Mauritius came in at the top, followed by Botswana, Cape Verde, the Seychelles, and Namibia. Three of the top 10 countries, however, saw their scores fall in this period, including South Africa, the continent's most industrialized country, and Ghana, which registered some of the largest drops. Zimbabwe, Rwanda, and Ethiopia, nations in which records on human rights and freedom of expression have continued to give cause for concern internationally, were ranked among the top 10 most improving African countries in terms of overall governance since 2006, mainly due to advances in the rural sector. However, despite gains, Zimbabwe (showing a 9.7 point increase) still ranked in the bottom half for overall governance, coming in 39th out of 54 countries. Rwanda (with an 8.4 point increase) was the only country to feature among the 10 most improved and the 10 highest scoring. Ivory Coast showed the most progress in overall governance since 2006, recording a 13-point improvement over the last decade, followed by Togo (9.7) and Zimbabwe (also 9.7). Liberia, Rwanda, Ethiopia, Niger, Morocco, Kenya, and Angola made up the remaining among the top 10 most improved.

These governance findings should be seen in the context of the latest ODA flows:

Preliminary data in 2020 show that net bilateral ODA flows from DAC members to Africa were USD39 bn, representing an increase of 4.1% in real terms compared to 2019. By contrast, net ODA to sub-Saharan Africa amounting to USD31 bn, fell by 1% in real terms.

By income group, net bilateral ODA flows from all DAC members to low-income countries were USD 25 bn, a decrease of 3.5% in real terms compared to 2019. By contrast, net bilateral ODA to lower-middle income was USD33 bn representing an increase of 6.9% in real terms. Net ODA to upper-middle countries also increased by 36.1% to USD18 bn. Net ODA flows to high-income countries more than tripled and stood at USD372 m. These trends, along with the increase in the share of loans in ODA would imply that part of the increase in ODA in 2020 is due to loans to middle-income countries.

Preliminary data showed that net bilateral aid flows from DAC members to the group of least developed countries were USD34 bn, and increased by 1.8% in real terms compared to 2019. (OECD 2021, 5)

Exit, Voice, and Accountability

Many of Hirschman's (1970) ideas on exit, voice, and accountability are relevant to the discussion of global governance. Hirschman argued that actors have two potential responses when confronted with a deleterious change in their environment—exit or voice—and that loyalty is a psychological characteristic that increases an actor's propensity to choose voice over exit. Others have modified some of Hirschman's original argument, treating loyalty as a potential behavioral response in its own right, on par with exit and voice. In other words, some models do not offer two different conceptualizations of the *Exit, Voice, and Loyalty* (Hirschman 1970).

Economists assume *exit*, similar to that from a market, to result from dissatisfaction with an organization's product or service, leading to a decline in demand for it. The United States reduced its contribution to the UN System in 2000 from 25 percent to 22 percent, promising to pay long-standing debts to the UN in exchange for the lower assessment (GPF 2020). During the Reagan administration, when the US had a number of reservations about the support for the UN, there were calls to reduce the then 25 percent cap, but the UN's active role in negotiating cease-fires and peace talks in the Persian Gulf eased the pressure to reduce payments in 1988 and led Reagan to promise to pay overdue dues (Shannon 1988). Political winds have again shifted, and President Trump's 2018 budget proposal called for major US cuts to UN peacekeeping operations and international aid—cuts that the UN said would make maintenance of essential operations impossible (Gladstone 2017). Similarly, the United States made a complete (albeit temporary) exit from the International Labour Organization (ILO) in 1977; and withdrew funding in 1984 from the United Nations Educational, Scientific and Cultural Organization (UNESCO), rejoined in 2003, and then again stopped funding in 2011, when UNESCO granted Palestinians full membership (US Department of State 2011; Rubin 2013).[11] On January 1, 2019, the United States officially withdrew from UNESCO. Notably, however, "officials estimate that the U.S. . . . has accrued $600 million in unpaid dues, which was one of the reasons for President Donald Trump's decision to withdraw" (*PBS News Hour* 2019).

The value of exit for large countries like the United States lies in the certainty that it provides in terms of the relationship between the customer or member and the firm (or organization) from which it exits. Political scientists think of how an actor/person/firm handles its response to customer dissatisfaction as the exercise of *voice* by stakeholders. The value of voice (which may take different forms, either in the form of lobbying or voting, or direct action as in Brexit) is that it can lead to changes that ultimately can bring about the

[11] The different attitude adopted by the United States toward ILO on the one hand, and UNESCO and WHO on the other, could be explained by a lack of a concerted and coordinated policy of the various US departments concerned with "their" UN agency; alternatively, this divergence may be explained by reasons widely reported in the international press, additional to those given by then US Secretary of State Henry Kissinger in 1975, who cited criticisms of politicization of ILO, disregard for due process, selective concern for human rights, and "the lack of autonomy of employers' and workers' representatives with respect to their own governments." Some press reports suggested that President Carter's decision to withdraw were political appeasements to labor and business in exchange for support of his energy legislation and Panama Canal treaties (Beigbeder 1979, 232).

firm's revival, or not, an idea also advanced by scholar Clayton Christensen (1997) in his book *The Innovator's Dilemma*. An understanding of the conditions under which exit and voice are exercised requires incorporation of the concept of loyalty. Loyalty makes voice more probable and exit less likely, but loyalty does not by itself make the exercise of voice more effective. Effectiveness of voice depends on the extent to which customers or members are willing to trade the certainty of exit against the uncertainties of improvement in the (deteriorating) product, and their ability to influence the organization—for example, through the use of trust funds to drive their own agenda, as we show in the cases of FAO and CGIAR in the next chapter. Recent global developments have brought these issues into sharper focus, lending renewed relevance to Hirschman's brilliant book (1970). It is an opportune time to examine issues of voice, contributions, and accountability in global governance.

The rule of "one country, one vote" in the UN, regardless of a country's GDP, population, or financial contribution to the system, means that large and rich countries have less voice in the General Assembly than they do in the Security Council, where, except for China, none of the world's populous developing and emerging countries have continuous representation. In the Bretton Woods institutions, discussed in the next chapter, changing shares of member countries also has been contentious, as voting rights of emerging countries, particularly China, have not increased relative to their economic power, as compared to that of European countries, despite the emerging countries' growing shares of global GDP or global population.

Changes in assessed contributions to the general budgets of the UN are marginal, even after the recent revisions in the assessed contributions of countries. So, some countries provide "trust funds" in support of activities of interest to their domestic constituencies, an issue explored more fully in Chapter 6 on the governance of the Big Five and in Chapter 7 on financing. The phenomenon of donor trust funds, and their increased role in global agenda setting since the mid-1990s, has fundamentally changed the voice and accountability of member governments and, hence, the governance of individual IOs and of global governance.[12] Various new ideas for leveraging public funds to raise private finance also are being proposed—for example, under IDA18—and in IFAD through public–private partnerships, other options are being exercised that will change the governance of these organizations, moving into an uncharted territory. IDA support for private sector development in IDA-eligible countries amounted to US$70 billion in the past four replenishments, and IDA18 participants endorsed the creation of an International Finance Corporation–Multilateral Investment Guarantee Agency (IFC–MIGA) Private Sector Window pilot in IDA18 to support direct private investment in IDA—only as additional to existing WBG programs. In December 12–13, 2019, in an IDA19 replenishment meeting in Stockholm, Sweden, global coalition of development partners agreed on a historic US$82 billion financing package for IDA countries for fiscal years 2021–3, representing a 3 percent increase in real terms, compared to IDA18 (IDA 2020a).

In light of opposition to Tobin tax, or tax on airlines, in the United States and the United Kingdom, several European countries have decided to introduce the tax, and it may be extended to all EU member countries. If imposed globally, it would raise billions of dollars.

In addition to financing gaps, many other gaps in global governance have been identified by champions of global public goods, notably by Inge Kaul et al. (2003) and various UN

---

[12] Although BMGF is not a member of IDA, it has contributed important ideas to the IDA18 Replenishment and, as noted earlier, is a member of GAFSP (IDA 2020b).

commissions that have examined provision of global public goods, including the Pearson Commission on International Development (Pearson 1969) and the World Commission on Environment and Development (WCED 1987; UN 2009; Zedillo 2009).

The theory gap arises when a case for the provision of global public goods is made without the benefit of a relevant, up-to-date theory in the rapidly evolving political and economic realities of globalization with new entrants and unexpected exits. Prevailing governance and decision-making are marked by a state-centric and nationally focused view, at a time when the globalized world entails a number of externalities and cross-border spillovers, such as climate change, risk of pandemics, and international financial instability. Some philanthropists are willing to contribute and help raise funds for the provision of some of these global public goods (Harvey 2011; Watson 2011). Bill and Melinda Gates, Warren Buffett, and others have been willing to finance health and climate change-related research; many have made commitments to the Giving Pledge, noted earlier in this chapter, with one report suggesting the Pledge could account for US$600 billion in donations by 2022 (Kotechi 2018a). Jeff Bezos, CEO of Amazon and often cited as the wealthiest individual in the world, notably had not joined the Giving Pledge as of 2018 and was criticized for his focus on short-term solutions[13]; CNBC, however, reports that Bezos was ranked at the top of the Philanthropy 50 in 2018, after announcing, among other philanthropy in the past year, the launch of a US$2 billion fund (the Bezos Day One Fund) in support of homeless families and education programs in underserved communities (Kotechi 2018b; Berger 2019; see also, https://www.bezosdayonefund.org). Should there be more concerted effort by the international community to raise funds from the new rich?

So, what should be the appropriate division of public and private sector funding and partnerships between them? It is a question that, of course, needs a context-specific discussion (Kaul et al. 2003). The CGD sponsored a report on multilateral development banks (MDBs) that addressed these concerns (Ahluwalia et al. 2016). While declaring MDBs a tremendous success of the 20th century, the report noted that new challenges call for global collective action and financing of the sort that MDBs are well suited to provide, but have been handicapped in addressing large global public goods issues.

The list of global challenges that the MDB report identified include major financial shocks, climate change, pandemic risk, resistance to antibiotics, poor management of international migration flows, and the welfare of displaced and refugee populations. Other areas include cross-border security and spillovers associated with growing competition for water and other renewable natural resources, and with climate change—an increase in the frequency and human cost of weather and other shocks in low-income countries, for which multilateral banks are poorly equipped to respond. There are direct or indirect food security dimensions. The report provided recommendations for a provision of a US$10 billion window to finance global public goods; additional financing of sustainable infrastructure at about US$200 billion annually; concessional lending of at least US$25 billion annually; crisis management and post-conflict reconstruction for rapid response and short-run humanitarian needs; and a shareholder-led MDB agenda (Ahluwalia et al. 2016). These recommendations, however, are not easy to implement in the face of other gaps of global governance, including a leadership gap, legitimacy gap, efficiency gap, policy coherence gap, and lack of representativeness, transparency, and political legitimacy (Thakur 2003). We demonstrate, in the case of the Big Five IOs, how these gaps play out in the next chapter.

---

[13] MacKenzie Bezos, the ex-wife of Jeff Bezos, signed the Giving Pledge in 2019, less than two months after finalizing her divorce (Schleifer 2019).

Unlike many democratically elected heads of national governments, leaders of IOs are not directly elected by their members, sometimes not elected at all but rather nominated: for example, in the case of the World Bank and WFP. The United States nominated three candidates for WFP to be endorsed by their boards; therefore, such organizations do not possess primary legitimacy. Representation of governments in IOs is too distant from the citizenry to effectively transform local rights into international rights and responsibilities, as in the case of common but differentiated responsibilities in multilateral environmental agreements, or adherence to the commitments made by the citizens' governments on trade rules. Global governance needs to be both more representative and more efficient to address issues of the legitimacy deficit and decision traps (Lamy 2012).

Challenges of Fairness in Global Governance

Two significant items on the WTO agenda illustrate the point of fairness, particularly affecting poor countries dependent on food imports. Tackling trade restrictions and removing distortions in agricultural markets would benefit least developed countries (LDCs) in achieving the 2030 Sustainable Goal of ending hunger and achieving food security. The US government provided US$14 billion in trade-distorting agricultural domestic support in 2014; China provided US$18 billion in equivalent support in 2010, and reported US$14 billion in 2012 (ICTSD 2017b). For well over a decade, reform of cotton subsidies in wealthier nations has been a central negotiating demand of LDCs from four West African countries—Benin, Burkina Faso, Chad, and Mali—known collectively as the Cotton 4 (ICTSD 2016). Three dozen of the 48 LDCs are WTO members, with another 8 negotiating to join the organization. The Ministerial Meeting of WTO in Argentina in December 2018 did not make much progress, as we discussed in Chapter 3.

Building Consensus: Formal and Informal Governance—International Responses since the 2007 Crisis and Their Rationale

Governance takes place through consensus building, reaching agreements, and taking concerted action to tackle identified problems. The 2007–8 food and financial crises, discussed in Chapter 3, provoked the concern that price volatility was here to stay, leading to a dizzying number of initiatives to address issues of food security and vulnerability of the poor to food shortages and price spikes (see Chapter 3, Figure 3.3). The sheer number of initiatives, which ensued after the 2007–8 food and financial crises, are shown in Box 5.4.

What Were the Outcomes of These Initiatives?

Food security returned to the front burner while price instability remained an issue: that is, from 2008 to 2012 (see Figures 3.2 and 3.3 in Chapter 3 of this volume). There were some important investment commitments: for example, the G8 (L'Aquila) investment of US$22 billion over three years (IIF 2009); the multilateral food security program (Global Food Security Program) (GAFSP 2018); and bilateral initiatives (Elliott and Dunning 2016; Feed the Future 2020); as well as the near doubling of funding for CGIAR, but only until 2014—funding stagnated again; establishment of an Agricultural Market Information System in

Box 5.4 International Initiatives in Response to the Food and Financial Crises

In chronological order, these initiatives fall into three phases: (1) the immediate post-crisis period; (2) 2010–14, when volatility appeared to return; and (3) 2015 and the post-2015 period. The initiatives fall into several different categories, for example:

(I) **30 initiatives related to global food security:**

(A) 17 in the immediate post-crisis period, including the:

(1) UN Secretary General's High Level Task Force on the Global Food Security Crisis, 2008;

(2–3) Two G8 summits (Japan, 2008; and L'Aquila Food Security Initiative [AFSI], 2009);

(4–6) Three G20 Conferences (Washington, 2008; London, 2009; and Pittsburgh, 2009);

(7) Global Agriculture and Food Security Program (GAFSP);

(8) Reform of the Committee on World Food Security (CFS), 2009;

(9) World Food Summit (Rome, 2009);

(10) Renewed Efforts against Child Hunger and Undernutrition (REACH), 2008;

(11) World Economic Forum's (WEF's) New Vision for Agriculture (NVA);

(12–13) Two sessions of the UN Commission on Sustainable Development (CSD) (New York, CSD-16, 2008, and CSD-17, 2009);

(14) Special Meeting of UN Economic and Social Council (ECOSOC) on Global Food Crisis (New York, 2008);

(15–16) Two FAO conferences (2008): a. High-Level Conference on "World Food Security: The Challenges of Climate Change and Bioenergy," and b. Thirty-fifth (Special) Session (Rome); and

(17) Madrid High-Level Meeting on Food Security for All (2009)

(B) 9 initiatives in 2010–14, involving the:

(1) Food Security Cluster (2010);

(2) Save Food (2011);

(3) Global Food Safety Partnership (GFSP) (2011);

(4) Agricultural Market Information System (AMIS) (2011);

(5) G20 Agriculture Ministers on Action Declaration entitled "Food Price Volatility and Agriculture" (Paris, 2011);

(6) Two G20 Presidencies (Cannes, 2011; Cabos, 2012) after the global food shortage and price spikes, with concerns that price instability was here to stay;

(7) AgResults (2012);

(8) Zero Hunger Challenge (2012); and

(9) Think.Eat.Save (2013).

(C) 4 initiatives in the 2015 and the post-2015 period, involving the:

(1–2) Two G20 Agriculture Ministers (China, 2016; Germany, 2017);

(3) United Nations Conference on Housing and Sustainable Urban Development (Habitat III) (Quito, Ecuador, 2016); and

(4) Milan Urban Food Policy Pact (2016).

(II) **6 initiatives related to global nutrition-related initiatives:**

(A) 3 initiatives in the 2010 to 2014 period, involving the:

(1) Scaling Up Nutrition Movement (SUN) (2010);

(2) Nutrition for Growth (N4G) Summit (London, 2013);

(3) Second International Conference on Nutrition (ICN2) (Rome, 2014).

(B) 3 initiatives in the 2015 and the post-2015 period, involving the:

(1) "Power of Nutrition" (2015), a new fund;

(2) Global Financing Facility (GFF) (2015) in support of "Every Woman Every Child"; and

(3) G7 Ise-Shima Leaders' Declaration (2015) restated as the *2015 Schloss Elmau G7 commitment* to "lift 500 million people in developing countries out of hunger and malnutrition by 2030."

(III) 7 environmental initiatives related to climate change, and to reducing deforestation and degradation:

(A) 2 initiatives in the immediate post-crisis period:

(1) Reducing Emissions from Deforestation and Forest Degradation (REDD) (2007); REDD+ (Reducing Emissions from Deforestation and Forest Degradation in Developing Countries) (2010); and

(2) The Green Economy Initiative (GEI) (2008).

(B) 3 initiatives in 2010–14:

(1) FAO coined the concept of Climate-Smart Agriculture (CSA) (Hague, 2010);

(2) CGIAR Research Program on Climate Change, Agriculture and Food Security (CCAFS) (2010); and

(3) The Global Alliance for Climate-Smart Agriculture (GACSA) (2014).

(C) 2 initiatives in the 2015 and the post-2015 period:

(1) UN Climate Change Conference (COP21)/The Paris Accord (2015); and

(2) UN Framework Convention on Climate Change (UNFCCC) COP22 (Bab Ighli, Marrakech, Morocco 2016).

(IV) 3 bilateral aid initiatives:

(A) 1 initiative in the immediate post-crisis period:

(1) The Millennium Challenge Corporation (MCC) and the UK Department for International Development (DFID) agreement (2008)

(B) 2 initiatives in 2010–14:

(1) Feed the Future (2010); and

(2) 1,000 Days (2010).

(V) 3 financial sector reforms and reform of the agricultural derivatives markets to curtail excessive speculation in the financial and commodity markets in the 2010–14 period:

(A) Basel III (2011);

(B) Dodd–Frank Wall Street Reform and Consumer Protection Act (2010); and

(C) Understanding and coping with food markets volatility towards more stable world and EU food systems (ULYSSES Project) (2013).

(VI) Global initiatives in the 2015 and the post 2015 period, include:

(A) Sustainable Development Goals (2015);

(B) Addis Ababa Action Agenda (2015);

(C) Paris Accord on Climate change in December 2015;

(D) World Humanitarian Summit (Istanbul 2016) brought some of these to culmination;

(E) More than 60 governments of developed and developing countries, committed to a record US$75 billion replenishment for the International Development Association

Continued

Box 5.4 Continued

(IDA18), for the poorest countries in 2016, and followed it up with US$82 billion IDA19 replenishment in 2019.

   Various regional and national initiatives, and numerous web-based initiatives on "how-to" in each of these areas have proliferated. They are too numerous to list, but are included as an illustration of the emergent tools of the digital revolution.

FAO (AMIS 2015), and zero hunger being etched into SDGs (UN 2020d; UN News 2012). (See a list of international initiatives since 2007 in Table A.5.1.) Nutrition came to the center stage on a global agenda through a concerted effort by the international nutrition community, via publications in *Lancet* (2008, 2011, 2013, 2015) and advocacy. In Africa, too, food and nutrition arrived at the center stage in Africa's Comprehensive Africa Agriculture Development Programme (CAADP) program with a commitment to invest 10 percent of government expenditures on agriculture (OSAA 2020).

   Since then, quite separately, IDA's capital was replenished by IDA donors in 2018 with a US$75 billion capital increase (IDA 2020b). This was followed by the capital increase of the World Bank Group, endorsed by its shareholders in April 2018, an ambitious package of measures that include a US$13 billion paid-in capital increase, a series of internal reforms, and a set of policy measures that could potentially strengthen the Bank Group's ability to scale up resources and deliver on its mission in areas of the world that need assistance the most (World Bank 2018).

   The package agreed to by the Development Committee of the Board of Governors consists of US$7.5 billion paid-in capital for the International Bank for Reconstruction and Development (IBRD) and US$5.5 billion paid-in capital for IFC, through both general and selective capital increases, as well as a US$52.6 billion callable capital increase for IBRD.

   Potentially, the capital available to the World Bank Group can greatly increase the overall investment of international institutions in food and agriculture both directly and indirectly, by leveraging private capital in a way that did not occur much through the various international initiatives beyond the 2007 food crisis, as discussed previously. The opportunities offered by the Bank group's capital increase are discussed in Chapter 6 on the governance of the five IOs. In the meantime, however, the President of the World Bank Group, Jim Yong Kim resigned, and he was replaced unanimously by David Malpass on April 9, 2019. Devesh Kapur (2019), notes a "growing clamor ... to eliminate the traditional arrangement in which the US picks the World Bank president and Europeans choose the managing director of the IMF." He further notes, "there was almost no opposition ... to Trump's selection of David Malpass to lead the World Bank, nor to Kristalina Georgieva's nomination to succeed Christine Lagarde at the IMF. This lack of pushback does not necessarily bode well for either institution. It signals resignation, foreshadowing the rise of other institutions."

Local Participation

Local participation is promoted to achieve a variety of goals, including better poverty targeting, improved service delivery, expansion of livelihood opportunities, and strengthening demand for good governance. In a quite different methodological approach to that pursued by Kaufmann, Kraay, and Mastruzzi (2011), Mansuri and Rao (2013) have explored the issues of decentralization and community participation, perhaps the most thoroughly over a number of years, basing their research on World Bank projects of CDD. By 2004, when they published their first paper, the World Bank had committed US $7 billion to community-based development (CBD) or CDD, or to social funds. In a systematic review of this early portfolio, they noted a dearth of well-designed evaluations of CDD projects (Mansuri and Rao 2004). The quantitative and qualitative evidence from studies published in peer-reviewed publications or conducted by independent researchers, however, showed that projects that rely on community participation have not been particularly effective at targeting the poor. Some CBD/CDD projects created effective community infrastructure, but not a single study established a causal relationship between any outcome and participatory elements of a CBD project. Most CBD projects are dominated by elites and, in general, the targeting of poor communities, as well as project quality, tend to be markedly worse in more unequal communities. A number of studies found a U-shaped relationship between inequality and project outcomes, highlighting a distinction between potentially "benevolent" forms of elite domination and the more pernicious types of "capture," important for understanding project dynamics and outcomes. Lele found a similar phenomenon in her study of *Cooperatives and the Poor* (Lele 1981). Whereas elite capture was pervasive, several examples could be found of a paternalistic approach to assisting the poor: for example, in Dr. Verghese Kurien's dairy development in India.

Mansuri and Rao (2013, 1) emphasized the need for a well-designed monitoring and evaluation systems, a question discussed later in Chapter 8 on the World Bank. Mansuri and Rao (2013), at a time when the World Bank had committed US$75 billion to community-based projects, noted the process was "still driven more by ideology and optimism than by systematic analysis, either theoretical or empirical" (Mansuri and Rao, 2013, 3). The researchers provided a theoretical framework of the factors underlying social failure.

Mansuri and Rao (2013) argued that whereas government and market failure are now widely recognized, there is less recognition of civil society failure at the local level, in which villages and municipal townships, drawing on a common, pooled resource, are unable to act collectively to reach feasible and preferable outcomes. Their findings help explain why the results of governance and performance, as presented here, suggest that East Asian countries perform better on economic growth and social indicators, as compared to SA countries. Voice and accountability is more present in SA, but government effectiveness is weaker. Lele observed a similar phenomenon in the case of performance in water management between China and India (GWP 2013).

Effective collective action is usually conditioned by a "cooperative infrastructure." It presupposes functional state institutions and is likely to be far more challenging in the absence of such institutions. Furthermore, while empowering civic groups may often lead to good outcomes, it is not clear that inducing civic empowerment is always superior to a pure market-based strategy, or a state-based strategy that strengthens the role of central bureaucrats. Participants in civic activities tend be wealthier, more educated, of higher social status (by class and ethnicity), male, and more politically connected than nonparticipants. Other World Bank projects have noted a similar phenomenon: for example, the projects in Andhra Pradesh (IEG 2008). This may reflect, to a degree, the higher opportunity cost of participation for the poor. However, it also appears that regardless of incentives to participate, the poor often benefit less from participatory processes absolutely, even though they may benefit more proportionately.

Democratic decentralization reduces the scope for capture, and community participation improves the quality of infrastructure. Much depends on the nature of electoral incentives, however, and the capacity of higher levels of government to provide oversight and to ensure downward accountability. Capacity also matters. As with participatory projects, more remote, more isolated, and less literate localities tend to do worse. Donors or NGOs alone cannot substitute for a nonfunctional state as a higher-level accountability agent. Induced participatory interventions work best when they are supported by a responsive state.

Appendix

Table A.5.1 International responses since the 2007 crisis

	Initiatives	Established/launched	Web link
	Food security-related initiatives		
1	UN Secretary-General's HLTF on the Global Food and Nutrition Security Crisis: 23 members, including UN specialized agencies, FAO, OECD, WFP, WHO, and the World Bank; leadership by UN Secretary-General and FAO Director General	April 2008, by UN's Chief Executive Board	http://www.un.org/en/issues/food/taskforce/
2	Zero Hunger Challenge: Led by UN Secretary-General Ban Ki-Moon and supported by UN System participants, non-UN participants, and UN departmental participants, including WHO, WTO, World Bank, DPI (Investment Centre Division, FAO), UN Department of Economic and Social Affairs (DESA), and Think.Eat.Save and supported by FAO, IFAD, WFP, UNICEF, the World Bank, and Bioversity International.	Announced by UN Secretary-General Ban Ki-Moon at Rio+20 on June 21, 2012	https://www.un.org/zerohunger/
3	16th session of the Commission on Sustainable Development (CSD–16)	3rd Implementation Cycle, May 5–16, 2008, New York	https://sustainabledevelopment.un.org/intergovernmental/csd16
4	17th session of the Commission on Sustainable Development (CSD–17)	3rd Implementation Cycle, May 4–15, 2009, New York	https://sustainabledevelopment.un.org/intergovernmental/csd17
5	Special Meeting of ECOSOC on Global Food Crisis	May 20–2, 2008, at UN, New York;	https://www.un.org/ecosoc/en/events/2008/global-food-crisis-2008
6	High Level Conference on World Food Security: The Challenges of Climate Change and Bioenergy	June 3–5, 2008, Rome	http://www.fao.org/foodclimate/conference/en/
7	Thirty-fifth (Special) Session, FAO Conference	November 18–21, 2008, Rome	http://www.fao.org/unfao/bodies/conf/c2008/Index_en.HTM

8	Madrid High Level Meeting on Food Security for All	January 6–27, 2009, Madrid	http://sdg.iisd.org/news/madrid-high-level-meeting-on-food-security-for-all-calls-for-exploring-options-for-a-global-partnership-for-agriculture-and-food-security/
9	G8 Summit, Japan	June 25–7, 2008, Hokkaido Toyako	http://japan.kantei.go.jp/summit/index_e.html
10	G8 Summit, L'Aquila Food Security Initiative (AFSI), Italy: US$22 billion pledged over 3 years. Endorsed by leaders of 26 countries and 15 organizations, including the HLTF, CFS, FAO, WFP, World Bank, and CGIAR.	July 8–10, 2009	http://iif.un.org/content/laquila-food-security-initiative
11	GAFSP: Supervised by the World Bank and resource allocation managed by an external Steering Committee. Works in partnership with AfDB, ADB, FAO, Inter-American Development Bank, IFAD, World Bank, and WFP. Allocated approximately US $1.4 billion to 30 LICs since its establishment in 2010.	September 2009, emerged as a multilateral mechanism to assist in the implementation of pledges made by G20 in Pittsburgh	http://www.gafspfund.org/
12	Reform of the CFS: Advisory group—FAO, WFP, IFAD, BMGF, HLTF, HLPE, and other private, research, philanthropic, and financial institutions.	October 2009, High Level Panel of Experts on Food Security and Security (HLPE), created as essential part of CFS	http://www.fao.org/cfs/en/
13	The World Food Summit: "Five Rome Principles for Sustainable Global Food Security" adopted	November 16–18, 2009	http://www.fao.org/wsfs/wsfs-list-documents/en/
14	REACH: established by FAO, UNICEF, WFP, and WHO to assist governments of countries with a high burden of child and maternal undernutrition, to accelerate the scale-up of food and nutrition actions. IFAD later joined REACH, extending an advisory role at the global level.	2008, with memorandum of understanding signed between the four leads in 2011	http://www.reachpartnership.org/
15	WEF's New Vision for Agriculture: Led by a Project Board selected from the World Economic Forum's Consumer Industries' Community; Advisory support from WEF's Global Agenda Council on Food Security, as well as high-level leaders of industry, government, institutions, and civil society	2009	https://www.weforum.org/projects/new-vision-for-agriculture
16	G20 conferences in Washington	November 14–15, 2008	http://www.g20.utoronto.ca/summits/2008washington.html

Continued

Table A.5.1 *Continued*

	Initiatives	Established/launched	Web link
17	G20 conferences in London	April 1–2, 2009	http://www.g20.utoronto.ca/summits/2009london.html
18	G20 conferences in Pittsburgh	September 24–5, 2009	http://www.g20.utoronto.ca/summits/2009pittsburgh.html
19	Interagency Report to the French (Cannes) G20 Presidency	2011	http://www.foodsecurityportal.org/sites/default/files/g20_interagency_report_food_price_volatility.pdf
20	Interagency Report to the Mexican (Cabos) G20 Presidency	2012	http://documents.worldbank.org/curated/en/788091468171845538/pdf/705060WP0P10650p0Small0Family0Farms.pdf
21	G20 Agriculture Ministers, France: Action Declaration entitled "Food Price Volatility and Agriculture"	June 22–3, 2011, Paris	http://www.g20.utoronto.ca/2011/2011-agriculture-plan-en.pdf
22	G20 Agriculture Ministers, China: discussed how G20 members can promote food security, nutrition, sustainable agricultural growth, and rural development worldwide and contribute to building an innovative, invigorated, interconnected, and inclusive world economy to fully achieve the 2030 Agenda for Sustainable Development, including eradicating hunger and extreme poverty	June 2016, Xi'an	http://www.g20.utoronto.ca/2016/160603-agriculture.html
23	G20 Agriculture Ministers, Germany: Action Declaration entitled "Towards Food and Water Security: Fostering Sustainability, Advancing Innovation"	January 22, 2017, Berlin	http://www.g20.utoronto.ca/2017/170122-agriculture-en.html
24	Agricultural Market Information System (AMIS): G20 initiative emerged out of the food crisis	June 2011	http://www.amis-outlook.org/
25	AgResults: A multi-donor, multilateral initiative incentivizing and rewarding high-impact agricultural innovations that promote global food security, health, and nutrition through the design and implementation of pull mechanism pilots. The governments of Australia, Canada, the United Kingdom, and the United States, in partnership with BMGF pledged US$118 million to establish AgResults through a Financial Intermediary Fund operated by the World Bank	Formerly known as the "Agriculture Pull Mechanism Initiative," mandate for this work originated at the June 2010 G20 Summit in Toronto. Renamed as AgResults, initiative, officially launched at the G20 Summit in Los Cabos, Mexico, June 18, 2012.	http://agresults.org/

Environmental initiatives

26	Reducing Emissions from Deforestation and Forest Degradation (REDD) and REDD+	REDD was formalized as an idea at 13th Session of the Conference of the Parties (COP13) to UNFCCC in Bali, 2007, and in 2010, at COP16, as set out in the Cancun Agreements, REDD became REDD+	https://www.un-redd.org
27	UNEP Green Economy Initiative (GEI)	October 2008	http://www.unsystem.org/content/green-economy-initiative-gei
28	CGIAR Research Program on Climate Change, Agriculture and Food Security (CCAFS): CGIAR Alliance Centers (Lead: International Center for Tropical Agriculture [CIAT]) and the Earth System Science Partnership (ESSP). Budget proposal US$63.2 million in 2011 (US$41.4 million from CGIAR Fund). Partnerships include government, civil society, and private sector, such as FAO, Forum for Agricultural Research in Africa (FARA), and WFP. Funded by CGIAR Fund, Canadian International Development Agency (CIDA), Danish International Development Agency (DANIDA), the EU and IFAD.	Officially launched during the UN climate negotiations at COP16 in Cancun, Mexico, on December 4, 2010, and scheduled to run through 2020	https://ccafs.cgiar.org/
29	The Global Alliance for Climate-Smart Agriculture (GACSA)	Launched in 2014 (September) at the UN Climate Summit	http://www.fao.org/gacsa/en/

International nutrition initiatives

30	Scaling Up Nutrition Movement (SUN): appointed by the UN Secretary-General in April 2012, the SUN Lead Group comprises 27 members from government, civil society, international organizations, donor agencies, business, and foundations. Current members include the executive director of UNICEF, the Chair of the Board of Directors, and the Partnership Council.	September 2010	http://scalingupnutrition.org/
31	Food Security Cluster (FSC): Based at WFP in Rome and co-led by FAO and WFP. The Global Support Team includes FAO, WFP, international NGOs, Red Cross, and Red Crescent members. Funding by Civil Protection and Humanitarian Aid Operations of the European Commission	The FSC was formally endorsed by the Inter-Agency Standing Committee (IASC) on December 15, 2010. Officially constituted in August 2011.	https://fscluster.org

Continued

Table A.5.1 *Continued*

Initiatives	Established/launched	Web link
(ECHO), the Protection Standby Capacity Project (ProCap), the Gender Capacity Project (GenCap), UKAid, Ministry of Foreign Affairs of Finland, and other donors.		
32 Save Food: Introduced by partners Messe Düsseldorf and FAO	January 27, 2011, Berlin	https://www.save-food.org
33 Global Food Safety Partnership (GFSP): World Bank is facilitating the establishment of a multi-stakeholder GFSP to build capacity in emerging and development markets, via an open community of practice and online knowledge-sharing platform. The GFSP builds on earlier efforts within the Asia–Pacific Economic Cooperation (APEC) forum and other organizations.	November 2011	http://fscf-ptin.apec.org/docs/final%20Global%20FS%20Partnership%20Brief%203%2029%202012.pdf
34 Think.Eat.Save: A partnership between the UNEP, FAO, and Messe Düsseldorf to eliminate food waste by promoting action and a global vision, through an online knowledge portal, highlighting initiatives, technical resources, and encouraging public commitments. This effort supports the UN Secretary-General's Zero Hunger Challenge.	January 2013	http://thinkeatsave.org/
35 Nutrition for Growth (N4G) Summit was endorsed by 90 stakeholders, including development partners, businesses, scientific, and civil society groups, to beat hunger and improve nutrition, with a US$4.15 billion financial commitment.	June 8, 2013, London	http://scalingupnutrition.org/news/an-historic-moment-for-nutrition-nutrition-for-growth-summit-in-london/
36 The Second International Conference on Nutrition (ICN2): UN endorsement of "Framework for Action" and launching of UN Decade of Action on Nutrition (2016–25) and first *Global Nutrition Report* (*GNR*). **Financial sector reforms and reform of the agricultural derivatives markets**	November 19–21, 2014	http://www.fao.org/about/meetings/icn2/en/
37 Basel III	June 2011	http://www.bis.org/bcbs/basel3.htm
38 The Dodd–Frank Wall Street Reform and Consumer Protection Act	July 21, 2010	https://www.gpo.gov/fdsys/pkg/PLAW-111publ203/pdf/PLAW-111publ203.pdf

39	Understanding and coping with food markets volatility towards more Stable World and EU food Systems (ULYSSES Project)	2013	https://cordis.europa.eu/project/id/312182/it
	Recent global initiatives (2015–present day)		
40	Power of Nutrition: A new fund, aims to unlock US$1 billion to help millions of children get proper nutrition and reach their full potential. The independent fund is supported by Children's Investment Fund Foundation, UBS Optimus Foundation, the UK's DFID, UNICEF, and the World Bank Group, and is open to private and public investors.	April, 2015	http://www.powerofnutrition.org/
41	Global Financing Facility (GFF) in support of "Every Woman Every Child": UN, WBG, and governments of Canada, Norway, and the United States joined country and global health leaders to launch it, announced US$12 billion.	Formally launched at the Financing for Development conference in Addis Ababa, Ethiopia, July 13–16, 2015.	https://www.globalfinancingfacility.org/
42	Sustainable Development Goals (SDGs)	September 25, 2015	http://www.un.org/sustainabledevelopment/
43	Paris Agreement on Climate Change (COP21)	November 30–December 12, 2015	http://unfccc.int/paris_agreement/items/9485.php
44	Addis Ababa Action Agenda	July 13–16, 2015, Ethiopia	http://www.un.org/esa/ffd/ffd3/press-release/countries-reach-historic-agreement.html
45	World Humanitarian Summit: Summit generated more than 3,000 commitments to action, launched more than a dozen new partnerships and initiatives to turn the Agenda for Humanity into meaningful change for the world's most vulnerable people.	May 23–4, 2016, Istanbul	https://www.agendaforhumanity.org/summit
46	UN Conference on Housing and Sustainable Urban Development (Habitat III)	October 17–20, 2016, Quito, Ecuador	https://sustainabledevelopment.un.org/?page=view&nr=1411&type=13&menu=1634
47	UNFCCC COP22, Marrakech Climate Change Conference	November 7–18, 2016, Bab Ighli, Marrakech, Morocco	https://unfccc.int/process-and-meetings/conferences/past-conferences/marrakech-climate-change-conference-november-2016/cop-22
48	G7 Ise-Shima Leaders' Declaration: The Leaders' Declaration highlighted important role that hunger and malnutrition play within the Global Goals for Sustainable Development and explicitly restated the 2015 Schloss Elmau G7 commitment to "lift 500	May 26–7, 2016	https://www.mofa.go.jp/files/000160266.pdf

Continued

Table A.5.1 *Continued*

	Initiatives	Established/launched	Web link
	million people in developing countries out of hunger and malnutrition by 2030."		
49	IDA18 Replenishment Meeting: More than 60 governments of developed and developing countries, committed to a record US$75 billion replenishment for IDA18 for the poorest countries **Regional initiatives** *Latin America and Caribbean*	December 14–15, 2016, Yogyakarta, Indonesia	http://ida.worldbank.org/financing/replenishments/ida18-replenishment
50	Hunger-Free Latin America and the Caribbean (HFLAC): Secretariat based at FAO and supported by all countries in the region. Funded by AECID (Spanish Agency for International Development Cooperation) *Asia*	First launched in 2005 by Brazil and Guatemala, later endorsed by all countries in the region in December 2008	http://www.fao.org/americas/prioridades/alc-sin-hambre/en/
51	Asia-Pacific Economic Cooperation) (APEC Food Safety Cooperation Forum: co-chaired by Australia (Food Standards Australia New Zealand) and China (General Administration of Quality Supervision, Inspection and Quarantine of the People's Republic of China).	Formally established under the APEC Sub-Committee for Standards and Conformance in the Hunter Valley, Australia, April 2007	http://www.foodstandards.gov.au/science/international/apec/pages/default.aspx
52	Association of Southeast Asian Nations (ASEAN) Integrated Food Security Framework (AIFS) and Strategic Plan of Action for Food Security (SPA–FS): ASEAN Secretariat and ASEAN Ministers on Agriculture and Forestry, potential donor support from FAO, World Bank, the International Rice Research Institute (IRRI), IFAD, and Asian Development Bank (ADB). Support also provided by ASEAN Development Fund and ASEAN Foundation.	ASEAN Summit 2009	https://www.asean-agrifood.org/?wpfb_dl=58
53	Cereal Systems Initiative for South Asia (CSISA): Led by the International Maize and Wheat Improvement Center (CIMMYT) and implemented jointly with the International Food Policy Research Institute (IFPRI) and IRRI and funded by BMGF and USAID.	2009	http://csisa.org/
54	South Asia Food and Nutrition Security Initiative (SAFANSI) established as a multi-donor trust fund by a joint undertaking of the World Bank, DFID, and AusAID *Middle East*	It was conceived in 2008 and formally commenced in 2010	http://www.worldbank.org/en/programs/safansi

55	The King Abdullah Initiative for Saudi Agricultural Investment Abroad: joint initiative by the Government of the Kingdom of Saudi Arabia and the Saudi private sector. Saudi private sector is the main investor with 3 billion Saudi Riyals (around US$800m).	January 2009	http://www.isdb.org/irj/go/km/docs/documents/IDBDevelopments/Internet/English/IDB/CM/Publications/IDB_AnnualSymposium/20thSymposium/8-AbdullaAlobaid.pdf
	Oceania		
56	Food Security through Rural Development (AUSAID): partnership led by AusAID works with Australian agricultural research organizations, governments, and civil society, and CGIAR. A US$464 million global food security initiative to assist countries in Asia, Pacific, and Africa.	May 12, 2009	http://reliefweb.int/sites/reliefweb.int/files/resources/34BAB0236CDC58B549257\651000E10D5-Full_Report.pdf
	European Union		
57	€1 billion EUFF: the European Parliament and the Council adopted a Regulation establishing the €1 billion "Food Facility," which constitutes the main EU response to the worsening global food security situation in 2007–8. Funding channeled through FAO, the United Nations Relief and Works Agency for Palestine Refugees in the Near East (UNRWA), UNICEF, IFAD, UNDP, the World Bank, and other country-specific UN agencies.	December 18, 2008	http://www.eubusiness.com/topics/food/food-facility.01/
58	EU Joint Programming Initiative on Agriculture, Food Security and Climate Change (FACCE–JPI): FACCE–JPI brings together 22 countries committed to building an integrated European Research Area addressing interconnected challenges of sustainable agriculture, food security, and impacts of climate change	Permanent governance was adopted at the Governing Board meeting, in Paris, February 9, 2012	https://www.faccejpi.com/
	Africa		
59	Grow Africa: Partnership was founded jointly by the African Union (AU), New Partnership for Africa's Development (NEPAD), and WEF	2011	https://www.growafrica.com/
60	Feed Africa: Strategy for Agricultural Transformation in Africa (2016–25) by African Development Bank Group (AfDB)	May 2016	https://www.afdb.org/en/news-and-events/feed-africa-afdb-develops-strategy-for-africas-agricultural-transformation-15875/

Continued

Table A.5.1 *Continued*

	Initiatives	Established/launched	Web link
61	The 6th Annual African Green Revolution Forum, Kenya: Pledged more than US$30 billion in investments to increase production, income, and employment for smallholder farmers and local African agriculture businesses over the next 10 years **Bilateral aid initiatives**	September 5–9, 2016, Nairobi	https://agrf.org/agrf2016/
62	The Millennium Challenge Corporation (MCC) and the UK's DFID signed a first-of-its-kind Memorandum of Understanding between the two organizations to increase coordination and make their poverty reduction efforts more effective in Africa and throughout the world	February 19, 2008	https://www.mcc.gov/news-and-events/release/release-021908-dfidmou
63	Feed the Future: US Government's initiative	May 2010	https://www.feedthefuture.gov
64	1,000 Days: Launched by US Secretary of State Hillary Clinton, then Irish Minister for Foreign Affairs Micheál Martin, and a community of global leaders	September 2010	http://thousanddays.org/

National-level initiatives (along with global and regional policy developments, individual countries initiated significant FSN policy changes in 2016)

France enacted anti-food waste actions and passed a law requiring supermarkets to donate unsold food.

China announced investments in agriculture of about US$450 billion to increase farm productivity and improve rural incomes, and outlined plans to reduce its citizens' meat consumption by 50 percent by 2030.

Malawi launched a new National Agricultural Policy to improve incomes, food security, and nutrition.

The Philippines finalized long-term development plans that include efforts to reduce poverty and to reach self-sufficiency in rice—the latter, a policy with potential drawbacks.

India continued to expand implementation of its 2013 National Food Security Act, aiming to allocate subsidized food grains to 800 million people across India's 36 states.

Web-based initiatives

Global Forum on Food Security and Nutrition (FSN Forum)	October 2007	http://www.fao.org/fsnforum/home
Agriculture–Nutrition Community of Practice (Ag2Nut CoP)	June 2010	https://www.unscn.org/en/forums/discussion-groups/ag2nut
Food Security Information Network (FSIN)	October 2012	http://www.fsincop.net/home/en/
National Information Platforms for Nutrition (NIPN)	2015	http://www.nipn-nutrition-platforms.org/

Source: Authors' construction.

References

Acemoglu, Daron, and James A. Robinson. 2012. *Why Nations Fail: The Origins of Power, Prosperity, and Poverty*. New York: Crown Publishers.

ADB (Asian Development Bank). 2013. *Asian Development Outlook 2013 Update: Governance and Public Service Delivery*. Mandaluyong City, Philippines: Asian Development Bank.

Agarwal, Manmohan. 2015. "South–South Economic Cooperation: Its Progress." In *World Scientific Reference on Asia and the World Economy*, Vol 1. *Sustainability of Growth: The Role of Economic, Technological and Environmental Factors*, edited by John Whalley and Manmohan Agarwal, 81–108. Singapore: World Scientific Publishing.

Ahluwalia, Montek Singh, Lawrence Summers, Andrés Velasco (co-chairs); Nancy Birdsall, and Scott Morris (co-directors). 2016. "Multilateral Development Banking for this Century's Development Challenges: Five Recommendations to Shareholders of the Old and New Multilateral Development Banks." Center for Global Development, Washington, DC.

Amadeo, Kimberly. 2019. "Dodd-Frank Wall Street Reform Act: 8 Ways a Repeal Hurts You." The Balance, August 21. https://www.thebalance.com/dodd-frank-wall-street-reform-act-3305688

Amadeo, Kimberly. 2020a. "Glass Steagall Act of 1933: Its Purpose and Repeal: This 1933 Law Would Have Prevented the Financial Crisis." The Balance, updated April 24. https://www.thebalance.com/glass-steagall-act-definition-purpose-and-repeal-3305850

Amadeo, Kimberly. 2020b. "Stock Market Crash of 1929: Facts, Causes, and Impact: The That Launched the Great Depression." US Economy, The Balance, updated April 28. https://www.thebalance.com/stock-market-crash-of-1929-causes-effects-and-facts-3305891

Amadeo, Kimberly. 2020c. "2008 Financial Crisis: Causes, Costs, and Whether It Could Happen Again." The Balance, updated May 7. https://www.thebalance.com/2008-financial-crisis-3305679

AMIS. 2015. Agricultural Market Information System. http://www.amis-outlook.org

Arndt, Christiane, and Charles Oman. 2006. *Uses and Abuses of Governance Indicators*. Paris: Organisation for Economic Co-operation and Development (OECD).

Bardhan, Pranab K., and Dilip Mookherjee. 2007. *Decentralization and Local Governance in Developing Countries: A Comparative Perspective*. New Delhi and New York: Oxford University Press.

Bartels, Lorand. 2016a. "Understanding the UK's Position in the WTO after Brexit (Part I—The UK's Status and Its Schedules)." International Centre for Trade and Sustainable Development (ICTSD), Opinion, September 26. http://www.ictsd.org/opinion/understanding-the-uk

Bartels, Lorand. 2016b. "Understanding the UK's Position in the WTO after Brexit (Part II—The Consequences)." International Centre for Trade and Sustainable Development (ICSTD), Opinion, September 26. http://www.ictsd.org/opinion/understanding-the-uk-0

Beigbeder, Yves. 1979. "The United States' Withdrawal from the International Labor Organization." *Relations industrielles/Industrial Relations* 34 (2): 223–40. https://www.riir.ulaval.ca/sites/riir.ulaval.ca/files/1979_34-2_1.pdf

Berger, Sarah. 2019. "Jeff Bezos Gave Away More Money than Bill Gates, Mark Zuckerberg Combined in 2018." CNBC.com, February 13. https://www.cnbc.com/2019/02/13/philanthropy-50-how-much-bezos-gates-zuckerberg-charities-gave-away.html

Besley, Timothy, Rohini Pande, Lupin Rahman, and Vijayendra Rao. 2004. "The Politics of Public Good Provision: Evidence from Indian Local Governments." *Journal of the European Economics Association* 2 (2–3): 416–26.

Besley, Timothy, Rohini Pande, and Vijayendra Rao. 2005. "Participatory Democracy in Action: Survey Evidence from Rural India." *Journal of the European Economic Association* 3 (2–3): 648–57.

Birdsall, Nancy, Christian Meyer, and Alexis Sowa. 2013. "Global Markets, Global Citizens, and Global Governance in the 21st Century." CGD Working Paper No. 329, Center for Global Development, Washington, DC.

Birner, Regina, and Jock R. Anderson. 2015. "Strengthening Agricultural Governance in an Interconnected World." 2015 IAAE Conference, International Association of Agricultural Economists, Milan, August 9–14.

BMGF (Bill and Melinda Gates Foundation). 2020. "Who We Are: Foundation Trust." https://www.gatesfoundation.org/Who-We-Are/General-Information/Financials/Foundation-Trust

Boughton, James M. 2012. "After the Fall: Building Nations out of the Soviet Union." In *Tearing Down Walls: The International Monetary Fund 1990–1999*, 349–408. Washington, DC: International Monetary Fund.

Bovaird, Tony, and Elke Löffler. 2003. "Evaluating the Quality of Public Governance: Indicators, Models and Methodologies." *International Review of Administrative Sciences* 69 (3): 313–28.

Buchanan, James, and William C. Stubblebine. 1962. "Externality." *Economica* 29 (116): 371–84.

CFS (Committee on World Food Security). 2017. "Evaluation of the Committee on World Food Security." Final Report, CFS, Rome. http://www.fao.org/fileadmin/templates/cfs/Docs1617/Evaluation/CFS_Evaluation_Final_Report__14_April_2017.pdf

CGIAR. 2017. "2016 CGIAR Financial Report." July 2017, CGIAR System Management Office, Montpellier, France. https://cgspace.cgiar.org/bitstream/handle/10947/4666/2016-CGIAR-Financial-Report.pdf

Christensen, Clayton. 1997. *The Innovator's Dilemma: When New Technologies Cause Great Firms to Fail*. Boston: Harvard Business School Press.

Dasgupta, Partha, and Karl-Göran Mäler. 1997. *The Environment and Emerging Development Issues*. New York: Oxford University Press.

Deaton, Angus, and Jean Drèze. 2009. "Food and Nutrition in India: Facts and Interpretations." *Economic and Political Weekly* 44 (7): 42–65.

Development Committee (Joint Ministerial Committee of the Boards of Governors of the Bank and the Fund on the Transfer of Real Resources to Developing Countries). 2015. "From Billions to Trillions: Transforming Development Finance Post-2015 Financing for Development: Multilateral Development Finance." Development Committee Discussion Note. Prepared jointly by African Development Bank, Asian Development Bank, European Bank for Reconstruction and Development, European Investment Bank, Inter-American Development Bank, International Monetary Fund, and World Bank Group, April 18.

DowDuPont. 2017. "DowDuPont™ Merger Successfully Completed." Press Release, September 1. http://www.dow-dupont.com/news-and-media/press-release-details/2017/DowDuPont-Merger-Successfully-Completed/default.aspx

Dubbudu, Rakesh. 2016. "How Much Do Various Countries Contribute to the UN Budget?" December 13, FACTLY, India. https://factly.in/united-nations-budget-contributions-by-member-countries/

Economist, The. 2015. "The 169 Commandments. The Proposed Sustainable Development Goals Would Be Worse than Useless." *The Economist*, Development, March 26. https://www.economist.com/news/leaders/21647286-proposed-sustainable-development-goals-would-be-worse-useless-169-commandments

Elliott, Kimberly, and Casey Dunning. 2016. "Assessing the US Feed the Future Initiative: A New Approach to Food Security?" CGD Policy Paper 075, March, Center for Global Development, Washington, DC.

European Parliament. 2016. "Speech of the President of the European Parliament, Martin Schulz at the European Council of 15 December 2016." European Parliament, Strasbourg. http://www.europarl.europa.eu/former_ep_presidents/president-schulz-2014–2016/en/pressroom/speech_of_the_president_of_the_european_parliament__martin_schulz_at_the_european_council_of_15_d

FAO (Food and Agriculture Organization of the United Nations). 2020. "Strategic Planning." About FAO. http://www.fao.org/about/strategic-planning/en/

Feed the Future. 2020. "A Strategy to End Hunger." The U.S. Government's Global Hunger and Food Security Initiative. https://www.feedthefuture.gov

Friedman, Lisa. 2017. "U.S. to Join Climate Talks Despite Planned Withdrawal from Paris Accord." *New York Times*, August 4. https://www.nytimes.com/2017/08/04/climate/us-to-join-climate-talks-despite-planned-withdrawal-from-paris-accord.html?mcubz=0

Furusawa, Mitsuhiro. 2017. "Opening Remarks at the 2017 IMF–JICA Conference." International Monetary Fund and Japanese International Cooperation Agency, Tokyo, February 2. https://www.imf.org/en/News/Articles/2017/02/01/SP02022017-Developing-Asia-and-the-Pacific-Fiscal-Risks

G20 (Group of 20). 2017. "Shaping an Interconnected World." G20 Summit, Hamburg. https://www.g20.org/Webs/G20/EN/Home/home_node.html

Gabaix, Xavier. 2016. "Power Laws in Economics: An Introduction." *Journal of Economic Perspectives* 30 (1): 185–206.

GAFSP (Global Agriculture and Food Security Program). 2018. GAFSP Fund. https://www.gafspfund.org

Gladstone, Rick. 2017. "U.N. Says Trump Budget Cuts Would 'Make It Impossible' to Do Its Job." *New York Times*, May 24.

GPF (Global Policy Forum). 2020. "Member States' Assessed Share of the UN Budget." UN Finance. https://www.globalpolicy.org/un-finance/tables-and-charts-on-un-finance/member-states-assessed-share-of-the-un-budget.html

GWP (Global Water Partnership). 2013. "Water and Food Security—Experiences in India and China." Technical Focus Paper, GWP, Stockholm. https://www.gwp.org/globalassets/global/toolbox/publications/technical-focus-papers/03-water-and-food-security—experiences-in-india-and-china-2013.pdf

Haddad, Lawrence. 2017. "The Geography of Malnutrition: Seemingly Worlds Apart (But Not Really)." Development Horizons blog, July 14. http://www.developmenthorizons.com/2017/07/the-geography-of-malnutrition-seemingly.html

Harvey, John. 2011. "Defining 'Global Philanthropy.'" *Alliance*, August 4. http://www.alliancemagazine.org/blog/defining-global-philanthropy/

Hawkins, Sonja. 2016. "Carbon Market Clubs under the Paris Climate Regime: Climate and Trade Policy Considerations." Climate Clubs, International Centre for Trade and Sustainable Development (ICTSD), Geneva, October 20.

Hirschman, Albert O. 1970. *Exit, Voice, and Loyalty: Responses to Decline in Firms, Organizations, and States.* Cambridge, MA: Harvard University Press.

ICTSD (International Centre for Trade and Sustainable Development). 2016. "US Announces US$300 Million in Payments for Cotton Producers." *Bridges* 20 (22): 17–18. https://www.ictsd.org/bridges-news/bridges/news/us-announces-us300-million-in-payments-for-cotton-producers

ICTSD (International Centre for Trade and Sustainable Development). 2017a. "TPP Signatories Consider Next Steps Following US Withdrawal." *Bridges* 21 (4): 12–13. https://www.ictsd.org/bridges-news/bridges/news/tpp-signatories-consider-next-steps-following-us-withdrawal

ICTSD (International Centre for Trade and Sustainable Development). 2017b. "US Reports Major Shift in Farm Subsidy Focus under 2014 Farm Bill." *Bridges* 21 (2): 7–9. https://www.ictsd.org/bridges-news/bridges/news/us-reports-major-shift-in-farm-subsidy-focus-under-2014-farm-bill

IDA (International Development Association). 2007. "The Role of IDA in the Global Aid Architecture: Supporting the Country-Based Development Model." Resource Mobilization Department, IDA, Washington, DC.

IDA (International Development Association). 2020a. "IDA19: Ten Years to 2030: Growth, People, Resilience." Additions to IDA Resources: Nineteenth Replenishment. Report from the Executive Directors of the International Development Association to the Board of Governors, February 11. http://documents1.worldbank.org/curated/en/459531582153485508/pdf/Additions-to-IDA-Resources-Nineteenth-Replenishment-Ten-Years-to-2030-Growth-People-Resilience.pdf

IDA (International Development Association). 2020b. Replenishments. IDA, World Bank Group. http://ida.worldbank.org/replenishments

IEG (Independent Evaluation Group). 2007a. "Strengthening World Bank Group Engagement of Governance and Anticorruption." IEG, World Bank Group, Washington, DC.

IEG (Independent Evaluation Group). 2007b. "Implementation Plan for Strengthening World Bank Group Engagement of Governance and Anticorruption." IEG, World Bank Group, Washington, DC.

IFAD (International Fund for Agriculture). 2017. "Annual Report 2016." IFAD, Rome. https://www.ifad.org/documents/38714170/39309732/AR2016.pdf/1f1a0e1e-6ebb-4480-a321-1da169f46198

IEG (Independent Evaluation Group). 2008. "An Impact Evaluation of India's Second and Third Andhra Pradesh Irrigation Projects: A Case of Poverty Reduction with Low Economic Returns." World Bank, Washington, DC. http://documents.worldbank.org/curated/en/440661468255272083/pdf/454060PUB0Box31UBLIC01June024102008.pdf

IEG (Independent Evaluation Group). 2009a. "Governance and Anticorruption in Lending Operations: A Benchmarking and Learning Review." Quality Assurance Group, World Bank, Washington, DC.

IEG (Independent Evaluation Group). 2009b. "Group of External Advisors for GAC Implementation: 2009 Report on the World Bank's Implementation of the Governance and Anticorruption Strategy." IEG, the World Bank Group, Washington, DC.

IEG (Independent Evaluation Group). 2009c. "Strengthening World Bank Group Engagement on Governance and Anticorruption: Second-Year Progress Report." IEG, the World Bank Group, Washington, DC.

IEG (Independent Evaluation Group). 2011. "World Bank Country-Level Engagement on Governance and Anticorruption: An Evaluation of the 2007 Strategy and Implementation

Plan." IEG, World Bank Group, Washington, DC. http://documents1.worldbank.org/cur ated/en/250021468169466128/pdf/794890PUB0WBCo00Box377372B00PUBLIC0.pdf

IFAD (International Fund for Agricultural Development). 2017. "Annual Report 2016." IFAD, Rome. https://www.ifad.org/documents/38714170/39309732/AR2016.pdf/1f1a0e1e-6ebb-4480-a321-1da169f46198

IIF (Integrated Implementation Framework). 2009. "L'Aquila Food Security Initiative." United Nations. http://iif.un.org/content/laquila-food-security-initiative

Kapur, Devesh. 2019. "What Next for the Bretton Woods Twins?" Project Syndicate, October 18. https://www.project-syndicate.org/onpoint/what-next-for-the-bretton-woods-twins-by-devesh-kapur-2019-10

Kaufmann, Daniel, Aart Kraay, and Massimo Mastruzzi. 2007. "The Worldwide Governance Indicators Project: Answering the Critics." Policy Research Working Paper, World Bank, Washington, DC.

Kaufmann, Daniel, Aart Kraay, and Massimo Mastruzzi. 2011. "The Worldwide Governance Indicators: Methodology and Analytical Issues." *Hague Journal of the Rule of Law* 3 (2): 220–46.

Kaul, Inge, Pedro Conceição, Katell Le Goulven, and Ronald U. Mendoza, eds. 2003. *Providing Global Public Goods: Managing Globalization*. United Nations Development Programme. New York: Oxford University Press.

KFF (Kaiser Family Foundation). 2016. "Terrorism, Human Rights, and Climate Change Top the Public's Priority List for U.S. Engagement in World Affairs; Other Issues, Including Health, Rated Important." KFF Newsroom, April 21. http://www.kff.org/global-health-pol icy/press-release/terrorism-human-rights-and-climate-change-top-the-publics-priority-list-for-u-s-engagement-in-world-affairs-other-issues-including-health-rated-important/

King, Julian, and Mariya Gabriel. 2019. "Facebook and Twitter Told Us They Would Tackle 'Fake News'. They Failed." *The Guardian*, February 28. https://www.theguardian.com/com mentisfree/2019/feb/28/facebook-twitter-fake-news-eu-elections

Klein, Aaron. 2018. "No, Dodd-Frank Was Neither Repealed nor Gutted. Here's What Really Happened." Series on Financial Markets and Regulation. Brookings, May 25. https://www. brookings.edu/research/no-dodd-frank-was-neither-repealed-or-gutted-heres-what-really-happened/

Knack, Steven. 2006. "Measuring Corruption in Eastern Europe and Central Asia: A Critique of the Cross-Country Indicators." Policy Research Department Working Paper 3968, World Bank, Washington, DC.

Kotechi, Peter. 2018a. "The Billionaire 'Giving Pledge' Signed by Bill Gates and Elon Musk Could Soon Be Worth up to $600 Billion." *Business Insider*, July 18. https://www. businessinsider.com/bill-gates-elon-musk-giving-pledge-may-reach-600-billion-2018-7

Kotechi, Peter. 2018b. "Jeff Bezos is the Richest Man in Modern History—Here's How He Spends on Philanthropy." *Business Insider*, September 13. https://www.businessinsider.com/ jeff-bezos-richest-person-modern-history-spends-on-charity-2018-7

Kurtz, Marcus J., and Andrew Schrank. 2007. "Growth and Governance: A Defense." *Journal of Politics* 69 (2): 563–9.

Lamy, Pascal. 2012. "Global Governance: From Theory to Practice." In *Multilevel Governance of Interdependent Public Goods: Theories, Rules and Institutions for the Central Policy Challenge in the 21st Century*, edited by Ernst-Ulrich Petersmann, 25–30. EUI Working Papers RSCAS

2012/23, Robert Schuman Centre for Advanced Studies, Global Governance Programme-18, European University Institute, Florence.

Lancet. 2008. Lancet Series: Maternal and Child Undernutrition. 371 (9608). http://www. thelancet.com/series/maternal-and-child-undernutrition

Lancet. 2011. Lancet Series: Obesity. 378 (9793). http://www.thelancet.com/series/obesity

Lancet. 2013. Lancet Series: Maternal and Child Nutrition. 382 (9890). http://www.thelancet. com/series/maternal-and-child-nutrition

Lancet. 2015. Lancet Series: Obesity 2015. 385 (9986). http://www.thelancet.com/series/obesity-2015

Lele, Uma. 1981. *Cooperatives and the Poor: A Comparative Perspective.* Washington, DC: World Bank.

Lele, Uma. 2009. "Global Food and Agricultural Institutions: The Cosmology of International Development Assistance." *Development Policy Review* 27 (6): 771–84.

Lele, Uma, and Sambuddha Goswami. 2017. "The Fourth Industrial Revolution, Agricultural and Rural Innovation, and Implications for Public Policy and Investments: A Case of India." *Agricultural Economics* 48 (51): 87–100.

Lele, Uma, Maggie Klousia-Marquis, and Sambuddha Goswami. 2013. "Good Governance for Food, Water, and Energy Security." *Aquatic Procedia* 1: 44–63. http://diamondh.co/Shape5/images/PDF/good_governance_for_food_water.pdf

Lele, Uma, Herve Plusquellec, and Richard Reidinger. 2015. "Policy Note: 'Water and Agriculture: Are We Ready for 2050?'" *Water Economics and Policy* 1 (1). DOI: 10.1142/S2382624X14710015

Lele, Uma, Ronald Ridker, and Jagadish Upadhyay. 2005. "Health System Capacities in Developing Countries and Global Health Initiatives on Communicable Diseases." Background paper prepared for the International Task Force on Global Public Goods, April 22. http://citeseerx.ist.psu.edu/viewdoc/download?doi=10.1.1.461.9789&rep=rep1&type=pdf

Lele, Uma, Aaron Zazueta, and Benjamin Singer. 2010. "The Environment and Global Governance: Can the Global Community Rise to the Challenge?" Lincoln Institute of Land Policy Working Paper WP10UL1, Cambridge, MA. http://www.ajfand.net/Volume13/No4/REPRINT-The%20environment%20and%20global%20governance.pdf

Levy, Brian. 2014. *Working with the Grain: Integrating Governance and Growth in Development Strategies.* Oxford and New York: Oxford University Press.

Live Mint. 2017. "United Nations Cuts Budget by $286 Million, US Claims Credit." December 27. http://www.livemint.com/Politics/v1nkW71gvyQpqQfgBQ9PXN/United-Nations-cuts-budget-by-286-million-US-claims-credit.html

Lowrey, Annie. 2012. "Transcript of 1944 Bretton Woods Conference Found at Treasury." *New York Times,* October 25. https://www.nytimes.com/2012/10/26/business/transcript-of-1944-bretton-woods-meeting-found-at-treasury.html

Luce, Edward. 2018. *The Retreat of Western Liberalism.* London: Abacus.

Mansuri, Ghazala, and Vijayendra Rao. 2004. "Community-Based and -Driven Development: A Critical Review." Working Paper No. 3209, February, World Bank, Washington, DC. http://documents1.worldbank.org/curated/zh/399341468761669595/pdf/wps3209community.pdf

Mansuri, Ghazala, and Vijayendra Rao. 2013. "Localizing Development: Does Participation Work?" Policy Research Report, World Bank, Washington, DC. http://documents.worldbank.org/curated/en/461701468150309553/pdf/NonAsciiFileName0.pdf

McGann, James G., ed. 2007. *Think Tanks and Policy Advice in the United States: Academics, Advisors, and Advocates*. New York: Routledge.

McGann, James G. 2016. "2015 Global Go To Think Tank Index Report." Think Tanks and Civil Societies Program (TTCSP), Global Go To Think Tank Index Reports. Paper 10. The Lauder Institute, University of Pennsylvania, Philadelphia. http://repository.upenn.edu/think_tanks/10

McGoey, Linsey. 2015. *No Such Thing as a Free Gift: The Gates Foundation and the Price of Philanthropy*. London: Verso.

MIF (Mo Ibrahim Foundation). 2016. *A Decade of African Governance: 2006–2015 Index Report*. London: Mo Ibrahim Foundation.

MIF (Mo Ibrahim Foundation). 2020. Ibrahim Index of African Governance (IIAG). http://mo.ibrahim.foundation/iiag/

Nagar, A. L., and Sudip Ranjan Basu. 2002. "Weighting Socioeconomic Indicators of Human Development: A Latent Variable Approach." In *Handbook of Applied Econometrics and Statistical Inference*, edited by Aman Ullah, Alan T. K. Wan, and Anoop Chaturvedi, eds., 609–42. New York: Marcel Dekker.

North, Douglass C. 1990. *Institutions, Institutional Change and Economic Performance*. Cambridge, UK: Cambridge University Press.

OECD (Organisation for Economic Co-operation and Development). 2017. "Development Aid Rises Again in 2016." April 11. OECD, Paris. https://www.oecd.org/dac/financing-sustainable-development/development-finance-data/ODA-2016-detailed-summary.pdf

OECD (Organisation for Economic Co-operation and Development). 2019a. "Launch of the Global Hub on the Governance for the SDGs." September 25. UN, New York. http://www.oecd.org/governance/pcsd/launchoftheglobalhubonthegovernanceforthesdgs.htm

OECD (Organisation for Economic Co-operation and Development). 2019b. Official Development Assistance (ODA). https://www.oecd.org/dac/financing-sustainable-development/development-finance-standards/official-development-assistance.htm

OECD (Organisation for Economic Co-operation and Development). 2021. "COVID-19 Spending Helped to Lift Foreign Aid to an All-Time High in 2020." Detailed Note, Paris, OECD, April 13. https://www.oecd.org/dac/financing-sustainable-development/development-finance-data/ODA-2020-detailed-summary.pdf

OECD.Stat. 2020. Organisation for Economic Co-operation and Development. Statistics. http://stats.oecd.org

Olson, Jr., Mancur. 1965. *The Logic of Collective Action: Public Goods and the Theory of Groups*. Cambridge, MA: Harvard University Press.

Onaran, Yalman. 2018. "1,000 Cuts to Dodd-Frank: Tracking Trump's Wave of Deregulation." *Bloomberg*, May 24. https://www.bloomberg.com/news/articles/2018-05-24/1-000-cuts-to-dodd-frank-tracking-trump-s-wave-of-deregulation

OSAA (Office of the Special Advisor on Africa). 2020. "Comprehensive Africa Agriculture Development Programme (CAADP)." United Nations. http://www.un.org/en/africa/osaa/peace/caadp.shtml

Ostrom, Elinor. 1990. *Governing the Commons: The Evolution of Institutions for Collective Action*. Cambridge, UK: Cambridge University Press.

Oxfam. 2017a. "An Economy for the 99 Percent." Oxfam Briefing Paper, January. https://www.oxfam.org/sites/www.oxfam.org/files/file_attachments/bp-economy-for-99-percent-160117-en.pdf

Oxfam. 2017b. "Just 8 Men Own Same Wealth as Half the World." Oxfam International, January 16. https://www.oxfam.org/en/pressroom/pressreleases/2017-01-16/just-8-men-own-same-wealth-half-world

Parks, Brad. 2015. "10 Essential Facts About Chinese Aid in Africa: Separating the Myths from the Research on China's $94 Billion in Africa Aid." *The National Interest*, November 30. http://nationalinterest.org/feature/10-essential-facts-about-chinese-aid-africa-14456

PBS News Hour. 2019. "U.S. and Israel Officially Withdraw from UNESCO." PBS, January 1. https://www.pbs.org/newshour/politics/u-s-and-israel-officially-withdraw-from-unesco

Pearson, Lester Bowles, ed. 1969. *Partners in Development: Report of the Commission on International Development*. New York: Praeger.

Petsonk, Annie, and Nathaniel O. Keohane. 2015. "Creating a Club of Carbon Markets: Implications of the Trade System." E15Initative, International Centre for Trade and Sustainable Development (ICTSD) and World Economic Forum, Geneva, August.

Piketty, Thomas. 2014. *Capital in the Twenty-First Century*. Translated by Arthur Goldhammer. Cambridge, MA, and London: The Belknap Press of Harvard University Press.

Popkin, Barry M. 2009. *The World Is Fat: The Fads, Trends, Policies, and Products That Are Fattening the Human Race*. New York: Avery.

PRS Group. 2016. *International Country Risk Guide (ICRG)*. East Syracuse, NY: PRS Group, Inc. http://epub.prsgroup.com/products/international-country-risk-guide-icrg

Rasmussen, Sune Engel. 2017. "Trump Policy Set to Hinder War on Polio in Pakistan." *The Guardian*, September 29. https://www.theguardian.com/global-development/2017/sep/29/trump-policy-set-to-hinder-war-on-polio-in-pakistan

Rubin, Alissa J. 2013. "U.S. Loses Voting Rights at Unesco." *New York Times*, November 8. http://www.nytimes.com/2013/11/09/us/politics/us-loses-voting-rights-at-unesco.html?mcubz=0

Schleifer, Theodore. 2019. "MacKenzie Bezos Signed the Philanthropic Commitment Her Ex-Husband Spurned." Vox, May 28. https://www.vox.com/recode/2019/5/28/18641623/mackenzie-bezos-giving-pledge-philanthropy-jeff-bezos-divorce

Schwab, Klaus. 2016. *The Fourth Industrial Revolution*. Geneva: World Economic Forum.

Sen, Amartya K. 1980. "Famines." *World Development* 8 (9): 613–21.

Sen, Amartya K. 1981. *Poverty and Famines: An Essay on Entitlement and Deprivation*. Oxford: Clarendon Press.

Sen, Amartya K. 1984. "Rights and Capabilities." In *Resources, Values, and Development*, 307–24. Cambridge, MA: Harvard University Press.

Sen, Amartya K. 1985. *Commodities and Capabilities*. Amsterdam: North-Holland.

Sen, Amartya K. 1999. *Development as Freedom*. Oxford: Oxford University Press.

Shannon, Don. 1988. "Reagan Releases U.N. Payments: Cites Fiscal Reforms, Peace Role; $188 Million Promised by Oct. 1." *Los Angeles Times*, September 14, 1988.

Strait Times. 2017. "China Expected to Take Over Japan's Second Spot in Contributions to United Nations." *Strait Times*, August 29. http://www.straitstimes.com/asia/east-asia/china-expected-to-take-over-japans-second-spot-in-contributions-to-united-nations

Thakur, Ramesh. 2003. "The United Nations in Global Governance: Rebalancing Organized Multilateralism for Current and Future Challenges." The United Nations Non-Governmental Liaison Service (NGLS). https://projects.iq.harvard.edu/violenceagainstwomen/publications/crisis-global-governance-challenge-united-nations-and-global

Thomas, Melissa A. 2010. "What Do the Worldwide Governance Indicators Measure?" *European Journal of Development Research* 22 (1): 31–54.

UN (United Nations). 2003. "The Human Rights Based Approach to Development Cooperation towards a Common Understanding among UN Agencies." UN Development Group Human Rights Working Group. https://undg.org/document/the-human-rights-based-approach-to-development-cooperation-towards-a-common-understanding-among-un-agencies/

UN (United Nations). 2004. "A More Secure World: Our Shared Responsibility." Report of the Secretary-General's High-level Panel on Threats, Challenges, and Change, A/59/565. UN, New York. https://documents-dds-ny.un.org/doc/UNDOC/GEN/N04/602/31/PDF/N0460231.pdf?OpenElement

UN (United Nations). 2009. "Report of the Commission of Experts of the President of the United Nations General Assembly on Reforms of the International Monetary and Financial System." September 21, Joseph E. Stiglitz, Chair, UN, New York. http://www.un.org/ga/econcrisissummit/docs/FinalReport_CoE.pdf

UN (United Nations). 2016. "Scale of Assessments for the Apportionment of the Expenses of the United Nations." A/Res/70/245, Resolution adopted by the General Assembly on December 15, 2015, 70th Session, Agenda Item 138, February 8, UN, New York. http://www.un.org/ga/search/view_doc.asp?symbol=a/res/70/245

UN (United Nations). 2017a. "Fifth Committee Recommends $5.4 Billion Budget for 2018–2019 Biennium as It Concludes Main Part of Seventy-Second Session." https://www.un.org/press/en/2017/gaab4270.doc.htm

UN (United Nations). 2017b. "Report of the Committee on Contributions." A/72/11, Seventy-seventh session, June 5–23. UN, New York.

UN (United Nations). 2019. Committee on Contributions. General Assembly. https://www.un.org/en/ga/contributions/index.shtml

UN (United Nations). 2020a. Sustainable Development Goals. https://sustainabledevelopment.un.org/sdgs

UN (United Nations). 2020b. Treaty Collection. Environment. Paris Agreement. Status. https://treaties.un.org/pages/ViewDetails.aspx?src=TREATY&mtdsg_no=XXVII-7-d&chapter=27&lang=en

UN (United Nations). 2020c. United Nations Food Systems Summit 2020. https://www.un.org/sustainabledevelopment/food-systems-summit-2021/

UN (United Nations). 2020d. Zero Hunger Challenge. http://www.un.org/en/zerohunger/challenge.shtml

UN News. 2012. "Rio+20: Secretary-General Challenges Nations to Achieve 'Zero Hunger.'" June 12, UN, New York. http://www.un.org/apps/news/story.asp?NewsID=42304#.WGPZVBTfTl4

UNFCCC (United Nations Framework Convention on Climate Change). 2014. Paris Agreement—Status of Ratification. http://unfccc.int/paris_agreement/items/9444.php

US Department of State. 2011. "About the U.S. and UNESCO." https://2009-2017.state.gov/p/io/unesco/usunesco/index.htm

Valdés, Raymundo, and Maegan McCann. 2014. "Intellectual Property Provisions in Regional Trade Agreements: Revision and Update." WTO Staff Working Paper No ERSD-2014–14, World Trade Organization (WTO), Economic Research and Statistics Division, Geneva.

Victor, David G. 2015. "The Case for Climate Clubs." E15Initiative, International Centre for Trade and Sustainable Development (ICTSD) and World Economic Forum, Geneva, January 19.

von Braun, Joachim, and Regina Birner. 2017. "Designing Global Governance for Agricultural Development and Food and Nutrition Security." *Review of Development Economics* 21 (2): 265–84.

Watson, Noshua. 2011. "When Taxpayers Are Fed Up, Philanthropists Can Meet Aid Needs." *The Guardian*, September 23. https://www.theguardian.com/global-development/poverty-matters/2011/sep/23/philanthropy-can-meet-aid-needs

WCED (World Commission on Environment and Development). 1987. *Our Common Future.* Brundtland Committee. Oxford and New York: Oxford University Press.

Weiss, Thomas G. 2013. *Global Governance: Why? What? Whither?* Cambridge, UK, and Malden, MA: Polity Press.

Weiss, Thomas G. 2014. *Governing the World? Addressing "Problems without Passports."* New York: Routledge.

Whalley, John, Manmohan Agarwal, and Jiahua Pan. 2015. *World Scientific Reference on Asia and the World Economy* (3 volumes). Singapore: World Scientific Publishing Company.

WHO (World Health Organization). 2007. "International Health Regulations Enter into Force." WHO Media Centre, June 14. http://www.who.int/mediacentre/news/releases/2007/pr31/en/

WHO (World Health Organization). 2019. "Poliomyelitis." Fact Sheet updated January 3, WHO Media Centre. http://www.who.int/mediacentre/factsheets/fs114/en/

World Bank. 2003. *World Development Report 2003: Sustainable Development in a Dynamic World: Transforming Institutions, Growth, and Quality of Life.* Washington, DC: World Bank. https://openknowledge.worldbank.org/handle/10986/5985

World Bank. 2004. *World Development Report 2004: Making Services Work for Poor People.* Washington, DC: World Bank. https://openknowledge.worldbank.org/handle/10986/5986

World Bank. 2005. *The Effectiveness of World Bank Support for Community-Based and -Driven Development.* Operations Evaluation Department. Washington, DC: World Bank.

World Bank. 2013. *Capital for the Future: Saving and Investment in an Interdependent World.* Global Development Horizons. Washington, DC: World Bank. http://siteresources.worldbank.org/EXTDECPROSPECTS/Resources/476882–1368197310537/CapitalForTheFuture.pdf

World Bank. 2016. "World Bank Board Approves New Environmental and Social Framework." Press Release, News Feature, August 4. https://www.worldbank.org/en/news/press-release/2016/08/04/world-bank-board-approves-new-environmental-and-social-framework

World Bank. 2017. Review and Update of the World Bank Safeguard Policies: World Bank Board Approves New Environmental and Social Framework. Consultations. https://consultations.worldbank.org/consultation/review-and-update-world-bank-safeguard-policies

World Bank. 2018. "World Bank Group Shareholders Endorse Transformative Capital Package." Press Release, April 21. https://www.worldbank.org/en/news/press-release/2018/04/21/world-bank-group-shareholders-endorse-transformative-capital-package

World Bank. 2020a. Enterprise Surveys. https://www.enterprisesurveys.org

World Bank. 2020b. World Development Indicators (database). http://data.worldbank.org/data-catalog/world-development-indicators.

Zedillo, Ernesto, Chair. 2009. "Repowering the World Bank for the 21st Century." Report of the High Level Commission on Modernization of World Bank Group Governance, World Bank Group, Washington, DC.

6

Governance of the "Big Five"

Uma Lele, Brian C. Baldwin, and Sambuddha Goswami

Summary

In this chapter, we outline key issues facing governance of international organizations (IOs) in the larger context of global governance of food and agriculture, as discussed in Chapter 5, and specifically, in the context of United Nations (UN) financing. We then discuss issues of governance of each of the Big Five IOs. We argue that underfinancing of food and agriculture can be addressed by using World Bank/International Development Association (IDA) resources differently, which are now exclusively country-directed, despite much rhetoric about the importance of global and regional public goods as complements to country assistance. This change will also require a different vision for the organizations that is more attuned to today's challenges, with stronger partnerships among them and with others around this new vision. To understand organizational governance and possibilities of changes within the organizations, we first need to understand how the organizations were originally structured and financed; how financing relates to their structure and governance; and how the formal and informal voices of members are exercised—for example, in the choice of leadership and the substantive content of what organizations do and how. We also selectively explore some issues of coordination *among* the organizations, for instance, among the Rome-based agencies (RBAs), the World Bank, and CGIAR. We review the myriad evaluations of IOs, but note that they rarely address the larger strategic issues concerning the individual organizations or collectively. In Chapter 5, we argued that the world is undergoverned in relation to the challenges of meeting the Sustainable Development Goals (SDGs) confronting climate change, conflict, natural resource degradation, income inequality, persistent poverty, and growing hunger. Solutions are increasingly intersectoral and not just agricultural. Important questions going forward are: how have the Big Five institutions, which we call the operating arms of global governance, responded to the challenges? Can they be more effective, or is there need to create new institutions and new funding mechanisms to improve global governance? With greater long-term support, the Food and Agriculture Organization of the United Nations (FAO) can translate its guidelines into operations to combat climate change and promote conservation agriculture and its Codex Alimentarius into food safety. With collaboration with the World Food Programme (WFP), the International Fund for Agricultural Development (IFAD), and the World Bank, FAO can help move fragile countries into rehabilitation, reconstruction, and development. CGIAR can use long-term funding, while the World Bank and IFAD can support the building of delivery systems.

Food for All: International Organizations and the Transformation of Agriculture. Uma Lele, Manmohan Agarwal, Brian C. Baldwin, and Sambuddha Goswami, Oxford University Press. © Uma Lele, Manmohan Agarwal, Brian C. Baldwin, and Sambuddha Goswami 2021. DOI: 10.1093/oso/9780198755173.003.0007

Governance of the Big Five Organizations

The Big Five—the World Bank Group (WBG), FAO, WFP, CGIAR, and IFAD—have been key players, the "operating arms" of the global governance of food and agriculture. They are a subset of a larger, dynamic system of global governance within which they operate, as we outlined in Chapter 5. They, therefore, provide a glimpse of how global governance works in practice. An FAO report (2017c, 119–21) spells out the six "salient" characteristics of the two recent global compacts on SDGs and the Paris Climate Change Accord, with respect to the governance of food and agriculture:

1. *Universal and inclusive nature*, involving developing and developed countries, not just initiatives directed at developing countries, as in the case of the Millennium Development Goals (MDGs). In this new spirit, in October 2017, the World Bank started publishing numbers on poverty for the Organisation for Economic Co-Operation and Development (OECD) countries (Silver and Gharib 2017). Angus Deaton (2018) made a case for direct assistance to the poor population in the United States, much as the developing countries' poor have received attention.
2. *Bottom-up approach*, as countries choose their own indicators to achieve SDGs from among 232 indicators.[1]
3. *Greater reliance on domestic resource mobilization*, with little or no expectation of new or additional official development assistance (ODA), except in the case of low-income countries (LICs). This has important implications for the World Bank and IFAD, each of which have already been moving in the direction of giving their concessional assistance to LICs.
4. *Policy coherence, laterally and vertically*: this area has been increasingly challenged, particularly since President Trump's election and the Brexit vote. As we have pointed out earlier, the United States either withdrew explicitly from many international agreements on trade, climate change, and aid, or effectively shown lukewarm support for them. Restoring global confidence in the US leadership under the Biden administration, and particularly its sustainability, is a challenge, given that Trumpism is alive and well.
5. *The "grand bargain"*—a term used in two different ways, the first calling for the increased role of the private sector in financing development (for example, from billions to trillions) and civil society (through impact financing by those interested in using financing to achieve social good), and the second arising out of the World Humanitarian Summit 2016[2]—namely, more efficiency from implementers of aid in return for more money from donors.
6. *Mutual accountability*: the past approach of donor-imposed conditionality is being replaced by *mutual responsibility* of recipient countries and donors, each following the rules for performance. As we have argued elsewhere in this book, donors have expected developing countries to change their behavior more than they have changed their own, often explaining their (non)actions in terms of their domestic parliaments and constituencies.

---

[1] The revised list of SDG indicators can be found at https://unstats.un.org/sdgs/indicators/indicators-list/. The list includes 232 indicators on which general agreement has been reached. The total number of indicators listed here is 244, but nine indicators repeat under more than one target.

[2] See World Humanitarian Summit, Istanbul, Turkey, May 23–4, 2016: http://whsturkey.org

With the global community's adoption of the 2030 SDGs and the Climate Change Accord in 2015, the financial resources needed to achieve global development goals have been recognized to far exceed current official international financial flows. In April 2015, the World Bank/International Monetary Fund (IMF) Development Committee published a report titled "From Billions to Trillions" about the dollars of financing needed to meet the challenge of promoting inclusive and sustainable growth, reducing poverty and inequality, and protecting the planet (Development Committee 2015). Multilateral development banks have proposed to leverage their capital base by borrowing from capital markets to increase their ability to finance development and catalyze greater private investment in several different ways: (1) promoting high-quality investment projects; (2) helping mitigate risk associated with investments; (3) mobilizing resources from and co-investing with traditional investors and through new sources of commercial financing for development; and (4) developing new financial products to help unlock additional flows (World Bank 2017). The World Bank is moving to fulfill this promise by courting Wall Street investors, including the recognition of the trillion-dollar infrastructure financing gap arrived at by consensus estimates from OECD by the Boston Consulting Group (Maier 2015; Thomas 2018). And IDA has the mandate to borrow on the capital market against its pledges, but progress has been slow.

As we have emphasized in previous chapters, investment in agriculture and rural development is critical to achieving structural transformation. Developing agriculture, however, increasingly calls for multisectoral investments in education, human and environmental health, energy, physical infrastructure, and communications. Underinvestment is a major impediment to structural transformation, and development is, first and foremost, the responsibility of the countries themselves, although international assistance can contribute in important ways, as we illustrate later in the book. Policies are often ineffective, institutions are weak, and appropriate technologies and financing are not easily accessible. More importantly, there is often underinvestment in research and development (R&D) and no consensus on key policy and institutional issues among donors and between donors and recipients. So, it is unclear if weak lending and technical assistance to agriculture and the rural sectors are a result of weak client country demand and capacity to utilize aid effectively and expeditiously, or if they are a result of weak supply of donor funds and expertise? How can the resources be increased and strengthened while also strengthening domestic resource mobilization, particularly in low-middle-income countries where funding must increasingly come from domestic resources, and how can aid coordination be increased among donors? Aid recipients have considered coordination to be "ganging up," in part, because they have seen the Bretton Woods institutions as Western-dominated in their governance and approaches. Where they have more voice, such as in FAO, the institutions have not elicited strong confidence in donor countries.

So, should such capital be delivered through existing multilateral channels or bilaterally, or through the creation of new global programs, as has often been done in the health sector? What should be the balance of assistance between providing global and regional public goods, as some argue for?[3] Clearly, there is scope to achieve both. IOs have the capacity to address these issues, but the recent trend has been toward a growing share of bilateral aid in total ODA, with a declining share of multilateral organizations, as we show in Chapter 7 on

---

[3] See, for example, Ahluwalia et al. (2016) and Kanbur (2017), whose argument for more support for global and regional goods, in part, is owing to their concerns about the growing irrelevance of IOs in providing country assistance.

financing. Multilateral banks have followed the principles of the Paris, Accra, Busan, and Rome Declarations more closely than have bilateral donors (OECD 2019a, 2019b, 2019c, 2019d). Bilateral aid has been described by some as "Trojan multilateralism" (Sridhar and Woods 2013). By appearing to pay allegiance to country ownership and country priorities, some argue, bilateral aid "creates 'the illusion of multilateral intent' while 'covertly introducing bilateral goals'"—using multilateral institutions as vehicles for their agendas (Browne and Cordon [2015, 1], quoting Sridhar and Woods [2013]). This raises the question of how priorities are determined among sectors, countries, and activities, and whose priorities do and should external assistance support. This is a particularly tricky issue in the case of assistance to low-income developing countries, which are eligible for concessional assistance. Typically, they display weak political will to support agriculture and weak capacity to set their own priorities, and particularly to carry them out, as a comparative study of Chinese and African development by a group of Chinese scholars documented (Xiaoyun et al. 2012). This situation implies the need for long-term development assistance to build capacity; but with some exceptions such as in the development of agricultural research and education in Asia during the Green Revolution, donors have been less effective in building capacity and have had increasingly shorter time horizons (Lele and Goldsmith 1989).

This chapter makes the case for multilateralism and continued country assistance, together with support for global public goods (GPGs). The argument here should also be seen as complementary to Chapter 7 on financing, wherein we provide evidence that, by and large, multilateral assistance is more transparent and more effective than bilateral assistance by several criteria, including: (1) the usefulness of advice (7 of the top 10 ranked by this criterion are multilateral donors); (2) agenda-setting influence (all of the top 10 are multilateral donors); (3) that more of their assistance actually is getting transferred to developing countries; (4) helpfulness, which earns IOs higher ratings in implementation; and (5) IOs tending to be more selective in terms of countries' assistance needs. More multilateral aid goes to low- and lower-middle-income countries (LMICs) than does bilateral aid. In addition, many of the GPGs cannot be realized without strong national and subnational capacities to deliver them. One cannot achieve GPGs of peace and security, contain transboundary spread of diseases, or respond to financial contagion or climate change, without also achieving those outcomes at the national and subnational levels. That calls for strong political will and domestic capacity, which many developing countries still lack.

Yet, the roles of multilateral assistance and the "Big Five" organizations have shrunk, not just in total capital flows, but as other financial flows have increased, including private finance, remittances, philanthropy, and South–South cooperation. Even in "official" flows, the share of multilateral aid has shrunk noticeably, with respect to food and agriculture—perhaps with the exception of WFP's share. This is because the need for humanitarian assistance has been growing more rapidly, in part, because of growing internal conflicts and climate change, compared to the demand for investment lending in food and agriculture. This is understandable in countries that are well advanced in structural transformation, but not in the case of countries at early stages of development.

In this chapter, we focus on the governance of each of the Big Five organizations: how these operating arms are governed, and how their governance and leadership matter for their continued relevance and coherence in the areas of food and agriculture, with each playing to their comparative advantage, as well as collectively. Furthermore, because governance and finance are closely related in a complex way, we provide an overview of the financing of the Big Five IOs, as it determines the supply of financial resources available to the organizations. Financing also affects the selection of leadership, as well as the abilities of their top leaders to mobilize resources. Regional banks are not discussed here, because, so far, they have not been significant players in lending to the agricultural sector, compared to their global counterparts such as the World Bank.[4] However, many of the issues discussed in this chapter would apply to regional banks, as they expand their development capacity generally and respond to the needs of agriculture and rural development, particularly some like the African Development Bank, which has traditionally focused on infrastructure, but has begun to gear up for expanded lending to agriculture.

Chapter 1 described the activities of the Big Five in general terms. Table A.1.2 in Chapter 1, and Table A.6.1 in this chapter present their missions, goals, strategic objectives, governance structures, business models, and funding cycles in greater detail. Chapters 8 through 12 describe their activities as organizations. In reality, there is considerable overlap among their declared objectives and activities, from their focus on eradication of poverty and hunger to new technologies and knowledge for farmers to increase productivity, from climate change mitigation to minimize impacts on food and agriculture to facilitating adaptation and resilience to climate change, and in addressing gender issues. The World Bank's focus on poverty and hunger came in the 1970s under its president, Robert McNamara, well before the MDGs were initiated in 1990, and the Bank expanded its objective to shared prosperity in 2013. As a multisectoral organization, it is able to address multiple SDGs in food, health, and, education. Nobel laureate Ronald Coase (in 1991) argued that companies establish their boundaries on the basis of transaction costs. When the cost of transacting for a product or service on the open market exceeds the cost of managing and coordinating the incremental activity needed to create that product or service internally, the company will perform the activity in-house. Coase also asked when should a firm (in this case, an international organization) "make" and when should it "buy" services? (*Economist* 2017). Venkat Atluri, Miklós Dietz, and Nicolaus Henke (2017), in their paper "Competing in a World of Sectors without Borders," noted, as digitization reduces transaction costs, it becomes economically desirable for companies to contract out more activities, and a richer set of more specialized ecosystems is facilitated. This should ideally occur across IOs, as it has in the private sector, but it has not yet happened. There is much scope for a new vision to emerge for global architecture, which enables faster evolution of IOs, so they become stronger complements to each other.

As documented in Chapter 5, as the number of actors has increased and development agendas have expanded, concerns have grown among development practitioners about mission creep within each organization: that is, taking on more functions and spreading activities too thinly, instead of relying on other organizations at the same time that partnerships have become an important part of the new lexicon. Proponents of expanding scope dismiss these concerns and argue that organizations have provided a legitimate response to the growing complexity of the development processes and interactions among different aspects of development: for example, climate change and resilience of food systems or food systems and nutrition. At the same time, with budget cuts, staff retirements, and attrition, capacity within individual organizations has declined. The overlapping nature of SDGs, documented in earlier chapters, further illustrates this problem. Cooperation *among* the five organizations and with other actors has waxed and waned, in part, because donors have helped spawn many different aid entities through the use of their trust funds, fostering

---

[4] The African Development Bank (AfDB); the Asian Development Bank (ADB); the European Bank for Reconstruction and Development (EBRD); and the Inter-American Development Bank (IDB) are examples of regional banks.

competition rather than cooperation (see McCalla [2007] for the impacts of such proliferation on FAO). It is also true that effective "supply chains" have not materialized. Organizations are not turning to each other for services, particularly to those with clearly demonstrated comparative advantages and efficiency. We cite some examples in this chapter, to the extent that they involve strategic choices at the level of governance and financing: for example, whether to give more resources to a multilateral organization or to rely on bilateral food aid; whether to rely on FAO for technical assistance in the provision of GPGs, such as statistics, food safety, and control of animal diseases and pests; and whether to rely on CGIAR for research, and if so, whether CGIAR should be focusing on global and regional public goods research while expecting national systems to build their own capacity to be stronger, more effective partners with CGIAR.

Key Financiers of the United Nations System and International Organizations

Governance and financing of IOs are interrelated in a complex way. IOs depend on their regular budget, based on assessed contributions in some organizations and trust funds, also known as voluntary contributions from donors, to supplement their operational activities. As budgets become increasingly more constrained, reliance on voluntary contributions has increased. When there are assessed contributions, voluntary contributions supplement them—in other cases, such as for WFP and CGIAR, their operations depend entirely on voluntary organizations. Table 6.1 provides information on voting power and financing shares of the top 10 assessed contributions (excluding trust funds) to the five organizations, plus the World Health Organization (WHO) and the UN System, as a whole. Together, 17 countries plus the European Union, the World Bank, and the Bill and Melinda Gates Foundation (BMGF)—in the case of CGIAR—play key roles. If trust funds and voluntary contributions are included, which constitute 61 percent of FAO's operational activity, then the picture changes substantially. FAO's financing is based on assessed contributions and voluntary contributions to carry out its program of work. Trust funds are, as their name suggests, given to FAO to use "in trust" for broad goals. The United Nations Development Programme (UNDP) once was an important contributor to FAO's trust funds in the 1960s and 1970s. As we indicate elsewhere, UNDP trust funds to FAO have now declined but other bilateral funding has increased and is now larger than FAO's assessed contributions.

In assessed contributions, the United States ranks first among donors for all organizations, and Japan, second, except for IFAD with lower assessed contributions (and to which the United States did not formally contribute to in 2018), and for WFP and CGIAR, which depend entirely on voluntary contributions. In both cases, the United States has been a major player. In terms of importance of donors, China's ranking has risen in assessed contributions to third in the International Bank for Reconstruction and Development (IBRD), WHO, and the UN, ahead of Germany; Germany's rank is either third or fourth for all except CGIAR. France ranks either fourth or fifth for all organizations, except WFP and CGIAR, and particularly, ranks tenth for IFAD. China's financing has, of course, expanded substantially outside of these institutions, as shown in chapter 7, dwarfing their role. The United Kingdom ranks between second and eighth for all organizations. The European Union is among the top 10 only for WFP (ranking second) and CGIAR (ranking seventh) (CGIAR 2012, 2013, 2014, 2015, 2016b; Wadsworth 2016; CGIAR 2017b; FAO 2017e; UN 2017a; IFAD 2019; WFP 2020a; WHO 2020; World Bank 2020).

Table 6.1 Ranking of top 10 member countries/donors in (assessed) contributions by their voting powers and voluntary contributions

Member countries/donors	By voting power					By assessed contributions to the regular budget			By contributions to the Fund		By voluntary contributions	
	IBRD	IDA	IFC	MIGA	IFAD	FAO	WHO	UN	WFP	CGIAR	FAO	World Bank Group Trust Fund
United States	1	1	1	1	1	1	1	1	1	3	2	1
Japan	2	2	2	2	4	2	2	3	6		7	3
China	3	10	10	6		3	3	2				
Germany	4	4	3	3	3	4	4	4	3		8	4
France	5	5	4	4	10	5	5	6				6
United Kingdom	6	3	5	5	8	6	6	5	4	2	3	2
India	7	7	6									
Russian Federation	8	6	7	9		9	9	9				
Saudi Arabia	9	9	8	7	6				9			
Italy	10	9	9	8	2	8	8	7				
Canada		8	8	10	7	10	10	10	5			5
Spain												
Brazil						7	7	8				
European Union									2	7	1	8
United Nations Central Emergency Response Fund (CERF)									7			
Sweden					9				8	9		
UN Other Funds and Agencies (excl. CERF)									10			
Netherlands					5					4		7
World Bank	n.a.	n.a.	n.a.	n.a.						5		
Bill & Melinda Gates Foundation										1		
Australia										6		10
Switzerland										8	10	
Norway										10	9	9
FAO Direct Access to Global Environment Facility (GEF) Funding											4	
Office for the Coordination of Humanitarian Affairs (UN–OCHA)											5	
United Nations Development Programme (UNDP)											6	
Administered Donor Joint Trust Fund												

Notes: n.a. means not applicable. The World Bank Group is comprised of IBRD, which lends to governments of middle-income and creditworthy LICs; IDA, which provides interest-free loans ("credits") and grants to governments in the poorest countries; the Multilateral Investment Guarantee Agency (MIGA), which promotes foreign direct investment (FDI) in developing countries and offers political risk insurance ("guarantees") to investors and lenders; and IFC, which is focused on the private sector, mobilizing capital and providing advisory services (see "About the World Bank," http://www.worldbank.org/en/about/.

Source: CGIAR (2012, 2013, 2014, 2015, 2016b, 2017a, 2017b); FAO (2017a, 2017b); Wadsworth (2016); FAO (2017a, 2017e); IFAD (2019); UN (2017a); Toma et al (2013); WFP (2020a); UN (2017e); WHO (2020); World Bank (2020).

When voluntary contributions are considered, however, in the case of the World Bank and FAO, then the European Union is important. The European Union ranked first for FAO and eighth for the World Bank Group Trust Fund in 2013, the latest year for which data were available (Toma et al. 2013). From FY09 through FY13, the United States and the United Kingdom made the largest contributions to WBG trust funds. Over that period, the United Kingdom was the largest development funder to the IBRD/IDA trust funds, followed by the United States, the European Union, Australia, and the Netherlands. Together, these five development funders accounted for almost half of the total cash contributions to IBRD/IDA trust funds since FY09. The United States remains the largest development funder to financial intermediary funds (FIFs), both cumulatively over five years and in FY13 (Toma et al. 2013).

Among developing countries other than China, based on assessments, Brazil, India, and Saudi Arabia are important contributors. CGIAR's donors are different. CGIAR's top 10 principal funders in 2017 are BMGF, United Kingdom, United States, the Netherlands, the World Bank, Australia, European Commission, Switzerland, Sweden, Norway (CGIAR 2017a, 52).

Data provide important insights into the financing of the UN System. The entire UN System's and individual organizations' assessed contributions are provided by a handful of countries (Figure 5.2), even though their ODA shares in their own gross national income (GNI) range vary widely, as shown in Figure 5.3 in Chapter 5. With 1.4 percent of its GNI, Sweden ranks at the top, and with 0.17 percent of its GNI, the United States ranks 22nd. As we discussed in the preceding chapter on global governance, collective action in a smaller group of countries has typically been easier, if there are shared objectives, leadership, and political will. The Group of Twenty (G20), which includes most of the large financiers of the UN, is another alternative, among others, to achieving long-term reforms and financing of the UN System and of individual organizations, as discussed later in this chapter. Even within this smaller group, however, collective action is a challenge. Germany has raised its aid levels, which may well reach 1 percent of GNI (Cheney 2017). The United States has been increasingly wary of aid (with a misperception in the public about how much larger a share of US GNI goes to aid, compared to the reality of 0.18 percent), as well as of nation building, even in countries in conflict, such as Afghanistan and Iraq, where the United States has engaged in the conflict, contributing to a hornet's nest of secondary collateral damage with global spillovers in refugees and terrorism. Given this larger context of global governance, how can the Big Five remain relevant and increase their effectiveness for an increasingly more complex agenda, where humanitarian assistance interacts with development needs and where sectoral silos are breaking down, as discussed in the previous chapter on governance? Or will they witness a slow decline, owing to the failure of their members and governance to respond to changing needs? With the level of instability and uncertainty in the world in 2020, it seems that IOs are needed more than ever. Yet, whether and how the Biden–Harris victory will report to multilateral institutions remains unclear.

In the pursuit of global poverty reduction, a Brookings study noted that a minority of about 30 countries risk being left behind, both in terms of their levels of deprivation and in the way that global progress is accounted for.[5] This risk suggests that the "leave-no-one-behind" principle on which the SDGs are built, originally intended to draw attention to

---

[5] Countries at most risk for being left behind include: Afghanistan, Benin, Burkina Faso, Burundi, Central African Republic, DR Congo, Djibouti, Equatorial Guinea, Eritrea, The Gambia, Guinea-Bissau, Haiti, DPR Korea, Lesotho, Liberia, Madagascar, Malawi, Mali, Mozambique, Myanmar, Niger, Nigeria, Rwanda, Somalia, South Sudan, St. Lucia, Syrian Arab Republic, Togo, Yemen, and Zambia (Chandy 2017, table 1, 7).

marginalized groups—ethnic, tribal, or religious minorities, or the disabled—might equally be applied to countries. It calls for new efforts to ensure these countries are not ignored and for further policy and implementation research that could help raise their performance. With this background, we now turn to the issues of governance faced in each of the five IOs.

The World Bank Group

WBG is the largest public lender to developing countries and to agriculture and the rural sector. Lending to the rural sector has been larger than to agriculture. With the multidimensional nature of rural poverty, it makes sense to support other complementary sectors to agriculture, including health, education, social safety nets, and infrastructure, to increase returns to agriculture.

Two opposite points of view prevailing on the future role of the World Bank have been resolved for the time being with the approval of a long-awaited general and selective capital increase (SCI) by the Development Committee, the ministerial platform which effectively constitutes the governance of the Bretton Woods institutions. A financial package of a US $13 billion paid-in capital increase, consisting of US$7.5 billion for the International Bank for IBRD and US$5.5 billion for the International Finance Corporation (IFC) of WBG, was agreed to at the April 2018 Spring Meetings of IMF and WBG (World Bank 2018). A pleasantly surprising development, given the reluctance of the Trump administration to approve a capital increase, the "transformative package" consists of capital measures as well as fundamental institutional and financial reforms for IBRD and IFC (Development Committee 2018, 1). A conservative Meltzer Commission, with whose views the Trump administration was aligned, had argued that the Bank should phase out of countries that have access to international capital markets. Rather, the Bank should (1) supply global goods, such as the elimination of tropical diseases or improvements in tropical agriculture; (2) promote economic and social development, using an incentive-based system that subsidizes institutional reform and gives incentives for maintaining reforms; and (3) use grants instead of loans to improve the quality of life in the poorest countries by inoculating children, providing sanitary sewers, bringing potable water to the villages, and in other ways.[6] The Commission proposed that the grants would be paid directly to contractors, on evidence of completion furnished by independent auditors. Grants would bypass corrupt governments; auditing results would improve performance (Meltzer 2000).

With the phasing out of development bank loans to middle-income countries (MICs) that have access to private international capital markets, the focus on grants and highly subsidized loans to poor countries implied that, within a few years, the vast bulk of the development banks' assistance would take the form of nonrepayable disbursements, essentially closing the operations of IBRD (Mikesell 2001).

More expansive views of the World Bank's continued roles were proposed by Ahluwalia et al. (2016) and Zedillo (2009) and are discussed later in this chapter. Before we turn to specific organizations, however, we first describe the financing of the UN System for a larger context in which the five IOs operate. We note the precarious financial role of the UN System as a whole and the towering role of the United States in it.

From a structural transformation perspective, the unique strength of WBG among development banks is its ability to provide the full menu of services and support, ranging

---

[6] See Scott Morris (2018a) on US National Security Advisor John Bolton's view of the multilateral system.

from customized global knowledge, analytics, and technical assistance to financing and implementation support, to convening of partnerships and crowding in contributions from diverse partners from the public and private sectors.

The establishment of the World Bank has been one of the important innovations of the 20th century (Ahluwalia et al. 2016). The final IDA19 replenishment of US$82 billion for fiscal years 2021–3, in December 2019, in Stockholm; the IDA19 replenishment represents a 3 percent increase in real terms compared to IDA18 (IDA 2020). Among the Bank's recent achievements was the largest replenishment ever approved for July 1, 2017 to June 30, 2020 in December 2016 (World Bank 2016; IDA 2017). Scott Morris (2018b) of the Center for Global Development (CGD) made five observations about the Development Committee's approval of the 2018 capital increase:

(1) It will enable the Bank Group to be a leader on climate finance, and more broadly, support GPGs, which CGD's 2016 High Level Panel on the Future of Multilateral Development Banking also recommended (Ahluwalia et al. 2016). Climate-related shares of IBRD's and IFC's portfolios will rise, and all bank projects will be screened for climate risks. For GPGs, more generally, the agreement will modestly increase IBRD's annual income to GPGs.

(2) It will introduce "the principle of price differentiation based on country income status, with higher income countries paying more than the bank's other borrowers," enabling additional revenues to be generated for the Bank. This approach will help the Bank to ask more from countries that have less financing need.

(3) The package will enable "IBRD's overall lending portfolio to channel 70 percent of the bank's resources to countries with per capita incomes below $6,895 and 30 percent to countries above this so-called 'graduation threshold.'" An additional good feature of this new package is that these targets would not affect crisis lending. China's access to World Bank loans will not be affected in the short run, "though over time, as more countries join the higher income category, the 30 percent share will be allocated across more borrowers."

(4) The package also identifies "a new financial framework that requires greater discipline when it comes to tradeoffs between lending volumes, loan pricing, and the bank's administrative budget."

(5) Finally, even while encouraging "greater differentiation [in the treatment] among countries, it reaffirms the World Bank's commitments to stay engaged with all its client countries, including China." There are no new proposals for graduation of MICs of the sort the United States has made before. Among current borrowers, the decision to graduate from assistance is expected to be theirs to make (Morris 2018b).

(6) A global coalition of development partners agreed on a historic US$82 billion financing package for IDA (IDA 2020).

The "graduation," particularly of India, the largest recipient of IDA, together with Vietnam and Sri Lanka, has freed large sums of resources for IDA to lend to other LICs, which are far smaller and/or have far less absorptive capacity than India did in its heyday of receipt of IDA assistance. IDA graduation has also created new opportunities for assistance outside IDA-eligible countries—for example, in support of migrants in Middle Eastern countries, such as Jordan and Lebanon in support of refugees—as the number of IDA-eligible countries has shrunk (Lele, Goswami, and Nico 2017; Manning 2017).

When IDA resources in the 1980s could not meet demand, based on the threshold for IDA eligibility established in 1964, IDA ceased to lend to countries at the upper end of the income scale, creating a second lower operational cutoff. The IDA cutoff in 1989 was 18 percent of the global GNI and 13 percent in 2013. Without this cutoff, its nominal value would have been 44 percent higher. More countries would have been eligible for IDA had the cutoff not been lowered over time to reduce IDA eligibility and graduate countries out of IDA to IBRD more rapidly (Lele, Goswami, and Nico 2017). Under IDA18, the Bank proposes to borrow against IDA, a step which Kapur and Raychaudhuri (2014) and Morris (2014) have argued has the potential not only to expand capital available to IDA-eligible developing countries, but also to transform the Bank from its historical dependence on the United States, with its virtual veto power, as described subsequently in this chapter.

Most of the World Bank capital for the loans to developing countries on near commercial terms and to other development banks is obtained from the sale of the bonds on world capital markets, while capital subscribed by member governments to the development banks constitutes a guarantee provided against default to the private holders of the bonds. As Keynes anticipated in 1944, this is a convenient way for member/developed countries to provide economic assistance to developing countries and share risk broadly (see Kanbur [2017] for the history of the Bank). Furthermore, their capital subscriptions are not disbursed or recorded in national budgets. The development banks currently rely on the interest and principal repayments of existing loans for financing new loans.

Concessional assistance, such as through IDA, comes from periodic replenishments of sovereign governments, an approach which provides stability and predictability to assistance, unlike the case of WFP and CGIAR, which depend entirely on voluntary contributions; FAO, which depends on voluntary contributions for a more than half of its resources; or most recently, the Global Agriculture and Food Security Program (GAFSP), established in 2010 in response to the 2007 food crisis as a self-standing program to minimize competition from other sectors for the limited IDA allocations, thereby, making more resources available to agriculture. Unlike IDA, the size and predictability of GAFSP replenishments has been a challenge. Demand for GAFSP resources exceeds supply, but unlike IDA, GAFSP is accessible to only a limited number of countries. A combination of the IDA18 replenishment, graduation of IDA countries, and GAFSP's financial challenges raise questions about whether the GAFSP model is scalable going forward or whether the well-established IDA should be reformed and made more flexible to introduce some of the features that GAFSP has adopted, such as greater inclusion of civil society and the private sector. IFC addresses these latter issues. (GAFSP 2009, 2015, 2018).

Three-year replenishments to IDA and GAFSP provide the stability and predictability to their operations, and yet, there are plenty of opportunities for the contributing donors to review their performance and suggest refinements. We argue that similar funding arrangements need to be adopted in the cases of CGIAR, FAO, and WFP.

Evolution of the World Bank

Not only has the World Bank's relative role in financing declined, compared to the past, three important changes in multilateral assistance have also taken place: (1) a change in the tone and interaction with client countries from being supply driven (during the

McNamara era)[7] to being demand driven, with client countries savvier than in the past, and in many cases, more experienced in the business of development than the Bank staff, particularly in high-income and middle-income countries—with an emphasis on country assistance strategies based on country dialogue and ownership, both on levels and allocation among sectors; (2) greater focus on results, relative to the past; and (3) increased reliance on trust funds to supplement stagnant or declining regular administrative budgets. In reality, the demand-driven concept is complicated. Typically, finance ministries negotiate country assistance with the World Bank's country directors. Sector ministries have weak voice vis-à-vis ministries of finance and are not always consulted in determining the allocation of resources. The same applied to project staff located in Global Practices, since changed, in the World Bank. Project staff and countries' sectoral ministries have considerable freedom in designing projects, working with their counterparts in developing countries, once the lending program is agreed upon, but not in the allocation of Bank resources among sectors. Given the limited IDA allocations per country, even after adjusting IDA eligibility criteria, as mentioned previously, demand for investment lending for food and agriculture from client countries has been weak, relative to the demand for infrastructure, education, or health, and unlike when the World Bank established targets for lending to the agricultural and rural sectors during McNamara's leadership. This poses a dilemma. Agricultural development is increasingly recognized to be a result of investments in other related sectors: for example, infrastructure, which determines market access education, and which influences the ability to adopt complex technologies and health resources, which in turn affect the quantity and quality of the labor supply. Resources committed by the World Bank, details of which are found in Chapters 7 and 8, provide evidence of the revealed preferences of client countries. Furthermore, as countries have more domestic resources to invest, the transaction costs of borrowing from the Bank may not seem worth the return. That was certainly the concern of China, leading to a call for addressing the high cost of doing business with the World Bank. Often these costs have been in the form of addressing the Bank's multiple safeguards and inspection panels, independent complaint mechanisms for people and communities who believe they have been, or are likely to be, adversely affected by World Bank-funded projects. Thus, the increased voice of developing countries does not seem to have led to increased demand for World Bank lending to agriculture and rural development. Taken together, factors determining commitments to a sector include overall country allocations, policy environment, competing demands from other sectors, the rate of disbursements (agriculture tends to be a slower disbursing sector compared to infrastructure), and the ability to implement projects that together determine commitments to a sector. This situation could well change for the better in the future, based on what was agreed to at the 2018 Spring Meetings:

- The Development Committee, the ministerial forum of WBG and IMF, approved a capital increase of US$13 billion for IBRD of US$7.5 billion and IFC of US$7.5 billion "to deliver development results more effectively while becoming more financially sustainable and efficient" (World Bank 2018).
- An additional innovation of IDA18 replenishment of US$75 billion, the World Bank's IDA fund for the poorest countries, was to leverage those resources in the capital market. It issued an inaugural bond that raised US$1.5 billion from investors around

---

[7] See Chapter 8 for the World Bank during the presidency of Robert McNamara.

the world in mid-April 2018. At the Spring Meetings, WBG President Jim Yong Kim stated, "IDA's entry to the global capital markets is historic—the latest transformational shift in how we approach development finance," adding that "IDA will be able to dramatically scale up financing to help countries meet the 2030 development goals, and deliver greater value to shareholders" (World Bank 2018).

- The power of the World Bank Board may be overestimated. The Board rarely blocks anything. The Board has little influence *ex ante* over strategic or tactical decisions made by staff—and not much influence *ex post* either.
- Funding allocations are made consultatively with countries, but in rather superficial ways, dominated by countries' Ministries of Finance and World Bank Country Management Units (CMUs). Both sector staff in the Bank and Ministries in countries complain that there is often no clear vetting of priorities among sectors and examination of trade-offs. One explanation often offered for the establishment of GAFSP after the 2007 financial crisis, as discussed in Chapter 5, was that the agricultural sector often could not compete with other sectors for IDA monies. Power resides with the CMUs, so holistic perspective is possible in principle, but technical depth is often not deep in allocation decisions (and the bias is toward country level, not GPGs or continental levels).
- In view of intersectoral competition, the World Bank sectoral units have relatively little power over allocations, but the Task Team Leaders (TTLs) typically have almost total control over project design, working with client counterparts. This is why the TTL's role in the Bank has traditionally been the most creative and satisfying, particularly when borrowers are interested and committed.
- World Bank instruments make it hard for the World Bank to lead on GPGs, or on continental or regional public goods (although, where there is funding or initiative from the World Bank, many partners are still willing to be convened by the World Bank and to follow and rely on its technical leadership). The very limited nature of grant-making instruments makes it very difficult for the World Bank to lead on global or regional public good issues for which it would otherwise have a lot to offer. Grants are preferable in this respect to loans or IDA credits, as governments who are part of a regional project have to agree to pay back their portion.
- World Bank technical depth is rapidly deteriorating and needs to be strengthened if its role in GPGs is to be sustained or strengthened; sectors need to be given more power within the World Bank.
- Collaboration with other agencies is possible and encouraged (at least in rhetoric from management). It requires individual initiative, however, as scarce resource envelopes and time constraints do not facilitate such collaborative efforts.

Would Greater Voice for Developing Countries Increase Demand for Resources for Rural Transformation? External Independent Assessments

The World Bank's governance reforms since the financial crisis of 2007–8 have marginally increased the voice and shares of developing countries and have been influenced by the external independent assessment of the World Bank's governance by Ernesto Zedillo, former President of Mexico, who was commissioned by WBG President Zoellick, with a panel of international experts (2007–12) (Linn 2009; Zedillo 2009). The reforms have helped the United States agree to increase the IBRD's capital base. More reforms are anticipated, but some of them could also be counterproductive and increase politicization of the Bank. For example, the United States is opposed to lending to China and other MICs, and under Trump, did not support the Bank's climate action. With Biden's 2020 election, the new administration has already announced a Climate Czar and are likely to be very proactive on climate change. With single borrower limits on large borrowers, both in the case of IBRD for maintaining the Bank's creditworthiness and of IDA for increasing access to all eligible countries, client countries are hesitant to borrow loans for sectors like agriculture, which tend to be small in size, slow in disbursing, and without many visible impacts to show in the short run—unlike in the cases of infrastructure, education, or health investment. The growth of development lending (what was once called program lending or balance of payments support, albeit for reforms already adopted rather than for conditioned lending), relative to investment lending, is getting around some of these constraints. The Zedillo reforms had focused on five issues: (1) the need to change voting shares to accord greater "voice" for developing countries, as "voice" in governance in the Bretton Woods institutions is in part determined by the member countries' share according to their subscribed capital;[8] (2) the need for increased capitalization of the Bank; (3) the high cost of safeguards to developing countries (China, India, and other emerging countries have stressed the high cost of doing business with the Bank and suggested national safeguards should be used and improved to come closer to international standards); (4) the need for shifting the Bank lending to GPGs, to respond to climate change and pandemics and to promote financial stability; and (5) the recommendation for doing away with the resident Executive Board, which approves every project, to instead using the finance ministers of member countries to address longer term strategic issues that the World Bank faces.

The underlying theme of the WBG reforms has been rooted in the discussions of shareholding structure and voting power, along with the conceptually separate but linked issue of the size of its capital base, in a shared vision of the role of WBG in the context of the complex and evolving development landscape. Under SCI, the size, allocation rules, and other adjustments related to one another will likely change. In 2008 following the financial crisis, a two-phase package of reforms was initiated by the Bank. Termed "The Voice Reform," it had three pillars: (1) voice as shareholding, (2) voice as responsiveness, and (3) voice as effective representation on the Board, with goals of increasing developing and transition countries' (DTCs) share in IBRD to 45.8 percent (and beyond that in IDA) (Figure 6.1); increasing basic votes marginally, by expanding field presence in sub-Saharan Africa (SSA); and expanding the Board from 24 to 25 seats, allocating the additional seat to the SSA region.[9,10] From a historical perspective, the Bank's Board had consisted of 12 members in earlier times, but Bank membership increased from the original 43 to 189 countries in 2017. The expansion reflects both a growing differentiation among member states, as well as greater importance attached to inclusiveness. Reforms also increased IFC capital by US$200 million, while also increasing the IFC voting power of DTC members from 33.41 percent to 39.41 percent, assuring a greater role of diversity in management and staff for women and developing country nationals.

[8] For example, in the case of IBRD, each member receives votes consisting of share votes (one vote for each share of the Bank's capital stock held by the member), plus basic votes (World Bank 2020).

[9] The total shift to DTCs in both phases is to 4.59 percentage points, when the current SCI is fully subscribed.

[10] How can a balance be struck between representation and efficiency in decision-making, including the relationship between the size of the Board and its constituency structure?

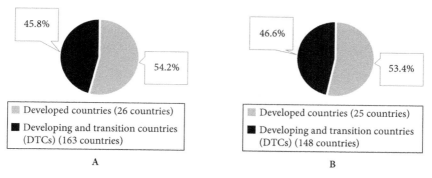

Figure 6.1 Voting shares

A. IBRD: Voting share by developed and developing and transition countries (as of March 29, 2017) (total number of votes by 189 countries = 2,350,174)

Source: Based on data from World Bank (2020).

B. IDA: Voting share by developed and developing and transition countries (as of January 31, 2017) (total number of votes by 173 countries = 26,862,188)

Source: Based on World Bank (2020).

In 2011, the Bank broadened its corporate goal from ending extreme poverty to include shared prosperity in a sustainable way. Concurrently, a far-reaching reorganization has brought the World Bank (IBRD and IDA), the IFC, MIGA, and the International Centre for Settlement of Investment Disputes (ICSID) under a single umbrella. It is slowly paving the way for increased public–private partnerships in policy analysis, advice, and lending beyond IFC's traditional "deal-making" approach. Due to the breadth of its business, WBG has more active partnerships with the UN agencies than the agencies often do among themselves, including the RBAs, as we discuss at the end of this chapter.

Internal Reforms

Internal reforms brought all technical staff under 13 Global Practices in August 2014, in an effort to better leverage global knowledge while still maintaining a system of matrix management—a two-headed animal in which the technical staff reported to their Global Practice management, as well as to regional management. With the Global Practices, a different, eternal challenge of silos emerged. For example, the Agriculture Global Practice had a narrower scope, while irrigation and water, rural development, forestry, biodiversity, and rural infrastructure were housed in other Global Practices. Beginning in 2019, the Bank, under President Malpass, abandoned these reforms, with technical staff (and respective budgets) solely under Regional Management. Global Practices are continuing to ensure quality in technical expertise, but with greatly reduced staff directly reporting to their management and severely reduced budgets. It is too early to know if the more fragmented organization is better suited to the intersectoral/interdisciplinary and multilevel needs: for example, in effecting productivity growth, while also achieving improved nutrition and sustainable landscape management. Internally, the Bank's new Country Engagement Model is called Program-for-Results.

The proposed periodic Shareholding Reviews are a way to address issues of voice, a way for the World Bank to maintain legitimacy and dynamism, and to reflect global economic changes in IBRD and IFC shareholding, as occurred in the context of the SCI.

Voice and Shareholder Influence

The US voting shares stood at 15.4 percent in 2017, still the largest in the Bank after the latest reforms, compared to 35 percent at the Bank's inception in 1945. The United States has an effective veto power on all policies of importance to the institution, including the Bank's capitalization (Gwin 1997; Kapur, Lewis, and Webb 1997). According to the Bretton Woods Project (2016): "Votes on substantive issues need 85 percent approval, granting the US (with its 16.46 percent quota) effective veto power over any major decisions." Most decisions are made by consensus, and formal votes are rarely taken, but through bilateral consultations between the shareholders and Bank management, the wishes of major shareholders are often accounted for before matters come to the Executive Board for consideration. Substantial literature exists that suggests, since the World Bank's establishment, the US government has used the World Bank to serve its strategic interests in variety of ways, including with membership and in the way veto power has been exercised formally, barring countries, such as Nicaragua, Vietnam, Iran, and Zimbabwe, from receiving World Bank assistance (Toussaint 2014). The United States' Executive Director is one of five appointed by major shareholders: that is, individual member countries (in line with the Articles). The remaining shareholders are elected by countries, after forming constituencies. While initially opposed to the idea of trust funds, the United States has become the largest contributor to the Afghanistan Trust Fund and other trust funds, as multilateral organizations can achieve certain bilateral objectives more effectively than bilaterals (Kharas 2007, 2008, 2009; Birdsall and Kharas 2010; Isenman and Shakow 2010; DFID and UK Aid 2011; Isenman 2011, 2012; Kanbur and Sumner 2012; DFID and UK Aid 2013; Custer et al. 2015; DFID and UK Aid 2016; Gulrajani 2016).

The concentration of economic power makes such influence inevitable but also strengthens ownership of those who have power. The top 25 member states in IBRD contribute 73.5 percent of the total subscriptions, and the remaining 164 countries contribute only 26.5 percent (Figure 6.2). In IFC, the top 25 member states contribute 78.4 percent. IDA voting power is less unequal: the top 25 member countries contribute 66.6 percent, and another 148 contribute 33.4 percent. Several developing countries, some of the largest recipients of IDA like India and China, now contribute to IDA and CGIAR. Keenly aware of the risk of exit of MICs, IBRD imposes less conditionality than IDA expects from its recipients on such issues as gender and governance. Since IDA recipients include many conflict-affected countries, more conditionality is understandable. This "pushing-on-the-string" approach, however necessary, is not sufficient. Empowerment of key groups in IDA countries in support of more robust participatory development is necessary, but may not yield quick visible results (World Bank 2011).

Will the World Bank's resident board be dissolved? It has been a matter of much debate, but it is not very likely. The Zedillo report (2009) noted the prohibitive cost of a resident board—US$70 million in 2009—and suggested that instead of approving individual projects, the Board should move upstream, involving finance ministers to address strategic issues facing the Bank. The issue of resident boards also applies to some of the RBAs. The

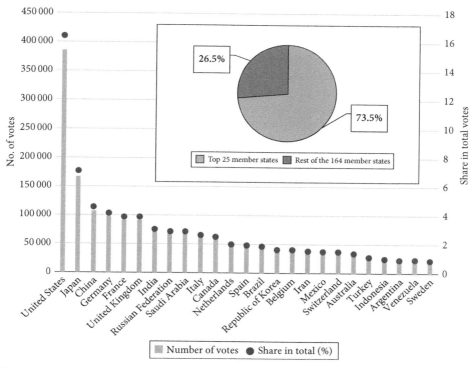

Figure 6.2 International Bank for Reconstruction and Development: Number of votes and percentage share in total by top 25 member states (as of March 29, 2017) (total number of votes = 2,350,174)

Note: The number may differ from the sum of individual percentages shown because of rounding.

Source: Based on data from World Bank (2020).

effectiveness of the boards in taking on and tackling strategic challenges is mixed and has rarely been evaluated.

Organizational Leadership, Influence, and Financial Contributions

The United States nominates a single American candidate for the Bank's president after informal consultations with other shareholders. Not all appointments have been illustrious in the World Bank and the IMF. Despite considerable debate on merit-based selections of World Bank presidents (reserved for the United States) and IMF Managing Directors (reserved for Europeans, regardless of nationality), and some flawed appointments in both organizations, competitive selection did not materialize in the World Bank in 2012, nor in 2019.[11] Even in the renewal of President Kim's second term, which occurred amid the 2016 US election fever, in advance of the July 2017 official reappointment, there was no competition. And his successor, David Malpass, was appointed unanimously in April 29 without any contest. In the "America First" argument, if the Bank were to be headed by a

---

[11] See Ottenhoff (2011); Weiss (2011); Wheeler (2007, 2011); and Beattie (2012) for discussions concerning the selection of World Bank presidents and IMF Managing Directors.

non-US national, the US Congress might lose interest in financing the World Bank, located a block away from the White House and the US Treasury. Expanding the capital base is also related to power sharing, however. Emerging countries, such as China, in particular, have expressed a strong interest in expanding the World Bank's capital base, and emerging countries are willing and able to contribute to it. Expanding the subscribed capital will open the issue of raising the share of emerging countries, like China, further in the Bank's governance, and the European donors are reluctant to lose their shares. Having their representation by a single EU representative, much like the United States, does not appeal to them (Zedillo 2013). China's voting share would increase by 1 percentage point under the new capitalization, a relatively minor adjustment. However, the Development Committee has accepted the need to correct the distribution of votes from the currently very unequal situation.

In a rapidly changing world, the Bank's strengths have been underutilized in expanding its capital base to provide more capital to countries for the badly needed investments in physical infrastructure. The World Bank–IMF report on financing "From Billions to Trillions," estimated infrastructural needs to be nearly a trillion dollars each for South Asia (SA) and SSA (Development Committee 2015). Needs of the rural sector and for capacity building are similarly large for small LICS to escape the vicious circle of poverty. As we will show in the chapters on the five organizations, however, the challenge is not simply one of mobilizing finance. Indeed, large amounts of funding committed to countries lacking internal capacity can be counterproductive. And donors' records on capacity building have been mixed when client countries have lacked political will or enabling environments.

Yet, the Bank's approved capital increase of US$13 billion must be applauded. In the past, major shareholders—the United States and European members—have been reluctant to make the transition to increasing overall subscriptions and including emerging countries in return for their increased access to the much needed capital and their increased voice in the governance of the WBG. The IDA graduation process has demonstrated the success of IDA, although it was achieved over more than half a century. Are SDGs too ambitious and unrealistic in terms of time, effort, preconditions, and patience?

The Obama administration's opposition to the establishment of the Asian Infrastructure Investment Bank (AIIB), even in the face of huge unmet infrastructure needs of developing countries, was difficult to understand in this context, except as a way to delay acknowledging the decline in the US (soft) power. Europeans rushed to join AIIB, even while Europe was cool to the idea of a capital increase for the World Bank. It is a choice to be a big fish in a small pond or a small fish in a large, globalized pond.

IFAD and WFP are examples of modified shareholder models, and FAO is a stakeholder model. Shareholder models have smaller governance, although are larger than in the private sector.

The Food and Agriculture Organization of the United Nations

FAO is a unique global knowledge organization, a provider of global and regional public goods, serving as a platform for arriving at international agreements on norms and standards; developing and promoting voluntary guidelines and agreements; generating knowledge and providing statistics; maintaining efficient market monitoring and early warning systems (Global Information and Early Warning System [GIEWS], Emergency Prevention System [EMPRES], etc.); and providing capacity development across a wide area of knowledge products and information activities. FAO monitors cross-border pests and diseases and has a demonstrated record in helping to eradicate or contain them (for example, rinderpest virus, peste des petits ruminants, or avian influenza).[12] It is also a global platform for establishing norms and standards for different aspects of food and agriculture, including food safety. Importantly, it hosts, together with WHO, the secretariats of the Joint FAO/WHO Food Standards Programme and the Codex Alimentarius Commission, which provides internationally binding standards to protect the health of consumers and to ensure fair practices in the food trade.[13] The Intergovernmental Panel on Climate Change (IPCC) relies on FAO's estimates of land use and land use changes; FAO's greenhouse gas (GHG) emission estimates have been used in IPCC assessment reports. Even the harshest critics of FAO would like to see FAO as a valuable provider of GPGs and related capacity development functions. In tandem with its traditional GPG function, which is funded chiefly by assessed contributions, FAO has developed an increasingly important development function. The development functions have seen a steady expansion and by 2019, have exceed the assessed contributions by about 60 percent. As a result of frozen nominal "regular" budget, FAO's GPG functions are underfunded. The disjuncture between FAO's GPG functions, performed by using its very modest assessed contributions, and its technical assistance function, provided entirely by stitching together robustly growing voluntary contributions, has continued to be a fault line.

Since the adoption of the SDGs, FAO has become a "custodian," responsible for monitoring 21 of the total 232 unique SDG indicators,[14]—for example, indicators for SDG2 (zero hunger), SDG5 (gender equality), SDG6 (clean water and sanitation), SDG12 (responsible consumption and production), SDG14 (life below water), and SDG15 (life on land), and as a contributing agency, for four more indicators (FAO 2017b). FAO has adopted SDG targets and indicators as the targets and indicators of its own five Strategic Objectives, as has IFAD for its own Strategic Framework. As a result, FAO is harmonizing its work with the SDGs and has declared it will contribute to 40 targets, measured through 53 unique SDG indicators of the 15 out of 17 SDGs, as part of the proposed Strategic Objective Results Framework for 2018–21 (FAO 2017a).

FAO will continue to provide data and statistical support to some 200 countries (FAO 2017d).

It is unclear how FAO's governance manages these demanding strategic objectives on a small budget. With a membership of 194 countries, two associate members, and the EU, FAO's Governing Bodies consist of the Conference of member countries, the Council, and supporting committees. Within their respective mandates, they contribute to the definition of the overall policies and regulatory frameworks of FAO and the establishment of the Strategic Framework, Medium-Term Plan, and Programme of Work and Budget. They also exercise or contribute to oversight of the administration of FAO. The Conference, the sovereign governing body of 194 member nations, the European Union, and two associate

---

[12] See FAO pages on peste des petits ruminants (http://www.fao.org/ppr/en/) and rinderpest (http://www.fao.org/ag/againfo/programmes/en/rinderpest/home).

[13] The General Principles of the Codex Alimentarius state: "The publication of the Codex Alimentarius is intended to guide and promote the elaboration and establishment of definitions and requirements for foods to assist in their harmonization and in doing so to facilitate international trade." Codex standards are the basis for adjudicating food safety-related questions under the SPS (Sanitary and Phytosanitary Measures) and TBT (Technical Barriers to Trade) agreements of the World Trade Organization (see http://www.fao.org/3/y7867e/y7867e08.htm).

[14] See the Revised List of Global Sustainable Development Goal indicators: https://unstats.un.org/sdgs/indicators/indicators-list/

members (Faroe Islands and Tokelau) is chaired by an elected member state representative and meets once per biennium. The Council acts as the executive organ of the Conference between sessions and usually meets at least five times per biennium. The Council consists of representatives of 49 member nations elected by the Conference for staggered three-year terms. It is chaired by an Independent Chairperson who is appointed by the Conference for a two-year renewable term.

Members meet every two years to elect a Council of 49 members, one of the largest governance bodies, particularly when considered in relation to its small, assessed contributions, of which the governing bodies have any control, chaired by a person other than the director-general (DG) (see http://www.fao.org/unfao/govbodies/gsb-definition/en/).

As noted earlier, FAO's overall program of work is funded by assessed and voluntary contributions. The assessed contributions are set at the biennial FAO Conference. The total FAO Budget for 2018–19 was US$2.6 billion, most (US$1.6 billion) of which came from. voluntary contributions and the rest (US$1.006 billion) from assessed contributions. Both parts of the budget are integrated under the Organization's results framework prepared by FAO management and submitted by the FAO Council to the biannual FAO Conference for approval.

The FAO Conference does not allocate funding for trust funds/voluntary contributions. Given the large share of voluntary contributions, an important question for FAO is the appropriate balance between voice, efficiency, relevance, and clarity in accountability: for example, to the individual donors who provide voluntary funds and enter into agreements with management versus the executive councils of the organization. Here, there has been even a difference among donors as to the extent to which the large current structure should manage only the small, assessed contributions, or be accountable for FAO's total work program. Some wonder if a modified shareholder model, weighted by contributions—such as that in IFAD, which manages its affairs almost entirely using its administrative budget without any trust funds, and WFP, which depends entirely on trust funds—should be adopted in FAO. CGD's work on FAO raised these thorny issues of the balance between FAO's GPG function versus its technical assistance/emergency work and the extent to which FAO's GPG function was being undermined by its technical assistance/emergency functions.

Having a long-standing mandate to provide all agriculture-related technical expertise under one roof, and having been given a large responsibility under the SDGs since 2015, FAO needs to be the true center of scientific and technical excellence for food and agriculture under climate change. It is not yet clear if FAO has sufficiently well positioned itself for this role. Indeed, within FAO, there is no consensus on the need for FAO to become a center of excellence, though, it is clear that the new management at FAO sees this as a significant and immediate challenge. This may reflect the current funding reality and the risk of making the gap between aspiration and reality explicit, or the funding reality reflecting a low level of aspiration.

Over the years, FAO has provided organizational leadership with a signature role in setting global goals for hunger reduction at the national and global levels, while traditionally, the United Nations Children's Fund (UNICEF) and WHO have been the champions of the issues of maternal and child care and food security at the household level. Despite the progress achieved for the SDGs, some statistics concerned with health are still appallingly high: infant and child mortality rates; wasting and stunting indicators; and incidence of anemia among young girls and women. The Rome Declaration, the outcome of the World Food Summit in 1996, organized by the FAO and attended by 112 heads or deputy heads of state and government, formed the basis of MDG1 and SDG2 (FAO 1996). FAO has increased its work at the household level, working with UNICEF and WHO, and expanded its partnerships overtly, including the issuance of a joint report, *The State of Food Security and Nutrition in the World 2017*, with IFAD, UNICEF, WHO, and WFP (FAO et al. 2017).

The SDGs' focus on results on the ground poses a tension between FAO's GPG functions in improving delivery of just-in-time, high quality statistics, ensuring food safety, and preventing pandemics. FAO's management challenges the widely shared internal and external views that its skills base is eroded, and a tension continues to haunt FAO— between the provision of GPGs and country assistance, both of which are needed with resources that are limited, fractionated, and unpredictable. In Chapter 9 on FAO, we further review this evidence, based on a CGD study that criticizes FAO on similar grounds. Again, within FAO there is no consensus about FAO's eroded skills base or the tension between the need to focus on FAO's mandated GPG function versus its technical assistance role at the country level, in the face of its very limited core budget.

2007 Independent External Evaluation

The Independent External Evaluation (IEE), for which Uma Lele served as a panel member, called for reform with growth. It noted that if FAO did not exist, it would have had to be invented. The panel also made well over 100 recommendations for reforms. The IEE kick-started reforms, which formally ended in 2013, but there has been no significant increase in resources for FAO to achieve growth. The first of its kind in the organization's history, the evaluation concluded that FAO's financial and programmatic crisis was rooted in its conservative and slow-to-adapt, bureaucratic leadership, with declining organizational capacity and many imperiled core competencies. It recommended a new Strategic Frame-work, an institutional culture change, and reform of administrative and management systems (FAO 2007a). A background paper on FAO's governance, written for the IEE, noted that FAO's overall budget was spread too thinly over a wide range of topics and many program entities had lost the critical mass necessary to be effective.[15] Decentralization of staff and resources risked reducing certain technical programs at headquarters below critical mass. The Technical Cooperation Programme (TCP) activities underwent real budget cuts, and other activities had to shrink even more, further aggravating the underfunding in normative activities. The programs implemented by the technical departments at head-quarters reached a disproportionately low share in FAO's overall resources, while admin-istration, communication, representation, and liaison received a high share. We present the trends and breakdowns of these resources in Chapter 9. As a result of these budgetary constraints, FAO was not using its full technical potential to participate actively and visibly, or take the lead in newly emerging initiatives. Extra-budgetary funds accounted for a growing share of the organizations' overall resources. However, at that time, there was no formal institutional mechanism that would help coordinate the use of these funds, bundle them, and seek synergies with the regular program.

The FAO management adopted IEE's advice to undertake "reform with the growth" in resources so as to have an FAO "fit for this century" in its official response (FAO 2007a, 2, 11; 2007b). The staff also supported "a radical shift in management culture and spirit,

---

[15] For the chapter on "Governance" in the IEE report, a note indicates: background "working papers were prepared by Abdelaziz Megzari, Sholto Cross and Martin Piñeiro" (FAO 2007a, 169).

depoliticization of appointments, restoration of trust between staff and management, [and] setting strategic priorities of the organization."[16] With a one-time injection of US$42.6 million (€38.6 million) and a three-year Immediate Plan of Action for "reform with growth," FAO spent US$21.8 million overhauling its financial procedures, hierarchies, and human resources management (*Economic Times* 2008). In January 2012, FAO DG José Graziano da Silva acted upon the commitment made during his campaign to bring the reform to completion, but FAO's critics have argued it is far from complete. The DG shifted the focus of the reform process to realization of its benefits and mainstreaming the reform into the work of the organization (FAO 2011).

The DG improved appointments in country offices, which in earlier times were riddled with political appointments. A number of highly qualified staff were moved to the fields. The shortage of staff at headquarters in critical areas, however, such as in water and in AQUASTAT[17] management, are obvious. Additionally, when high-quality staff members retire, or are moved to country offices, while it bolsters FAO in the field in the latter case, its headquarters staffing is thinned.

The creation of a matrix management structure took an additional toll on FAO's already thinned-out technical capacity. More than 50 critically important technical staff were absorbed by the new horizontal layer of the matrix, the so-called Strategic Programmes (SPs), without providing the technical divisions with the necessary replacements or compensatory funding. Worse, most of the staff seconded to the SPs continue to be financed through the budgets of the technical divisions, which made the critics of this matrix move refer to it as adding "insult to injury" to FAO's technical work. A recent internal audit report took stock of a hiring spree that started in December 2016. The findings of the report are not in the public domain; even FAO country missions can only view it on dedicated computers, with no files, not even screenshots, taken. Some of the salient findings of the audit report corroborate the idea that appointments were increasingly undertaken on a political rather than a meritorious basis, further undermining FAO's technical capacity.

Issues of Leadership

At FAO, the DG is elected democratically, although regional rotation does enter into consideration: that is, the turn of a region, as others have had their turn. Yet, the DG's position was occupied for 36 years by only two autocratic leaders (Edouard Saouma, 1976–93, and Jacques Diouf, 1994–2011), with complaints that the elections entailed political horse trading, senior-level appointments, and other benefits for countries' officials in return for votes—a phenomenon for which the UN is also criticized, more so than the World Bank or the IMF. The IEE recommended no more than two 6-year terms. FAO's main governing body, the Conference, reduced the term of office to two 4-year terms for FAO's DG.

Historically, FAO's culture has been one of top down governance, in contrast to the World Bank's, but this culture has changed for the better under the current DG. The shortage of resources, outlined in this chapter, has led to a tension between the provision of GPGs and country assistance. The loss of retiring staff, combined with recruitment of

---

[16] "For a Renewal of FAO," online petition, November 2007.

[17] AQUASTAT is the global water information system of FAO, which collects, analyzes, and disseminates data and information by country on water resources, water uses, and agricultural water management (see "About AQUASTAT": http://www.fao.org/nr/water/aquastat/About_us/index.stm).

new staff on contracts, has led to a loss of institutional memory and lack of trust between staff and management, potentially risking FAO's professional reputation (FAO 2017e). This challenge, however, is not unique to FAO. The spate of "express" appointments in 140 professional posts boosted the statistics in the face of criticism from members about the high rate of vacancies, but increased the possibility of detrimental effects on the organization's technical capacity in the long term (FAO 2016). The fact that FAO needs in-house skills and access to state-of-the-art measurement tools, including GIS and other wide-ranging tools, as well as a good knowledge of its clients, is indisputable. Therefore, the review of FAO's technical capacity was much anticipated. Although carried out by three veterans of IOs (Cleaver, Golan, and Sood 2017), the FAO's Council and management lost a major opportunity to do a thorough review of the quality and not just the quantity of staff in relation to demand or need for skills in rapidly changing technical areas. The debate on the quantity vs. the quality of staff, in relation to needs of FAO's functions, came perilously close to the old North–South debates, with the Northern side being in favor of seniority and quality of staff. Some in FAO argue that such old North–South tension has disappeared in the context of the SDGs, since donor resources are small and increasingly fractionated, relative to government expenditures of developing countries. The need for help is still great in least developing countries, however, and expectations MICs for international staff knowledge have increased, given that their own internal capacity is now much higher than it was 50 years ago. IOs are not able to keep up with this reality, in the face of their shrinking core budgets and changing needs.

The World Bank faces a similar challenge. One-third of its staff is long-term, regular employees. Another third has fixed-term contracts, and still another third are short-term consultants. Mentoring has declined. Both institutions need to be centers of excellence, but reputational risk is greater for FAO than the World Bank. FAO is exclusively a knowledge organization, and its services are not accompanied by millions of dollars of loans and grants.

Donors' Role in Governance

FAO's total assessment is small in relation to its vast public goods agenda and the stewardship of the largest number of SDG indicators. FAO assessments are concentrated among donors, as indeed they are in other organizations we review: for example, WFP, for which 88 percent of its funding comes from 15 donors, as we discuss here. As much as 79.24 percent of FAO's *assessed* contributions come from 15 member countries, and as much as 88.35 percent is from 25 member countries. The remaining 154 countries contribute only 11.65 percent of the assessed contributions (Figure 6.3). With its heavy reliance on voluntary contributions, donors understandably want to drive the agenda, but their own fragmentation has led them to move to bargaining in the retail business of aid, largely at the country level, rather than on the larger global or regional levels. Many member countries, including several developed countries and some developing countries, continue to prefer for FAO to focus on its GPG functions, whereas other member countries prefer technical assistance and emergency assistance. However, unlike the World Bank in which the Country Policy and Institutional Assessment (CPIA) is used to allocate resources among countries using transparent, relatively more objective criteria (IEG 2009), FAO's allocations of technical assistance and emergency resources and their actual use appear to be less subject to clear rules, rather achieved on a country-by-country, project-by-project, donor by donor basis, leading to much debate and criticism among member countries. Demand-driven

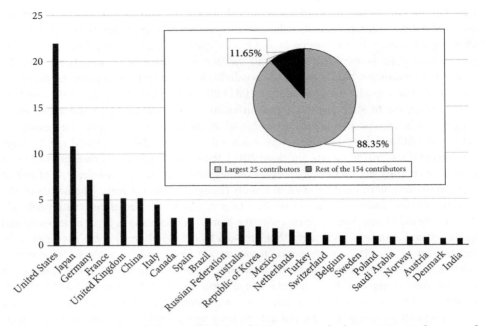

Figure 6.3 Assessment rate (%) to the FAO Regular Programme by largest 25 contributors and percentage share in total, 2016–2017

Source: Authors' construction. Data from "Regular Programme Contributions of Largest 25 Contributors," http://www.fao.org/about/strategic-planning/country-contributions/en/

technical assistance is often cited as an example of a potential for matching supply with needs. The Africa Solidarity Trust Fund, funded by African governments with a steering committee with clear roles and responsibilities, and the lightly earmarked FAO Multipartner Programme Support Mechanism (FMM), supported by the Netherlands, Belgium, and Sweden, could benefit from such a perspective.[18]

The demand-driven focus of FAO on results on the ground to meet SDGs also raises another important issue, with a parallel to CGIAR's downward orientation, and may be diverting attention from achieving excellence in FAO's GPG function, much as we have argued it does in the case of CGIAR. Can a GPG function, whether in FAO or in CGIAR, be addressed in a purely demand-driven, results-on-the-ground approach? To date, FAO's statistics work is largely supported by donors, including BMGF, and in the 2018–19 budget, the Codex Initiative has had to rely on reallocations of unspent funds from the budget rather than a predetermined allocation from the administrative budget supported by assessed contributions.

To summarize, it is unclear if FAO's member states and management have the commitment and consensus to address both its GPG function and technical assistance/emergency function at the country level at its best. Chapter 9 on FAO, in which we review a number of recent FAO evaluations, confirms this tension about the need for stronger staff, both at

---

[18] "FAO uses unearmarked funding strategically... The FMM is a funding mechanism for partners willing to contribute unearmarked funds or slightly earmarked funds. Created in 2010, the FMM is currently supported by the Kingdoms of Belgium, the Netherlands and Sweden" (http://www.fao.org/partnerships/resource-partners/news/news-article/en/c/451561/).

headquarters and country offices, with a proposal for the establishment of a center of excellence and with necessary resources, if FAO is to assist countries effectively.

The World Food Programme

> Our compassion is boundless...But our budgets, unfortunately, are limited. Matching our funding to our vision remains our long-term objective.
>
> (WFP 2016b)

WFP received the Nobel Peace Prize in 2020 for its extraordinary effort to match funding to its vision in the context of the growing refugee population.

Matching demand with supply of resources, however, is also one of WFP's biggest challenges, particularly as the funding is totally voluntary, and 88 percent of it comes from 15 countries (WFP 2016a). The number of people affected by humanitarian crises has more than doubled over the past decade (Development Initiatives 2016).

WFP in its report, "World Food Assistance 2017: Taking Stock and Looking Ahead," noted, "Crises are growing in complexity and duration. Funding needs are climbing sharply. Humanitarian principles are under threat, with humanitarian response constantly at risk of being co-opted by political objectives. These challenges apply in full to food assistance agencies. As is the case for all areas of humanitarian action, food assistance agencies face significant challenges linked to funding levels and conditions, access to beneficiaries, protection of beneficiaries and security of staff" (WFP 2017b, 106).

WFP is the brainchild of the former US President Eisenhower, who established the Food for Peace program to use massive food surpluses for emergency and development programs. Senator George McGovern played a key role in 1961, in establishing an emergency response program within FAO, using US surpluses. WFP, as an entity in its own right, became operational in 1963, and soon evolved into a program of repute, addressing emergencies in Iran, Sudan, Thailand, and Ethiopia (Glauber, Nabil, and Smith 2017).

As the need for agility and flexibility of emergency response challenged FAO's more deliberate administrative procedures, WFP obtained more autonomy in 1978. Like other heads of UN funds and programs, the WFP executive director is appointed by the UN secretary-general, but in WFP's case, jointly with the FAO DG, a historical legacy.

Through food assistance, WFP seeks to address the causes for hunger, ranging from lack of resilience to climate change to gender inequality and market failures, using "the full range of instruments, activities, and platforms that empower vulnerable and food-insecure people and communities so they can regularly have access to nutritious food" (WFP 2017b, 8).

WFP has begun to take a broader view of food assistance, going beyond the short term, through in-kind food transfers, cash-based transfers, local and regional procurement of food and food system services, technical assistance measures, and numerous support activities. It also seeks to combat the root causes of hunger (climate change, conflict, gender inequality, urbanization) in the medium term and long term. Further, the frequency, scale, and severity of humanitarian crises are increasing (OCHA 2016). WFP's direct food assistance expenditures increased from US$2.2 billion in 2009 to US$5.3 billion in 2015 (WFP 2017b, 11). And, although WFP has been innovative in deploying a range of tools to address the varied challenges it has faced, it was able to serve a smaller number of needy during this period than previously. In 2017, WFP helped 91.4 million people in 83 countries, about 11 percent of the 815 million hungry estimated by FAO, compared to 109 million in 75 countries in 2010 (WFP 2010; FAO 2017f).

The declining number serviced, despite more than doubling of WFP's expenditures during this period, as well as the declining share of in-kind food transfers from 54 percent to a less than 40 percent, is noteworthy. The share of cash-based transfers saw the most increase from less than 1 percent to 20 percent, the fastest in Latin America and the Caribbean and slowest in Central Africa. The increased share and role of cash-based transfers reduced the cost of delivery, relative to in-kind food transfers. The share devoted to logistics also fell from 32 percent to 20 percent, reflecting the contraction in the share of in-kind food transfers (WFP 2017b).

WFP has been innovative in its approach to food assistance, more so than the US bilateral food aid. It has been adopting a blend of approaches, ranging from in-kind food aid to cash-based transfers and triangular purchases in countries closer to places of action. In contrast, US bilateral food aid is procured domestically, shipped in US ships, and every tax dollar spent on US food aid yields only 35–40 cents of food commodities available to hungry or disaster-affected people. Canada has no such restrictions and makes far more extensive use of local and regional purchases, cash, and vouchers. As a result, its taxpayers see roughly twice as much—almost 70 cents' worth of food—from every food aid dollar spent (Barrett 2017).

Many facing emergencies are in MICs, such as Nigeria and Syria. This assistance involved the handling of six Level 3 emergencies (the most severe of large-scale humanitarian disasters), including a famine in South Sudan and emergencies in northern Nigeria, Somalia, and Yemen.[19] Level 3 emergencies, the highest classification for the most severe and large-scale humanitarian crises, require mobilization of global-, regional-, and country-level response capabilities—dominated by food assistance funding and expenditures, most of which is earmarked. This earmarking diverts attention from other protracted, but lower-level emergencies. This reflects broader trends in humanitarian funding.[20]

WFP's voluntary funding tends to be uncertain, insufficient, delayed, restricted, and unpredictable. Over the past five years, 88 percent of voluntary contributions to WFP have come from just 15 countries (see Figure 6.4). There is an urgent need to expand and diversify the funding base for internationally facilitated food assistance (IASC 2013) or to reallocate existing funding differently: for example, from bilateral to multilateral organizations.

This diversification or reallocation is needed because WFP has been more agile and more efficient than the US bilateral assistance, due in large part to absence of lobbying pressure of domestic interests, such as the shipping industry, the community of nongovernmental organization (NGOs), or members of Congress with agricultural interests.

WFP has responded well to the growing criticism of in-kind food aid as being a disincentive to food production and to the reality of declining food surpluses—changing its strategy from food aid to food assistance beginning around 2005. It has positioned itself well by, first, linking its activities to MDGs, and later, to the SDGs and climate change. Finally, WFP has been better able to deal with different kinds of emergencies and to participate in the continuum from emergencies and humanitarian assistance to development, although there is

---

[19] To declare a Phase 5 Famine, the UN Integrated Food Security Phase Classification, or IPC scale, must indicate that, "Even with any humanitarian assistance at least one in five HHs [households] in the area has an extreme lack of food and other basic needs where starvation, death, and destitution are evident." A famine is declared when 1 in 10,000 people are dying every day (see "IPC and Famine": http://www.ipcinfo.org/ipcinfo-website/resources/resources-details/en/c/1129202/).

[20] For more information on humanitarian system-wide emergency activation (L3 activation), see IASC (2012).

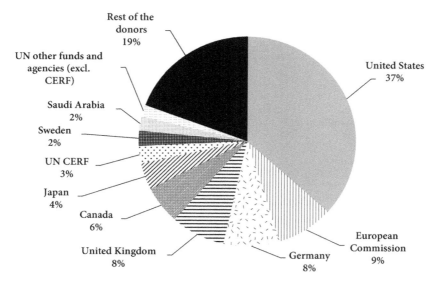

Figure 6.4 Total contributions to the World Food Programme by top 10 donors, 2013–2017* (total = US$22.1 billion)

Note: *As of March 19, 2017. Contribution data may be subject to change, as a result of retroactive adjustments. CERF = Central Emergency Response Fund (UN).

Source: World Food Programme, Funding and Donors (WFP 2020a).

scope for improvement in WFP playing to its comparative advantage in emergency assistance and partnering more actively with development actors.

Governance

A 36-member executive board oversees WFP's humanitarian and development food aid activities. Board seats are determined by election, divided equally between the UN Economic and Social Council (ECOSOC) and FAO. Of the 36 total seats, 21 are from developing countries, the majority selected by FAO, and 15 are from developed country donors, the majority selected by ECOSOC (WFP 2014a). This partial shareholder model differs from than the "one country, one vote" model of FAO. It gives donors considerable voice and power. The composition of the executive board ensures that developing nation members have a stake in decision-making (see Table 6.2). In 2014, all but two developing countries on the board were contributing governments or had contributed in the preceding five-year period (with the exceptions being Ghana and Equatorial Guinea; see Table A.6.1). The WFP Board, like the boards of other multilateral organizations, strives to make all decisions by consensus, and the board is expected to work to achieve such consensus before a matter is put to a vote.

In 2016, WFP adopted a new corporate architecture to support national governments in their efforts to achieve their goals for food security. This "Integrated Road Map" was adopted to change the way WFP plans, manages, and reports on programs, with a view to improving operational effectiveness, so as to maximize impact for beneficiaries and to align more closely with countries' priorities. It will take a lot of internal capacity to achieve the objectives of WFP's 2030 Agenda. This is an area in which there is considerable scope for

Table 6.2 World Food Programme governance

Countries		FAO selection	ECOSOC selection	Totals
Developing country[a] lists	A	4	4	8
	B	3	4	7
	C	3	2	5
	Rotating[b]	1		1
Developing country members		11	10	21
Developed country lists	D	6	6	12
	E	1	2	3
Developed country members		7	8	15
Total members		18	18	36

Notes: [a] For a definition of developing countries, see https://executiveboard.wfp.org/state-members-and-distribution-seats

[b] "One additional member rotating among the states included in lists A, B, and C to be elected by the Council of the Food and Agriculture Organization of the United Nations; the pattern of rotation shall be as follows: (i) A State from list A to be elected to occupy the additional seat every other term, starting from 1 January 2012; (ii) A State from list B to be elected to occupy the additional seat every fourth term, starting from 1 January 2015; (iii) A State from list C to be elected to occupy the additional seat every fourth term, starting from 1 January 2021" (WFP 2014a, appendix B(f), 30).

Source: Table by authors, derived from "WFP Governance and Leadership" (https://www.wfp.org/governance-and-leadership) and WFP (2014a).

RBAs to cooperate with FAO, which is often lacking in funding to provide technical assistance that can serve WFP's needs. IFAD and the World Bank can fund the programs in their effort to develop a joint path from disasters to humanitarian aid to rehabilitation and development, as discussed later in this chapter, in the context of RBA collaboration.

A large share of WFP funding has come from the United States (Figure 6.4), and as its largest donor, with a few exceptions, US nationals have led the organization, for the most part, since the 1990s. Internationalizing food aid has made its distribution more efficient and less political. As the world ran out of food surpluses around 2005, WFP made its strategic transition from supplying food aid to providing food assistance and cash transfers. There was also a growing consensus at that time of the distortionary effects of in-kind food aid on local and regional markets and the disturbance of local dietary traditions, with unintended negative consequences. Hence, receiving cash from donors, local purchase of food for distribution, and cash transfers to recipients have become the preferred instruments.

Governance Reforms

The WFP Executive Board approved a new, considerably strengthened Evaluation Policy in November 2015, to increase its accountability and to be comprehensively incorporated into all WFP's policies and programs (WFP 2020b). The work under the accountability framework started as early as 2000, and has expanded and evolved beyond the original recommendations accepted by the Board, as a result of a dialogue between the Board, the Secretariat, and the External Auditor. As a major step forward in governance reforms, with the Executive Board, WFP's working group's lengthy deliberations culminated in a report in 2005 on developing tools to support the four frameworks: strategy, policy, oversight, and accountability of WFP, as well as delineating the roles of the Board and the Executive Director (WFP 2005). With regard to information sharing, dialogue, consensus building, and decision-making, the assessment measures up well against best practices elsewhere in the international and public sectors. The tools have provided an effective basis for further evolution. The Executive Board and Management work together: for example, for swift implementation of emergency responses; unanimous decision-making, with growing delegation of responsibility to management; and increased transparency.

WFP's 2016 annual evaluation report, the first under the new policy, addressed WFP's performance at all three levels—global, country, and project. It reaffirmed WFP's capacity to quickly move to providing large-scale emergency assistance. The 2016 evaluation provided insights into the evolution of WFP's ability to move fluidly between implementing and enabling, using a range of activities and transfer modalities to respond to shocks in countries where development and humanitarian needs are constantly shifting. The displacement of 10 million refugees from Iraq in 2016 and the Ebola crisis in 2014 affirmed WFP's strategic reorientation under the Strategic Plan (2017–21). Evaluations make clear that highly demanding emergency responses take precedence over all other work. WFP's activities have stretched their capacity for addressing emergencies and building the Integrated Road Map. The Annual Report of the Inspector General in Rome, in June 2017, addressed these issues (WFP 2017a).

Key challenges going forward for WFP include the stretched capacity for emergencies, in addition to implementation of the Integrated Road Map. WFP's potential inability to handle several emergencies simultaneously presents major risks. Other important areas of work may not receive the attention or resources needed, given the high number of emergencies and transformation processes underway. "Gaps in workforce planning and talent management" also could prove problematic (WFP 2017a, 7), which is why WFP's collaboration with other RBAs and other IOs, including the World Bank, will be critical going forward. These collaborations are discussed in Chapter 12 on WFP.

The International Fund for Agricultural Development

One of the major responses to the food crises of the early 1970s, and a significant outcome of the 1974 World Food Conference, was the establishment in 1977 of IFAD, the 13th specialized agency of the UN.[21] The purpose in establishing IFAD was not only to increase investments in the poor, but also to recycle petrodollars, from the first oil shock, for development purposes. This initial commitment by the Organization of the Petroleum Exporting Countries (OPEC) led to an agreement that gave OPEC countries a role in the governance of IFAD, including equal voting power (on the basis of "one country, one vote") among the three categories of members: OECD, OPEC, and developing countries (IFAD and the OPEC Fund 2005). However, as IFAD's funding base has evolved, so, too, has its voting structure. Voting rights are distributed according to paid contributions, and as of July 2017, the List A category (primarily OECD members) has 48.7 percent of votes; List B (primarily OPEC members) has 12.5 percent; and List C (developing countries) member countries has 38.8 percent (Figure 6.5). Except for two, all presidents of IFAD have come from OPEC countries. In recent elections, the presidential election has been become an

---

[21] See IFAD, Governance, https://www.ifad.org/en/governance.

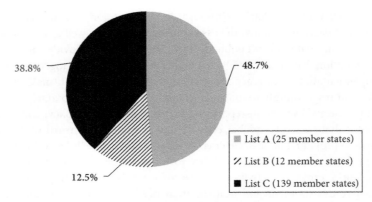

38.8%

48.7%

12.5%

■ List A (25 member states)

⁄ List B (12 member states)

■ List C (139 member states)

Figure 6.5 Voting rights of IFAD member states: Percentage share in total votes by List A (primarily OECD members); List B (primarily OPEC members); and List C (developing member states), as of March 10, 2017
Source: IFAD (2019).

increasingly competitive process, and Gilbert Fossoun Houngbo, former Prime Minister of Togo, took office as the sixth president of IFAD on April 1, 2017.

The big question for IFAD going forward is whether it will continue to assist poor in MICs or concentrate its resources in LICs. IFAD lending to MICs, at higher interest rates, has provided increased reflows to IFAD's capital base, ensuring longer term financial sustainability, and in addition, these countries are providing increased levels of contributions during the replenishment process, with both India and China increasing their contributions. Second, there can be cross-country learning, but transferring lessons across countries has been harder than typically argued. Third, lending to MICs gives IFAD a global status and ensures those countries' participation in broader governance decisions, whereas lending to poor countries only makes it more of a regional institution.

IFAD's funding history, ostensibly reflecting an OPEC–OECD funding accord, is discussed in Chapter 11 on IFAD. There have been no changes in IFAD's governance, apart from voting rights reform in 1995. Three major external evaluations led to some marginal improvements in IFAD's management. IFAD has been financed predominantly by OECD members, with a growing share, albeit small, from recipient members themselves. The perceived weakness in the original funding model led to the only major reform in governance in 1995, the switch from a "one country, one vote" to voting shares based on membership and levels of contribution. In 2001, the first president was elected from a non-OPEC country. Apart from the continued emphasis on co-financing, the concerns over the funding model has also initiated limited sovereign borrowing (in 2014), and a discussion (in 2017) at the ongoing 11th IFAD Replenishment of how IFAD could access capital markets to develop a larger capital base to source financing to facilitate the demand for and growth in lending to MICs for rural development (see https://webapps.ifad.org/members/repl/sessions). These discussions reflect some of the aspects of the Zedillo evaluation of the World Bank in 2009: changing voting shares to reflect membership's voice; reducing MIC lending from donor-sourced replenishment funds; and in the future, increased capitalization (Zedillo 2009). The Governing Council and Executive Board, with the exception of voting shares, retain the same membership categories, representation, functions, and authority, as conceived in 1977.

The reforms that have taken place since 2007–8, therefore, have been largely focused on operational and administrative activities, both internal and external, with an emphasis on effectiveness and efficiency in the business model and driven by the recommendations of the external evaluations and reviews. The development of a country presence strategy, a reform initiated and led by IFAD in 2011, had initially been conceived to support program implementation, but is now augmented with broader representational roles, so that with a zero-growth budget, the strategy means a trade-off with operational work. Further expansion of country presence, now underway, will require a substantive budget transfer to outpost operations (that is, not just staff costs, and as of December 2017, agreed to by the Executive Board), together with real decision-making at the country level, as highlighted by the Multilateral Organisation Performance Assessment Network (MOPAN). Retaining senior staff and decision-making at headquarters, together with many support and ancillary departments, like FAO, can perpetuate the bureaucratic imperative of centralized headquarters management. UN reforms may address this issue of consolidation of country offices of RBA institutions (UN 2017b).

Within its focus on small-scale agriculture and mandate of rural poverty alleviation, IFAD, like others, has developed a broad menu of services to complement its investment functions. This includes knowledge management, technical assistance, partnerships, and in the case of farmer organizations and land tenure, advocacy work and the development of financial models to elicit financing from foundations and the private sector—including for the Adaptation for Smallholder Agricultural Programme (ASAP), a key climate change adaptation program for smallholder farmers, launched in 2012. Given both the complementarity of this menu and the specificity of IFAD's approach, there is scope for better development of synergies with the other four of the Big Five organizations, especially with CGIAR. Obviously, the proximity of the other RBAs provides a potential starting point, and FAO's technical services offer the most immediate potential, but WBG still remains key for both the financial services currently offered and the future growth in private sector financing. In IFAD's specific case, accessing financial markets to broaden financial products to meet the diverse financing needs of its membership, including MICs, reflects the role of IFAD as a mobilizer of funds for rural development and is in line with its founding charter.

The IFAD Eleventh Replenishment of its core financing for the 2019–21 period was concluded on February 12, 2018, prior to its meeting of the Governing Council but following a postponement of the final pledging session at the December 2017 replenishment meeting. Provisionally, total pledges made totaled US$845 million (compared to US$1,030 million for IFAD10), with some countries, particularly Germany, still to pledge. For the first time in IFAD's history, the United States did not pledge (IFAD10 pledge was US$90 million). This was partially offset by increased pledges from China (US$60–81 million) and the Netherlands (US$75–86 million).

The Replenishment target was US$1.2 billion to provide for a lending and grant program of up US$3.5 billion. IFAD will continue to use its Sovereign Borrowing Framework to borrow up to 50 percent of the replenishment target (from lenders such as the KfW Development Bank) and will consider concessional partner loan frameworks, similar to those introduced by IDA and the AfDB. Finally, as noted, IFAD will continue to explore possible market funding.

Following changes to its allocation framework, IFAD will allocate 90 percent of its core finance to LICs and LMICs, with 10 percent going to upper-middle-income countries (UMICs), such as China, Mexico, and Brazil, which will mean a decrease in levels of funding to UMICs. These strategic changes reflect the underlying financial constraints of the current IFAD model where, unlike the World Bank, IFAD cannot graduate highly concessional (IDA) members into IBRD resources, because IFAD, as a Fund, has no market-based lending facilities. In line with the Addis Ababa Financing for Development meeting, IFAD will try to further develop partnerships (and co-financing) with the private sector but recognizes that it will be challenging to increase private sector collaboration and co-financing (IFAD 2018). These critical issues are expected to be central in the discussions of the ongoing IFAD12 Replenishment.

CGIAR

Often described as the best investment that donors have made to increase food productivity and reduce hunger, and directly relevant to SDG2, CGIAR has contributed substantially to increasing world food production in food deficit countries since its inception in 1971. Its original business model was to provide global and regional public goods and to promote investment in building capacity of national agricultural research systems (NARS) in developing countries, so as to make them stronger partners to undertake essential downstream activities of applied and adaptive research and extension to achieve impacts at scale.

Among the five organizations, CGIAR is by far the most complex, and Chapter 10 on CGIAR discusses the three major and many minor reforms that it has undertaken to address issues of governance, management, financing, research priorities, and conduct during the 2001–3, 2008–15, and post-2015 periods. Funding of CGIAR had stagnated until 2005–6, then more than doubled from US$426 million (in 2006) to US$960 million (in 2016) in response to the food crisis. Since 2014 (US$1,057 million), its funding has declined again and has remained fragmented, short-term, and unpredictable. Accountability for the system-level performance is less clear.

The organization grew in response to donors' desires to expand the scope of research and the number of Centers, such as for agroforestry and forestry, livestock, water, and natural resource management. However, without the system being able to generate predictable funding—particularly unrestricted funding—funding increased only temporarily in response to the 2008 food crisis, and the degree of tying of the use of funding, subtly to the donor's own institutions, has increased again.

The CGIAR governance structure is distributed and layered with (1) System-wide governance at the top, (2) inter-Center governance, (3) governance at the level of Centers, and (4) governance at the level of CGIAR Research Programs (CRPs). The System Council and System Board have unclear lines of responsibility and accountability, a problem compounded by the continued fragmented funding.

Successive reforms over the history of CGIAR have, among other aims, been intended to increase accountability for results, set clearer priorities, and increase long-term, unrestricted funding. The reforms, as discussed in Chapter 10, have not yet been successful in increasing long-term, unrestricted funding. Increased restricted funding has moved research downstream to demonstrate greater evidence of impacts on poverty and hunger. There is no consensus among donors on the nature of long-term payoffs of CGIAR. Resources to maintain and utilize its vast germplasm collection is stretched. Because of their own weaknesses, NARS have been unable to perform some of the downstream work that still falls to CGIAR, and without their strong role scaled up, impacts cannot be achieved (McCalla 2017).

In 2016, the rapidly evolving organizational structure of CGIAR consisted of 15 research Centers and 16 System-wide CRPs. Consolidation has been a challenge historically, but with funding shortages by 2019, voluntary mergers of Centers were occurring: for example, the International Center for Tropical Agriculture (CIAT) and Bioversity, who in their first joint Board of Trustees meeting on November 27–8, 2018, signed a Memorandum of Understanding (MoU) in support of their plans to create an Alliance (Bioversity 2018). The two forestry Centers—the World Agroforestry Centre (ICRAF) and the Center for International Forestry Research (CIFOR)—merged on January 1, 2019, with the establishment of a common Board, but with CIFOR and ICRAF continuing to maintain their headquarters in Indonesia and Kenya, respectively (ICRAF 2019). With the number of Centers declining to 14, inter-Center programs were achieving more cooperation. With the founding principles of Center autonomy and donor sovereignty intact, the complex superstructures of Center Boards and CRP Advisory Committees continued. The System Council and System Board were each reconstituted as part of the latest reforms in 2016, replacing the two-pillared governance of "funders" and "doers," which were not working, as described in the chapter on CGIAR. The new reforms have moved the system in the right direction. Together, the new System-level entities are moving toward 3-to-4-year replenishment funding, much like that of IDA and IFAD, which will increase stability of research funding and release scientists' time to focus more on research.

The chairman of CGIAR has a four-year term. Traditionally held by the World Bank, which has been a major donor to the CGIAR, CGIAR members urged the Bank to nominate a senior Bank official as chair. The possible loss of the Bank as chair of the CGIAR in the future could mean a loss of an internal champion with clout to plead for Bank contributions to CGIAR. Bank funding, in turn, signals confidence among other donors to fund the system, and indeed, having the Bank chair has fulfilled an important function, providing stability to CGIAR, even when the Bank funding has been reduced annually from US$50 to US$30 million. The 9th Systems Council (November 2019) approved, by far, the most radical institutional innovation of a unified and integrated One CGIAR, to adapt to the rapidly changing global conditions, while also making the CGIAR System itself more relevant and effective. The move to One CGIAR, as agreed on at the Extraordinary General Assembly of the Centers (Rome, December 2019) includes a unified governance and management through a reconstituted System Management Board and new Executive Management Team. This should assist CGIAR in better prioritizing its research agenda; increasing ownership among emerging countries, such as Brazil, Russia, India, China, and South Africa (BRICS), to take more responsibility for financing; and for building capacity of the weaker NARS in Africa. Whether reforms will bring new and additional sources of funding remains to be seen. CGIAR constituted 2 percent of global research funding in 2020, compared to 4 percent of funding that it once was in the early 2000s (Beintema and Echeverría 2020). Besides BMGF, the sources of funding have not changed.

Collaboration among Rome-Based Agencies

Collaboration among the three RBAs has been an issue of perennial interest to donors, with periodic reports prepared by the three organizations, individually and collectively, on how the collaboration is working or should work (WFP 2009a, 2009b; Tutwiler 2012; FAO, IFAD, and WFP 2014; Global Landscapes Forum 2014; Shaw 2014; WFP 2014b;

FAO, IFAD, and WFP 2015; IFAD 2015; FAO, IFAD, and WFP 2016; FAO 2020).[22] In the Informal Joint Meeting of the Executive Boards of the RBA held on September 15, 2017, a number of members suggested the preparation of a Joint RBA "Rome Vision for Agenda 2030," in order to increase the visibility of the RBA's work for the implementation of the Agenda 2030 in the UN (especially in New York). The final version of the meeting report is available online (UN 2017b).

Bill Gates' speech in 2012 to the IFAD Governing Council received much attention, albeit with a widespread reaction among RBAs that it was overly simplistic and did not show an understanding of the mandates, financing, management, or accountability of the three organizations: He noted, "WFP runs nearly every aspect of the program, with a little guidance from FAO and a little funding from IFAD. But in an ideal world, you would collaborate to make a whole that is greater than the sum of its parts. WFP would focus on what it does best: logistics and procurement. IFAD would handle the financing. FAO would provide advice to the farmers, standards to make sure they produce high-quality food, and market information to facilitate negotiations" (Gates 2012).

Veterans of IOs thought Gates' remarks simplistic. They showed little understanding of how the three organizations are funded or what they do. Does it mean, for example, that IFAD should fund WFP? The target for contributions for IFAD's 11th Replenishment (2019–21) is US$1.2 billion, whereas WFP's annual budget is at least four times that large. Would FAO give up its small, assessed contributions and deviate from its many GPG functions for which it has few resources?

Why such an interest in RBA collaboration? First, in principle, their missions (concessional financing for rural development, emergency relief, agricultural technical skills, and global goods) are complementary. WFP was an internal program in FAO until tensions grew between FAO and WFP, so WFP increasingly obtained greater autonomy (Ingram 2006). There have been proposals to integrate the three RBAs from time to time, including from the Aspen Institute (Axworthy 2015), but in our view, a formal merger is not a workable solution. The organizations have very different financing, governance, organizational arrangements, and *modus operandi*, as discussed earlier in the chapter. In the case of WBG, collaboration between the World Bank, IFC, and MIGA is still a work in progress. A statement on RBA collaboration was based on the mandates, related comparative advantages, and distinctive strengths of each partner (FAO, IFAD, and WFP 2016). However, each organization is accountable to the constituency that established it and governs it. Even though, in several cases, the same members serve on the governing councils of more than one Rome-based organization, the member countries have not demanded such consolidation and/or integration.

The experience in Niger identifies issues that need to be addressed, more generally (Box 6.1).

The joint statement from FAO, IFAD, and WPF on collaboration between the RBAs to deliver the 2030 Agenda stated:

RBA collaboration should lead to a clear and mutually recognized added value in terms of results relevant to the goals and objectives set by the RBAs' Membership. Within this

---

[22] See, also, IFAD: "Partners," https://operations.ifad.org/web/ifad/partners/rome-based-un-agencies; WFP: "Rome-Based Agencies," https://www.wfp.org/news/rome-based-agencies-rbas-5013; FAO: "Resilience—Strengthening Resilience for Food Security and Nutrition in Contexts Facing Recurrent Shocks and Stressors," http://www.fao.org/resilience/news-events/detail/en/c/335041/

context, RBA collaboration should serve as a means for greater effectiveness in supporting international governance of agriculture, agricultural development, food security and nutrition, including through results-based monitoring and incorporating lessons learned. (FAO, IFAD, and WFP 2016, 6)

It remains unclear as to the extent this has been delivered. In its report on WFP and global food security, the International Development Committee (IDC) of Great Britain asserted:

There is a desperate need for a one-UN approach to meeting food security challenges. Roughly speaking, the model devised 30 years ago, assigns agriculture-for-food-production to FAO, agriculture-for-poverty-reduction-and-empowerment to IFAD, food access-for-children to UNICEF and food provision-in-emergencies to WFP... While there are exceptions, very few truly joint initiatives manage to transcend the institutional fights for resources and media limelight. (IDC 2008, 61)

Summarizing this discussion of RBA collaboration, MOPAN (2013, x) reported: "Donors, in particular, appear concerned that WFP's recent shift to food assistance may extend the organisation further into development programming and result in a duplication of roles and responsibilities with other United Nations agencies." That expansion impinges on FAO's

---

Box 6.1 SWOT Analysis for Collaboration in Niger

SWOT (strengths, weaknesses, opportunities, threats) analysis for an RBA collaboration with synergy toward resilience in Niger stressed as its **strengths** the credibility and good reputation of RBAs among Nigerien government partners, their complementary mandates, activities, and tools. Expertise and experience with collaboration could provide positive and promising results with multilevel, diverse partnerships.

Its **weaknesses** include different programming processes and cycles, leading to funding delays, lack of resources for resilience, lack of staff to focus on resilience, and a weak RBA coordination mechanism with different geographical targeting priorities.

Opportunities include strong support from the Government of Niger, UN agencies, and other financial and technical partners, fostering joint targeting and complementary interventions to operationalize resilience and measure impact in Communes de Convergence (C2Cs). Interest of financial partners toward integrated, multisectoral interventions to build resilience could offer opportunities (for example, the World Bank on social protection, USAID and EU on food security).

Threats include insufficient and lack of long-term, predictable funding for resilience activities, lack of government resources at the national and subnational levels (for example, for technical services), and recurrent shocks and insecurity in the subregion, North, and border areas.

The Nigerien review made a number of recommendations and discussed next steps for a strengthened RBA collaboration on resilience, including policy dialogue, analysis and planning, joint/complementary programming and implementation, and monitoring impacts and measuring resilience.

traditional responsibilities more than most. Being an emergency organization, WFP has had a strong comparative advantage and well-recognized expertise in logistics, and due to the nature of its mission, it is an agile organization. It is well connected with key donors, with the United States as its foremost champion. FAO has more staff on long-term basis, whereas most of WFP hires tend to be on short-term contracts. Over the years, donors and critics of FAO have expressed concerns about FAO providing small TCP projects to governments, rather than confining its efforts to the provision of GPGs (FAO 2007a; CGD 2015). FAO's assessed contributions are increasingly ring-fenced for its GPG functions, with voluntary contributions carrying on donors' preferred activities: for example, in transition from emergencies to rehabilitation of land rights, seed supply, and reconstruction. Consequently, there has been increasing overlap between WFP's and FAO's activities in the field, and while FAO has much of the technical expertise in these fields, WFP commands more financial resources. FAO's annual extra-budgetary resources of about US$800 million pale before WFP's US$5–6 billion voluntary contributions annually, although some of WFP's contributions are in-kind, voluntary, and never certain. Some commentators on this chapter have argued that this dichotomy between GPGs and projects is outdated, superseded by, among other things, the SDGs and Agenda 2030.

It is clear from the preceding discussion that organizations have grown in response to their own needs to be able to achieve expeditious responses and not necessarily based on their comparative advantages. In theory, FAO may have a strong comparative advantage, through its technical expertise, to work with WFP, but may have been unable to exercise its advantage, owing to its limited fragmented voluntary contributions rather than long-term funding that would enable FAO to build on it—a challenge compounded by FAO's slow bureaucratic approach, in part to conserve its limited resources, compared to the agility and speed of WFP's operations. This state of affairs can change only if there is assured long-term funding from donors for FAO and an agreement in principle that expertise matters.

The short answer to the RBA collaborative experience, thus far, is that it works better at the global level than at the country level—for example, (1) in publishing reports on food security, which are largely initiated by FAO but co-prepared and signed by WFP and IFAD; (2) in providing joint support for organizing the Committee on World Food Security (CFS) conferences, mostly driven by member countries; (3) for administrative collaboration in travel and security management; or (4) in meetings such as the Second International Conference on Nutrition (ICN2). Collaborations at the regional and country levels remain weak, even though each of the organizations has country operations and sometimes share offices or office compounds. The other ICN2-related initiatives, such as Scaling Up Nutrition (SUN), have begun to have more traction in countries.

The question in need of more systematic, independent evidence is at what level does collaboration work better and why. IFAD's regional presence is limited to a small number of regional grants, with the majority of IFAD's concessional financing being focused at the country level. Cooperation at the country level will improve if member countries, while recognizing the different operational modalities of RBAs, both support and demand their collaboration for specific initiatives, and if dedicated programs do not compete with the already stretched budgets and current programming of the RBAs, or be met with strong expectations from donors that they each show results on the ground for their own brands. The extent to which the "One UN" idea works in practice at the field level is unclear. We hesitate to suggest another evaluation, because far too often, evaluation findings are not implemented, though the parameters of the forthcoming Food Systems Summit 2021 may offer the broad terms of reference for such a study.

Partnerships between the World Bank Group and United Nations Agencies

The UN agencies and WBG have a long history of partnerships on all matters related to the SDGs and climate change, ranging from formal, long-term legal arrangements to more informal and ad hoc forms of engagement and exchange in the areas of research, policy development, and knowledge sharing, as well as operational cooperation at regional and country levels through programs, projects, and technical assistance. Between 2006 and 2016, WBG provided US$3.4 billion in direct and indirect financing to UN funds, programs, and agencies with the largest share going to UNICEF (US$1.5 billion), followed by the United Nations Office for Project Services (UNOPS), the United Nations Population Fund (UNFPA), WHO, WFP, FAO, and the UNDP.[23] World Bank's borrowers engage UN agencies for implementation of project-specific activities at the country level, using standard financial and fiduciary agreements. FAO's Cooperative Programme with the World Bank, since 1964, provides technical services to member countries. In partnership with the World Bank, it provides policy, advisory, analytical investment project formulation and implementation support, and capacity development, involving between 55–65 percent of World Bank projects in the areas of agriculture, environment, water, and land.

The Food and Agricultural Organization of the United Nations, the International Fund for Agricultural Development, the World Bank, and the International Labour Organization

FAO, IFAD, and the World Bank are partnering on GAFSP, which illustrates what can be achieved in terms of programmatic collaboration and are actively engaged at the regional and country levels in 145 investment projects, with IDA and IBRD cofinancing, for a total amount of US$3.8 billion. IFAD also has participated, since 1996, in the Heavily Indebted Poor Country Debt Initiative (HIPC–DI). It has provided US$445.1 million, in nominal terms, in debt relief to the 35 completion-point countries and collaborated closely with the World Bank and regional development banks in the implementation of the program.

To improve the design of public works programs, the Bank has contributed US$45.5 million over six years to support the International Labour Organization's (ILO) technical assistance through grants and loans to Afghanistan, Egypt, Ghana, Guinea, Kenya, Mali, Burkina Faso, Sierra Leone, Cambodia, India, Indonesia, Nepal, Yemen, and Paraguay.

The World Food Programme and the World Bank

WFP and the World Bank have collaborated on national social protection systems in 25 countries for well over a decade. WFP has received over US$360 million from the Bank for technical cooperation on school feeding, as well as shock-responsive social protection systems in food security and agriculture, national social protection and safety net systems,

---

[23] See https://www.worldbank.org/en/about/partners#3

future pandemic preparedness, and on issues related to the humanitarian development–peace nexus in fragile and conflict-affected contexts.

The World Health Organization and the World Bank

WHO and the World Bank co-lead the group of UN organizations and major donors' development agencies that work in global health, including an agreement for the provision of WHO technical assistance in Bank-financed projects and output delivery on health-related issues. They also provide joint secretariat support to the International Health Partnership of Universal Health Coverage 2030.

The United Nations Children's Fund and the World Bank

The World Bank and UNICEF partner on issues related to early childhood development; service delivery for children; social protection; youth and adolescents; and fragility-affected refugee, and migrant children. Through an alliance to advance early childhood development, WBG and UNICEF invite governments, development partners, civil society, foundations, and the private sector to make early childhood development a global and national development priority, including on childcare and nutrition in the "early years" in nutrition.

The Bank is also a founding cosponsor of the Joint United Nations Programme on HIV/AIDS (UNAIDS) and supports the development of strategic, prioritized, and costed multi-sectoral national AIDS plans, undertaking investment research to underpin resource allocation. The institutions are working together to integrate HIV sensitivity in the Bank's new billion-dollar loan portfolios on social protection and education.

The Economic Commission for Africa (ECA), the Ministry for Economic Cooperation and Development (BMZ) of Germany, and the World Bank are working together to strengthen advisory capacities for land governance in Africa with special attention to the rights of marginalized groups, such as small-scale farmers, pastoralists, and women through the Network of Excellence on Land Governance in Africa (NELGA). The World Bank is also a key partner of the Global Land Tool Network, which aims to promote development and use of pro-poor and gender-sensitive land tools, including the Social Tenure Domain Model, widely used by diverse stakeholders. As part of this partnership, the United Nations Human Settlements Programme (UN-Habitat) is actively involved in the organization of the annual World Bank Global Land and Poverty Reduction Conference, which is held in Washington, DC, every year for researchers, practitioners, and policy-makers in the land sector.

The Bank is also a member of the Global Migration Group (GMG), a forum of 22 UN System entities that promotes the wider application of all international and regional instruments and norms relating to migration, developing the adoption of coordinated approaches to the issue of international migration.

These are some of the examples of cooperation among IOs. Given the overlap in some specific functions that IOs carry out and with limited resources at their disposal, how should they specialize, bring the best knowledge, and cooperate further to improve their individual and collective effectiveness, and where should they collaborate?

A Fractionated Record of Donor Evaluations of International Organizations: The Need to Separate the Forest from the Trees

The evidence base to improve governance and management of individual organizations remains less than satisfactory. Donor-led assessments of IOs have proliferated (Achamkulangare and Bartsiotas 2017). Some 205 bilateral assessments in the sense of evaluations by Development Assistance Committee (DAC) members of the OECD were conducted during 2012–14 alone, with the UN having to create a response apparatus just to introduce some order and discipline. Given that 70 percent of the UN financing comes from voluntary contributions (Jenks and Topping 2017), with funds and programs such as WFP and UNICEF almost totally financed by voluntary contributions, increased taxpayer awareness and concerns about aid effectiveness and accountability of IOs in OECD donor countries explains this growth in donor-led assessments, despite increases in transparency and accountability in the IOs over time. The treatment of organizations is uneven. Three Paris Declaration surveys provided evidence of how the five Paris Declaration principles were being implemented and gave good marks to the World Bank, IFAD, and regional banks (and these surveys were, in turn, used by MOPAN; see Box 6.2 for more about MOPAN). Assessments are typically short-term snapshots, occasionally helping with reforms within individual organizations, but overall, to us, the benefits of individual bilateral assessments do not seem commensurate with the resources that donors spend on them. Most importantly, they do not address larger, strategic questions—huge funding challenges in the face of ambitious agendas of work, the need for renewal of skill sets and incentives, and the growing competition for funds—the sorts of issues that we explore here.

Evaluating the Governance Processes of the Big Five

It is next to impossible to collapse the assessments of IOs into something manageable, because each bilateral donor looks at the IOs in terms of fulfilling the expectations of their taxpayers, which vary among donors. The bilateral assessments offer donors a view of the complex world of IOs to make more informed decisions about levels and allocations of aid, but taken together, they make huge demands on IOs to respond to the information needs of individual donor countries (Government of Australia 2012), entailing staff and management costs and with duplication of efforts across evaluations. Since IOs are more effective, transparent, and accountable, in terms of use of resources and outcomes, than their bilateral aid counterparts, this chapter issues a call for action to bilateral donors to place greater trust in the collective assessment process: consolidate resources; focus on critical questions of global importance; abandon a "one-size-fits-all" approach to evaluation methodologies; devote resources to a few, high quality evaluations; reduce the transaction costs of external evaluations to IOs; and help mobilize increased funding for them to be more effective in filling the huge gap between need and supply (Birdsall and Kharas 2010).

Lindoso and Hall (2016) have also argued that the academic literature on the evaluation of IOs has been carried out in parallel with donor assessments, with little interaction among them. They pointed to the need for further research and coordination. We argue, on the other hand, that assessments of IOs need to address larger strategic issues of the type that we address in this chapter from the available evidence, extensive interviews, and our own experience. The two governance issues we focus on are financing and effectiveness.

Box 6.2 Multilateral Organisation Performance Assessment Network

MOPAN[a] is a network of 18 bilateral donor countries,[b] which contribute 95 percent of ODA to and through the multilateral system and share concerns about the effectiveness of multilateral organizations and the organizations' accountability to donor countries' taxpayers. The 2013 independent evaluation of MOPAN by the Swedish Institute of Public Administration noted that MOPAN's common approach across organizations was supply-led and not very useful to IOs in improving their performance (Balogun et al. 2013). MOPAN 3.0 has since improved its methodology and coverage of organizations, adding four dimensions of organizational effectiveness—strategic management, operational management, relationship management, and knowledge management—to also cover development effectiveness (MOPAN n.d.). Due to the diversity of the organizations' mandates and structures, MOPAN does not compare or rank them. Because MOPAN's assessments do not coincide with aid cycles of individual donors and do not meet their home constituencies' specific needs, AusAID, like other bilateral donors, continue to conduct their own assessments. MOPAN's focus on field- or country-level results and information (and the efforts taken to ask questions at that level) is said to have focused agency attention on having those decision-making and reporting structures in place at the country level. Donors argue that their assessments are usually linked to parliamentary approval processes for budgets and are "supplements" to MOPAN.

MOPAN assessments of FAO, in 2011 and 2014, noted improvement in virtually every performance indicator. In four important areas linked to delivery—corporate strategy based on clear mandate, country focus on results, support of national plans, and contributing to policy dialogue—the rating was raised from "inadequate or below" to "strong or above" (MOPAN 2011, 2014). MOPAN (2014), which referred to the Jacques Diouf era (1994–2011), prior to José Graziano da Silva taking over FAO leadership in 2010, cited two areas of continued concern: results-based budgeting and management of human resources. The 2016 Multilateral Development Review (MDR) of the UK Department for International Development (DFID) confirmed MOPAN's findings, noting that FAO has turned its performance around, crediting the leadership, modernized management structure, and efficiency savings for the positive outcome. The MDR rated FAO as "good," on a four-step scale of weak, adequate, good, or very good (DFID and UK Aid 2016). The Norwegian Agency for Development Cooperation, on the other hand, decided to reduce their funding of FAO in 2012, based on outdated evidence. FAO convinced MOPAN to use more up-to-date evidence for evaluation (personal communication, Daniel Gustafson, Deputy Director- General, FAO, August 21, 2017). FAO's MOPAN (2018, 9) was even stronger on its positive performance, as a "highly effective" organization, but noted its growing reliance on voluntary contributions and concluded, "FAO may need to engage member nations in identifying options for new, more sustainable forms of funding for activities that have traditionally relied on core funding" (MOPAN 2018, 43).

Notes:

[a] MOPAN has assessed 27 organizations since 2003, and has done so multiple times, using three different approaches (Annual Survey, Common Approach, and MOPAN 3.0). Their selection follows a dual-track process of (1) identification of member preferences through a process orchestrated by the MOPAN Secretariat; and (2) a sampling process, based on clear criteria, conducted by International Organisation Development Ltd (IOD PARC), as part of its inception work for assessments. MOPAN members select when and what organizations to assess on a consensus basis (see "MOPAN assessments: who do we assess?" http://www.mopanonline.org/ourwork/whodoweassess)

[b] The countries include Australia, Canada, Denmark, Finland, France, Germany, Ireland, Italy, Japan, Luxembourg, The Netherlands, Norway, Korea, Spain, Sweden, Switzerland, the United States, and the United Kingdom.

Appendix

Table A.6.1 Governance of international organizations in 2016

	World Bank	IFAD	CGIAR	FAO	WFP
Voice and participation: Shareholder or stakeholder model	*Shareholder*	*Modified shareholder*	*Hybrid shareholder/stakeholder*	*Stakeholder*	*Modified shareholder*
Head of the organization	Governors	Governing Council	System Council (governed by the CGIAR System Framework [see CGIAR (2016a)]) and System Management Board of the CGIAR System Organization (governed by the System Organization Charter)	FAO Conference, includes all members	Executive Board
Delegated to board	Yes	Yes; to Executive Board	Yes	Yes; to Council	Yes
Number in board	25+1 (from Africa proposed as part of 2015 reforms)	18 elected members; 18 Alternates	20 voting members + observers	49	36
Elected	5 large shareholders nominated by their governments, the rest by forming constituencies of countries. Voice reforms in 2010 increased the voting power of developing countries in IBRD to 47.19 percent, bringing the total shift to DTCs in both Phases to 4.59 percentage points once the current Selective Capital Increase is fully subscribed. Also, Governors agreed to conduct periodic IBRD and IFC Shareholding Reviews, every five years, beginning in 2015, as a way to maintain legitimacy and dynamism and to reflect global economic	List A: 8 Members; 8 Alternates (OECD) List B: 4 Members; 4 Alternates (OPEC) List C1: 2 Members; 2 Alternates (Africa) List C2: 2 Members; 2 Alternates (Europe, Asia, and the Pacific) List C3: 2 Members; 2 Alternates (Latin America and the Caribbean)	1. System Council consists of:(a) Up to 20 voting members as follows:i. Up to 15 representatives of Fundersii. Five developing country representatives that are either Funders, or countries hosting a Center, or countries with significant national agricultural systems(b) Ex-officio non-voting members as follows:i. Chair of the System Council, so far by consensus from WB, but nominated by WBii. Co-Chair of the System Council, to be elected at each meetingiii. Chair of the System Management Boardiv.	YesBy region:Africa 12Asia 9Europe 10Latin America and the Caribbean 9Near East 6North America 2Southwest Pacific 1	18 by the Economic and Social Council and 18 by the FAO Council

Continued

Table A.6.1 *Continued*

World Bank	IFAD	CGIAR	FAO	WFP
changes in IBRD and IFC shareholding according to the weight of all members in the world economy; to review contributions to the WBG development mission; and to make progress toward equitable voting power between developed and developing members. On responsiveness to increase diversity in management and staff, accelerating decentralization of operations and field presence, as well as internal governance reforms undertaken.		Executive Director of the System Organization.v. Two Center representatives to be appointed by the Centersvi. One representative from each of the following entities, provided that if any such entity is a voting member or an alternate of the System Council such entity may not also participate as an ex-officio:FAO, IFAD, World Bank.Each voting member, non-voting member, and active observer may appoint an alternate that may attend System Council meetings and, if necessary, serve in their stead.2. System Management Board comprise the following nine (9) voting members, as follows:(a) Seven Center Board members or Directors General, as appointed by the Centers(b) Two independent members, one of which should, whenever possible, be the Chair.i. System Management Board shall appoint a Chair from among its members.ii. Executive Director of the System Organization will serve on the System Management Board as an ex-officio non-voting member.iii. The process and criteria for the selection and appointment of voting members of the System Management Board shall be defined by the Centers.		

Name of leader	President	President	The System Management Board will include at least one expert in organizational management and one expert in financial management. Chairman (and Rotating Co-chair) of the System	Director-General	Executive Director
Selection of leader	Chosen by United StatesVoting weighted by quota	President elected by Governors at Governing Council. Votes per member are proportional to historical financial contribution.	The System Council appoints a Chair. The World Bank has a standing invitation to nominate a System Chair. The System Council appoints a Co-Chair for each meeting from among its voting members. Executive Director of the System Office, as chief executive officer, appointed by the System Management Board, selected on basis of merit, in an open and competitive manner. The Executive Director may be appointed to a term of four years, which can be renewed once by the System Management Board.	Elected by ConferenceStrive for consensus; one vote per country, majority of voters	Executive Director (so far. with one exception, from major contributing countries) appointed by the UN Secretary-General and FAO Director General Board (1 vote per person)
Terms of appointment	Six years	Four years		Four years	Five years
Financial contributions	Share capital and contributions to IDA	Replenishment every four years	Voluntary contributions, but minimum contribution to be funders member and higher contribution to be eligible to be member of Council	Assessed and voluntary contributions	Voluntary contributions
Decision-making processes		All decisions are made by Executive Board, Annual Programme of Work and Budget given final approval by Governing Council			

Continued

Table A.6.1 *Continued*

	World Bank	IFAD	CGIAR	FAO	WFP
State members	188 countries	176 countries	64 members worldwide (25 developing and 22 industrialized countries, 4 private foundations, and 13 regional and international organizations)	194 countries, 2 associate members, 1 member organization (European Union)	195 countries
Key organizational components		Four departments: Financial Operations	DepartmentCorporate Services DepartmentProgramme Management DepartmentStrategy and Knowledge Department	CGIAR's Research Centers: Africa Rice, Bioversity International, Center for International Forestry Research (CIFOR), International Center for Agricultural Research in the Dry Areas (ICARDA), International Center for Tropical Agriculture (CIAT), International Crops Research Institute for the Semi-Arid Tropics (ICRISAT), International Food Policy Research Institute (IFPRI), International Institute of Tropical Agriculture (IITA), International Livestock Research Institute (ILRI),	Six departments: Agriculture and Consumer ProtectionEconomic and Social

Continued

International Maize and Wheat Improvement Center (CIMMYT), International Potato Center (CIP), International Rice Research Institute (IRRI), International Water Management Institute (IWMI), World Agroforestry Centre (ICRAF), WorldFish, and other bodies of the CGIAR: Global Forum on Agricultural Research (GFAR), Independent Evaluation Arrangement (IEA), and Independent Science and Partnership Council (ISPC). *Note:* ICRAF and CIFOR merged Jan. 1, 2019: CIAT and Bioversity signed MoU in November 2018 for alliance.

DevelopmentFisheries and AquacultureForestryCorporate ServicesTechnical Cooperation Programme Management

Table A.6.1 *Continued*

	World Bank	IFAD	CGIAR	FAO	WFP
Offices	More than 120 offices worldwide	46 offices worldwide under "Country Presence" initiative approved by Executive Board	CGIAR's Research Centers implement large-scale CGIAR Research Programs (CRPs) conducted in more than 60 countries, collaboratively with academia, NGOs, and the private sector	5 regional offices, 9 subregional offices, 80 country offices (excluding those hosted in regional and subregional offices), 3 offices with technical officers/FAO Representatives, and 38 countries covered through multiple accreditations. In addition, the FAO has 6 liaison offices and 2 information offices in developed countries.	76 offices worldwide
Staff	More than 10,000	More than 530	1,846 international and 9,509 others	1,795 professional staff (including Junior Professional Officers, Associate Professional Officers and National Professional Officers), and 1,654 support staff. Figures only refer to staff holding fixed terms and continuing	Employs about 14,700, 90 percent of whom worked in the field, delivering food and monitoring its use. Not included: temporary contracts of 11 months or less for short-term, international professionals, consultants, short-term general service,

appointments (as of November 1, 2013).

special service agreements, interns, author's contract, fellowship, WFP volunteers, or casual laborers.

Source: Authors' construction.

References

Achamkulangare, Gopinathan, and George A. Bartsiotas. 2017. "Donor-Led Assessments of The United Nations System Organizations." JIU/REP/2017/2, Joint Inspection Unit, United Nations, Geneva.

Ahluwalia, Montek Singh, Lawrence Summers, Andrés Velasco (co-chairs); Nancy Birdsall, and Scott Morris (co-directors). 2016. "Multilateral Development Banking for this Century's Development Challenges: Five Recommendations to Shareholders of the Old and New Multilateral Development Banks." Center for Global Development, Washington, DC.

Atluri, Venkat, Miklós Dietz, and Nicolaus Henke. 2017. "Competing in a World of Sectors without Borders." *McKinsey Quarterly*, July. https://www.mckinsey.com/business-functions/mckinsey-analytics/our-insights/competing-in-a-world-of-sectors-without-borders

Axworthy, Lloyd. 2015. "Reforming International Governance of Food Security." The Aspen Institute, November 9. https://www.aspeninstitute.org/aspen-journal-of-ideas/reforming-international-governance-food-security/

Balogun, Paul, Paul Isenman, Derek Poate, and Viktoria Hildenwall. 2013. "Evaluation of MOPAN." Swedish Institute for Public Administration (SIPA), Stockholm. http://www.mopanonline.org/otherproducts/items/EVALUATION%20OF%20MOPAN%20Final%20vol.%201.pdf

Barrett, Christopher B. 2017. Testimony before the United States Senate Committee on Foreign Relations Hearing on "Modernizing the Food for Peace Program." Room 419, Dirksen Senate Office Building, October 19. http://barrett.dyson.cornell.edu/presentations/Senate%20Foreign%20Relations%20Oct%202017%20Barrett%20testimony%20final.pdf

Beattie, Alan. 2012. "World Bank: An Exercise of Influence." *Financial Times*, April 2. https://www.ft.com/content/15b9d4d8-7ca6-11e1-8a27-00144feab49a

Beintema, Nienke M., and Ruben G. Echeverría. 2020. "Evolution of CGIAR Funding." ASTI Program Note, September, International Food Policy Research Institute (IFPRI), Washington, DC. https://www.ifpri.org/publication/evolution-cgiar-funding

Bioversity. 2018. "Bioversity International and CIAT Sign Memorandum of Understanding that Establishes the Alliance Foundations." News, December 11. https://www.bioversityinternational.org/news/detail/bioversity-international-and-ciat-sign-memorandum-of-understanding-that-establishes-the-alliance/

Birdsall, Nancy, and Homi Kharas, with Ayad Mahgoub and Rita Perakis. 2010. "Quality of Official Development Assistance Assessment." QuODA Report, Brookings Institution and Center for Global Development (CGD), Washington, DC.

Bretton Woods Project. 2016. "IMF & World Bank Decision-making and Governance." IFI Governance, Inside the Institutions, March 31. http://bwp.handsupdev.com/2016/03/imf-world-bank-decision-making-and-governance-existing-structures-and-reform-processes/

Browne, Stephen, and Roberto Cordon. 2015. "Vertical Funds: Lessons for Multilateralism and the UN." Briefing 25, January, Future United Nations Development System, Ralph Bunche Institute for International Studies, CUNY Graduate Center, New York.

CGD (Center for Global Development). 2015. "Time for the FAO to Shift to a Higher Gear." A Report of the CGD Working Group on Food Security (originally published October 2013 and updated January 2015), CGD, Washington, DC. https://www.cgdev.org/publication/time-fao-shift-higher-gear

CGIAR. 2012. "CGIAR Financial Report for Year 2011." A joint collaborative effort between the International Rice Research Institute (IRRI), the CGIAR Consortium Office, and the Fund Office. CGIAR Consortium Office, Montpellier, France. https://cgspace.cgiar.org/bitstream/handle/10947/2707/2011_CGIAR_Financial_Report.pdf

CGIAR. 2013. "CGIAR Financial Report for Year 2012." September 20. CGIAR Consortium Office, Montpellier, France. https://library.cgiar.org/bitstream/handle/10947/2869/2012_CGIAR_Financial_Report.pdf

CGIAR. 2014. "CGIAR Financial Report for Year 2013." June 18. Prepared by the CGIAR Consortium Office, Montpellier, France. https://library.cgiar.org/bitstream/handle/10947/3069/CGIAR%20Finance%20Report%202013.pdf

CGIAR. 2015. "CGIAR Financial Report for Year 2014." October 1. Prepared by the CGIAR Consortium Office and the CGIAR Fund Office, Montpellier, France. https://library.cgiar.org/bitstream/handle/10947/4018/2014%20CGIAR%20Financial%20Report.pdf

CGIAR. 2016a. "CGIAR System Framework." Approved by System's Funders and Centers June 17. http://library.cgiar.org/bitstream/handle/10947/4371/CGIAR%20System%20Framework%20-%20WEB.pdf?sequence=4

CGIAR. 2016b. "2015 CGIAR Financial Report." June 2016, CGIAR Consortium Office and CGIAR Fund Office, Montpellier, France, and Washington, DC. https://library.cgiar.org/bitstream/handle/10947/4452/2015%20CGIAR%20Financial%20Report.pdf

CGIAR. 2017a. "CGIAR System Annual Performance Report 2017." https://www.cgiar.org/wp/wp-content/uploads/2018/10/CGIAR-Annual-Performance-Report-2017.pdf

CGIAR. 2017b. "2016 CGIAR Financial Report." July, CGIAR System Management Office, Montpellier, France. https://cgspace.cgiar.org/bitstream/handle/10947/4666/2016-CGIAR-Financial-Report.pdf

Chandy, Laurence. 2017. "No Country Left Behind: The Case for Focusing Greater Attention on the World's Poorest Countries." Global Economy and Development, Brookings Institution, Washington, DC.

Cheney, Catherine. 2017. "German Foreign Aid Is at a Record High and Rising. Here Is How It Works." Devex, February. https://www.devex.com/news/german-foreign-aid-is-at-a-record-high-and-rising-here-is-how-it-works-89366

Cleaver, Kevin, Amnon Golan, and Anil Sood. 2017. "An Independent Assessment of FAO's Technical Capacity." FAO, Rome. http://www.fao.org/3/a-ms760e.pdf

Custer, Samantha, Zachary Rice, Takaaki Masaki, Rebecca Latourell, and Bradley Parks. 2015. "Listening to Leaders: Which Development Partners Do They Prefer and Why?" AidData, Williamsburg, VA. http://aiddata.org/sites/default/files/execsummary_2.pdf

Deaton, Angus. 2018. "The U.S. Can No Longer Hide from Its Deep Poverty Problem." Opinion, *New York Times*, January 24. https://www.nytimes.com/2018/01/24/opinion/poverty-united-states.html

Development Committee (Joint Ministerial Committee of the Boards of Governors of the Bank and the Fund on the Transfer of Real Resources to Developing Countries). 2015. "From Billions to Trillions: Transforming Development Finance Post-2015 Financing for Development: Multilateral Development Finance." Development Committee Discussion Note. Prepared jointly by African Development Bank, Asian Development Bank, European Bank for Reconstruction and Development, European Investment Bank, Inter-American Development Bank, International Monetary Fund, and World Bank Group, April 18.

Development Committee (Joint Ministerial Committee of the Boards of Governors of the Bank and the Fund on the Transfer of Real Resources to Developing Countries). 2018. "Sustainable Financing for Sustainable Development." DC2018-0002/P, April 21, Report to the Governors at the 2018 Spring Meetings, World Bank Group, Washington, DC.

Development Initiatives. 2016. "Global Humanitarian Assistance Report 2016." Development Initiatives Ltd, Bristol, UK. http://devinit.org/wp-content/uploads/2016/06/Global-Humanitarian-Assistance-Report-2016.pdf

DFID (Department for International Development) and UK Aid. 2011. *Multilateral Aid Review: Ensuring Maximum Value for Money for UK Aid through Multilateral Organisations.* London: DFID. http://www.who.int/country-cooperation/what-who-does/DFID_multilateral_aid_review.pdf?ua=1

DFID (Department for International Development) and UK Aid. 2013. *Multilateral Aid Review: Driving Reform to Achieve Multilateral Effectiveness.* London: DFID. https://www.gov.uk/government/uploads/system/uploads/attachment_data/file/297523/MAR-review-dec13.pdf

DFID (Department for International Development) and UK Aid. 2016. *Raising the Standard: The Multilateral Aid Review 2016.* London: DFID. https://www.gfdrr.org/sites/default/files/publication/evaluation-dfid-multilateral-development-review-2016.pdf

Economic Times. 2008. "UN Food Agency Approves US$42.6 Million Reform Plan." *India Times,* November 22. http://economictimes.indiatimes.com/news/international/un-food-agency-approves-42-6-million-reform-plan/articleshow/3745635.cms

The Economist. 2017. "Six Big Ideas: Coase's Theory of the Firm." Economics brief, July 27.

FAO (Food and Agriculture Organization of the United Nations). 1996. "Rome Declaration on World Food Security and World Food Summit Plan of Action." World Food Summit, November 13–17, Rome. http://www.fao.org/docrep/003/w3613e/w3613e00.htm

FAO (Food and Agriculture Organization of the United Nations). 2007a. "The Challenge of Renewal." Report of the Independent External Evaluation of the Food and Agriculture Organization of the United Nations (FAO), submitted to the Council Committee for the Independent External Evaluation of FAO (CC–IEE), September 2007.

FAO (Food and Agriculture Organization of the United Nations). 2007b. "Official FAO Response to Evaluation Report." FAO Newsroom, Rome, October 29. http://www.fao.org/newsroom/en/news/2007/1000692/

FAO (Food and Agriculture Organization of the United Nations). 2011. "FAO Reform: Looking Forward." FAO, Rome. http://www.fao.org/docrep/018/mg881e/mg881e.pdf

FAO (Food and Agriculture Organization of the United Nations). 2016. "2015 Annual Report of the Inspector General." FC 161/10, Finance Committee, FAO, Rome, May 16–20.

FAO (Food and Agriculture Organization of the United Nations). 2017a. "The Director-General's Medium Term Plan 2018–21 and Programme of Work and Budget 2018–19." FAO, Rome.

FAO (Food and Agriculture Organization of the United Nations). 2017b. "FAO and the SDGs Indicators: Measuring up to the 2030 Agenda for Sustainable Development." FAO, Rome. http://www.fao.org/3/a-i6919e.pdf

FAO (Food and Agriculture Organization of the United Nations). 2017c. "The Future of Food and Agriculture. Trends and Challenges." FAO, Rome. http://www.fao.org/3/a-i6583e.pdf

FAO (Food and Agriculture Organization of the United Nations). 2017d. "Informal Seminar on SDG Indicators." A statement by FAO Director-General José Graziano da Silva, FAO, Rome, March 1. http://www.fao.org/about/who-we-are/director-gen/faodg-statements/detail/en/c/472444/

FAO (Food and Agriculture Organization of the United Nations). 2017e "Regular Programme Contributions as at 31 October 2017." About FAO/Strategic Planning. http://www.fao.org/about/strategic-planning/country-contributions/en/

FAO (Food and Agriculture Organization of the United Nations). 2017f. Verbatim Records of Plenary Meetings of the FAO Council, 156th Session, Rome, April 24–8. http://www.fao.org/about/meetings/council/cl156/en/

FAO (Food and Agriculture Organization of the United Nations). 2020. "Rome Based Agencies Work Together to Ensure Food Security in Mozambique." FAO Projects. http://www.fao.org/in-action/rome-based-agencies-work-together-to-ensure-food-security-in-mozambique/en/

FAO (Food and Agriculture Organization of the United Nations), IFAD (International Fund for Agricultural Development), UNICEF (United Nations Children's Fund), WFP (World Food Programme), and WHO (World Health Organization). 2017. *The State of Food Security and Nutrition in the World 2017. Building Resilience for Peace and Food Security.* Rome: FAO.

FAO (Food and Agriculture Organization of the United Nations), IFAD (International Fund for Agricultural Development), and WFP (World Food Programme). 2014. "Food Security, Nutrition and Sustainable Agriculture in the Post-2015 Agenda: Priority Targets and Indicators Identified by FAO, IFAD and WFP." March 27, Rome. http://www.fao.org/fileadmin/user_upload/post-2015/Targets_and_indicators_RBA_joint_proposal.pdf and http://www.fao.org/fileadmin/user_upload/post-2015/RBA_Target_indicator_box.pdf

FAO (Food and Agriculture Organization of the United Nations), IFAD (International Fund for Agricultural Development), and WFP (World Food Programme). 2015. "Strengthening Resilience for Food Security and Nutrition." A Conceptual Framework for Collaboration and Partnership among the Rome-based Agencies, April. https://www.wfp.org/rba-joint-resilience-framework

FAO (Food and Agriculture Organization of the United Nations), IFAD (International Fund for Agricultural Development), and WFP (World Food Programme). 2016. "Collaboration among the United Nations Rome-based Agencies: Delivering on the 2030 Agenda." CL 155/12 Rev.2, November, Rome. http://www.fao.org/3/a-mr918rev1e.pdf

GAFSP (Global Agriculture and Food Security Program). 2009. "Framework Document for a Global Agriculture and Food Security Program (GAFSP)." Sustainable Development Network, December 7.

GAFSP (Global Agriculture and Food Security Program). 2015. "Executive Minutes: Joint GAFSP Steering Committee/Private Sector Window Donor Committee Meeting." https://www.gafspfund.org/sites/default/files/inline-files/SC%20Meeting%20Apr%202018%20Executive%20Minutes_0.pdf

GAFSP (Global Agriculture and Food Security Program). 2018. "Ending Poverty and Hunger." Who We Are. https://www.gafspfund.org

Gates, Bill. 2012. Prepared Remarks to International Fund for Agricultural Development Governing Council, February 23. https://www.gatesfoundation.org/media-center/speeches/2012/02/bill-gates-ifad

Glauber, Joseph W., Ryan Nabil, and Vincent H. Smith. 2017. "Food for Peace Reform Act." *Inside Sources/Politics*, May 17. http://www.insidesources.com/food-peace-reform-act/

Global Landscapes Forum. 2014. "A Paradigm Shift in Agriculture: Rome Based Agencies Push for SDGs that Target Whole Food Systems, Consumption and Waste Reduction." http://www.landscapes.org/paradigm-shift-agriculture-rome-based-agencies-push-sdgs-target-whole-food-systems-consumption-waste-reduction/

Government of Australia. 2012. *Australian Multilateral Assessment*. March. Canberra: Commonwealth of Australia. https://dfat.gov.au/about-us/publications/Documents/ama-full-re port-2.pdf

Gulrajani, Nillma. 2016. "Bilateral versus Multilateral Aid Channels: Strategic Choices for Donors." ODI Report, Overseas Development Institute, London.

Gwin, Catherine. 1997. "U.S. Relations with the World Bank, 1945–1992." In *The World Bank, Its First Half Century*, Volume 2, edited by Devesh Kapur, John P. Lewis, and Richard Webb, Richard, 195–274. Washington, DC: Brookings Institution Press.

IASC (Inter-Agency Standing Committee). 2012. "Humanitarian System-Wide Emergency Activation: Definition and Procedures—IASC Transformative Agenda Reference Document." PR/1204/4078/7, April 13. https://reliefweb.int/report/world/humanitarian-system-wide-emergency-activation-definition-and-procedures-iasc

IASC (Inter-Agency Standing Committee). 2013. "Common Framework for Preparedness." October 18, UN, New York. https://interagencystandingcommittee.org/system/files/com mon_framework_for_preparedness.pdf

ICRAF (World Agroforestry Centre). 2019. "ICRAF & CIFOR Merger: Accelerating Impact for a Sustainable World." About Us. http://www.worldagroforestry.org/about/icraf-cifor

IDA (International Development Association). 2017. "Towards 2030: Investing in Growth, Resilience and Opportunity." Report from the Executive Directors of the International Development Association to the Board of Governors, Additions to IDA Resources: Eighteenth Replenishment, IDA, Washington, DC.

IDA (International Development Association). 2020. "IDA19: Ten Years to 2030: Growth, People, Resilience." Additions to IDA Resources: Nineteenth Replenishment. Report from the Executive Directors of the International Development Association to the Board of Governors, February 11. http://documents1.worldbank.org/curated/en/459531582153485508/pdf/Additions-to-IDA-Resources-Nineteenth-Replenishment-Ten-Years-to-2030-Growth-People-Resilience.pdf

IDC (International Development Committee). 2008. *The World Food Programme and Global Food Security: Tenth Report of Session 2007–2008*, Vol. II: *Oral and Written Evidence*. Ordered by The House of Commons. London: The Stationery Office Ltd.

IEG (Independent Evaluation Group). 2009. "Governance and Anticorruption in Lending Operations: A Benchmarking and Learning Review." World Bank, Washington, DC. http://siteresources.worldbank.org/EXTLAWJUSTINST/Resources/GAC_review_2009.pdf

IFAD (International Fund for Agriculture). 2015. "Collaboration of the United Nations Rome-based Agencies." EB 2015/115/R.23, IFAD Perspective Position Paper, August 18, IFAD, Rome. https://webapps.ifad.org/members/eb/115/docs/EB-2015-115-R-23.pdf

IFAD (International Fund for Agriculture). 2018. "Report of the Consultation on the Eleventh Replenishment of IFAD's Resources. Leaving No One Behind: IFAD's Role in the 2030 Agenda." IFAD/11/5/INF.2, Governing Council, Forty-first Session, Rome, February 13–14. https://webapps.ifad.org/members/repl/11/05

IFAD (International Fund for Agriculture). 2019. "Voting Rights of IFAD Member States 06/11/2017." https://webapps.ifad.org/members/static/Countries-Voting-Rights.pdf

IFAD (International Fund for Agriculture) and OPEC Fund. 2005. "A Partnership to Eradicate Rural Poverty." September, Rome. https://www.ifad.org/documents/10180/4ad78b11-9a35-4d97-9af7-28eba6127c94

Ingram, James. 2006. *Bread and Stones: Leadership and the Struggle to Reform the United Nations World Food Programme.* North Charleston, SC: BookSurge.

Isenman, Paul. 2011. "Architecture, Allocations, Effectiveness and Governance: Lessons from Global Funds." ODI Meeting on Climate Change, May 5, Overseas Development Institute, London.

Isenman, Paul. 2012. "Learning from Assessments of Overall Effectiveness of Multilateral Organisations." Paper submitted to the Swedish Agency for Development Evaluation (SADEV), Stockholm.

Isenman, Paul, and Alexander Shakow. 2010. "Donor Schizophrenia and Aid Effectiveness: The Role of Global Funds." IDS Practice Paper No. 5, Institute of Development Studies (IDS), University of Sussex, Brighton, UK.

Jenks, Bruce, and Jennifer Topping. 2017. "Financing the UN Development System: Pathways to Reposition for Agenda 2030." September, Dag Hammarskjöld Foundation and United Nations Multi-Partner Trust Fund Office, Uppsala, Sweden. http://www.daghammarskjold. se/wp-content/uploads/2017/10/Financing-UNDS-2017_2oct.pdf

Kanbur, Ravi. 2017. "What is the World Bank Good For? Global Public Goods and Global Institutions." CEPR Discussion Paper No. DP12090, Center for Economic Policy Research, London.

Kanbur, Ravi, and Andy Sumner. 2012. "Poor Countries or Poor People? Development Assistance and the New Geography of Global Poverty." *Journal of International Development* 24 (6): 686–95.

Kapur, Devish, John P. Lewis, and Richard Webb, eds. 1997. *The World Bank: Its First Half Century,* Vol. 1: *History* and Vol. 2: *Perspectives.* Washington, DC: Brookings Institution Press.

Kapur, Devesh, and Arjun Raychaudhuri. 2014. "Rethinking the Financial Design of the World Bank." Working Paper 352, Center for Global Development, Washington, DC.

Kharas, Homi. 2007. "Trends and Issues in Development Aid." Working Paper 1, Wolfensohn Center for Development, Brookings Institution, Washington, DC.

Kharas, Homi. 2008. "Measuring the Cost of Aid Volatility." Working Paper 3, Wolfensohn Center for Development, Brookings Institution, Washington, DC.

Kharas, Homi 2009. "Action on Aid: Steps toward Making Aid More Effective." Report, Brookings Institution, Washington, DC.

Lele, Uma, and Arthur A. Goldsmith. 1989. "The Development of National Agricultural Research Capacity: India's Experience with the Rockefeller Foundation and Its Significance for Africa." *Economic Development and Cultural Change* 37 (2): 305–43.

Lele, Uma, Sambuddha Goswami, and Gianluigi Nico. 2017. "Structural Transformation and the Transition from Concessional Assistance to Commercial Flows: The Past and Possible Future Contributions of the World Bank." In *Agriculture and Rural Development in a Globalizing World: Challenges and Opportunities,* edited by Prabhu Pingali and Gershon Feder, 325–52. London and New York: Routledge.

Lindoso, Vinicius, and Nina Hall. 2016. "Assessing the Effectiveness of Multilateral Organizations." BSG Working Paper 2016/013, April, Blavatnik School of Government, University of Oxford. https://www.bsg.ox.ac.uk/sites/www.bsg.ox.ac.uk/files/documents/2016-04_Hall_Lindoso-Multilateral_Effectiveness.pdf

Linn, Johannes F. 2009. "The Zedillo Commission Report on World Bank Reform: A Stepping Stone for the G-20 Summits in 2010." Brookings Institution, Washington, DC, November 18.

https://www.brookings.edu/articles/the-zedillo-commission-report-on-world-bank-reform-a-stepping-stone-for-the-g-20-summits-in-2010/

Maier, Thomas. 2015. "Toward an Effective PPP Business Model: An Eight-Point Plan for Closing the Infrastructure Gap." World Bank blog, September 15. http://blogs.worldbank.org/ppps/toward-effective-ppp-business-model-eight-point-plan-closing-infrastructure-gap

Manning, Richard. 2017. "Multilateral Development Aid. Assessing the Major Replenishments of 2016." WIDER Working Paper 2017/172, United Nations University World Institute for Development Economics Research (UNU–WIDER), Helsinki.

McCalla, Alex F. 2007. "FAO in the Changing Global Landscape." Working Paper No. 07–006, University of California Davis. http://ageconsearch.umn.edu/bitstream/190919/2/WP07-006.pdf

McCalla, Alex F. 2017. "The Relevance of the CGIAR in a Modernizing World. Or Has It Been Reformed *ad infinitum* into Dysfunctionality?" In *Agriculture and Rural Development in a Globalizing World: Challenges and Opportunities*, edited by Prabhu Pingali and Gershon Feder, 353–69. London and New York: Routledge.

Meltzer, Allan H. 2000. "The Report of the International Financial Institution Advisory Commission: Comments on the Crisis." Research Showcase at CMU, Tepper School of Business, Carnegie Mellon University, Pittsburgh, PA. http://repository.cmu.edu/cgi/viewcontent.cgi?article=1029&context=tepper

Mikesell, Raymond F. 2001. "Review Article: The Meltzer Commission Report on International Institutions." *Economic Development and Cultural Change* 49 (4): 883–94.

MOPAN (Multilateral Organisation Performance Network). n.d. "MOPAN 3.0: A Reshaped Assessment Approach." http://www.mopanonline.org/ourwork/ourapproachmopan30/

MOPAN (Multilateral Organisation Performance Assessment Network). 2011. "Organisational Effectiveness Assessment: Food and Agriculture Organization (FAO) of the United Nations." http://www.mopanonline.org/assessments/fao2011/index.htm

MOPAN (Multilateral Organisation Performance Assessment Network). 2013. "Institutional Report, World Food Programme, 2013." http://www.mopanonline.org/assessments/wfp2013/index.htm

MOPAN (Multilateral Organisation Performance Assessment Network). 2014. "Synthesis Report: Food and Agriculture Organization of the United Nations (FAO), 2014." https://www.state.gov/documents/organization/244675.pdf

MOPAN (Multilateral Organisation Performance Assessment Network). 2018. "MOPAN 2017–18 Assessments: Food and Agriculture Organization (FAO)." http://www.mopanonline.org/assessments/fao2017-18/index.htm

Morris, Scott. 2014. "Shaking Up the Donor Shakedown at the World Bank." Center for Global Development, Washington, DC.

Morris, Scott. 2018a. "John Bolton Wants to Shut Down the World Bank." Center for Global Development, Washington, DC.

Morris, Scott. 2018b. "Trump's Treasury Delivers at the World Bank: More Capital for Climate, Solid Policy Framework." Center for Global Development, Washington, DC.

OCHA (United Nations Office for the Coordination of Humanitarian Affairs). 2016. "World Humanitarian Data and Trends 2016." OCHA. http://interactive.unocha.org/publication/2016_datatrends/

OECD (Organisation for Economic Co-operation and Development). 2019a. Fourth High Level Forum on Aid Effectiveness. http://www.oecd.org/dac/effectiveness/fourthhighlevelforumon aideffectiveness.htm

OECD (Organisation for Economic Co-operation and Development). 2019b. HLF1: The First High Level Forum on Aid Effectiveness, Rome. http://www.oecd.org/dac/effectiveness/hlf-1thefirsthighlevelforumonaideffectivenessrome.htm

OECD (Organisation for Economic Co-operation and Development). 2019c. Second High Level Forum on Aid Effectiveness (HLF-2), 28 February to 2 March 2005, Paris, France. http://www.oecd.org/dac/effectiveness/secondhighlevelforumonjointprogresstowardenhancedaid-effectivenessharmonisationalignmentandresults.htm

OECD (Organisation for Economic Co-operation and Development). 2019d. Third High Level Forum on Aid Effectiveness. http://www.oecd.org/dac/effectiveness/theaccrahighlevel forumhlf3andtheaccraagendaforaction.htm

Ottenhoff, Jenny. 2011. "Leadership Selection at the International Financial Institutions." CGD Brief, Center for Global Development, Washington, DC.

Shaw, D. John. 2014. "A Global Partnership Program to End World Hunger." Briefing 18, Future United Nations Development System, Ralph Bunche Institute for International Studies, CUNY Graduate Center, New York. https://www.futureun.org/media/archive1/briefings/FUNDSBriefing18-FoodSecurity-Shaw.pdf

Silver, Marc, and Malaka Gharib. 2017. "What's the Meaning of the World Bank's New Poverty Lines?" Goats and Soda: Stories of Life in a Changing World/Poverty, National Public Radio, October 25. https://www.npr.org/sections/goatsandsoda/2017/10/25/558068646/whats-the-meaning-of-the-world-banks-new-poverty-lines

Sridhar, Devi, and Ngaire Woods. 2013. "Trojan Multilateralism: Global Cooperation in Health." *Global Policy* 4 (4): 325–35.

Thomas, Jr., Landon. 2018. "The World Bank Is Remaking Itself as a Creature of Wall Street." Business Day, *New York Times*, January 25. https://www.nytimes.com/2018/01/25/business/world-bank-jim-yong-kim.html

Toma, Valentina (team leader), Amreeta Regmi, David Gray, Tingting Guo, Deborah Schermerhorn, Carina Pernia, Tatiana Nikolskaya, Luzviminda Tatlonghari, Natalia Antsilevich, Fernando J. Machado, Galina Menchikova, Aleksandre Revia, and Milagros Reyes. 2013. "2013 Trust Fund Annual Report." Concessional Finance and Global Partnerships Vice Presidency, World Ban Group, Washington, DC. http://documents1.worldbank.org/cur ated/en/618651468159591695/pdf/897860AR0P14680Box0385294B00PUBLIC0.pdf

Toussaint, Eric. 2014. "Domination of the United States on the World Bank." September 1, Committee for the Abolition of Illegitimate Debt (CADTM), Liege, Belgium.

Tutwiler, Ann. 2012. "Joint Statement by the Rome-based Agencies (FAO, IFAD, and WFP) on CSW 56 Priority Theme: Empowering Rural Women to Reduce Poverty and Eradicate Hunger." Presentation, Opening Meeting, February 27, Rome. http://www.un.org/womenwatch/daw/csw/csw56/statements/statement-Tutwiler.pdf

UN (United Nations). 2017a. "Report of the Committee on Contributions." A/72/11, Seventy-seventh session, June 5–23. UN, New York.

UN (United Nations). 2017b. "Repositioning the United Nations Development System to Deliver on the 2030 Agenda: Ensuring a Better Future for All." Report of the Secretary-General. General Assembly, Economic and Social Council, United Nations, New York. http://undocs.org/A/72/124

Wadsworth, Jonathan. 2016. "Brief History of the CGIAR Fund." Discussion Paper, April, CGIAR, Washington, DC. http://www.cgiar.org/wp-content/uploads/2016/03/Brief-history-of-the-CGIAR-Fund.pdf

Weiss, Martin A. 2011. "International Monetary Fund: Selecting a Managing Director." CRS Report, Congressional Research Service, Washington, DC. https://pdfs.semanticscholar.org/a0e1/7c10c2f408e590271d4585d18e25a5f222dc.pdf

WFP (World Food Programme). 2005. "Final Report on the Governance Project." WFP/EB.2/2005/4-C/Rev.1, November 9, WFP, Rome. http://one.wfp.org/eb/docs/2005/wfp076984~2.pdf

WFP (World Food Programme). 2009a. "Directions for Collaborations among the Rome-based Agencies." CL 137/INF/10, August, WFP, Rome. ftp://ftp.fao.org/docrep/fao/meeting/017/k5809e.pdf

WFP (World Food Programme). 2009b. "Three Rome-based UN Agencies Launch Food Security Strategy On Eve of World Food Summit." News, November 16, WFP, Rome. https://www.wfp.org/news/news-release/three-rome-based-un-agencies-launch-food-security-strategy-eve-world-food-summit

WFP (World Food Programme). 2010. "Fighting Hunger Worldwide." Annual Report 2010, WFP, Rome. http://ja.wfp.org/sites/default/files/ja/file/2010_ann_rep_english.pdf

WFP (World Food Programme). 2014a. "General Rules, Financial Regulations Rules of Procedure of the Executive Board." January. WFP, Rome.

WFP (World Food Programme). 2014b. "Update on Collaboration among the Rome-based Agencies." WFP/EB.2/2014/4-C, October 16, WFP, Rome.

WFP (World Food Programme). 2016a. "Key Extracts of the Draft Management Plan 2016–2018." WFP, Rome.

WFP (World Food Programme). 2016b. "The Year in Review 2016." WFP, Rome. https://www.wfp.org/content/wfp-year-review-2016

WFP (World Food Programme). 2017a. "Annual Report of the Inspector General." WFP/EB.A/2017/6-F/1, Executive Board Annual Session, WFP, Rome, June 12–16. http://www.fao.org/3/a-mt088e.pdf

WFP (World Food Programme). 2017b. "World Food Assistance 2017: Taking Stock and Looking Ahead." July, WFP, Rome. https://www.wfp.org/content/2017-world-food-assistance-taking-stock-and-looking-ahead

WFP (World Food Programme). 2020a. "Funding and Donors." http://www1.wfp.org/funding-and-donors

WFP (World Food Programme). 2020b "Independent Evaluation." http://www1.wfp.org/independent-evaluation

Wheeler, David. 2007. "It's One World Out There: The Global Consensus on Selecting the World Bank's Next President." CGD Working Paper No. 123, June, Center for Global Development, Washington, DC. https://www.cgdev.org/files/13861_file_World_Bank_President_Survey.pdf

Wheeler, David. 2011. "Unity in Diversity: A Global Consensus on Choosing the IMF's Managing Director—Evidence from CGD's Online Survey." CGD Working Paper No. 267, September 15, Center for Global Development, Washington, DC. https://www.cgdev.org/publication/unity-diversity-global-consensus-choosing-imf's-managing-director—evidence-cgd's-online

WHO (World Health Organization). 2020. "Assessed Contributions." About WHO. http://www.who.int/about/finances-accountability/funding/assessed-contributions/en/

World Bank. 2011. World Development Report 2011: Conflict, Security, and Development. Washington, DC: World Bank.

World Bank. 2016. "Global Community Makes Record US$75 Billion Commitment to End Extreme Poverty." Press Release, December 15, World Bank, Washington, DC. http://www.worldbank.org/en/news/press-release/2016/12/15/global-community-commitment-end-poverty-ida18

World Bank. 2017. "Mobilization of Private Finance by Multilateral Development Banks." 2016 Joint Report, WBG, Washington, DC.

World Bank. 2018. "A Strong Foundation for Greater Impact." News. Feature story, April 21. http://www.worldbank.org/en/news/feature/2018/04/21/a-strong-foundation-for-greater-impact

World Bank. 2020. "Voting Powers." World Bank/Who We Are/About/Organization. http://www.worldbank.org/en/about/leadership/votingpowers

Xiaoyun, Li, Qi Gubo, Tang Lixia, Zhao Lixia, Jin Leshan, Guo Zhanfeng, and Wu Jin. 2012. *Agricultural Development in China and Africa: A Comparative Analysis.* London and New York: Routledge.

Zedillo, Ernesto, Chair. 2009. "Repowering the World Bank for the 21st Century." Report of the High Level Commission on Modernization of World Bank Group Governance, World Bank Group, Washington, DC.

Zedillo, Ernesto. 2013. Interview, July 30, 2013, by Jeffrey E. Garten, Yale School of Management, International Center for Finance. http://som.yale.edu/interview-ernesto-zedillo

7

Financing for Sustainable Structural Transformation

Uma Lele and Sambuddha Goswami

Summary

Unlike developed countries, developing countries tend to spend a small share of public expenditures on agriculture, and as their per capita income increases, they have been known to spend a larger share on agricultural support (that is, "Amber Box"), and yet, as documented in Chapter 2, overall evidence suggests they spend a lower share of total expenditures on agriculture, unlike their industrial counterparts. This means that once "Amber Box" support to agriculture, largely in the form of input subsidies, is excluded, their support for public goods, particularly to research, extension education, and transportation that would link farms to markets, is limited indeed (WTO 2020b).

Official development assistance (ODA) volumes and multilateral shares of them, as well as domestic expenditures of developing countries on food and agriculture, are often too small, even though ODA has increased in 2020, relative to needs or for stimulating private investment, and they are suboptimally allocated, in terms of choice of activities, including, in particular, too little to agricultural education, research, and extension. Learning and evaluation of impacts, while advancing, also need to improve and expand to keep up with the complexity of the challenges facing farming households.

In earlier chapters, we emphasized two issues: (1) the need to balance the priority to agriculture in a development strategy, relative to other sectors, to achieve equitable and sustainable structural transformation from agriculture to nonagriculture—for example, through infrastructure, education, and the ability to adapt to climate change; and (2) the need to promote the development of agriculture, particularly smallholder agriculture. We demonstrated that the concept of agriculture itself has become multisectoral: for example, to include concerns about nutrition and environmental management. This means financing of agriculture must also be seen in a multisectoral context. Nutritional status is determined by an individual's dietary intake, but it also interacts with the individual's health status, and these variables are determined by underlying household- and community-level drivers (including access to healthy foods, health services, water and sanitation, education, and child caring capacity and practices); and additional structural drivers relating to the amount, control, and the use of various types of resources. We discussed these multidimensional aspects of poverty in Chapter 2 (on structural transformation) and Chapter 4 (on food security to nutrition security) and showed how they determine the extent of favorable social, economic, and political conditions, broadly termed the "enabling environment." They are important for food security and nutrition, as well as for structural transformation. Agriculture is both a contributor to adverse environmental impacts— for example, to greenhouse gas (GHG) emissions and loss of biodiversity through land

Food for All: International Organizations and the Transformation of Agriculture. Uma Lele, Manmohan Agarwal, Brian C. Baldwin, and Sambuddha Goswami, Oxford University Press. © Uma Lele, Manmohan Agarwal, Brian C. Baldwin, and Sambuddha Goswami 2021. DOI: 10.1093/oso/9780198755173.003.0008

use changes, as well as agricultural practices leading to soil degradation, water pollution, and emissions—and yet, conversely, the protector of the environment. Through improved policies and practices of the landscape as a whole, agriculture can protect the environment in each of these respects. This multisectoral nature of agriculture means that financing for agriculture and rural spaces must be viewed, in the broad context, as consisting of multiple components for each of these three dimensions of financing: not just domestic or international, but in each case consisting of resources that are (1) public, (2) private (household), and (3) private (external to household), coming from multiple channels in each of the six categories: public—domestic and international; private—domestic and international; and household—savings and remittances.

Information on the "traditional" ODA sources of financing for agriculture is much better than for nontraditional ODA: for example, from emerging countries, including particularly China's growing involvement in Southern countries, private investments in value chains, land purchases, and private philanthropy. In 2011, leading donors committed in Busan to make their aid transparent by the end of 2015. Only 10 donors, accounting for 25 percent of total aid, have met this commitment to aid transparency. Outside the notable exception of the Bill and Melinda Gates Foundation (BMGF), there is hardly any philanthropist reporting aid to the Organisation for Economic Co-operation and Development/Development Assistance Committee (OECD DAC). However, even in the case of BMGF, its rating, according to the Aid Transparency Index (ATI), improved from a "very poor" rating of 18.1 percent out of 100 in 2013 to 47.3 percent in 2018 ("fair"). Although this indicates an improvement, there was very little improvement in its rating since 2014 to 2018, as we will see later. The 2020 ATI, however, reported significant improvement in aid donors' overall transparency compared to 2018, but while revealing an improvement in overall transparency among the major aid agencies, there is less transparency on the impact of aid projects (ATI 2014, 2018, 2020).

The new themes, including nutrition and the environment, also pose challenges to estimating sources of resource flows in support of adaptation of agriculture to these new concerns. We will show in this chapter that available aid resources are very small indeed, relative to needs and the extent of advocacy.

With rapid economic growth, direct public expenditures of developing countries are of increasing importance in developing agriculture, relative to external aid, but once again there are several challenges. First, information is spotty. Second, there are conceptual issues in determining which expenditures are supportive for creating an enabling environment, and third, productive investments in agriculture by developing countries are very limited. Trade economists define support for agriculture as consisting of two categories of domestic support—support with no, or minimal, distortive effects on trade (often referred to as "Green Box" measures), and trade-distorting support (often referred to as "Amber Box" measures). For example, government-provided agricultural research or training is considered to be of the "Green Box" type, while government buying-in at a guaranteed price ("market price support") falls into the latter category. Under the World Trade Organization (WTO) Agreement on Agriculture, all domestic support in favor of agricultural producers is subject to rules, and the maximum levels of such support are bound in the WTO. In addition, the aggregate monetary value of "Amber Box" measures is, with certain exceptions, subject to reduction commitments as specified in the schedule of each WTO member providing such support (WTO 2016, 2020b).

Twenty-eight members (including the European Union [EU]) "had non-exempt domestic support during the base period and hence reduction commitments specified in their schedules. The reduction commitments are expressed in terms of a 'Total Aggregate

Measurement of Support' (Total AMS) which includes all product-specific support and non-product-specific support in one single figure" (WTO 2020a). Developed country members "with a Total AMS have to reduce base period support by 20 percent over 6 years," and developing country members have to reduce it by "13 percent over 10 years" (WTO 2020a). Beyond a few emerging countries, which the OECD DAC includes in its estimates of agricultural support, such as China and Indonesia, little such information is available for developing countries at large.

Similarly, information on private investments tends to be weak and anecdotal. Notwithstanding these limitations, we attempt to provide orders of magnitude for each category.

Introduction: Why Give Aid, and Particularly, Multilateral Aid?

There is much skepticism about aid and its effectiveness. This has led to widespread aid fatigue. Additionally, OECD countries that have been the principal donors of ODA have faced slow growth, increasing fiscal woes, and a perception of uncontrolled immigration among voters, a phenomenon compounded since 2020 by the COVID-19 pandemic. All of these factors explain Brexit, the fateful British referendum on June 23, 2016, in support of exiting from the EU (Lele 2016). While threatening the integrity of the EU, in a way that even the 2007–8 global food and the financial crises had not done, Brexit has also triggered ascendant politics of division, xenophobia, anti-trade, and anti-open border rhetoric in Europe and North America, exemplified in the 2016 US presidential election. Some have worried that under the Trump administration the international order established after the Second World War is under threat of unraveling. It is too early to know what the impact of Brexit will be on the EU and Britain. Although the COVID-19 pandemic has led to an increase in ODA in 2020 over 2019, the increase also included support of refugees in donor countries. So net flows *to developing countries* were not larger. Politics have implications for international capital flows as well as for the support of the "Big Five" international organizations generally, including those concerned with food and agriculture: namely, the World Bank Group (WBG) (1945); the Food and Agriculture Organization of the United Nations (FAO) (1945); the World Food Programme (WFP) (1961); the Consultative Group for International Agricultural Research (CGIAR)[1] (1971); and the International Fund for Agricultural Development (IFAD) (1976).[2] Paradoxically, they were established in the post-Second World War period, by seizing the various crises as opportunities to avoid mistakes of the years following the First World War. By enhancing international cooperation, they have contributed to the longest period of economic expansion.

Such continued economic cooperation is needed because, as documented in previous chapters, growth has not lifted all boats despite rapid progress in developing countries. Most of the poverty in the world now is found in lower middle-income countries (LMICs) and low-income countries (LICs). Poor households and poor countries have low savings and investment capacity. Substantially greater investment is needed, targeted at poor countries and the poor populations in the middle-income countries (MICs) (Kanbur and Sumner 2012). Also, the world has seen the largest displacement of population since the Second

---

[1] CGIAR, originally known as the Consortium of International Agricultural Research Centers, was established in April 2010 to coordinate and support the work of the 15 international agricultural research centers supported by the CGIAR.

[2] Year of founding for each international organization shown in parentheses after organizational acronym.

World War, so that the need for humanitarian and development assistance exceeds the supply of aid. If the World Health Assembly (WHA) targets (outlined in Chapter 4) are to be achieved by 2025, and the Sustainable Development Goals (SDGs) (outlined in Chapter 4) by 2030, not only do domestic policies need to improve, but substantially greater investment is needed and targeted at poor countries and the poor populations in the MICs. Additional problems on the horizon include the growing incidence of obesity throughout the world that is associated with income growth, urbanization, and unhealthy dietary changes. To contain obesity, investments in improved information, and an improved regulatory environment and its implementation are needed to contain the fiscal burden of poor health on countries.

Even after 70 years of work of the Bretton Woods institutions, capital markets today still face problems of uninsured risk and risk of another crisis (Ravallion 2016). Despite substantial accumulated savings in the world, with perceived risks, the private sector tends to be reluctant to lend to poor countries (World Bank 2013a) and to poor populations in MICs. Multilateral lending helps directly to fill this gap and thereby assists in creating the enabling conditions for private sector investments (Ravallion 2016). Multilateral lending also directly provides positive signals to the private sector and generates the necessary macroeconomic and sectoral information on an objective basis that can help private actors to make informed decisions.

Furthermore, there is growing consensus that international assistance should provide global public goods (GPGs), such as climate mitigation and adaptation, the control of communicable diseases, financial stability, and an open and fair trading system. Such assistance can slow climate change, control communicable diseases, and contain conflicts (Birdsall and Kharas 2010; Deaton 2013). All three are priorities of WBG's International Development Association (IDA)18 replenishments approved in 2016. Developing countries have argued, however, that GPG financing should not come at the cost of development assistance, but should be additional to it at the country level.

There are other reasons to support multilateral lending. It is less politicized, it is more efficient per dollar disbursed, and more equitable. Typically, going to poorer countries and populations, it is more transparent in terms of the amounts delivered and the purposes for which they are spent, and it is usually more selective than bilateral assistance. Multilateral agencies generally give, on average, 55 percent of their aid to LICs, whereas non-DAC and DAC bilateral agencies give only about 19 percent (Gulrajani 2016).

Developing countries prefer multilateral aid to bilateral aid. Gulrajani (2016, 11) noted: "There has long been an assertion that aid-receiving countries view multilateral institutions as more legitimate and trustworthy partners than their bilateral brethren. In the postwar period, the multilateral system seemed to guard against the coercive interests of Western powers overwhelming newly independent states (Andreopoulos et al. 2011; Mills 1964)." Multilateral aid is less fragmented and delivered on a larger scale, and more of the reported aid resources are actually transferred to developing countries because of less tying and lower costs of delivery (Rondinelli 1993; Kharas 2007, 2008, 2009; Birdsall and Kharas 2010; Custer et al. 2015).

Multilateral institutions are able to develop knowledge, which is a public good. Supporters of aid have argued that the World Bank, for example, is a source of the "soft power" of knowledge, citing examples in the areas of agriculture, education, health, social safety nets, trade, and fiscal policies in which the Bank's analytical capacity has made a difference (Rodrik 1996; Kanbur 2004; Radelet 2006; Kharas 2007, 2008, 2009; Birdsall and Kharas 2010; Isenman and Shakow 2010; Isenman 2011, 2012; Clemens et al. 2012; Kanbur and Sumner 2012; Clemens and Kremer 2016). The World Bank and, increasingly, the regional banks contain the world's largest collection of expertise in development economics. There are economies of scale in generating large-scale information. It requires substantial initial capital, which international organizations have invested over the years, establishing decades of record, trust, and experience. Their near universal membership gives them legitimacy and access to global expertise, in addition to access to governments. Except for the largest multinationals, the private sector, on the other hand, has little interest, breadth, or depth of reach, and most importantly, little incentive to collect, analyze, and share information with the public. Not only can multilateral institutions play a more effective role in providing GPGs of information and knowledge, norms, and standards, as well as achieve international consensus and agreements, but they also can help contain regional public "bads," such as pandemics, involuntary migration, and climate change—which have cross-border spillovers and contribute to poverty.

There are also many critics of aid, however (Lal 2006; Easterly and Pfutze 2008; Easterly and Williamson 2011; Deaton 2013; Easterly and Pfutze 2013). Easterly (2006), by far the most vocal critic of aid, has argued that billions of dollars spent on aid in developing countries have had very little impact. Deaton (2013), too, asserted that aid has had little impact in Africa, because governments receive too large a share of their expenditures as aid, which makes them more accountable to donors and less accountable to their poor constituents. In contrast, he argued, aid to China and India has been successful: that is, poverty has declined and social indicators have improved. This is because aid has been a small share of gross domestic product (GDP), and governments have not spent most of their time being accountable to donors rather than to their own people (Easterly 2006). We also provide further evidence in the chapters on the World Bank, IFAD, and CGIAR that aid to China has been even more effective than that to India, and project performance in LICs has typically been lower than in MICs.

Bilateral aid politicizes aid giving. Although tying has diminished, some bilateral donors tie aid to the procurement of goods and services of their own country. and aid can be unstable, depending on the bilateral political relationships, which distort aid in the direction of interests of the domestic constituencies. Allocation of aid by bilaterals differs greatly from that which would maximize poverty impacts (Collier and Dollar 2002).

Most of the top 10 donors, with high rankings on transparency and who are meeting Busan commitments, are multilateral organizations. The exceptions are the US's Millennium Challenge Corporation (MCC) and the UK's Department for International Development (DFID), but the MCC gives aid to a relatively small number of countries, as compared, for example, to the World Bank's lending to countries.

These positive observations do not mean international organizations are free of political influence. In Chapter 5 (on global governance), we noted that the nationality of the leaders of Bretton Woods Institutions is determined by historical agreements. Even where the leadership is not so formally determined, contributions have a heavy influence on the choice of leaders, such as in WFP. Reinhart and Trebesch (2015) and Eichengreen and Woods (2016) cited several examples of the influence of the United States and Europe on the activities of the International Monetary Fund (IMF): for example, US pressure to privatize industry during the Asian Crisis, the European influence on the standby arrangements in Greece, and, more generally, the influence of the larger shareholders on IMF and World Bank policies. The World Bank's safeguard policies have been heavily influenced by international nongovernmental organizations (INGOs) directly and through the influence of the executive directors of the larger shareholders. Yet, there is considerable evidence that multilaterals typically delivers multilateral aid based on a relatively more transparent, well laid out criteria, and perform better than bilaterals across three dimensions: usefulness of advice (seven of the top 10 donors here being multilateral); agenda-setting influence (all of the top 10 are multilateral); and helpfulness in implementation (eight of the top 10 are multilateral) (Custer et al. 2015), based on an extensive survey conducted by Aid Data of 6,750 development policymakers and practitioners in 126 LICs and MICs. Bilaterals are more selective in giving aid to countries which meet their political objectives such as the US aid to Israel and Egypt; however, multilaterals give aid in terms of country needs—for example, based on per capita income or level of poverty—but not always necessarily in terms of the quality of governance.

Key Messages

This chapter presents the financial commitments of the Big Five international organizations in the context of the overall financial flows to developing countries. It outlines the declining role of multilateral assistance, and the rise of multi-bi funding in international organizations, which has fundamentally transformed OECD's external assistance and has been accompanied by the rise of the Global South in funding.[3] The chapter also situates the very small financial flows going directly to agriculture and the need to increase both the quantity and quality of international and national public investment in agriculture. This is done for several reasons (UNCTAD 2019b):

(1) traditional sources of OECD ODA are shrinking relative to other sources, for example, private finance, remittances, philanthropy, South–South cooperation;

(2) competition from other sectors, in need of large-scale capital and promising quick disbursements, is crowding out investment in agriculture, with the result that public goods in agriculture have been, and continue to be, underfunded by donors and governments alike;

(3) rapid growth in the domestic revenues of developing countries has not necessarily resulted in more resources to agricultural development;

(4) until recently, there was a substantial increase in private sector funding, South–South cooperation, and remittances, but private sector funding and remittances have declined, and information is limited on how they benefit agriculture; and

(5) innovative sources of financing, such as taxes on transactions, airlines, and auctions, have not been explored much in areas such as climate change, biodiversity conservation, and water management.

Agriculture and Intersectoral Priorities

Financing needs of developing countries amount to trillions of dollars. Infrastructure investments tend to be large, capital intensive, and relatively rapidly disbursing, as compared to agricultural investments. There is strong demand for infrastructure development. In theory, international public and private sectors can help finance. Also, many of these

---

[3] The OECD publication, "Multilateral Development Finance" defines non-core/earmarked/multi-bi contributions as "resources to ODA-eligible multilateral agencies over which the donor retains some degree of control on decisions regarding disposal of the funds. Such flows may be earmarked for a specific country, project, region, sector, or theme. They are bilateral resources channelled through a multilateral agency, and therefore technically qualify as part of bilateral ODA. These resources can be administered through trust funds, either as single or multi-donor trust funds" (OECD 2015, 255).

investments are complementary: for example, availability of infrastructure being critical for value chains. When considered individually, these investments often have high rates of return, similar to or higher than in agricultural research and extension, even though, as shown in Chapter 10 (on CGIAR), hundreds of studies produced by CGIAR and others show high rates of return to the adoption of improved crop varieties.

There is also the more complex challenge of developing "softer" infrastructure, in terms of institutions and human capital. This latter development poses very different challenges than the establishment of physical capital, and human and institutional capital is often a prerequisite to achieving high rates of return on infrastructure, agriculture, water and sanitation, or nutrition. Hence, policymakers face a tension between complementarity of investments among sectors—the old Rosenstein–Rodan argument of the "Big Push" (Hoff 2001; see, also, Akber and Paltasingh 2019). Hoff famously argued that, at an early stage of development, the investments of industrializing firms in one sector could increase the profitability of other sectors throughout the economy. Simultaneous industrialization of many sectors could be profitable for all of them, but no sector would be profitable industrializing alone. As a result, an underdevelopment equilibrium was possible: even the market may not succeed in coordinating the activities needed to ensure development. She explained the big push argument in modern, theoretical terms as a "coordination" challenge (Hoff 2001). Hoff asserted that modern economic theory has broadened our view of the sources of spillovers that could lead to underdevelopment as an equilibrium. She argued for an "ecological perspective" (Hoff 2001, 147) on development, which also applies to rural development, where the influences from others in one's environment are a critical determinant of outcomes, and many interaction effects are not mediated by markets. She thus distinguished between deep interventions that change underlying forces and shallow interventions, which do not, but may actually make things worse.

With globalization and interconnectedness, the need for public goods in a range of areas has increased. Global food and financial crises, and pandemics like the Ebola outbreak, spread rapidly, whereas, existing international and domestic institutions that could help contain the crises tend to be weak, and rigid in making the adjustments needed to respond to the speed of transmission of challenges. This has implications for investments in public goods, capacity building, and institutional adjustments at all levels. The Center for Global Development's (CGD) multilateral development banking report (Ahluwalia et al. 2016), referred to in Chapter 5 (on global governance), makes a strong case for investment in GPGs based on this reason.

Not all the reported aid goes to developing countries, but rather to the ecosystem of organizations, which, in addition to nation states, include UN agencies, multilateral organizations, INGOs, and think tanks seeking to use those same limited resources to advance their agendas. Those agendas range from short-term humanitarian assistance to long-term development, policy advice, technical assistance, and advocacy.

As shown in Chapter 5 (on global governance), the production or generation of global, regional, national, and local public goods is often closely intertwined vertically from the local to the global levels and, horizontally, across sectors. Furthermore, although in principle, and often, even in practice, production or generation of public goods and their delivery tends to be independent of financing, with financing closely related to the level at which the public goods are provided.

The supply of development finance to agriculture and to overall development should focus on the sorts of public goods listed in Box 7.1 at all levels: global, regional, and national. A GPGs agenda of direct relevance to food and agriculture should be contrasted with the gaps that currently exist.

Box 7.1 International, Transboundary, and National Public Goods of Relevance to Food and Agriculture

Here we list only the very direct public goods—activities of relevance to agriculture that should receive high priority in funding. Global Platforms are useful in exchanging information and points of view, but they should be seen as complementary to building the capacity of countries to generate and use information. Most of these latter capacity-building activities are underfunded: clean air, clean water, landscape, green transport infrastructure (such as footpaths, cycleways, greenways, etc.), public parks, urban parks, rivers, mountains, forests, and beaches are a subcategory of nonmarket public goods.

1. *Information and Knowledge*: Generation of quality information for users at local, subnational, national, regional, and global level tends to be of highest priority. Policymakers at the subregional and national levels need information, which would likely overlap with the data for global monitoring, for example, of SDGs. International organizations provide far too little technical assistance, training, capacity-building, and oversight to assure quality and comparability of data collected at the national level with both that at the sectoral and subsectoral level and, as appropriate, at the household and local levels on agricultural production systems, forests, fisheries, water, land, diseases and pests, and genetic resources; nor do they monitor adherence to global agreements. Beyond countries' own systems, international organizations collect household and other microeconomic and macro data to conduct research and report on key emerging issues.

2. *Early Warning Systems*: These are needed to address potential emergencies and to avoid cross-border spillover of "global public bads," such as hunger, disease, and pests.[a] Here, too, together with national organizations, international organizations need the funding and partnerships to help build such systems and the necessary capacities at the national and subnational levels on a consistent, long-term, cross-country basis.

3. *Neutral Forum for Policy and Scientific Dialogue and Exchange*: Food security and agriculture issues require platforms to discuss policy and strategy issues with and across countries and regions. The international organizations of FAO and CGIAR provide networked organizations. The Committee on World Food Security (CFS), discussed in Chapter 9 on FAO, provides one such important platform since it was reformed in 2009. At present, however, CFS does not have the mandate and the resources to translate its resolutions, or the recommendations of technical working papers and other material to put into practice, monitor the adopted practices on the ground, and report back progress on implementation to member countries. Still, there is considerable potential for the CFS to work with FAO, including to follow up on a variety of nonbinding agreements, such as the following:
   a. Nonbinding international instruments and guidelines;
   b. The Code of Conduct for Responsible Fisheries;
   c. Voluntary Guidelines to Support the Progressive Realization of the Right to Adequate Food in the Context of National Food Security;
   d. Voluntary Guidelines on the Responsible Governance of Tenure of Land, Fisheries, and Forests in the Context of National Food Security;
   e. The Principles for Responsible Investment in Agriculture and Food Systems.

Continued

Box 7.1   Continued

f. FAO's EU-funded Pilot Monitoring Program: This program needs to be refined and institutionalized, with the World Bank, IFAD, regional banks, and CGIAR supporting it and building their operational work and lending operations around it. CGIAR and the National and Regional Research and Development Systems need effective partnerships to lift millions of out of poverty, which is CGIAR's declared mission. A Global Conference on Agricultural Research for Development (GCARD) is meant to provide a global platform for concerned stakeholders and promote partnerships.

4. *Food Safety Standards*: WTO recommends countries adhere to standards for regional and international trade. As private food standards have proliferated, countries must adhere to meeting import requirements in advanced countries, and reconciling requirements of Codex Alimentarius and private standards has become an increasing challenge (Clarke 2010). Countries need assistance to implement these. The World Bank is leading multisectoral global partnership on food safety. An international reporting system is also needed to assess progress and what further help the countries need (WBG 2015).

5. *Management of Genetic Resources*: FAO, together with CGIAR, have had responsibility for the International Treaty on Plant Genetic Resources, which is now an independent trust.[b] A recent independent evaluation notes that the agreement has had a positive impact on making the CGIAR centers' genetic resources available and suggests that more research is needed to see how the CGIAR collection could be made more accessible in view of climate change, political instability, and the need for adaptation to climate change adaptation (Gotor, Caracciolo, and Watts 2010). There is also need to conserve ex-situ biodiversity in tropical countries, which is being lost at a rapid rate. SDG2 includes biodiversity conservation with very limited specification of how it would be motivated or monitored.

6. *Generation and Mobilization of Agricultural Technologies*: New challenges require new technologies with global and regional public goods characteristics, such as high-yielding varieties attuned to production systems and to new climate change challenges of higher temperatures, variable rainfall, floods and droughts, pests and diseases. The private sector now produces technologies for major, internationally traded crops and livestock, such as maize, wheat, soybeans, and edible oils; and four or five multinationals now control most of the intellectual property rights on improved genetic material. CGIAR cannot replicate their resources, science, or market instinct. In the health sector, intellectual property rights in vaccines have been negotiated to produce vaccines that can be delivered to poor people. Agriculture has greater complexities and will require effective partnerships between CGIAR and the private sector to provide a huge jump in the availability of technologies to 500 million small farmers in developing countries in the face of climate change. Norman Borlaug's message "take it to the farmer" requires a new and different strategy in 2016 than in 1966, a strategy that involves the private sector, national systems, civil society, and value chains, as well as extension systems that exist. This issue is discussed in Chapter 10 on CGIAR.

Notes: [a] The PREDICT Consortium (2014) report, produced for the United States Agency for International Development, "Pandemic Risk and Promoting Global Health," cited Murray and Aviso (2011): "Despite increasing endorsement of One Health by agency officials and policy makers globally, the lack of cross-sectoral and transboundary collaboration coupled with siloed resources have limited widespread implementation of the approach" (PREDICT Consortium 2014, 79). The report also mentioned the partnership between FAO, the World Health Organization (WHO) and the World Organisation for Animal Health (OIE) under One Health. The Independent Evaluation Group report on avian influenza (containing "global bads"), however, saw no prospect of support for it in Bank operations unless there was another emergency (IEG 2013b). For more information on PREDICT's shutdown, see KFF (2019); Carlson (2020); Global Biodefense (2020).

b In 1994, an agreement between CGIAR, FAO, and the UN established the "In-Trust Agreements" (ITAs) that formalized the legal status of ex-situ germplasm collections held by the CGIAR gene banks. These agreements facilitated germplasm flows and institutionalized open access to germplasm from CGIAR Centers under the auspices of the ITAs, contributing to policymaking and the exchange of the germplasm.

Most GPGs in Box 7.1 call for capacity at the national and subnational levels. There has not only been increased emphasis in the traditional country assistance literature on the need to enhance the provision of GPGs at the national and subnational level, but increasingly, there is tendency to promote the use of traditional country assistance to enhance the capacity of developing countries to generate the supply of global and regional public goods. Many developing countries have resisted, arguing instead that financing for the provision of GPGs should involve additional resources and different mechanisms outside country assistance financing and instruments to finance GPGs (see, for example, discussion starting IDA13 to 17) (IDA 2020a). Again, the CGD report on the multilateral development banks makes a case for why the World Bank should become a major source of financing, to the tune of US$10 billion annually, approved by the Bank's shareholders, together with reforms in the governance of the Bank (Ahluwalia et al. 2016). The prospect of such financing from the World Bank, however, does not seem likely.

Financing Needs for Food and Agriculture

Although not immediately obvious, the activities of the Big Five international organizations span all three areas of the UN System: Peace and Security, Humanitarian Assistance, and Development. All five are working at the edges of all three of these larger-than-life issues confronting humanity. Most recently, the largest number and growth of human displacement since the Second War has occurred, showing us that without peace and security, and law and order for the 60 million people directly affected by displacement and for others in whose countries they have had to take shelter, there can be no food security, environmental or social safety, and no development. The largest growth in the UN budget in recent years has been for humanitarian assistance, the size of which has grown due to emergencies that had not been anticipated only a few years ago. All humanitarian funding raised is from voluntary contributions. A combination of underfunding and short-term appeals determines the effectiveness of the Big Five organizations.

As the Development Committee Discussion Note (prepared jointly by the African Development Bank [AfDB], Asian Development Bank [ADB], European Bank for Reconstruction and Development [EBRD], European Investment Bank [EIB], Inter-American Development Bank [IDB], IMF, and World Bank) on financing needs of developing countries for the Addis Ababa Financing meeting in June 2015 stressed, the financing needs to fill the infrastructure and energy deficits in South Asia (SA) and sub-Saharan Africa (SSA) alone amount to well over a trillion dollars each (Development Committee

2015). Infrastructure investments are critical and, indeed, overdue for transforming agriculture and overall economies. Similarly, for the billion poor who lack access to energy, water, and sanitation, energy investments are critical to promote agriculture and education. The report of the Development Committee (a joint ministerial committee of the World Bank and IMF), entitled "From Billions to Trillions: Transforming Development Finance," emphasized that most of the financing will have to come from the private sector, but public policies and regulatory frameworks can help. The Bretton Woods Institutions can assist in creating an enabling environment, in the same way that peace and security can be established under the UN umbrella to create an enabling environment for development (Development Committee 2015). Financing issues are far less settled, however. A separate World Bank report (2013b) stressed that future financing for these sectors is likely to come from East Asia and, particularly China, indicative of the growing role of China. (See also Bussalo, Lim, and Maliszewska 2013.)

South–South Cooperation

Growth in developing countries, as a group, since the 1990s, has changed the donor–recipient relationship in a significant way. Rapid growth in demand for raw materials in large developing economies has led to a commodity boom that has benefited exporters in Latin America and SSA. The role of external aid has declined. Developing country governments have more revenues to spend from increased growth. Many enjoy investment-level credit ratings and increased access to international private capital. Emerging economies have also been offering large government-to-government aid, most notably China (Agarwal 2015).

The rise of China as a global donor and investor serves, perhaps, as the most powerful illustration of the changed landscape for the World Bank and other international institutions. Citing McKinsey & Company, Runde (2015) noted that "while the total level of loans outstanding from the world's five biggest multilateral development banks stood at US$500 billion in 2013, total Chinese outstanding foreign loans and deposits were a staggering US$838 billion at the end of 2011. Foreign direct investment totaled US$1.45 trillion in 2013, with US$778 billion of that total heading to developing countries." Separately, Brazil's National Development Bank (BNDS) alone disbursed US$60 billion in 2013, compared to the World Bank's annual disbursements of US$27 billion. Runde (2015) concluded, "Clearly organizations like the World Bank which previously were juggernauts in an empty playing field are now minority shareholders in a system that is much larger than them."

Emerging Countries Are Becoming Big Players in Other Respects as Well

In agriculture, China is now priming itself to supply the US$16 billion seed market, hoping to surpass traditional multinational seed companies, such as Monsanto, Syngenta, and Pioneer. It is already a big investor in Africa and in other developing countries.

We present recent evidence on China's involvement and impacts in SSA and Latin America later in the chapter.

Recent Trends in Financial Flows to Developing Countries

Many of the GPGs have a strong national and subnational public goods dimension. One cannot achieve peace and security, a free and fair trading system, financial stability or food security, or contain climate change, without also achieving those outcomes at the national and subnational levels, and further, with countries have systems in place, which maximize good cross-border spillovers and minimize bad ones. Some countries' mismanagement can have disproportionate adverse spillovers across borders: for example, in the case of the financial crisis or avian influenza. Therefore, achieving GPGs requires all countries to participate; it is more than a sum of its parts, whether a weighted sum or not. Formal or informal rules and regulations, their implementation, and modes of human behavior determine outcomes as well as the capacity of the countries and institutions to generate them and to benefit from them, including particularly those of the weakest among them.

Sources of Trillion Dollar Flows to Developing Countries: Shrinking Roles of Official Development Assistance

Financing sources have grown and diversified in recent years, with multiple channels of financing into agriculture; for example, support for nutrition comes through direct nutrition programs, as well as through cash transfers; and for the environment, through financing for biodiversity conservation, climate mitigation and adaptation, forest and landscape management. The role of ODA has declined in relative, and in some cases, absolute terms. Increased financing has come from: (1) domestic sources of financing of developing countries from their own economic growth; (2) growth of private (legal and illegal) capital flows from developed to developing countries; (3) philanthropic organizations; (4) growing South–South cooperation; and (5) the extraordinary growth of remittances.

Figure 7.1 shows overall financial flows, including remittances to developing countries from 2002 to 2017, which reached a trillion dollars in 2010, 3.6 times greater than 2002, and peaked in 2016 at US$1.5 trillion (in 2016 constant prices). Over recent years, growth has been driven by rapid increases in remittances, growing almost 4.4 times since 2002, and in private resource flows, predominantly foreign direct investment (FDI). The slowdown in the world economy, followed by the COVID-19 pandemic, led to decline in all resource flows except ODA. According to the January 2021 "Investment Trends Monitor" of the United Nations Conference on Trade and Development (UNCTAD), "Global foreign direct investment (FDI) collapsed in 2020, falling by 42% to an estimated US$859 bn, from US$1.5 trillion in 2019" (UNCTAD 2021). Such a low level was last seen in the 1990s and is more than 30 percent below the investment trough that followed the 2008–9 global financial crisis (UNCTAD 2021).

Due to the COVID-19 pandemic, ODA increased by 3.5 percent over 2019, and stood at 3.2 percent combined gross national income (GNI) of OECD countries, compared to 3 percent in 2015. Over the past two decades, developing countries steadily increased their share of global FDI receipts. FDI now represents one of the largest sources of developing countries' external financing. The decline in FDI in 2020 was concentrated in developed countries, where flows plummeted by 69 percent to an estimated US$229 bn. Flows to North America declined by 46 percent to US$166 bn, with cross-border mergers and acquisitions (M&As) dropping by 43 percent. Announced greenfield investment projects

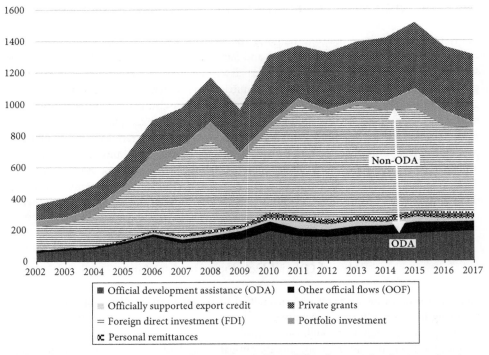

Figure 7.1 Shrinking roles of ODA financing in trillion-dollar flows to developing countries: Total dollar receipts, 2002–2017 (ODA + non-ODA + remittances, US$bn, constant 2016 prices)

Note: ODA: Official development assistance in the figure includes bilateral ODA and multilateral concessional flows. Other non-ODA flows include: other official developmental flows (OOF) and multilateral concessional flows, officially supported export credits, private grants, FDI, and portfolio investment. Official flows, officially supported export credits and private grants are adjusted gross disbursements. Personal remittances, FDI, and portfolio investments are net flows. All flows are in 2016 prices.

Source: Based on data from http://www.oecd.org/dac/stats/beyond-oda.htm

also fell by 29 percent and project finance deals tumbled by 2%. The United States recorded a 49 percent drop in FDI, falling to an estimated US$134 bn. The decline took place in wholesale trade, financial services, and manufacturing. Cross-border M&A sales of US assets to foreign investors fell by 41 percent, mostly in the primary sector. On the other side of the Atlantic Ocean, investment to Europe dried up. Flows fell by two-thirds to –US$4 bn. In the United Kingdom, FDI fell to zero, and declines were recorded in other major recipients (UNCTAD 2021).

FDI flows to developing economies decreased by 12 percent in 2020 to an estimated US$616 bn, but they accounted for 72 percent of global FDI—the highest share on record. The fall was highly uneven across developing regions: –37 percent in Latin America and the Caribbean, –18 percent in Africa and –4 percent in developing countries in Asia. FDI to transition economies declined by 77 percent to US$13 bn. While developing countries in Asia weathered the storm well as a group, attracting an estimated US$476 bn in FDI in 2020, flows to members of the Association of Southeast Asian Nations (ASEAN) contracted by 31 percent to US$107 bn, due to a decline in investment to the largest recipients in the subregion. China was the world's largest FDI recipient, with flows to the Asian giant rising by 4 percent to US$163 bn (UNCTAD 2021).

High-tech industries saw an increase of 11 percent in 2020, and cross-border M&As rose by 54 percent, mostly in ICT and pharmaceutical industries (UNCTAD 2021).

"A return to positive GDP growth (+2.3 percent) and the government's targeted investment facilitation programme helped stabilize investment after the early lockdown," the UNCTAD report says.

India, another major emerging economy, also recorded positive growth (13percent), boosted by investments in the digital sector. (UNCTAD 2021)

Although one of the largest sources of developing countries' external financing, FDI to developing countries has already dropped by about a third over 2016–17, following a 12 percent drop in overall external finance from 2013–16, as well as project finance down 30 percent in the first quarter of 2018. External finance to poor countries is also declining, despite a promise by the international community three years ago to increase development finance flows, in particular through private investment (OECD 2018b). It is interesting to see how the picture changes from year to year.

A 2019 OECD report noted that ODA from advanced economies was below target and had fallen as a share of total resources received by many developing countries, while other flows such as remittances and philanthropy were increasing but comparatively small in recent years (OECD 2019i).[4]

In overall financial flows, over 46 percent was from private flows,[5] nearly one-third as personal remittances, only 15 percent from ODA and remaining 6 percent as other official flows (OOF),[6] including export credits in 2017. Total official and private flows (in constant

---

[4] ODA includes bilateral ODA and multilateral concessional flows. ODA is defined as those "flows to countries and territories on the DAC List of ODA Recipients and to multilateral development institutions that are: (i) provided by official agencies, including state and local governments, or by their executing agencies; and (ii) concessional (i.e., grants and soft loans) and administered with the promotion of the economic development and welfare of developing countries as the main objective" (OECD 2019i).

[5] From the "DAC Glossary of Key Terms and Concepts" (https://www.oecd.org/dac/stats/dac-glossary.htm):

Private flows consist of flows at market terms, financed out of private sector resources (i.e. changes in holdings of private, long-term assets held by residents of the reporting country) and private grants (i.e. grants by non-governmental organizations and other private bodies, net of subsidies received from the official sector). In data presentations which focus on the outflow of funds from donors, private flows other than foreign direct investment are restricted to credits with a maturity of greater than one year and are usually divided into:

- Foreign direct investment: Investment made to acquire or add to a lasting interest in an enterprise in a country on the DAC List of ODA Recipients;
- Private export credits: Loans for the purpose of trade and which are not represented by a negotiable instrument;
- Securities of multilateral agencies: The transactions of private non-bank and bank sector in bonds, debentures, etc., issued by multilateral institutions; and
- Bilateral portfolio investment and other: Includes bank lending and the purchase of shares, bonds and real estate.

[6] From the "Other Official Flows (OOF)" (https://data.oecd.org/drf/other-official-flows-oof.htm):

Other official flows (OOF) are defined as official sector transactions that do not meet official development assistance (ODA) criteria,... [include] grants to developing countries for representational or essentially commercial purposes;... official bilateral transactions intended to promote development, but having a grant element of less than 25%;... [or are] export credits; the acquisition...of securities issued by multilateral development banks at market terms; subsidies (grants) to the private sector to soften its credits to developing countries; and funds in support of private investment.

2016 US dollars) were US$878.2 billion in 2017,[7] of which total official flows (ODA + OOF, including export credits) was US$265.3 billion and total private flows to developing countries reached US$612.9 billion (OECD.Stat 2020b). Grants from philanthropic organizations like BMGF amounted to US$5 billion in 2018, of which 8 percent went to agricultural development.[8] Today, remittances represent the largest source of external finance for many developing countries and also an important contributor to resilience in the face of economic or humanitarian crises. Both the estimates of remittances and their uses have been a matter of considerable debate, we discuss further in this chapter.

Role of International Organizations Concerned with Food, Agriculture, and Nutrition

The latest available statistics on the total flows to developing countries from the public and the private sector, and those going into agriculture from OECD countries, make three facts clear. First, the role of "traditional OECD ODA" has been shrinking with respect to the overall flows to developing countries from all sources to all sectors (Figure 7.1). Second, the 2007–8 food and agriculture crisis has had little positive effect on increasing ODA going to agriculture (see Figure 3.4, Chapter 3). On the contrary the share of all ODA going to agriculture has shrunk in total ODA, as compared to the peaks reached in the 1980s. Third, the role of international organizations' financing with respect to total ODA going to agriculture has been shrinking, the Rome 2003, Paris 2005, Accra 2008, and Busan 2011 Declarations produced at High Level Forums (HLF), notwithstanding (HLF-1 2003; HLF-2 2005; HLF-3 2008; and HLF-4 2011) (OECD 2019h).

Together, the Big Five organizations spent or committed only about US$21.3 billion annually on food and agriculture (of which about one-third is humanitarian or emergency assistance assistance) in 2018–19, which is miniscule, but potentially catalytic annual activity focused mainly on agriculture production and livelihood, as compared to annual investment of developing countries in agriculture, excluding investment needed in other sectors (OECD 2019h). According to the World Bank (2014a), developing countries spent about US$1 trillion a year on infrastructure. A more recent World Bank report found that investments of 4.5 percent of GDP will allow developing countries to achieve their infrastructure-related SDGs and stay on track to limit to meet the goal of limiting climate change to up to 2°C (Rozenberg and Fay 2019). These expenditure numbers provide orders of magnitude and are not strictly comparable.

WBG and IFAD are financing institutions whose funds go directly to developing countries in the form of loans, credit, and grants, but they operate at different scales. WBG's annual commitments, including the International Finance Corporation's (IFC), to

---

[7] Official and Private or Concessional and Non-Concessional flows in OECD DAC statistics. [Non-ODA flows mean (Other Official Flows + Private Grants + Private Flows at Market Terms)]:

	Concessional	Non-Concessional
Official	ODA	Other Official Flows
Private	Net Private Grants	Private Flows at Market Terms (FDI + Other Securities)

Source: http://www.oecd.org/dac/stats/beyond-oda.htm#understanding

[8] DAC statistics include activity-level data from BMGF on aid grants, loans, and equities by recipient and by sector since 2009. These activities are classified as financial flows from the private sector (that is, private grants and private flows at market terms) and should be excluded from analyses of Official Development Finance.

food and agriculture amounted to about US$9.9 billion in 2019, with US$5.4 billion in (only 8.5 percent of the total) commitments to the public sector made by the World Bank (International Bank for Reconstruction and Development [IBRD]/International Development Association [IDA]) and US$4.5 billion in commitments to food and agriculture by the private sector development arm, the IFC, mostly to agribusiness value chains.[9]

IFAD's total loan and grant operations was nearly US$1.2 billion in 2018 (last year of the IFAD10 replenishment period. In 2019, new approvals for IFAD projects and programs increased to a record US$1.67 billion, to do more in improving the lives of rural people, as well as building a sustainable future for their families and communities (IFAD 2018a, 2018b, 2019).

CGIAR committed about US$836 million in 2019 to its long-term research program in its 15 international research centers (CGIAR 2019).

FAO's biannual budget was US$2.6 billion. This means its annual budget was only about US$1.3 billion in 2018–19, about the same as IFAD. Of this amount, 39 percent comes from assessed contributions paid by member countries, which is available on a long-term predictable basis, while 61 percent is mobilized through voluntary contributions, through the phenomenon of donor trust funds, from members and other partners. The FAO regular biennium budget for the 2018–19 is US$1,005.6 million, which means an annual budget of about US$503 million. The voluntary contributions provided by members and other partners support technical and emergency (including rehabilitation) assistance to governments for clearly defined purposes linked to the results framework, as well as directly support FAO's core work. The voluntary contributions are expected to reach approximately US$1.6 billion in 2018–19.[10]

The largest amount, outside WBG, was WFP's humanitarian and emergency assistance. Unlike in the case of other four organizations that either provide development assistance or GPGs, WFP's humanitarian and emergency assistance amounted to around US$8.1 billion in 2019. It was funded almost entirely by voluntary contributions, unlike the assessed contributions that fund FAO and WHO. The data on humanitarian needs have been highly fragmented.[11]

It is in this broader context that the trends in the World Bank, IFC, and IFAD lending in support of investment in food and agriculture, and the activities of FAO in providing GPGs of norms and standards, and statistics, as well as CGIAR's investments in R&D and WFP's humanitarian and emergency assistance and their impacts should be seen.

The World Bank's focus on the objectives of poverty reduction and increased prosperity has incorporated increased IFC lending to agribusinesses since 2000, addressing a wide range of private sector activities in land and water, nutrition, and value chains. Whereas WFP has been traditionally known for its food-for-work and school-feeding programs, increasingly, it has had to focus on emergencies to save lives in fragile and conflict areas. It is

---

[9] See World Bank, "Agriculture and Food." https://www.worldbank.org/en/topic/agriculture/overview#2
[10] See "Strategic Planning": http://www.fao.org/about/strategic-planning/en/
[11] A paper on the financing of humanitarian assistance notes:

Better reporting would improve transparency in terms of:

1) the *totality* of funding, including resources beyond humanitarian assistance;

2) *traceability* beyond the first-level recipient to see the transaction chain from donor to crisis-affected person and the time it takes for the money to work its way through the system 3) *timeliness* to allow real-time data on available resources in fast-moving humanitarian settings.... Improvements to the IATI [International Aid Transparency Initiative] standard currently in progress mean that by the end of 2015 it will be fully compatible and interoperable with the UN Office for the Coordination of Humanitarian Affairs (OCHA)'s Financial Tracking Service (FTS) and other aid coordination platforms. (Lattimer 2015, 2)

the leading humanitarian organization delivering food and assistance, with two-thirds of WFP's work occurring in conflict-affected countries. FAO's five objectives focus on eradication of hunger and food insecurity, while managing natural resources; CGIAR's research focuses on connections between food and health, and between food and the environment. CGIAR's declared objective is to contribute to the SDGs, by achieving 150 million fewer hungry people by 2030, and restoring 190 million degraded lands. Measurement of these achievements and, particularly, attribution of the results to international organizations is a challenge. IFAD, too, increasingly presents its activities as addressing SDGs and mentions a range of objectives with a focus on enhancing poor people's assets to help them address issues of resilience to climate change, gender, natural resource management and microfinance as a way to move them out of poverty.

Official Development Assistance from Development Assistance Committee Member Countries

According to preliminary data, in 2018, net ODA flows from member countries of the DAC fell 2.7 percent from 2017, with a declining share going to the neediest countries. The drop was attributed largely to less aid spent on hosting refugees, as arrivals slowed and rules were tightened on which refugee costs could come from official aid budgets. ODA from the 30 members of OECD's DAC totaled US$153 billion in 2018 and US$161 billion in 2020, representing 0.31 and 0.32 percent of the DAC donors' combined GNI, respectively, as calculated using a "grant-equivalent" methodology, to obtain a more accurate count of the donor effort in development loans. We discuss the methodology later in this section (OECD 2019d, 2021).

The ODA was comprised of US$150.4 billion in the form of grants, official aid loans, or contributions to multilateral institutions; US$1.5 billion to development-oriented private sector instrument (PSI) vehicles, US$1.0 billion in the form of net loans and equities to private companies operating in ODA-eligible countries and US$0.2 billion of debt relief.

According to an OECD report:

In 2020, official development assistance (ODA) by member countries of the Development Assistance Committee (DAC) amounted to US$161.2 bn, representing 0.32% of their combined GNI...This total included US$158.0 bn in the form of grants, loans to sovereign entities, debt relief and contributions to multilateral institutions (calculated on a grant-equivalent basis); US$1.3 bn to development-oriented private sector instrument (PSI) vehicles and US$1.9 bn in the form of net loans and equities to private companies operating in ODA-eligible countries.

Total ODA in 2020 rose by 3.5% in real terms compared to 2019....

The United States continued to be the largest DAC donor of ODA (US$35 bn), followed by Germany (US$28.4 bn), the United Kingdom (US$18.6 bn), Japan (US$16.3 bn), and France (US$14.1 bn). The following countries met or exceeded the United Nations' ODA as a percentage of GNI target of 0.7%: Denmark (0.73%) Germany (0.73%), Luxembourg (1.02%), Norway (1.11%), Sweden (1.14%) and the United Kingdom (0.70%). (OECD 2021, 1, 2)

OECD countries provided $11.0 billion of COVID-19-related aid. Previously, the October 2019 news release from OECD had noted a similar pattern, although with slightly lower aid commitments:

The grant-equivalent ODA figure for 2018 is equivalent to 0.31% of the DAC donors' combined gross national income, well below the target ratio of 0.7 percent ODA to GNI. Five DAC members—Sweden [1.04%], Luxembourg [0.98%], Norway [0.94%], Denmark [0.72%], and the United Kingdom [0.7%]—met or exceeded the 0.7% target. Non-DAC donors Turkey and the United Arab Emirates, whose ODA is not counted in the DAC total, provided 1.10% and 0.95% respectively of their GNI in development aid. (OECD 2019d)[12]

On the grant-equivalent basis, G7 countries provided three-quarters of total ODA; and DAC–EU countries provided 56.5 percent of the total, representing 0.47 percent of their combined GNI (OECD 2019e).

The grant-equivalent methodology, which the DAC agreed upon 2014, was first adopted with the 2018 ODA release. The methodology provides a more realistic comparison between grants (83 percent of bilateral ODA in 2018), and loans (17 percent). ODA comprises over two-thirds of external finance for least-developed countries (LDCs). The DAC is pushing for ODA to be leveraged to generate more private investment and domestic tax revenue in poor countries to help them to achieve the UN SDGs (OECD 2019d).

As noted previously, "the 'grant equivalent' headline figures are not comparable with the historical series on a 'cash basis.' For the sake of transparency and analysis of trends over time, the OECD will continue to publish ODA data on a cash basis" (OECD 2019e, 2). The data in this chapter all refer to net ODA flows on a cash basis.

Using the "cash-flow basis" methodology, net ODA flows by DAC member countries of US$161 billion were higher in 2020 compared to US$149.3 billion in 2018, representing a fall of 2.7 percent in real terms, as compared to 2017. This drop reflected a reduction of in-donor refugee costs for many DAC members, but in 2020, the costs were US$8.98 billion. If these costs were excluded, net ODA levels amounted to US$152.19 billion in 2020, higher by less than US$3 billion, whereas they were stable in 2018, compared to 2017. The number of refugees entering Europe peaked in 2015–16 and has dropped since. In-donor refugee costs of US$10.6 billion were reported by DAC countries in 2018, a fall of 28.4 percent in real terms compared to 2017. These costs represented 5.6 percent in 2020, compared to 7.1 percent of total net ODA in 2018, 9.6 percent in 2017, and 11.0 percent in 2016, when in-donor refugee costs were highest. These costs represented more than 10 percent of the total ODA for seven of the DAC countries; for two countries, the costs were over 20 percent (OECD 2019e, 2021).

The OECD brief of April 10, 2021 stated:

Net ODA flows for bilateral projects, programmes and technical assistance, which represent just over half of total net ODA, rose by 8 percent in real terms in 2020 compared to 2019. Contributions to multilateral organisations, which represent about a third of total ODA, increased by 9%. Humanitarian aid amounted to US$18 bn and rose by 6% in real terms compared to 2019. Debt relief grants also rose to US$554 m.

In 2020, 22% of gross bilateral ODA by DAC members was provided in the form of non-grants (loans and equity investments), up from a level which hovered around 17% in previous years. The remaining bilateral ODA is provided in the form of grants.

---

[12] Bracketed percentages in the indented quote are found in OECD (2019e).

Preliminary data in 2020 show that net bilateral ODA flows from DAC members to Africa were US$39 bn, representing an increase of 4.1% in real terms compared to 2019....

By income group, net bilateral ODA flows from all DAC members to low-income countries were US$25 bn, *a decrease of* 3.5 percent in real terms compared to 2019. By contrast, net bilateral ODA to lower-middle income was US$33 bn representing an increase of 6.9% in real terms. Net ODA to upper-middle countries also increased by 36.1% to US$18 n. Net ODA flows to high-income countries more than tripled and stood at US$372 m. *These trends, along with the increase in the share of loans in ODA would imply that part of the increase in ODA in 2020 is due to loans to middle-income countries.*

Preliminary data showed that net bilateral aid flows from DAC members to the group of least developed countries were US$34 bn, and increased by 1.8% in real terms compared to 2019 (Emphasis added). (OECD 2021, 5)

As performance by bilateral donors, 2018 ODA outflows rose in 17 donor countries, with the largest increases recorded in Hungary, Iceland, and New Zealand. In contrast, ODA fell in 12 countries, with the largest drops in Austria, Finland, Greece, Italy, Japan, and Portugal. Most of these falls were due to lower in-donor refugee costs. Net ODA flows from DAC-EU countries were US$87.4 billion, representing a decrease of 1.2 percent in real terms, as compared to 2017. Excluding in-donor refugee costs, ODA flows increased by 3.9 percent in real terms (OECD 2019e).

Country programmable aid (CPA), also known as "core" aid, is the portion of an aid donor's program for individual countries, and over which partner countries could have a significant say. CPA is much closer than ODA to capturing the flows of aid that go to a partner country, and in several studies, has been proven to be a good proxy of aid recorded at the country level (OECD 2019i). DAC countries' total CPA was US$57 billion in 2014, a 4 percent decrease in real terms from 2013. This volume represents 53 percent of DAC countries' gross bilateral ODA. CPA as a share of total bilateral ODA has been fairly stable since 2004, apart from a temporary drop in 2005 and 2006 due to exceptional debt relief to Iraq and Nigeria (OECD 2019c).

Within the renewed global partnership, it is vital that the role of ODA is reexamined so that this unique resource can be used effectively within the post-2015 development agenda. There is need for both more and better ODA—for commitments to be met, including for ODA equivalent to 0.7 percent of DAC donors' GNI and the 0.15–0.20 percent of GNI as ODA to least developed countries' (LDCs) target and allocations improved for better development results.[13]

Donors Unlikely to Meet 0.7 Percent Aid Target

ODA levels have been a long-standing source of contention between developed and developing countries. While the debate continues in the context of SDGs and the financing of GPGs, including, especially, climate change (see CGD's 2016 report on multilateral development banks [Ahluwalia et al. 2016]), the debate on country-level assistance has become mute, particularly as the distinction between aid recipients and donors has blurred with

---

[13] UN definition of LDC: Per capita income < US$1,035; Human Asset Index (HAI) < 60 and Economic Vulnerability Index (EVI) < 36.

emerging countries such as China, Brazil, and India becoming aid donors. Nobel Prize-winning economist, Jan Tinbergen, as Chairman of the United Nations Committee on Development Planning in 1964, developed guidelines that suggested transfer of 0.75 percent of gross national product (GNP) of rich countries annually to developing countries to finance development, an idea championed by every major head of a commission concerned with global affairs.[14] However, in view of the unlikely changes in OECD ODA levels, increased allocation of ODA to agriculture is a zero-sum game—what goes to agriculture comes from other priorities. Therefore, the catalytic role of the current ODA to priorities for expenditures, as well for enhancing the quality of expenditures and influencing resource allocation in developing countries, is of critical importance. Like everything else, discussion of financing, in the context of these different categories, has tended to become mixed due to the interconnectedness of the issues. One's perception of ODA depends on whether it is viewed in nominal or real terms, absolute amounts or shares of OECD GNI of developing countries' GNI, or total investment or as shares of government expenditures—how it is allocated and whether it is used effectively.

Net ODA disbursement by DAC member countries, as a percentage of GNI in 2018, was 0.31 percent. This looks good when compared to the all-time low of 0.21 percent in 2001, before rising to 0.32 percent in 2005, and then settling down to 0.3 percent in the most recent period. However, ODA was 0.54 percent in 1961, and declined steadily to 0.21, reaching an all-time low share of GNI in 2001 before rising again (Figure 7.2).

A handful of OECD countries have consistently exceeded the 0.7 percent of GNI. Five of DAC's 29 member countries—Sweden, Luxembourg, Norway, Denmark, and the United Kingdom—met or exceeded the United Nations (UN) ODA target of 0.7 percent of GNI (OECD 2019d).

Yet, ODA has become highly fragmented. There are 29 bilateral donor members within the OECD's DAC, and a growing group of non-DAC donors consists of at least 28 states, with this aid channeled through over 210 major organizations and funds, with numerous smaller trust funds providing aid (OECD 2012).[15]

More Aid for the Least Developed Countries: 0.15 to 0.2 Percent of Gross National Income in Official Development Assistance

There are 47 LDCs (as of December 2018), home to over 1 billion people (13.2 percent of world's population), a quarter living in extreme poverty (38 percent of the world's poor).[16] More than 75 percent of the population in LDCs still live in poverty. LDCs account for less

---

[14] This was echoed by Lester Pearson, prime minister of Canada in 1968, in the Pearson Commission report (Pearson 1969), and was an idea that was actively promoted by Robert McNamara, president of the World Bank. Developing countries adopted the target in the meeting of the G77 in Algiers in 1967, and later, in the United Nations Conference on Trade and Development (UNCTAD) meeting in New Delhi in 1968, but with pushback from developed countries, they accepted the concessional ODA target level of 0.7 percent of GNP, adopted by the UN General Assembly in 1970. In 1980s, Willy Brandt, the German chancellor, reinforced the need for ODA at such a level, as did the Brundtland Report (WCED 1987).

[15] The EU is also a full member of the Committee, bringing the total membership to 30. Among nonmembers, 18 currently report their financial flows to the OECD, while 10 conduct their own statistical reporting, which is then used by the OECD to estimate development spending (see http://www.oecd.org/development/stats/non-dac-reporting.htm).

[16] Extreme poverty is defined here as the proportion of people living on less than US$1.90 per day. See the United Nations' Committee for Development Policy (CDP) List of Least Developed Countries: https://www.un.org/development/desa/dpad/wp-content/uploads/sites/45/publication/ldc_list.pdf

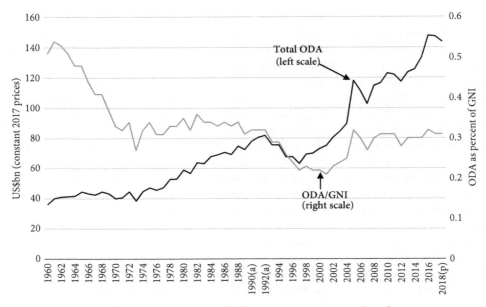

Figure 7.2 Overall aid trends: Net ODA (US$bn, constant 2017 prices) and as a percentage share of GNI, 1960–2018

Note: (a) Total ODA excludes debt forgiveness of non-ODA claims in 1990, 1991 and 1992; (p) Preliminary data.

Source: Based on OECD International Development Statistics (database) (OECD.Stat 2020a) http://stats.oecd.org/viewhtml.aspx?datasetcode=TABLE1&lang=en

than 2 percent of world's GDP and around 1 percent of world trade. LDCs are comprised of more than 31 countries in SSA, small island states, Haiti (the only such country in the Americas), fragile states such as Yemen and Afghanistan, and 6 other countries in Asia (including Nepal and Bangladesh). Since the LDC category was defined, only five countries have "graduated"—Botswana in 1994, Cape Verde in 2007, the Maldives in 2011, Samoa in 2014, and Equatorial Guinea in 2017 (UNCTAD 2019a).

Since the beginning of the 21st century, external finance to LDCs has increased significantly, from US$24 billion in 2000, to US$163 billion in 2017, largely due to the rising weight of remittances, FDI, and external debt. Following the global upward trend, remittances have surged to become the second largest source of external finance for LDCs, rising to a record high of US$42.4 billion in 2017, behind ODA at US$49 billion. FDI inflows to LDCs also recorded a sharp increase, from US$3.9 billion in 2000, to US$37.6 billion in 2015, then receding somewhat to US$20.7 billion and US$23.8 billion, respectively, in 2017 and 2018. Despite the recent decline, the amount of FDI inflows, although six times higher than in 2000, is now the third largest source of external finance for LDCs (UNCTAD 2019a).

Unlike for other developing countries, LDCs remain heavily reliant on ODA, "underscoring the challenges in attracting market-based external financial resources" (UNCTAD 2019a, 17). Concessional finance continues to represent the bulk of external development financial resources for LDCs—one-third of total external finance supplied by OECD economies in 2014–17, compared to merely 4.5 percent for other developing countries. In contrast:... the importance of FDI as a source of external finance was the reverse for these two groups of countries. While in LDCs it accounted for one fifth of the total, in other developing countries, it contributed almost half of total external finance. Interestingly, personal remittances had a broadly similar weight for both country groups: approximately one third of total external finance. (UNCTAD 2019a, 17)

"Among LDCs, the significance of ODA relative to other sources of foreign finance is even starker when assessed at an individual country level" (UNCTAD 2019a, 18). LDCs received approximately 22 percent of the total official support (UNCTAD 2019a, 32). In 2018, net ODA to LCDs increased from US$48.9 billion in 2017 to US$51.6 billion in 2018 (constant 2015 US dollars), showing a mildly upward trend, recorded since 2014. The share of total net ODA for LDCs decreased from 34 percent, at its peak in 2010, to a low of 32.2 percent in 2018 (Figure 7.3). Their share of global OOF has slightly risen but remains marginal by global standards, accounting for roughly 4.4 percent of gross disbursements to LDCs.

According to UNCTAD's "The Least Developed Countries Report 2019":

> ODA flows have continued to be distributed more evenly across individual LDCs than other official flows or other sources of external finance, such as FDI and remittances. This holds true, despite the fact that donors' aid allocation is not only affected by country needs, but also by additional factors ranging from geopolitical considerations to historical and cultural links, especially in the case of bilateral flows (Alesina and Dollar 2000; Anderson 2008; Bermeo 2017). (UNCTAD 2019a, 32)

At the third International Conference on Financing for Development held in Addis Ababa in 2015, and the Development and Programme of Action for the Least Developed Countries for the Decade, 2011–2020 (Istanbul Programme of Action), the donor

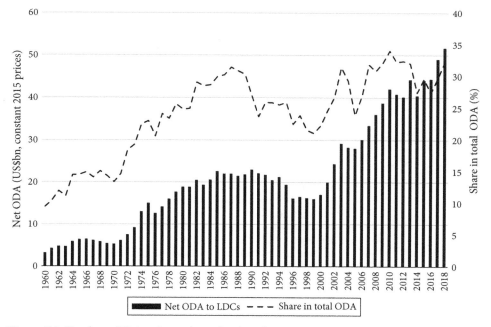

Figure 7.3 Total net ODA going to least developed countries, 1960–2018 (US$bn, constant 2015 prices)

Source: Based on World Bank's World Development Indicators (World Bank 2020b).

community reaffirmed the UN target, set in 1990, of providing between 0.15 percent and 0.2 percent of their GNI of ODA to LCDs (in parallel to a commitment to provide the equivalent of 0.7 percent of GNI in ODA to developing countries) (WFP 2011; UN 2015). In 2017, only seven of the 29 DAC member countries fulfilled this commitment: . . . namely, Denmark, Luxembourg, Norway, Sweden, Switzerland, and the United Kingdom—have met the Sustainable Development Goal 17.2 target related to LDCs. (With the exception of Switzerland, these very countries are also the ones that provided aid equivalent to at least 0.7 percent of their GNI to all developing countries.) Others, including some of the world's largest donors, remain far from the internationally agreed targets. (UNCTAD 2019a, 35)

In total, DAC countries provided 0.09 percent of their GNI as ODA to least developed countries in 2017, down from 0.10 percent in 2013 (OECD.Stat 2020a). To meet the SDG target 17.2, there is need for an additional US$33–58 billion assistance (UNCTAD 2019a).[17]

Some multilaterals tend to spend too little aid in the poorest countries. For example, the EU spends only 27 percent of its aid in LICs (the biggest recipients of EU aid are Turkey, Serbia, Morocco, Tunisia, and Ukraine). The World Bank/IDA, by contrast, does well on this measure, spending 55 percent of its ODA in LICs. The UK's bilateral aid program is somewhere in between, with 38 percent spent in LICs (Barder and Juden 2016).

As a share of GNI, ODA has been declining steadily in all regions except SSA, where it reached a peak in 1994, mainly because of the Heavily Indebted Poor Country (HIPC) settlement and has declined since 2003 (Figure 7.4).

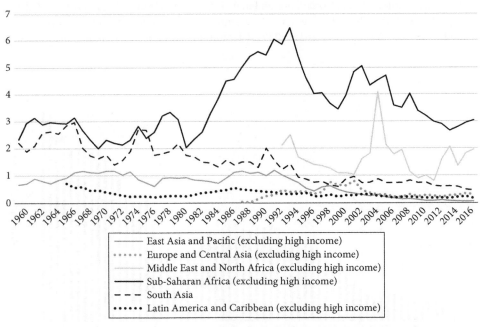

Figure 7.4 Declining ODA share as percentage of GNI by region, 1960–2018
Source: Based on World Bank's World Development Indicators (World Bank 2020b).

---

[17] The SDG target 17.2 specifies: "Developed countries to implement fully their official development assistance commitments, including the commitment by many developed countries to achieve the target of 0.7 percent of ODA/GNI to developing countries and 0.15 to 0.20 percent of ODA/GNI to least developed countries; ODA providers are encouraged to consider setting a target to provide at least 0.20 percent of ODA/GNI to least developed countries." See https://sustainabledevelopment.un.org/sdg17

Untying Aid

Untied aid is defined by the DAC as loans and grants whose proceeds are fully and freely available to finance procurement from all OECD countries and substantially all developing countries. All other loans and grants are classified either as tied aid (procurement open only to suppliers in the provider country) or as partially untied aid (procurement open to a restricted number of countries, which must include substantially all developing countries and can include the provider country). These definitions apply whether aid is tied formally or through informal arrangements.

Aid has traditionally been tied by source of procurement or source of delivery. Tied aid is inefficient. The most long-standing case is that of food aid. Studies show that, in most circumstances, financial aid rather than food aid in-kind is the preferable option, not only for providing project assistance or budgetary support for general development, but also for the distribution of food. Context-specific rationale, however, is always required for relying on food aid in-kind, in preference to financial aid. Furthermore, for the donor, food aid is often relatively expensive if the aid is tied. The costs to the donor of providing tied food aid, instead of financing commercial imports, tends to be at least 30 percent. The actual cost of tied direct food aid transfers was, on average, approximately 50 percent more than local food purchases, and 33 percent costlier than procurement of food in developing countries. For the recipients, too, food aid can be a disincentive to domestic production and a real loss of opportunity to develop local production and agro-processing, compared to financial aid (Barrett and Maxwell 2005; OECD 2006; Lentz and Barrett 2013). Thus, there is scope for considerable efficiency gains in switching to less restricted sourcing, and this has been shown again and again the case of development aid—hence, the push for untying.

The DAC has focused on the issue of the tying status of aid since its inception in 1961. The purpose of reporting tying status items is to show how much of members' aid is open for procurement through international competition. Internationally competitive procurement promotes cost-effective sourcing of aid inputs, promotes free and open trade, and facilitates the implementation of commitments under the Paris Declaration on Aid Effectiveness in areas such as coordination and alignment (OECD 2008b). DAC, reporting on tying status, does not include multilateral ODA (core contributions to multilateral agencies), as this is treated as untied by convention. In this field, as in others, the DAC has for many years given special consideration to the needs of least developed countries. In 2001, the DAC agreed to the Recommendation on Untying ODA to the Least Developed Countries. In 2008, it expanded this Recommendation to include those HIPCs that were not included as least developed countries (OECD 2020a).

The Paris Declaration committed OECD–DAC providers "to continue making progress to untie aid as encouraged by the 2001 DAC Recommendation on Untying ODA to the Least Developed Countries" (OECD 2016, 156; 2019j), while the Accra Agenda for Action encouraged cooperation providers to "elaborate plans to further untie aid to the maximum extent" (OECD 2016, 156; 2019k). The Busan Partnership agreement urges providers to "accelerate efforts to untie aid" and to "improve the quality, consistency and transparency of reporting on the tying status of aid" (OECD 2016, 156; 2019g).

OECD summarized the progress in untying aid:

DAC Members have made considerable progress in untying aid. From 1999–2001 to 2018, the proportion of ODA covered by the Recommendation that was untied rose progressively from 47% to 88%.

The adherence to transparency provisions, aimed at providing transparency that de jure untied aid is also de facto untied, has also significantly improved. The percentage of Members who reported on ex post contract awards has increased from 55% in 2013 to 80% in 2016 which is the highest level recorded historically. (OECD 2020b)

Bilateral Official Development Assistance Allocations to and through Civil Society Organizations

Civil society organizations (CSOs) are playing a major role in the framework of sustainable development: namely, for improving economic, social, and political conditions in developing countries. In 2017, DAC countries channeled about US$20 billion (disbursements, constant 2016 prices) in ODA to and through CSOs (Figure 7.5). This accounted for a little over 17 percent of total bilateral aid. While the share of bilateral aid allocated to and through CSOs differs widely among DAC members, the average share of total bilateral aid for all DAC countries over the last three years has been 16.7 percent (OECD 2019a).

• The total number of INGOs operating in the sector is too numerous to count. Only data for US-based organizations are available in a cross-comparable manner.

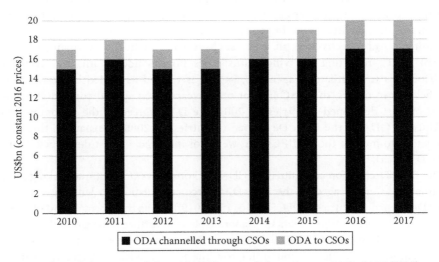

Figure 7.5 Bilateral ODA to and through CSO gross disbursements, 2010–2017 (US$bn, constant 2016 prices)

Note: CSOs: civil society organizations; ODA: official development assistance.

Source: Based on data from OECD (2019a).

- Most INGOs rely on traditional donors for a large share of their in-country expenditures. Barrett and Maxwell (2005) noted that INGOs are hardly a progressive force in the delivery of food aid, since many depend on the delivery of food aid as a source of revenue. Budgetary dependence on food aid tempers their willingness to publicly challenge a system that many privately acknowledge underperforms its potential.
- Limited, shared characteristics exist across this clustering of organizations but LICs, except for the Philippines, India, and Nicaragua, are popular destinations for work.
- Eighty-two organizations in the United States were operating 2,373 projects during 2007–14.

Official Development Assistance to and through the Multilateral Aid System: The Rise of Multi-Bi Aid

A growing number of aid recipients compete for this fragmented aid, including nation states, UN agencies, multilateral organizations, INGOs, and think tanks wishing to use those same limited resources to advance their agendas.[18]

Total use of the multilateral aid system means all funds channeled to and through multilateral organizations, or the sum of "core" and "non-core" resources. It, therefore, encompasses multilateral ODA/core contributions (that is, official contributions to multilateral agencies, whether negotiated, assessed, or voluntary, for which the governing boards have the unqualified right to allocate as they see fit within organizations' charters) and non-core/earmarked/multi-bi contributions, discussed previously (see Note #3) (OECD 2015).

The trend to provide voluntary funding to complement "core" budgets originated with the creation of several of the large UN development funds and programs in the 1960s, allowing donors to assert influence "through the backdoor" (Reinsberg, Michaelowa, and Eichenauer 2015). Non-core/earmarked/multi-bi, by contrast, began in the early 1990s, and has grown over time, in response to several developments in the external environment, leading to the fragmentation of aid, with allocation of resources largely in response to the priorities of aid donors. It is a result of a combination of the emergence of civil society in donor countries as a significant force, combined with the decline of bilateral aid-giving agencies. Parking funds with multilateral agencies allowed stakeholders in developed countries to exercise an influential voice in aid priorities through the multiplicity of donor-funded programs outside multilateral aid agencies; to have a seat at the table of trust-funded programs; and gain access—while also creating new challenges for global governance, including diminished transparency and accountability—than international agencies have provided. Most of these funds have gone to the health and environmental sectors, but in agriculture, CGIAR is also a large recipient of donor trust funds.

Contributions to multilateral organizations by DAC countries represented about one-third of total ODA in 2020. an increase of 9 percent. This compared, on average, for 2015 and 2016, of 39.3 percent of their *ODA to and through the multilateral aid system* (core + multi-bi/non-core/earmarked), a slight increase from the 2009–10 average of 36.8 percent, from only 24.6 percent in 2004–5 (OECD 2021).

---

[18] Core resources are unearmarked contributions to multilateral organizations, known as multilateral ODA (OECD 2012). Non-core resources are contributions to multilateral organizations that are earmarked for specific purposes, sectors, regions or countries, which include contributions to trust funds and joint programming, also referred to as "multi-bi" aid (OECD 2012).

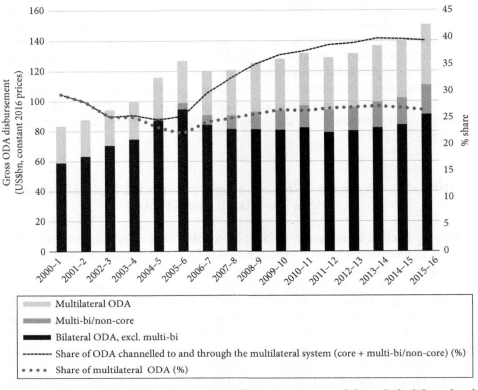

Figure 7.6 The rise of multi-bi aid: Gross ODA disbursements to and through the bilateral and multilateral aid system, 2000–1 to 2015–16 (US$bn, constant 2016 prices)

Note: Data collection on multi-bi/non-core funding started in 2004.

Source: Based on OECD/DAC Creditor Reporting System (CRS) data and OECD (2018a).

This increase was mainly due to larger ODA shares tied to projects for specific regions, countries, themes, or sectors (multi-bi/non-core/earmarked). OECD data suggest multi-bi assistance rose from 10.3 percent in 2009–10 to 12.9 percent in 2015–16, and from only 1.5 percent of total DAC ODA in 2004–5. Share of multi-bi assistance in total multilateral (core + multi-bi/non-core/earmarked) spending rose from 27.9 percent in 2009–10 to 32.9 percent in 2015–16, and from only 5.6 percent in 2004–5. The share of core contributions in gross ODA disbursements increased only marginally, from 26.5 percent in 2009–10 to 26.4 percent in 2015–16 (peaking in 2013–14 at 27.2 percent and then showing a downward trend), down from a high of 29.4 percent in 2000–1 (OECD 2019a) (Figure 7.6). Nevertheless, a new data set suggests that these figures may be gross underestimates, with multi-bi aid standing at over 20 percent of total ODA and almost 60 percent of total multilateral contributions (Reinsberg, Michaelowa, and Eichenauer 2015).

Investment Flow Methodology in the Agriculture Sector

Investing in agriculture is essential for reducing hunger and promoting sustainable agricultural production. Those parts of the world where agricultural capital per worker and public investments in agriculture have stagnated are the epicenters of poverty and hunger, as FAO rightly noted in 2012 (FAO 2012). There are five indicators typically mentioned in the literature for measuring investment in agriculture and assessing attention to or priority to agriculture using OECD/DAC Creditor Reporting System (CRS) database, the International Food Policy Research Institute's Statistics of Public Expenditure for Economic Development (IFPRI's SPEED database), and FAO's Government Expenditure on Agriculture (GEA) database:

1. ODA to Agriculture as a Share of Total ODA;
2. Per capita government expenditure in agriculture;
3. Government agricultural expenditure as a share of agricultural value-added;
4. Government agricultural expenditure as a share of total government expenditure; and
5. Agriculture Orientation Index (AOI), as the share of government expenditure to agriculture in total government expenditure divided by the share of agricultural value-added in total GDP.

Most of the analysis focuses on the public financing in agriculture—that is, either domestic official financing or international official financing—not on private financing, which has significant and increasingly more important role in agricultural financing. The multisectoral nature of agriculture means that financing for agriculture must be viewed in the broad context, consisting of multiple components for each of the following dimensions of financing: public and private and their domestic and foreign flows. Financing in agriculture is captured in the following framework (Figure 7.7), along with the associated indicators for measurement with their data sources; it is based on the "FAOSTAT's Agricultural Investment Data Framework," the most complete framework (see FAO–OEA/CIE–IICA Working Group [2013]). It uses all the financing sources to agriculture, but it's one main limitation is the absence of data on the largest components of private investment financing: private equity or savings of agricultural producers; foreign remittances received; and informal borrowing, which includes borrowing from family, friends, local moneylenders, landowners, and input suppliers. Such information is likely best collected through agricultural surveys, and may require significant financial investments (marked in italics in the framework; see Figure 7.7).

Findings from Different Indicators

We next show the performances of the different economies/regions based on the different measurements: that is, indicators on investment in agriculture.

Gross Fixed Capital Formation in Agriculture, 1991–2014

Over the period 2005–14, global annual physical investment flows in agriculture—as measured by gross fixed capital formation (GFCF) in agriculture—rose by almost 50 percent from US$259 to US$378 billion in constant 2005 US dollars (FAO 2020b). LICs and MICs, as a group, invest almost as much in agriculture, in absolute terms, as high-income countries—around US$190 billion in both country groups.

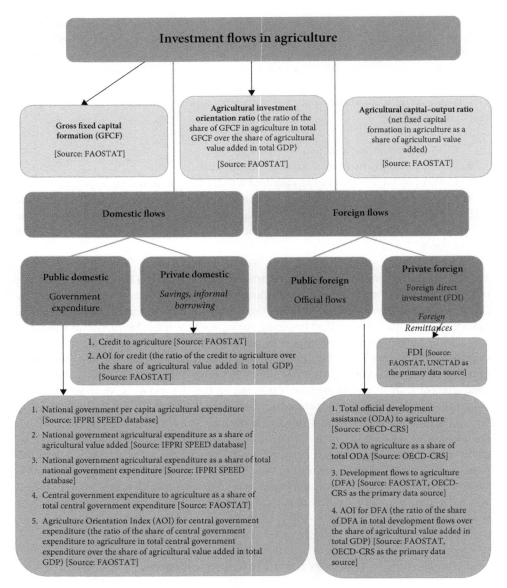

Figure 7.7 Agricultural investment framework

Source: Authors' construction. Based FAOSTAT's Agricultural Investment Data Framework, FAO–OEA/CIE–IICA Working Group (2013).

According to FAO's 2017 publication, "The Future of Food and Agriculture. Trends and Challenges":

In the period 1991–2014, agricultural investment levels increased in all country groupings, although at different rates. In high-income countries, investment increased from around US$120 billion to US$190 billion. . . . In China, it grew from less than US$10 billion to US$75 billion, . . . while investment in agriculture in the remaining low- and middle-income countries grew from US$45 billion to US$115 billion. (FAO 2017, 23)

Among the low- and middle-income regions, SA's growth has been highest, followed by East Asia and the Pacific (EAP) (excluding China). GFCF in the Middle East and North Africa (MENA) is lowest, behind SSA and Latin America and Caribbean (LAC) (FAO 2017). Over the period 2005–14, annual flows of physical investment in the agriculture sector doubled in Asia and Pacific region; it remained stagnant in Europe and in the other developed regions, but increased by around 62 percent in North America. For the remaining regions, agricultural physical investment flows increased by around 54 percent in LAC and 34 percent in Africa. These diverging regional trends in investment directly translated into the agricultural capital stock, because the investment flows add up to build capital stocks after adjustment for depreciation (FAO 2020b).

Significantly, similar interregional diverging patterns on investment in physical capital are present when the overall economy is considered (all sectors together). GFCF was a key driver of GDP growth, as it rose from US\$3.6 trillion (2005 US\$) to US\$13.8 trillion between 1970 and 2014. The investment ratio—GFCF as a proportion of GDP—remained relatively stable at around 22 percent throughout the period globally. At the regional level, the investment ratios for Africa (from 0.25 in 1970–9 to 0.22 in 2010–14); Europe (from 0.25 in 1970–9 to 0.20 in 2010–14); and LAC (from 0.24 in 1970–9 to 0.22 in 2010–14) present downward trends, while Asia and Pacific and North America, to the contrary, saw investment ratios increasing from 0.2 in 1970s to 0.35 in 2010–14, and 0.18 in the 1970s to 0.20 in 2010–14, respectively (FAO 2020b).

Agricultural Investment Orientation Ratio, 1991–2014

The agricultural investment orientation ratio is the ratio of the share of GFCF in agriculture in total GFCF over the share of agricultural value-added in total GDP. It provides a measure of how the investment intensity in agriculture compares to that of the total economy. From this definition, it appears that countries with a higher investment intensity in agriculture, compared to overall economy, will have a value greater than 1, indicating that on average a larger share of each unit of value-added is spent on GFCF in agriculture, as compared to the other sectors of the economy (FAO 2020b).

According to FAO:

> In the last two decades, high-income countries have always devoted a larger share of investment to agriculture than the share of the sector in GDP. This is reflected in the fact that the "agricultural investment orientation ratio" has remained consistently above 1. In low- and middle-income countries, in contrast, this ratio is much lower, at around 0.4.... While the investment orientation ratio is increasing in East Asia and the Pacific (including China), South Asia, Europe and Central Asia, it is decreasing in the Middle East, North Africa, sub-Saharan Africa and, to some extent, Latin America and the Caribbean. (FAO 2017, 24–5)

Agricultural Capital–Output Ratio, 1991–2014

The agricultural capital–output ratio is the net fixed capital formation in agriculture as a share of agricultural value-added. The FAO notes:

Degrees of capital intensity in agriculture sectors also vary.... [A]griculture in high-income countries is significantly more capital intensive than in low- and middle income countries—it requires 4 units of capital to generate one unit of value added, compared to around 1.5 in low- and middle-income countries. However, in East Asia and the Pacific (including China), South Asia, Europe and Central Asia, [where surface irrigation has been the primary source of water, capital intensity has been high, compared to when groundwater is used, and whereas China's area under irrigation is about the same as India's, China's irrigation is substantially more capital intensive, as described in the forthcoming paper on water scarcities in China and India (Lele 2021)]. Overall, the capital-intensity of agricultural production is increasing [in Asia]...in the Middle East and North Africa, sub-Saharan Africa, and Latin America and the Caribbean, capital-intensity has fallen. (FAO 2017, 25)

Notably, the Green Revolution was capital intensive if one took account of the need for fertilizer and water. Surface irrigation is quite capital intensive—groundwater is not so capital intensive.

Public Domestic Financing to the Agriculture Sector

Next, we discuss the public domestic financing to the agriculture sector based on the different measurements.

National Government per capita Agricultural Expenditure and National Government Agricultural Expenditure as a Share of Agricultural Value-Added, 1995–2016

Trends differ in different parts of the world and between developing and developed countries. For developed countries, despite their large volume of investments, agriculture represents only a marginal portion of the economy. Per capita agricultural expenditure (2011 PPP dollars) for high-income European countries and other high-income countries (US$83.5 to US$69.5) declined from 1995 to 2016 (US$199.7 to US$94.2 in high-income European countries and US$83.5 to US$69.5 in other high-income countries). The ratio of agricultural expenditure to agricultural GDP also declined in both countries, 25.9 percent to 17.9 percent in high-income European countries and 18 percent to 12.1 percent in other high-income countries from 1995 to 2016, respectively (IFPRI 2019). In developing countries, on the other hand, although agriculture accounts for a larger share of the economy, per capita agricultural expenditure is considerably lower. In addition, per capita agricultural expenditure in developing countries remained flat until the early 1990s, and showed a recovery after that (IFPRI 2017).

Comparing performance across the world's developing regions, per capita agricultural public spending has increased most rapidly in EAP, especially following the 2008/09 food crisis (US$38.8 in 1995 to US$66.6 in 2005 to US$ 318.2 in 2016), largely driven by rapid growth in agricultural spending in China since 2005 (IFPRI 2018, 2019). EAP increased spending relative to the size of their agricultural economies (6.4 percent in 1995 to 9.2 percent in 2005 to 26 percent in 2016). MENA as well as Europe and Central Asia (ECA) regions have spent large amounts on agriculture and showed increasing trend both per capita (US$73.6 to US$212.6 in MENA and US$26.2 to US$105 in ECA from 1995 to 2016) and as a share of agricultural GDP (5.9 percent to 16.7 percent in MENA and 2.9 percent to 10.7 percent in ECA from 1995 to 2016). SA and SSA lag behind in terms of both per capita agricultural expenditure and ratio of agricultural expenditure to agricultural GDP, while LAC showed a declining trend. Among developing regions, agricultural public spending per capita and as a share of agricultural GDP in 2016 was lowest in SSA followed by SA. In SSA, agricultural public spending per capita and as a share of agricultural GDP increased very little, from US$16.3 to US$25.9, and from 3.2 percent to 3.9 percent from 1995 to 2016. Performance was slightly better in SA than SSA: agricultural public spending per capita and as a share of agricultural GDP increased from US$15 to US$48, and from 2.9 percent to 5.2 percent from 1995 to 2016. In LAC, agricultural public spending per capita and as a share of agricultural GDP, decreased from US$69.6 to US$52.5, and from 10.2 percent to 6.8 percent from 1995 to 2016 (IFPRI 2019).

The 2017 *Global Food Policy* report noted that:

> By two measures, developing regions spend less than developed regions on agriculture. Both per capita spending and the ratio of public expenditure to agricultural GDP are lower across all developing regions. But the gap has shrunk over time.... Structural adjustment programs implemented in the 1980s and 1990s in developing countries curtailed government spending on agriculture, but since the early 2000s, many developing country governments have increased allocations to the sector.

> Several regions showed a strong recovery in the most recent period (1995–2014), while others experienced further declines in spending. This disparity reflects differences in levels of resources, economic performance, demographic shifts, and development priorities. For example, South Asia and Africa south of the Sahara, which have the lowest level of resources and overall economic performance in terms of GDP per capita, have lagged behind other developing regions in both per capita spending and the ratio of public expenditure to agricultural GDP. (IFPRI 2017)

National Government Agricultural Expenditure as a Share of Total National Government Expenditure, 1995–2016

The SPEED database on public expenditures indicates that expenditures in productive sectors, such as infrastructure and agriculture, lagged behind social sectors in most regions. On average, developing countries channeled more funds to education and defense; defense spending has been high in the Middle East, SA, and Africa. It is unclear if it is directed toward containing terrorism and conflict or simply for buying weapons from arms-exporting countries, and therefore, is a diversion from development expenditures, of which social protection dominates public resources in developed countries. The growth of social protection spending in developed countries is much more pronounced than developing countries. ECA and Latin America and LAC were the top two developing regions followed by MENA in social protection expenditure share. The share was the lowest in EAP, SSA, and SA, among the six sectors. Education attracted the largest share in EAP, LAC, and SSA and was in second position after defense in MENA and SA. On average, except for ECA, developing regions spent 10–17 percent of their total expenditures on education, with EAP at the top and SA at the bottom. The share of health sector spending was highest in LAC followed by EAP, SSA, MENA, ECA, and SA (IFPRI 2015b).

Globally, agriculture and infrastructure (transportation and communication) received the least amount of attention among the six sectors, with social protection at the top, followed by education, defense, and health. Public resources allocated to agriculture have increased alongside total spending, but agricultural spending has not kept pace with the total increases in budgets (IFPRI 2015b).

The share of agriculture in total public spending performed the worst and declined over time in all regions for the period from 1980. Since 1995, as the share of total spending, agricultural spending showed the largest drop in LAC (dropping from 4.1 percent in 1995 to 1.6 percent in 2016), followed by SSA (dropping from 2.7 percent in 1995 to 2.2 percent in 2016) (IFPRI 2018). Agricultural spending in EAP appears to be rising with overall public spending, though not as fast as aggregate spending. In EAP the ratio increased from 8.1 percent in 1995 to 9.3 percent in 2016; in SA the ratio increased from 4.4 percent to 5.4 percent; in ECA the ratio increased from 0.5 percent to 1.4 percent, and in MENA, from 2.4 percent to 2.7 percent. In developed countries, the ratio was decreasing, in high-income European countries, it dropped from 1.4 percent in 1995 to 0.5 percent in 2016, and in other high-income countries, from 1.3 percent to 0.6 percent, respectively (IFPRI 2019).

In SA and SSA, infrastructure and agriculture ranked third and fourth, above health and social protection, below education and defense expenditures. In 2014, agricultural spending, as a share of overall public spending, Africa, as a whole, has underperformed. Notably, the heads of state and government in Africa adopted the Comprehensive Africa Agriculture Development Programme (CAADP) in 2003 and committed to spend at least 10 percent of their national budgets on agriculture. Almost all African countries fell short of the 10 percent target of public spending, with the region reaching an average of 2.9 percent per year between 2003 and 2014. The average share was higher (3.3 percent) prior to the 2009 global financial crisis. Only Burkina Faso, Malawi, Mozambique, and Zimbabwe had barely met or surpassed the 10 percent target (Malawi and Mozambique consistently surpassed it). Three countries—Niger, Rwanda, and Zambia were close behind at 9 percent (Goyal and Nash 2017).

Central Government Expenditure to Agriculture as a Share of Total Central Government Expenditure, 2001–2017

FAO's GEA Statistics website noted:

> From 2001 onwards, governments allocated less than 2% of their central government expenditure to agriculture. The agriculture share of total expenditure fluctuated around 1.6%, with a peak of 1.85% in 2008 during the food price crisis, remaining, on average, under almost one-third of the sector's contribution to GDP, which increased in the same period [2001–17] from 4.13% to 6.15%.

> The public underinvestment in agriculture, and the sector's importance to economic growth and poverty alleviation, particularly in Africa, was acknowledged in the African Union's Maputo Declaration of 2003, under which signatory nations committed to allocate 10% of government expenditures to agriculture and rural development. Though several countries were unable to attain this goal, the importance of public expenditures in agriculture was recognized in the Malabo Declaration of 2014, in which signatory nations re-committed to the 10% goal. Increasing investments in agriculture is also crucial at attainment of Goal 2 of the 2030 Agenda for Sustainable Development, which is monitored through Agriculture Orientation Index (AOI) for Government Expenditures. . . .

> Asia & the Pacific has been the region providing the highest percentage of central government spending to agriculture between 2001 (3.85%) and 2017 (3.03%), followed by Africa, where the share has progressively declined from 3.66% (2001) to 2.30% (2017). The developed regions (Europe and other developed, which refers to Australia, Canada, New Zealand and United States) allocated the lowest share of central government expenditure to agriculture, both series fluctuating around 1%.

In 2008, during the food price crisis, all the regions (except Europe) experienced an increase in the agriculture share of central government expenditure. In particular, Asia & the Pacific and Latin America & the Caribbean registered the highest value of their whole series (respectively, 4.38% and 2.51%). (FAO 2019)

Asian and African countries lead GEA share of government expenditures. Overall, Asia and the Pacific (A&P) and Africa had the highest GEA share of central government spending, and included 9 of the top 10 countries between 2012 to 2016—Malawi (16.4 percent), Bhutan (13.0 percent), Uzbekistan (11.9 percent), Ethiopia (9.0 percent), Bangladesh (8.7 percent), Nepal (8.7 percent), Zambia (7.6 percent), Belarus (7.1 percent), Thailand (7.0 percent) and Togo (6.3 percent) (FAO 2019).

Agriculture Orientation Index for Government Expenditure, 2001–2017
The FAO GEA database website notes further:

> SDG Indicator 2.a.1—Agriculture Orientation Index (AOI) for Government Expenditures, compares the central government contribution to agriculture with the sector's contribution to GDP [that is, a ratio of the agriculture share of central government spending to agriculture's contribution to GDP]. An AOI less than 1 indicates a lower orientation of the central government towards the agriculture sector relative to the sector's contribution to the economy, while an AOI greater than 1 indicates a higher orientation of the central government towards the agriculture sector relative to the sector's contribution to the economy.

> At global level, the AOI consistently declined from 0.42 (2001) to 0.26 (2017). During this period, most of the regions remained stably under 0.5, in particular, sub-Saharan Africa and Oceania (excluding Australia and New Zealand) registered the lowest values, with time series never exceeding 0.35. The regions that experienced the highest values are Eastern & South-eastern Asia, Northern America & Europe, and Western Asia & Northern Africa. Even though, in the most recent years, the trends in these regions decreased, and their values are more in line with the other regions. (FAO 2019)

Private Domestic Financing to the Agriculture Sector

We next discuss the private domestic financing to the agriculture sector based on the different measurements.

Credit to Agriculture, 1991–2017
In its notes to readers, FAO's Credit to Agriculture database describes this data set as:

> Credit to Agriculture measures loans to agriculture producers provided by commercial bank credit. This dataset is built by compiling official country data published on-line by national central banks in their monetary and financial statistics publications, either through annual or quarterly reports. As a new series, the data begins from 1991 to 2017, inclusive. (FAO 2020c)

Globally, the total credit to agriculture disbursed by commercial banks operating in the countries, increased from 2.4 percent in 2016 to 2.9 percent in 2017, while the agriculture sector contributed over 4 percent of GDP. This means that agricultural producers received a lower share of credit than producers in other sectors. Access to credit enables farmers to purchase inputs, such as feed, seed, and machinery without using personal savings, borrowing from relatives or friends, or paying high interest loans from informal lenders. The lack of access to reasonable credit presents a particular problem for farmers who face a time lag between income spent in sowing crops and raising livestock, and realizing income from postharvest and livestock sales. During the last decade, the share of agriculture in total credit supply has slightly increased from 2.2 percent in 2006 to 2.9 percent in 2017.

During the 1990s, Latin America provided the highest percentage of credit to agriculture among the regions, but it declined from over 10 percent in 1991 to little over 4 percent during 2011 and little over 2 percent in 2017. This sharp decline was also visible in Asia (nearly 8 percent in 1991 to nearly 5 percent in 2017) and Africa (nearly 9 percent in 1991 to above 4 percent in 2017) during this period.

FAO's Credit to Agriculture database website noted:

Traditionally, the share of credit supply to agriculture has been relatively low, 3–4% of total credit, in European and other developed countries. Since these countries account for bulk of the global credit flows, the global percentage of credit to agriculture is quite low despite higher shares of agriculture in Latin America, Asia and Africa.

From 2003 onwards, the agriculture sector in most regions received between 2 to 4% of total credit. Following the food price crisis of 2007–08 and the increased policy attention to food security and agriculture, most regions witnessed a slow revival of credit to agriculture, with higher growths observed in Asia and the Pacific and Africa regions. (FAO 2020c)

In the most recent five-year period, 2013–17, the top 10 countries in terms of highest share of agriculture in total credit included three Asian, three African, three Latin American and one Oceania country: of total credit, the countries were Malawi (21 percent); Kyrgyzstan (19 percent), Zambia (18 percent), Sudan (16 percent), Uruguay (15 percent), New Zealand (15 percent), Nicaragua (13 percent), India (13 percent), Tajikistan (12 percent), and Belize (12 percent) (FAO 2020c).

Agriculture Orientation Index for Credit, 2012–2016

The AOI is the ratio of the credit to agriculture (C2A share) over the share of agricultural value-added in total GDP. As the Credit for Agriculture database website notes:

The Agriculture Orientation Index (AOI) for credit normalizes the share of credit to agriculture (C2A share) by taking into account the economic contribution of the sector (ratio of the C2A share over the Agriculture share in GDP). As such, it can provide a more accurate measure of the relative importance commercial banks place on financing this sector. An AOI less than 1 indicates that the agriculture sector receives a credit share less than its economic contribution, while an AOI greater than 1 indicates a credit share to the agriculture sector greater than its economic contribution. (FAO 2020c)

The AOI for Credit of developed countries is generally higher than that of developing countries, perhaps due to large organized farming in developed countries compared to the preponderance of smallholder farms in developing countries.

The Credit for Agriculture database reported in 2018:

> In general, developed countries tend to have a higher AOI than developing countries. This may be due to the fact that agriculture is dominated by large producers; more commercial production; existence of agribusinesses; higher degrees of mechanization and greater capacity to provide collateral....
>
> Among developing countries, the AOI was particularly low for many sub-Saharan African countries, starting with Togo (0.01%), Niger (0.02%) and Guinea-Bissau (0.02%). This may be explained by a larger prevalence of small agricultural producers with little or no capacity to provide collateral to access loans from formal financial sector. (FAO 2020c)

Public Foreign Financial Flows to the Agriculture Sector

Next, we discuss the public foreign financing to the agriculture sector based on the different measurements.

Overall Development Flows to Agriculture, 2001–2017

In 2017, US$18 billion was committed globally as development flows to agriculture (DFA), accounting for 5.3 percent of total development flows.[19] Donors disbursed US$11 billion to agriculture, in the same period, 4.4 percent of the total disbursed flows. While commitments to agriculture increased by US$4 billion from 2016, disbursements to agriculture only increased by US$0.6 billion. "The share of commitments and disbursements to agriculture increased from in 2016 by 4.8 percent to 5.3 percent and from 4.2 percent to 4.4 percent, respectively" (FAO 2020d).

While total development assistance increased over time, the share to agriculture fell, with a slight rise following the food price crisis of 2007–8. "Between 2002 and 2017, donors disbursed to Africa and the Asia & Pacific together more than 70 percent of the total DFA. Asia and Pacific received relatively more than Africa until 2010, but Africa saw a continuous increase of its portion, which reached 42 percent of total DFA in 2017," while Asia & the Pacific received 37 percent (FAO 2020d). For 2002–17, IDA, the United States and the EU, IBRD, Japan, and Germany were among the most important donors. BMGF ranked 8th in 2015 and 10th in 2017 among donors (Table 7.1).

Agriculture Orientation Index for Development Flows to Agriculture, 2001–2017

The AOI for DFA measures the share of flows to agriculture relative to the sector's contribution to the GDP. An AOI greater than 1 indicates a donor preference for the agriculture sector, keeping in view the contribution of various sectors of economy, while an AOI less than 1 indicates less emphasis on agriculture.

Global development assistance has been less oriented to agriculture over time. According to the FAO's DFA database website:

> Globally, between 2002 and 2017, the share of development flows received by agriculture was lower compared to the contribution of the sector to GDP....

---

[19] The DFA data published in FAOSTAT are composed of ODA flows, OOFs, and Private Grant/Flows reported by donor countries, multinational organizations, and private entities to the OECD DAC Directorate.

Table 7.1 Development flows to the Agriculture, Forestry and Fishing sector by top 10 donors and recipients*

Rank	Top 10 donors (2017)	Top 10 recipients (2017)
1	IDA	Indonesia
2	United States	India
3	EU institutions	China, mainland
4	IBRD	Morocco
5	Japan	Pakistan
6	Germany	Ethiopia
7	United Kingdom	Malawi
8	Asian Development Bank	Kenya
9	France	Uzbekistan
10	Bill & Melinda Gates Foundation	Vietnam

Note: *Development assistance provided by a multilateral agency includes only those expenditures from its core budget, while country contributions exclude contributions to core budgets of multilateral agencies. This is done to avoid double counting of total expenditure flows.
Source: FAO (2020d).

Only few countries reported an average 2013–17 AOI larger than 1, indicating that in most cases the share of assistance devoted to agriculture is smaller than the contribution of the sector to GDP.... There are seventeen countries showing an average AOI larger than 1 in the 2013–17 period: Antigua and Barbuda, Saint Lucia, Botswana, Seychelles, Montserrat, Saint Vincent and the Grenadines, Cuba, Palau, Zambia, Peru, Argentina, Swaziland, Belize, Uruguay, Djibouti, Timor-Leste and Republic of Moldova. Most of these are countries in which the Value Added of agriculture is small, both relative to GDP and in absolute terms. (FAO 2020d)

Official Development Assistance to Agriculture, Forestry and Fishing, 1995–2018

In 2018, total aid commitments to Agriculture, Forestry and Fishing (AFF) amounted to US $11.2 billion (constant 2017 US dollars) (Figure 7.8), of which bilateral ODA from DAC countries amounted to US$6.1 billion, slightly more than half, 54.8 percent.[20] Multilaterals contributed nearly US$5 billion, or 44.2 percent, and non-DAC contributed only US$0.1 billion, or nearly 1 percent, assuming that this reporting on non-DAC is complete. The share of multilaterals declined from 50.4 percent in 1995 to 44.2 percent in 2018.[21]

Among DAC members, the largest donors to the AFF sector in 2018 were the United States (US$1.2 billion, 19.6 percent of the total DAC contribution to AFF); Japan (US$1.1 billion, 17.9 percent); United Kingdom (US$780 million, 12.7 percent); Germany (US$706 million, 11.5 percent); France (US$393 million, 6.4 percent); and Canada (US$209 million, 3.4 percent). On the multilateral side, IDA was the predominant agency, accounting for 35.4 percent of total multilateral aid to AFF in the last three years, with EU institutions accounting for 29.1 percent, followed by IFAD (12 percent).

[20] The DAC definition of aid to agriculture excludes rural development (classified as multisector aid), developmental food aid (general program assistance), and emergency food aid (humanitarian assistance). The DAC definition of aid to agriculture includes "agriculture," "forestry," and "fishing." The definition of aid to agriculture excludes aid to other sectors, which may have a direct or indirect effect on food security: for example, rural development, developmental food aid, and emergency food aid.

[21] Since 1995, the OECD Creditor Reporting System (CRS) has published the ODA to Agriculture data by DAC and multilateral donors.

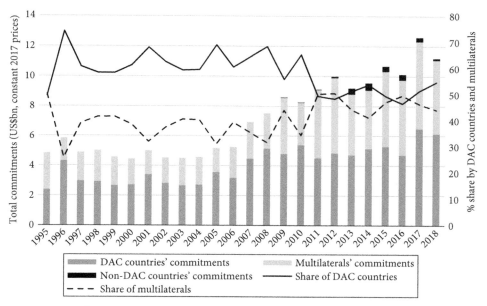

Figure 7.8 Total ODA to Agriculture, Forestry and Fishing (commitments in US$bn, constant 2017 prices) and changing nature of the bilateral and multilateral aid (%), 1995–2017

Source: Based on http://stats.oecd.org/, Creditor Reporting System (CRS).

Declining Share of Official Development Assistance to Agriculture, Forestry and Fishing, 1967–2018

Since the mid-1980s, aid to agriculture has fallen to US$11.4 billion (constant 2017 US dollars) from US$20.8 billion (constant 2017 US dollars), but post-2007–8 crisis data indicate a slowdown in the decline, and in 2017, the aid to agriculture reached a peak among recent years of US$2.8 billion (constant 2017 US dollars). The share of aid to agriculture in total ODA has declined sharply from 20.2 percent in 1983, to 5.7 percent in 2018 (see Figure 3.4, Chapter 3). Over the period 2009–18, aid flows to agriculture primarily targeted SSA (39.3 percent) and South and Central Asia (19 percent).

Official Development Assistance (Total Commitments) to Agricultural Research, Extension, and Education/Training, 1995–2018

Returns to R&D have consistently been shown to be high, and yet, investments in R&D both by donor and developing countries have been lackluster and fragmented. Total commitment to agricultural research, extension, and education/training reached US$1.07 billion (in constant 2017 US dollars) in 2017, but declined to US$0.9 billion (in constant 2017 US dollars) in the next year. Share in total AFF ODA gradually increased until 2006, reaching a peak at 17.6 percent, from only 4.1 percent in 1995, but the trend has been declining since, dropping to only 6.8 percent in 2014, increasing to nearly 8 percent in 2018 (Figure 7.9). Over the period 1995–2018, total commitment to agricultural research, extension, and education/training was 14.9 billion (in constant 2017 US dollars), of which 10.3 billion was by DAC countries (69 percent) and 4.6 billion by multilateral donors (31 percent) (Figure 7.10).

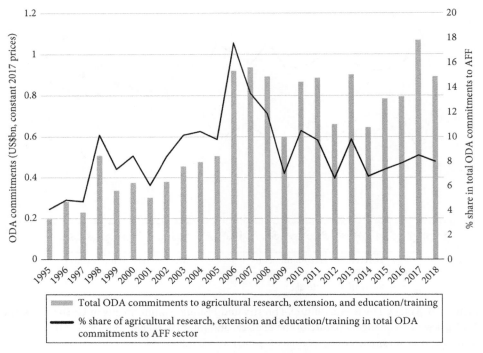

Figure 7.9 Total ODA to agricultural research, extension, and education/training (commitments in US$bn, constant 2017 prices) and share in total Agriculture, Forestry and Fishing sector (%), 1995–2018

Source: Based on http://stats.oecd.org/, Creditor Reporting System (CRS).

Official Development Assistance to Other (Rural Development, Developmental Food Aid/Food Security Assistance, and Emergency Food Aid) Related Sectors by Development Assistance Committee Countries and Multilaterals

The DAC definition of aid to AFF excludes rural development (classified as multisector aid), developmental food assistance (classified as general program assistance), and emergency food aid (classified as humanitarian assistance). Table 7.2 shows data including these sectors, but such data are available only from 1995 for all donors. Using this broader measure, aid to agriculture and rural development (ARD) and food security amounted to US$18.8 billion (constant 2017 US dollars) per year, on average, in 2016–19, from US$8.3 billion per year in 1995–2000 (constant 2017 US dollars). Bilateral ODA typically focuses on countries and sectors of strategic importance to their own countries. International agencies tend to have more clearly defined rules for allocation of resources, and a larger share of their resources reach developing country governments than is often the case with bilateral assistance, unless the latter is completely untied. Bilateral aid to ARD and food security rose from US$5.2 billion per year in 1995–2000 to US$12.1 billion per year in 2016–18, and multilateral aid rose from US$3.2 billion per year in 1995–2000 to US$6.7 billion per year in 2006–18 (Figure 7.11).

Humanitarian Assistance

Humanitarian action saves lives, alleviates suffering, and maintains human dignity following conflict, shocks, and natural disasters. For this reason, it is a high priority for donors.

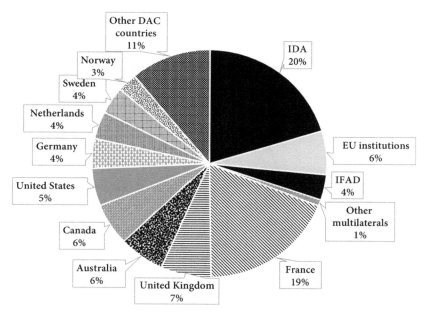

Figure 7.10 Share in total ODA to agricultural research, extension, and education/training by major donors, 1995–2018 (%)

Source: Based on http://stats.oecd.org/, Creditor Reporting System (CRS).

Table 7.2 ODA to agriculture and other (rural development, developmental food aid/food security assistance and emergency food aid) related sectors, 1995–2018 (annual average commitments in US$bn, constant 2017 prices)

	1995–2000	2001–2007	2008–2015	2016–2018
DAC countries				
Agriculture/forestry/fishing	3.0	3.3	5.2	5.8
Rural development	0.6	0.7	0.8	0.8
Developmental food assistance	1.1	1.4	1.2	1.4
Emergency food assistance	0.4	1.8	2.9	4.2
Total aid to ARD and food security-related sectors	5.2	7.2	10.1	12.1
Multilaterals				
Agriculture/forestry/fishing	1.9	1.9	4.3	5.3
Rural development	0.6	0.6	1.0	0.7
Developmental food assistance	0.6	0.5	0.3	0.4
Emergency food assistance	0.0	0.2	0.3	0.3
Total aid to ARD and food security-related sectors	3.2	3.2	5.9	6.7
Total				
Agriculture/forestry/fishing	4.9	5.1	9.5	11.0
Rural development	1.2	1.3	1.8	1.5
Developmental food assistance	1.7	1.9	1.5	1.8
Emergency food assistance	0.5	2.0	3.2	4.4
Total aid to ARD and food security-related sectors	8.3	10.4	16.0	18.8

Source: Based on http://stats.oecd.org/, CRS.

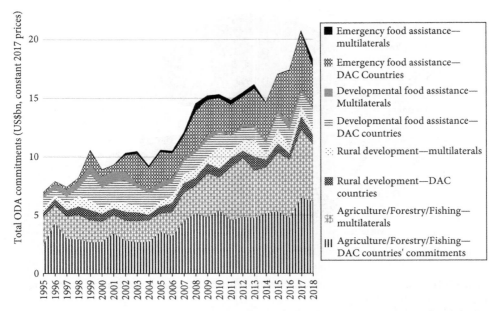

Figure 7.11 ODA to agriculture and other (rural development, developmental food aid/food security assistance, and emergency food aid) by DAC countries and multilaterals, 1995–2018 (total commitments in US$bn, constant 2017 prices)

Source: Based on http://stats.oecd.org/, Creditor Reporting System (CRS).

Humanitarian aid amounted to US$18.2 billion in 2018 (constant 2017 US dollars), up from US$2.7 billion in 1995 (constant 2017 US dollars), but declined 12.9 percent from 2017.[22] Humanitarian aid by DAC donors rose from US$1.6 billion in 1995 to US$14.2 billion in 2018 (but declined from US$16.9 billion in 2017), and by multilaterals from US$1.1 billion in 1995 to nearly US$4 billion in 2017.[23] Share of multilaterals declined from 40.2 percent in 1995 to only 22 percent in 2017 (Figure 7.12). Net debt relief grants was US$801 million in 2018 and represented about 0.5 percent of total net ODA by DAC countries in 2018, compared to about 20 percent in 2005 and 2006, when debt relief was at its highest level due to exceptional measures for Iraq and Nigeria (FAO 2020a).

Private Foreign Financing to the Agriculture Sector

We now discuss the private foreign financing to the agriculture sector based on the different measurements.

---

[22] Humanitarian aid includes emergency and distress relief in cash or in-kind, including emergency response, relief food aid, short-term reconstruction relief and rehabilitation, and disaster prevention and preparedness; and excludes aid to refugees in donor countries.

[23] WFP is not included in the OECD CRS database.

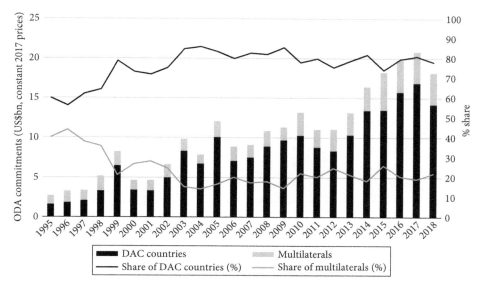

Figure 7.12 Humanitarian-related ODA by DAC countries and multilaterals, 1995–2018 (total commitments in US$bn, constant 2017 prices)

Source: Based on http://stats.oecd.org/, Creditor Reporting System (CRS).

Foreign Direct Investment to Agriculture, Forestry and Fishing

From 1991 to 2011, FDI inflows to AFF increased from US$0.33 billion in 1991 to US$1.8 billion in 2017, with significant year-to-year volatility.[24] FDI inflows to AFF peaked in 2007, when they reached a record high of US$11.6 billion (all prices are in constant 2010 US dollars) (Figure 7.13) (FAO 2020e).

The AFF share of total FDI inflows remained below 0.45 percent throughout the period, except in 2007, with a peak of 0.56 percent. By contrast, the food, beverages, and tobacco (FBT) share of global FDI inflows averaged 2 percent. In the AFF industry, FDI inflows are largely aimed at resource control, mostly land (Hallam 2009). In Africa, FDI focuses largely on rice, wheat, oilseed, and floriculture production; in Asia, the focus is on rice, wheat, meat, and poultry productions; and in South America, the focus is on sugarcane, fruits, flowers, and soybeans (UNCTAD 2009). Other investors are engaged in producing agricultural inputs such as equipment, fertilizer, and seeds.

Developing regions were the main destinations for AFF FDI inflows, accounting for almost 85 percent of all inflows between 1991 and 2017, or a total of US$61 billion. Countries in A&P were the largest recipients, receiving 45 percent of the total inflows to

---

[24] FDI is defined as an investment that aims to acquire a lasting management influence (10 percent or more of voting stock) in an enterprise operating in a foreign economy (IMF 1993; OECD 1996). FDI can be decomposed into two types of investments: M&A and greenfield investments. The latter results in the creation of new entities and setting up of offices, buildings, plants, or factories in a foreign economy. FDI is the sum of equity capital, reinvested earnings, and other FDI capital, whereas other FDI capital includes the borrowing and lending of funds. The FAOSTAT FDI database (obtained from UNCTAD, the International Trade Centre [ITC], the World Bank, and OECD, with UNCTAD as the primary data source) likely underestimates actual levels of FDI and inflows to agriculture because of country undercoverage. Country undercoverage is a key challenge facing the Agriculture FDI database, as there is limited access by FAO and other users to the global FDI database compiled by UNCTAD.

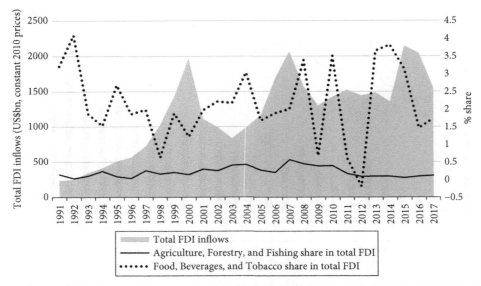

Figure 7.13 Total foreign direct investment inflows (US$bn, constant 2010 prices) and Agriculture, Forestry and Fishing, and Food, Beverages and Tobacco shares in total FDI (%), 1991–2017

Source: FAO (2020e). Statistics. Foreign Direct Investment to Agriculture, Forestry and Fishing, http://www.fao.org/economic/ess/investment/fdi/en/

AFF. Inflows to Africa also grew rapidly during the period 2001 to 2011, rising from 2.1 percent to 23.7 percent of total FDI inflows to AFF, but declined sharply afterward.

In 2007, all regions experienced an increase in FDI inflows to AFF, rising to a record high of US$11.6 billion. Increases were highest in A&P, where they increased more than five times over the previous year to a record high of US$7.3 billion (Figure 7.14). After 2007–8, FDI inflows to AFF began to decline in all regions, and despite increases in some years, remained below the 2007 highs. The 2007 highs can be explained by the food price crisis, during which food price increases attracted transnational corporations and institutional investors looking to acquire land and a larger share of the agro-food export market (McNellis 2009). Part of the large 2007 growth in A&P can be attributed to large domestic consumer markets and a productive agricultural sector, and the trend reversal after 2007, to food export restrictions and currency appreciation (Sharma 2011).

Between 2007 and 2017, the top 10 recipients of FDI inflows to AFF included China (US$522 million annually), followed by Indonesia (US$379 million), Argentina (US$328 million), Brazil (US$293 million), and Malaysia (US$232 million). The top five source countries for FDI outflows to AFF included Japan (US$307 million), Malaysia (US$257 million), the United States (US$200 million), China (US$195 million), and Spain (US$58 million).

FDI outflows to AFF from developing countries may be motivated by increasing domestic agro-food prices and lower agricultural production costs elsewhere, as in the case of China and the Republic of Korea, who invested in foreign agricultural production to help meet growing domestic demand (McNellis 2009).

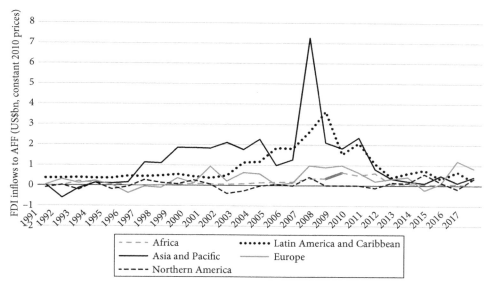

Figure 7.14 Foreign direct investment inflows to Agriculture, Forestry and Fishing by region, 1991–2017 (US$bn, constant 2010 prices)

Source: FAO (2020e). Statistics. Foreign Direct Investment to Agriculture, Forestry and Fishing, http://www.fao.org/economic/ess/investment/fdi/en/

Underinvestment in Food and Agriculture Relative to Needs

Estimates of amounts required to end hunger vary widely, ranging from as little as US$7 billion to as much as US$265 billion per year, depending on the assumptions made. According to estimations in FAO, IFAD, and WFP's "Achieving Zero Hunger," 0.3 percent of global GDP is needed annually to bring global hunger near (but not actually to) zero (Box 7.2) (FAO, IFAD, and WFP [2015]).

Laborde et al. (2016) provided an alternative approach to estimating the cost of reducing hunger, using a representative sample of seven countries in Africa south of the Sahara: Ghana, Malawi, Nigeria, Senegal, Tanzania, Uganda, and Zambia and identifying five spending categories that are critical to ending hunger (social safety nets, support for farmers to expand production and boost incomes, rural development to reduce inefficiencies along agricultural value chains and spur productivity, enabling policies, and nutrition). In their analysis, they focused only on the first three of those categories, because "there is a clear and measurable link to between these expenditures and increased calorie consumption" and excluded the last two factors, though they are important, because of the lack of data and the complexities of estimating their costs (Laborde et al. 2016, 4). The analysis, based on the MIRAGRODEP economic model (Laborde 2013) (to simulate national and international markets and key economic, biophysical, and socioeconomic trends that impact agriculture), combined with household surveys (to identify changes in the consumption and production of major food items, and in nonfarm sources of income) and satellite accounts (to identify the costs of different development interventions). Laborde et al. (2016) identified 74 countries that would still have hunger levels above 5 percent of the population in 2030, of which 18 would be expected to have sufficient domestic funds to address hunger without additional donor support. They estimated it will cost, on average, an extra US$11 billion per year

---

Box 7.2 FAO Estimates of the Cost of Abolishing Hunger by 2030

FAO recently estimated incremental investment requirements to achieve zero hunger during 2016 and 2030 (FAO, IFAD, and WFP 2015). Based on current trends, FAO estimates that around 650 million people would still suffer from hunger, or will have chronically inadequate dietary energy in 2030 beyond such investments. That is a very small decline from the 795 million estimated to be hungry in 2015. Indeed, as we have noted in earlier chapters, FAO's estimates suggest hunger has declined more slowly than poverty. To achieve zero hunger through social protection and targeted investments to the poor, FAO estimates an average of US$267 billion per year, 0.3 percent of the gross world product, will be required each year from 2016 to 2030, compared to the 0.3 percent of OECD GNI as ODA. This means just to address a single SDG will call for investments twice the size of today's ODA. Of this investment, rural areas would need US$181 billion a year. Even with this level of funding, an estimated 338 million people would still be unable to earn enough to overcome hunger or chronic (dietary energy) undernourishment after 2030. Meeting the Minimum Dietary Energy Requirement (MDER) of those "left behind" would cost US$14 billion.

---

of public spending from now until 2030 to end hunger (defined in this study as reducing the undernourished population in each country to 5 percent or lower), and of that total, US$4 billion would need to come from international donors each year, while the remaining US$7 billion would come from the affected countries.

Both of these studies ("Achieving Zero Hunger" by FAO, IFAD, and WFP [2015] and Laborde et al. [2016]) consider investments in and outside of agriculture and do not include the impacts of climate change. Mason-D'Croz et al. (2019, 49), "instead of costing the eradication of hunger, attempt[ed] to estimate the potential hunger reduction from investments only in the agriculture sector and includes the potential impacts of climate change on hunger eradication efforts."

In their paper, the researchers noted:

> Under baseline productivity scenarios, direct investments in agriculture (excluding infrastructure) across developing countries average US$20 billion annually from 2010 to 2030. Including infrastructure, the total baseline investments across developing countries is about US$45.5 billion.... [A]dditional investments [needed] are US$52 billion annually from 2015 to 2030 and are allocated to agricultural R&D, expanding irrigation, improved water use efficiency and soil management, and improved transportation and energy infrastructure. Most of the additional investments needed in agricultural R&D takes place in SSA while investments in some other sectors are more evenly spread among regions. (D'Mason-Croz et al. 2019, 49)

In short, efforts are underway to construct theories of change and to estimate the cost of eradicating hunger by 2030, exploring implications for domestic investment strategies and aid modalities. There are vast differences in estimates, however, of the cost of eradicating hunger that need to be reconciled. Also, whether such investments would need to be funded on a long-term, consistent basis either by countries or donors remains to be seen.

There continues to be considerable underinvestment in food, agriculture, and the rural sector generally, not just to transform agriculture but to transform economies out of agriculture, particularly in SA and SSA, even as the available government revenues and private sector resources in these countries exceed those of the past. In a passionate open letter to African leaders just before the 23rd African Union Summit in June 2014, Kanayo Nwanze, President of the IFAD, conjured the image of two Africas, in a way only an African could do: "the new land of opportunity... offering limitless possibilities to investors.... [and] a starving and hopeless continent, hungry and poor, corrupt and prey to foreign exploiters" (Nwanze 2014). He added:

> More than 10 years have passed since the Maputo Declaration, in which you, as African leaders, committed to allocating at least 10 percent of national budgets to agriculture and rural development—key sectors in the drive to cut poverty, build inclusive growth and strengthen food security and nutrition.
>
> Today, just seven countries [out of 54] have fulfilled the Maputo commitment consistently, while some others have made steps in the right direction. Ten years is a long time to wait...
>
> Don't just promise development, deliver it, and make it happen now. Make real, concrete progress toward investment that reaches all Africans. Investments that prioritize rural people. (Nwanze 2014)

In a way, he was also speaking for South Asian and other fellow citizens of the developing world, where cities exist side by side with the poor and the wretched living in slums.

The challenge for donors is to leverage national government interventions to increase the quantity and improve the quality of government expenditures, to promote well-coordinated expenditures across multiple sectors that are germane to agricultural productivity growth and the reduction of poverty and hunger—for example, addressing constraints of energy supply, transport, and information to agriculture. Agriculture was neglected for nearly three decades. The increase in donor commitments in the aftermath of the food crisis and the types of those commitments do not match the magnitude of the accumulated investment deficit.

Nutrition Financing

Advocacy in support of nutrition has increased considerably in the last decade as we discussed in earlier chapters. In 2017, led by the World Bank and supported by 1,000 Days, the Investment Framework for Nutrition was created, as a roadmap toward achieving the WHA nutrition targets by 2025, with financial investments needed from domestic governments, donors, and other sources. The World Bank's "Investment Framework for Nutrition" report estimated that an additional US$7 billion would be needed annually to scale up a core package of nutrition-specific interventions in order to achieve four (decreasing stunting, anemia, and wasting, and encouraging breastfeeding) of the six WHA targets (outlined in Chapter 4) by 2025, in addition to the world's current spending on nutrition annually (Shekar et al. 2017). Closing this additional resource gap will result in 3.7 million children's lives saved, with at least 65 million fewer stunted children, and 265 million fewer women suffering from anemia, as compared to the 2015 baseline

(Shekar et al. 2017). Alongside this scale-up of nutrition-specific interventions, achieving the WHA targets would also require improvements in the underlying determinants of undernutrition through nutrition-sensitive programs in sectors such as water, sanitation, and hygiene (WASH); agriculture; and education. Only about US$3.9 billion is currently being spent annually on the costed package of interventions by governments in LMICs and donors, of which about US$1 billion is provided by ODA for nutrition interventions. Of the ODA, 53 percent or US$531 million is allocated to treat severe and acute malnutrition. Another US$358 million (36 percent) is allocated to the interventions costed for the target to reduce stunting. Much lower amounts are directed to interventions to increase exclusive breastfeeding (US$85 million or 8.5 percent) and to reduce anemia in women of reproductive age (US$78 million or 7.8 percent).[25]

According to a Save the Children report (2018), a shift could increase global funding goals from US$7 billion annually to as much as US$23 billion. It concluded that "an additional US$23.25 billion is required per year to meet the challenge of SDG2—more than three times the US$7 billion that the World Bank Investment Framework suggests" (Save the Children 2018). While these calculations are rudimentary (as mentioned, the nutrition-sensitive data here are almost nonexistent), the underlying message is clear and unequivocal: the current nutrition financing paradigm cannot provide that sort of financing—we need a step change in how we fund the fight against malnutrition. The report sets out what needs to be done to address the financing gap. The first element is a diversification and refocusing of nutrition finance, including:

- uplifting the primary standing of domestic resource mobilization and the necessity for progressive tax reform;
- scaling up innovative financing mechanisms, such as the Global Financing Facility and Power of Nutrition;
- using ODA to fill the gaps, focusing on the most excluded and catalyzing new domestic resources (Save the Children 2018).

The *Global Nutrition Report* (*GNR*) for 2018 noted:

Aid for basic nutrition reported by donors and multilateral agencies amounted to US$856 million in 2016—almost 0.5% of total ODA. Other estimates of nutrition-specific spending are higher, at US$1.12 billion [see D'Alimonte et al. 2018]. Even at the higher figure, this amounts to less than 1% of global ODA.

… [B]asic nutrition disbursements from ODA donors for 2007 to 2016 [showed] a four-fold rise from 2007 to 2013, [after which] spending has stalled. Moreover, as a percentage of total ODA, basic nutrition ODA has declined annually since the spending peak in 2013.

---

[25] Note that the amounts across targets cannot be summed to the total owing to some intervention overlap within targets.
The *Global Nutrition Report 2016* notes:

> Reporting on nutrition spending is patchy, at best. Government spending data on nutrition-related NCDs [noncommunicable diseases] and obesity are fragmented across multiple departments and often bundled in with non-nutrition items. The Organisation for Economic Co-operation and Development's Development Assistance Committee does not monitor donor nutrition-sensitive spending or nutrition-related NCD spending. Governments and donors do not always take consistent approaches to tracking their nutrition spending. (IFPRI 2016a, 77)

Basic nutrition ODA now represents *less than half of 1%* of total ODA—a relatively small share of all development assistance compared with other sectors: in 2016, 6.8% of ODA was spent on education, 4.1% on agriculture and 1.0% on malaria control. (IFPRI 2018, 104–5)

In 2016, the United Kingdom, the United States, the EU, and Canada continued to be the largest DAC donors, providing for 60 percent of global basic nutrition ODA. "Some donors report significantly less spending in 2016 than 2015 on basic nutrition ODA. The US, for example, cut spending through the basic nutrition code by 50 percent. Germany has also cut spending via the basic nutrition code (by 65%) and Japan by 89%" (IFPRI 2018, 107).

The *GNR* 2018 also noted:

Some of these decreases may be partly due to the recent changes to the basic nutrition purpose code.... Some may also be attributable to greater spending on nutrition-sensitive approaches....

Looking beyond the purpose code,... nutrition-specific spending is aligned with the stunting and wasting targets.... An estimated US$1.12 billion was spent on nutrition-specific interventions in support of the global nutrition targets in 2015. Most of those funds were spent on stunting reduction (US$495 million) and wasting (US$224 million) and were allocated to sub-Saharan Africa and South Asia. The majority of funding was allocated to micronutrient supplementation, treatment of acute malnutrition, nutrition counselling and research. (IFPRI 2018, 107–8)

The United States has been the largest donor for nutrition-sensitive approaches by far over the past few years; the EU, Canada, and the United Kingdom are also significant contributors. Nutrition-sensitive spending totaled US$6.08 million in 2016, an increase from US$5.48 million spent in 2015 (IFPRI 2018).

Until 2018, it was not been possible for donors to report their ODA to combating obesity and diet-related NCDs. The *Global Nutrition Report* developed methodology to track spending, reporting results for the past three years. *GNR* (2018) showed very low levels of spending. In 2016, "just 0.018% of ODA was allocated to obesity and diet-related NCDs. Disbursements increased in 2016—from US$25.3 million to US$32.5 million but were still lower than in 2014.... Commitments for future spending were at their highest level for three years—albeit at just US$51.2 million" (IFPRI 2018, 116).

GNR 2018 notes that Australia, with a contribution of US$8.7 million, is among donors investing the most in combating diet-related NCDs, which accounts for more than a quarter of global spending. Other large donors include the EU, the United Kingdom, Switzerland, Canada, Italy, and New Zealand. Furthermore, in tracking donor financing for obesity and NCDs, the *GNR* found that just over half went to UMICs, 20 percent to LMICs, and less than 3 percent to the LICs (IFPRI 2018).

The increased financing need among all sources is substantial—scaling up all nutrition-specific interventions would require a 4.5-fold increase in total donor contributions by 2021 through ODA, and a 3.5-fold increase in total government contributions by 2025. About US$13.5 billion in additional financing, on top of current investments, is expected to be contributed over the next 10 years if "business as usual" (extrapolating current spending growth trends for nutrition forward) continues. However, such a scenario would result in falling far short of the global nutrition targets with a resource gap of US$56 billion (D'Alimonte, Rogers, and de Ferranti 2017).

The SUN Movement Strategy and Roadmap (2016–20) calls for improved access and use of financial resources for nutrition. As a step toward the SUN Movement's pursuit of this objective, a mapping was undertaken in 2016 of multilateral external (non-domestic) investments to improve awareness and understanding of nutrition funding sources and how to access them. The work was overseen by the SUN Donor Network, with the assistance of an independent consultant and the financial support of the Bill & Melinda Gates Foundation (SUN 2015).

Scaling up nutrition investments is still a high-impact, high-return proposition, with a benefit–cost ratio of 16:1 and a compound rate of return of more than 10 percent (IFPRI 2014, 2015a).

The *GNR 2016* details financing gaps:

- Analysis of 24 low- and middle-income governments' spending shows the mean allocation to nutrition at 2.1 percent, compared with 33 percent to agriculture, education, health, and social protection.
- NCDs, many of which are linked to nutrition, cause 49.8 percent of death and disability in low- and middle-income countries. But less than 2 percent of donor health spending goes to NCDs per year ($611 million in 2014). And nutrition-related NCDs received only US$50 million of donor funding in 2014, compared with nearly US$1 billion spent on nutrition-specific interventions.
- Donor allocations to all nutrition-specific interventions are stagnating at US$1 billion, although their allocations to nutrition via other sectors are increasing (IFPRI 2016a, 77).

As Lawrence Haddad stated: "Where leaders in government, civil society, academia and business are committed—and willing to be held accountable—anything is possible. Despite the challenges, malnutrition is not inevitable—ultimately it is a political choice: one which we need leaders across the world to make" (IFPRI 2016b).

The *GNR 2015* noted:

Steps to create more enabling political environments, healthier food environments, and nutrition-friendly food systems, as well as to promote nutrition in children's first 1,000 days, all offer opportunities for addressing both kinds of malnutrition synergistically. (IFPRI 2015a, xxiv)

So, although much has been accomplished in bringing nutrition to the center stage, clearly much remains to be done if the history of trends in aid is not to be repeated.

Multilateral development banks have provided only US$38 billion annually in 2013, out of well over a trillion dollars in flows to developing countries (World Bank and IMF 2015). Again, the net flows were far smaller than gross, owing to repatriation and repayments on past loans.

According to the *GNR 2018*:

1. Government spending on nutrition has increased in some developing countries, the Nutrition for Growth (N4G) financial commitment of US$19.6 billion has been met and there are initiatives with the potential to deliver finance at scale. However, official development assistance (ODA) to address all forms of malnutrition remains unacceptably low....
2. Nutrition-specific spending is particularly low.... Donors need to prioritise investing in nutrition-specific and nutrition-sensitive programmes equally.

3. Domestic spending remains opaque and difficult to track and funding levels vary widely from country to country. Clear targets need to be set...
4. New ways of tracking financial flows are being implemented...
5. ...Innovative mechanisms and business investment are needed to supplement government finance [such as the] Power of Nutrition initiative...
6. There is strong momentum to address malnutrition through commitments made globally—Sustainable Development Goals (SDGs), the UN Decade of Action on Nutrition 2016–2025 and the Milan Global Nutrition Summit in 2017.... (IFPRI 2018, 97)

Looking ahead to 2020, the *GNR 2018* noted that new financial commitments were made in 2017: In Milan, at the Global Nutrition Summit, three of the largest original donors, together with four new ones pledged "US$640 million to be disbursed along with other commitments (both financial and non-financial) from countries, businesses and civil society organisations" (IFPRI 2018, 119). In 2018, the High Level Meeting on NCDs in September brought together 23 heads of government and state and 55 ministers of health, who made 13 new commitments on NCDs. In December 2020, the N4G Summit in Tokyo was planned to present a new opportunity for countries, donors, and other organizations "to pledge new and SMART [specific, measurable, achievable, relevant, time-bound] commitments..." (IFPRI 2018, 122).

The Dramatically Changed External Environment for Assistance of International Institutions: The New Actors

We outlined the substantial changes in the global architecture with a proliferation of actors in Chapter 5. We now outline these changes in the context of financing.

The Big Five within the Changed International Aid Architecture

A useful overview of the aid architecture and changes, within which to view the aid to food and agriculture, is provided by the UN Secretary General's Report (UN 2019). It shows a significant increase from the low level of aid in 2002. The fastest increase has been in humanitarian aid, a category to which WFP belongs. In 2017, 46 percent of the UN System's operational activities for development (UN–OAD) consisted of shorter-term humanitarian assistance. Longer-term development objectives were addressed by 59 percent of total UN–OAD in 2017. Expenditure on UN–OAD amounted to US$34.3 billion in 2017, which represented about 71 percent of the US$48.3 billion in expenditure on all United Nations system-wide activities. Peacekeeping operations accounted for just under a fifth of total expenditures, while global norm- and standard-setting, policy, and advocacy, including the activities of FAO and WHO, among other functions made up the remaining 10 percent.

Total Contributions for UN–OAD amounted to US$33.6 billion in 2017, which equals 23.3 percent of ODA.[26] The US$33.6 billion received in funding for UN–OAD in 2017

---

[26] OAD is operational activities for development. This amount of US$33.6 billion differs slightly from the US $34.3 billion expended by the United Nations development system in 2017, since contributions are not necessarily expended in the same calendar year as they are received.

represents an increase of 12.6 percent, compared with the level in 2016. Core funding increased by 3.4 percent and non-core funding by 15.3 percent from 2016 to 2017, resulting in a decline in core funding as a share of the total, from 22.4 percent to an all-time low of 20.6 percent. The rate of growth in funding for operational activities for development followed a track similar to that of overall global ODA since 2002. In the five years from 2013 to 2017, however, United Nations development system funding exceeded the ODA growth rate.[27] Core funding for the development system grew at a significantly slower pace than ODA over the 15-year period. Looking at the longer-term trends, growth in core resources has been minimal compared to growth in non-core resources for both development-related activities and humanitarian assistance activities.

The UN report noted:

> Non-core funding for the United Nations development system nearly doubled from 2007 to 2016, while core funding grew at a rate of approximately one fifth of the non-core rate. Non-core funding for humanitarian assistance activities was particularly robust, increasing by 185 per cent, nearly tripling over the decade. Core funding for development-related activities grew by 8 percent over the same period. (UN 2019, Funding Analysis, 4/29)

The UN report, in a discussion of the distribution of funding across entities, noted:

> In 2016, the top eight (the World Food Programme (WFP), the United Nations Development Programme (UNDP), the United Nations Children's Fund (UNICEF), the Office of the United Nations High Commissioner for Refugees (UNHCR), the World Health Organization, the United Nations Relief and Works Agency for Palestine Refugees in the Near East (UNRWA), the Food and Agriculture Organization of the United Nations (FAO) and the United Nations Population Fund (UNFPA)) accounted for 83 per cent of all contributions. The other 35 development system entities account for the remaining 17 per cent of funding for operational activities for development. (UN 2019, Funding Analysis, 7/29)

Core and non-core contributions received by the eight largest UN development system entities in 2017 (relative to 2007) are described here. The UN report notes:

> System-wide, only nine entities received over 30 per cent of their voluntary contributions [excluding assessed contributions] in the form of non-earmarked core funding, which creates challenges for many of them, as it limits their ability to reallocate funding to underfunded areas in their strategic plans. That issue is at the heart of the funding compact, particularly commitment 4 [in which Member States pledge to predictable funding to specific requirements of SDG entities]. (UN 2019, Funding Analysis, 7/29)

The UN report further notes:

> The growth in humanitarian disasters resulting from the impacts of climate change as well as the increase in conflicts in recent years has accelerated the growing imbalance between core and non-core resources (since humanitarian funding tends to be primarily non-core

---

[27] The designation "United Nations development system" refers to 43 UN entities that undertake operational activities for development and are eligible for ODA.

in nature). Apart from that, Member States have been increasingly earmarking their funding for development-related activities for decades. The funding compact aims to reverse that long-term trend and bring about a better balance between core and non-core resources so that United Nations development system entities can effectively deliver on their strategic objectives and provide the holistic development solutions required by the 2030 Agenda for Sustainable Development. (UN 2019, Funding Analysis, 8/29)

For the five largest entities, the non-core component exceeded the core component by a significant margin. In Chapter 5 (on global governance), we demonstrated the increased reliance of FAO and WHO on voluntary contributions and why and how that is driven by what donors wish to finance, rather than what might be needed. For example, until now in the case of WHO, donors mostly financed investment in communicable diseases. The challenges of FAO and the World Bank are better understood in the context of this overall aid picture. One of the biggest challenges that the international architecture faces is the near stagnation of assessed contributions.

On the subject of burden-sharing, the UN report notes:

Government contributors account for nearly three quarters of the funding [74 percent] for operational activities for development.... Among government contributors to the United Nations development system, there is heavy reliance on a few countries. In 2017, three donors—the United States of America, the United Kingdom ... and Germany—accounted for half of all funding for operational activities for development received from Governments, and just seven contributors accounted for over two thirds of all government contributions. (UN 2019, Funding Analysis, 8/29–9/29)

Finally, in terms of allocation of resources, with an overview of expenditures, the UN report noted:

Spending on operational activities for development totaled US$34.3 billion in 2017. Some US$25.2 billion, or 73 per cent, was spent at the country level, and another US$3.3 billion, or 10 per cent, was spent at the regional level. Accordingly, 17 percent of total expenditures concerned either global activities, programme support and management or activities that could not be attributed to any other category.... Just over half, or 54 per cent, of expenditures were for development-related activities, while the other 46 per cent was spent on humanitarian activities....

In terms of the regional distribution of country-level expenditures in 2017, US$11.9 billion, or 42 per cent, was spent in Africa. The largest change in terms of the regional allocation of expenditures in recent years occurred in Western Asia. In 2011, that region accounted for only 6 per cent of spending on country-level operational activities for development. By 2017, the share had increased to 28 per cent, most of which was spent on humanitarian activities. (UN 2019, Funding Analysis, 17/29–18/29)

Growth of Trust Funds from OECD Donors

The trend of issue-specific financing by donors, called vertical funds, shows no sign of abating, in part, because donors are more inclined to give money to specific agendas they support. The Development Committee Communiqué of the 2015 Spring Meetings of IMF and the World Bank encouraged the possible creation of a Pandemic Financing Facility to mobilize and leverage public and private resources, including insurance mechanisms, to help countries receive rapid funding in the face of an outbreak, based on strong preparedness plans; the creation of the Catastrophe Containment and Relief Trust; the Global Financing Facility in Support of Every Woman, Every Child to be launched in Addis Ababa; and other initiatives for addressing hunger and malnutrition (World Bank and IMF 2015). Bilateral donors are also allocating more of their funds through their own programs, changing the share of bilateral and multilateral funding and modifying established governance arrangements.

What the countries do themselves, with or without these funds, and whether and how the donor demand for quicker and more demonstrable impacts contributes to the better, long-term uses of national funds, human resources, and institutions is the central issue. Yet short-term, unpredictable, and uncertain funding tied to issues of particular interest to the donors, albeit without an overarching strategy, does not merely reduce the impact of external aid, but can distract developing countries from the main business at hand and often substitute for the functions that developing countries must perform to achieve sustained impacts on poverty, as we will demonstrate in Chapter 10 in the case of CGIAR. Aid fatigue and erosion of confidence in the ability of international institutions to address rapidly evolving challenges have played a role in the way that donor funding is tied to results, rather than through the old-style three-year replenishments, as in the case of IDA, or to subscribed capital, and other long-term forms of contributions to multilateral institutions. In view of how small development aid is, key questions are: (1) is it helping to leverage domestic resources of developing countries; and (2) is it having scaled-up impacts?

Trust Funds in the Aid Architecture

While trust funds may at times fill gaps in the multilateral system, the strengths of the multilateral system (vis-à-vis bilateral aid) play an important role in driving the establishment of trust funds. For instance, donors' limited presence in some developing countries, or limited funds management and implementation capacity in certain sectors, may account for the use of multilateral platforms (that is, in the role of trustee or implementing agency) to achieve bilateral objectives. The use of trust funds gives donors more visibility and influence, reduces transaction costs, and allows them to target countries where their bilateral presence is limited (IEG 2011a). Regular trust funds represent bilateral aid channeled through non-core contributions to the multilateral system (so-called multi-bi aid). They roughly account for 11 percent of ODA disbursements, financial intermediary funds' (FIFs) support programs, or funds that are typically recorded as multilateral aid (and which account for an estimated 5 percent of ODA); their funding is more likely to compete with that for other multilateral channels.

There is now increased reliance on multi-donor trust funds (MTDFs), greater alignment of recipient-executed trust funds (RETFs) with WBG policies for IBRD/IDA lending, improved data analysis and risk management, and increased cost recovery. While progress has been made in reforming the management of trust funds (for example, enhanced multi-year budget frameworks, foreign exchange risk management, board engagement and oversight of the Bank's trust fund portfolio, and annual reporting), further changes are needed, and reforms continue to evolve.

World Bank management has noted that it would have liked to have seen a more systematic treatment of the political economy factors (both internal and external) that underlie the creation of trust funds. The creation of new global programs (and FIFs supporting these) is often linked to G7/G20 initiatives. Bank management has acknowledged that there are multiple interests at play at the level of donors—involving several constituencies, from parliaments to executive powers, with a wide variety of decision-making processes, from centralized to very decentralized.

Trust Funds' Contribution to Aid Fragmentation

The huge growth of partnerships fueled by donor "trust funds" from traditional OECD donors, non-core funds, or funds provided outside of the regular budgets of international organizations has been the new norm, starting about the mid-1990s. Whereas much of the discussion here is focused on the World Bank, trust fund issues are generic. In all but the large, mostly MICs, such as China, India, or Brazil, this growth has eroded old-style multilateralism and the earlier roles of international organizations in development finance and development advice.

Donors' seemingly ad hoc behavior in creating trust funds, often responding to the need for visibility on issues of national interest, explains the swift action they expect from the Bank. Although the Bank has been successful in meeting donor demands and trust funds are basically aligned with the Bank's broad strategy, trust funds are contributing to aid fragmentation. These factors make improving the Bank's trust fund framework very challenging.

Additionality and Effectiveness of Trust Funds

Determining additionality of trust funds is complex, and there is no agreement. The IEG evaluation of Trust Funds (2011a) concluded that trust funds may not mobilize additional ODA resources, but World Bank management argued that they could leverage funds from non-ODA sources. In addition, trust funds channeled through multilaterals may be more effective than funds provided bilaterally (which are sometimes tied or support political agendas, and are less coordinated).

Consistency with Aid-Effectiveness Principles

There are other paradoxes. The majority of country-specific trust funds are better aligned with country priorities than thematic or sector-focused trust funds. There have also been assertions in the literature, however, that the value-added of trust funds is more evident in the financing of GPGs than when they finance country priorities. Trust funds could benefit from greater evaluation of impacts.

According to the IEG evaluation of trust funds:

> [Programs that trust funds finance range] from huge global programs with their own governance structures [such as the Global Environment Facility (GEF) or CGIAR] to conventional development projects; debt relief operations; and studies, technical assistance, and project preparation carried out by the World Bank or recipients.... While the channeling of aid resources through trust funds has grown in response to perceived limitations of bilateral and multilateral aid mechanisms in meeting changing development challenges, the use of the trust fund vehicle has raised strategic issues for the effectiveness, efficiency, and coherence of the international aid system. (IEG 2011a, vii)

WBG is trusted by OECD donors for its fiduciary management, proven by its being the largest manager of trust funds. They fund a wide range of projects and activities, either freestanding or programmatic, which can be country-specific, regional, or global in scope.

The Independent Evaluation Group noted:

> To address limitations in bilateral aid, donors [also] use trust funds to pool funds for particular programs, tap into the capacities and systems of the trustee organization, and distance themselves from politically controversial activities. The choice is made primarily for political reasons to direct aid to particular countries or issues, and large global funds are created typically at the initiative of high-level government officials. (IEG 2011a, vii)

The IEG assessed trust funds, noting trust funds "have enabled the Bank to enhance its development role, [and] the Bank would continue to accept them. But changes are needed to foster more effective, efficient, and accountable use of trust funds." The IEG evaluations have recommended over the years that "the World Bank adopt a more structured and disciplined approach to the mobilization and deployment of these funds" (IEG 2011a, xi). When partners select the option of global programs, the Bank should continue to participate and require that each partnership program have a charter, a governing body, a management unit, and terms of reference to guide the Bank's participation.

WBG managed 984 trust funds (in FY2014), holding a total of US$30.09 billion, and supported activities of particular interest to the domestic constituencies of donors, in part due to the desire of bilateral donors to have a direct voice in these organizations. From FY09 through FY13, the United States and the United Kingdom made the largest contributions to WBG trust funds. Over that period, the United Kingdom was the largest development funder to the IBRD/IDA trust funds, followed by the United States, the EU, Australia, and the Netherlands. Together, these five development funders accounted for almost half of the total cash contributions to IBRD/IDA trust funds since FY09. The United States remains the largest development funder to FIFs, both cumulatively over the five years and in FY13. Sovereign development funders remain the major contributors to the WBG trust funds, accounting for 80 percent of total cash contributions received in FY13 for IBRD/IDA trust funds, 95 percent for FIFs, and 67 percent for IFC trust funds. In Chapter 10 on CGIAR, we demonstrate that after the 2008 reforms, which were intended to provide funds in Windows 1 and 2. Growth in those windows did not materialize as was intended, as described in Chapter 10 in detail. Windows 1 and 2 are not tied to specific research agendas. From the perspective of the Fund Council, Window 1 and 2 funds are restricted only in the sense that money must be spent on CGIAR Research Programs (CRPs) as contracted. Window 3 contributions consist of funds that donors wish to allocate to specific Centers and bilateral funding that goes directly to the Centers. Several Centers contend that Window 3 provides them more freedom than do Windows 1 and 2, and that they could not deliver on the CRPs without Window 3 funding (Figure 10.2, Chapter 10). Reforms in the funding of research has not accomplished the change the reformers intended. In the meantime, new donor funds that use multilateral institutions as vehicles continue to proliferate. The transaction costs to developing countries in accessing these funds relative to their impact on development, unlike the past long-term roles of the Rockefeller or the Ford Foundations, must be questioned. Bezanson and Isenman (2012) noted several weaknesses in the new partnerships:

1. Weakness or absence in strategic direction, accountability mechanisms, monitoring and evaluation systems, and management of risk
2. Lack of clarity on the roles and responsibilities of trustees or host organizations
3. Confusion between the roles of management versus governance
4. Inadequate attention to resource mobilization and to the human resources required to deliver programs and achieve objectives.

Multi-Donor Trust Funds

An MDTF is a multi-entity funding mechanism designed to support a clearly defined, broad programmatic scope and results framework, through contributions that are comingled, not earmarked for a specific UN entity and held by a UN fund administrator.[28] In these UN interagency funds, the organization also takes the lead in making fund allocation decisions, as well as fund implementation, and thus, these types of funds are a more flexible and higher quality form of noncore contributions. They include the One United Nations funds, which were established to address underfunded areas of a program country's One United Nations country program, through unearmarked or loosely earmarked contributions.

Contributions to UN-administered MDTFs, including One United Nations funds, totaled US$2.3 billion in 2014, a significant increase over the US$1.4 billion in contributions in 2013. More than half of this increase is attributable to the Saudi Humanitarian Fund for Iraq and funds for the Ebola response. Commitments to One United Nations funds also increased by 35 percent, surpassing US$87 million in 2014. Contributing to this increase was the launch of the "Delivering Results Together" fund, which channeled more than US $13 million to One United Nations country funds (OECD 2016).[29]

During the first phase of the Economic and Social Council dialogue, it was suggested that development-related MDTFs were not being used to their full potential to support UN coherence and to reduce fragmentation, and that one option to make them more attractive to donors could be to have fewer funds with broader scope.

Global Thematic and Vertical Funds

Single-donor and program- and project-specific funds include resources received through global funds, sometimes referred to as vertical funds. They have become a significant resource channel for the UN development system over the last decade. These funds focus on specific issues or themes, just like global MDTFs, but they are not directly administered by a UN entity and do not require the UN to play a leading role in the fund allocation process. They usually have their own trustee, funding, governance, policy, and programming arrangements. Thus, global funds are a form of pooled funding, from the perspective of the organization, but the funds are often tightly earmarked for particular projects, with the UN playing the role of the implementing organization. Examples are the GEF, the

---

[28] In September 2015, three entities reported administering MDTFs: the UNDP Multi-Partner Trust Fund Office, UNFPA, and the United Nations Office for Project Services.
[29] The "Delivering Results Together" fund, managed by the UN Development Group, is a global pooled funding facility for delivering as one country, with funding flowing through the operational One United Nations funds.

Global Fund to Fight AIDS, Tuberculosis and Malaria, the Multilateral Fund for the Implementation of the Montreal Protocol, and the Global Alliance for Vaccines and Immunization. In 2014, an estimated US$1.0 billion, or some 8.6 percent, of all non-core contributions for development-related activities of the UN System came from global funds, a 41 percent increase in volume since 2011 (OECD 2016).

World Bank Group Trust Funds

WBG identified five global issues as its institutional priorities: climate change, crisis response, jobs, gender, and infrastructure. Trust funds play a vital role, complementing IBRD, IDA, and IFC, for each of these areas of focus (World Bank 2019b). The Executive Summary of the "2018–2019 Trust Fund Annual Report" highlights the role of trust funds in WBG in working toward its goals of ending extreme poverty and promoting shared prosperity:

> WBG trust funds and financial intermediary funds (FIFs) are among the WBG's main channels of development assistance (along with IBRD and IDA), and the WBG holds a substantial portfolio of such funds: the amount of WBG funds held in trust (FHIT) (for World Bank, IFC, and MIGA [Multilateral Investment Guarantee Agency] trust funds as well as FIFs, FHIT comprises cash, investments, and promissory notes receivable) as of end-FY19 is estimated at US$12.1 billion for trust funds and US$23.1 billion for FIFs. These funds provide significant and predictable multiyear funding for the WBG to utilize in support of flexible and customizable development solutions that serve client countries [and] ... finance about two-thirds of the World Bank's advisory services. (World Bank 2019b, xiii)

With respect to FHIT (FY15–FY19), the Trust Fund report noted, "Among the trust funds that had significant increases in FY19 were Afghanistan Reconstruction Trust Fund (ARTF) (US$264 million), Global Financing Facility (US$203 million), Carbon Finance (US$186 million), and Sint Maarten Recovery, Reconstruction, and Resilience Trust Fund (US$145 million)" (World Bank 2019b, 34).

Disbursements and cash transfers from trust funds and numbers of IBRD/IDA, IFC trust funds, multi-donor trust funds (MDTFs), single-donor trust funds (SDTFs), and programmatic freestanding IBRD/IDA trust funds were detailed by the 2018–19 Trust Fund Report, with the key points being:

> Total WBG disbursements and cash transfers fluctuated over the past five years between US$4.2 billion in FY15 and US$3.7 billion in FY19 for IBRD/IDA trust funds, and between US$300 million and US$260 million for IFC trust funds....
>
> The total number of IFC trust funds declined from 249 as of end-FY15 to 195 as of end-FY19. (World Bank 2019b, 38, 40)

Contributions to IBRD/IDA trust funds by governments and by top ten trust fund donors are included in the Trust Fund Report:

> Sovereign governments remain the largest contributors to IBRD/IDA trust funds, accounting for 78 percent of total cash contributions received in FY19 (US$3.0 billion),

an increase of over US$800 million compared to FY18. Intergovernmental institutions contributed 15 percent (US$572 million) in FY19, an increase of US$210 million from FY18.... The European Union contributed 82 percent of total intergovernmental institution cash contributions in FY19, while the Bill & Melinda Gates Foundation contributed 65 percent of total private nonprofit entity cash contributions.

... The top three donors for FY19 continued to be the United Kingdom, the United States, and the European Union, with increased contributions from the United States (US$341 million, compared to US$308 million in FY18) and the European Union (US$467 million, compared to US$331 million in FY18). (World Bank 2019b, 45–6)

RETFs were the other major chunk of funds:

Total disbursements from all RETFs, which include stand-alone RETFs, cofinancing RETFs, and other RETFs, remained steady at around US$3.4 billion between FY15 and FY16, and then started to decline, reaching US$2.6 billion in FY19. This decline was primarily due to a decrease in disbursements by [several] programs.... On average, RETFs accounted for 76 percent of total trust fund disbursements over the past five years.

In FY19, of total RETF disbursements (US$2.6 billion), 39 percent (US$1.0 billion) were from stand-alone RETFs. Stand-alone RETF disbursements decreased from US$1.6 billion in FY15 to US$1.5 billion in FY17 and to US$1.0 billion in FY19. Over the past five years, 37 percent of the stand-alone RETF disbursements were from ARTF (US$2.7 billion), 17 percent from IBRD as an IE for GPE, and 5 percent from IBRD as an IE for CIFs (World Bank 2019b, 47–8).

The Trust Fund Report detailed RETF disbursements:

Cumulative total RETF disbursements were US$15.1 billion between FY15 and FY19, with the highest annual level of US$3.4 billion in FY15, decreasing 24 percent to US$2.6 billion in FY19. The IDA countries continue to receive the largest share of RETF disbursements year after year—63 percent of total RETF disbursements in FY19. Over the past five years, approximately US$1 out of every US$7 disbursed to IDA-only and blend countries was from RETFs, whereas RETF disbursements to IBRD countries were equivalent to 2 percent of IBRD disbursements.

... RETF disbursements in FCS [fragile and conflict-affected states] decreased from US$1.5 billion in FY16 to US$1.2 billion in FY19. The share of RETF in FCS out of total RETF disbursements also declined, from 50 percent in FY18 to 45 percent in FY19. Disbursements to Afghanistan in FY19 continued to account for a significant portion—65 percent—of total RETF disbursements in FCS (US$0.8 billion). RETF disbursements to FCS other than Afghanistan averaged around US$0.5 billion over the past five years. In FY19, besides Afghanistan, the five FCS that received the highest RETF disbursements were the West Bank and Gaza (US$96 million), Somalia (US$55 million)...

The majority of RETF disbursements went to the following three sectors: (a) public administration (which includes the World Bank's work on governance and anticorruption), 19 percent; (b) agriculture, fishing, and forestry, 16 percent; and (c) education, 14 percent. Together, the three sectors accounted for 49 percent of total RETF disbursements in FY19. Even so, in FY19 disbursements in the public administration and education sectors decreased significantly (US$156 million and US$222 million, respectively) as compared to FY18, primarily because of decreased disbursements in GPE (by US$177 million) and ARTF (by US$219 million). Disbursements in the social protection sector increased by US$120 million in FY19 over FY18, and disbursements in the industry, trade, and services sector increased by US$72 million because of increased disbursements in the Global Concessional Financing Facility (by US$36 million) and ARTF (US$68 million). (World Bank 2019b, 50–2)

In terms of regional shares of RETF disbursements (FY15–FY19), the Trust Fund Report stated:

Among the World Bank's Regional units, South Asia (SAR) was the largest beneficiary of RETFs in FY19 with US$1 billion, primarily because of [Afghanistan], the ARTF. The Africa Region (AFR, US$840 million) was the second-largest beneficiary, followed by the Middle East and North Africa (MENA, US$345 million). RETF disbursements in East Asia and Pacific (EAP), Latin America and Caribbean (LCR), and Europe and Central Asia (ECA) were US$126 million, US$187 million, and US$166 million, respectively. Compared with FY18, RETF disbursements decreased in AFR; and in EAP, RETF disbursements decreased by 39 percent from US$207 million in FY18 to US$126 million in FY19, primarily because of the decrease in disbursement from the IBRD as an IE of Clean Technology Fund (CTF) (US$37 million), the Indonesia Program for Community Empowerment (US$18 million), and Pacific Catastrophe Risk Assessment and Financing Initiative (US$12 million). (World Bank 2019b, 54)

The Trust Fund Report also detailed bank-executed trust fund (BETF) disbursements:

BETF disbursements increased by 38 percent (US$306 million), from US$770 million in FY15 to US$1.1 billion in FY19. In FY19, 59 percent of BETFs were disbursed for country engagement work and 16 percent for global engagement work, up from 58 percent and 14 percent, respectively, in FY15. More than half of BETF disbursements in FY19 went to support regional work (such as the Global Facility for Disaster Reduction & Risk Trust Fund for Africa) or global work (such as the Consultative Group to Assist the Poorest Trust Fund) and non-members such as the West Bank and Gaza. Out of approximately US$4.8 billion in BETF disbursements over the last five years, about US$965 million were for activities that support IDA countries. During FY15–FY19, BETF disbursements for activities to support IDA countries grew by 40 percent to US$217 million in FY19; BETF disbursements for activities to support blend countries grew by 22 percent to US$66 million in FY19; and BETF disbursements for activities to support IBRD countries grew by 67 percent to US$205 million in FY19.

During FY15–FY19, country engagement activities (largely ASA [advisory services and analytics]) accounted for the largest share of total BETF disbursements (59% in FY19). Global engagement activities (including global knowledge, research and development and global advocacy) accounted for the second-largest share (16% in FY19). (World Bank 2019b, 55–6)

IFC Advisory Services program expenditures was described also in the Trust Fund Report:

IFC trust funds are the main instrument for financing IFC Advisory Services, with funding coming from development partners, IFC, and clients. As of end-FY19, there were 195 IFC active trust fund accounts. Through 783 active projects (as of end-FY19), IFC is providing advisory solutions for private sector clients in about 100 countries, focusing on fragile and conflict-affected areas and on IDA countries.

IFC trust funds are the main instrument for financing IFC Advisory Services. Program expenditures for IFC Advisory increased from US$273 million in FY18 to US$295 million in FY19, the highest level in the five-year period. IDA countries accounted for 59 percent of the Advisory Services program expenditures in FY19. (World Bank 2019b, 57, 62)

MIGA trust funds were also reviewed in the Trust Fund Report:

> MIGA, one of the five WBG organizations, has a mission to promote foreign direct investment in developing countries to help support economic growth, reduce poverty, and improve people's lives. MIGA provides political risk insurance to private sector investors and lenders. Since its inception in 1988, MIGA has issued more than US$45.0 billion in guarantees in support of over 800 projects in 110 of its member countries. In FY18, MIGA issued US$5.3 billion in guarantees for projects spanning four strategic priority areas—IDA countries, FCS, climate change, and innovations.
>
> ...MIGA's portfolio consisted of four trust funds...[that] offer support to fragile and conflict-affected situations and promote the stability and growth of countries in FCS by catalyzing private capital flows from investors and financial institutions to FCS through mobilizing political risk insurance products to these countries, from both MIGA and the global political risk insurance industry. (World Bank 2019b, 63)

FIFs are:

> ...financial arrangements that typically leverage a variety of public and private resources in support of international initiatives, enabling the international community to provide a direct and coordinated response to global priorities like agriculture and food security, environment and climate change, and natural disasters. Through FIFs the World Bank can support the international community in providing targeted and coordinated responses that focus on the provision of global public goods, such as preventing communicable diseases, responding to climate change, and improving food security. (World Bank 2019b, xiv)

The report notes that the World Bank has a large and growing portfolio of FIFs:

> Since the establishment of the first FIF in 1971, total cumulative funding to FIFs as of end-FY19 has amounted to US$104.4 billion, of which US$7 billion was contributed in FY19. The number of active FIFs has more than doubled from 12 at end-FY08 to 27 at end-FY19. The World Bank serves as limited trustee of all FIFs, providing a set of agreed financial services that include receiving, holding, and investing contributed funds, and transferring them when instructed by the FIF governing body. (World Bank 2019b, xvi–xvii)

FIFs play a significant role in international aid architecture, with transfers from FIFs to implementing entities (IEs): "The average amount of annual transfers from FIFs over FY15–FY19 was US$6.5 billion; annual transfers from FIFs to IEs declined from US$7.1 billion to US$5.9 billion from FY18 to FY19, primarily because of a decline in transfers from GFATM, which decreased by US$0.8 billion from FY18 to FY19" (World Bank 2019b, 104).

Notably, "the World Bank hosted 18 FIF secretariats in FY19, an increase from 14 in FY15. The overall increase in the number of FIFs, each with its own independent governance structure and terms of access to funds, can contribute to aid fragmentation and increased complexity for client countries and IEs" (World Bank 2019b, 106).

Remittances

The world's migrants send huge amounts of money to their families through cross-border money transfers, called remittances, and are of considerable interest from the perspective of economic transformation of countries from agriculture to the service and the manufacturing sector. Half of the agricultural labor force in the US consists of migrant labor of 11 million people, mostly from Mexico and Central America. According to the United Nations Department for Economic and Social Affairs, the worldwide number of international migrants (including refugees) was 272 million in 2019, up from 153 million in 1990. "Europe hosts the largest number of international migrants (82 million), followed by Northern America (59 million) and Northern Africa and Western Asia (49 million). The regional distribution of international migrants is changing, with migrant populations growing faster in Northern Africa, Western Asia and sub-Saharan Africa than in other regions" (UNDESA 2019, iv). In the coming decades, demographic forces, globalization, and climate change will increase migration pressures both within and across borders (World Bank 2014b, 2017).

The World Bank estimated that remittances inflows totaled US$706.6 billion in 2019, of which US$550.5 billion went to LMICs (an increase of about 4.7 percent over the previous year), and these flows are projected to reach US$574 billion in 2020 and US$597 billion by 2021, involving some 272 million migrants (Ratha et al. 2019). The remittances are a significant share of the macroeconomic story by a variety of measures: three times the size of ODA since the mid-1990s, several times the earnings of developing countries from exports, and are growing rapidly. In 2019, they are on track to overtake FDI flows to LMICs (Ratha et al. 2019). The April 2019 publication of WBG and the Global Knowledge Partnership on Migration and Development (KNOMAD) on "Migration and Remittances" noted, "Remittance flows grew in all six regions, particularly in South Asia (12.3 percent) and Europe and Central Asia (11.2 percent)" (WBG and KNOMAD 2019, vii).

In 57 countries, remittances exceeded 5 percent of GDP last year in 2019. The money went mostly to low-income households. Against the background of the current health crisis, the need for that income is acute. In April, 2020, the World Bank estimated that remittances would fall by 20 percent in LICs and MICs (World Bank 2020a). This is broadly consistent with projections derived from applying the elasticity of remittances to growth—observed during the 2008 global financial crisis—to the June 2020 forecasts of the IMF's World Economic Outlook (IMF 2020). However, growth remained reasonably strong in low-income developing countries during the financial crisis, so the need for remittances in recipient countries was not as urgent as it is now.

Despite the COVID-19 pandemic and its likely impact on remittances, the picture is not unconditionally bleak. Remittances often hold up in response to adverse shocks in recipient countries. This possibly explains why they were surprisingly resilient in many countries in the first half of the year. Although there is a great deal of diversity, remittances largely fell from March, then started to stabilize in May, before picking up. This pattern was broadly in line with the stringency of virus containment policies in advanced countries, where strict measures were put in place in March and slowly relaxed, starting in May. The bounce back in remittances could be driven by a greater need to send money back to families, as the countries receiving remittances now struggle with the pandemic and collapse in external demand (Gurara, Fabrizio, and Wiegand 2020). This illustrates the countercyclical role of remittances.

However, if migrants are dipping into their meager savings to support families back home, this may not be sustainable over time, especially if the recession in host economies becomes protracted. A second outbreak of COVID-19 in the latter part of the year in host economies, for example, could jeopardize remittance flows further (Quayyum and Kpodar 2020).

The top recipients of remittances in 2019 were India (US$82.2 billion), with more than US$77 billion earned from the country's flagship software services exports. China (US$70.3 billion), Mexico (US$38.7 billion), the Philippines (US$35.1 billion), and Egypt (US$26.4 billion) follow among top recipients of remittances. Other large recipients included Nigeria, Egypt, Pakistan, Bangladesh, Vietnam, and Indonesia. However, as a share of GDP, remittances were larger in smaller and lower income countries; top recipients, relative to GDP, in 2019 were Tonga (38.5 percent), Haiti (34.3 percent), Nepal (29.9 percent), Tajikistan (29.7 percent), and the Kyrgyz Republic (29.6 percent) (Ratha et al. 2019).

For many developing countries, remittances are an important source of foreign exchange, surpassing earnings from major exports, and covering a substantial portion of imports. For example, in Nepal, remittances are nearly double the country's revenues from exports of goods and services, while in Sri Lanka and the Philippines, remittances are over 50 percent and 38 percent, respectively. In Uganda, remittances are double the country's income from its main export of coffee (World Bank 2014c).

Ratha et al. (2019) noted the sharpness of the slowdown in growth of remittances in 2019 for all regions, except LAC and SSA:

> In 2019, Latin America and the Caribbean would see the fastest pace of remittance growth at 7.8 percent due to the continued robustness of the US economy. Remittances would increase moderately in South Asia (5.3 percent), sub-Saharan Africa (5.1 percent) and East Asia and Pacific (3.8 percent) due to the buoyancy in inflows from the US being offset by slower growth of receipts from the Euro area and the GCC [Gulf Cooperation Council countries]. (Ratha et al. 2019)

The global average cost of sending remittances (that is, US$200 to LMICs) was 6.8 percent of each transaction in the second quarter of 2019, only slightly below previous quarters (7 percent), according to the World Bank's Remittance Prices Worldwide database.[30] The WBG and KNOMAD brief on migration and remittances noted:

> This is more than double the Sustainable Development Goal (SDG) target of 3 percent by 2030 (SDG target 10.c). The cost was the lowest in South Asia, at around 5 percent, while sub-Saharan Africa continued to have the highest average cost, at about 9.3 percent.... Remittance costs across many African corridors and small islands in the Pacific remain above 10 percent. (WBG and KNOMAD 2019, 5)

---

[30] See Remittance Prices Worldwide, https://remittanceprices.worldbank.org/en

Banks were the costliest channel for transferring remittances, at an average cost of 10.9 percent.... Opening up national post offices, national banks, and telecommunications companies to partnerships with other MTOs could remove entry barriers and increase competition in remittance markets. (WBG and KNOMAD 2019, viii)

At the household level, an estimated 40 percent of Somalia's population depends on remittances and uses the cash to buy food and medicine. Dilip Ratha, Manager of the Migration and Remittances Team at the Bank's Development Prospects Group noted that additionally, "migrants living in high income countries are estimated to hold savings in excess of US$500 billion annually," representing "a huge pool of funds developing countries can do much more to tap into." "Nigeria is readying a diaspora bond issue to mobilize diaspora savings and boost financing for development" (World Bank 2014c).

Despite the hardships encountered by many migrants due to the policies of countries receiving migrants, remittances are more stable, predictable, and the least controversial aspect of international capital flows, both from the perspectives of recipients and senders. Remittances are becoming an important part of the strategies of international organizations to harness them for development. The World Bank, IMF, and the UN organizations concerned with labor are actively working on the issues of migration and capital flows.

Two Views of the Impact of Remittances on Growth and Development

More research is urgently needed on the direct and systematic evidence of remittances on impact on poverty of households. It comes from a cross-country regression based on 74 countries by Adams and Page (2005), who showed that a 10 percent increase in the share of remittances in a country's GDP can lead to an average 1.2 percent decline in the poverty headcount. Household survey data, confirmed this result using Adam's work on Guatemala (Adams 2006), and Yang's study on the Philippines (Yang 2005). Orozco (2006) provided evidence on the mobilization of migrants' (and their relatives') savings and investments at home (through the acquisition of land, property, or small businesses), which can spur economic growth in areas neglected by the public and private sectors (Maimbo and Ratha 2005). Kaushik Basu, Senior Vice President and Chief Economist of the World Bank, noted that these flows act as an antidote to poverty and promote prosperity. Remittances "act as a major counter-balance when capital flows weaken as happened in the wake of the US Fed announcing its intention to reign in its liquidity injection program." (*Economist* 2014). Money sent from abroad, Basu added, can also work as an automatic stabilizer when a recipient nation's currency weakens, which makes it more expensive to import, but also cheaper for foreign workers to remit. So even if the effect on economic growth may turn out to be negligible, helping migrants to remit could still have a greater impact in developing countries than many other policies. "Remittances and migration data are also barometers of global peace and turmoil and World Bank's KNOMAD initiative to organize, analyze, and make available these data is important" (*Economist* 2014).

Basu's view is not shared universally by all economists. Michael Clemens of CGD and David McKenzie of the World Bank asked why such a rapid growth in remittances has not led to any discernible growth in GDP and provided three possible answers (Clemens and McKenzie 2014). First, the growth in remittances may actually be an illusion because of measurement error or reflect change in measurement error: for example, for Nigeria. Clemens and McKenzie (2014) estimated that about 80 percent of the reported growth in remittances received by developing countries between 1990 and 2010 simply reflects changes in measurement. Irrespective of measurement errors and insufficient statistical methods, the effect on growth may in fact be fairly small and can be negative. The cash may flow back but the human capital has left. If those who emigrated were not working anyway, then the flow of remittances will have a positive effect. The effect of remittances on GDP growth depends upon how the money is spent by the recipients. Nevertheless, Clemens argues remittances "have big effects—on things other than national GDP growth at the home country. For example, remittances do have important and easily measurable effects on poverty at the home country" (Clemens 2014).

> There is by no means consensus on the role of remittances in economic development. Adolfo Barajas of the IMF and his co-authors pointed out:... decades of private income transfers—remittances—have contributed little to economic growth in remittance-receiving economies...the most persuasive evidence in support of this finding is the lack of a single example of a remittances success story: a country in which remittances-led growth contributed significantly to its development.... [N]o nation can credibly claim that remittances have funded or catalyzed significant economic development. (Barajas et al. 2009, 16–17)

Foreign Direct Investment: Inflows and Outflows

In 2002, the Monterrey Consensus fundamentally transformed the development agenda by explicitly recognizing that, rather than being part of the problem, FDI can play an important role in financing development objectives.[31] The global FDI slump continues. FDI fell slightly fell slightly from US$1.41 trillion in 2018 to US$1.39 trillion in 2019. UNCTAD's Investment Trends Monitor notes that this has occurred "against the backdrop of weaker macroeconomic performance and policy uncertainty for investors, including trade tensions" (UNCTAD 2020). The UNCTAD publication further noted:

> FDI flows to developed countries remained at a historically low level, decreasing by a further 6% to an estimated US$643 billion. FDI to the European Union (EU) fell by 15% to US$305 billion, while flows to the United States remained stable at US$251 billion.... Flows to developing economies remained unchanged at an estimated US$695 billion. FDI increased by 16% in Latin America and the Caribbean and 3% in Africa. Despite a decline of 6%, flows to developing Asia continued to account for one-third of global FDI in 2019. Flows to transition economies rose by two thirds to US$57 billion. (UNCTAD 2020, 1–2)

FDI inflows remaining at 28 percent below the levels reached in 2007—the decline due mainly to "the fragility of the global economy, policy uncertainty for investors, and elevated geopolitical risks. New investments were also offset by some large divestments. The decline

---

[31] The Monterrey Consensus includes the final text of agreements and commitments adopted at the UN International Conference on Financing for Development in Monterrey, Mexico, on March 18–22, 2002 (UN 2002).

in FDI flows was in contrast to growth in GDP, trade, gross fixed capital formation, and employment" (UNCTAD 2015, 2).

FDI Inflows

Trends in FDI inflows into the developing economies as a group have not generally followed the global trends outlined above. At the peak of the FDI boom in 2007, OECD countries received around 70 percent of all FDI inflows. In a span of only seven years, however, this share dropped to around 40 percent, with inflows to non-OECD countries overtaking those of the OECD country grouping for the first time, in 2012. According to UNCTAD's "Investment Trends Monitor":

> Global FDI flows remained flat in 2019, at an estimated US$1.39 trillion, down 1% from a revised US$1.41 trillion in 2018. Flows declined in Europe and developing Asia, remained unchanged in North America and increased in Africa, Latin America and the Caribbean and transition economies. The impact of the 2017 US tax reform which reduced US outward FDI flows and global FDI in 2018 appear to have diminished in 2019.
>
> Developing economies continue to absorb more than half of global FDI flows and half of the top 10 largest recipients of FDI fall in this category. The United States remained the largest recipient of FDI, attracting US$251 billion in inflows, followed by China with flows of US$140 billion and Singapore with US$110 billion.
>
> FDI flows to developed economies fell by 6% to an estimated US$643 billion from their revised US$683 billion in 2018. FDI remained at a historically low-level, at half of their peak in 2007. Equity investment flows exhibit sluggishness....
>
> FDI flows to developing economies remained stable at an estimated US$695 billion. Latin America and the Caribbean saw an increase of 16%, with growth concentrated in South America. Africa continued to register a modest rise (+3%) while flows to developing Asia fell by 6%.
>
> FDI flows into developing Asia reached an estimated US$473 billion in 2019. The overall decline was driven mostly by a 21% drop in investment in East Asia. Investment to Hong Kong, China almost halved to US$55 billion as divestments continued through the year. Flows to the Republic of Korea also saw a decline of 46% to US$7.8 billion, attributed to trade tensions and investment policy changes. Inflows to China remained stable at US$140 billion.
>
> South-East Asia continued to be the region's growth engine; FDI rose to an estimated US $177 billion, a 19% increase from 2018. Singapore, the biggest FDI host country in the region, continued to grow in 2019—by 42% to US$110 billion, driven by deals in the information and communication sector. Investments into Indonesia rose 12% to US$24 billion with significant flows going into wholesale and retail trade (including the digital economy) and manufacturing.
>
> South Asia recorded a 10% increase in FDI to US$60 billion. The growth was driven by India, with a 16% increase in inflows to an estimated US$49 billion. The majority went into services industries, including information technology. Inflows into Bangladesh and Pakistan declined by 6% and 20%, respectively, to US$3.4 billion and US$1.9 billion.

...FDI to Latin America and the Caribbean increased by 16% in 2019, reaching an estimated US$170 billion. In South America, flows grew by 20% to an estimated US $119 billion, with decreases in Argentina and Ecuador offset by growing flows to Brazil, Chile, Peru and Colombia....

Flows to Central America grew by 4% to an estimated US$46 billion. FDI to Mexico increased by 3% to an estimated US$35 billion; the new trade agreement USMCA lifted expectations for easier economic relations....

In the Caribbean (excluding offshore financial centres), inflows grew by 49% to an estimated US$4.2 billion led by growing investments in the Dominican Republic where FDI reached an estimated US$2.7 billion and in Trinidad and Tobago where inflows turned positive to an estimated US$600 million.

FDI flows to Africa amounted to an estimated US$49 billion—an increase of 3%. Persistent global economic uncertainty and the slow pace of reforms seeking to address structural productivity bottlenecks in many economies continue to hamper investment in the continent. Egypt remained the largest FDI recipient in Africa with a 5% increase in inflows to US$8.5 billion....

FDI flows to East Africa remained steady totaling US$8.8 billion. Flows to Ethiopia, Africa's fastest growing economy, slowed down by a quarter to US$2.5 billion. China was the largest investor in Ethiopia in 2019, accounting for 60% of newly approved FDI projects. Inflows to Uganda increased by almost 50% to US$2 billion due to the continuation of the development of major oil fields and an international oil pipeline. Flows to West Africa increased by 17% to an estimated US$11 billion as investment surged in Nigeria by 71% to US$3.4 billion. FDI to the continent's largest economy was buoyed by resource seeking inflows in the oil and gas sector. (UNCTAD 2020, 2–5)

FDI Outflows

Before the food and financial crises of 2007–8, as opposed to the pandemic-driven crisis in 2020, OECD countries accounted for around 87 percent of global outflows, reaching US$1.9 trillion in 2007. By 2018, OECD country outflows had declined by US$585 billion, to 66 percent. In contrast, non-OECD country outflows more than tripled between 2005 and 2014, from US$125 billion to US$302 billion. OECD's "FDI in Figures" noted: "In the first half of 2019, major sources of FDI worldwide were Japan, the United States, Germany, the United Kingdom and China. The United States recorded negative outflows in Q1 2019 but returned to its position as the major source of FDI worldwide in Q2" (OECD 2019f, 3–4).

As with inflows, China stands out as a special case, accounting for just under 20 percent of all emerging market FDI outflows over the same period (OECD 2016). Investment by MNEs [multinational enterprises] from developing and transition economies continued to grow. Developing Asia became the world's largest region for investment. In 2014, MNEs from developing economies alone invested US$468 billion abroad, a 23 percent increase from the previous year. Their share in global FDI reached a record 35 percent, up from 13 percent in 2007. Among developing economies, MNEs from Asia increased their investment abroad, while outflows from LAC, and Africa fell. For the first time, MNEs from developing Asia became the world's largest investing group, accounting for almost one-third of the total. Outward investments by MNEs based in developing Asia increased by

29 percent to US$432 billion in 2014. Outward investments by MNEs in Africa decreased by 18 percent in 2014 to US$13 billion. South African MNEs invested in telecommunications, mining, and retail, while those from Nigeria focused largely on financial services. These two largest investors from Africa increased their investments abroad in 2014. Intra-African investments rose significantly during the year.

Despite the broader involvement of developing countries in global investment, capital flows have started to decelerate, and economic vulnerabilities seem to be growing (IMF 2015). As the inevitable tightening of quantitative easing programs in the advanced economies is expected to result in capital outflows from the emerging markets, it could likewise result in some turnaround in the rebalancing trend of FDI described here (OECD 2016).

There has been a marked drop in project financing, too. Similarly, even as FDI inflows to the emerging markets have been increasing, project financing has dropped by around 40 percent since 2009.[32] After reaching a record high of US$240 billion in 2009, this financing is expected to reach its lowest level since 2006 (US$142 billion). Over the past two years, the equity component of project finance has also declined by 80 percent. While the least developed countries account for a relatively small share of total developing country project finance (consistently less than 5 percent), these flows are especially important to them, given their small size (economically) and their considerable infrastructure needs. Yet, the decline in project financing has been particularly severe in these countries: after reaching a record high in 2008 (US$13 billion), it fell to US$2 billion in 2015, its lowest level in over a decade. Furthermore, much as in developing countries in general, the equity component of project financing for the least developed countries has fallen to insignificant levels, meaning that infrastructure projects in the least developed countries are now financed almost wholly via debt (OECD 2016).

Increased Role of Philanthropic Foundations

Philanthropy is often thought of as "the rich giving to the poor." Modern philanthropy emerged at the beginning of the 20th century in the United States when Rockefeller and Carnegie set up the first large American foundations. As early as the First World War, these foundations began to engage beyond national borders, indicating an interest and willingness to invest in social progress overseas, particularly in developing countries (OECD 2014).

Because foundations' strategic priorities and activities vary greatly—ranging from advocacy to implementing their own projects (OECD 2003)—it is difficult to formulate a global definition that encompasses their diverse natures. Yet, they can be broadly described as independent, nonprofit organizations with their own resources that work locally, regionally, and internationally to improve the lives of citizens. They fund and run activities in numerous areas, from youth empowerment and education to health and climate change (EFC n.d.). Philanthropists have fundamentally altered the role of external assistance and traditional international organizations, and, in many ways, they are influencing the global agenda, raising issues of accountability.

It was only in 2011, in the Busan Partnership agreement, that philanthropic foundations were recognized as significant contributors to development, although only from a financial

---

[32] Although there is no precise definition for what constitutes "project financing," usually this takes the form of investments in either infrastructure or extractive industries.

perspective: as providers of additional funding for development cooperation.[33] Today, foundations' broader role in global development efforts is increasingly acknowledged and valued. The report of the High Level Panel of Eminent Persons on the Post-2015 Agenda acknowledges that their role as central actors in development cooperation goes far beyond the financial (HLP 2013). This recognition was confirmed at the First High Level Meeting of the Global Partnership for Effective Development Co-operation (GPEDC), which acknowledged the "added value that philanthropic foundations bring to development co-operation" (GPEDC 2014). This is reflected in the decision of the Steering Committee of the Global Partnership to offer philanthropists full member seats, as of June 2014.[34] Philanthropists increasingly recognize the power of involving governments and other development stakeholders, such as the private sector, in partnerships to enable systemic change, ensure increased sustainability, and scale up their efforts (OECD 2016).

Although the philanthropic contribution to development is hard to quantify, available data suggest that it has nearly multiplied by 10 in less than a decade (OECD 2014). Outside of the notable exception of BMGF, it is difficult to track. Concerns about nutrition and the environment entail new sources of flows into agriculture: for example, through climate funds and nutrition programs.

BMGF is by far the most significant player among philanthropists, in global advocacy and financing of humanitarian and development causes, and the only philanthropist whose assistance is listed in the OECD DAC database. To date, BMGF committed more than US$2 billion to agricultural development efforts, primarily in SSA and SA (BMGF 2020). In 2018, of the total grants of US$5 billion made by BMGF, US$1.8 billion went to global development, and US$1.4 billion to global health—with over 60 percent of it to communicable or infectious diseases, US$646 million went to global growth and opportunity, US$501 million went to global policy and advocacy, and only US$493 million went to United States programs. Of the US$1.8 billion spent on global development, 6 percent was given nutritional improvement, and out of the US$646 million to global growth and opportunity, 61 percent was allocated for agricultural development, including large support to CGIAR and the Alliance for the Green Revolution in Africa (AGRA) (BMGF 2018). BMGF was the third largest provider in the health sector (including reproductive health) in 2014 (OECD 2017). Commitments to agriculture are smaller than for health, but nonetheless significant, given the Foundation's high profile and increasing influence in shaping international organizations and the aid architecture as a whole. From 2007 to 2014, AGRA gave 673 grants worth US$386 million to 16 countries with a mission to transform Africa's agriculture. Whereas BMGF has urged transparency and accountability of international organizations, it have not applied the same standards for its own philanthropy. Independent evaluation of AGRA is not available to the public.

With his US$40 billion endowment, Bill Gates has had a profound influence on global expenditures on health and will continue to do so in a variety of other areas. Besides managing Warren Buffet's philanthropic grants, Gates has been working on convincing 100

---

[33] The Busan Partnership agreement was the outcome of the Fourth High Level Forum on Aid Effectiveness held in Busan, Korea, in 2011 (OECD 2011). This new broad and inclusive partnership for development cooperation sets out four common principles: (1) ownership of development priorities by developing countries; (2) a focus on results; (3) inclusive development partnerships; and (4) transparency and accountability to each other.

[34] GPEDC was formed following the Fourth High Level Forum on Aid Effectiveness in Busan (OECD 2019g) to act as a forum for advice, shared accountability, and shared learning and experiences to support the implementation of the Busan Partnership agreement principles. See http://effectivecooperation.org.

other billionaires to make philanthropic contributions to eradicate poverty and hunger. It is hard to get a handle on the international activities and expenditures of philanthropists, many of whom act alone and learn by making their own mistakes, and, unlike BMGF, their expenditures are not included in the OECD database (Kotechi 2018).

If income and wealth inequalities continue to grow and if differential tax laws toward dividends from capital investments and (wage) income remain in place, as they are likely to do during the Trump administration in the United States, private philanthropy would become even more significant, relative to the traditional ODA of OECD countries, which will likely stagnate with slow growth in OECD countries. How much of the philanthropic assistance will go to agriculture, compared to other competing activities, will depend on the power of advocacy and potential for markets—for example, there is a huge market for children's vaccinations, drugs for AIDS, tuberculosis, malaria, Ebola, and increasingly, to contain NCDs. Philanthropists such as Bill Gates are creating a demand for drugs and vaccines by supporting research for their development and also by cofunding programs jointly with OECD donors to meet the needs of developing countries governments for the drugs and vaccines, once developed. Since the poor cannot afford to pay market prices, how sustainable these programs are will depend on the level of aid. Already there is evidence that the World Bank experts in the health sector have expressed their concern about the cost and the lack of sustainability of the Global Alliance for Vaccines and Immunizations (GAVI) program, even though the World Bank helped raise funds in its support. Since then, tensions between GAVI and the World Bank increased, and GAVI moved its headquarters to Geneva (IEG 2015). Yet, the influence of BMGF has increased through:

- significant amounts of funding in support of specific development issues pertaining to poverty, food and nutrition, women empowerment, and children's health;
- contributing investments in global and regional, as well as national public and private goods;
- fostering results orientation, measurement of impacts, promotion of "corporate score cards" and other private sector "business" models to the operations of international organizations;
- establishing partnerships that complement but also influence resource allocation of official donors in certain directions.

Some of these contributions have been positive. In other cases, such as the focus on the private sector business models for children's vaccines, attention has been diverted from the importance of public goods and the lack of sustainability of the model among poor households.

Decisions to increase and allocate development assistance, largely from official sources, still are vested in the hands of career professionals in countries giving aid. In our interviews, some felt that the recent philanthropists, unlike their earlier counterparts, may be favoring "feel-good" humanitarian assistance, which will have immediate, demonstrable impacts rather than supporting long-term assistance, which will help transform policies and institutions and create capacity in developing countries to address their own problems on a large scale, whether in the public or the private sector. (See Box 7.3 on changes in demands for and expectations from development assistance.)

Competition between multinationals of OECD countries and emerging countries will likely accelerate to capture growing markets for agricultural inputs, food, and health-related products in developing countries. The pharmaceutical industry in developing countries

---

Box 7.3 Changes in Demands and Expectations from "Aid"

- Linking aid to delivery of outputs (such as Cash for School Attendance, Carbon Sequestration, REDD [reducing emissions from deforestation and degradation] readiness—fundamentally changing the character of aid)
- Increasing focus on outcomes and impacts as a condition for receiving aid
- Shifting focus from aid effectiveness to development effectiveness
- Shifting from macro growth indicators to household outcomes and impacts, such as nutrition and child survival
- Shifting from MDGs to SDGs
- Scorecards for (1) countries, (2) international organizations, and (3) donors
- Conditional cash transfers

---

already plays a major role through partnerships, given their lower production costs of drugs, vaccines, and equipment such as bed nets. India's Serum Institute provides an example of such a public–private partnership through GAVI, WHO, and the Program for Appropriate Technology in Health (PATH). Serum institute's partnership with external actors is an important example of capacity-building of a developing country with private enterprise to produce vaccines of interest to the poor. Serum and other Indian pharmaceuticals do not yet have the resources to do fundamental research, but they are able to produce drugs once their patents have expired. The Chinese have shown tremendous inclination for reverse engineering of technology and have purchased Syngenta, one of the five big pharmaceutical companies. Gates is similarly training scores of Africans under AGRA, but the human capital deficit is so large, as we show in the case of national agricultural research systems (NARS) in Africa, that substantially larger and long-term investment is needed. Whether these small businesses can provide service without the dedication of the nationals and some initial subsidies and support is too early to tell. Both are likely to be more lasting contributions, particularly if BMGF also creates and supports centers of excellence, as did the Rockefeller and Ford Foundations did earlier. However, US and European producers are also vying for these same markets; for example, the United Kingdom and United States were both developing an Ebola vaccine, as they and others have raced to develop a COVID-19 vaccine.

Individual Initiatives

Celebrities, like Bono, are not billionaires but command considerable persuasive power to get the likes of Jesse Helms, former conservative US senator from North Carolina, to increase American aid for HIVAIDS to Africa. Working with individual leaders, even conservative leaders opposed to aid, and through his "One" campaign, Bono has addressed specific issues, such as eradication of hunger, HIV/AIDS, trafficking of girls, and other causes, and influenced ODA allocations of the US government. In 2000, Helms co-authored a bill authorizing US$600 million for international AIDS relief efforts and became a proponent of fighting the spread of AIDS, lending support to the efforts of African leaders such as President Yoweri Museveni of Uganda. Bono may also have dissuaded Helms from working to disband the United States Agency for International Development (USAID) and convinced European leaders, such as German Chancellor Angela Merkel and British prime ministers to continue supporting poverty reduction.

Think Tanks and Consulting Firms

Internationalization of Western think tanks, with active support from bilateral donors, is an important development since the early 2000. A variety of institutions in developed countries, such as the Brookings Institution, CGD, and McKinsey, have become major competitors of traditional multilateral organizations like the World Bank in diagnosis and advice, in such areas as the role of conditional cash transfers in safety nets, policies, and implementation of climate change programs. In food and agriculture, this development has greatly increased competition, as well as collaboration in research and policy analysis, between the think tanks and the World Bank. Like the World Bank and IMF, the think tanks have become major suppliers of policy advisors to developing countries. Developing countries appreciate these alternative sources of supply, which come without the loan obligations that often go with the World Bank's traditional analytical and advisory services.

The Impact of the Aid Effectiveness Agenda

In 2005, donor governments, a few recipient governments, and some INGOs, agreed to a set of principles for how to make aid better support development. These came to be known as the Paris Declaration on Aid Effectiveness (OECD 2008b). Five principles were agreed to—ownership, alignment, harmonization, managing for results, and mutual accountability. Global targets correspond to these principles, which are now a touchstone for effective recipient–donor relations in any setting. They provide a common agenda for both global and country dialogue on aid effectiveness and have inspired attempts to localize global commitments through country-based action. Measurable targets were outlined, and a deadline was set to meet them: 2010, supported by a series of surveys to monitor progress, administered by the recipient countries themselves.

So how have donors performed? The general consensus and the evaluation of the Paris Declaration suggest not very well, except for some aid untying and some better aid coordination. While the Declaration has been generally applauded for enshrining the Paris Principles in matters related to aid, there have been many criticisms. Among the criticisms are that the principles focused on bureaucratic processes, rather than on political decision-making in donor countries to change aid modalities, and they did not include new emerging country donors. Although some criticism suggested that the indicators that were difficult to measure and follow, they did form the basis for three successive surveys on monitoring the Paris Declaration, covering 34 partner countries with data from 60 donors, which the Multilateral Organisation Performance Assessment Network (MOPAN) used as a basis for their subsequent analyses.

The 2008 Accra Agenda for Action attempted to improve on the Paris Declaration (OECD 2008a, 2008b), and the 2011 Busan Declaration reinforced the principles of ownership of development priorities by developing countries, including a focus on results, inclusive development partnerships recognizing the different and complementary roles of all actors, and transparency and accountability (OECD 2011). However, these would hardly seem to be the principles that developing countries would demand, particularly, aid coordination, where there are pros and cons from the perspective of the recipient. The more it is done by the recipients, the more they have a sense of ownership, as aid coordinated around a well-defined strategy by a government can put a country in the driver's seat and can potentially reduce transaction costs.

The aid effectiveness agenda has also highlighted accountability mechanisms, but governments of many developing countries have mixed views about the civil society and media in their countries, despite legislation, such as India's "Right to Information Act of 2005," which has made a sea change in the way the civil society uses information to hold government accountable. External aid needs to support such legislative and regulatory reforms, working with the nationals of the countries, rather than the kind of governance agenda of looking into the procurement of their own projects, which the donors typically support. Such a narrow approach to governance and to safeguards has had very limited success, according to IEG's evaluation of the Bank's involvement in improving governance (IEG 2011b, 2014).

The importance of the aid effectiveness agenda, and particularly the principle of country ownership, is now widely acknowledged. The country ownership principle is reflected in virtually all donor initiatives to boost food security and support agriculture—including the five Rome Principles for Sustainable Global Food Security issued at the World Food Summit of November 2009 (FAO 2009). More broadly, it is a principle that has become intrinsic to the work of donor agencies and international financial institutions. It would be fair to note, however, that developing countries, including even the less developed, are less inclined to accept terms dictated by donors. In that sense, their self-assurance with respect to policy reforms and lessons learned has increased. Yet, donors' willingness to accommodate this capacity in their own aid modalities is less clear.

Aid Effectiveness and Transparency in Development Cooperation

The basic principles of transparency, accountability, and citizen engagement are now accepted as central to more effective development and are reflected in the current discussions on the Post-2015 Development Agenda and calls for a data revolution. As the development community looks to the future to define its goals over the coming years, it is important to reflect on progress to date, particularly on the commitments made and the lessons learned from delivering them.

Over the past decade, donors have repeatedly committed to improving aid effectiveness and transparency in development cooperation. At the second HLF in Paris in 2005, donors committed to "take far-reaching and monitorable actions and to reform the way we manage and deliver aid," including by improving predictability, ownership and integration, and reducing duplication and fragmentation (OECD 2008b). This was followed by pledges at the third HLF in Accra in 2008 to "make aid more transparent" and "to publicly disclose regular, detailed and timely information on volume, allocation and, when available, results of development expenditure to enable more accurate budget, accounting and audit by developing countries" (OECD 2008a). The IATI was also launched in Accra, providing a practical approach for publishing aid information in a comparable, open format. Further-more, one of the most significant and concrete commitments to come out of the fourth HLF, in Busan in 2011, was for donors to "implement a common, open standard for electronic publication of timely, comprehensive and forward-looking information on resources pro-vided through development cooperation operation," with endorsers undertaking to fully implement this common standard, including IATI, by December 2015 (OECD 2011). The international donor community needs to work together to provide a full picture of devel-opment flows. All donors should ensure the inclusion of transparency and open data as an integral part of the Post-2015 Agenda and share lessons learned from the development effectiveness agenda. While reporting has improved, it still remains poor. Indeed, donors are not practicing what they preach to developing countries and expect from multilateral organizations where the record of transparency is much higher, particularly IDA. The 2014 Aid Transparency Index report noted, "Much of the information available is scattered across websites and it is difficult to join the dots between the descriptive, financial and performance information related to individual activities, making the data difficult to use. This means that there is still a long way to go in obtaining a full picture of all development flows, without which development effectiveness and improved donor coordination will be difficult to achieve" (ATI 2014, 4).

At the first High Level Meeting of the GPEDC in Mexico in 2014, donors reaffirmed their past commitments to publish information to a common, open standard, incorporating the IATI, by the end of 2015 (GPEDC 2014).

Significant findings from the 2016 Index (ATI 2016) were as follows:

- The 2016 ATI results demonstrate that 10 donors (UNDP, MCC, UNICEF, DFID, Global Fund, World Bank–IDA, IDB, ADB, Sweden's Ministry for Foreign Affairs–International Development Cooperation Agency [MFA–Sida], and AfDB), which account for 25 percent of total aid, are included in the "very good" category. Each scores above 80 percent and is publishing "timely, comprehensive, and forward-looking" data in an open and comparable format, meeting the 2011 Busan commit-ment to aid transparency (OECD 2011). UNDP "tops the Index for the second time with an excellent score of 93.3%, the only organisation to score above 90% ... UNICEF enters the 'very good' category for the first time, jumping into third place" (ATI 2016, 1). "Since 2013, UNICEF has made the most progress, jumping from 'poor' to 'very good' in three years and performing well in each year" (ATI 2018, 10)
- "Information at the activity level on finances (such as budgets), on performance (such as results) and on documents (such as evaluations and contracts), which is important to both aid providers and recipient countries for planning purposes is not always published. For example, thirty providers do not get points for results, meaning either that the information is not published at all or that it is not published consistently" (ATI 2016, 8).
- "The provision of forward-looking budgets information is insufficient.... Over half of the organisations [out of 46] included in this Index do not publish forward-looking budgets in the IATI Standard, including a breakdown by countries...." (ATI 2016, 8).
- Multilaterals as a group continue to perform well, with 11 of the 18 placed in the "very good" or "good" categories, whereas bilaterals as a group, only 7 are in these categories. As a group, bilaterals continue to perform poorly; 9 out of 12 are placed in the "poor" or "very poor" categories (ATC 2016).

- As in 2016, international financial institutions (IFIs), as a subset of multilaterals, placed 4 (World Bank IDA, IDB, ADB, and AfDB) out of 10 in "very good," 2 (EIB and EBRD) out of 18 in "fair" and 2 (IMF and World Bank IFC) out of 7 in "poor" categories (ATC 2016).

According to the 2016 ATI Index: "Based on these findings, the report recommends that all publishers should recognise the right to information enshrined in the SDGs. Publishers should improve the quality and comprehensiveness of their data to provide a full picture of all development flows" (ATI 2016, 1).

The 2020 Aid Transparency Index report made these recommendations:

- Donors should share comprehensive data about the results and impact of their projects.
- Donors should publish project budget documents, project procurement information (contracts and tenders), and sub-national locations.
- Regional development banks should publish their private sector portfolios.
- DFIs should publish financial and performance data about their private sector portfolios.
- Donors remaining in the "fair" category should prioritise transparency—all donors need to pull their weight.
- Donors should engage directly with stakeholders in partner countries to raise awareness about the available data, build trust, and establish feedback loops for continuous improvement (ATI 2020, 5).

IDA Graduation and Likely Implications for Aid to Food and Agriculture

"IDA is one of the largest sources of assistance for the world's 76 poorest countries," 39 of which are in Africa. IDA is also "the single largest source of donor funds for basic services in these countries" (IDA 2020b). Among 59 IDA-only countries, 29 countries were in the low-income category, 26 countries in the lower middle-income category, and 4 countries in upper middle-income category but heavily indebted. An estimated 1.3 billion people lived in IDA-only countries in 2015. Of the 77 countries eligible to receive IDA resources in 2016, 59 were IDA-only, and 18 were blend countries (eligible to receive IDA and IBRD). In addition, India, the largest recipient of IDA since its establishment, is receiving transitional support since having graduated from IDA in 2014. Since 1960, IDA has provided US$328 billion to 112 countries. Annual commitments have increased steadily and averaged about US$19 billion over the last three years (2014, 2015 and 2016), with about 50 percent of that going to Africa. In fiscal year 2016 (which ended June 30, 2016), IDA commitments totaled US$16. billion (including IDA guarantees), of which 12 percent was provided on grant terms. New commitments in FY16 comprised 161 new operations. Unlike bilateral funding, which has grown in recent years, IDA is a transparent, non-politically driven, cost-effective platform for achieving results. The financial viability and future supply of IDA is of considerable importance to development assistance, including, particularly to ARD and economic transformation.

The World Bank has undergone several transitions of interest to transforming economies. One is the graduation of a number of LICs from being IDA recipients to IBRD countries, as their per capita GNI has been rising and they are reaching the threshold of US $1,215 in fiscal year 2016 (was initially set at US$250 in 1964—now known as the "historical cutoff"), below which they qualified for concessional assistance. So, there is the so-called "poor country"–"poor people debate" started by Kanbur and Sumner (2012), among others. As shown in Chapters 1 and 2, the bottom billion people, in terms of poverty, are mostly in MICs, and external analysts have raised a question as to whether countries with large incidence of poverty should be excluded from receiving concessional assistance, simply because they have crossed a predetermined income bar, or whether the lending criteria should be modified. They have pleaded for concessional assistance on three grounds: first, there are large pockets of poverty, even in the countries such as China and India where incomes have risen, and second, there are spillover effects of poverty, such as pandemics, food crises, and cross-border migration that need to be contained. Kanbur has shown that with low per capita incomes, countries such as India are unable to raise enough domestic resources to pay for the consequences of global public bads, such as climate change and disaster relief and preparedness. Kanbur and Summer (2012) estimated an increase in the marginal rates of taxation that would be needed in India. This is one important reason, they argued, developing countries with large incidence of poverty need greater access to development finance. They also noted that these countries need additional finance to undertake GPGs, that provision of GPGs should not come at the cost of development expenditures. Further, there is huge scope for knowledge transfers from MICs to LICs or subregions within countries, with the issue of knowledge transfers. Finally, there is a moral obligation in addressing poverty, and international assistance should play a role in that process. In the chapters on the World Bank and IFAD, we will discuss the extent to which we can demonstrate any impact of the World Bank–IDA and IFAD lending on food and nutrition security and agriculture, poverty reduction, and sustainability. We will explore why the 70-year-old project model, embraced by all "Banks"—since the World Bank has been a standard setter—is outmoded. And we explain why development banks need to drastically change their approach to poverty reduction if they wish to remain relevant, whether they are using IDA or IBRD as instruments of lending, an issue those writing on the IDA do not consider.

Increasingly, discussions about IDA include considerations of financing for adaptation to climate change, disaster preparedness, and disaster relief, all an outcome of global public bads (for example, disaster preparedness as a consequence of climate change). In addition to the direct impacts of climate change on crop losses, loss of coastal areas, increased risk and uncertainty, developing countries incur the cost of disaster preparedness. The poor are the most adversely affected. IDA17 financing already includes support for such activities, and going forward, there is an active debate on including criteria for IDA lending beyond the traditional GNI, to account for a broader set of criteria, such vulnerability to disasters or the multidimensional nature of poverty. This is the so-called "poor countries" vs. "poor people" (even within MICs) debate discussed earlier.

There is a fourth, related debate about the Bank's capital base, and whether there is enough headroom for the Bank to grow and lend money without a capital increase. Finally, there is the issue of the voting rights of the new emerging shareholders. As discussed in Chapter 6 on the governance of the five organizations, in the World Bank, shares were determined historically by their contributions to the share capital, and they have been adjusted too slowly since the Bank was established. Now emerging countries not only want to remain members of the World Bank, but would like to see the Bank changing from a "lender's bank" as one executive director described it, to a "borrower's bank," whereby emerging countries (1) increase their own share capital in the Bank; (2) get higher voting shares with greater voice in the Bank's governance; (3) benefit from the leveraging of the World Bank's subscribed capital by going to the market with a safe gearing ratio, as the World Bank already does; and (4) have access to international capital on IBRD terms. These changes potentially have implications for demand from the IDA-graduating developing countries, for borrowing for the "softer" sectors, including for agricultural and rural development. The past record of IBRD–IDA borrowing suggests that this demand will not be strong in IBRD countries. Changing from a lender's bank to a borrower's bank will also mean adjustment of the European shares in the Bank to make room for the greater share for emerging countries, something which Europeans are reluctant to do.

In the fourth IDA18 replenishment meetings (December 14–15, 2016, Indonesia), a coalition of more than 60 donor and borrower governments agreed to ratchet up the fight against extreme poverty with a record US$75 billion commitment for the IDA, the World Bank's fund for the poorest countries (World Bank 2016).

The World Bank also noted:

The IDA18 replenishment period, which runs from July 1, 2017 to June 30, 2020, is expected to support:

- Essential health and nutrition services for up to 400 million people
- Access to improved water sources for up to 45 million people
- Financial services for 4–6 million people
- Safe childbirth for up to 16–20 million women through provision of skilled health personnel
- Training for 9–10 million teachers to benefit 300+ million children
- Immunizations for 130–80 million children
- Better governance in 30 countries through improved statistical capacity
- An additional 5 GW of renewable energy generation capacity. (World Bank 2016)

The funds will also help governments strengthen institutions, mobilize resources needed to deliver services, and promote accountability.

A total of 48 countries pledged resources to IDA; additional countries are expected to pledge in the near-term. WBG is continuing the tradition of contributing its own resources to IDA.

Proposals for Alternative Uses of IDA "Savings" from Graduation of IDA Countries

There are several options for IDA savings:

1. Not to raise IDA funds as large as in the past, because countries have graduated—in essence, returning them to the treasuries of rich countries;
2. Allocate "savings" to remaining (mostly, fragile and conflict-affected) IDA countries who have limited absorptive capacity and less good performances;

3. Allocate funds to all countries with large poor populations (including now graduating countries), regardless of their incomes;
4. Use funds to produce GPGs, described in Box 7.1; and
5. Plough funds into IBRD to increase assistance to graduating emerging countries on IBRD terms.

The following discussion should be seen in the context of the list of GPGs in Box 7.1 and related evidence in the rest of this book. Whereas there was a general consensus in the literature in the late 1990s and early 2000s, when the GPGs literature began to explode, that financing of GPGs should come from "outside" ODA, Inge Kaul, among others, has been a strongest protagonist and an early advocate of this point of view, increasingly advancing arguments that development assistance should be used for such things as adaption to climate change, disaster relief, and disaster preparedness (Kaul, Grunberg, and Stern 1999).

At the same time, some have suggested that the World Bank should transform itself and partially or fully become a provider of GPGs (Birdsall and Subramanian 2007), and indeed, as we point out throughout this book, in several cases it is hard to distinguish between the traditional development assistance provided by the World Bank and the provision of GPGs, for example, in agricultural research—in avoiding pandemics, adaptation to climate change, or replacing coal-based energy with renewable sources of energy to reduce emissions. Donors have argued for a considerable time that there was no need for a separate adaptation fund, since adaptation is development and development aid can finance it.

In practice, both financing the provision of GPGs through development aid and turning development organizations into GPGs organizations has turned out to be challenging for both conceptual and practical reasons. Development "aid," including the case of the IBRD and IDA, is country assistance. Provision of GPGs, as reflected in Box 7.1 or in the 117 World Bank partnerships, discussed in Chapter 8, have had to account for a variety of cross-border GPGs features for which countries tend to be reluctant to borrow from the Bank. Increasingly, country assistance strategies, more recently called "country partnership strategies" (country programmable aid, or CPA) have emphasized country ownership, and IBRD allocations have been determined by countries' finance ministries. Furthermore, development-oriented staff tend not to be more equipped than their clients to provide the kind of inputs needed in the provision of GPGs, as highlighted in Box 7.1.

Many of the global programs supply GPGs for which there is no realistic alternative source. As we showed in Chapter 3, some of the major existing partnerships are not achieving strategic objectives, have weak governance, lack ownership of all stakeholders, and they have not shown impacts. They tend to be sustainable as long as donor support lasts, but without an assurance that they are the right mix for the highest priority activities in which international organizations should be engaged. IEG evaluations suggest, perhaps, they are not.

The partnerships are not funded adequately at the global level either to generate the global or the regional public goods, and in some cases, such as in the Global Agriculture and Food Security Program (GAFSP), they are generally complementing the existing mechanism that is working well in IDA, the governance structure of which is discussed in Chapter 8 on the World Bank. GAFSP carries out functions that IDA already performs, although it has different contributors, including BMGF. As an intergovernmental organization, IDA does not accept subscriptions from foundations. So, should one include NGOs, such as BMGF, as part of the future for IDA? Among all the discussions we noted on the future of IDA, we did not see any discussion of the role of philanthropists like BMGF in the future of IDA.

Poor Countries vs. Poor Populations in Aid Giving: Bretton Woods Institutions Face a Cap on Growth

WBG, including IDA and IFC, have been the largest sources of external assistance to developing countries by far, in support of food, agriculture, forestry, education, health, and social safety nets among other sectors. IFC has provided advice and invested in private sector projects, and its overall commitments to agriculture have increased considerably, particularly since 2012 (World Bank 2015a). Through their own policies, investments, and access to concessional IDA resources, low-income, "IDA-only" countries have typically tended to transform themselves from agricultural to industrial economies and "graduate" from low- to low-middle and middle-income countries. Once they have reached an income threshold and other allocation criteria, they lose their eligibility for IDA and qualify for IBRD loans.[35] Eventually, countries experiencing economic growth tend to become lenders to the World Bank, thereby helping to retain and enhance the status of World Bank as a truly international organization. China graduated in 1999. India, by far the largest borrower, graduated from IDA in 2014, after benefiting from the largest amount of concessional finance, knowledge, and expertise from the World Bank, albeit small in per capita terms, given its size.

In a paper on "The World Bank at 75," Morris and Gleave (2015) called IDA a remarkably effective fundraising model over many decades. Using triennial replenishments of the IDA, the Bank's arm provides grants and highly concessional loans to the world's poorest countries. The World Bank has also been a model on methods and tools, such as CPIA, to other multilateral banks.

As a result, the Bank is becoming increasingly more dependent on trust funds, a phenomenon well documented in various OED/IEG reviews (OED 2003, 2004; IEG 2011a, 2011c). Morris and Gleave (2015) argued, that in a highly changed world, the Bank's traditional shareholders and emerging countries will be encouraged to embrace alternatives. And, indeed, except for a handful of close US allies (the United Kingdom, Germany, France, and Japan), countries are already doing just that. They have joined the Asian Infrastructure Investment Bank (AIIB) and the BRICS' New Development Bank (NDB), despite resistance by the World Bank and the United States to the establishment of those institutions—although Bank President Jim Yong Kim offered his hand of cooperation to the AIIB in Singapore in 2015 (see Box 7.4). Certainly, developing countries have welcomed the establishment of AIIB and to a lesser extent the NDB with enthusiasm, as a possible new source of finance where it is much needed. The AIIB is also considering investment in agriculture.

---

[35] World Bank's Country Policy and Institutional Assessment (CPIA) is a tool that measures the extent to which a country's policy and institutional framework supports sustainable growth and poverty reduction, and consequently, the effective use of development assistance. The CPIA rates countries against a set of 16 criteria grouped in four clusters: (1) economic management; (2) structural policies; (3) policies for social inclusion and equity; and (4) public sector management and institutions, including Transparency, Accountability, and Corruption in the Public Sector. The World Bank's IDA Resource Allocation Index (IRAI) is based on the results of the annual CPIA exercise (World Bank 2011, 2019a).

Box 7.4 The BRICS New Development Bank and the Asian Infrastructure Development Bank

The leaders of Brazil, Russia, India, China, and South Africa met at the seventh annual BRICS Summit held on July 8–9, 2015, in the Russian city of Ufa. The theme of the summit was "BRICS Partnership: A Powerful Factor for Global Development." The members discussed two major initiatives that had been formalized at their previous meeting in Fortaleza, Brazil, in July 2014: the creation of the New Development Bank (NDB) and a Contingent Reserve Arrangement to compete with the IMF facility. The development bank, headquartered in Shanghai, was expected to be operational by the first quarter of 2016, with an initial capital base of US$50 billion to fund infrastructure and other development projects in BRICS and other developing economies. The Contingent Reserve Arrangement, a US$100 billion fund to help countries forestall short-term liquidity pressures, was operational in 2015.

The World Bank and ADB estimate that developing countries will need trillions of dollars in financing to develop infrastructure. The World Bank's assumption that private capital would flow to developing countries for this purpose has not occurred at the level expected. The United States opposed the establishment of the Asian Infrastructure Investment Bank (AIIB), however, on grounds that it will not meet environmental and fiduciary standards, will lend to sectors that the United States considers undesirable, such as investment in coal, and for other reasons. By not becoming a shareholder in the AIIB, the United States is seen to be losing influence in setting the rules of the new bank, and the US response is widely seen as petulant (*The Economist* 2015). That is one of several reasons why the Trans-Pacific Partnership (TPP) trade agreement was being watched with interest, but the Trump administration decided to drop support for it. In the meantime, the World Bank established a Global Infrastructure Facility of its own. The Development Committee Communiqué of the 2015 IMF World Bank Spring 2015 urged the Bank Group to enhance its support for sustainable infrastructure development and financing, creating an enabling environment to mobilize private long-term finance for commercially viable projects, and strengthening public and private partnerships, including through the Global Infrastructure Facility (Development Committee 2015).

The United States had initially also opposed the establishment of the BRICs bank. Informed critics wondered why it would oppose a BRICS bank, when there is AfDB, ADB, EBRD, EIB, and IDB, which work in close cooperation with IMF and the World Bank on the SDG agenda and its financing (Chhibber 2015). The impetus for the BRICS bank came from the slow action on the decision reached in 2010 to change voting rights in IMF to give more voice to developing countries.

China has not been reporting its aid to OECD-DAC, and therefore, the numbers are difficult to obtain, and come with much speculation. We were fortunate to find the numbers in a research paper by (2019), and they are presented here (see, also, Kitano and Miyabayashi 2020). Net foreign aid increased steadily to US$6.1 billion, followed by another increase in 2018 to US$6.4 billion (Figure 7.15), mainly due to the increase in grants and interest-free loans.

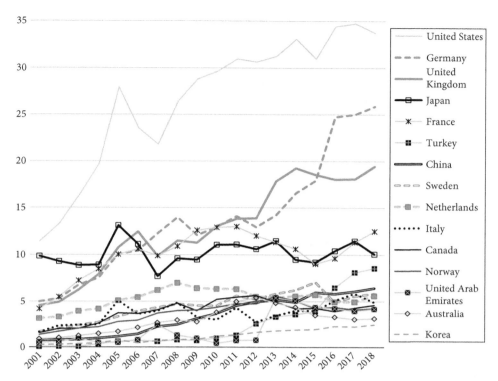

Figure 7.15 Net ODA disbursements from DAC and other countries and China's net disbursement of foreign aid, 2001–2018 (US$bn)
Source: Adapted from Kitano (2019, 15, fig. 6).

According to Kitano (2019, 2): "The grant equivalent system introduced by the DAC assesses the level of concessionality of concessional loans based on discount rates differentiated by income group (OECD 2019b). China's foreign aid on a grant equivalent basis was estimated at US$5.3 billion in 2017 and US$5.7 billion in 2018."

The World Bank noted, "China Development Bank's 'full participation' in the G-20 Africa's debt relief effort ... was important to make the initiative work, especially since it has played *such an important role in providing development assistance to Africa* [emphasis added]" (Brautigam 2020).

In her article, "China, the World Bank, and African Debt: A War of Words," Deborah Brautigam (2020) further notes:

> With the important exception of Angola, however, CDB [China Development Bank] is *not* a significant lender in the group of African countries that are participating in the DSSI [Debt Service Suspension Initiative]....China's two largest overseas lenders are China Export Import Bank (Exim Bank) and China Development Bank...China Exim Bank has provided close to 75 percent of all Chinese loan commitments in the DSSI-eligible African countries.

As a Southern country, China has had a policy of not interfering in the domestic policies of countries and not tying its aid to conditionality. A comparative assessment of the impacts of

Chinese involvement in SSA and Latin America is summarized in Table 7.3. China largely buys raw materials and exports manufactured goods to Africa and Latin America, but Chinese goods have been much more a threat to the domestic industry in Latin America, which is more industrialized, than in SSA, with the exception being South Africa, the most industrialized country in SSA. So, the premature deindustrialization has been more a real adverse impact on Latin America than in SSA. There has been a less favorable view of Chinese imports among South American policymakers, some of which have led to WTO's disputes, and some have led to WTO decisions in favor of Latin America. It suggests that, by and large, the international rule of law has been working.

Table 7.3 Summary of China's major impacts on sub-Saharan Africa and on Latin America and the Caribbean

	Sub-Saharan Africa	Latin America and the Caribbean
Economic impacts		
Growth of commodity exports	Benefiting fuel and mineral exporters	Benefiting fuel, mineral, and temperate agricultural exporters
Competition in export markets	Limited to a few garment-exporting countries	Particularly affected are Mexico, CAFTA–DR,[a] and more industrialized South American countries
Competition from imports from China	Mainly displacing imports from other countries	Significant impacts on some industries in more industrialized countries
Infrastructure	Significant boost	Limited up to 2015 but may increase in future
Social impacts		
Employment	Some job creation by Chinese companies but concerns exist over use of Chinese workers	Job losses in manufacturing as a result of Chinese competition; limited employment creation from exports
Wages and working conditions	Weak trade unions and enforcement of labor rights by government permitting low wages and poor conditions	Stronger trade unions and regulation in the more industrialized countries, providing more protection for workers
Local communities	Little effective opposition to effects of extractive industries and dams	Conflicts where civil society is mobilized on extractive issues
Political impacts		
"One China policy"	Accepted by all but one country	Nine countries still recognize Taiwan
Type of regime	No evidence that China has promoted corruption or authoritarianism	No evidence that China has promoted anti-US regimes
Policy space	Increased resources not necessarily used to promote development	Increased policy space for progressive governments to pursue alternative economic strategies
Environmental impacts		
Environmental degradation	Weak environmental regulation allowing firms to cause substantial degradation	Mobilization around environmental issues to counter worst aspects
Wind and solar power	China playing a significant role	Up to now, limited involvement apart from in Chile

[a] Dominican Republic–Central America Free Trade Agreement.

India's aid to SSA has been smaller than China's and, in general, India has aided Africa more on the basis of Africa's need, although more recently India, too, has begun to look at its domestic economic interest in aiding Africa (Agarwal and Kumar 2020).

Shared Governance Integrally Related to Legitimacy and Finance

Governance and finance of the Big Five organizations are closely related. The capital increase of the World Bank in 2010 was accompanied by change in the voting power. The US$86.2 billion for IBRD and US$200 million increase in capital for IFC were accompanied by increased voting power for developing and transition countries. In IBRD the power of those countries increased by 3.13 percentage points, bringing them to 47.19 percent; in IFC the increase in voting power was increased to 39.48 percent. This was accompanied by an agreement to review IBRD and IFC shareholdings every five years and a commitment to equitable voting power between developed countries and developing and transition countries over time. WBG President Robert B. Zoellick stated, "The change in voting-power helps reflect better the realities of a new multi-polar global economy where in which developing countries are now key global players" (World Bank 2010).

How Is Financing Affecting the Transformation Underway in the Other Four Institutions?

Since 2007's Independent External Evaluation, FAO has undergone a major reorganization and restructuring of its strategic framework after years of stagnation and decline. WFP has been transformed from being a food aid agency to a food assistance agency, aiming to help countries by merging short-term emergency and longer term development assistance—and giving food assistance beneficiaries a voice, particularly with the use of cash-based transfers (CBTs), in choosing what food they receive and how it is received. CGIAR has undergone a major revamping since 2008 and began yet another change in its governance in 2015 and in 2019. IFAD, among other reforms, has embarked on borrowing from sovereign governments to increase its capital base.

Financing for the development of both physical and human capital are critical for transformation and for linking small farmers to international markets. The strategies needed to develop each tend, of course, to be quite different. Some have argued that building human capital is more difficult than building physical infrastructure, since the latter typically entails design of the infrastructure and large-scale contracts based on procurement of contracting services and equipment. Yet, often issues of land acquisition, entailing safeguards, tend to be intensively complex and often controversial in land-short countries. Although we discuss issues in terms of financing and volumes, it is clearly insufficient. Human capital is about developing capacities. It requires opening opportunities, mentoring, training, and building links with other actors in the relevant networks and markets. We discuss these issues in Chapter 9 on developing human capital for research and development in Africa and SA. While physical capital may remain intact, human capital faces the risk of obsolescence and needs to be upgraded continuously, or it deteriorates rapidly if not used. Trade literature acknowledges that there is more to expanding trade than tariff and non-tariff barriers and trade liberalization (World Bank 2015b). For example, it costs US

$14,000 to move cargo 2 km on a river in the Democratic Republic of Congo, compared to US$1,000 to move cargo for well over 250 km in the port of Kuala Lumpur. Investments needed to improve domestic infrastructure and institutions to reduce internal costs of doing business tend to run into trillions (Copley 2015).

New and Innovative Sources of Financing beyond Official Development Assistance

It is clear from the preceding discussion that developing countries' financial needs to transform their economies are large. The sources of financing have grown and diversified and the relative role of the World Bank has shrunk, and yet, the current sources of funding are not sufficient to meet the needs. This was the conclusion even before the COVID-19 crisis, and now with COVID-19, financial needs have increased substantially.

The United Nations Department of Economic and Social Affairs noted:

> The need for additional and more predictable development financing has led to a search for alternative, innovative sources. The Monterrey Consensus [2002] recognized "the value of exploring innovative sources of finance provided that those sources do not unduly burden developing countries," and encouraged "exploring innovative mechanisms to comprehensively address debt problems of developing countries, including middle-income countries and countries with economies in transition." (UN 2012)

The need for financing GPGs to contain climate change, cross-border pests and diseases, financial contagion and trade rules have been repeatedly made by economists and documented throughout this book. ODA, currently the primary source of financing for GPGs at the country level, remains very limited. With competing demands, it becomes a zero-sum game. What is funded internationally comes at the cost of what, therefore, cannot be funded in support of developmental or humanitarian needs. Furthermore, it forces us to ask whether all possible sources of financing GPGs are currently being exploited. As Tobin, Stiglitz, Sachs, Collier, and many others have argued, there are different ways of raising additional resources while avoiding public bads and promoting public goods. Possibilities include: (1) auctioning permits to exploit already overexploited ocean fisheries; (2) increasing IMF's Special Drawing Rights and using them to finance high priority national and GPGs; (3) imposing airline or financial transaction taxes, as Europeans are doing by taxing their airlines in the case of UNIT AID; (4) replacing fossil fuel subsidies with carbon taxes; or (5) taxing international arms trade, among others. The Climate Finance Study Group (CFSG) of G20, among others, have developed alternatives for financing climate-related GPGs outside of ODA (CFSG 2014), but that process seems to be fraught with difficulties. Several G20 members from developing countries have emphasized that, given the United Nations Framework Convention on Climate Change (UNFCCC) principles and provisions, public finance from developed countries to developing countries should be a key issue considered in the analysis. Other members (not identified in the report) "noted that the G20 had no legitimacy to intervene in UNFCCC discussions and thus cannot provide guidance over commitments taken in such fora" (CFSG 2014). These alternatives for financing GPGs have yet to attract attention in the places, such as the G20, where they might be taken further.

Private Sector Financing, Public–Private Partnerships, and Cross-Border Trade

FAO is often considered a "producer" of national agricultural statistics and often blamed for not undertaking quality assurance of these data and, therefore, for the poor quality of these statistics (CGD 2015). Developing countries are responsible for generating food and agriculture statistics at the national level. FAO assembles and reports the data it receives from countries, devising comparable concepts and definitions, which allows for global reporting and monitoring. International organizations use that information for global monitoring, including for international discussions or agreements, or for helping to address short- and long-term issues of food and financial crisis, food security-related resolutions, and climate agreements. They typically provide guidelines on standards and norms, quality assurance, timeliness, and international comparability. Their legitimacy needs to be combined with the quality and accuracy of their reporting.

Data need to be collected at the national government level and used for policymaking. In a study of early warning after the 2007–8 food crisis, Babu (2014) explored the policy-making processes followed in developing responses to the food price crisis to draw lessons for improving and strengthening these processes for the future. He developed a combined framework that could be applied to food policymaking in developing countries across countries, using empirical analysis of processes in selected countries. A key lesson is that: "by strengthening the role of various players and actors, and empowering them by increasing their capacity for research, analysis, communication, and advocacy, their capacity in food policy-making processes can be enhanced (Babu 2014, 97). Their participation depends, however, on the nature of the political institutions in the country. "A broader insight from the review of the policy processes is that not one theory alone can fully explain the food policy-making process" (Babu 2014, 97). Policy processes are affected by political, socioeconomic, and cultural contexts of the countries. Babu concluded: "Understanding the nature and magnitude of these factors will help in devising strategies that could help development partners and policy makers to guide the development of open, transparent, and effective policy processes that can result in better policies" (Babu 2014, 97). For example, India not only had data and machinery in place for information gathering but also a policymaking process, which was active (personal conversations with B. Ramaswami, June 23, 2017). Bangladesh turned to India to learn lessons. Several African countries including Malawi, Angola, and Mozambique not only lacked data but also the internal processes. The gap in estimates between satellite data and on-the-ground estimates need to be closed by bringing the best of science and technology to developing countries.

Financing to Support Global Public Goods

There is now considerably greater global consensus on:... the role of international public goods in determining the well-being of the poor.... Whether couched in terms of cross-border spillovers of environmental externalities or financial instability; or in terms of the central role of basic research into tropical agriculture and tropical diseases, the recognition was clearly abroad that public intervention is needed in these areas. The emerging importance of this issue was instinctively grasped by most. It may well be that this happy state of affairs is due precisely to the fact that this is a relatively new issue in the policy arena, that once we get into the details, divisions will grow. (Kanbur 2005, 16)

The provision of GPGs requires cooperative action by all parties. Information, laws, rules, institutions, and incentives are needed at appropriate levels to form policies and plans and to ensure their sustainable use in pursuit of food security and nutrition. This requires responsible stewardship of public goods management.

Future Sources of Financing

Next, we explore some recent efforts at mobilizing financing.

International Monetary Fund and World Bank Estimates: From Billions to Trillions

The IMF–World Bank report on overall financing (Development Committee 2015) was a major effort to identify financing needs for SDGs, although it does not include sectoral breakdowns. It argues that public investment is important because the most substantial development spending happens at the national level and below, in the form of public resources. To achieve the transformative vision of the SDGs, the report contends, requires achieving the trajectory from billions to trillions, which, each country and the global community must support together to finance. The "From Billions to Trillions" report is also a way to deflect from the 0.7 percent target. It "is shorthand for the realization that achieving the SDGs will require more than money. It needs a global change of mindsets, approaches and accountabilities to reflect and transform the new reality of a developing world with highly varied country contexts" (Development Committee 2015, 1). The role of IMF and the World Bank in mobilizing these trillions is seen as helping developing countries to improve their own resource mobilization strategies. The largest potential for further investment, argues the report, is from private sector business, finance, and investment. Kharas and McArthur (2019) have since criticized this global approach, arguing that more disaggregated country-by-country estimates are needed, and LICs most in need of finances receive the least.

The European Parliament Committee's Report Seems More Realistic on Its Assessment on Financing

The European Parliament's Committee on Development report on "Financing for Development Post-2015: Improving the Contribution of Private Finance" (European Parliament 2014) noted that while government spending is not sufficient, it is the largest domestic resource in most developing countries and is growing rapidly; but in per capita terms, it is very little. More than three billion people live in countries where government spending is extremely low—less than purchasing power parity (PPP) US$1,000 per person each year.

The European Parliament report is also skeptical of private sector resource flows, particularly to LICs:

> Most [outflows of private financial resources] are not productive investments. . . . but repayments on loans (over USD 500 billion in 2011), repatriated profits on foreign direct investment (FDI) (USD 420 billion) or illicit financial flows (USD 620 billion).

...FDI is the largest resource flowing to developing countries, but outflows of profits made on FDI were equivalent to almost 90 % of new FDI in 2011.

...By contrast, 70 % of FDI in developing countries in 2011 went to just 10 countries, with China alone accounting for over a quarter of total FDI. (European Parliament 2014, 4)

Hence, the European Parliament report argues that ODA is the largest flow to least developed countries and those with the lowest levels of domestic resources. Both donor aid and governments have been fickle in their investments in agriculture, much like the private sector, slowing their investments in agriculture when real food prices showed a steady decline, which encouraged complacency. Large and small aid-dependent countries have behaved differently, but most have spent more resources on not-so-smart subsidies, rather than on productive investments. The European Parliament report argued that aid should be targeted at the poorest countries, where private investment flows are weak to nonexistent, and that without public investment in education, health and infrastructure, regulatory systems "for profit" sector will not thrive (European Parliament 2014).

Promotion of the use of public resources to leverage private finance suggests a belief that the two are interchangeable, but, in reality, they are complementary. Similarly, the AGRA Status Report 2016 acknowledges limited success in getting the private sector to invest more in SSA, in the absence of public investment by the countries themselves (AGRA 2015). Bill and Melinda Gates and Warren Buffet increasingly stress the importance of the governments scaling up their pilot efforts.

Will China Be the Main Financier of Future Global Development?

The World Bank study *Capital for the Future* noted that deficits in the balance of payments in India and SSA, will be financed, not by the North, but by the newly industrialized East Asian countries, most notably China (World Bank 2013a). China and the oil-exporting Middle Eastern countries have already been financing investments in developed countries. The household-level evidence they gather suggests that the poor save little, and these two continents will need to pursue policies that will substantially increase investments in their own countries and attract inflow from East Asia (Babu et al. 2015). By 2030, developing countries' share in global saving and investments will have increased from 20 percent to 50 percent, and developing countries will account for two-thirds of every dollar saved and 50 percent of the capital stock, compared to the 30 percent today (Bussolo, Lim, and Maliszewska 2013). This emergence of developing countries in savings and investments is a result of productivity catch-up, integration into global markets, and better macroeconomic policies. COVID-19 has changed this situation as China's economic growth declined substantially, for the first time realizing negative growth rate in 2020, but China's economy has also been one of the first to recover from COVID-19-related recession.

Policy Issues Going Forward

Remittances, as we documented earlier, have amounted to about US$500 billion worth of flows to developing countries, but have declined by 20 percent since the COVID-19 pandemic in 2020.[36] Dilip Ratha, Manager of Migration and Remittances Team at the Bank's Development Prospects Group argued that in the context of SDGs, "Continued efforts are required to lower the cost of sending money through official channels, although inroads are being made.... The closure of bank accounts of money transfer operators serving Somalia and other fragile countries is also worrying,... 'particularly exorbitant fees paid by low-skilled workers to recruitment agents to secure jobs overseas'" (World Bank 2014c). Concerns over money laundering are keeping costs high by increasing compliance costs for commercial banks and money transfer operators, and delaying the entry of new players and the use of mobile technology. Thus, the World Bank and IMF are focusing on increasing transparency, inclusion of migrants in the financial system, increased use of core principles in financial transfers, and reducing the cost of transfers to the poor migrants given the regulatory obstacles at the receiving end. Global deliberations on financing the implementation of post-2015 development goals, migration, and remittances can be leveraged to raise development financing via reducing remittance costs, lowering recruitment costs for low-skilled migrant workers, and mobilizing diaspora savings and diaspora philanthropic contributions. Remittances can also be used as collateral, through future-flow securitization, to facilitate international borrowings with possibly lower costs and longer maturities. And they can facilitate access to international capital markets by improving sovereign ratings and debt sustainability of recipient countries. To improve transparency in immigration policies, Bhagwati (2003) proposed a World Migration Organization that would codify immigration policies and spread best practices. Rodrick (2001) proposed "multilateralizing" immigration rules so that two countries participating in a special arrangement to share workers would not generate adverse spillover effects on other countries.

WFP and other humanitarian organizations are exploring how they might link with the migrants' remittances, benefiting from strong connections with families in countries needing help. They can help in starting small enterprises or supporting existing enterprises with know-how.

Recognizing the close links between migration and development, WBG is deepening its engagement on the issue. Central to its involvement is its leading role in establishing and advancing the KNOMAD program, which is envisaged as a hub of knowledge and policy expertise on migration. KNOMAD's work program is undertaken through 12 thematic working groups: data; skilled labor; low-skilled labor; integration issues in host communities; policy and institutional coherence; security; migrant rights and social aspects of migration; demography; remittances; diaspora resources; environmental change; and internal migration. It also covers four crosscutting themes: gender, monitoring and evaluation, capacity-building, and public perceptions.

From Inputs to Outcomes and from Dependency to Increased Accountability

There is considerable consensus on the principles of macroeconomic management. Controversies surrounding the Washington Consensus in the era of structural adjustment have given way to the need for better macroeconomic policies, open trade, and more receptivity

---

[36] See https://www.worldbank.org/en/topic/labormarkets/brief/migration-and-remittances

to foreign investment in developing countries. Donors generally accept the need for better outcomes for the poor. IMF and the donors support and actively promote the use of safety nets, particularly in SSA. The World Bank reports a sharp growth in social protection programs throughout the developing world (IEG 2013c). The largest such programs are in MICs, funded largely from the countries' own resources. The growth is largest in SSA, and most of it is funded by donors. Although attention to health and education has increased since the HIPC initiative, agriculture has been neglected.

More generally rapid growth in large developing countries, such as China, India, and Brazil has come to be seen by developing countries as offering a range of development models, perhaps more than the former East Asian miracles. The growth in large countries has increased markets for Africa's primary commodities, raising their export earnings, and increased and diversified the sources of aid to Africa. A departure from the dependency syndrome and the "default" position of resistance to the traditional "northern" prescriptions emanating from the Bretton Woods institutions, have given way to fresh thinking. An important question is whether the increased domestic resources in SA and SSA are also leading to better and more stable domestic policies toward their food and agricultural sectors and to rural development, generally, for which there have not been the kind of powerful champions as there have been for health and education.

Reflecting this new reality of a globalized multipolar world, the inclusion of SDGs for both developing as well as developed countries is necessary in order to get better and fairer agreements in the areas of international agricultural trade and aid, norms and standards, climate change, international capital movements, conflict and emergencies, as well as more broadly shared international rules, standards, and norms in which emerging countries have a larger role.

The dramatically changed external environment means developing countries and international institutions have to manage multiple sources of information, knowledge, capital, and competition.

OECD official financial resources need to increase significantly, unless alternative solutions are embraced. Developing countries will be largely on their own, facing an increasingly complex set of challenges. Currently, though, many countries lack the capacity to respond so as to maximize these opportunities. They can learn from the examples of successful developing countries.

The future role and relevance of the Big Five international institutions has been premised on their strong legitimacy, in turn through their post-Second World War founding principles of a liberal, globalist world order, which have determined their missions and mandates, governance, and financing—and made the organizations themselves international and increasingly evolving towards the provision of GPGs. Those in turn have influenced their evolving practices and the choices each of them face going forward. With much more autarkic, inward looking views of the world among the emerging governments in the United States, the United Kingdom, and Western Europe, the future missions and financing defined decades ago, and modified only at the margins, is increasingly unclear.

The Big Five will still be needed and be of future relevance and value for providing policy analytics and advice, which smaller think tanks, philanthropists, and bilateral governments cannot do. How their key member countries come together to respond to the institution specifically and the overall options and how they work together will determine their individual and collective contributions.

In the chapters that follow, we explain the architecture of the Big Five international organizations, starting with their founding principles, which have determined their membership, finance, models of shareholder or stakeholder governance. We examine how these features have led to each organization's operating principles, choice of leadership, the standards by which they operate, their access to international finance and human capital, and their flexibility to manage complexity in the context of the rapidity of technical change and the emergence of developing countries.

A large majority of the poverty and food insecurity is now found in MICs (albeit lower-middle income), with the rest in weak fragile states. The numbers of fragile states has grown at an unexpected speed from just a decade ago, each with its own internal dynamics. In neither stable emerging countries nor conflicted countries do donors and external actors wield the kind of influence they once exercised and that led, for example, to the generation of the Green Revolution.

In the next chapters, we illustrate the roles of the Big Five "traditional" international organizations with the current global context. Dramatic changes in the global aid environment since the five organizations were established have led to several new models of development assistance since the mid-1990s. A spate of new global and regional partnerships are competing with the traditional international organizations, resulting in their own partnerships being overextended as they seek to be relevant the context of the changing environment, to be more effective, but also to "capture" more resources as aid budgets tighten.

References

Adams, Richard H., Jr. 2006. "Remittances and Poverty in Ghana." Research Working Paper 3838, World Bank, Washington, DC.

Adams, Richard H., Jr., and John Page. 2005. "Do Internal Migration and Remittances Reduce Poverty in Developing Countries?" *World Development* 33 (10): 1645–69.

Agarwal, Manmohan. 2015. "South–South Economic Cooperation: Its Progress." In *World Scientific Reference on Asia and the World Economy*, Vol. 1. *Sustainability of Growth: The Role of Economic, Technological and Environmental Factors*, edited by John Whalley, Manmohan Agarwal, and Jiahua Pan, 81–108. Singapore: World Scientific Publishing.

Agarwal, Manmohan, and Sushil Kumar. 2020. "Development Assistance from India: An Econometric Analysis." Research and Information System for Developing Countries (RIS), New Delhi, India.

AGRA (Alliance for a Green Revolution in Africa). 2015. *Africa Agriculture Status Report 2016: Youth in Agriculture in sub-Saharan Africa.* Nairobi: AGRA.

Ahluwalia, Montek Singh, Lawrence Summers, Andrés Velasco (co-chairs); Nancy Birdsall, and Scott Morris (co-directors). 2016. "Multilateral Development Banking for this Century's Development Challenges: Five Recommendations to Shareholders of the Old and New Multilateral Development Banks." Center for Global Development, Washington, DC.

Akber, Nusrat, and Kirtti Ranjan Paltasingh. 2019. "Is Public Investment Complementary to Private Investment in Indian Agriculture? Evidence from NARDL Approach." *Agricultural Economics* 50 (5): 643–55.

Alesina, Alberto, and David Dollar. 2000. "Who Gives Foreign Aid to Whom and Why?" *Journal of Economic Growth* 5 (1): 33–63.

Anderson, Edward. 2008. "Practices and Implications of Aid Allocation." Background study for the 2008 Development Cooperation Forum, UN Economic and Social Council (ECOSOC). https://www.un.org/en/ecosoc/newfunct/pdf/revised%20draft(anderson).pdf

Andreopoulos, George, Giuliana Campanelli Andreopoulos, and Alexandros Panayides. 2011. "Multilateral vs Bilateral Aid: Addressing Some Puzzles." *European Journal of Management* 11 (4): 73–8.

ATI (Aid Transparency Index). 2014. "2014 Report: Aid Transparency Index 2014." Publish What You Fund, London. https://www.publishwhatyoufund.org/wp-content/uploads/2016/12/2014-Aid-Transparency-Index.pdf

ATI (Aid Transparency Index). 2016. "2016 Report: Aid Transparency Index 2016." Publish What You Fund, London. https://www.publishwhatyoufund.org/wp-content/uploads/2016/12/2016-Aid-Transparency-Index.pdf

ATI (Aid Transparency Index). 2018. "Aid Transparency Index 2018." Publish What You Fund, London. https://www.publishwhatyoufund.org/reports/2018-Aid-Transparency-Index.pdf

ATI (Aid Transparency Index). 2020. "Aid Transparency Index 2020." Publish What You Fund, London. https://reliefweb.int/sites/reliefweb.int/files/resources/PWYF_AidTransparency2020_Digital.pdf

Babu, Suresh Chandra. 2014. "Policy Processes and Food Price Crises: A Framework for Analysis and Lessons from Country Studies." In *Food Price Policy in an Era of Market Instability: A Political Economy Analysis*, edited by Per Pinstrup-Andersen, 76–101. Oxford: Oxford University Press.

Babu, Suresh Chandra, Jikun Huang, P. Venkatesh, and Yumei Zhang. 2015. "A Comparative Analysis of Agricultural Research and Extension Reforms in China and India." *China Agricultural Economic Review* 7 (4): 541–72.

Barajas, Adolfo, Ralph Chami, Connel Fullenkamp, Michael T. Gapen, and Peter Montiel. 2009. "Do Workers' Remittances Promote Economic Growth?" IMF Working Paper No. 09/153, International Monetary Fund, Washington, DC.

Barder, Owen, and Matt Juden. 2016. "Aid Isn't Reaching the Very Poorest Countries." Views from the Center blog, Center for Global Development (CGD), London. http://www.cgdev.org/blog/aid-isnt-reaching-very-poorest-countries

Barrett, Christopher B., and Daniel G. Maxwell. 2005. *Food Aid After Fifty Years: Recasting Its Role.* London: Routledge.

Bermeo, Sarah Blodgett. 2017. "Aid Allocation and Targeted Development in an Increasingly Connected World." *International Organization* 71 (4): 735–66.

Bezanson, Keith A., and Paul Isenman. 2012. "Governance of New Global Partnerships: Challenges, Weaknesses, and Lessons." CGD Policy Paper 014, Center for Global Development, Washington, DC. https://www.cgdev.org/publication/governance-new-global-partnerships-challenges-weaknesses-and-lessons

Bhagwati, Jagdish. 2003. "Borders Beyond Control." *Foreign Affairs* 82 (1): 98–104.

Birdsall, Nancy, and Homi Kharas, with Ayad Mahgoub and Rita Perakis. 2010. "Quality of Official Development Assistance Assessment." QuODA Report, Brookings Institution and Center for Global Development (CGD), Washington, DC.

Birdsall, Nancy, and Arvind Subramanian. 2007. "From World Bank to World Development Cooperative." Center for Global Development Essay, CGD, London.

BMGF (Bill and Melinda Gates Foundation). 2018. "Annual Report 2018." https://www.gatesfoundation.org/Who-We-Are/Resources-and-Media/Annual-Reports/Annual-Report-2018

BMGF (Bill and Melinda Gates Foundation). 2020. "Agricultural Development." Strategy Overview. What We Do. https://www.gatesfoundation.org/what-we-do/global-growth-and-opportunity/agricultural-development

Brautigam, Deborah. 2020. "China, the World Bank, and African Debt: A War of Words." Pacific Money, *The Diplomat*, August 17. https://thediplomat.com/2020/08/china-the-world-bank-and-african-debt-a-war-of-words/

Bussalo, Maurizio, Jamus Jerome Lim, and Maryla Maliszewska. 2013. "Structural Transformations and the Future of Saving and Investment." Technical background paper, World Bank, Washington, DC. http://siteresources.worldbank.org/EXTDECPROSPECTS/Resources/476882-1,368,197,310,537/PRWPsub2.pdf

Carlson, Colin J. 2020. "From PREDICT to Prevention, One Pandemic Later." Comment, May 1. *Lancet Microbe* 1 (1): E6–7. https://www.thelancet.com/journals/lancet/article/PIIS2666-5247(20)30002-1/fulltext

CFSG (Climate Finance Study Group). 2014. "G20 Climate Finance Study Group Report to the Finance Ministers." September. http://www.g20australia.org/sites/default/files/g20_resources/library/g20_climate_finance_study_group.pdf

CGD (Center for Global Development). 2015. "Time for the FAO to Shift to a Higher Gear." A Report of the CGD Working Group on Food Security (originally published October 2013 and updated January 2015), CGD, Washington, DC. https://www.cgdev.org/publication/time-fao-shift-higher-gear

CGIAR. 2019. "CGIAR Financial Report for Year 2018." CGIAR System Organization, Montpellier, France. https://cgspace.cgiar.org/bitstream/handle/10568/105573/CGIAR-Financial-Report-2018.pdf

Chhibber, Ajay. 2015. "New World Bank Order: China's Asian Infrastructure Investment Bank Extends Its Regional and Global Strategy." *Indian Express*, April 3. http://indianexpress.com/article/opinion/columns/new-world-bank-order/

Clarke, Renata. 2010. "Private Food Safety Standards: Their Role in Food Safety Regulation and Their Impact." Presentation and discussion, 33rd Session of the Codex Alimentarius Commission, July 5–9, Geneva. http://www.fao.org/3/ap236e/ap236e.pdf

Clemens, Michael A. 2014. "Remittances Are Blowing Up, but Economic Growth Isn't. What Gives?" Center for Global Development, Views from the Center blog, June 4. https://www.cgdev.org/blog/remittances-are-blowing-economic-growth-isnt-what-gives

Clemens, Michael A., and Michael Kremer. 2016. "The New Role for the World Bank." *Journal of Economic Perspectives* 30 (1): 53–76.

Clemens, Michael A., and David J. McKenzie. 2014. "Why Don't Remittances Appear to Affect Growth?" World Bank Research Working Paper No. 6856, Development Research Group, Finance and Private Sector Development Team, World Bank, Washington, DC.

Clemens, Michael A., Steven Radelet, Rikhil R. Bhavnani, and Samuel Bazzi. 2012. "Counting Chickens When They Hatch: The Short-Term Effect of Aid on Growth." *Economic Journal* 122 (561): 590–617.

Collier, Paul, and David Dollar. 2002. "Aid Allocation and Poverty Reduction." *European Economic Review* 46 (8): 1475–500.

Copley, Amy. 2015. "Africa In the News: AGOA Forum Held, Zimbabwe Asks for Economic Support, South Africa Fears Recession, and South Sudan Peace Deal Signed." Brookings Institution, Washington, DC, August 28. https://www.brookings.edu/blog/africa-in-focus/2015/08/28/africa-in-the-news-agoa-forum-held-zimbabwe-asks-for-international-economic-support-south-africa-fears-recession-and-south-sudan-peace-deal-signed/

Custer, Samantha, Zachary Rice, Takaaki Masaki, Rebecca Latourell, and Bradley Parks. 2015. "Listening to Leaders: Which Development Partners Do They Prefer and Why?" AidData, Williamsburg, VA. http://aiddata.org/sites/default/files/execsummary_2.pdf

D'Alimonte, Mary Rose, Hilary Rogers, and David de Ferranti. 2017. "Financing the Global Nutrition Targets." In *An Investment Framework for Nutrition: Reaching the Global Targets for Stunting, Anemia, Breastfeeding, and Wasting*, edited by Meera Shekar, Jakub Kakietek, Julia Dayton Eberwein, and Dylan Walters, 187–215. Washington, DC: World Bank.

D'Alimonte, Mary, Emily Thacher, Ryan LeMier, and Jack Clift. 2018. "Tracking Aid for the WHA Nutrition Targets: Global Spending in 2015 and a Roadmap to Better Data." Results for Development (R4D), Washington, DC. http://www.r4d.org/wp-content/uploads/R4D-tracking-aid-to-WHA-nutrition-targets-April-2018_final.pdf

Deaton, Angus. 2013. *The Great Escape: Health, Wealth, and the Origins Of Inequality*. Princeton, NJ: Princeton University Press.

Development Committee (Joint Ministerial Committee of the Boards of Governors of the Bank and the Fund on the Transfer of Real Resources to Developing Countries). 2015. "From Billions to Trillions: Transforming Development Finance Post-2015 Financing for Development: Multilateral Development Finance." Development Committee Discussion Note. Prepared jointly by African Development Bank, Asian Development Bank, European Bank for Reconstruction and Development, European Investment Bank, Inter-American Development Bank, International Monetary Fund, and World Bank Group, April 18.

Easterly, W. 2006. "Why Doesn't Aid Work?" Cato Unbound, April 2 2006. http://www.cato-unbound.org/2006/04/02/william-easterly/why-doesnt-aid-work.

Easterly, William, and Tobias Pfutze. 2008. "Where Does the Money Go? Best and Worst Practices in Foreign Aid." *Journal of Economic Perspectives* 22 (2): 29–52.

Easterly, William, and Tobias Pfutze. 2013. "Comment: Response from William Easterly and Tobias Pfutze." *Journal of Economic Perspectives* 23 (1): 243–6.

Easterly, William, and Claudia R. Williamson. 2011. "Rhetoric versus Reality: The Best and Worst of Aid Agency Practices." *World Development* 39 (11): 1930–49.

Economist, The. 2014. "Remittances and Growth: Gone Missing. Why Has the Growth in Remittances Not Led to Growth in GDP?" Free exchange blog by S.H., August 1. http://www.economist.com/blogs/freeexchange/2014/08/remittances-and-growth

Economist, The. 2015. "The Asian Infrastructure Investment Bank. The Infrastructure Gap. Development Finance Helps China Win Friends and Influence American Allies." March 19. http://www.economist.com/news/asia/21646740-development-finance-helps-china-win-friends-and-influence-american-allies-infrastructure-gap

EFC (European Foundation Centre). n.d. Data on Foundations. http://www.efc.be/philanthropy-sector/foundations-in-europe/

Eichengreen, Barry, and Ngaire Woods. 2016. "The IMF's Unmet Challenges." *Journal of Economic Perspectives* 30 (1): 29–52.

European Parliament. 2014. "Financing for Development Post-2015: Improving the Contribution of Private Finance." Directorate-General for External Policies, European Parliament's Committee on Development, Brussels. https://eurodad.org/files/pdf/1546190-financing-for-development-post-2015-improving-the-contribution-of-private-finance.pdf

FAO (Food and Agriculture Organization of the United Nations). 2009. "Declaration of the World Summit on Food Security." WSFS 2009/2, Rome, November 16–18. http://www.fao.org/fileadmin/templates/wsfs/Summit/Docs/Final_Declaration/WSFS09_Declaration.pdf

FAO (Food and Agriculture Organization of the United Nations). 2012. "The State of Food and Agriculture 2012: Investing in Agriculture for a Better Future." FAO, Rome. http://www.fao.org/3/i3028e/i3028e.pdf

FAO (Food and Agriculture Organization of the United Nations). 2017. "The Future of Food and Agriculture. Trends and Challenges." FAO, Rome. http://www.fao.org/3/a-i6583e.pdf

FAO (Food and Agriculture Organization of the United Nations). 2019. Statistics. Government Expenditure on Agriculture. http://www.fao.org/economic/ess/investment/expenditure/en/

FAO (Food and Agriculture Organization of the United Nations). 2020a. FAO in Emergencies. Funding. http://www.fao.org/emergencies/about/funding/en/

FAO (Food and Agriculture Organization of the United Nations). 2020b. Statistics. Capital Stock and Investment in Agriculture. http://www.fao.org/economic/ess/ess-economic/capitalstock/en/

FAO (Food and Agriculture Organization of the United Nations). 2020c. Statistics. Credit to Agriculture 2018. http://www.fao.org/economic/ess/investment/credit/en/

FAO (Food and Agriculture Organization of the United Nations). 2020d. Statistics. Development Flows to Agriculture. FAO Investment Financing Dataset. June 2019. http://www.fao.org/economic/ess/investment/flows/en/

FAO (Food and Agriculture Organization of the United Nations). 2020e. Statistics. Foreign Direct Investment to Agriculture, Forestry and Fishery. http://www.fao.org/economic/ess/investment/fdi/en/

FAO (Food and Agriculture Organization of the United Nations), IFAD (International Fund for Agricultural Development), and WFP (World Food Programme). 2015. *Achieving Zero Hunger: The Critical Role of Investments in Social Protection and Agriculture.* Rome: FAO. http://www.fao.org/3/a-i4951e.pdf

FAO–OEA/CIE–IICA Working Group (FAO Statistics Division) 2013. "FAO Statistical Initiatives in Measuring Investment in Agriculture: Global Investment Dataset and Country Investment Profiles." Session 6: Recent advances in agricultural economic statistics, FAO–OEA/CIE–IICA Working Group on Agricultural and Livestock Statistics for Latin America and the Caribbean, 26th Session, Port of Spain, Trinidad and Tobago, June 5–7. http://www.fao.org/fileadmin/templates/ess/documents/meetings_and_workshops/IICA_2013/papers/IICA_Investment.pdf

Global Biodefense. 2020. "Shutdown of PREDICT Infectious Disease Program Challenged by Senators Warren and King." February 4. https://globalbiodefense.com/2020/02/04/shutdown-of-predict-infectious-disease-program-challenged-by-senators-warren-and-king/

Gotor, Elisabetta, Francesco Caracciolo, and Jamie Watts. 2010. "The Perceived Impact of the In-Trust Agreements on CGIAR Germplasm Availability: An Assessment of Bioversity International's Institutional Activities." *World Development* 38 (10): 1486–93.

Goyal, Aparajita, and John Nash. 2017. *Reaping Richer Returns: Public Spending Priorities for African Agriculture Productivity Growth.* Africa Development Forum. Washington, DC: World Bank and Agence Française de Developpement. https://openknowledge.worldbank.org/bitstream/handle/10986/25996/9781464809378.pdf

GPEDC (Global Partnership for Effective Development Co-operation). 2014. "First High Level Meeting of the Global Partnership for Effective Development Co-operation: Building Towards an Inclusive Post-2015 Development Agenda." Mexico High Level Meeting Communiqué, April 16, GPEDC. http://effectivecooperation.org/wp-content/uploads/2016/08/Communique-Mexico-HLM-16.4.14.pdf

Gulrajani, Nillma. 2016. "Bilateral versus Multilateral Aid Channels: Strategic Choices for Donors." ODI Report, Overseas Development Institute, London.

Gurara, Daniel, Stefania Fabrizio, and Johannes Wiegand. 2020. "COVID-19: Without Help, Low-Income Developing Countries Risk a Lost Decade." IMFBlog, August 27. https://blogs. imf.org/2020/08/27/covid-19-without-help-low-income-developing-countries-risk-a-lost-decade/?utm_medium=email&utm_source=govdelivery

Hallam, David. 2009. "Foreign Investment in Developing Country Agriculture—Issues, Policy Implications and International Response." OECD Global Forum on International Investment VIII, Paris, December 7–8.

HLP (High-level Panel on the Post-2015 Development Agenda). 2013. "A New Global Partnership: Eradicate Poverty and Transform Economies through Sustainable Development." Report of the HLP of Eminent Persons on the Post-2015 Development Agenda, United Nations, New York.

Hoff, Karla. 2001. "Beyond Rosenstein-Rodan: The Modern Theory of Coordination Problems in Development." In *Proceedings of the Annual World Bank Conference on Development Economics*, 2000 (Supplement to the *World Bank Economic Review*), 145–88. Washington DC: World Bank.

IDA (International Development Association). 2020a. Replenishments. http://ida.worldbank. org/replenishments

IDA (International Development Association). 2020b. "What is the IDA?" IDA, World Bank Group, Washington, DC. http://ida.worldbank.org/about/what-is-ida

IEG (Independent Evaluation Group). 2011a. "Trust Fund Support for Development: An Evaluation of the World Bank's Trust Fund Portfolio." IEG, World Bank Group, Washington, DC. https://ieg.worldbankgroup.org/evaluations/trust-fund-support-development

IEG (Independent Evaluation Group). 2011b. "World Bank Country-Level Engagement on Governance and Anticorruption: An Evaluation of the 2007 Strategy and Implementation Plan." IEG, World Bank Group, Washington, DC.

IEG (Independent Evaluation Group). 2011c. "The World Bank's Involvement in Global and Regional Partnership Programs: An Independent Assessment." World Bank, Washington, DC. http://ieg.worldbankgroup.org/Data/reports/grpp_eval.pdf

IEG (Independent Evaluation Group). 2013a. "Knowledge-Based Country Programs: An Evaluation of the World Bank Group Experience." World Bank, Washington, DC. http://documents.worldbank.org/curated/en/201041468152102121/pdf/812570WP0v10Kn00Box379835B00PUBLIC0.pdf

IEG (Independent Evaluation Group). 2013b. "Responding to Global Public Bads: Learning from Evaluation of the World Bank Experience with Avian Influenza 2006–13." IEG, World Bank Group, Washington, DC. https://ieg.worldbankgroup.org/sites/default/files/Data/reports/avian_flu1.pdf

IEG (Independent Evaluation Group). 2013c. "The World Bank Group and the Global Food Crisis: An Evaluation of the World Bank Group Response." IEG, World Bank Group, Washington, DC. http://documents.worldbank.org/curated/en/543311468323944900/The-World-Bank-Group-and-the-global-food-crisis-an-evaluation-of-the-World-Bank-Group-response

IEG (Independent Evaluation Group). 2014. "Results and Performance of the World Bank Group 2014." An Independent Evaluation. IEG, World Bank Group, Washington, DC. https://ieg.worldbankgroup.org/Data/Evaluation/files/rap2014.pdf

IEG (Independent Evaluation Group). 2015. "Global Program Review: The GAVI Alliance—The World Bank's Partnership with the GAVI Alliance." Washington, DC: World Bank. https://ieg.worldbankgroup.org/Data/Evaluation/files/wbp_gavi_alliance2.pdf

IFAD (International Fund for Agricultural Development). 2018a. "IFAD Annual Report 2018." IFAD, Rome. https://www.ifad.org/documents/38714170/41203357/AR2018_e_LONG.pdf/ e64a6026-9092-5080-4da3-300e95c7bcd1

IFAD (International Fund for Agricultural Development). 2018b. "Report of the Consultation on the Eleventh Replenishment of IFAD's Resources. Leaving No One Behind: IFAD's Role in the 2030 Agenda." IFAD/11/5/INF.2, February 12, Rome. https://www.ifad.org/ documents/38714174/40306705/Report+of+the+Consultation+on+the+Eleventh+Replenish ment+of+IFAD%27s+Resources.pdf/3819f1bc-d975-45ce-9770-8f673e26caa0

IFAD (International Fund for Agricultural Development). 2019. "IFAD Annual Report 2019." IFAD, Rome. https://www.ifad.org/documents/38714170/41784870/AR2019+EN. pdf/ba495c3d-7db8-a688-08d2-1589ade15f4f

IFPRI (International Food Policy Research Institute). 2014. *Global Nutrition Report 2014: Actions and Accountability to Accelerate the World's Progress on Nutrition.* Washington, DC: IFPRI.

IFPRI (International Food Policy Research Institute). 2015a. *Global Nutrition Report 2015: Actions and Accountability to Advance Nutrition and Sustainable Development.* Washington, DC: IFPRI.

IFPRI (International Food Policy Research Institute). 2015b. "Statistics on Public Expenditures for Economic Development (SPEED)." https://doi.org/10.7910/DVN/INZ3QK, Harvard Dataverse, V3

IFPRI (International Food Policy Research Institute). 2016a. *Global Nutrition Report 2016: From Promise to Impact: Ending Malnutrition by 2030.* Washington, DC: IFPRI.

IFPRI (International Food Policy Research Institute). 2016b. Press Release—"Global Nutrition Report: Malnutrition Becoming the 'New Normal' Across the Globe." June 14, IFPRI, Washington, DC. https://www.ifpri.org/news-release/global-nutrition-report-malnutrition-becoming-"new-normal"-across-globe

IFPRI (International Food Policy Research Institute). 2017. *Global Food Policy Report* 2017. Washington, DC: IFPRI.

IFPRI (International Food Policy Research Institute). 2018. *2018 Global Food Policy Report.* Washington, DC: IFPRI. https://www.who.int/nutrition/globalnutritionreport/2018_Global_ Nutrition_Report.pdf

IFPRI (International Food Policy Research Institute). 2019. *2019 Global Food Policy Report.* Washington, DC: IFPRI. http://ebrary.ifpri.org/utils/getfile/collection/p15738coll2/ id/133129/filename/133348.pdf

IMF (International Monetary Fund). 1993. *Balance of Payments Manual.* Fifth Edition. Washington, DC: IMF.

IMF (International Monetary Fund). 2015. *World Economic Outlook (WEO):* Adjusting to Lower Commodity Prices, October, IMF, Washington, DC.

IMF (International Monetary Fund). 2020. "A Crisis Like No Other, An Uncertain Recovery." World Economic Outlook Update, June, IMF, Washington, DC. https://www.imf.org/en/ Publications/WEO/Issues/2020/06/24/WEOUpdateJune2020

Isenman, Paul. 2011. "Architecture, Allocations, Effectiveness and Governance: Lessons from Global Funds." ODI Meeting on Climate Change, May 5, Overseas Development Institute, London.

Isenman, Paul. 2012. "Learning from Assessments of Overall Effectiveness of Multilateral Organisations." Paper submitted to the Swedish Agency for Development Evaluation (SADEV), Stockholm.

Isenman, Paul, and Alexander Shakow. 2010. "Donor Schizophrenia and Aid Effectiveness: The Role of Global Funds." IDS Practice Paper No. 5, Institute of Development Studies (IDS), University of Sussex, Brighton, UK.

Kanbur, Ravi. 2004. "Cross-Border Externalities and International Public Goods: Implications for Aid Agencies." In *Global Tensions: Challenges and Opportunities in the World Economy*, edited by Lourdes Benería and Savitri Bisnath, 54–64. London: Routledge.

Kanbur, Ravi. 2005. "Economic Policy, Distribution, and Poverty: The Nature of Disagreements." In *Growth, Inequality, and Poverty: Prospects for Pro-poor Economic Development*, edited by van der Hoeven. Rolph, and Anthony F. Shorrocks, World Institute for Development Economics Research, 13–28. Oxford: Oxford University Press.

Kanbur, Ravi, and Andy Sumner. 2012. "Poor Countries or Poor People? Development Assistance and the New Geography of Global Poverty." *Journal of International Development* 24 (6): 686–95.

Kaul, Inge, Isabelle Grunberg, and Marc A. Stern, eds. 1999. *Defining Global Public Goods.* New York: Oxford University Press, published for United Nations Development Programme (UNDP).

KFF (Kaiser Family Foundation). 2019. "U.S. Government Shutting Down USAID's Predict Program." KFF Daily Global Health Policy Report, October 25. https://www.kff.org/news-summary/u-s-government-shutting-down-usaids-predict-program-investigating-disease-jumps-from-animals-to-humans/

Kharas, Homi. 2007. "Trends and Issues in Development Aid." Working Paper 1, Wolfensohn Center for Development, Brookings Institution, Washington, DC.

Kharas, Homi. 2008. "Measuring the Cost of Aid Volatility." Working Paper 3, Wolfensohn Center for Development, Brookings Institution, Washington, DC.

Kharas, Homi 2009. "Action on Aid: Steps toward Making Aid More Effective." Report, Brookings Institution, Washington, DC.

Kharas, Homi, and John McArthur. 2019. "How Much Does the World Spend on the Sustainable Development Goals?" Future Development blog, July 29, Brookings Institution, Washington, DC. https://www.brookings.edu/blog/future-development/2019/07/29/how-much-does-the-world-spend-on-the-sustainable-development-goals/

Kitano, Naohiro. 2019. "Estimating China's Foreign Aid: 2017–2018 Preliminary Figures." October 20. Global Center for Science and Engineering, Waseda University and Japanese International Cooperation Agency (JICA) Research Institute, Tokyo. https://www.jica.go.jp/jica-ri/publication/other/l75nbg000018z3zd-att/20190926_01.pdf

Kitano, N., and Yumiko Miyabayashi. 2020. "Estimating China's Foreign Aid: 2019–2020 Preliminary Figures." Ogata Sadako Research Institute for Peace and Development, Japanese International Cooperation Agency (JICA) Research Institute, Tokyo. https://www.jica.go.jp/jica-ri/publication/other/20201214_01.html

Kotechi, Peter. 2018. "The Billionaire 'Giving Pledge' Signed by Bill Gates and Elon Musk Could Soon Be Worth up to $600 Billion." Business Insider, July 18. https://www.businessinsider.com/bill-gates-elon-musk-giving-pledge-may-reach-600-billion-2018-7

Laborde, David. 2013. "MIRAGRODEP Model: Modelling International Relationships under Applied General equilibrium for agRODEP." African Growth and Development Policy Modeling Consortium (AGRODEP), facilitated by International Food Policy Research Institute (IFPRI). http://www.agrodep.org/model/miragrodep-model

Laborde, David, Livia Bizikova, Tess Lallemant, and Carin Smaller. 2016. "Ending Hunger: What Would It Cost?" International Institute of Sustainable Development (IISD), Winnipeg. http://www.iisd.org/library/ending-hunger-what-would-it-cost

Lal, Deepak. 2006. "Reply to Easterly: There Is No Fix for Aid." Cato Unbound, April 3, 2006. http://www.cato-unbound.org/2006/04/06/deepak-lal/there-no-fix-aid.

Lattimer, Charlotte. 2015. "Making Financing Work for Crisis-Affected People." Position paper for The World Humanitarian Summit (WHS), Istanbul, May 2016.

Lele, Uma. 2016. "Exit, Voice, and Loyalty: Lessons from Brexit for Global Governance." Future Development: Economics to End Poverty blog, The Brookings Institution, Washington, DC, July 7. http://www.brookings.edu/blogs/future-development/posts/2016/07/07-brexit-global-governance-lele

Lele, Uma. 2021. "Growing Water Scarcities: Responses of India and China." Forthcoming, *Applied Economic Perspectives and Policy*.

Lentz, Erin C., and Christopher B. Barrett. 2013. "The Timeliness and Cost-Effectiveness of the Local and Regional Procurement of Food Aid." *World Development* 49: 9–18.

Maimbo, Samuel Munzele, and Dilip Ratha. 2005. *Remittances: Development Impact and Future Prospects*. Washington, DC: World Bank.

Mason-D'Croz, Daniel, Timothy B. Sulser, Keith Wiebe, Mark W. Rosegrant, Sarah K. Lowder, Alejandro Nin-Pratt, Dirk Willenbockel, Sherman Robinson, Tingju Zhu, Nicola Cenacchi, Shahnila Dunston, and Richard D. Robertson. 2019. "Agricultural Investments and Hunger in Africa Modeling Potential Contributions to SDG2—Zero Hunger." *World Development* 116: 38–53.

McNellis, Patrick E. 2009. "Foreign Investment in Developing Country Agriculture—The Emerging Role of Private Sector Finance." FAO Commodity and Trade Policy Research Working Paper No. 28, Trade and Markets Division, Food and Agriculture Organization of the United Nations, Rome.

Mills, Lennox A. 1964. *Southeast Asia: Illusion and Reality in Politics and Economics*. Minneapolis: University of Minnesota Press.

Morris, Scott, and Madeleine Gleave. 2015. "The World Bank at 75." CGD Policy Paper 058, Center for Global Development, Washington, DC.

Murray, Gardner, and Sharie Aviso. 2011. "Policy Opportunities for Linking Animal and Human Health." Paper presented at: Animal Health and Biodiversity Preparing the Future. Compendium of the OIE Global Conference on Wildlife, Paris, France, February 23–5, 2011.

Nwanze, Kanayo F. 2014. "Open Letter to African Heads of State." International Fund for Agricultural Development. https://www.ifad.org/en/event/tags/y2014/14219933

OECD (Organisation for Economic Co-operation and Development. 1996. *Detailed Benchmark Definition of Foreign Direct Investment*. Third Edition. Paris: OECD.

OECD (Organisation for Economic Co-operation and Development). 2003. "Philanthropic Foundations and Development Co-operation." *OECD Journal on Development* 4/3. DOI: http://dx.doi.org/10.1787/journal_dev-v4-art23-en

OECD (Organisation for Economic Co-operation and Development). 2006. "The Development Effectiveness of Food Aid. Does Tying Matter?" OECD, Paris.

OECD (Organisation for Economic Co-operation and Development). 2008a. "The Accra Agenda for Action." OECD, Paris. http://www.oecd.org/dac/effectiveness/34428351.pdf

OECD (Organization for Economic Co-operation and Development). 2008b. "Paris Declaration on Aid Effectiveness." 2006. In *Paris Declaration on Aid Effectiveness and the Accra Agenda for Action*, 1–13. Paris: OECD. https://www.oecd.org/dac/effectiveness/34428351.pdf

OECD (Organisation for Economic Co-operation and Development). 2011. "Busan Partnership for Effective Development Co-Operation." Fourth High Level Forum on Aid Effectiveness, Busan, Republic of Korea, November 29–December 1. http://www.oecd.org/dac/effective ness/49650173.pdf

OECD (Organisation for Economic Co-operation and Development). 2012. "What Do We Know About Multilateral Aid? The 54 Billion Dollar Question." OECD, Paris. http://www. oecd.org/development/aid-architecture/13_03_18%20Policy%20Briefing%20on%20Multi lateral%20Aid.pdf

OECD (Organisation for Economic Co-operation and Development). 2014. *Development Co-operation Report 2014: Mobilising Resources for Sustainable Development*. Paris: OECD Publishing.

OECD (Organisation for Economic Co-operation and Development). 2015. *Multilateral Aid 2015: Better Partnerships for a Post-2015 World*. Paris: OECD Publishing.

OECD (Organisation for Economic Co-operation and Development). 2016. *Development Co-operation Report 2016: The Sustainable Development Goals as Business Opportunities*. July 18. Paris: OECD Publishing.

OECD (Organisation for Economic Co-operation and Development). 2017. OECD–DCD Survey on Global Private Philanthropy for Development. Results of the OECD Data Survey as of 3 October 2017. http://www.oecd.org/dac/financing-sustainable-development/development-finance-standards/Philanthropy-Development-Survey.pdf

OECD (Organisation for Economic Co-operation and Development). 2018a. *Development Co-operation Report 2018: Joining Forces to Leave No One Behind*. Paris: OECD Publishing, Paris. https://doi.org/10.1787/dcr-2018-en

OECD (Organisation for Economic Co-operation and Development). 2018b. *Global Outlook on Financing for Sustainable Development 2019: Time to Face the Challenge*. Paris: OECD Publishing. https://www.oecd-ilibrary.org/docserver/9789264307995-en.pdf

OECD (Organisation for Economic Co-operation and Development). 2019a. "Aid for Civil Society Organisations." Statistics based on DAC Members' reporting to the Creditor Reporting System database (CRS), 2016–2017. January 2019, OECD, Paris. https://www.oecd.org/dac/financing-sustainable-development/development-finance-topics/Aid-for-CSOs-2019.pdf

OECD (Organisation for Economic Co-operation and Development). 2019b. "China's Progress Report on Implementation of the 2030 Agenda for Sustainable Development." https://www.fmprc.gov.cn/mfa_eng/topics_665678/2030kcxfzyc/P020190924780823323749.pdf

OECD (Organisation for Economic Co-operation and Development). 2019b. "Converged Statistical Reporting Directives for the Creditor Reporting System (CRS) and the Annual DAC Questionnaire." DAC Working Party on Development Finance Statistics. DCD/DAC/STAT(2018)9/ADD3/FINAL, March 18. https://one.oecd.org/document/DCD/DAC/STAT(2018)9/ADD3/FINAL/en/pdf

OECD (Organisation for Economic Co-operation and Development). 2019c. Country Programmable Aid (CPA). Aid Architecture. Development Co-operation Directorate (DCD–DAC). http://www.oecd.org/dac/aid-architecture/cpa.htm

OECD (Organisation for Economic Co-operation and Development). 2019d. "Development Aid Drops in 2018, Especially to Neediest Countries." October 4, OECD, Paris. https://www.oecd.org/newsroom/development-aid-drops-in-2018-especially-to-neediest-countries.htm

OECD (Organisation for Economic Co-operation and Development). 2019e. "Development Aid Drops in 2018, Especially to Neediest Countries: OECD Adopts New Methodology for Counting Loans in Official Aid Data." April 10, OECD, Paris. https://www.oecd.org/dac/financing-sustainable-development/development-finance-data/ODA-2018-detailed-summary.pdf

OECD (Organisation for Economic Co-operation and Development). 2019f. "FDI in Figures." October, Foreign Direct Investment Statistics: Data, Analysis and Forecasts, OECD, Paris. http://www.oecd.org/investment/FDI-in-Figures-October-2019.pdf

OECD (Organisation for Economic Co-operation and Development). 2019g. Fourth High Level Forum on Aid Effectiveness. http://www.oecd.org/dac/effectiveness/fourthhighlevelforum onaideffectiveness.htm

OECD (Organisation for Economic-Co-operation and Development). 2019h. "The High Level Fora on Aid Effectiveness: A History." OECD/Development Co-operation Directorate (DCD–DAC)/Effective Development Co-operation. http://www.oecd.org/dac/effectiveness/thehighlevelforaonaideffectivenessahistory.htm

OECD (Organisation for Economic Co-operation and Development. 2019i. Official Development Assistance (ODA). https://www.oecd.org/dac/financing-sustainable-de velopment/development-finance-standards/official-development-assistance.htm

OECD (Organisation for Economic Co-operation and Development). 2019j. Second High Level Forum on Aid Effectiveness (HLF-2), 28 February to 2 March 2005, Paris, France. http://www.oecd.org/dac/effectiveness/secondhighlevelforumonjointprogresstowardenhancedaid effectivenessharmonisationalignmentandresults.htm

OECD (Organisation for Economic Co-operation and Development). 2019k. Third High Level Forum on Aid Effectiveness. http://www.oecd.org/dac/effectiveness/theaccrahighlevel forumhlf3andtheaccraagendaforaction.htm

OECD (Organisation for Economic Co-operation and Development). 2020a. "DAC Recom-mendation on Untying Official Development Assistance." OECD/LEGAL/5015, OECD, Paris. https://legalinstruments.oecd.org/public/doc/140/140.en.pdf

OECD (Organisation for Economic Co-operation and Development). 2020b. "Untied Aid." https://www.oecd.org/dac/financing-sustainable-development/development-finance-standards/untied-aid.htm

OECD (Organisation for Economic Co-operation and Development). 2021. "COVID-19 Spend-ing Helped to Lift Foreign Aid to an All-Time High in 2020." Detailed Note, Paris, OECD, April 13. https://www.oecd.org/dac/financing-sustainable-development/development-finance-data/ODA-2020-detailed-summary.pdf

OECD.Stat. 2020a. Organisation for Economic Co-operation and Development. Statistics. http://stats.oecd.org

OECD.Stat. 2020b. Organisation for Economic Co-operation and Development. Statistics. Total Flows by Donor (ODA + OOF + Private) [DAC1]. http://stats.oecd.org/viewhtml.aspx? datasetcode=TABLE1&lang=en

OED (Operations Evaluation Department). 2003. "The CGIAR at 31: An Independent Meta-Evaluation of the Consultative Group on International Agricultural Research." Revised Edition. OED, World Bank, Washington, DC. https://openknowledge.worldbank.org/bit stream/handle/10986/15041/281310PAPER0CGIAR0at0310see0also025926.pdf

OED (Operations Evaluation Department). 2004. "Addressing the Challenges of Globalization: An Independent Evaluation of the World Bank's Approach to Global Programs." World Bank, Washington, DC.

Orozco, Manuel. 2006. "Conceptual Considerations, Empirical Challenges, and Solutions in Measuring Remittances." Report presented in the Launching Seminar of the Improving Central Bank Reporting and Procedures on Remittances Program, developed in the CEMLA facilities, in Mexico, D.F. October 12–14, 2005 CFRM-B001, Centre for Latin American Monetary Studies, Multilateral Investment Fund. http://w.thedialogue.org/ PublicationFiles/conceptual.pdf

Pearson, Lester Bowles, ed. 1969. *Partners in Development: Report of the Commission on International Development.* New York: Praeger.

Quayyum, Saad Noor, and Roland Kangni Kpodar. 2020. "Supporting Migrants and Remittances as COVID-19 Rages On." IMFBlog, September 11. https://blogs.imf.org/2020/09/ 11/supporting-migrants-and-remittances-as-covid-19-rages-on/?utm_medium=email& utm_source=govdelivery

Radelet, Steven. 2006. "A Primer on Foreign Aid." CGD Working Paper Number 92, Center for Global Development, Washington, DC. http://www.cgdev.org/files/8846_file_WP92.pdf

Ratha, Dilip, Supriyo De, Eung Ju Kim, Sonia Plaza, Ganesh Seshan, and Nadege Desiree Yameogo. 2019. "Data Release: Remittances to Low- and Middle-Income Countries on Track to Reach \$551 Billion in 2019 and \$597 Billion by 2021." World Bank blog, October 16. https://blogs.worldbank.org/peoplemove/data-release-remittances-low-and-middle-income-countries-track-reach-551-billion-2019

Ravallion, Martin. 2016. "The World Bank: Why It Is Still Needed and Why It Still Disappoints." *Journal of Economic Perspectives* 30 (1): 77–94.

Reinhart, Carmen M., and Christopher Trebesch. 2015. "The International Monetary Fund: 70 Years of Reinvention." NBER Working Paper No. 21805, National Bureau of Economic Research, Cambridge, MA.

Reinsberg, Bernhard, Katharina Michaelowa, and Vera Z. Eichenauer. 2015. "The Rise of Multi-bi Aid and the Proliferation of Trust Funds." In *Handbook on the Economics of Foreign Aid*, edited by B. Mak Arvin and Byron Law, 527–44. Cheltenham: Edward Elgar Publishing.

Rodrik, Dani. 1996. "Why Is There Multilateral Lending?" In Annual World *Bank Conference on Development Economics 1995*, edited by Michael Bruno and Boris Pleksovic, 167–205. Washington DC: IBRD.

Rodrik, Dani. 2001. "Comments at the Conference on Immigration Policy and the Welfare State," unpublished paper delivered at the Third European Conference on Immigration Policy and the Welfare State, Trieste, June 23, 2001.

Rondinelli, Dennis A. 1993. *Development Projects as Policy Experiments: An Adaptive Approach to Development Administration.* Development and Underdevelopment Series. London and New York: Routledge.

Rozenberg, Julie, and Marianne Fay. 2019. "Beyond the Gap: How Countries Can Afford the Infrastructure They Need while Protecting the Planet." Sustainable Infrastructure, World Bank, Washington, DC. https://openknowledge.worldbank.org/handle/10986/31291

Runde, Daniel. 2015. "Ensuring The World Bank's Relevance." *Forbes*, March 16. http://www. forbes.com/sites/danielrunde/2015/03/16/ensuring-world-bank-relevance/#4e0127507ffe

Save the Children. 2018. "Nutrition Boost: Why the World Needs a Step Change in Finance for Nutrition—and How It Can Be Achieved." Save the Children, London. https://www. savethechildren.org.uk/content/dam/gb/reports/health/nutrition-boost.pdf?_ga=2.190007083. 1201801319.1586025789-1289203846.1586025789

Sharma, Ramesh. 2011. "Food Export Restrictions: Review of the 2007–2010 Experience and Considerations for Disciplining Restrictive Measures." FAO Commodity and Trade Policy Research Working Paper No. 32, Trade and Markets Division, Food and Agriculture Organization of the United Nations, Rome.

Shekar, Meera, Jakub Kakietek, Julia Dayton Eberwein, and Dylan Walters, eds. 2017. *An Investment Framework for Nutrition: Reaching the Global Targets for Stunting, Anemia, Breastfeeding, and Wasting.* Washington, DC: World Bank.

SUN (Scaling Up Nutrition). 2015. "Sun Movement Strategy and Roadmap (2016–2020)." https://scalingupnutrition.org/wp-content/uploads/2016/09/SR_20160901_ENG_web_pages.pdf

UN (United Nations). 2002. "Monterrey Consensus of the International Conference on Financing for Development." Monterrey, Mexico, March 18–22, United Nations Department of Economic and Social Affairs, New York. http://www.un.org/esa/ffd/monterrey/MonterreyConsensus.pdf

UN (United Nations). 2012. "Innovative Finance for Development." Department of Economic and Social Affairs. https://www.un.org/esa/ffd/topics/innovative-finance.html

UN (United Nations). 2015. "Addis Ababa Action Agenda of the Third International Conference on Financing for Development." Department of Economic and Social Affairs, Financing for Development Office, New York. http://www.un.org/esa/ffd/wp-content/uploads/2015/08/AAAA_Outcome.pdf

UN (United Nations). 2019. Implementation of General Assembly Resolution 71/243 on the Quadrennial Comprehensive Policy Review of Operational Activities for Development of the United Nations System, 2019: Monitoring and Reporting Framework. Report of the Secretary-General. Economic and Social Council 2019 session. https://digitallibrary.un.org/record/3803212?ln=en

UNCTAD (United Nations Conference on Trade and Development). 2009. *World Investment Report 2009: Transnational Corporations, Agricultural Production and Development.* New York and Geneva: UN.

UNCTAD (United Nations Conference on Trade and Development). 2015. *World Investment Report 2015: Reforming International Investment Governance.* Geneva: UN.

UNCTAD (United Nations Conference on Trade and Development). 2019a. "The Least Developed Countries Report 2019." United Nations, New York. https://unctad.org/en/PublicationsLibrary/ldcr2019_en.pdf

UNCTAD (United Nations Conference on Trade and Development). 2019b. *World Investment Report 2019: Special Economic Zones.* New York and Geneva: UN. https://unctad.org/en/PublicationsLibrary/wir2019_en.pdf

UNCTAD (United Nations Conference on Trade and Development). 2020. "Investment Trends Monitor." Issue 33, January. United Nations. https://unctad.org/en/PublicationsLibrary/diaeiainf2020d1_en.pdf

UNCTAD (United Nations Conference on Trade and Development). 2021. "Investment Trends Monitor." Issue 38, January. United Nations. https://unctad.org/webflyer/global-investment-trend-monitor-no-38

UNDESA (United Nations. Department of Economic and Social Affairs). 2019. "International Migration 2019: Report." ST/ESA/SER.A/438, Population Division, United Nations, New York. https://www.un.org/en/development/desa/population/migration/publications/migrationreport/docs/InternationalMigration2019_Report.pdf

WBG (World Bank Group). 2015. *The World Bank Group A to Z.* Washington, DC: World Bank.

WBG (World Bank Group) and KNOMAD. 2019. "Migration and Remittances. Recent Developments and Outlook." Migration and Remittances Team, Social Protection and Jobs, World Bank, Washington, DC. https://www.knomad.org/sites/default/files/2019-04/Migrationanddevelopmentbrief31.pdf

WCED (World Commission on Environment and Development). 1987. *Our Common Future.* Brundtland Committee. Oxford and New York: Oxford University Press.

WFP (World Food Programme). 2011. "Istanbul Programme of Action for the Least Developed Countries for the Decade 2011–2020." WFP/EB.2/2011/4-C, Executive Board Second Regular Section, Rome, November 14–17. https://documents.wfp.org/stellent/groups/public/documents/eb/wfpdoc061607.pdf

World Bank. 2010. "World Bank Reforms Voting Power, Gets $86 Billion Boost." Press Release, April 25. http://www.worldbank.org/en/news/press-release/2010/04/25/world-bank-reforms-voting-power-gets-86-billion-boost

World Bank. 2011. "CPIA 2011 Criteria." Country Policies and Institutional Assessments, World Bank Group, Washington, DC. http://siteresources.worldbank.org/IDA/Resources/73153-1,181,752,621,336/CPIAcriteria2011final.pdf

World Bank. 2013a. *Capital for the Future: Saving and Investment in an Interdependent World.* Global Development Horizons. Washington, DC: World Bank. http://siteresources.worldbank.org/EXTDECPROSPECTS/Resources/476882-1,368,197,310,537/CapitalForTheFuture.pdf

World Bank. 2013b. "Financing for Development Post-2015." World Bank, Washington, DC. http://documents.worldbank.org/curated/en/206701468158366611/pdf/828000WP0Finan0Box0379879B00PUBLIC0.pdf

World Bank. 2014a. "Global Infrastructure Facility." Brief, October 8. World Bank, Washington, DC. https://www.worldbank.org/en/topic/publicprivatepartnerships/brief/global-infrastructure-facility-backup

World Bank. 2014b. "Migration and Remittances: Recent Developments and Outlook." Migration and Development Brief 22, April 11. Migration and Remittances Team, Development Prospects Group, World Bank, Washington, DC.

World Bank. 2014c. "Remittances to Developing Countries to Stay Robust This Year, Despite Increased Deportations of Migrant Workers, Says WB." Press release, April 11, World Bank, Washington, DC. http://www.worldbank.org/en/news/press-release/2014/04/11/remittances-developing-countries-deportations-migrant-workers-wb

World Bank. 2015a. "The State of Social Safety Nets 2015." World Bank, Washington, DC. http://documents.worldbank.org/curated/en/415491467994645020/pdf/97882-PUB-REVISED-Box393232B-PUBLIC-DOCDATE-6-29-2015-DOI-10-1,596,978-1-4648-0543-1-EPI-1464805431.pdf

World Bank. 2015b. "World Bank Group at the World Trade Organization's 5th Global Review for Trade." July 21, News, World Bank, Washington, DC. http://www.worldbank.org/en/news/feature/2015/07/21/world-bank-group-at-the-world-trade-organizations-5th-global-review-of-aid-for-trade

World Bank. 2016. "Global Community Makes Record $75 Billion Commitment to End Extreme Poverty." Press Release, December 15, World Bank, Washington, DC. http://www.worldbank.org/en/news/press-release/2016/12/15/global-community-commitment-end-poverty-ida18

World Bank. 2017. "Migration and Remittances." April, World Bank, Washington, DC. http://pubdocs.worldbank.org/en/992371492706371662/MigrationandDevelopmentBrief27.pdf

World Bank. 2019a. *Country Policy and Institutional Assessment.* International Development Association (IDA). Washington, DC: World Bank.

World Bank. 2019b. "Trust Fund Annual Report for 2018–2019." World Bank, Washington, DC. http://documents.worldbank.org/curated/en/461611570786898020/pdf/Trust-Fund-Annual-Report-for-2018-2019.pdf

World Bank. 2020a. "COVID-19 Crisis Through a Migration Lens." Migration and Development Brief, No. 32, World Bank, Washington, DC. https://openknowledge.worldbank.org/handle/10986/33634

World Bank. 2020b. World Development Indicators (database). http://data.worldbank.org/data-catalog/world-development-indicators

World Bank and IMF (International Monetary Fund). 2015. World Bank/IMF Spring Meetings 2015: Development Committee Communiqué, Washington, DC, April 18. http://www.worldbank.org/en/news/press-release/2015/04/18/world-bank-imf-spring-meetings-2015-development-committee-communique

WTO (World Trade Organization). 2016. "Members' Participation in the Normal Growth of World Trade in Agricultural Products," Article 18.5 of the Agreement on Agriculture. Note by the Secretariat. G/AG/W/32/Rev.15, WTO, Geneva.

WTO (World Trade Organization). 2020a. "Agriculture: Domestic Support." https://www.wto.org/english/tratop_e/agric_e/ag_intro03_domestic_e.htm

WTO (World Trade Organization). 2020b. "Domestic Support: Amber, Blue and Green Boxes." Agriculture Negotiations: Backgrounder. https://www.wto.org/english/tratop_e/agric_e/negs_bkgrnd13_boxes_e.htm

Yang, Dean. 2005. "International Migration, Human Capital, and Entrepreneurship: Evidence from Philippine Migrants' Exchange Rate Shocks." RSIE Discussion Paper No. 531, Research Seminar in International Economics, Gerald R. Ford School of Public Policy, The University of Michigan, Ann Arbor.

PART II

INTERNATIONAL ORGANIZATIONS

8

The World Bank

Uma Lele and Sambuddha Goswami

Background and Summary

In the 1960s and 1970s, a professional consensus emerged around a "package" approach to agricultural development. The package consisted of improved seeds, fertilizers, irrigation, research and extension, and farmers' access to inputs, knowledge, and output markets. This involved a combination of provision of public goods and service delivery. Because markets did not exist for many of these services, governments were nudged to provide them. Over time, however, trust in the ability of governments to deliver services dissipated. The World Bank experimented with privatization, farmers' organizations, and bottom-up participatory approaches to each of these services, as well as "smart" subsidies. It also experimented with rural development, going beyond agriculture.

Today's reigning paradigms are sustainable agriculture and healthy diets. Effective ways to address them is a challenge, and indeed, there is much debate about the meanings of the terms sustainable agriculture and healthy diets. Moreover, differentiation among countries is large today, as are their variations in agricultural technologies, institutional capabilities, farm sizes, and productivities. So, other than a few exceptions, there is little consensus on what works and how to assess their complex, multidimensional impacts. Concurrently, there are growing environmental challenges affecting agriculture, including climate change, depletion of water tables, and soil degradation, with few, easily scalable, universally applicable solutions. In the meantime, the fourth industrial revolution is offering many possibilities in the current and future developing environment, as well as disruptive technologies and trends, such as the Internet of Things (IoT), robotics, virtual reality (VR), and artificial intelligence (AI). They are changing the way we live and work, with huge scope for their application but requiring massive investments. Does the Bank's past experience offer lessons on responding to the rapidly changing external environment, including increased technological options?

The World Bank's history volumes described the Bank in the mid-1990s as one of the strongest of the multilateral banks, owned by governments but rooted in political realism. Unlike the United Nations, the World Bank is described as a benign hegemon where all nation states are not equal. A world's premier multilateral with a broader agenda than the IMF, the Bank chose to rely on the bond market for capital, with only minimum intrusion on taxpayers for aid in the International Development Association (IDA). It was able to bring other bilateral donors along at the least cost. It successfully transitioned from reconstruction to development, covering all regions and most sectors (Kapur, Lewis, and Webb 1997).

The International Bank for Reconstruction and Development (IBRD) and IDA, commonly and hereafter referred to as the World Bank, have together lent approximately US $161 billion in real terms (Manufactures Unit Value [MUV] Index 2010 = 100), in 159 countries, since 1960 to 2018, to develop the Agriculture, Forestry and Fishing (AFF) sector,

Food for All: International Organizations and the Transformation of Agriculture. Uma Lele, Manmohan Agarwal, Brian C. Baldwin, and Sambuddha Goswami, Oxford University Press. © Uma Lele, Manmohan Agarwal, Brian C. Baldwin, and Sambuddha Goswami 2021. DOI: 10.1093/oso/9780198755173.003.0009

which we will refer to in the aggregate as agriculture. The agriculture sector share in total lending has varied from a peak of 38.5 percent of total lending in FY1978 to a trough of 4.9 percent in FY2010, and up again to 8.5 percent in 2018, as we detail later in Figure 8.2.

The World Bank's lending is the largest assistance to food, agriculture, and rural development ever given by any international organization, even without including the roles of the International Finance Corporation (IFC) and the Multilateral Investment Guarantee Agency (MIGA). Increasingly, it is a small share of investments needed in developing countries, and therefore, their catalytic and leveraging effect is of particular importance going forward. Including IFC and MIGA with IBRD and IDA constitutes the World Bank Group (WBG). The World Bank Group's experience is of considerable relevance, given the growing concern about underfunding of Sustainable Development Goals (SDGs), and particularly SDG2.[1] Many countries are already off-track in achieving SDG2, and some, particularly small, low-income countries (LICs), mainly in sub-Saharan Africa (SSA), are projected to remain off track in 2030 (Kharas, McArthur, and Rasmussen 2018). Additionally, food and nutrition security are increasingly seen as important, as the world population is projected to reach 8 billion by 2030 and more than 9 billion by 2050. Africa will exceed South Asia (SA) in total population, and Africa's urban population will exceed Asia's by 2050 (UN 2016). Future production will need to be resilient to climate change and natural resource degradation, with more balanced nutrition from a diverse diet, which includes fruits, vegetables, meat, fish, poultry, in place of simply increased calories from four major grains (rice, wheat, maize, and soybeans) to improve health linkages, as outlined in previous chapters. Incorporation of environmental and nutritional concerns makes this a multidimensional phenomenon, requiring multisectoral and multilevel approaches. Vertically, the required approaches range from local to macroeconomic and trade policies, and horizontally, across sectors, such as infrastructure, education, and finance. Being a multisectoral international organization, unlike the four other organizations reviewed in this book, WBG has had a unique role in contributing to structural transformation by promoting agricultural development in countries.[2] It provides multisectoral assistance to education, infrastructure, and health, which is often critical to developing agriculture. WBG is the only international organization in a position to provide multisectoral assistance with a holistic view of its clients' economies. The paradigms of climate-resilient agriculture and healthy food systems are relatively new.

Bank commitments are, however, a small share of overall official development assistance (ODA) relative to the past and are an even smaller share of investments made in agriculture by developing countries themselves, particularly considering the big, emerging developing countries like India, the World Bank's largest recipient of lending. Furthermore, World Bank's commitments are small when considered in terms of the amounts needed to achieve sustained, faster, and equitable growth. IFC committed US$4.5 billion in support of agribusiness, food companies, and banks in 2019, but leveraging effects of WBG on investments by the public or private sector flows into agriculture are not known.[3]

---

[1] SDG2 is "End hunger, achieve food security and improved nutrition and promote sustainable agriculture." See https://sustainabledevelopment.un.org/sdg2

[2] Although there are other multisectoral international organizations (IOs), most notably the United Nations Development Programme (UNDP), it is not a lending organization, and it is not included in this book.

[3] Notably, in 2019, 53 percent of the Bank's agricultural investments were in directly financing climate mitigation and adaptation measures. This is an increase of 28 percent over four years. See "World Bank: Food and Agriculture Overview" (last updated September 23, 2019): https://www.worldbank.org/en/topic/agriculture/overview#2

Given the growing importance of raising private finance, the experiences of IFC and MIGA, too, are of considerable interest. This story, however, is focused primarily on the IBRD and IDA, with a brief coverage of IFC and MIGA activities, due to the limited amount of information on private sector activities in the public domain. The World Bank is often seen as potentially in a strong position to scale up, leverage, or mobilize other sources of funding to increase investments.

The lending experience contained in this chapter is reviewed, with specific focus on food and agriculture, and with a view to the implicit or explicit theory of development that this assistance entailed. The broad sweep and relationship of this chapter with the rest of the book is described, to outline the ideas that drove World Bank lending and policy dialogue. It identifies lessons the World Bank learned from its own experience, as well as those it could have learned but did not, and the implications going forward for the development community as a whole, particularly in the areas of capacity building, human capital, and institutions.

Assistance to India and the rest of Southeast Asia in the 1960s, and to Bangladesh, starting in 1970, is a good example of support to LICs that have become emerging countries. Assistance to Bangladesh, in particular, soon after its independence, seemed "humanitarian" in nature at the time, with a concern in the Bank's top management that it could hurt the Bank's reputation as a development bank. With the passage of time, that support transformed the country into an emerging country. Admitting China into the Bretton Woods system in 1980, similarly, was a decision of considerable importance, contributing to a dramatic reduction in global poverty and to global growth (Kapur, Lewis, and Webb, 1997).

Nearly 60 percent of the poverty now is in SSA. A question going forward is whether project lending is a sufficient instrument, in view of low project performance ratings of African projects for well over 40+ years, relative to other regions and given the challenges of difficult agroecological conditions, environmental degradation, limited human and institutional capital, and high aid dependence?

Introduction

The evidence for this chapter comes from the World Bank Group's archives and oral histories; evaluations of the Operations Evaluation Department/Independent Evaluation Group (OED/IEG); the Bank's databases and publications, including histories of the World Bank (Kapur, Lewis, and Webb 1997) and *IDA in Retrospect* (World Bank 1982a); the *World Development Reports* (*WDRs*); the authors' years of experience in research, operations, and evaluation in the World Bank; and conversations with former colleagues and client country nationals who have dealt with the World Bank. Policy advice and lending is reviewed, including the interplay of internal factors within the Bank and external factors and shocks affecting member countries (for example, commodity prices, debt crises, and climate disasters). The Bank's diversified lending instruments are considered over time. A chronology of the World Bank is included in Appendix A.

Did the Bank have an agricultural development strategy? We argue that at least initially the strategy of an integrated agricultural development, with complementarity of seed, fertilizer, irrigation, and market access to farmers was much clearer in Asia, particularly in the 1960s with the start of the Green Revolution, than it was in Africa or Latin America. The strategy vacillated over time between agricultural development and rural development. The Bank experimented with privatization and farmers organizations, among other solutions. While the Bank decidedly embraced a community-driven development approach, that strategy affected rural development more than agricultural development. Furthermore, the Bank's focus was on poverty reduction, and that on food security and nutrition was spotty, changing from time to time, and impacts were not well monitored.

In view of the scope of the World Bank's activity, described in this chapter, its content is complementary to the content of virtually all other chapters: the broad agriculture and rural development strategy framework needed to achieve structural transformation and the slow progress needed to achieve it should be recalled in viewing the treatment of the World Bank's approach to food and agricultural policy advice and lending described in this chapter. Chapter 3 contains an in-depth discussion of the nature of the global food crisis during the 2007–12 period and the response of the global community to that crisis. This chapter describes the Bank's response to that crisis and its lessons. Chapter 4 on food security and nutrition addresses a broad swath of issues, including changing food systems and impacts of multidimensional poverty and gender on food security. There has been a long history in the Bank on the merit of spending more on poorer areas (Beegle and Christiansen 2019). Chapters 5 and 6 discuss global governance of food and agriculture, in which the World Bank has been an important player, but again, the voting rights have changed only marginally in the Bank's governance, and the leadership selection process remains unchanged. A US national heads the Bank, despite the debate that occurred on leadership selection in 2012, when there was growing pressure from member countries, particularly in the southern hemisphere, for selection of a candidate from an emerging market country. This did not occur at all in the recent appointment of President Malpass in April 2019.

The Bank's role in total financial flows and in ODA to developing countries has been by far the most significant, including particularly of the IDA, but has declined. Upper middle-income countries (UMICs), including, most notably, China, are graduating faster than occurred historically (*Economist* 2019), and demand from them for support for food and agriculture has declined. The question going forward is whether the Bank will continue to remain an important player, as it was in the past? Did it use its pivotal position to achieve accelerated, equitable, and sustainable agricultural growth and mobilize more resources?

Chapter 7, on international and domestic financial flows to agriculture and related sectors, shows that private flows (that is, foreign direct investment [FDI] and remittances) now tower over public/concessional and non-concessional (for example, IBRD) official flows. As also noted in Chapter 7, international financing of the SDGs probably fell in nominal terms in 2018 to US$669 billion, compared to an estimate of US$748 billion in 2017, largely driven by a sharp reduction in private lending to developing country governments through banks and bond markets (Kharas 2020). In addition, there is considerable uncertainty in the size of private and non-Development Assistance Committee (DAC) official flows. Also, there is no formal international statistical system to record them.

Focus on Smallholder Agricultural Development

IOs, including the World Bank, have steadfastly accorded priority to the development of smallholder agriculture for well over a half century, notwithstanding the academic debates on the pros and cons of smallholder development in the last decade. Specifically, in Table 2.1 in Chapter 2, we outlined what transformation of agriculture needs and the frequent political economy challenges in getting to the right mix of policies, institutions, investments, and human capacity at all levels, from the grassroots to subregional, national, and international levels. Box 2.3 then outlined the stages of development at which different issues tend to be addressed, and the rest of the chapter described how different countries have performed in transformation.

Smallholder development is essentially a private sector activity involving millions of small farmers to increase their productivity, improve food security, develop their capacity to deal with the risks, and generally, increase agriculture's resilience. Supply of public goods are critical in the effective delivery of services to farmers, and they range widely from transport and communication, technological packages, regulatory framework, policies, and institutions. As an institution that only lends to governments, the Bank has a comparative advantage in the provision of public goods. For public sector investment, regulation and implementation of essential services is critical to fostering private investment.

The Bank has brought investment finance to agriculture and the rural space, often accompanied by new technologies in the form of varietal improvements, seed, and fertilizers, agricultural finance, improved farmers' market access, and the capacity of the public sector to manage agricultural services, monitor progress, and learn from the experience of planning and implementation.

Against this background, this chapter illustrates choices the Bank made to finance specific activities in the public and private sector, such as seeds and mechanization, and how these choices have differed across countries and over time, and the lessons they offer. Overall, it is clear that governments have a clear role to play in policy, in the provision of public goods, such as research and development, education and training, and the development of human capital, generally, as well as helping to foster an investment climate that encourages private sector investment.

The International Development Association in the Context of Bank Instruments

WBG has four instruments at its direct disposal: IDA, IBRD, IFC, and MIGA. Founded in 1960, IDA has been the workhorse for support of agriculture and rural development in LICs (World Bank 1982a) (see Appendix C on the Role of the Multilateral Investment Guarantee Agency).

Since the articles of agreement of the IBRD were drawn up at the United Nations Monetary and Financial Conference, at Bretton Woods, New Hampshire, July 1–22, 1944, the founders, recognizing the scale of resources IBRD needed, had to demonstrate institutional creditworthiness to private lenders in the financial community in New York, and to persuade them that the Bank's borrowers were pursuing sound policies. Projects were seen as instruments. These were discrete, finite investments, which were distinct from sector policies, designed by high-quality professional experts of "good professional pedigree," to reassure bond holders that both project lending and good policies were being pursued (Kapur, Lewis, and Webb 1997, Vol. 1, 9). The pressure to fund "bankable projects" on harder terms with IBRD funding would have made many countries and investment projects ineligible for financing. The issue of fungibility was recognized early on by economists, such as Paul Rosenstein-Rodan and Albert Hirschman, associated with the World Bank, but, perhaps for reasons of simplicity and optics, those issues remained subordinate in selling the Bank to investors (Kapur, Lewis, and Webb 1997).

No country quotas on staffing were necessary. Search for excellence meant technical expertise could be recruited from around the world. Economics homogenized recruitment from the best universities (Kapur, Lewis, and Webb 1997).

Establishment of the IDA in 1960, as concessional window became necessary, as we explain later, for the Bank to able to provide soft loans of long duration. IDA turned the Bank into a premier development organization and leader, from a staid infrastructure Bank, a role it could not have claimed without IDA. IDA remains the largest and most important innovation for poorest countries, one which has had a large role in LICs and will continue to in SSA going forward. Examples of India, China, and Bangladesh show that, with appropriate support, countries previously considered "basket cases" can become thriving emerging economies, but it is long-term endeavor, requiring long-term presence that only the Bank has been able to provide on a consistent basis. It does not mean however that the Bank's strategy has been consistent over the years (World Bank 1982a; IDA 2020).

Autonomy diminished with IDA in the 1980s, with more demands on the Bank from IDA donors, particularly the United States, and to a lesser extent, the United Kingdom. The key issue that Jiajun Xu (2017) argued in her book, *Beyond US Hegemony in International Development: The Contest for Influence*—written from the Chinese perspective—is that the policymaking power, which was in the hands of Executive Directors shifted to the IDA Deputies, an informal group, when the group effectively argued that net income from IBRD should be allocated to IDA. It overtook the powers of the Executive Board (since they were the superiors of the Executive Directors) and with whom the Bank Management had to negotiate policy and management issues. For China, this became problematic, not so much because of substantive policy issues, of which there were a few, but because China was left out of a process where the major donors had their say, and ultimately, the US Treasury and Congress had the casting votes. China argued that the net income of the Bank could have been used to reduce interests to middle-income countries (MICs), and similarly, later when the income was used in support of the Heavily Indebted Poor Countries (HIPC) initiative. China first reacted by becoming an IDA donor, but then decided (after much interministerial debate in Beijing), that they should set up multilateral development banks (MDBs) of their own where they had a central position—the Asian Infrastructure Investment Bank (AIIB) and the New Development Bank (NDB). The early presidents of the Bank and the US-led (and other) executive directors—that is, the Bank management—preserved its operational/policy-setting independence. Much later, IDA deputies moved into the space carved out by the early presidents, and the IDA replenishment process became the key strategic policy process in the Bank. Just what influence the IDA deputies have had on the agriculture/rural development agenda, if any, is not clear, but it is recognized that IDA deputies imposed more conditionalities on IDA borrowers over time and those conditionalities typically applied to IBRD borrowers.

Also, with the push for structural adjustment, the Bank could no longer buy itself a "seat at the policy table" in the old-fashioned way of borrower persuasion (Kapur, Lewis, and Webb 1997, vol. 1, 217).

Since IDA's establishment, 44 low-income IDA-recipient countries have "graduated" (are no longer eligible for IDA's concessional resources).[4] Nine fell back due to various reasons, such as external shocks, poor macroeconomic management, or conflict, but Egypt, Indonesia, and the Philippines have climbed back.

---

[4] For more information, see "IDA Graduates," http://ida.worldbank.org/about/ida-graduates

Although the terms of IDA credit are soft, over the years, the Bank has emphasized that IDA projects are generally identical in scope and rigor to IBRD projects. Because IDA countries are less developed, a larger proportion of IDA lending has financed agriculture and rural development. IDA credits have also tended to finance a larger share of total project costs than IBRD loans, with the share higher in the poorest countries. The remaining share of total IDA project costs (56 percent), according to *IDA in Retrospect* (World Bank 1982a), has been financed partly by the recipients and by other donors. In general, IDA credits have financed a larger share of local costs than IBRD projects. This is, in part, because IDA projects typically involve more local costs, as well as finance a higher share of total project costs. IDA has also contributed to addressing balance of payments deficits to investments; physical capital, most notably, in the form of irrigation and rural roads; and technical assistance.

In 2019, 75 countries (59 IDA-only and 16 blend countries) remained IDA-eligible, with populations of 1.6 billion (Box 8.1). Since half of the global poverty and hunger (undernutrition) is in low- and middle-income countries (LMICs), those that have graduated from IDA eligibility still need investments in meeting SDG2. Kanbur and Sumner (2012) have argued that international assistance should go to poor people, rather than only to poor countries. This means the eligibility closely tied to per capita income should be replaced by other criteria. This would mean continued concessional aid to India, a LMIC, and to China, a UMIC—the two countries with the largest incidence of global poverty, despite its rapid decline, particularly in China (Lele, Agarwal, and Goswami 2018). Their argument was based, first and foremost, on the spillover effects of benefits for the poor to others. Donors may also gain knowledge, which they can transfer to other countries, and finally, they also raised moral and ethical issues of exclusion of populations, using income criteria—issues

---

Box 8.1 World Bank Lending

Operational lending categories: Economies are divided into IDA, IBRD, and "blend" countries, based on the operational policies of the World Bank. IDA countries are those with low per capita incomes that lack the financial ability to borrow from IBRD. Blend countries are eligible for IDA loans but are also eligible for IBRD loans, because they are financially creditworthy.

Eligibility for IDA support depends on a country's relative poverty, defined as gross national income (GNI) per capita below an established threshold and updated annually (US$1,145 in fiscal year 2019). IDA also supports some small island economies, which are above the operational cutoff but lack the creditworthiness needed to borrow from IBRD. Some countries, such as Nigeria and Pakistan, are IDA-eligible based on per capita income levels and are also creditworthy for some IBRD borrowing. They are referred to as "blend" countries. Seventy-five countries (59 IDA-only and 16 blend countries) are eligible to receive IDA resources in 2019.

IDA countries are those that lack the financial ability to borrow from IBRD. IDA credits are deeply concessional—interest-free loans and grants for programs aimed at boosting economic growth and improving living conditions. IBRD loans are non-concessional.

Source: http://ida.worldbank.org/about/borrowing-countries

which Angus Deaton (2018) has also raised in making a case for including poverty alleviation in developed countries, as we discuss elsewhere in the book. Kanbur and Sumner (2012) predicted that where the poor live will shape the debate. Under IDA18, some aid has gone to MICs receiving large numbers of refugees, such as Jordan and Lebanon, but overall this argument has been hard to sell, either to the donor shareholders or to developing countries (IDA 2018). Some of the Bank's shareholders, most notably the United States, have objected to continuing lending to China, and other conservatives, such as Meltzer, who argued against lending to MICs, as we have discussed in Chapter 6 (Meltzer 2000). Starting with similar initial conditions to India around 1960, China has reduced poverty and hunger rapidly, more so than India, although it has received much less ODA, including from IDA. China's domestic policy reforms were more robust than India's, and reflected more of the Bank's analysis of its economy in the 1980s, until its agricultural subsidies increased to a level larger than all that of the Organisation of Economic Co-operation and Development (OECD), as shown in Chapter 3. Their performance offers important lessons to others. Their emerging country status is already leading to more South–South cooperation. We explore these arguments later in this chapter, drawing lessons for SDG2 financing and support going forward.

Another vexing issue is about fragile or conflict-affected states. About half the world's poor live in a fragile, conflict, and violence (FCV) group. In 2019, out of 36 "fragile situations," 29 countries are IDA-only, three are blend countries, and one territory and three countries are IBRD-only, according to World Centre on Conflict, Security and Development (CCSD).[5] Fragility, conflict, and violence threaten efforts to end extreme poverty, in both LICs and MICs, the share of the extreme poor who live in conflict-affected situations is expected to rise by around half by 2030. Conflicts also drive 80 percent of all humanitarian needs and reduce gross domestic product (GDP) growth by 2 percentage points per year, on average (World Bank 2020b). Yet, on average, a country that experienced 20 years of violence also experienced twice the volatility in aid of a country that did not experience violence. Volatility of revenues has considerable costs for all governments, but particularly so in fragile situations, in which it may derail reform efforts and disrupt institution-building (World Bank 2011c). According to the IEG, the Bank's comparative advantage is in long-term development, but as of 2011, at least, its operational response (to conflict-affected countries) was constrained by its limited menu of instrument choices. Moreover, institutional and staff incentives to engage in conflict situations and to take risks lagged behind the spirit of its strategic approach, as expressed in various Bank documents, including the 2011 *WDR: Conflict, Security, and Development* (World Bank 2011c; IEG 2016c).

The Bank acknowledges:

Violent conflict has spiked dramatically since 2010, and the fragility landscape is becoming more complex. Climate change, rising inequality, demographic change, new technologies, illicit financial flows and other global trends may also create fragility risks. The World Bank Group is focused on addressing FCV, emphasizing prevention and acting early...[and] remaining engaged during active conflict, and in countries going through transitions to peace. Stronger collaboration with humanitarian, development, peace and security partners is critical for delivery in challenging environments, such as in the Bank's response to famine. (World Bank 2020b)

---

[5] See the "Harmonized List of Fragile Situations FY 19": http://pubdocs.worldbank.org/en/892921532529 834051/FCSList-FY19-Final.pdf

Since 1991, the same 10 conflicts have accounted for the majority of the forcibly displaced persons, who have been consistently hosted by about the same 15 countries. The host countries are largely developing countries (WBG 2017b). How is today's World Bank addressing these issues? The policy has evolved since the tenure Robert McNamara, president of the World Bank from 1968 to 1981, based on lessons of experience, but upon reviewing extensive evidence, we conclude it has not evolved enough to fit future needs.

Early Strong Foundations

The Bank's experience in food and agriculture illustrates how its approaches have reflected personalities of its presidents, but have also been path dependent, responding to the changing external environment and internal pressures in the Bank's client countries, shaping Bank policy analysis and advice. We start with an overview of the role of the Bank's presidents.

World Bank Presidents and McNamara's Defining Influence

After the Bretton Woods conference was held in July 1944, and signature of the Bank's articles of agreement were inked, the first two presidents, Eugene Meyer (1946) and John McCloy (1946–9) had much to do with the Bank's initial selection and organization of personnel and operational procedures to establish the World Bank's strong foundations. The very short duration of President Meyer seemed curious to us. Archives suggested that it was due to the US pressure exerted on him to expand the Bank more rapidly than Meyer felt the Bank was ready for, and despite his early departure, his desire to maintain the Bank president's independence from the board left a strong legacy of separation of the board from the executive, which has been only occasionally violated.[6] In *The World Bank Since Bretton Woods*, the authors described Meyer's frustration and resignation:

> Meyer was confronted by a strong board of directors, led by the young, well informed, energetic, and ambitious U.S. executive director. Much of Meyer's time and energy was spent in battling with the board for leadership of the institution.... The principal frustration of the Bank's first president was his feeling of having responsibility without authority, of having to battle the U.S.-led executive directors for stewardship of the institution. His explanation [for his abrupt resignation] was that he had accepted the presidency initially on the understanding that he would remain only until the Bank had been organized... Weariness, unwillingness to engage in bureaucratic infighting, and dissatisfaction with his anomalous position as president appear to be more plausible explanations. (Mason and Asher 1973)

Eugene Black (1949–62) was a much-admired CEO, and George Woods (1962–8) had extensive knowledge of SA. Each paved the way for increased support to macroeconomic

---

[6] In oral history, Richard Demuth, a highly respected veteran of the World Bank, explained that after careful search for a top-notch President, Meyer resigned after six months, because of excessive pressure from the US executive director, unbeknownst to the State Department, to expand World Bank operations too quickly. President McCloy negotiated hard terms of noninterference by the board in Bank management, setting a high standard for subsequent presidents about independence of management from the board (Demuth 1961).

policy reforms and food and agriculture policy, going beyond looking at individual projects, and this was well before the era of structural adjustment, a contribution that is often overlooked, with the relatively greater credit given to McNamara for his dynamic leadership.[7]

The period of the 1960s offers insights into understanding the interactions between external shocks, macroeconomic balances, and effectiveness of sector and project performance. Those lessons also stress the importance of learning from history, which were not always absorbed, as the later structural adjustment experience illustrates.

Eugene Black played a pivotal role in the Indus Waters Treaty, signed in 1960, between India and Pakistan for sharing waters from five northern rivers.[8] Water scarcity remains a source of acute concern today with climate change, growing demand, and inefficient use. The agreement was signed after 10 years of negotiations (Kraske 1996). The Bank's signature achievement is that the agreement still stands today, despite the fact that Indians were reluctant to have the Bank involved, and despite three wars and recurrent tensions between the two countries.

During President Black's tenure, the Bank acquired AAA bond rating. This enabled the Bank to borrow capital in bond markets at competitive interest rates. President Black also played a pivotal role in the establishment of IDA, as a multi-donor concessional window and as an integral part of the World Bank. India, the largest developing country, with its strong commitment to development, was an important client, although India viewed the Bank with suspicion, as a creature of Western powers (Kraske 1996). IDA arose out of the need to pledge resources to India's growing foreign exchange gaps annually, through a consortium of donors, following India's 1958 foreign exchange crisis and its growing capital needs. In retrospect, the strategic success to host IDA, a multi-donor fund, expanded the Bank's role in the development community in a way that is qualitatively different than, when in the 1990s, the Bank began to agree to host an assortment of multi-donor trust funds. The latter contributed to the fragmentation of aid and fundamentally changed the aid architecture (OED 2005b).[9] Other achievements of Black's tenure include the establishment of IFC in 1956 to promote private enterprise. Today, it lends as much to agribusiness (about US$4.5 billion annually) as do the World Bank and IDA combined. Under Eugene Black, the Economic Development Institute (EDI) was established in 1956, and later restructured as the World Bank Institute. EDI became the training ground for World Bank staff and

---

[7] In a World Bank archives' oral history interview of Stanley Please, on August 26, 1986, he noted:

George Woods' contribution there has been grossly underrated, particularly against that of [Robert] McNamara, who is known to have been greatly interested in development policy. But when you look back, some of the major departures in the Bank were made under George Woods, including building up the economic staff, moving into agriculture, into education, into industry as areas in which the Bank had to move in a big way, the appointment of Irving Friedman as the Economic Adviser to the President. Woods' involvement in the Indian exercise is also of interest in this regard. After the period of the 1950s when all the Western world thought India did everything right and could do nothing wrong in terms of development policy, suddenly in the 1960s everybody felt that it was all going sour, population was growing too rapidly, production was going down. Woods clearly recognized that he had a major development problem on his hands in the next to the largest country in the world and he set up the Bell Mission to try to provide guidance from the Western world to the Indians, and to the Bank itself.... [I]n terms of how he saw the Bank evolving in its responsibilities,... he has to be given credit for major steps forward in the 1960s, steps forward which McNamara was then able to build upon. (Please 1986, 11)

[8] See World Bank (2018a): "Fact Sheet: The Indus Waters Treaty 1960 and the Role of the World Bank."

[9] Donor pressure to create several different, independent trust funds, in the form of global programs, separated them from the Bank's primary mission, and the fragmented financing arrangement diluted the World Bank's influence, creating today's aid scenario. Supporters of trust funds have argued that additional aid would not have been mobilized had the Bank not played the role of a trustee.

developing country policymakers in the techniques of project appraisal, which were the bread and butter of the World Bank's lending business. Indonesia became the 56th member of the Bank, at the request of the government of the Netherlands to support the newly independent country needing help. The Bank wrote an important economic report and lent to a number of sectors, including agriculture. Black had been personally involved in Indonesia before becoming World Bank president.

In its early years, under Black, the Bank was also increasingly invited to be part of international financial diplomacy; for example, at the request of Governments of the United Kingdom and Egypt, the Bank worked on the Suez Canal Compensation Agreement in 1958, related to the expropriation of property. This long track record helped the Bank to be a credible international actor in matters related to international finance and negotiations.

George Woods followed Black. During his tenure, the Bank expanded further, as 18 African countries joined the World Bank in 1963, and although Indonesia withdrew its membership in 1965, it rejoined the Bank in 1967, and in 1968, became one of the largest recipients of IDA credits and World Bank loans.

President Wood initiated the Bell Mission to India in 1964 in response to India's second balance of payments crisis. The balance of payments crisis in 1958 had already led to the establishment of IDA. India was the largest client. Having invested in its development, stakes were as high for India's success to the Bank, as they were to India, as discussed later.

More generally, Woods also initiated a concerted effort to identify bankable projects and entered into an agreement with FAO to establish the cooperative program with the World Bank, FAO–CP in 1964 to help augment the Bank's capacity to respond to the growing client demand. FAO–CP is different than FAO's technical cooperation program, known as TCP, for which support comes from FAO's regular program budget and stood at 14 percent of the budget share in recent years. FAO–CP serves the needs of a number of IOs and support for it comes from IOs (see Chapter 9). The FAO–CP decision was not popular among Bank staff and managers, who felt that the Bank was giving away some of its prerogative to identify and appraise projects. The Bank retained the responsibility to appraise projects, but turned to FAO for project identification and preparation, and increasingly, to perform several other functions, including project supervision and project completion reports. It was a way to address issues of growing demand for Bank services from client countries, and FAO–CP has continued to play that role since. Bank attention to mount the Green Revolution was well underway in the mid-1960s, during George Wood's presidency, when Robert McNamara became the next president in 1968.

The substantive issues related to the Green Revolution and its lessons are discussed later. With the force of his personality, a strong intellect, adherence to modern management principles, and dedication to poverty alleviation, McNamara played a defining role in shaping the World Bank, as William Clark, the Bank's Director of External Relations, described in a 1981 article in *Foreign Affairs* (Clark 1981). McNamara's influences on the World Bank have been many and varied: for example, putting poverty eradication at the center stage of the Bank's mission, asserting the link of small farm agriculture to poverty reduction, and operationally, making use of IDA resources strategically to support a big push on the generation of the Green Revolution in India and Asia. He brought in new members such as Bangladesh (despite US opposition), expanded Bank activities in Indonesia and Egypt, and played a key role in the entry of the People's Republic of China (PRC) into the World Bank in 1980, paving the way for China's opening up of its economy and extraordinary growth.

Smallholder approaches, however, were underway well before McNamara under President George Woods. Robert Ayres, in his 1985 book, *Banking on the Poor: The*

World Bank and World Poverty, noted that, in reality, McNamara's attack on poverty was more an illusion than a reality. Ayres put it well: "While the Bank under McNamara was no longer a bastion of developmental traditionalism, it was a long way from adopting the more radical implications of attempting to mount an attack on poverty. The concern that the Bank might desert the poor must depart from a realization that under McNamara it never totally embraced them" (Ayres 1985, 235). McNamara was also early to note intersectoral linkages and complexity—for example, in the relationship between health and development, and nutrition and development—supporting WHO's onchocerciasis program (commonly known as "river blindness").[10] McNamara opened up lending to rural development in SSA, while greatly expanding the Bank's assistance to population, health, and nutrition. Methodologically, he popularized targeting aid to the lowest 40 percent of the income distribution, although operationally, targeting by income groups has not been easy, as we discuss later.

McNamara promoted research on growth and income distribution, and measurement of income and multidimensional poverty. He opened a resident mission in Jakarta, headed by Bernard Bell, to help Indonesia recover from the tattered Sukarno economy. Bell's tenure was more influential in Indonesia than in India, showing the importance of personal chemistry and country specificity in achieving results (Bell 1990), but it could also be that while the Bell mission was short-term, he was head of Indonesia's resident mission for several years, thus permitting the establishment of more enduring relations.

McNamara championed IDA replenishments and general capital increases for IBRD, even when they were not popular. By actively supporting the Pearson Commission led by the former Prime Minister of Canada, he drummed up support for aid in the broader development community (Pearson 1969). Similarly, he supported the Brandt Commission, the independent commission on international development issues, which released its report in 1980 (World Bank 1980). McNamara established the Consultative Group on International Agricultural Research (CGIAR), and more generally, turned the World Bank from a relatively obscure infrastructure bank into a central player and an intellectual leader in the international development community.

The Bank shifted abruptly from project lending (excessive in relation to country capacity) in the 1970s, particularly in Africa, to structural adjustment lending (SAL) in the 1980s during President Alden "Tom" Clausen's regime (1981–6). McNamara advocated this shift from project lending to a macroeconomic perspective in his farewell speech. Although he had been a banker of one of the largest banks, Clausen was not suited temperamentally to lead the Bank at a complex time in the Bank's history. With the benefit of hindsight, the Bank had overlooked lessons of the 1950s and 1960s of interactions between India's balance of payments crisis in managing project lending and need to support it with program lending while operating in Africa in the 1970s. At McNamara's behest, the Bank had expanded lending to state enterprises in Africa until commodity prices and poor project performance led to a debt crisis. Adjustment lending followed the Berg Report, but the Bank was also slow to address the debt crisis, which was crippling investments in agriculture and other social sectors (health and education)—the beginning of the "lost decade" (World Bank 1981).

Barber Conable (1986–91), a former Republican US congressman, is, ironically, the one known for the greening of the Bank, establishing the environment department and increasing lending to environmental projects. Road building, which caused deforestation in the

---

[10] See https://www.who.int/news-room/fact-sheets/detail/onchocerciasis

Amazon in Brazil, and other environmental impacts, such as the irrigation dams like the one on the Narmada River in India, began to be viewed through the lens of environmental and social safeguards. The Bank proactively participated in the Conference on Environment and Development in Rio de Janeiro in 1992, and hosted the Global Environmental Facility (GEF), which was born out of the conference.

Lewis Preston (1991–5), a brilliant banker, made the Bank client-oriented, helping to shift the Bank's approach from a supply-side to a demand-oriented approach—which, perhaps, also explains why there is not more lending to agriculture, as client demand for this sector is weak. He mounted the most ambitious review of Bank operations under veteran Vice President Willi Wapenhans, as the World Bank celebrated its 50th anniversary at the end of the 1980s, the "lost development decade," in the wake of structural adjustment and the debt crisis (World Bank 1992).

James Wolfensohn (1995–2005) brought renewed focus on poverty reduction and actively promoted the much needed, bottom-up, inclusive community and social development. He changed the Bank's culture by expanding partnerships with civil society and the private sector. The HIPC program was only approved in 1996, under Wolfensohn, even though the debt problem was evident in the 1980s (World Bank 2018b).[11] President Wolfensohn rightly considered it one of his crowning achievements.

Coming to the Bank on the heels of a failed presidency for President Paul Wolfowitz, Robert Zoellick (2007–12) restored confidence in the Bank. He recapitalized the Bank, introduced an open data policy—an important gift to the development community, including the Living Standards Measurement Study (LSMS) household surveys, now being extended under the 50 × 2030 initiative (discussed in Chapter 9 on FAO)—while ramping up the Bank's crisis response during the 2007–8 food and financial crises, making the Bank more agile and able to provide a speedier response in times of crisis. He also commissioned the Zedillo report (Linn 2009; Zedillo 2009), discussed in Chapter 6.

Jim Yong Kim's tenure (2012–19) brought record replenishments of IDA and with recapitalization of the Bank, made sizable investment in climate funds, and promoted a human capital index. Jim Yong Kim, a Korean-American physician and anthropologist, served as the 12th President of the World Bank from 2012 to 2019. He resigned prematurely February 1, 2019. During his first term, the Bank established the twin goals to end extreme poverty by 2030, and to boost shared prosperity, focusing on the bottom 40 percent of the population in developing countries. During his term, the Bank achieved record IDA replenishments, while also launching several innovative financial instruments, including facilities to address infrastructure needs, prevent pandemics, and help the millions of people forcibly displaced from their homes by climate shocks, conflict, and violence. The Bank also announced a human capital index.

President David Malpass took over as World Bank president in April 2019, from Kristalina Georgieva, CEO of the World Bank since 2017 and the first woman Acting President from February to April 2019; Georgieva became Managing Director of the International Monetary Fund (IMF) in 2019 (Kapur, Lewis, and Webb 1997; WBG 2014a).

---

[11] In oral history, Anne Krueger described the debt issue thusly: "the Bank was clearly in there for the developing countries and was concerned about the long-term growth impacts and development impacts, but to a first approximation the first part of the problem was simply getting immediate financing, and for that it was either the U.S. or the G7 or the IMF, or some combination of those. The Bank would then contribute to it, especially, with structural adjustment loans" (Krueger 2010, 7).

Malpass's appointment was the first in recent history when there were no serious contenders outside the United States for the position. Nomination of a candidate with a deep background in Treasury was pleasant surprise, although Malpass, like Jim Kim, had been opposed to the World Bank. President Malpass outlined a number of challenges in his address to the 2019 meeting of the Board of Governors, including, particularly, a proposed increased lending to climate change issues (World Bank 2019b). He announced, in January 2020, the division of the Africa region consisting of 54 countries into two regions "Eastern & Southern Africa" and "Western & Central Africa," effective July 1, 2020, as well as greater decentralization of Bank staff to field offices to increase country focus (Edwards 2019). Since 2000, Africa was subdivided at the World Bank into the "Middle East and North" and another region called "Africa," which included all of SSA. President Jim Kym's leadership changed the Bank from country to global practices, a step which has now been reversed (Kumar 2020). The global pandemic and the need for country action means that in a globalized world, the Bank cannot choose between country and global emphasis. It needs to balance both.

Reorganizations are costly in terms of staff disruption, and in reality, their role in achieving cost savings or development effectiveness is unclear. Furthermore, decentralization of the technical expertise from headquarters to the field increases staff costs and raises questions of development effectiveness when the numbers of technical staff have dwindled and their global knowledge is critical in country assistance. Later, we provide evidence that operational budgets per dollar lent have declined, meaning efficiency per dollar lent has increased, but whether it has increased development effectiveness using outcome indicators is unclear. A larger share of economic and sector work now comes from donor trust funds. And reorganizations have been like moving boxes around on an organizational chart.

A big and positive difference in the World Bank (and IMF), compared to the 1980s and 1990s, is that in March 2020, the Bank already had emergency operations underway in 60 countries, and its Board was considering the first 25 projects, valued at nearly US$2 billion under a US$14 billion fast-track facility to help fund immediate health care needs.

Country Performance

This long review makes clear that throughout the decades, a country's own development strategies, if well-defined and country-owned, have made a difference in outcomes in terms of decline in poverty and hunger, agricultural productivity, and participation of smallholders in the process, as has the quality of the Bank's (and donors') input. Furthermore, country performance can vary from one decade to the next. This is illustrated by South Korea and Thailand (both have graduated from the World Bank), as well as China. India's economic growth has increased steadily from one decade to the next, although less spectacularly than China's, to which the World Bank has contributed fewer resources. Ethiopia has shown more variable performance over the decades, given its changing political situation, but has shown promise in recent years. Commodity exporters in Latin America and SSA have experienced much greater external shocks, but they have managed those shocks less well, for example, than Indonesia, except during the 1997 crisis. Agricultural productivity growth has been critical in economic transformation in each of these countries, albeit those achievements have entailed some early wins, as in the case of India, followed by prolonged but slow growth until a dramatic turnaround in policy, in India in 1991, and more recently, also in Ethiopia. Absent domestic political will and action, even the best and the brightest in development economics, many of whom are employed by the Bank, have brought little in the way of increased development effectiveness. We counted 60 such economists who contributed to analysis of agriculture over the years. Attribution of impacts to any single event, project, policy, or piece of analysis, however, is always a challenge. Given this context, what contributions can an institution like the World Bank make going forward to the realization of the SDG2 goals, based on its long experience? We believe, first and foremost, in building human capital and institutional capacity of the countries to address their complex challenges, but interpretation of history has also varied.

Montague Yudelman, the first Director of Rural Development appointed by McNamara, noted that in the period prior to McNamara's presidency, smallholder agriculture was not seen as a problem area worthy of focus (but as we have indicated earlier in this chapter, the reality does not bear out this thinking, at least not in Asia) (Yudelman 1986). The Green Revolution was well underway in the 1960s, with active World Bank support. To continue with the Yudelman narrative, the Bank provided foreign exchange loans for building large-scale infrastructure, such as dams and railways, based on the Two Gap Model (the gap between investment and savings and imports and exports, which Hollis Chenery, the Bank's chief economist had articulated; see Chenery and Strout [1966]). Few people coming from developed countries, outside of those with colonial experience, knew much about tropical agriculture, and McNamara wanted to change the Bank's colonial image. As a member of the Ford Foundation board of directors, McNamara had seen modern technology brought to small farmers in Asia. He was fascinated by the idea of shaping the World Bank to deliver technology to small farmers to address the growing food shortages, brought on by recurring droughts, balance of payments difficulties, depletion of the US grain stocks with sales to Russia, and the first oil shock in 1972. Gathering development experts from around the world, including Mahbub ul-Haq from Pakistan, Paul Streeten from Britain, Chenery from Harvard University, and Yudelman from South Africa, McNamara embarked on the pursuit of a poverty eradication mission and reshaping the Bank to deliver on his program of action. Throughout this period, the tension between opting for growth advocated by Chenery and distribution advocated by Mahbub ul-Haq was clear (ul-Haq 1982). Ul-Haq contributed to McNamara's Nairobi speech, given on September 24, 1973, not long after the first global energy crisis began:

Absolute poverty is a condition of life so degraded by disease, illiteracy, malnutrition, and squalor as to deny its victims basic human necessities. It is a condition of life suffered ... by hundreds of millions of the citizens of the developing countries ... And are not we who tolerate such poverty, when it is within our power to reduce the number afflicted by it, failing to fulfill the fundamental obligations accepted by civilized men since the beginning of time?

Experience demonstrates that in the short run there is only a limited transfer of benefits from the modern to the traditional sector. Disparities in income will simply widen unless action is taken which will directly benefit the poorest.... [T]herefore, there is no viable alternative to increasing the productivity of small-scale agriculture if any significant advance is to be made in solving the problems of absolute poverty in the rural areas.... Without rapid progress in smallholder agriculture throughout the developing world, there is little hope either of achieving long-term stable economic growth or of significantly reducing the levels of absolute poverty. (McNamara 1973)

The Nairobi speech was a watershed in the history of the Bank. It shaped the Bank's vision and a mission of a world without poverty, making the Bank into an institution that champions poverty eradication, proactively pursuing development interventions to achieve impacts. The speech made a strong case for development assistance to reduce poverty, admonishing donors, including McNamara's own country, for not raising aid to 0.7 percent of GDP, when the aid environment was not propitious.

Ahead of its time, the Nairobi speech was rich in content; it emphasized increasing agricultural productivity of small farmers, and espoused views on the interconnectedness of population, health, and nutrition among each other and with agriculture and rural development. To achieve productivity growth among small farmers, it emphasized secure land tenure, rural finance, and infrastructure—envisioning that, if productivity of poor people and agriculture increased by 5 percent for 15 years, developing countries' economies would be transformed. Box 8.2 describes some of the solutions the Bank deployed.

Food Prices and Incentives to Invest in Food and Agriculture

We noted in previous chapters that donors and national governments often respond to crises, albeit with a lag. Typically, the crisis is reflected in international food prices (although recently, more direct measures of food insecurity have become available, such as FAO's Food Insecurity Experience Scale/Voices of the Hungry, discussed in Chapter 4). World Bank responded to the crises strongly from the 1960s until the mid-1980s with a rise in lending, followed by a sharp decline in lending from the mid-1980s, as shown in Figure 8.1. This response has been less intense over time since then. Thus, the lagged value of the Grain Price Index to IBRD lending to agriculture in a Granger causality test is only 0.04, which confirms the direction of causality over the 59-year period, covering 1960 to 2018 and the weakening strength of response. Food prices reached a peak in 1974, and the strongest World Bank response followed, reaching the first lending peak in 1975 and soaring to higher levels until 1986, before showing a precipitous decline in lending—in turn, a result of declining food prices and disincentive to investment. Food prices reached the first bottom in 1996, and with it, a bottom in lending. Agricultural prices showed the first slight rise in 1996, followed by a lending increase that reached a peak in 1998, before prices declined once again but then rose from 2007–8 to 2012, then again declining and remaining low until 2019. The lending response, as well as the overall role of the World Bank in global agricultural investments, has been less important as the share of assistance over time, as we show in this chapter.

Public and donor investments respond, often after farmers have responded to price rises and markets have calmed down. They need to provide a steady rate of investments in public goods, such as research and education, information, communications, and infrastructure, regardless of prices.

The Start of Rural Development

Yudelman produced the first official policy paper on rural development (World Bank 1975b). He also delivered a series of "new-style" rural development projects. In an account for the oral history project, Yudelman described it as a US$10 billion experiment (Yudelman 1986). He noted the enormous pressure he felt to lend for agriculture and

Box 8.2 McNamara's Bank Reorganized to Deliver Solutions in Agriculture and Rural Development

Although developing countries in Africa had asked for support for agriculture and rural development, Bank's presidents, prior to McNamara, had not responded to the call, perhaps because Black and Woods had been addressing major issues in Asia. This changed under McNamara. Based on advice from McKinsey, the Bank was reorganized. An all-powerful director, James Evans, who had been effectively vested with the Bank's entire technical brain trust prior to the reorganization, was replaced by Montague Yudelman, a South African economist dedicated to rural development. Regional vice-presidencies were established, and a bulk of the technical staff was moved out of the centralized Project Department to the newly formed regional vice-presidencies. This organizational shift affected the focus of Bank activities, making it more attuned to the demands of developing countries. The Bank succeeded beyond expectations, in South and Southeast Asia in the 1960s and 1970s, by contributing to the Green Revolution and establishing CGIAR in support of it. By all internal accounts of senior Bank managers during this time, reported in oral histories,[a] the Bank, however, had limited success in its efforts in Africa.

India contains the largest number of the world's poor and hungry and remains a continued battleground for SDG2. Although India received the largest amount of IDA lending in support of poverty and hunger, the lending was small in per capita terms or as share of domestic investment.[b] Politically, India was supported by Western countries as a bulwark against Communist China. It has remained a strong democracy, and its economic growth has been higher in every successive decade than the preceding one, but growth has not been accompanied by equity, and agricultural performance has been mixed since the heyday of the Green Revolution, with more complex challenges of groundwater exploitation and climate change in achieving sustainable intensification. We explore the reasons and the limits of the Bank's role in the sections that follow.

Agricultural growth has picked up in Africa in the new millennium, mostly from area expansion, but with slowest productivity growth among continents, and little or no growth in per capita income, as shown in Chapter 2 on transformation. We explore the reasons why, including their implications for future World Bank assistance.

Notes:

[a] See WBG (2019), the WBG Archives Oral History Program at https://oralhistory.worldbank.org, and particularly, the transcripts of interviews with Stanley Please (Please 1986); Willi Wapenhans (Wapenhans 1993); and Montague Yudelman (Yudelman 1986).

[b] External aid constituted slightly less than one-third (28–25 percent of total investment outlays during the third five-year plan [1961–2 to 1965–6]). By 1984–5, during the sixth plan, external aid had already declined to 7.7 percent. The Bank ranked third in grant-in-aid to India in 2017. The top ranked donors were the United Kingdom, followed by the Global Fund to Fight AIDS, Tuberculosis and Malaria (GFATM). The Bank, and specifically, IDA, ranked low for grants-in-aid, once India graduated from IDA in 2017.

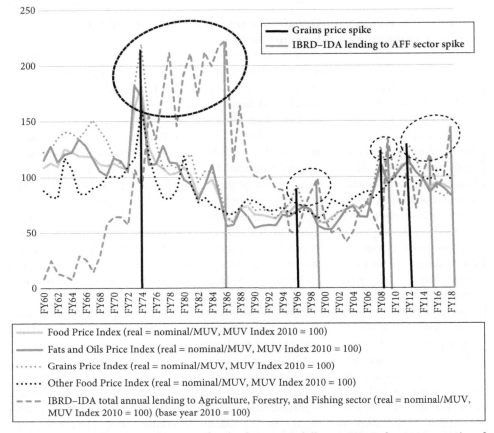

Figure 8.1 World Bank Food Price Index (real 2010 US dollars, MUV Index 2010 = 100) and IBRD–IDA total annual lending to the Agriculture, Forestry and Fishing sector (MUV Index 2010 = 100, base year 2010 = 100), FY1960–FY2018

Source: Based on data from https://www.worldbank.org/en/research/commodity-markets and http://data.worldbank.org/data-catalog/projects-portfolio

rural development, given McNamara's personal interest in agriculture (see World Bank [1988b] for a review of World Bank experience with rural development from 1965 to 1986). The Bank increased commitments; recruited a pool of technical staff; and put agriculture, population, and nutrition at the center stage of human development, while also establishing a department of Population, Health, and Nutrition (PHN).[12] It also added a social

---

[12] The review, "Learning from World Bank History" noted: "There has been no well-articulated vision about what, operationally, agriculture can and should be accountable for regarding nutrition, and how such action is integral to agriculture's goals. This is strongly related to an *absence of targets for success and accountability* that make sense for agriculture" (WBG 2014a, xii). Further:

> Meerman (1997) reported that only 6 out of 50 Agriculture Sector Adjustment Loans (AGSECALs) addressed food security issues (Jamaica, Kenya, Madagascar [1986], Mauritania, Mexico [1992], Morocco).... [T]hree other AGSECALs (Burkina Faso, Mexico [1988], and Somalia) also dealt with issues of food security as loosely defined by OED as 'the degree to which an individual or group has adequate nutrition at all times.' Therefore, we consider that out of 50 AGSECALs between 1979 and 1995, at least nine AGSECAL addressed food security in some way, and some also addressed nutrition explicitly. (WBG 2014a, 20)

dimension by recruiting its first rural sociologist. Since then, the number of sociologists at the Bank has increased, following Wolfensohn's push for bottom-up, community-driven development in the mid-1990s. The "new-style" integrated rural development projects, operating side-by-side with operations in regions of Latin America, Asia, and SSA, where regional vice presidencies continued to expand conventional lending to agriculture and rural development. This included transmigration projects in Indonesia and agricultural credit projects in Brazil. Many of them were of questionable quality and quantity, approved under the guideline from top management that at least 20 percent of the lending should go to agriculture and rural development. As we showed in Chapter 4, nutrition was in ascendancy in lending in the 1970s, but also subsequently experienced a spectacular fall, before rising again after 2007. Support to population also declined, overtaken by support to health. The PHN department was renamed Health, Nutrition and Population (HNP) in 1997.

Although Bank lending recognized the multisectoral nature of poverty reduction and interventions needed to achieve it, Yudelman acknowledged in an oral history interview that the concept of rural development remained elusive well into the 1990s (Yudelman 1991). There was also considerable skepticism among the frontline operational staff about the merits of rapidly expanding lending and reporting data on all aspects of agriculture and rural development, which McNamara demanded. This included the number of people reached by Bank projects, increase in crop yields, and number of beneficiaries from new water sources, among others. McNamara set a demanding tone for numbers to show impacts, but often data did not exist. The demand for evidence of benefits first manifested itself in a new push for social rates of return in place of the traditional economic rates of return, and much later, in a big surge in impact analysis through randomized trials. The ubiquitous nature of cell phones, the speed of remote sensing, the data revolution, AI, and speed of broadband through 5G, and more are together bringing down the cost of data collection and analysis. An important question going forward is whether more data are improving our understanding of the development process.

As the Bank announced a policy toward rural development, a study, *The Design of Rural Development: Lessons from Africa* (Lele 1975), was commissioned by the Africa region of the Economics Research department. The impetus for the study came in response to a request made by Tanzania's Finance Minister Cleopa Msuya, at the Annual Meetings of the World Bank in 1972, that the Bank should expand lending to African agriculture. After reviewing 13 donor-funded projects in depth in seven African countries, Lele concluded that, except for a few well-conceived export crop schemes (such as smallholder tea and coffee projects in Kenya), integrated rural development projects, as practiced by donors at the time in Africa, had limited impacts and even bigger questions about their sustainability. They were too costly and too complex in relation to the countries' capacities to plan and implement them. The implementation targets were too ambitious, and the projects' sustainability was in question because of their fiscal, institutional, and human capital requirements. The study recommended a sequential approach to project design and implementation. Its message was: identify the most critical constraints, establish priorities for interventions via active local participation, and build capacity of indigenous institutions to deliver services that people prioritized *before* expanding the project scope horizontally to other sectors or before

Nevertheless, during the 23 years (1972–95) of Alan Berg's tenure (the World Bank's former Senior Nutrition Advisor), the size of nutrition operations generated by the Bank (freestanding nutrition projects and nutrition components of health, education, agriculture, rural development, and social protection projects) totaled US$2.1 billion, significantly more than the spending of all other donors combined (WBG 2014a).

scaling up vertically. The Bank publication of *Design of Rural Development*, with McNamara's foreword, became a bestseller on US and European campuses as a teaching resource. It also reached African policymakers widely, giving its author a few months of renown, but the study had little impact internally on the Bank's thinking or lending. Local participation did emerge as a popular tool in the World Bank in the 1990s, widely known as social funds projects, community-based development (CBD), and community-driven development (CDD), terms developed by the World Bank under President Wolfensohn's promotion of a global compact. According to the Operations Evaluation Department (OED), now called the Independent Evaluation Group (IEG), the concepts were being applied to at least nine different types of sectors/interventions (OED 2005b). The rural development sectors—roads, water, health, education, energy—received much attention on a large scale, but agriculture received little.

McNamara's Nairobi speech generated so much intellectual and bureaucratic energy that it led to very rapid growth in both IBRD and IDA commitments to agriculture and "integrated rural development" in the 1970s and 1980s (Figure 8.2). With IBRD lending in MICs and regions (Latin America and the Caribbean [LAC], Middle East and North Africa [MENA], and East Asia) and IDA lending in SA and SSA, Bank assistance was soon followed by an increased share of the entire ODA going to agriculture during the decade of 1973–84. The 1973 Annual Meetings resulted in a pledge by the WBG of US$22 billion for nearly 1,000 projects over the next five years to target the problems of the rural poor in developing countries.

The Bank's research department, led by Hollis Chenery, the World Bank's chief economist, initiated an ambitious research program on growth and income distribution, measurement of poverty levels, and the causes of changes in them, many of which have been mainstreamed now. McNamara was assiduous about programming and budgeting to ensure that staff increases were accompanied by increased numbers of projects, which assured real resource transfers. Figure 8.3 shows the long record of demonstrating the relationship between administrative budget and number of operations to measure efficiency of Bank operations. McNamara also established the Bank's Operations Evaluation Department, now the IEG.

Agriculture's share in total lending increased from 3.9 percent (lowest) in 1964 to a peak of 38.5 percent (highest) in 1978, before declining significantly (Figure 8.2). After reaching second and third peaks of lending in 1981 and 1986, respectively, and after a decade of disappointing performance, both the share of Bank lending going to agriculture and the share of donor aid to agriculture declined precipitously (Figure 8.2). The Bank led in the decline of donor aid to agriculture. The share of aid to agriculture did not recover again until around 2005, but as we will show, IDA lending began to show green shoots in Africa in 2000 and rose sharply after 2008, as it did similarly in SA. Yet, overall Bank/IDA lending never achieved the shares in total lending that it had reached in the 1970s and 1980s, and as shown in Figures 8.5 and 8.6, IBRD lending to agriculture showed a precipitous decline, whereas IDA has remained in business in agriculture.

IBRD–IDA total annual commitments to the AFF sector increased, from a low of US $0.21 billion in 1964 to a peak of US$6.3 billion in 1986, before declining significantly (Figure 8.2). By 2003, lending to agriculture sector had reached its lowest level. Attention had moved to other related themes. IBRD–IDA annual commitment to the AFF sector was above US$4 billion in 2018, for the first time since 1988.

Overall, the IBRD and IDA together lent US$1,077 billion in nominal terms and US$1,337 billion in real terms (MUV Index 2010 = 100) between 1960 and 2018, of which nearly US $114 billion in nominal terms and US$161 billion in real terms (MUV Index 2010 = 100)

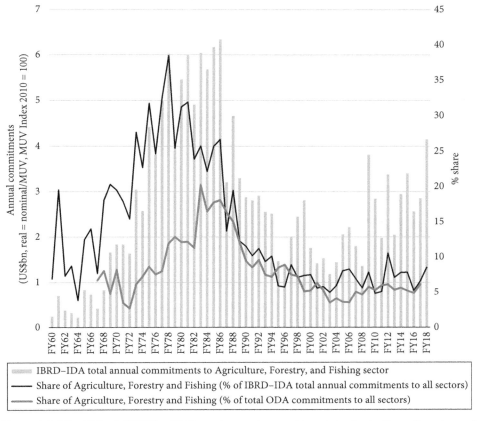

Figure 8.2 World Bank (IBRD + IDA) total annual commitments to Agriculture, Forestry and Fishing sector (US$bn, real = nominal/MUV, MUV Index 2010 = 100) and agriculture share in total aid down: Share of ODA and World Bank (IBRD + IDA) commitments to Agriculture, Forestry and Fishing as a percentage of total commitments to all sectors, 1960–2018

Note: ODA data is available up to 2017.

Source: Based on data from https://datacatalog.worldbank.org/dataset/world-bank-projects-operations and https://stats.oecd.org/

went to the AFF sector in 159 countries located in six regions (East Asia and Pacific [EAP], Europe and Central Asia [ECA], LAC, Africa, MENA, and SA).

SA ranked at the top, with shares of about 24 percent, and with 20 percent to EAP, 19 percent to LAC, 10 percent to ECA, and 8 percent to MENA, but with huge variations, of course, between peak and trough periods across regions (Figure 8.4). The lending to the agricultural sector was only 12 percent of the overall lending by IBRD and IDA together for the whole period. The Bank (IBRD + IDA) annual commitments to the AFF sector since 1960 to 2018, by region, is shown in Figure 8.5.

The shares of IBRD and IDA were 56 percent and 44 percent, respectively, in total commitments to AFF sector for the entire period (1960–2018) for all six regions, where the share of IDA increased significantly from 40 percent (initial period 1960–80) to 56 percent (2000–18), and the share was 38 percent for the period 1980–2000, which was lowest among all periods. From Figures 8.6 and 8.7, it is clear that, since 2000, IDA's role to the agricultural sector became more prominent and surpassed IBRD in the last few years.

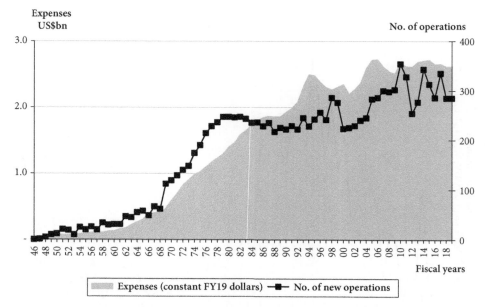

Figure 8.3 World Bank (IBRD/IDA) number of operations and administrative expenses, FY1946–FY2019 (constant FY2019 US dollars)

Note: For FY18 and FY19 the budget is applied for expenses. FY19 operations are notionally indicated at the FY18 level.

Source: World Bank (2019c). Data provided by Bill Katzenstein on May 31.

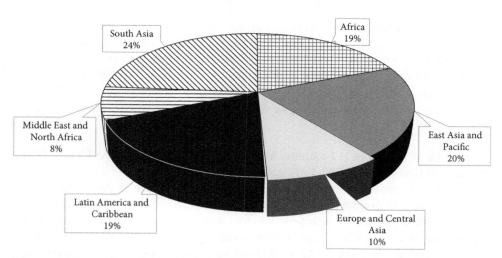

Figure 8.4 Share of IBRD–IDA total commitments to the Agriculture, Forestry and Fishing sector by region, FY1960–FY2018 (total = US$161bn, real = nominal/MUV, MUV Index 2010 = 100)

Source: Based on data from https://datacatalog.worldbank.org/dataset/world-bank-projects-operations.

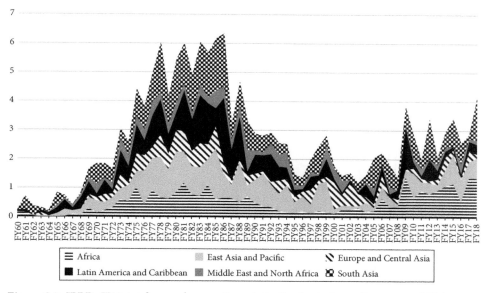

Figure 8.5 IBRD–IDA total annual commitments to the Agriculture, Forestry and Fishing sector by region, FY1960–FY2018 (US$bn, real = nominal/MUV, MUV Index 2010 = 100)

Source: Based on data from https://datacatalog.worldbank.org/dataset/world-bank-projects-operations

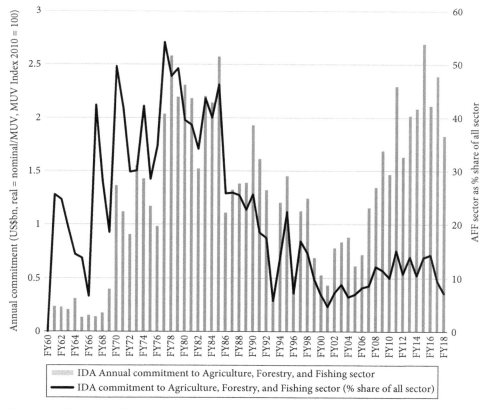

Figure 8.6 IDA annual commitment to the Agriculture, Forestry and Fishing sector (US$bn) and AFF sector share as a percentage of total commitment to all sectors, FY1960–FY2018 (real = nominal/MUV, MUV Index 2010 = 100)

Source: Based on data from https://datacatalog.worldbank.org/dataset/world-bank-projects-operations

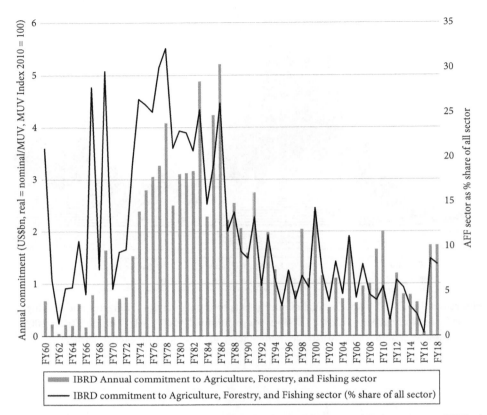

Figure 8.7 IBRD annual commitment to the Agriculture, Forestry and Fishing sector (US$bn) and AFF sector share as a percentage of total commitment to all sectors, FY1960–FY2018 (real = nominal/MUV, MUV Index 2010 = 100)

Source: Based on data from https://datacatalog.worldbank.org/dataset/world-bank-projects-operations

SA and India, in particular, received the largest share of IDA lending to the AFF sector for the whole period 1960–2018—45 percent of total commitments. India is and has long been the recipient of the largest share of World Bank loans and credits. IDA also dominated in Africa, with an average share of 32 percent of total commitments to AFF for the period 1960–2018, whereas IBRD lending went mostly to LAC (33 percent), followed by EAP (24 percent), ECA (16 percent), MENA (11 percent), SA (9 percent), and Africa (7 percent) (Figures 8.8 and 8.9).

As the overall ODA increased, World Bank (IBRD + IDA) lending remained almost constant in real terms during the years 1983 to 2008, except for the brief period during the 1997 East Asian financial crisis, when lending to Indonesia increased. Then, in 2009–10, once again, the financial crisis resulted in a substantial growth in lending and in the number of investment operations (Figure 8.10). Since 2013–14, World Bank (IBRD + IDA) lending trend has been increasing. Figure 8.10 also shows a big decline in WBG lending, relative to ODA over time and to the extent that the Bank has more to contribute in terms of development policy and institutions, it should try to get its share up in ODA. ODA is also smaller relative to the overall financial flows to developing countries, which have grown greatly over the past 50 years, as discussed in Chapter 7. In the case of SSA, too, external

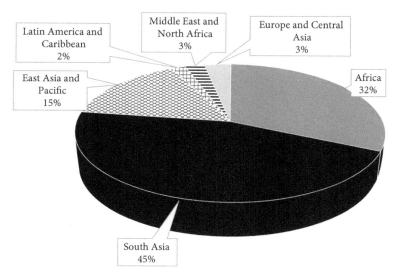

Figure 8.8 Share of IDA annual commitment to the Agriculture, Forestry and Fishing sector by region, FY1960–FY2018 (%, total = US$74.4bn, MUV Index 2010 = 100)

Source: Based on data from https://datacatalog.worldbank.org/dataset/world-bank-projects-operations

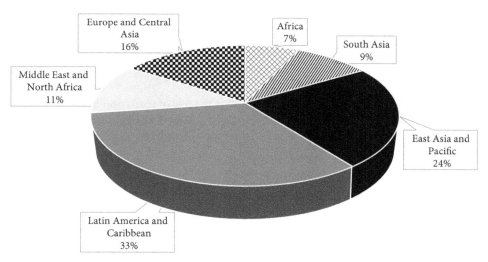

Figure 8.9 Share of IBRD annual commitment to the Agriculture, Forestry and Fishing sector by region, FY1960–FY2018 (%, total = US$94.9bn, MUV Index 2010 = 100)

Source: Based on data from https://datacatalog.worldbank.org/dataset/world-bank-projects-operations

financial flows (that is, the sum of gross private capital flows, ODA, and remittances to the region) have not only grown rapidly since 1990, from US$20 billion in 1990 to above US $120 billion in 2012, but their composition has changed significantly. Most of this increase in external flows is due the increase in private capital flows and the growth of remittances, especially since 2005 (Sy and Rakotondrazaka 2015).

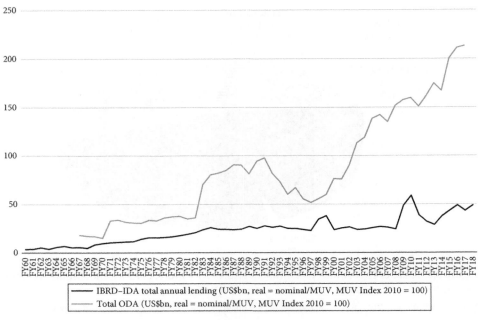

Figure 8.10 ODA and IBRD–IDA total annual commitments to all sectors, FY1960–FY2018 (US$bn, real = nominal/MUV, MUV Index 2010 = 100)

Note: ODA data are available up to 2017.

Source: Based on data from https://datacatalog.worldbank.org/dataset/world-bank-projects-operations and https://stats.oecd.org/

At a more micro level, in this chapter, we discuss the role of the World Bank illustratively in fostering seed companies, IFC's activity in agriculture, and foreign purchases of agricultural land in Africa. In infrastructure, too, FDI is many times larger than ODA and has been growing rapidly since 1990.

Asia Was the Place of Action, Drama, and Results

Agricultural strategies raise important, "stage appropriate" roles of markets and states, and strategic investments in technology, infrastructure, institutions, and human capital—issues which have been faced in lending to SSA. In Asia and, particularly, in India, by force of circumstances—the Bank strategy in the 1960s emerged from India's second balance of payment crisis, which prompted the unpopular Bell Mission to India in 1964. India's poor agricultural performance, food shortages, and increased food aid dependence combined with the poor macroeconomic performance during the Third Plan were leading concerns in the World Bank about India's slowing macroeconomic and agricultural performance. Between 1962 and 1972, 40 percent of India's aid flows were in the form of food aid. The US administration was concerned about declining US food stocks and the United States' inability to continue sending food aid on a large scale, straining India's port capacity. Uniquely, the Bell mission reported to the World Bank's President George Woods and turned out to be deeply unpopular in India.[13] However, the Bell mission's agricultural sector strategy, headed by Sir John Crawford, was most impactful. It had been, with input from W. David Hopper, Wolf Ladjinsky, and Louis Goreux, a model builder. The Bell Report noted:

> Accelerated growth of agricultural output calls for policies substantially different from those which prevailed during most of the Third Plan period. Strong and stable price incentives to producers must be provided and sustained; much larger and genuinely adequate supplies of the major physical inputs must be supplied. These include most importantly fertilizers, irrigation water, improved seed and plant protection materials. Industrial production and allocations of scarce domestically produced and imported materials must be geared to provide these even if this should require alteration in the pattern of industrial investment and foreign exchange allocation. Farm credit must be made available in adequate amounts and to all classes of cultivators. We emphasize these as the major factors which are likely to affect output in the immediate future. Proper balance in policy must, however, give concurrent attention to better organized and directed research, to reorganization and strengthening of extension work and of administration, to better gearing of irrigation planning and operation to agricultural production requirements, to enforcement of security of tenure and fair rents, and to the speeding of consolidation of fragmented holdings. (World Bank 1965a, 22–3)

The lasting value of this diagnosis of India, made in the 1960s, can be seen in a more recent African context: for example, on the decision of Ethiopia to adopt seed and fertilizer distribution, as interrelated for at least three reasons and with spectacular success in transforming agriculture (Rashid et al. 2013; Bachewe et al. 2018). First, average yield increases tend to be higher when the inputs are adopted simultaneously than when adopted separately, due to complementarity effects (Feder 1982). Second, the combined use of two or more inputs can be risk-reducing, since the synergistic use leads to better outcomes. Third, agricultural input supply strategies in the last decade have encouraged African farmers to adopt chemical fertilizers and improved seeds as a package, at times bundled with input credit, making adoption of these two inputs an inherently simultaneous decision or one made between sets of possible technology bundles.

For the same reason, the Bank sector strategy in India in the 1960s injected a technology-driven package approach to the languishing Intensive Agricultural Development Program (Herdt 2012). Its focus was on modern crop varieties and complementary external inputs of seed, fertilizer, irrigation, credit, and assured minimum prices. The mission made a strong case for more aid to India, and it was backed by wide-ranging interventions in the entire agriculture sector, involving public sector delivery systems, promoted by the World Bank

---

[13] Woods knew India intimately, admired its development effort, and recognized the need for the Bank to exercise leadership by undertaking sound analysis of India's economy at a time when India, the Bank's largest borrower, was facing difficulties. In 1962, India had lost a border war with China, and due to crop failures, was importing massive amounts of food aid. The United States, the principal source of food aid, was running out of food surpluses. India's criticism of the Vietnam War was not well received by President Johnson, then deeply escalating the United States' role in the war. Prime Minister Nehru passed away in 1964. India was facing an acute balance of payments crisis and the demand for a major devaluation (Lele and Agarwal 1991). India needed help. The Bell Mission, sent by Woods to comprehensively review India's economy, was interpreted by Indian policy-makers as undue interference in its sovereignty at a time when India was vulnerable and sensitive to criticism, after having been treated as a country that could do no wrong. Having invested a great deal of the World Bank and donor funds in India, Woods considered it the Bank's responsibility to enhance India's performance through policy advice, to be able to make a case for continued high levels of lending.

and backed by the US government, with the personal involvement of US President Lyndon Johnson and scientists from US foundations. Copying the US agricultural strategy, including support prices that generated food surpluses and land grant universities, these actions were followed by a significant and predictable infusion of World Bank financing in support of agriculture for nearly a decade, while McNamara was Bank president. India was the largest recipient of IDA and of lending for fertilizer imports, seed production, and irrigation. Internally, India was better governed prior to the declaration of emergency by Prime Minister Indira Gandhi in 1975 to 1977. Most importantly, despite opposition to the strategy by Indian intellectuals (for example, T. N. Srinivasan [1991]), the strategy was owned by the influential policymakers, the secretary of agriculture, and the scientists from the Indian Council of Agricultural Research (ICAR), who were in key positions in the government and who ensured speedy implementation. Norman Borlaug actively supported India's powerful political commitment to achieve food security, by first contributing 18,000 tons of hybrid seed from Mexico, until India had developed its own seed production and distribution system. The adoption of the strategy was driven by a national sovereignty imperative, influenced by what is referred to, even today, as the then "ship-to-mouth" existence in India, when President Johnson personally threatened to hold back shipments of food aid, week by week, if India made a critical statement on the Vietnam War (Lele and Goldsmith 1989; Lele and Bumb 1994).

Whether India could have pulled off the Green Revolution without public sector seed companies remains debated.[14] The Crawford team stressed that without the "all-hands-on-deck" policy of the government, which the Crawford team promoted, the Green Revolution would not have occurred (Raj Paroda, former Director General, ICAR, personal communication, August 15, 2019).

Now, despite these and subsequent achievements, such as that of genetically modified (GM) cotton turning India into the second largest producer of cotton in the world, the Indian seed sector faces enormous challenges of productivity gap, low replacement rates under quality seeds of high-yielding varieties (HYVs)/hybrids, lack of effective public–private partnership, poor access to genetic resources, declining R&D investments in plant breeding, and above all, the uncertain policy environment for scaling innovations such as GM technology. Paroda notes that these need to be addressed on a priority basis (Raj Paroda, personal communication, August 15, 2019). Indian public policy is clearly critical to

[14] Byerlee and Pray, in personal exchanges on August 13, 2019, suggested that India had an active private sector, but the Bell Mission Report, Annex 3 (World Bank 1965b, paras. 53–4) indicates Rockefeller Foundation scientists helped develop India's joint government–private sector-controlled Seed Corporation, under the Seed Act, to create a modern seed industry to produce foundation seed, which would go to the private seed producers. The 4th Five Year Plan had a target of 274 million acres under improved seed by 1971. Assuming seed replacement by farmers every five years, it would require 1.3 million acres under improved seed production (Derek Byerlee and Carl Pray, personal communication, August 13, 2019).

There was considerable interest in foreign seed companies, according to Paroda: "In the sixties, there was hardly a private seed industry. Thanks to the World Bank, under National Seed Project Phase 1, 2 and 3, a system of seed production under public domain was established and required human resources created through SAUs [state agricultural universities] in the seventies and eighties. The private sector came into it in a big way only in nineties and after" (Raj Paroda, former Director General, ICAR, personal communication, August 15, 2019). Chauhan et al. (2016, 578), in their paper on the seed industry in India, also stressed the need for a "strong and vibrant seed production system" for India's food security. Consistent decline through the years has reduced seed supply. The authors suggest that timely availability of breeder seed is possible if the farmers place orders three years in advance to ICAR and SAUs, allowing time for breeder seed to be converted to foundation and certified seed. The authors conclude that in addition to increasing demand for quality seed among farmers, "policy support from government such as tax exemption, credit on soft terms, duty free import of equipment and integrated approach towards seed security through nationwide seed science research are the growth drivers for a vibrant seed sector [with] potential to raise India from 6th to 3rd position in global seed trade" (Chauhan et al. 2016, 578).

addressing these long overdue policy reforms, but it has not made much headway. Policy uncertainty discourages investment.

Borlaug tried an approach, similar to that used in India, through the Sasakawa Africa Association (SAA) in the 1980s, but there was no appetite among donors to create a policy framework with a strong role for the public sector until the private sector could be developed, a strategy that the Alliance for a Green Revolution in Africa (AGRA) has followed. The tolerance of the public sector role, however, has increased, perhaps, in the post-2000 period, as illustrated by continued donor support for Ethiopia, whose performance has improved significantly with a strong role for the public sector in the delivery of inputs, and one that the government has been slow to give up. Recent analytical findings suggest that more competition between the public and private sector is now warranted to reduce fiscal burden (Rashid et al. 2013). Thus, the dilemma remains: whether to scale up rapidly, using public sector's broad reach, albeit recognizing that it will build vested interests and reforms will be difficult to achieve, or to build a private sector delivery system, which will admittedly be slower, particularly if farmer demand does not increase with the lack of access of the farming community to inputs.

The Bank invested heavily in irrigation and drainage—the largest investment in irrigation in the world and once again, India was the largest beneficiary of this investment (see Figures 8.11 and 8.12). In retrospect, the World Bank's irrigation portfolio does not look as good as it did at the time of the Green Revolution for reasons that we will discuss later in the chapter.

US agricultural scientists, with the Rockefeller Foundation in India, encouraged the Indian government to establish public sector seed companies in the 1960s, when quality

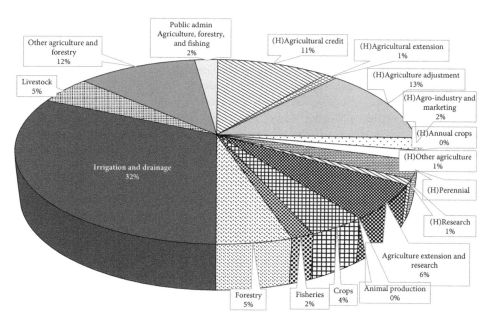

Figure 8.11 Share of IBRD–IDA total commitments to the Agriculture, Forestry and Fishing sector by subsector, FY1960–FY2018 (%, total = US$161bn, real = nominal/MUV, MUV Index 2010 = 100)

Source: Based on data from https://datacatalog.worldbank.org/dataset/world-bank-projects-operations

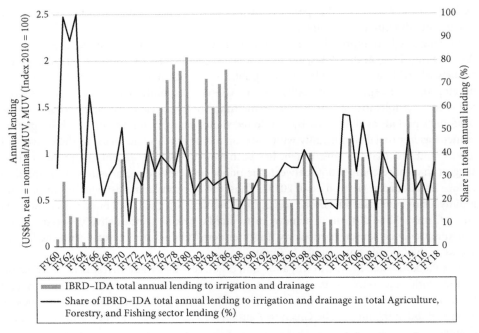

Figure 8.12 IBRD–IDA total annual commitments to irrigation and drainage and percentage share in total lending to the Agriculture, Forestry and Fishing sector, FY1960–FY2018 (US$bn, real = nominal/MUV, MUV Index 2010 = 100)

Source: Based on data from https://datacatalog.worldbank.org/dataset/world-bank-projects-operations

seed supply was critical for the generation of the Green Revolution (Lele and Goldsmith 1989). The World Bank financed and Rockefeller scientists helped with the Seed Law, seed standards, regulations, and human resource development of the public sector seed corporations. The World Bank's financing of seed companies enabled delivery of quality seed on the scale needed during the Green Revolution period, spawning a thriving seed industry. Between 1965 and 1985, private seed, pesticide, and agricultural machinery industries grew, stimulated mainly by public sector research and development. Pray and Nagarajan (2014) documented that, since the end of the 1980s, a combination of general economic liberalization and changes in the structure of Indian agriculture could explain the growth of the private sector Indian input industry, including public sector research by ICAR and CGIAR centers; increase in FDI of input industries; the demand pull from the growth of high-value agricultural exports; improved intellectual property rights; consolidation of seed, pesticides, and mechanical industries, with the larger size being associated with increased research; and exports of pesticides, machinery, and seed, as well as output. Some of the largest seed companies in India are private sector companies. Spielman et al. (2014) noted that, without restrictive public policies toward the pricing of rice and wheat and an interstate movement of seed, growth of the private sector input industry would be even larger. An important take-home message from the work of Pray and Fuglie (2015) is that both international and domestic public sector research, in all types of input industries— that is, seed, chemical, and mechanical—has stimulated private sector research and development, but now is the time for a sharper distinction to be made in the role of the public sector in the provision of public goods, such as agricultural research, while engaging in service delivery, as an infant industry, and then turning it over to the private sector once developed, leaving service delivery then to the private sector. The fertilizer industry has not seen such reform, and public sector research is faltering in many countries, as shown elsewhere in this book, because fiscal resources are being frittered away in formal or informal subsidies to input delivery.

In a study of 10 African governments, Jayne and Rashid (2013, 547) showed that collectively, the 10 African governments "spent roughly US\$1 billion annually on input subsidy programs (ISPs), amounting to 28.6% of their public expenditures on agriculture," and using microlevel evidence since the mid-2000s, they showed:

> The costs of the programs generally outweigh their benefits. Findings from other developing areas with a higher proportion of crop area under irrigation and with lower fertilizer prices—factors that should provide higher returns to fertilizer subsidies than in Africa—indicate that at least a partial reallocation of expenditures from fertilizer subsidies to R&D and infrastructure would provide higher returns to agricultural growth and poverty reduction.... [They noted, however, that because input subsidy programs] enable governments to demonstrate tangible support to constituents, they are likely to remain on the African landscape for the foreseeable future. (Jayne and Rashid 2013, 547)

Among the most important efforts needed to minimize the adverse effects of subsidies are "efforts to reduce the crowding out of commercial fertilizer distribution systems and programs to improve soil fertility to enable farmers to use fertilizer more efficiently. The challenges associated with achieving these gains are likely to be formidable" (Jayne and Rashid, 2013, 547). In short, there is huge scope for growth of the input industry and value chains (World Bank 2020d) in the private sector going forward. Countries, however, have been less willing or able to shake off vested interests rapidly.

As a result of and despite a range of multinational and national private seed companies operating in India (Pray and Nagarajan 2012), an estimated 70 percent of the seed supply in recent years has come from the informal sector, including farmers' own seed (Gulati, Ferroni, and Zhou 2018).

What are the generalizable lessons from this evidence?

Value chains have been going through a revolution on a global scale. Despite much literature on the supermarket revolution, their transformative role in increasing smallholder agricultural productivity in developing countries is not clear. Yet, countries that have limited value chains in their domestic food and agricultural production cannot be expected to break through in developing global value chains (GVCs) (see Figure 4.8). According to the 2020 WDR: Trading for Development in the Age of Global Value Chains: "A global value chain breaks up the production process across countries. Firms specialize in a specific task and do not produce the whole product" (World Bank 2020d). GVCs are more efficient than manufacturers who produce whole products, and they create employment, increase income, and contribute to the quality of production. As a result, GVCs are associated with structural transformation in developing countries, drawing "people out of less productive activities and into more productive manufacturing jobs" and service activities (World Bank 2020d, 78). "Firms in GVCs are unusual in another respect: across a wide range of countries, they tend to employ more women than non-GVC firms. They contribute therefore to the broader development benefits of higher female employment" (World Bank 2020d, 3).

GVCs are not growing, however, at the same speed everywhere, as the Indian example of the lagging seed sector, previously discussed, shows. Nearly 60 percent of the final price paid by consumers in rice markets in Bangladesh and India is in off-farm value (Reardon et al. 2013). As urban demand is increasing for higher quality and more diversified food products, whether for rice in Bangladesh, dairy in Kenya or *injera* (flat bread) in Ethiopia, for example, with it the demand for quality produce, storage, transport, handling, processing, and packaging is increasing, as well as demand for labor and capital off-farm. This growth calls for more investment of capital: for example, to blend fertilizers in a more fine-tuned way to meet farmer demand in Ethiopia.

Through five Bank-supported operations from 1974 to 1995, milk production quadrupled in India between 1974 and 2006, while per capita milk availability more than doubled over the same period, in part due to the Operation Flood programs implemented by the National Dairy Development Board (NDDB) (World Bank 2011a). "To date, over 3.7 million milk producers have benefited from overall NDP [National Dairy Plan-1] interventions in breed improvement, animal nutrition, and bulk milk collection" (World Bank 2019a, 2).

The Bank has also supported NDDB's 15-year, US$3.5 billion National Dairy Plan. The first phase of 2012–19 entailed a total investment of US$290 million across 18 participating states (responsible for nearly 95 percent of India's milk production) for breed improvement, feed optimization, nontraditional fodder production, and farmer mobilization through dairy cooperative societies and dairy producer companies (World Bank 2019a).[15]

The World Bank can substantially expand its investments in value chains, increasing off-farm employment for millions of rural and urban households.

Policy lending was in ascendancy in the 1980s, with policy distortions, such as overvalued exchange rates and high implicit and explicit taxation of agricultural exports (Krueger, Schiff, and Valdés 1988, 1991); the large role of government in agricultural input and output markets; prices that deviated considerably from the free market; and subsidies on fertilizer, credit, and other inputs. The distortions have declined in SSA, and there has been a return to project/investment lending. Yet, we know more about how investment lending has performed in specific terms than about policy-based lending. Impacts are known only by looking at indicators—SDG outcomes and productivity growth-related indicators—to know how the Bank may have contributed to them.

As we discussed in earlier chapters, agricultural reforms were relatively weak, even in the face of macroeconomic reforms in Africa, starting in the 1980s, and in India, starting in the 1990s. Policy frameworks remain weak to date in many countries. In terms of thematic issues, food security was a clear concern in Asia in the 1960s and 1970s, leading to substantial Bank lending. As Asia achieved a measure of national self-sufficiency, a sense

---

[15] According to the Implementation Status & Results Report for the World Bank's National Dairy Support Project:

> The Ration Balancing Program (RBP)...is reducing both feed cost and methane emissions by about 12% while increasing net daily income per animal by nearly 25 Rs. RBP coverage now reaches 2.8 million milch animals owned by two million farmers across 33,000 villages.... Some 43,000 villages have been newly organized or strengthened for dairy under NDP-I, enrolling an additional 925,000 milk producers. Dairy Cooperative Societies have been strengthened by equipping them with capital items such as Bulk Milk Chilling Units (BMCUs), Automated Milk Collection Units or Data Processor Milk Collection Units. Such automation of the milk procurement process has substantially increased transactional transparency and confidence, as dairy producers are able to view both weight and fat content of their milk. Overall, more milk is being procured as a result of this technological intervention. (World Bank 2019a)

of complacency developed, particularly as food and agricultural prices remained low, challenging returns to investments in agriculture in the 1980s and 1990s.

Concerns about issues of access to and utilization of food or the sustainability of natural resources were relatively weak. It has taken a long time to begin addressing issues of agricultural diversification. Commitment to food security was reflected largely in self-standing nutrition projects and nutrition components, with shifting emphasis on nutrition throughout the years, as shown in Chapter 4. The Bank's objective in support of agriculture was as a means of poverty reduction, with a focus on productivity growth. The pendulum swung from time to time between agriculture and rural development, and more recently to rural–urban linkages (the latter entailing multisectorality and complexity). When demand grew for simplicity of projects, agricultural lending focused on productivity increase. Demand for simplicity, in turn, was a reaction against project complexity, which integrated rural development and multisectoral nutrition projects entailed. Demand was implicitly also seeking clarity of objectives, which productivity growth entailed. On the other hand, rural development had come into ascendancy when complexity and multisectorality of the development process was recognized as inevitable. In practice, achieving multisectorality has been difficult. It is a lesson for today's SDG discourse, which, once again, extols the virtues of multisectorality and multidisciplinary approaches.

Certain themes have risen and then fallen in popularity in Bank lending: agricultural credit, integrated rural development, T&V extension (a training-and-visit agricultural extension approach). These changes are most obviously noted in the changes in lending codes used to maintain lending data, with certain codes having disappeared and others emerged, suggesting that changing thoughts on development (or fashions, depending on one's point of view) played a role in the Bank's lending, more than a vision of a strategy for agricultural development.[16] Furthermore, it takes time to see results on the ground, and even in the face of evidence and after billions of dollars of commitments, sometimes there is reluctance to acknowledge failures: for example, with agricultural credit (von Pischke 1992); integrated rural development (World Bank 1988b); and T&V extension (Gautam and Anderson 1999; Gautam 2000). A later study by three respected analysts confirmed these same concerns on a much larger scale (Anderson, Feder, and Ganguly 2006). Extension and research, as a share of lending, peaked at the end of the 1980s Figure 8.13), until T&V projects reached a limit of unpopularity.

Community-based or community-driven participatory approaches came into ascendancy in the 1990s, when Bank President Wolfensohn promoted a Comprehensive Development Framework (CDF): a concept based on four mutually reinforcing principles—a long-term holistic framework for development; country ownership; country-led partnership; and results- orientation.

A number of developing countries and international cooperation agencies were simultaneously seeking to put it into practice these same principles through the Millennium Development Goals (MDGs). CDF principles were meant to reverse the top-down nature of the approaches in the 1970s and 1980s, which had disregarded empirical evidence that

---

[16] Directed credit was considered desirable in the 1950s and 1960s. With lending pressures under McNamara and subsequently, credit to agriculture was easy to push, but repayments turned out to be poor. Lending to agricultural credit as self-standing projects disappeared, as did the practice as a lending code. It turned out to be difficult to achieve consensus on the new financial sector policy. The Bank tried to promote saving mobilization, but not very proactively. Developing countries and Japan, on the executive board, continued to support directed credit (von Pischke 1992), and developing countries have continued to practice debt forgiveness, much to the detriment of the financial sector. (See, for example, Kotwal and Sen 2019.)

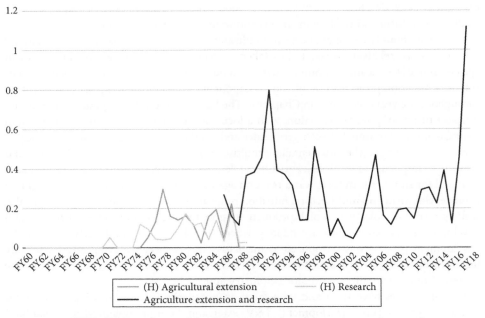

Figure 8.13 IBRD–IDA total annual lending to agricultural extension and research, FY1960–FY2018 (US$bn, real = nominal/MUV, MUV Index 2010 = 100)

Note: The codes with an "(H)" are historical codes that were discontinued in 1990.

Source: Based on data from https://datacatalog.worldbank.org/dataset/world-bank-projects-operations

bottom-up, participatory approaches were necessary to design interventions relevant to intended beneficiaries (Lele 1975). CDF had limited impact, however (Hanna 2000; McEuen 2003), and the 2000–2001 *WDR*, which contained the ideas of balancing voice [empowerment, based on the study, *Voices of the Poor* (Narayan 2000)], opportunity, and security led to an internal debate in the Bank on whether to prioritize voice or opportunity (World Bank 2001). Opportunity won out over voice (Stern 2006).

The 2008 *WDR* on agriculture dispelled old ideas of government interventions and subsidies and made a case for market-based investment in agriculture, based on three worlds of agriculture (World Bank 2007). Developing countries in Asia, including China and India, have continued with subsidies and government interventions. Did the 2008 *WDR* have impact on investment in agriculture? It is difficult to discern, since the its publication coincided with the global food and financial crisis, but increase in donor funding turned out to be temporary, as we discussed in previous chapters.

In view of the growing interest in diversified farming systems, it is noteworthy that crop development has dominated in lending, relative to livestock, forestry, and fisheries. Irrigation has been the largest recipient among subsectors, playing a key role in the Green Revolution, but also implicitly seeking resilience of production systems. Yet, effectiveness of irrigation has diminished over time, particularly where lending has been the highest, such as in India. Groundwater development went virtually unnoticed for a long time, while surface irrigation received most of the attention. A thorough analysis of the water sector—not just World Bank projects but also the country environment, including water governance, is needed. Past irrigation sector reviews appear to have had little impact on improving project outcomes, aside from the exceptions discussed in the body of this chapter.

Back to Africa

After the rise of lending in the 1970s, the results in Agriculture and Rural Development (ARD) projects in Africa were particularly disappointing, but they varied across regions (see Figure 8.14). In SSA, project performance deteriorated sharply by the end of the 1970s. It was a result of high oil prices, balance of payment difficulties, fiscal pressures, and overvalued exchange rates, more in in Tanzania than in Kenya (see Lele and Meyers [1989]). Even where there were successes, as in Nigeria or Malawi, Yudelman noted that the collapse of the economy changed that, but there is a more complex history behind these observations (Yudelman 1986).

The 1975 "Tanzania Basic Economic Report" strongly endorsed integrated rural development projects as a key strategy (World Bank 1977). A Bank report on Tanzania's agricultural sector in the 1980s noted that donors were part of the problem. Vice President for Economic Research Anne Krueger created a program of research on aid and development in 1982, and invited Lele to lead it; the study, "Managing Agricultural Development in Africa" (MADIA) was a part. It examined the role of country policies, external shocks, and behavior of eight donors (Lele 1989).

Analysis of the IEG-evaluated project ratings outcomes, by region and by sector board, for the entire period is shown in Table 8.1. It shows that the percentage share of outcomes in the satisfactory range is lowest in Africa for almost all the sector board, except Social Protection (just above SA), Urban Development (just behind EAP), and Water (behind EAP and ECA). SA's performances are poor in Financial and Private Sector Development, Public Sector Governance, Urban Development and Water sectors, compared to other sector board performances. LAC showed poor performances in Agriculture and Rural Development; Financial Sector; Health, Nutrition and Population; and Water sector boards. MENA performed poorly in Agriculture and Rural Development; Economic Policy; Energy

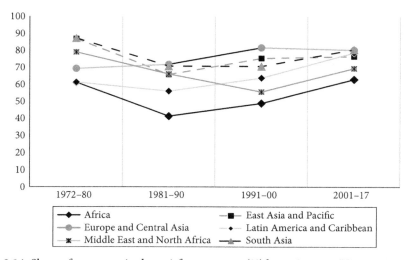

Figure 8.14 Share of outcomes in the satisfactory range (%) by region, exit FY1972–2017 (2,185 Agriculture and Rural Development projects evaluated by the Independent Evaluation Group)

Source: Based on the data from https://finances.worldbank.org/Other/IEG-World-Bank-Project-Performance-Ratings/rq9d-pctf

Table 8.1 Project rating outcomes evaluated by the Independent Evaluation Group by region by sector board, exit FY1972–2017

Number of projects evaluated by the Independent Evaluation Group

Region	Agriculture and Rural Development	Economic Policy	Education	Energy and Mining	Environment	Financial and Private Sector Development	Financial Sector	Global Information/ Communications Technology	Health, Nutrition and Population	Poverty Reduction	Private Sector Development	Public Sector Governance	Social Development	Social Protection	Transport	Urban Development	Water	Grand Total
Africa	672	255	272	270	81	136	85	53	174	44	6	181	21	93	381	117	125	2,973
EAP	404	75	162	238	38	39	59	35	76	7	2	53	18	18	240	92	80	1,637
ECA	237	150	72	218	70	120	42	9	59	1	2	81	15	87	141	46	65	1,423
LAC	343	122	192	246	117	104	66	25	108	8	6	149	14	81	237	126	123	2,069
MENA	175	27	101	118	28	37	36	18	38	1	1	37	6	38	89	80	81	913
SA	354	69	95	184	23	49	35	26	70	5	1	34	4	11	101	42	57	1,166
Grand total	2,185	698	894	1,274	357	485	323	166	525	66	18	535	78	328	1,189	503	531	10,181

Share of outcomes in the satisfactory range (%)

Region	Agriculture and Rural Development	Economic Policy	Education	Energy and Mining	Environment	Financial and Private Sector Development	Financial Sector	Global Information/ Communications Technology	Health, Nutrition and Population	Poverty Reduction	Private Sector Development	Public Sector Governance	Social Development	Social Protection	Transport	Urban Development	Water
Africa	54	68	69	61	59	61	54	79	57	68	50	55	57	81	75	81	72
EAP	77	81	90	86	72	69	76	89	72	100	100	68	78	89	91	82	75
ECA	78	87	69	74	77	82	81	100	75	100	100	75	87	82	88	70	75
LAC	68	74	78	75	70	77	68	92	66	88	100	75	71	85	79	73	64
MENA	69	67	70	66	79	76	78	89	61	0	0	62	100	82	80	73	64
SA	77	86	83	70	91	61	80	100	73	80	100	65	100	73	76	67	68

Source: Based on the data from https://finances.worldbank.org/Other/IEG-World-Bank-Project-Performance-Ratings/rq9d-pctf

and Mining; Health, Nutrition and Population; Public Sector Governance; and Water sectors, compared to other sector board performances.

Weaknesses of the McNamara Strategy

Its accomplishments notwithstanding, the McNamara approach had some notable weaknesses. Most prominent among them was the project approval culture that was created by setting lending targets and focusing on disbursements, a culture which is understandably alive and well in the institution, which is, after all, a bank. In addition, McNamara's demand for numbers, as a means of measuring results, led to an obsession with poverty headcounts, and spurious and misleading indicators of accuracy in the social rates of return which were then introduced to encourage poverty targeting. Even Little and Mirrlees (1991), the fathers of the social cost–benefit analysis, acknowledged that the extent to which such analysis was used and had real influence was not great (Devarajan, Squire, and Suthiwart-Narueput 1997). The two issues for which cost–benefit analysis was considered important—whether public sector investment should be justified in a project and whether it should be funded by foreign aid—became obsolete as the role of governments and foreign aid declined. A big challenge remains today: how to devise quantitative and qualitative measures that enable us to capture progress on outcomes that matter, without a huge cost in data collection. This issue remains unanalyzed or is analyzed mostly by academics to prove to donors that aid works or does not.

As Devarajan, Squire, and Suthiwart-Narueput (1997) and Stern and Ferreira (1997) noted, the social funds and the CDD movement led by sociologists in the Bank in the late 1980s and 1990s was prompted by growing aversion to top-down, technocratic approaches that used social rates of return. Technocrats in agriculture, on the other hand, continue to argue that CDDs ignored technical sectoral issues of agriculture, health, and education, creating a parallel universe of community structures adjacent to the local governments, and mostly financed small infrastructure with few links to the sectoral ministries of agriculture, education, or water—observations that we gathered as part of the IEG Indonesia Country Assistance Evaluation (IEG 2006). Thus, critics argue that the CDDs were less a proactive means of decentralized development through line ministries to reach the poor, than a new development trend—although over time in Brazil, India, and Indonesia, among others, there have been attempts to "absorb" CDD efforts into local governments with mixed success (IEG 2015a, 2015b).

Had McNamara's approach continued with investments in agriculture, infrastructure, population, and health, putting a stronger focus on local institutions and taking a bottom-up stance in the 1980s, one is left to wonder would it have helped the countries with the greatest amount of poverty today, particularly those in Africa? We believe the prospects could have been brighter. Would Africa have been better off had the mistakes been corrected, rather than relinquishing investments in agriculture altogether? Sustainability remains the real challenge. Many of the 13 projects reviewed in the *Design of Rural Development* (Lele 1975) vanished by the 1980s, when field visits to some of the same countries for the MADIA study found little memory among local people of the existence of the previous projects. Lending to the agriculture and rural sector continued in Asia at a brisk pace in the 1980s, but effectiveness of the irrigation sector, on which the Green Revolution rested, had begun to deteriorate (Lele et al. 2011; Lele, Klousia-Marquis, and Goswami 2013).

Lending and Administrative Budget Pressures

Bank net administrative expenses since 1946 are meticulously maintained by Bill Katzenstein, a retired budgeting veteran, and are shown in Figure 8.3 They relate only to lending activity and that constitutes only 20 percent of the Bank's total administrative expenses. Lending expenses only slightly exceed the level of the early 1990s. The share of Bank staff time and other expenses devoted to lending and supervision have decreased from 45 percent in 1980 to about 20 percent in this decade. Increases in nonlending activities, deemed operational, made up the difference.

Katzenstein suggests lending activity has become more efficient over time, largely due to technology benefits, due to repeat projects, and possibly to decentralization. Concurrently, staff time and other resources for nonlending work considered as operational expenses have increased for activities, such as resource mobilization, knowledge management, and institutional outreach. Katzenstein also notes that three out of four reorganizations and attempted downsizings since 1987 have had mixed results in terms of cost savings. This has occurred owing to a lack of institutional discipline in follow-through. Staff morale has suffered because of the appearance of capricious management (Katzenstein 2011).

These are sobering findings. Reorganization is rarely a solution to improve efficiency, but the analysis also raises questions as to whether the Bank is devoting enough resources to its operational activities, compared to other activities, in view of the portfolio issues raised here.

In the past several years, the Bank has done more lending work overall and significantly increased assistance to conflict-affected states (particularly costly with high security expenses). Although cost-reduction measures introduced with the 2013 reorganization did not result in significant bottom-line savings, the Bank has taken on challenging activities while averting budget increases.

Project Performance through the Decades

In 1993, Will Wapenhans, while leading a portfolio review of 1,800 projects, including interviews with developing country policymakers, and with 400 pages of notes, stated:

> There is a declining trend in project performance, highly concentrated in IDA countries and the Bank is contributing to it because of the presence of an approval culture. To remain the leading and preeminent institution that it is, it needs to reverse, and it can reverse to its earlier emphasis on performance. It should not resort to more bureaucracy, to a further invitation to promote compliance. It should not invite its staff, including its managers, to protect their rear. Such an emphasis would further foster risk aversion, not only of staff but also of managers. If not contained, it could retard development. (Wapenhans 1993, 39)

The IEG of WBG provides the independent evaluations and project ratings, which are the only comprehensive source of World Bank project performance data with a long time series. IEG is an independent unit within WBG, reporting directly to the Board of Executive Directors, which oversees IEG's work through its Committee on Development

Effectiveness.[17] IEG uses a six-point rating scale: Highly Satisfactory, Satisfactory, Moderately Satisfactory, Moderately Unsatisfactory, Unsatisfactory, and Highly Unsatisfactory. The ratings methodologies have been refined periodically, based on lessons learned and have become a standard for other multilateral organizations. Simply put, they rate projects on the extent to which the declared objectives of investment lending were achieved, based on detailed implementation completion reports, prepared by operational staff in the World Bank who are responsible for overseeing project implementation (IEG 2014b). Project ratings are carried out soon after projects are closed, and therefore, their sustainability is unclear.

The lack of evidence of impact of IOs' interventions is a relatively new, but growing concern has led to the increased use of randomized control trials (RCTs) to assess impacts of the investment portfolios in the international financial institutions, including the World Bank and the International Fund for Agricultural Development (IFAD) (CGD 2006).

Angus Deaton and Nancy Cartwright, in "Understanding and Misunderstanding Randomized Controlled Trials," argued that:

> The lay public, and sometimes researchers, put too much trust in RCTs [randomized controlled trials] over other methods of investigation. Contrary to frequent claims in the applied literature, randomization does not equalize everything other than the treatment in the treatment and control groups, it does not automatically deliver a precise estimate of the average treatment effect (ATE), . . . At best, an RCT yields an unbiased estimate, but this property is of limited practical value. Even then, estimates apply only to the sample selected for the trial, often no more than a convenience sample, and justification is required to extend the results to other groups, including any population to which the trial sample belongs, or to any individual, including an individual in the trial. (Deaton and Cartwright 2018, 2)

Impact evaluations are growing rapidly, and a vast literature is emerging, which shows the popularity of RCTs. Awarding of the 2019 Nobel Memorial Prize in Economic Sciences to Abhijit Banerjee, Esther Duflo, and Michael Kremer will in all likelihood increase the popularity of RCTs, but an equally significant literature questions how effective the RCT is as a tool in helping to reduce global poverty. Nobel laureate Angus Deaton and Nancy Cartwright also raised the issue of "external validity" (generalizability of the findings of an RCT to other circumstances). They noted, "RCTs can play a role in building scientific knowledge and useful predictions but they can only do so as part of a cumulative program, combining with other methods, including conceptual and theoretical development, to discover not 'what works', but 'why things work'" (Deaton and Cartwright 2018, 2).

In a similar vein, Ravallion (2012, 104) also noted in his review of Banerjee and Duflo's (2012) book, *Poor Economics: A Radical Rethinking of the Way to Fight Global Poverty*: "Randomized experiments are not new to economic analysis and policy evaluation. What is new is (first) the degree to which experiments are seen to be the only credible approach and (second) their extensive application in developing countries." RCTs are still a small share of the total investment portfolio of IOs, and the findings of existing studies have not had much operational impact. In a subsequent paper Ravallion (2018) argued, "The statistical case is unclear on *a priori* grounds; a stronger ethical defense is often called for; and there is a risk

---

[17] See the IEG website: http://ieg.worldbankgroup.org

of distorting the evidence-base for informing policymaking.... [P]ressing knowledge gaps should drive the questions asked and...answer[s], not the methodological preferences of some researchers. The gold standard is the best method for the question at hand."

The share of projects that IEG rated, using its methodology, as satisfactory or higher (in the satisfactory range), summarized by regions and by decades, is shown in Figure 8.14.[18] SA's projects received the highest ratings in the 1970s around the time of the Green Revolution. Project performance of all regions (except ECA) declined in the 1980s, as macroeconomic difficulties and debt problems rocked the developing world, particularly in SSA and Latin America. Ratings recovered somewhat in the 1990s, as economic performance improved, but never really recovered fully in SA from the heights reached in the 1970s. Africa's performance has remained consistently the lowest among all regions, even as it improved; and lending to SSA, particularly IDA lending to agriculture, has increased considerably since 2000 (see Figure 8.15). African indebtedness has also risen, as Africa's overall economic performance has slowed (IMF 2019b).

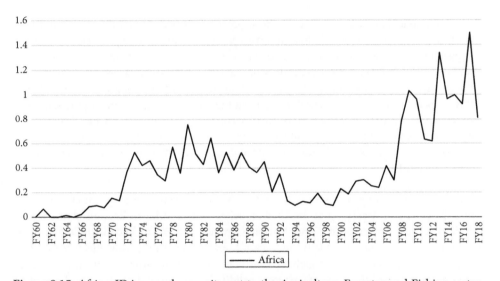

Figure 8.15 Africa: IDA annual commitment to the Agriculture, Forestry and Fishing sector, FY1960–FY2018 (US$bn, real = nominal/MUV, MUV Index 2010 = 100)

Source: Based on data from https://datacatalog.worldbank.org/dataset/world-bank-projects-operations

[18] Inter-year comparisons are not without issues. The categories for ratings have been expanded from 4 to 6. Some task managers whom we interviewed argued that the assessments of the criteria for ratings have become more stringent, so that fewer projects get classified as marginally satisfactory or satisfactory. Others argued that project ratings do not necessarily reflect improved project performance, but result in pressure from Bank management on IEG to show that performance has improved. According to Indre Sud and Jane Olmstead-Rumsey:

> The database contains assessments of project performance in various dimensions. The data from this database were used to verify the published assessments of the World Bank. The analysis points to significant doubt about the reported improvement in performance and suggests that the reported improvement appears to have been mostly a result of pressures of management targets and less than full independence of the World Bank's evaluation function. (Sud and Olmstead-Rumsey 2012, 1)

The Bank established a Quality Assurance Group to oversee quality of design and implementation after the Wapenhans Report, discussed in this chapter (World Bank 1992). The reasons for seemingly improved performance may also be because nonperforming components of projects were often dropped during implementation.

In addition to looking at the performance ratings by regions, as shown in Figure 8.14, we considered the same ratings by categories of countries: low-income, low-middle-income, and upper-middle-income, and by individual countries (Figure 8.16). Generally, LICs performed less well than LMICs and UMICs. IFAD's evaluation of the performance of MICs, discussed in Chapter 11, on the other hand, found no significant difference in the performance of LICs and MICs. IFAD explains this result based on the fact that, even in MICs, IFAD projects are targeted to the poorest populations or poorest regions, perhaps, more so than the World Bank's projects. In countries, such as Brazil and China, World Bank projects have consistently been targeted to the poorest regions, such as the southwestern region in China and the northeastern region in Brazil, although this has not always been the case, as in India. Ravallion argued, in the case of China, beyond targeting to the poor regions, targeting specifically to low-income households is often not possible (Ravallion 2009). Findings of the Asian Development Bank (ADB) support Ravallion's observations. Between 2 and 3 percent of GDP in Asian countries is spent on targeting: that is, "the use of policy instruments and interventions to channel resources to a target group identified below an agreed national poverty line" (Weiss 2004, 2). So, the issue needs more than passing mention. ADB undertook surveys of the experiences with poverty targeting in a number of large Asian economies in SA (India), Southeast Asia (Thailand, the Philippines, and Indonesia) and in PRC. According to John Weiss, in his paper on experiences from India, Indonesia, the Philippines, PRC, and Thailand:

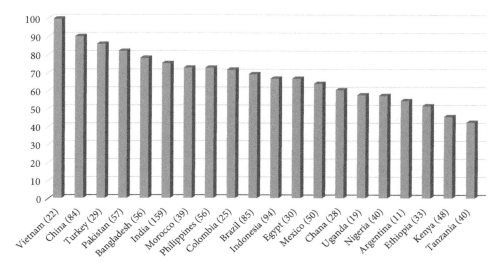

Figure 8.16 Share of outcomes in the satisfactory range (%) of the Agriculture and Rural Development projects in the top 20 recipient countries by IBRD–IDA commitments to the Agriculture, Forestry and Fishing sector, exit FY1972–2017 (1,005 Agriculture and Rural Development projects evaluated by the Independent Evaluation Group in the top 20 recipient countries)

Note: ( ) shows number of evaluated projects.

Source: Based on the data from https://finances.worldbank.org/Other/IEG-World-Bank-Project-Performance-Ratings/rq9d-pctf

Poverty targeting is used by all governments in Asia in one form or another, either to 'protect' the poor from adverse shocks or 'promote' their long-run move out of poverty. Such measures typically include reaching the poor with credit, food, employment, access to health and other social facilities and occasionally cash transfers.... In some of these countries poverty targeting has a relatively lengthy history stemming from long-standing social welfare concerns (India, the Philippines and PRC), whilst elsewhere it originated principally in the late 1990s in response to the impact of the regional Financial Crisis (Thailand and Indonesia). (Weiss 2004, 2)

Weiss provides examples of classifications of targeting:

Measures to reach the poor can be classified in different ways. For example:
- *Targeting by activity*, such as primary health care and primary education ...
- *Targeting by indicator*, where alternatives to income... [are] correlated with poverty [and] are used to identify the poor. These can include lack of, or size of, ownership of land, form of dwelling, and type of household, for example number of children or gender of the head of family.
- *Targeting by location*, where area of residence becomes the criteria for identifying the target group,... a central element in poverty reduction initiatives in PRC
- *Targeting by self-selection or self-targeting*, where programs are designed to be attractive only to the poor. An example is employment creation or 'workfare,' where payment is either in cash or in food,... and therefore only of interest to those with no opportunity to work at the market wage. Another self-selection procedure is the subsidization of low quality foodstuffs (like high-broken rice). (Weiss 2004, 2–3)

Experiences in the five countries suggested that "errors in targeting have been very significant, leakage rates have been high and many of the poor have not been covered, with the implication that in some cases these programs have had only a minor impact on poverty reduction" (Weiss 2004, 2).

The "consistent picture," which the ADB study noted, based on the available evidence, "is that while some schemes may have had a modest positive effect on the poor,... trends in poverty reduction have been driven principally by macroeconomic developments—the rate and pattern of economic growth—rather than by targeted interventions" (Weiss 2004, 10).

The ineffectiveness of public delivery systems has led Banerjee, Duflo, and Kremer to use experimental economics, using RCTs as a "gold standard," but Ravallion, Deaton, and others caution against their external validity.

The fact that LICs perform poorly and projects targeted to the poor in MICs also do poorly has implications, however, for the global community's ambition and strategy to eradicate poverty and hunger by 2030.

Among the 20 top recipients of World Bank (IBRD + IDA) assistance to agriculture, for which the World Bank evaluated a total of 1,005 AFF projects, exiting during 1972 and 2017, China has consistently been one of the best performers in overall ratings, as well as the country with the largest number (12 out of 84 rated projects) of highly satisfactory projects (Figure 8.16). Brazil also has had a number of highly satisfactory projects (3 out of 85 rated projects). The three African countries, all LICs (Ethiopia, Kenya, and Tanzania), had the lowest ratings.

Lele, Goswami, and Nico (2017), in their chapter in *Agriculture and Rural Development in a Globalizing World*, noted:

> There is a huge range in the performance of satisfactory projects over the entire period. Armenia had 100 percent of the IEG-rated projects in the satisfactory range, albeit from a small portfolio, followed by China and Azerbaijan at 92.6 percent each...In China, however, as many as 94 projects were evaluated by the IEG, compared to 18 projects in Albania and 13 in Azerbaijan. Brazil, India, Pakistan, and Bangladesh each had large portfolios and had ratings of satisfactory in the case of about 70 percent of the projects; the least well performing projects were in African countries: Ethiopia, Tanzania, Cameroon, Republic of Congo, and Côte d'Ivoire....On the whole, agricultural projects [in Africa] have performed less well than the World Bank's overall project portfolio, but they have also performed differently in different regions. East Asia was on top in overall project performance, and Eastern Europe's and South Asia's agricultural performance was on par with each region's overall portfolio performance, although in each case, the performances were less than East Asia's. Upper income countries, classified by World Bank criteria, had higher performance ratings of about 73 percent in agriculture, with lower-middle-income countries having about 67 percent, followed by low-income countries of about 53 percent. The same phenomenon is noted in the International Finance Corporation's (IFC) lending performance of its agricultural portfolio. It performed least well in sub-Saharan Africa, and performance was weaker in agriculture than in other sectors in Africa. Other sectors (4 percent of total) had higher shares of "highly satisfactory" projects than did the ARD sector (2 percent of total). (Lele, Goswami, and Nico 2017, 343–4)

Fragile Country Borrowers Perform Less Well than Others

Lele, Goswami, and Nico (2017) reported on the performance of fragile countries:

> The IEG...rated 702 ARD sector projects in 44 of the 55 fragile countries containing 20 percent of the world's population. Fifty-eight percent were rated satisfactory and above, compared to the Bank-wide average for all countries of 67 percent satisfactory and above. Yet, fragile countries are going to need much more and better quality investment on a continuous, long-term basis by the international community as a whole, than accorded thus far, while keeping expectations of good outcomes low, and a focus on institution and capacity building. (Lele, Goswami, and Nico 2017, 344)

In the 2019 WBG Spring Meetings, humanitarian agencies urged the Bank to give more authority to the field staff to make commitments on behalf of the Bank to expedite decision-making, and develop genuine lasting partnerships with civil society organizations, rather than just working with whomever happens to be at the table. Their argument is supported by evidence generated in the Bank (Devex 2019).

In an econometric study, Fardoust and Flanagan (2011) argued that project performance tends to be consistent with the quality of the World Bank's economic and sector work. Another econometric study by IEG concluded that project ratings improved as countries liberalized their economies (Fardoust and Flanagan 2011; IEG 2013a). These are important findings.

The World Bank's Contribution to Agricultural Sector Performance

IEG's Country Assessment evaluation methodology has been careful not to attribute country performance of the sector or the economy to Bank assistance. Furthermore, although the methodology expects Bank assistance performance to be generally consistent with overall country performance, in practice, the two can diverge significantly.[19] In the MADIA study, Lele and Meyers (1989) noted that although Kenya performed well in the 1970s, the World Bank funded project portfolio performed quite poorly. In Tanzania, both Tanzanian agriculture and the World Bank project portfolio performed poorly in the 1970s.

In the India country assistance evaluation in the 1990s, IEG cited a case study of India by Lele and Bumb (1994), which showed that the Bank contributed to sustaining agricultural growth in India through the development of a holistic strategy during the Green Revolution, as well as contributing to increased investments and policy dialogue in the 1980s. Both India's performance and that of Bank projects, however, have been more mixed; since the 1980s, project ratings have not regained their earlier level.[20] A World Bank study on India, "Accelerating Agricultural Productivity Growth," highlights India's variable agricultural performance over time and in the various states and explains the reasons why, including India's lagging behind in structural transformation relative to China and Indonesia (World Bank 2014). Unlike in SSA, both India and the World Bank initially had a poverty reduction strategy grounded in agriculture. Over time, India has become less engaged.

Lele, Goswami, and Nico (2017) addressed the contribution of the World Bank to structural transformation:

> Over the entire period, 1960–2015, during which the World Bank has been active in most of these countries, excluding China, which joined in 1980, and Eastern Europe that joined in 1990, smaller countries typically received a higher share of GDP as World Bank loans and credits (1.4 percent in constant 2005 dollars in Honduras and Tanzania each), compared to mega countries—0.14 percent in China, 0.25 percent in Brazil, and 0.54 percent in India. On a per capita basis, too, China, India, Nigeria, Bangladesh, and Ethiopia ranked lower than middle-income countries, like Turkey and Mexico. Lending to large countries was more stable than small countries—that is, the standard deviation of year-to-year commitments as a share of GDP was only 0.2 in China, compared to 2.6 in Tanzania. Armenia, and Republic of Congo at the high end of the variability in World

---

[19] From "Appendix B: Guide to IEG's Country Program Evaluation Methodology":

If a Bank Group assistance program is large in relation to the country's total development effort, the program outcome should be similar to the country's overall development progress. However, most Bank Group assistance programs provide only a fraction of the total resources devoted to a country's development [that are provided] by development partners, stakeholders, and the government itself. In CPEs [country program evaluations], IEG rates only the outcome of the Bank Group's program, not the country's overall development outcome, although the latter is clearly relevant for judging the program's outcome....

Subsequently, IEG makes an assessment of the relative contribution to the results achieved by the Bank Group, other development partners, the government and exogenous factors. (IEG 2014a, 101, 103)

[20] The share of outcomes in the satisfactory range (%) in India (Exit FY1972–2017) for ARD sector projects:

1972–80	100.0 percent
1981–90	67.7 percent
1991–2000	64.9 percent
2001–17	87.8 percent

Bank assistance, compared to China, Brazil, Mexico, and India.... This variability was even greater on a per capita basis in small countries than in large countries. Large countries offer more investment opportunities than small countries, but it is also apparent that many low-income and small countries, such as Tanzania, Republic of Congo, Ethiopia, and Côte d'Ivoire, have also had much more unstable macroeconomic and/or political environments over the last 50 years, as compared to countries like China and India. Turkey, Brazil, and Mexico fall in the middle of the pack. And this shows up in the absence of lending activity over long stretches in countries with macroeconomic or political problems. (Lele, Goswami, and Nico 2017, 343).

The World Bank's Contribution to Country Performance

How does one demonstrate the Bank's contribution to country performance, except by using independent observation, combined with statistical indicators, mixed methods, country- and Bank-specific knowledge and insights?

Country capacity to prepare and implement its own projects is a necessary condition for the Bank's contribution. Country proposals reflect their own priorities and ownership. Because African countries lacked the capacity to develop "bankable" projects, the Agricultural Development Service was established in Nairobi in the 1960s, largely staffed by expatriates. Bank-funded projects in Nigeria and Malawi had especially large numbers of expatriates to implement them. Although the Bank prepared agricultural sector reports in Africa in the 1970s and 1980s, the reports were largely devices to identify bankable projects, rather than strategies for developing agriculture, unlike in the case with the Bell Mission's Agricultural Annex on India, which provided a country strategy. The MADIA study and the book, *Aid to African Agriculture: Lessons from Two Decades of Donor Assistance*, made a strong case for countries preparing their own country agricultural development strategies and the need for substantial investment in capacity building in Africa (Lele 1992). Clearly, capacity has increased a great deal in Africa, but not nearly what is needed.

From Integrated Rural Development to Structural Adjustment: China vs. Africa

Investment projects fell out of favor for Africa in the 1980s, and the Bank and bilateral donors abandoned integrated rural development in favor of SAL. The concept of integrated rural development became discredited, and little domestic capacity or institutions remained when project lending resumed later in the 1990s, in the form of CBD and CDD. However, the difference was not simply one of top-down or bottom-up approaches; there was a difference in the way agriculture was (or more likely, was not) supported, including the multisectoral nature of developing agriculture.

In China, on the other hand, both the World Bank and IFAD invested in Integrated Rural Development Programs (IRDPs), and IRDP projects performed well in China. An IEG report on China noted:

Bank lending [to China] accounts for only a small share of China's resource flows—about 0.6 percent of GDP at its maximum in the early 1990s. The Bank has therefore not tried to achieve its objectives primarily through the direct impact of its lending or through conditionality. Rather, the Bank has relied mostly on variants of persuasion and example. These included a dual-track approach of (i) building trust through [project] lending while promoting policy dialogue through sector work and (ii) relying on the demonstration effect of successful project experience in introducing new technologies, management methods, or policy reforms to leverage policy outcomes. (IEG 2005, ix–x)

China attributes its success in agriculture to a series of reforms in institutions, infrastructure, technology, market liberalization, and delivery systems, starting in 1979 (Huang 2014).

In contrast to China, an IEG country assistance evaluation of Rwanda, covering the years 1989–2001, noted, "The most notable shortcoming of the Bank's program throughout the 1990s was the absence of a concerted effort to promote agricultural development. A weakness of the IDA program was the scarcity of analytical work. . . . OED rates the outcome of IDA assistance overall as unsatisfactory for the pre-genocide period" (IEG 2004, vi).

Long-term strategies can result in sustained provision of public goods in agriculture and rural development, such as research and extension, agricultural education, finance, regulatory policies and institutions, seed production, and distribution capacity (Babu and Joshi 2019). This was the case in China where, like in India and unlike in Africa, the Bank did not take an ideological stand. The two largest borrowers are quite capable of showing it the door.

The absence of the countries' own long-term strategies and a sense of ownership, and the lack of institutions and internal capacity within the countries has led to an ebb and flow of assistance.

The 1980s: Structural Adjustment and the Debt Crisis Legacy

In the words of Ravi Kanbur, there was a shift in the 1980s from "a situation where the state could do no wrong to one where the state could do no right" (Kanbur 2005, 13).

The 1981 Berg Report, the 1982 *World Development Report*, and Shift to Adjustment Lending

African agriculture came into focus with the publication of the Berg Report, named after for its coordinator Elliot Berg of the African Strategy Review Group, titled *Accelerated Development in Sub-Saharan Africa: An Agenda for Action* (World Bank 1981). This was followed by the *WDR* (World Bank 1982b) on the theme of agriculture. The Berg Report helped move African countries away from state-run economies and toward free market systems at a time when Africa's economies were drastically underperforming. It was the Bank's first study of development in SSA. The Berg Report argued that African governments could increase exports and better develop rural economies through swift implementation of better governance and market reforms in exchange rates, liberalization of domestic markets, and cuts in subsidies. The report asserted that, in much of Africa, domestic policies were biased against agriculture. Exchange rates and the high cost of domestically produced inputs reduced competitiveness in world markets and were at the heart of the failure to provide adequate incentives for increased agricultural production and exports (World Bank 1981). These findings were later confirmed by the Krueger, Schiff, and Valdés (1988, 1991) study on agricultural price distortions. Their study was updated by Kym Anderson on the changing extent of price distortions across countries and commodities globally. Evaluating the degree of distortion reduction since 1984, compared with how much still remained, Anderson's study noted a huge reduction in distortions, using a global, economy-wide model (Anderson 2010). At issue was not so much the policy ideas, but how the Bank implemented them.

The Berg Report was critical of African governments for corruption and bloated bureaucracies. It recommended a significantly smaller role for governments in the national economies and proposed more private sector involvement in key industries. A major weakness of the Berg report was that it did not acknowledge the role the donor community had played in reinforcing the worst tendencies of African policies in the 1970s under McNamara's leadership (World Bank 1981). A Tanzanian agricultural sector report, prepared in the project department of the African region, in contrast, documented a number of price and non-price factors that were inhibiting growth. The report argued that the "getting prices right" mantra of the 1980s, via structural adjustment packages, including exchange rates, was unlikely to get a response from the export sector. Tanzania needed substantial injection of capital to increase agricultural input supply, in the short run, and in the medium run, to shore up the development of the dilapidated physical infrastructure, as well as massive investment in human capital. The report had a substantial following in IMF, which was ready to mount a mission to Tanzania (World Bank 1983a). The World Bank approved an export credit loan to Tanzania in 1980s, which was necessary, but not sufficient.[21]

The publication of the Berg Report also coincided with the adoption the Organization of African Unity (OAU) and the Economic Commission for Africa (ECA) of the *Lagos Plan of Action for the Economic Development of Africa 1980–2000*, at a conference of African Heads of State and Government in Lagos, Nigeria, in April 1980 (OAU 1980). The "Adedeji Report," known for Adebayo Adedeji, the United Nations Under Secretary-General and Executive Secretary of the ECA, was highly critical of the approach being adopted by the Bank and its donors under structural adjustment programs (SAPs) (UNECA 1989). So, there were pressures and arguments being placed on African governments in both directions.

More generally, the World Bank embarked on placing conditions on aid packages through SAPs, which emphasized liberalization of markets, exchange rates, and other reforms. The demand for extensive reforms led many African governments to reduce subsidies to public sector health and education programs and to agriculture, in return for needed developmental assistance. In the absence of meaningful political and economic reforms, however, efforts to modernize continued to flounder in Africa, while debt burden increased. As we showed in Chapter 2, growth in Africa has not been rapid enough to increase per capita income (Gill and Karakülah 2018). The Berg Report's legacy remains

---

[21] In a review of draft of this chapter, Stephen O'Brien, a veteran at the World Bank, noted:

Clearly, we overestimated government capacity, and even interest, in the reforms, and underestimated the corruption/vested interest that delayed or defeated reforms. I agree that adjustment programs neglected poverty and related issues, but I think that we thought this was a temporary fix, clearing the decks of all the policy mistakes, which would be followed by a return to project lending that would be much more productive. Of course, it was never a quick fix; we underestimated the time required for such major policy adjustments, even in semi-willing countries, so the criticism grew. (Stephen O'Brien, personal communication, email dated July 19, 2019)

In a conversation on July 22, 2019, this same sentiment was also supported by Jochen Kraske, who was country director for Southern Africa at the time the Tanzania report was prepared.

mixed—a story of a glass half full and half empty. Liberalization of economies accelerated economic growth in Africa and helped to rein in government spending through "improved governance, better policy management, and a new generation of skilled leaders in government and business" (Radelet 2016, 6). The author argued that these "are likely to persist into the future" (Radelet 2016, 6). Since 1995 to 2005:

> GDP growth across the continent...averaged about 4.3 percent a year, 3 percentage points higher than in the previous two decades. [Growth rates] varied widely, with about half the countries in the region moving forward and others changing little. In the 20 fastest growing countries—excluding oil exporters—GDP growth averaged a robust 5.8 percent for two decades, and real incomes per person more than doubled. But in other countries, growth was much slower, and in eight countries, income per person actually fell. Some of the differences are stark: in Rwanda real income per person more than doubled; in Zimbabwe it fell 30 percent. (Radelet 2016, 7)

The percentage of population living on less than US$1.90 declined from 60 percent to 40 percent, and child mortality declined substantially. At the same time, much needed investment in agriculture and related sectors, particularly infrastructure to facilitate market operation, did not occur, and absent a government role, the institutional vacuum in services remained.

The 2016 African Development Bank report, "Feed Africa: Strategy for Agricultural Transformation in Africa 2016–2025," noted:

> The total cost for agricultural transformation for the priority commodities and agroecological zones in the strategy is between US$315bn and US$400bn over 10 years, equivalent to US$32bn–$40bn per year. Current sources of finance for agricultural development are primarily from three areas: funds from sovereign and non-sovereign investments into agriculture from the multi-lateral and bilateral development partners including the AfDB; public sector spending; and private sector investments into agriculture. Overall these total ~ $9bn per year of investments into African agriculture (of the AfDB's level of spend[ing] is assumed to be $2.4bn per year, rather than the current $0.6bn per year), leaving a gap of $23bn to $31bn per annum to be mobilized in order to drive transformation. (AfDB 2016, 31)

> Africa needs a multi-stakeholder, public sector-enabled, but private sector-led transformation that will allow it to realize the potential of agriculture as a business and create a foundation for prosperity, nutrition, and quality of life for all Africans. (AfDB 2016, 40)

In most African countries, there was little private sector left in rural areas that could respond, but over the past several decades, it has been in development. The Bill and Melinda Gates Foundation's AGRA, established in 2006, has a program to support the development of input distributors in 11 priority countries, but there is not yet an independent evaluation of the program to know what has been achieved, whether it is sustainable without continued external support, and whether it is helping to establish national policy frameworks that are clear and predictable.

A related question is how much has agricultural policy been liberalized and does it matter whether the public or the private sector plays roles? Ethiopia is an example of impressive growth in total factor productivity (TFP) since 2005. Modern input distribution has almost exclusively been in the hands of the public sector in Ethiopia. Use of chemical fertilizer in Ethiopia has grown remarkably since the official elimination of subsidies in the 1990s, and under a new set of policies adopted in 2008, which: (1) granted monopoly control over fertilizer imports to the Agricultural Input Supplies Corporation (AISCO), the government's input marketing agency; and (2) carried out marketing and distribution of fertilizer, exclusively through farmers' organizations. Rashid et al. (2013) showed:

> ... (a) fertilizer use in major cereal is profitable; (b) while there is no official subsidy program, fertilizer promotion has involved large fiscal costs—estimated at US$40 million per year since 2008; and (c)...a mismatch between government's policy targets and the effective fertilizer demand, resulting in large carryover stock with estimated implicit costs of US$30 million per year during 2008–2011. (Rashid et al. 2013, 595)

The Ethiopian government turned to the experience of Asian countries to set up its Agricultural Transformation Agency (ATA) and remains in charge of managing donor aid. The expansion of the input use, increasing the adoption of chemical fertilizers and improved seeds, "appears to have been driven by high government expenditures on the agriculture sector, including agricultural extension, but also by an improved road network, higher rural education levels, and favorable international and local price incentives" (Bachewe et al. 2018, 286).

The agricultural growth over the 2004–14 period has been accompanied by poverty reduction. In 2004, the International Food Price Research Institute (IFPRI) established the Ethiopia Strategy Support Program (ESSP), to provide direct support to the Government of Ethiopia. An independent impact assessment concluded that "relatively few of the wide range of ESSP outputs appear to have produced tangible outcomes in Ethiopia...[and had] languished without inspiring action, reflecting ideological barriers" (Renkow and Slade 2013, xii). The assessment cited IFPRI's most important influences in Ethiopia, beyond ESSP, in the establishment of institutions, notably, the Productive Safety Net Program (PSNP) and ATA (Renkow and Slade 2013, xii). In 2005, the government set up the PSNP, covering 7 million people throughout the country, which included a Public Works component, for creating employment to improve rural roads, irrigation systems, and other needed infrastructure. Access to markets was significantly improved, as was access to education, with a significant decrease in illiteracy among rural populations (Bachewe et al. 2018).

The 1982 *WDR* contained extensive discussion of adjustment issues, finding the prospects for many LICs to be of critical concern (World Bank 1982b). The low-income, sub-Saharan countries were the least able to make structural adjustments rapidly, and Jayne noted many of the proposed reforms were not implemented in Africa (Jayne, Chamberlin, and Benfica 2018).

In India and China, with large, relatively self-sufficient economies and smaller debt burdens, the effect of adverse external events was more than offset by rising domestic investment and good agricultural performance. Vulnerability to balance of payments deficit, however, continued in the case of India, requiring it to approach the IMF for a stabilization program in 1991. China had embarked on agricultural reforms of its own since 1979, with the introduction of its household responsibility system and continued reforms sequentially with acceleration in the growth rate, which various studies have documented (Rozelle and Swinnen 2004; Gulati and Fan 2007; Huang 2014; Gulati and Saini 2016; Huang 2017;

Huang and Yang 2017). The Chinese state has played a critical role in the development of Chinese agriculture, including investment in irrigation, transportation and communication, human capital, and in R&D, several times that of India. Its support to agriculture was larger than that of all OECD countries together, as shown in Chapter 3.

Stanley Please, the principal champion of structural adjustment and director of the East Africa Department, argued that, in Africa, moving to macroeconomic lending, which adjustment loans entailed, was not only the right approach for the developing world to correct imbalances, but, also, as a general strategy for the World Bank. It was the beginning of the primacy of macroeconomic and sector policy work and lending in the Bank and the weakening of the project approach to lending. (World Bank 1981). Please and Amoako said of the Berg Report in their "A Critique of Some of the Criticism" in 1984:

> Emphasis should be placed on the tradeables sectors in African economies, and particu-larly to agriculture. This priority can only be achieved through a combination of, first, a switch in the internal terms of trade in favor of the tradeable sectors and against the service sectors (most obviously in African circumstances this means against government employ-ment). Secondly, government expenditures should shift in favor of agricultural services and against such other services as administration and defense. (Education, health, water supply, etc., should, in this connection, be thought of as necessary inputs into agricultural production . . .) (Please and Amoako 1984, 49)

The World Bank spent considerable time, energy, and resources to develop acceptance and legitimacy of structural adjustment among Africans and Europeans, given the resistance of African policymakers.

Carole Lancaster reported Africans' concerns in her chapter, "The World Bank since 1980: The Politics of Structural Adjustment Lending" as follows:[22]

> Adjustment programs were intrusive . . . Africans were sensitive to the appearance (and reality) of having their policy choices dictated by outside powers or institutions. . . . [including] complaints about the tendency of Bank staff to preach to Africans and at times to appear to be giving instructions to them. (These criticisms were also echoed by various officials of bilateral aid agencies based in African countries). . . .

> Africans have argued that structural adjustment—however extensive—is unlikely to contribute to a brighter economic future for their countries as long as their debt burdens remain so great. (Lancaster 1997, 169–70)

The African Development Bank's "Feed Africa" emphasized that without governments taking the lead and inviting the private sector to invest more in Africa's structural trans-formation, the continent will continue to lag (AfDB 2016).

---

[22] Carole Lancaster, former Deputy Administrator of the United States Agency for International Development (USAID), who had served as Deputy Assistant Secretary of State for African Affairs (1980–81) and as a member of the Policy Planning Staff of the Department of State (1977–80), endorsed the Please view. The Berg Report called for much needed attention to the deepening economic problems facing Africa—recommending a doubling in aid to the region—but more importantly, it argued that economic policy reform was critical to any economic recovery in Africa, because "state-led development had been a failure" (Lancaster 1997, 167).

Debt Burden

Nicholas Stern, former Chief Economist of the Bank, noted: "There was...fairly universal agreement that the Bank has been slow to respond to the debt issue" (Stern and Ferreira 1997, 600). An external evaluation of the World Bank's research program, led by Abhijit Banerjee, Angus Deaton, Nora Lustig, and Ken Rogoff (2006), also reiterated this finding of the prolonged neglect of the debt issue.

Adjustment with a Human Face

Some of the most influential voices in support of reducing poverty as an ethical and pragmatic good were Giovanni Andrea Cornia, Richard Jolly, and Frances Stewart, editors of *Adjustment with a Human Face*, a 1987 United Nations Children's Fund (UNICEF) study (Cornia, Jolly, and Stewart 1987). They have had a profound impact on the approaches of IMF and the World Bank to development in the new millennium, including with respect to safety nets, an important part of public policy. They called "for a more people-sensitive approach to adjustment" (Cornia, Jolly, and Stewart 1987, 3) and criticized the way that structural adjustment affected the social sectors, most notably, health and education. The book argued that the social sectors often bore massive budget cuts, because most structural adjustment projects involved balancing budgets and eliminating deficit spending while requiring investment in a number of industrial and commercial sectors. School programs, health programs, environmental programs, and various social safety systems have all been eliminated or severely reduced. Using 10 country case studies, the study outlined ideas for how to minimize the negative impacts of structural adjustment and showed working models to improve the lives of everyday people in the nations being adjusted. Ultimately, *Adjustment with a Human Face* led to a massive overhaul of adjustment lending at both IMF and the World Bank, with more attention paid to social sectors through Poverty Reduction Strategy Papers (Cornia, Jolly, and Stewart 1987).

World Bank Evaluation Findings on Structural Adjustment

The Bank undertook several evaluations of adjustment programs (Yagci, Kamin, and Rosenbaum 1985; World Bank 1988a; Corbo and Rojas 1991; OED 1996). With growing criticism of the Washington Consensus,[23] social safety nets became an important part of the Bank's support to countries, in response to the concerns about the social impacts of adjustment.[24] Lending to social sectors and to social safety nets increased (Figure 8.17), but agriculture did not

---

[23] See Chapter 2 for a definition of the Washington Consensus.

[24] In its publication, *The State of Social Safety Nets 2018*, WBG notes:

> The global focus on social protection and jobs in general and on the role of SSN [social safety nets] in particular has intensified. For the first time, social protection is part of a comprehensive agenda of the Sustainable Development Goals (SDGs). SDG1 calls to end (extreme) poverty in all its manifestations by 2030, ensure social protection for the poor and vulnerable, increase access to basic services, and support people harmed by climate-related extreme events and other economic, social, and environmental shocks and disasters. Target 1.3 (Goal 1) seeks to implement nationally appropriate social protection systems and measures for all, including floors, and by 2030 achieve substantial coverage of the poor and the vulnerable. (WBG 2018, xi)

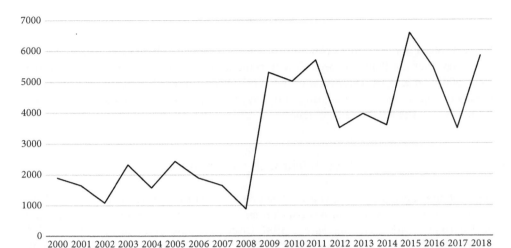

Figure 8.17 World Bank (IBRD and IDA) lending to social protection and risk management, 2000–2018 (US$m)

Note: From FY2017, the World Bank theme was changed, so that FY2017 and FY2018 values are for Social Development and Protection, instead of Social Protection and Risk Management.

Source: Based on World Bank Annual Reports data.

receive much attention in the World Bank until the early years of the new millennium, and even then, too weakly. Two major policy papers on agriculture, from "Vision to Action" in 1997 and "Reaching the Rural Poor" in 2003 had little impact on increasing lending to agriculture (Ayres and McCalla 1997; World Bank 2003b). Bank evaluations helped lead to the incorporation of mechanisms to assist segments of society adversely affected by adjustment in the short run (Jayarajah, Branson, and Sen 1996). In addition, the Bank devoted a larger share of lending and advice to central government reform, based on the identification of governmental capability as a central obstacle to successful development outcomes.

Institutional development began to gain recognition as a part of adjustment lending between 1983 and 1989, notably, first appearing as a central development issue in the 1983 *WDR*, with Part II entitled "Management in Development" (World Bank 1983b). The theme also occurred in OED evaluations and external analysis. The OED evaluation of the Bank's public sector reforms noted that there was little treatment of institutions in the Bank's work (Girishankar 2001). There are a few notable exceptions, including in the book, *The Design of Rural Development* (Lele 1975). The OED evaluation noted:

> Most of the CAEs [Country Assistance Evaluations] in the sample concluded that the Bank lacked a coherent strategy on public sector reform or country-level ID [institutional development], even when sectoral ID objectives were deemed relevant. In evaluating relevance, the reports did not adequately differentiate between structural and capacity constraints. Most CAEs, however, did go beyond the stated objectives of projects and considered whether the relevance of country programs was preserved in the details of operational design, and their "goodness of fit" to institutional setting. Some evaluations in turn attributed flaws in both strategy and design to internal disincentives within the Bank itself. (Girishankar 2001, 24)

John Staatz and Niama Nango Dembélé, in their background paper for the 2008 *WDR* (World Bank 2008), discussed the "comprehensive approach" needed in SSA, citing Lele's findings in the *Design of Rural Development*:

> In contrast to Asia during its Green Revolution (which had much of its infrastructure, substantial human capital, administrative capacity and other institutions in place), SSA is weaker in all these dimensions. Therefore, SSA needs a more comprehensive approach to address many of the challenges that require coordinated actions by different actors to spur productivity and rural income growth [Poulton et al. 2008]. Yet, top-down integrated rural development approaches to address these multiple challenges all at once have not worked well in SSA (Lele [1975], 1979 [3rd printing cited]). (Staatz and Dembélé 2008, 54)

Mosley and his colleagues (Mosley, Harrigan, and Toye 1991) noted that structural adjustment went through several stages and varied across regions. The first adjustment loans in SSA were uncompromising on the speed of reforms that they expected, without regard to the social impacts of the reforms. Asia and Latin America had very different experiences. The big difference was that the Asian countries, such as South Korea and Thailand, had already recognized the need to adjust and had the necessary capacity and sense of ownership of the reforms. South Korea was the most adept in making use of different public and private instruments flexibly (Kharas and Shishido 1991). They negotiated with the Bank on their terms and adjusted, using balance of payment support from the Bank. In Latin America, aid was unimportant, with each country having their own history and political economy of macroeconomic management. In Mexico, Díaz noted that Mexico's role in the establishment of the Bretton Woods institutions and prior good record of borrowing from IMF, the Inter-American Development Bank (IDB), and the World Bank led to a situation in which the Bank "practically suspended (the institutional flows) in crisis years (1976–82)," thinking Mexico had good macroeconomic capability, "only to play an important role later in the adjustment process" (Gil Díaz 1991, 241). Mexico's excessive borrowing from commercial banks was solely the responsibility of the governments toward the population they ruled. Carvalho (1991) discussed the history of Brazil's historical swings between export promotion and import substitution "at any cost" from the 1940s. In contrast, during the period 1974–85, combined with a combination of oil price shocks and interest rate shocks, Brazilian authorities began borrowing abroad, rather than accepting FDI for nationalistic reasons, increasing its debts, with very high interest rates and shorter term payment schedules. It was late to come on board with FDI and was done so only after a huge debt crisis (in contrast to Africa's public borrowing debt). The book, *Transitions in Development: The Role of Aid and Commercial Flows*, edited by Uma Lele and Ijaz Nabi, explored the cases of a number of countries in Latin America, Asia, and the Middle East and Africa (Lele and Nabi 1991).

OED/IEG evaluations of the Bank's experience with SAL and sectoral adjustment lending (SECAL) supported adjustment generally (IEG 1992; Jayarajah, Branson, and Sen 1996; IEG 2008).[25] The evaluations stressed the need for a long-term outlook regarding social impacts,

---

[25] The OED 1992 evaluation noted the primacy of economic growth as the most significant factor affecting poverty alleviation, in both countries that received SAL and "non-adjuster" countries. A sound macroeconomic policy framework was important in promoting growth and poverty reduction. In the agriculture sector, particularly, sector-specific adjustment operations (agriculture sector adjustment loans, or ASALs) did not perform where there were no corresponding macroeconomic policies (IEG 1992; Jayarajah, Branson, and Sen 1996).

noting that safety net instruments (cash transfers, consumer subsidies, employment generation) should not be thought of in terms of short-term compensatory measures, but rather as longer-run goals of enhanced productivity and reduced poverty through the positive, long-term impacts of safety nets (Jayarajah, Branson, and Sen 1996).[26]

Commenting on the country-level experience with SALs and SECALs, Jayarajah, Branson, and Sen (1996, 2) stated: "Countries that possessed a trained and highly mobile labor force and supporting economic infrastructure were well positioned to exploit the new market opportunities." Middle-income and Asian "adjusters" were most successful. The principal message from the OED study was that the social impact of adjustment was more positive for countries that had favorable macroeconomic policy and supply-side reforms, "good macroeconomic policies and measures—combined with relevant sectoral policies and appropriate public expenditure allocation—provide a favorable environment for accelerating savings and investment, both necessary for sustained economic growth and poverty reduction" (Jayarajah, Branson, and Sen 1996, 1).

Need for Stage-Appropriate Assistance and Nurturing Development of Institutions

How to assess the role of the Bank's advice and impact remains a thorny issue. The Berg Report (World Bank 1981) blamed Africa's and developing countries' problems almost exclusively on bad domestic policies, without acknowledging that many of those policies had been put in place by the colonial governments and extended to include more African farmers with the advice and funding of external donors and their advisors. In Kenya, many of the state interventions—for example, a large farm strategy—were inherited from the colonial past, condoned, and even promoted by external advisors (see, for example, Hazelwood [1991]). The lack of functioning markets in many developing countries, particularly in SSA, led to state interventions. Parastatal marketing boards, inventions of colonial governments originally created to support white farmers, were expanded by newly independent countries with burgeoning aid to provide services to African farmers. Import-substituting industrialization strategies, however, compounded the balance of payments problems, because they came at the expense of exports and made countries vulnerable to external shocks (Collier 1991). To the extent that foreign aid facilitated these poor policies, it contributed to the problems (Carvalho 1991; Hazelwood 1991). Even after the structural adjustment period, it took a long time internally in the World Bank to acknowledge that, in Africa, ethnic issues also mattered: for example, with regard to the curtailment of the role of Asian and Lebanese traders and discouragement of their activities by governments, which were typically overlooked.

A 1989 MADIA study chronicled the role of aid in African agriculture, external shocks, and domestic policies, many of which were overlooked in the Bank's single-minded pursuit of SALs and during Africa's public sector growth (Lele 1989). Owning up to the role of the donors and the World Bank was a challenging part of the MADIA study. Donors who participated in carrying out parallel studies of their own assistance to African agriculture

---

[26] The "Social Dimensions" evaluation noted programs, including public works programs, which generate both income for beneficiaries and contribute to infrastructure: food distribution through health centers/primary schools that contribute to both nutrition and education (Jayarajah, Branson, and Sen 1996). We discuss this further in Chapter 12.

were concerned that acknowledging lack of impacts would either be considered disloyal to their aid institutions, or worse, would imply liability for debt forgiveness, with the risk that the problems would be seen as the fault of outsiders, with no need to pay back the borrowed funds—the so-called moral hazard (Lele 1989).

After the fall of the Berlin Wall and the breakup of the Soviet Union, the Bank also initiated assistance to Eastern Europe. Karen Brooks, one of the few Russian-speaking agricultural economists at the World Bank was in demand for designing assistance programs to Eastern Europe, as she noted in personal communication with Uma Lele:

> The Bank was most effective in the initial advice on loosening the administrative pricing system to avoid the feared catastrophic breakdown in food markets in the winter of 1991–1992. This so-called "price liberalization" is unpopular with many people who lived through it, but it was needed and effective, and not badly implemented. The other aid organizations did not have any guidance on pricing when the shortages appeared in fall of 1991, and the Soviet Union asked the Bank formally for US$14.5 billion in food aid. The Bank mission made the case for price liberalization in the food sector, and it was accepted by the Russian government in January 1992, and subsequently by the other newly independent republics to varying degrees.

> The Bank also carried out a lot of work advising on land issues and farm restructuring, and offered general agricultural policy advice in the form of sector reviews for each of the newly independent countries. Acceptance of the advice was very mixed, and the agricultural sector evolved in haphazard ways throughout the transition. In Russia, the sixfold devaluation of the ruble in August 1998 was quite instrumental in adjusting the competitiveness of agriculture, and spurred consolidation of assets in the hands of the old farm managers and *nomenklatura*—that had already been under way, but it accelerated after the devaluation. The Central Asian countries and Belarus were very slow to change. (Karen Brooks, personal communication with Uma Lele, August 31, 2019)

For more details on the reforms in Eastern Europe, see Rozelle and Swinnen (2004).

Differences between Structural Adjustment in the 1980s and in the New Millennium

Contrary to the early 1980s, the governments' responses in 2008–9 were characterized by the adoption of Keynesian fiscal stimulus packages, in which an increase in social spending was one of the main components (Martorano, Cornia, and Stewart 2014). Nonetheless, in 2010–11, fear of debt default and continuous pressures from the financial markets pushed many policymakers to introduce austerity packages and cut public social expenditure, thereby offsetting part of the prior policy decisions, as was already noted in the early 1980s. Econometric evidence shows that the factors explaining the difference in policy approaches between the early 1980s and in 2008–9 include greater country autonomy compared to the past, the spread of democracy, and greater attention paid to human development by policymakers designing fiscal adjustments (Martorano, Cornia, and Stewart 2014).

Martorano, Cornia, and Stewart (2014) also noted that the financial crisis of the 2000s affected more regions of the world, but its effects on particular countries were more heterogeneous, varying according to countries' dependence on different sources of foreign capital. Southern and Eastern Europe and Latin America were affected the worst. Because of heavy aid dependence and less integration with financial markets, SSA was less severely affected. In contrast, in the 1980s, SSA and Latin America suffered most. In aggregate terms, the fall in GDP was much greater in the 2000s than the 1980s. Yet, taken as a whole, the impact on poverty appears to have been less in the later period. One major difference between the 1980s and 2000s was the greater autonomy that countries had in policymaking, with less dependence on IMF, allowing countries to follow more expansionary policies. Government expenditure, as a proportion of GDP, was generally sustained in 2000s, compared to the severe cuts in the 1980s. Moreover, there were more extensive social support programs in the 2000s, which acted as mild protection against economic downturn. The crisis of the 2000s was shorter than that of the 1980s, so that people and governments could draw upon their savings to protect their livelihoods (Martorano, Cornia, and Stewart 2014).

The 1990s: "The Lost Decade"—The Wapenhans Report and Debt Relief

The 1990s were the "lost decade" for economic growth, in general, and for agriculture, in particular. Developing countries experienced slow growth and mounting debt. The 1980s had radically transformed the Bank's relationship with developing countries, with far-reaching impact on the Bank's declining presence in overall resource transfers and even more so in the agricultural sector, a decided shift from projects to macroeconomic and sector lending—leading to the establishment of a Poverty Reduction and Economic Management (PREM) vice-presidency in the Bank.

In 1992, World Bank President Lewis Preston appointed a senior vice-president, Willi Wapenhans, to lead an ambitious Bank-wide Portfolio Management Task Force to address issues of poor portfolio performance. Some 1,800 projects were reviewed in 113 countries, with a total portfolio of US$138 billion for implementation performance. It was an authoritative, thorough, and devastating critique of the Bank operations. Wapenhans noted that 37.5 percent of the projects completed in 1991 were deemed unsatisfactory at completion, up from 15 percent in 1981, and 30.5 percent in 1989. Bank staff also reported that 30 percent of projects in their fourth or fifth year of implementation in 1991 had major problems. The worst affected sectors were Water Supply and Sanitation, where 43 percent of the projects were said to have major problems, and Agriculture, with 42 percent of those problematic. Geographically, the African region had the most severe performance problems, and two countries in Latin America had 50 percent of the problems in that region. The report noted that, far from being isolated sector phenomenon, the problems were spreading: "traditionally strong performing sectors are now affected too: among them (in FY91), telecommunications (18%), power (22%), industry (17%), and technical assistance (27%). New areas of lending are also encountering major problems: poverty (28%), environment (30%), and private and public sector reform (23%)" (World Bank 1992, 4).

The task force made 87 recommendations to improve effectiveness. The report recommended linking country portfolio performance to the Bank's core business practices, reflecting portfolio performance in country assistance strategies (CASs), preparing an annual report on portfolio performance, providing more active project and portfolio restructuring, assuring country commitment and broad-based participation in project preparation, performing a rigorous analysis of project risks, emphasizing the Bank's role in improvement of management of project performance, and monitoring and more independent evaluation by OED. It also urged decisiveness in portfolio management and a review of procurement issues and guidelines (World Bank 1992). In 1993, the executive directors approved "A Program of Actions," based on management proposals of how to implement the recommendations of the Wapenhans task force. The program's main objective was to ensure that the Bank obtained better results on the ground, thereby increasing the development impact of its operations (World Bank 1993).

Lessons from the Wapenhans Report: Challenge of Implementation and Desire for Greater Country Ownership and Longer Time Horizon

The most critical lesson to emerge from the Wapenhans Report was that without borrower commitment and capacity to design and implement reforms, Bank supervision of its loans could not be effective. Borrower commitment can, of course, exist without the necessary institutional capacity. In such cases, capacity building should be an integral part of the adjustment process. This has implications for both the content and pace of reforms. The gestation period will be much longer—a consideration not sufficiently recognized in the design and supervision of policy-based loans. In the absence of borrower commitment, the adjustment lending process should focus on developing commitment and ownership through country economic and sector work and dialogue. Rushing a policy loan to the Board may impose an unacceptably heavy burden of supervision and monitoring of the program. It should be followed with greater rigor than had been evident in the recent past. The report admonished borrowers to be involved in developing program content, supervision, and monitoring of the impact of policy loans to build capacity, increase ownership, and provide information and analysis on the basis of which midterm corrections could be made. It urged flexibility in design and for procedures; multiple tranches were considered desirable since they provide opportunities for systematic discussion with the borrower and within the Bank. There were detailed recommendations along these lines, including on the management of dialogue on economic reform, macroeconomic monitoring by the Bank, guidelines on public expenditure reviews, and, particularly, the link between expenditures and social sectors, including compensatory measures to reduce social cost on the directly affected and vulnerable in society that may require expenditures. Among the recommendations was the need to adopt at least a 10-year framework for policy lending, with active involvement of borrowers and monitorable targets ensuring joint ownership and better supervision (World Bank 1992).

Rising Debt and Debt Relief for Heavily Indebted Countries

In the early 1990s, concern about the rising debt of poor African countries further reinforced focus on the social sectors and safety nets, but once again ignored the role of the food and the agricultural sector. Wolfensohn, Bank president from 1995 to 2005, considers debt relief one of his singular achievements. The concern prompted a few international players, including UK Prime Minister Tony Blair, some OECD government leaders, and nongovernmental organizations (NGOs), to advocate for effective debt relief for LICs.[27] In 1996, with the World Bank and the IMF launching the Debt Initiative for HIPC, a framework for all creditors was created, including multilateral creditors, to provide debt relief to the world's poorest and most heavily indebted countries—with the aim of ensuring that no poor country faced a debt burden that it could not manage. Assistance was conditional on national governments meeting a range of economic management and performance targets, making a commitment to poverty reduction through policy changes, and demonstrating a record of good economic management over time. The Fund and Bank provided interim debt relief in the initial stage, and when a country met its commitments, full debt relief was provided. The initiative was enhanced in three ways in 1999:

- *Deeper and Broader Relief*: External debt thresholds were lowered from the original framework. As a result, more countries became eligible for debt relief and some countries became eligible for more relief.

- *Faster Relief*: A number of creditors began to provide interim debt relief immediately at the decision point. Also, the new framework permitted countries to reach the completion point faster.

- *Stronger Link between Debt Relief and Poverty Reduction*: Freed resources were to be used to support poverty reduction strategies through Poverty Reduction Strategy Papers, which are developed by national governments in consultation with civil society. (World Bank 2018b)

The modifications strengthened the HIPC initiative. However, the initiative is not a panacea for all the problems of heavily indebted poor countries. Even without debt, most still depend on significant levels of external development assistance. Most of the ODA now goes to low-income developing countries. The Bank had focused more on agricultural productivity growth and poverty reduction than on food security. In 1993, however, organized by Ismail Serageldin, the World Bank held a conference on food security at the American University entitled "Overcoming Global Hunger." The proceedings were edited and published in 1994, by Serageldin and Pierre Landell-Mills, as *Overcoming Global Hunger: Proceedings of a Conference on Actions to Reduce Hunger Worldwide*, part of the World Bank's Environmentally Sustainable Development Series (Serageldin and Landell-Mills 1994). See more in Chapter 4 on food security.

The 1997 Rural Development Policy: Getting Back on the Agenda with "From Vision to Action"

After a long hiatus, the Bank formed a new rural development policy, directed by Alex McCalla, then Director of Rural Development, with large active role played by Hans Binswanger, two brilliant economists, highly respected internationally. After a few years,

[27] President Carter proposed debt forgiveness for Guyana in 1993 to IMF and the World Bank, when Uma Lele served as the founding Director of the Global Development Initiative of the Carter Center and the Carnegie Endowment (while on leave from the World Bank from 1991 to 1995). Lele had recruited Ravi Gulhati, former Chief Economist of the Bank's Africa Region to help develop a stabilization program for Guyana in 1993. The United States, Germany, and Japan were opposed to debt rescheduling or debt forgiveness. When the British Prime Minister Tony Blair came up with a debt initiative, the HIPC Debt Initiative began to gather momentum and became a reality in 1997 (Copson 2005).

the effort was frequently described as long on vision and short on action. It showed how difficult it has been to motivate action on agriculture and rural development from the Bank, with McNamara's top-down period having been a singular exception. Key elements of "Vision to Action" involved working with partner countries and the international community to integrate rural development into Country Development Strategies, "addressing long-ignored issues," and "addressing old issues in new ways" (Ayres and McCalla 1997, viii). Land reform, gender equality, and food and nutrition were highlighted as "ignored" (Ayres and McCalla 1997, 18). The strategy suggested implementing new ways to deliver rural financial services, promote sustainable resource use, and proposed involving the entire WBG in promoting rural development, rather than only the Agricultural and Rural Development Global Practice.

The strategy identified four major challenges: (1) poverty and hunger reduction; (2) raising economic growth; (3) increasing global food production; and (4) halting natural resource and environmental degradation. A "broad and complex" strategy called for growth not only to expand food output, but also to be "widely shared and sustainable" (Ayres and McCalla 1997, 3). Eliminating poverty had been the central tenet of McNamara's 1973 speech to the World Bank's Annual Meeting. The executive summary of "Vision to Action" asked why these critical issues were not being addressed. It cited a lack of attention from three sources—the country, international agencies, and WBG. The strategy noted weak demand from countries ("agricultural underperformers or even dropouts") (Ayres and McCalla 1997, 3) and the international community's complacency in the face of declining food prices, as well as the significant decline in lending to agriculture by the World Bank. The underperformers were characterized by the Bank as having institutional frameworks and agricultural policies that discriminated against the rural sector and private sector initiatives; underinvesting in technology development and in its dissemination, and in health and education; having inappropriate agrarian structures; and showing a tendency to undervalue natural resources and, therefore, to waste them (Ayres and McCalla 1997, 3). In developing countries, agriculture was seen as a declining sector in the economy and, therefore, not worth prioritization. This perception was coupled with a lack of voice for the poor dispersed in rural areas, relative to a growing urban population with increased political power.

"Vision to Action" also acknowledged that the deterioration in project and program performance in the Bank's agricultural and rural development portfolio played a role. Only 52 percent of the completed projects in the 1980s were rated satisfactory. IFC was disorganized, and the performance of its agribusiness portfolio was poor, too. It had reorganized into a single department in 1992, thus bringing its performance in this area rapidly in line with the rest of IFC work. Since 1997, performance of completed Bank projects improved, according to the "Vision to Action" policy document. The policy document also outlined lessons learned from failed approaches, such as in the case of integrated rural development projects. For instance, "most decisions . . . were made by central government officials, and communities were rarely involved in project design, implementation, or monitoring" (Ayres and McCalla 1997, 5):[28]

- Sector-specific projects, such as offering of agricultural credit through parastatals, had not worked—they had poor repayments, benefited richer farmers, and distorted financial markets through subsidies.

---

[28] In reality, in many cases, particularly in SSA and Latin America, Bank-funded projects were designed by external actors, and many of those in Africa were implemented by expatriates.

- Resettlement projects tended to be centralized, costly, and unsustainable.
- Large-scale irrigation was centrally driven, tending to experience delays in construction, cost overruns, and environmental problems, such as salinization and soil degradation.
- Public sector involvement in seed production, supply, and marketing through parastatals had caused problems—the private sector was thought to be able to perform better and more efficiently.

There was little mention of support for agricultural technology in the "Vision to Action" report, and the few references to it were made in the context of the work being done by CGIAR or regional interventions. In terms of improved Bank business, "Vision to Action" outlined: (1) research and extension through NGOs; (2) sector policy lending in support of policy reforms that governments had undertaken; (3) sector investment lending, which in some cases helped consolidate donor projects into public expenditure support programs; (4) rural development through NGOs and CDD—for example, the transfer of responsibilities for irrigation and drainage (as in northeast Brazil) to communities at risk of reliance on overcentralized bureaucracies; (5) rural finance focused on increased savings; and (6) increased use of microfinance, reduced subsidies, increased competition, and land reform through market-assisted policies. It noted that these innovations were yet to be monitored and introduced into problem projects. Except for China and Brazil, progress in developing countries was mixed at best in these areas (Ayres and McCalla 1997).

The strategic checklist was utopian, envisioned by an enlightened, well-informed agricultural policymaker. "Vision to Action" set out to achieve 80 percent "satisfactory" project ratings by 2002, through regular portfolio reviews. ECA achieved that level by 2000, while African rates still remained below all others in 2017. The report acknowledged the perpetual tension between improved portfolio performance and innovation and risk. To address this challenge, pilot experimental projects were proposed to learn lessons before investments were scaled up. Qualitative outcomes were also proposed: (1) perceived Bank leadership in the fight to reduce rural poverty and improve natural resource management; (2) progress toward freer and fairer world trade; and (3) reversal of the low-growth trends of underperforming countries through country ownership and political will.

"Vision to Action" was launched in 1997 with considerable fanfare, following extensive consultations, with support from the Bank's top management and a complement of 470 staff in rural development, including 100 long-term consultants. It optimistically proclaimed, "This rural sector strategy is not business as usual!" (Ayres and McCalla 1997, 17). Yet, 2003 turned out to be the year with the lowest level of lending to agriculture by the World Bank (Figures 8.2 and 8.5).

The 2000 OED evaluation of the "Vision to Action" strategy found that it failed to provide an enabling framework for effective action. "Since *From Vision to Action* was prepared, the Bank's effectiveness at rural development is perceived to have increased— but it is still less than satisfactory . . . Partners express skepticism about the scope for market-based solutions and decentralization" (OED 2000, 1–2). The evaluation concluded that the Bank's rural work was not sufficiently focused on poverty reduction. The Bank has not been effective at communicating its corporate rural strategy, and better articulation of the strategy was required—including attention to cross-sectoral issues and the nexus between urban and rural development—in CASs (OED 2000).

The 2000s: Toward a Food and Financial Crisis

The new millennium saw the development of new strategies to address continuing problems.

The 2003 Rural Development Strategy

The Bank's new rural development strategy, described in its 2003 publication, "Reaching the Rural Poor: A Renewed Strategy for Rural Development," again attempted to refocus effort on rural development, but again without much emphasis on agriculture, the sector most of the rural poor continue to depend upon for their livelihoods. In his foreword, Bank President James Wolfensohn declared the strategy as "our 'battle-plan' for such a renewed focus, and our commitment to reverse the downward trend in rural lending" (World Bank 2003b, v). He noted in his foreword: "Over the last decade lending to rural development, and especially to agriculture, has been in unprecedented decline—both at the World Bank and among our development partners. This situation cannot continue. We must renew our focus on agriculture and rural development" (World Bank 2003b, v).

Development of the strategy began with regional action plans and dialogue with Bank clients, civil society organizations, the private sector, academia, and other IOs and policy leaders—over 2,000 people in all. A series of regional and corporate strategy consultations began in 2001 throughout Asia, Europe, Africa, and Latin America and continued through 2002. Early on, the Bank launched a website to solicit public comments. As with "Vision to Action," the 2002 World Summit for Sustainable Development presented an opportunity for world leaders to pledge support for rural development; other international forums have also provided platforms for stakeholder discussion (for example, the World Food Summit of FAO and IFPRI's program, 2020 Vision).[29]

As with the previous strategy, the new strategy recognized past disappointments. In fact, the fundamentals and context largely carried over from the previous "Vision to Action"— compounded with five years of additional experience. "Reaching the Rural Poor" concluded that "Vision to Action" had a decisive influence on global thinking, but produced little results.[30] It reported, in 2001, that lending for agricultural projects was the lowest in the World Bank's history—for fiscal years 1999 to 2001, amounting to US$5 billion annually, or 25 percent of total Bank lending. Of the US$5 billion in rural lending in fiscal year 2002, agricultural sector investment was only US$1.5 billion, or 7.9 percent of total Bank lending. By comparison, it was at over 30 percent in the 1980s (World Bank 2003b, xiv).

The strategy rested its case on the connection between agricultural growth and poverty reduction, citing the literature and evidence documenting and linking GDP and per capita income changes to agricultural growth, presenting a number of illustrative examples,

---

[29] See https://sustainabledevelopment.un.org/milesstones/wssd for more information about the World Summit for Sustainable Development, and see http://www.fao.org/WFS/for FAO's World Food Summit and https://www. ifpri.org/program/2020-vision to read more about the IFPRI 2020 Vision program.

[30] Annex I of "Reaching the Rural Poor" evaluated the three projected outcomes of "Vision to Action," concluding: (1) the Bank did not lead in reducing rural poverty due to a decline in lending and limited institutional capacity; (2) the limited authorizing environment in dealing with OECD country subsidies limited progress in trade liberalization; and (3) a focus on 15 countries led to variable results in promoting increased economic growth (World Bank 2003b, 96–7).

particularly from India and East Asia.[31] It designated agriculture as the "leading sector within the rural economy, with significant forward and backward linkages to the non-farm sector" (World Bank 2003b, 43). The agenda of "Reaching the Rural Poor" pays specific attention to agriculture, with proposed shifts from:

- Narrow agricultural focus to a global policy context for agriculture growth and poverty reduction;
- A focus on yields to market demands and outcomes;
- Staples to high-value crops;
- Primary production to the food chain as a whole;
- A single-farm approach to heterogeneity (later, a core feature of the 2008 *WDR* [World Bank 2007]);
- Public to public–private partnerships and CDD;
- Avoidance of issues to a head-on approach to biotechnology, forestry, and water, and other key issues (World Bank 2003b, 44).

Food security, which has become a major focus for the global community since 2007, was included under the objective of improving social well-being and mitigating risk. The approach suggested new types of insurance to navigate weather changes and commodity prices and the use of more cost-effective, targeted programs over generalized subsidies. The evidence on crop insurance in the United States suggests it is heavily subsidized (Smith 2017), and it is unlikely to operate differently in developing countries (Raju and Chand 2007; Binswanger-Mkhize 2012; Sahu 2018). The promotion of certain ideas, whether social rates of return or crop insurance, tend to be driven by a momentum behind certain ideas of economic entrepreneurs.

The strategy also notes the importance of comprehensive nutrition programs for women and children, an area that has received, in particular, an international boost since 2007–8. Chapter 4 describes the complexity of the nutrition challenge and why the efforts of the Bank have had limited impacts (World Bank 2003b). The latest research on India shows that the idea of a multisectoral platform, agreed to in principle in India's nutrition policy to address a multisectoral challenge, is not working (Menon et al. 2019).

In hindsight, the language, argumentation, and evidence in "Reaching the Rural Poor" seemed familiar to authors and readers of previous reports. The new strategy sought to distinguish itself from past approaches, in that it was results-oriented and stressed practice, implementation of "attainable actions," monitoring, and empowerment of the people who it was designed to help (World Bank 2003b, xiv). In outlining strategic objectives, "Reaching the Rural Poor" highlights essential elements of an appropriate macroeconomic policy environment and supportive institutional framework, including agricultural trade liberalization; good governance, including decentralization and transfer of responsibility for services to the political and administrative level closest to (rural) users; and a better understanding of the relation between financial services and poverty, as well as a shift from supply-driven agricultural credit (World Bank 2003b).

Unlike "Vision to Action," "Reaching the Rural Poor" did not set specific targets, noting that the demand-driven nature of the strategy would result in differing regional benchmarks and goals. It suggested a results-based management approach and tracking of country

---

[31] The strategy document noted the average real income of small farmers in southern India rose by 90 percent between 1973 and 1994, as a result of the Green Revolution (World Bank 2003b, xix).

indicators in rural development and poverty reduction to monitor and evaluate results over a five-year period. The identified risks to successful strategy implementation were lack of multisectoral adoption of the strategy, failure to address institutional arrangements and staffing, failure of institutional learning and innovation to materialize, lack of country buy-in, and long-term growth unrealized in client countries.

In 1998, the Bank's Agriculture and Rural Development department established an Agriculture and Knowledge Information System (AKIS), a Bank-wide network of practitioners, also involving practitioners in other agencies and produced a number of knowledge products. Noting that agricultural lending had declined precipitously from the peak of 1991 to a bottom in 2003, the *Agriculture Investment Sourcebook* identified the changing investment climate and assembled a collection of examples from Bank projects and country policies, providing good practices from around the developing world in 11 different areas (World Bank 2005a). In its Review of World Bank activities, "Putting Social Development to Work for the Poor," OED noted:

> Only after President Wolfensohn's first annual meetings address, "New Directions and New Partnerships," did the Bank make rapid progress in mainstreaming attention to social concerns. The culmination of this effort came in 1996, when President Wolfensohn convened a Social Development Task Force to address the role of social assessment in Bank lending instruments and Country Assistance Strategies. Then, through the 1997 Strategic Compact, the Bank provided additional resources for social development capacity building, as well as funds to help execute the Regional Social Development Action Plans. As a result of these initiatives, Bank social scientists began to provide social analysis and to take steps to understand the social impacts of both traditional Bank projects and the Bank's growing portfolio of social service projects. (OED 2005b, ix)

See Box 8.3 for a discussion of CDD.

Approximately 105 IBRD and IDA countries had undertaken projects with a CDD approach as of 2011. Between 2002 and 2011, IBRD and IDA approved 734 projects, which used CDD approaches, either for the entire projects or in selected components. Total Bank lending for CDD, managed and controlled directly by communities and local governments, was US$22.5 billion over the period, with an average of US$2.2 billion per year, and including several large projects approved in Africa and East and SA (World Bank 2013a).

As lending has increased, the big challenge, particularly in the second and third generation of projects, was to mainstream CDDs into the body politic of the local governments, into specific sectors, and to make them sustainable.

"Agriculture" or "Agriculture and Rural Development"?

One of the vexing issues in the Bank, over the past 50 years, has been how best to achieve agricultural development: that is, whether by lending to agriculture alone, through specialized activities, or to agriculture and rural development, using an integrated development strategy. In certain circumstances, specialized loans or credits—for example, for agricultural research and education or for agricultural finance—are essential and make sense. Overall, however, it does not make sense to think of agriculture in a narrow sense, omitting the critical importance of transport, irrigation, power, and communications in determining

Box 8.3 Community-Driven Development

Community-driven development (CDD) is meant to support empowerment of the poor to make interventions, which are more relevant to their needs, by giving communities control of subproject resources and decisions. Community-based development (CBD) "emphasizes collaboration, consultation, or sharing information" with communities on project activities, while giving them less responsibility (OED 2005a, ix). Since the late 1990s, the Bank has favored CDD, though many CDD projects also include CBD components. The share of projects that include a CBD or CDD component grew from about 2 percent in fiscal 1989 to 25 percent in 2003 (OED 2005a, xiii).

Mansuri and Rao (2013) in a comprehensive review of 500 studies, "Localizing Development," noted the Bank had committed over US$85 billion to participatory projects over the previous decade.

The OED study on "The Effectiveness of World Bank Support for Community-Based and -Driven Development" noted:

> Over the 1994–2003 period, the outcome ratings of CBD/CDD projects have been better than those for non-CBD/CDD projects on quantitative goals such as construction of infrastructure than on qualitative goals, such as capacity enhancement. Sustainability ratings for the projects have improved over time, but there is considerable room for improvement. Bank interventions have often failed to provide the consistent, long-term support needed for an activity to become sustainable (for example, in a forestry project, support should be provided until the forest starts yielding adequate returns from timber and non-timber products). (OED 2005a, ix)

In his recent book, *Why Counterinsurgency Fails: The US in Iraq and Afghanistan*, Dennis de Tray argues in favor of bottom-up, decentralized development in fragile and conflict-affected countries, such as Afghanistan and Iraq, because fragile states' governments do not or cannot serve their people, and people in fragile states neither believe in nor support their government. The only government most people know is local government. Local governors know more about what their people need than either the coalition forces or Kabul would ever know, and they knew how to get things done in their local environment (de Tray 2019). So, what happens if we give local governors resources, accountability, and responsibility and insist only on transparency? It works better. De Tray came to many of these conclusions, as did Mansuri and Rao (2013): leadership matters. Programs worked best in districts with competent and engaged leadership. One size does not fit all. Local conditions dictated different approaches to development and the uses of development resources. Provinces and districts have weak capacity, but that is not the same thing as zero capacity. Given a chance, provincial and district governments were capable of making local development happen.

Mansuri and Rao (2013) documented how community participation is highly context-specific, depending on history, geography, cultural, and political factors. Success depends on careful, independent monitoring. Task managers, who were surveyed, highlighted several problems, including:

> ... lack of management support, the lack of an adequate project supervision budget, and the fact that most World Bank managers believe that governments see monitoring

systems as a box to be checked off in order to qualify for a loan rather than as an instrument to help improve the effectiveness of projects. Given their sense that country counterparts have little incentive to implement good M&E [monitoring and evaluation] systems, explicit support from the World Bank may be critical. (Mansuri and Rao, 2013, 303)

Additional concerns, including increased access to infrastructure, does not always translate into effective service delivery. The poorest do not always benefit from these projects. There is little evidence on the poverty-reducing and community capacity-enhancing impacts of the projects.

TFP and in the development of value chains in agriculture, or of clean water and sanitation and gender empowerment in achieving household food security and nutrition. Effective agriculture and rural development calls for holistic, intersectoral approaches, for which the Bank has a unique advantage.

The 2007 and 2010 IEG evaluations of "World Bank Assistance to Agriculture in Sub-Saharan Africa" argued that, from time to time, when the Bank has chosen to opt for agriculture or rural development, it has neglected either agriculture while shifting to rural development, or ignored complementarities with related sectors, such as rural roads, while focusing on agriculture (IEG 2007). "The central finding of the study is that the agriculture sector has been neglected both by governments and the donor community, including the World Bank. The Bank's strategy for agriculture has been increasingly subsumed within a broader rural focus, in which its importance has suffered" (IEG 2007, xi). AFF sector lending peaked in FY 2018, compared to FY1990, increasing from the low of only US $1.8billion in FY2003 to US$4.2 billion in FY2018, all in real terms (nominal/MUV Index, 2010 = 100), while lending to rural development peaked in FY2010, since FY1990, at US$7.8 billion and has increased more significantly from US$1 billion in FY2002. Recently, lending to rural development showed a declining trend while the trend of lending to the AFF sector is increasing (Figure 8.18). The Agriculture versus Rural Development debate stresses the importance of area development going forward, rather than narrowly conceived "agricultural" projects, given the increasing interdependence of agriculture with water, energy/power, transportation, and information. Also, it calls for a decentralized development approach that increases the role of local governments. It is only through area development approaches that the need for intersectoral coordination can be addressed: within the World Bank and within governments, with a need to break down silos. Silos—sectoral staff and project and program staff working in isolation of each other—have long been a long-standing challenge within the Bank, which Stanley Please described well in his oral history account, cited previously (Please 1986). It is unclear if the Bank has eliminated silos or created new ones. Much will depend on how budgeting is done and what incentives will be set up for cross-sectoral staff to collaborate in a solution mode. The 2019 "Realignment" appears to have significantly weakened Global Practices, which were created in 2014 under Jim Kim, increasing his unpopularity. The latest reorganization strengthened the regions relative to Global Practices, as both budgets and work programs are under regional directors (IEG 2019).

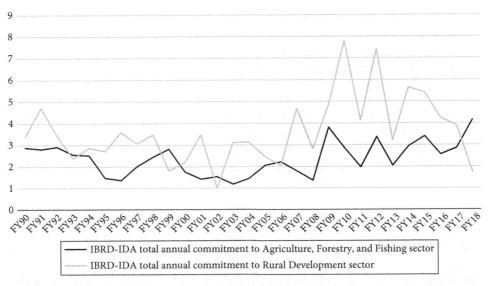

Figure 8.18 IDA and IBRD annual commitment to the Agriculture, Forestry and Fishing sector and Rural Development sector, FY1990–FY2018 (US$bn, real = nominal/MUV, MUV Index 2010 = 100)

Source: Based on data from https://datacatalog.worldbank.org/dataset/world-bank-projects-operations

It is hard to say what these moving of boxes on an organizational chart means to the Bank's performance, as we noted earlier.

The Bank's Gender Strategy and Implementation

In his speech to the Plenary Session of the 2019 Annual Meetings of the Board of Governors, World Bank President Malpass stated: "We're investing in human capital. More than half of all 10-year-olds in low- and middle-income countries can't read, which is unacceptable. In this week's education and learning announcements, we set a target of at least cutting learning poverty in half," and "We're putting substantial resources into closing the gender gap. In fiscal 2019, over 60 percent of combined IBRD and IDA operations helped address gender gaps and encouraged full incorporation of women in economies" (World Bank 2019b).

The development community has realized for several decades that gender parity, empowering women and improving women's access to factors of production while giving them voice in decision-making of matters that affect their lives and those of their households, and indeed, of nation states, is critical to achieve development.

In an IMF Staff Discussion Note, "Women, Work and the Economy: Macroeconomic Gains from Gender Equity," it was asserted:

Women make up a little over half the world's population, but their contribution to measured economic activity, growth, and well-being is far below its potential, with serious macroeconomic consequences. Despite significant progress in recent decades, labor markets across the world remain divided along gender lines, and progress toward gender equality seems to have stalled. Female labor force participation (FLFP) has remained lower than male participation, women account for most unpaid work, and when women are employed in paid work, they are overrepresented in the informal sector and among the poor. They also face significant wage differentials vis-à-vis their male colleagues. In many countries, distortions and discrimination in the labor market restrict women's options for paid work, and female representation in senior positions and entrepreneurship remains low. The challenges of growth, job creation, and inclusion are closely intertwined ... (Elborgh-Woytek et al. 2013, 4)

Notably, IMF was headed by French economist Christine Lagarde, who served as the first woman Managing Director and Chairman of the Executive Board of the IMF from 2011 to September 2019. As noted earlier, Kristalina Georgieva, former CEO of the World Bank, assumed this position on October 1, 2019. IMF's research on gender makes a number of recommendations to address the challenge: "the constraints preventing women from developing their full economic potential, [and] implementing policies that remove labor market distortions and create a level playing field for all will give women the opportunity to develop their potential and to participate in economic life more visibly." The Staff Discussion Note was "based on research undertaken in academia and by other international financial institutions, in addition to the IMF's own surveillance and research work" (Elborgh-Woytek et al. 2013, 4).

The World Bank's approach has been slow to evolve with limited impact on outcomes. The Bank appointed the first Women in Development Advisor as early as in 1977, but the progress was slow. In 2001, the Bank produced an operational strategy on gender that required CASs, later called country partnership strategies, to comment on the countries' own policies and plans on gender and the Bank's proposed response through assistance in various sectors (World Bank 2002). Successive IDA replenishments and later MDGs reinforced attention to gender. The Bank has also had an operational policy, OP 4.20 on gender and development, since 2003, which was revised in March 2012, and is still in effect.[32] The IEG evaluation of the 2001 strategy noted that, after an initial spurt, implementation tapered off due to absence of monitoring and accountability. CASs did not have a systematic treatment of gender, and there was frequently weak follow-up of the strategies in Bank assistance to countries and unclear prioritization of assistance by sectors in which it would have the biggest impact (IEG 2010). In 2007, the Bank prepared the Gender Action Plan, with resources for analytical work and policy dialogue, which went beyond project lending and provided an input into the Bank's 2012 *WDR: Gender Equality and Development* (World Bank 2012). The Bank has also become more active in other gender-related platforms. Its latest strategy for 2016–23 proposes to move beyond mainstreaming gender to outcomes based on enhanced, country-level diagnostics, building capacity of countries' statistical offices to improve "data collection in four priority areas: (1) physical and financial asset ownership and control, (2) time use, (3) employment, and (4) welfare. Each area has three components: methodological research, data production, and data dissemination and usability" for assistance and monitoring of results (WBG 2015, 66). The Gender Strategy FY2016–23 states that in SSA, "the Bank Group will focus on the

---

[32] See OP 4.20 – Gender and Development. https://policies.worldbank.org/sites/ppf3/PPFDocuments/1680090224b08231c012.pdf and http://web.worldbank.org/archive/website01541/WEB/0__-1909.HTM

gender gap in agricultural productivity and agribusiness operations, whereas in South Asia the focus will be on nutrition-sensitive and safe food systems and sustainable livelihoods, as well as on linking smallholder farmers to value chains" (WBG 2015, 43). The Bank is also working in partnership with IFC's initiative, described in the section on IFC in Appendix B. The World Bank Group's *Gender Strategy (FY16–23): Gender Equality, Poverty Reduction and Inclusive Growth* describes the IFC partnership, *She Works* (WBG 2015).

The World Bank's Work on Land Policy

In Chapter 2, we discussed debates on agricultural productivity growth by farm size and the role of factor markets, particularly labor market failures, in explaining the inverse relationship between farm size and productivity at early stages of development. In that chapter, we also provided some recent evidence that productivity growth may be showing a U-shaped pattern of farm size and productivity, with respect to growth in per capita income (Muyanga and Jayne 2019). Typically, as factor markets develop, labor finds alternative employment in the nonagricultural sector at wages equal to or more than the marginal product of labor in agriculture, and labor moves out of agriculture, causing labor shortages and leading to increased capitalization of agriculture—that is, substitution of machines for labor—consolidation of land, and increase in farm size. This process is aided by the development of land and capital markets in a synergetic way. Good public policy toward land and finance can accelerate this process. Economists in the Bank have argued that secure property rights enable access to capital, using land as collateral; promote land rental markets to facilitate more intensive land use; or use underutilized land, thereby creating more employment and increased efficiency.

Hans Binswanger was at the forefront of these issues and has had considerable influence in placing the issue of property rights on the World Bank's agenda of agriculture and rural development. Klaus Deininger, his mentee, has helped spawn a huge program of work on land, illustrating what a combination of intellectual leadership, entrepreneurship, and the Bank's convening power can do to mobilize research resources, attract other analysts, and influence the Bank's policy dialogue and operations. Since their first paper in 1993 (Binswanger and Deininger 1993), Deininger has organized 20 annual Land and Policy conferences, attended by over 1,500 professionals, donors, and national policymakers, and in 2019, with influence on more than US$1.8 billion of the Bank's operating funds.

Together, Binswanger and Deininger documented the impact of institutions in governing access to use of land and on socioeconomic development. They broke new ground by demonstrating that benefits from secure land rights and good land governance can be large, pro-poor, and multifaceted for many reasons. Clearly, their thinking evolved considerably, based on reality on the ground, as can be seen from their papers. In their 1999 paper, Deininger and Binswanger identified "three guiding principles: (1) the desirability of owner-operated family farms; (2) the need for markets to permit land to be transferred to more productive users; and (3) the importance of an egalitarian asset distribution. In the 25 years since that paper [the World Bank's (1975a) "Land Reform Policy Paper"] was published, these guiding principles have remained the same ... " (Deininger and Binswanger 1999, 247).[33] In reality, the policies did change quite a bit with experience. Whereas the World Bank had "recommended

---

[33] See Chapter 2: we note that the definition of what constitutes a family farm varies in the literature.

communal tenure systems be abandoned in favor of freehold titles and the subdivision of the commons," in the 1975 paper, the researchers noted a growing recognition in the Bank that some "communal tenure systems can be more cost-effective than formal [an Anglo-Saxon concept of a land ownership] title, that titling programs should be judged on their equity as well as their efficiency" (Deininger and Binswanger 1999, 247–8). In the same vein, they argued:

> The potential of land rental markets has often been severely underestimated, that land-sale markets enhance efficiency only if they are integrated into a broader effort at developing rural factor markets, and that land reform is more likely to result in a reduction of poverty if it harnesses (rather than undermines) the operation of land markets and is implemented in a decentralized fashion. Achieving land policies that incorporate these elements requires a coherent legal and institutional framework together with greater reliance on pilot programs to examine the applicability of interventions under local conditions. (Deininger and Binswanger 1999, 247)

Realities on the ground, however, can be quite different.

In 2009, based on the review of the literature on the impact of land administration interventions in specific contexts, Deininger and Feder (2009, 234) noted, outcomes depend on "the governance environment, the effectiveness of the state apparatus, and the distribution of socio-economic power." The authors noted: "If property rights are secure, well-defined, and publicly enforced, landowners need to spend less time and resources guarding them" (Deininger and Feder 2009, 236). Enhanced tenure security through land registration results in higher levels of investment and productivity and a reduced need to defend land rights, but the evidence is not uniform. "Land registration has also been shown to increase activity in land rental markets, leading to higher efficiency overall" (Deininger and Feder 2009, 233). However, there is little "evidence of improved access to credit, due to formalization of land rights...Even in situations where land registration had positive benefits, the literature contains little rigorous analysis of cost-effectiveness and long-term sustainability of impacts....[F]ormalization of land rights should not be viewed as a panacea" (Deininger and Feder 2009, 233), a major turn-around from the Bank's position in 1975, and perhaps even in 1999. They further noted that "interventions should be decided only after a careful diagnosis of the policy, social, and governance environment" (Deininger and Feder 2009, 233).

The Bank has conducted economic and sector work on Mexico, Colombia, Nicaragua, India, Malawi, Zambia, Ethiopia, China, Philippines, Vietnam, and Ukraine, among others; all of the work is in the Bank's Image Bank.[34] Most of these have resulted in projects, but increasingly this is shifting to development policy loans (in Malawi and Ukraine) and P4Rs (Program-for-Results financing) (out of a recently approved US$200 million P4R for Ukraine, US$160 million is for land, including (1) establishment of a farmer register (linked to the land and animal registry) to target subsidies and provide information for private sector (for example, banks and insurance); (2) land use planning by local governments; (3) free legal aid and awareness campaigns and establishment of an ombudsman to allow land owners, especially women, effectively enforce their rights.

---

[34] See https://archivesphotos.worldbank.org/en/about/archives/photo-gallery

Beyond the Bank, Deininger and his colleagues are evaluating efforts undertaken by governments without Bank assistance (Deininger et al. 2008), or funded by other donors (as in Rwanda; Ali, Deininger, and Goldstein 2014), and pushed methodological innovations: in particular, assessing gender-differentiated demand for land title (in Tanzania; Ali et al. 2016); linking to administrative data to assess land registry sustainability (in Rwanda; Ali, Deininger, and Duponchel 2017; and Ali et al. forthcoming); assessing large farm investment (in Ethiopia; Ali, Deininger, and Harris 2017; and in Malawi; Deininger and Xia 2018); using freely available satellite imagery to assess effects of soil and water conservation measures (in Ethiopia; Ali, Deininger, and Monchuk 2020); potential for tax revenue (in Rwanda; Ali, Deininger, and Wild 2020); and urban expansion (in Vietnam; Goldblatt, Deininger, and Hanson 2018).

If intervention is justified, the performance of land administration systems needs to be benchmarked in terms of coverage, cost effectiveness, and quality of service provision. Some country experiences of Bank interventions are worth noting.

In Brazil, a pilot project was undertaken to support market-based land reform for 15,000 farmers, initiated in 1997 and completed in 2001, with a US$90 million loan. The outcome was rated satisfactory. The number of farmer beneficiaries was slightly more than targeted, and their actual income was significantly higher than projected (World Bank 2003a). Whether it has led to scaling up the program in a significant way to make a difference at the macroeconomic level is unclear. The Brazilian economy has gone through considerable gyrations, growing unemployment, changes of governments—including one impeachment, and unrelatedly, since coming to power in 2017, the Bolsonaro government has opened up the Amazon for slash and burn agriculture with considerable adverse environmental impacts on greenhouse gas emissions (Canuto 2019a, 2019b; CFI 2019; IMF 2019a).

In South Africa, the World Bank intervention to introduce a land market to foster smallholder agriculture had had limited success, if any. There was little buy-in from white commercial farmers who took over massive areas of land from black farmers, pushing them into their homelands. Essentially, there was no "surplus" land, as the project assumed. South Africa's underlying common law also had an influence on how property rights work. Because all of Southern Africa works with Roman-Dutch law, and because South Africa's common law was heavily discriminatory against black people and women generally, it was never going to be possible to merely transfer lessons from the global experience to South Africa. "Unfortunately, government officials were (and still are) unaware of the importance of this distinction, so no pressure has been put on South African courts to start using a broader interpretation of what the Constitution allows (where our Constitution almost begs them to do so!), and the result has been fewer and weaker property rights for South Africans and a whole host of missed opportunities" (Nick Vink, personal communication with Uma Lele, October 22, 2019).

John Heath, another former World Bank colleague, recently wrote a paper on the challenge, in Colombia, posed by the skewed pattern of land ownership and the underuse of land suitable for farming (Heath 2019), which was tackled by the famed Albert Hirschman (1970) and later in the 1990s by the World Bank. In the early 1960s, Hirschman backed an administrative approach to land reform, led by a state agency. In the mid-1990s, the World Bank championed a new, market-assisted approach to land reform, building on legislation introduced by the Colombian government (Aiyar, Parker, and Van Zyl 1995). Both attempts failed. They neither reduced the level of concentration of landholding, nor did they help to reduce rural poverty and create a new class of prosperous small farmers.

With rapid changes in technologies, such as remote sensing, 5G, and cell phones, and with the World Bank and donors helping developing countries to address their own challenges of class structure and policy capture, the countries will hopefully have brighter futures than the examples related here, although Ethiopia has achieved much in giving land titles to women. So, there is hope yet.

Agricultural Pricing, Subsidies, and Trade

Three issues have been of particular interest in Bank work: (1) pricing/subsidy and trade policies of developing countries and changes in those policies; (2) the role the World Bank has played through its bilateral discussions/analysis of individual client country policies, and its impact on country policies; and (3) the Bank's support to trade liberalization and elimination of distortions, more generally.

Kym Anderson, writing about agricultural and trade policy reform historically, noted:

> Governments in the past have tried to alter not only the trend level of farm prices but also to reduce their year-to-year fluctuations. Typically, this was done by varying the restrictions on international trade according to seasonal conditions domestically and changes in prices internationally. Effectively this involves exporting domestic instability and not importing instability from abroad. When many countries indulge in such insulating behavior it 'thins' international markets for farm products, making them more volatile and thereby encouraging even more countries to insulate. (Anderson 2010, 19)

Distortions to agricultural incentives for developing countries have diminished since the mid-1980s, with the important exceptions of rice and wheat—cereals in which India and China are the largest producers and consumers. As we discussed in Chapter 3, in times of price volatility, countries have imposed temporary trade restrictions to insulate domestic prices from international markets. Virtually all Asian countries have imposed trade restrictions following increased price volatility, starting in 2007.

The World Bank has taken a very different approach to influencing policies and investment strategies in China and India, its two biggest borrowers—mostly by persuasion and demonstration, rather than by conditionality or a "sledge hammer" approach. For understandable reasons, however, it has had very little, if any, influence on the issues of agricultural pricing subsidies and trade, either in India or China. India's Food Bill, which passed in 2013, was a politically charged effort, based on a "rights" approach. Even though the World Bank stayed out of this controversial issue, over the years, it has consistently pointed out the direct cost of agricultural subsidies for growth and distribution: for example, by causing distortions in food production in favor of cereals, and thereby, arresting agricultural diversification. Also, the Bank noted indirect costs arising from the diversion of funds from the much needed physical and institutional infrastructure to support agricultural productivity growth, in which India has lagged behind other East and Southeast Asian countries, as shown in Chapter 2.

The World Bank has frequently advocated agricultural trade liberalization. The outcome of the Bali Ministerial Conference (9th WTO Ministerial Conference in December 2013) was the Trade Facilitation Agreement (TFA). The TFA, as part of a wider "Bali Package," provides for faster and more efficient customs procedures, through effective cooperation between customs and other appropriate authorities on issues of trade facilitation and customs compliance. It also contains provisions for technical assistance and capacity building in this area: WTO members concluded negotiations on the landmark TFA, effective February 22, 2017, following its ratification by two-thirds of the WTO membership at the Bali Conference (WTO 2020).

Bank support to WTO on the Doha Round is evident in various ways. Danny Leipziger, the Bank's Vice President for PREM, urged urgent action on the Doha Round of trade talks to deliver on its promise for the world's poor: "Only by giving the poorest people a chance to get jobs and generate income will the world become more equitable and more stable" (World Bank 2005d).

Bank research has also demonstrated global gains from trade reforms and the Doha development agenda implemented after 2004: the abolition of tariffs, subsidies, and domestic support programs could boost global welfare by nearly US$300 billion per year by 2015. Productivity increases from the reforms could generate even more gains (Anderson and Martin 2005, 11).

Since 2005, US and EU subsidies have declined but have not gone away, and have come in different garbs. The United States still supports individual commodities. In Europe, there are income subsidies. At a seminar at IFPRI on US and EU pricing and subsidies, the conclusion of the speakers was that not only are subsidies extensive, but quite complex for developing country policymakers to keep track of and untangle for negotiations (Zulauf and Orden 2014).

World Development Report 2008: Agriculture for Development

It is interesting to look at the 2008 *WDR* (World Bank 2007), in view of the implementation record of World Bank assistance. *WDR*s are, of course, written for an external audience but also receive considerable attention internally. The 2008 *WDR* was the first one with an agriculture focus in 25 years (the previous one being 1982's *Agriculture and Economic Development* [World Bank 1982b]). The 2008 *WDR* arrived at the height of the 2007–08 global food price crisis and five years after "Reaching the Rural Poor" had laid out the World Bank's five-year rural and agricultural development strategy. As with "Vision to Action" and "Reaching the Rural Poor," the 2008 *WDR* sought to "place agriculture afresh at the center of the development agenda," but this time for a larger development community (World Bank 2007, 1), and took stock of disappointments and failures since the last agriculture-oriented *WDR*—primarily, in terms of political will.

The 2008 *WDR* pointed out two challenges to the agriculture-for-development agenda: (1) managing the political economy of agriculture policies to overcome bias and under-management or incorrect investment; and (2) strengthening governance for policy implementation. These observations directly followed the demand emphasis of the Bank's two rural and agricultural strategies for its lending that preceded it and served to further underscore that successful implementation rests on the political will of client countries, and potentially, the motivation and capacity of regional and country teams. The report especially blamed "insufficient attention to these political economy and governance challenges" for slow progress on trade liberalization, lack of investment in African infrastructure and research and development, and poor delivery of rural education and health services since 1982. One need not look that far back, however, as the 1997 and 2003 agendas had both failed to deliver in these areas (World Bank 2007, 22).

The 2008 *WDR* highlighted achievements, governance reforms, and stronger roles of rural civil society organizations and the private sector in agricultural value chains for improved prospects for agricultural development outcomes, in comparison to the 1982 context. The report also outlined preconditions for success, including strengthened state capacity to work with new stakeholders and coordinate across sectors; further "third sector" empowerment to better represent the rural poor; a mix of centralized and decentralized services to bring government services closer to rural populations; improved donor effectiveness; and reformed global institutions (World Bank 2007, 23–4). The latter two recommendations are particularly important. The 2008 *WDR* noted the influence of donors, who at that time represented between 28 and 80 percent of agricultural development spending in given sub-Saharan countries. CASs, poverty reduction strategies (PRSs), and the Comprehensive Africa Agriculture Development Programme (CAADP) provided priorities for coordinated donor investment and alignment with governments' expenditures, but implementation was slow. Regarding the changing global architecture for agricultural development, the 2008 *WDR* characterized global institutions as "inadequately prepared" and of a "narrow sectoral focus" (World Bank 2007, 24).

Agriculture for Development defined agriculture as socially and economically heterogeneous in nature, outlining "three distinct development worlds," which inform the relevant agricultural and economic development agendas (Table 8.1) (World Bank 2007, 1). The report addressed how agriculture can further develop in these distinct worlds—agriculture-based, transforming, and urbanized countries—what the best instruments are to use agriculture for development—particularly in terms of increasing smallholder farmer productivity and raising households out of poverty—and how agricultural development agendas, policies, and decision-making should be designed and tailored to best govern agricultural development (see Box 8.4). The 2008 *WDR* described how agriculture contributes to development in various ways: "as an economic activity, as a livelihood, and as a provider of environmental services, making the sector a unique instrument for development" (World Bank 2007, 2–3). Hence, its contributions to development differ in the three rural worlds: agricultural production is "particularly critical in a dozen countries of sub-Saharan Africa," critical for food security because it the primary source of income for the rural poor (World Bank 2007, 3). For transforming countries in South and Southeast Asia, MENA, and urbanized areas, mainly in Latin America, Europe, and Central Asia, "agriculture is no longer a major source of economic growth . . . but poverty remains overwhelmingly rural (82 percent of all poor)" (World Bank 2007, 4). Different agricultural worlds can also coexist within a country, adding to the complexity of prescribing appropriate national policies and instruments. The report recommended productivity gains and market access for agriculturally based countries in SSA, diversification to high-value crops in South and Southeast Asia, and the need to contain the environmental footprint for urbanized countries.

Setting and Implementing the 2008 *World Development Report: Agriculture for Development* Agenda

According to the 2008 *WDR*, agriculture agendas require policy frameworks anchored in an understanding of agents within food chains, effective governance, political will (demand), and implementation capacity. Using agriculture for economic growth also requires a sound macroeconomic base. The 2008 *WDR* laid out a "policy diamond" for applying four policy objectives to a given country type to create an agenda that has "established preconditions

---

Box 8.4 Instruments for Agriculture for Development

The 2008 *WDR* identified several instruments in using agriculture for development:

- *Increase access to assets*—land, water, and human capital, including rural education and health of rural populations.
- *Make smallholder farming more productive and sustainable*—improve price incentives and increase public investment; improve the functioning of produce markets; improve access to financial services and reduce exposure to risk; enhance producer organization performance; promote innovation; and make agriculture more sustainable and a provider of environmental services.
- *Promote a dynamic rural economy*—create agriculture and nonfarm sector rural employment opportunities; and provide safety nets, such as targeted food aid or cash transfers, or work programs.

Source: World Bank (2007, 8–10, 17).

(social peace, adequate governance, and sound macro fundamentals)" and is "comprehensive," "differentiated," "sustainable," and "feasible." (World Bank 2007, 19). The four policy objectives of the "diamond" are:

1. Improve market access; establish efficient value chains.
2. Enhance smallholder competitiveness; facilitate market entry.
3. Improve livelihoods in subsistence agriculture and low-skill rural occupations.
4. Increase employment in agriculture and the rural nonfarm economy; enhance skills.

(World Bank 2007, 19, figure 9)

Investment in agriculture increased after 2007 until about 2017, in part, as a response to the food and financial crises, in which the *WDR*'s plea for political will to invest in agriculture also contributed, but the effect has not been lasting (Figure 8.18).

Achieving these objectives rests on the behavior of agents—of the state, producers and their agents (civil society), the private sector, donors, and global institutions—that must also adapt to new roles in a rapidly changing global context. The burgeoning food crisis provided an immediate test for each stakeholder in the food and agriculture value chain.

Notwithstanding these many lofty reports, IEG's two agricultural sector evaluations, on SSA and on the Bank's overall assistance to agriculture (IEG 2007), were critical of the Bank's engagement in agriculture. The IEG evaluation of the Bank's response to the 2008 food crisis, on the other hand, was much more laudatory (IEG 2013b).

Crisis Response

We discussed the complex genesis of the 2007 food crisis, the domino effect of crop failures and stock depletions on trade policies of developing countries, and the relatively weak response of the international community to the crisis in Chapter 4. While the Bank provided an extraordinary, short-term response, the long-term issues of capacity, infrastructure, skills, and technology linger.

Although the 2008 price crisis response was believed to be something of an exceptional event, a number of lessons that emerged from it have led to a faster, more coordinated and more institutionalized response by the Bank to food price shortages in 2017, in some of the same set of countries—for example, Ethiopia, Sudan, Somalia, and Northern Nigeria—as we show in this section.

The price spikes in 2008 were unexpected and large, and the impact on developing countries was also large. They were estimated by the World Bank to have kept or pushed 105 million people into poverty in LICs. In mid-2008, the World Bank Food Price Index (Figure 8.19) rose by 60 percent over just a few months, and international prices of maize, rice, and wheat increased by 70 percent, 180 percent, and 120 percent, respectively, compared to mid-2007 (World Bank 2013b).

From a forward-looking perspective, there is every expectation that such crises, prompted by climate change or other unexpected disasters, will likely occur more frequently. The experience from the 2008 crisis, perhaps, can help to keep in place the machinery that can be activated more effectively, now that much learning by doing has taken place.

International development partners marshaled a response to the global food crisis in 2008, to counter the immediate impact on the poor—who were said to be particularly hard hit, due to the larger proportion of household earnings spent on food—and to address the longer-term implications for human and economic development (Townsend et al. 2013). In April 2008, the UN established a High Level Task Force on Global Food Security to coordinate responses and guide the UN response (with the Bank as a member), sparking parallel actions in the G8 and G20. Clients requested fast-disbursing financial support and

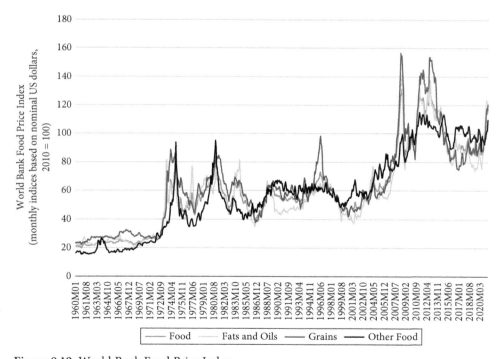

Figure 8.19 World Bank Food Price Index

Source: https://www.worldbank.org/en/research/commodity-markets

urgent policy advice to help them cope with the crisis; this led the World Bank to create the Global Food Crisis Response Program (GFRP). Bank management endorsed the GFRP Framework Document, providing a menu of interventions and outlining guidance to staff on responding to client needs through budget support, social protection, and short-term agricultural support (World Bank 2013b).

In 2012 and 2013, the IEG reviewed and evaluated the Bank Group's Response to the Food Crisis of 2007–8, paying special attention to developments from mid-2008 to 2013. The resulting evaluation, *The World Bank Group and the Global Food Crisis: An Evaluation of the World Bank Group Response* was released in June 2013, and aimed to inform continued and future actions by the Bank Group and its global partners (IEG 2013b).

Although forecasters within the Bank, FAO, and other agencies raised concerns about escalating food prices in 2007, countries and IOs had "no cause to expect" the severity of the crisis, nor adjust staffing, budgets, and instruments to rapidly changing circumstances (IEG 2013b, xxvii). Lulled into complacency after a period of low and stable food prices, governments were unprepared for the economic and political implications of the crisis and ensuing domestic unrest—riots related to food price increases occurred in more than 60 countries in early 2008. Affected client countries made an urgent appeal for help at the 2008 Spring Meetings of the Bank, and the IMF and Bank management responded by calling for "a New Deal for Global Food Policy, combining immediate assistance with medium- and long-term efforts to boost agricultural productivity in developing countries ..." (IEG 2013b, xi). Bank management encouraged WBG to strengthen its engagement in agriculture and called on donors to support WFP to provide for immediate relief (IEG 2013b).

Many of the issues identified in the Bank's evaluation of the crisis, now seen as a perfect storm, were discussed in Chapter 3. On the demand side, rising population and incomes leading to diverse demand; demand for biofuels and financial speculation and credit tightening on the supply side; growing pressure on land and water; underinvestment in agriculture, and rising energy prices leading to increased fertilizer prices; adverse weather; and depletion of grain stocks were all contributing factors to the storm.

The Bank's Extraordinary Emergency Response to the 2007 Food Crisis

In 2008, the Bank's Board of Executive Directors endorsed the GFRP initially, as a US$1.2 billion, rapid-financing facility to provide financial assistance and policy and technical advice to the poorest and most vulnerable countries. Included in this assistance, management approved a US$200 million Food Price Crisis Trust Fund from the IBRD surplus. In April 2009, the size of the facility was increased to US$2 billion, and the program was extended until June 2012, to allow for a swift response to calls for assistance from countries hard hit by price spikes. From July 2012 onward, the Bank's emergency response was channeled through the IDA Crisis Response Window,[35] and the IDA Immediate Response Mechanism that will provide emergency assistance in the future (IEG 2013b, xii; World Bank 2013b). It was a major story for the humanitarian community when the Bank became involved.

The GFRP was designed with a short- to long-term view to accomplish three things. First, it would reduce the impact of food price volatility on the poor. Second, it would support

---

[35] See IDA Crisis Response Window: http://ida.worldbank.org/financing/crisis-response-window

governments in designing sustainable policies to mitigate the immediate impact of high prices on poverty, while minimizing longer-term market distortions. Third, it would support broad-based growth in productivity and market participation in agriculture for future food security (a familiar refrain since "Vision to Action," though made more acute by crisis). The framework document laid out the Bank's perceived comparative advantage in meeting the challenges of the food crisis, citing its multisectoral expertise, presence in the countries most affected, and expertise in providing integrated solutions, as well as its capacities in policy analysis and program design. The framework also identified potential risks, such as limited availability of resources, client capacity, oversight arrangements and coordination between multiple partners, leakage in targeting beneficiaries, and inadequate component design (IEG 2013b).

The Bank response consisted of support for operations to enhance a food supply response, support for private sector activities and investments, scaled-up lending for agriculture and social protection, as well as IFC's increased access to liquidity for agribusinesses and agricultural traders, and new incentive programs for agricultural market participants. GFRP's operations were to be processed as emergency projects with special preparation, appraisal, and approval procedures, while expanded agricultural and social protection coverage in country programs fell under normal processing requirements. "The Bank's short-term assistance to agriculture [included] input subsidy and distribution operations to increase food supply. Short-term support for social safety nets mainly consisted of in-kind transfers and public works programs. Existing public works and school feeding programs were continued or expanded, often in partnership with the World Food Programme (WFP)" (IEG 2013b, ix). More countries became eligible for IDA support, although there was some question of whether this entailed additionality to their IDA allocations (IEG 2013b).[36]

A 2005 Agriculture and Rural Development Department report, entitled "Managing Food Price Risks and Instability in an Environment of Market Liberalization," anticipated that there would be occasions that required short-term interventions, such as the use of publicly held strategic reserves and adjustments in variable tariffs. It warned that such short-term interventions should avoid undermining long-run market development (World Bank 2005c).

IEG's evaluation of the Global Food Crisis addressed social safety nets:

> Extensive analyses and lessons relating to the social impacts of and policy responses to previous economic crises indicated that, in the short term, the causes, transmission channels, and main poverty impacts of a crisis need to be assessed at the country level. They also indicated that the response needs to focus on protecting pro-poor social expenditures and on expanding large and effective safety net programs to operate in a "countercyclical" fashion as "automatic fiscal stabilizers." The studies also found that

---

[36] According to the IEG evaluation of the World Bank's trust fund portfolio, with respect to additionality:

There is no clear evidence that trust fund resources have added to global ODA, although a few have helped introduce nontraditional ways of mobilizing finance. Typically, each donor country establishes its overall aid envelope and channels some portion of it through trust funds. The growth in the use of trust funds appears to be increasing, at the margin, the proportion of aid channeled multilaterally, while contributing to fragmentation of the aid architecture where they support separate global programs, and to an increase in earmarked (as distinct from core) funding, entrusted to multilateral institutions. (IEG 2011c, viii)

safety net programs, comprising cash transfers, public works programs, and human development interventions, needed to be country-specific.

Overall, a lack of data at the country level for assessing the welfare impacts of the crisis and hence for targeting specific interventions represented a significant constraint for the development of crisis responses in most GFRP countries. (IEG 2013b, xv–xvi)

IEG argued "analytical work to underpin social safety net lending was limited due to insufficient prior Bank engagement" (IEG 2013b, xvii). In many of these countries, the Bank had little previous engagement or analytic work in social protection, which limited the choice of interventions and their ability to target vulnerable groups. Yet, staff working on social protection contend that the Bank had been very active in the area of social protection in the 1990s, including in Africa, and there was, perhaps, a failure of communication and a silo mentality, resulting in insufficient drawing on existing work. Before launching these operations, there was limited use of rapid assessments; rather, the Bank used existing, more general economic and sector work. "In the poorest countries, such as Liberia, Madagascar, and Nepal, there was considerable fragmentation across donors and donor programs— especially on safety net programs. According to partners interviewed by the evaluation team, in these situations the Bank played a constructive role, adding muscle to country authorities' efforts to establish greater coherence across donor-supported programs" (IEG 2013b, xx). The IEG evaluation also noted:

> The social protection safety net lending most frequently supported by the GFRP were in-kind transfers and public works programs, while cash transfers and direct nutritional support to young children and pregnant and breastfeeding women saw limited use. This mix of interventions reflects the dominance in the program of sub-Saharan Africa, which accounted for more than half of GFRP operations with social safety net activities and almost a third of GFRP social safety net commitments. (IEG 2013b, xvii)

The social protection interventions are also discussed in the chapter on WFP, as a partner in the GFRP. The IEG report discusses coordination further:

> In agriculture, coordination with other donors worked relatively well. At the level of the individual project or program, coordination was the norm for food and agricultural activities, especially with the Rome-based agencies. For the most part, coordination with FAO and International Fund for Agricultural Development (IFAD) covered the provision of agricultural inputs—or in the case of WFP, school feeding programs—as the Bank and others provided only limited support for policy reform in the agriculture sector, given the very complex political economy of reform in the sector and country authorities' reluctance to tackle vested interests during the crisis.

> In social protection, coordination was more challenging. The partnership situation was different for social protection, for which there were far more donors and donor-supported programs seeking to help the poor and the vulnerable. In low-income countries, a common denominator was the school feeding programs pioneered by WFP and used by a number of UN agencies and bilateral donors—and by the Bank in Sierra Leone and other countries. The Bank approach in IDA-eligible countries also included food-for-work, social action funding, and support for the beginnings of social protection programs. (IEG 2013b, xx)

Beyond GFRP, special programs to implement the Bank response included:

- *Global Food Initiative*: IFC short-term program to support the agribusiness value chain in IDA and IDA/IBRD (blend) countries, consisting of investment lending (US$600 million) and advisory services (US$300 million).
- *Global Agriculture and Food Security Program* (GAFSP): A multiple-donor, grant-based partnership launched in April 2010, providing a multilateral mechanism to support agricultural development and food security-enhancing activities by governments and national/regional organizations. On September 6, 2013, the GAFSP Steering Committee allocated US$254 million in grant funds to 8 countries: Burkina Faso, Honduras, the Kyrgyz Republic, Mali, Nicaragua, Uganda, Yemen, and Zambia. By 2019, GAFSP had lost funding support, however, in the United States. With support from the Bill and Melinda Gates Foundation and Germany, GAFSP was working toward replenishments in August 2019.
- *Agricultural Price Risk Management*: A US$4 billion, IFC-led program announced in June 2011 to provide protection from volatile food prices to farmers, food producers, and consumers in developing countries via hedging instruments.
- *Horn of Africa Program*: A US$500 million package, scaled up to US$1.9 billion in 2011, to assist drought victims via short- and long-term food security, social project, and agricultural development activities—not a direct response to the food crisis, but targeting the same countries. (IEG 2013b, 5–6; GAFSP 2018)

Via the GFRP, the Bank supported operations in 35 countries through 55 operations, one-third of which focused on food supply and pricing, social protection, and a mix of objectives. Sixty percent of total funding went to SSA, while the majority of the funding supported just four countries—Bangladesh, Ethiopia, the Philippines, and Tanzania.[37] Twenty-seven operations were freestanding to support the food crisis response, and 28 were add-ons to ongoing Bank activities (IEG 2013b, ix, xiii; GAFSP 2018).

Evaluating the World Bank's Response to the Crisis

It is a useful examination of how an institution involved in long-term assistance adapted to shorter-term crisis response. The Bank adapted its internal procedures and relied on other organizations to perform functions for which it was less equipped. Out of the crisis came new ways to work together and a more tangible sense of how global partners could or should collaborate—not to mention how this partnership should work in tandem with the needs and demands of the countries they help. The task at hand for the Bank, post-crisis, as previewed in the Action Plan 2013–15, is how to best use these lessons, as the Bank returns to a long-term approach that will contribute to sustainable pathways out of poverty (World Bank 2013c).

The GFRP and other new instruments to mainstream the lessons learned, such as the IDA Crisis Response Window and the IDA Immediate Response Mechanism, helped to reposition the Bank as a key player in agriculture and food security matters. The IEG concluded:

[37] For a bilateral perspective, the Chicago Council on Global Affair's *2012 Progress Report on U.S. Leadership in Global Agricultural Development* examined US activities in Ethiopia and Bangladesh (Chicago Council on Global Affairs 2012).

The Bank Group's short-term response program in May 2008 was unique among global financial institutions in speedily articulating a comprehensive, concrete, and fast-disbursing financial support program to provide hard-hit clients with a menu of options for crisis mitigation. Along with the Bank Group's longer-term regular agricultural and social protection programs, and knowledge-based policy advice, the GFRP helped solidify the Bank's place as a key player in food security matters. The Bank's constructive participation in the UN High-Level Task Force and contribution to G-7 and G-20 meetings helped the international community to initiate several food security programs. (IEG 2013b, xv)

Lessons

At the time of the IEG review, two-thirds of 21 closed GFRP operations were rated "moderately satisfactory or higher on outcome"—in line with outcomes for projects in Africa and LICs in the Bank-wide (non-GFRP) portfolio (IEG 2013b, xiv). With expedited processing rules for emergency projects, the Bank was able to hasten project preparation by 70 percent, reducing the time required from 236 for all Bank projects over the same period to 71 days (IEG 2013b, xxviii). GFRP strategy was informed by Bank cross-disciplinary skills and policy capacity. However, resource constraints hampered design and implementation of specific operations, resulting in varied outcomes. Perhaps unavoidably, resource (staff and funding) constraints limited overall Bank impact. GFRP funding was effectively diluted, averaging out to less than US$11 million for each of the 35 GFRP client beneficiaries (IEG 2013b, 19).

The IEG found that risks identified in the GFRP Framework Paper were relevant and became a factor in GFRP implementation. Trade-offs between speed, flexibility, and quality were evident (IEG 2013b, xiv). The IEG reports more emphasis on nonlending technical assistance, to the detriment of analytical and advisory activities, with potential implications for the Bank's knowledge base. The IEG evaluation reveals crisis-related strains that underscore issues predating the food crisis—namely, declines in the Bank's technical expertise—historically, a comparative advantage for the Bank (IEG 2013b, xix).

IEG identifies several findings with long-term impacts for the Bank, as it navigates agricultural development support in the new global context (IEG 2013b):

- *"The implementation of the short-term support program helped build experience for broader institutional crisis response mechanisms within the World Bank Group"* (IEG 2013b, xv). New instruments included the IDA Crisis Response Window and the IDA Immediate Response Mechanism.
- *"The GFRP helped to reposition the Bank as a key player in agriculture and food security matters"* (IEG 2013b, xv).
- *"World Bank agricultural lending expanded significantly after the crisis and is now more directly focused on support to productive agriculture"* (IEG 2013b, xix). Building on increases called for in the FY2010–12 and FY2013–15 Action Plans, the latest lending figures indicate that the World Bank Group is increasing its support for agriculture to US $8–10 billion annually in FY2013–15, from US$6.2–8.3 billion annually in FY2010–12.[38]

---

[38] See the Agriculture: Sector Results Profile: http://www.worldbank.org/en/results/2013/04/15/agriculture-results-profile

In its response to the IEG evaluation, Bank management also noted that the Bank has increased its visibility and effectiveness in global discussions on food crisis issues since 2008, and that the food crisis was a catalyst for a strategic assessment of IFC's agricultural engagement, resulting in the 2011 Agribusiness Strategic Action Plan (IEG 2013b, xxvi).

Findings on the Bank's response to short-term effects of the crisis have pointed out the Bank's lack of experience or resources in some areas (debunking its own perception of its comparative advantage). In the policy advice realm, the creation of the GFRP tacitly acknowledged that crisis demanded quick and sometimes "second-best" solutions. Although the Bank cited its country presence as an advantage, in most GFRP countries, insufficient prior Bank engagement limited the analytical work available to inform social safety net projects. Indeed, the Bank increased its engagement with LICs as a result of GFRP.

It relied on WFP for in-kind transfers, public works, and school feeding programs, and its engagement with LICs increased as a result of GFRP. By doing so, and expanding existing programs, the Bank and its global partners missed targeting some of the most vulnerable people (particularly infants and pregnant women) with critical nutrition support. Only the Kyrgyz Republic, Lao Peoples Democratic Republic, Liberia, Moldova, Nepal, Senegal, Sierra Leone, and Tajikistan focused on infant and maternal nutrition in their GFRP social safety net operations. This lack of attention appears to be driven both by Bank capacity constraints and client demand (IEG 2013b, xviii). From its chapter on Bank support to social safety nets, the IEG discusses the Bank's response to the nutrition gap:

> A startling gap in the response of governments and the Bank has been nutrition inter-
> ventions for infants and mothers. Only a few countries appear to have emphasized
> nutrition support to this population as part of their response to the food crisis... This
> finding is the more startling as 22 of the 36 countries with 90 percent of the global burden
> of stunted growth in children, and 21 of the 32 smaller countries with more than
> 20 percent child stunting or underweight are among the countries "most vulnerable" or
> "vulnerable" to a food price crisis according to the index used by this evaluation. This
> finding underscores the challenges the Bank and client countries face to address the
> operational complexities arising from the multisectoral nature of both determinants of
> malnutrition and nutrition interventions. It is also indicative of the low priority given to
> nutrition by client countries as well as the institutional barriers to cross-sector collabora-
> tion both inside the Bank and in client countries. Finally, the Bank also has traditionally
> had few nutrition experts on its staff. (IEG 2013b, 78)

Throughout GFRP implementation, partnership with other donors and multilaterals and promotion of country ownership was dynamic. The very nature of the crisis and the heterogeneity of the countries meant differing levels of country capacity and donor cohe-sion. In the poorest areas, donor programs were platforms for coordination and supple-mented weak government direction. On the other hand, in Nicaragua and the Philippines, strong government oversight led to friction between partners and donors over the govern-ment-dictated division of labor between donors within the countries.[39] Partnership in the social sector was reportedly most challenging, an effect of donor crowding and mission creep. In the food and agricultural sector, however, the IEG evaluation stated that overall, "coordination was the norm... especially with the Rome-based agencies" (IEG 2013b, xx).

---

[39] The example provided in the IEG report is the geographic division of labor between the Bank and WFP on school-feeding programs (IEG 2013b, xx).

FAO and IFAD provided agricultural inputs or programs, and WFP provided school feeding programs. Bank support for agricultural policy reform was limited by client reluctance to counter vested interests during the crisis.

Comments from Bank management in response to the IEG evaluation indicate an eagerness on the Bank's part to reflect on the future of the organization in a changed global context. While it "broadly agrees" with findings, management noted the failure of the evaluation to take into account "less tangible" aspects of implementation that would inform Bank knowledge and learning (IEG 2013b, xxx). While the IEG correctly reviews outcomes of projects for beneficiaries, management had also begun to think about what GFRP did to build trust and facilitate collaboration—issues at the heart of addressing agricultural development and poverty alleviation in the 21st century.

Strategic crisis response framework is necessary but not sufficient to ensure effective interventions. Administrative budgets are required to support emergency operations. Increased lending depends on adequate staff capacity to conduct critical analytical work and design interventions. Having social safety net systems in place before a crisis hits is crucial to protecting vulnerable populations. The Bank support to safety nets increased considerably during the 1990s, while lending to productivity-enhancing operations stagnated. As such, emergency responses may be needed more frequently, particularly if there is not enough investment in agriculture. Countries should be prepared well in advance of emergencies. For example, there is growing consensus that safety nets should be in place and routinely functional, and emergency responses should enhance them. The poorest countries typically have the weakest safety nets.

An important lesson learned by IOs, including the World Bank, are evident here. According to the Fact Sheet, "The World Bank Group's Response to the Famine Crisis" (WBG 2017a):

> More than 20 million people in North-East Nigeria, Somalia, South Sudan, and Yemen are facing famine or the risk of famine over the coming six months, according to the United Nations. Deteriorating conditions in parts of Kenya and Ethiopia were also of concern.
>
> An estimated 1.4 million children were at imminent risk of death from severe acute malnutrition. For others, especially children, famine can have lasting impacts—including on health, ability to learn, and to earn a living, which can hinder development progress.
>
> Resolving this crisis called for close collaboration across humanitarian–development–peace partners, such as governments of the affected countries, UN agencies, and CSOs [civil society organizations].
>
> On March 8, 2017, President Jim Yong Kim announced that the World Bank Group is mobilizing an immediate response to the devastating food insecurity for Ethiopia, Kenya, North-East Nigeria, Somalia, South Sudan, and Yemen.
>
> The WBG implemented a US$1.8 billion famine response package consisting of 17 projects to build social protection systems, strengthen community resilience, and maintain service delivery to the most vulnerable. More than US$870 million from existing projects will be redirected to help communities threatened by famine. About US$930 million will be used for emergency food security projects, safety net programs, and agriculture and water programs in South Sudan, Yemen, North-East Nigeria, Ethiopia, and Kenya. Total disbursement as of August 2017 is US$632 million.
>
> The International Development Association (IDA), the Bank's fund for the poorest countries, is currently funding four emergency and crisis response projects in Yemen through grants totaling US$983 million.... (WBG 2017a)

In Ethiopia, the Bank supported Ethiopia's PSNP to provide assistance in Eastern Ethiopia on an emergency basis that it was unable to do before.[40]

The Bank's Assessment of Its Performance in Agriculture

IEG Evaluations: The Challenges of African Agriculture

In 2019, Africa is at the third phase of development cooperation. The first phase was when western donors had considerable influence through ideas and financial assistance. Governments had weak capacity and weak commitment to agriculture. Donors tried integrated rural development, T&V extension, and structural adjustment with mixed results. The period of adjustment lending and the post-global financial crisis have led to healthy skepticism about traditional external assistance and advice. African policymaking has been exposed to information, advice, and finance from a far broader range of sources, including emerging countries, Western think tanks and universities, philanthropists such as the Bill and Melinda Gates Foundation, and international NGOs.

Governments have to sift through knowledge and experience of these wide variety of actors to develop their own agricultural policies. Unlike in Asia, however, there are limited irrigation possibilities, and climate change is at the doorstep (or already over the threshold, according to some experts). Capacity and confidence have been bolstered considerably from learning by doing, from the benefit of such hindsight.

In 2007, IEG conducted an evaluation of "World Bank Assistance to Agriculture in Sub-Saharan Africa," covering fiscal years 1991–2006. It found that governments and donors, including the World Bank, had neglected the agriculture sector. "The Bank's strategy for agriculture has been increasingly subsumed within a broader rural focus, which has diminished its importance.... [T]he technical skills needed to support agricultural development have also declined over time" (IEG 2007, xxiii). By 2007, the number of Bank staff engaged in agriculture had diminished precipitously, and it is lower still today.

IEG argued that the Bank's limited and declining support (until 2009) for addressing the constraints on agriculture "has not been used strategically to meet the diverse needs of a sector that requires coordinated intervention across a range of activities" (IEG 2007, xxiii). The lending support from the Bank has been spread across various agricultural activities, including research, extension, credit, seeds, and policy reforms, but with little recognition of the potential linkages among them to contribute effectively to agricultural development. "As a result, though there have been areas of comparatively greater success—research, for example—results have been limited because of weak linkage with extension and limited availability of such complementary and critical inputs as fertilizers and water" (IEG 2007, xxiii). Hence, the Bank has had limited success in contributing to the development of African agriculture. The evaluation made 10 different recommendations to effectively focus on agricultural development as a key priority, including: (1) focusing on expansion of irrigation and productivity of rainfed agriculture through improvements in land quality, as well as water and drought management; (2) public–private partnerships to improve service delivery; (3) development of marketing infrastructure; (4) development of transport infrastructure; (5) quantity and quality of analytical work so that policy advice and lending are

---

[40] For details, see https://www.worldbank.org/en/topic/fragilityconflictviolence/brief/fact-sheet-the-world-bank-groups-response-to-the-famine-crisis

grounded in the findings; (6) public expenditure analyses to assess resource availability for agriculture and to help set Bank priorities; (7) building technical skills; (8) improving data systems; (9) improvement of monitoring and evaluation; and (10) increasing intersectoral coordination (IEG 2007, xxviii). Indeed, the "to do" list was so long that one wonders whether and how priorities were set, and what could be achieved.

A more optimistic view was envisioned when the World Bank released a report on "Unlocking Africa's Agricultural Potential" in early September 2013 (Box 8.5).

Box 8.5 Unlocking Africa's Agricultural Potential

In the World Bank's report, "Unlocking Africa's Agricultural Potential," economists, policy analysts, and researchers detailed "a unique confluence of factors" positively affecting agriculture in Africa (World Bank 2013e, Foreword). The report, one of the first in the Africa Region Sustainable Development Series, explored how the World Bank can help Africa take advantage of these factors to begin its own green revolution and create an agricultural industry that is a powerful engine of development. It noted that a number of factors have changed Africa's farming environment for the better and set the stage for the continent's green revolution. These include a steady rise in the prices of agricultural products, a booming urban food market that is projected to triple in size by 2030, and significant improvements in government policies directed at agriculture, such as reduced or eliminated taxes and revised exchange rate policies. "Across Africa, south of the Sahara, agriculture is the predominant sector in the economies of most countries," and provides jobs "for over two-thirds of Africa's population," according to Jamal Saghir, the World Bank Director for Sustainable Development in the Africa Region. The Bank wants "to galvanize action and forge new partnerships that can help Africa to achieve a vibrant farm economy that contributes to more growth, more jobs, better food and an overall improvement in the quality of livelihoods, particularly for poor people" (World Bank 2013e, Foreword). The plan to help Africa achieve increased agriculture production will require a long-term strategy that delivers "simultaneously on productivity growth and market connections, while enhancing resilience to climate change" (World Bank 2013e, 17). Over the next 10 years, the plan includes scaling up Bank lending to about US $3 billion per year, with ambitious targets in five areas (World Bank 2013e, 17–19):

- *Irrigation*: Double irrigated areas to 40 percent of arable land by 2030; the Bank and Western donors have indeed started promoting small-scale, farmer-led irrigation in Africa;
- *Land administration*: Move from small-scale projects to larger, systematic projects and push to scale up best practices and improve tenure security;
- *Technology and education*: Improve access to technology, climate-smart agriculture, and other yield-enhancing inputs such as fertilizers and insecticides; investment in these activities has increased;
- *Market competitiveness*: Reduce trade barriers and improve market performance to double trade in 10 years; Africa has adopted a policy of trade liberalization across the entire continent, a huge policy advance; and
- *Financial services*: Unlock lending and long-term financing, diversify commercial bank portfolios, and provide financial services through information and communication technology platforms.

According to John Nash, Lead Economist of Africa Region's Sustainable Development Department:

Increasing investments in the farm economy can deliver high-impact development returns such as increasing rural incomes, boosting food security, making cheap and more nutritious food available to Africa's bustling cities and protecting the environment through innovations such as climate smart agriculture. Despite the many challenges, now is the time for Africa to realize the full potential of its agriculture sector. (World Bank 2013d)

Saghir further stated, "A country's economic, environmental and social well-being is intricately linked to a healthy, well-performing agricultural sector. With this report, we want to seed solutions that can help accelerate the fight to end poverty in Africa" (World Bank 2013d).

Source: World Bank (2013d, 2013e).

Overall Challenge of Agriculture through IEG's 2011 Evaluation of Agriculture

IEG's main recommendation, in its 2011 "Growth and Productivity in Agriculture and Agribusiness. Evaluative Lessons from World Bank Group Experience," echoed similar sentiments as in its 2007 evaluation of African agriculture. Additional observations and recommendations are highlighted below:

- "To increase the effectiveness of its support for agricultural growth and productivity in agriculture-based economies, notably sub-Saharan Africa." IEG argued that SSA's "needs are the greatest and success there is the most elusive" (IEG 2011b, xiv).
- The evaluation recommended that IFC's engagement in SSA should be increased (IEG 2011b, 22–7).
- IEG considered setting up a knowledge network involving the entire Bank Group, as both necessary, more possible, and more likely under the latest reorganization. "Agriculture and agribusiness supply-chain specialists across the World Bank Group can be linked to strengthen communication and collaboration among sector departments within the Bank and IFC, as well as across the World Bank Group" (IEG 2011b, xiv). While collaboration between IFC and the World Bank has increased on a project-by-project basis, such a Bank–IFC wide network appears not to have been established. The evaluation strongly advocated the need for WBG to more effectively work with the CGIAR system. These links still remain weak.
- IEG noted that Bank staff strength had dwindled and the Bank was under pressure from key shareholders to reduce the budget by US$400 million in the next three years.
- Budget retrenchments in all IOs, including FAO, IFAD, CGIAR, call for pooling staff, expertise, and resources more systematically, and regularly to do more with less, reducing duplication and competition, and increasing areas of collaboration. Progress has been slow.

- Asked to "enhance IFC support to the development and application of internationally accepted commodity certification systems" (IEG 2011b, xv). FAO has Voluntary Guidelines on the Responsible Governance of Tenure of Land, Fisheries and Forests in the Context of National Food Security (FAO 2012). They outlined principles and practices that governments can refer to when making laws and administering land, fisheries, and forests rights. The World Bank, the Institute of Development Studies (IDS), and many other institutions have been investigating the role of FDI in land, but the information base is still poor (Deininger and Byerlee 2011). An article in the *National Geographic* noted that, with the rapid increase in world prices of corn, soybeans, wheat, and rice, big corporations, such as Wanbao and other Chinese and Japanese firms, are leasing or buying large tracts of land in SSA, ignoring land rights in coordination with governments. Mozambique has leased 7 percent of its arable land; Ethiopia and Liberia have also been mentioned in the context of land grabs (von Braun and Meinzen-Dick 2009; Bourne 2014). It is unclear if this is a widespread phenomenon or what would be the costs and benefits of this approach to Africa. Will IFC's guidelines be adopted? More importantly, will they be implemented and monitored, and information on their adherence shared with the public on a routine basis?
- IEG found overall World Bank agricultural project performance ratings to equal or surpass portfolio averages in most regions, but they were well below average in SSA throughout the 40-year period. IEG attributed it, in part, to inconsistent client commitment and weak capacity, in addition to constraints on staffing and internal coordination in the Bank (IEG 2011b, x) (see Appendix D).

The World Bank Group's Agriculture Action Plans 2010–2012 and 2013–2015

Given the disappointing implementation of the "Vision to Action" and "Reaching the Rural Poor" strategies, the "return" to agriculture in the new millennium was presented as an action plan, rather than as a strategy. Action Plans 2010–12 and 2013–15 were devised, because the tremendous energy that the Bank had expended to prepare the previous strategies was not matched by follow-through in implementation (World Bank 2009, 2013c).

Agriculture Action Plan 2010–2012: Crisis Response versus Long-Term Development

The FY2010–12 Agriculture Action Plan assumed a renewed World Bank Group commitment to agriculture, based on the foundation of 2003's "Reaching the Rural Poor" and the 2008 *WDR* (World Bank 2003b, 2007). The action plan, which operationalizes the three worlds approach of the 2008 *WDR*, was based on cited client demand and a "new phase of the World Bank Group's commitment to support client countries [to] improve agriculture's contribution to food security, raising the incomes of the poor, facilitating economic transformation, and providing environmental services" (World Bank 2009, xiii). It pledged to increase collective Bank Group support (IDA, IBRD, and IFC) to agriculture and related sectors to between 13 and 17 percent of total projected commitments.[41] Released in 2009 between the two food crises, the Action Plan followed the Bank's 2008 launch of GFRP (see World Bank [2013b]). The now common call to heed a "changing global context" was underscored by a new urgency and a more immediate awareness of how exogenous pressures linked to and affected the food and agriculture sector (World Bank 2009, xiii):

- High price volatility dampened supply price, affecting poor producers and consumers.
- The financial crisis slowed trade and growth.
- Declining government revenue impeded governments' response to the crises.
- Exchange rate depreciations kept food prices high.
- Tighter commercial bank lending practices raised interest rates for farmers and agribusiness.
- Lower remittances and migration to rural areas put pressure on poor households.

The FY2010–12 action plan outlined the Bank's comparative advantage in responding to these challenges in comparison to other donors and international donors. In addition to the largest number of country-level programs, strong in-country representation, technical expertise, links to country ministries, institutional memory, and analytical capacity—attributes to which other organizations can also lay claim—the Bank noted that it retained a larger share of support for agriculture relative to the social sectors, including health and social science. IFAD seems to have a presence in many of these areas and, perhaps, presence in a larger number of countries. However, compared to IFAD, the World Bank has, perhaps, a stronger complement of economists. These strengths aside, claimed capacity is one thing and past implementation failures of agricultural strategies, quite another. However, the backdrop of the food crisis provided a real-time proving ground for multilaterals to adapt to the crisis (World Bank 2009).

With no choice but to get involved, the Bank laid out its plan to pair short-term crisis response with longer-term vision in addressing five "action areas":

1. Raise agricultural productivity growth
2. Link farmers to markets and strengthen value chains.
3. Reduce risk and vulnerability
4. Facilitate agriculture entry and exit, and rural nonfarm income
5. Enhance environmental services and sustainability. (World Bank 2009, xv)

The Action Plan recommended a differentiated mix of support for these areas, consistent with the three worlds of agriculture in the 2008 *WDR* (World Bank 2007). For agriculture-based worlds of Africa and some parts of Asia, the Bank would focus on agricultural productivity growth, particularly in food staples, including support for technology adoption, improved extension services, water management and irrigation, strengthened property rights and land rental markets, and development of standards on foreign investment. Ongoing CGIAR reforms also fall under global actions for raising agricultural productivity growth.

The Action Plan for 2010–12 reflected lessons learned from "Reaching the Rural Poor." It would keep the MDGs central to the development agenda and prioritize regions with the

---

[41] The commitment was to start from the baseline average support in FY2006–8 of US$4.1 billion annually, rising to between US$6.2 and US$8.3 billion annually over the next three years (World Bank 2009, xiii).

largest number of rural poor (SSA, SA, and EAP). In addition, the Bank aimed to continue its trade liberalization efforts, where it has had no success; strengthen donor alignment at the country level, where success has been limited; and improve its own project modalities to improve country assistance. The plan paid special attention to the latter two in its plan to strengthen local ownership (through CAADP, PRSs, and CASs), and to leverage donor partnerships. The plan recognized the existence of donor fragmentation and the potential to worsen the situation, especially in countries that relied most on development assistance—where donor support is the major share of public support for agricultural development. The Bank pledged to integrate with government-led efforts, consistent with the Paris Declaration and Accra Agenda, and to leverage FAO and CGIAR synergies (World Bank 2009).

Agriculture Action Plan 2013–2015

The World Bank Group Agriculture Plan for 2013–15 retained the focus on the five action areas presented for 2010–12, but sought to return to longer term actions, in light of the longer-term nature of agricultural price volatility. Going forward, the Bank would emphasize support for climate-smart agriculture, long-term risk management, and better nutritional outcomes, as a means to improving the resilience of agricultural systems and rural livelihoods, with additional items on the agenda. Forced into an emergency response in 2006, by the avian flu and food crises, the Bank is now consciously moving back to a long-term view, cognizant of the need for a longer-term approach for economic growth. In institutional terms, this means less work through GFRP; larger project size (as dictated by resource constraints); and integrated projects in lieu of freestanding crop or forest projects. This view also seems to acknowledge challenges implicit in responding on too many fronts at once, with an aim to improving portfolio quality by concentrating or consolidating available staff and budget resources. On the heels of the food crisis response, the 2013 Action Plan calls for more strategic, efficient, and effective global partnerships. Client demand will dictate targets for specific action areas (World Bank 2013c).

In a positive development, the Action Plan 2013–15 reported delivering on the promise of the previous plan to raise collective Bank support (IDA, IBRD, and IFC) to agriculture and related sectors. By FY2010–12, aggregate support increased by 70 percent to US$7 billion from the US$4.1 billion annual average in FY2006–8 (World Bank 2013c, xvi). Table 8.2 compares the two action plans.

Going Forward

What should be the role of the World Bank in agriculture going forward? To address the multiple challenges that agriculture faces, the global food system requires an alternative paradigm in which the main goal of policymakers would be to ensure better health, with all being stakeholders (individuals, biodiversity). Macroeconomic problems may yet once again scuttle agricultural and rural development, as they did in the 1980s with the build-up of debt and the 2007 Great Recession.

Table 8.2 A comparison of action plans

Action plan thematic areas, FY2010–15		Increased emphasis in FY2013–15	Implementation
Raise agricultural productivity and improve resilience		Climate-smart agriculture	Strengthen planning and investment prioritization in poorest countries
Link farmers to markets, strengthen value chains		Private sector response	Facilitate scale-up of irrigation and land tenure projects
Increase rural nonfarm income		Private sector response	Better link IDA/IBRD/IFC/MIGA support at country level
Cross-cutting	Reduce risk, vulnerability, and gender inequality	Reduce gender inequality	Strengthen analytical work, including impact evaluations to guide sector dialogue and project identification
		Risk management	Improve project quality
		Nutrition	
		Governance	
	Enhance environmental services and sustainability	Landscape approaches	

Source: World Bank (2009, 2013e).

In his 2019 address to the Board of Governors, World Bank Group President David Malpass stated:

> A big obstacle to investment is the amount of a country's sovereign and SOE [state-owned enterprises] debt and the lack of transparency surrounding the debt. Public debt in emerging markets and low-income countries has risen to levels not seen since the 1980s, and too much of that debt isn't transparent. Some lenders, including Non-Paris Club lenders and private creditors, have imposed strict non-disclosure clauses on government borrowers; required liens and collateralization that violate the negative pledge clauses in the Bank's loan contracts; employed weaker procurement, environmental and social standards; placed guaranteed debt in state-owned enterprises and special purpose vehicles that undermine debt sustainability and paid insufficient attention to non-concessional borrowing policies that are key to emerging from poverty.
>
> ... Fewer than half of the countries we've reviewed meet minimum requirements for debt recording, monitoring and reporting. Lenders need to be more transparent, eliminating confidentiality clauses in their lending to sovereign borrowers. (World Bank 2019b)

Malpass continued, noting that in addition to the Bank's commitment to closing the gender gap, as discussed previously in this chapter, WBG in Fiscal Year 2019 committed US$17.8 billion to climate-related investments. The WBG is now the largest funder of climate action among MDBs and other IOs, providing almost half of such climate-related financing. Malpass stated: "Over 30 percent of IBRD/IDA and IFC commitments included climate co-benefits in fiscal 2019, surpassing our target. We've doubled its own climate commitment targets for fiscal years 2021–2025 to US$200 billion" (World Bank 2019b).

The Bank Group launched PROGREEN and PROBLUE, umbrella trust funds "to boost efforts to stop deforestation, restore degraded lands, and improve livelihoods in poor, rural communities [and] to help countries sustainably develop their blue economies" (World Bank 2019b).

According to President Malpass:

We're aggressively expanding our work on marine plastics and the prevention of marine pollution, [to help] countries provide clean air and water, healthy oceans, resilient cities, and sustainable food and agriculture systems. To scale up climate-related investments, we've launched initiatives such as Scaling Solar, which is helping countries accelerate development of utility-scale solar-energy plants. We're one of the biggest financers of renewable energy and energy-efficiency projects in developing countries. During IDA's current three-year funding cycle, we'll contribute more than US$1billion annually to grid and off-grid solutions for electricity access in countries with the high electricity deficits. Advances in digital technologies are another critical development path. A decline in transaction costs is particularly beneficial for new entrants to markets, women, small businesses and the poor. We're almost at the point of having systems that would allow the poor to electronically receive remittances, foreign aid, and social safety net payments as well as their earnings, and then be allowed to save and transact freely. Once more countries enable these technologies, the innovation may turn out to be as big an advance in development policy as the ones that allowed people to move from a barter economy to a market economy. A key challenge is to make new systems compatible with the world's interest in anti-money laundering and counter terrorism efforts. We're helping client countries preserve correspondent banks and interact with FATF [Financial Action Task Force], the financial action task force, and helping FATF-style regional bodies interact with developing countries.

Financial inclusion and liberalization are core steps in development. We're using Program-for-Results financing in a host of countries to encourage concrete outcomes and ensure accountability. We're expanding our work to support to correspondent banking relationships for developing countries, a key task in building stronger financial systems as well as helping to leverage technology-based solutions to improve financial inclusion. (World Bank 2019b)

The 2020 *WDR* explains how the expansion of global supply chains is helping countries to reduce poverty and is boosting shared prosperity (World Bank 2020d).

A first policy priority would then be to reorient away from sector-specific goals and toward integration of sectoral priorities into a more climate-sensitive food system and to consider spillover impacts across sectors. A second policy priority would be changing the focus of the scientific community from designing strategies to increase calories to strategies that improve nutritious diets.

That will depend on global food supply and demand, in turn influencing world agricultural prices, and the need for investments and knowledge. If the WTO's Doha Round of multilateral trade negotiations were to be concluded—if there were substantial cuts in agricultural tariffs and subsidies, ending protectionism in agricultural markets—world food prices would depend on global supply and demand as determined by the market. Supply would depend in part on whether technological progress could keep pace with the growth in global demand for farm products, as has occurred since the 1970s, and whether investment in agricultural research, infrastructure, human capital, and irrigation will continue and could be more effectively directed toward increasing the access of the poor to food. Now, there is growing pressure on land and water. Irrigation efficiency has declined considerably in India. The pace of climate change and the recent growth in demand for biofuels will determine demand for infrastructure investments, if agricultural research does not generate new technologies and if resistance to GM food continues. China and India would become more food import-dependent, as the countries continue to rapidly industrialize. There will be huge need for investments in SSA.

If the Doha Round does not succeed, developing countries like India will maintain agricultural protection with suboptimal levels of production. In that case, fewer domestic resources will be released for investments and will require more external investments.

How sustainable is the demand for Bank or IDA investments going forward, as distinct from demand for knowledge? The past experience, when Bank lending to agriculture reached its lowest level, suggests that both governments' willingness to invest in agriculture and donors' willingness to supply aid to agriculture may be explained by the behavior of food prices.

Until the 2007 food crisis, the decline in agriculture's share in aid was closely related to real international prices of food, and future demand for aid may be influenced by food prices. Ironically, increased investment in irrigation in Asia resulted in a decline in the real price of rice and a decline in demand for Bank involvement in agriculture. Increased food prices and concerns about climate change have changed that to some extent.

Grant resources will be needed. It is unlikely that demand for Bank involvement will be high on IBRD terms. The experience of GAFSP suggests that demand may be stronger than implied by the World Bank experience—if funding is provided as grants, if project concept and design is left entirely to countries and approved subject to a technical review, and if there is no competition for funding from other sectors, a problem regular IDA or IBRD funding faces.

Two good outcomes of the crisis with regard to partnerships are worth stressing. First, the Bank had to revise its procedures for operating in an emergency. Second, it had to turn to other organizations to perform functions that it could not or did not have the time or capacity to do. The Bank relied upon partner organizations and gave credit to organizations, such as WFP, for their comparative advantage in operations and field response. The food crisis, in some respects, provided a model for how these institutions could optimally work together. More such long-term, effective partnerships need to be fostered. For example, the Bank could forge a stronger operational relationship with CGIAR in the projects its funds, as well as with FAO. Throughout its institutional history, the Bank has produced high-quality knowledge products, including on agriculture, but often these products are underutilized (IEG 2016b.) The Bank also needs to draw upon the work of other institutions.

How Should the Impacts of Bank Interventions Be Assessed?

Impacts of Bank lending have been difficult to discern beyond project ratings. Monitoring and evaluation (M&E) has been weak, because borrowers have not taken M&E seriously, certainly not as a means of managing projects, but rather as a tool for accountability in donor countries (Székely 2014). M&E has now been made mandatory before projects go to the World Bank's board for approval.

Understanding the impacts of World Bank interventions remains a challenge. IEG routinely rates 20 percent of World Bank completed projects in each sector and shares those rating results individually and collectively with the regions and in the annual performance reviews that IEG produces. It also conducts sector and regional assessments, such as on the World Bank's assistance to African agriculture, or to agriculture more generally, and in doing so, it conducts portfolio reviews and some in-depth case studies. Findings of a few major OED/IEG evaluations are presented here.

IEG undertook an evaluation in 2016 on the self-evaluation systems of the Bank, "Behind the Mirror," which noted that although self-assessment "lies at the heart of the World Bank Group's results measurement system," to assess outcomes. It found that knowledge gained from self-evaluation "is rarely valued or used and there is little effort to extract and synthesize evidence and lessons to inform operations" (IEG 2016a, xii).

The report further noted:

Learning has taken a backseat to accountability. The systems' focus on accountability drives the shape, scope, timing, and content of reporting and limit the usefulness of the exercise for learning. If the self-evaluation systems had been set up to primarily serve learning, they would have been more forward-looking (how can we do better?), more selective (which projects offer the greatest learning opportunities?), more programmatic (are there synergies across activities and countries?), attuned to unintended positive and negative consequences, and more often done in real-time. (IEG 2016a, xii)

By and large, the Bank has avoided assessment of its own contributions to the country sectors or subsectors, even when the amount of lending is large, as in the case of irrigation. Twenty five percent of all irrigation lending by the World Bank (IBRD + IDA) went to India, and while it made important contributions at the outset over time, irrigation performance deteriorated in India in part due to declining governance. The Bank's support for maintenance and operations may have unwittingly encouraged government neglect. Similarly, in the case of agricultural extension and nutrition, problems in projects become visible only when projects are implemented, and also have become unpopular among operational staff.

At times, assessment of the Bank's own strategies—for example, in forests or water— have led to questions posed by the Bank about whether it had the right strategy at the outset. External stakeholders, when not convinced by World Bank's evaluations—for example, in the case of dam construction—have developed their own point of view, such as with the establishment of the Commission on Dams (McCully 1997; World Commission on Dams 2000). There is growing concern, however, that the real impacts of Bank interventions on the lives of people are not known, and while there have been repeated attempts to improve M&E, this remains a weak area. Most governments do not use M&E in a way that they should. An interesting insight from IFAD's attempt at impact evaluations was that it led to the realization of the faulty design of projects in which results chain in inputs and outcome and impacts were not clear, which helped to improve project design.

Impact assessments, based on experimental design, counterfactual, and the use of RCTs, have become increasingly popular, in application to individual investments but their broad application to the portfolio as a whole has been limited due to the cost, time, data intensity and issues of external validity, However, since 2013 IFAD has begun to apply these methods to 15 percent of its portfolio to assess its overall effectiveness (see Chapter 11). With the reduced cost of data collection and the awarding of the 2019 Nobel Prize in Economics to Banerjee, Duflo, and Kremer, as noted earlier in the chapter, application of these methods to impact assessment will likely expand their application.

Knowledge Bank

The Bank once had a strong agricultural economic research base in the Development Economics Department in the 1970s. This capacity was occasionally made available to central project staff and regions to produce policy papers on agriculture and rural development or to conduct operationally relevant research. Over the years, the agricultural economic research division was decimated and from time to time came up in another garb. For example, a new Agriculture Division was created in the Research Group in the early 2000s but was later merged with the Energy and Environment Group to match the merger in Operations in the mid-2000s.

After 2007, Agriculture took on a higher profile, and in 2009, teams were established of Agriculture and Rural Development and Environment and Energy. There is a huge amount of outstanding work on land, factor markets, and a range of other topics in a relatively unstable environment.

Over the last decade, the World Bank has steadily allocated a larger share of its administrative budget for core knowledge work. In 2011, this reached 31 percent of its budget, compared with 24 percent in 2002 (World Bank 2011b, 2). The 2013 IEG evaluation of the World Bank's Knowledge-Based Country Programs found that Bank Group knowledge activities have been relevant, especially in countries that do not rely much on its financial services: "Clients value the Bank Group's ability to convey international best practice, act as a trusted knowledge broker, customize knowledge to the local context, and take a sensible approach to important multisectoral development issues" (IEG 2013a, 64).

The World Bank's "Knowledge for Development" report noted:

> Knowledge products and services are creatively responding to a swiftly changing development knowledge landscape . . . It is providing more technical assistance, a service highly valued by clients. At the same time, it is producing fewer of the longer analytical pieces and shorter just-in-time policy notes for clients.[42] Trust funds and fee-based services are becoming more important. Trust funds now support 40 percent of core knowledge, and fee-based services are becoming the predominant practice for some countries. The Bank's knowledge services are becoming more open. The Open Data Initiative and the Knowledge Platforms are just two examples.

> Surveys show that clients cite knowledge services as the Bank's most valuable contribution, more than twice as often as financial resources. Yet the Bank's knowledge work is not seen internally, or by independent evaluators, as having the impact it could. Managers and staff see limited internal support for their knowledge work and some of them feel that such work is undervalued. This gives rise to a knowledge paradox. Most staff feels, despite the growing importance of knowledge work, that the Bank's main internal incentives are still . . . [loaded in favor of] lending. One reason for this apparent contradiction may be the lack of robust and systematic evidence that knowledge work brings demonstrable and measurable returns. By contrast, lending has built-in metrics. Lending volumes and disbursement rates are easily understood and communicated (even though money spent may not be a valid measure of impact). (World Bank 2011b, 2)

---

[42] McKinsey has moved in the opposite direction to producing larger, more complex products. See, for example, the McKinsey & Company report of Gupta et al. (2014).

The Bank is working to "create better two-way connections inside and outside the Bank, so that the best expertise and the most relevant experiences, wherever they may be, can be brought to bear on specific challenges of development" (World Bank 2011b, 3).

The food crisis was a wake-up call to developing nations. They realized that they had neglected agricultural development relative to macroeconomic development goals, temporarily igniting heightened demand for agricultural development. Whether this demand will be sustained is unclear, but it is clear that if countries are not interested, an approach to development based on SDG-type goals of the international community is not sufficient. Success of World Bank lending, based on action plans such as in 2013–15, depend on country involvement in ensuring that demand for agricultural development remains at or above its current level. The food crisis effectively forced the Bank (and developing nations) to focus anew on agriculture and, particularly, on long-term agricultural development and economic growth. The price rise abated after 2012, however, and so did interest in agriculture (Figures 8.1 and 8.19).

The use of impact evaluation using counterfactuals to assess causal effects of development interventions and complement other evaluation approaches has expanded rapidly over the past decade, as the development community has focused more sharply on measuring results with and without interventions. At the IDA replenishment discussions, there have been calls to institutionalize the use of such evaluations under a World Bank strategic framework.

IEG noted limitations of impact evaluations recognized by others. They tend to be expensive, compared to other types of evaluation (IEG 2012). Across WBG, funding, staff capacity, and incentive issues still constrain the scope and coverage of impact evaluations. They lack quality control and "appear to have had limited use and influence for various reasons: poor timing, underdeveloped operational linkages, failure to engage project teams and decision makers, or lack of dissemination" (IEG 2012, xii). On impact evaluations, and particularly RCTs, a huge issue is the generalizability of results to other circumstances, the so-called "external validity" challenge that Deaton, Ravallion, and others have pointed to, as we discussed earlier in this chapter. If the institutional setting of the project/intervention plays a role in the response to the intervention, generalizability is highly suspect unless the institutional setting is explicitly included in a RCT. Additionally, most RCTs tend to be single-country efforts, so generalizability to another country tends to be difficult.

The IEG assessment does not answer questions about the "impact" and cost-effectiveness of impact evaluations, their contribution relative to other evaluation approaches, forms of knowledge production, or the strategic scope of the Bank Group's impact evaluation work. The study also does not formally evaluate specific initiatives or models of impact evaluation conducted at WBG, but with growing interest in accountability and establishment of independent evaluation offices in developing countries, impact evaluation issues will continue to be debated—hopefully, with larger voice from policymakers in developing countries.

President Malpass, in his 2019 to the Board of Governors identified important knowledge products of the Bank: the 2020 WDR (World Bank 2020d), which explains how countries can reduce poverty and have shared prosperity through global supply chains; a report on "Women, Business, and the Law" (World Bank 2020c) that helps identify barriers women experience in gaining full inclusion in societies and economies; IFC's "Creating Impact" report (IFC 2019) that surveys markets for impact investing; and the semi-annual Global Economic Prospects report (World Bank 2020a) that tracks economic trends (World Bank 2019b).

Solutions for Sustainable Agriculture and Food Systems

Given the huge diversity of agriculture and multiple starting points for change, there can be no solution that fits all situations. Countries need to follow the most suitable path and timelines for addressing their specific challenges. The world needs to concentrate its efforts on science-based, actionable, socioculturally relevant solutions, tailored to local contexts. In practice, workable options—actionable "solutions"—must address the existential threat of climate change to agriculture and focus on raising the diversity, productivity, efficiency, resilience, value, and therefore, the overall profitability of farming. This is the entry point for moving from the vicious circles trapping rural people in poverty or creating environmental problems toward virtuous circles of agriculture for sustainable development.

A variety of recent reports address challenges of sustainable, climate-smart agriculture.

The Bank Going Forward in a Changed Context

At the 2019 Annual Meetings of the World Bank Group, President Malpass noted "the weak global economic outlook," "trade and geopolitical uncertainty, sluggish investment rates and frozen capital in low-yielding bonds" as grave challenges for development (World Bank 2019b). Poverty is increasingly more concentrated in fragile and conflict-affected states, with falling medium incomes and many refugees fleeing to countries that already are struggling to deliver basic services, security, and peace to their citizens.

Investment rates in developing countries are insufficient:

> ... to meet development needs; health systems, learning outcomes and technology are falling further behind needs; climate changes and extreme weather are taking a heavy toll; for some countries populations are expanding much faster than resources and capacity; and many countries are facing fragility, conflict and violence, making development even more urgent and difficult.... Globally, countries are losing US$160 trillion in wealth due to differences in lifetime earnings between men and women. (World Bank 2019b)

Going forward, the Bank's development tools and products, such as loans, credits, guarantees, grants, equity investments, insurance, and advisory and risk-management services, will need to work harder to help "broad-based growth, transparency, the rule of law, and private sector expansion" (World Bank 2019b). How is the Bank responding?

Replenishment of IDA's and IBRD's Capital Increase Package

The Bank has doubled IDA allocations for countries affected by fragility, conflict, and violence to more than US$14 billion under IDA18. "The Global Concessional Financing Facility (GCFF) has provided around US$500 million in grants to unlock more than US$2.5 billion in concessional financing for Jordan and Lebanon to help address the influx of Syrian refugees, as well as for Colombia to help address the needs of more than 1.4 million displaced Venezuelans and their host communities" (World Bank 2019b).

The IDA19 replenishment process has progressed well. It is based on five themes:

... jobs and economic transformation; fragility, conflict and violence; climate change; gender and development; and governance and institutions. It will also incorporate four cross-cutting issues: addressing debt vulnerabilities, exploiting opportunities from digital technology, investing in people to build human capital, and promoting inclusion of people with disabilities. The package includes a significant scale up of the regional program, as well as a further increase in FCV resources. The Private Sector Window, introduced in IDA18 together with IFC and MIGA, will help mobilize private capital and scale up private sector development, particularly in fragile situations. (World Bank 2019b)

IDA19 will increase its support of the Horn of Africa, the Sahel, and development goals around the world. In addition to scaling up commitments to countries affected by fragility, conflict and violence, the Bank is bolstering the Crisis Response Window. The Bank is working closely with Ethiopia, Sudan, Somalia, Kenya, Rwanda, Egypt, South Sudan, Eritrea, and Djibouti.

As to IBRD, the Bank is implementing the capital increase package, endorsed by share-holders in 2018. It is working toward targeting IBRD loans more sharply to IBRD borrowers who are below the graduation threshold, while accelerating IBRD graduation policy for higher-income IBRD borrowers, such as China. It is addressing issues of net income by adjusting loan pricing, and other financial measures to improve IBRD's financial sustain-ability. It has a board-approved crisis buffer amount, but also an annual limit on lending to ensure that IBRD remains financially sustainable *without additional capital increases*. It is cutting costs to increase efficiency, as well as anchoring administrative expenses to business revenues with demanding goals. This will certainly have implications for lending to poorer countries and weak sectors, such as agriculture with high transaction costs.

President Malpass noted:

IBRD, IDA, IFC and MIGA are working together to [be] more effective, efficient and accountable [in] ... coordinating country programs, co-locating offices, aligning staffing with country programs, adjusting the global footprint of the WBG to increase [the Bank's] presence in lower income countries, providing employee benefits and developing country platforms that will help governments work more effectively with the entire investor community. [The Bank is] encouraging more staff exchanges between the WBG entities and more joint teams working together on a problem to create better solutions for clients. Successful implementation of these processes is critical [for the Bank's] mission. (World Bank 2019b)

Malpass further stressed the importance of:

Coordination with other MDBs, ... encouraging better implementation of graduation and price differentiation to avoid undercutting each other's work, covenants and standards, [including in launching] country platforms. They can help countries prioritize their key development issues and encourage donors ... to engage [programs] tailored to the coun-tries and their needs, and increase the focus on private sector involvement and engage-ment. The goal is for the World Bank Group and the broader development community to be as effective as possible in helping countries achieve good development outcomes.

... Strong leadership [is critical] to choose a path that works economically, socially and politically. (World Bank 2019b)

As the Bank works close the gender gap, President Malpass noted that some of the goals include "preventable maternal and child mortality, ensuring that women and children can access comprehensive health services, and reducing childhood stunting" (World Bank 2019b).

With rapid urbanization, WBG has proposed to help to build sustainable cities "by investing directly in urban infrastructure and helping national and municipal governments develop fiscal and financial systems to expand revenues and provide access to private capital" (World Bank 2019b).

As we have noted previously in this chapter, WBG has made climate and environment investments a key part of its work. In Fiscal 2019, the Bank committed US$17.8 billion to climate-related investments, doubling climate commitment targets for fiscal years 2021–5 to US$200 billion.

A New Service to Assess Public Policies and Interventions

Two areas specific to food and agriculture need clear attention going forward. First, project outcomes are weakest in Africa and in LICs. Given the length of time that this state of affairs has persisted, the Bank and the international community need to find ways to achieve better outcomes—for example, to:

- Help with the development of and adherence by governments and donors alike of strong, holistic, and long-term agricultural and rural development strategies;
- Achieve better aid coordination with the country in charge;
- Improve capacity of aid recipient countries' own systems of technology generation and delivery institutions, policies and infrastructure: that is, teaching to fish rather than giving fish.

Second, developing countries have adopted a number of public policies and interventions on their own (Dutta et al. 2012, 2014). Many need improvements to increase their effectiveness. They entail large public sector outlays and a national commitment, such as India's National Rural Employment Guarantee Act (MGNREGA) and its National Food Security Act.[43] Can the same policies be implemented more cost effectively and with better results on the ground? Are there alternative ways of achieving the same objectives? The Bank and the international community need to take up Prime Minister Modi's challenge of being an Ideas Bank, to help improve the quality of the implementation of these policies by undertaking comparative analysis across countries (*Economic Times* 2014). This is important because government commitment over the long haul is critical; election cycles, planning and implementation deficit, silos with fragmented approaches, and corruption all

---

[43] In total, data from the MGNREGA website shows that until July 13, approximately 227,233 households out of the 47.8 million were provided jobs under the act and had completed their mandatory 100x days employment. Also, around 55.5 million households have sought work under the act (until July 13, 2020), while 47.8 million households have been provided work (86 percent). In 2019–20, 57.4 million people had sought work under the scheme in the full year (Mukherjee 2020).

In May 2020, India's Finance Minister Nirmala Sitharaman announced an increase in allocation of Rs 40,000 crores to the MGNREGA budget to ensure migrants do not face unemployment, as laborers move back to their villages, during the national lockdown during the pandemic (*India Today* 2020). An increase in the minimum wage under MNREGA from Rs.182 to Rs.202 was announced by the Rural Development Ministry, but wages need to increase further (*National Herald* 2020). An increase in the number of guaranteed days of work from 100 to either 150 or 200 days for MGREGNA was under consideration by the government in April 2020 (Sharma 2020).

make a strong case for multisectoral, area-based, nationally owned rural development strategies, based on the experience of the past 50 years. The Bank has wavered on agricultural and rural development. The wholesale shift to social sectors has led to a lack of attention to productive investments in agriculture, research and extension, and education. Irrigation faces huge challenges. Constraints imposed by institutional weaknesses and weaknesses in other sectors have also been largely ignored—for example, the role of subsidies in the power sector in improving irrigation efficiency. The CDD approach has had weak linkages with productive sectors. These weaknesses have been well documented. Participatory approaches have not wrestled sufficiently with governments' own decentralization efforts. A long-term, 10-year approach should be adopted to deliver on clear goals/destinations, a road map, and milestones along the way, the progress of which can be judged with unambiguous indicators from well-defined baselines.

Where is there scope for improving clarity of policies, better public–private partnerships, learning across countries from successful examples? How can new technology, such as remote sensing, digital technology, and drones improve outcomes?

The current project-by-project approach needs to help mainstream effective policy and institutional reforms in the operation of governments—the reason why structural adjustment was justified in the start of 1980s.

Latest Readjustment for the World Bank

To meet challenges that we have identified in this chapter, including slowing global growth, climate change, and the number of countries affected by fragility, conflict, and violence, the World Bank initiated organizational adjustments in 2019 to increase its country focus and its contribution to country outcomes—actions intended to strengthen the Bank's development impact and reinforce its delivery of global expertise (World Bank 2019b).

Beginning July 1, 2020, Regional Directors (RDs) will report directly to the Regional Vice President, realigned with a dotted line to the Practice Group Vice President. Practice Group Managers and their staff, who had been reporting to RDs, will be also realigned to report to the Regional VP. Strengthening the link between the practice staff and the region will allow the Bank to be more responsive to client needs, reduce cross-group silos, and enhance delivery to the region and countries. Strong Global Practice Boards and Practice Councils will ensure that regional staff maintain their group identities. Also, Global Directors will continue to report to Practice Group VPs; they will be expected to play even greater roles in delivering global expertise. The Accountability and Decision Making (ADM) framework will be revised to ensure that Practice Group staff have a greater role in the corporate review of operations (finance, analytical services, and advisory services) (World Bank 2019b).

Based on the Bank's several reorganizations since 1972, it is unclear what they have achieved in organizational effectiveness. This review has shown that the Bank has been, perhaps, the largest source of development thinking including on agriculture and rural development, but some of the more innovative thinking, including the adoption of MDGs and SDGs occurred outside the Bank. The Bank's project lending has increasingly proven to be a less effective instrument to deal with the complex, rapid multisectoral changes taking place. They call for building capacity in the form of human and institutional capital in the countries to address them and to mobilize substantial resources. It is unclear if the Bank's "project lending" model is sufficient to deal with the new reality. It calls for longer term, consistent presence in countries, effective partnerships, and genuine mutual trust between the Bank and countries.

Appendix A: Chronology of the World Bank

For more information, see the World Bank Group Timeline: https://timeline.worldbank.org/#event-bretton-woods-conference-begins

---

1940s   In 1944, the Bretton Woods Conference, of 44 governments, held in Bretton Woods, New Hampshire from July 1–22, gave birth to both the International Monetary Fund and the International Bank for Reconstruction and Development.

In 1945, IBRD Articles of Agreement entered into force on December 27.

In March 1946, the first annual meeting of the World Bank and IMF held in Savannah, Georgia, from March 1–18.

The first meeting of the World Bank executive directors addressed a number of fundamental issues, including the nomination of a president on May 6, 1946.

Eugene Meyer became the first World Bank President on June 18, 1946. World Bank staff started their first day of work and the World Bank opened for business on the 10th floor of 1818 H St. NW, Washington, DC, June 25.

The World Bank Governors held their first meeting from September 27 to October 3, 1946, in Washington, DC.

In March 1947, the Working Party on the Polish Loan Application was released (March 27). The report, authored by the Bank's Research Department, focused much of its attention on the country's Four-Year Plan of Economic Reconstruction (1946–9).

The World Bank approved the first loan for reconstruction on May 9, 1947. The World Bank's first loan, to Credit National of France in the amount of US$250 million was for general reconstruction purposes.

In July 1947, in response to demand for investment by client countries, the World Bank entered the bond market with a US$250 million offering (July 15).

The World Bank instituted group health insurance for staff on September 1, 1947.

In 1947, London was the site of the Second Annual Board of Governors Meetings (September 11). The Second Annual Board of Governors Meeting was attended by World Bank governors and their alternates from 44 of the Bank's 45 member countries.

The United Nations and the World Bank formalized their relationship. The agreement with the United Nations was initially approved by the World Bank's Board of Governors in September, and then by the United Nations General Assembly on November 15, 1947. The agreement, which named the Bank as a specialized agency of the United Nations, defined the Bank as an independent organization and outlined its freedom in matters of lending and financial management.

In April 1948, the World Bank established a liaison with the Organisation for European Economic Cooperation (OEEC) (April 16).

In June 1949, the World Bank's Annual Report discussed the impact of the Marshall Plan on operations (June 30).

1950s   In 1952, the World Bank implemented its first reorganization on October 1. Prior to the 1952 reorganization, operations staff were organized along functional lines, with loan officers working separately from country and technical specialists. The new organization arranged staff geographically; each new operational department maintained operational relationships with a particular geographical group of the World Bank's member countries. A new Department of Technical Operations was responsible for assessing the economic, financial, and technical merits of proposed projects and for following the progress of approved projects.

In March 1955, the World Bank established the Economic Development Institute (March 11), with the purpose of building country capacity by providing training for officials concerned with programs and projects in developing countries. Initially, courses were general in nature and offered exclusively in Washington, DC. Over time, more intensive courses on, such as project preparation and sector planning were developed and offered outside of the United States.

In 1956, the International Finance Corporation was founded on July 20. The IFC was created as an affiliate of the World Bank and was designed to further economic development by encouraging the growth of private enterprise. IFC was initially authorized to have a total capital of US$100 million but was restricted from involvement in equity financing.

In November 1956, the World Bank Group increased activities with development banks. Investment in Development Finance Corporations (DFCs), since 1949, allowed the World Bank Group to invest in relatively small-scale private enterprise. As part of an expansion of its activities in this sector, the Bank published a report on the topic in 1957 that assessed the operating records of DFCs and discussed the establishment of new institutions. Subsequent activity in the sector resulted in a significant increase in assistance to DFCs by 1960.

In 1957, IFC made its first investment on June 20.

In February 1958, Senator Mike Monroney proposed the creation of an International Development Association (February 24).

In 1959, World Bank Governors asked, on October 1. that the IDA charter be drafted.

1960s The Bank functioned largely as a project lending organization for large-scale infrastructure.

Developing countries requested lending to agriculture and rural development.

In 1960, India and Pakistan signed Indus Waters Treaty on September 19.

IDA was created on September 24, 1960, launched in response to calls by those member countries not deemed sufficiently creditworthy to borrow from the World Bank Group. Eligible countries would receive loans, called "credits," on terms more favorable than conventional loans offered by the Bank. IDA does not raise its funds in the capital markets like IBRD, but instead raises its funds through members' subscriptions, loan repayments, and periodic replenishments by the World Bank Group's wealthier members.

In 1961, the first IDA credit was approved on May 12. During its first year of operations, IDA extended credits totaling US$101 million to four countries: Sudan, Chile, India, and Honduras. The US$9 million credit to Honduras was the first transportation sector funding approved by IDA. The investment assisted a program of highway development and maintenance, including a 62-mile extension of the Western Highway, the continuation for two years of a highway maintenance program, and a highway planning survey.

Robert S. McNamara was appointed President of the Bank, IDA, and IFC in April 1968.

1970s First Global Public Goods Program.

CGIAR was established—described in World Bank archives as the "brainchild" of McNamara (WBG 2014b, 174).

A 1972 "Agriculture" Sector Working Paper outlined the key role of agriculture in development outcomes: greater production and exports, more employment, better distribution of income, and highlights of policy issues facing developing countries and the Bank Group's past activities in agriculture, with projections of increased lending. For the first time, lending for agriculture exceeded that of any other sector.

In 1972, the Bank underwent the largest structural change, since establishment, with McKinsey's advice. Regional Vice-Presidencies were established, with a shift from a centralized, "technical brain trust" project department to regional entities with country departments, macroeconomists, and loan officers.

In 1973, McNamara's Nairobi speech coined the term "the absolute poor" and reshaped the Bank's vision to abolish absolute poverty, "a condition of life so degrading as to insult human dignity" (McNamara 1973)

In 1975, the World Bank, FAO, and UNDP began the Consultative Group on Food Production and Investment in Developing Countries (CGFPI), as requested by the World Food Conference of 1974 (WBG 2014b, 186).

In 1975, *The Design of Rural Development: Lessons from Africa,* a World Bank Research publication by Uma Lele, was published. According to World Bank archives, the book was "the centerpiece in the Bank's search for ways to counter food shortages and unequal income distribution."

In 1975, the Bank's "Rural Development" Sector Policy Paper announced that the Bank planned to greatly increase its assistance for agriculture and rural development, with US$7.2 billion committed for the five-year period fiscal 1975–9 (World Bank 1975b).

In 1976, the Bank approved the first nutrition loan, a US$19 million loan for Brazil.

In 1978, the "Rural Enterprise and Nonfarm Employment" and "Agricultural Land Settlement" were published, with focus on poverty alleviation and distribution of the benefits of growth to the poorest. McNamara, in the 1978 Annual Meetings, emphasized, "the only feasible hope for reducing poverty is to assist the poor to become more productive" (WBG 2014b, 1998).

Lending to agriculture increased rapidly in the 1970s, but two oil price shocks, in 1973 and 1979, hit developing countries of Latin America and Africa particularly hard, leading to the beginning of a debt crisis, with profound impacts on domestic development.

By the late 1970s, Bank project performance deteriorated but with regional differences: SA performed best, whereas Africa's performance, already low, deteriorated.

In August 1978, the first *World Development Report* was issued with the theme of accelerating growth and alleviating poverty and identified major policy issues affecting those prospects.

On July 24, 1979, proposals to begin lending operations in health were approved by the Executive Directors.

1980s Agricultural performance dropped, except in Asia. Overall, Bank lending remained flat, and lending to agriculture declined, but administrative expenses increased. leading to what was later called a "lost decade" for agriculture.

In May 1980, the People's Republic of China joined the Bank, replacing Taiwan, becoming one of the Bank's largest borrowers, opening up and systematically learning from the Bank in a way no other developing country has done.

In 1980, the era of Structural Adjustment Loans began with a shift in attention from project lending to macroeconomic lending; the first SAL was approved in March for Turkey for US$200 million, to increase "export orientation," increase "mobilization of domestic resources," and foster "a self-reliant State Economic Enterprise sector" (WBG 2014b, 206). According to Stanley Please, who called himself the "mother and the father of SALs," the lending led the Bank to face a barrage of criticism from all sections of the development community inside and outside the Bank.

In 1981, Robert McNamara ended his tenure as President of the World Bank Group. His final speech to Board of Governors radically departed from the Nairobi approach, making the case for the pursuit of macroeconomic reform.

In July 1981, A. W. Clausen became the sixth World Bank Group President. President Clausen summarized the fiscal year to staff: reduced budget contributions to IDA6 meant an austere budget for the World Bank with implications for lending.

In August 1981, Elliot Berg's *Accelerated Development in Sub-Saharan Africa,* the so-called "Berg Report," was published. It was the first in a series of Bank reports that focused on development problems of SSA.

In May 1982, Anne Krueger became the first woman appointed Vice President, to replace retiring Hollis B. Chenery, as VP of Economics and Research.

In 1982, planning for IDA7 commenced. The front-end fee on IBRD loans was introduced; changes in borrowing operations were approved, with continued lending toward the poorest segments of society: agriculture and rural development, and energy constituted 50 percent of the lending program.

In 1984, an acute famine in Ethiopia led to worldwide efforts at fundraising for famine relief.

In 1984, the "Joint Program of Action for Sub-Saharan Africa," released by the Bank highlighted the need for domestic policy reforms to accelerate growth and placed emphasis on donor assistance strategy as essential to supporting these reforms. In September, a Special Office for African Affairs was established, and the report "Toward Sustained Development in Sub-Saharan Africa" was released.

In 1985, the World Bank granted US$3 million to the World Food Programme for emergency food supplies to drought-stricken SSA.

In 1986, Barber Conable became World Bank President and helped to nearly double US Congressional appropriations for the Bank. In his inaugural address, he identified the "central challenge" of the Bank as "to mobilize the will and the resources of the affluent and of the afflicted alike in the global battle against poverty" (WBG 2014b, 229).

In 1986, the Special Program for African Agricultural Research (SPAAR) Secretariat was established to improve the effectiveness of investments in agricultural research by governments and multilateral and bilateral donors. SPAAR's main tasks were to coordinate donor activities, collect, assess and disseminate information on promising technologies, and to develop national research strategies and regional research programs.

In 1986, the *World Development Report: Trade and Pricing Policies in World Agriculture— The Need to Reform Policies in Developed and Developed Countries* was released; it examined the potential for large gains from more liberal trade in agriculture and suggested that liberalization of trade should be a high priority for international action in agriculture (World Bank 1986).

In September 1986, President Conable addressed world trade leaders at the Ministerial Meeting of the General Agreement on Tariffs and Trade (a) in 1987 in Punta de Este, Uruguay.

In December 1986, a "Poverty Task Force" was established to bring together senior staff to review the Bank's poverty work and recommend new programs.

In 1987, President Conable, in an address to the World Resources Institute, announced the creation of the Environment Department. The new Bank measures, including environmental assessments of 30 of the most vulnerable developing nations, initiatives against desertification and forest destruction, and promotion of conservation of tropical forests, were taken in response to strong negative public reaction to several bank projects that had had adverse environmental and social impacts. It led to an increase of Bank environmental staff, introduction of the environmental safeguard policies, and a program of environmental lending (WBG 2014b, 234).

In February 1987, the World Bank, together with WHO and the UN Fund for Population Activities, sponsored a conference on Safe Motherhood in Nairobi. President Conable established the Safe Motherhood Initiative to focus on women's health needs.

In 1987, *Adjustment with a Human Face: Protecting the Vulnerable and Promoting Growth* (Cornia, Jolly, and Stewart 1987) detailed the negative impact of SAPs on health and education; its title is now used commonly to describe policy recommendations that came out of the study.

In September 1987, the Social Dimensions of Adjustment (SDA) initiative was launched with the African Development Bank and UNDP. The World Bank also issued "Education in Sub-Saharan Africa: Adjustment, Revitalization and Evaluation," an education policy paper in September. (World Bank 1987).

In June 1988, the Bank approved a US$175 million emergency loan to assist reconstruction in Rio de Janeiro following floods and landslides in February 1988. President Conable issued a statement, urging support for Brazil's debt relief efforts.

In September 1988, President Conable pledged reconstruction assistance to Bangladesh, following flooding.

In December 1988, Conable addressed the GATT trade negotiations in Montreal, warning against the trend of protectionism, as a threat to the growth of both rich and poor nations. The World Debt Tables 1988–9 were issued by the World Bank.

In June 1989, the Bank adopted operational guidelines for debt and debt-servicing payments.

In August 1989, the Debt-Reduction Facility for IDA-only countries was established.

In November 1989, the Bank published "Sub-Saharan Africa: From Crisis to Sustainable Growth," which analyzed development experiences since independence in SSA and explicated long-term development strategies (World Bank 1989).

The UNICEF *Adjustment with a Human Face* report detailed negative impact of SAPs on health and education; its title is now used commonly to describe policy recommendations that came out of this study.

In November 1989, the study, "Managing Agricultural Development in Africa" (MADIA) by Uma Lele was published. The study chronicled the relative roles of external shocks, domestic policies, and aid to African agriculture in explaining performance in selected African countries (Lele 1989).

1990s   Called the "lost decade" for developing countries with slow growth and mounting debt, the OED Country Assistance Evaluation for Brazil (OED 2004b), for example, noted the 1980s radically transformed the Bank's relationship with developing countries, with far-reaching impact on the Bank's declining presence in overall resource transfers, and even more so, in the agricultural sector—a decided shift from projects to macroeconomic and sector lending; leading to the establishment of a PREM network in 1998.

In the 1990s, partnerships and trust funds began to proliferate in response to major international initiatives, such as the Montreal Protocol and the United Nations Conference on the Environment and Development (UNCED) in June 1992, leading to the establishment of Ozone Trust Fund and Global Environment Facility (GEF). Additional initiatives in the latter half of the 1990s—the Heavily Indebted Poor Countries Initiative in 1996, and the Consultative Group to Assist the Poor (CGAP)—further expanded the scope and boosted momentum for partnerships. There was little or no interaction between these initiatives and agriculture—GEF's forestry and biodiversity initiative and agriculture; HIPC, with its focus on social sectors almost to the exclusion of agriculture; and CGAP's focus microfinance.

In 1990, the Bank's first *World Development Report* on poverty was published, focusing on poverty reduction promotion of economic opportunities for the poor, delivering social services to the poor, and provision of transfers and safety nets (World Bank 1990).

In 1990, Eastern Europe became an active recipient of Bank loans; the first loans to Croatia, Slovenia, and Poland were approved in February.

In November 1990, the Global Environment Facility, jointly administered by the World Bank, UNDP, and the United Nations Environment Programme was launched. Later in the month, Conable traveled to Moscow, as the first World Bank president to visit the Soviet Union, to discuss ways in which the Bank could help the Soviet Union, as it moved to a market economy.

In December 1990, President Conable issued a statement on GATT negotiations: "Many developing countries, already struggling with debt burdens, environmental crises and chronic poverty, have made difficult political and economic choices in their efforts to liberalize their trade regimes." He again warned against protectionism, which he predicted would "increase international tension and diminish prospects for world economic growth" (WBG 2014b, 261).

In 1991, the World Bank reorganized again, becoming more fractionated. The Vice Presidency for Sector and Operations Policy was replaced by three new vice presidencies:

Human Resources Development and Operations Policy, Finance and Private Sector Development, and Environmentally Sustainable Development. All research was consolidated under the Chief Economist and Vice President for Development Economics. Regional Technical Departments were made smaller, and the sector operations divisions were strengthened.

In 1991, the Bank published a "Forest Policy" strategy paper, the first on the subject since 1978, declaring that it would not finance commercial logging in tropical forests (World Bank 1991).

In September 1991, Lewis Preston became the 8th Bank president.

In December 1991, the first grant from GEF was approved, a US$4.5 million project to protect the biological diversity of two endangered forest ecosystems in Poland.

In 1992, the Portfolio Management Task Force Report was issued on "*Effective Implementation: Key to Development Impact*," known commonly as the Wapenhans Report, a mammoth effort to identify steps needed to improve project implementation, leading to the establishment of the Quality Assurance Group (World Bank 1992).

In April 1992, President Preston announced the World Bank Governors had approved the membership of 13 of 15 republics of the former Soviet Union, with approval expected for remaining two shortly thereafter.

In May 1992, President Preston declared, "Sustainable poverty reduction is the overarching objective of the World Bank. It is the benchmark by which our performance as a development institution will be measured" (WBG 2014b, 272).

In October 1992, the World Bank announced US$20 million in grant funds for famine relief to East Africa.

In the 1993 reorganization under President Lewis Preston, Agriculture and Natural Resources Department (AGR), Environment Department (ENV), and the Consultative Group for International Agricultural Research Secretariat (CGIAR) were established as separate entities, with relatively little interaction among the three.

In July 1993, the Executive Directors approved the recommendations of the Wapenhans Report. The bank introduced "a country-by-country approach into the management of it lending operations ... the Bank began collaborating with authorities in borrowing countries to review the performance of the portfolio in each country and resolve systemic problems ... [which] represented an important shift in the Bank's business practices ... to a greater concern with development results in the field of Bank-supported operations" (WBG 2014b, 286).

In November 1993, the World Bank hosted a conference on world hunger. President Preston announced the Bank would expand support for microlevel credit programs.

In June 1994, the World Bank issued *Governance: The World Bank's Experience,* which argued that good government is critical to economic development (World Bank 1994).

In June 1995, James Wolfensohn was appointed the 9th World Bank president, following the death of President Preston in May 1995. Between 1995 and 2005, Wolfensohn brought renewed focus on poverty reduction and actively promoted the much needed, bottom-up, inclusive community and social development.

In November 1995, following the peace agreement between Bosnia and Herzegovina, Croatia, and Serbia, the World Bank and the European Commission announced plans for a donor conference to mobilize resources for postwar reconstruction and economic normalization.

In December 1995, the World Bank participated in World AIDS Day. At this time, the Bank had already invested US$700 million in prevention and control health projects, 49 percent in SSA. Also, the African Programme for Onchocerciasis Control, a joint international partnership program of governments, NGOs, bilateral donors, and international agencies, was launched at ceremonies in Washington.

In February 1996, President Wolfensohn launched the *World Bank Participation Sourcebook*. Moving beyond traditional cooperation with member governments, he sought "to include participation in decision-making by nongovernmental organizations, the private sector, community groups, cooperatives, women's organizations, and the poor and disadvantaged. He called for empowerment of stakeholders—including borrowers, directly affected groups, indirectly affected groups, and the Bank itself—in development decision-making" (WBG 2014b, 305).

In March 1996, Wolfensohn and UN Secretary-General Boutros Boutros-Ghali announced the UN Special Initiative for Africa, a joint expanded program of assistance to SSA.

In April 1996, the World Bank sponsored a conference on Early Childhood Development, following upon its report, "Early Child Development: Investing in the Future" (Young 1996).

The 1996 *WDR: From Plan to Market* analyzed successes and failures in transition economies (World Bank 1996).

In September 1996, the conference, "Rural Well-Being: From Vision to Action" was held in Washington, DC. In the following month, the Bank urged member countries "to place rural development at the top of their policy agendas. ... [S]ince most of the world's poor lived in rural areas, the strategy for reducing poverty, achieving food security, and protecting the environment depended upon the rural development" (WBG 2014b, 311).

In January 1997, the World Bank issued the report, "Poverty Reduction and the World Bank: Progress and Challenges in the 1990s." (World Bank 1997c).

In 1997, the Bank's "Vision to Action" report was issued by the Agriculture Department, in an attempt to revive Bank lending to agriculture (Ayres and McCalla 1997).

In June 1997, Wolfensohn addressed the UN Earth Summit, urging "revitalization of environmental goals" and prioritizing "climate change, protecting biodiversity, ozone depletion, desertification, and clean water" (WBG 2014b, 318).

In August 1997, the Bank issued *Everyone's Miracle? Revisiting Poverty and Inequality in East Asia* and *India: Achievements and Challenges in Reducing Poverty*, two publications that showed that, despite the "East Asian Miracle," poverty and inequality remained serious problems (Ahuja et al. 1997; World Bank 1997b).

In November 1997, the Bank issued "Confronting AIDS: Public Priorities in a Global Epidemic" (World Bank 1997a)

In April 1998, the first meeting of the full assembly of GEF was held in New Delhi.

In November 1998, the World Bank report, "Assessing Aid: What Works, What Doesn't and Why," advocated for "more foreign aid and for open trade, secure private property rights, the absence of corruption, respect for the rule of law, social safety nets, and sound macroeconomic and financial policies" (WBG 2014b, 337).

In December 1998, the World Bank released *Global Economic Prospects and the Developing Countries 1998–99*, which described how developing countries will be most vulnerable to the global economic slowdown (World Bank 1999).

In January 1999, Wolfensohn called for adoption of a Comprehensive Development Framework.

In April 1999, the World Bank, together with the AfDB and IMF, agreed to establish the Joint Africa Institute (JAI) to provide training to government officials and private sector participants on macroeconomic policies, poverty alleviation, gender issues, good governance, and environmental and reform policies.

In September 1999, the World Bank launched a new strategic plan on HIV/AIDS: "Intensifying Action Against HIV/AIDS in Africa: Responding to a Development Crisis." Also, in September, Wolfensohn was appointed to a second term as president.

On September 30, 1999, the World Bank warned that the fight against poverty was failing, based on poverty data and consultations, published later as *Voices of the Poor* (Narayan 2000).

The Bank announced a joint production of IMF and client governments, the Poverty Reduction Strategy Paper (PRSP) to focus on client "ownership" of the development process.

In October 1999, Wolfensohn communicated to World Bank staff a broader approach to development—a shift in focus from lending to a knowledge bank model of assistance.

2000s   The Bank increased its focus on corruption and governance and potentially, an important initiative for agriculture; it announced removal of three staff members and debarring of three Swedish firms from contracts in December 2000.

In March 2000, the Meltzer Commission Report (Meltzer 2000) was "highly critical of the Bank and the Fund, and urged they be radically reduced and restructured" (WBG 2014b, 358). Also released in March was the World Bank's study, *Voices of the Poor: Can Anyone Hear Us?* (Narayan 2000).

On March 22, 2000, President Wolfensohn addressed the Second World Water Forum, The Hague.

In April 2000, the World Bank announced a plan to "jumpstart governments into providing free basic education for all children" by 2015, at the World Education Forum in Dakar, which convened government partners, UN agencies, the Bank, NGOs, and academia (WBG 2014b, 361).

In July 2000, the Bank pledged US$500 million to assist AIDS prevention and treatment in Africa at the XIIIth International AIDS Conference in Durban, South Africa. In September, the Bank pledged increased support to combat HIV/AIDS in Caribbean countries.

In 2001, Wolfensohn and Commonwealth Secretary-General Don McKinnon issued a joint statement calling for reduction in agricultural subsidies in the developed world, saying that the subsidies were preventing exports from the developing world to the rich countries.

In 2001, the *WDR* again focused on "Attacking Poverty" (World Bank 2001).

In January 2001, President Wolfensohn pledged Bank support for reconstruction work in Gujarat, India, following an earthquake.

In February 2001, the Bill and Melinda Gates Foundation pledged US$20 million for elephantiasis elimination, to be channeled through a World Bank trust fund.

In April 2001, the World Bank and the IDB signed a Memorandum of Understanding to strengthen their collaboration.

In July 2001, the Bank's Executive Directors endorsed a new environmental strategy to ensure environmental concerns are integrated in all projects and programs, developed after consultation with over 30 stakeholders throughout the world.

In September 2001, the Bank announced it would join the UN as a full partner in implementing MDGs, endorsed by 189 countries at the September 2000 UN General Assembly.

In October 2001, Joseph Stiglitz, the World Bank's Chief Economist and Senior Vice President from 1997–2000 was awarded the Nobel Prize in Economic Sciences.

In October 2001, WHO and the Bank launched the *Global Plan to Stop TB*.

In January 2002, the World Bank and IMF launched the Poverty Reduction Strategy Conference.

In May 2002, the Bank launched the Afghanistan Reconstruction Trust Fund.

In August 2002, donor countries agreed to highest replenishment (US$2.92 billion) for GEF. Also, in August, the Bank joined governments and multilateral institutions in launching the Global Village Energy Partnership, with the aim of reducing poverty in rural areas, by doubling the number of people who gain access annually to lighting, heating, mechanical energy, and electrical power.

In September 2002, the Bank partnered with the International Emissions Trading Association (IETA) on the Community Development Carbon Fund (CDCF) initiative, a US$100 million fund to reduce GHG emissions in small developing countries and rural areas of all developing countries.

On September 27, 2002, the World Bank and the WTO established a Standards and Trade Development Facility, to link aid to trade opportunities in the fight against poverty.

In September 2002, the World Bank/IMF Annual Meetings opened amid growing anti-globalization protests. Wolfensohn called on rich countries to improve donor coordination, untie aid, and agree on a *"fixed timetable"* for the elimination of agricultural subsidies (WBG 2014b, 400).

In October 2002, the Bank announced a new revised forest policy and strategy, with a more balanced approach toward forests on conservation, poverty reduction, and growth, rather than the exclusive focus on conservation, as in the 1991 Forest Strategy. The reformulated 2002 forest strategy aimed to increase focus on the livelihoods of people living in extreme poverty and who depend on forests, while improving the environmental protection of forests in the developing world with increased focus on forest governance.

In November 2002, the first BioCarbon Fund was launched to focus on land use, allocating resources to projects that transform landscapes and directly benefit poor farmers, as they earn income from sequestering or conserving carbon.

In 2003, the revised agricultural and rural development strategy, *Reaching the Rural Poor,* was released, after consultations with government officials, civil society organizations, academics, the business community, and donor agencies (World Bank 2003b).

In March 2003, the World Bank released "Water—A Priority for Responsible for Growth and Poverty Reduction: An Agenda for Investment and Policy Change" to reemphasize the role of water as key to growth and poverty reduction.

In May 2003, the World Bank released "Breaking the Conflict Trap: Civil War and Development Policy," a report that asserted that ethnic tensions and old political feuds are rarely the cause of civil wars, but rather poverty, heavy dependence on natural resource exports, and other economic forces lead to conflicts (Collier et al. 2003).

In July 2003, a new set of indicators, Worldwide Governance Indicators, tracking quality of governance, covering 200 countries were published by the Bank.

In October 2003, the Grant Facility for Indigenous Peoples was established to fund projects initiated and managed by Indigenous Peoples in developing countries.

In January 2004, the World Bank established a US$25 million trust fund to build capacity and strengthen institutions in Low-Income Countries Under Stress (LICUS).

In June 2004, the World Bank, together with UNDP, UNEP, and the World Resources Institute, issued a landmark report, "World Resources 2002—2004: Decisions for the Earth—Balance, Voice, and Power" (UNDP et al. 2004), which called for "fundamental changes in how decisions are made concerning the world's natural resources," and stressed the need "for changes to arrest the accelerating deterioration of the world's environment and to address the crisis of global poverty" (WBG 2014b, 446).

In 2004, OED issued the first phase of the "Addressing the Challenges of Globalization: An Independent Evaluation of the World Bank's Approach to Global Programs," addressing issues of global partnerships, recommending improved management of the growing trust fund portfolio (OED 2004a).

In September 2004, the first two World Bank Public Information Centers (PICs) in Vietnam were launched to share knowledge and provide access to a rich source of information on various topics of development.

In April 2005, the World Bank released a new study, "Economic Growth in the 1990s: Learning from a Decade of Reform," which reviewed the impacts of policy and institutional reforms introduced in the 1990s on economic growth (World Bank 2005b; see, also, Rodrik 2006).

In May 2005, the World Bank, after consultation with the Governments of India and Pakistan, announced an agreement for the appointment of a Neutral Expert to address differences concerning a project governed by the Indus Waters Treaty.

In June 2005, Paul Wolfowitz became the 10th World Bank president.

In August 2005, the World Bank, FAO, the International Union for Conservation of Nature (IUCN), WorldFish, and developing countries launched a Global Program on Fisheries, "PROFISH," to reverse the trend toward fish depletion (see https://www.worldbank.org/en/topic/environment/brief/global-program-on-fisheries-profish).

In September 2005, the World Bank publication *Where is the Wealth of Nations?* provided new estimates of total wealth, which included produced capital, natural resources, and human skills values and capabilities, noting that measures such as GDP ignore resource depletion and environmental damage (World Bank 2005e).

In October 2005, TerrAfrica, a new partnership to address land degradation and increase sustainable land management throughout the Africa region was announced at the UN Conference of the Parties on Desertification in Nairobi. TerrAfrica was developed after calls for action from the UN Convention to Combat Desertification (UNCCD), as well as from the New Partnership for Africa's Development (NEPAD) and the CAADP/NEPAD Environmental Action Plan, and the G8 Gleneagles Summit Africa statement (World Bank 2015).

In November 2005, the World Bank study, *Reducing Poverty on a Global Scale* drew on more than 100 case studies of poverty reduction to identify factors for successful reduction, including leadership, commitment, institutional innovation, learning, experimentation, and donor assistance (Moreno-Dodson 2005).

In December 2005, at WTO Trade Talks in Hong Kong, the Bank engaged in strong advocacy to resume agricultural trade talks, reduce protectionism, and increase market access.

The December 2005 Bank report, "Reaching the Poor: What Works, What Doesn't, and Why," examined health, nutrition, and population programs that often fail to reach the poor who most need them (Gwatkin, Wagstaff, and Yazbeck 2005).

In 2006, the Bank Group worked closely with the World Organisation for Animal Health (OIE), the World Health Organization (WHO) and FAO, as well as partner countries and private donors and IMF, to develop initiatives at both the regional and international levels to prevent the spread of avian influenza and reduce the risk of outbreaks turning into pandemics. Two vice presidents were appointed to coordinate the Bank's external response and an internal one, to examine and improve, as needed, the existing contingency plans for Bank staff and families.

In February 2006, the AfDB, ADB, IDB, European Investment Bank, European Bank for Reconstruction and Development, IMF, and the World Bank agreed on policies and practices to address internal and external problems of corruption.

In March 2006, the World Bank published the report, "Reengaging in Agricultural Water Management: Challenges and Options," which called for doubling rural irrigation investment to improve agricultural productivity and avert a global food crisis in the next 20 years (World Bank 2006).

In September 2006, the World Bank launched a four-year, US$24.5 million plan, Gender Equality as Smart Economics, to increase economic potential of women in areas such as infrastructure, agriculture, and finance in developing countries.

In October 2006, the World Bank released *The Other Half of Gender*, a book on gender equality, arguing for a focus on relations between men and women (Bannon and Correia 2006). It also released the report, "Close to Home: The Development Impact of Remittances in Latin America," a study that examined who the money that migrant workers send back increased growth, reduces poverty, and improves education and health in their home regions (Fajnzylber and López 2007).

In 2007, the World Bank launched a new framework to speed response to disasters and emergencies with initial funding for start-up activities and more effective long-term support for recovery efforts.

In May 2007, the Executive Directors of the World Bank accepted the resignation of President Paul Wolfowitz, amid scandal. Robert Zoellick was nominated to replace him. Paul Wolfowitz's failed Presidency with scandal diminished the Bank's stature.

In July 2007, President Robert Zoellick became the 11th World Bank president. He restores focus on crisis response to the dual food and financial crisis (food crisis spreads first in Ethiopia and the Horn of Africa, followed by the global food crisis of 2007–8).

In October 2007, the *World Development Report 2008: Agriculture for Development* was released, stressing the need to place the agriculture sector at the center of the development agenda to meet MDGs (World Bank 2007).

In 2007, Zoellick pushed for a Bank response to the food and financial crisis in partnership with IOs, most notably WFP and FAO. Zoellick increased emphasis on conflict-affected countries.

In August 2008, the World Bank released new poverty estimates and sets a new poverty line of US$1.25/day.

In October 2008, the World Book published *Gender in Agriculture Sourcebook*, that related underinvestment in women and agriculture, with gender disparities in knowledge, access to credit, and land, result in higher levels of poverty and greater food insecurity (World Bank 2008). The Bank also joined with governments and the private sector to launch the Adolescent Girls Initiative (AGI) to promote the economic empowerment of girls in poor and post-conflict countries. See https://www.worldbank.org/en/programs/adolescent-girls-initiative

In November 2008, the Bank increased support for developing countries in the financial crisis. Between 2008–13, overall lending and lending to agriculture increased.

In December 2008, the World Bank and the Bill and Melinda Gates Foundation (BMGF) launched the Living Standards Measurement Study—Integrated Survey on Agriculture (LSMS–ISA) to establish household panel surveys in six African countries, to generate high-quality and consistent data on rural households.

In March 2009, the Bank published *Moving out of Poverty: Success from the Bottom Up*, a study carried out in 15 countries, including interviews with more than 60,000 people (Narayan, Pritchett, and Kapoor 2009).

In April 2009, the World Bank announced it would triple investments in safety nets and other social protection programs in health and education over the next two years, to protect the most vulnerable from the global economic crisis.

In June 2009, the WBG established the Agriculture Finance Support Facility, to expand rural finance in the developing world, with a US$20 million contribution from the BMGF.

In September 2009, the 2010 *WDR: Development and Climate Change* was published, reporting that development goals are threatened by climate change, with heaviest impacts on poor countries and poor people, and calling for quick action toward a "climate-smart" agriculture (World Bank 2010).

In November 2009, President Zoellick launched a global urban strategy at an Infrastructure Finance Summit, to work with developing countries undergoing rapid urbanization.

In December 2009, the Bank's Board of Executive Directors approved a US$1.3 billion Crisis Response Window for IDA to protect LICs from crises. Also, in December, the World Bank launched the Carbon Partnership Facility at the UN Climate Change Conference in Copenhagen to help develop programmatic approaches to assist countries "to pursue low-carbon growth and to accelerate greenhouse gas emission reduction" (WBG 2014b, 698).

In January 2010, the World Bank and Microsoft announced partnership to leverage information and communication technology in Africa to support social and economic development.

In March 2010, the World Bank report, "Women, Business and Law" was the first to measure gender gap using quantitative and objective data (see World Bank 2020c).

In April 2010, WBG's Open Data Initiative created data.worldbank.org for data access. On November 8, 2010, on World Statistics Day, President Zoellick stated, "It's important to make the data and knowledge of the World Bank available to everyone. Statistics tell the story of people in developing and emerging countries and can play an important part in helping to overcome poverty."[44]

In December 2010, the World Bank and IMF launched online the Quarterly Public Sector Debt Database, to provide statistics for 30 emerging markets and developing countries.

In 2011, IEG issued its evaluation of the World Bank's lending to agriculture and agribusiness in 2011, "Growth and Productivity in Agriculture and Agribusiness. Evaluative Lessons from World Bank Group Experience," which covered a 10-year period, 1998–2008 (IEG 2011b).

In April 2011, the *World Development Report: Conflict, Security and Development* (World Bank 2011c) examined the causes of organized violence in the 21st century, noting "risks of violence are greater when high stresses combine with weak capacity or lack of legitimacy in key national institutions" (WBG 2014b, 736).

In June 2011, the first "World Bank Report on Disability" provided an estimate of more than one billion persons with disabilities globally (WHO and World Bank 2011).

In September 2011, the *World Development Report 2012: Gender Equality and Development* (World Bank 2012) noted that gender equality "could raise productivity, improve outcomes for children, make institutions more representative, and advance development prospects for all" (WBG 2014b, 747). Also published in September, *The State of the World Bank Knowledge Services: Knowledge for Development* was the first institution-wide review of the Bank's knowledge work—research, economic and sector reports, technical assistance, and training (World Bank 2011b).

In April 2012, the World Bank announced its Open Access Policy for Research and Knowledge and launch of its Open Knowledge Repository.

In July 2012, Jim Yong Kim became the World Bank president.

In August 2012, the sourcebook, *Getting to Green—A Sourcebook of Pollution Management Policy Tools for Growth and Competitiveness* was published, to serve as a reference and technical guide for policymakers and development practitioners (Ahmed 2012).

In October 2012, President Kim called for the World Bank to become a "Solutions Bank" to work with partners to eliminate extreme poverty. President Kim also spoke of the concept of "Science of Delivery" in several speeches, with the general message that the world has invested too much in *what* to deliver and too little in *how* to deliver it.

In December 2012, the World Bank report, "The Future of Water in African Cities: Why Waste Water?" was aimed at changing policymakers' thinking about urban water management and planning in Africa (Torres 2012).

In April 2013, the World Bank published *The State of the Poor: Where Are the Poor and Where are the Poorest?* which used World Development Indicators to examine extreme poverty headcount rates (Beegle et al. 2013). The World Bank also announced the establishment of the Global Knowledge Partnership on Migration and Development (KNOMAD), to provide a hub for knowledge and policy expertise on migration issues.

In November 2013, the World Bank report, "Building Resilience: Integrating Climate and Disaster Risk into Development," examined gradual or slow-onset effects of climate change—sea-level rise, salinization, droughts, as well as extreme weather events such as floods, cyclones, and heat waves (World Bank and GFDRR 2013).

In 2013, the World Bank's Agriculture Action Plan 2013–15 was focused on increasing agricultural productivity and resilience, especially for smallholder farmers (World Bank 2013c). More emphasis was given to climate-smart agriculture, gender mainstreaming, and nutrition (World Bank 2019b). The department's name was changed from Agriculture and Rural Development to Agriculture and Environmental Services.[45]

---

[44] https://blogs.worldbank.org/opendata/world-statistics-day-recognized-important-role-official-statistics-policy-making-development

[45] Previously called: Agriculture division (1953–68), Agriculture Projects Department (1968–77), Agriculture and Rural Development Department (1977–92), Agriculture and Natural Resources Department (1993–7), Rural Development Department (1997–2002), Agriculture and Rural Development Department (2002–13), and from 2013, the Agriculture and Environmental Services Department.

Appendix B: Role of the International Finance Corporation

IFC's mission is to create opportunities for people to escape poverty. IFC's approach has evolved over the years: from support to private sector-led growth, in general, to promoting environmentally and socially sustainable growth, to beginning to pay explicit attention to inclusive growth. There have been different perspectives of how IFC's support for private-sector development is helping to tackle poverty. Yet, there was not enough clarity about what poverty means within the IFC context, and how IFC's interventions reach and affect the poor.

IFC's "IFC 3.0 strategy" is embedded in the Bank Group's Forward Look vision (discussed in Chapter 5). It recognizes that to achieve impact at scale, IFC must leverage the strengths of the entire World Bank Group and other development partners to create markets and mobilize private sector resources at a greater scale. There is huge potential to this effect, which is still unrealized despite rapid growth of IFC.

This new strategy follows IEG's 2011 evaluation of IFC's impacts on poverty. Reviewing the decade 2000–10, the evaluation noted that priority given to what it calls "frontier markets" has led to increases in IFC investments in IDA countries, but that these investments need to be spread around in more than the few IDA countries in which they are currently concentrated. IFC investments in targeted sectors need to also be expanded "beyond financial markets where trade finance had contributed most to expansion," particularly after the financial crisis when international trade finance dried up (IEG 2011a, xi). The evaluation also recommended that "IFC needs to continue to strengthen its partnership with the World Bank to enhance its poverty focus and results" (IEG 2011a, xi).

The report noted further that patterns of growth are important, "including making development impact a key driver of strategy, testing development goals in operational activities, and participating in funding the IDA. But it can more fully exploit the vast potential for poverty orientation in its growth supporting activities" (IEG 2011a, xiii).

The evaluation assessed IFC "in terms of how its strategies, projects, and results measurement framework contribute to growth and to distributional patterns of growth that create opportunities for the poor" (IEG 2011a, xiii).

At the strategic level, the sectors were defined so broadly as to be consistent with a pro-poor orientation, but the strategic sectors needed "to be designed and implemented in ways that actually enhance opportunities and the impact on poor people" (IEG 2011a, xiii).

The IEG report noted that at the project level:

> It has been challenging for IFC to incorporate distributional issues in interventions. Fewer than half of projects reviewed included evidence of poverty and distributional aspects in project objectives, targeting of interventions, characteristics of intended beneficiaries, or tracking of impacts. Where projects reflected distributional aspects, targeted the poor, and monitored the results, they were more likely to achieve better poverty outcomes. Projects that paid attention to distribution issues performed as well, if not better than, other projects on development and investment outcomes; this suggest that poverty focus need not come at the expense of financial success. A broad range of IFC's interventions can therefore be simultaneously pro-growth and pro-poor, but this link is neither universal nor automatic. . . .

> On development results, most IFC investment projects generate satisfactory returns but do not provide evidence of identifiable opportunities for the poor to participate in, contribute to, or benefit from the economic activities that the project supports. The fact that projects do not provide evidence of enhanced opportunities for the poor does not necessarily mean that they do not contribute to poverty reduction. Achieving satisfactory economic returns suggests that they make a positive contribution to growth and therefore most likely to poverty reduction. However, the relatively high proportion of projects that do not generate identifiable opportunities for the poor suggests the primary reliance on the pace of growth for poverty reduction, at a time when IFC's strategies point to more attention to the pattern of growth that it supports. Greater effort is needed in translating the strategic intentions into actions in investment operations and advisory services to enhance IFC's poverty focus. (IEG 2011a, xiv)

With respect to defining frontier regions, IFC needs to consider "the incidence of poverty, spatial distribution of the poor, and non-income dimensions of poverty" (IEG 2011a, xiv). The evaluation recommended the need to sharpen the definition of poverty "and shared understanding of poverty and poverty impact within the IFC context, and providing guidance to staff on how to operationalize it within the development effectiveness framework at the strategy and project level" (IEG 2011a, xiv). The evaluation recommended adoption of "more nuanced concepts of poverty when defining frontier regions" and "a consultative framework, including the participation of relevant networks of the World Bank Group and partner organizations to deepen understanding and develop innovative approaches for understanding, measuring, and reporting of poverty impacts within the IFC context" (IEG 2011a, xiv).

The evaluation further recommended:

> At the project level, there is a need to re-examine the stakeholder framework to address distributional and poverty issues in project design. IFC needs to make explicit in its interventions the underlying assumptions about how projects can contribute to growth and patterns of growth that provide opportunities for the poor.
>
> On measuring results, for projects with poverty reduction objectives, poverty outcomes ought to be defined ex-ante, then monitored and reported. For projects that focus primarily on growth ... (IEG 2011a, xiv)

The World Bank Group's *Gender Strategy (FY16–23): Gender Equality, Poverty Reduction and Inclusive Growth* describes IFC's work in advancing gender equality via partnerships with the private sector:

> The Partnerships with the private sector are critical to advancing economic opportunities for women and including men in supporting gender equality in the workplace. One such partnership led by the IFC is *SheWorks*, a global private sector partnership to improve employment opportunities and working conditions for more than 360,000 women by 2016 through knowledge sharing and best practices. In its first year, the partnership recruited 13 leading private sector companies (in nine countries and 20 sectors, including traditionally male-dominated industries such as financial services, real estate, telecommunications, construction, petrochemicals, energy, and information technology) that have pledged to implement a minimum of three measures to support women in the workplace: flexible work, effective anti-sexual-harassment mechanisms, and programs to accelerate women in leadership. The EDGE Certified Foundation, the International Labor Organization, and UN Global Compact provide knowledge support and facilitate implementation of best practices. Early results show increases in women's employment numbers. This model will be used to consolidate learning and best practices for replication by other companies, industries, and regions in the years to come. (WBG 2015, 43)

Similar to the IBRD, IFC is acting to execute a capital increase plan, "shifting its focus to working 'upstream' to open markets and create projects that will increase private investment in all countries, especially the poorest ones" (World Bank 2019b). The IFC and the World Bank have developed "the 'Cascade' approach, which looks for private-sector solutions to development challenges and directs World Bank programs to overcome obstacles in the private sector framework. This approach is key to attracting new investment and boosting the impact of every development dollar" (World Bank 2019b).

Historical Evolution of the International Finance Corporation

Highlights of IFC's chronology are summarized here (World Bank 2016, 2017):

1956: IFC was established under Robert Garner's leadership with US$100 million in capital.
1957: IFC's first loan of US$2 million was made to help Siemens' Brazilian affiliate manufacture electrical equipment.
1971: IFC Capital Markets Department was created to strengthen local banks, stock markets, and other financial intermediaries, eventually becoming IFC's largest area of emphasis.

1972–4: IFC's advisory services and field offices grew in the 1970s, helping to build Indonesia's first securities markets.

1973: IFC's first housing finance project: IFC became a founding shareholder in a start-up in Colombia, later adopting same model in 1978, with HDFC Bank in India.

1974: IFC's US$17.3 million investment and advice to Korea's LG Electronics helped it become one of the first globally competitive, emerging-market companies.

1976: IFC created first small- and medium-sized enterprise (SME) finance project, a US$2 million loan for Kenya Commercial Bank to lend to smaller local companies.

1980: IFC made its first investment in the Tata Group, India: Tata Iron and Steel Company borrowed US$38 million from IFC.

1981: IFC coined the phrase "emerging markets," changing the financial world's perception of developing countries and defining a new asset class. IFC created the Emerging Markets Database, the basis of the world's first emerging markets stock index.

1984: IFC launched the first publicly traded emerging-market country fund, the NYSE-listed Korea Fund.

1985: IFC provided investment-climate reform advice to China.

1988: During the Latin American debt crisis, IFC helped several Mexican conglomerates reduce their debt.

1989: IFC received its first triple-A credit rating, a key to a major multicurrency borrowing program that, by 2016, topped US$15 billion a year.

1992: IFC coined the phrase "frontier markets." IFC led one of Russia's first privatization programs, auctioning 2,000 businesses in Nizhny Novgorod.

1996: IFC entered the microfinance sector with a US$3 million stake in Profund, focused on LAC. In one of their first investments in a conflict-affected state, IFC helped to launch Bosnia's microfinance pioneer (now ProCredit Bank). IFC led Africa's largest privatization, the US$70 million sale of the government's stake in Kenya Airways to KLM.

1998: IFC adopted new environmental and social review procedures and safeguard policies. Responding to the Asian financial crisis, IFC began a five-year, nearly US$1 billion counter-cyclical investment and advisory package to strengthen clients in Korea.

2002: Amid worsening economic conditions in Argentina, IFC started a series of countercyclical investments, beginning with US$60 million for the agribusiness client AGD.

2003: Leading commercial banks launched the Equator Principles, modeled on IFC's standards.

2004: IFC launched its first large-scale gender initiative, encouraging projects to help local women-owned businesses. IFC oversaw creation of the Emerging Market Private Equity Association (EMPEA).

2006: New Performance Standards were adopted by IFC.

2007: IFC's US$5 million investment in FINO, a start-up Indian IT firm, helped expand access to finance for people in rural areas.

2009: The G20 launched its Financial Inclusion initiative, naming IFC its SME finance adviser. Responding to the global financial crisis, IFC provided €2 billion to an international effort to maintain commercial bank lending in Central and Eastern Europe. Having decentralized to be closer to clients, IFC had more than 50 percent of its staff in the field.

2010: IFC launched a private sector window in the US$1.25 billion Global Agriculture and Food Security Program, a new World Bank Group initiative formed at the request of the G20.

2012: A year after the end of conflict in Côte d'Ivoire, IFC financed the expansion of the country's largest thermal power plant, Azito.

2013: World Bank Group launches its twin goals—ending extreme poverty and boosting shared prosperity. The People's Bank of China pledges US$3 billion to IFC's new Managed Co-Lending Portfolio Program, becoming the first investor in the new syndications program.

2014: IFC's first offshore Masala bond in Indian rupees was issued in London. The program has grown to US$3 billion.

2014: IFC's partnership with Goldman Sachs, 10,000 Women began with the 2014 launch of the Women Entrepreneurs Opportunity Facility (WEOF), which *expands access to capital for women entrepreneurs*. To date, WEOF has supported the deployment of over US$1.4 billion to financial institutions, reaching over 53,000 women across 32 countries.

2015: IFC has played a key role in highlighting the importance of the private sector in achieving the SDGs. As part of the coordinated World Bank Group response to the Ebola crisis in West Africa, IFC provided US$225 million to help local banks maintain lending to local SMEs. IFC was a thought leader in Paris at historical international climate change talks. IFC showcased emerging-market clients with innovative climate-smart solutions.

Appendix C: Role of the Multilateral Investment Guarantee Agency

MIGA, a member of the World Bank Group, was composed of 181 member governments as of August 2016—of which 156 nations are developing countries and 25 are industrialized countries. MIGA was created to complement both public and private investment insurance sources against noncommercial risks in developing countries. Its multilateral character and sponsorship by advanced and developing nations bolstered confidence in foreign investment.

In September 1985, the World Bank endorsed the idea of a multilateral political risk insurance provider and established MIGA as a part of the World Bank Group in April 1988. MIGA started out with US$1 billion worth of capital and 29 original member states.

As described in the MIGA Brief, "MIGA: Cultivating Agribusiness Growth":

Agricultural investments are risky business.... Unclear or incomplete laws on property ownership may affect profit. Restrictions on revenue repatriation could disrupt a project's finances adding to the imbalance between foreign-denominated debt and locally denominated revenue. Threats such as revolution or terrorism add an additional layer of uncertainty...

MIGA provides political risk insurance (guarantees) and credit enhancement support against certain noncommercial risks to investments in developing countries. In collaboration with our World Bank Group colleagues, we work with investors to structure deals in ways that benefit all parties and foster positive relationships with the communities where they invest.

MIGA guarantees [mitigate] the noncommercial risks of agribusiness investments, thereby lowering the cost of capital and helping secure financing. Our guarantees reassure lenders that their investments are protected and help equity owners overcome hesitations that may loom large prior to deal signing, particularly for costly investments in high-risk countries. Once a deal is in place, MIGA guarantees, backed by the World Bank Group, bring companies peace of mind, providing an added measure of security that can stabilize a project's risk profile and reinforce positive relations with host governments.

MIGA can also help guide agribusiness companies as they face challenges related to the environmental and social aspects of their investments. For example, key natural resources need to be managed effectively while yields are increased to meet market demand. Investments in agriculture can play a significant role in poverty reduction, but only if local production needs are met and high labor standards are practiced. MIGA has the experience to advise its agribusiness clients in implementing social and environmental best practices in their operations. (MIGA 2015)

Some of the areas in which MIGA has provided guarantees include: (1) currency inconvertibility and transfer restrictions; (2) expropriation; (3) war, civil disturbance, terrorism, and sabotage; (4) breach of contract; (5) non-honoring of financial obligations. MIGA also provides dispute resolution services for guaranteed investments to prevent disruptions to developmentally beneficial projects (MIGA 2015).

Since 1988, MIGA has issued more than US$30 billion worth of political risk insurance globally for more than 750 projects in various sectors. Among the agribusiness guarantees that MIGA has extended is its support for Agrivision Africa in Zambia, a business operating grain-related agribusinesses and related value-chain assets. In 2011, MIGA initially backed an investment in two commercial farms in Zambia's Central Province. In South Africa, MIGA provided coverage for EcoPlanet's first investment there in 2015. In the Eastern Cape Region, MIGA provided a guarantee of US$8.6 million to cover an equity investment for converting degraded land in an impoverished area into bamboo plantations for the production of activated carbon and bio-charcoal to be sold to local and export markets. In Ethiopia, MIGA has supported a fruit processing plant, adding to the value chain.

Administering the West Bank and GAZA Investment Guarantee Trust Fund, MIGA is providing guarantees for investors developing Medjool date palm farms in Jericho (MIGA 2015).

MIGA's significant growth under the FY18–20 strategy has been driven by "a deepening partnership with the Bank and IFC, an increasing focus on business development and product innovation. MIGA has expanded its reinsurance to seventy percent of gross exposure. This will allow MIGA to sustain its growth in the medium term as global macro and business conditions evolve" (World Bank 2019b).

Appendix D: Independent Evaluation Group and World Bank Project Performance Ratings

IEG independently validates all completion reports that the World Bank prepares for its projects (known as Implementation Completion and Results Report, or ICRs). For more information, see https://ieg.worldbankgroup.org/methodology and https://ieg.worldbankgroup.org/data#

References

AfDB Group (African Development Bank Group). 2016. "Feed Africa—Strategy for Agricultural Transformation in Africa 2016–2025." AfDB Group, Abidjan, Côte d'Ivoire. https://www.afdb.org/fileadmin/uploads/afdb/Documents/Generic-Documents/Feed_Africa-_Strategy_for_Agricultural_Transformation_in_Africa_2016-2025.pdf

Ahmed, Kulsum. 2012. *Getting to Green: A Sourcebook of Pollution Management Policy Tools for Growth and Competitiveness*. Washington, DC: World Bank. http://documents.worldbank.org/curated/en/560021468330349857/pdf/716080WP0Box370Getting0to0Green0web.pdf

Ahuja, Vinod, Benu Bidani, Francisco Ferreira, and Michael Walton. 1997. *Revisiting Poverty and Inequality in East Asia*. Washington, DC: World Bank.

Aiyar, Swaminathan, Andrew Parker, and Johan Van Zyl. 1995. "Market-assisted Land Reform: A New Solution to Old Problems." AGR Dissemination Notes No. 4, August, Agriculture and Natural Resources Department, World Bank, Washington, DC.

Ali, Daniel Ayalew, Matthew Collin, Klaus Deininger, Stefan Dercon, Justin Sandefur, and Andrew Zeitlin. 2016. "Small Price Incentives Increase Women's Access to Land Titles in Tanzania." *Journal of Development Economics* 123: 107–22.

Ali, Daniel Ayalew, Klaus Deininger, and Marguerite Duponchel. 2017. "New Ways to Assess and Enhance Land Registry Sustainability: Evidence from Rwanda." *World Development* 99 (C): 377–94.

Ali, Daniel Ayalew, Klaus Deininger, and Markus Goldstein. 2014. "Environmental and Gender Impacts of Land Tenure Regularization in Africa: Pilot Evidence from Rwanda." *Journal of Development Economics* 110 (C): 262–75.

Ali, Daniel Ayalew, Klaus Deininger, and Anthony Harris. 2017. "Using National Statistics to Increase Transparency of Large Land Acquisition: Evidence from Ethiopia." *World Development* 93 (C): 62–74.

Ali, Daniel Ayalew, Klaus Deininger, Godfrey Mahofa, and Rhona Nyakulama. Forthcoming. "Sustaining Land Registration Benefits by Addressing the Challenges of Reversion to Informality in Rwanda." *Land Use Policy* (online November 9, 2019).

Ali, Daniel Ayalew, Klaus Deininger, and Daniel Monchuk. 2020. "Using Satellite Imagery to Assess Impacts of Soil and Water Conservation Measures: Evidence from Ethiopia's Tana-Beles Watershed." *Ecological Economics* 169: 106512.

Ali, Daniel Ayalew, Klaus Deininger, and Michael Wild. 2020. "Using Satellite Imagery to Create Tax Maps and Enhance Local Revenue Collection." *Applied Economics Applied Economics* 52 (4): 415–29.

Anderson, Jock R., Gershon Feder, and Sushma Ganguly. 2006. "The Rise and Fall of Training and Visit Extension: An Asian Mini-drama with an African Epilogue." Policy Research Working Paper

No. 3928, World Bank, Washington, DC. http://documents.worldbank.org/curated/en/190121468140386154/pdf/wps3928.pdf

Anderson, Kym. 2010. "Krueger/Schiff/Valdés Revisited: Agriculture Price and Trade Policy Reform in Developing Countries since 1960." Policy Research Working Paper No. 5165, January, World Bank, Washington, DC. https://openknowledge.worldbank.org/handle/10986/19952

Anderson, Kym, and Will Martin, eds. 2005. *Agricultural Trade Reform and the Doha Development Agenda*. Washington, DC: World Bank and New York: Palgrave MacMillan.

Ayres, Robert L. 1985. *Banking on the Poor: The World Bank and World Poverty*. Cambridge, MA: MIT Press.

Ayres, Wendy Schreiber, and Alexander F. McCalla. 1997. "Rural Development: From Vision to Action." Environmental and Socially Sustainable Development Studies (ESSD) and Monograph Series No. 12. World Bank, Washington, DC. http://documents.worldbank.org/curated/en/445541468326432599/Rural-development-from-vision-to-action

Babu, Suresh C., and Pramod K. Joshi, eds. 2019. *Agricultural Extension in South Asia: Status, Challenges, and Policy Options*. London: Academic Press.

Bachewe, Fantu, Guush Berhane, Bart Minten, and Alemayehu S. Taffesse. 2018. "Agricultural Transformation in Africa? Assessing the Evidence in Ethiopia." *World Development* 105: 286–98.

Banerjee, Abhijit, Angus Deaton, Nora Lustig, and Ken Rogoff. 2006. "An Evaluation of World Bank Research, 1998–2005." World Bank, Washington, DC. https://openknowledge.worldbank.org/handle/10986/17896

Banerjee, Abhijit, and Esther Duflo. 2012. *Poor Economics: A Radical Rethinking of the Way to Fight Global Poverty*. New York: PublicAffairs.

Bannon, Ian, and Maria C. Correia, eds. 2006. *The Other Half of Gender: Men's Issues in Development*. Washington, DC: World Bank. http://documents.worldbank.org/curated/en/673491468313860266/pdf/365000Other0ha101OFFICIAL0USE0ONLY1.pdf

Beegle, Kathleen, and Luc Christiaensen, eds. 2019. *Accelerating Poverty Reduction in Africa*. Washington, DC: World Bank Group. https://openknowledge.worldbank.org/handle/10986/32354

Beegle, Kathleen G., Pedro Olinto, Carlos E. Sobrado, and Hiroki Uematsu. 2013. "The State of the Poor: Where Are the Poor, Where Is Extreme Poverty Harder to End, and What is the Current Profile of the World's Poor?" Economic Premise No. 125, October, World Bank, Washington, DC. http://documents.worldbank.org/curated/en/311511468326955970/pdf/818010BRI0EP120Box0379844B00PUBLIC0.pdf

Bell, Bernard R. 1990. Transcript of Oral History Interview, November 20. Conducted by John Lewis, Richard Webb, Devesh Kapur, World Bank Group Archives Oral History website. https://oralhistory.worldbank.org/transcripts/transcript-oral-history-interview-bernard-r-bell-held-november-21-1990

Binswanger, Hans P., and Klaus Deininger. 1993. "South African Land Policy: The Legacy of History and Current Options." *World Development* 21 (9): 1451–75.

Binswanger-Mkhize, Hans P. 2012. "Is There Too Much Hype about Index-based Agricultural Insurance?" *Journal of Development* Studies 48 (2): 187–200.

Bourne, Joel K., Jr. 2014. "The Next Breadbasket: Why Big Corporations Are Grabbing Up Land on the Planet's Hungriest Continent." *National Geographic*, July. http://www.nationalgeographic.com/foodfeatures/land-grab/

Canuto, Otaviano. 2019a. "Brazil Must Hold to Structural Reforms While Undergoing Slow Economic Recovery." Center for Macroeconomics & Development, August 7. https://www.cmacrodev.com/brazil-must-hold-to-structural-reforms-while-undergoing-slow-economic-recovery/

Canuto, Otaviano. 2019b. "Why Brazil Must Build a (Fiscal) Wall." *Americas Quarterly*, January 30. https://www.americasquarterly.org/content/why-brazil-must-build-fiscal-wall

Carvalho, José L. 1991. "Aid, Capital Flows, and Development in Brazil." In *Transitions in Development: The Role of Aid and Commercial Flows*, edited by Uma Lele and Ijaz Nabi, 295–328. San Francisco: ICS Press.

CFI (Capital Finance International). 2019. "Otaviano Canuto, Center for Macroeconomics and Development: How to Heal the Brazilian Economy." cfi.co, February 27. https://cfi.co/finance/2019/02/otaviano-canuto-center-for-macroeconomics-and-development-how-to-heal-the-brazilian-economy/

CGD (Center for Global Development). 2006. "When Will We Ever Learn? Improving Lives through Impact Evaluation." Report of the Evaluation Gap Working Group, May, Co-chaired by William D. Savedoff, Ruth Levine, and Nancy Birdsall, CGD, Washington, DC.

Chauhan, Jitendra S., S. Rajendra Prasad, Satinder Pal, P. R. Choudhury, and K. Udaya Bhaskar. 2016. "Seed Production of Field Crops in India: Quality Assurance, Status, Impact and Way Forward." *Indian Journal of Agricultural Sciences* 86 (5): 563–79.

Chenery, Hollis B., and Alan M. Strout. 1966. "Foreign Assistance and Economic Development." *American Economic Review* 56 (4): 679–733.

Chicago Council on Global Affairs. 2012. "2012 Progress Report on U.S. Leadership in Global Agricultural Development." Catherine Bertini and Dan Glickman, co-chairs, Chicago Council on Global Affairs, Chicago. https://agriknowledge.org/downloads/9p290938x

Clark, William. 1981. "Reconsiderations: Robert McNamara at the World Bank." *Foreign Affairs* 60 (1): 167–84.

Collier, Paul. 1991. "Aid and Economic Performance in Tanzania." In *Transitions in Development: The Role of Aid and Commercial Flows*, edited by Uma Lele and Ijaz Nabi, 151–71. San Francisco: ICS Press.

Collier, Paul, V. L. Elliott, Håvard Hegre, Anke Hoeffler, Marta Reynal-Querol, Nicholas Sambanis. 2003."Breaking the Conflict Trap: Civil War and Development Policy". A World Bank policy research report, World Bank, Washington, DC. https://openknowledge.worldbank.org/handle/10986/13938

Copson, Raymond W. 2005. "Africa, the G8, and the Blair Initiative." CRS Report for Congress. Congressional Research Service, Washington, DC. https://fas.org/sgp/crs/row/RL32796.pdf

Corbo, Vittorio, and Patricio Rojas. 1991. "World Bank-Supported Adjustment Programs: Country Performance and Effectiveness." Policy, Research, and External Affairs Working Paper No. 623, March, Country Economics Department, World Bank, Washington, DC. http://documents.worldbank.org/curated/en/340781468739253079/pdf/multi0page.pdf

Cornia, Giovanni Andrea, Richard Jolly, and Frances Stewart, eds. 1987. *Adjustment with a Human Face: Protecting the Vulnerable and Promoting Growth*. A Study by UNICEF. Oxford: Oxford University Press.

de Tray, Dennis. 2019. *Why Counterinsurgency Fails: The US in Iraq and Afghanistan*. Cham, Switzerland: Palgrave Macmillan.

Deaton, Angus. 2018. "The U.S. Can No Longer Hide From Its Deep Poverty Problem." Opinion, *New York Times*, January 24. https://www.nytimes.com/2018/01/24/opinion/poverty-united-states.html

Deaton, Angus, and Nancy Cartwright. 2018. "Understanding and Misunderstanding Randomized Controlled Trials." *Social Science & Medicine* 210: 2–21.

Deininger, Klaus, Daniel Ayalew Ali, Stein Holden, and Jaap Zevenbergen. 2008. "Rural Land Certification in Ethiopia: Process, Initial Impact, and Implications for Other African Countries." *World Development* 36 (10): 1786–812.

Deininger, Klaus, and Hans Binswanger. 1999. "The Evolution of the World Bank's Land Policy: Principles, Experience, and Future Challenges." *World Bank Research Observer* 14 (2): 247–76.

Deininger, Klaus, and Derek Byerlee, with Jonathan Lindsay, Andrew Norton, Harris Selod, and Mercedes Stickler. 2011. "Rising Global Interest in Farmland: Can It Yield Sustainable and Equitable Benefits?" Agriculture and Rural Development (ARD), World Bank, Washington, DC. https://siteresources.worldbank.org/DEC/Resources/Rising-Global-Interest-in-Farmland.pdf

Deininger, Klaus, and Gershon Feder. 2009. "Land Registration, Governance, and Development: Evidence and Implications for Policy." *World Bank Research Observer* 24 (2): 233–66.

Deininger, Klaus, and Fang Xia. 2018. "Assessing the Long-term Performance of Large-scale Land Transfers: Challenges and Opportunities in Malawi's Estate Sector." *World Development* 104: 281–96.

Demuth, Richard H. 1961. Transcript of Oral History Interview Held on August 10. Conducted by Robert Oliver, World Bank Group Archives Oral History website. http://documents.worldbank.org/curated/en/623541468147539954/pdf/789850TRN0Demu0view0August010001961.pdf

Devarajan, Shantayanan, Lyn Squire, and Sethaput Suthiwart-Narueput. 1997. "Beyond the Rate of Return: Reorienting Project Appraisal." *World Bank Research Observer* 12 (1): 35–46.

Devex. 2019. "World Bank Meetings." https://www.devex.com/focus/world-bank

Dutta, Puja, Rinku Murgai, Martin Ravallion, and Dominique van de Walle. 2012. "Does India's Employment Guarantee Scheme Guarantee Employment?" Policy Research Working Paper No. 6003, World Bank, Washington, DC. http://documents.worldbank.org/curated/en/464991468051015810/Does-Indias-employment-guarantee-scheme-guarantee-employment

Dutta, Puja, Rinku Murgai, Martin Ravallion, and Domnique van de Walle. 2014. *Right to Work? Assessing India's Employment Guarantee Scheme in Bihar.* Equity and Development Series. Washington, DC: World Bank. https://documents.worldbank.org/en/publication/documents-reports/documentdetail/104331468266411269/right-to-work-assessing-indias-employment-guarantee-scheme-in-bihar

Economic Times. 2014. "Rather than Dollars, We Need Ideas, Knowledge: Narendra Modi to World Bank Chief Jim Yong Kim." *India Times*, July 23. http://economictimes.indiatimes.com/news/politics-and-nation/rather-than-dollars-we-need-ideas-knowledge-narendra-modi-to-world-bank-chief-jim-yong-kim/articleshow/38936984.cms

Economist, The. 2019. "America Wants the World Bank to Stop Making Loans to China." Finance and Economics, December 12. https://www.economist.com/finance-and-economics/2019/12/12/america-wants-the-world-bank-to-stop-making-loans-to-china

Edwards, Sophie. 2019. "In Decentralization Push, World Bank to Relocate Hundreds of DC Staffers." Devex, October 25. https://www.devex.com/news/in-decentralization-push-world-bank-to-relocate-hundreds-of-dc-staffers-95875

Elborgh-Woytek, Katrin, Monique Newiak, Kalpana Kochhar, Stefania Fabrizio, Kangni Kpodar, Philippe Wingender, Benedict Clements, and Gerd Schwartz. 2013. "Women, Work, and the Economy: Macroeconomic Gains from Gender Equity." IMF Staff Discussion Note, September, International Monetary Fund, Strategy, Policy, and Review Department and Fiscal Affairs Department, Washington, DC.

Fajnzylber, Pablo, and J. Humberto López. 2007. "Close to Home: The Development Impact of Remittances in Latin America." World Bank, Washington, DC. http://documents.worldbank.org/curated/en/869061468266372115/pdf/489110WP0Close1Biox338933B01PUBLIC1.pdf

FAO (Food and Agriculture Organization of the United Nations). 2012. "Voluntary Guidelines on the Responsible Governance of Tenure of Land, Fisheries and Forests in the Context of National Food Security." FAO, Rome. http://www.fao.org/docrep/016/i2801e/i2801e.pdf

Fardoust, Shahrokh, and A. Elizabeth Flanagan. 2011. "Quality of Knowledge and Quality of Financial Assistance: A Quantitative Assessment in the Case of the World Bank." World Bank, Washington, DC.

Feder, Gershon. 1982. "Adoption of Interrelated Agricultural Innovations: Complementarity and the Impacts of Risk, Scale, and Credit." *American Journal of Agricultural. Economics* 64 (1): 94–101.

GAFSP (Global Agriculture and Food Security Program). 2018. Ending Poverty and Hunger. https://www.gafspfund.org

Gautam, Madhur. 2000. "Agricultural Extension: The Kenya Experience." OED Précis No. 198. World Bank, Washington, DC. http://documents.worldbank.org/curated/en/972111468758711518/pdf/multi0page.pdf

Gautam, Madhur, and Jock R. Anderson 1999. "Reconsidering the Evidence on the Returns to T&V Extension in Kenya." Operations Evaluations Department, World Bank, Washington, DC.

Gil Díaz, Francisco. 1991. "Mexico's Experience with Foreign Aid." In *Transitions in Development: The Role of Aid and Commercial Flows*, edited by Uma Lele and Ijaz Nabi, 225–64. San Francisco: ICS Press.

Gill, Indermit S., and Kenan Karakülah. 2018. "Has Africa Missed the Bus? The Condescending Consensus on the Continent's Growth." Duke Center for International Development, Durham, NC. https://www.brookings.edu/wp-content/uploads/2018/06/Africa-Growth-Paper_Gill-and-Karakulah_June-15.pdf

Girishankar, Navin. 2001. "Evaluating Public Sector Reform: Guidelines for Assessing Country-Level Impact of Structural Reform and Capacity Building in the Public Sector." Operations Evaluation Report (OED), World Bank, Washington, DC. http://documents.worldbank.org/curated/en/104421468780318696/pdf/11370279340PublicSect.pdf

Goldblatt, Ran, Klaus Deininger, and Gordon Hanson. 2018. "Utilizing Publicly Available Satellite Data for Urban Research: Mapping Built-Up Land Cover and Land Use in Ho Chi Minh City, Vietnam." *Development Engineering* 3: 83–99.

Gulati, Ashok, and Shenggen Fan, eds. 2007. *The Dragon and the Elephant: Agricultural and Rural Reforms in China and India*. Baltimore: Johns Hopkins University Press for the International Food Policy Research Institute.

Gulati, Ashok, Marco Ferroni, and Yuan Zhou. 2018. *Supporting Indian Farms the Smart Way*. New Delhi: Academic Foundation.

Gulati, Ashok, and Shweta Saini. 2016. "From Plate to Plough: Raising Farmers' Income by 2022." *Indian Express*, March 28. https://indianexpress.com/article/opinion/columns/from-plate-to-plough-raising-farmers-income-by-2022-agriculture-narendra-modi-pradhan-mantri-fasal-bima-yojana/

Gupta, Rajat, Shirish Sankhe, Richard Dobbs, Jonathan Woetzel, Anu Madgavkar, and Ashwin Hasyagar. 2014. "From Poverty to Empowerment: India's Imperative for Jobs, Growth, and Effective Basic Services." Report, February, McKinsey Global Institute, McKinsey & Company. http://www.mckinsey.com/global-themes/asia-pacific/indias-path-from-poverty-to-empowerment

Gwatkin, Davidson R., Adam Wagstaff, and Abdo S. Yazbeck. 2005. *Reaching the Poor with Health, Nutrition, and Population Services: What Works, What Doesn't, and Why*. Washington, DC: World Bank. https://openknowledge.worldbank.org/handle/10986/7393?locale-attribute=en

Hanna, Nagy. 2000. "Implementation Challenges and Promising Approaches for the Comprehensive Development Framework." Operations Evaluation Department (OED) Working Paper No. 13. World Bank, Washington, DC. http://documents.worldbank.org/curated/en/294911468761428989/pdf/multi0page.pdf

Hazelwood, Arthur. 1991. "Foreign Aid and Economic Development in Kenya." In *Transitions in Development: The Role of Aid and Commercial Flows*, edited by Uma Lele and Ijaz Nabi, 125–50. San Francisco: ICS Press.

Heath, John Richard. 2019. "'Possibilist' Ventures in Land Reform: Albert Hirschman, the World Bank and a Colombian Lost Cause." Presented at the Third Albert Hirschman Conference, Berlin, October.

Herdt, Robert W. 2012. "People, Institutions, and Technology: A Personal View of the Role of Foundations in International Agricultural Research 1960–2010." *Food Policy* 37 (2): 179–90.

Hirschman, Albert O. 1970. *Exit, Voice, and Loyalty: Responses to Decline in Firms, Organizations, and States*. Cambridge, MA: Harvard University Press.

Huang, Jikun. 2014. "China's Grain Policy and the World." Presentation at the Borlaug Summit on Wheat for Food Security, Ciudad Obregón, Mexico, March 25–8.

Huang, Jikun, and Guolei Yang. 2017. "Understanding Recent Challenges and New Food Policy in China." *Global Food Security* 12: 119–26.

Huang, Yukon. 2017. *Cracking the China Conundrum: Why Conventional Economic Wisdom Is Wrong*. New York: Oxford University Press.

IDA (International Development Association). 2018. "IDA 18 Mid-Term Review: Implementation and Results Progress Report—Towards 2030: Investing in Growth, Resilience and Opportunity." October 24, IDA, World Bank Group, Washington, DC. http://documents.worldbank.org/curated/en/462921542812670940/pdf/ida18-mtr-implementation-and-results-progress-report-10252018–636762749999422339.pdf

IDA (International Development Association). 2020. "What is the IDA?" IDA, World Bank Group, Washington, DC. http://ida.worldbank.org/about/what-is-ida

IEG (Independent Evaluation Group). 1992. "Adjustment Lending: Lessons from a Decade of Experience (SAL/SECAL Overview)." No. 32, June 1, World Bank, Washington, DC.

IEG (Independent Evaluation Group). 2004. "Rwanda: Country Assistance Evaluation." Report No. 27568-RW, January 5, World Bank, Washington, DC. http://documents.worldbank.org/curated/en/239451468759916593/pdf/275680RW.pdf

IEG (Independent Evaluation Group). 2005. "China: An Evaluation of World Bank Assistance." World Bank, Washington, DC. http://documents.worldbank.org/curated/en/983471468025155179/pdf/32332.pdf

IEG (Independent Evaluation Group). 2006. "Indonesia: Country Assistance Evaluation." Approach Paper, World Bank, Washington, DC. http://documents.worldbank.org/curated/en/630791468039060742/pdf/822380IEGAppro00Box382092B00PUBLIC0.pdf

IEG (Independent Evaluation Group). 2007. "World Bank Assistance to Agriculture in Sub-Saharan Africa: An IEG Review." World Bank, Washington, DC. https://openknowledge.worldbank.org/handle/10986/6907

IEG (Independent Evaluation Group). 2008. "Public Sector Reform: What Works and Why?" An IEG Evaluation of World Bank Support, World Bank, Washington, DC. http://siteresources.worldbank.org/EXTPUBSECREF/Resources/psr_eval.pdf

IEG (Independent Evaluation Group). 2010. "An Evaluation of Bank Support, 2002–08: Gender and Development." World Bank, Washington, DC. http://documents.worldbank.org/curated/en/197201468139492803/pdf/533190PUB0REPL10Box345607B01PUBLIC1.pdf

IEG (Independent Evaluation Group). 2011a. "Assessing IFC's Poverty Focus and Results." World Bank, Washington, DC. http://ieg.worldbankgroup.org/evaluations/assessing-international-finance-corporations-ifc-poverty-focus-and-results

IEG (Independent Evaluation Group). 2011b. "Growth and Productivity in Agriculture and Agribusiness. Evaluative Lessons from World Bank Group Experience." World Bank, Washington, DC. http://siteresources.worldbank.org/EXTGPAA/Resources/Agribusiness_eval.pdf

IEG (Independent Evaluation Group). 2011c. "Trust Fund Support for Development: An Evaluation of the World Bank's Trust Fund Portfolio." IEG, World Bank Group, Washington, DC. https://ieg.worldbankgroup.org/evaluations/trust-fund-support-development

IEG (Independent Evaluation Group). 2012. "World Bank Group Impact Evaluations: Relevance and Effectiveness." June, World Bank Group, Washington, DC. https://openknowledge.worldbank.org/handle/10986/13100

IEG (Independent Evaluation Group). 2013a. "Knowledge-Based Country Programs: An Evaluation of the World Bank Group Experience." World Bank, Washington, DC. http://documents.worldbank.org/curated/en/201041468152102121/pdf/812570WP0v10Kn00Box379835B00PUBLIC0.pdf

IEG (Independent Evaluation Group). 2013b. "The World Bank Group and the Global Food Crisis: An Evaluation of the World Bank Group Response." IEG, World Bank Group, Washington, DC. http://documents.worldbank.org/curated/en/543311468323944900/The-World-Bank-Group-and-the-global-food-crisis-an-evaluation-of-the-World-Bank-Group-response

IEG (Independent Evaluation Group). 2014a. "Appendix B. Guide to IEG's Country Program Evaluation Methodology." In Brazil Country Program Evaluation, *FY04–11: Evaluation of the World Bank Group Program*, 101–5. Washington, DC: World Bank.

IEG (Independent Evaluation Group). 2014b. "Guidelines for Reviewing World Bank Implementation Completion and Results Reports: A Manual for Evaluations." Last updated

August 1, 2014 (a living document under ongoing revision). IEG, World Bank Group, Washington, DC. http://ieg.worldbankgroup.org/sites/default/files/Data/ICRR_EvaluatorManual August2014.pdf

IEG (Independent Evaluation Group). 2015a. "Project Performance Assessment Report—Brazil." Report No. 92270-BR, IEG, World Bank, Washington, DC.

IEG (Independent Evaluation Group). 2015b. "Project Performance Assessment Report—India: Ten Million Women and Counting: An Assessment of World Bank Support for Rural Livelihood Development in Andhra Pradesh, India." Report No. 95274, March 30, IEG, World Bank, Washington, DC. http://documents.worldbank.org/curated/en/107971468033309842/pdf/ 952740PPAR0P04020Box385455B00OUO090.pdf

IEG (Independent Evaluation Group). 2016a. "Behind the Mirror: A Report on the Self-Evaluation Systems of the World Bank Group." World Bank, Washington, DC. https://ieg.worldbankgroup. org/evaluations/roses

IEG (Independent Evaluation Group). 2016b. "Knowledge-Based Country Programs. An Evaluation of World Bank Group Experience." World Bank, Washington, DC. http://documents.worldbank. org/curated/en/436361469075535538/pdf/107156-PUB-PUBLIC-PUBDATE-11–16.pdf

IEG (Independent Evaluation Group). 2016c. "World Bank Group Engagement in Situations of Fragility, Conflict, and Violence." World Bank, Washington, DC. https://ieg.worldbankgroup.org/ evaluations/fragility-conflict-violence

IEG (Independent Evaluation Group). 2019. "Knowledge Flow and Collaboration under the World Bank's New Operating Model." An Independent Evaluation, April 8, World Bank Group, Washington, DC. https://ieg.worldbankgroup.org/sites/default/files/Data/reports/kfc.pdf

IFC (International Finance Corporation). 2019. "Creating Impact: The Promise of Impact Investing." April, World Bank Group, Washington, DC. https://www.ifc.org/wps/wcm/connect/66e30dce-0cdd-4490-93e4-d5f895c5e3fc/The-Promise-of-Impact-Investing.pdf?MOD=AJPERES&CVID= mHZTSds

IMF (International Monetary Fund). 2019a. "Brazil: 2019 Article IV Consultation-Press Release; Staff Report; and Statement by the Executive Director for Brazil." IMF Country Reports 19/242, July, IMF, Washington, DC.

IMF (International Monetary Fund). 2019b. "Regional Economic Outlook. Sub-Saharan Africa: Recovery Amid Elevated Uncertainty." April, IMF, Washington, DC. https://www.imf.org/en/ Publications/REO/SSA/Issues/2019/04/01/sreo0419

India Today. 2020. "Rs 40,000 Crore Increase in Allocation for MGNREGA to Provide Employment Boost: Nirmala Sitharaman." New Delhi, May 17. https://www.indiatoday.in/business/story/ increase-mgnrega-provide-employment-boost-finance-minister-nirmala-sitharaman-coronavirus-economic-package-5th-tranche-1678920-2020-05-17

Jayarajah, Carl, William Branson, and Binayak Sen. 1996. "Social Dimensions of Adjustment: World Bank Experience, 1980–93." A World Bank Operations Evaluation Study, World Bank, Washington, DC. http://documents.worldbank.org/curated/en/788671468765930053/pdf/multi-page.pdf

Jayne, Thomas S., Jordan Chamberlin, and Rui Benfica. 2018. "Africa's Unfolding Economic Transformation" *Journal of Development Studies* 54 (5). https://doi.org/10.1080/00220388.2018.1430774

Jayne, Thomas S., and Shahidur Rashid. 2013. "Input Subsidy Programs in sub-Saharan Africa: A Synthesis of Recent Evidence." *Agricultural Economics* 44 (6): 547–62.

Kanbur, Ravi. 2005. "The Development of Development Thinking." Lecture delivered at the Institute for Social and Economic Change, Bangalore, June 10, 2004. http://services.iriskf.org/data/articles/ Document13082005400.6939966.pdf

Kanbur, Ravi, and Andy Sumner. 2012. "Poor Countries or Poor People? Development Assistance and the New Geography of Global Poverty." *Journal of International Development* 24 (6): 686–95.

Kapur, Devish, John P. Lewis, and Richard Webb, eds. 1997. *The World Bank: Its First Half Century*, Vol. 1: *History* and Vol. 2: *Perspectives*. Washington, DC: Brookings Institution Press.

Katzenstein, Bill. 2011. "Gauging World Bank Productivity Over the Long Term." Special Historical Supplement to *The 1818 Society Bulletin* 3 (5): 18–23.

Kharas, Homi. 2020. "International Financing of the Sustainable Development Goals." Unpublished paper, Brookings Institution, Washington, DC.

Kharas, Homi, John McArthur, and Krista Rasmussen. 2018. "How Many People Will the World Leave Behind?" Report, September 14, Brookings Institution, Washington, DC. https://www.brookings.edu/research/how-many-people-will-the-world-leave-behind/

Kharas, Homi J., and Hisanobu Shishido. 1991. "The Transition from Aid to Private Capital Flows." In *Transitions in Development: The Role of Aid and Commercial Flows*, edited by Uma Lele and Ijaz Nabi, 401–28. San Francisco: ICS Press.

Kotwal, Ashok, and Pronab Sen. 2019. "What Should We Do about the Indian Economy? A Wide-Angled Perspective." *India Forum*, October 4. https://www.theindiaforum.in/article/what-should-we-do-about-indian-economy

Kraske, Jochen. 1996. *Bankers with a Mission: The Presidents of the World Bank, 1946–91.* Washington, DC: Oxford University Press.

Krueger, Anne O. 2010. Transcript of Oral History Interview, January 29, 2010. Conducted by Marie T. Zenni, World Bank Group Archives Oral History website. https://oralhistory.worldbank.org/transcripts/transcript-oral-history-interview-anne-o-krueger-held-january-29-2010

Krueger, Anne O., Maurice Schiff, and Alberto Valdés. 1988. "Agricultural Incentives in Developing Countries." *World Bank Economic Review* 2 (3): 255–72.

Krueger, Anne O., Maurice Schiff, and Alberto Valdés. 1991. *The Political Economy of Agricultural Pricing Policy*, Vol. 1: *Latin America*; Vol. 2: *Asia*; and Vol. 3: *Africa and the Mediterranean*. Baltimore, MD: Johns Hopkins University Press, for the World Bank.

Kumar, Raj. 2020. "Exclusive: With Lending to Africa Up, Malpass Splits World Bank Africa Department in Two." Devex, February 5. https://www.devex.com/news/exclusive-with-lending-to-africa-up-malpass-splits-world-bank-africa-department-in-two-96515

Lancaster, Carole. 1997. "The World Bank in Africa since 1980: The Politics of Structural Adjustment Lending." In *The World Bank: Its First Half Century*, Vol. 2: *Perspectives*, edited by Devesh Kapur, John P. Lewis, and Richard Webb, 161–94. Washington, DC: Brookings Institution Press. http://documents.worldbank.org/curated/en/405561468331913038/pdf/578750PUB0v20W10Box353775B01PUBLIC1.pdf

Lele, Uma. 1975. *The Design of Rural Development: Lessons from Africa*. Baltimore, MD: Johns Hopkins University Press for the World Bank.

Lele, Uma. 1989. "Managing Agricultural Development in Africa: Three Articles on Lessons from Experience." Managing Agricultural Development in Africa (MADIA) Discussion Paper No. 2, World Bank, Washington, DC. Presented at a symposium at the World Bank conference on "Agricultural Development Policies and the Economics of Rural Organization," Annapolis, MD, June 13–16. http://documents.worldbank.org/curated/en/546901468767433513/pdf/multi-page.pdf

Lele, Uma, ed. 1992. *Aid to African Agriculture: Lessons from Two Decades of Donors' Experience.* Baltimore: Johns Hopkins University Press for the World Bank.

Lele, Uma, and Manmohan Agarwal. 1991. "Four Decades of Economic Development in India and the Role of External Assistance." In *Transitions in Development: The Role of Aid and Commercial Flows*, edited by Uma Lele and Ijaz Nabi, 17–42. International Center for Economic Growth. San Francisco: ICS Press.

Lele, Uma, Manmohan Agarwal, and Sambuddha Goswami. 2018. *Patterns of Structural Transformation and Agricultural Productivity Growth (with Special Focus on Brazil, China, Indonesia and India).* Pune, India: Gokhale Institute of Politics and Economics.

Lele, Uma, Manmohan Agarwal, Peter Timmer, and Sambuddha Goswami. 2011. "Patterns of Structural Transformation and Agricultural Productivity Growth with Special Focus on Brazil,

China, Indonesia and India." Paper prepared for "Policy Options and Investment priorities for Accelerating Agricultural Productivity Growth" organized jointly by Indira Gandhi Institute of Development Research (IGIDR) and Institute for Human Development (IHD) and supported by the Planning Commission (India), the Food and Agriculture Organization of the United Nations (FAO) and the World Bank, New Delhi, November 9–11.

Lele, Uma, and Balu Bumb. 1994. *South Asia's Food Crisis: The Case of India*. Washington, DC: Banco Mundial.

Lele, Uma, and Arthur A. Goldsmith. 1989. "The Development of National Agricultural Research Capacity: India's Experience with the Rockefeller Foundation and Its Significance for Africa." *Economic Development and Cultural Change* 37 (2): 305–43.

Lele, Uma, Sambuddha Goswami, and Gianluigi Nico. 2017. "Structural Transformation and the Transition from Concessional Assistance to Commercial Flows: The Past and Possible Future Contributions of the World Bank." In *Agriculture and Rural Development in a Globalizing World: Challenges and Opportunities*, edited by Prabhu Pingali and Gershon Feder, 325–52. London and New York: Routledge.

Lele, Uma, Maggie Klousia-Marquis, and Sambuddha Goswami. 2013. "Good Governance for Food, Water, and Energy Security." *Aquatic Procedia* 1: 44–63. http://diamondh.co/Shape5/images/PDF/good_governance_for_food_water.pdf

Lele, Uma, and L. Richard Meyers. 1989. "Growth and Structure Change in East Africa: Domestic Policies, Agricultural Performance, and World Bank Assistance, 1963–86, Parts 1 and II." Managing Agricultural Development in Africa (MADIA) Discussion Paper No. 3, World Bank, Washington, DC.

Lele, Uma, and Ijaz Nabi. 1991. *Transitions in Development: The Role of Aid and Commercial Flows*. San Francisco: ICS Press.

Linn, Johannes F. 2009. "The Zedillo Commission Report on World Bank Reform: A Stepping Stone for the G-20 Summits in 2010." Brookings Institution, Washington, DC, November 18. https://www.brookings.edu/articles/the-zedillo-commission-report-on-world-bank-reform-a-stepping-stone-for-the-g-20-summits-in-2010/

Little, Ian M. D., and James A. Mirrlees. 1991. "Project Appraisal and Planning Twenty Years On." In *Proceedings of the World Bank Annual Conference on Development Economics 1990*, 351–95. Washington, DC: World Bank.

Mansuri, Ghazala, and Vijayendra Rao. 2013. "Localizing Development: Does Participation Work?" Policy Research Report 73762, World Bank, Washington, DC. http://documents.worldbank.org/curated/en/461701468150309553/pdf/NonAsciiFileName0.pdf

Martorano, Bruno, Giovanni Andrea Cornia, and Frances Stewart. 2014. "Human Development and Fiscal Policy: Comparing the Crises of 1982–85 and 2008–11." In *Towards Human Development: New Approaches to Macroeconomics and Inequality*, edited by Giovanni Andrea Cornia and Frances Stewart, 221–44. Oxford: Oxford University Press.

Mason, Edward S., and Robert E. Asher. 1973. *The World Bank Since Bretton Woods: The Origins, Policies, Operations, and Impact of the International Bank for Reconstruction and Development and the Other Members of the World Bank Group*. Washington, DC: The Brookings Institution.

McCully, Patrick. 1997. "A Critique of 'The World Bank's Experience with Large Dams: A Preliminary Review of Impacts.'" International Rivers, April 11. https://www.internationalrivers.org/resources/a-critique-of-the-world-bank's-experience-with-large-dams-a-preliminary-review-of-impacts

McEuen, Caroline, ed. 2003. "Toward Country-led Development: A Multi-partner Evaluation of the CDF." Operations Evaluation Department (OED), Précis no. 233. World Bank, Washington, DC. http://documents.worldbank.org/curated/en/898741468176050536/pdf/276520Precis2330English.pdf

McNamara, Robert S. 1973. "The Nairobi Speech: Address to the Board of Governors," World Bank Group, Nairobi, September 24. http://www.juerg-buergi.ch/Archiv/EntwicklungspolitikA/EntwicklungspolitikA/assets/McNamara_Nairobi_speech.pdf

Meerman, Jacob. 1997. "Reforming Agriculture: The World Bank Goes to Market." Operations Evaluation Department Study, World Bank, Washington, DC. http://documents.worldbank.org/curated/en/290141468766478117/pdf/multi-page.pdf

Meltzer, Allan H. 2000. "The Report of the International Financial Institution Advisory Commission: Comments on the Crisis." Research Showcase at CMU, Tepper School of Business, Carnegie Mellon University, Pittsburgh, PA.

Menon, Purnima, Rasmi Avula, Shinjini Pandey, Samuel Scott, and Alok Kumar. 2019. "Rethinking Effective Nutrition Convergence: An Analysis of Intervention Co-Convergence Data." *Economic and Political Weekly* 54 (24): 18–21.

MIGA (Multilateral Investment Guarantee Agency). 2015. "MIGA: Cultivating Agribusiness Growth." Agribusiness MIGABRIEF, July, World Bank Group, Washington, DC. https://www.miga.org/sites/default/files/2018–06/agribusinessbrief.pdf

Moreno-Dodson, Blanca, ed. 2005. *Reducing Poverty on a Global Scale: Learning and Innovating for Development. Findings from the Shanghai Global Learning Initiative.* Washington, DC: World Bank.

Mosley, Paul, Jane Harrigan, and F. J. Toye. 1991. *Aid and Power: The World Bank and Policy-based Lending*, Vol. 1. London: Routledge.

Mukherjee, Sanjeeb. 2020. "Over 55 Million Households Demand Work under MGNREGA This Year So Far." *Business Standard*, July 15. https://www.business-standard.com/article/economy-policy/over-55-million-households-demand-work-under-mgnrega-this-year-so-far-120071400372_1.html

Muyanga, Milu, and Thomas S. Jayne. 2019. "Revisiting the Farm Size–Productivity Relationship Based on a Relatively Wide Range of Farm Sizes: Evidence from Kenya." *American Journal of Agricultural Economics* 101 (4): 1140–63.

Narayan, Deepa. 2000. *Voices of the Poor: Can Anyone Hear Us?* Oxford: Oxford University Press for the World Bank.

Narayan, Deepa, Lant Pritchett, and Soumya Kapoor. 2009. *Moving Out of Poverty: Success from the Bottom Up.* Washington, DC: World Bank. http://documents.worldbank.org/curated/en/653631468043174245/pdf/481040PUB0Movi101Official0use0only1.pdf

National Herald. 2020. "FM Nirmala Sitharaman's Announcement of Wage Increase for MNREGA Workers Misleading." March 23. https://www.nationalheraldindia.com/india/fm-nirmala-sitharamans-announcement-of-wage-increase-for-mnrega-workers-misleading

OAU (Organization of African Unity). 1980. *Lagos Plan of Action for the Economic Development of Africa, 1980–2000.* Addis Ababa: OAU.

OED (Operations Evaluation Department). 1996. "Structural Adjustment in India." OED Précis, June, World Bank, Washington, DC. http://documents.worldbank.org/curated/en/923271468750298112/pdf/28681.pdf

OED (Operations Evaluation Department). 2000. "Rural Development. From Vision to Action? Phase II." Report No. 20628, June 22, Sector and Thematic Evaluation Group, Operations Evaluation Department, World Bank, Washington DC. http://documents.worldbank.org/curated/en/395421468052452228/pdf/multi-page.pdf

OED (Operations Evaluation Department). 2004a. "Addressing the Challenges of Globalization: An Independent Evaluation of the World Bank's Approach to Global Programs." World Bank, Washington, DC.

OED (Operations Evaluation Department). 2004b. "Country Assistance Evaluation: Brazil." March 16, World Bank, Washington, DC. http://documents.worldbank.org/curated/en/241981468770133499/pdf/29406.pdf

OED (Operations Evaluation Department). 2005a. "An Evaluation of the Effectiveness of World Bank Support for Community-Based and -Driven Development." World Bank, Washington, DC. http://documents.worldbank.org/curated/en/660951468152956553/pdf/347730Effectiv101OFFICIAL0USE0ONLY1.pdf

OED (Operations Evaluation Department). 2005b. "Putting Social Development to Work for the Poor: An OED Review of World Bank Activities." World Bank, Washington, DC. https://openknowledge.worldbank.org/bitstream/handle/10986/7374/344270PAPER0So101Official0use0only1.pdf

Pearson, Lester Bowles, ed. 1969. *Partners in Development: Report of the Commission on International Development.* New York: Praeger.

Please, Stanley. 1986. Transcript of Oral History Interview on August 26. Conducted by Charles Ziegler, World Bank Group Archives Oral History website. http://documents.worldbank.org/curated/en/751941468149396355/pdf/790940TRN0Plea0view0August026001986.pdf

Please, Stanley, and K. Y. Amoako. 1984. "The World Bank's Report on Accelerated Development in Sub-Saharan Africa: A Critique of Some of the Criticism." *African Studies Review* 27 (4): 47–58.

Poulton, Colin, Geoff Tyler, Peter Hazell, Andrew Dorward, Jonathan Kydd, and Mike Stockbridge. 2008. "All-Africa Review of Experiences with Commercial Agriculture: Lessons from Success and Failure." Background paper for the Competitive Commercial Agriculture in Sub-Saharan Africa (CCAA) Study, Centre for Environmental Policy, Imperial College, London for the World Bank.

Pray, Carl E. and Keith Fuglie. 2015. "Agricultural Research by the Private Sector." *Annual Review of Resource Economics* 7 (1): 399–424.

Pray, Carl E., and Latha Nagarajan. 2012. "Innovation and Research by Private Agribusiness in India." IFPRI Discussion Paper 01181, May, Environment and Production Technology Division, International Food Policy Research Institute, Washington, DC.

Pray, Carl E., and Latha Nagarajan. 2014. "The Transformation of the Indian Agricultural Input Industry: Has It Increased Agricultural R&D?" Agricultural *Economics* 45 (S1): 145–56.

Radelet, Steven. 2016. "Africa's Rise—Interrupted?" *Finance & Development* 53 (2): 6–11.

Raju, S. S., and Ramesh Chand. 2007. "Progress and Problems in Agricultural Insurance." *Economic and Political Weekly* 42 (21): 1905–8.

Rashid, Shahidur, Nigussie Tefera, Nicholas Minot, and Gezahegn Ayele. 2013. "Can Modern Input Use Be Promoted Without Subsidies? An Analysis of Fertilizer in Ethiopia." *Agricultural Economics* 44 (6): 595–611.

Ravallion, Martin. 2009. "How Relevant is Targeting to the Success of an Antipoverty Program?" *World Bank Research Observer* 24 (2): 205–31.

Ravallion, Martin. 2012. "Fighting Poverty One Experiment at a Time: Poor Economics: A Radical Rethinking of the Way to Fight Global Poverty." Review Essay. *Journal of Economic Literature* 50 (1): 103–14.

Ravallion, Martin. 2018. "Should the Randomistas (Continue to) Rule?" Working Paper No. 492, August, Center for Global Development, Washington, DC. https://www.cgdev.org/sites/default/files/should-randomistas-continue-rule.pdf

Reardon, Thomas, Bart Minten, Kevin Z. Chen, and Lourdes Adriano. 2013. "The Transformation of Rice Value Chains in Bangladesh and India: Implications for Food Security." ADB Economics Working Paper No. 375, Asian Development Bank, Manila. https://www.econstor.eu/bitstream/10419/109491/1/ewp-375.pdf

Renkow, Mitch, and Roger Slade. 2013. "An Assessment of IFPRI's Work in Ethiopia 1995–2010: Ideology, Influence, and Idiosyncrasy." Independent Impact Assessment Report No. 36, International Food Policy Research Institute, Washington, DC.

Rodrik, Dani. 2006. "Goodbye Washington Consensus. Hello Washington Confusion? A Review of the World Bank's 'Economic Growth in the 1990s: Learning from a Decade of Reform.'" *Journal of Economic Literature* 44 (4): 973–87.

Rozelle, Scott, and Johan F. M. Swinnen. 2004. "Success and Failure of Reform: Insights from the Transition of Agriculture." *Journal of Economic Literature* 42 (2): 404–56.

Sahu, Prasanta. 2018. "Crop Insurance Scheme: Still Too Early to Judge, Let It Stabilise, Says NITI Aayog Member Ramesh Chand." *Financial Express*, New Delhi, July 14.

Serageldin, Ismail, and Pierre Landell-Mills, eds. 1994. *Overcoming Global Hunger*. Washington, DC: World Bank.

Sharma, Yogima. 2020. "Raising Guaranteed MGNREGS Days Are on the Cards." *Economic Times*, New Delhi, April 30. https://economictimes.indiatimes.com/news/economy/policy/raising-mgnregs-days-on-the-cards/articleshow/75479563.cms

Smith, Vincent H. 2017. "The US Federal Crop Insurance Program: A Case Study in Rent-Seeking." Mercatus Working Paper, Mercatus Center at George Mason University, Arlington, VA. https://www.mercatus.org/system/files/smith-farm-bill-wp-mercatus-v1.pdf

Spielman, David J., Deepthi E. Kolady, Anthony Cavalieri, and N. Chandrasekhara Rao. 2014. "The Seed and Agricultural Biotechnology Industries in India: An Analysis of Industry Structure, Competition, and Policy Options." *Food Policy* 45 (2014): 88–100.

Srinivasan, T. N. 1991. "Food Aid: A Cause or Symptom of Development Failure or an Instrument for Success." In *Transitions in Development: The Role of Aid and Commercial Flows*, edited by Uma Lele and Ijaz Nabi, 373–99. San Francisco: ICS Press.

Staatz, John M., and Niama Nango Dembélé. 2008. "Agriculture for Development in Sub-Saharan Africa." Background Paper for *World Development Report 2008*, World Bank, Washington, DC. https://openknowledge.worldbank.org/handle/10986/9043

Stern, Nicholas. 2006. Transcript of Oral History Interview with Nicholas H. Stern Held on April 5 and 16. Conducted by William Becker, World Bank Group Archives Oral History website. https://oralhistory.worldbank.org/transcripts/transcript-oral-history-interview-nicholas-h-stern-held-april-05-and-16-2005

Stern, Nicholas, and Francisco Ferreira. 1997. "The World Bank as 'Intellectual Actor'." In *The World Bank: Its First Half Century*, Vol. 2: *Perspectives*, edited by Devesh Kapur, John P. Lewis, and Richard Webb, 523–610. Washington, DC: Brookings Institution Press. http://documents.worldbank.org/curated/en/405561468331913038/pdf/578750PUB0v20W10Box353775B01PUBLIC1.pdf

Sud, Inder, and Jane Olmstead-Rumsey. 2012. "Development Outcomes of World Bank Projects: Real or Illusory Improvements?" IGIS Working Paper, Institute for Global and International Studies, George Washington University, Washington, DC.

Sy, Amadou, and Fenohasina Maret Rakotondrazaka. 2015. "Private Capital Flows: Official Development Assistance, and Remittances to Africa: Who Gets What?" Policy Paper 2015–02, Global Economy and Development, Brookings Institution, Washington, DC. https://www.brookings.edu/research/private-capital-flows-official-development-assistance-and-remittances-to-africa-who-gets-what/

Székely, Miguel. 2014. "Closing the Circle for Results-Based Management in Social Policy." The Nuts & Bolts of M&E Systems, No. 32, World Bank Group, Washington, DC. http://www.worldbank.org/content/dam/Worldbank/document/Poverty%20documents/Nuts-and-Bolts32-Closing-Circle-final.pdf

Torres, Carolina Dominguez. 2012. "The Future of Water in African Cities: Why Waste Water? Urban Access to Water Supply and Sanitation in Sub-Saharan Africa." Directions in Development, Environmental and Sustainable Development, World Bank, Washington, DC. https://openknowledge.worldbank.org/bitstream/handle/10986/12276/NonAsciiFileName0.pdf

Townsend, Robert F., Iride Ceccacci, Sanjiva Cooke, Mark Constantine, and Gene Moses. 2013. "Implementing Agriculture for Development: World Bank Group Agriculture Action Plan (2013–2015)." World Bank Group, Washington, DC. http://documents.worldbank.org/curated/en/331761468152719470/pdf/779110WP0Ag0Ac0than0the0Board0paper.pdf

ul-Haq, Mahbub. 1982. Transcript of Oral History Interview, December 3. Conducted by Robert Asher, World Bank Group Archives Oral History website. https://oralhistory.worldbank.org/transcripts/transcript-oral-history-interview-mahbub-ul-haq-held-december-3-1982

UN (United Nations). 2016. "World Population Prospects: Key Findings and Advance Tables." 2016 Revision. Department of Economic and Social Affairs, UN, New York.

UNDP (United Nations Development Programme), UNEP (United Nations Environment Programme), World Bank, and World Resources Institute. 2004. *World Resources 2002–2004: Decisions for the Earth: Balance, Voice, and Power.* Washington, DC: World Resources Institute.

UNECA (United Nations Economic Commission for Africa). 1989. *African Alternative Framework to Structural Adjustment Programmes for Socio-Economic Recovery and Transformation (AAF-SAP).* New York: UNECA. http://repository.uneca.org/pdfpreview/bitstream/handle/10855/5670/Bib-44783.pdf

von Braun, Joachim, and Ruth Meinzen-Dick. 2009. "'Land Grabbing' by Foreign Investors in Developing Countries: Risks and Opportunities." IFPRI Policy Brief 13, International Food Policy Research Institute, Washington, DC.

von Pischke, John. 1992. Transcript of Oral History Interview, January 29. Conducted by John Lewis and Devesh Kapur, World Bank Group Archives Oral History website. https://oralhistory.worldbank.org/transcripts/transcript-oral-history-interview-john-von-pischke-held-january-29-1992

Wapenhans, Willi A. 1993. Transcript of Oral History Interview. Second interview session, August 19. Conducted by William Becker and David Milobsky, World Bank Group Archives Oral History website. https://oralhistory.worldbank.org/oral_search?search_api_views_fulltext=will+wapenhans

WBG (World Bank Group). 2014a. "Learning from World Bank History: Agriculture and Food-Based Approaches for Addressing Malnutrition." Agriculture and Environmental Services Discussion Paper 10, World Bank Report No. 88740-GLB, June, World Bank, Washington, DC.

WBG (World Bank Group). 2014b. *World Bank Group Archivists' Chronology 1944–2014.* Washington, DC: World Bank. https://www.worldbank.org/en/about/archives/history/chronology

WBG (World Bank Group). 2015. *World Bank Group Gender Strategy (FY16–23): Gender Equality, Poverty Reduction and Inclusive Growth.* World Bank Group, Washington, DC. http://documents.worldbank.org/curated/en/820851467992505410/pdf/102114-REVISED-PUBLIC-WBG-Gender-Strategy.pdf

WBG (World Bank Group). 2017a. "Fact Sheet: The World Bank Group's Response to the Famine Crisis." November 28. https://www.worldbank.org/en/topic/fragilityconflictviolence/brief/fact-sheet-the-world-bank-groups-response-to-the-famine-crisis

WBG (World Bank Group). 2017b. *Forcibly Displaced: Toward a Development Approach Supporting Refugees, the Internally Displaced, and Their Hosts.* Washington, DC: International Bank for Reconstruction and Development, World Bank. https://openknowledge.worldbank.org/bitstream/handle/10986/25016/9781464809385.pdf

WBG (World Bank Group). 2018. *The State of Social Safety Nets 2018.* Washington, DC: World Bank. http://documents.worldbank.org/curated/en/427871521040513398/pdf/124300-PUB-PUBLIC.pdf

WBG (World Bank Group). 2019. World Bank Group Archives Oral History website. https://oralhistory.worldbank.org

Weiss, John. 2004. "Poverty Targeting in Asia: Experiences from India, Indonesia, the Philippines, People's Republic of China and Thailand." ADBI Institute Research Bank Institute, Tokyo. https://www.adb.org/sites/default/files/publication/157277/adbi-rpb9.pdf

WHO (World Health Organization) and World Bank. 2011. "World Report on Disability." WHO, Geneva. https://www.who.int/disabilities/world_report/2011/report.pdf

World Bank. 1965a. *Report to the President of the International Bank for Reconstruction and Development and the International Development Association on India's Economic Development Effort,* Vol. 1 (Main Report), 1964–65 Economic Mission headed by Bernard R. Bell, October 1. Washington, DC: World Bank.

World Bank. 1965b. *Report to the President of the International Bank for Reconstruction and Development and the International Development Association on India's Economic Development Effort,* Annex 3, 1964–65 Economic Mission headed by Bernard R. Bell, October 1. Washington, DC: World Bank.

World Bank. 1975a. "Land Reform." Sector Policy Paper, May, World Bank, Washington, DC. http://documents.worldbank.org/curated/en/911161468153545471/pdf/PUB4400PUB0Lan00Box-365739B00PUBLIC0.pdf

World Bank. 1975b. "Rural Development." Sector Policy Paper, February, World Bank, Washington, DC. http://documents.worldbank.org/curated/en/688121468168853933/Rural-development-sector-policy-paper

World Bank. 1977. "Tanzania Basic Economic Report." Report No. 1616-TA, East Africa Country Programs, World Bank, Washington, DC. http://documents.worldbank.org/curated/en/911211468341057583/pdf/multi-page.pdf

World Bank. 1980. "Brandt Commission Proposals of Relevance to the World Bank: A Progress Report." World Bank, Washington, DC. http://documents.worldbank.org/curated/en/768581468161104977/Brandt-commission-proposals-of-relevance-to-the-World-Bank-a-progress-report

World Bank. 1981. *Accelerated Development in Sub-Saharan Africa: An Agenda for Action*. African Strategy Review Group coordinated by Elliot Berg. Washington, DC: World Bank.

World Bank. 1982a. *IDA in Retrospect: The First Two Decades of the International Association*. New York: Oxford University Press for the World Bank. http://documents.worldbank.org/curated/en/547941468762296226/pdf/multi-page.pdf

World Bank. 1982b. *World Development Report 1982*. International Development Trends. Agriculture and Economic Development. World Development Indicators. Washington, DC: World Bank Group. http://documents.worldbank.org/curated/en/948041468152100530/pdf/108870REPLACEMENT0WDR01982.pdf

World Bank. 1983a. "Tanzania: Agricultural Sector Report." Report No. 4052-TA, August 19, Eastern Africa Projects Department, Southern Agriculture Division, World Bank, Washington, DC. http://documents.worldbank.org/curated/en/470811468116659028/Tanzania-Agricultural-sector-report

World Bank. 1983b. *World Development Report 1983: World Economic Recession and Prospects for Recovery*. Management in Development. World Development Indicators. Washington, DC: Work Bank. https://openknowledge.worldbank.org/handle/10986/5966

World Bank. 1986. *World Development Report 1986: Trade and Pricing Policies in World Agriculture*. Washington, DC: World Bank. https://openknowledge.worldbank.org/bitstream/handle/10986/5969/WDR%201986%20-%20English.pdf?

World Bank. 1987. "Education Policies for Sub-Saharan Africa: Adjustment, Revitalization, and Expansion." Report No. 6934, September 15, World Bank, Washington, DC. http://documents1.worldbank.org/curated/en/276651468193498631/pdf/multi-page.pdf

World Bank. 1988a. "Adjustment Lending: An Evaluation of Ten Years of Experience." Policy and Research Series No. 1, Country Economics Department, World Bank, Washington, DC. http://documents.worldbank.org/curated/en/604231468740963424/pdf/multi-page.pdf

World Bank. 1988b. *World Bank Experience with Rural Development: 1965–1986*. Washington, DC: World Bank Group. http://documents.worldbank.org/curated/en/265431542121876931/World-Bank-Experience-with-Rural-Development-1965–1986

World Bank. 1989. "Sub-Saharan Africa: From Crisis to Sustainable Growth." A Long-Term Perspective Study, World Bank, Washington, DC. http://documents1.worldbank.org/curated/en/498241468742846138/pdf/multi0page.pdf

World Bank. 1991. "The Forest Sector." A World Bank Policy Paper, Report No. 9965, World Bank, Washington, DC. http://documents.worldbank.org/curated/en/256211468139769817/pdf/multi0page.pdf

World Bank. 1990. *World Development Report: Poverty*. New York: Oxford University Press. https://openknowledge.worldbank.org/handle/10986/5973

World Bank. 1992. *Effective Implementation: Key to Development Impact*. (Wapenhans Report). Washington, DC: World Bank. http://documents.worldbank.org/curated/en/596521467145356248/pdf/multi0page.pdf

World Bank. 1993. "Portfolio Management: Next Steps—A Program of Actions." Memorandum to the Executive Directors, June 15, Operations Policy Department, World Bank, Washington, DC. http://documents.worldbank.org/curated/en/177411468178127024/pdf/multi-page.pdf

World Bank. 1994. *Governance: The World Bank's Experience*. Washington, DC: World Bank. http://documents1.worldbank.org/curated/en/711471468765285964/pdf/multi0page.pdf

World Bank. 1996. *World Development Report 1996: From Plan to Market*. New York: Oxford University Press. https://openknowledge.worldbank.org/handle/10986/5979

World Bank. 1997a. "Confronting AIDS: Public Priorities in a Global Epidemic." A World Bank Policy Research Report, World Bank, Washington, DC.

World Bank. 1997b. *Inequality in East Asia* and *India: Achievements and Challenges in Reducing Poverty*. Washington, DC: World Bank.

World Bank. 1997c. "Poverty Reduction and the World Bank. Progress and Challenges in the 1990s." January, World Bank, Washington, DC. http://documents1.worldbank.org/curated/en/703821468766779072/pdf/multi0page.pdf

World Bank. 1999. *Global Economic Prospects and the Developing Countries 1998–99*. Washington, DC: World Bank. https://openknowledge.worldbank.org/handle/10986/32393

World Bank. 2001. *World Development Report 2000/2001: Attacking Poverty*. New York: Oxford University Press, for the World Bank. http://documents.worldbank.org/curated/en/230351468332946759/pdf/226840WDR00PUB0ng0poverty0200002001.pdf

World Bank. 2002. "Integrating Gender into the World Bank's Work: A Strategy for Action." January, World Bank, Washington, DC. http://siteresources.worldbank.org/INTGENDER/Resources/strategypaper.pdf

World Bank. 2003a. "Brazil—Land Reform and Poverty Alleviation Pilot Project." World Bank, Washington, DC. http://documents.worldbank.org/curated/en/124361468744102792/Brazil-Land-Reform-and-Poverty-Alleviation-Pilot-Project

World Bank. 2003b. "Reaching the Rural Poor: A Renewed Strategy for Rural Development." World Bank, Washington, DC. https://openknowledge.worldbank.org/bitstream/handle/10986/14084/267630REACHING0THE0RURAL0POOR0.pdf

World Bank. 2005a. *Agriculture Investment Sourcebook*. Washington, DC: World Bank. http://documents.worldbank.org/curated/en/633761468328173582/pdf/343920PAPER0Agl01OFFICIAL0USE0ONLY1.pdf

World Bank. 2005b. *Economic Growth in the 1990s: Learning from a Decade of Growth*. Washington, DC: World Bank

World Bank. 2005c. "Managing Food Price Risks and Instability in an Environment of Market Liberalization." Agriculture and Rural Development Department, World Bank, Washington, DC. http://siteresources.worldbank.org/INTARD/Resources/ManagingFoodPriceRisks.pdf

World Bank. 2005d. "Needs of Poor Still Not Met at Trade Talks in Hong Kong." News Release No. 2006/206/PREM, Hong Kong, December 15.

World Bank. 2005e. *Where is the Wealth of Nations? Measuring Capital for the 21st Century*. Washington, DC: World Bank.

World Bank. 2006. "Reengaging in Agricultural Water Management: Challenges and Options." Directions in Development. Washington, DC: World Bank. https://openknowledge.worldbank.org/bitstream/handle/10986/6957/355200PAPER0Re1water01OFFICIAL0USE1.pdf

World Bank. 2007. *World Development Report 2008: Agriculture for Development*. Washington, DC: World Bank. https://openknowledge.worldbank.org/handle/10986/5990

World Bank. 2008. *Gender in Agriculture Sourcebook: Agriculture and Rural Development*. Washington, DC: World Bank. http://documents.worldbank.org/curated/en/799571468340869508/pdf/461620PUB0Box3101OFFICIAL0USE0ONLY1.pdf

World Bank. 2009. "Implementing Agriculture for Development: World Bank Group Agriculture Action Plan—FY 2010–2012." World Bank, Washington, DC. http://documents.worldbank.org/curated/en/800771468157515420/pdf/512130WP0Agric10Box342021B01PUBLIC1.pdf

World Bank. 2010. *World Development Report 2010: Development and Climate Change.* Washington, DC: World Bank. https://openknowledge.worldbank.org/handle/10986/4387

World Bank. 2011a. "National Dairy Support Project." Project Information Document (PID). Report No AB6495. World Bank, Washington, DC.

World Bank. 2011b. "The State of World Bank Knowledge Services: Knowledge for Development." World Bank, Washington DC. http://documents.worldbank.org/curated/en/353931468337483106/pdf/651950Revised0box361556B00PUBLIC005.pdf

World Bank. 2011c. *World Development Report 2011: Conflict, Security, and Development.* Washington, DC: World Bank.

World Bank. 2012. *World Development Report 2012: Gender Equality and Development.* Washington, DC: World Bank.

World Bank. 2013a. "Community-Driven Development: Results Profile." April 14, Projects & Operations, World Bank, Washington, DC. http://www.worldbank.org/en/results/2013/04/14/community-driven-development-results-profile

World Bank. 2013b. "Global Food Crisis Response Program," April 11, World Bank, Washington, DC. http://www.worldbank.org/en/results/2013/04/11/global-food-crisis-response-program-results-profile

World Bank. 2013c. "Implementing Agriculture for Development: World Bank Group Agriculture Action Plan (2013–2015)." World Bank, Washington, DC. http://documents.worldbank.org/curated/en/331761468152719470/pdf/779110WP0Ag0Ac0than0the0Board0paper.pdf

World Bank. 2013d. "Seeding Solutions for Agricultural Growth to End Poverty in Africa." World Bank News, Feature Story, April 24, World Bank, Washington, DC. http://www.worldbank.org/en/news/feature/2013/04/24/seeding-solutions-for-agricultural-growth-to-end-poverty-in-africa

World Bank. 2013e. "Unlocking Africa's Agricultural Potential: An Action Agenda for Transformation." Africa Region. Sustainable Development Series, World Bank, Washington, DC. https://openknowledge.worldbank.org/bitstream/handle/10986/16624/769900WP0SDS0A00Box374393B00PUBLIC0.pdf;sequence=1

World Bank. 2014. "Republic of India: Accelerating Agricultural Productivity Growth." May 21, World Bank Group, Washington, DC. http://documents.worldbank.org/curated/en/587471468035437545/pdf/880930REVISED00ivity0Growth00PUBLIC.pdf

World Bank. 2015. "TerrAfrica: Building the Resilience of Land and Livelihoods in a Changing Climate." Feature Story, December 1, World Bank, Washington, DC. https://www.worldbank.org/en/news/feature/2015/12/01/terrafrica-building-the-resilience-of-land-and-livelihoods-in-a-changing-climate

World Bank. 2016. "IFC: The First Six Decades: Leading the Way in Private Sector Development—A History." World Bank Group, Washington, DC. http://documents.worldbank.org/curated/en/668851478627391927/pdf/109806-WP-IFC-History-Book-Web-Version-OUO-9.pdf

World Bank. 2017. "IFC Annual Report 2016." World Bank Group, Washington, DC. http://documents.worldbank.org/curated/en/861141527851540865/pdf/126705-WBAR-v1-PUBLIC-IFC-AR16-Full-Volume-1.pdf

World Bank. 2018a. "Fact Sheet: The Indus Waters Treaty 1960 and the Role of the World Bank." Where We Work/South Asia. https://www.worldbank.org/en/region/sar/brief/fact-sheet-the-indus-waters-treaty-1960-and-the-world-bank

World Bank. 2018b. Heavily Indebted Poor Country (HIPC) Initiative. https://www.worldbank.org/en/topic/debt/brief/hipc

World Bank. 2019a. "National Dairy Support Project (P107648)." Implementation Status & Results Report. Revised Closing Date: November 29, 2019. World Bank, Washington, DC.

World Bank. 2019b. World Bank Group President David Malpass: Speech to the Plenary Session of the Annual Meetings of the Board of Governors, October 18. https://www.worldbank.org/en/news/speech/2019/10/18/world-bank-group-president-david-malpass-speech-to-the-plenary-session-of-the-annual-meetings-of-the-board-of-governors

World Bank. 2019c. World Bank Legacy Budget and Operations Record, FY1946–2019: Annual Update, History Thematic Group, World Bank, Washington, DC. Data provided by Bill Katzenstein on May 31.

World Bank. 2020a. *Global Economic Prospects: Slow Growth, Policy Challenges.* Washington, DC: World Bank. https://www.worldbank.org/en/publication/global-economic-prospects

World Bank. 2020b. "Overview." Fragility, Conflict and Violence. Understanding Poverty. World Bank. https://www.worldbank.org/en/topic/fragilityconflictviolence/overview

World Bank. 2020c. "Women, Business and the Law 2020." World Bank, Washington, DC. https://openknowledge.worldbank.org/bitstream/handle/10986/32639/9781464815324.pdf

World Bank. 2020d. *World Development Report 2020: Trading for Development in the Age of Global Value Chains.* Washington, DC: World Bank. https://www.worldbank.org/en/publication/wdr2020

World Bank and GFDRR (Global Facility for Disaster Reduction and Recovery). 2013. "Building Resilience: Integrating Climate and Disaster Risk into Development. Lessons from World Bank Group Experience." World Bank, Washington, DC. http://documents.worldbank.org/curated/en/762871468148506173/pdf/826480WP0v10Bu0130Box37986200 OUO090.pdf

World Commission on Dams. 2000. *Dams and Development: A New Framework for Decision-making.* The Report of the World Commission on Dams, November 20. London and Sterling, VA: Earthscan Publications Ltd. https://www.internationalrivers.org/sites/default/files/attached-files/world_commission_on_dams_final_report.pdf

WTO (World Trade Organization). 2020. "Trade Facilitation." Trade Topics. https://www.wto.org/english/tratop_e/tradfa_e/tradfa_e.htm

Xu, Jiajun. 2017. *Beyond US Hegemony in International Development: The Contest for Influence at the World Bank.* Cambridge, UK: Cambridge University Press.

Yagci, Fahrettin, Steven Kamin, and Vicki Rosenbaum. 1985. "Structural Adjustment Lending: An Evaluation of Program Design." World Bank Staff Working Paper 735, World Bank, Washington, DC. http://documents.worldbank.org/curated/en/213291468740376951/pdf/multi-page.pdf

Young, Mary Eming. 1996. "Early Child Development: Investing in the Future." World Bank, Washington, DC. https://inee.org/system/files/resources/ECD_investing_in_the_future.pdf

Yudelman, Montague. 1986. Transcript of Oral History Interview, July 18. Conducted by Robert Oliver, World Bank Group Archives Oral History website. http://documents.worldbank.org/curated/en/121111468340259318/pdf/860330TRANSCRI0LBox382163B00PUBLIC0.pdf

Yudelman, Montague. 1991. Transcript of Oral History Interview, September 12. Conducted by John Lewis and Devesh Kapur, World Bank Group Archives Oral History website. http://documents.worldbank.org/curated/en/743241468149085280/pdf/860350TRANSCRI00Box382163B00PUBLIC0.pdf

Zedillo, Ernesto, Chair. 2009. *Repowering the World Bank for the 21st Century.* Report of the High Level Commission on Modernization of World Bank Group Governance. Washington, DC: World Bank Group.

Zulauf, Carl, and David Orden. 2014. "US Agricultural Act of 2014: Reaffirming Countercyclical Support." Presentation at IFPRI Seminar, "21st Century Agricultural Policies: The 2013 EU CAP & US Farm Bill," Washington, DC, July 16

9

The Food and Agriculture Organization of the United Nations

Uma Lele and Sambuddha Goswami

Summary

The Food and Agriculture Organization of the United Nations (FAO) is the only international organization charged with comprehensive responsibility for all aspects of agriculture.[1] Hence, it has a critical role in addressing the emerging global challenges of food and
agriculture's impacts on the environment and on human health. Climate change and its
impacts on agriculture is one of the many environmental challenges. It also has a key role to
play in the rapidly transforming food systems and its impacts on human health. FAO's
"Save and Grow—A Policymaker's Guide to the Sustainable Intensification of Smallholder
Crop Production" described the challenge as: "To feed a growing world population,... to
grow, agriculture must learn to save" (FAO 2011c, vii). This implies farming systems that
provide a balance of "productivity, socio-economic and environmental benefits to producers and to society at large," while ensuring soil health and managing crop diversity and
plant protection to suit a variety of agroecosystems confronting climate change, requires
policies and institutions conducive to meet these challenges (FAO 2011c, vii). (See Box 9.1.)

What are FAO's specific roles and how well has it been performing them? How can it be
strengthened to meet the daunting challenges going forward, including those which will
emanate from the UN Food Summit in 2021? Can it become a global center of excellence to
help countries achieve the needed transformative changes in their agriculture, as they face
growing environmental and human health challenges? This story explores FAO's evolving
roles and reforms since the 2007 Independent External Evaluation (IEE), the FAO Director-
General (DG) José Graziano da Silva in 2019, and the initial year and a half of the new DG,
Qu Dongyu's tenure, in which FAO has made a substantial culture change. What it needs
now are resources to go with change to fulfill its considerable potential to make a difference
to the outcomes.

IEE was the first comprehensive independent external evaluation of any international
organization, on which Uma Lele served and was responsible for review of all of FAO's
technical work, and therefore, provides a useful baseline derived from her firsthand
evaluative experience. This period of a near decade and a half has witnessed a global food
crisis, the transition from Millennium Development Goals (MDGs) to Sustainable

---

[1] Uma Lele was a member of the Independent External Evaluation of FAO in 2006–7 and was responsible for
overseeing assessment of FAO's technical work in all areas, including policy, food and nutrition, livestock,
research and extension technical assistance, the FAO–Cooperative Programme with the World Bank, emergency
assistance, forestry, fisheries, soils, water, and statistics. In 2012, she chaired an external panel of experts that
reviewed independent external evaluations of FAO's work on forestry.

Food for All: International Organizations and the Transformation of Agriculture. Uma Lele, Manmohan Agarwal, Brian C. Baldwin, and
Sambuddha Goswami, Oxford University Press. © Uma Lele, Manmohan Agarwal, Brian C. Baldwin, and Sambuddha Goswami 2021.
DOI: 10.1093/oso/9780198755173.003.0010

Development Goals (SDGs), and the Paris Agreement to combat climate change, and now a proposed Food Summit, following the tragedy of COVID-19. During this period, FAO has responded to more than 100 recommendations of the IEE, an unusually high number of recommendations to address its known weaknesses. This chapter outlines how FAO's adoption of a strategic framework and matrix management has enabled it to meet the goals it has adopted for itself, toward SDGs, particularly SDG2 ("zero hunger"). It is a substantially expanded but necessary agenda. The chapter concludes that FAO has made considerable progress in its vision and strategy and laid the groundwork with a framework for being accountable for results. The chapter identifies four issues for FAO going forward.

The first is the old debate on the balance between FAO's normative, public goods function and the embrace of SDGs to help member countries advance them. The debate represents an old fight between developed and developing countries. And even today, there is no consensus, even within FAO's staff and Council, and certainly among its external supporters, on FAO's relative role in country assistance, which is increasingly used to forward the SDG agenda, compared to its role in the provision of global public goods (GPGs).

What are these GPG functions, how different are they from national public goods, and how well has FAO been able to discharge them? There are multiple GPGs, each requiring a specific approach to its delivery. We define public goods and how and why GPGs are different from national public goods, how they are delivered differently depending on the nature of each, and then discuss implications of their delivery needs later in the chapter.

Second, matrix management is a challenge, which is by no means unique to FAO. It calls for working across departments at headquarters and with a decentralized system in the field to achieve shared organizational objectives. Graziano's top-down management style, which also prevailed under two former DGs, may have inhibited management effectiveness, despite the strength of the logical framework he helped to establish. This challenge has already been addressed by DG Qu Dongyu. He reorganized FAO and has moved to an "executive director" style, with revisions in the management structure. In July 2020, Qu Dongyu proposed a second set of reforms to achieve "four betters"—better production, better nutrition, a better environment, and a better life by further transparent, open, innovative, responsible, and effective reform. The FAO Council agreed to eliminate departments and have the division directors, and their divisions, directly report to one of the five members of the "cabinet": three Deputy Directors-General (DDGs), the Chief Economist, and the Chief Scientist, a new position created and announced at the 35th Regional Conference for the Near East in September 2020. (The titles of most divisions have also been adjusted.) The DG also announced his intention to minimize silos, encourage cross-divisional cooperation, and reduce hierarchy and "kingdoms" with team work. The proposals also included creation of the office of Sustainable Development Goals and a new division of Food Systems and Food Safety, as well as strengthening of the country and regional offices. The Assistant Directors-General (ADGs) remain in place as special advisors and thought leaders in their respective areas. The reforms also proposed strengthening three partnerships—an investment center that collaborates with international financial institutions (IFIs); the Joint FAO/IAEA Centre, which reflects the long-standing strategic partnership in sustainable agriculture development and food security, using nuclear science and technology; and the Joint FAO/WHO Centre that will house the Codex Alimentarius Commission (CAC) and address issues related to zoonotic diseases. The DG also announced his intention to strengthen the capacities of FAO country and regional offices, and a number of responses in support of COVID-19, working with the G20 and World

Economic Forum among others, promoting digital agriculture and South–South cooperation.

Morale in the organization had reportedly improved since the new DG's regime, with staff being regarded more as a core asset rather than an expense, maternity leave being lengthened, and staff entitlements brought back in line with UN standards. Long-term morale will depend on how the DG works with his managers and staff to manage the organization and works with member states to strategically plan and resource the organization. A new Strategic Plan should be reviewed by the FAO Council in December 2020 and be approved by the FAO Conference in June 2021, but the initial signs have been positive.

Third, a big challenge is increasing resources in the context of FAO's assessed contributions. They have remained flat in nominal terms since 2010–11, shown later in Figure 9.4, and have declined in real terms, albeit with a slightly increased share of emerging countries in total assessments based on their rapid economic growth, while FAO's agenda has grown and FAO's dependence on voluntary contributions has increased. It is part of the generic underfunding of the United Nations (UN) System documented in this book, in the cases of the International Fund for Agricultural Development (IFAD) and the World Food Programme (WFP), and unlikely to change in the foreseeable future. Furthermore, the UN System has been facing a cash crunch with only 70 percent of the assessments having been paid. This, too, is not a new issue for the UN System. Therefore, other sources of funding are needed, including the increased reliance on South–South cooperation as a cost-effective way of delivering services to developing countries. There is need for further expansion of resources to meet FAO's current obligations.

Finally, the chapter makes a case for establishing FAO as a center of excellence to achieve a transformative, sustainable food system and to address its GPGs and SDG functions, supported by predictable funds to be accorded to FAO, well beyond its current level of assessed and voluntary contributions, with expected transparency in the use of resources.

Introduction

Climate change, including increased frequency and intensity of weather extremes, has adversely impacted food production and terrestrial ecosystems, contributing to desertification and land degradation in many regions. The Intergovernmental Panel on Climate Change (IPCC 2019) predicted resultant food shortages and likely increased flow of migrants, which is already redefining politics in North America, Europe, and other regions. Chapter 12 on WFP is dedicated to the issues of emergency assistance.

Widely recognized, also, is the growing damage caused by food production to the global resource base and to human health, leading to a growing incidence of noncommunicable diseases and a focus on shifting sustainable food systems.[2] Food production is leaving a growing footprint on the world's natural resource base, weighing on biodiversity, contributing to soil erosion and groundwater depletion. It has been driving deforestation and the overexploitation of fish stocks, and is responsible for a quarter of global greenhouse gas (GHG) emissions. In addition, modern food systems, laden with salt, sugar, and fats, have been recognized increasingly as harmful to human health. With these challenges, food and agriculture must adapt to climate change, help lower a stubbornly high level of

---

[2] Food production in the broadest sense includes fish, forestry, fiber, and fuel.

undernourishment, while producing increased and more diversified food with less resources. The challenges of food and agriculture have brought together several international organizations concerned with global food supply, the stewardship of the world's natural resources, and human health. FAO is at the heart of this focus, and its roles is expected to increase with the proposed global food summit in 2021.[3]

A strengthened FAO will help respond to these challenges more effectively than it has thus far. Of course, a systems approach, combining food supply, natural resources, and human health into a single concept, is relatively new for all of us. FAO has been a leader in starting to move in this direction and to advocate a shift, as evidenced, for example, by its Strategic Objective 4 (SO4), discussed in this chapter. These are recent ideas, and they will be at the center stage in the forthcoming UN Food Summit in 2021.

Countries had not demanded this approach until recently, and it is still far from clear if this broader approach is widely understood, endorsed, or used by international organizations and member countries, as we demonstrate in the case of other international organizations in other chapters. FAO will have to continue to lead in responding to these challenges, as the challenges will call for a more integrative approach across sectors and disciplines than the one FAO and others have pursued in the individual specific elements of sustainable management: for example, of crops, livestock, and others. In 2019, FAO, working with the Rome-based IFAD and WFP, as well as the United Nations Children's Fund (UNICEF), and the World Health Organization (WHO), reported rising levels of undernourishment for the third year in a row, mostly in conflict-affected countries and countries suffering from El Niño. Out of the 815 million estimated to be hungry, 489 million were hungry due to conflict, mostly in the Middle East and North Africa (MENA) region, as discussed further in Chapter 12 on WFP (FAO et al. 2019).

FAO's aggregate estimate of Prevalence of Undernourishment (PoU) declined from 821 million in 2019, to 690 million in 2020, prior to the pandemic (FAO et al. 2020, viii). The decline is mainly because undernourishment estimates for China were adjusted by over 100 million people, based on using a newly available series of household data going back to 2000, which resulted in a substantial downward shift of the number of undernourished in the world. China's undernourished decreased from 10 percent of its population to 2 percent. The new PoU estimates of 690 million hungry represent 8.9 percent of the world population, but it is still up by 10 million people in one year and by nearly 60 million over five years from 2014 to 2019, confirming the trend reported in past editions, even as the number has changed from that published in recent reports (FAO et al. 2020, 5–6). Food insecurity, measured as calorie deficit, is now concentrated in South Asia and Africa, although malnourishment and obesity remain extensive challenges. The OECD–FAO 2020–9 Outlook predicts that most of the hunger will remain in these two regions, driven by population growth, climate change and conflict, keeping SDG2 off track and posing a continuing challenge for FAO (OECD–FAO 2020).

FAO was founded in 1945 as a UN Agency for Food and Agriculture to promote agricultural development and food security. Australian nutritionist Frank McDougall had long advocated for an international forum to address hunger and malnutrition, and his proposals were taken up by Eleanor Roosevelt, who organized a meeting with President

---

[3] This chapter draws on information from the 2007 IEE and the Immediate Plan of Action (FAO 2007a, 2008a), as well as findings from other internal and external evaluations of FAO since 2007, a review of literature, and personal communications and interviews with professionals familiar with FAO. The shortcomings, however, are our own.

Franklin D. Roosevelt. A year later, President Roosevelt convened the United Nations Conference on Food and Agriculture at Hot Springs, Virginia, in 1943, bringing together representatives from 44 governments. The Conference ended with a commitment to establish a permanent organization for food and agriculture. On October 16, 1945, in Château Frontenac, Quebec, 34 governments signed the constitution for the organization, and by the end of the first session, held from October 16 to November 1, FAO had 42 members (FAO 2015).

FAO is the only institution with a global mandate to monitor and help eradicate hunger and improve nutrition by acting as "a neutral forum where all nations meet as equals to negotiate agreements and debate policy."[4] To this end, it provides knowledge and information related to all aspects of food and agriculture (UNESCO 1984). FAO has had a long track record of policy advocacy, as discussed in Chapter 4. In addition to offering perspectives and leadership in monitoring trends and challenges and, at times, being in the center of a perfect storm, as discussed in Chapter 3 on the food crisis, which extended from 2007 to 2011, FAO is expected to provide policy advice, information, and practical solutions to address these challenges. We discussed the global initiatives that emerged after the crisis in Chapter 5 on global governance and considered them all too inadequate, with a few exceptions such as the establishment of the Agricultural Market Information System (AMIS) and the Global Agriculture and Food Security Program (GAFSP), detailed in Chapter 5. Since then, with the 2030 Agenda on Sustainable Development, FAO was given a pivotal role in monitoring the SDGs, including custodianship of 21 SDG indicators.

FAO, in its 2011 publication "Save and Grow," proposed a new approach to crop production that would be environmentally sustainable and holistic (Box 9.1).

These emerging challenges prompted a major rethinking in FAO, starting in 2012, with the arrival of DG José Graziano da Silva, leading to a new strategic framework in 2013, well before the SDGs were adopted in 2015. FAO had also actively contributed to the MDGs, and then to their transition to SDGs, playing a key role in setting the global goals of reducing hunger, both in the MDGs and SDGs, albeit with a more expansive goal in the transition from MDGs to SDGs, particularly SDG2.

The new DG, Qu Dongyu, will continue the focus on SDGs, which is likely to be further accentuated by the dialogues leading up to, and the conclusions of, the Food Systems Summit 2021 (UN 2020a). The greater alignment with the SDGs and SDG indicators is likely to drive a focus on ensuring the cross-cutting nature of FAO's contributions to the SDGs, built into the responsibilities of division directors and their respective divisions. This chapter takes stock of where FAO stood at the time of this leadership transition. It explores why FAO is critical to our collective efforts to reach Zero Hunger (UN 2020b). FAO's strategic framework, discussed here, offers a foundation for a clear, logical path to achieving SDG2 by 2030. Therefore, it is relevant for all actors to fulfill their respective roles, although certainly the framework and its functioning, including its matrix management can be improved for the reasons outlined in this chapter. We conclude that the FAO framework has established a strong foundation for the anticipated changes of a new Strategic Framework to be approved by FAO Conference in June 2021, which will guide FAO and its member states over the next 6–8 years. FAO's current structure, as already noted, has changed following the FAO Council session in July 2020.

---

[4] http://www.fao.org/in-action/inpho/links/detail/en/c/214/

Box 9.1 Save and Grow

The challenge: "To feed a growing world population, we have no option but to intensify crop production. But farmers face unprecedented constraints. In order to grow, agriculture must learn to save" (FAO 2011c, vii).

Farming systems: "Crop production intensification will be built on farming systems that offer a range of productivity, socio-economic and environmental benefits to producers and to society at large" (FAO 2011c, vii).

Soil health: "Agriculture must, literally, return to its roots by rediscovering the importance of healthy soil, drawing on natural sources of plant nutrition, and using mineral fertilizer wisely" (FAO 2011c, viii).

Crops and varieties: "Farmers will need a genetically diverse portfolio of improved crop varieties that are suited to a range of agro-ecosystems and farming practices, and resilient to climate change" (FAO 2011c, viii).

Water management: "Sustainable intensification requires smarter, precision technologies for irrigation and farming practices that use ecosystem approaches to conserve water" (FAO, 2011c, ix).

Plant protection: "Pesticides kill pests, but also pests' natural enemies, and their overuse can harm farmers, consumers and the environment. The first line of defense is a healthy agro-ecosystem" (FAO 2011c, ix).

Policies and institutions: "To encourage smallholders to adopt sustainable crop production intensification, fundamental changes are needed in agricultural development policies and institutions" (FAO 2011c, x).

Source: FAO (2011c).

Structure at Headquarters, Challenges of Central vs. Decentralized Structure, and Declining Funding Structure

FAO's structure follows the content of its work and consisted, until July 2020, of seven main departments:[5]

1. Agriculture and Consumer Protection
2. Climate, Biodiversity, Land and Water Department
3. Corporate Services
4. Economic and Social Development
5. Fisheries and Aquaculture
6. Forestry
7. Technical Cooperation and Programme Management

Since then, the organization has changed as shown in Figure 9.1. The Management Committee now consists of three DDGs under the DG, the Chief Economist, and a Chief

---

[5] See http://www.fao.org/about/who-we-are/en/

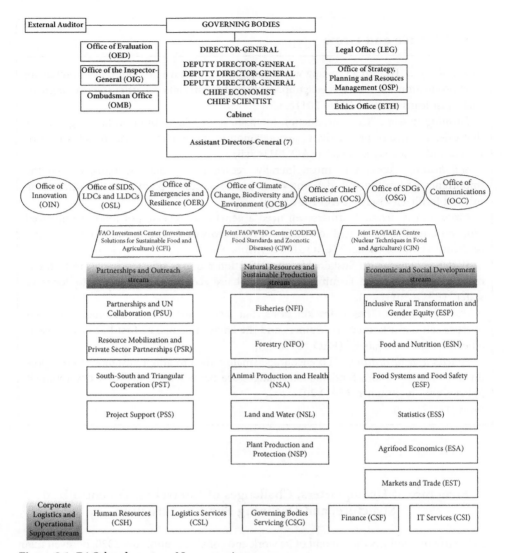

Figure 9.1 FAO headquarters: New organigrammes

Source: FAO Structure, http://www.fao.org/faoterm/collection/fao-structure/en/

Scientist, a position created in July 2020. ADG positions remain the same, and there has been some adjustment of the departments below them. There is also some reorganization of country and regional offices.

FAO has a field presence in more than 130 countries (see Table 9.1). The decentralized network includes 5 regional offices, 10 subregional offices, 74 country offices, and 8 offices with technical officers or FAO Representatives. In addition, FAO has 5 liaison offices and 4 information offices in developed countries. This has been the situation for some time, except for more recently, with expanded field representation in Papua New Guinea, Mongolia, Tajikistan, Kyrgyzstan, and the Democratic People's Republic of Korea. FAO, like many other international organizations, faces the challenge of striking the right structural and budgetary balance between fieldwork and the headquarters.

Table 9.1 International organizations' country presence

Organization	Country presence (estimates)
FAO	130
World Bank	130
WFP	80
IFAD	40
CGIAR	15

Notes: CGIAR has Center headquarters in 15 countries, but the Centers have offices in more than 75 countries.

Source: Based on organizational websites as of 2019 (except for IFAD):
FAO: http://www.fao.org/about/who-we-are/en/
World Bank: https://www.worldbank.org/en/who-we-are
WFP: http://jo.one.un.org/en/partner/wfp/15
IFAD: https://webapps.ifad.org/members/eb/117/docs/EB-2016-117-R-4.pdf
CGIAR: https://storage.googleapis.com/cgiarorg/2019/02/CGIAR-Business-Plan-Web.pdf

Decentralized Offices

This structure (Figure 9.2) should be seen in the context of flat assessed contributions in nominal terms over a long time and have declined in real terms.

The share of voluntary contributions in total has increased from 58 percent to 66 percent at the time of completion of this chapter in 2019. One FAO reviewer noted that "the

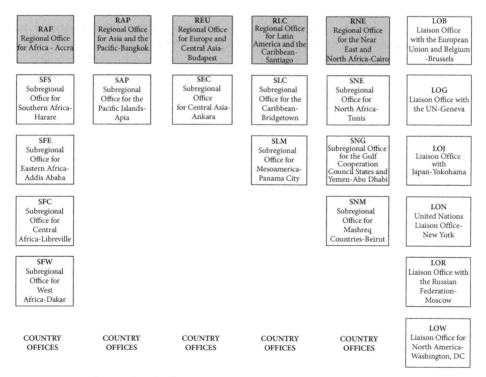

Figure 9.2 FAO decentralized offices: New organigrammes
Source: FAO Structure, http://www.fao.org/faoterm/collection/fao-structure/en/

characterization of the [FAO] funding as precarious and fragmented...does not tell the whole story." It is remarkable in many ways that FAO (and some others in the UN) continue to have guaranteed funding that member countries are required to pay. Member countries would not agree to such guaranteed funding if FAO had started up in 2019. The UN Funds and Programs do not have the requirement of assessed contributions, for example, and financing for the UN as a whole is precarious, notwithstanding its growing needs, including the "cash crisis" because of delayed payments mentioned earlier. The fundamental dilemma that underpins this problem and other issues that the chapter raises has three parts: (1) the assessed contribution portion of the budget is not growing, and there are no indications that members will agree to a substantial increase in assessed contributions at any time in the foreseeable future; (2) almost all funding of FAO activities at the country level comes from voluntary funding, through specific projects; and (3) FAO's Results Framework and the Strategic Objectives (SOs), initially built around the SDGs as called for by members, and the SDG indicators all represent changes at the country level, *without much of any room to accommodate normative work.* As a result, an improved trend in independent assessments of FAO reforms, since the IEE in 2007, appear to have had little impact on increased and predictable (assessed) financial support to FAO, needed to enable it and its partners to the realization of SDG2 on a wider scale, shown later in Table 9.5. This is notwithstanding the fact that FAO has defined its program of work and budget largely in support of SDGs, and particularly SDG2. The one significant difference is that the share of emerging countries, and particularly China, in the assessed contributions has increased, because their GDP has grown more rapidly than that of developed countries, with a big jump particularly in China's assessed contribution—its biannual assessed contribution in 2018 was US$120 million compared to the US contribution of US$220 million. In the interim, their voluntary contributions have increased, including through South–South cooperation. The Chinese assessed contribution has increased significantly over the past several UN budgets (UN System and FAO), to an almost a fourfold increase, so that China is now the second largest contributor (replacing Japan). The new scale of contribution was approved by the FAO Conference in 2019. China's contribution amounts to 12.01 percent for 2019–21, compared to 7.92 for 2016–18 (*Strait Times* 2018).

FAO's Visions and Goals

FAO's vision is "A world free from hunger and malnutrition where food and agriculture contribute to improving the living standards of all, especially the poorest, in an economically, socially and environmentally sustainable manner" (UN News 2016).

The three Global Goals that FAO members have adopted are:

(1) eradication of hunger, food insecurity, and malnutrition, progressively ensuring a world in which people, at all times, have sufficient safe and nutritious food that meets their dietary needs and food preferences for an active and healthy life;

(2) elimination of poverty and the driving forward of economic and social progress for all, with increased food production, enhanced rural development and sustainable livelihoods; and

(3) sustainable management and utilization of natural resources, including soil, land, water, air, climate and genetic resources for the benefit of present and future generations

[for internal reforms and a strategic framework introduced in 2012, with a fundamental change in the way it works through matrix management]. (FAO 2019a, 17)

FAO's core functions include: first and foremost, providing a neutral platform for all member countries to arrive at international agreements, develop long-term perspectives and leadership in monitoring and assessing global trends in food security and agriculture, fisheries, and forestry, and in all aspects of natural resources pertaining to agriculture; stimulating the generation and dissemination of information and knowledge on all things relating to agriculture, including, particularly, statistics and international instruments; setting norms and standards and voluntary guidelines; supporting the development of national legal frameworks; articulating policy and strategy options; and providing advice, technical support, technology transfer, and capacity building; and providing emergency assistance.

FAO operates globally, regionally, and nationally in 130 countries and is governed by a Conference, comprised of 194 members.[6] FAO's data and numerous flagship publications including the *State of Food and Agriculture* (*SOFA*) and the *State of Food Insecurity and Nutrition*, as well as those on forestry and fisheries, are routinely drawn upon by international organizations, such as the World Bank, the IPCC, and the UN System as a whole, as well as scholars in developed and developing countries, the civil society, and the private sector.

Evolution of FAO since Inception

In 1943, years before the Bretton Woods institutions were established, 44 governments met in Hot Springs, Virginia, in the United States, to create a permanent international organization for food and agriculture, FAO. In 1945, the first session of the FAO Conference took place in Quebec City, Canada, and established FAO as a specialized UN agency. In 1951, FAO moved its headquarters from Washington, DC, to Rome (FAO 1996b). The Preamble of the FAO Constitution, as adopted in 1945, states:

> The Nations accepting this Constitution, being determined to promote the common welfare by further separate and collective action on their part for the purpose of: raising the levels of nutrition and standards of living of the peoples under their respective jurisdictions; securing improvements in the efficiency of the production and distribution of all food and agricultural products; bettering the condition of rural populations; and thus contributing toward an expanding world economy and ensuring humanity's freedom from hunger; . . . .[7] (Phillips 1981a, 9)

FAO uniquely serves both developed and developing countries, unlike the World Bank, WFP, the International Fund for Agriculture Development (IFAD), and CGIAR, which were established to assist developing countries with contributions coming largely from developed countries. This feature is both an asset and a source of tension in FAO, as discussed earlier, when the expectations of developed and developing countries differ and often diverge.

---

[6] As the European Union (EU) is a member of FAO, we use "members" rather than "member nations" or "member states."

[7] "Ensuring humanity's freedom from hunger" was added in an amendment in 1965.

FAO was created amid concern about food shortages in postwar Europe. It was called the Food and Agriculture Organization, with "Food" coming first, intentionally. The idea of "Freedom from Want," from Roosevelt's Four Freedoms speech was key.[8] The Founders were also concerned with nutrition and rural development and with overproduction, or at least with problems of marketing and lack of markets for farm production, coming out of the experience of the Great Depression.

Hence, governments on both sides of the Atlantic decided to support and reinforce the agricultural sector and farm production. FAO was instrumental in assessing the food situation, projecting what would be needed to fend off starvation, and recommending how production could be increased to meet that need. At the time, FAO had little international competition in nutrition, food, and agriculture. It focused on increasing local food production by improving farmers' education and providing farmers with improved technology. FAO was tasked to collect, analyze, interpret, and disseminate information internationally, as well as provide technical assistance, if requested by its members (McCalla 2007b).

By the early 1950s, when industrial countries began to grow again, the World Bank, which had been engaged in reconstruction, was able to withdraw from that effort, as the countries it had assisted began to access international capital markets. The World Bank then evolved to address capital market failures in developing countries and, in 1960, established the International Development Association (IDA) to assist the poorest developing countries, which could not afford loans on the terms of the International Bank for Reconstruction and Development (IBRD). FAO, on the other hand, has always been an organization of developed and developing country members with diverse expectations; for example, the nutrition focus in the original FAO mandate was to address hunger, not only in Europe, but over time, both the membership and the needs of developing countries increased, as they became more differentiated. While the World Bank developed different lending instruments for the differing needs of borrowers, FAO never created different approaches to deal with different members, or moved members from one income category to another, as they advanced and their development needs changed. For example, as emerging countries' agricultural trade increased, their need for food safety standards increased to meet the level of standards in the industrial countries with whom they traded, whereas many poor countries remain dependent on food imports and that dependence has, in some cases, even increased. FAO needed to be equipped to deal with clientele of different levels of sophistication. For example, during IEE, Latin American countries expressed their disappointment that FAO lacked the skill set to deal with their needs in trade and food safety standards.

In the 1960s, FAO helped establish several important conventions: among them, the International Plant Protection Convention (IPPC); international food standards, guidelines, and codes of practice (Codex Alimentarius); an early warning system (Global Information and Early Warning System, or GIEWS); and comprehensive data collection systems (AGROSTAT, now called FAOSTAT). (See FAOSTAT 2019; FAO 2020b; FAO and IPPC 2020; FAO and WHO 2020.) FAO became known as the world's center for data on food and agriculture. The 1974 World Food Conference, held during a period of food shortages in the southern Sahara, pressed FAO to promote programs related to world food security at a time when other donor-funded players began to emerge.

---

[8] See https://www.fdrlibrary.org/four-freedoms

Responsibility for scientific, social, and policy research, originally an FAO priority, was shifted to CGIAR, when it was established in 1972, on the initiative of private foundations, the United States Agency for International Development (USAID), and the World Bank, among others. The rapid expansion of CGIAR over the next two decades may have been viewed within FAO as competition for donor support of traditional research and extension activities, which FAO had been charged to promote. At the same time, other UN organizations (such as WFP, discussed in Chapter 12, and IFAD, the United Nations Environment Programme [UNEP], and the United Nations Development Programme [UNDP]); international nongovernmental organizations (INGOs, including Oxfam, CARE, and Save the Children); and private sector entities and foundations (including the Rockefeller and Ford Foundations and, later, the Bill and Melinda Gates Foundation [BMGF]) were born or expanded, and the mandates of these organizations complicated FAO's ability to ascertain its comparative advantage (Kharas 2007; Lele 2007; McCalla 2007b). FAO went along with and helped to establish CGIAR (Warren Baum [1986], as quoted in McCalla 2007b). FAO was granted the status of cosponsor, and the secretariat of the Technical Advisory Committee of CGIAR was placed in FAO's governing structure. Along the way, FAO's previous DG fought and lost many battles for control, such as over the selection of the chair of CGIAR's Technical Advisory Committee. Meanwhile, CGIAR's various attempts to consolidate its research—for example, through inter-Center programs, System-wide programs, Ecoregional Programs, and Challenge Programs—have so far had limited success (see Chapter 10 on CGIAR). The recent CGIAR reforms propose to do more.

The election of FAO's DGs with "one country, one vote," unlike the case of other organizations that we have reviewed in this book, is a more common approach in UN agencies and means donors may have less direct influence but does emphasize more consensual decision-making and, in these times, needed dialogue. Major reforms have introduced term limits for the DG, later reducing the term length from six years to four years, with a limit of two terms that a DG may serve (UN 2003).

As we discussed in various earlier chapters (Chapters 3, 7, and 8), in the 1980s and 1990s, developing countries tried to keep food security at the forefront of international attention by promoting the World Food Council, established by the UN General Assembly in December 1974, based on the recommendation of the World Food Conference. The effort failed. The Council became the only UN organization ever to be abolished in 1993—donors saw little merit in paying for an agency to plead for aid to agriculture in which they had lost interest. As we discuss in Chapter 8 on the World Bank, even as the World Bank's various attempts to revive interest in agricultural investments failed to elicit support among its country directors and developing country governments, FAO kept food security on the global agenda, most notably at the 1996 World Food Summit, which adopted a universal definition of food security and set the goal of halving world hunger (FAO 1996a). Such global goals, not common in that era of complacency about agriculture, heightened attention to health and education sectors. To its credit, FAO's continued focus on hunger contributed to the eventual adoption of halving hunger, together with poverty reduction, as MDG1 in 2000. The twin goals have since been divided into two, in SDG1 and SDG2.[9]

The big picture contribution of FAO, discussed in Chapter 4, was to the 1996 definition of food security, which was the foundation for MDG1, reducing incidence of hunger by half,

---

[9] In "A New Profile of the Global Poor," Castañeda et al. (2018, 251) of the World Bank Data for Goals Group, note that the world's poor "tend to be rural and young." They find that "About 80% of the extreme poor and 76% of the moderate poor live in areas classified ... as rural."

the setting of the global goal to meet the hunger gap, and the establishment of the Comprehensive Africa Agriculture Development Programme (CAADP). CAADP was heavily criticized outside of FAO at the time, as top-down and externally driven; with appropriate modifications by African governments, the program has been embraced by African policymakers and donors, many of whom have forgotten that FAO's strong push led to the establishment of CAADP (FAO 2006).

FAO's five SOs currently provide a larger view of FAO's mission activity, and the evaluations of SOs offer some important insights, including the use of safety nets, as in Brazil's *Fome Zero*, rather than just focus on agricultural production and productivity. This received some push back in-house in FAO in 2012, but, of course, this was not true in 2019, as documented earlier in references to the Multilateral Organisation Performance Assessment Network (MOPAN) 2017–18 Assessment, UK's Department for International Development (DFID) Multilateral Development Review, and the OED Synthesis report on the evaluation of SOs (DFID and UK Aid 2016; MOPAN 2018; FAO 2019g). Although FAO's estimates of the resources it would take to reduce hunger have included the cost of safety nets, the evaluation notes that donors and countries have not seen it as FAO's comparative advantage. Also, they have seen the strategic framework as an internal FAO exercise, rather than change in the way FAO operates.

FAO's other important asset is the unfailing trust of countries' ministries of agriculture. Recent assessments of FAO suggest that FAO has successfully reached out to other ministries and stakeholders, addressing its perceived traditional limitation of being exclusively oriented toward ministries of agriculture. Increasingly, agriculture operates in a larger space, involving other parts of governments, as well as stakeholders outside government, civil society, and the private sector in which FAO has been less well known. Its strategic framework has opened up its agenda.

Ad Spijkers, former FAO Resident Representative, provides an example of Vietnam. After a long war, the challenges facing the reunified country in 1976 were huge. FAO started operations there in 1979, and the FAO Country Office in Hanoi worked to expand the country program during the time of the US embargo; and in the absence of the World Bank, the International Monetary Fund (IMF), and regional development banks, FAO was an important partner and the main contributor of technical assistance for the country's agriculture sector. According to Spijkers: "There were 21 Chief Technical Advisors (CTA) on UNDP-financed projects executed by FAO in 1990. In the 1980s, FAO's programme in Vietnam was its third largest in the world after India and China, still remembered today by the [Vietnamese] government" (Ad Spijkers, personal communication with Uma Lele, February 8, 2020).

FAO's adoption of a wider approach to reducing food insecurity that involves a variety of other interest groups who are affected by food insecurity is a good development, as evident in the joint FAO–International Food Policy Research Institute (IFPRI) conference on Zero Hunger in Bangkok in December 2018.[10] The technical focus of FAO on agriculture, often perceived as its strength as well as a limitation, has given way to partnerships in developed and developing countries to overcome FAO's narrow technical expertise, address the multidisciplinarity of food insecurity, malnutrition, and obesity, although there is scope to expand this line of work.

---

[10] See https://www.ifpri-faobangkokconference.org

Performance and Progress on Implementation of Evaluation Recommendations: Old and New Issues in a Changing Context

Over the years, various bilateral organizations, think tanks, and journals publicly criticized FAO as irrelevant, overly bureaucratic, and ineffective. However, many internal and external evaluations and assessments conducted over the past decade, such as MOPAN 2017–18 (MOPAN 2018) and DFID (DFID and UK Aid 2016) have reaffirmed FAO's critical role in the food and agriculture sector. The 2007 IEE was the first such evaluation, commissioned by donors in 2004.

The 2007 Independent External Evaluation and Its Overarching Messages

Published in 2007, the IEE was presented to DG Jacques Diouf, who was serving a third term, as the donors had been unable to influence the slate of candidates or outcome of the 2005 election. The IEE noted that FAO had many accomplishments: it continued to furnish a range of essential goods and services that no other organization could and had made significant contributions to global governance on food and agriculture issues.

The IEE report made more than 100 recommendations (with many more sub-recommendations), starting with the formulation and adoption of an immediate action plan (FAO 2007a). In November 2008, a Special Conference of FAO Member Countries agreed to a US$42.6 million, three-year Immediate Plan of Action, which called for an overhaul of the financial procedures, organizational structure, and human resources (HR) management (FAO 2008a). Specifically, the plan outlined the need for:

- A new strategic framework;
- Investments in governance;
- Institutional culture changes and reform of administrative and management systems; and
- Restructuring for effectiveness and efficiency in both the headquarters and the field.

In its official response to the evaluation on October 29, 2007, FAO management said that it: "supports the principal conclusion in the report of the IEE on the need for 'reform with growth' so as to have an FAO 'fit for this century' ... " (FAO 2007c).

The central conclusion of the evaluation was that, "If FAO did not exist, it would need to be invented" (FAO 2007a, Summary, 59), but that the organization required "reform with growth" (FAO 2007a, 2). The evaluation offered fifteen messages:

1. FAO needs "reform with growth" (12).
2. FAO is in a "state of crisis which imperils the future of the Organization" (12).
3. "If FAO were to disappear tomorrow, much of it would need to be reinvented" (15).
4. "The world needs FAO to fulfil the potential it has to contribute to the 21st century, but that potential [can only be realized] ... if a new political consensus is reached, based on renewed trust and mutual respect" (15).
5. "The goal posts must shift—FAO's future relevance and effectiveness will depend on enhanced strategic and policy capabilities focused both on new realities confronting food and agriculture and on creating the large enabling environments that will be needed to address them" (16).

6. "FAO urgently needs to make tough strategic choices" (17).
7. "FAO must become a more flexible Organization while continuing to be a responsible manager of public funds. It needs to break out of its risk-averse culture, creating greater efficiency and effectiveness" (18).
8. "As a knowledge organization, FAO's job is to support Members in ensuring that the needs of the world within its area of mandate are fully met—not necessarily to undertake each task itself" (20).
9. "FAO must strengthen its global governance role as a convener, a facilitator and a source of reference for global policy coherence and in the development of global codes, conventions and agreements" (21).
10. "FAO's governance is weak and is failing the Organization.... [It] has not ensured an adequate corporate strategy with realistic priorities,..." (21).
11. "FAO has many talented staff with a deep commitment to the mission of the Organization, but they are stifled by the fragmented structures of FAO and rigidly centralized management systems" (21).
12. "There is a widespread... [willingness] within FAO for major and fundamental change, but an almost equal cynicism about whether senior management and the Governing Bodies can make this happen" (22).
13. "There is scope for FAO to achieve further major efficiency gains" (22).
14. "FAO does not deserve the generally 'bad name' it has as a partner [organization]" (22).
   "There is serious misperception in some quarters as to the size and resources of FAO" (23) (FAO 2007a, Summary, 5–23).

FAO's Response: The Immediate Plan of Action for FAO Renewal, 2009–2011

FAO's official response to the IEE was issued in October 2007. The response noted "that the report contained both positive and critical assessments of the Organization" and concluded, "Overall, the underlying analysis and resulting recommendations provide a good basis for objective discussion of the issues, challenges and opportunities pertaining to the future of the Organization" (FAO 2007c). The response continued, noting that FAO management accepted the need for a new strategic framework, welcomed the introduction of measures to make governance more cohesive and effective, and agreed with the vast majority of recommendations.

The first step in the post-IEE reform was the adoption of the Resolution 1/2008 and the preparation of the Immediate Plan of Action, which was discussed and approved by the 35th Special Session of the FAO Conference in November 2008. The plan provided for enhancing FAO governance and improving its performance through streamlined management, and by focusing more closely on core objectives and functions through 274 action items. The plan introduced a results-based framework for all of FAO's work, consisting of global goals, SOs, organizational results, and core functions. It also laid out strategies and timetables for reforming governing bodies, systems, and organizational structures, as well as further actions to improve the effectiveness of governance. The plan required funding by extra-budgetary contributions under the 2010–11 Programme of Work and Budget, and member countries were urged to contribute extra-budgetary resources of a provisional amount of US$21.8 million for 2009 to a special trust fund established for this purpose

(FAO 2008a). Strong support from FAO headquarters to field offices can help mobilize donor funds in support of field operations, as some experienced FAO representatives have stressed.

Center for Global Development's Assessment of the Immediate Plan of Action Achievements and Challenges

In 2012, the Center for Global Development (CGD) organized a Working Group on Food Security, comprised of experts in food and agricultural policy and nutrition, funded by BMGF. From a governance point of view, this was an interesting exercise. Such assessments are entirely outside the processes of the UN, in general, and other governmental and intergovernmental bodies, in particular. The only ones who have a voice are the members, although such assessments as well as the work of influential INGOs and think tanks can affect opinions of key member governments. Much of what we have reported in this chapter relates to what members say, or to evaluations and reports that have been conducted on their behalf, the IEE, MOPAN, FAO Office of Evaluation (OED) reports, the DFID reviews, etc. Outside authors, of course, are entitled to their opinions on matters, but they are entirely outside of the governing body processes. CGD's task was to take stock of the Rome-based UN food agencies in the context of the current challenges to agricultural development and food security. The working group focused on FAO and issued a report in 2013, with two messages: FAO should shift focus to GPGs and improve its institutional governance (CGD 2013).

The CGD report said that FAO "is the only entity that can provide many of the needed 'global public goods' in the area of its mandate (such as basic research, global analysis, statistics, international standards, and advocacy). And historically, FAO has proven to be a valued repository of knowledge and capacity for national development efforts" (CGD 2013, xii). However, the report also argued that FAO's capacity to deliver on GPGs is constrained by its institutional governance: that is, its dependence on voluntary funds.

While FAO is doing a better job of "ensuring that voluntary contributions do not divert resources from the main program, and in providing new mechanisms for more flexible voluntary financial support," increased reliance on voluntary funds imposes costs on FAO's ability "to make strategic budgetary choices" (CGD 2013, xii). CGD recommended that FAO's member states ensure that financing is aligned with the organization's priorities for its core activities (particularly, statistics), rather than provide funding earmarked for short-term projects: "member governments should relinquish short-run, locally visible FAO projects in exchange for a greater role in policy formulation, advocacy, and development activities that offer more substantial but longer-term dividends" (CGD 2013, xi). However, as we note later, this advice has not been heeded.

Regarding the shift to GPGs, the CGD assessment recommended that member governments should reallocate budgets away from the local level to focus on the global level, with about 50 percent of FAO resources, compared to current levels of 35 percent on GPGs, including: "assembling, publishing, and analyzing data on food production and consumption; developing early warning systems related to hunger, disease, and pests; and providing a neutral forum for policy dialogue on issues related to food security and agriculture" (CGD 2013, xi). CGD argued that these goods are "FAO's most visible and influential contribution, and the reality is that there is no realistic alternative source of supply for them" (CGD 2013, xi).

CGD also highlighted the tension between FAO's core operational work and its field activities, with high-income countries often arguing for more focus on statistics and policy guidelines, at the same time that developing countries are requesting more country-level technical assistance.

The Assessment of FAO's Achievements and Challenges through FAO's Post-2007 Independent Evaluations

The Intermediate Plan of Action led to a number of changes, including restructuring at the headquarters, reformed delegation of authority, modernized and streamlined administrative and operational processes, and greater autonomy of FAO's decentralized offices. And sources in FAO suggest the management style under the new DG is already changing rapidly, with greater delegation of responsibility and accountability in place of micromanagement. With an acceleration of reform activities in 2012, led by the DG, 92 percent of the reforms were reportedly completed by the end of that year. Only 22 (out of 274) actions have been abandoned or "parked" for later consideration. The full effect of these changes is as yet unknown, but the progress made should be considered in terms of the range of follow-up that FAO has implemented, and not only on the basis of steps completed.

Since 2007, the need for global attention to agriculture and food security has increased, as efforts to combat hunger have faced challenges, such as climate change, higher energy and fuel prices, and growing populations. Several evaluations have looked at various aspects of FAO's work and role in agriculture and food security. After the IEE, FAO created its own evaluation capacity, the OED, which regularly assesses FAO projects, the portfolio of all FAO work in a given country, and broad areas of the FAO program. The evaluations have improved in quality and increasingly emphasize themes of critical importance to FAO's work. As of July 2020, the OED will report directly to the FAO DG.

External evaluations included the British Multilateral Aid Review, MOPAN's Organisational Effectiveness Assessment of FAO, and the 2012 Australian Multilateral Assessment (DFID and UK Aid 2011, 2016; MOPAN 2011, 2014, 2018, Government of Australia 2012). Most of these evaluations reiterated the messages of the IEE. With the passage of time, IEE has rightly faded into the background.

Based on a review of the post-IEE evaluations, FAO has a strong role to play at the national level and has made significant improvements in the effectiveness of its work at the country level. Consistent messages from the recent external evaluations include:

- FAO has a clear mandate and a strategy that links to that mandate.
- It commands strong legitimacy and trust at the country level.
- It is highly valued by its direct partners.
- It consistently delivers a wide range of global and regional public goods.
- Its policy work at the global level is excellent and influential.
- The Investment Centre provides FAO with an essential door to the world of investment.
- FAO continues to be an active advocate of food security.

- Its impact in on epidemic disease control, including work on rinderpest and avian influenza is unparalleled.
- It is a global leader on forestry and water.

Problems identified in the evaluations include the tension between FAO's normative GPGs function and its field operations, complex governance and structural issues and related corporate culture, and weak impact at the country level. These problems are institutional and grounded in long-standing management issues such as decentralization. One of the sources of tension remains over the GPGs function. The difference in the priorities of developed and developing members has also been an important issue. Issues of interest to advanced (and even to some developing countries) are not necessarily those that are of the greatest need to the least developed countries; the countries' demands or FAO's supply of assistance have not been consistent always with real needs for agricultural development, including policies, strategies, and investment climate. However, evaluations suggest that FAO has substantially improved its global work, and they all stress the importance of bringing FAO's global knowledge to bear at the country level.

FAO Reforms

As noted earlier, FAO initiated a series of organizational reforms in 2009, following the first IEE (FAO 2007a), with the launch of the Immediate Plan of Action. The process continued with the introduction of "transformative changes" introduced in 2012 by the new DG. A number of reform initiatives since have been instrumental in shaping FAO. Key among these initiatives was FAO's revised Strategic Framework 2010–19 and the associated shift to a matrix management model. They have led to a major change management project, requiring significant changes in the way in which FAO has operated. The reform initiatives were designed to increase FAO's effectiveness and the needs of the operating environment. The process continued to evolve and has aligned itself with the SDGs, launched in late 2015 under the 2030 Agenda.

FAO's SOs were reduced from 11 to 5 and are articulated within the context of its vision, attributes, and core functions:

1: *Contribute to the eradication of hunger, food insecurity and malnutrition*

2: *Make agriculture, forestry and fisheries more productive and sustainable*

3: *Reduce rural poverty*

4: *Enable more inclusive and efficient agricultural and food systems*

5: *Increase the resilience of livelihoods to threats and crises* (FAO 2017c, 25)

At its 120th session, FAO's Programme Committee endorsed the 2017–19 Indicative Rolling Work Plan of Evaluations, which included a synthesis of findings and lessons from the SO evaluations for consideration by the Committee at its spring 2019 session (FAO 2016). The findings and lessons were based on the five separate independent evaluations of SOs and extrapolated how and to what extent the FAO Strategic Framework (SF) has been effective as a programming tool in support of the

Organization's greater development contribution since 2014. The synthesis presented "14 key messages that reflect the lessons learned from, and the challenges and constraints of, the conceptualization, operationalization and results of the SOs, in addition to a consideration of deliberations on recent global developments of importance to the Strategic Framework" (FAO 2019g, 1):

- Conceptualization: How relevant are the SOs?
- Operationalization: What were the enabling and limiting factors for the implementation of the SOs?
- Results: How and to what extent have the SOs strengthened FAO's contribution to sustainable development results?
- Looking ahead: What are the main considerations in terms of the 2030 Agenda, UN Reform, and the SDGs? (FAO 2019g, 1)

This section draws heavily on FAO's own evaluative description of the design of FAO's results framework, the alignment of the SOs and their programs to address the SDGs, and an overview of the Strategic Programmes, including context, theory of change, and the related outcomes and outputs to be achieved by FAO and its members. It paints a picture of FAO substantially different than the one we had developed in earlier drafts of this chapter, based on FAO's IEE of 2007, and therefore, is reported first followed by findings of other external independent evaluations of FAO by its donors. They suggest an organization on the move, compared to where it stood in 2007 when the IEE was completed, albeit with some continued long-standing challenges.

FAO Results Framework

Based on a "results chain" model, FAO's results framework links objectives, outcomes, and outputs. The results framework provides a guide to plan and monitor FAO's work. In its "Overview of FAO's Strategic Objective Programme," in April 2018, FAO noted:

Three levels of results contribute to the *Global Goals of Members*:

- *Strategic Objectives* express the development outcomes in countries, regions and globally. They are expected to be achieved over a long-term timeframe by Members with FAO's contributions.
- *Outcomes* describe changes in the country, regional or global enabling environment and in capacities available to achieve a specific Strategic Objective.
- *Outputs* are FAO's direct contributions to Outcomes. They result from the delivery of FAO's interventions at the national, regional and global levels, using both regular and extrabudgetary resources. (FAO 2018d, 1–2)

Cross-cutting themes on hunger, poverty resilience, etc., is a great idea and innovation. They need to be empowered, in terms of resource allocation and evaluation of staff from various departments.

FAO's Normative Work

A major issue facing FAO going forward, as it has been in the past regarding normative work, is that the SDG indicators (and hence, FAO's results framework) relate to aggregated changes at the country level, making it very difficult to accommodate normative work in a results framework built around direct contributions to these SDG indicators. Members, including both G77 and OECD countries, demand both normative work and country-level SDG support activities, but there are no indications that they will be very interested in increasing their assessed contributions. FAO's normative work provides public goods. What are these public goods? Public goods are like clean air. They benefit all. They are non-rivalrous. Consumption by one person does not diminish the supply for another, and they are non-excludable. No one can be barred from consuming the good.

The kinds of GPGs that FAO provides include (but are not limited to) international agreements and establishment of norms and standards—for example, adopting the IPPC (1951) and the framework for rules to prevent the spread of plant pests by international trade; food safety (working jointly with WHO) through the establishment of the CAC with the WHO (1961) and regulating international food safety standards; monitoring and control of cross-border pests and diseases; developing global information, analysis, and statistics on the state of the food, agriculture, forests, fisheries; developing the Early Warning System for plant, animal, bird diseases, locusts, and other disasters, which call for timely response (1975); and advocacy on food and agricultural policies, broadly defined and agricultural development to help reduce global poverty and hunger. FAO pioneered Integrated Pest Management—for reducing losses to pests without exposure or reliance on excessive pesticides—and the farmers' field school (FFS) approach to disseminate the pest management techniques through farmer participation (1980s). FAO contains experts in a variety of fields, including agriculture, nutrition, economics, forestry, fisheries, and social sciences, and it uses this expertise in networks of other world experts, to provide the essential services of agreements, data, and knowledge on good practices.

FFS, an adult education intervention, uses intensive discovery-based learning to promote skills. An International Initiative for Impact Evaluation (3IE) Systematic Review noted:

> [It] has been used to train 12 million farmers in over 90 countries across Asia, Africa, and Latin America, the effectiveness of this approach has long been a subject of debate. Drawing on a systematic review of over 500 documents, this study finds that FFSs have changed agricultural practices and raised yields in pilot projects, but they have not been effective when taken to scale. The FFS approach requires a degree of facilitation and skilled trainers, which are difficult to sustain beyond the life of the pilot programmes. (Waddington and White 2014)

In contrast, retired FAO Country Manager, Ad Spijkers noted, based on his firsthand experience in initiating an interregional programme on Integrated Pest Management, IPM/FFS in Asia, Cambodia, and China (1990–2000): "we can say in hindsight that this was one of the most successful FAO field programs with millions of farmers who have been trained with support from, among others, Australia and the Netherlands." He speculated that if the training had been linked with policy change with respect to pesticide use, the impact of the program would have been long lasting (Ad Spijkers, personal communication with Uma Lele, February 8, 2020). Spijker's remarks make one wonder: Would it have been the result of change in policy or due to program intervention?

"The Strategic Programmes (SPs) [facilitated] the achievement of results at the country level in the context of each of the five Strategic Objectives" (FAO 2018d, 2). The shift from 11 discipline-oriented SOs (animal health, crop production, fisheries, forestry, nutrition, etc.) to the five cross-cutting SOs predated the SDGs, but come out of the same wave of thinking (which FAO also influenced) to look at the interconnected nature of big objectives that need to be addressed together. Hunger eradication is one, but so is sustainable production (SO2), social protection—livelihoods and extreme poverty eradication (SO3), sustainable food systems (SO4), and resilience (SO5). These look natural now, but they were groundbreaking in 2012, not necessarily understood or endorsed by FAO staff or the membership. The resilience agenda, linked to the humanitarian–development nexus, and sustainable food systems are now similarly common currency, but they were both quite controversial among Members when they were proposed, as was the idea that FAO and rural and agriculture programs had anything to do with social protection, also now widely accepted.

Beyond the five, large interconnected SOs, consideration of internal needs of FAO to meet these goals leads to another objective:

> To ensure a robust and practical results-based approach to all of the work of the Organization, FAO must ensure that it has the internal technical capacity and integrity to achieve the expected results. Therefore, the Strategic Framework includes a sixth objective, *Technical quality, statistics and cross-cutting themes (climate change, gender, governance, and nutrition)*, to ensure technical leadership and integration of statistics and the cross-cutting issues of climate change, gender, governance and nutrition in the delivery of the Strategic Objective programmes (SPs). (FAO 2018d, 2)

Alignment with Sustainable Development Goals

The "Overview of FAO's Strategic Objective Programme" further describes how the 2030 Agenda for Sustainable Development defines the context for FAO's work toward the SDGs: "The main innovation in the MTP 2018–21 has been to identify and use exclusively the SDG targets and indicators that relate to each SO ... [resulting] in a new set of SDG-based SO level indicators that will be monitored biennially to report trends and progress toward global targets" (FAO 2018d, 2).

This exclusive focus on SDGs poses some challenges in balancing FAO's GPGs functions, which we note that donors have demanded, with developmental functions that the developing country members expect. The issue pertains not only to FAO. In essence, by adopting the SDGs, whose indicators are almost all linked to verifiable changes at the country level, it is difficult to fit in the normative work of FAO and others. This was always going to be an issue for FAO and its own SF and reporting, but it is exacerbated by the UN System Reform and the heightened importance of aligning all of the UN's work at the country level to the SDGs.[11] We discuss this further later in the chapter.

The "Overview of FAO's Strategic Objective Programmes" further noted that at the level of Outcomes, entire indicators have been replaced with SDG indicators: "Outcome

---

[11] For more information, see "UN Development System Reform 101": https://reform.un.org/content/un-development-system-reform-101

indicators will continue to measure the biennial level of change achieved and ... [countries'] progress in those areas where FAO more directly contributed through its work. Overall, FAO's work [contributes] to 40 SDG targets measured through 53 SDG indicators as part of the proposed FAO Strategic Objective results framework for 2018–21" (FAO 2018d, 2).

Operationalization

The SOs have introduced cross-sectoral, interdisciplinary approaches and conceptual frameworks for FAO's engagement in relation to emerging, interconnected challenges to food security, nutrition, and well-being, while maintaining environmental and natural resource sustainability. These are clearly major achievements.

The synthesis concluded, "The Strategic Framework entailed significant investment in operationalization and implementation arrangements with a view to translating normative work and knowledge products into tangible policy and practices at country level" (FAO 2019g, 2). How wide is the acceptance of the SOs, internally and externally, which are now well embedded in FAO's architecture? FAO's external stakeholders have sometimes considered the reforms and SOs to be largely for its internal audience and operationalization, whereas the staff do not consider them fully integrated internally. So, it should be considered work in progress. A few other external evaluations, reported and discussed later in this chapter, have had different views of the extent to which the framework pays attention to FAO's normative work.

FAO recognized the need for stronger integration of Strategic Programme 3 activities with the other Strategic Programmes in order to maximize its contribution to poverty reduction and SDG1. The Strategic Programmes are: SP1 for the eradication of hunger, food insecurity, and malnutrition; SP2 to make agriculture, forestry and fisheries more productive and sustainable; SP3 to reduce rural poverty; SP4 for enabling more inclusive and efficient agricultural and food systems; and SP5 to increase resilience of livelihoods to threats and crises (FAO 2018d).

As highlighted in the "Evaluation of FAO's Contribution to Reduction in Rural Poverty," FAO would benefit from deepening its multisectoral, cross-strategic program initiatives, such as nutrition-sensitive social protection and zero hunger (SP1–SP3), shock responsive social protection (SP3–SP5), migration (SP3–SP5), inclusive value chain/food systems (SP3–SP4), and decent employment and improved livelihoods in agriculture, including family farming (SP2–SP3). Until now, policy-related work was embedded in the three outcomes of SP3.[12] During the preparation of the Medium Term Plan 2018–21, and in the context of the SDGs, it became apparent that a stronger, multisectoral effort to support countries in making progress towards SDG1 was needed. As a response, FAO added a fourth outcome to the 2018–19 SP3 framework to support countries' capacities to implement multisectoral and gender equitable policies, strategies, and programs for poverty reduction (FAO OED 2017b). Specific emphasis on "addressing the political economy of

[12] According to the OED's "Evaluation of FAO's Contribution to the Reduction of Rural Poverty through Strategic Programme 3":
Strategic Programme 3 (SP3) was set up to lead the delivery of SO3 under three main work streams aimed to achieve three main organizational outcomes (OOs):

OO3.1 Rural poor are empowered through improved access to resources and services.
OO3.2 Improved opportunities to access decent farm and non-farm employment.
OO3.3 Strengthened social protection systems to reduce rural poverty. (FAO OED 2017b, 1)

rural poverty reduction through policy work, advocacy, stakeholder participation, [multi-sectoral coordination, South–South cooperation,] and partnerships" will be essential for success (FAO 2018d, 14). MOPAN has highlighted some of these issues, and reportedly, the new DG has begun to address them, also.

Challenges and Constraints

The Synthesis addressed the challenges and constraints in implementation, faced by the SF, "largely in relation to skills and technical capacity, resource mobilization, monitoring and results reporting, operational and administrative procedures" (FAO 2019g, 3). We should also add that the constraints have resulted from FAO's assessed contributions, which have not grown in nominal terms and are declining in real terms in the budget, combined with retirement of senior staff and their replacements with younger, inexperienced staff and consultants, as we discuss later.

The Synthesis further noted:

> Despite strong conceptualization and commitment, the Strategic Framework encountered a number of implementation challenges and constraints, particularly in relation to the balance and distribution of skills and technical capacity (overall and in new thematic areas), resource-mobilization strategy, structure and mechanisms to deal with the decentralization of donor funding, the transaction and opportunity costs of operational and administrative procedures, and conceptual issues in defining, monitoring and reporting results. (FAO 2019g, 3)

Results

In November 2019, FAO issued an evaluation of FAO's SF, which was designed in 2013, to better strategically position FAO and "to address the facts that the Organization's programmatic activities were defined along silo-like disciplinary lines and that corporate efforts were not clearly aligned with the country programme priorities agreed with Members" (FAO OED 2019a, vii). The SF was well conceived to address these goals, and the value of establishing SOs, as has been confirmed by recent evaluations, employing FAO's technical advantage and engagement at the country level in achieving the SDGs.[13]

The evaluation makes clear that FAO has made "commendable efforts" toward managing "substantial transformation" of its organizational structure so as to "prepare it for the emerging landscape," and has considerable achievements to its credit (FAO OED 2019a, vii). For example, FAO has decentralized and become a more "strategically oriented" organization since 2013, applying a "learning-by-doing" approach and promoting "more multidisciplinary work across technical departments at headquarters level" (FAO OED 2019a, vii).

The evaluation urged the new leadership to "fast-track its transformation" by addressing the issues identified in the evaluation report and "preparing the ground for FAO to adopt a strategic orientation that has expertise-based engagement and agile implementation as its new organizational culture" (FAO OED 2019a, 6). The evaluation noted that the SF had led

---

[13] See "Our Priorities: The FAO Strategic Objectives" (http://www.fao.org/3/a-mg994e.pdf).

to FAO's adoption of an approach based upon "interconnected and cross-sectoral objectives." Still, FAO needs to "to better support Country Offices in light of the United Nations Sustainable Development Cooperation Framework (UNSDCF)" (FAO OED 2019a, vii). Further, the evaluation recommended that FAO update "the theory of change underpinning the Results Framework to identify more tangible, issue-based programmatic objectives" (FAO OED 2019a, viii). The OED stresses the need for FAO to "articulate the result chains of its normative work" involving GPGs and development objectives (FAO OED 2019a, viii).

In examining the effectiveness of management arrangements, the evaluation notes:

> The matrix-type structure was suited to fostering cross-sectoral thinking and led to more interdisciplinary work at headquarters. However, it did not have the expected positive effects on FAO country programmes, in particular, as the matrix did not percolate down to decentralized levels of delivery. (FAO OED 2019a, viii–ix)

The Evaluation further recommended placing FAO's Country Offices central to its programme delivery structure, by "bringing multidisciplinary teams closer to country level" and directly engaging "the decentralized and headquarters-based technical teams, also contributing to FAO's normative mission,...to ensure that FAO warrants the highest technical inputs to the UNSDCF and country programmes." Such engagement further facilitates the integration of FAO's normative and development missions, in line with the original vision of the SF (FAO OED 2019a, ix).

New skill sets are called for by the Revised Strategic Framework "to support programmatic thinking, interdisciplinary approaches, and investment mobilization" (FAO OED 2019a, ix). The Evaluation recommends that FAO "establish mechanisms to ensure its staff profiles match needs at all levels," adjusting capacities to changing demands (FAO OED 2019a, ix).

The SF's programmatic orientation was designed "to strengthen FAO's mark in establishing the centrality of food and agriculture to country development agendas" (FAO OED 2019a, x). SPs have had "limited influence on FAO's large field programme [due to] the disconnect to the field, or the top-down orientation of corporate planning systems and disconnect between the Results Framework and field priorities" (FAO OED 2019a, x). Other reasons for the failure of SPs to become "programmatic pillars" was the unclear delineation of FAO's technical and SP functions, with "the extent by the staffing of SP teams with technical experts, prompting SP teams to divert to other functions" (FAO OED 2019a, x). Donors and governments do not follow a programmatic logic. There has been limited donor support for programmatic approaches and low levels of lightly earmarked funding.

Country priorities have been progressively integrated with normative technical work in FAO's corporate planning and work. The Evaluation notes improvements toward "bottom-up planning, based on country priorities, [but] work planning is still excessively oriented towards regular budget allocations, while significant pieces of technical/normative work and country programming supported by extra-budgetary resources remain poorly reflected in planning and reporting" (FAO OED 2019a, x).

The Evaluation described the FAO's results monitoring and reporting systems (the Programme Planning, Implementation Reporting and Evaluation Support System, the Field Project Management Information System, and the Country Office Information Network) as fragmented. Although these systems are able to generate huge amounts of information, the Evaluation points to the need for "stronger structures and processes for strategic and qualitative programme monitoring and review of organizational performance and development contributions" (FAO OED 2019a, xi).

To improve FAO's ability to respond to country's needs, the Evaluation recommended increasing the efficiency of its administrative procedures "by increasing delegation of authority to decentralized offices, while establishing the appropriate accountability mechanisms to ensure the sound management of risks" (FAO OED 2019a, xi).

Looking Ahead: The 2030 Agenda, UN Reform, and Climate Change

Addressing the future, the Synthesis noted:

> Implementing the Strategic Framework has steered FAO in a new direction and better prepared the Organization for the 2030 Agenda, which will call for similar interdisciplinary approaches, cross-sectoral thinking and collaboration with diverse partners, but on a much bigger scale. FAO will need to assess the implications for FAO and the next Strategic Framework of the 2030 Agenda and the SDGs, UN System Reform and the repositioning of the UN Development System to deliver the SDGs, as well as the growing profile of climate change in the development landscape....
>
> Because of the potential programming and resource implications, the new Strategic Framework [due to be approved by FAO Conference in June 2021] should strike the right balance between the normative aspects of FAO's work as a specialised agency and its contributions to and support for countries in achieving the SDGs. (FAO 2019g, 4)

If we consider support to countries in achieving the SDGs, noted here, as country-level work, then almost all of this work (with the exception of the Technical Cooperation Programme's US$70 million per year) is funded by donor projects and not by the Regular Programme (RP) financing. The SF encompasses both, of course, but reporting on results is much easier—in terms of SDG indicators—for country-level work than for the normative work.

The Synthesis identified some crucial challenges:

> With the SDGs central to the evolving development dialogue, *the new Strategic Framework and its results chain will need to reflect more explicitly FAO's contributions to and support for countries in attaining their SDG targets* [emphasis added by the author]. The narrative will need to be sharpened to reflect FAO's comparative advantages and role as a custodian agency. At the same time, *specialized agencies like FAO have global obligations in relevant normative areas that have been approved and funded by their global and regional governing bodies, in addition to policy and technical programmes, which may not be adequately reflected in the UN System response, which is rooted entirely within the SDGs and mapped to SDG targets and indicators.* [author's italicization]
>
> The status of the new United Nations Development Assistance Framework (UNDAF) [now known as the UN Sustainable Development Cooperation Framework (UNSDCF)], as the primary UN System-wide support for delivering the SDGs will have implications for the CPF [country program framework], FAO's country-level programming mechanism. CPFs have the potential to become even more important in capturing the priorities,

specific targets and indicators in national SDG plans to which FAO can contribute. However, *CPFs should also position relevant normative areas and scope out FAO's potential role in areas that may not be specified in UNDAF* [now, UNSDCF], *but are requested by governments in keeping with FAO's mandate* [After considerable debate, this duality was agreed upon within the context of UN Development System Reform.] *Consequently, strengthening decentralized office capacity to effectively engage with UN Country Teams will become increasingly important* [authors' italics added for emphasis].

The rising profile of climate change, not only as major development challenge, but also as a major funding/financing theme, merits a re-examination of its prominence and position as a cross-cutting issue within the Strategic Framework. ...

Stepping up FAO's resource-mobilization capacity at decentralised levels will become increasingly important and require greater attention to the packaging, communication and marketing of FAO's offerings, comparative advantages and UNDAF-linked contributions to resource partners and governments. [Most resource mobilization is already done at the country level, where most of the donor funding decisions are made.[14] Some country offices are much better at it than others.]

As SDG implementation is nationally owned and led, a large proportion of resources needs to be leveraged at country level for national SDG implementation plans. For countries to achieve the SDGs, far more financing needs to be raised than at present. A large portion of that financing will need to come from government funds, both revenue and debt, as well as private-sector investment. The scope and budgetary envelopes of CPFs will be informed by SDG targets and prioritized by Members and the extent to which FAO can contribute in terms of resource mobilization and investment operations. All of these things will necessitate an increase in FAO resource mobilization and investment operational capacity at the decentralized level. Regional and headquarters-based teams will also be a need to backstop programme preparation, marketing communication and business development support.

The shift in focus from development funding to financing will require FAO to focus on investment impact beyond resource mobilization. The financial resources required to achieve the SDGs call for substantial diversification of and innovation in financing options. Development flows are transitioning from "funding" to "financing" and there has been greater focus on alternative financing methods, including blended financial instruments. (FAO 2019g, 4–5)

FAO has considerable experience in investment support through the Investment Centre, working with the World Bank since in the 1960s, with the European Bank for

---

[14] An example of a positive spin-off was the work at the country level in Bangladesh, in 2010, of the development of the Country Investment Plan for Agriculture, in which the FAO Investment Centre was heavily involved as well as USAID. A FAO representative was the chair of the donor meeting/coordination. It was a prerequisite for a successful application for GAFSP, the multi-donor fund hosted by the World Bank. USAID/Feed the Future played a crucial role. Work was divided among six technical papers, which were coordinated by IFPRI, and the Country Investment Plan was developed and prepared by the FAO Investment Centre. USAID and the European Commission's Dhaka offices funded it. It was a participative process of government, scientists, technicians, universities, the private sector, farmers' organizations, and NGOs. Bangladesh received a grant of US$52 million from GAFSP, and soon after, the Danish International Development Agency (DANIDA) approved an additional US$75 million, while USAID worked on an additional investment program based on the Center for Innovation and Partnership (CIP). The World Bank followed the process closely, and there was strong involvement of the African Development Bank (AfDB), IFAD, and the Inter-American Development Bank (IDB).

Reconstruction and Development (EBRD), now the second largest partner, and with IFAD and regional development banks. There is more to be done, particularly with regard to the private sector, but due to the work of the Investment Centre, FAO is well positioned in this regard. For example, the work with EBRD is all private-sector related. A new evaluation, FAO's "Evaluation of FAO's Private Sector Partnership Strategy" makes many of these same points (FAO OED 2019b). The evaluation notes that, at the time of its adoption in 2013, FAO's Strategy for Partnerships with the Private Sector contributed to more private sector collaboration and resulted in several formal agreements being signed, but this has been ad hoc and one-off, rather than systematic, long-term partnerships. The Evaluation asks FAO to ensure its role in setting and applying policies, norms, and standards are safeguarded, demonstrate concrete and tangible impact for SDGs, seek effective resource mobilization from the private sector, and ensure an open, fair, and transparent process for engagement with the private sector.

Following the adoption of the 2030 Agenda and the SDGs, several UN organizations shifted gear and established deeper and more proactive partnerships with the private sector. FAO has not positioned itself to fully capitalize on such potential and maintains a more conservative approach. Meanwhile, those partnerships formalized by FAO with private sector entities have yielded positive but limited results, and appear to have been more opportunistic and reactive. FAO should strategize on its engagement with the private sector by identifying priority thematic areas for collaboration.

The Multilateral Organisation Performance Assessment Network: Findings and Conclusions

As we discussed in Chapter 6, MOPAN is a network of 18 countries with a shared interest in assessing the effectiveness of the major multilateral organizations they fund (MOPAN 2017). MOPAN undertakes periodic assessments. The latest MOPAN 2017–18 assessment noted that "FAO has strengthened its performance since the last MOPAN assessment in 2014.... [It has] an enhanced strategic focus; stronger operational management, including of fiduciary risk; and a stronger commitment to partnerships" (MOPAN 2018, 7).

The assessment identified several key strengths of FAO including:

1. ...a clear, compelling and focused strategic vision that bodes well for the future.

2. ...a strong commitment to working in partnerships, [including] through South–South co-operation and the private sector.

3. ...the refocusing of FAO's strategic direction...[to] a more integrated, multidisciplinary way of working. The associated shift to a matrix management model has had profound implications for the way in which FAO operates and organises and staffs itself.

4. ...a sound, high-quality financial management systems and improved...systems of internal control.   (MOPAN 2018, 8)

MOPAN identified five major areas for improvement:

1. "Insufficient attention paid to strategic risk management";
2. "Operational and reputational risk" of HR management;
3. Tardiness of FAO's "administrative and operational processes for delivery";

4. *"Insufficient visibility to the organisation's crucial normative work*...Its corporate results framework (CRF)...does not do justice to FAO's key role as a knowledge provider...against the organisation's CRF for 2016–17" (authors' italicization for added emphasis);

5. Reporting of corporate performance is insufficiently integrated and incomplete. "Evidence points to important gaps in FAO's whole-of-organisation view and oversight of performance. Interviews and FAO's own evaluation reports indicate that the tools and approaches used have limited utility for management.... FAO's ability to manage and communicate its performance will be important in the future" (MOPAN 2018, 8–9).

MOPAN stressed that FAO's "key challenge" is that "its normative functions and its role as a provider of global public knowledge rely on a core budget that has nominally stayed flat throughout the review period.... [T]he bigger debate may revolve around how to sustainably fund activities that have traditionally been core-funded in ways that are acceptable to members" (MOPAN 2018, 9). Later, in this chapter, we review these challenges from a historical perspective. How to find sustainable funding for normative work that should remain core activities of FAO, but for which the members are not willing to pay, hoping that someone else will pick up the tab through some creative project-funding, poses a challenge.

FAO is a more complex organization than the other four international agencies and uses a stakeholder model, again, unlike the other four shareholder organizations (see Chapter 6). While all five agencies dealt with in this book are membership organizations, each member of FAO, regardless of size or economic importance, has one vote (with the exception of the European Union); and all, including some that are not members of the Bretton Woods institutions, are members of FAO. Singapore has been a member of the UN since 1965, but joined FAO in 2013.[15]

FAO was founded to achieve agreements among its members on important issues related to food security and nutrition faced by all member countries and to serve as a repository of information and knowledge. This feature was and remains FAO's main asset, although in several areas, there are now alternative sources of information and knowledge. Hence, FAO, like all other international organizations, has been challenged, in a changing external environment, to define those areas in which it has a comparative advantage and a unique niche. Developed countries attach considerable importance to FAO's standard-setting functions, but many developing countries, including China, also increasingly attach importance to FAO's normative work, such as FAO's Codex Alimentarius, or "Food Code" for international standards, guidelines, and codes of practice adopted by the CAC to protect consumer health and promote fair practices in food trade.[16] Developing countries look to FAO for knowledge as freestanding input, not associated with capital transfers and commercial interests. In addition, there are a variety of cross-border issues—such as food safety standards, control of pests and diseases, and national information systems on food and agriculture—that pertain to the World Trade Organization (WTO), which an international organization such as FAO with its necessary legitimacy, expertise, and access to governments can address, even as many informal standards have evolved. While FAO remains the standard- and norm-setting organization and a key source of information and knowledge

---

[15] See "Membership of FAO": http://www.fao.org/legal/home/membership-of-fao/en/

[16] The CAC is a central part of the joint FAO/WHO Food Standards Programme and was established by FAO and WHO in 1963. See http://www.fao.org/fao-who-codexalimentarius/en/

on global food security, it is much less able to operate as effectively at the country level as it did in the 1970s, when UNDP funding facilitated a considerable field presence and generally high-quality staff in the field. Ministry officials who interacted with FAO, who were interviewed during the IEE (FAO 2007a) and for this chapter by Lele, reported that the presence of FAO helped developing countries put into place needed systems for soil surveys and field trials for agricultural crops, among other assistance. Member countries reported their appreciation for these past services of FAO but noted a decline in FAO's presence after withdrawal of UNDP funding.

Organizationally, the erosion of FAO's responsibilities started slowly in the 1970s; for example, the end of UNDP financing nearly 25 years ago was a blow to FAO's high-quality field presence, and a funding issue that is relevant today, with the organization's complex, expanded agenda and stretched field presence. In addition to the emergence of other organizations such as CGIAR in 1972, and the evolution of CGIAR Centers (discussed in Chapter 11), as well as problems with bureaucratic management and the loss of critical expertise at FAO, CGIAR Centers took on the responsibility for crop trials and the International Service for National Agricultural Research (ISNAR), established in 1979, was charged with the function of building the capacity of the national agricultural research systems. FAO had advised developing countries on the relevance of building their national agricultural research and extension systems before ISNAR was established. FAO's capacity to provide knowledge at scale and of the quality, as it once did, was noted by IEE. Many have denied this early critical role of FAO, but a recent paper by Byerlee and Lynam (2020) documents FAO's critical role, together with that of USAID, before CGIAR Centers were established. FAO, similarly, once conducted field trials on crops before the activities of CGIAR's crop Centers (the International Rice Research Institute [IRRI], the International Maize and Wheat Improvement Center [CIMMYT], and the International Institute of Tropical Agriculture [IITA]) expanded. As noted earlier, other external evaluations also noted the need for field presence and country-level results: for example, the DFID Multilateral Aid Review 2013 (DFID and UK Aid 2013). MOPAN 2017–18 noted, "FAO's decentralisation agenda, ... designed to maintain and enhance the organisation's relevance and agility, remains a work in progress" (MOPAN 2018, 24).

Upon taking over the agricultural research function from FAO in 1979, CGIAR established the International Service of the National Agricultural Research (ISNAR), ultimately closing it in 2004, when the Center was merged with IFPRI. Since then, IFPRI has largely focused on monitoring of data and research on investments in agricultural research and has not taken up many of the support functions for national agricultural systems that ISNAR was meant to perform. Building capacity of the national systems, carried out so ably by the Rockefeller Foundation and USAID in the 1960s and 1970s (Lele and Goldsmith 1989), now occurs through the investments by multilateral organizations, such as the World Bank, the Inter-American Development Bank (IDB), and bilateral donors, such as USAID, and increasingly, Germany. World Bank investments in research and development (R&D) are important but much too small, relative to needs, as discussed in Chapter 8. The United States has been, by far, the largest trainer of human capital in agriculture with its rich land grant university tradition, more recently under its "Feed the Future" initiative (see Elliott and Dunning 2016). That assistance, however, is now much smaller than the needs. Indeed, capacity for R&D of developing countries remains one of the largest gaps from the viewpoint of increasing productivity growth, particularly sustainably (Beintema and Stads 2017).

With growing realization of the importance of the provision of GPGs, including its embrace as an authorized mission of the World Bank since 2000, competition for GPG-type goals and global partnership programs has grown, many with overlapping objectives. Most of them are advocacy and knowledge partnerships. It is useful to consider FAO's distinct and complementary role in the provision of public goods, in such areas as food safety standards, control of transboundary pests and diseases, and agricultural statistics, in the context of this rapidly evolving area.

Among the key challenges that the IEE recognized was the governance and management of the organization. Specifically, trust in the leadership of FAO had gradually declined among developed countries over nearly three decades.[17] The fact that only two people had been elected as FAO DGs for 36 years, 18 years each, and that the leadership had come from only two regions of the world, contributed to the tension. The last two DGs were elected in free and fair elections. Graziano was elected uncontested the second time around and did not continue beyond his prescribed two four-year terms. There is every expectation that these terms will be honored by the current DG.

Second, over the long history of FAO and WFP, it is not surprising that there has been tension off and on. WFP was initially part of FAO, and later became a separate entity, in part because of the different imperatives of their missions. WFP needed to be flexible and able to respond quickly. FAO's rules and regulations made it difficult to be agile.[18] More recently, the peak of tension between FAO and WFP was at the end of Ertharin Cousin's term as WFP's Executive Director, subsiding under the current leadership of David Beasley, Executive Director of WFP, appointed in June 2017. Recognizing that there is much to do for each organization, without stepping on each other's toes, FAO and WFP seem to have more clearly carved out their respective responsibilities, with more cooperation and less competition and overlap. There are also tensions between developed country members, particularly the United States, and developing country members, which was at its peak prior to the IEE in 2006 (Shaw 2014).

The dynamics between developed and developing countries has also played out very differently in FAO in recent years. With the emergence of middle-income developing countries, the old Group of 77 (G77) versus OECD country dynamics no longer works. Developing countries have become more stratified, and their capabilities and interests are no longer always aligned closely with the erstwhile, seemingly homogenous G77, whose numbers have been closer to 130 and whose interests have been less homogenous than generally acknowledged. Nevertheless, their interests vary more today, depending on the issue, with ever changing alliances on specific issues, and how they will vote on any issue is less predictable and more complex than in the past. FAO was headed by a Brazilian, and since 2019, by a Chinese leader. Other emerging countries are playing important leadership and contributory roles. Most G77 members voted for China in the last election and most OECD countries voted for France, and although this is a noticeable divide, it was nothing like the old days. Even on budget matters, with the growth of middle-income economies, the assessed contributions of many G77 countries have grown substantially, in some case more than doubling, so their interest in a zero growth budget is now shared with the United States

---

[17] Some reviewers of an earlier version of this chapter noted that critics considered the process flawed because of one-country, one-vote, and some did not like the outcome and would have preferred some type of qualified voting. There was also grumbling in June 2019 by OECD members when the French candidate did not win, but the Chinese candidate won by a very large margin, on the first round. The US-backed candidate got 12 votes out of 194. Was it a flawed process?

[18] The appointment letter of the WFP director is still issued by the UN secretary-general and the FAO DG.

and Japan. The EU members saw a decline in their assessed contributions, so they may have been more open to budget increases, but it was not pressed. These changes have largely removed the old North–South divide on the budget, but it is even more difficult to envisage a significant increase in regular program funding through increase in assessed contributions.

In this vein, assessments, including the UK's DFID and MOPAN 14 upgraded the rating of FAO's performance in four important areas: corporate strategy based on clear mandate, country focus on results, support of national plans, and contribution to policy dialogue—the rating was raised from "inadequate or below" to "strong or above" (MOPAN 2011, 2014; DFID and UK Aid 2011, 2016). MOPAN (2014), but expressed concerns about results-based budgeting and management of HR.[19] According to MOPAN 2017–18, too, results-based budgeting has improved, but not management of HR. As stated earlier, HR management is getting more attention.

Staff and Council members have stressed FAO's "controlling" management style, with relatively little internal consultation with and leeway for senior managers and staff to take initiatives forward. This management style, too, has begun to change under the leadership of the new DG, and it has lifted morale.

In the new DG's first year, he took immediate, corrective action, starting with a change of the HR director and a reset in the roles of ADG, with division directors now all reporting directly to one of the DDGs, or to the (new) Chief Scientist and Chief Economist, as approved by the FAO Council (July 2020).

FAO and Global Public Goods

The IEE performed another important function by articulating the nature and sources of the tension between GPGs and FAO's field operations, and the steps needed to address them. This tension has been attenuated, but it has not gone away and, indeed, the most recent MOPAN 2017–18 flags that same issue, as shown earlier in this chapter.

Given the complexities of FAO's mission, its membership structure, and governance, as well as the fact that it is not a financing institution, generating consensus is often a challenge. Getting consensus on global policy priorities has been a source of tension over the years, as has agreement on the role of FAO and the strategies and actions necessary to generate global outcomes. Some critics have argued that FAO should fulfill its GPGs function at the global level and divest from performing country activities (see CGD [2013]). With the advent of the SDGs, however, it is unlikely that any knowledgeable critic would put forward a view such as this today.

Global Public Goods, the Technical Cooperation Programme, and Sustainable Development Goals

FAO cannot deliver on its GPGs function in many areas without effective capacity at the country level to deliver GPGs. Developing countries look to FAO for technical

---

[19]   MOPAN 2017–18 noted:

New recruitment rules designed to promote the representativeness of FAO staff (in relation to members) over time, risk disrupting field activities in the short term, if not carefully introduced. More generally, a number of changes have been instituted in ways perceived as arbitrary or lacking transparency. (MOPAN 2018, 25)

assistance as a trusted partner. Who will help developing countries to build such a capacity and how? Evaluations of the World Bank's global programs, many of which are donor-funded to generate GPGs, raise similar issues (World Bank 2002). Without capacity in developing countries and financing, developing countries often are unable to deliver on public goods. FAO, with its regional and country office presence, has a comparative advantage in performing the function of creating capacity in developing countries. Therefore, in certain areas, FAO should take the lead, in a partnership with others, such as with the World Bank, to command more funding, and with others who may have specific expertise, such as some of the US or European agencies on food safety standards, but which may lack FAO's global reach, infrastructure, and broad legitimacy among member countries.

The 2017 Evaluation of FAO's contribution to inclusive and efficient agricultural and food systems (SO4) supports this conclusion. It notes:

> FAO has a comparative advantage in supporting the formulation of standards, providing authoritative data, and promoting enabling environments for value chain development. However, SO4 faces capacity gaps in the areas of food safety, trade, value chain development, agribusiness, investment support at the regional level, and value chain finance at headquarters that constrain the ability of the programme to reach the ambition of the Objective. These gaps pose reputational risks, as well as limit capacities to backstop and scale-up field projects. [FAO's production data have come under criticism, and elsewhere in this book, we point out data issues.] (FAO OED 2017a, 38–9)

All international staff at the country level, with the exception of a FAO Representative and one or two staff members funded by assessed contributions, are funded by projects. If there are few SO4 projects, by definition, there are few field-level technical resources. Similarly, resource mobilization for SO4 has been quite difficult, particularly relative to other more traditional and easily understood SOs. The vast majority of voluntary resources (which the report finds already high) are mobilized at the country level, as that is where the donor decision-making is located.

FAO's progress on the reforms related to the performance of its GPGs functions continues to be work in progress. That work contributes to its flagship reports on the *State of the Food and Agriculture*, *State of the Food Insecurity*, and the *State of the World's Forests and Fisheries*, as well as the work of the Committee on World Food Security (CFS). These activities and products have acquired increasing importance in a globalized, interconnected world. Yet, the efficiency, effectiveness, and quality of FAO's operational assistance to developing countries, even in these specific areas of GPGs, has been hampered by a limited budget, lingering internal organizational and management issues, and lack of support from members to synergistically achieve long-term, sustainable results.

Debates surrounding FAO's global data sets, assembled from data from member countries and using standard concepts, have related to the timeliness and reliability of data on food security or forest degradation, discussed in Chapters 2, 3, and 4. The evaluations (including the IEE) have noted the lack of reliability of data, particularly due to limited capacity, especially among low-income countries (LICs) to generate high-quality data.[20]

[20] See Morten Jerven's *Poor Numbers: How We are Misled by African Development Statistics and What to Do About It* (Jerven 2013).

Hence, the new "50 × 2030" initiative is significant. It is "the biggest effort made to date to fund agricultural data collection, with a target of raising more than $500 million in support of that cause." The initiative will emphasize three priorities: "First, to scale up current activities, second, to strengthen collaboration with multiple stakeholders, and third, to have the commitment of country authorities and the donor community" (FAO 2018c). Two existing and tested survey approaches will form "the backbone" of the "50 × 2030" initiative: FAO's Agricultural Integrated Surveys (AGRISurvey)[21] and the World Bank's Living Standards Measurement Study's Integrated Surveys on Agriculture (LSMS–ISA). The "50 × 2030" initiative brings together the two tools "within a multi-institutional partnership . . . to make improved agricultural data available in 35 countries by 2025 and in 50 countries by 2030" (FAO 2018c).

An important innovation of FAO on the measurement of food insecurity is the Food Insecurity Experience Scale (FIES), one of the SDG2 indicators, which was discussed in Chapter 4.

According to then DG Graziano da Silva: "FAO's AGRIsurvey allows countries to track progress on at least four SDG targets, such as labour productivity and income of small scale holders (SDG2.3), agricultural sustainability (SDG2.4), women's ownership on agricultural land (SDG5.a) and food losses (SDG12.3)" (FAO 2018c).

In some cases, such as water, forests, or fisheries, member countries have either lacked systematic data collection systems or have been reluctant to share data with FAO. With rapid improvement and reduced costs in geographic information systems (GIS), information technology (IT), and other technologies, a surge in data is expected. Still, unless developing country policymakers attach the importance of data in policymaking and maintain and build relevant in-country capacities—and unless donors cooperate and do not fund short-term efforts that compete with and undermine long-term capacity building—little high-quality data, which FAO can assemble and disseminate, will be generated by countries. Furthermore, technologies, such as GIS, the Internet, nanotechnologies, and cell phones will result in "big data" from multiple sources, and may make the type of data that FAO has been assembling from member countries' governments irrelevant in years to come. In the meantime, FAO will continue to have a critical GPG function in generating information and knowledge.

FAO has untapped potential to be more effective at the country level, given its unique and multifaceted knowledge of food and agriculture in interrelated areas of land, water, soils, forests, and fisheries. Evaluations of FAO programs have noted that FAO is spread thin, despite the developing world's need for FAO to be more effective at the country level. FAO's evaluations have been divided on this subject. Some have noted the lack of sufficient attention and resources to its GPG function such as food safety regulations, control of transboundary pests and diseases; and others have lamented weak work at the country level. There is no hard and fast rule that can be applied to allocations between these two types of activities, but it is clear that currently both are under-provisioned for all of the activities in a country, with the exception of Technical Cooperation Programme (TCP) projects, which are funded through voluntary contributions.

TCP was set up under DG Saouma to use RP funds (assessed contributions) for technical assistance at the country level: that is, where FAO self-funds country-level activities rather than relying on voluntary donor funds. This amount is set at 14 percent of the overall RP

---

[21] See http://gsars.org/wp-content/uploads/2017/01/AGRIS-POSTER-700x1000-01-11-FINAL.pdf

budget, so around US$140 million per biennium. A major evaluation of TCP was underway when this chapter was being finalized. The Investment Centre, which we discuss later in the chapter, is the division that implements the Cooperative Programme with the World Bank, and other project formulation work with the IFIs. Overall, the shares turn out to be something like 60 percent IFIs and 40 percent FAO RP contributions, which are essentially pooled for work on projects in agreement with the IFIs. In the World Bank's case, there is an agreed number of staff weeks of Investment Centre staff (or consultants hired by FAO) charged at a standard rate, for support to a series of projects agreed upon by the relevant units in the Bank.

The findings of the TCP evaluation will be presented to the Programme Committee in November 2020.

There has never been a proposal by management or members to increase the size of the RP-funded country office staff. Recent reports from the Caribbean, the Gulf Cooperation Council States (GCCS), and other subregional offices suggest that the level of country activity depends on project resource mobilization at the country level.

Some interesting questions are raised. Developing countries consider FAO to be the most trusted international organization, without an agenda of its own. Skeptics see greater trust in FAO, resulting from the fact that FAO does not offer "tough" advice that is critical of developing countries' policies.

Challenges to improving FAO's performance at the country level have been intertwined with its weak priority setting at headquarters. For a long time, the debates in the Council over normative work have been about specific regular program allocations to certain aspects of FAO's normative work: antimicrobial resistance (AMR), Codex, and biodiversity being the most prominent examples over the last several years. The amounts called for in each case are quite small, a few million dollars for AMR in the food chain and Codex, for example, with a total price tag for all three of about US$4–5 million. There was never a suggestion that this money should come at the expense of keeping country offices open, as opposed to other cost savings in other technical areas.

G77 members often advocate for regular program budget increases. They expect that the increased budget will lead to more activities in their country (or as a group), but it does not. The way to increase country-level activities is either to increase the size of the TCP budget, which is set at 14 percent of the total, as we have noted previously, or to raise more voluntary funding.

How does the previous discussion relate to FAO's organizational strategy? FAO has had a clearer set of priorities since 2007 and, particularly since 2012, FAO has fully embraced SDGs in its program of work and SF. The organization has been shaped to address these priorities, including its approach to decentralization. And yet, the need to fund its GPG agenda has not received the attention it deserves.

FAO's HR strategy also needed attention. A new director of personnel was appointed in December 2019. FAO has had considerable turnover of country representatives, some with qualified recruits (MOPAN 2018). FAO continues to be constrained by lack of growth in assessed contributions and the need to raise voluntary resources, combined with its recruitment practices. All of the UN that is funded by assessed contributions has essentially the same geographic representation guidelines, with the definitions of underrepresented, equitably represented, or overrepresented by staff numbers, tied to the volume of their assessed contributions, based on country income. It does not apply to voluntarily funded projects.

It needs long-term, assured financing—either through increased assessed contributions from member countries or an endowed trust fund, in return for demonstrated and independently evaluated results—for it to be the center of excellence that it could be. An endowed trust fund would not be the only option. Pooled funding for a certain thematic area (smaller than one of the SPs, this funding could support normative work at headquarters, country-level activities, and provide additional resources for backstopping that work. With rapid growth in international trade and changing commodity markets; complex effects on the outlook for food security and poverty; the growing pressure on land, water, and genetic resources; and climate change, the world deserves nothing less.

Divided Governance: Southern Leadership with Challenges—Hierarchical and Authoritarian

FAO's governance structure of "one country, one vote" was designed as a forum where all member countries could debate global issues and reach agreements with respect to food and agriculture policy on an equal basis. FAO is more inclusive than Bretton Woods Institutions. Some of FAO's members are not members of the Bretton Woods institutions and are members of FAO by virtue of their membership in the UN.[22] The "one country, one vote" model engenders a high level of trust from FAO's developing country members, but it is unclear as to the extent to which this view is shared by developed country members candidates.

FAO Conference

FAO is directed by the Conference of Member Nations, which meets every two years. Early on, the Conference met annually, but in 1949, the constitution was amended so that sessions would be held every two years. The Conference is responsible for acting on applications for FAO membership, electing the members of the Council, reviewing and approving the organization's work program, deciding the level of its budget, setting the scale of contributions, reviewing the state of food and agriculture, making decisions on administrative and constitutional questions, and appointing the DG and the Independent Chairperson of the Council.[23]

FAO Director-General

The Conference elects a DG.[24] The FAO Constitution (Article VII) provides, "There shall be a Director-General of the Organization who shall be appointed by the Conference..." and further, that "Subject to the general supervision of the Conference and the Council, the Director-General shall have full power and authority to direct the work of the Organization" (FAO 1945).

---

[22] For a list of members that is searchable by accession date and participation, see FAO's site: http://www.fao.org/unfao/govbodies/gsb-membershipandbureau/search-by-region/en/

[23] See FAO's Governing and Statutory Bodies website: http://www.fao.org/unfao/govbodies/gsbhome/gsb-home/en/

[24] Qu Dongyu of China was elected DG of FAO during the 41st session of the FAO Conference on June 23, 2019.

The Conference decided to limit the terms of office of future FAO DGs, starting with the election in 2005, so that FAO DGs "should be appointed for a term of six years, renewable only once for a further term of four years" (UN 2003). In 2009, Article VII was amended again to reduce the term limits of FAO DGs to four years, eligible for reappointment only once for a further term of four years (FAO 2009a). The norm of two terms of four years for the DG and more frequent rotation would help renew and refresh the organization.

Clear Wins through Partnerships

In the long history preceding Graziano da Silva, there have been a number of clear wins for global outcomes, centered on FAO, which are often overlooked. Such was the case when WFP (discussed in Chapter 12) was first formally established within FAO in 1960 to internationalize emergency food aid. With strong support from the United States, the Cooperative Programme was established between the World Bank and FAO in 1964. It has enabled the World Bank, and later, other international organizations, including IFAD and the Global Environment Facility (GEF) to draw on FAO's technical expertise to expand their investment operations. Founded in 1964, FAO's Investment Centre partners with governments, IFIs, national organizations, the private sector, and producer organizations to provide investment support services to developing and transition countries in food security, nutrition, agriculture, rural development, and sustainable natural resources management (FAO 2014a).[25]

FAO worked with the World Bank to establish CGIAR in 1972 (Baum 1986, 125–6), during the avian flu outbreaks, and in addressing the global food crisis in 2008, discussed in Chapter 8 on the World Bank, as well as on the collaborative "50 × 2030" initiative on data, discussed earlier.

The Consequences of Leadership Style

In the case of FAO, both Saouma and Diouf were widely described as autocrats, with centralized leadership and long tenures becoming problems, but their leadership also had considerable following. WHO evolved differently. It introduced two 5-year term limits on leadership in 1996, following the tenure of an ineffective DG. Many in WHO attribute the establishment of the Joint United Nations Programme on HIV/AIDS (UNAIDS) and the Global Fund to Fight AIDS, Tuberculosis and Malaria (GFATM) to the failure of WHO leadership to respond to the demand from donor countries' constituencies to expand interventions in HIV/AIDS. WHO also experienced substantial rotation of DGs, and they came from both developed and developing country nationalities. Few completed more than a single term, with the exception of Dr. Margaret Chan. WHO's leadership selection, with greater voice given to the regional directors has had both positive and negative effects. Its delayed response to Ebola was seen as a result of greater dominance of regional leaders relative to the global director general, and the emergence of SARs prior to that provided an altogether different challenge. Some considered WHO's response altogether too quick, and others, not quick enough. In any case, the leadership rotation helped restore WHO's global

---

[25] FAO's Investment Centre supported about 70 countries in 2017 (FAO 2018b).

leadership in health to a degree. WHO has also accepted far greater dependence on trust funds to pursue its health agendas of interest to donors than did FAO until recently, largely in the areas of communicable diseases, recognizing that donor countries traditionally have had little interest in increasing the WHO budget to address endemic, noncommunicable diseases in poor countries (see Figure 9.3, WHO's Biennial Program Budget). The new debate on nutrition and health and life-cycle effects of poor food choices on health, however, has changed the balance of attention donors are giving to noncommunicable diseases.

Unfortunately, for international organizations, FAO and WHO are not the only organizations that have faced leadership challenges. The World Bank, in 2011, and IMF in 2012, each went through leadership changes accompanied by controversy and outright scandal, which emphasized the importance of selecting qualified leaders of integrity, regardless of nationality, for international organizations. Both of these institutions faced open lobbying for non-OECD candidates for leadership from established entities within OECD countries, issues of voting shares of developing countries, and the criteria for future leadership successions, away from the traditional reservation of positions to US and EU nationals. While traditional patterns of leadership have ensured funding from OECD countries for now, it has also jeopardized ownership of the Bretton Woods institutions in a changed world in which the role of emerging countries has increased.[26]

FAO's SF will take time to show greater impacts. Nevertheless, the rapid pace of change in the other organizations has given FAO a significant challenge: on the one hand, of substantial costs of the reform process to make the necessary changes, and on the other, of making a convincing case to the donors that the reforms are worth supporting with large

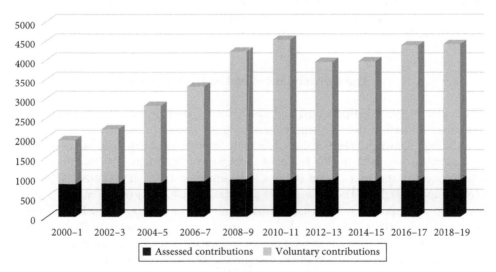

Figure 9.3 WHO's biennial program budget: Voluntary contribution and regular budget, 2000–1 to 2018–19 (US$m)

Source: https://www.who.int/about/finances-accountability/budget/en/

---

[26] Devesh Kapur (2019) noted that global governance of intergovernmental organizations was so weakened under the Trump administration that there was no serious discussion of alternative candidates in the most recent selection of leaders at the helm in 2019 in the World Bank and IMF.

enough sums—to turn it into a premier organization, a center of excellence that FAO deserves to be and one that the world needs, if it is serious about world food security.

It is clear that a sizeable amount of untied funds would be needed annually, together with organizational reforms proposed by the new DG to turn FAO into a center of excellence as a way to increase FAO's impact. The sad reality is that few donors are willing to contribute unearmarked or slightly earmarked voluntary funds. This could change, as tightly earmarked voluntary contributions are now subject to a 1 percent levy, an element of the reformed funding mechanisms for new UN country teams, to fund the repositioned United Nations Development System (UNDS).

FAO is working towards less earmarked voluntary contributions through a new "business portfolio." The idea is that donors choose certain areas of work where their voluntary contributions should go while leaving it to the FAO secretariat to determine for which specific projects these funds would be used. The advantage of these almost unearmarked voluntary contributions is that FAO can pool funds from several donors so as to implement much bigger programmatic approaches that evaluations call for reducing significantly the transaction and administrative costs. The buy-in from donors is still rather lukewarm.

The previous DG's Brazilian nationality ensured geographic diversification in leadership; his experience as a key player in Zero Hunger in his own country and his knowledge of FAO were important assets, although his managerial style was unpopular for being top-down and centralized, with micromanagement leaving no voice and scope for innovation at lower levels. Some noted, for Graziano "geographical distribution" had become a mantra, which has led to serious negative impacts on the technical capacity. In the Audit of the on Recruitment and Onboarding of Professional Staff, submitted in November 2018, the Inspector General made a number of very critical remarks. For instance, a survey of hiring managers found that 74 percent of the managers disagreed (28 percent strongly disagreed) that recruitment objectives in terms of geographical distribution did not diminish the technical suitability of appointees. Furthermore, diversity requirements were thought to give preference to less qualified candidates from target groups. The 2018 Annual Report of the Inspector General observed: "Most recruitment actions ran smoothly and resulted in the hiring of technically competent candidates in line with recruitment objectives and guiding principles (geographic and gender balance). However, there was room for improvement in some phases of the regular recruitment and onboarding process" (FAO 2018e, 49). The report noted, "Several hiring managers indicated that in the majority of cases the appointed candidate is not the person considered most suitable by the PSSC [Professional Staff and Selection Committees] and this has had an impact on their units' technical capacity" (FAO 2018e, 8).

FAO Council

The FAO Conference also elects a council of 49 member states (serving three-year rotating terms), which provides executive oversight of program and budgetary activities. Article V of the Constitution, covering the FAO Council, states that each member has one representative and one vote.[27] The Council membership reflects the seven regional groups. Usually more

---

[27] See FAO Governing and Statutory Bodies website: FAO Council: http://www.fao.org/unfao/govbodies/gsbhome/council/en/

than two-thirds of the Council members are from developing countries (currently 34 out of the 49 members). The Council is FAO's second-level governing body, and its work is carried out under an Independent Chairman (also elected by the Conference), unlike at the World Bank and IFAD, where the CEO also chairs the board. In the case of the World Bank, the Zedillo Commission considered this arrangement to be unhealthy and suggested reforms (Linn 2009; Zedillo 2009). Article V also provides the Council with the assistance of eight committees tasked with most of the substantive and detailed work.

The Program & Finance Committees work well, are member state-chaired and are central to FAO's operations. The Committee on Agriculture (COAG), open to observers from civil society and private sector, is also a venue for the review of the FAO Work Programme and suggestions for changes in scope and emphasis of programs (see Figure 9.4).

Figure 9.4 still reflects old thinking. New issues, such as climate change and food systems, and the need for an integrated approach to problem solving, will need to be given more attention, even if the organizational structure reflects silos, particularly of the Technical Committees.

Funding

Figures 9.5 and 9.6 show FAO's regular and voluntary contributions.[28] The assessed contributions (for core technical work, cooperation, and partnerships) are member countries' contributions, confirmed at the biennial FAO Conference. The voluntary contributions provided by members and other partners tend to support technical and emergency (including rehabilitation) assistance to governments, although some voluntary funds also support FAO's core work. With the advent of SP5 on resilience and the global developments in looking at the humanitarian–development nexus, almost all of this work takes place in crisis

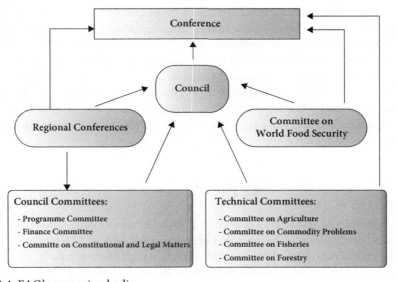

Figure 9.4 FAO's governing bodies
Source: http://www.fao.org/unfao/govbodies/gsbhome/gsb-home/en/

[28] See http://www.fao.org/about/strategic-planning/en/

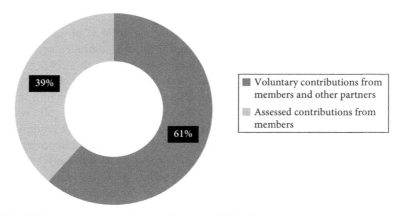

Figure 9.5 FAO assessed and voluntary funding, 2018–2019

Source: http://www.fao.org/about/strategic-planning/en/

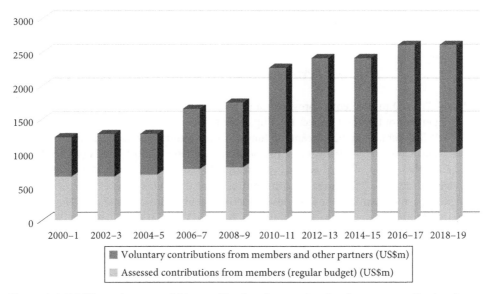

Figure 9.6 FAO's total approved biannual budget (assessed and voluntary contributions), 2000–1 to 2018–19 (US$m)

Source: Based on data from the Director-General's Medium Term Plan and Program of Work & Budget Reports (FAO 2017a) and http://www.fao.org/about/strategic-planning/en/

countries, although not all of it is "emergency-related," as in the past. The issues of emergencies are discussed in Chapter 12.

The total FAO budget planned for 2018–19 was US$2.6 billion. Sixty-one percent of FAO's funding came from voluntary contributions from members and other partners, an increase in recent years, as assessed contributions (39 percent paid by member countries) have remained unchanged for years and declined in real terms (FAO n.d.; CGD 2013).[29]

---

[29] See FAO website: About FAO/Strategic Planning: http://www.fao.org/about/strategic-planning/en/

The decline in assessed contributions in real terms has been accompanied by a rise in voluntary contribution resources from US$1 billion in 1996–7 to US$1.6 billion for 2018–19. In 2018, US$1.14 billion was mobilized through voluntary contributions, of which 55 percent was for development (down from 59 percent in 2017). Because these figures come from two different biannual programs of work and budget, they should be treated with caution. Without additional assessed contributions, a major shift in allocating the RP resources to technical support and backstopping would likely require reducing the number of country offices, and perhaps scaling down staffing in the regional offices— neither of which has ever been seriously contemplated or even raised by member governments or management. So, some kind of an endowment or pooled funds earmarked for thematic programs, such as response to climate change, might be needed in the future. FAO's largest donors over the past few years have been the European Union, the United States, the UN Office for Coordination of Humanitarian Affairs (OCHA), GEF, the United Kingdom, Japan, Norway, Germany, UNDP, and the World Bank. These resources are generally earmarked for fixed-period projects that are directed by donor priority. There is limited core operational work at the country level. High-income countries often argue that FAO should focus on statistics and policy, while developing countries call for more in-country technical cooperation assistance.

Programs and Projects

In 2016–17, FAO implemented programs and projects with a total value of US$1.6 billion. About 8 percent of the total project funding came from assessed contributions through the FAO TCP. The remaining 92 percent are funded from voluntary contributions, through the Government Cooperative Programme (34 percent), Unilateral Trust Funds (UTFs) (5 percent), and other forms of Trust Funds (53 percent) that include UN Joint Programmes. The "Regular Programme," the assessed contributions, are flat; those funds cover only a very small portion of the work in the field (less than 10 percent of project funding). The rest is all donor-funded projects, now approaching two-thirds of the overall budget. The RP budget only covers the salary of the FAO representatives, two national professional staff, some administrative staff, and the rent, lights, and overhead. All other work at the country level, which is often substantial, needs to funded by projects.[30]

Operations

According to the "Programme Implementation Report 2016–17," RP expenditures accounted for 44 percent of total expenditures, including 5 percent for the TCP. Extrabudgetary expenditures, accounting for 56 percent of total expenditures, were reported by type: emergency assistance projects (44 percent), non-emergency field and global projects (40 percent), and global and interregional projects (16 percent). Fifty-eight percent of RP resources were spent at headquarters, a 1 percent decrease over 2014–15, "demonstrating the financial consequences of increasing decentralization of activity within FAO" (FAO 2019e, 102). Table 9.2 shows that a large portion of FAO's funding is for

---

[30] From "About FAO/Who We Are": http://www.fao.org/about/who-we-are/en/

emergency assistance (the 2010–11 budget for emergency assistance was three times that for non-emergency activities), and the FAO/Government Cooperative Programme, while funding for the (non-emergency) TCP (technical support and training) declined. From the Forty-first Session, June 22–9, 2019, in Rome, the DG's Foreword for the Program Implementation Report 2016–17 noted: "the continued flat budgets since 2012–13 put FAO in a very delicate situation that may, in the near future, impact our delivery of results" (FAO 2019e, 2).

In practice, there is not much competition for RP resources between normative work and country-level work. The latter is not funded by RP, except for keeping the offices open. There is competition for RP resources between headquarters (HQ) and regional offices, which perform somewhat similar functions and are staffed with technical people that correspond with, and report to, HQ divisions through the matrix management approach. There is also a problem with the lack of RP financial resources and RP-funded staff time to backstop project work, but the problem has always been woeful underfunding and lack of attention to this work. This issue, however, has not been high enough on the members' or management's radar, and that needs to change.

In reality, this was never an important issue for RP resource allocation (as almost all country-level work is donor project-funded), although it has always surfaced in debates around the budget. An increased RP budget does not translate into increased country-level work, and it never has.

The Government Cooperative Programme is a financing modality in which a resource partner provides funds to FAO for the provision of technical assistance services (such as policy advice and normative activities) for a specific developing country or group of countries. Other modalities that received significant funding in recent years include UTFs, the FAO/EU Food Facility, the UN Joint Programme, and the Multilateral Trust Funds. UTFs are agreements arranged between FAO and a recipient country, whereby funds are provided by the beneficiary country to FAO for its technical expertise. The FAO/EU Food Facility, a three-year program set up in 2009, in response to the soaring food prices in developing countries, also received a large amount of funding for 2010–11. The facility focused on improving access to agricultural inputs and services, such as fertilizers and seeds, safety net measures to maintain or increase agricultural production capacity, and vocational training and support for agricultural professionals. The UN Joint Programme is a multi-donor funding mechanism for support of nationally led and owned programming processes, such as the FAO/IFAD/WFP/UN Women's collaborative program entitled "Accelerating Progress towards the Economic Empowerment of Rural Women," which fosters policies such as gender mainstreaming (FAO 2012a). Multilateral trust funds typically assist developing countries and multilateral organizations to identify and plan effective and sustainable agricultural policies, program, and projects, and to monitor their implementation (FAO 2008c, 2019e).

Since the launch of FAO's TCP in 1976, projects have been approved primarily to put FAO's technical knowledge at the disposal of its member countries. The TCP is financed only through the RP, and therefore, under FAO's direct control. It is much smaller than voluntary contributions. The TCP focuses on improving household or national food security and rural livelihoods, as well as on reducing poverty, through short-term, quick-impact technical support and training. Historically, the largest percentage of FAO's TCP resources has gone to the Africa region. In 2016–17, 786 TCP projects totaling US$151.9 million were approved, as shown in Table 9.2, compared to 501 projects that totaled US$145.7 million in 2014–15. "Overall, the level of approvals and number of projects approved

Table 9.2 Distribution of approved Technical Cooperation Programme resources by region, 2016–17

Region	Total budget (US$m)	Number of projects	Percentage of total approved budget
Africa	65.3	274	43
Near East	12.8	54	8
Asia and the Pacific	34.0	194	22
Europe	12.3	73	8
Latin America and the Caribbean	25.0	184	16
Inter-regional	2.6	7	2
Total	**152.0**	**786**	**100**

Source: FAO (2019e, table 4, 93).

has increased by 4% and 57% respectively as compared to the previous biennium. The increase in number of projects is mainly due to a change in how TCPR [TCP Facility] projects are captured... 68% of the approved budget allocation is for national projects" (FAO 2019e, 92).[31]

As expected, two-thirds of technical cooperation funds are spent in Africa and in Asia and the Pacific. The biggest need is in Africa. TCP projects address both development support and emergency assistance needs. The distribution by category of project intervention is provided in Table 9.3.

"During the biennium [2016–17], delivery reached US$135.6 million, compared to US$125.8 million during 2014–15. [Table 9.4] illustrates the distribution of the TCP assistance delivered during the biennium appropriation. by category of project" (FAO 2019e, 94).

"The distribution of TCP assistance by Strategic Objectives is illustrated in [Table 9.5]. Over 61% of delivery falls under two Strategic Objectives: *Increase and improve provision of goods and services from agriculture, forestry and fisheries in a sustainable manner* (SO2) and *Increase the resilience of livelihoods to threats and crises* (SO5)" (FAO 2019e, 94).

Delivery of Global Public Goods

It is worth recalling that FAO is considered the only entity that can provide many of the needed GPGs in the areas of its mandate (such as global analysis, statistics, international standards, and advocacy). "The Codex Alimentarius or 'Food Code' is a collection of standards, guidelines, and codes of practice adopted by the Codex Alimentarius Commission," a body established in 1961 by FAO, and joined by WHO in June 1962. The Commission's goals are "to protect consumer health and promote fair practices in food trade." The Codex Alimentarius is recognized by WTO as an international reference point

---

[31] Reference to the TCP evaluation is made *inter alia* in Table 1 in Annex 1 to the Report of the 127th Session of the Programme Committee (Rome, November 4–8, 2019) and in the Report on the 163rd Session of the Council of FAO (December 2–6, 2019) in para. 11.e: "[The Council] looked forward to reviewing the comprehensive evaluation of the TCP in 2020 to be presented to the Council through the Finance and Programme Committees" (FAO 2019f, 4).

Table 9.3 Technical Cooperation Programme project approvals by category

Project category	2014–15		2016–17	
	Total budget (US$m)	Number of projects	Total budget (US$m)	Number of projects
Emergency assistance[a]	27.4	61	24.4	57
Support to development[b]	95.7	304	105.4	367
TCP facility[c]	22.6	136	22.1	362
Total	145.7	501	151.9	786

Notes:

[a] Emergency assistance—During the 2016–17 biennium, 57 emergency projects for a total of US$24.4 million were approved. This compares with 61 emergency projects for a total of US$27.4 million in 2014–15. Projects were approved, in particular, in response to droughts and floods caused by El Niño and cyclones.

[b] Development support—In 2016–17, 367 projects amounting to a total of US$105.4 million were approved for development support, an increase of 21 and 10 percent, respectively, from the 304 projects for a total of US$95.7 million which were approved in 2014–15. Given the requirements for technical support, projects responding to the outbreak of the Fall Armyworm in African countries are included in this category.

[c] The TCP Facility is used to respond to requests for limited technical expertise, formulation of project proposals, and documents for interaction with resource partners, and strengthening program planning. Since 2016, each TCP Facility is recorded as an individual project rather than a component under a single umbrella project in each country. This allows for better management of resources and oversight, but has resulted in more than doubling the number of TCP Facility projects from 136 in 2014–15 to 362 in 2016–17, despite slightly reducing the overall resources allocated through this modality from US$22.6 million to US$22.1 million. Out of 389 TCP projects with budgets above US$100,000 active in 2016–17, 59 percent addressed gender equality, exceeding the target of 30 percent for Standard 15.

Source: FAO (2019e, table 5, 93–4).

Table 9.4 Technical Cooperation Programme delivery by project category, 2016–17

Project category	US$ million	Percentage
Emergency assistance	20.8	15.3
Support of development	95.5	70.4
TCP Facility	19.3	14.2
Total	135.6	100.0

Source: FAO (2019e, table 6, 94).

for the resolution of disputes concerning food safety and consumer protection (FAO and WHO 2020).

The Commission on Genetic Resources for Food and Agriculture, an intergovernmental forum, was established in FAO in 1983, to deal with issues related to plant genetic resources.[32] Over time, it has also come to cover other components of biodiversity relevant to food and agriculture, such as animal genetic diversity, forest genetic diversity, aquatic genetic diversity, microorganisms, and invertebrates. It is the only permanent forum for governments to discuss and negotiate matters specifically relevant to biological diversity for

---

[32] See http://www.fao.org/cgrfa/en/

Table 9.5 Technical Cooperation Programme delivery by Strategic Objectives, 2016–17

Strategic Objective	Delivery in 2016–17(US$m)	Percentage oftotal delivery
1. Contribute to the eradication of hunger, food insecurity and malnutrition	19.3	14.2
2. Increase and improve provision of goods and services from agriculture, forestry and fisheries in a sustainable manner	50.2	37.0
3. Reduce rural poverty	16.4	12.1
4. Enable more inclusive and efficient agricultural and food systems	16.9	12.5
5. Increase the resilience of livelihoods to threats and crises	32.2	23.7
OB6 Technical quality, knowledge and services, including the cross-cutting theme on gender	0.6	0.4
Total	135.6	100.0

Source: FAO (2019e, table 7, 94).

food and agriculture, including policies for the sustainable use and conservation of genetic resources for food and agriculture, and the fair and equitable sharing of benefits derived from their use. In 2001, after seven years of negotiations in the Commission, the FAO Conference adopted the International Treaty on Plant Genetic Resources for Food and Agriculture (Resolution 3/2001), a legally binding treaty covering all plant genetic resources for food and agriculture, recognizing farmers' rights and establishing a multilateral system to facilitate access to plant genetic resources for food and agriculture, and to share the benefits derived from their use in a fair and equitable way.

Since its establishment, the Commission has overseen global assessments of the state of the world's plant and animal genetic resources for food and agriculture and negotiated major international instruments, including the International Treaty on Plant Genetic Resources for Food and Agriculture, an important tool for the management of genetic resources, and the latter has acquired growing importance, as the focus has shifted from food production to food systems in which the various parts of GPGs for which FAO is responsible can form a cohesive whole (FAO 2009b; see, also, http://www.fao.org/plant-treaty/overview/en/). The discussion of GPGs and how to look at them are germane to FAO's restructuring going forward.

How GPGs are delivered, depending on their nature, has implications for financing and country capacity critical for them to achieve impacts. Delivery typically uses one of three approaches: the "best shot" approach, the summation approach, or "the shoring up of the weakest link" approach (Sandler 1992).

The "best shot" approach brings to bear the best scientific know-how and expertise, regardless of where it is located in the world, and usually addresses issues of interest to humanity or the environment. The Gates Foundation's support for children's vaccines is an example, as is CGIAR's work, which develops and delivers advanced plant breeding technologies to the world. FAO has not been in the business of mobilizing scientific know-how to generate technologies since CGIAR was established in 1972, but it continues to provide information on best practices, such as integrated pest management. FAO also addresses global public policy issues: for example, on plant genetic resources, food safety (Codex), and voluntary agreements on land and water resources.

There are still other global public policy issues for which FAO could foster international agreements, such as with respect to biosafety of genetically modified organisms; intellectual property rights; information and knowledge on global production, trade, prices and stocks; and monitoring of the implementation of international agreements. FAO uses the other two approaches—namely, the summation approach and the weakest link approach—for the generation of GPGs to a far lesser extent and could do much better in support of these two other types of interventions. The summation approach involves helping countries to develop the capacity to deliver a national public good, the sum of which is aggregated into a GPG, such as FAO's agricultural statistics that are vital for national as well as global policymaking. Conservation of genetic resources at the country level could also use a summation approach to achieve better global outcomes.

The "weakest link" approach helps contain a "public bad" in the weakest, institutionally least-developed countries, thereby preventing its spread to other countries, as is the case of avian flu and other bird and animal diseases. FAO needs internal capacity, not only for early warning of such hazards but also for mobilizing technical assistance to help the weakest developing countries to contain communicable diseases, as it has done successfully with rinderpest and avian flu—much in the same way that WHO is relied upon by developing countries to help contain risks to human health before they become epidemics. Yet, recent experience with avian flu demonstrates that such a function cannot be performed solely with emergency assistance. It requires assisting countries to establish long-term capacity in areas that are politically and socially less "sexy" than gender or environmental issues. Agriculture, in general, seem to be a less popular area, so international organizations recruit more food security experts and fewer agronomists, water engineers, livestock specialists, or foresters.

Understanding the nature of countries' needs is fundamental for FAO to be able to meet the needs of its members. The worst locust invasion has hit East Africa in decades, causing massive amounts of food loss. FAO has launched an emergency appeal for US$76 million to help governments in East Africa to combat the locust invasion. Conflict and climate change contribute to the increase in the problem, and timely addressing of the locust problem is critical (OCHA 2020).

FAO has 194 members today, compared to 39 members at the end of the First Session of the FAO Conference in 1945 (see Box 9.2) (Phillips 1981b, 13). How countries articulate their needs and how they are grouped strategically may help FAO to better understand and respond to the countries' demands through exchange of transcontinental expertise, based on the percentage of people dependent on agriculture and natural resources for livelihoods, the importance of agriculture and rural development to their stage of economic transformation, their human capital and institutional capacity, the extent of their market orientation, or their ability to pay for services or contribute to South–South cooperation—rather than simply by pursuing a supply-driven, regional, or subregional approach.

In the more advanced of developing countries in Asia, Latin America, Eastern Europe, and the Middle East, the demand for high-quality knowledge is considerable, but there are also many alternative sources of information, often from their own neighborhoods: for example, among the Southern Cone countries of the southernmost South America. In contrast, in the least developed countries of sub-Saharan Africa and parts of Asia, slow growth, organizational decline, weak regional neighborhoods, and increased reliance on international assistance suggest a larger role for FAO. Increased institutional diversity offers the opportunity to leverage FAO's limited resources through active partnerships at all levels to a greater extent than FAO has pursued.

Box 9.2 The FAO's Diverse Membership Calls for Different Responses Depending on Internal Capacity[a]

Emerging economies[b]—Large and middle-income, urbanized, or fast-growing countries, such as Argentina, Brazil, Chile, China, India, Mexico, Morocco, Thailand, Tunisia, and Turkey.

Economies in transition[c]—Countries with specific political and institutional legacies, such as Central Asian countries.

Other countries—Countries with considerable internal capacity to absorb new information and knowledge, such as Bangladesh, Central American countries, Egypt, Indonesia, and Pakistan.

Low-income, food-deficit countries[d]—51 small, aid-dependent, slow-growing countries with limited capacity, including most of sub-Saharan Africa and small Asian countries, such as Nepal and the Lao People's Democratic Republic.

Fragile and conflict-affected areas[e]—Countries with ongoing or recently ended conflicts and those in fractious political situations, such as Afghanistan, Central African Republic, Somalia, South Sudan, Yemen, and Syria.

Small island developing states[f]—Countries such as Haiti, East Timor, and Tuvalu.

Notes:

[a] There are a total of 197 members, consisting of 194 member nations, 1 member organization (the European Union), and 2 associate members.
http://www.fao.org/legal/home/membership-of-fao/en/

[b] The term "emerging market economy" was first used in 1981 by Antoine W. van Agtmael of the IFC of the World Bank. Emerging market countries are those that are striving to become advanced countries and are generally on a more economically disciplined track to become more sophisticated, including increased fiscal transparency, focus on production, developing regulatory bodies and exchanges, and acceptance of outside investment. Although some countries like China and India have high production and industry, other factors like low per capita income or a heavy focus on exports lead to the classification of even large countries as emerging markets.

According to the Morgan Stanley Capital International (MSCI) Emerging Market Index, 24 developing countries qualify as emerging markets—including Brazil, Chile, China, Colombia, Czech Republic, Egypt, Greece, Hungary, India, Indonesia, Korea, Malaysia, Mexico, Pakistan, Peru, Philippines, Poland, Qatar, Russia, South Africa, Taiwan, Thailand, Turkey, and United Arab Emirates. The index follows the market caps of the companies on the countries' stock markets.

Additionally, the IMF has a similar list of 23 countries, although there are some discrepancies in the list, compared to the MSCI list. Among the IMF and the MSCI, the S&P, Dow Jones, and Russell all have lists of emerging markets that follow similar strains, although with some variation (see https://unctadstat.unctad.org/EN/Classifications/UnctadStat.EconomicGroupings.Criterias_EN.pdf).

[c] The group of transition economies accounts for the particular circumstances of a group of economies shaped by socialism and now in transition to a market economy. Transition economies are involved in a process of moving from a centrally planned economy to a mixed or free market economy. This group includes Albania, Armenia, Azerbaijan, Belarus, Bosnia and Herzegovina, Georgia, Kazakhstan, Kyrgyzstan, Montenegro, Republic of Moldova, Serbia, Tajikistan, Turkmenistan, Ukraine, Uzbekistan, and the former Yugoslav Republic of Macedonia. Starting in 2010, data for the Ukraine exclude the temporarily occupied territory of the Autonomous Republic of Crimea and Sevastopol (UNCTAD 2018; UN 2019).

[d] Low-income, food-deficit countries (LIFDCs): List for 2018: The list of the LIFDCs stands at 51 countries, one country less than previously, but with some changes in the composition of the list. Three countries have graduated from the list: Nigeria, Pakistan, and Papua New Guinea. Nigeria and Papua New Guinea graduated based on the income criterion, while Pakistan graduated based on the net food-exporter criterion. Two countries, Congo and Vietnam, have been added to the list for not meeting the three criteria for exclusion, discussed next (see http://www.fao.org/countryprofiles/lifdc/en/).

The classification as LIFDC, used for analytical purposes by FAO, is traditionally determined by three criteria. First, a country should have a per capita gross national income (GNI) below the "historical" ceiling used by the World Bank to determine eligibility for IDA assistance and for 20-year IBRD term applied to countries included in World Bank's categories I and II. The 2018 LIFDC list is based on the GNI for 2016 (estimated by the World Bank using the Atlas method) and the historical ceiling of US$1,905 for 2016. The second criterion is based on the net food trade position (that is, gross imports less gross exports) of a country averaged over the preceding three years, for which statistics are available—in this case from 2014, 2015, and 2016. Trade volumes for a broad basket of basic foodstuffs (cereals, roots and tubers, pulses, oilseeds, and oils other than tree crop oils, meat, and dairy products) are converted and aggregated by the calorie content of individual commodities. Thirdly, the self-exclusion criterion is applied when countries that meet the above two criteria specifically request FAO to be excluded from the LIFDC category. In order to avoid countries changing their LIFDC status too frequently, typically reflecting short-term exogenous shocks, an additional factor was introduced in 2001. This factor, called "persistence of position," would postpone the "exit" of a LIFDC from the list, despite the country not meeting the LIFDC income criterion or the food-deficit criterion, until the change in its status is verified for three consecutive years. In other words, a country is taken off the list in the fourth year, after confirming a sustained improvement in its position for three consecutive years.

[e] See https://www.worldbank.org/en/topic/fragilityconflictviolence/brief/harmonized-list-of-fragile-situations; http://pubdocs.worldbank.org/en/892921532529834051/FCSList-FY19-Final.pdf

[f] UN members (38); Non-UN members/Associate members of regional commissions (20). See https://sustainabledevelopment.un.org/topics/sids/list

Source: Adapted from Lele (2007).

There is no scientific way to allocate resources between these competing demands of GPGs and country programs, but more resources to FAO, along with other reforms and a clearer demonstration of FAO's impacts will dampen this debate. A great deal of FAO's work is on GPGs, such as statistics, environment and climate change, information systems for transboundary animal diseases, forest resource assessments, and analysis of trade in agricultural products. "This work is vital because it creates the background against which investors—small or large, public or private—make their decisions" (FAO OED 2013, xxxvii). Most important of these GPGs is FAO's work in statistics. Several organizations, institutes, and governments generate "agricultural, forestry and fisheries data … None, however, provide global statistics in such a wide range of areas as FAO" (FAO 2008b, 6). FAO is unique in assembling, maintaining, analyzing, and disseminating the world's largest and most influential statistical data set on agriculture, broadly defined to include area, yields, and production of crops, livestock, forestry, and fisheries. It is the provider of statistical inputs into debates on many key global and national issues related to sustainable and broad-based development.

Indeed, FAO's position as an international leader in agriculture information and statistics is increasingly under threat, as other governmental and nongovernmental organizations, institutions, foundations, and private sector entities, with larger budgets and growing legitimacy, seek to compete in this area. FAO's efforts have been hindered by insufficient resources to perform this function, and even though donor support for its statistical work has increased, the resources are not nearly what are needed. Donor financing of short-term data collection efforts to meet their own needs may also hamper the long-term efforts (Lele 2007).

The 2008 independent evaluation of FAO's role and work in statistics concluded that the FAO statistics program had challenges, such as the quality of the collection methods, the quality of the data coming to FAO from national sources, and the quality of FAO data reaching the user. The evaluation also concluded that critical human and financial resource and capacity limitations affect the ability of FAO to develop new methods and techniques for use in national statistical systems, as well as provide direct institutional support to its members. This evaluation echoed the IEE's finding in noting that the "most pressing 'emerging' data need is actually a 're-emerging' need: to improve the capacity of member countries for collection and dissemination of country data in order to make the best data available for use in analytic and decision support tools, with priority on the poorest countries, particularly those in Africa" (FAO 2008b, 8). The evaluation concluded that FAO must renew its commitment to improving national statistical capacity and better promote its position of leadership of agricultural statistics at the international level (FAO 2008b).

There has been considerable progress on the allocation of additional resources in FAO's Programme of Work and Budget, although the allocations are not as transparent as they could be, particularly in the use of voluntary contributions. In the 2011 document, for example, resources were provided for the development of the Statistical Working System and a Statistical Data Warehouse; the creation of the Impact Focus Area on capacity building in information and statistics; and the development and implementation of a Global Strategy to Improve Agricultural and Rural Statistics. Furthermore, a Statistics Programme Steering Committee and a Statistics Coordination Working Group were established to coordinate FAO's statistical activities (FAO 2011a).

Key accomplishments have included preparation of the first FAO Statistical Programme of Work 2010–11 (FAO 2013b), re-engineering of FAOSTAT, and development of CountrySTAT (FAO 2010). The 2010 Global Strategy to Improve Agricultural and Rural Statistics was also a significant effort by FAO, World Bank, and the United Nations Statistical Commission to strengthen agricultural statistics. A Chief Statistician was appointed and supported by the Inter-Departmental Working Group on Statistics. The Chief Statistician leads FAO's work in statistics and seeks to improve the quality of the data that FAO produces, collects, and distributes. The position is also tasked with improving coordination of activities within the international statistical community. The International Advisory Group on FAO Statistics (IAGFS) was subsequently formed, and the first meeting was held at FAO headquarters in September 2013. "The mandate of the IAGFS is to advise FAO on statistical priorities, best practices in data compilation, analysis and dissemination, and on the design and implementation of major FAO statistical projects and capacity development programmes" (FAO 2019d). This action will lead to increased transparency, better quality and methodology, and investment in upgrading software and hardware.

Unfortunately, FAOSTAT and FishSTAT (FAO's Fisheries and Aquaculture Statistics) are still not integrated, although it is not clear why. It does make it harder to use the two together, which is unfortunate, given the increasing attention given to fish as a nutritious food.

Thus, our understanding is that statistics were not entirely recognized as a core function of the organization. Large shares of the internal finance of statistical activities have been made dependent upon the SF. The 50 × 2030 initiative, discussed earlier in this chapter, is a good initiative (FAO 2018c), but it does not go far enough. Data improvement related to all matters that FAO is responsible for, using state-of-the-art technology, is essential, and new technology is now making data accessible to all actors.

Policy Work

Policy work and support for investment will be the cornerstone of economic progress. Support of qualified staff is critical. If the management does not put in place competent staff, the risk of nonperformance is high, with all its consequences. FAO cannot fail and needs to maintain the support of its development partners.

The 2012 "Evaluation of FAO's Role and Work in Food and Agriculture Policy," led by Jock R. Anderson, reported that FAO's work on global policy in food security was excellent, consistent, of high quality, and very influential, but that its work on country-level policy was lacking in quality, quantity, impact, and accountability. "Policy work, in its many and varied dimensions, is among the most important things that FAO does" (FAO OED 2012a, x). This view was also shared by the 2013 "Evaluation of FAO's Role in Investment for Food and Nutrition Security, Agriculture and Rural Development," led by Roger Slade: "FAO headquarters' work on global policy issues in FNSARD [Food and Nutrition, Agriculture and Rural Development] is unequalled … and is used by governments in developing investment strategies" (FAO OED 2013, xxxvii). Anderson and his team found that, globally, FAO has delivered—despite a large, complex, increasingly uncertain, and multifaceted world of food and agriculture—and they highlighted several key achievements, including the annual *State of Food and Agriculture* and *State of Food Insecurity* reports, "global instruments (Voluntary Guidelines, International Treaty on Plant Genetic Resources) and the effective servicing of a revitalized Committee on World Food Security" (FAO OED 2012a, x).

FAO's comparative advantage for country-level policy work is markedly less than that of its global-level work, or in comparison with IFPRI, which has a larger presence at the country level. Country visits by the evaluation team found that, although FAO does not provide a leading role in policy support at the country level (even as FAO is very close to governments), it is still:

> … better suited than any other organization to help developing countries identify, adopt and implement the policies that address hunger, poverty and sustainability. … because it enjoys unmatched trust, access and ownership, as well as presence in all countries; and it has technical knowledge in all fields of agriculture, livestock, forestry and fisheries that no other organization has and it can play the role of a global knowledge broker. (FAO OED 2012a, xi).

The evaluation argued that the inadequacy of the country-level policy work was due to a level of support for FAO in-country representation that was insufficient to allow engagement in high-quality policy dialogue; to reliance on consultants who produce work of uneven quality; to lack of organizational accountability and incentives to deliver policy advice at country level; and to fragmented institutional arrangements for policy (also noted in the IEE) (FAO OED 2012a).

One major strategy to combat the challenges at the country level has been to further decentralize, so as to simplify processes and make FAO less hierarchical. Evaluation findings indicated that FAO's decentralization reform increased rather than decreased FAO's problems with delivering high-quality policy assistance at the country level. The evaluation attributed this increase to the limitation of the decentralization recommendation put forth by the IEE. The evaluation argues that the IEE should have recommended a way to maintain quality control and technical supervision of the work in decentralized offices. Following the 2007 IEE, FAO experts, from the various fragmented departments that were responsible for policy work, prepared a paper to outline how they could improve country-level policy work. The evaluation reported that management did not pay attention to issues highlighted in this paper, and therefore, concluded that decentralization has a "strong potential for improving policy work if *appropriate mechanisms to create accountability* for policy work are put in place" (FAO OED 2012a, 93).

Helping Developing Countries to Mobilize Additional Resources for Investments in Agriculture

Help to developing countries is needed to mobilize resources from unconventional sources—not just to prepare donor projects—such as from carbon financing and from private sector and national and international philanthropies, and generally, to create an investment-friendly, enabling environment in agriculture and related sectors, along the lines described in Table 2.1 in Chapter 2 on structural transformation. The new DG's "Hand-in-Hand" Initiative highlights this investment approach to connect the different stakeholders involved—for example, the rich and the poor provinces in China—to promote investments.[33] Linking up with IFAD in this initiative would be mutually beneficial.

FAO's Investment Centre (TCI), established in 1964 to support World Bank investments in agriculture, is mandated to support and serve the governments of member countries in the preparation of agricultural investment projects. The two institutions agreed: "to co-operate together in ... assisting countries of common membership in the identification and preparation of agricultural projects of types which fall within the framework of the economic development objectives and general policies of the Bank and FAO and which the Bank is willing to consider for financing ... " (FAO 1964 [1a]). The agreement provided for FAO and World Bank to arrange for "technical assistance required for the implementation of Bank financed projects" (FAO 1964 [1d]). The result was the creation of one of FAO's largest divisions, TCI, which has seen its structure and functions evolve with time, including the negotiation of several more Cooperative Agreements with other IFIs—though, the one with the World Bank remains the largest by far.

If increasing investments in developing countries' agriculture is critical, then FAO's TCI calls for a closer look. It has helped to design and implement over 2,000 investment operations, valued at more than US$116 billion, across 170 countries, that have involved some 95 international experts in various regions of the world. Working mainly in three-way partnerships, TCI works with member countries and international financing institutions, including the World Bank, but also IFAD and regional development banks. TCI also partners with other national and international organizations, lending institutions, the private sector, and producer organizations.[34]

Over the years, other IFIs and some bilateral donors (partners) joined the Cooperative Programme, which was originally established between FAO and the World Bank. For example, FAO is one of 10 agencies through which countries can request GEF funds. TCI coordinates FAO's collaboration with both the GEF Secretariat and other GEF agencies. It helps member countries identify, develop, and implement GEF-eligible projects. These projects include co-financing from governments, collaborating agencies, bilateral donors, IFIs, and FAO, including TCP. The TCI also supports implementation of CAADP, the strategic agricultural framework of the African Union and New Partnership for Africa's Development (NEPAD), by participating in the national roundtable process, by sharing

---

[33] See "Hand-in-Hand Initiative Creates a New Business Model for Partners to Work Together to End Poverty and Hunger." http://www.fao.org/news/story/en/item/1253626/icode/

[34] See FAO, Support to Investment: http://www.fao.org/support-to-investment/en/

knowledge through studies and reports, and by facilitating donor coordination, especially through its role in the Global Donor Platform for Rural Development (GDPRD) (FAO OED 2013).

The IEE found that the TCI has contributed significantly to agricultural development investments over the years in member countries. A majority of the stakeholders interviewed for this evaluation noted that the product quality of what was formerly called Technical Cooperation Investment, now called Programme Support (FAO 2014a), has been on par with the quality of investment documents prepared by international financial organizations or with those prepared by others for them. The IEE made a number of observations and suggestions regarding FAO's support for investment, of which not all were accepted by management. These observations were reinforced by several subsequent studies and evaluations. Since 2007, despite some changes, FAO's and the Investment Centre Division's progress on the IEE's and others' priorities has been mixed. In 2018, US$6 billion of US $7.2 billion total investments made by governments were World Bank-related. Most were public sector investments. The Investment Center will need to develop capacity to mobilize private sector resources (FAO 2019b).

Although Slade et al. in their 2013 "Evaluation of FAO's Role in Investment for Food and Nutrition Security, Agriculture and Rural Development," confirmed FAO's "unrivalled advantage, the legacy of the skills and knowledge it commands" (FAO OED 2013, vi), their major findings suggested that FAO needs to do a lot more to increase investments. Among the actions FAO could take were: "expand support to investment, as demand for its services outstrips supply, by relaxing binding budgetary constraints [and] move investment work more effectively to the field where it can assist and guide member governments in building the skills to do better for themselves" (FAO OED 2013, vi). For example, developing and implementing a clear and concise, results-based strategy for support to investment had not yet been accomplished. Nor had FAO leveraged its mandate and comparative advantage to generate new and innovative partnerships (both internally and externally) focused, especially on investment. This could be done through farmers and farming enterprises, the public sector (governments, international and nongovernmental organizations, or official development assistance), and the private sector (domestic and foreign philanthropic institutions and private companies). Each type of investment is different and calls for a completely different strategy, with new and more inclusive development partnerships: for example, with the International Federation of Red Cross and Red Crescent Societies and the International Cooperatives Alliance.[35] FAO also set up a multi-donor trust fund to allow private sector companies to financially contribute to the organization's work and support FAO projects and programs (FAO 2013a), but this has had limited effect and has rarely been implemented by FAO. FAO has detailed codes of conduct to ensure that the interests of the food and chemical industries are assessed, administered by the Partnerships Division. A new Private Sector Strategy is under development, closely followed by a newly appointed DDG, who had carried out a series of consultations with the private sector (May–June 2020), signifying a new approach to interaction with all stakeholders in agriculture, livestock, and fisheries, and less focused on financial contributions but rather on credible and tangible engagement. This is also intended to support a more proactive

---

[35] See "FAO Partners with the International Federation of Red Cross and Red Crescent": https://www.ifrc.org/en/news-and-media/press-releases/general/fao-partners-with-the-international-federation-of-red-cross-and-red-crescent/

"match-making" by FAO with private and public sector financial institutions to get needed engagement and investment in place.

The "Evaluation of FAO's Contribution to Inclusive and Efficient Agricultural and Food Systems (SO4)" recommended:

> *Mechanisms and policies to partner with the private sector and IFIs should be reviewed so that there are no unnecessary bottlenecks.* There is a need for more practical and calibrated approaches that recognise the wide spectrum of private sector profiles—from transnational conglomerates down to district-level small enterprise associations. Accordingly, there is merit in delegating decisions to decentralised levels to pursue limited, short-term, localised opportunities which do not pose corporate reputation risks. The posting of partnership officers in some regional offices is a positive step in this direction. (FAO OED 2017a, 44)

Advocacy

While Roger Slade and his evaluation team reaffirmed FAO's position as a highly regarded knowledge organization and neutral global platform, they argued that FAO "has tended to serve more as a trusted technical advisor than as a pro-active advocate" for food security (FAO OED 2013, iii). Jock Anderson and his evaluation team were more favorably disposed, indicating "areas where FAO was most active in advocacy" (FAO OED 2012a, 43):

- food security (household and national) [also supported by the 2010 Water Evaluation],
- fisheries management, both inland and marine,
- forestry management,
- importance of the agricultural sectors in rural development and livelihoods,
- pesticides and pest management, and
- food safety and standards (FAO OED 2012a, 43)

Food Security

The 2012 policy evaluation also stated that FAO has provided "effective servicing of a revitalized Committee on World Food Security" (FAO OED 2012a, x), which provides "an opportunity for FAO to exercise global leadership on important policy issues, such as food security" (FAO OED 2012a, 26).

The intergovernmental CFS was set up in 1974 to be a forum for review and to follow up on food security policies with a vision to "strive for a world free from hunger where countries implement the voluntary guidelines for the progressive realization of the right to adequate food in the context of national food security" (FAO 2009c, 2). The permanent secretariat is at FAO, and all three Rome-based food agencies fund and are members of the secretariat. Food security was not explicitly mentioned in FAO's original mandate in the way that nutrition was; yet, food security is an expected outcome of all that FAO does (FAO 2012b). The IEE recognized that the World Food Summits (organized by FAO) are considered milestones in the global fight against hunger and malnutrition. The two

World Food Summits helped to keep the hunger on the global agenda, and the inclusion of the term "hunger" in the first MDG is attributed to FAO's leadership. Similarly, FAO's contribution is justifiably acknowledged for the inclusion of the role of agriculture in NEPAD, including its leadership of the development of the CAADP proposals—subjects that, by some accounts, were being overlooked or forgotten (FAO 2007a).

The 2011 "Evaluation of FAO's Role and Work in Nutrition," led by Nigel Nicholson, reported that FAO's technical assistance on policy, principally related to agriculture and food security, its advocacy work on the Right to Food, and its technical assistance in support of policies and legislation in food security and nutrition have been effective, particularly across the Latin American and Caribbean region. The evaluation noted that its advocacy in other regions has been less influential, but that this can be attributed to tensions between the various international actors at the field level (FAO 2011b; FAO OED 2011).

Nutrition

Nutrition is enshrined in FAO's Constitution, current SOs, and global goals and has always been central to its mandate. Following the outcome of the IEE and the subsequent Immediate Plan of Action (FAO 2007a, 2008a), FAO launched its Strategic Framework 2010–19, which acknowledged, "the main challenges facing food, agriculture and rural development are the large and increasing number of undernourished in the world, the prospect of rising inequality and problems of access to food by the most vulnerable populations, and the increased scarcity of natural resources worsened by climate change" (FAO 2009d, 3) and approved a vision for FAO: "a world free of hunger and malnutrition where food and agriculture contributes to improving living standards of all, especially the poorest, in an economically, socially and environmentally sustainable manner" (FAO 2009d, 14). Certainly, since the Global Nutrition Conference in 2014, FAO has increased attention to nutrition. Lawrence Haddad, Executive Director of the Global Alliance for Improved Nutrition (GAIN) and a World Food Prize winner and a former critic of FAO's limited advocacy of nutrition, in delivering the 2019 "Nutrition Inspiration Award" to former FAO DG Graziano da Silva, praised his role on several counts, including the "global zero hunger" campaign, inspired by his Brazilian experience, the introduction of the FIES (FAO 2020c), FAO's increased partnerships, and for holding FAO to account for its effort (Haddad 2019).

However, the place and role of nutrition in the activities of FAO have varied, and in recent years, it has been severely constrained by a declining budget that is "unacceptably low in view of FAO's mandate in nutrition" (FAO OED 2011, 13). During former DG Graziano's leadership, FAO certainly placed Zero Hunger front and center on the agenda. Graziano's Brazilian experience gave him an edge in moving beyond production to safety nets, traditionally not FAO's focus. FAO's SOs contained objectives that came to the center stage during 2012–19. The 2011 evaluation of FAO's work in nutrition noted that FAO's global and national leadership in nutrition had declined, primarily because it was not prioritized by senior management. Since that time, though, nutrition has been rising in importance on international and national agendas. The evaluation confirmed the prominence of nutrition concerns within FAO's goals and the recognition of malnutrition as a distinct issue, but argued that FAO's analysis of nutrition, in terms of "under-nourishment" embedded as a separate set of activities, creates a "silo" effect within the organization (FAO OED 2011, 42). This effect had also been reported by the IEE (FAO 2007a).

The IEE and OED's "Evaluation of FAO's Role and Work in Nutrition" also agreed that there does not appear to be an integrated approach to nutrition across sectors (in particular, linkages to agriculture and food security efforts and linkages between normative and field work). The report notes, "a key role for FAO is to articulate the importance of linking nutrition and agriculture" (FAO OED 2011, 17). Other SOs barely refer to nutrition, and linkages between the field program and normative work in nutrition are weak. Consequently, there is very little coordination across technical areas in relation to nutrition (FAO OED 2011, 13). Nonetheless, a program of work has been maintained, and thin resources are spread over a broad range of activities, principally in Africa, Asia, and Latin America.

The 2011 evaluation of FAO's work in nutrition, as previously noted, pointed to FAO's distinct advantages, but it also concluded, "FAO lacks the vision and corporate commitment accorded to nutrition in its original mandate. Furthermore, it falls short of the expectations of key stakeholders in addressing increased nutrition concerns worldwide from the perspective of agriculture and food-based intervention" (FAO OED 2011, 19). The evaluation strongly recommended that FAO place nutrition high on its agenda and demonstrate how its contribution can make a difference against global malnutrition, in order to keep its relevance and influence in this important area (FAO OED 2011).

The "2012 Strategy and Vision for FAO's Work in Nutrition," published in response to the "Evaluation of FAO's Role and Work in Nutrition," repositioned and prioritized FAO's work in nutrition and asserted FAO's "leadership role in bringing stakeholders together, in generating and communicating knowledge to build political commitment and guide actions, and in strengthening the capacities of governments and other implementing partners to act effectively" (FAO 2012b, 2).

In recent years, FAO has carried out substantial work on nutrition strategy, vision, and guidelines. "FAO's Role in Nutrition" notes: "Emerging challenges, such as climate change, environmental sustainability and rapid technological shifts, are transforming food systems and raising questions about how to feed a growing world population in sustainable ways."[36] The 2014 "Strategy and Vision for FAO's Work in Nutrition" recognized the need for a "holistic approach, bringing the potential of food and agricultural systems to bear on the problem, joining with those working on health and care" to address malnutrition (FAO 2014b, 3). FAO's unique role is one of sharing knowledge, bringing stakeholders in nutrition together, and strengthening the capacity of countries to evaluate and monitor their nutrition situations, and through working with partners, achieve the greatest impact. FAO provides scientific advice to member countries and international organizations on nutrient requirements and recommendations,[37] and expertise and to support countries in collecting, and disseminating information on diet and nutrition and nutrition assessment to evaluate whether nutritional needs are being met.[38] Through its policies and programs, FAO provides technical assistance to member states and partners to "create an enabling environment for the eradication of hunger and all forms of malnutrition."[39]

Partners include the Scaling Up Nutrition movement (SUN), the Reach Partnership (Ending Child Hunger and Undernutrition), the Global Panel on Agriculture and Food Systems for Nutrition (GLOPAN), the New Partnership for Africa's Development

---

[36] See http://www.fao.org/nutrition/en/
[37] See http://www.fao.org/nutrition/requirements/en/
[38] See http://www.fao.org/nutrition/assessment/en/
[39] http://www.fao.org/nutrition/policies-programmes/en/

(NEPAD), UNICEF, WHO, WFP, IFAD, and the World Bank.[40] FAO's Nutrition and Food Systems Division (ESN) coordinates its work to protect, promote and improve sustainable food systems, focusing on the link between agriculture and nutrition. Jointly with WHO's Nutrition Department, ESN leads the Technical Secretariat of the UN Decade of Action on Nutrition 2016–25—a 10-year commitment by UN member states for implementation of policies, programs, and increased investments to eliminate all forms of malnutrition.[41]

Resilience to Emergencies

Under its Strategic Objective 5, FAO has adopted a proactive approach to dealing with the growing number of emergencies that the world faces from multiple sources: climate shocks, economic shocks, conflict and-post conflict situations, and the growing influx of refugees, by building resilience in countries, communities, and individuals. FAO defines *resilience* as "The ability to prevent disasters and crises as well as to anticipate, absorb, accommodate or recover from them in a timely, efficient and sustainable manner."[42]

Under its resilience agenda, FAO's ambition is to act in seven areas:

- FAO helps countries develop and implement appropriate legal, policy and institutional systems including, for example, food chain crisis management, disaster risk reduction and management for the agricultural sectors and the Framework for Action for Food Security and Nutrition in Protracted Crises.

- FAO builds national and local capacities to reduce the risks and impacts of natural and climate hazards, food chain threats, conflicts and protracted crisis, to enhance the resilience of agricultural livelihoods.

- FAO promotes knowledge, guidelines, standards and good practices of disaster and crisis risk governance, risk monitoring and early warning, vulnerability reduction measures, preparedness and response to shocks.

- FAO helps countries and communities to develop mechanisms for the collection, analysis and dissemination of data to monitor, warn and act on crises risks and threats to agriculture, food safety and food security and nutrition.

- FAO advocates and provides assistance to protect the livelihoods of vulnerable farmers, herders, fishers and tree-dependent communities before, during and after emergencies.

- FAO builds and promotes partnerships and synergies with academic, UN, civil, and private sector agencies to join forces for increasing resilience of agricultural livelihoods in order to achieve sustainable development.

- FAO supports countries and regions to mobilise adequate resources for risk reduction and crisis management, regular information and early warning, risk and vulnerability reduction at community and household level and emergency preparedness and response to disasters and crises. (FAO 2017d, 3)

---

[40] See http://www.fao.org/nutrition/policies-programmes/en/
[41] See http://www.fao.org/economic/nutrition/en/; https://www.un.org/nutrition/
[42] See http://www.fao.org/emergencies/how-we-work/resilience/en/

This is a vast agenda that FAO conducts in three areas: food chain crises, natural hazards, and violent conflicts and protracted crises. Natural hazards and related disasters include floods, droughts, and earthquakes. Food chain threats are caused by transboundary plant pests and diseases and animal diseases, as well as food safety threats, such as nuclear contamination or avian flu. FAO establishes normative standards and technical guidelines, and it covers all of FAO's departments, ranging from Agriculture and Consumer Protection; Climate, Biodiversity, Land and Water; Economic and Social Development; Fisheries and Aquaculture, Forestry; and Technical Cooperation (FAO 2017d; 2018a; see, also, http://www.fao.org/about/who-we-are/departments/en/).

Are international organizations and bilateral aid agencies translating the principles they outline that were listed here? The Intergovernmental Authority on Development (IGAD) initiative formed in 1986 to monitor food insecurity situation in eight East African countries (Djibouti, Ethiopia, Eritrea, Kenya, Somalia, the Sudan, South Sudan, and Uganda.)[43] provides an example.

The third annual "Global Report on Food Crises," of the Food Security Information Network (FSIN 2019b), with its regional focus on the member states of IGAD, marked another major collaborative effort between agencies in the international humanitarian and development community to share data, analysis, knowledge, and expertise regarding people facing food crises. A reference document on the latest estimates of acute hunger in the world, "it is a public good prepared collectively by 15 leading global and regional institutions," including, among others, FAO, WFP, USAID, FEWSNET, IFPRI, and UNICEF.[44]

The crisis is a result of poor climate, economic problems, as in Sudan, and protracted conflict and displacement. "Climate shocks, conflict and economic turbulence were the main drivers of food insecurity" in the seven countries that constitute the IGAD region in East Africa in 2018 (FSIN 2019b, 2). The precise reasons are different, however, even within this microcosm. "Adverse climate was the primary driver in Ethiopia, Kenya, Uganda and Djibouti where ... 11.9 million people were acutely food insecure. Prolonged dry conditions and flash floods negatively affected pastoral and agro-pastoral livelihoods by damaging crop production, pasture, browse, as well as limiting water sources for both domestic and livestock usage" (FSIN 2019b, 2).

The Productive Safety Net Programme (PSNP) of Ethiopia, which has been in existence for 15 years, is intended to be a permanent safety net, operating both in the Highlands and also the Lowlands, including Afar and Somali. The program underwent a substantial evaluation by IFPRI in 2013, which noted that it does not work as well as it should in the Lowlands (Knippenberg and Hoddinott 2017). This is and rightly ought to be the subject of considerable interest and concern for both government and the development partners who support the PSNP and are concerned about resilience. Design work on the fifth phase of the program is starting now and strengthening implementation in Afar and Somali is a priority. In contrast, IGAD report recommends instead a number of short-term initiatives to address a series of successive food insecurity events (John Hoddinott, personal communication, October 17, 2019).

The Food and Nutrition Security Resilience Programme (FNS-REPRO) of FAO, funded by the Government of the Netherlands, is the first program in Eastern Africa designed specifically to:

---

[43] See https://www.uneca.org/oria/pages/igad-intergovernmental-authority-development
[44] See FSIN (2019a): http://www.fsinplatform.org/report/global-report-food-crisis-2019/

...foster peace and food security at scale. The programme will employ a livelihood and resilience-based approach in some of the least stable regions, where interventions are normally exclusive of a humanitarian nature. Its design will allow FAO and partners to set good examples of how to build food system resilience in protracted crises and strengthen cooperation across the humanitarian–development–peace nexus towards this end. (FAO 2019c)

In Chapter 8 on the World Bank in the section on the Berg Report, we show that the Bank's emergency assistance to the East African countries fortunately provided fast considerable assistance to the countries in support of these emergencies, including to shore up the PSNP.

A recent IMF paper provides a sobering account of possibilities of dealing with emergencies created just by temperature rise. The authors explored how "macroeconomic policies, structural policies, and institutions can mitigate the negative relationship between temperature shocks and output in countries with warm climates. Empirical evidence and simulations... [Models] reveal that good policies [such as low public-debt-to-GDP, foreign aid, and remittances] can help countries cope with negative weather shocks...," as policy buffers in the short run (Mejia et al. 2019, 2).

The IMF economists assert that only curbing greenhouse gas emissions, to mitigate further global warming, could have a long-lasting effect in limiting the adverse macroeconomic consequences of weather shocks. They note, however, that none of the adaptive policies they have considered "can fully eliminate the large aggregate output losses that countries with hot climates experience due to rising temperatures" (Mejia et al. 2019, 2).

FAO's work in emergencies, in the single area of climate change alone, is thus an uphill task. It is funded almost exclusively from extrabudgetary resources, which are provided by member countries and intergovernmental organizations, such as the European Union, IFIs, or other UN agencies (FAO 2020a).

FAO is known for its contributions and impact on epidemic disease control, including the near elimination of rinderpest and management of the highly pathogenic avian influenza. FAO's work in emergencies is almost exclusively funded from extra-budgetary resources, provided by its member countries and intergovernmental organizations. In 2004, a Special Fund for Emergency and Rehabilitation Activities was established to enhance FAO's capacity to respond quickly to an emergency. These trust funds provide FAO with the flexibility and financial resources to react to emergencies before additional donor funding is secured. Contributions in 2012 slightly declined from US$400 million in 2011 to US$378 million, with the United States, the European Union, OCHA/Central Emergency Response Fund (CERF), and the United Kingdom as the top contributors (FAO 2020a). In general, FAO performs two roles with respect to emergencies and rehabilitation: monitoring, coordinating, and implementing measures to counter epidemics such as avian influenza; and assisting with immediate recovery from natural disasters or the consequences of economic changes (price rises), involving agriculture, fisheries, or forestry (FAO 2007b). FAO describes its emergency program in 2016:

In 2016, FAO's emergency programme exceeded US$300 million, with contributions from over 40 resource partners, including 22 FAO member countries and the European Union, as well as numerous pool funding mechanisms such as the Central Emergency Response Fund (CERF), and other UN Trust Funds at country level. FAO's main resource partners for emergency activities in 2016 were (in order of importance): the United States of America, the United Kingdom, the European Union, the UN Office for the Coordination of Humanitarian Affairs, Canada, the Netherlands, Belgium, Norway, Sweden, Japan,

Germany, and UN trust funds at country level, of which the main one is The Common Fund for Humanitarian Action in Sudan. (FAO 2020a)

The second role has become a major task for FAO, with strong financial support from member states. This role comes with some consequences, however, as emergency response is, by definition, a specific, focused response to a given situation, which may not necessarily fall within the "sustainable" focus of FAO's Strategic Programme Objectives, aligned as they are to the SDG Agenda. The funds provided, furthermore, are not available for allocation to FAO's operations, which are focused on the organization's current SOs—although this situation is expected to change under the new DG. As such, the 2017 "Evaluation of FAO's Contribution to the Reduction of Rural Poverty through Strategic Programme 3" concluded, "In spite of demonstrating the relevance and appropriateness of the SP3 approach, FAO has not been very successful in mobilizing extra-budgetary resources for SP3 themes" (FAO OED 2017b, 3). The Evaluation recommends, "FAO should develop a customized resource mobilization strategy that includes global, regional and country level dimensions and considers the identification of new funding streams within donor institutions more relevant to SP3" (FAO OED 2017b, 3). Table 9.6 shows FAO expenditures by the source of funds.

Table 9.6 Expenditure summary by source of funds

Funding source	2014–15 (US$m)	2016–17 (US$m)	Difference (US$m)	Difference (%)
General and related funds:Regular Programme expenditure versus budget of US$1,005.6 million[a]	1,000.1	1,001.8	1.7	0.2
Jointly financed investment activities	35.5	38.5	3.0	8
Voluntary contributions and funds received under inter-organizational arrangements	131.7	138.0	6.3	5
Government cash contributions and other sundry income	21.4	20.4	(1.0)	(5)
TCP, Capital Expenditure and Security Expenditure Facility Adjustments	(28.6)	(9.2)	19.4	(210)
Currency variance[b]	(30.7)	(33.9)	(3.2)	10
Other[c]	(20.6)	(22.6)	(2.0)	9
Subtotal	1,108.8	1,132.9	24.1	2.1
Trust Funds and UNDP				
Trust Funds/UNDP (excluding emergency projects)	770.7	816.6	45.8	6
Special relief operations (emergency projects)	616.8	661.8	45.0	7
Subtotal	1,387.5	1,478.4	90.8	6
Total expenditures	**2,496.3**	**2,611.3**	**115.0**	**4**

Notes:

[a] Regular Programme expenditure for 2016–17 excludes US$5.6 million funded from carry-over of unspent balance of the 2014–15 appropriations authorized by the Conference Resolution 6/2015.

[b] Currency variance represents adjustments to the actual to reflect the translation of euro-denominated transactions at the budget rate of exchange rather than the UN operational rate of exchange in effect at the date of the transactions.

[c] Under the line "Other," the main item represents US$21.5 million for health insurance premiums, which is recorded as a reduction of After-service Medical Coverage (ASMC) liability for financial reporting.

Source: FAO (2019e, table 9, 99).

The first case of highly pathogenic avian influenza (H5N1) was identified in Asia; other cases followed in Europe and Africa. "FAO responded within weeks of the initial outbreaks by implementing small regional and national TCP projects with its own funds while seeking to raise [additional] donor funds" (FAO 2007b, 6). Meanwhile, FAO collaborated with the World Organisation for Animal Health (OIE) and WHO to develop technical strategies for controlling the disease (FAO–OIE–WHO 2011). The Global Highly Pathogenic Avian Influenza Programme became a major program for FAO, characterized by high exposure, complex interagency coordination, management challenges, and large amounts of extra-budgetary funding (FAO 2007b).

"The First Real-Time Evaluation of FAO's Work on Highly Pathogenic Avian Influenza (HPAI)," in 2007, led by Anthony Wilsmore, recognized the importance of FAO in addressing this emergency with the creation of the Special Fund for Emergency and Rehabilitation Activities, the rapid mobilization of governments, and the presence of FAO in isolated areas, where it was the first, and for some time, the only presence assisting governments in their response to the outbreak or threat of avian influenza. *These successes were achieved within severe resource constraints* (FAO 2007b).

CERF, an important contributor to FAO's emergency activities, was created in December 2005, and launched in March 2006. CERF was established to support more timely and reliable assistance to those affected by armed conflicts and natural disasters, through a grant facility of up to US$450 million per year and a loan facility of approximately US$50 million. This financial instrument provides FAO with early funding, allowing it to respond to the most pressing needs shortly after a sudden-onset disaster or early enough during a slow-onset disaster to be effective (FAO OED 2010c). FAO has been one of the largest recipients of CERF grant funding (FAO OED 2010a). The 2010 "Evaluation of FAO Interventions Funded by the CERF," led by Olivier Cossée, looked at FAO emergency activities using this grant funding and found that, for the most part, FAO in-country technical teams were doing "excellent work" in their disaster response activities (FAO OED 2010a, 18). FAO, the report found, provides "an important humanitarian contribution to communities affected by crises by supporting their self-reliance and local food availability through time-critical agricultural interventions" (FAO OED 2010a, 67). The report concluded, "The work of FAO in support of both development and disaster risk management over many decades allowed the Organization to forge strong links with perennial institutions and actors" (FAO OED 2010a, 67).

The main concern of the CERF evaluation team pertains to efficiency and timeliness, particularly the slow information exchange between headquarters and the field and the variable capacity of in-country staff implementing emergency projects. Although not unique to FAO, the evaluation attributes these challenges to its information management and decentralization architecture, which does not permit a rapid and flexible flow of budgetary and implementation information from the field to headquarters (FAO OECD 2010a).

FAO's strong capacity to deal with transboundary animal diseases (zoonosis and corona viruses) is undisputed. In 2013, FAO quickly responded to the occurrence of the A(H7N9) influenza virus in China. It monitored the situation through its wide network of country and regional offices and key partners, including WHO and OIE (FAO 2013c). FAO and the OIE Reference Center, the Harbin Veterinary Research Institute of the Chinese Academy of Agricultural Sciences, led the laboratory analysis. The scientific community and FAO experts in the Animal Production and Health Section of the Joint FAO/International Atomic Energy Agency (IAEA) Division of Nuclear Techniques in Food and Agriculture worked to optimize diagnostic approaches to better detect this new strain of influenza virus. They delivered much needed avian flu detection training courses "to contribute to the early detection of this virus and early reaction capabilities in Member States." FAO organized training for multiple sets of countries from Asia (IAEA 2013).

The FAO Emergency Centre for Transboundary Animal Diseases (ECTAD) plans and delivers veterinary assistance to FAO member countries that are responding to transboundary animal health threats.[45] By building animal capacity, ECTAD works to respond to animal disease outbreaks at the source and prevent their spread. ECTAD teams facilitate the Global Health Security Agenda and Emerging Pandemic Threats, two USAID-funded programs.

Locusts (a collection of certain species of short-horned grasshoppers) are an important source of food chain crises in many parts of the world. Heavy rains and cyclones triggered a surge in Desert Locust populations, causing an outbreak to develop in Sudan and Eritrea, rapidly spreading along both sides of the Red Sea to Saudi Arabia and Egypt, FAO warned in February 2019. FAO operates a centralized Desert Locust Information Service (DLIS), monitoring the Desert Locust situation throughout the world, providing information on the general locust situation to the global community, and gives timely warnings and forecasts to countries in danger of invasion A locust plague threatened the livelihoods of 13 million people in Madagascar. In March 2013, FAO called for US$41 million of donations to fight locusts. Under the proposed aid plan, US$22 million would be delivered by June for pest control efforts, and US$19 million were devoted to a three-year plan to keep the insect in check. The FAO plan called for large-scale aerial operations to spray pesticides over 1.5 million hectares (3.7 million acres) of land from 2013 to 2014.[46]

Forestry

The promotion of the sustainable management of forests and trees has been part of FAO's mission since its founding in 1945, when it was mandated to sustain forest timber values to ensure "continuous productivity of existing forests" (FAO OED 2012b, x). The 2007 IEE report said, "no other global organization matches FAO's comprehensive mandate for food, agriculture, forestry and fisheries, including the production and provisioning of such a broad range of global goods and services" (FAO 2007a, 21). The OED "Evaluation of FAO's Role in Investment for Food and Nutrition Security, Agriculture and Rural Development," said FAO's "Forestry Department's understanding of forest governance, institutions and forest management in different countries is often crucial for investment decisions" (FAO OED 2013, xxxvi).

In the 2012 "Strategic Evaluation of FAO's Role and Work in Forestry," team leader Jürgen Blaser noted that FAO is renowned globally for its combination of technical knowledge in forests and forestry and a visible role as a "steward of the world's forests" (FAO OED 2012b, xi). The evaluation reported that FAO is "visible" within the international forestry sector, "relevant" in its forestry activities (work related to supporting forest governance reform, tenure reform, national forest policy and program development, and supporting capacity building for relevant institutions), and known as a "timely,"

[45] See http://www.fao.org/emergencies/fao-in-action/ectad/en/
[46] See http://www.fao.org/emergencies/crisis/madagascar-locust/en/

"extensive," and "effective" generator and disseminator of statistics on the state of forest resources and forest products (FAO OED 2012b, xi–xii).

The evaluation argued that FAO's comparative advantages—as an impartial global leader in forestry, as well as a source for technical expertise in forest resource assessment and monitoring, global forest-related information services, forest sector policies and planning, and some aspects of forest resources management—can secure its position as the international leader in forestry contributions to food security and poverty reduction. As in other areas of FAO's work, however, the evaluation found that FAO faces competition from new entities in the field who can now offer similar services in places where FAO was once the sole provider. The emergence of two CGIAR centers, the World Agroforestry Center and Center for International Forestry Research, as well as the GEF, the International Tropical Timber Organization, United Nations Forum on Forests, International Union for the Conservation of Nature, World Wildlife Fund, Conservation International, and UNEP have fragmented the global forestry agenda (FAO 2007a; Lele, Zasueta, and Singer 2010). There are now many other entities that can do the same activities as FAO, and yet, the FAO OED report argued that there is "more need than ever for an impartial global leader looking at forests and forestry in a holistic sense, linking global, regional and national levels and relating forests and forestry to other land use sectors" (FAO OED 2012b, xiv). In this regard, FAO is well positioned and could once again become an international leader in forestry, given its ability to provide a neutral platform and to meet the cross-sectoral needs related to forestry contributions to watersheds, food security, poverty reduction, and climate change, as well as its expertise and capacity to deal with technical issues in forestry and other activities related to land and natural resources.

Now in its third phase of collaboration, FAO's Forestry Department, together with the EU–FAO Forest Law Enforcement, Governance and Trade (FLEGT) program, and the UN Reducing Emissions from Deforestation and Forest Degradation in Developing Counties (REDD+) program partnered, in 2003, to start an initiative that aims to identify linkages and opportunities for synergies between their respective processes. To facilitate coordination, the initiative also aims to support the integration of REDD+ and FLEGT activities into national forest planning processes. Although these processes have specific objectives, they have similar activities. In particular, both processes aim to strengthen forest governance through work with policy, legislative, and institutional frameworks, and to implement activities at national and subnational levels.[47]

Water

The third Global Goal of the FAO Strategic Framework 2000–15 was "the conservation, improvement and sustainable utilization of natural resources, including land, water, forest, fisheries and genetic resources for food and agriculture" (FAO 1999).

The *Climate, Biodiversity, Land and Water Department* has gone through a considerable evolution over the past 20 years from the department of natural resources, and for a time when there was no department at all, to now when climate is included in the title. It will de-emphasize and realign work on the water footprint of food loss and waste in food value

---

[47] See the UN–REDD Programme site: http://www.un-redd.org/and the FAO–EU FLEGT Programme site: http://www.fao.org/forestry/eu-flegt/en/

chains, following the completion of the study on the methodologies to quantify the water embedded in food products that are lost or wasted in the food value chain. The follow-up will be handed over to partners with higher comparative advantages for such analysis. FAO's water-related work will concentrate on increasing and improving water productivity in agriculture and food systems, water accounting and auditing, water quality and food safety, water governance, and the interlinkages of water and other sectors, including the nexus approach. The SF includes water scarcity, pollution, salinization, and integrated natural resources management within the old Strategic Objective D1: Integrated management of land, water, fisheries, forest, and genetic resources. FAO's work related to water is anchored in the Water Development and Management Unit, part of the Division of Land and Water in the Natural Resources Department. Like food security, policy, and forestry, water is also an important aspect of the work of at least eleven other units (FAO OED 2010b).

In 2017, FAO established a portal for water monitoring, developing:

WaPOR, a publicly accessible near real time database using satellite data that will allow monitoring of agricultural water productivity. The beta release of WaPOR was launched on April 20, 2017. Based on the methodology review process, a new version WaPOR 1.0 became available in June 2018, focusing first on the coarser resolution level (Level 1), covering the whole of Africa and the Near East at 250 m ground resolution and then the national / river basin (Level 2) at 100 m resolution. (FAO 2020d)

FAO's committees have repeatedly emphasized the importance of water use and management for sustainable agriculture, forest, and food security efforts. "Over the last decade, FAO's Governing Bodies have frequently discussed issues related to water in agriculture, given its paramount importance" (FAO OED 2010b, viii). In 2003, the Committee on Forestry highlighted the forest and water theme. In 2007, COAG discussed a proposal on "Agriculture and Water Scarcity" and welcomed "the proposal for a multidisciplinary integrated framework to address water scarcity" (FAO 2007d, 1). The Committee on World Food Security also repeatedly stressed that FAO should pay particular attention to water scarcity and drought, and the IEE concluded that FAO was in a weak position in the water sector (FAO 2007a, CFS 2015). The IEE commissioned a background working paper on Water Management and Irrigation. The IEE's core recommendation for water focuses on the need for "significant realignment of existing resources together with the securing of new ones, both human and financial," as well as a "different strategic approach that would enable [FAO] to contribute to integrated policies and programmes which bring together engineering, tenure, economics, management and legislation" (FAO 2007a, 158). The findings of the IEE triggered a complex reform process that was supported by, among others, the undertaking of an "Evaluation of FAO's Role and Work Related to Water," led by Andrew Bullock (FAO OED 2010b). FAO has moved toward exploiting remote sensing data to map water productivity (FAO 2020d). Meanwhile, Google Earth is offering Evapotranspiration (ET) maps.[48] So, things are moving along, and new technology is replacing AQUASTAT, which was what water experts had hoped, in supporting the water prize for AQUASTAT.

Bullock and his team found that, at the global level, FAO's work related to water since 2004 has been relevant to the Global Goals and MDGs, but limited at the country level, due

---

[48] See https://eeflux-level1.appspot.com

to both resource constraints and the absence of an institutional framework for intervention. The evaluation said that FAO "has a clearly defined role in water and agriculture and related issues of global relevance," (FAO OED 2010b, x) and that it has contributed to raising the profile of agriculture in the international debate on water through active participation in international forums, such as the World Water Forum and UN–Water, and is recognized for its good work in maintaining the AQUASTAT global database. Water professionals, on the other hand, were concerned that FAO was underfinancing AQUASTAT.

Some have expressed concern about the quality of the database, but AQUASTAT has been frequently nominated and shortlisted for the World Water Award (Chris Perry, personal communication).The evaluation reported that FAO's work in water is "unique and recognised as such" and that FAO's services in the water sector are in high demand "as the Organization is recognized as a reliable source of information, technical advice and support" (FAO OED 2010b, x). Positive results are also reported at the normative level in publications and training materials, the interface between freshwater management and aquaculture, and watershed management. Similarly, in policy and legal advice in support of water policies and strategies, FAO has reportedly been valuable. The evaluation also said that FAO is "appreciated by partners and participating countries" (FAO OED 2010b, xi).

The evaluation points out that the membership of FAO is diverse, its needs and expectations complex, and the organization's contribution at the country level has been "less than fully coherent and coordinated" (FAO OED 2010b, x). This is attributed to its complexity and the fact that it cuts across sectors and ministries, including agriculture, water resources, irrigation, energy, environment, forest and watershed management, health, and municipalities. Although the IEE found that FAO "lost its overall leadership role" (FAO 2007a, 119) in water, the 2010 OED evaluation concluded that FAO is still "clearly the lead institution within the United Nations system on water in the context of food and agriculture" (FAO OED 2010b, x) (see Box A.9.1 for additional evaluations of FAO).

Implications for the Future

Transforming FAO is a tough but an important task, and under the new leadership of DG Qu Dongyu, this has already begun. FAO members should provide the strategic guidance and human and financial resources needed to achieve the improvements intended to serve the organizational mission and strategy. This will be a central dialogue as the new SF is reviewed by FAO Council in December 2020, and approved by the FAO Conference in June 2021. Despite improvements in FAO and articulation of a vision and a strategy, there has been no real increase in the regular budget, with funds increasingly provided as additional voluntary contributions, often for emergency assistance. Member countries have approved only a nominal increase, which compares well with the UN's zero growth. FAO's current, regular budget expenditures include 75 percent in staff-related costs. It is difficult to assess if this is ratio is appropriate in a knowledge organization. It is not so much the ratio as the fragmentation and unpredictability of voluntary contributions that makes its use less efficient than it could be.

With an emphasis on SDG monitoring, FAO faces an expanded agenda and growing competition from international agencies, initiatives, and emerging partnerships. Its strengths are its legitimacy, access to global data, and knowledge base; and it is highly valued by its partners. Its long-term prospects, however, depend on its ability to remain relevant with qualified, effective staff.

High-level evaluations confirm that FAO is more trusted by developing countries than IFIs, for its neutrality and for the perception of an absence of any agenda of its own. FAO's substantial convening power (McCalla 2007b) and access to global knowledge and expertise, combined with its ability to produce or mobilize global and regional databases in key areas of food, agriculture, and natural resources are important assets. FAO also boasts a highly committed and internationally well-known staff with specialized expertise in agriculture, forestry, fisheries, international law, and soils that does not exist in other global or regional institutions. It needs to communicate better and promote its expertise. Notwithstanding all these assets, for a variety of external and internal reasons, FAO's performance is less than the vision of its founders, its potential, or that demanded by the contemporary challenges of the global food, agriculture, and natural resource system. FAO was expected to work toward its mandate; when it was founded, the circumstances were very different than the way the external and the internal environment has evolved (Lele 2007).

Building FAO as a Center of Scientific and Evidence-Based Excellence

We end this chapter by making a case for why FAO needs to be a center of excellence.

In the 2007 report "FAO and the International Financial Institutions: The World Bank and the Regional Development Banks," by Alex McCalla and his collaborator David Nielson, a Senior Economist from the World Bank, now retired, had asserted that in marketing itself to the world, FAO should strive to be an esteemed knowledge bank in rural development with multiple centers of excellence within it. Observations that McCalla made are even more relevant in 2020 than they were in 2007. Not only have the demands on food and agriculture increased and become more complex, but the technical capacity within international organizations and bilateral organizations to help developing countries develop agriculture sustainably and equitably has declined even further compared to 2007. McCalla noted:

> Development agencies are doing less themselves and relying more on others. Rural staff of the bilateral and multilateral development agencies have much in common with the interests of the staff of the Investment Centre, but the focus of their working environment is increasingly on managing the instruments of financial support. Less and less staff time is available to engage in the underlying sectoral issues and processes. Technical gravitas within the development agencies is becoming startlingly scarce. (McCalla 2007a, Annex 2, 22)

However, as a 2017 evaluation of FAO's contribution to SO4 noted:

> Main external partners for TCI are the World Bank, IFAD, EBRD, the International Finance Corporation (IFC) and the Inter-American Development Bank (IDB). The 2013 *Evaluation of FAO's Role in Investment for Food and Nutrition Security, Agriculture and Rural Development* [FAO OED 2013] noted important limitations of TCI to find partners beyond its current ones, particularly the difficulties in working with ADB [Asian Development Bank], AfDB, and EIB [European Investment Bank], mainly due to the need for regular tendering processes with the latter, while this is not necessary for the other IFIs. (FAO 2017b, 37)

And, indeed, such partnerships between FAO and IFC, and FAO and GEF have been well underway.

Some commentators inside FAO have disagreed with this characterization of FAO by its own OED.

Yet, there is a need for developing countries to mobilize investment resources beyond technical assistance and beyond investment of traditional donors FAO serves. Except for LICs, developing countries are now the major investors in agriculture and related sectors. They are similarly mobilizing private sector funding. International expertise is needed not just to prepare donor-aided projects but to help shape countries' own investment strategies for environmentally resilient and human health-sensitive agriculture.

In this regard, David Nielson, a veteran World Bank staff member who McCalla had interviewed in the course of IEE, and later by Lele in the course of this FAO study, had complimentary observations to make, based on his firsthand experience about the Investment Centre and its considerable potential going forward:

> The Investment Centre has an enormous (still not fully realized) potential to contribute to rural development initiatives throughout the world.... When the Investment Centre is at its best, the competition cannot really compete. Private sector consultants do not offer the same access to a critical mass of technical and conceptual support. Academics do not usually enjoy the same degree of familiarity with the development agencies and the programs they support in the field. In-country experts in client countries often do not possess the same degree of exposure to global developments, and cannot claim the same degree of objectivity for assignments in their own countries as can the staff of the Investment Centre. (McCalla 2007a, annex 2, 20, 21–2)

Nielson, who has collaborated with TCI many times, highlighted successful World Bank–FAO collaboration projects in Ethiopia, Mozambique, and Uganda: "We mention these specific initiatives because they illustrate the potential of the [core staffing of the entire FAO (as financed by the assessed contributions), including but not confined to the] Investment Centre" (McCalla 2007a, annex 2, 21).

Other areas of FAO have played similar roles, and they are pushing envelopes. A recent example is the guideline for responsible private investments using sustainable practices developed by FAO and OECD and promoted through the CFS.

As we have described in this chapter, FAO is the center of expertise on all matters concerned with food and agriculture, the only international organization charged with such responsibility. FAO plays a critical role in helping Member States to design and implement food systems in the broader context of rural development (in agricultural services, rural finance, irrigation, natural resource management, among others), with the aim of helping governments and development institutions by providing guidance and assistance in the field, as they design and implement transformative approaches to mitigating climate change and promoting healthy food systems. This entails creating an institutional culture as a knowledge bank. The evidence reviewed in this chapter and FAO's various evaluations suggest that this process has been well underway in FAO, but that it needs to be further supported and strengthened in view of the evidence we have provided. FAO's staffing and hiring may be driven less by search for excellence than by concern for diversity. Its ability to assist countries is fostered by energetic entrepreneurial field staff, who can mobilize resources working with donors and governments at the country level. It shows:

- Systematic internal discussions and reviews (by colleagues from FAO and from partner organizations) of staff outputs stimulate joint thinking and establish a culture of accountability for quality, both internally and for external clients.
- Building on the work of the SF to establish communities of practice within FAO can and do establish strategic areas (such as agricultural services, land tenure, rural finance, water, and natural resource management, among others), which would create synergies among the technical expertise that exists in the rest of FAO, thereby increasing its technical expertise.
- Enhancing the integrative skills and the intellectual leadership of FAO staff through aggressive and strategic staffing, and investing in the development of the staff.

Arguments in favor of this approach include:

- As proposed investments in agriculture increase, so will demand for a broad skills mix.
- Most international organizations and bilateral donors have lost technical capacity—the World Bank, for example, may now have only 200 staff in the agriculture network, half of them short-term consultants, compared to 495 in the 1990s, and FAO, too, has lost technical capacity—all need a center from which they can borrow it.
- Project complexity and processing requirements have increased, leaving little time for those who manage projects to think and address substantive issues.
- Continuity is needed, rather than simply reliance on employment of short-term consultants with little institutional memory.
- The aspiration of the World Bank and regional banks aspire to deal with climate change, to scale up successful programs by governments, and link farmers to markets. It calls for going beyond project investments to country strategies.
- The need for multidisciplinary expertise has increased at all levels.
- University academics bring to bear analytical skills, but they need complementary operational skills to meet the operational challenges, and bilateral donors have lost capacity, too.
- FAO has long-standing experience in preparing investment projects for the World Bank and the regional banks. Of the US$7.2 billion of investment projects in 45 countries in 2018, US$6 billion were World Bank projects in 30 countries (FAO 2019b).
- In some areas—such as participatory water management, water users' associations, gender, and FFSs—FAO has been ahead of the curve.
- In other areas, it would be worth conducting surveys of developing countries and international organizations to assess demand for technical skills.
- Rather than duplicating efforts, international organizations could determine demand and skill mix needs collectively, to ensure that FAO assembles and supplies skills that are needed.
- FAO recruits people of the highest caliber, regardless of their nationalities. The de facto quota system makes recruitment difficult, and FAO's salaries may not attract top-notch professionals if the external audits have validity.
- In such areas as participatory forest management, value chains, and nutrition, there is no reason why FAO could not or should not be able to recruit people and build top notch capacity.
- FAO has instituted new staff training, coaching, and performance assessment processes using external consultants.

Appendix: FAO Evaluations

Box A.9.1 Other Evaluations of FAO

Other evaluations included, among others, the following:

- Evaluation of FAO's Contribution to Integrated Natural Resource Management for Sustainable Agriculture (SO2) (FAO OED 2018)
- Evaluation of FAO's Contribution to the Reduction of Rural Poverty through Strategic Programme 3 (FAO OED 2017b)
- Evaluation of FAO's Contribution to the Strategic Objective 4: Enabling Inclusive and Efficient and Agricultural and Food Systems (FAO OED 2017a)
- Evaluation of the Financial Support by the World Bank Group with the Development Grant Facility to Support the "Partnership for Agricultural Market Information System (AMIS)" (FAO OED 2017c)
- Evaluation of the FAO Multipartner Programme Support Mechanism (FMM) (FAO OED 2016a)
- Evaluation of FAO Strategic Objective 5: Increase the Resilience of Livelihoods to Threats and Crises (FAO OED 2016b)
- Evaluation of FAO's Work in Genetic Resources. (FAO OED 2016c)
- Final Evaluation of the Improved Global Governance for Hunger Reduction Programme (FAO OED 2016d)
- Mid-term Evaluation of the Forest and Farm Facility Programme (FAO OED 2016e)
- Evaluation of FAO's Contribution to Climate Change Adaptation and Mitigation (FAO OED 2015a)
- Evaluation of FAO's Contribution to Knowledge on Food and Agriculture (FAO OED 2015b)
- Evaluation of FAO's Role in Investment for Food and Nutrition Security, Agriculture, and Rural Development (FAO OED 2013)
- Evaluation of FAO's Role and Work in Food and Agriculture Policy (FAO OED 2012a)
- Strategic Evaluation of FAO's Role and Work in Forestry (FAO OED 2012b)
- Evaluation of FAO's Role and Work in Nutrition (FAO OED 2011)
- Evaluation of FAO Interventions Funded by the Central Emergency Response Fund (FAO OED 2010a)
- Evaluations of FAO's Role in Water (FAO OED 2010b)
- Evaluation of FAO's Role and Work in Statistics (FAO 2008b)

References

Baum, Warren C. 1986. *Partners Against Hunger*. Washington, DC: World Bank.

Beintema, Nienke, and Gert-Jan Stads. 2017. "A Comprehensive Overview of Investments and Human Resource Capacity in African Agricultural Research." Agricultural Science and Technology Indicators (ASTI) Synthesis Report, International Food Policy Research Institute, Washington, DC. http://ebrary.ifpri.org/utils/getfile/collection/p15738coll2/id/131191/filename/131402.pdf

Byerlee, Derek, and John K. Lynam. 2020. "The Development of the International Center Model for Agricultural Research: A Prehistory of the CGIAR." Unpublished draft.

Castañeda, Andrés, Dung Doan, David Newhouse, Minh Cong Nguyen, Hiroki Uematsu, and Joao Pedro Azevedo, World Bank Data for Goals Group. 2018. "A New Profile of the Global Poor." *World Development* 101: 250–67. https://www.sciencedirect.com/science/article/pii/S0305750X17302735

CFS (Committee on World Food Security). 2015. "Water for Food Security and Nutrition." HLPE Report 9, The High Level Panel of Experts on Food Security and Nutrition, CFS, Rome. http://www.activeremedy.org/wp-content/uploads/2015/10/HLPE_Report_9_EN.pdf

CGD (Center for Global Development). 2013. "Time for the FAO to Shift to a Higher Gear." A Report of the CGD Working Group on Food Security, CGD, Washington, DC. https://www.cgdev.org/sites/default/files/FAO-text-Final.pdf

DFID (Department for International Development) and UK Aid. 2011. *Multilateral Aid Review: Ensuring Maximum Value for Money for UK Aid through Multilateral Organisations.* London: DFID. https://www.gov.uk/government/uploads/system/uploads/attachment_data/file/67583/multilateral_aid_review.pdf

DFID (Department for International Development) and UK Aid. 2013. *Multilateral Aid Review: Driving Reform to Achieve Multilateral Effectiveness.* London: DFID. https://www.gov.uk/government/uploads/system/uploads/attachment_data/file/297523/MAR-review-dec13.pdf

DFID (Department for International Development) and UK Aid. 2016. *Raising the Standard: The Multilateral Aid Review 2016.* London: DFID. https://www.gfdrr.org/sites/default/files/publication/evaluation-dfid-multilateral-development-review-2016.pdf

Elliott, Kimberly, and Casey Dunning. 2016. "Assessing the US Feed the Future Initiative: A New Approach to Food Security?" CGD Policy Paper 075, March, Center for Global Development, Washington, DC.

FAO (Food and Agriculture Organization of the United Nations). n.d. "FAO Renewal, Budget and Staff." FAO, Rome. http://www.fao.org/docrep/014/am859e/am859e13.pdf

FAO (Food and Agriculture Organization of the United Nations). 1945. Constitution of the Food and Agriculture Organization of the United Nations. Appendix III.D in Report of the Conference of FAO, First Session, City of Quebec, Canada, October 16–November 1. http://www.fao.org/docrep/x5584E/x5584e00.htm

FAO (Food and Agriculture Organization of the United Nations). 1964. "Memorandum of Understanding with Respect to Working Arrangements between the Food and Agriculture Organization of the United Nations and the International Bank for Reconstruction and Development and the International Development Association." Appendix C, Report of the Council of FAO, 43rd Session, Rome, October 5–16. http://www.fao.org/docrep/meeting/007/22512E/22512E12.htm

FAO (Food and Agriculture Organization of the United Nations). 1996a. "Rome Declaration on World Food Security and World Food Summit Plan of Action." World Food Summit, November 13–17, Rome. http://www.fao.org/docrep/003/w3613e/w3613e00.htm

FAO (Food and Agriculture Organization of the United Nations). 1996b. What is FAO. A Short History of FAO. http://www.fao.org/UNFAO/histo-e.htm

FAO (Food and Agriculture Organization of the United Nations). 1999. "A Strategic Framework for FAO 2000–2015." Version 2.0, FAO, Rome. http://www.fao.org/unfao/fao2000/x0870e.htm#P.168_13671

FAO (Food and Agriculture Organization of the United Nations). 2006. *Comprehensive Africa Agriculture Development Programme: Integrating Livestock, Forestry and Fisheries Subsectors into the CAADP*. Rome: New Partner for Africa's Development (NEPAD) and FAO. http://www.fao.org/3/a0586e/a0586e00.htm

FAO (Food and Agriculture Organization of the United Nations). 2007a. "The Challenge of Renewal." Report of the Independent External Evaluation of the Food and Agriculture Organization of the United Nations (FAO), submitted to the Council Committee for the Independent External Evaluation of FAO (CC–IEE), September 2007. http://www.oecd.org/derec/finland/40800533.pdf (Summary) and http://www.fao.org/unfao/bodies/IEE-Working-Draft-Report/K0489E.pdf

FAO (Food and Agriculture Organization of the United Nations). 2007b. "The First Real-Time Evaluation of FAO's Work on Highly Pathogenic Avian Influenza, February–June 2007." September, FAO, Rome. http://www.fao.org/fileadmin/user_upload/oed/docs/HPAI%201st%20RTE%20final%20rpt%2014sep07.pdf

FAO (Food and Agriculture Organization of the United Nations). 2007c. "Official FAO Response to Evaluation Report." FAO Newsroom, Rome, October 29. http://www.fao.org/newsroom/en/news/2007/1000692/

FAO (Food and Agriculture Organization of the United Nations). 2007d. "Report of the Twentieth Session of the Committee on Agriculture." CL132/9, Rome, April 25–8. http://www.fao.org/tempref/docrep/fao/meeting/012/j9941e.pdf

FAO (Food and Agriculture Organization of the United Nations). 2008a. "Follow-up to the Independent External Evaluation of FAO. Resolution 1/2008 and Immediate Plan of Action for FAO Renewal (IPA)." 35th Special Session of the FAO Conference, Rome. http://www.fao.org/fileadmin/user_upload/IEE/Resolution_IPAEnglish.pdf

FAO (Food and Agriculture Organization of the United Nations). 2008b. "Independent Evaluation of FAO's Role and Work in Statistics." Programme Committee, 100th Session, Rome, October 6–10.

FAO (Food and Agriculture Organization of the United Nations). 2008c. "Mobilizing Resources for Food and Agriculture. FAO Trust Funds." Rome, FAO. http://www.fao.org/tc/docs/tf_web.pdf

FAO (Food and Agriculture Organization of the United Nations). 2009a. "Appointment and Term of Office of the Director-General." Committee on Constitutional and Legal Matters, 85th Session, Rome, February 23–4, 2009.

FAO (Food and Agriculture Organization of the United Nations). 2009b. "International Treaty on Plant Genetic Resources for Food and Agriculture. A Global Treaty for Food Security and Sustainable Agriculture." FAO, Rome. http://www.fao.org/3/a-i0510e.pdf

FAO (Food and Agriculture Organization of the United Nations). 2009c. "Reform of the Committee on World Food Security." Final Version. 35th Session, FAO, Rome, October 14, 15, and 17. http://www.fao.org/fileadmin/templates/cfs/Docs0910/ReformDoc/CFS_2009_2_Rev_2_E_K7197.pdf

FAO (Food and Agriculture Organization of the United Nations). 2009d. "Strategic Framework 2010–2019." Conference, FAO, Rome, November 18–23. http://www.fao.org/uploads/media/C2009K5864EnglishStrategicFr_1.pdf

FAO (Food and Agriculture Organization of the United Nations). 2010. "Follow-up to the Independent Evaluation of FAO's Role and Work in Statistics." Programme Committee, 104th Session, Rome, October 25–9. http://www.fao.org/docrep/meeting/019/k8827e.pdf

FAO (Food and Agriculture Organization of the United Nations). 2011a. "The Director-General's Medium-Term Plan 2010–13 (Reviewed) and Programme of Work and Budget 2012–13." 37th Session of the Conference, FAO, Rome. June 25–July 2. http://www.fao.org/docrep/meeting/021/ma061e.pdf

FAO (Food and Agriculture Organization of the United Nations). 2011b. "Evaluation of FAO's Role and Work in Nutrition." 108th Session, Rome, October 10–14. http://www.fao.org/3/mb663E01/mb663E01.pdf

FAO (Food and Agriculture Organization of the United Nations). 2011c. "Save and Grow: A Policymaker's Guide to the Sustainable Intensification of Smallholder Crop Production." FAO, Rome. http://www.fao.org/3/a-i2215e.pdf

FAO (Food and Agriculture Organization of the United Nations). 2012a. "FAO, IFAD, WFP and UN Women Launch a Five-Year Multi-Agency Programme to Empower Rural Women." Gender News, FAO, Rome. http://www.fao.org/gender/gender-home/gender-news/gender-newsdet/en/c/155576/

FAO (Food and Agriculture Organization of the United Nations). 2012b. "Strategy and Vision for FAO's Work in Nutrition." 112th Session of FAO Programme Committee, Rome, November 5–9. http://www.fao.org/docrep/meeting/026/me902e.pdf

FAO (Food and Agriculture Organization of the United Nations). 2013a. "FAO Director-General Asks Private Sector to Support Anti-Hunger Trust Fund." News, Partnerships, FAO, Rome. http://www.fao.org/partnerships/news-archive/news-article/en/c/208953/

FAO (Food and Agriculture Organization of the United Nations). 2013b. "FAO Statistical Programme of Work 2012/2013." FAO, Rome. http://www.fao.org/3/a-aq147e.pdf

FAO (Food and Agriculture Organization of the United Nations). 2013c. "Strong Biosecurity Measures Required in Response to Influenza A(H7N9) Virus." FAO News, April 5, FAO, Rome. http://www.fao.org/news/story/en/item/173655/icode/F

FAO (Food and Agriculture Organization of the United Nations). 2014a. "FAO Investment Centre: An Overview, 1964–2014." FAO, Rome. http://www.fao.org/3/a-i4235e.pdf

FAO (Food and Agriculture Organization of the United Nations). 2014b. "Strategy and Vision for FAO's Work in Nutrition." FAO, Rome. http://www.fao.org/3/a-i4185e.pdf

FAO (Food and Agriculture Organization of the United Nations). 2015. *70 Years of FAO (1945–2015)*. Rome: FAO. http://www.fao.org/publications/card/en/c/efeddfc5-0be1-4010-8aeb-24e6c1979566/

FAO (Food and Agriculture Organization of the United Nations). 2016. "Indicative Rolling Work Plan of Evaluations 2017–2019." PC 120/8, 120th Session, Programme Committee, Rome, November 7–11. http://www.fao.org/3/a-mr719e.pdf

FAO (Food and Agriculture Organization of the United Nations). 2017a. "The Director-General's Medium Term Plan 2018–21 and Programme of Work and Budget 2018–19." FAO, Rome. http://www.fao.org/3/a-ms278e.pdf

FAO (Food and Agriculture Organization of the United Nations). 2017b. "Evaluation of FAO's Contribution to Inclusive and Efficient Agricultural and Food Systems (SO4)." PC 122/3, October 2017, 122nd Session, Rome, November 6–10. http://www.fao.org/fileadmin/user_upload/bodies/Progr_Comm/PC_122-documents/MU657e.pdf

FAO (Food and Agriculture Organization of the United Nations). 2017c. "Reviewed Strategic Framework". C 2017/7 Rev.1, 40th Session, Rome, July 3–8. http://www.fao.org/3/a-ms431reve.pdf

FAO (Food and Agriculture Organization of the United Nations). 2017d. "Strategic Work of FAO to Increase the Resilience of Livelihoods." FAO, Rome. http://www.fao.org/3/a-i6463e.pdf

FAO (Food and Agriculture Organization of the United Nations). 2018a. "EMPRES. About Us." Agricultural and Consumer Health Department, Animal Production and Health, Emergency Prevention System for Animal Health (EMPRES-AH). http://www.fao.org/ag/againfo/pro grammes/en/empres/about.html

FAO (Food and Agriculture Organization of the United Nations). 2018b. "FAO Investment Centre: Annual Review 2017." CA1898EN/1/10.18. FAO, Rome. http://www.fao.org/3/CA1898EN/ca1898en.pdf

FAO (Food and Agriculture Organization of the United Nations). 2018c. "Global Push to Stamp Out Hunger Hinges on Better Data." FAO News, September 25. http://www.fao.org/news/story/en/item/1154013/icode/

FAO (Food and Agriculture Organization of the United Nations). 2018d. "Overview of FAO's Strategic Objective Programmes." APRC/18/6 Web Annex 1, March, for FAO Regional Conference for Asia and the Pacific, 34th Session, Nadi, Fiji, April 9–13. http://www.fao.org/3/MW154en/mw154en.pdf

FAO (Food and Agriculture Organization of the United States). 2018e. "2018 Annual Report of the Inspector General." Finance Committee, 175th Session, Rome, March 18–22. http://www.fao.org/aud/48421-0353d94f7776e6f0991133063b331953b.pdf

FAO (Food and Agriculture Organization in the United Nations). 2019a. "FAO Framework on Rural Extreme Poverty. Towards Reaching Target 1.1 of the Sustainable Development Goals." FAO, Rome.

FAO (Food and Agriculture Organization of the United Nations). 2019b. "FAO Investment Centre: Annual Review 2018." FAO, Rome. http://www.fao.org/3/ca5343en/CA5343EN.pdf

FAO (Food and Agriculture Organization of the United Nations). 2019c. "Food and Nutrition Security Resilience Programme: Building Food System Resilience in Protracted Crises." Briefing Note, FAO, Rome. http://www.fao.org/3/ca6159en/ca6159en.pdf

FAO (Food and Agriculture Organization of the United Nations). 2019d. "A Key Milestone for FAO Statistics—First Meeting of the IAGFS." FAO News, FAO, Rome. http://www.fao.org/statistics/news/en/

FAO (Food and Agriculture Organization of the United Nations). 2019e. "Programme Implementation Report 2016–17." C2019/8, April 2018, for the Conference of the 41st Session, FAO, Rome, June 22–9. http://www.fao.org/fileadmin/user_upload/bodies/Progr_Comm/PC_124-documents/MV543e.pdf

FAO (Food and Agriculture Organization of the United Nations). 2019f. "Report of the Council of FAO." CL 163/REP, 163rd Session, Rome, December 2–6. http://www.fao.org/3/nb990en/nb990en.pdf

FAO (Food and Agriculture Organization of the United Nations). 2019g. "Synthesis of Findings and Lessons Learnt from the Strategic Objective Evaluations." FAO, Rome. http://www.fao.org/3/ca3774en/ca3774en.pdf

FAO (Food and Agriculture Organization of the United Nations). 2020a. FAO in Emergencies. Funding. http://www.fao.org/emergencies/about/funding/en/

FAO (Food and Agriculture Organization of the United Nations). 2020b. GIEWS—Global Information and Early Warning System. Country Briefs. http://www.fao.org/giews/coun trybrief/index.jsp

FAO (Food and Agriculture Organization of the United Nations). 2020c. Voices of the Hungry. The Food Insecurity Experience Scale. http://www.fao.org/in-action/voices-of-the-hungry/fies/en/

FAO (Food and Agriculture Organization of the United Nations). 2020d. "WAPOR–FAO Portal to Monitor Water Productivity through Open Access of Remotely Sensed Derived Data." http://www.fao.org/land-water/databases-and-software/wapor/en/

FAO (Food and Agriculture Organization of the United Nations), IFAD (International Fund for Agricultural Development), UNICEF (United Nations Children's Fund), WFP (World Food Programme), and WHO (World Health Organization). 2019. "The State of Food Security and Nutrition in the World 2019. Safeguarding against Economic Slowdowns and Downturns." FAO, Rome. http://www.fao.org/publications/sofi/en/

FAO (Food and Agriculture Organization of the United Nations), IFAD (International Fund for Agricultural Development), UNICEF (United Nations Children's Fund), WFP (World Food Programme), and WHO (World Health Organization). 2020. *The State of Food Security and Nutrition in the World 2020: Transforming Food Systems for Affordable Healthy Diets*. Rome: FAO. http://www.fao.org/3/ca9692en/CA9692EN.pdf

FAO (Food and Agriculture Organization of the United Nations) and IPPC (International Plant Protection Convention). 2020. "International Plant Protection Convention." https://www.ippc.int/en/

FAO (Food and Agriculture Organization of the United Nations), and WHO (World Health Organization). 2020. Codex Alimentarius. International Food Standards. http://www.fao.org/fao-who-codexalimentarius/en/

FAO OED (Office of Evaluation). 2010a. "Evaluation of FAO Interventions Funded by the CERF." Final Report. Food and Agriculture Organization of the United Nations, Rome. https://www.alnap.org/system/files/content/resource/files/main/cerf-fao-evaluation-final-version.pdf

FAO OED (Office of Evaluation). 2010b. "Evaluation of FAO's Role and Work Related to Water." Final Report. Food and Agriculture Organization of the United Nations, Rome. https://www.alnap.org/system/files/content/resource/files/main/water-evaluation-final-report.pdf

FAO OED (Office of Evaluation). 2010c. "Second Real-Time Evaluation of FAO's Work on Highly Pathogenic Avian Influenza (HPAI)." http://www.fao.org/docrep/meeting/019/k8501e.pdf

FAO OED (Office of Evaluation). 2011. "Evaluation of FAO's Role and Work in Nutrition." Final Report. Food and Agriculture Organization of the United Nations, Rome. http://www.fao.org/docrep/meeting/023/mb663E01.pdf

FAO OED (Office of Evaluation). 2012a. "Evaluation of FAO's Role and Work in Food and Agriculture Policy." Food and Agriculture Organization of the United Nations, Rome. http://www.fao.org/fileadmin/user_upload/oed/docs/1_Evaluation%20of%20FAOs%20role%20and%20work%20in%20food%20and%20agriculture%20policy_2012_ER.pdf

FAO OED (Office of Evaluation). 2012b. "Strategic Evaluation of FAO's Role and Work in Forestry." Final Report. Food and Agriculture Organization of the United Nations, Rome. http://www.fao.org/3/me685e/me685e.pdf

FAO OED (Office of Evaluation). 2013. "Evaluation of FAO's Role in Investment for Food and Nutrition Security, Agriculture and Rural Development." Food and Agriculture Organization of the United Nations, Rome. http://www.fao.org/docrep/meeting/027/mf599e.pdf

FAO OED (Office of Evaluation). 2015a. "Evaluation of FAO's Contribution to Climate Change Adaptation and Mitigation." Final Report, Thematic Evaluation Series, October. Food and Agriculture Organization of the United Nations, Rome. http://www.fao.org/3/a-bd903e.pdf

FAO OED (Office of Evaluation). 2015b. "Evaluation of FAO's Contribution to Knowledge on Food and Agriculture." Final Report, Thematic Evaluation Series, September. Food and Agriculture Organization of the United Nations, Rome. http://www.fao.org/3/a-bd904e.pdf

FAO OED (Office of Evaluation). 2016a. "Evaluation of FAO Multipartner Programme Support Mechanism (FMM)." Project Evaluation Series, March. Food and Agriculture Organization of the United Nations, Rome. http://www.fao.org/3/a-bd457e.pdf

FAO OED (Office of Evaluation). 2016b. "Evaluation of FAO Strategic Objective 5: Increase the Resilience of Livelihoods to Threats and Crises." Thematic Evaluation Series, October. Food and Agriculture Organization of the United Nations, Rome. http://www.fao.org/3/a-bq613e.pdf

FAO OED (Office of Evaluation). 2016c. "Evaluation of FAO's Work in Genetic Resources." Thematic Evaluation Series, October. Food and Agriculture Organization of the United Nations, Rome. http://www.fao.org/3/a-bq613e.pdf

FAO OED (Office of Evaluation). 2016d. "Final Evaluation of the Improved Global Governance for Hunger Reduction Programme." Project Evaluation Series, April. Food and Agriculture Organization of the United Nations, Rome. http://www.fao.org/3/a-bd492e.pdf

FAO OED (Office of Evaluation). 2016e. "Mid-term Evaluation of the Forest and Farm Facility Programme." Project Evaluation Series, July. Food and Agriculture Organization of the United Nations, Rome. http://www.fao.org/3/a-bq504e.pdf

FAO OED (Office of Evaluation). 2017a. "Evaluation of FAO's Contribution to the Enable Inclusive and Efficient and Agricultural and Food Systems (SO4)." Thematic Evaluation Series, PC 122/3, October. Food and Agriculture Organization of the United Nations, Rome. http://www.fao.org/evaluation/highlights/highlights-detail/en/c/1045813/

FAO OED (Office of Evaluation). 2017b. "Evaluation of FAO's Contribution to the Reduction of Rural Poverty through Strategic Programme 3." Thematic Evaluation Series, March. Food and Agriculture Organization of the United Nations, Rome. http://www.fao.org/3/a-bd600e.pdf

FAO OED (Office of Evaluation). 2017c. "Evaluation of the Financial Support by the World Bank Group with the Development Grant Facility to Support the 'Partnership for Agricultural Market Information System (AMIS)'." Project Evaluation Series, July. Food and Agriculture Organization of the United Nations, Rome. http://www.fao.org/evaluation/evaluation-digest/evaluations-detail/en/c/1105557/

FAO OED (Office of Evaluation) 2018. "Evaluation of FAO's Contribution to Integrated Natural Resource Management for Sustainable Agriculture (SO2)." Food and Agriculture Organization of the United Nations, Rome. http://www.fao.org/3/CA2164EN/ca2164en.pdf

FAO OED (Office of Evaluation). 2019a. "Evaluation of FAO's Strategic Results Framework." Food and Agriculture Organization of the United Nations, Rome. http://www.fao.org/3/ca6453en/ca6453en.pdf

FAO OED (Office of Evaluation). 2019b. "Evaluation of Strategy for Partnerships with the Private Sector." Food and Agriculture Organization of the United Nations, Rome. http://www.fao.org/3/ca6678en/ca6678en.pdf

FAO–OIE–WHO (Food and Agriculture Organization of the United Nations–World Organisation for Animal Health–World Health Organization). 2011. "FAO-OIE-WHO Technical Update: Current Evolution of Avian Influenza H5N1 Viruses." September 7. http://www.oie.int/doc/ged/D11128.PDF

FAOSTAT. 2019. Food and Agriculture Organization of the United Nations. Statistics Division. Definitions and Standards Used in FAOSTAT. http://www.fao.org/faostat/en/#definitions

FSIN (Food Security Information Network). 2019a. "Global Report on Food Crises 2019." March. http://www.fsinplatform.org/global-report-food-crises-2019

FSIN (Food Security Information Network). 2019b. "Regional Focus on the Intergovernmental Authority on Development (IGAD) Member States." Global Report on Food Crises 2019, September. http://fsinplatform.org/sites/default/files/resources/files/IGAD%202019%20online.pdf

Government of Australia. 2012. "Assessment Summary: Food and Agriculture Organization of the United Nations." In *Australian Multilateral Assessment*, 84–91. Canberra: Commonwealth of Australia. https://dfat.gov.au/about-us/publications/Documents/ama-full-report-2.pdf

Haddad, Lawrence. 2019. "Dr. Graziano Da Silva: The Quiet FAO Revolutionary." Global Alliance for Improved Nutrition (GAIN). https://www.gainhealth.org/knowledge-centre/dr-graziano-da-silva-the-quiet-fao-revolutionary/

IAEA (International Atomic Energy Agency). 2013. "IAEA and FAO Help Member States Detect Deadly Avian Influenza." IAEA News, September 13. https://www.iaea.org/newscenter/news/iaea-and-fao-help-member-states-detect-deadly-avian-influenza

IPCC (Intergovernmental Panel on Climate Change). 2019. "Climate Change and Land." An IPCC special report on climate change, desertification, land degradation, sustainable land management, food security, and greenhouse gas fluxes in terrestrial ecosystems. https://www.ipcc.ch/report/srccl/

Jerven, Morten. 2013. *Poor Numbers: How We Are Misled by African Development Statistics and What to Do About It.* Ithaca, NY: Cornell University Press.

Kapur, Devesh. 2019. "What Next for the Bretton Woods Twins?" ry, October 18.

Kharas, Homi. 2007. "The New Reality of Aid." Report, August 1, Wolfensohn Center for Development, Brookings Institution, Washington, DC.

Knippenberg, Erwin, and John F. Hoddinott. 2017. "Shocks, Social Protection, and Resilience: Evidence from Ethiopia." ESSP Working Paper No. 109, August, Strategy Ethiopian Support Program, Ethiopian Development Research Institute (EDRI) and International Food Policy Research Institute. http://www.ifpri.org/publication/shocks-social-protection-and-resilience-evidence-ethiopia

Lele, Uma. 2007. "Assessment of Technical Work: FAO as A Knowledge Management Organization." FAO, Rome.

Lele, Uma, and Arthur A. Goldsmith. 1989. "The Development of National Agricultural Research Capacity: India's Experience with the Rockefeller Foundation and Its Significance for Africa." *Economic Development and Cultural Change* 37 (2): 305–43.

Lele, Uma, Aaron Zasueta, and Benjamin Singer. 2010. "The Environment and Global Governance: Can the Global Community Rise to the Challenge?" Lincoln Institute of Land Policy Working Paper WP10UL1, Cambridge, MA. http://www.ajfand.net/Volume13/No4/REPRINT-The%20environment%20and%20global%20governance.pdf

Linn, Johannes F. 2009. "The Zedillo Commission Report on World Bank Reform: A Stepping Stone for the G-20 Summits in 2010." Brookings Institution, Washington, DC, November 18. https://www.brookings.edu/articles/the-zedillo-commission-report-on-world-bank-reform-a-stepping-stone-for-the-g-20-summits-in-2010/

McCalla, Alex F. 2007a. "FAO and the International Financial Institutions: The World Bank and the Regional Development Banks." Unpublished background paper for the "The Challenge of Renewal." Report of the Independent External Evaluation of the Food and Agriculture Organization of the United Nations (FAO), 2007.

McCalla, Alex F. 2007b. "FAO in the Changing Global Landscape." Working Paper No. 07–006, University of California Davis. http://ageconsearch.umn.edu/bitstream/190919/2/WP07-006.pdf

Mejia, Sebastian Acevedo, Claudio Baccianti, Mico Mrkaic, Natalija Novta, Evgenia Pugacheva, and Petia Topalova. 2019. "Weather Shocks and Output in Low-Income Countries: Adaptation and the Role of Policies." IMF Working Paper WP/19/178, International Monetary Fund, Washington, DC. https://www.imf.org/en/Publications/WP/Issues/2019/08/16/Weather-Shocks-and-Output-in-Low-Income-Countries-The-Role-of-Policies-and-Adaptation-48554

MOPAN (Multilateral Organisation Performance Assessment Network). 2011. "Organisational Effectiveness Assessment: Food and Agriculture Organization (FAO) of the United Nations." http://www.mopanonline.org/assessments/fao2011/index.htm

MOPAN (Multilateral Organisation Performance Assessment Network). 2014. "Synthesis Report: Food and Agriculture Organization of the United Nations (FAO), 2014." http://www.mopanonline.org/assessments/fao2014/FAO-2014-Synthesis_Report-eng.pdf

MOPAN (Multilateral Organisation Performance Assessment Network). 2017. "Methodology Digest. MOPAN 3.0." http://www.mopanonline.org/ourwork/ourapproachmopan30/Mopan%20Methodology%20Digest%202017.pdf

MOPAN (Multilateral Organisation Performance Assessment Network). 2018. "MOPAN 2017–18 Assessments: Food and Agriculture Organization (FAO)." http://www.mopanonline.org/assessments/fao2017-18/index.htm

OCHA (United Nations Office for the Coordination of Humanitarian Affairs). 2020. "East Africa Locust Infestation." https://www.unocha.org/east-africa-locust-infestation

OECD–FAO (Organisation for Economic Co-operation and Development–Food and Agriculture Organization of the United Nations). 2020. *OECD–FAO Agricultural Outlook 2020–2029*. Rome: FAO and Paris: OECD Publishing. https://www.oecd-ilibrary.org/docserver/1112c23b-en.pdf

Phillips, Ralph W. 1981a. "The Constitutional Expression of the FAO Idea." In *FAO: Its Origins, Formation and Evolution 1945–1981*. Rome: Food and Agriculture Organization of the United Nations (FAO). http://www.fao.org/3/a-p4228e.pdf

Phillips, Ralph W. 1981b. *FAO: Its Origins, Formation and Evolution 1945–1981*. Rome: Food and Agriculture Organization of the United Nations (FAO).

Sandler, Todd. 1992. *Collective Action: Theory and Applications*. Ann Arbor: MI: University of Michigan Press.

Shaw, D. John. 2014. "A Global Partnership Program to End World Hunger." Briefing 18, Future United Nations Development System, Ralph Bunche Institute for International Studies, CUNY Graduate Center, New York. https://www.futureun.org/media/archive1/briefings/FUNDSBriefing18-FoodSecurity-Shaw.pdf

Strait Times. 2018. "China Rises to Second Largest Contributor to United Nations Budget." *The Strait Times*, Singapore Press Holdings, December 24. https://www.straitstimes.com/asia/east-asia/china-rises-to-second-largest-contributor-to-united-nations-budget

UN (United Nations). 2003. "FAO Conference Ends 32nd Session: Term Limits Set for Future Directors-General." Meetings Coverage and Press Releases, December 10. http://www.un.org/press/en/2003/sag200.doc.htm

UN (United Nations). 2019. "World Economic Situation and Prospects 2019." Statistical Annex. https://www.un.org/development/desa/dpad/wp-content/uploads/sites/45/WESP2019_BOOK-ANNEX-en.pdf

UN (United Nations). 2020a. United Nations Food Systems Summit 2020. https://www.un.org/sustainabledevelopment/food-systems-summit-2021/

UN (United Nations). 2020b. Zero Hunger Challenge. http://www.un.org/en/zerohunger/challenge.shtml

UN News. 2016. "Agriculture Must Transform to Feed a Hotter, More Crowded Planet, UN says on World Food Day." October 16, FAO OED, UN, New York.

UNCTAD (United Nations Conference on Trade and Development). 2018. *Handbook of Statistics*. New York: UNCTAD.

UNESCO (United Nations Educational, Scientific and Cultural Organization). 1984. *Guide to the Archives of International Organizations. I. The United Nations System.* Paris: UNESCO. http://unesdoc.unesco.org/images/0005/000591/059141eo.pdf

Waddington, Hugh, and Howard White. 2014. "Farmer Field Schools: From Agricultural Extension to Adult Education." Systematic Review Summary 1. International Initiative for Impact Evaluation (3ie), New Delhi. https://www.3ieimpact.org/evidence-hub/publications/systematic-review-summaries/farmer-field-schools-agricultural-extension

World Bank. 2002. "The World Bank's Approach to Global Programs: An Independent Evaluation." World Bank, Washington, DC.

Zedillo, Ernesto, Chair. 2009. "Repowering the World Bank for the 21st Century." Report of the High Level Commission on Modernization of World Bank Group Governance, World Bank Group, Washington, DC.

10

CGIAR

Uma Lele and Sambuddha Goswami

Summary and Implications Going Forward

CGIAR is by far the most complex of the five organizations that we have reviewed in this book.[1] Uncertain year-to-year funding and lack of growth in funding since 2014 have challenged CGIAR's continued ability to contribute to Sustainable Development Goal 2 (SDG2). Successive waves of reforms, detailed in this chapter, have responded to the need to broaden the research agenda on food security by incorporating the growing complexity of CGIAR's agenda: poverty reduction, food security, nutrition, gender equity, environmental concerns about climate change, and pressure on natural resources threatening yield growth and production stability, concurrently with the need to promote diversification of production by explicitly incorporating biodiversity in the farming systems to increase their resilience to climate change and resource pressures. This means incorporation of legumes, agroforestry, livestock, fisheries, fruits, vegetables, and nuts. This agenda has been recently described by international organizations as broadly encompassing sustainable food systems. Diversification of farming systems implies it is an effective way to address the triple burden of hunger, micronutrient deficiencies, and obesity. The growing complexity of the research, however, has to be achieved in the face of the growing gap in the funding of public sector research and development (R&D). Public funding of research has had high rates of return, but funding shortages are occurring, despite this evidence, and even in the face of the reversal of the long-term trend in hunger reduction demonstrated elsewhere in this book.

The need to increase productivity while building the resilience of agriculture is urgent. Diversified integrated farming systems are needed to improve environmental and human health and to curtail excessive reliance for the food security of the poor on a handful of cereals, such as wheat, rice, maize, and root crops.

CGIAR is based on voluntary funding, but CGIAR's mission is complex, scientific, and long-term, conducting research to develop technologies for small farmers to increase their productivity and manage their resources sustainably. It takes between 5 and 25 years to deliver technologies and show results at scale. Historically, CGIAR has engaged in capacity building with developing countries' national agricultural research systems (NARS), while also focusing CGIAR research on essential global and regional public goods—that is, research with a long time horizon, research with substantial spillovers, yet research on the problems of poor farmers with limited scope to achieve scaled-up demand for inputs or services relatively quickly. Somewhere along the way, however, this model of global and regional public goods, through CGIAR and NARS conducting applied and adaptive

---

[1] Uma Lele was on the founding board of the Center for International Forestry Research, a member of the Technical Advisory Committee (TAC), and a leader of CGIAR's meta-review, titled "CGIAR at 31," carried out by the World Bank's Independent Evaluation Group.

Food for All: International Organizations and the Transformation of Agriculture. Uma Lele, Manmohan Agarwal, Brian C. Baldwin, and Sambuddha Goswami, Oxford University Press. © Uma Lele, Manmohan Agarwal, Brian C. Baldwin, and Sambuddha Goswami 2021. DOI: 10.1093/oso/9780198755173.003.0011

research, has fallen apart. With the exceptions of China and Brazil, developing countries are not investing, and donors are not financing sufficient resources in their own R&D systems, with the result that CGIAR has moved downstream to carry out activities that NARS should do. We suggest some remedies in this chapter.

Many countries are off track in achieving SDG2 and related targets, and only 10 years are left to reach the goal by 2030. Hence, there is a particular urgency in CGIAR fulfilling its promise.

Using a historical approach, this chapter explains how CGIAR's mission has grown over time, based on changing donor support and expectations, while funding has stagnated. To meet SDG2 targets among small and marginal farmers, CGIAR has established the target of US$2 billion annual funding in nominal terms by 2030, as part of its recent reforms. If realized, it will slightly more than double and stabilize research funding. Increased funding and its certainty will reduce the distraction of valuable staff time by fundraising activities, curtail inter-Center competition, and allow researchers to focus on research and its impact, engaging actively in outreach, as they have done in the past.

CGIAR's latest reorganization, known as "One CGIAR," is a major restructuring, described in this chapter against the background of history of reforms. It is also responding to the funding challenges creatively. The proof will be in increased funding support under this new reorganized structure. The System Board, newly named after "unified governance" became effective on October 1, 2020, and replaces the old System Management Board (SMB). It is a self-governing mechanism of the System and Centers, intended to work better under the troika of managing directors that report to the unified System Board. In addition, inter-Center research collaborations have been occurring through bottom-up Center-driven efforts, with benefits of lower operational costs and better ability to improve the quality of research through skill mixes. CGIAR has focused on crop research on cereals, roots, and tubers; livestock; trees; land and water management; and policy research. Still, new strategic partnerships are needed, including with the private sector and civil society, to promote faster diversification of healthy food production and diversified diets through agricultural value chains that do no harm, and by greater focus on land and water management. Greater focus on diet diversification also requires greater engagement with women in production, food processing, and in consumer awareness and with civil society. We review the history of CGIAR's new gender platform, as a positive development.

Partnerships with advanced country institutions have strengthened, as well as those with developed countries. Partnerships with developing countries were the foundation of CGIAR's success during the Green Revolution, but over time, they have weakened in part due to a shortage of resources and a growing research agenda. Stronger partnerships are also needed with the private sector. The increasing involvement of private foundations, such as the Bill and Melinda Gates Foundation (BMGF), provides CGIAR with opportunities to achieve transformative change. Nevertheless, CGIAR needs to open up its System to new funding sources, and with the private sector and to qualified researchers, whether inside or outside the CGIAR System, to lead research programs to accelerate the delivery of technologies, thereby creating competition and enhancing the quality of research and outreach. Developing countries, the intended beneficiaries of CGIAR's research, still lack sufficient voice, a phenomenon that is not unique to CGIAR, as discussed in Chapters 5 and 6 on global governance. Stronger and more responsible voice for developing countries will increase their sense of ownership and the effectiveness of CGIAR. The chapter makes a case for the uses of the International Development Association (IDA) and the International Bank for Reconstruction and Development (IBRD) to substantially increase investments in

R&D among World Bank borrowers as well—in the case of IDA, to increase core contributions to CGIAR.

Introduction

Organizational and cultural change is key to keeping up with the disruptive changes underway in the global environment. Change is never easy in complex organizations with growing agendas and competing interests, posing inevitable collective action challenges, as we have discussed in Chapters 5 and 6 on global governance. CGIAR has been undergoing considerable change since its establishment and, particularly, since the beginning of the new millennium and will likely have changed further by the time this study emerges. It is an organization based entirely on voluntary finance, like the World Food Programme (WFP).

There are key differences between CGIAR and WFP, however. WFP's mission to provide emergency assistance to populations in urgent need of food is easily understood and appealing to donors, and the link between its operations and outcomes are direct and easy to see for its financiers in a relatively short time, although measuring impacts of WFP's activities has been a challenge (Brück et al. 2018). In contrast, whereas CGIAR's research has had an extraordinary impact—documented once again in a recent, exhaustive study of returns to research by Alston, Pardey, and Rao (2020), that with a benefit–cost ratio (BCR) of 10:1, CGIAR's research is a long-term endeavor. Earlier, Pardey and Beintema (2001) had described agricultural research and development (AgR&D) as "slow magic." It takes at least 5–20 years from the inception of research to demonstrate results on the ground, because there are many intervening factors between research and final outcomes, over which CGIAR has no control. Research, by its nature, is uncertain and usually nonlinear. Although extraordinary scientific advances are speeding up the research process, to deploy new scientific methods requires engagement in complex partnerships. Engaging in meaningful enduring partnerships involves issues of intellectual property and resolutions of attribution. For that reason, this chapter is more than about CGIAR's research impact. It is about the political economy of foreign aid, in a context in which the giving of aid is increasingly driven by short-term pressures to show development impacts rather than by expertise, with understanding of what it takes to achieve those impacts.

A recent report of the Food and Agriculture Organization of the United Nations (FAO), *The State of the World's Biodiversity for Food and Agriculture*, noted that only nine crops produce two-thirds of the world's food supply,[2] and biodiversity has declined, in part, due to the success of CGIAR's research (FAO 2019). Such concentration of the world's food supply in a few crops is a high-risk strategy. Yet, the long gestation lags in conducting research is also inconsistent with short-term funding and increasing donor demand for results, including how the results are generated and what activities donors are willing to finance. The number of actors in CGIAR has grown, and successive reforms have been intended to make CGIAR more attuned to changing times and more effective in delivering on its declared mission. The mission, too, has evolved—to fit the Sustainable Development Goals (SDGs) and the Paris Accord on Climate Change (see Table A.10.1 in the Appendix). CGIAR's latest mission and multiple internal and external stakeholders are listed in Box 10.1.

---

[2] Sugarcane, maize, rice, wheat, potatoes, soybeans, oil palm fruit, sugar beet, and cassava.

Box 10.1 CGIAR's Vision, Mission, and Internal and External Stakeholders

---

CGIAR's Vision

"A world free of poverty, hunger and environmental degradation" (CGIAR 2017f).

As part of its latest (2019–20) reforms, CGIAR adopted a new mission:

1. Ending hunger by 2030—through science to transform food, land and water systems in a climate crisis (CGIAR 2019e, 4).

2. "We work to advance agricultural science and innovation to enable poor people, especially women, to better nourish their families, and improve productivity and resilience so they can share in economic growth and manage natural resources in the face of climate change and other challenges."[a]

CGIAR stakeholders include management of the System-wide CGIAR research programs (CRPs), management and staff of the Centers, 15 until 2020, some of which are in the process of formal or informal alliances, their boards of CRPs and Centers and oversight bodies (Independent Science and Partnership Council [ISPC, renamed the Independent Science for Development Council or ISDC]; Independent Evaluation Arrangement [IEA]; Standing Panel on Impact Assessment [SPIA]); and CGIAR management and governance at the System level (System Council and System Management Board and Office). Two pairs of the Center—that is, four of the 15 Centers—recently merged/aligned into formal or informal cooperation, and others are in dialogue about closer cooperation. The International Center for Research in Agroforestry (ICRAF) and the Center for International Forestry Research (CIFOR) are formally aligned, merging officially on January 1, 2019, albeit with only one Director-General (DG) and one board each yet (CIFOR 2019), whereas the International Center for Tropical Agriculture (CIAT) and Bioversity International signed a Memorandum of Understanding in November 2018 to form an alliance and since both DGs were leaving, the two Boards appointed Juan Lucas Restrepo to become Bioversity International's DG and the Chief Executive Officer (CEO) Designate of the Alliance (CIAT 2018). The International Rice Research Institute (IRRI) and AfricaRice (the Africa Rice Center) are similarly in dialogue about closer cooperation (CGIAR 2018a). Other related CGIAR actors include the Global Forum on Agricultural Research and Innovation, donors and international organizations that support CGIAR through financial support and perform other functions such as trusteeship, developing countries, the private sector, civil society, the scientific community, and producers and consumers of food.

[a] See "CGIAR: How We Work: Strategy": http://www.cgiar.org/how-we-work/strategy

---

Have the changes in CGIAR been the right ones, and enough in the context of a rapidly changing external environment? How do we know if they have "worked"? If these were easy questions to answer, they would have already been tackled. One relatively unambiguous indicator of success is when introduced changes pass the test of time. The more difficult task is to assess change in terms of its effectiveness, using different criteria: for example, the ability to mobilize other partners with special assets and additional funding, to achieve scientific excellence, and to be primed for larger impacts on the lives of the intended beneficiaries in terms of scale and scope.

The CGIAR story should be seen in the context of its extraordinary contribution to the Green Revolution and subsequently to the spread of new technologies through crop improvement and other technologies and policies, documented later in this chapter. However, rapid population growth, urbanization, changing diets, slow economic transformation, climate change, soil degradation, water shortages, growing obesity, and the need to create youth employment, particularly in sub-Saharan Africa (SSA) and South Asia (SA), pose new challenges, as we discussed in earlier chapters.

There are also other global trends. Despite substantial accumulated evidence on very high internal rates of return on investments, public R&D spending in developed and developing countries (with the exceptions of China, Brazil, and India) has slowed (Hurley et al. 2016). Beintema and Echeverría (2020) also showed current slowing trends in public sector research, but most of the growth in global agricultural research spending (excluding the private for-profit sector) from US$31 to US$47 billion during 2000–16 occurred during 2000–10, and in middle-income countries (MICs). China accounted for about half of the increase. Combined with growth in other large MICs—their share in global research expanded from 40 to 59 percent of the global total. In sharp contrast to the growth in public investment in MICs, however, agricultural research has slowed in the United States and Europe. It was 0.7 percent during 2000–10, and 0.8 percent during 2010–16. Furthermore, 122 countries out of the sample of 179 countries invested less than US$100 million in agricultural research in 2016, and 52 of these spent less than US$10 million. The five top-ranked countries were China (US$8 billion), the United States (US$5 billion), India (US$4 billion), Brazil (US$3 billion), and Japan (US$3 billion). Yet, underinvestment, while significant in developed countries, is particularly prevalent among countries with small- and medium-sized research systems. Countries with both small research systems and low potential to increase their investment in agricultural research will need to adopt alternative strategies—such as collaboration with countries and regions that share mutual research needs and goals—in order to acquire the knowledge and technologies they need to achieve agricultural development and growth in the coming decades. We will return to the implications of these findings at the end of this chapter.

There is increased reliance on private sector research in developed countries. Part of the reason for decline in public sector research in the United States, for example, is the assumption that the private sector will investment more. Fuglie (2016), however, has shown that private research concentrates on only a few commodities, and responds to market prices. Current slowing trends in public sector research portend slower agricultural productivity growth, a phenomenon that is particularly disconcerting, given the proprietary nature of private sector research.

CGIAR's quintessential comparative advantage has been in high-quality research, particularly on germplasm, and in its broad presence throughout the developing world. What, then, is and will be the role of CGIAR in research and technology development in this new world, including in genetically engineered crops? What about the strong resistance to genetically modified crops, even though there has been no evidence found of adverse impacts on human health (NASEM 2016; Brody 2018)?[3] What would happen if CGIAR,

---

[3] The Cartagena Protocol on Biosafety to the Convention on Biological Diversity, an international agreement, was adopted January 29, 2000, and entered into force on September 11, 2003. It seeks to ensure the safe handling, transport, and use of living modified organisms (LMOs), derived from biotechnology, that could have adverse effects on biological diversity or present risks to human health. See the "Convention on Biological Diversity": https://bch.cbd.int/protocol/

which has conducted research using conventional means disappeared, as some have feared it could do without a stable, predictable level of international financing for agricultural research and further structural reforms? How will countries at very different stages of development be affected?

We argue that the new scientific frontiers call for CGIAR to raise its game scientifically to take advantage of the opportunities provided upstream by the fourth industrial revolution, while diversifying its research portfolio. It also means "substantially more emphasis on priority setting [and risk taking], both at the System and the CGIAR Research Program (CRP) level, if the CGIAR wants to realize its own goal to be at the forefront on how the international development community should allocate resources for international agricultural research," as noted in the lessons from evaluations of 15 CRPs (Birner and Byerlee 2016, x). The Birner and Byerlee synthesis of evaluations also noted that "legacy research and bilateral funding played a large role in CRP resource allocation.... [S]uch bilateral funding often drives CRPs toward [downstream] development activities in which they do not have comparative advantage" (Birner and Byerlee 2016, x). A recent CGIAR paper noted, however, that "through W3 (Window 3) and bilateral funding individual Funders steer approximately 80% of the portfolio directly" (CGIAR 2017e, 2). This suggests the need to develop a strategy toward bilateral funding, which achieves CGIAR's strategic objectives, rather than allowing funding to drive the downstream development research agenda. Indeed, the intention in setting up the System Council (SC) and Window 1's unrestricted funding, was precisely to achieve increased stable funding, but such unrestricted funding has become scarcer.[4]

The principle of subsidiarity is often invoked in research management. It means performing only those tasks that cannot be performed more effectively at a more local level. This action should be pursued ideally by actors in developing countries who are entering in partnership with CGIAR to maximize their joint impacts. This is the way that CGIAR began in Asia in the 1960s, in partnership with bilateral donors—particularly, the United States Agency for International Development (USAID) and the Rockefeller and Ford Foundations—by building the capacity of Asian NARS to undertake applied and adaptive research, while supplying the international public goods of plant material of high-yielding varieties from CGIAR Centers.

---

[4] For more information about funding windows, see the section "CGIAR Fund," later in this chapter. The concept of "restricted funding" has changed over time. Before CGIAR's 2015–16 reforms:

> Restricted funds ... [were] restricted either by attribution (to a particular research program or region) or by contract (to a project, subproject, or activity). An allocation to one Center as opposed to another is not restricted funding by the CGIAR's definition. While a Center's funds can be allocated to any program or cost according to a particular Center's institutional needs or priorities, these cannot be switched from one Center to another. Different degrees of restriction result in part from donors allocating funds to the Centers from their various units and budgets. (OED 2003, 188)

The World Bank is the only donor that allocates its resources exclusively to the overall system (that is, to Window 1 [W1]) (Personal communication, Jonathan Wadsworth, former Executive Secretary of CGIAR with Uma Lele, January 29, 2019). There are other contributors to W1, but they also make other contributions to W2 and W3, and/or bilaterally. Bank staff sometimes contract Centers for small specific studies, and some IBRD or IDA borrowers may contract CGIAR to do significant work—however, this latter item is effectively on behalf of the borrower, not the World Bank. The differences in the three windows are discussed in more detail later in this chapter.

Notably, even World Bank funding has diminished from US$50 million annually to US$30 million (see Hagstrom Report [2015]).

According to the 2016 CGIAR System Framework, unrestricted funding is defined as "funding from the CGIAR Trust Fund that has not been designated by a Funder for a specific Center or research program" (CGIAR 2016a, 4).

Alston, Pardey, and Rao (2020), in their latest study, noted that in 2016 present value terms, the costs of the entire CGIAR portfolio over the period 1960–2010 was US\$59.7 billion (2016 dollar values). They noted:

> If we attribute just one-quarter of the benefits reported in the nine high-payoff projects to CGIAR (with the remainder to national partners and others), the BCR is 7.5:1; if we count only the costs of the CGIAR Centers that conducted the relevant R&D, the BCR is 10:1.
>
> If one-half the value of all the reported agricultural TFP growth from 1960–2016 in developing countries is taken as a measure of the benefit from research investments by both CGIAR and public agencies in developing countries, a BCR on the order of 10:1 is implied for research CGIAR and national partners combined. (Alston, Pardey, and Rao 2020, iv)

The 18,000 tons of wheat seed delivered to India by CGIAR's International Maize and Wheat Improvement Center (CIMMYT), under Norman Borlaug's leadership when India lacked the capacity to produce quality seed, led to the start of the Green Revolution. Most importantly, private foundations and external bilateral and multilateral assistance helped build India's capacity (Lele and Bumb 1995; Lele and Goldsmith 1989). In a 2017 publication, "Improving System Financing Modalities," CGIAR addressed this same issue of restricted funding and its relationship to upstream or downstream research (CGIAR 2017e). For CGIAR to move upstream, developing countries will need to provide complementary investments in research in their own NARS and be capable of producing appropriate applied and adaptive technologies suited to their local circumstances, while relying on the CGIAR Centers to conduct upstream, state-of-the-art, international or regional public goods research. Except for China, Brazil, and to a lesser extent India, by and large, developing countries have not been investing enough in agricultural research and innovation systems to keep up with the growing challenges, as we discussed in Chapter 7 on financing for sustainable structural transformation.

This recent growth of agricultural research in the private sector and emerging countries presents an underexploited opportunity and challenges for CGIAR and governments of donor and developing countries to carve out a new niche for CGIAR research and technology. Partnering with the private sector poses a challenge of trade secrecy and intellectual property rights. It can be managed and overcome through innovative licensing approaches and by organizations such as the African Agricultural Technology Foundation (AATF), a not-for-profit organization that facilitates and promotes public–private partnerships to access, develop, adapt, and deliver appropriate agricultural technologies for sustainable use by smallholder farmers in SSA.[5] Even American farmers warn that consolidation of big agrochemical companies, like Bayer and Monsanto, will make matters worse for them, with declining commodity prices and increasing input costs, particularly with the weakened voice of public sector research entities, even in developed countries, as noted here (Varinsky 2018).

CGIAR's internal partnerships among its Centers have improved, as well as steps to consolidate centers; for example, as detailed in Box 10.1, the International Center for Tropical Agriculture (CIAT) and Bioversity International have formed an alliance, the International Center for Research in Agroforestry (ICRAF) and the Center for International

---

[5] See https://www.aatf-africa.org

Forestry Research (CIFOR) have merged, and other such ideas are being actively explored. Partnerships with advanced country institutions are also increasing, as donors make their funds increasingly available in-kind, in the form of domestic research capacities for collaboration with CGIAR rather than in cash. However, CGIAR has a long way to go in improving partnerships with the private sector and with emerging countries. CGIAR entities need to become leaders of different "themes," establishing global and regional digital platforms and networking globally with key actors, many of whom are not currently part of CGIAR, rather than CGIAR Centers primarily being the small-scale "doers" of research. Such evolution, which is already underway, could be faster and wider through the "One CGIAR" approach.

A third major new and disruptive change prompts the need to promote balanced diets in the face of rapidly changing food habits and needs of consumers—that is, in the context of the growth of ultra-processed junk food and sugary beverages—and changes in the structure of agricultural production and value chains accompanying them. As we discussed in Chapter 4, some have attributed these changes in food demand structure directly to the outgrowth of value chains and foreign direct investment (FDI) in the food industry. Going forward, it is conceivable that new digital platforms such as "Uber eateries"[6] could provide healthier food, while creating more flexible employment for youth and women. Indeed, the COVID-19 pandemic has worsened the employment and food situation for the poorest while accelerating the use of digital tools. In Chapter 4, we showed how small and marginal Mexican farmers are being absorbed into the process of farm consolidation and have been moving out of agriculture to nonfarm employment, where their reliance on purchased food has increased. Concurrently, Mexico was exporting healthy fruits and vegetables to North America under the North American Free Trade Agreement (NAFTA). "Few predicted when Mexico joined the free-trade deal that it would transform the country in a way that would saddle millions with diet-related illnesses" (Jacobs and Richtel 2017). Vegetables are an important source of micronutrients, and making active alliances with all relevant providers, such as the World Vegetable Center (AVRDC),[7] is critical. The Center's location in Taiwan has, for decades, been controversial for its inclusion in the CGIAR System, due to the objection of the People's Republic of China to a Center based in Taiwan. CGIAR can help diversify agricultural production from its cereal-centric past and crowd-in all possible technologies and know-how for fruits, vegetables, fisheries, and poultry, by involving relevant concerned actors to help farmers produce and consumers eat healthy food. CGIAR's future relevance, effectiveness, and impact depend critically on such a new vision, strategy, and donor behavior (see Table A.10.1 in the Appendix). Developing countries will also need to change their cereal-centric food policies, as discussed in Chapters 2 and 3.

Once the Heart of the International System

CGIAR's story is one of growing organizational complexity and declining share of global expenditures, from 4 percent in the 1990s to less than 2 percent in 2020, evolving in a changing context, which makes reforms difficult. We examine the history of its partnerships and its prospects of establishing more partnerships, in a new context of a rapidly emerging

---

[6] A "virtual" online restaurant, with food available for delivery. See Garsd (2018).
[7] AVRDC was formerly known as the Asian Vegetable Research and Development Center and was established in 1971 in Taiwan. See https://avrdc.org

number of actors, providing an opportunity to establish a new platform with the private sector and NARS—as highlighted at the end of the chapter—to enhance the prospects of CGIAR's contribution to world food security going forward. A related theme of this story is CGIAR's unpredictable financing with unrestricted funding, despite its extraordinary impact on the world's food supply, particularly in developing countries, but also benefiting countries such as the United States and Australia, and paradoxically, despite substantially increased donor funding of CGIAR since 2008 until 2014, when it peaked. In the past, CGIAR has sought increased funding without regard to its quality, meaning, certainty, predictability, timeliness, and restrictions. Evidence thus far suggests that its large funding volume, without certainty, predictability, and timeliness, is not necessarily good for planning CGIAR's long-term research activities or, in particular, for their execution and, therefore, only of short-term benefit for its intended beneficiaries.

Even with only 4 percent of the global share of agricultural research, CGIAR was described by the World Bank's Operations Evaluation Department (OED) in 1999 as "at the heart of an international system linking developing and industrial nations" (Anderson and Dalrymple 1999, vii). That share had declined to less than 2 percent of total agricultural research funding by 2020 (Beintema and Echeverría 2020). In celebrating its own achievements, CGIAR noted that, with the near doubling of the world population from 3.8 billion since its establishment in 1971 to 6.8 million in 2011, the world would not have been able to feed itself without CGIAR's contributions (CGIAR 2011b).[8] Although a counterfactual is impossible to construct—if the world would have found alternative ways to increase its food supply, several independent reviews and impact studies over the years have credited CGIAR with being one of the best investments that donors have made (OED 2003; FAO 2007; CGIAR 2008, 2011a, 2020c). (See Box A.10.2 in the Appendix.)

In addition to improved germplasm, CGIAR has also delivered knowledge about policies and institutions, conserved biodiversity for germplasm improvement, contributed to human capital through collaborative research and training of developing country nationals, and been a credible policy advocate for global food and nutrition security. Strategic partnerships, even in which CGIAR's presence is small, can have a huge leveraging effect on the entire CGIAR System, and this lesson has implications for partnerships going forward. Now, though, it faces several strategic challenges. First, while it has had a loyal base of funders, it needs to attract new sources of funding, as it did in early 2000, with BMGF; second, short-term funding has posed challenges in conducting long-term research; and third, increased funding for Africa has come at the cost of investments in other regions, with implications for CGIAR's impacts of its overall research.

CGIAR Growth and Consolidation

Since its establishment in 1971, CGIAR has grown from 4 Centers—the International Rice Research Institute (IRRI), CIMMYT, CIAT, and the International Institute of Tropical Agriculture (IITA)—to 15 Centers, headquartered in 12 developing and 2 developed countries on 5 continents, with many stations and offices of the 15 Centers located in more than 60 countries and how with mergers of two sets of Centers (CIAT and Bioversity, and CIFOR and ICRAF)—13 Centers. Much of the System's growth of Centers occurred in

---

[8] In 2017, the population had reached 7.5 billion (UN 2019).

the 1980s, adding Centers on water, agroforestry, and forestry. While there were good reasons for expansion, the need for two separate centers for forestry and agroforestry was much debated, as were the two livestock centers, which eventually merged. The expansion of these Centers occurred at the instigation of donors, with CGIAR's hope that acceding to donors' wishes for expansion would lead to increased donor funding (McCalla 2017). Funding did not materialize, however, on the scale envisaged until the 2007–8 food and financial crises, which also coincided with the beginning of major reform efforts of CGIAR, to be discussed later in this chapter. Governance and management reforms were meant to bring a more organized structure to a system, which its stakeholders considered unwieldy. It was an informal organization of Centers and a growing number of members (64 members in 2009, consisting of donors, international organizations, and developing countries intended to be the System's contributors and beneficiaries). Developing countries contributed land, forests, biodiversity, and generous access to their societies. (See Table A.10.1 in the Appendix on the evolution of CGIAR's mission, centers, and membership.)

In 2017, some of the 15 Centers—independent, nonprofit research organizations—were in the process of merging of their own volition, in part due to the inability of the System to raise adequate funds. The 15 Centers are AfricaRice, Bioversity International, CIFOR, International Center for Agricultural Research in the Dry Areas (ICARDA), CIAT, International Crops Research Institute for the Semi-Arid Tropics (ICRISAT), International Food Policy Research Institute (IFPRI), IITA, International Livestock Research Institute (ILRI), CIMMYT, International Potato Center (CIP), IRRI, International Water Management Institute (IWMI), ICRAF, and WorldFish (see Figure 10.1). As previously noted (see Box 10.1), some of the Centers are in the process of merging or forming alliances, aligning their research to strengthen their capacities and accelerate impacts.

CGIAR is present in 70 countries. Funding in nominal terms has grown from US$19.5 million in 1972 to US$1,057 million in 2014, the peak year of funding, after which it declined (excluding the Centers' own income). Despite the unpredictability, uncertainty, and often, restricted nature of funding, which inhibits high priority and high-quality research, CGIAR is still the world's leading research partner on crops, livestock, aquaculture, and forestry, with approximately 11,000 staff in 96 countries (CGIAR 2016c). Of those, 2,072 were internationally recruited staff. To put CGIAR funding and staffing in perspective, China's annual expenditures in 2013 for agricultural research were US$9.4 billion (constant 2011 purchasing power parity [PPP] dollars), with the full-time equivalent (FTE) number of researchers at 43,200; in 2008, Brazil's expenditures were US$2.7 billion (constant 2011 PPP dollars), with FTE researchers of 5,869 in 2013; and India's expenditures were US$3.3 billion (constant 2011 PPP dollars) in 2014, with FTE researchers of 12,747 (IFPRI 2016).

The Overarching Context: Sustainable Development Goals and CGIAR's Strategy and Results Framework—An Attempt at Results Orientation and Accountability

Adoption of SDGs in 2015, by all member countries, led international organizations to align their work and strategy with SDGs and their targets. CGIAR is no different. CGIAR acknowledges that its Strategy and Results Framework (SRF) is ambitious. By 2030, its proposed action, together with its partners, is expected to result in three System Level

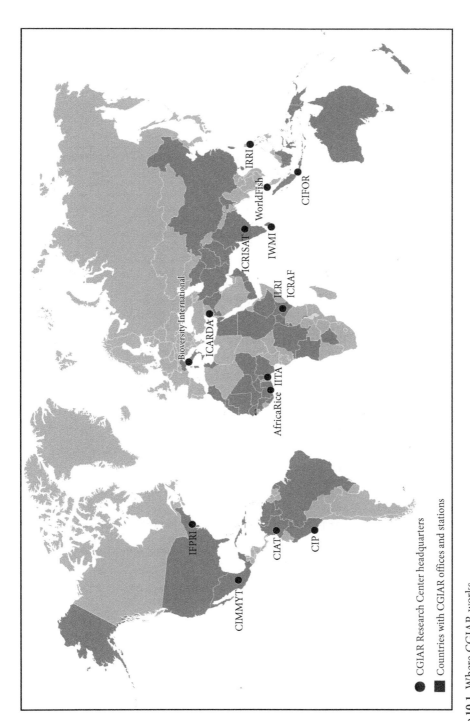

Figure 10.1 Where CGIAR works

Source: Provided by the CGIAR System Management Office.

Outcomes (SLOs), shown in Table 10.1. This is a considerably more articulated set of goals than previously.

Clearly, some donors appreciate this approach, as the Norwegian assessment of CGIAR illustrates (see Chapter 6 on the governance of the Big Five) (Government of Norway 2014).

Table 10.1 CGIAR's three System Level Outcomes and 10 targets with their 2022 intermediary and 2030 final values

Three goals or System Level Outcomes	Ten targets	
	Descriptions and intermediary 2022 values (to align with the CRP II portfolio)	**2030 values (to align with the SDGs)**
1. Reduce poverty	1. One hundred million more farm households have adopted improved varieties, breeds, or trees, and/or improved management practices*Links to SDG1, SDG2, SDG12, SDG14, and SDG17.*	350 million
	2. Thirty million people, of whom 50 percent are women, helped out of poverty*Links to SDG1, SDG2, SDG5, SDG8, SDG10, and SDG17.*	100 million
2. Improve food security and nutrition for health	3. Improve the rate of yield increase for major food staples from current < 1 to 1.2–1.5 percent/year*Links to SDG1, SDG2, SDG12, and SDG17.*	< 2.0 to 2.5 percent/year
	4. Thirty million more people, of whom 50 percent are women, meeting minimum dietary energy requirements*Links to SDG1, SDG2, SDG3, SDG5, SDG6, SDG12, and SDG17.*	150 million
	5. One hundred fifty million more people, of whom 50 percent are women, without deficiencies of one or more of the following essential micronutrients: iron, zinc, iodine, vitamin A, folate, and vitamin B_{12}*Links to SDG2, SDG5, SDG12, and SDG17.*	500 million
	6. Ten percent reduction in women of reproductive age who are consuming less than the adequate number of food groups*Links to SDG2, SDG3, SDG12, and SDG17.*	33 percent
3. Improve natural resources and ecosystem services	7. Five percent increase in water and nutrient (inorganic, biological) use efficiency in agroecosystems, including through recycling and reuse*Links to SDG2, SDG5, SDG6, SDG12, SDG14, SDG15, and SDG17*	20 percent
	8. Reduce agriculturally related greenhouse gas emissions by 0.2 Gt CO2-e yr^{-1} (5 percent), compared with business-as-usual scenario in 2022*Links to SDG13, SDG15, and SDG17.*	0.8 Gt CO2-e yr^{-1}
	9. Fifty-five million hectares (ha) degraded land area restored*Links to SDG 15, SDG16, and SDG17.*	190 million
	10. Two and one-half million ha of forest saved from deforestation*Links SDG13, SDG15, SDG16, and SDG17.*	5 million ha

Source: CGIAR (2015b, adapted from table 1, 5); CGIAR (2017b); CGIAR Strategy (https://www.cgiar.org/how-we-work/strategy/)

The SC's 5th meeting paper shows that CGIAR is moving to nine results indicators (CGIAR 2017c), and the CGIAR 2016–30 SRF has three SLOs, with CRPs focusing, variously, on 10 intermediate targets (as relevant to them) (CGIAR 2015b).

Since the CGIAR Centers were established in the 1970s and 1980s, their work has always supported objectives similar to those of SDGs, which were devised and adopted in 2015, but in the past the Centers did not *formally* align their objectives to some larger goals. Since its establishment in 1972, the first-ever effort to develop a CGIAR System-level, results-oriented SRF was initiated in 2010. Several economists closely associated with CGIAR were critical of the approach, which they considered mechanistic when applied to research (for example, see Binswanger [2011] in an internal review of one of the early CRPs in 2010, and Alex McCalla [2014, 2017]).

The Strategy and Results Framework

CGIAR's SRF is an overarching structure, increasingly used to define the System's strategic directions. It has evolved over time, based on consultations and lessons learned. The latest SRF (2016–30) has three goals: (1) reduce poverty, (2) improve food security and nutrition, and (3) improve natural resources and ecosystem services (CGIAR 2015b). The SRF links 11 CRPs in 2020 (1. Agriculture for nutrition and health; 2. Climate change and food security; 3. Forests, trees and agroforestry; 4. Fish and agri-food systems; 5. Maize; 6. Livestock; 7. Policies, institutions, and markets; 8. Wheat; 9. Rice; 10. Roots, tubers, and bananas; and 11. Land, water, and ecosystems) to seven SDGs, to which the research results are targeted: for example, no poverty (SDG1), zero hunger (SDG2); good health and well-being (SDG3); gender equality (SDG5); clean water and sanitation (SDG6); climate action (SDG13); and life on land (SDG15); and moderately, to the 5 SDGs targeted at decent work and economic growth (SDG8); reduced inequalities (SDG10); responsible consumption and production (SDG12); peace, justice, and strong institutions (SDG 16); and partnerships for the goals (SDG17).

CGIAR's various external observers often note, as did the external review panel of Hayami, Lipton, and Mule (2003), appointed for the CGIAR Meta Review in 2002, that an entire new vocabulary continues to emerge in CGIAR, which is difficult even for veteran CGIAR observers to keep track of, so as to understand how it operates—a phenomenon not unique to CGIAR. External panels often note the steep learning curve in understanding an institution's vocabulary, with the alphabet soup of frequently changing acronyms, with implications for whether and how short-term consultants and advisors can be useful in contributing to decisions that have long-term effects. Equally, or even more challenging, donors or developing country officers, new to CGIAR, need to understand what it all means and how the System operates. To ground the SLOs at the level of research activities, CGIAR has also introduced the concept of Intermediate Development Outcomes (IDOs), to empower researchers to think through the contexts in which their outputs might contribute to development outcomes. Below this level are Sub-Intermediate Development Outcomes (Sub-IDOs), which represent research outcomes adopted by immediate users, such as researchers of NARS and national policymakers. In the latest SRF (2016–30), 10 IDOs and 30 Sub-IDOs are aligned with 3 SLOs, 4 IDOs, and 16 Sub-IDOs, which are, in turn, aligned with 4 crosscutting themes: (1) Climate Change, (2) Gender and Youth, (3) Policies and Institutions, and (4) Capacity Development, which are critical to attaining their goals and targets. The SRF is a "living document and will be periodically updated with new challenges and opportunities that reflect lessons learnt" (CGIAR 2015b, 15). By 2030, according to the latest SRF, the action of CGIAR and its partners will result in, among other attained goals, 150 million fewer hungry people, 100 million fewer poor people—at least 50 percent of whom are women, and 190 million ha less degraded, while mitigating and adapting to climate change risks and shocks, ensuring gender and youth equity and inclusion, strengthening the policy and institution-enabling environment, and developing the capacity of national partners and beneficiaries (CGIAR 2015b).

CGIAR's and its partners' contributions to the achievement of their global goals have been quantified by 10 targets (allied with three SLOs), summarized in Table 10.1, for two time periods: by 2022, to reflect outcomes from the six-year next generation of CGIAR CRPs commenced in 2017 (CRP II 2017–22), and by 2030 to align with the SDGs.

How incremental benefits are measured—for example, 100 million more households, of whom 50 percent are women—raises a number of measurement and attribution issues, when CGIAR is increasingly involved in complex multi-actor, multilevel partnerships. These are issues explored later in the chapter.

Successive Waves of Reforms and the Tragedy of the Commons

In view of the rapidly changing external environment, CGIAR deserves credit for having gone through frequent reforms. Important questions are: did CGIAR make decisions that have had long shelf lives, and how beneficial have these reforms been in mobilizing more and stable funding and improving CGIAR's effectiveness?

Three distinguished development experts who were members of the external review panel of CGIAR's Meta Review, carried out in the World Bank's Evaluation Department in early 2000 (OED 2003), called the situation a "Tragedy of Commons"—a term coined by Garrett Hardin in an article in *Science* in 1968, to describe what happens to common pooled resources when they are overused and eventually depleted, as a result of the self-interest of individual stakeholders, without regard to the common good (Hardin 1968). The Meta Review showed that donors, Centers, and CGIAR Center scientists and managers acted in pursuit of their interests at the cost of CGIAR as a system (Hayami, Lipton, and Mule 2003). Indeed, as discussed later, some of our interlocutors have wondered if CGIAR is a system at all, or still an assortment of Centers that do not constitute a system (personal communication, Greg Traxler, September 28, 2015).

The characterization—the "Tragedy of Commons," applied in 2003—and continued into 2017 (CGIAR 2017d).[9] The 2003 Meta Review identified several issues, some of which CGIAR continued to face in 2017 (OED 2003). By 2002, CGIAR's funding for productivity-enhancing agricultural research—a global or regional public good ideally suited to a publicly funded global network—had declined by 6.5 percent annually in real terms between 1992 and 2001, whereas expenditure on policies and protection of the environment increased by 3.1 percent annually during the same time. Overall, CGIAR funding stagnated in nominal terms during that same 1992–2001 period, declining in real terms by 1.8 percent annually.

---

[9] In "Improving System Financing Modalities—A Scoping Note," issued April 28, 2017, it was noted: "CGIAR's funding system—like the natural landscapes we work in—faces a constant risk of the 'tragedy of the commons,' whereby incentives at an individual (funder, Center, CRP or ISC) [level] do not always align with the collective benefit of maintaining system funding" (CGIAR 2017d, 9).

Most importantly, the degree of restricted funding earmarked to specific projects increased from 36 percent of total funding in 1992 to 57 percent in 2001.

The characterization of Professors Yujiro Hayami, Michael Lipton, and Mr. Harris Mule, of CIGAR as a "tragedy of commons" provides a useful backdrop against which to review changes in the external environment that CGIAR has faced and its reforms during 2003, 2008–11, and since 2015 (Hayami, Lipton, and Mule 2003).

Centralized and Decentralized Models of International Agricultural Research and Its Financing

The Meta Review of 2003 noted that the great successes in the 1970s and early 1980s achieved by the original two CGIAR Centers—IRRI focused on rice research based in the Philippines and CIMMYT focused on wheat in Mexico—occurred because the two CGIAR Centers had substantial scientific autonomy, but also had a *core scientific strategy* at both Centers, which maintained high standards for research. The two Centers submitted proposals, which were vetted by a strong scientific authority based on the System's priorities (originally, the Technical Advisory Committee [TAC] and in 2003, the interim Science Council, discussed later in the chapter). The System supported research of high priority and high quality by making *financial allocations* to the Centers. The Centers carried out the research with considerable *scientific autonomy*. The panel noted that the CGIAR of 2000 was *formally* similar to this original model. It had "a System-level hierarchy and institutions, incurring substantial associated costs" (Hayami, Lipton, and Mule 2003, 1). Yet, in practice, the near autonomous Centers did not look to the CGIAR System for finances. Instead, they raised "an increasing majority of their funds bilaterally, tied to specific uses or projects" and activities that donors preferred (Hayami, Lipton, and Mule 2003, 1–2). The Centers had little incentive to agree on a common "System-level" strategy. Even if they did, it could not be enforced, because the scientific body had lost its power to allocate funds. Instead CGIAR's new funding policy was to reward the Centers, who had raised funds directly from donors, with matching grants that the donors, rather than the scientific committee, approved. Donors were interested in an immediate impact of research and, therefore, increasingly opted for downstream operational research, more like development projects. This was the beginning of the process of dilution of the role of science in priority setting in CGIAR with an increasing focus on direct development impacts.

The most recent proposals for improving System funding put it differently:

The system-funding model and associated CRP modality is perhaps imbalanced in terms of being:
a. over-determined on how system-level funding is received, and how research is managed across the system and over time; and
b. under-determined on how system-level financing is allocated and its results framework, expected added value/quality, and funding cycle. (CGIAR 2017d, 3)

CGIAR's *"loss of strategic focus"* and *"drift downstream,"* were already evident in the CGIAR System's natural resource management (NRM) research (Hayami, Lipton, and Mule 2003, 3). Even if returns were high, such research was location-specific and better accomplished by involving the active participation, and even the leadership, of NARS. The meta reviewers, in their Advisory Committee Report, continued, "Also, adoption of NRM advice by farmers often depends on productivity gains, which are larger with good germplasm, attuned to sustainable high productivity under specific environmental constraints. Therefore, falling CGIAR funds for germplasm research and conservation can undermine the usefulness of NRM research" (Hayami, Lipton, and Mule, 3). This makes partnerships with NARS, in the conduct of NRM research, even more critical than germplasm research. The highly variable agroecosystems into which new varieties and hybrids must be targeted, developed, and fitted make it essential that NARS be actively involved, if not take the lead in such research.

To correct the decline in funding for germplasm, the Meta-Evaluation recommended in the report, "The CGIAR at 31" that CGIAR should:

- "Increase funding for conventional germplasm enhancement and plant and animal breeding research, in which CGIAR possesses a comparative advantage; ... and devolve that portion of CGIAR's applied and adaptive NRM research program that does not constitute global or regional public goods research to national and regional agencies ... "
- Substantially raise the share of CGIAR outlay devoted to the core competencies— germplasm collection and improvement—on which gains from other CGIAR activities rest; the Bank and bilateral donors should act to reverse the collapse in external assistance to agriculture and to increase unrestricted funding to CGIAR (OED 2003, 38).

How have CGIAR's reforms in 2001–3, 2009–11, and 2015–16 built on these previous findings? All three sets of reforms are detailed in Table A.10.2 in the Appendix.

As a background to understanding these reforms, we quote the latest 2020 study of returns to CGIAR research by Alston, Pardey, and Rao. They echo the findings of 2003 Meta Review and observations of Hayami, Lipton, and Mule of 2003:

In round figures, over the past five decades the CGIAR has spent about $60 billion in present value terms. This investment—mainly through its contributions to enhancing yields of staple food crops—has returned tenfold benefits (i.e., a benefit-cost ratio of 10:1), manifest as less-easily measured payoffs for poor people from greater food abundance, cheaper food, reduced rates of hunger and poverty, and a smaller geographical footprint of agriculture. This does not count substantial benefits accruing in high-income countries. (Alston, Pardey, and Rao 2020, i)

Alston, Pardey, and Rao (2020) noted further:

... the greater part of the evaluation evidence pertains to research directed at improving crop and livestock productivity—especially staple food grains (e.g., wheat, rice, maize) and crops (e.g., cassava, edible beans, and pulses). This was the narrow focus of the founding four centers and, albeit to a lesser extent, the early expansion centers added in the 1970s. Much less of the evidence pertains directly to the broader agenda of the centers added since 1980, which accounted for more than 40% of the total CGIAR budget in the mid-1980s and still accounted for almost 30% of the budget in 2017. The lack of evidence on the economic returns to research conducted by the post-1980 expansion centers may reflect a lack of measurable impact, but it may also reflect conceptual and empirical challenges in measuring the benefits—for instance, as the studies reported by Pardey and Smith (2004) describe regarding policy-oriented R&D (POR) conducted by IFPRI, other CGIAR centers, and other policy researchers (e.g., Pannell et al. 2018). (Alston, Pardey, and Rao 2020, 27, 29)

Writing in 2003, Barrett pointed to evaluation complexities as one explanation for "...a dearth of ex post impact assessment of CGIAR NRM research" (Barrett 2003, 25). Barrett (2003, p. 24) also noted:

> ...given the relatively recent launch of most of the CGIAR's NRM research and the excessively diffuse nature of some of the early research in this area in the early-to-mid 1990s, it seems unreasonable to expect to see significant aggregate level evidence of any impact just yet. The absence of clear, quantitative evidence of impact to date does not imply the absence of current, much less likely future impact; it merely means we simply do not know yet.

More recently, the CGIAR Standing Panel on Impact Assessment (SPIA) commissioned various studies seeking to rectify the dearth of evidence of impact in certain understudied areas, including NRM and policy-oriented research. Subsequently, Stevenson and Vlek (2018) reviewed nine studies of the adoption of NRM practices commissioned by SPIA. In a foreword to that review report (p. iv), Karen Macours, the chair of SPIA, noted that the adoption rates for NRM practices were consistently and surprisingly lower (often much lower) than expected, and accordingly expressed some pessimism about the associated flows of benefits (Alston, Pardey and Rao 2020, 27, 29–30).

2001–2003 Reforms: Introduction of Challenge Programs and Some Organizational Centralization

The reforms, commenced in 2003, established an Executive Committee consisting of donors, Centers, and other stakeholders, moving in the direction of formality, more akin to the one that exists in 2017 and 2020. It was the first major attempt to improve CGIAR governance and management, and to transform CGIAR's Center-based research to globally visible Challenge Programs (CPs). CPs, in some ways the antecedents of today's CRPs, were a way for CGIAR to elevate its game, open the System to outside researchers, strengthen partnerships with NARS and other research actors, and mobilize additional funds, while avoiding consolidation or elimination of Centers which, from experience, had turned out to be politically difficult and diverted attention from the business of conducting research (Özgediz 2012). The changes set in motion have continued in subsequent reforms, albeit too slowly.

Lessons of three of the four CPs approved—on water and food, biofortification, climate change, and one submitted by the Forum for Agricultural Research in Africa (FARA)—have influenced subsequent CGIAR reforms. CPs worked around the issue of System-wide priorities, an issue that has remained with CGIAR, while promoting inter-Center collaboration. The CP on Water for Food showed that if the Science Council vetting continued to be preempted by the raising of "tied" money, in support of large CPs, then it would subvert the scientific process and affect science quality (CGIAR Science Council 2008). Creation of the Executive Committee showed that it could increase efficiency in decision-making and delegation by the membership at large to the Executive Committee members' works. Conversion of the TAC to the interim Science Council stripped TAC of the onerous reviews of Center's programs and management function. Establishment of a CGIAR System Office to provide common shared services to all the Centers showed mixed results, as Centers were not enthusiastic about the idea of centralization. Adoption of a formal Charter of the CGIAR System paved the way for *formalization of the System*—a System to measure performance, reduce the number of CGIAR meetings from two to one per year, and invest in strategic communications to improve efficiency. Paralleling these initiatives, the Centers advanced their capacity to work together, taking collective action by forming an informal alliance.

What Did Not Work in the 2003 Reforms?

An issue that still affects today's reforms is that Centers viewed, as a threat, the opening of the System with the introduction of CPs, without restrictions on who could submit proposals. Separately, the Centers were also concerned that CPs were taking money from their budgets. Responding to internal pressures, three CPs were selected from among proposals submitted by the Centers themselves, as lead institutions. Importantly, this shut off the opening of CGIAR to external competition, a phenomenon that has also influenced the latest reforms. CGIAR points out that Center leadership of CRPs and Platforms has many advantages (fiduciary responsibility, trust of donors, performance management and CGIAR-wide risk management, and adherence to CGIAR policies). The CP experiment did not achieve full traction, never coming close to the original intent of placing half of all CGIAR research under CPs within five years (Özgediz 2012), but it paved the way for achieving this aim in the post-2008 reforms. With the exception of the Genebank Platform with its six-year partnership (2017–22) between the Global Crop Diversity Trust and CGIAR, CGIAR Centers are lead centers of CRPs and Platforms. Proposals were submitted by the Centers and the Global Crop Diversity Trust, and the development of the proposals involved partnerships.

The CPs brought in some additional funding, but also diverted other funding, including some of the World Bank's that otherwise would have gone to the core Centers' programs. It created winners and losers among the Centers, as only a few Centers coordinated CPs. The major benefit of these reforms was in demonstrating how the CGIAR System could run multi-institutional global research programs, thereby helping to prepare mindsets for an even bolder application of this principle in reforms starting in 2008.

The 2003 reforms helped improve CGIAR business processes. The Executive Council initiative showed how the Donor Group could manage its affairs through delegation. The Performance Measurement System focused on results and efficiency of Centers, but the Centers disliked it because of the additional burden of generating the data required. The "virtual" System Office experiment did not generate much integration but helped with inter-unit communication. The new Science Council could develop a new set of priorities but was unable to mobilize the scientific community toward the goals of CGIAR and had no resource allocation authority, unlike in the past.

2009–2011 Reforms and Evolution to 2020

The period 2008–15 was the time of the most far-reaching reforms, which in turn provided the foundation for the post-2015 reforms. As noted in a section titled "Governance ambiguities" in the "Final Report from the Mid-Term Review Panel of the CGIAR Reform," in 2016:

> The entities in the reformed CGIAR include the Fund Council (FC) and Fund office (FO), the CB [Consortium Board], and CO [Consortium Office], the ISPC [Independent Science and Partnership Council], the IEA [Independent Evaluation Arrangement], and the 15 Centers each with their own respective Boards. There are also currently 16 CPRs— partnerships with their own governance structure and systems. (CGIAR 2016b, 24)

The CGIAR Fund was established in 2010 and remains a key component of the reforms even in 2020. The creation of the Consortium of International Agricultural Research Centers, which operated under the name *CGIAR Consortium*, set up initially as a contractual joint venture and then as an international organization in 2012. The CGIAR Consortium has since, with the 2015–16 reform, changed its name to CGIAR System Organization. The CO, based in Montpellier, France, is now called the CGIAR System Management Office (SMO). The FO was based in Washington, DC, and the IEA and the renamed ISPC, formerly the Science Council and now the ISDC, were and are still based in Rome. Governance reform in 2010 created the FC, CB, and Funders Forum to replace the previous Executive Council and Annual Business Meeting. Programmatically, an overall CGIAR SRF was put into place, providing the overarching themes in which a set of large CRPs was started. The totality of CRPs involved essentially covered much of the CRP in all Centers, each with a Lead Center and many participating Centers and other partners.

According to Wadsworth (2016), then Executive Secretary of the FC and Head of the CGIAR FO:

> The fundamental rationale of the Fund was influenced by . . . the Paris Declaration with its emphasis on donor harmonization, alignment, reduced conditionality, transparency, untied aid, predictability of funding and mutual accountability. The Fund had three main objectives which have been identified as solutions to current difficulties faced by CGIAR, namely: a) to increase the overall level of funding which was not growing in line with the increased need for research and CGIAR's ambition to do more, b) to improve the predictability of funding for research in order to plan and carry out long term research initiatives which require known budgets over 5–10 year time horizons and to attract and retain top researchers, and c) to provide stability of funding and fund use flexibility through timely disbursements, with a greater proportion as unrestricted funding, and to ensure continuity of research which if stopped cannot be easily restarted. (Wadsworth 2016, 1)

A new vision was adopted: "to reduce poverty and hunger, improve human health and nutrition, and enhance ecosystem resilience through high-quality international agricultural research, partnership and leadership" (CGIAR 2011d, 10–11), along with four strategic outcomes enshrined in the first results-oriented SRF, developed in 2010, which were later reduced to three in the 2016–30 SRF (CGIAR 2016a) and remained in the latest SRF available in 2020: 1. Reduced poverty; 2. Improved food and nutrition security for health; 3. Improved natural resource systems and ecosystem services.

Key features of the 2009–11 reform included:

- The 2009 reform, intended as a move away from the fragmented and restricted projects and Center-based programming and funding, pursued funding in support of major program areas (CRPs), drawing on the existing competencies of the relevant Centers and partners to achieve results. The reform sought to define distinct roles for "doers" ("suppliers" of research) and "funders" to establish clear accountabilities, and to move away from a complex overlay of reporting and funding relationships, which led to heavy oversight and micromanagement by funders, yet without accountability for results from the CGIAR Centers, leading to frustration on both sides.

- A new consortium of CGIAR Centers (then named CGIAR Consortium and modified into a System Management Board in 2016 [CGIAR 2019b]), and System Board in 2020, working with partners and the ISPC's advice, was given responsibility for overseeing the development of the strategic research agendas set out in the SRFs, programs that came to be known as CRPs, and for implementation of results. A reinvigorated partnership culture, supported by incentives and processes, could promote partnership approaches and instill new dynamism into the agenda with a research environment, which would attract, develop, and support the best scientists. Stable funding for Centers to invest in the development of scientists and in their facilities would support great science. Incentives for partnership and openness could allow CGIAR scientists to work with peers in agricultural research institutes, NARS, UN agencies, and the private sector with more fluidity, and to see their research translated into results. The Consortium was to evaluate the organization against the CRPs and move to reduce overlaps, including merging of Centers, as appropriate, to optimize the governance and management units, while CGIAR infrastructure and campuses remained similar or increased.

Linking CGIAR Research Programs to System-wide Priorities

The SRF emphasized program financing with provisions for institutional support to the Centers (CGIAR 2008). The idea that the SRF would be setting the priorities, against which CRPs would be approved, turned out to be a myth. Rather, in the first round, approved CRPs were based on legacy research, but the latest round refined the CRPs, with input from independent reviews by ISPC on the quality of research proposals submitted by the Centers, which then resubmitted after reviews. In short, science quality, rather than alignment with strategic priorities, became the driving criteria for approval. Who sets the priorities, and on what basis, remains a debated question since the focus remains on cereals and root crops, when consumption patterns have changed, leading to malnutrition and obesity. More balanced diets require livestock, poultry fruits, vegetables, and nuts. While there is some shift in this direction, much more needs to change in CGIAR if the quality of consumption is to be a concern. The key questions have been what types of CRPs should CGIAR promote, when should it partner with others, and what are the implications of competition for the limited funding.

In its June 2017 report, "An Overview of Links between Obesity and Food Systems: Implications for the Food and Agriculture Global Practice Agenda," the World Bank identified entry points for action:

Agricultural Research Subsystem

1. Incentivize more public sector research on high quality and underserved foods (legumes, fruits, vegetables) to increase productivity and shift relative prices.
2. Ensure that cereal research and provision on inputs include a nutrition focus, and not just a yield focus, and that results are communicated to producers.

3. Encourage private sector advances in research favoring high quality and underserved foods.

Production Subsystem

1. Ensure that bio-fortified cereals are the norm, where they are available and agronomically competitive, rather than the exception.
2. Eliminate subsidies and other production/price support measures for production of unhealthy ingredients for food processing.
3. Encourage production (and consumption) of fruits, vegetables, and pulses. (World Bank 2017, xi)

Since then, the evaluation of ISPC by IEA noted that, despite having delivered a substantial body of work, there is considerable debate at the SC, its standing committee—the System Integrated Monitoring and Evaluation Committee (SIMEC)—the SMB, and among donors, about what exactly should be the role of the ISPC in the future (O'Kane and Pehu 2017). There is general agreement that a strong capability to identify the research challenges to delivering on CGIAR's goals is needed, as well the ability to identify new research developments and directions (foresight analysis).

Seraj and Pingali (2018) edited *Agriculture and Food System to 2050*, the first systematic foresight assessment by CGIAR to bring together state-of-the-art knowledge on the CGIAR System. There are few surprises for those familiar with the agricultural development literature. Yet, it is a comprehensive reference book for researchers and research leaders in developed and developing countries. How this will affect CGIAR's priorities going forward to achieve transformative change is unclear. There is also agreement that measuring and evaluating the impact of research in the System is vital, but there is debate about the utility of other roles currently carried out by the ISPC, and whether some of the ISPC outputs would be better delivered through other mechanisms. Another part of the debate is whether the ISPC is value for money. Those familiar with the System say that the issue of value for money of ISPC is not just a supply side issue but also one of the demand side. The SC has not clearly articulated what it wants from its advisory body.

CGIAR Fund

The original intent was to finance the agreed upon CRPs through only two funding windows, one for unrestricted (pooled) contributions to be allocated to CRPs by the FC (Window 1), and the other for contributions that targeted specific CRPs (Window 2). The plan did not materialize on the scale expected. Altogether, there are 80 donors (see "CGIAR Funders," http://www.cgiar.org/about-us/our-funders/). New funding arrangements through Windows (that is, Window 1 [W1], Window 2 [W2], and Window 3 [W3]) were introduced in 2011, as part of the 2008 reforms. Initially, only W1 and W2 were conceived, but donors preferred the option of channeling contributions directly to specific Centers. So, a third window was added to the CGIAR Fund structure.

A notable shift between funding windows/bilateral for the top 10 W1 and W2 donors was observed between 2012 and 2015. The top 10 donors, who collectively represented over 90 percent of the total W1 and W2 funding in 2012, reduced their W1 and W2 funding by US $62 million, a 20 percent reduction from the 2012 level (CGIAR 2017d).

In 2017, fund transfers to Centers from the CGIAR Fund (Windows 1, 2, and 3) represented 56 percent, or US$475 million of total funding. Bilateral project grants represented as much as 41 percent, or US$348 million of total funding. The remaining 3 percent, or US$25 million came from Centers. W1 and W2 funding declined from US$262 million in 2015 to US$220 million in 2016, and further to US$161 million in 2017, a 39 percent decrease, or US$101 million in 2015 to 2017. By contrast, in 2016, W3 funding increased to US$321 million from US$291 million in 2015, in 2017 it decreased slightly to US$314 million, representing about 8 percent growth in 2015 to 2017, or US$22 million. Bilateral project grants declined by 10.5 percent, or US$41 million, from US$388 million in 2015 to US$348 million in 2017. Centers continued to use more of their own funding, decreasing the Center contribution by 14 percent, from US$29 million in 2015 to US$25 million in 2017 (CGIAR 2018c). We explain the differences between Windows 1, 2, and 3 later in this section.

The "Improving System Financing Modalities" paper issued October 2017, requests the SMB to "manage within-cycle funding adjustments to CRPs to enable CGIAR's research agenda to respond when relevant to an evolving environment." It also asks the SC to consider introducing "the possibility of earmarking of Window 2 funding contributions for individual flagship projects, in the event that this modality is the means by which a Funder wishes to make contributions to W2" (CGIAR 2017e, 1). Some noted a further shift away from System and CRP funding, reflecting a lack of confidence in the System and CRP modalities to get allocations "right."

To build the System-wide structure now, some suggest that, perhaps, 10 or 20 percent of all funds raised by Centers be contributed to the System-wide infrastructure; this idea should have been considered in the 2008 and 2015 reforms, but was not. Already, there is the System cost percentage (SCP) levy on W2, W3, and bilateral funds, which are collected and transferred to W1 to provide funds for the CGIAR SMO, the Independent Science for Development Council (ISDC), IEA, and SMB costs of operation. There is a formula for calculating the percentage value, but 2 percent has been close to the actual costs of these System entities. It can be adjusted if the percentage becomes too large or too small. SMO has done a good job at ensuring that Centers pay their percentage on bilateral funds (W2 and W3 levies are automatically deducted by the trustee). The actual recovery rate is probably close to 90 percent. Thus, many of the original financing issues and their relationship to the organizational structure tend to be complex and need to be tackled. Figure 10.2 shows contributions to the CGIAR Fund by major donors through W1, W2, and W3 and bilateral channels for the 2011–17 period. The 10 largest CGIAR Fund donors in the period 2011–15 (the United States, BMGF, United Kingdom, World Bank, the Netherlands, Australia, Sweden, Canada, Switzerland, and the European Commission) accounted for over 65 percent of total CGIAR income and over 90 percent of CGIAR Fund income (Wadsworth 2016, 8). Few donors chose a single channel; 10 donors funded via all four streams (that is, W1, W2, W3, and bilateral), and 32 donors contributed to one or more of the three funding windows:

Window 1: Thirteen donors contributed to this window of completely untied funds. Contributions of some donors to W1 have declined from the past for various reasons. The World Bank, the United Kingdom, Sweden, Norway, Canada, Denmark, New Zealand, and France "made contributions exclusively or primarily through W1" (Wadsworth 2016, 9). The decline may be explained that in the donor trust in W1. Some say that Centers have been fairly transparent in saying that they treat W1 as core funding and use it to subsidize under-funded bilateral and W3 contracts with donors. Understandably, W1 donors object to such practices and have moved to W2 (or even W3) to ensure they get value for money. The Centers may have abused the System, rather than it being a flaw in the System itself.

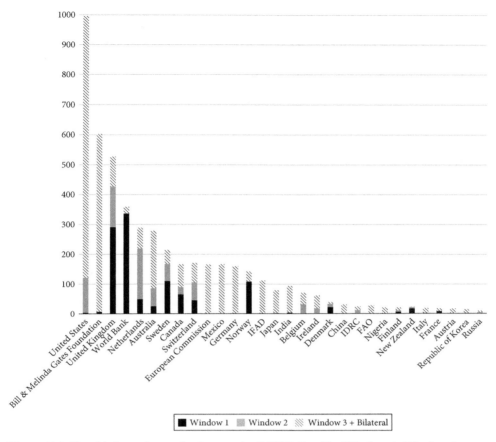

Figure 10.2 Top 30 donors' contributions to the CGIAR Fund by Window 1, Window 2, Window 3, and bilateral, 2011–2017 (US$m)

Source: CGIAR Financial Reports.

Window 2: Of the 12 donors contributing to W2, four were also W1 donors. The Netherlands, Australia, Switzerland, Belgium, Ireland, Russia, and International Development Research Centre (IDRC) "placed greater emphasis on W2 in their overall contributions mix" (Wadsworth 2016, 9).

Window 3: Twenty-five donors contributed to W3 by allocating their contributions to specific CGIAR Centers. The United States, BMGF, the European Community, Japan, India, the International Fund for Agricultural Development (IFAD), and China "made contributions exclusively or primarily through W3" (Wadsworth 2016, 9). BMGF has indicated that it is looking to move more funding into W2 and W1—contingent on seeing real signs of current reform proposals being enacted. USAID may follow suit, but more than half of USAID money comes from country office budgets, so will that will invariably be project dictated. The Washington-derived USAID funds could move to W1/W2 once a new "system collective" funding regime is agreed upon for a new more targeted and focused research portfolio.

Bilateral donors: 73 bilateral donors contribute to the CGIAR Fund.

Establishing a contractual relationship between the FC represented by the World Bank and the Consortium, based on program performance, lasted six years (2011–16) but was problematic. So, the separation of the governance and management roles of the System was replaced in another round of reforms starting in 2015. The clear decision-making and accountability mechanisms, as proposed in the 2008–15 organization, did not work. There were issues in the relationship between the CB and the CO, as well as between CO and the Centers. The Chair and the CEO of the CO were observers in the deliberations of the FC. The terms of reference of CEO and chair vis-à-vis the Centers and donors were also not clearly defined, leading to personalities rather than functions, according to some commentators of this chapter, including work style, micromanagement, and authoritarian tendencies of the previous CEO, contributing to effectiveness, among the many features that needed revision.

The reformed CGIAR SC of 2016 was intended to be more of a stakeholder model, rather than the shareholder model that it was prior to reforms, but the outcome may be more of a shareholder model. Together with its chair, appointed for a four-year term, the SC has a co-chair elected at each meeting. Every three years, eligible funders and developing countries consult and agree upon their constituencies, which may be composed of one or more governments or organizations. Each constituency determines the rules and procedures to govern how it operates. The 20 voting members of the Council for the period July 2016–June 2019, which includes 11 bilateral donors, are the African Development Bank, Australia, BMGF, Canada, East Asia and the Pacific, the European Commission, Germany and Belgium (one constituency), Japan, Latin America and the Caribbean, Mexico, The Netherlands, Norway, SA, SSA, Sweden, Switzerland, United Kingdom and Northern Ireland, the United States, and the World Bank.[10]

The SC had a relatively more balanced constituency system. Earlier, some commented that, before the recent reorganization, the FC was close to a shareholder model and the CB with Center representation had seemed very "Western." FAO was a founding cosponsor, and its financial contributions, through the waving of overheads and in the past with direct contributions to ISPC/IEA budgets, accorded it skin in the game. CGIAR severed its relations with FAO and moved ISPC and its new incarnation, ISDC, out of FAO headquarters. By moving CGIAR offices out of the World Bank to Montpellier, France, this premier international System has essentially moved to a provincial place, although France is proud to have increased its influence, as discussed in this chapter.

Other than BMGF, there is no representation of either the private sector or civil society. Developing country board members have not played a proactive role, so it is largely a traditional donors' club and has not helped to increase a sense of ownership, even among emerging countries. The governance structure of the SMB and SC, which came into effect on July 1, 2016, impressed many of CGIAR's funders and the Centers themselves with the changes that took place (CGIAR 2017g). It was an improvement over the very confrontational CB approach, which prevailed in the past and which seemingly defended the interests of the Centers, but Centers did not see it that way. They saw the approach as serving the interests of the CB.

---

[10] For more information about the composition of the System Council, see https://www.cgiar.org/how-we-work/governance/system-council/sc-composition/

CGIAR Research Program Governance and Management Review

The CRP Governance and Management Review of 2014 identified a total of 23 active CRP governance bodies, varying in terms of composition, size, function, and degree of independence. Some CRPs had a single governance body, while others were found to have the functional equivalent of two or more, and overall, CRP governance was found to be heavily influenced by lead and participating Centers. External partners had limited roles at the governance level, and women and individuals from target regions were significantly underrepresented. The imbalance in representation and participation in CRP governance undermines confidence in the legitimacy and fairness of decision-making. The review also noted the increased potential for conflicts of interest for Lead Center boards between their duty to their Centers and their accountability to the Consortium for CRPs. A key finding of the review was the lack of a common understanding about roles and relative authority at the System level among the FC, the Consortium, and the Centers (Robinson et al. 2014). Some readers of the chapter draft, familiar with CGIAR, have commented that these shortfalls were predictable and predicted.

The review also considered the extent to which CRP leaders had the authority to manage for results. It found the current "reporting line for CRP leaders, which for most is through the lead center DG, does not provide the CRP leader with authority to manage for results" (Robinson et al. 2014, 12). The number and structure of CRP governance and management committees also limit the scope and authority of CRP leaders. The shift in investment from Centers to programs, uncertainty about the levels and flow of W1 and W2 funds, and the relative imbalance between resources generated by the Fund and those generated by the Centers have heightened the sense of risk on the part of the Centers, sharpening concerns about a loss of standing within the System as a whole. The review also noted that while the basic accountability framework for CRPs was functional, the governance bodies closest to CRPs were less so (Robinson et al. 2014).

Eight recommendations emerged from the review, which were intended to highlight a core group of principles that support good governance and effective management, rather than a rigid set of structures.

The recommendations were informed by the need to:

- streamline structures,
- strengthen the [independence and] legitimacy of decision making,
- provide CRP leaders with the authority to manage for results,
- strengthen accountability and transparency, and
- recognize the need to sustain the institutional capacity of centers. (Robinson et al. 2014, 78)

In terms of CRP leadership, governance, and reporting, the CGIAR Consortium generally agreed with the review and its recommendations, except for one important difference: namely, that it believed the CRP leader should report administratively to the Lead Center DG, and programmatically to the Independent Steering Committee (Robinson et al. 2014).

Consolidation of Research Programs

If the objective of CGIAR going forward is diet diversification, then it needs to establish or bring in the System Centers, such as the AVRDC, to promote production diversification, including toward fruits and vegetables. The 2008 reforms led instead to the establishment of 16 relatively conventional CRPs based on CGIAR's traditional research. By all accounts, inter-Center collaboration increased, with several Centers involved in individual CRPs, but true consolidation of research has not yet been achieved, and CGIAR's own evaluations of CRPs noted the mixed quality of research proposals (Birner and Byerlee 2016). The initial 16 CRPs coincided with the 15 Research Centers. In CRP Phase 1, 12 Centers were involved in multiple CRPs, but three Centers (Bioversity International, ICRAF, and AfricaRice) did not lead any CRPs. All CRPs except CRP4 had continued legacy research and selectivity exercised through ISPC reviews to improve quality—a very worthy and necessary development—but not sufficient for priority setting.

After some months of implementation, this dysfunctional arrangement was already viewed by many with buyers' remorse and thought to be less effective than the Executive Council, which it had replaced. This dissatisfaction led to the establishment of the SC and the System Board.

Top-Heavy Administrative Superstructure of CGIAR Research Programs

Each CRP has a program management committee with an average of 10 members, thus engaging 150 people at management level (15 CRPs with 10 members each), who meet, on average, four times each year. Also, for each CRP, there is an advisory committee/panel/board of another 10 people, so that is another 150 people at the advisory/governance level meeting, on average, twice yearly. The joint submission of the Centers to the Panel described "ambiguity about whether the Centers are part of the Consortium or not and the uncertainty concerning the obligations in both directions [having] severely impeded the building of trust and cohesion between the Centers and the CB/CO" (CGIAR 2014b, 24). Even with a single board, this governance ambiguity between Center management and CRP management would continue, unless steps are taken to streamline governance.

2014 Mid-Term Review Panel of CGIAR Reform

The Mid-Term Review Panel was appointed in mid-2013 to assess progress in the implementation of the 2008 reforms. It called for the importance of a clear mission and vision as a global network, together with a high-quality SRF, developed by wide consultation with stakeholders to develop a keen sense of ownership focused on outcomes. A lack of an effective SRF leads to an inability to prioritize research and its outcomes, so that budgets can be allocated to the highest priority research activities. Also, it is difficult to establish robust metrics across the research portfolio (beyond the individual project) to be able to assess the System's value. Some stakeholders agreed with the Mid-Term Review recommendation that the preparation of the SRF should not be rushed, so that donors and Centers can be fully engaged and that priorities should be based on scientific considerations (CGIAR 2014b).

The review made many recommendations on the substance of the research strategy: for example, on greater emphasis on nutrition, reduction of food wastage, restoration of degraded lands, increased resilience, and investments in big data. Specifically, it recommended:

- the establishment of a broadly representative single board, which includes the private sector and civil society; the latter has not yet been achieved;
- the replacement of the FC and the CB with a single CGIAR Board supported by one Administrative Unit, thereby replacing the FO and CO and eliminating the prevailing ambiguity in the governance structure;
- the strengthening of CGIAR's ability to deliver its research mission and development impact; and
- the acceleration and scaling up of partnerships that are solution-driven, public–private collaborations (CGIAR 2014b).

Financing Prospects

The 2014 Mid-Term Review was not optimistic about improving financing:

> While the balance between Windows 1 and 2 and the contributions channeled through Window 3 and other bilateral funding may not be ideal for maximizing the focus on CRPs, the Fund Council and other CGIAR partners should be primarily focused on maximizing the total amount of funding available for high-quality, high-priority research.…
>
> Several donors indicated to the Panel that continued funding is conditional on performance and highlighted the difficulty of securing long-term, predictable commitments to fund CGIAR Research Programs, as well as the uncertainties around maintaining, let alone significantly increasing, funding. (CGIAR 2014b, 9)

The Review Panel urged the pursuit of innovation in funding, such as green bonds and public–private partnerships.

Comments on the Consultation Draft of the Mid-Term Review urged caution to the Panel, suggesting that both a slower pace and more minor changes were preferred to major changes in governance that the Panel had proposed. The Panel argued that those comments "seriously underestimate the urgency of the need for such change and the significant problems that were identified in the evidence that the Panel was able to review" (CGIAR 2014b, 7).

2015–2016 Reforms: Which Reforms Were Abandoned?

A significant difference in the new SC, from the earlier FC established during the 2008–15 period, was that a unitary structure was introduced to replace the dual structure of funders and doers, which the former CGIAR Fund governance framework had created as recommended by the external review in 2008, but which had not worked well (CGIAR 2019b).

The FC decided to transition to a new governing arrangement and put in place a transition team at the 13th FC Meeting, April 28–30, Bogor, Indonesia.[11] Over the period of May 2015 to May 2016, the FC's governance committee stewarded the work of the (largely) independent transition team. However, final decisions on the actual organizational structure (very different from the April 2015 decision in Bogor) were made by electronic decision in mid-June 2016. The new organizational structure of CGIAR announced by the

---

[11] A meeting summary is available at: https://cgspace.cgiar.org/bitstream/handle/10947/3942/FC13%20Summary%20FINAL.pdf

FC reflected the lessons learned from the major reorganization undertaken, beginning in 2008 and continuing until 2011. The SC became the strategic decision-making body of the CGIAR System, under the CGIAR System Framework (CGIAR 2016a). Reformed governance and advisory bodies include the CGIAR SC; the CGIAR SO with a CGIAR SMB, and the SMO; a General Assembly of the Centers; System-wide advisory bodies (ISPC termed ISDC in 2019, IEA, and Internal Audit Function, clearly different from the historical Centers' CGIAR Shared Services Internal Audit Unit); and a newly conceived Partnership Forum to replace the Funders Forum (CGIAR 2019b). Funders and the Centers also agreed that they would review the role of ISPC and IEA after the transition. ISPC was renamed as the Independent Science for Development Council in 2019. Figure 10.3 presents the latest CGIAR System Framework. We include in part to show the complexity of the organization.

A new organizational structure to reflect the One CGIAR reforms in 2019–20 was issued in 2021.

The former FC decided to radically transform the administrative support arrangements for the new governing arrangements—into a single office, by building on the existing legal personality of the formerly titled CGIAR Consortium as an effective transition. Some bilateral donors were not enthusiastic about the relocation to Montpellier, France. The location was selected through open competition of governments and a committee led by the

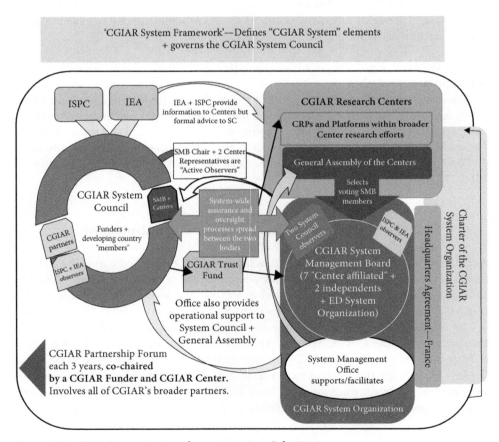

Figure 10.3 CGIAR organizational structure since July 2016
Source: Courtesy of CGIAR.

incoming SMB Chair, who visited all proposed sites and made the final selection. India, Kenya, France, and Canada put in bids (Canada subsequently retracted its bid). The bid from France included substantial investment in the form of a custom-built office complex at the Agropolis Campus in Montpellier and the usual expat privileges (Personal communication, Jonathan Wadsworth, former Executive Secretary of CGIAR with Uma Lele, January 29, 2019). What does the merger and physical move away from other international organizations mean to CGIAR? It remains to be seen.

CGIAR entities charged with different responsibilities include ISPC/ISDC; the SPIA, which is part of ISPC/ISDC; Strengthening Impact Assessment in CGIAR (SIAC), which was a project of SPIA, and the CO and Board, now the SMO and SMB; as well as CRP independent advisory committees and Center Boards.

In July 2016, the CGIAR Consortium was transformed into the CGIAR System Organization, and the CGIAR Consortium's constitution was replaced by the Charter of the CGIAR System Organization (CGIAR 2019b). Taking note that the role of the SMO is to provide administrative support to the SC, SMB, and the General Assembly of the Centers, the annual priorities and work plan of the SMO are shared across all three—in November in advance of a new year to the SC for budget ceiling approval and SMB approval of key themes, and then to the General Assembly in January of the current year, with the General Assembly of Centers created as part of the revised CGIAR governance structure that came into being on July 1, 2016, and the General Assembly Meeting serves as a forum for Centers to discuss issues related to the CGIAR System and the CGIAR System Office. Functional responsibilities of the General Assembly regarding the SMB provide "additional clarity on the accountability lines between the SMB and the General Assembly, and potentially explor[e] additional rules of procedure to enhance transparency and effective relationships, for consultation with the General Assembly in advance of formal adoption by the Board" (CGIAR 2019c, 3).

The SC composition that was finally agreed to was more akin to a shareholder board, with participation of developing country members also, subject to the level of their weighted contribution, based on a formula. Also, BMGF is now represented on the SC.

To incentivize W1 and W2 funding windows, funding is weighted as follows: $W1 \times 3$; $W2 \times 2$; W3, and bilateral $\times 3$—funders were ranked in weighted order, and the top 15 were allocated donor seats (bilateral donors pushed hard to have same weighting as W3 and won the argument—that was a mistake) (Personal communication, Jonathan Wadsworth, former Executive Secretary of CGIAR with Uma Lele, January 29, 2019).

In the governance reforms, the Centers also gained more voice with the establishment of the SMB, until it was changed again. Of the nine voting members, six were Center-affiliated members (who could be either Center Board of Trustee members or Directors General).[12] Critically, the Center-affiliated members serve as voting members, representing the CGIAR System and not the specific Centers with which they are affiliated.

Comprised of eight voting members, two ex-officio non-voting members, and six active observers, the One CGIAR System Board is responsible for providing leadership and governance for CGIAR in the delivery of its mission and for appointing and overseeing the Executive Management Team (EMT), which currently consists of three managing directors.[13] "Working in partnership with the CGIAR System Council, the new System

---

[12] For more information about the governance of the SMB, see https://www.cgiar.org/how-we-work/governance/system-organization/system-management-board/smb-composition/

[13] See "Executive Management Team," https://www.cgiar.org/how-we-work/governance/emt/

Board reviews the effectiveness of the CGIAR System, striving for excellence, and adopts and monitors compliance with CGIAR policies, procedures, and guidelines, with a view to ensuring results and the continued relevance of CGIAR's agricultural research for development."[14]

Until August 31, 2020, the Board of the CGIAR System Organization was known as the "CGIAR System Management Board," or SMB. For this reason, some related documents still contain this terminology, which are anticipated to be adjusted through relevant approvals by the end of 2020.

One reason offered for a single board in 2016 was to overcome conflicts of interest across Centers, but was this goal achieved? Under the previous reform, the Centers only appointed one observer to the CB to represent the Centers' interests. Since July 2016, the Centers gained more direct access to the donors, as two Center representatives were ex-officio non-voting members of the SC until August 2020. Therefore, they no longer had to rely exclusively on the Executive Director of the CGIAR System Organization and the Chair of the SMB (as was the case under the previous reform), to speak on their collective behalf. The General Assembly of the Centers enables Center Board of Trustee Chairs and Directors General to come together to address a variety of issues related to the CGIAR System and CGIAR System Organization. In practice, the Centers began to use the General Assembly mechanism to appoint a co-convener of each of the Board Chairs and Directors General groups, and these two individuals also served as the ex-officio non-voting members of the SC (CGIAR 2019b).

What Did the 2009–2011 and 2015–2016 Reforms Achieve?

Important achievements during the 2009–11 and 2015–16 reform periods have been realized in three areas: (1) increased inter-Center collaboration; (2) advancement in the application of the theory of change (TOC) to CRPs; and (3) greater transparency in partnerships involving advanced country institutions.

Although CGIAR has retained almost all its founding principles, such as Center autonomy and donor sovereignty, the most significant and potentially rewarding development, since CGIAR was established, was the adoption of a new, more formal, organizational structure, starting in 2008, which it has since transformed into One CGIAR. It is too early to know how One CGIAR will perform. The SMO had underway a major effort to reduce the bureaucratic superstructure of the System, consisting of Center management and boards and CRPs and their superstructure, as the initial optimism about reforms in 2008 gave way to skepticism. The new management of the 2020 System Board hopes to turn that around, conveying a greater sense of optimism about the way forward.

Growing Skepticism about CGIAR Began Giving Way to Cautious Optimism and Continued Donor Demand for Impacts
Despite the increase in funding and reforms in the System since 2003, or perhaps because of the way reforms were engineered, the 2008–15 reforms were viewed as reorganizing chairs on the deck, and CGIAR was thought to be becoming a marginal player, with a concern that

---

[14] See "CGIAR System Board," https://www.cgiar.org/how-we-work/governance/system-organization/system-board/

the System could disappear altogether—with individual Centers surviving as independent entities. Skeptics have included Alex McCalla, veteran of CGIAR and chair of CGIAR's TAC from 1988 to 1994, and thereafter, Director of Agriculture in the World Bank, starting in the mid-1990s; and Gordon Conway, an eminent biologist who has played leadership roles internationally and in CGIAR (Conway 2012; McCalla 2017). McCalla and Conway have attributed the risk of irrelevance to several factors: fiddling with the bureaucratic super-structure of the organization; vested interests; unwillingness to respond to the changing science; and, in response to donor demands, a downward drift toward development objectives oriented toward service delivery.

The organization and leadership of the SMB in 2018 resulted in a positive view that the governance arrangement was working well. Donor demand for demonstrating impacts is not new. The demand has been persistent at least since the early 1990s, when CGIAR faced its first major financial crisis. The System has been responding to those expectations, through major System-level reforms in 2001–3, 2009–11, 2015–16, and 2019–20, and several mini-reforms, as well as with publications of impact studies. In the meantime, while the tools to understand pathways to impacts have improved considerably in recent years, there remain many challenges in assessing impacts outside of germplasm, such as those related to policy research or research on NRM (Renkow 2016).

Convincing evidence on the impacts of NRM interventions, other than zero tillage, is limited (as was noted at the Conference on Impacts of International Agricultural Research: Rigorous Evidence for Policy, Nairobi, July 8, 2017). IWMI, one of the CGIAR Centers, was instrumental in making "more crop per drop" a household slogan and highlighting the groundwater crisis, particularly in India. There is a growing consensus, however, that "more crop per drop," while necessary, is not enough. Total water use in agriculture at the basin level needs to be reduced. Packages of technological, institutional, and policy solutions to these challenges, however, are needed, and they have been more difficult to develop, for example, from participatory management to water accounting and monitoring. NRM research is location-specific, so that the development of tools to address certain kinds of generic issues are distinct from applied problem-solving research and need a careful examination. In a recent review article on CGIAR's environmental impacts, Garcia (2020) described the challenge well. The literature is currently inadequate to guide innovation and policy. In particular, few studies employ the necessary rigorous research designs: that is, approaches that isolate causal relationships rather than correlational associations.

Isolating causal relationships is always a challenge for empirical work, and particularly so when the underlying relationships are complicated. Agricultural intensification can affect the environment through different channels. Changes to the inputs that often accompany intensification, such as fertilizers or crop varieties, may have direct impacts on the imme-diate environment through contamination of groundwater or run-off. Indirect impacts may also arise from changes in the profitability of agriculture, or adjustments in prices if output increases. This may change where it is profitable to grow crops or raise livestock, which could lead to either more or less land under production. The specific locations where agricultural land expands or contracts will, in turn, affect other environmental outcomes. While the impacts of intensification on land use are relatively well studied, effects on greenhouse gases, water quality, and biodiversity remain largely devoid of causal evidence that accounts for changes in farmer behavior and the adjustment of related markets.

Funders have a role to play in filling this gap in the evidence: supporting research that pins down the causal impact of agricultural intensification on the environment will—by the logic of supply and demand—lead to more research in this area. SPIA, in a call for proposals issued in collaboration with the Environmental Market Solutions Lab (emLab) at the University of California–Santa Barbara, is taking this approach, albeit at a very modest scale relative to the need. Several new SPIA-funded empirical studies of different agricultural innovations are underway, each rigorously estimating a causal relationship between the rollout of an agricultural innovation and environmental outcomes, such as air quality, rangeland health, and land-use and land-cover change. While these empirical questions were difficult to address to begin with, they now face additional implementation challenges amid the COVID-19 pandemic. Each study has a strong measurement strategy centered on remote sensing, which not only offers the possibility of measurement at a large scale but also makes socially distant COVID-resilient data collection possible. So, we are optimistic that, despite the many challenges posed by the pandemic, these projects will still deliver the high-quality evidence that is sorely needed (Garcia 2020).

Donors, on the other hand, have continued to keep funding tied, fractionated, and less predictable. In turn, a combination of complexities about the research agenda, CGIAR's growing organizational complexity, and the multiplicity of vested interests has affected the pace of reforms and their outcomes (Lele 2020).

Addressing New Research Challenges: CGIAR Research Portfolio of CGIAR Research Programs and Platforms, 2017–2022

Synchronization and extension of the first set of CRP portfolios (2010–16) and development of a new CGIAR SRF continued in 2014, with the FC approving the extension of the 15 CRPs to the end of 2016. The new draft SRF was discussed during November 2014 and approved March–April 2015. Each CRP proposal describes a more coherent research program associated with at least one SLO, while also describing how it would consider unintended consequences on the other two SLOs.

Table 10.2 shows that the new CGIAR Research Portfolio (CRP 2) builds substantially on the 2010–16 portfolio, but differs in key aspects:

- *CRP 2 proposals "demonstrate greater synergy"* within and among them and propose to "deliver impact that is greater than the sum of their parts," and this process could be taken substantially further (CGIAR 2015c).
- *With greater experience and with the review process,* the scientific quality of proposals, the monitoring of programmatic outputs, and mentoring have improved, although this is a work in progress. There are significant differences among proposals in terms of quality. The ISPC's assessment of revised proposals in 2016 rated Fish; Forests, Trees, and Agroforestry (FTA); and Livestock as weaker than the others. Even within a single CRP, there are differences in ISPC ratings that are assigned to specific flagship programs.
- *The portfolio has a focus on outcomes,* "with all programs expected to be based on a clearly defined theory of change, well defined impact pathways, and identified outputs, as well as research outcomes, and specified targets toward (sub-) intermediate development outcomes as defined in CGIAR's 2016–2030 SRF" (CGIAR 2015c).
- *The portfolio "makes explicit the collaboration among the agri-food system CRPs in* defined geographies via Site Integration Plans, [reportedly] developed in close consultation with national partners and each other, and with well-defined coordination

Table 10.2 CGIAR Research Programs (CRPs): CRP I (2010–2016) vs. CRP II (2017–2022)

CRP I (2010–2016) [16 CRPs]	CRP II (2017–2022) [12 CRPs + 3 Platforms]	
CRP 3.1: Wheat	1: Wheat	*8 Agri-Food Systems*
CRP 3.2: Maize	2: Maize	*(AFS) programs*
CRP 3.3: Rice (Global Rice Science Partnership, GRiSP)	3: Rice	
CRP 3.4: Root, Tubers, and Bananas (RTB)	4: Roots, Tubers and Bananas (RTB)	
CRP 6: Forests, Trees, and Agroforestry (FTA)	5: Forests, Trees and Agroforestry (FTA)	
CRP 3.7: Livestock and Fish	Livestock Fish	
CRP 3.5: Grain Legumes	Grain LegumesDryland Cereals	
CRP 3.6: Drylands Cereals		
CRP 1.1: Dryland Systems		
CRP 1.2: Humidtropics		
CRP 1.3: Aquatic Agricultural Systems (AAS)		
CRP 4: Agriculture for Nutrition and Health (A4NH)	1:Agriculture for Nutrition and Health (A4NH)	*4 Global Integrating Programs (GIPs)*
CRP 7: Climate Change, Agriculture, and Food Security (CCAFS)	Climate Change, Agriculture, and Food Security (CCAFS)	
CRP 2: Policies, Institutions, and Markets (PIM)	Policies, Institutions, and Markets (PIM)	
CRP 5: Water, Land, and Ecosystems (WLE)	Water, Land, and Ecosystems (WLE)	
CRP 8: Genebanks	GeneBank Platform	*3 Platforms*
	Platform for Big Data in Agriculture	
	Excellence in Breeding Platform	

Source: CGIAR website, Research Portfolio: https://www.cgiar.org/research/research-portfolio/

mechanisms, led by a specified center or CRP in each country or site" (CGIAR 2015c). This is an area that requires far more work, as the consultations about the Site Integration Plans indicate. There are many management issues on leadership, coordination, funding, and collaboration with NARS yet to be sorted out.

- *The four crosscutting, global-integrating CRPs* "will work closely with each other and with the *8 agri-food CRPs* to leverage best practices across the portfolio" (CGIAR 2015c). The question is whether the decision-making and resource allocation structures and processes now in place facilitate and incentivize these types of collaboration, or instead impose unintended barriers.
- The proposed Managing Directors (MDs) of the EMT will call the shots and instruct DGs what they need to do (like vice-presidents in the World Bank). Of course, DGs do not like the idea of taking orders from anyone—many DGs have been able to get their Boards to follow the directions proposed by the DGs, so doing what one common board decides through the executive powers of the MDs is an alien concept for them.
- *The new portfolio also promotes three crosscutting platforms:* (1) GeneBank Platform, (2) Platform for Big Data in Agriculture, and (3) Excellence in Breeding Platform. Also, it "addresses gender, capacity development, and monitoring, evaluation and learning as functions coordinated by specific Centers or Communities of Practice to ensure integration and coordination across the CRPs" (CGIAR 2015c).

The Gender Platform has had a complicated history and is described in the Appendix (see Box A.10.1).

Gender research was underway in CGIAR from at least the 1980s, but due to lack of funding, it died several times, yet with a significant amount of research ongoing as part of CRPs, particularly since 2017. It survived mainly due to donor pressure, but also died due to lack of donor funding, and a full-fledged Gender Platform was formally launched only in January 2020. Its implementation has been slow for the reasons discussed in the Appendix.

The outputs and outcomes of CGIAR research and related activities span the entire target sub-IDOs of the SRF (at the portfolio level, a total of 953 key outputs were listed in 2017). Eighteen percent of key outputs are principally linked with Capacity Development, while 10 percent and 4 percent of those were principally linked with Gender and Youth, respectively. Across all platforms, significant levels of outputs are targeted to Capacity Development, while the Genebank Platform did not indicate any key outputs tagged with Gender and Youth, due to the nature of the activities. At the aggregate portfolio level, the total budget for year 2018 will be US$762 million, comprised of W1–W2 funding of only US$199 million (26 percent) and W3-Bilateral funding of US$559 million (73 percent). The W1/W2 total funding was rather sad and approaching an untenably low level, but Centers understandably tend to be almost unanimously unwilling to share their W1/W2 funding. Centers find W1/W2 to be a precious resource, but those who favor reforms say Centers may have squandered the good will of donors and have only themselves to blame. If the Centers want to return to the past, this is an excellent strategy to bring it about.

Sixty-four percent (US$484 million) of the portfolio budget is made up of Agri-Food System CRPs, with 31 percent (US$234 million) and 6 percent (US$43 million) made up of Global Integrating CRPs and Platforms, respectively (Table 10.3 shows the Planned Budget for 2018 for CRPs). In CRPs, the share of W1–W2 funding is around 12–37 percent (average 23 percent). Among platforms, Big Data is fully dependent at start-up on W1–W2 funding, while the Excellence in Breeding Platform and Genebanks maintained 49 percent and 30 percent W3 and Bilateral funding, respectively.[15]

Role of National Agricultural Research Systems in Gender Research

NARS should ideally address issues of gender and youth, but they have not been sufficiently proactive, despite international initiatives, such as the Global Conference on Women in Agriculture, jointly co-sponsored by GFAR, the Indian Council of Agricultural Research (ICAR), the Asia–Pacific Association of Agricultural Research Institutions, and many donors in New Delhi, March 13–15, 2012 (GFAR 2012). How CGIAR can stimulate NARS research remains a question. The emphasis on TOCs has been a welcome one and has compelled scientists to think through the pathways by which their work achieves impacts. Scientists and Centers are also being asked to *quantify* the contribution of their research to the various outcomes along the development pathway—often all the way down to poverty reduction in numbers. This is a tall order and an unreasonable one to meet in a rigorous way. Many things can happen downstream to mediate impact, or even negate it, but that does not necessarily mean the technology was not worth developing. This is

---

[15] See "Annual Plan of Work and Budget Reports" for each of the CRPs: https://www.cgiar.org/research/annual-plan-work-budget/page/2/

Table 10.3 Summary of CGIAR Research Programs (CRPs) planned budget, 2020 (US$m)

CRPs	W1+W2	W3/Bilateral	Own funds	% share in total	% share in total
Grain Legumes and Dryland Cereals (GLDC)[a]	9.2	35.3		44.5	6
Fish[b]	5.96	25.46		31.42	4
Forests, Trees and Agroforestry (FTA)[c]	9.99	76.89		86.88	12
Livestock[d]	21.34	34.26	0	55.6	7
Maize[e]	11.68	54.42		66.1	9
Rice	13.92	45.81		59.73	8
Roots, Tubers and Bananas (RTB)	20.09	47.4	0.7	68.19	9
Wheat[f]	14.2	39.1		53.3	7
Total [8 Agri-Food Systems (AFS) Programs]	*106.38*	*358.64*	*0.7*	*465.72*	*62*
Agriculture for Nutrition and Health (A4NH)[g]	20	65.06		85.06	11
Climate Change, Agriculture and Food Security (CCAFS)[h]	20.95	41.87		62.82	8
Policies, Institutions, and Markets (PIM)[i]	16.29	40.24		56.53	8
Water, Land and Ecosystems (WLE)[j]	9.2	21.15	0.53	30.88	4
Total [4 Global Integrating Programs (GIP)]	*66.44*	*168.32*	*0.53*	*235.29*	*32*
Platform for Big Data in Agriculture	3.5	0		3.5	0
Excellence in Breeding Platform[k]	1.7	6.21		7.91	1
Genebank Platform	15.27	13.35		28.62	4
Gender Platform[l]	4.46	0		4.46	1
Total [4 Support Platforms]	*24.93*	*19.56*		*44.49*	*6*
Grand total	197.75	546.52	1.23	745.5	100

Notes: [a] The provisional budget for 2020 allocated by SMO is US$9.2 million, which includes 2 percent CSP. The budget in the table is expressed at 100 percent spending levels. For operation purposes, CRP–GLDC is currently planning to spend 90 percent of this budget until further guidance is received from SMO.

[b] This reflects the revised CGIAR Research Financing Plan 2020–1, as submitted to the SMB 16th meeting and is subject to approval by that meeting. The 2020 W1 and W2 budget is based on guidance provided in the 2020–1 FINPLAN for 90 percent of W1 target (US$1.959 million) and W2 (US$3.998 million). Cross-program investments are also funded by W3/bilateral. However, the figure for cross-program investments is embedded under the FP1 and FP2 W3/bilateral budget.

[c] Includes CRP management, program-level communication and outreach, foresight, monitoring, evaluation, learning and impact assessment, and support to program integration (for example, cross-FP integrative operational priorities).

[d] Total CRP budget for 2020 has increased by approximately 37 percent, compared to the Annual Plan of Work and Budget (POWB) 2019, due to both an increase in W3/bilateral funds and use of unallocated or unspent W1/2 funds from the CRP Strategic Investment Fund from previous years.

[e] Includes M-MC buffer for 2020 W1&2 volatility and FX risk; **Best estimate based on 2018/2019 data. Figures updated quarterly and sent to SMO.

[f] W1&2 incudes carryover within CIMMYT Res (FP 1-4). W3/Bilateral are best estimates, will be updated in 1st quarter reporting to SMO.

[g] Planned contribution in 2020 of non-CGIAR partner in Flagship 1, Wageningen University and Research and in Flagship 5, London School of Hygiene and Tropical Medicine, is US$5,826,029 and US$515,730, respectively.

[h] Planned W1/W2 funds total US$20.953 million, comprising US$19.306 million as per the 2019–21 Financial Plan (US$19.7 million for year 2020 gross of 2 percent CSP) and extraordinary additional W2 funding from Norwegian Agency for Development Cooperation (NORAD) for US$1.647 million allocated to IITA directly.

Continued

Table 10.3 *Continued*

CRPs

W1+W2

W3/Bilateral

Own funds

% share in total

% share in total

[i] PIM implemented a policy allowing carryover of up to 10 percent of each participating Center's 2019 budget by flagship upon justification. Amounts to be finalized after audit confirmation of 2019 expenses.

[j] Financial reporting for 2019 has not been completed, therefore carry-forward funds are estimated; the carry-forward budget provided here is intended for use in 2020. Remaining 2018–19 funds will be carried forward for use in 2021; all W1/W2 figures are net of CSP; all gender-related funding is included in Flagship budgets; this budget includes confirmed bilateral, W3, and Center funding as of January 2020. Incoming information suggests that the total bilateral funding will increase; as requested, we note that the bilateral contribution from Water, Land, and Ecosystem's core non-CGIAR partner, RUAF (FP3), will be approximately US$200k in 2020.

[k] This budget does not include use of the expected W1&W2 carry-over funds. They will be allocated to Module 1 (US$420,000), Module 2 (US$533,600), Module 3 (US$543,000) 4 (US$514,400), and 5 (US$450,000).

[l] A call was made for proposals for a fourth research support Platform, the CGIAR Gender Equality in Food Systems Research Platform, approved by the SMB. This Platform began its implementation period in January 2020.

Source: CGIAR website, Annual Plan of Work and Budget: https://www.cgiar.org/research/annual-plan-work-budget/

creating an unhealthy pressure to show unreasonably big numbers. Of course, accountability is necessary, but expectations also need to be reasonable. And, it is important to acknowledge that not all research will yield winners, and that good science needs the freedom and space to learn from its mistakes. Furthermore, although all CRPs focus on the TOC and downstream impacts, evidence of the precise nature of links to developing countries' NARS in CRPs is very limited; there are occasional references to the 20 site selections, also discussed variably as country focus. This casual approach to partnerships with NARS of developing countries contrasts to the treatment of partnerships with developed countries' institutions provided in the CRPs.

An important emerging trend is the greater role of developed country institutions in CRPs. Donors are expecting CGIAR Centers to be vehicles, through partnerships, for increased access of developed country institutions to developing countries to conduct research. Whereas this has been the US approach bilaterally for decades—helping to generate the Green Revolution—this is a recent phenomenon in the case of other bilateral donors: for example, in the case of UK's Department for International Development (DFID) or the Netherlands. As resources become more limited, and the need to engage domestic constituents for continued support to CGIAR has increased, this is indeed an effective way to employ science in developed countries, provided the process is transparent and competitive. This is useful as a complementary arrangement but not at the cost of the core CGIAR funding, and there must be a strong presence of developing countries' NARS. Perhaps increased South–South cooperation can help foster this bilateral support in place of the currently very fragmented, ad hoc approach.

Growth of private sector investments in agricultural R&D in emerging countries is relatively recent. The investments are a result of a combination of advances in genetic engineering: "an unprecedented convergence of advances in biology, agronomy, plant and animal science, digitization and robotics ... often referred to collectively as 'digital agriculture,' 'precision farming,' or 'smart farming'"—or as part of the fourth industrial revolution technologies, and increasing marketization of the agricultural supply chains (Jaruzelski, Staack, and Johnson 2017, 90). Together, they "are creating the foundation for a new, more productive and sustainable future of agriculture" (Jaruzelski, Staack, and Johnson 2017, 90). To grow, emerging countries will have to follow the path of the more advanced knowledge powerhouses, such as Japan and South Korea, where private sector investments are nearly four times the public sector R&D.

There is also a structural change underway in farm ownership patterns in emerging countries, which we outlined in Chapter 2. It is leading to land consolidation and the creation of "a multiplier effect because farmers who automate are able to manage larger fields and greater numbers of animals" (Jaruzelski, Staack, and Johnson 2017, 90). Such consolidation is occurring more rapidly in countries that have good infrastructure—only one-third of the farms in Africa are located near a road. And, as we noted in Chapter 2 on structural transformation, countries which have been able to create off-farm jobs are growing more rapidly—for example, in East and South East Asia—as compared to SA where the average farm size is declining (ICRISAT 2017).

In their chapter in *The Global Innovation Index 2017*, Barry Jaruzelski, Volker Staack, and Tom Johnson note:

> Much of this new wave of innovation is enabled by the shift in corporate R&D towards software, advanced hardware, and service offerings. The integration of embedded software and sensors in farm equipment, in the soil, and on the animals—as well as the ability to reliably and inexpensively connect and network agricultural producers, suppliers, products, and customers using cloud-based systems and shared analytics—has significant potential to increase output. Such innovations are enabling major gains in yields, asset productivity, and sustainability that will be key factors in meeting the escalating demand for food. (Jaruzelski, Staack, and Johnson 2017, 90)

A CGIAR Imperative: Stable, Predictable, Unrestricted Funding

CGIAR, like all of the big five has continually sought to address it funding sources, methods of financing, and linkage to the design and implementation of its programs.

CGIAR's Financing Challenge

The fast growth in CGIAR financing from 2010 to 2014 had led to great optimism (Figure 10.4).

The latest dashboard indicates that System revenue and expenses were not only lower by about US$200,000 in 2019, compared to the peak revenue of US$1,067,000 reached in 2014, but there was a deficit with revenue of US$828,000, compared to the expense of US$836,000, a deficit CGIAR has experienced since 2016.

Jonathan Wadsworth, the former Executive Director of CGIAR made a number of perceptive observations. "Existence of the Fund probably had a major effect on accelerating growth of CGIAR and passing the $1bn/yr target by providing a multilateral approach and

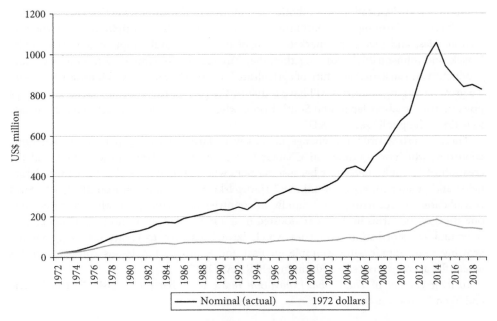

Figure 10.4 CGIAR: Evolution of funding (nominal and in 1972 US dollars), 1972–2019 (US$m)

Note: Excludes Center own income.

Source: Based on data from CGIAR Financial Reports; 2017 CGIAR Research Financing Plan (CGIAR 2017i); CGIAR Center Financial Result – 2016 (CGIAR 2017a).

new funding channels" (Wadsworth 2016, 2). Whether the 2007–8 food and financial crisis or the reforms, however, caused the fast growth in post-2008 funding remains a debated issue. Perhaps both played a part. In 2017, funding declined to US$840 million from the 2014 peak (CGIAR 2017h). Importantly, the reform "did not achieve the objective of attracting the majority of CGIAR funding through pool means (W1 & W2) which would have enabled a truly multilateral approach to international agriculture research through the CGIAR CRPs" (Wadsworth 2016, 2). Finally, the fragmented funding has kept the transaction costs of fundraising for CGIAR high and the aid quality low. Wadsworth noted, "Centres continued with the heavy burden of fundraising resulting in *many hundreds of bilateral projects* persisting across the CGIAR with all the concomitant inefficiencies both programmatic and administrative. This may have limited CGIAR's potential for uniquely transformational research, impact and change that is needed in the global food and agriculture system" (Wadsworth 2016, 2 [emphasis added]). A 64 million dollar question is why is this the case, and whether and how the donor behavior described here can be changed.

The decline in the share of unrestricted (core) funding over time is closely related to priority setting, the changing role of technical advice, and the fragmented funding and program of work. Before the 2008 reforms, the 15 CGIAR Centers had 3,500 bilaterally funded programs of assorted sizes, time horizons, and scopes of research. After the reforms, the number of programs was reduced by 900, but there were still 2,600 such programs outside the purview of CGIAR in 2015.

Over seven years (2011–17), the distribution of contributions across the Fund windows changed strikingly; the share of unrestricted W1 + W2 dropped dramatically from 84 percent of the Fund receipts in 2011 to 36 percent in 2017, with the W1 funding (completely unrestricted) falling from a high 66 percent to 19 percent of the Fund receipts over the same period. Correspondingly, W3 grew from 16 percent of the Fund receipts in 2011 to 65 percent in 2017 (see Figure 10.5) (CGIAR 2018c).

In the meantime among developing country partners, only Brazil was enjoying a generous level of investment, increasing from 1 percent to nearly 2 percent of agricultural gross domestic product (GDP) in agricultural research from 1980 to 2016 (Figure 10.6). China's funding as share of agricultural GDP was less than 0.5 percent but showed a clearly increasing trend. India's funding level while the increase was not nearly as great as China's, only half that amount according to latest numbers. Finally, sub-Saharan Africa's share of agricultural research in agricultural GDP among its approximately 46 countries has shown a clear declining trend since the 1980s (Figure 10.6).

Unrestricted funding to the Centers, therefore, makes a big difference in their ability to partner with developing countries.

In 2010, prior to establishment of the CGIAR Fund, unrestricted core funding to Centers was around 34 percent of the total CGIAR funding, significantly reduced from the 84

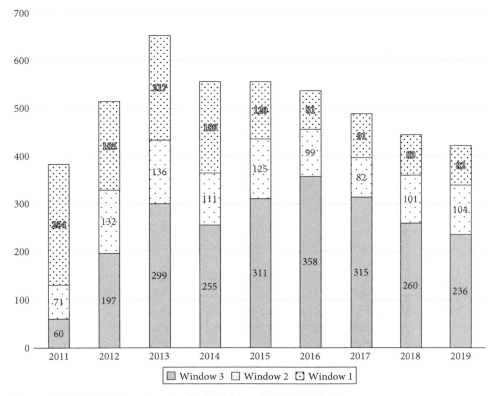

Figure 10.5 CGIAR Fund receipts by Windows, 2011–2019 (US$m)

Source: Based on data from CGIAR Financial Reports 2011 (CGIAR 2012); 2012 (CGIAR 2013); 2013 (CGIAR 2014a); 2014 (CGIAR 2015a); 2015 (CGIAR 2016c); 2016 (CGIAR 2017h); 2017 (CGIAR 2018c); CGIAR (2020e); CGIAR Financial Report Dashboards (https://www.cgiar.org/food-security-impact/finance-reports/dashboard/).

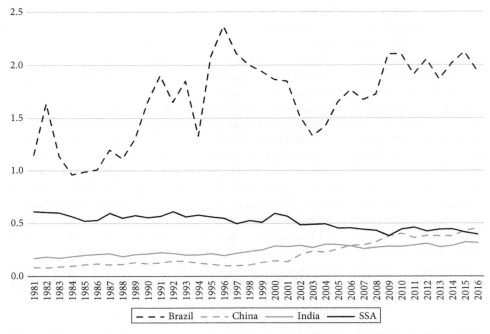

Figure 10.6 Agricultural research spending as a share of AgGDP: Brazil, China, India, and SSA, 1981–2016 (%)

Source: Based on data from ASTI/IFPRI (https://www.asti.cgiar.org)

percent in 1988, whereas restricted funding increased from 16 percent (US$33 million) in 1988 to 81 percent (US$446 million) in 2011 (Figure 10.7).

In short, prospects in 2017 did not seem as good for the level, stability, or predictability of funding (through multi-year pledges that CGIAR has sought), as they did a just few years earlier. As late as 2013–14, plans were underway to double CGIAR annual funding to US$2 billion.

Wadsworth noted, and we agree, that CGIAR's fragmented funding approach is unique for an international organization of its size and achievements, and:

> A more existential question for CGIAR is to ask why other multilateral initiatives such as the Global Fund to fight AIDS, Tuberculosis and Malaria [GFATM and the GAVI Vaccine Initiative (GAVI), both "vertical funds" but often used by CGIAR's 2015 Transition Team, as two of several identified comparator organizations] are able to function at much higher levels of long term pledged funding with a policy that severely restricts earmarking of funds by contributors, while CGIAR seemingly cannot, despite having the financial support of many of the very same donors? (Wadsworth 2016, 4)

We therefore investigated alternative funding models.

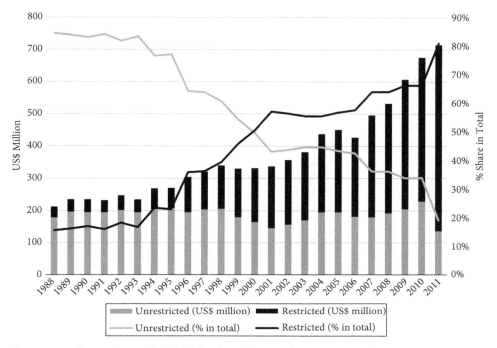

Figure 10.7 Composition of CGIAR funding: Restricted vs. unrestricted, 1988–2011

Notes: Restricted vs. unrestricted data are available up to 2011, and since then, the data are available by W1, W2, W3, and Bilateral.

Source: Based on CGIAR Financial Reports.

Vertical Funds: A Possible Model?

The Global Fund to Fight AIDS, Tuberculosis and Malaria (GFATM) is frequently mentioned as a possible model for CGIAR financing. Richard Manning, who has helped raise funds for a number of international organizations, told us that the Global Fund is not a relevant model. It is mainly financing country programs of commodities with big economies of scale, so the incentives for donors are very different. Research systems in other areas such as health are better comparators (Richard Manning, personal communication, October 2, 2017). Despite the World Health Organization's (WHO) best efforts, there is no real equivalent to CGIAR that has been successful in developing a coordinated approach from the outset. In health, a set of sector- or issue-specific initiatives exists (the Medicines for Malaria venture, heavily backed by BMGF, in much the same way, it is putting money into CGIAR, even if it is via W3). Tropical agriculture is rather unusual in having achieved a more coordinated approach. The challenge is how to sustain it. The System Financing Modalities paper presents several ideas for discussion, including a large-scale commitment push, separate GeneBank funding, and changes in the way funds are raised for individual CRPs and allocated among CRPs, delinking W1 and W2 funding, and instead of "salami slicing," allocating resources across CRPs in a more discriminating way (CGIAR 2017d, 2017e).

Those familiar with the financing of the Global Fund argue the comparisons are not valid. GFATM makes grants to countries to achieve health outcomes, which are achievable in a relatively short period. On the other hand, according to some estimates, only 10 percent of all medical research is devoted to conditions that account for 90 percent of the global disease burden. Moreover, due to limited support for research that addresses some of the most neglected diseases and populations, the world's best scientists are not sufficiently engaged. Research, in the health sector on tropical diseases, established under the aegis of WHO, has had difficulty attracting funding from donors in the same way that agricultural research has difficulty attracting resources (WHO 2020). The same is true for CGIAR.

BMGF's Discovery & Translational Sciences program aims to create and improve preventive, diagnostic, and therapeutic interventions for infectious diseases, as well as other conditions that affect mothers, infants, and children (BMGF 2020). Being selective under W3, BMGF is providing considerable support for agricultural research within CGIAR, but has so far been reluctant to provide predictable, sizable, long-term funding in return for reform of the System as a whole.

Replenishment Model

CGIAR could have put in place—and it still can do—a system of three-year replenishments at the time of the 2008 reforms. However, replenishments have been hard to achieve, as examples of Global Agriculture and Food Security Program (GAFSP), IFAD, and regional banks can testify. So, CGIAR is trying to obtain longer term commitments, even without replenishments.

The final IDA19 replenishment meeting took place in Stockholm, Sweden, December 12–13, 2019. A global coalition of development partners agreed on a historic US$82 billion financing package for IDA countries for fiscal years 2021–3, representing a 3 percent increase in real terms, compared to IDA18 (IDA 2020). An additional new approach, in view of the successful US$82 billion IDA19 replenishments over three years, would be to support African countries' national and regional research through IDA funds. With graduation of big IDA borrowers like India, and the new ability of IDA to borrow on the commercial market, based on IDA subscriptions, there is more money in IDA, than it can, perhaps, usefully commit.

IDA, a coalition of more than 60 donor and borrower governments is ratcheting up the fight against extreme poverty with a record US$75 billion commitment to the World Bank's fund for the poorest countries. IDA needs to be deployed actively to support R&D at the country and regional levels. There is substantial aid and goodwill toward SSA, from which a global vision of partnership built upon a CGIAR-run platform can emerge. The IDA's potential recipients can individually and regionally commit to contributing up to US$1 billion annually and predictably to help build a joint program.

CGIAR in the World Bank and the International Development Association

The Bank has had a key role in the establishment of CGIAR as a founding member.[16] It has traditionally contributed net income from IBRD loan repayments to CGIAR, first justified

[16] We are grateful for comments from Jonathan Wadsworth, Karen Brooks, and Will Martin. Views and shortcomings are entirely our own.

by Robert McNamara at the founding of CGIAR in 1972. Such contribution of IBRD net income was justified on grounds that CGIAR research is long-term, requires bulky capital, and the best of scientific talent—on a global scale. CGIAR achieves benefits with substantial cross-border spillovers. CGIAR investments have been spectacularly successful, particularly in contributing to the Green Revolution in Asia, containing cassava mealybug in Africa, and in biofortified crops all over, documented recently by a comprehensive study of returns to CGIAR research (Alston, Pardey, and Rao 2020), but its mission of food security and nutrition remains unfulfilled. Indeed, the number of undernourished and extremely hungry—that is, those persons whom WFP supports—has increased substantially. Thus, the challenge of food security and nutrition has expanded and become more complex with the need to address climate change, natural resource degradation, conflict, rainfed agriculture, and a diversified food production system, many areas that IDA supports, in contrast to the research on monoculture focusing on a handful of crops, such as rice, wheat, and maize that CGIAR has conducted in the past.

Relatedly, the need for more public goods investment in CGIAR has increased, as its resources have diminished, particularly since 2014 (Figure 10.4), and they become more fragmented, unpredictable, and tied to small, short-term projects.

The Scale and Need for Agricultural Research in IDA Countries

IDA countries are the poorest and least food secure. According to the various background papers prepared in support of IDA19, 500 million people live in extreme poverty in the currently IDA-eligible countries, and their numbers have not diminished over successive IDA replenishments. There are more violent conflicts in IDA countries than at any time in the past 30 years. Economic growth has often been accompanied by inequalities, also leading to exclusion. Gender gaps remain high in education and employment. Around 20 million jobs need to be created in IDA countries *annually* for the next decade, according to IDA19 background papers, simply to meet the growing number of young men and women entering the labor market. High unemployment contributes to growing involuntary displacement of people.

Total factor productivity growth in agriculture has been the slowest in SSA, compared to other regions, whether it is considered by regions or by income categories (see Figure 2.1). This is, in part, because their investment in R&D, already low as share of agricultural GDP, has declined over time (Figure 10.6). Given the small size of their R&D establishments, there are diseconomies of scale in research. They need to collaborate with other neighboring countries to take advantage of scale economies. That is why regional cooperation in R&D is needed. And partnership with CGIAR can help promote it.

CGIAR has allocated a sizeable share of its own funding to Africa, in situation where its own funding has not grown, and indeed, has declined since the peak was reached in 2014, and with a sizable share of the funding in W3 (Figure 10.5), it is restricted, fragmented, and unpredictable reducing its overall impact.

CGIAR has currently set a target of US$2 billion by 2030, but in the current fiscal environment, CGIAR's traditional donors are fiscally strapped, so that raising new additional funding is difficult. Several of CGIAR's donors are also IDA contributors. After reaching a peak in 2013, the flow of official development assistance (ODA) grants to IDA countries has declined, largely due to the shift in official grant financing toward non-IDA countries due to natural disasters and humanitarian assistance to refugees.

The Potential of IDA Funding Both to IDA Countries and to CGIAR

IDA19 replenishment of US$82 billion is a testimonial to the confidence donors have placed in IDA as an institution since its establishment in 1960. IDA has proven to be successful in supporting enhanced food security in Asia, contributing to reducing poverty by nearly one billion people, and contributing to the graduation of several IDA countries. No other multilateral institution has the record of stable fundraising and performance as does IDA. Evidence of more than 2,000 World Bank and IDA-funded agricultural projects from 1970 to 2018 (Figures 8.14 and 8.16; Table 8.1) shows that OED/IEG performance ratings of completed projects in low-income countries (LICs) are systematically lower than those of low-middle-income countries (LMICs) and MICs, even when the performance of LICs improves, and increasingly, completed Bank-funded projects lack estimates of returns on investment because of the difficulty of quantifying many investments (IEG 2010). Contrast this with the high rates of return realized by funding CGIAR research, which are widely documented. The latest study shows a benefit cost ratio of 10:1 for CGIAR investments (Alston, Pardey, and Rao 2020). Despite these clear benefits, IDA borrowers have limited capacity to meet the investment requirements.

More funding for CGIAR, so mobilized by using IDA as the demand pull, will require it to create programs in greater consultation with developing countries. It will bring a cascading combination of global, regional, and national public goods research, scientific rigor, training, and institution building, assuring relevance, particularly if the funding is used in partnership with scientists in advanced, developed, and developing countries. IDA for CGIAR will require support of major IDA deputies/CGIAR donor countries in addition to agreement in principle of IDA-eligible countries both at the broader strategic level as well as on specific research programs of mutual interest.

Potential Scope and Use of IDA Funding to CGIAR

Allocation of IDA to CGIAR of up to US$1 billion annually, out of a total of US$82 billion over three years, arguably, is an insignificant amount for IDA but a substantial increment for CGIAR. Its funding was US$870 million in 2020. IDA funding can support CGIAR activities downstream to applied and adaptive research, and even extension activities of the kind national systems should perform.

With more predictable and diversified financial support to IDA countries, these collective tendencies can strengthen NARS. They can also create obvious demand for complementarity of global or regional GPGs from CGIAR, as it did during the Green Revolution with improved germplasm or with cassava mealybug, or more recently, with biofortified crops.

Relatedly, additional IDA resources would make the reorganization successful from the vantage point of view of donors and recipients as a whole, so CGIAR can deliver global and regional public goods for which CGIAR was established: that is, research with large spillovers, and economies of scale and scope.

IDA funding to CGIAR, from US$500 million to up to US$1 billion annually, can ensure a triple win: (1) success of the latest CGIAR reorganization to achieve its larger stated global and regional public goods functions; (2) getting the global development community closer to achieving SDG2 (food security and nutrition) and other related SDGs (gender equality, climate change, water management) by 2030, given that many LICs are currently off track; and (3) helping low-income, IDA-eligible countries to build their R&D capacity, raise their investments in R&D, and by strengthening their food and agricultural sectors, achieve broad-based sustainable growth, thereby helping them graduate from IDA eligibility.

Nevertheless more funding for CGIAR from IDA should be more flexible and yet tied to increased funding from IDA to the national-level institutions to build national capacity, as an essential element of "IDA for CGIAR" for delivery and impact on the ground. IDA funding is necessary but will not be sufficient. Some of the big global R&D issues of interest to CGIAR, such as climate change, necessarily involve big non-IDA countries. Ideally, IDA funds would be matched by pooled funding from traditional donors plus emerging countries to ensure the range of GPGs that are needed. A combination of stimulating demand from borrowing countries and pooled funding from other partners will increase the ownership of CGIAR in developing countries.

In short, as CGIAR pivots toward its rearticulated mission of transforming agro-food systems for climate resilience and healthy diets, funding will be critical. CGIAR is still uniquely positioned and equipped to play a major role in enabling and accelerating the transformation of the world's food system. It will call for modifying some of the restrictive IDA procurement and safeguarding rules. It will call for strong, creative, collective leadership of donors, of the kind that led to the establishment of CGIAR under McNamara's leadership in which profits on IBRD loans were used to cross-subsidize CGIAR.

Funding of the CGIAR Windows on a Multi-Year Basis

None of the proposals discussed here directly addresses the core funding problem. The traditional donors are key to this. There is a good case for a more formal, periodic replenishment system, so that the three windows (not the bilateral funding) are replenished on a multi-year basis. That could also be the venue for trying to get a better balance between the windows, as well as reaching out to new donors.

Thus, for example, W3 was and remains essentially a pass-through mechanism to channel donor funds to individual Centers. The World Bank as Trustee of the CGIAR Fund entered into W3 transfer agreements directly with the Centers receiving the W3 funds. However, the legal agreements between the FC, represented by the World Bank, and the CGIAR Consortium also had terms that governed the use of W3 funds. These requirements flowed down through the CGIAR Consortium to the Centers in Program Implementation Agreements, along with W1 and W2 requirements. The new arrangements came into effect on January 1, 2017.

The FC did not enter into any contractual relationships with the System Board of the group of Centers or the individual Centers, with respect to the use of W3 funds, and it did not take part in setting CGIAR priorities. Indeed, a review of the continuation of W3 was planned after a two-year transitional period of reforms, but W3 continues. The creation of W3 defeated the purpose of a consolidated research agenda under a System-level umbrella, with both the increasing share of W3 financing and the creation of a considerable amount of uncertainty and instability in the funding, as different Centers have different abilities to raise resources (Özgediz 2012). W1 and W2, taken together to mean unrestricted program funding, as a replacement for the previously defined unrestricted Center core funding declined to 19 percent (US$161 million) of CGIAR's total revenue in 2017, from the 2014 peak of US$383 million (35 percent of the total), while bilateral funding fell from 69 percent in 2011 to 41 percent in 2017 (CGIAR 2017h) (see Figure 10.7). Unless this imbalance can be dramatically reversed, the newly proposed reforms will fail, because there will be no incentives and discipline to get Centers to conduct research collaboratively and within the System's framework of priorities.

Independent scientific advice and priority setting have taken the biggest tolls in successive reorganizations of CGIAR. Our interviews suggest that donors do not appear to want independent scientific advice, and neither do the Centers. While there are a few notable exceptions, by and large, donors also do not seem to want to see priority-setting efforts, perhaps because it would disturb their ongoing bilateral relationship, and they would have less control over resource mobilization. This is contrary to the argument made by Hayami, Lipton, and Mule (2003), or that implied in the funding reforms of 2008, in creating two windows, even though the current arrangement of three windows entails high transaction costs, with each Center doing their own fundraising, as the Mid-Term Review emphasized (CGIAR 2014b).

Growth of Window 3 Funding

The most significant change has been the rapid growth of W3, which exhibited more than a 18-fold increase from US$17 million in 2011 to US$314 million in 2017, which was 37 percent of CGIAR's total revenue in 2017, and an increase from only 2 percent in 2011 (see Figure 10.8; CGIAR 2018c). W3 and bilateral projects are intended to contribute to the achievement of the CGIAR SRF through alignment with CRP activities and objectives. However, most are project-specific (Wadsworth 2016). While bilateral funding is likely to remain an important component of overall CRP financing, the extent to which CRPs are reliant on bilateral support, whether through the Fund or through Centers, has the potential to distort priority setting within the CRPs and limit the flexibility to allocate resources. At the System level, coherent and integrated strategy for resource mobilization reportedly exists but reinforces a hyperawareness of boundaries and distinctions in standing among organizational entities intended to be complementary and collaborative (Robinson et al. 2014).

The new CGIAR Trust Fund was set up in 2017. It had to be set up for legal reasons, but essentially remains the same as the old trust fund. According to One CGIAR's Resource Mobilization, Communication and Advocacy Strategy:

> The year 2017 was the first of Phase 2 of the CRP portfolio, and although revenue for 2017 was below the peak revenue for 2013, pooled investments stabilized.... [I]n 2019, coordinated advocacy around CGIAR's climate agenda and momentum around One CGIAR generated the first—albeit moderate—increase in pooled funding since 2013. (CGIAR 2020c)

ODA has been the main source of CGIAR funding. More than 50 percent of the funding comes from the Organisation for Economic Co-operation and Development–Development Assistance Committee (OECD–DAC) countries. Other sources of funding include foundations and the private sector, multilateral development banks (MDBs), and international financial institutions (IFIs), and other non-DAC countries sources.

"System Council Funders (all sources) provide more than 70% of all funding to CGIAR.... They also provide 99% of the pooled funding to the shared research agenda. All other sources of funding are contributed through Window 3 and bilateral" (CGIAR 2020c, 6).

One CGIAR's 2020 multi-channel action area approach entails strengthening relations with existing SC funders, growing emerging markets, tapping climate funds and finance,

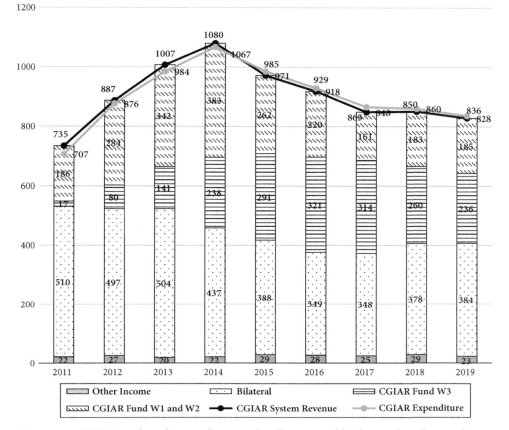

Figure 10.8 CGIAR total implemented revenue by all sources of funding and total expenditure, 2011–2019 (US$m)

Source: Based on data from CGIAR Financial Reports 2011 (CGIAR 2012); 2012 (CGIAR 2013); 2013 (CGIAR 2014a); 2014 (CGIAR 2015a); 2015 (CGIAR 2016c); 2016 (CGIAR 2017h); 2017 (CGIAR 2018c); CGIAR (2020e); CGIAR Financial Report Dashboards (https://www.cgiar.org/food-security-impact/finance-reports/dashboard/).

engaging country partners and IFIs, and cultivating innovative and private finance (CGIAR 2020c, 10).

Effects of Levels of Fragmented Funding on the Research Program

The drop in Windows 1 and 2 affected System-wide CRPs differently. CRPs were created under the 2008 reforms. "Seven CRPs exceeded or came close to achieving full total budgets; five CRPs achieved 75–90% full budgets; and four CRPs fell below 75% full funding despite two of the latter receiving close to their approved W1+W2 budgets" (Wadsworth 2016, 2). There are suggestions that CRPs, which had directors who were particularly skilled at fundraising or which had themes that were appealing to donors, kept their funding intact. As noted earlier, CGIAR set up a Trust Fund in 2017.

The Need for Multi-Year Funding

CGIAR has sought multi-year contribution agreements from donors to increase stability and predictability of funding and assure timely disbursements to research programs. Only 40 percent of Fund receipts in 2014, however, reached formal multi-year agreements. "Timely disbursements from the Fund were only possible when the Fund carried sufficient resources over from one year to the next to enable smoothing of the skewed nature of Fund receipts, which occurred mainly in the final quarter of the year" (Wadsworth 2016, 2). Such funding was at the lowest level in September 2017.

Funding uncertainty has affected the quality of partnerships with NARS. Centers are hesitant to make commitments on collaborative research when they are uncertain of the flow of funds; this is a particularly significant issue with developing countries' NARS, which depend on external resources for collaborations, given their own underfunding, more so than in developed countries. These funding prospects must be seen in the larger context in which CGIAR operates and its ability to deliver on promised results.

Several external factors beyond the control of CGIAR in recent years explain its funding challenge: for example, with the huge refugee crisis, the largest human displacement since the Second World War, aid budgets were reallocated to refugee management at home and for the humanitarian crisis abroad in several European countries. In 2017, Syria, Yemen, South Sudan, Somalia, and northern Nigeria each experienced emergency demands for food and other forms of aid. Strong anti-globalization movements that swept Western countries, as reflected in the Brexit vote and the 2016 US election, have also taken a toll on aid budgets. Now, stimulus packages in response to the COVID-19 pandemic and slower growth in OECD countries have stretched their resources. However, these challenges call for a stronger, not weaker CGIAR. As part of the G20 Summit in July 2017, "the Merkel plan" called for more investment in Africa, as a way of stemming the anticipated tide of an estimated 100 million African migrants to Europe if nothing was done, according to the German Foreign Minister Gerd Muller. Chancellor Merkel vowed to invest some US$335 million to attract foreign investors to Africa and vowed to convince the other 19 nations attending the July 2017 G20 summit to show greater commitment to the continent's struggling economies (G20 2017). Although more resources have been committed to Africa in recent years, needs are even greater, as we showed in Chapter 5 on global governance and Chapter 7 on finance.

CGIAR's Need to Adeptly Change and Develop Its Priorities

CGIAR, by its very definition, needs to be able to restate its priorities, based on the rapidly changing science and technology, on the one hand, and the changes in CGIAR:

1. *Climate-smart agriculture*, focusing on urgently needed adaptation and mitigation options for farmers and other resource users.
2. *Genetic improvement* of crops, livestock, fish and trees, to increase productivity, resilience to stress, nutritional value and efficiency of resource use.
3. *Nurturing diversity*, ensuring that CGIAR in-trust plant genetic resources collections are safely maintained, genetically and phenotypically characterized to maximize the exploitation of these critical resources for food security, productivity, nutrient rich crops and resilient farming systems.

4. *Natural resources and ecosystem services*, focusing on productive ecosystems and landscapes that offer significant opportunities to reverse environmental degradation and enhance [sustainable intensification of] productivity.

5. *Gender and inclusive growth*, creating opportunities for women, young people and marginalized groups.

6. *Nutrition and health*, emphasizing dietary diversity, nutritional content and safety of foods, and development of value chains of particular importance for the nutritional benefit of poor consumers.

7. *Agricultural systems*, adopt a systems approach to optimize economic, social and environmental co-benefits in areas with high concentrations of poor people.

8. *Enabling policies and institutions* to improve the performance of markets, enhance delivery of critical public goods and services, and increase the agency and resilience of poor people. (CGIAR 2015b, 4)

These clearly are not operational priorities. Some reviewers of this chapter have argued that the lack of such priorities, operationally defined so that compliance can be enforced, is one of the main reasons that donors are hesitant to provide funding to W1 and W2. They have little idea as to how their funds would be deployed. Has ISPC/ISDC been too timid in setting priorities, or have donors been reluctant to encourage ISPC to set priorities, because they would rather allocate resources according to the wishes of their officials and domestic constituencies?

CGIAR Activities and the Challenge of Alignment with a Proliferation of Global Agendas

The goals and targets of CGIAR's SRF reflect and are aligned with increasing worldwide political convergence on necessary actions to meet the competing demands of global development. CGIAR's new SRF is expected to achieve global ambition, reflected in many different initiatives (CGIAR 2015b): SDGs, United Nations' Zero Hunger Challenge, G8 Nutrition for Growth Compact, the Global Alliance for Climate-Smart Agriculture's (GACSA) commitment, the Bonn Challenge on Landscape Restoration of the International Union for Conservation of Nature (IUCN), and the Aichi Biodiversity Targets of the Convention on Biological Diversity. CGIAR has signed the G8's Nutrition for Growth Compact, which has committed, *inter alia*, to reaching 500 million pregnant women and children with effective nutrition interventions by 2030; preventing at least 20 million children under the age of 5 from having stunted growth; and saving at least 1.7 million lives by reducing stunting, increasing breastfeeding, and treating severe acute undernutrition. CGIAR also cofounded the 2014 Global Alliance for Climate-Smart Agriculture, which has undertaken to reach 500 million farms with climate-smart interventions by 2030.

CGIAR and the Global Conference on Agricultural Research for Development

CGIAR relied upon the Global Conference on Agricultural Research for Development (GCARD), an innovative platform introduced in 2008, to open itself to outside partners, including, in particular, the NARS of developing and developed countries. GCARD 1 in 2010 replaced CGIAR's annual general meeting. A Roadmap, based on a theme paper prepared by Lele et al. (2010) and negotiated heavily by regional organizations and the Global Forum on Agricultural Research (GFAR) Steering Committee, was adopted. The Roadmap clearly needed to evolve over time and be monitored, but like many other such well-intentioned roadmaps, its implementation was never systematically overseen or monitored. The agendas and the participation of stakeholders in subsequent GCARD meetings on the opening of the CGIAR System to outside stakeholders did not materialize. Regional research organizations are weak and do not always represent the interests of disparate national systems of different sizes and clout.

Our interviews of CGIAR stakeholders suggested a loss of confidence in the GCARD process in organizing effective interactions between national and regional stakeholders and CGIAR. GFAR's leadership, in turn, was disappointed that it did not have the opportunity to play an effective role. Whatever the underlying reasons, including leadership and money, it seems GCARD did not realize the potential it held, when CGIAR replaced its annual general meetings with the format of GCARD in 2009, to open itself to global consultations. This is unfortunate but inevitable, because it had no decision-making power and very little influence.

Learning from the lessons of the CPs, CGIAR leadership did not open the leadership of CRPs to non-CGIAR actors, avoiding the creation of competition for the CGIAR Centers. Opening the System could have increased research quality by receiving proposals from developed or emerging countries. The Brazilian Agricultural Research Corporation (EMBRAPA), for example, provides a case of a cutting-edge research program on soils, Bt cotton, and biotechnology and is already engaged in partnership with several African countries (Reifschneider et al. 2016). How well the Brazilian partnership and other such South–South collaborations are working and the strength of their commitments to play roles in multilateral agencies need an independent review to build larger, more inclusive scientist-to-scientist and farmer-to-farmer global partnerships.

SRF Priorities: Disconnect between Stated Priorities and Research Allocation

In the CRP 1 process, Birner and Byerlee (2016, x), in the CGIAR report on the "Synthesis and Lessons Learned from 15 CRP Evaluations," noted that the priorities of the 2010–16 SRF were "so generic that they provided little guidance either to the choice of a CRP portfolio or the relative importance among CRPs within a portfolio. Nonetheless, all evaluations concluded that the CRPs align well with CGIAR SLOs." Further, the Centers built on the ongoing historical legacy research, thus turning to somewhat of an "old wine in a new bottle" approach, not necessarily bringing new science to old research programs or new research programs, except for climate change, which was started in 2003 as a Challenge Program, and the CRP4 on food and nutrition also started as a challenge program HarvestPlus, subsequently incorporated into the broader CRP on Agriculture for Nutrition and Health (A4NH).

Priorities are meaningful if they influence resource allocation, but should the priorities be determined by the size of the "bang for the buck"—that is, return to investment—or driven by what are "desirable outcomes," regardless of whether CGIAR has a comparative advantage in them? There are also other issues in assessing impacts—impacts of germplasm research are relatively easy to measure, whereas those from processes in NRM are difficult to measure. Also, where outcomes materialize only over time, even if CGIAR is not able to achieve them acting alone and certainly not on a large scale, it is not easy to figure out what has been spent against each "priority"—and even harder to do *ex ante* allocations against them.

There are funding problems at various levels. In 2017, funding in W1 and W2 was only one-third of the funding from bilateral donors. Donors provide funding dependent on which objective is appealing to their domestic constituencies, as we show in Chapter 6 on the governance of the Big Five. There is no mechanism to make Centers or donors abide by the priorities or outlaw objectives that do not fall inside the priorities. Priorities have been a well-meaning list—not to be taken literally. Better scientific advice from an independent scientific board may help to improve priorities by having them based more on rapidly advancing science and changing consumer demand.

The Role of the Scientific Advisory Board in Establishing Priorities

CGIAR needs a broad-based, multidisciplinary scientific advisory body with international reputation, equivalent to the National Academies of Sciences of advanced countries, with deep knowledge of development. CGIAR needs scientific advisors with knowledge and expertise in research organizations in advanced and emerging countries, the private sector, and poorest countries that can go outside the traditional CGIAR approaches. One of the recommendations of the Independent Evaluation of ISPC is to do just that, including renaming ISPC to ISDC (CGIAR–IEA 2017). There has been a history of relabeling entities, from TAC to Science Council to ISPC, and now ISDC, but changing functions and behavior remain a challenge. Effective January 1, 2019, the ISDC was established as "an external, impartial standing panel of experts in science and development subject matters (including food systems innovation matters that extend beyond the agricultural sector) appointed by the System Council and accountable to it, with the responsibility of providing rigorous, independent strategic advice to the System Council..." (CGIAR 2018d, 1). Some of our interlocutors remained cautiously pessimistic that this change would not make any difference if the underlying power structure and funding system remains the same.

The Benefits of Opening the CGIAR System to All Qualified Researchers

CGIAR needs to open its System to allow all qualified researchers, whether from the inside or outside the CGIAR System, *to lead* research programs to accelerate delivery of technologies, thereby creating competition and enhancing the quality of research and outreach. This was one of the key recommendations from the Structure and Governance Working Group in 2009, but it faced strong center opposition, and little or no support among donors. SMO states that CRPs have steering committees with a majority of external members, but that is not the same as external researchers conducting research. This has been a contentious issue in CGIAR. Centers are happy to form partnerships, but fear that opening up the System will accelerate its demise, particularly if advanced countries' universities are more at the cutting edge of science, and as the Centers' scientists argue, not necessarily as committed to development objectives, compared to publishing and more resource mobilization.

The Increasing Requirement for Monitoring and Impact Assessment of CGIAR Research Implementation

A monitoring system for the implementation of CGIAR research needs to be established with the monitored output routinely reviewed by an independent scientific body with clout and credibility, and with regular reporting to the CGIAR donors and intended beneficiaries. The monitoring must be done not only for accountability but, more importantly, as a tool of learning, providing feedback information on successes and failures to guide adjustments in research objectives and methods.

Measurement of Impacts and Capacity Development

Approaches to measure both impacts of technology generation and capacity development in institutions need to be strengthened to scale up impacts. In addition to the most recent impact assessment by Alston, Pardey, and Rao (2020), retrospective studies of CGIAR's impacts have attributed 0.7–1.0 percent yield growth annually between 1965 and 2000 to genetic gains, with about half of that attributable to CGIAR (Byerlee 2016). In aggregate, without CGIAR's genetic improvements, world food production would have been 5 percent lower and food prices 18–21 percent higher (Evenson and Gollin 2003; Byerlee 2016). Nearly 90 percent of all the reported gains that CGIAR attributes to its research is attributable to germplasm improvement of rice, wheat, and maize alone and, to a lesser extent, to several other rainfed crops, as well as biological control of cassava mealybugs (see Box A.10.3 in the Appendix).

Questions about Extraordinary CGIAR Impacts

It should be noted that in exhaustive reviews of returns to food and agricultural R&D, new questions have been raised on these extraordinary estimates. Hurley et al. (2016), using 2,829 estimates throughout the world, and Pardey et al. (2016a), reviewing internal rate of return (IRR) estimates and the corresponding 129 BCRs averaged in SSA from 1975 to 2014, have both questioned the credibility of previous estimates:

> The large dispersion in the reported IRRs and BCRs makes it difficult to discern meaningful patterns in the evidence. Moreover, the distribution of IRRs is heavily (positively) skewed, such that the median value...is well below the mean....The weight of commodity-specific evaluation evidence is not especially congruent with the composition of agricultural production throughout Africa, nor, to the best that can be determined, the commodity orientation of public African agricultural R&D. (Pardey et al. 2016a, 1)

Hurley et al. (2016) observed that it is not difficult to see how policymakers may question the credibility of such evidence. In Africa, although Pardey et al. (2016a) found research investment evidence to be worrisomely small, they noted further:

> Many countries throughout SSA are failing to sustain the long-run commitments to investments in [their own] R&D (and associated educational and science-based regulatory capabilities) required to develop the local innovation and institutional capacities that have

been pivotal to the agricultural productivity performance of countries elsewhere in the world. This is in spite of the growing body of IRR and BCR estimates reported here, which suggests that overall, governments throughout the region are continuing to underinvest in research directed to their food and agricultural sectors. (Pardey et al. 2016a, 7)

Observers of African research argue that underfunding of agricultural research in Africa is in part because governments in SSA see the CGIAR Centers as a sufficient substitute for their own NARS. At the end of the chapter, we note this same unintended consequence in many other developing countries, particularly in countries where CGIAR Centers are located.

The impacts of research on policies and on NRM are harder to measure and demonstrate than those of germplasm research. Particularly in the case of NRM research, the focus has to be more on learning and less on end results. IFPRI's research has been widely lauded, and it has been one of the fastest growing research centers, among CGIAR's 15 Centers, suggesting donors believe policy research is important, regardless of the difficulty of garnering evidence on impacts. Despite a flurry of activity, starting around 2007, there has been a distinct lull since in the production of quantitative *ex post* impact assessments of policy-oriented research within CGIAR. Impact assessment is costly in terms of both time and money, so the most obvious explanation for this lull is that from the perspective of CGIAR researchers and administrators managing that research. The costs of meaningfully deriving such quantitative assessments outweigh the benefits that such assessments confer on their institutions (Hazell and Slade 2016; Renkow 2016).

Strengthening Impact Assessment in CGIAR

Currently, a special grant program financed by several of CGIAR's funders supports the SIAC work program of the SPIA, a subgroup of the ISPC. Evaluation of SIAC was meant to "demonstrate accountability to SIAC donors for Phase 1 (2013–2016); and to draw lessons and make recommendations [to] inform the second phase of SIAC and future directions of SPIA" (CGIAR–IEA 2016, vi). The evaluation notes several areas for improvement:

First, the theory of change of SIAC needs revisiting in depth before taking major decisions on the scope and activities of any further phase of SIAC—with a focus on how SIAC activities and outputs can be best designed to lead to institutional strengthening of impact assessment in the CGIAR. Second, more work needs to be done to agree on the comparative advantage of SIAC/SPIA and its priority activities vis-à-vis impact assessment conducted by Centers and CRPs. We believe this is a priority for the forthcoming evaluation of ISPC/SPIA....

Another area for possible improvement is to broaden out external partnerships, in particular to get greater involvement of nationals of countries where the work is taking place....[T]he Fund Council has been unable to exercise effective governance of SPIA/SIAC to date, and...the new System Council [needs to address this] through its "Strategic Impact, Monitoring and Evaluation Committee" and/or through the ISPC. Furthermore,...despite the commitment and hard work of its members, the Project Steering Committee (PSC) is not appropriately composed and configured for either a management or a governance role, and [we] suggest that this be revisited before a second phase. (CGIAR–IEA 2016, vi–vii)

The Development of Theories of Change for CGIAR

The CGIAR System has systematically moved to adopt a theory framework (Box 10.2).

Box 10.2 Theory of Change

"Theory of Change (TOC)—presents an explicit identification of the ways by which change is expected to occur from [intervention to] output to outcome and impact. The TOC questions the assumptions about causality underlying the relationships between [interventions,] outputs, outcomes and impact. In TOC the assumptions present the mechanisms of change. There is no single method or presentational form agreed for TOCs." (ISPC 2012, 2)

This approach is not altogether accidental. The idea of the TOC was conceived in the context of donor-funded development projects, and its application to research proposals have been questioned by many, but its adoption may be explained by the downward drift of CGIAR research (McCalla 2014, 2017; Birner and Byerlee 2016). Some note that TOCs are often done as window dressing to check a box. Moreover, many TOCs share the fatal flaws of the old log frame mindsets from which they have evolved. They ignore the complexity, uncertainty, and nonlinearity of change in a real life context.

TOCs are highly context-specific and require a high degree of participation of all concerned stakeholders to determine if the theory mimics reality closely. If applied carefully, it can stimulate micromanagement of downstream processes beyond the control of CGIAR several years forward. Often, the causal chain is not unidirectional, with much learning involved in achieving ultimate impacts, if what Howard White and David Raitzer (2017) call the "funnel of attrition" is to be avoided.[17] This is why a culture of learning and adaptive management is key. Many unanticipated factors intervene in the adoption process, which affect impacts. Going back to the earlier processes to correct links—for example, inappropriate targeting of nutrition interventions and the mother-in-law factor that White outlined—is typically the role of NARS.[18] We show this schematically in Figure 10.9; see, particularly, the box for site selection of countries. Most importantly, the adoption process takes place in countries at the local and regional level. The approach of the CRPs cannot materialize without the active participation of NARS. Yet, since the reforms started in 2008, our interviews suggested that partnerships with NARS have weakened and, particularly, their participation in the design of CRPs. An enormous amount of time is spent by CGIAR scientists on templates of programs of work and budgets, and reporting with the help of IEA and ISPC/SPIA, piloted in 2017. The intent is to bring annual planning and reporting into closer alignment for the better planning and assessment of program progress toward

---

[17] White and Raitzner (2017, 23) describe funnel attrition: "The motivation behind the funnel is that participation rates and effect sizes diminish along the causal chain, so that final effects are not as large as project designers often envision . . . There may be substantial attrition because exposure is not universal, participation may be partial, behavior change may not always occur, and conditions for full effects may not always be present."

[18] According to White (2014, 6), "And for women in joint households—meaning they live with their mother-in-law—as a sizeable minority do, then the mother-in-law heads the women's domain. Indeed, project participation rates are significantly lower for women living with their mother-in-law in more conservative parts of the country."

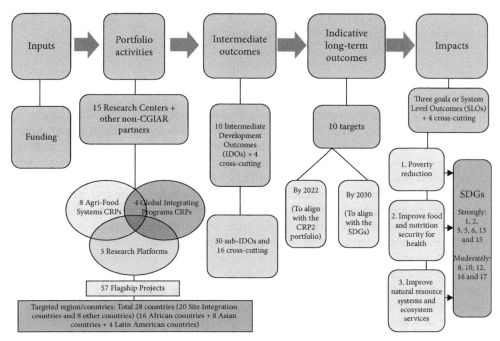

Figure 10.9 CGIAR: Theory of change (TOC)

Source: Authors' depiction.

CGIAR's 2022 targets, for learning and adapting by management and, potentially, for portfolio or resource adjustment in the future. Owing to great funding uncertainties, scientists have been distracted from conducting science, but also this is due to the dependence on bilateral funding, and contrary to when there was more unrestricted funding available without micromanagement and forms to complete so as to report on research. Only a fifth of resources now come from Windows 1 and 2 (see Figure 10.7). Standardization of the language of program descriptions, the common vocabulary of TOCs, CRP/Flagship programs and clusters of activity, annual milestones, outputs, program outcomes, indicators, and targets have become a common language and are providing clarity to administrators in framing research effort and results. The year 2017 was an experimental one for performance management design and implementation, and further improvements to this interim program of work and budget template are being made for 2018, based on recent experience.

For illustrative purposes, we provide a stylized TOC, shown in Figure 10.9. Individual CRPs and their 57 flagship programs, in which the 16 CRPs were divided, involve numerous CRP-specific Intermediate and Sub-Intermediate Outcomes that should lead to SLOs. The major impact pathways should be supported by a thorough and realistic TOC. The independent review process has helped to improve the quality of proposals of the initial four SLOs in the first SRF. The TOC approach has similarly been turned into a mechanistic approach. Our own interviews suggest that a genuine systematic involvement of NARS in a partnership mode on a routine basis is costly. There are no resources for them to engage in partnerships or to conduct the downstream activities needed to realize results on the ground, unless they allocate resources from their own NARS' budgets, which are short of funds, as discussed earlier. Many whom we interviewed have called TOC "window dressing"—a good idea in principle, but one that does not account for the complexity of the innovation process involved in the course of implementation.

A New Vision for CGIAR

CGIAR made a big impact when hunger was the only challenge and an exclusive focus on increasing calorie supply made sense. At midlife, CGIAR has evolved, but it has not nearly reached the transformation needed to respond to the two radical paradigm shifts in agriculture, combined with a highly changed external environment: environmentally sustainable food production and healthy nutritious food for an expanding, urbanizing, and more prosperous population, without leaving behind the billion poor and hungry. These new challenges are accompanied by extraordinary changes in the world. Encapsulated in the fourth industrial revolution, the far-reaching technological changes in scope and speed, and the new tools accompanying them from the emerging countries, have profound implications for how and where food is produced and consumed (Lele and Goswami 2017). Today, meat and milk can be produced without animals, and urban food with vertical farming. Climate change, the growing incidence of obesity, the risk of pandemics, zoonosis, food safety issues, the threat of antimicrobial resistance are all part of the system. To solve problems at scale, we need to harness technologies through markets and public sectors of "the system" to achieve public good based on coordinated global approaches.

Can CGIAR be the prime mover to radiate change out into the community of stakeholders—that is, donors, NARS, nongovernmental organizations (NGOs), national governments, and the private sector—around a new vision beyond hunger eradication, important as that is? Without the large-scale mobilization of all concerned actors, CGIAR will not be able to continue its impact in the future. Why do we believe the time is right for such an initiative? And what would motivate stakeholders to participate around clearly defined objectives? They all should want to be part of the two sets of global goals: namely, the SDGs and climate change mitigation and adaptation.

Some possible objectives of the transformed CGIAR could be:

(1) An expanded dual research agenda on sustainable production food and healthy food consumption with strong health linkages.
(2) A platform for broadly shared, easily accessible information to match supply from a wide range of sources with demand/need.
(3) Large-scale mobilization of talent wherever it exists.
(4) Public–private partnerships/funds to achieve accelerated impact on the quality of the environment and health through science.
(5) The "newly transformed organization" would be a marketplace for matching demand (and need) for technology with the supply of technology generation and delivery. Wadsworth previously described this concept as CGIAR becoming a "chassis" to which the best science from anywhere in the world could be attached and supported.

CGIAR research needs to move upstream to generate essential international and regional public goods of importance to developing countries, which only CGIAR can provide, and offer an alternative proposal based on public–private partnerships. It would be a global movement for collaboration on technology generation and adoption, which CGIAR could spearhead, coordinate, and facilitate to address the downstream challenges of SDG2, eradicating hunger and malnourishment sustainably. It needs to actively and transparently solicit participation of all types of technology providers and users from the public, private, and NGO sectors, including international, regional, and national providers.

Defining CGIAR's Niche Based on Its Comparative Advantage

In a dynamic world, CGIAR needs to clearly define its niche and priorities, based on its comparative advantage and relative to new entrants as providers of technologies, particularly the private sector and emerging countries and research universities.

CGIAR's share in total public and private expenditures on AgR&D has shrunk to 1 percent, down to 1.7 percent of the public expenditures in 2011, from 4 percent in 1999 (Pardey 2017). At the same time, the gap between poor and rich countries for public AgR&D has widened considerably. In per capita terms, the difference has increased from 7.7-fold in 1980 to 11.7-fold in 2011. In 2011, high-income countries spent US$17.73 per person, compared to US$1.51 in LICs. Also, regions of the world experiencing the highest rates of population growth are the places where per capita investment in AgR&D is among the lowest in the world. The population in SSA has nearly tripled since 1980 (372 million) to 1,023 million people today and will increase by 2030 to 1,418 million and by 2050 to 2,168 million. The top 10 countries, however, accounted for 70 percent of AgR&D worldwide in 2011.The bottom 100 countries contributed just 9 percent of their spending in that year's total. These 100 countries include some of the poorest and are home to 22 percent of the world's population (Pardey et al. 2016b, 2016c). So how should public–private roles be viewed?

In the case of the United States, "private R&D is commercially oriented. Companies, which must hold down costs, concentrate R&D funds on research that is likely to result in sales and profits, preferably on research that will lead to intellectual property that can be protected by patents" (NIFA 2004, 48). According to Fuglie et al. (1996, iii): "More than 40 percent of private agricultural R&D budgets is for product development research, compared with less than 7 percent of public agricultural research."

Public sector investments can serve a critical role in promoting innovation in specific areas, where the private sector cannot justify the investment, such as important basic research that may yield benefits only in the longer term (GHI 2011).

Joachim von Braun and Philip G. Pardey noted perceptively in 2006:

> Recent developments in both the developed and developing worlds mean that poor countries may no longer be able to depend as they have in the past on spillovers of new agricultural technologies and knowledge from richer countries, especially advances related to enhanced productivity of staple foods.

> As a consequence of these changes, simply maintaining their current agricultural R&D policies may leave many developing countries as agricultural technology orphans in the decades ahead. Developing countries may have to become more self-reliant and perhaps more dependent on one another for the collective benefits of agricultural R&D and technology. Some of the more advanced [former] developing countries like South Korea, Brazil, China, and India seem to be gaining ground, with productive and self-sustaining local research sectors taking hold. (Foreword by Joachim von Braun, Director General, IFPRI, in Pardey, Alston, and Piggott [2006, xix–xx])

Confirming their observation, India's gross expenditure on R&D in 2015 was about 90 percent of the combined investment of 35 low-income and 55 low-middle-income countries (personal communication, T. Ramasami, July 5, 2017). Evidence specific to the 54 countries of the African continent, including many small and least developed countries, provided by Beintema and Stads (2017) also confirms this story (discussed in Chapter 7 on financing). Further, Reifschneider et al. (2016) described Brazil's partnership with Africa.

Regionally, CGIAR research is concentrated where the majority of the world's poor and hungry live: Africa receives over 50 percent of the investments, Asia receives about 30 percent, and poverty hot spots in Latin America receive about 20 percent. With all the hallmarks of downstream research, CGIAR in its SRF states:

> We must redouble our focus on women and young people, extend our efforts to improve dietary quality among the poor and vulnerable, and intensify our work on climate-smart agriculture—all given new prominence in our research agenda. At the same time we will continue to build on our long record of achievement in research to improve the productivity of staple foods, livestock and fish, and to restore and protect the natural resources used to produce them—our traditional areas of strength. (CGIAR 2015b, 1)

CGIAR's demonstrated traditional strengths, however, have not been in gender or NRM, and going forward they cannot be realized without CGIAR putting some of its own money where it says its priorities are and engaging in active, long-term, high-quality partnerships with NARS, as shown in the Appendix.

The SRF makes clear the research program "reflects the collective expectations of the donor community" (CGIAR 2015b, 1). It lacks an exploration of the rapidly changing science—how it is currently incorporated into CGIAR's research and its implications for CGIAR strategy going forward. Similarly, the SRF lacks a discussion of the objective reality in developing countries, such as the changing structure of agriculture with the dual growth of unviable holdings and the rising role of commercial farmers. How it will focus on the reduction of hunger and poverty is unclear. Malnourishment and the growing incidence of micronutrient deficiencies are now substantially larger and a faster growing problem than that of hunger (filling the calorie gap by increasing supply, which has been CGIAR's demonstrated impact, rather than improving or changing consumption). The newer need for diversification of diets calls also for diversification of farming systems and NRM—going beyond research on traditional cereals and roots and tubers, which has been CGIAR's forte. CGIAR's focus on biofortification of many crops provides a powerful strategy (discussed in Box A.10.2 in the Appendix), as well as on value chains (again, an area in which its research has been very limited).

Recognizing Strengths, Weaknesses, Opportunities, and Threats: A SWOT Analysis

SWOT analysis of Strengths, Weaknesses, Opportunities, and Threats will help us summarize the preceding discussion in the chapter of the global research system, thus allowing us to evaluate these four elements as an input into structured planning.

Strengths

CGIAR is the logical candidate to operate a global platform, as the largest (US$1 billion) global research network with a presence in more than 70 countries and supported by 65 principal donors It has the largest collection of germplasm, a well-proven track record in increasing food security and nutrition, providing policy research, and fostering institutional development. It undertakes research on some of the major commodities and natural resources of forestry and agroforestry, soils, water, and climate change. It is engaged in thousands of partnerships with research and development institutions at the global, regional, and national levels throughout the developing world. Some of these partnerships are genuine, and others are ghost partnerships. CGIAR has a demonstrated track record of impact, trust, and credibility, and it is one of the Big Five international organizations concerned with food and agriculture, with long-standing partnerships. (See Box A.10.2 in the Appendix on CGIAR's achievements.)

Weaknesses

CGIAR's research funding of less than US$1 billion is not nearly enough to make a dent on poverty and hunger among a billion people, most of them women and children. There is a huge funding gap at the national level and in CGIAR. Most important is the deficit of political commitment and leadership at all levels. The original intent in establishing CGIAR in 1971, was that all countries would develop effective NARS within 20–30 years, and indeed, the Rockefeller Foundation and USAID in the 1960s and 1970s and the World Bank in the 1980s worked actively toward this goal by investing in agricultural research and educational institutions at the national level and supporting regional organizations. CGIAR has built capacity mainly through collaborative research involving NARS partners and establishing research networks. Bilateral and multilateral organizations and, particularly, investments by the United States in universities have strengthened institutions at the national and subnational levels. Donor interest in institution building has declined, however. It is a long-term task, whereas donors have increasingly shorter time horizons, and often, political commitment is lacking in developing countries where such attempts were made and where a strong sense of ownership is critical to sustain efforts. Countries go through cycles—India had strong political commitment when it was in a food deficit status. In Ethiopia, the University of Oklahoma was engaged in an attempt to build Haramaya College in the 1950s. After a series of ups and downs in the new millennium, Ethiopia is taking its AgR&D seriously with good outcomes (Bachewe et al. 2018).

One objective of this networked platform would be to "leave no NARS behind"—with a serious intent to graduate some NARS into quality NARS—like that of China, Brazil, and India, or smaller ones, like those of Chile or Uruguay—while choices will have to be made about which NARS have the capacity and scale to graduate into lead research organizations, and which ones should develop advanced capacities to select, borrow, and adapt technologies developed by others, and also to establish global norms and standards for scientific partnerships. If we do not aspire for something big, we will not get there.

Under the Comprehensive Africa Agriculture Development Programme (CAADP), African policymakers undertook to allocate 10 percent of their national budgets to the agricultural sector, with a growth of 6 percent annually, but, in reality, only a few have done so—an argument that the former president of IFAD, Kanayo Nwanze, emphasized at the Malabo summit in an open letter to the African Union heads of state (see more discussion in Chapter 4 on food security and Chapter 7 on financing) (Nwanze 2014).

Donor expectations from CGIAR are unrealistic. The funding remains fragmented and unpredictable, more focused on development and less on basic and strategic research, while the scope and ambition of its research has expanded. Not surprisingly, partnerships with lagging developing countries—those with large incidence of hunger—are far weaker today than they were in the 1970s and 1980s. Despite 55 percent of CGIAR's research effort already in Africa, the impacts there have been modest. Donors have become obsessed with targets and performance that is tangible, visible, and can be measured each year, thus dealing with the symptoms rather than the underlying causes of limited performance. Africa's research challenges are great, and its research systems are weak and fragmented, with great underinvestment. The spectacular successes of biological control of the cassava mealybug, dryland maize, orphan crops, and, more recently, biofortified orange-fleshed sweet potatoes and some varieties of rainfed rice show that there is huge unrealized potential. Unlike in Asia, CGIAR has not been able to devolve applied and adaptive research downstream to African countries, or to regional organizations in cases where NARS are too weak or too small, under-resourced, and face diseconomies of scale because of prolonged underinvestment in agricultural R&D. Even in Asia, there is greater scope for NARS, such as India's efforts to be more effective, and context for CGIAR to follow the principle of subsidiarity: that is, using an organizing principle that posits that activities should be handled by the lowest or least centralized competent authority. This principle will recognize the greater role of NARS, and World Bank loans and credits could proactively promote NARS–CGIAR collaborations.

Opportunities

Agriculture is key to growth. GDP growth in SSA slowed sharply to 1.2 percent in 2016, down from 4.8 percent in 2013—the lowest level of growth in more than two decades. The World Bank forecasts an increase in growth to 2.6 percent in 2017, to 3.2 percent in 2018 in SSA, predicated on moderately rising commodity prices and reforms to tackle macroeconomic imbalances. Per capita output is projected to shrink by 0.1 percent in 2017, and to increase to a modest 0.7 percent pace of growth over 2018–19. At these rates, growth will be insufficient to achieve poverty reduction goals in the region, particularly if constraints to more vigorous growth persist (WBG 2017).

Per capita income growth was negative, –1.5 percent in 2016, weighed down by population growth (2.7 percent in 2016). Positive per capita income growth returned in 2017, 2018, and in 2019. An important contributor to the slower growth in both GDP and agriculture was conflict and climate change in several major African countries. There is variation across countries, particularly between resource-rich and resource-poor countries, but overall, the region's economic growth trend remains below pre-financial crisis levels, with greater inequality than anywhere else in the world. Slower growth deepens the challenge of reducing poverty. Despite progress, the share of the population living on US$1.90 a day or less remains very high, estimated at 41 percent in 2013, and has increased by 112 million since 1990, although the prevalence has declined from 54 percent (World Bank 2020).

Science is advancing very rapidly, and to keep pace and maintain relevance, CGIAR must have access to cutting-edge scientific infrastructure and scientific skills by augmenting North–South and South–South collaborations—thereby increasing ownership of and access to developing countries' farmers and consumers, with increased transparency, accountability for results, and on a scale that even CGIAR's expanded research program cannot realistically provide. Underinvestment in CGIAR and NARS remains widespread. Although agricultural research spending in SSA grew by nearly 50 percent between 2000 and 2014, the accumulated backlog of underinvestment in research and education is so considerable that it would take years of consistent effort to build capacity, even if investment in R&D increased considerably (Traxler 2004; Blackie et al. 2010). Thirty-three out of 40 countries (for which data were available to Beintema and Stads [2017]) spent less than 1 percent of their AgGDP on agricultural research. Across SSA, although the numbers of agricultural researchers increased by 70 percent during 2000–14, the very large share of senior, PhD-qualified researchers approaching retirement is a problem. Without adequate succession strategies and training, significant knowledge gaps will emerge.

Threats

The gap between new science needing human resource capacity to take the science forward is widening rapidly over time both at the national level and the level of CGIAR, and the drop-off of current cohorts of trained staff in Africa will be exponential, as a large proportion reach retirement in next 5–10 years (ASTI, IFPRI, and FARA 2011). Education systems and capacity development of young researchers needs to be revamped in NARS, and both need much more investment. A number of crosscutting issues are in need of resources to address. For example, issues involving gender and youth; data management; monitoring, evaluation, and learning (MEL); and capacity development have to be incorporated within the allocated resources of a scientific project, and the resources are stretched very thinly for that process in most projects. Therefore, additional investments are needed in support of these crosscutting aspects.

Threats to CGIAR are caused by donor policies and changes in donor priorities that lead, in turn, to CGIAR's inability to attract and retain qualified experienced staff.

Donor dependence and funding volatility also remain critical in Africa. Outdated research facilities and equipment impede the conduct of productive research, compromising the number and quality of research outputs, ultimately translating into reduced impacts. Again, the issues with small NARS LICs are not new. External support for African agriculture and African NARS was considerable in the 1970s, then declined precipitously, but now seems to be on a growth trajectory again. However, at the recent rate of growth in African research expenditures, it will take years to get back to the old level.

It is time to rethink how to leverage limited CGIAR resources to have a far larger impact on SSA, by pursuing a consistent, long-term, predictable strategy, more along the lines of what the Rockefeller Foundation pursued in India to help achieve a Green Revolution, albeit using recent technologies and tools more appropriate to Africa—beyond the misnomer of the Green Revolution.

Key Perspectives for a Transformed CGIAR

CGIAR's entire Global Platform in 2020 consisted of the CGIAR Portfolio of 2017–22, of the 12 CRPs and 3 research support platforms plus the newly launched gender platform that underpin the research of the whole System. The CRP is restricted by legacy activities of the past 40+ years. There is a huge gap in research on vegetables, fruits, and nuts (that should compose 50 percent of our daily diets for health and nutrition). There are hundreds of young start-up enterprises, using new technology—for example, dairy and meat industries without cows, vertical farming, insect farming (for animal and human feed), microbes, and bacteria, etc. Many of these venture capital-based enterprises will fail, often lacking sufficient capital and access to other delivery mechanisms. Some will go on to set the pace. They are unlikely to have the public good at heart; some may even create considerable unemployment in agriculture—thus, CGIAR and others need to be in these emerging spaces and new tech fields to conduct public goods research as a counterweight to commercial disruptive research with consequences for environment, the poor, and disadvantaged.

From such a perspective, some of CGIAR's new initiatives are promising: big data in agriculture, excellence in breeding, and gene banks to conserve and make available 750,000 accessions of crops and trees under the International Plant Treaty, thereby improving efficiency, enhancing use, and ensuring compliance with international policy. Also, there are four crosscutting themes (Climate Change, Gender and Youth, Policies and Institutions, and Capacity Development), which are intended to interact closely together and with the CRPs to leverage best practices across the portfolio. The platform will include many other actors, however, with whom CGIAR and NARS will collaborate. The following list is illustrative, rather than comprehensive.

There are a large number of bilateral donors, international and regional organizations, philanthropic organizations such as BMGF's Alliance for a Green Revolution in Africa (AGRA), universities in advanced countries, and NARS of emerging countries. NARS of large emerging countries such as China, Brazil, and India already play a significant role through South–South collaboration bilaterally—but much is bureaucratic and political, and not results-oriented—or through triangulated arrangements involving multilateral or UN organizations, such as WFP and a strengthened FAO, along the lines recommended. They should be invited to be a part of a global network, led by CGIAR. This will entail a very substantial and different partnership effort than exists today.

AGRA, established by BMGF and the Rockefeller Foundation in 2006, has already given 778 grants to 18 countries for agricultural development, with a total commitment of US$430 million between 2006 and 2016. Building on the systems and tools for Africa's agriculture—quality seeds, soil health, access to markets, and credit—coupled with stronger farmer organizations and agricultural policies, countries have gained experience in a decade working with AGRA in many areas: strengthening agricultural input systems; technology and its adoption; building resilience through growth of structured markets for quality produce and operational capacity of output systems; strengthening business growth, finance, and risk management in national- and regional-level systems; and reducing impact of agricultural volatility. Unfortunately, no independent evaluation of AGRA activities is available to the public, despite a decade of aid, unlike the aid by multilateral organizations that undergo independent impact evaluations, which even BMGF has often actively supported for external aid (AGRA 2016b). AGRA has also worked with the University of KwaZulu-Natal's African Center for Crop Improvement (ACCI) and with the West African Center for Crop Improvement (WACCI) of the University of Ghana, Legon, to train hundreds of NARS breeders from across the continent in applied breeding methods. On the less positive side, organizational constraints have siloed their programs, making it difficult for them to deliver integrated programs of support to individual countries and subregions in which work on crops, soils, and markets are brought together synergistically for greater impact and sustainability. AGRA is moving in this direction, but we are not aware of the actual progress.

More than US$30 Billion Expected in Commitment to African Agriculture

At the sixth African Green Revolution Forum in September 2016, AGRA announced commitments totaling more than US$30 billion to boost production, income, and employment for smallholder farmers and agricultural businesses on the African continent over the next 10 years. The initiative is backed by the African Union Commission, the New Partnership for Africa's Development (NEPAD), AfDB, AGRA, key NGOs, companies, and donor countries.

As part of the "Feed Africa" campaign, AfDB has committed US$24 billion over 10 years—a 400 percent increase over its previous commitments—to help drive agricultural transformation on the continent. Through the flagship program called the Technologies for African Agricultural Transformation (TAAT), the AfDB works with CGIAR to support the "Feed Africa" campaign by providing the needed and proven agricultural and food processing technologies and implementation strategies for inclusion within the Bank's loans to Regional Member Countries (RMCs). BMGF pledged at least US$5 billion to development initiatives on the continent over the next five years, including at least US$1 billion for agriculture, with a focus on the Foundation's ongoing efforts to "expand crop and livestock research, strengthen data collection for decision-making, and improve systems to deliver better tools, information and innovations for farmers" (AGRA 2016a). The Foundation also pledged to match other development partner support for AGRA programs on a one-to-one basis. AGRA's links to CGIAR are not clear, although BMGF is one of the largest donors to CGIAR (Wadsworth 2016). The original position of AGRA was that NARS were grossly underfunded and needed more support than the CGIAR Centers.

The Rockefeller Foundation announced US$50 million in new funding, in addition to US$105 already committed to AGRA. In addition, the Foundation committed US$130 million to the YieldWise initiative: "work directed by AGRA and other partners that is deploying better storage, handling and processing capabilities to reduce the significant post-harvest losses on African farms due [to] spoilage or pests" (AGRA 2016a). IFAD pledged more than US$3 billion to Africa, with a focus on efforts to generate jobs in farming and food production and value chains, particularly for African youth and African women. And WFP pledged to purchase at least US$120 million of the agricultural products that it distributes annually—10 percent of its annual procurement budget—from smallholder farmers through a partnership called the Patient Procurement Platform (AGRA 2016a).

In a single fiscal year, the World Bank approved US$9.3 billion (20 percent of its total commitment) for Africa for 109 projects in 2016–17. This amount includes US$669 million in IBRD loans and US$8.7 billion in IDA commitments, of which US$200 million was from the IDA Scale-up Facility. "Key focus areas include raising agricultural productivity, increasing access to affordable and reliable energy, building resilience to climate change, strengthening fragile and conflict-affected areas, and promoting good-quality education" (World Bank 2016, 24). Procurement issues would need to be addressed.

South–South Research Cooperation Is Thriving

Thriving South–South cooperation is not always viewed favorably by Northern actors. It seems to be partly a result of apprehension and competition, partly a genuine sense of superiority about Western modes of bilateral cooperation, and partly a lack of knowledge. It might be well worth doing systematic comparative studies of how Northern and Southern countries cooperate in order to identify their strengths and weaknesses, because cooperation is here to stay and should grow.

In the *Agricultural Innovation Marketplace*, Reifschneider et al. (2016) described the South–South collaboration established by Brazil's EMBRAPA with African countries in an upbeat, optimistic way. Since 2010, the Africa–Brazil Agricultural Innovation Marketplace (MKTPlace) has implemented 82 projects around the world. A new program, *Building on the Successes of the Marketplace* (M-BoSs), was developed; it focuses on previously fruitful MKTPlace projects in order to provide extended financing and wider adoption of positive practices. The MKTPlace has been supported by an open group of some of the same partners that have made cash and in-kind contributions totaling approximately US$21 million. Partners include: FARA, Inter-American Institute for Cooperation on Agriculture (IICA), EMBRAPA, the Brazilian Cooperation Agency of the Ministry of Foreign Relations of Brazil (ABC/MRE), UK's DFID, BMGF, IFAD, the World Bank, FAO, and the Inter-American Development Bank (IDB). MKTPlace has organized four major international events, several partner policy dialogues, and funded 82 R&D projects, with 42 under implementation. It has also paved the way for successful projects to be scaled up through the new joint initiative, M-BoSs, which has already mobilized over US$9 million (Reifschneider et al. 2016).

China and India each have substantial bilateral and trilateral programs on the continent of Africa, including collaboration in agriculture and climate change. The launching of a new agriculture partnership (Feed the Future–India Triangular Training Program [FTF–ITT]) between the United States and India was announced in July 2016, "to achieve Ever Green Revolution to address Global Food Security" (Government of India 2016). Originally announced during a state visit by then US President Barack Obama to India in November 2010, this collaboration sought to establish a long-term farmer-to-farmer exchange. According to the Indian Ministry of Agriculture's press bureau, "The effort included Triangular Cooperation adapting technological advances and innovative solutions to address Food Security Challenges in Africa. This pilot stage focused on three African Countries i.e., Kenya, Liberia and Malawi with potential to expand throughout the African Continent in [the] future" (Government of India 2016). South Korea and Taiwan similarly have cooperation on rice with Africa.

Such a platform will enhance the Northern donors' gradual efforts to (1) overcome fragmented, North–South bilateral aid to African agriculture and research; (2) greatly complement the allocation of over 50 percent of the CGIAR research expenditures to SSA around a strategic framework; and (3) strengthen applied and adaptive research downstream, which ideally NARS should conduct. Most importantly, it will greatly enhance CGIAR's impacts on two major continents.

CGIAR's 2020 Reforms

CGIAR underwent reorganization once again in 2019–21, at a time when this chapter was being finalized. Box 10.3 contains the key elements of reforms. Proposed reforms build on the changes already made to System governance in 2016 (and indeed, some instituted well before for nearly two decades, as the history of CGIAR outlined in this chapter illustrates). Ambitious in their nature and described as the biggest change in CGIAR's history by some, the SRG's vision for "One CGIAR" is that of a global leader and recognized brand, both of which CGIAR already possesses, but the proposal seems to be to do more and better through five interconnected elements (CGIAR 2019d).

Box 10.3 Five Key Elements of CGIAR's Proposed Reforms

---

1. One Mission: Ending Hunger by 2030—through science to transform food, land, and water systems in a climate crisis, focused on nutrition, poverty, gender, climate, and environment. Target date: 2030, to be reflected in agreed mission, by end of 2020.
2. Unified governance—Common Board to provide unified governance. Target date: July 1, 2020.
3. Institutional integration:
   a. Integrated operational structure—three managing directors in place by April 2020
   b. One CGIAR policies and services. Target date: 2021–2
   c. One CGIAR at the country and regional level. Target date: End 2020.
4. New research modality. Target date: January 2022.
5. More and pooled funding: 50 percent pooled funding to be achieved by end of 2022.

Source: CGIAR (2019e, 4–5).

In June 2020, CGIAR announced the appointment of its inaugural CGIAR EMT, composed of three Managing Directors who are collectively charged with stewarding the creation of a more unified "One CGIAR"—a CGIAR that is impactful partner for our funders, national research systems, the agricultural community, and global and regional agencies.

The Executive Management Team consists of, first, a Team Convener and Managing Director, Research Delivery and Impact. A second Managing Director is responsible for Institutional Strategy and Systems, and a third Managing Director is responsible for Global Engagement and Innovation (CGIAR 2020c).

Two of the three appointees are highly experienced women. Collectively, the three bring demonstrated experience in transforming the way that institutions think, work, and partner. The appointments are another key implementation step, of the unanimous decision taken by CGIAR's SC in November 2019, to endorse a bold set of recommendations to create One CGIAR. These recommendations, developed by CGIAR together with its funders and partners, outline the key elements of a unified One CGIAR (CGIAR 2019e, 2020c):[19]

1. A sharper mission statement and impact focus to 2030, aligned with the SDGs;
2. Unified governance under a "CGIAR System Board";
3. Institutional integration, including more aligned management under an empowered EMT, common policies and services, and a unified country and regional presence;
4. A new research modality; and
5. More, and pooled, funding.

---

[19] See, also, "CGIAR System Reference Group," https://www.cgiar.org/how-we-work/strategy/cgiar-system-reference-group/

One CGIAR's New Mission is "Ending hunger by 2030—through science to transform food, land and water systems in a climate crisis," focused on five impact areas: (1) nutrition and food security; (2) poverty reduction, livelihoods, and jobs; (3) gender equality, youth, and social inclusion; (4) climate adaptation and greenhouse gas reduction; and (5) environmental health and& biodiversity (CGIAR 2019e, 8).

These are high expectations from CGIAR to chart a new course for CGIAR—based on the extensive leadership experience, complementary skills, and access to scientific expertise and resources—to ensure that CGIAR can deliver on its mission of ending hunger by 2030.

One CGIAR is expected to be much more than the sum of its parts, "reaching out across CGIAR with a systems lens, listening to and working with the Director Generals and scientists of every Center to bring CGIAR's incredible expertise, partnerships, and resources together to deliver innovation on the ground and impact at a systems level" (CGIAR 2020c).

The inaugural EMT was appointed for an initial term of two years to drive transformational change at pace and report collectively to the SMB. "A key element of its role will be to identify how to best leverage CGIAR's nearly 10,000-strong staff and its diversity of talent and brands to deliver as One CGIAR" (CGIAR 2020c).

The new CGIAR System Board, with 50 percent male/female representation has broad diversity across eight voting members. Center boards are represented by this common slate of members with a minimum two-thirds majority. Centers were in process of changing their Charters to adopt new Board construct, expected October 2020.[20]

As part of reforms CGIAR has adopted US$2 billion as an aspirational target by 2030, targeting a sustainable US$2 billion investment in research (CGIAR 2020c). CGIAR held public consultation on its Research Strategy from October 16–26, 2020, and this will be shared to a targeted group of partners and open for feedback on *cgiar.org*.

Based on various recent reports, CGIAR has assumed that there is strong evidence of global will for an improved CGIAR. It cites the 2019 EAT-*Lancet* report (Willett et al. 2019); the IPCC Report to the 2019 UN Climate Action Summit (IPCC 2019); key themes on food systems presented at the 2020 World Economic Forum (WEF 2020); Global Nutrition Report (GNR 2020), and related planning discussions for the 2021 UN Food Systems Summit (UN 2020a, 2020b).

As an integral part of the CGIAR System and the governance body of the CGIAR System Organization, the CGIAR System Board ("System Board"), comprising eight Voting members, two Ex-Officio Non-Voting members and six Active observers, is responsible for providing leadership and governance for CGIAR in the delivery of its mission, and for appointing and overseeing the Executive Management Team.

Working in partnership with the CGIAR SC, the System Board keeps under review the effectiveness of the CGIAR System, its reputation for excellence, and adopts and monitors compliance with CGIAR policies, procedures and guidelines, with a view to ensuring results and the continued relevance of CGIAR's agricultural research for development.

The System Board may recommend actions that may be considered to better respond to the evolving challenges of international agricultural research, taking into account any recommendations of the SC.

---

[20] For more information, see "CGIAR System Board," https://www.cgiar.org/how-we-work/governance/system-organization/system-board/

Appendix: Mainstreaming Gender Platform—An Example of Collective Action Challenge in CGIAR

Increased incomes in the hands of women and their greater control of assets is known to increase their decision-making power, their productivity, food security, and nutritional outcomes, as well as the outcomes for their children. Societal preferences and norms about gender influence women's participation in household decision-making, processes of technological change in agriculture, and women's opportunities to work outside their homes. Women comprise nearly half of the world's agricultural labor force, yet their unequal access to economic opportunities results in less benefits to them than to men from their participation. Also, persistent gender gaps in access to resources and markets and in decision-making are widely understood in the development literature as a constraint on overall agricultural productivity and growth and as factors contributing to the persistence of hunger and undernutrition, with adverse impacts on children, such as underweight, high infant and child mortality, stunting and wasting—all with life-cycle effects on future generations. We explored some of these issues in Chapter 4.

Here, we showed that CGIAR's research on gender received a kickstart from the 2008 External Review, including its mainstreaming and outreach. CGIAR has produced a considerable body of research, but the progress has been slow and uneven across Centers, halting and scattered due to lack of a coherent strategic vision and collective action challenges, and reinforced by shortage of funding. In 2020, CGIAR finally launched a crosscutting gender platform, much as it has done with other such platforms. Whether it will lead to a coherent program will depend on the platform leader providing strategic direction and leadership, combined with predictable resources to the program.

Research must be distinguished from other gender-related programs in CGIAR, which have an early history. They are not covered here—for example, CGIAR's Gender & Diversity Program and a program on Gender, Diversity Inclusion in Workplaces in CGIAR. Both started in the 1980s.[21]

Post-2008 History of Gender Research

The CGIAR Independent Review Panel Report of 2008 noted that the CGIAR System had not built "on best practice institutional accountability approaches to mainstream gender and to devise special measures, where necessary, to address the specific needs of women and girls" (CGIAR 2008, 4). The Review Panel Report of the CGIAR System devoted an entire chapter (chapter 4) to the issues of gender and diversity, and recommended that "the Consortium and the Fund adopt a gender strategy based on accountability for integrating gender in the work of partnerships" (CGIAR 2008, 12).

This does not mean that CGIAR was not addressing gender issues in the 1980s and 1990s. For example, Joachim von Braun published several important pieces of research on commercialization of agriculture, food aid, and famines in which gender was one of several dimensions, and therefore, that research did not get "tagged" as gender research, with some exceptions—for example, his research on The Gambia.[22] Agnes Quisumbing's research on property rights, and Ashby's research on participatory technology development and adoption at CIAT also included treatment of gender, but such research declined because of lack of funding and attrition of qualified staff (see, for example, Quisumbing and Kumar [2014]; Lilja and Ashby [1999]).

---

[21] Based on email exchange with Vicki Wilde, who became the first director of the Gender and Diversity program in 1999. In 2017, the CGIAR conducted an independent review of its history of work in this area. For the CGIAR's new Framework for Gender, Diversity and Inclusion in CGIAR's Workplaces, see CGIAR (2020d), and for the approved Action Plan for Gender, Diversity and Inclusion in CGIAR's Workplaces (2020–2021), see CGIAR (2020a).

[22] Some of the examples of this research include:
On commercialization: von Braun, Hotchkiss, and Immink (1989); von Braun, Puetz, and Webb (1989); von Braun and Webb (1989); von Braun, de Haen, and Blanken (1991); von Braun and Kennedy (1994). On famine: Webb and von Braun (1994); von Braun, Teklu, and Webb (1998).

Recent evidence suggests that mainstreaming across CGIAR is occurring in number of places. CGIAR's CRPs use "OECD–DAC gender equality policy markers" (OECD 2016) to classify CGIAR research outcomes. (CGIAR 2018b, 11, 42). CRPs have been reporting on these markers to the System Management Organization annually since 2017, providing independent verification of the supporting evidence. The proportion of reported research outcomes in which gender was recorded as "significant" increased from 16 percent in 2017 to 33 percent in 2019. Conversely, the proportion of outcomes in which gender was recorded as "not targeted" fell from 77 percent in 2017 to 57 percent in 2019 (information courtesy of CGIAR SMO and Programs).[23]

Recently, three independent reviews of CRPs—namely, of A4NH, Wheat and Grain Legumes, and Dryland Cereals—also confirm these findings of greater treatment of gender (CAS Secretariat 2020a, 2020b, 2020c), but it has taken a long time to get to this point because of collective action problems within CGIAR.

In 2009, following the external review's findings of the CGIAR Independent Review Panel in 2008 of inattention to gender (CGIAR 2008), Canada's International Development Research Centre (IDRC) funded IFPRI to conduct a consultation about what should be done—whether there should be a "gender program" like the four other CRPs then funded: Climate Change, HarvestPlus, Water for Food, and Sub-Saharan Africa. A structured e-consultation at each Center, followed by a longer discussion, came up with the recommendation for a platform that would support gender across all the CRPs, but one of the Center directors (of CIP, headed by a woman) opposed the idea, arguing that gender work would divert resources away from the CRPs. Although her male counterparts among Center directors supported the idea, the SMB dropped it. So, the CRPs proceeded without any requirement for gender. Yet, every time the issue of gender was raised, the then ISPC expected gender specialists in CGIAR to address the issue, but without assigning any resources.

The gender mainstreaming assessment of CRPs in 2013 (Assessment of the Status of Gender Mainstreaming in CRPs commissioned by the FC and submitted by the CO at the FC 10th meeting, Nairobi, November 6–7, 2013) noted that the reform of CGIAR, following the 2008 external evaluation, had not tackled the problems identified by the "Stripe Review on Social Sciences": namely, the weaknesses of the social science capacity (Barrett et al. 2009; Ashby, Lubbock, and Stuart 2013). And those issues continued to prevail in gender research in 2013. Mainstreaming gender effectively into CGIAR research depended fundamentally on strong social science and the appropriate mix of disciplines. While that assessment looked at the integration of gender into CRPs, the context, the status, and the use of social science in CGIAR had not improved.

ISPC suggested the gender platform be housed in PIM (a CRP called Policy, Institutions and Markets, an entity that was certain to be funded), rather than as a separate platform (with no history in CGIAR and possibly more uncertain budget). However, fund allocation rules soon handcuffed the gender platform while others were able to thrive. Ashby, Lubbock, and Stuart (2013) noted that allocated funds were divided in 13 Centers, and the precise source and certainty of amounts are unclear from the reporting. Some CRPs earmarked a significant percentage of their total budget for gender, while others provided little (as shown in Ashby, Lubbock, and Stuart 2013, 16, table 2).

Thus, whereas in 2012–13, most CRPs did not include gender in their original proposals or budgets, CRPs varied greatly as to the extent to which gender was mainstreamed. Those CRPs relatively advanced in gender implementation were the research programs concerning Aquatic Agricultural Systems (AAS); Policies, Institutions and Markets (PIM); Agriculture for Nutrition and Health (A4HN); Climate Change; Agriculture and Food Security (CCAFS); and Forests, Trees and Agroforestry (FTA). These CRPs prioritized research themes and defined sites to undertake gender-relevant research and data collection.

Although the CO expected CRPs to mainstream gender in their own programs, it recruited a senior advisor on gender in research in its own office in 2013. She, in turn, established standards for integration of gender in all of the CRPs, an important contribution.

The notion of a Gender Platform was proposed as early as April 2010 by gender experts within CGIAR, when the CRPs were being set up, and again in 2015, when three platforms—the Big Data Platform, Excellence in Breeding, and Gene Bank—were approved. To qualify as a platform, a

---

[23] I am grateful to Julia Compton for mustering this evidence.

program had to work across Centers around common themes and also involve external partners. In principle, the gender program qualified on those grounds.[24]

Yet, in 2015, for the CO's call for proposals for platforms on various topics, including gender, gender outcomes were not among the 10 core intermediate development outcomes (IDOS) in CGIAR's SRF, approved May 2015 for implementation in the 2016–30 period. Gender was among the four "cross-cutting" outcomes. That helped to set the stage for more serious attention to gender in impact pathways, and 2022 outcome targets and milestones. Also, annual reporting on gender findings and outcomes was formalized. Most platforms were turned down, with only Big Data, Excellence in Breeding, and Gene Banks accepted. A full gender proposal was not accepted. ISPC asked PIM to host a gender platform as part of Phase 2 of the CRPs (starting in 2016), as a flagship platform on Gender, without the responsibility and financial resources to support gender across the whole System. PIM contracted two external specialists in gender to lead the Gender flagship program. The PIM Gender flagship had two clusters, one of which was the gender platform, coordinated by the Royal Tropical Institute (KIT). The other was a PIM research-focused cluster led by an IFPRI staff member, and the larger flagship was led by faculty at University of Oxford.

The 2016–17 Independent Evaluation of Gender in CGAIR, IEA (CGIAR–IEA 2017) focused on CRPs for the period 2011–16, but considered the new framework of the second phase of CRPs and substantial changes to the overall governance architecture of CGIAR during 2016.

Evolution of the CGIAR SRF is evident from these SRFs. The 2010–15 SRF identified gender inequality as a critical area that directly affects CGIAR's likelihood of success in all areas (CGIAR 2011d), but the 2016–30 SRF made an explicit commitment to tackle gender equity throughout CGIAR, including by closing the gender gap in equitable access to resources, information, and power in the agri-food system by 2030 (CGIAR 2015b). Women featured as 50 percent of the targets for 2010–15 SRF System-Level Outcomes and specific targets to reduce women's micronutrient malnutrition. Additionally, "gender and inclusive growth" became one of eight strategic research priority areas (CGIAR 2011d). (See discussion on CGIAR priorities, Table 10.1.)

The "Evaluation of Gender in CGIAR" was the first independent, System-wide evaluation on this topic. It turned out to be timely and influential. Its main purposes were:

• accountability to the CGIAR system as a whole on progress at system, Center, and CRP levels: in developing appropriate gender strategies in pursuit of the objectives contained in the SRFs; integrating gender analysis in their research and engaging in appropriate gender research and impact analysis; and in achieving *gender equity and inclusiveness at the workplace* [emphasis added]. (Baden et al. 2017)

While a single evaluation covering both gender in research and gender at the workplace was first envisaged, both contributing to the common objective of gender equity, the distinct set of issues and actors of these two led to different impact pathways. The evaluation noted the significant progress towards gender equity, attributing it at least in part to pressure from key System donors. Key institutions were strengthened, and gender mainstreaming was incorporated across all research programs, resulting in a growing body of gender research, but with different degrees of treatment and different quality of research, due, in part, to differences in the extent and quality of gender staffing. It called for renewed System-level leadership and an updated framework that reflects a clear System-level commitment on both gender in CGIAR research and at the workplace, the appropriate balance of effort and investment between gender-specific research, capacity building, and mainstreaming (or integration of gender) across different flagships (Baden et al. 2017).

The evaluation noted, however, that using gender analysis to inform overall priority setting remains a key challenge. It recognized that for those CRPs with more limited resources and capacities investments in gender-specific research will require collaboration with other CRPs with shared interests and more experience, and/or with specialist strategic partners (Baden et al. 2017).

The evaluation noted that cross-CRP collaboration and learning was needed:

---

[24] For recent history, see: CGIAR Gender Platform: About Us: https://gender.cgiar.org/genderplatform/

A few CRPs—notably, PIM, CCAFS—enabled by the Gender Network have played an important role in fostering collaboration on gender research and promoting the adoption of new tools and methods for gender research, notably on value chains and climate change. External partnerships and funding have also been key enablers of more formal collaboration, alongside long-standing professional relationships between leading gender researchers and Centers. (Baden et al. 2017, xvi)

Putting Gender under PIM with PIM's proposal for a sixth flagship on Gender, the platform's resources were subject to limitations, owing to overall funding amounts to PIM and sharing of those among six flagships. Yet, PIM convened an annual conference and supported calls for research on topics, like seed systems and feminization of agriculture, with KIT supporting other Centers to address gender.

The evaluation suggested that the SMB should maintain or strengthen the capacity of System-level bodies, notably the SMO and the Gender Platform, to be able to carry out their respective budgeting, monitoring, and accountability, and learning and coordination functions, within the reformed system, with regard to integrating gender in CGIAR research. Of the 11 recommendations for future, action included need for a clearer vision and action plan for gender equity; greater consistency in gender research; stronger systems for monitoring and evaluations of outputs and outcomes; and support to gender capacity and expertise (Baden et al. 2017).

At the Consortium meeting in Berlin in 2018, donors noted again that having a platform under PIM was not sufficient—it did not have enough resources or profile at the System level.[25] The gender platform under KIT was also very under-resourced, but an impression was also created at the Berlin meeting that the donors were upset because the platform was not performing (putting the blame on the platform rather than on the System for not supporting it). Eventually, they put out a call for a new Gender Platform around March 2019. Had a platform been established early on—for example, in 2011—gender research would have advanced more rapidly (CGIAR 2018b).

CGIAR Has Promoted More Inter-Center Competition than Coherence

Many gender researchers within CGIAR would have preferred to design one joint proposal, but CGIAR opted instead for competition. ILRI led the development of one proposal on behalf of a consortium of eight CGIAR Centers: Africa Rice, CIMMYT, CIP; ICARDA, ICRISAT, IITA, and IRRI. IFPRI led a proposal including the Alliance of Diversity International and CIAT, CIFOR/ICRAF, IWMI, WorldFish, African Women in Agricultural Research and Development (AWARD), KIT, Self-Employed Women's Association (SEWA), and the ISEAL Alliance. The ISPC selected the ILRI-led proposal, with a note that they should draw on the other proposal as well, a decision officially adopted in November 2019, in Chengdu (CGIAR 2019e).

Some Examples and Achievements of CGIAR's Gender Research

CGIAR's body of literature on gender covers a range of economic, social, anthropological, political, and technological issues, such as legislation aimed at eliminating gender-based discrimination and gender parity in property rights, and the extent to which these laws and policies have been enforced.

IFPRI has been a leader in gender research, some say, because it was taken up by (male) economists with serious credentials, so it was not dismissed as "lightweight" or merely "advocacy." IFPRI has had two DGs with serious gender research credentials. In other Centers, often junior women (frequently without gender training) undertook research. IFPRI also set up the Gender Task Force and extended gender work across the Institute, not just in the Poverty, Health, and Nutrition division.

---

[25] 6th CGIAR System Council Meeting, Berlin, Germany, May 16–17, 2018: https://www.cgiar.org/meeting-document/6th-cgiar-system-council-meeting/

Other early work on gender and participatory management outside IFPRI was at CIAT by Lilja, Ashby, and Sperling (2001) on assessing impact of participatory research and gender analysis.

IFPRI continues to publish prolifically on gender, some of it imbedded in other development work, such as on water, property rights, technology adoption, but not always tagged as gender-related papers, so it is hard to identify key outputs from the website. Its public policy influence has also been considerable, the 20th anniversary of the Beijing conference, led to a series of blogs on the key publications, grouped by topics (Theis, Quisumbing, and Meinzen-Dick 2015a, 2015b, 2015c, 2015d).

IFPRI worked closely with FAO on the 2011 *State of Food and Agriculture* (*SOFA*) (FAO 2011), and produced a book based on the background paper (Quisumbing et al. 2014).

Since that time, the development of the project-level Women's Empowerment in Agriculture Index (WEAI) is probably the biggest "seller." Originally released in 2011, there are now four different versions of the aggregate index, which quantifies women's empowerment and measures gender parity, with the different versions modified for different purposes, including the abbreviated WEAI (A-WEAI), the Project WEAI (pro-WEAI), and the project-level WEAI for market inclusion (pro-WEAI+MI).[26]

Additional relevant works include:

- The Regional Strategic Analysis and Knowledge Support System (ReSAKSS) Annual Report on gender (Quisumbing, Meinzen-Dick and Njuki 2019).
- A forthcoming IFPRI publication on "Advancing Gender Equality through Agricultural and Environmental Research," from the PIM flagship support, is a good summary of the state of the art (Anisimova 2019).
- A big initiative involving several Centers includes the GENNOVATE (Enabling Gender Equality in Agricultural and Environmental Innovation) project. An article by Badstue et al. (2018) provides an overview.[27]

Other communities of practice in other Centers include breeding, water, and forestry, in which gender is an important part—for example, in CIMMYT, IRRI, ICRAF, and CIFOR. The breeding initiative also includes a gender initiative.

Some of the key coordinated works on gender in 2019 include dynamics in seed systems, feminization of agriculture, and gender transformative approaches (GTAs). A synthesis of CGIAR gender research in agriculture fostered several gender communities of practice, and CGIAR co-organized the Seeds of Change Conference in Canberra, Australia, where nearly 60 CGIAR scientists drove the global agricultural research for development agenda forward.[28]

A4NH is the one CRP that has explicitly had "inclusion" in its work.[29] And CIFOR has a good set of guidelines for addressing intersectionality. Much of the gender work does include some attention to intersectionality, but the System itself does not seem to seriously consider whether it would prioritize, for example, dominant farming communities or marginalized groups (pastoralists, indigenous, etc.). The CGIAR Performance Report 2019 (CGIAR 2020b) and the 2017 Annual Performance Report (CGIAR 2018b) have sections on gender and other social issues.[30]

Critics argue that one weakness of focusing on gender is the overlooking of other social exclusion issues, such as ethnicity or caste (Doss and Kieran 2013). Discussion can be found in the A4NH 2015 evaluation (Compton et al. 2015); it has led to taking up wider social equity issues, but the gender community in CGIAR offers strong pushbacks.

---

[26] For more information, see WEAI: Versions, https://weai.ifpri.info/versions/

[27] Other papers are available at https://agrigender.net/all_issues.php

[28] CGIAR Gender Platform: "Seeds of Change" Annual Scientific Conference 2019. https://gender.cgiar.org/annual-conference-2019/

[29] See the 2015 publication, "Independent CRP-Commissioned External Evaluation of the CGIAR Research Program on Agriculture for Nutrition and Health (A4NH)" for the background paper on Gender and Equity: http://www.a4nh.cgiar.org/files/2015/01/Background-papers-for-the-A4NH-evaluation.pdf

[30] See, also, "CGIAR Gender Platform": https://www.cgiar.org/research/program-platform/cgiar-gender-platform/

Another weakness was that the mechanism of allocating funds to CRPs was not adjusted to recognize the special status of the Gender Platform, with the result that donors wishing to support the platform directly had difficulty doing so. Within a fixed allocation to PIM, funds directed to the Gender Platform were subtracted dollar for dollar from support to the other flagships addressing policy and institutional issues. Inflexibility of the funding mechanism combined with a perception that a platform hosted within a program to signal a lack of priority to gender and impeded the visibility of the work.

A Gender Platform at Last

CGIAR launched a Gender Platform in January 2020. It puts gender equality at the forefront of global agricultural research for development and is based in ILRI.[31] The platform was rebuilt in 2019 as a freestanding entity within CGIAR, comparable to the other existing platforms (CGIAR 2019a). This platform was too slow to get off the ground, in part, due to lack of confirmed budget for the platform in 2020.[32] Three "modules" are being set up: (1) Evidence led by IRRI; (2) Methods led by IFPRI; and (3) Alliances by CIAT.

The stakeholders of Gender Research are Coordinators from each of the CGIAR Centers, Research Programs and Platforms, and core members of the Platform include gender scientists and postdoctoral fellows from across the CGIAR System. The Platform is also intended to serve external partners, including NARS, university partners, NGOs, multilateral institutions, and governments with which CGIAR collaborates.

Research on GTAs was a key focus for the platform and CRPs in 2019 (Wong et al. 2019). Also a significant work on GTA has been carried out by WorldFish (with Helen Keller International and others), led by Cynthia MacDougall.[33]

The Platform published a discussion paper on GTAs in agriculture to support a European Commission project that aims to embed GTAs in policy dialogue, programs, and working modalities of FAO, IFAD, and WFP (Wong et al. 2019). While the initial Gender flagship at PIM was led by KIT, the new Gender Platform has moved entirely within CGIAR. On women's empowerment, in 2019, A4NH entered the second phase of the Gender, Agriculture, and Assets Project (GAAP2).[34] While this is one of the big, exciting areas of gender work with over 100 organizations in 55 countries using WEAI or its variations, it is mostly IFPRI's work, not CGIAR-wide. GAAP2 developed a project-level Women's Empowerment in Agriculture Index (pro-WEAI) in 2017, with integrated quantitative and qualitative work, to measure women's empowerment and inclusion in agricultural development projects.[35] Following the launch of the pilot version of pro-WEAI in 2018, two papers on pro-WEAI development were published in *World Development* (Malapit et al. 2019; Yount et al. 2019).

Lessons from the Gender Research Experience: Toward A Stronger Mainstreaming of Gender in CGIAR?

Gender and inclusion are one of the Results Areas of the One CGIAR. This is a positive step. How will that translate into accountability for serious attention to gender? Will gender be built into the DNA of each of the areas of research or will it be treated as an icing on the cake, nice to have if there are "extra" resources? A stronger accountability at the System level is expected under One CGIAR, with two champions of gender on the Executive Team.

[31] See CGIAR Gender Platform: About Us: https://gender.cgiar.org/genderplatform/
[32] Personal communication, email exchange between PIM director, Frank Place, and Uma Lele.
[33] See "Crafting the Next Generation of CGIAR Research—Beyond Gender and Development/Gender Transformative Approaches," CGIAR Gender Platform, January 14: https://gender.cgiar.org/nextgen-gender-gta/
[34] See "Agriculture, and Assets Project (GAAP)": About GAAP2, https://gaap.ifpri.info/about-gaap2/
[35] See "GAAP2: Project-level WEAI": https://gaap.ifpri.info/resource/project-weai/

A cross-cutting platform would help support gender work, to make sure it is of high quality, and would draw together gender work from across the System/programs, so that the whole is greater than the sum of the parts. The unit should also have resources for some strategic gender research—for example, on methods development—that may not be undertaken by individual areas of research, regardless of whether they are conducted by women or men.

Key donors have been BMGF, USAID, IDRC, the Government of Canada, and the Australian Centre for International Agricultural Research (ACIAR). They need to continue to insist that the Gender program is supported financially to thrive, and SMB and the CO need to be much more proactive in supporting Gender.

Box A.10.1 What is Gender Mainstreaming?

The Gender Mainstreaming evaluation (Baden et al. 2017) defined mainstreaming as:

'[T]he process of assessing the implications for women and men of any planned action...and the strategy for making women's as well as men's concerns and experiences an integral dimension of the design, implementation, monitoring and evaluation of policies and programs in all political, economic and societal spheres so that women and men benefit equally and inequality is not perpetrated' (UN 1999, 24). Mainstreaming gender in research refers to the use of the analysis of gender differences to inform the entire research cycle: targeting, priority setting, research design, implementation, research adoption/utilisation, monitoring, evaluation and impact assessment (CGIAR 2011c, 3). (Baden et al. 2017)

Box A.10.2 In CGIAR's Own Words, Extraordinary Impacts of CGIAR's Productivity-enhancing Research in the Developing World

"A 2008 study estimated the overall annual economic benefits of CGIAR research on the three main cereals alone, and just in Asia, at US$10.8 billion for rice, $2.5 billion for wheat and $0.8 billion for maize..." (CGIAR 2011b, 8).

"As a result of crop improvement research within and beyond the CGIAR, 65% of the total area planted to the world's 10 most important food crops is sown to improved varieties" (CGIAR 2011b, 8).

"About 60% of the food crop area planted to improved varieties is occupied by many of the approximately 7,250 varieties bred using genetic materials from the CGIAR" (CGIAR 2011b, 8).

"According to a 2008 study on potato improvement, varieties originating in the CGIAR were planted to more than 1 million hectares, double the area documented just 5 years before" (CGIAR 2011b, 9).

"Research to maintain resistance to a single major disease of wheat—leaf rust—generated benefits from 1973 to 2007 that are currently worth $5.4 billion" (CGIAR 2011b, 9).

"CGIAR research on yield stability estimated that the global economic value of genetic resistance to various wheat diseases amounts to as much as $2 billion annually" (CGIAR 2011b, 9).

Continued

Box A.10.2 Continued

"More than 50 new maize varieties with drought tolerance have been adopted on a total of 1 million hectares across East and Southern Africa..." (CGIAR 2011b, 9).

"A novel approach to seed dissemination has put a new flood-tolerant rice variety in the hands of 100,000 Indian farmers..." (CGIAR 2011b, 9).

"A landmark 2003 study on the impact of crop improvement research from 1965 to 1998 painted a counterfactual scenario of what the global food system would be like without CGIAR research:

- Developing countries would produce 7–8 percent less food.
- Their cultivated area would be 11–13 million hectares greater, at the expense of primary forests and other fragile environments.
- Their food consumption per capita would be 5% lower on average.
- Some 13–15 million more children would be malnourished" (CGIAR 2011b, 10).

Through reduced food prices and increased employment, CGIAR has had huge impacts on reducing poverty and providing training for hundreds of scientists in developing countries. "The overall economic benefits of the CGIAR were estimated to range from US$14 billion to more than $120 billion" (CGIAR 2011b, 10).

"A 2007 review of investments in agricultural research carried out by five CGIAR Centers and their partners in South Asia since the end of the Green Revolution period in the early 1980s found average annual benefits of more than $1 billion from research on maize, rice and wheat alone, far above the CGIAR's total annual expenditures in the region" (CGIAR 2011b, 10–11).

"The economic returns—reaching a current value of US$9 billion on research on just one of the pests, the cassava mealybug—far exceed the CGIAR's total investment in Africa since 1971" (CGIAR 2011b, 11).

Improved varieties of maize and cowpeas, and gains with improved common beans have been registered in Africa. "New Rice for Africa, branded NERICA rice, combines the high yields of Asian rice with African varieties' resistance to local pests and disease. It has spread to 250,000 hectares in upland areas [West Africa], helping reduce the rice import bills and generating higher incomes in rural communities" (CGIAR 2011b, 12).

"Recent research has begun to document the nutritional benefits from improved crop varieties. In Mozambique, the introduction of new orange-fleshed sweet potato rich in beta-carotene significantly increased the intake of this vegetable precursor of vitamin A among young children in 850 households, according to a 2007 study" (CGIAR 2011b, 12).

Impacts of research on natural resources have been difficult to measure and demonstrate. The examples that "CGIAR at 40" included were: In Zambia, the spread of an agroforestry system known as "fertilizer tree fallows," to renew soil fertility; in Malawi, successes in aquaculture; in Benin, adoption of the leguminous climbing shrub *Mucuna pruriens* as a cover crop by 10,000 farmers; in the Indo-Gangetic Plains of SA, zero or reduced tillage in the rice–wheat systems reducing costs of cultivation among adopters by 10 percent while increasing yield by 10 percent (CGIAR 2011b, 12).

In policy research, which has been growing rapidly, notable benefits cited include liberalization of rice price policies in Vietnam, a food-for-education program in Bangladesh, and improved pesticide policies in the Philippines (CGIAR 2011b, 14).

CGIAR's gene banks: CGIAR spends US$6 million annually to protect its gene banks, holding the collections in trust on behalf of humanity. "In 2006, the 11 Centers with genebanks signed superseding agreements that placed the collections under the International Treaty on Plant Genetic Resources for Food and Agriculture and adopted its standard contract for exchanging genetic materials" (CGIAR 2011b, 16).

Box A.10.3 The New Frontier of Biofortification to Address Hidden Hunger

Breakthroughs in biofortification, beyond the achievements reported in Box A.10.1, are an illustration of new frontiers, in which CGIAR could make huge contributions. At the time of writing this chapter, biofortification was benefiting more than 20 million people in farm households in developing countries, which are now growing and consuming biofortified crops, again a global public good par excellence. It is a cost-effective and sustainable tool in the fight against hunger and micronutrient deficiencies, and CGIAR has been at the forefront of this technology, demonstrating important results, with four researchers, Maria Andrade, Robert Mwanga, Jan Low, and Howarth Bouis, receiving the 2016 World Food Prize for biofortification. There is huge scope to mainstream biofortification work throughout CGIAR's breeding work and beyond, since CGIAR does not do research on many commodities, including edible oils, fruits, and vegetables that are important for changing diets and contribute to reduction of poverty and hunger, and improving nutrition.

HarvestPlus, a part of the CGIAR Research Program on Agriculture for Nutrition and Health, started as a Challenge Program in 2003, and now included in CRP 4, has focused on three micronutrients identified by the WHO (see also Chapter 4 on food security and nutrition security):

- Vitamin A deficiency—Approximately 30 percent of preschool-age children are deficient; nearly 5.2 million preschool-aged children suffer from night blindness caused by vitamin A deficiency; and over 19 million pregnant women in developing countries are vitamin A deficient.
- Zinc—Over 17 percent of the world's population is at risk of inadequate zinc intake, which causes stunting and worsens diarrhea and pneumonia, the most common cause of death among children in developing countries. Globally, approximately 23 percent of preschool-aged children are stunted. Inadequate zinc intake is estimated to be greater than 25 percent in SSA and 29 percent in SA.
- Iron—Iron deficiency is the most common micronutrient deficiency in the world, impairing mental and physical capacity. Twenty-five percent of anemia in preschool children and 37 percent in women of reproductive age is attributable to iron-deficiency; worldwide, 800 million women and children are affected by anemia. Iron-deficiency is the leading cause of anemia in developing countries (HarvestPlus 2020).

The movement to scale up biofortification into an action-oriented agenda, which Bouis and Saltzman (2017), and Norman Borlaug well before them, have advocated, is gathering momentum to improve nutrition globally. Bouis and Saltzman (2017, 49) asserted:

To reach one billion people by 2030, there are three key challenges: 1) mainstreaming biofortified traits into public plant breeding programs; 2) building consumer demand; and 3) integrating biofortification into public and private policies, programs, and investments. While many building blocks are in place, institutional leadership [and financial support] is needed to continue to drive towards this ambitious goal.

Source: Bouis and Saltzman (2017); HarvestPlus (2020).

Table A.10.1 Evolution of CGIAR's mission, Centers, and membership

Year	Center and members	Mission/mandate/vision
1971	• 4 CGIAR Centers • 18 members	To stave off hunger by increasing the productivity of dominant staple grains (rice, wheat, and maize). Strategic, science-based focus on increasing "the pile of rice on the plates of food-short consumers" (OED 2003, 3).
1980	• 13 CGIAR Centers • 35 members (including 4 developing countries)	The research portfolio was later broadened to include cassava, chickpea, sorghum, potato, millet, and other food crops, as well as pasturage. CGIAR's original mission statement, in its First System Review of 1977, was "…to support research and technology that can potentially increase food production in the food-deficit countries of the world" (IEG 2002, 7).In 1985, the mission statement was amended, for the first time, by the TAC Review of CGIAR Priorities and Future Strategies (TAC37 Los Baños) to include the notion of sustainability "…to contribute to increasing sustainable food production in developing countries in such a way that the nutritional levels and general economic well-being of low income people is improved" (IEG 2002, 7).
1990	• 13 CGIAR Centers • 35 members (including 4 developing countries)	Food security and poverty eradication in developing countries through research, partnerships, capacity building, and policy support, promoting sustainable agricultural development based on the environmentally sound management of natural resources.In the early 1990s, the CGIAR mission statement was reformulated at the TAC Review (MTM92 Istanbul) as follows: "…in partnership with national research systems, to contribute to sustainable improvements in the productivity of agriculture, forestry and fisheries in developing countries in ways that enhance nutrition and well-being, especially of low-income people" (IEG 2002, 7).
2000	• 16 CGIAR Centers • 58 members (including 22 developing countries)	CGIAR's mission statement was again updated at the 1995 Ministerial-Level meeting in Lucerne: "…to contribute, through its research, to promoting sustainable agriculture for food security in the developing countries" (IEG 2002, 7)."The Third System Review in 1998 [ICW98, Washington] recommended formal amendment of the mission statement to include explicit reference to poverty and environmental sustainability. The Group responded with a decision to change the statement to read: '…to contribute to food security and poverty eradication in developing countries through research, partnership, capacity building, and policy support, promoting sustainable agricultural development based on the environmentally sound management of natural resources'" (IEG 2002, 7).

2009	• 15 CGIAR Centers
	• 64 members (including 25 developing countries)

Vision: "To reduce poverty and hunger, improve human health and nutrition, and enhance ecosystem resilience through high-quality international agricultural research, partnership and leadership" (CGIAR 2011d, 10–11).

2010	• New CGIAR business model
	• 15 CGIAR Centers
	• CGIAR Fund
	• Fund Council (FC)
	• Fund Office (FO)
	• CGIAR Consortium
	• Consortium Board (CB)
	• Consortium Office (CO)

2015	• 15 CGIAR Centerso CGIAR System Council (SC)
	• CGIAR System Organization (SO)
	• CGIAR System Management Board (SMB)
	• CGIAR System Management Office (SMO)
	• 14 CGIAR Centers

Vision: "A world free of poverty, hunger and environmental degradation" (CGIAR 2017f).
Mission: "To advance agricultural science and innovation to enable poor people, especially women, to better nourish their families, and improve productivity and resilience so they canshare in economic growth and manage natural resources in the face of climate change and other challenges" (CGIAR 2016a, 10).*Vision*: "A world free of poverty, hunger and environmental degradation" (CGIAR 2017f).

2019	• CGIAR's System Council endorsed a bold set of recommendations in November 2019 to create One CGIAR. A new organizational structure to reflect the One CGIAR reforms in 2019–20 will be issued in 2021.
	• The System Board, new name after "unified governance" became effective on October 1, 2020, replacing the old "System Management Board."

Mission: "Ending hunger by 2030—through science to transform food, land and water systems in a climate crisis" (CGIAR 2019e, 8).Five Impact Areas:*i. Nutrition and food securityii. Poverty reduction, livelihoods and jobsiii. Gender equality, youth and social inclusioniv. Climate adaptation a d greenhouse gas reductionv. Environmental health and biodiversity* (CGIAR 2020e)

Note: CGIAR "Members" changed to "Fund Donors" with the new business model in 2010.

Source: See IEG 2002; CGIAR 2011d; CGIAR 2016a; CGIAR 2017f; CGIAR 2019e; CGIAR 2020e; https://www.cgiar.org/how-we-work/strategy/

Table A.10.2 CGIAR's reforms in 2001–2007, 2008–2015 (June) and post-2015

Time period	Governance structure	Advisory bodies	Accountability	Financing/funding arrangement	Organization of research	Communication
2001 to 2007 First steps to formalization of govern- ance and management: Movement toward centralized model	1. 21-member Executive Council appointed: 13 rotating and 8 permanent members. 2. Virtual System Office, like corporate office, to bring together CGIAR Secretariat, Science Council Secretariat, Future Harvest Foundation, and other entities; common services to Centers 3. Shorter, streamlined business processes of CGIAR, increased accountability of the units 4. CGIAR Formal Charter adopted in 2004, after 33 years of informal status	Transformation of Technical Advisory Committee (TAC) into the Science Council (SC)	Performance Measurement System introduced with the Centers, the SC, the Secretariat, and external experts involved in its development		Introduction of Challenge Programs (CPs) Center Organization: Merger of Centers— International Service for National Agricultural Research (ISNAR) became a division of the IFPRI and relocated to Ethiopia, carrying out some functions of the former Center.	Communications adviser position created at the Secretariat, and a strategic, science-based communications program, developed with strong collaboration with Centers
2008 to 2015 (June) Transforma- tional change in governance	1. A New Vision: Transition to the "New CGIAR" in 2008 with four strategic outcomes: – *reduced rural poverty*	1. Independent Science and Partnership Council (ISPC) Standing panel of experts to independently advise	**Binding results-based program performance agreements** between Fund and Consortium defined funding and results-based	New funding arrangements through Windows. Two funding windows, Window 1 for unrestricted (pooled)	The Strategy and Results Framework (SRF) developed by the Consortium and endorsed by Funders Forum provided	The first Global Conference on Agricultural Research for Development, Montpellier, France, March 2010; and first

| and management | - *improved food security*
 - *improved nutrition and health*
 - *sustainably managed natural resources*
 2. "New CGIAR" built on different organizational model. Two of four principles of the old CGIAR, donor sovereignty and independent technical advice, less pronounced, and one principle, decision-making by consensus, remained in force in the Fund Council with less significance. The fourth principle, center autonomy, was retained
 3. Three new founding principles:
 - *separation of funders and doers*
 - *harmonization of research funding and implementation*
 - *managing for results*
 4. "New CGIAR" adopted two-pillar structure to separate | SC on science and research matters, including strategies for effective partnerships along research for development continuum.
 - Functionally independent from SO and organization hosting ISPC Secretariat. Standing Panel on Impact Assessment (SPIA)
 2. Independent Evaluation Arrangement (IEA): Advises SC, providing accountability, contributing to learning, supporting decision-making through the conduct of independent, external evaluations to provide CGIAR System with objective, contemporary, cost-effective information on overall performance of CGIAR research and functions and structures of CGIAR | operational dimensions of each CRP. Results-based contracts + accountability through streamlined monitoring and evaluation mechanism, with new Independent Evaluation mechanism set up by Fund Council as its anchor. CGIAR endorsed changes in December 2009, adopting declaration outlining essential elements of reform, approving three founding documents, and appointing the first Fund Council to assume executive responsibility for the donor group. | contributions to be allocated to CRPs by Fund Council and Window 2 for contributions targeting specific CRPs. Donors preferred contributing directly to specific Centers through CGIAR Fund. Window 3 added to Fund structure for this purpose. Fund Council not to contract Consortium or individual Centers for use of Window 3 funds; Window 3 essentially a pass-through for donor funds to individual Centers.
 - BMGF joined CGIAR
 -CGIAR Trust Fund established at World Bank, January 2010. Contributions to Fund made as per development of legal instruments between individual donors and World Bank as trustee of the CGIAR Fund, | roadmap to achieve new vision and strategic outcomes. The Consortium approved set of global programs called CGIAR Research Programs (CRPs) and requested financing for each CRP from Fund. The SRF implemented through a portfolio of 15 CRPs, each led by a CGIAR Center. | Funders Forum, FAO headquarters. Rome, July. |

Continued

Time period	Governance structure	Advisory bodies	Accountability	Financing/funding arrangement	Organization of research	Communication
	"doers" and "funders": - CGIAR Fund (established January 2010, in Washington, DC) - Fund Council (FC) - Fund Office (FO) - The Consortium of International Agricultural Research Centers (established as an international organization in 2012) - Consortium Board (CB) - Consortium Office (CO) (set up in March 2010 and located at Agropolis Campus, Montpellier) "New CGIAR" operational in 2010.	System. Functionally independent from SO and organization hosting IEA Secretariat. 3. CGIAR Internal Audit Unit (IAU): Shared service unit; all Centers are members and exercise authority over IAU.		disbursed under agreements, between Fund Council represented by the World and the CGIAR Consortium. - Inaugural meetings of Fund Council, Consortium Board		
2015 (June) to 2016 (July) to present: Further changes to governance	1. June 2015: Decision to reform governance structure adopted; June 2016: CGIAR established Unified CGIAR System Framework (SF); July	Advisory bodies continued with stronger mandate to ISPC; introduced Centers' General Assembly for CGIAR Research			2016–2030 Strategy and Results Framework (SRF): CGIAR is guided by 2016–30 SRF, aligned with global development targets,	Introduced CGIAR Partnership Forum into CGIAR's operating environment in July 2016 • Brings together diverse group of

and manage-ment	2016: Consortium's Constitution replaced by Charter of the CGIAR System Organization (SO) 2. CGIAR System - CGIAR System Council (SC) - CGIAR SF defines SC functions. - Overarching themes: • Vision, Strategic Direction, Advocacy • Governance • Partnership Engagement, Resource Mobilization • Financial, Programmatic Performance • Evaluations and Impact Assessment - Up to 20 voting members - Up to 15 funders' representatives - 5 developing countries' representatives - Ex-officio non-voting • SMB chair • SMO executive	Centers to discuss issues related to CGIAR System and CGIAR SO: - Centers meet at least once in each calendar year as a General Assembly - Functions of General Assembly:- Nominate for election all candidates for members of System Management Board in accordance with agreed upon process and criteria - Elect Chair of General Assembly of Centers - Approve mechanism based on a proposal from SMB for determining contribution of each Center to SO operating budget - Receive reports of Chair of the System Management Board and of Executive Director of SO - Consider proposed	providing overall strategic direction and result framework for second generation of CRPs. CGIAR SRF: By 2030, action of CGIAR and partners will result in 150 million fewer hungry people, 100 million fewer poor people, at least 50 percent of whom are women, and 190 million ha less degraded land. Three goals, or System Level Outcomes (SLOs): 1. Reduce poverty 2030 TARGETS: - 350 million more farm households adopted improved varieties, breeds or trees, and/or improved management practice - 100 million people, of whom 50 percent are women, assisted to exit poverty 2. Improve food and nutrition security	stakeholders actively supporting CGIAR System to express views on CGIAR operations—Funders, Centers, advisory bodies—most importantly, national agricultural research and extension systems, universities and advanced research institutes, policy bodies, global and regional fora, IGOs, NGOs, private sector companies, farmers/ producers and consumers. • Convened by CGIAR SO at least once every 3 years, a key area of focus of the Partnership Forum is to consider ongoing trends, signals and risks in local, regional, and global contexts in science and in the field of agricultural research for development.

Continued

Table A.10.2 *Continued*

Time period	Governance structure	Advisory bodies	Accountability	Financing/funding arrangement	Organization of research	Communication
	director • 2 Centers' representatives • FAO and IFAD – Active observers • GFAR, IEA, ISPC – Chair: Previously by Consensus from World Bank, but nominated by World Bank • CGIAR System Organization (SO) – *CGIAR System Management Board (SMB)* • CGIAR System Management Board (SMB) with Greater Voice to CG Centers – Responsible for providing strategic direction, effective governance, leadership of CGIAR SO. SMB provides mechanism for CGIAR's 15 member Centers to participate in decisions impacting operations	amendments to this Charter – Approve the Center representatives to serve on SC			2030 TARGETS – Improve the rate of yield increase for major food staples from current <2.0 to 2.5 percent per year. – 150 million more people, of which 50 percent are women, meeting minimum dietary energy requirements – 500 million more people, of which 50 percent are women, without deficiencies of one or more of these essential micronutrients: iron, zinc, iodine, vitamin A, folate, and vitamin B_{12} – 33 percent reduction in women of reproductive age consuming inadequate number of food groups 3. Improve natural resources and ecosystem services *2030 TARGETS*	

Continued

– 20 percent increase in water and nutrient (inorganic, biological) use efficiency in agroecosystems, including through recycling and reuse

– Reduce agriculturally-related greenhouse gas emissions by 0.8 Gt CO2-e year^{-1} (15 percent) compared with a business-as-usual scenario in 2030

– 190 million hectares (ha) degraded land area restored

– 7.5 million ha of forest saved from deforestation

• Goals contribute strongly to the Sustainable Development Goals (SDGs) targeted at no poverty, zero hunger, good health and well-being, gender equality, clean water and sanitation, climate action and life on land. They also moderately

of CGIAR SO and CGIAR System overall.

– Functions are defined by the CGIAR System Charter

• 9 voting members

• Board Chair (DG CIMMYT)

• 2 independent members

• 6 Centers' representatives (DG, Board members)

– 1 non-voting ex-officio member (EC SMO)

– 5 active observers

• 1 CRP Director

• 2 SC voting members

• IEA Director

• ISPC Chair

– *CGIAR System Management Office (SMO)*

Support the SMB, SC.

– Coordinate development of CGIAR SRF.

– Develop, with CGIAR Centers, guidelines, research standards for CGIAR Portfolio

Table A.10.2 *Continued*

Time period	Governance structure	Advisory bodies	Accountability	Financing/funding arrangement	Organization of research	Communication
	– Strategically promote the mission, reputation, and activities of CGIAR System – Monitor and report on implementation of CGIAR System-wide risk management framework – Prepare annual analyses of CGIAR Portfolio with Centers – Monitor implementation of decisions arising from evaluations of CGIAR Research				contribute toward quality education, good jobs, and economic growth, reduced inequalities, responsible consumption, life below water, peace and justice, and partnerships. *Four Crosscutting Issues:* 1. Climate change 2. Gender and youth 3. Policies and institutions 4. Capacity development *Eight Research Priorities:* 1. Climate-smart agriculture 2. Gender and inclusive growth 3. Genetic improvement of crops, livestock, fish and trees 4. Nutrition and health 5. Nurturing diversity 6. Agricultural systems	

Continued

7. Natural resources and ecosystem services 8. Enabling policies and institutions. CGIAR CRP 2 Portfolio (2017–22) SRF and SDGs provide strategic direction, research priorities, and results framework for CGIAR CRP 2 Portfolio 2017–22. Portfolio developed and informed by former Fund Council, CGIAR's System Council, advice from CGIAR's ISPC, Centers, and other stakeholders. The CGIAR CRP 2 Portfolio 2017–22 builds on CGIAR CRP 1 Portfolio 2010–16 to maintain momentum in selected areas, but emphasizes integrated agri-food systems-based approaches, nutrition and health, climate change, soils and degraded land, reducing food systems

Table A.10.2 *Continued*

Time period	Governance structure	Advisory bodies	Accountability	Financing/funding arrangement	Organization of research	Communication
					waste, food safety, global stewardship of genetic resources, and big data, and information and communication technologies. The CGIAR CRP 2 Portfolio 2017–22 is structured around two interlinked clusters of challenge-led research: 1. Innovation in Agri-Food Systems, involving adoption of integrated, agricultural systems approach to advancing productivity, sustainability, nutrition, and resilience outcomes at scale. *The 7 Agri-Food Systems CRPs are:* • Fish • Forests, Trees and Agroforestry • Livestock • Maize	

- Rice
- Roots, Tubers and Bananas
- Wheat

2. Four crosscutting Global Integrating Programs framed to work closely with 8 Agri-Food Systems Programs within relevant agroecological systems:

- Agriculture for Nutrition and Health
- Climate Change, Agriculture and Food Security
- Policies, Institutions, and Markets
- Water, Land, and Ecosystems

These CRPs will consider influence of rapid urbanization and other drivers of change to ensure that research results deliver solutions at the national level that can be scaled up and out to other countries and regions.

Continued

Table A.10.2 *Continued*

Time period	Governance structure	Advisory bodies	Accountability	Financing/funding arrangement	Organization of research	Communication
					The scope of the CGIAR CRP 2 Portfolio 2017–22, in addition to programs, also includes research support Platforms, underpinning research of the whole System. *There are three such Platforms:* • Platform for Big Data in Agriculture • Excellence in Breeding Platform • Genebank Platform While CRPs and Platforms will be led by CGIAR Research Centers, each will work with strategic partners, both CGIAR Research Centers and other institutions. Partners from outside CGIAR can lead Flagship Projects within CGIAR Research Programs, depending on their comparative advantages and track record.	

Source: Özgediz (2012) and http://www.cgiar.org/about-us/our-governance/

References

AGRA (Alliance for a Green Revolution in Africa). 2016a. "More than US $30 Billion in Commitment to African Agriculture." AGRA Digital, Nairobi, September 8. https://agra. org/news/more-than-us-30-billion-in-commitment-to-african-agriculture/

AGRA (Alliance for a Green Revolution in Africa). 2016b. "Transforming Africa's Agriculture for Sustainable Inclusive Growth, Improved Livelihoods, and Shared Prosperity." July 15, Voices of the Alliance—The AGRA Blog. https://agra.org/news/transforming-africas-agriculture-for-sustainable-inclusive-growth-improved-livelihoods-and-shared-prosperity/

Alston, Julian M., Philip G. Pardey, and Xudong Rao. 2020. "The Payoff to Investing in CGIAR Research." October, SOAR Foundation. https://supportagresearch.org/assets/pdf/Payoff_to_Investing_in_CGIAR_Research_final_October_2020.pdf

Anderson, Jock, and Dana G. Dalrymple. 1999. "The World Bank, the Grant Program, and the CGIAR: A Retrospective Review." OED Working Paper Series No. 1, March, World Bank Operations Evaluation Department, World Bank, Washington, DC. http://documents.wor ldbank.org/curated/en/699361468163156017/pdf/319670Cgiar0oed0wp1.pdf

Anismova, Evgeniya. 2019. "Advancing Gender Equality through Agriculture and Natural Resource Management." Policies, Institutions, and Markets, November 20. https://pim. cgiar.org/2019/11/20/advancing-gender-equality-through-agriculture-and-natural-resource-management/

Ashby, Jacqueline A., Annina Lubbock, and Hendrika Stuart. 2013. "Assessment of the Status of Gender Mainstreaming in CGIAR Research." July 30, Working Document presented at the Fund Council 10th Meeting, Nairobi, November 6–7. https://cgspace.cgiar.org/bitstream/han dle/10947/3097/4%20Assessment%20of%20the%20Status%20of%20Gender%20Mainstreaming %20in%20CGIAR%20Research%20Programs%203.pdf

ASTI (Agricultural Science & Technology Indicators), IFPRI (International Food Policy Research Institute), and FARA (Forum for Agricultural Research in Africa). 2011. "How to Address Training Needs to Tackle Human Resource Capacity Challenges in African Agri-cultural R&D." Panel Discussion with Ekwamu Adipala, Ralph Christy, Mark Laing, Agnes Mwang'ombe, and August Temu at "Agricultural R&D: Investing in Africa's Future: Analyz-ing Trends, Challenges, and Opportunities," ASTI/IFPRI–FARA Conference, Accra, Ghana, December   5–7.   https://www.asti.cgiar.org/pdf/conference/Theme2/Summary-training-panel-session.pdf

Baden, Sally, Lynn Brown, Deborah Merrill-Sands, Rachel Percy, and Federica Coccia. 2017. "Evaluation of Gender in CGIAR, Volume I." Report of the Evaluation of Gender in CGIAR Research commissioned by the Independent Evaluation Arrangement (IEA), CGIAR. https:// cas.cgiar.org/sites/default/files/pdf/REPORT-CGIAR-Gender-in-Research-Vol-I-1.pdf

Bachewe, Fantu, Guush Berhane, Bart Minten, and Alemayehu S. Taffesse. 2018. "Agricultural Transformation in Africa? Assessing the Evidence in Ethiopia." *World Development* 105: 286–98.

Badstue, Lone, Patti Petesch, Shelley Feldman, Gordon Prain, Marlène Elias, and Paula Kantor. 2018. "Qualitative, Comparative, and Collaborative Research at Large Scale: An Introduction to GENNOVATE." *Journal of Gender, Agriculture and Food Security* 3 (1): 1–27.

Barrett, Christopher B. 2003. "Natural Resources Management Research in CGIAR: A Meta-Evaluation." The CGIAR at 31: An Independent Meta-Evaluation of the Consultative Group on International Agricultural Research, Thematic Working Paper, World Bank, Washington, DC.

Barrett, Christopher B., Arun Agrawal, Oliver T. Coomes, and Jean-Philippe Platteau. 2009. "Stripe Review of Social Sciences in the CGIAR." CGIAR Independent and Partnership Council, CGIAR, Rome.

Beintema, Nienke M., and Ruben G. Echeverría. 2020. "Evolution of CGIAR Funding." ASTI Program Note, September, International Food Policy Research Institute (IFPRI), Washington, DC. https://www.ifpri.org/publication/evolution-cgiar-funding

Beintema, Nienke, and Gert-Jan Stads. 2017. "A Comprehensive Overview of Investments and Human Resource Capacity in African Agricultural Research." Agricultural Science and Technology Indicators (ASTI) Synthesis Report, International Food Policy Research Institute, Washington, DC. http://ebrary.ifpri.org/utils/getfile/collection/p15738coll2/id/131191/filename/131402.pdf

Binswanger, Hans P. 2011. "On the Wrong Path: CGIAR Strategy and Results Framework." Agriculture and Rural Development blog, March 29. http://hansvins.blogspot.com/2011/03/on-wrong-path-cgiar-strategy-and.html

Birner, Regina, and Derek Byerlee. 2016. "Synthesis and Lessons Learned from 15 CRP Evaluations." Independent Evaluation Arrangement (IEA) of CGIAR, Rome. http://iea.cgiar.org/wp-content/uploads/2016/10/Synthesis2016web.pdf

Blackie, Malcolm J., Reuben Blackie, Uma Lele, and Nienke M. Beintema. 2010. *Capacity Development and Investment in Agricultural R&D in Africa.* Kampala, Uganda: Regional Universities Forum for Capacity Building in Agriculture.

BMGF (Bill and Melinda Gates Foundation). 2020. "Discovery & Translational Sciences." Strategy Overview. What We Do. https://www.gatesfoundation.org/What-We-Do/Global-Health/Discovery-and-Translational-Sciences

Bouis, Howard E., and Amy Saltzman. 2017. "Improving Nutrition through Biofortification: A Review of Evidence from HarvestPlus, 2003 through 2016." *Global Food Security* 12 (2017): 49–58.

Brody, Jane E. 2018. "Are G.M.O. Foods Safe?" *New York Times*, April 23. https://www.nytimes.com/2018/04/23/well/eat/are-gmo-foods-safe.html

Brück, Tilman, Neil T. N. Ferguson, Jérôme Ouédraogo, and Zacharias Ziegelhöfer. 2018. "Impacts of the World Food Programme's Interventions to Treat Malnutrition in Niger." Impact Evaluation Report 80, International Initiative for Impact Evaluation (3ie), New Delhi.

Byerlee, Derek. 2016. *The Birth of CIMMYT: Pioneering the Idea and Ideals of International Agricultural Research.* Mexico: CIMMYT.

CAS Secretariat (CGIAR Advisory Services Shared Secretariat). 2020a. "CGIAR Research Program 2020 Reviews: Agriculture for Nutrition and Health." CAS Secretariat Evaluation Function, Rome. https://cas.cgiar.org/sites/default/files/images/news/A4NH%20CRP%20Review%202020.pdf

CAS Secretariat (CGIAR Advisory Services Shared Secretariat). 2020b. "CGIAR Research Program 2020 Reviews: Grain Legumes and Dryland Cereals." CAS Secretariat Evaluation Function, Rome. https://cas.cgiar.org/sites/default/files/images/news/GLDC%20CRP%20Review%202020.pdf

CAS Secretariat (CGIAR Advisory Services Shared Secretariat). 2020c. "CGIAR Research Program 2020 Reviews: WHEAT." CAS Secretariat Evaluation Function, Rome. https://cas.cgiar.org/sites/default/files/images/news/WHEAT%20CRP%20Review%202020.pdf

CGIAR. 2008. "Bringing Together the Best of Science and the Best of Development." CGIAR Independent Review Panel, chaired by Elizabeth McAllister, Report to the Executive Council. Washington, DC. https://cgspace.cgiar.org/handle/10947/4945

CGIAR. 2011a. "Annual Report 2011: Celebrating 40 Years of Progress." CGIAR, Montpelier, France and Washington, DC. https://library.cgiar.org/bitstream/handle/10947/2789/CGIAR_Annual_Report_2011.pdf?sequence=1

CGIAR. 2011b. "The CGIAR at 40 and Beyond: Impacts that Matter for the Poor and the Planet." CGIAR, Washington, DC. https://cgspace.cgiar.org/handle/10947/2549

CGIAR. 2011c. "Consortium Level Gender Strategy." CGIAR Consortium Board, November, CGIAR, Montpellier, France. https://cgspace.cgiar.org/bitstream/handle/10947/2630/Consortium_Gender_Strategy.pdf

CGIAR. 2011d. "A Strategy and Results Framework for the CGIAR." For submission to the CGIAR Funders Forum, February 20. http://www.cgiar.org/wp-content/uploads/2011/08/CGIAR-SRF-Feb_20_2011.pdf

CGIAR. 2012. "CGIAR Financial Report for Year 2011." A joint collaborative effort between the International Rice Research Institute (IRRI), the CGIAR Consortium Office, and the Fund Office. CGIAR Consortium Office, Montpellier, France.

CGIAR. 2013. "CGIAR Financial Report for Year 2012." September 20, 2013. CGIAR Consortium Office, Montpellier, France. https://library.cgiar.org/bitstream/handle/10947/2869/2012_CGIAR_Financial_Report.pdf

CGIAR. 2014a. "CGIAR Financial Report for Year 2013." June 18, 2014. Prepared by the CGIAR Consortium Office, Montpellier, France. https://library.cgiar.org/bitstream/handle/10947/3069/CGIAR%20Finance%20Report%202013.pdf

CGIAR. 2014b. "Final Report from the Mid-Term Review Panel of the CGIAR Reform." CGIAR Consortium Office, Montpellier, France. https://library.cgiar.org/handle/10947/3368

CGIAR. 2015a. "CGIAR Financial Report for Year 2014." October 1, 2015. Prepared by the CGIAR Consortium Office and the CGIAR Fund Office, Montpellier, France. https://library.cgiar.org/bitstream/handle/10947/4018/2014%20CGIAR%20Financial%20Report.pdf

CGIAR. 2015b. "CGIAR Strategy and Results Framework 2016–2030: Redefining How CGIAR Does Business Until 2030." CGIAR Consortium, Montpellier, France. https://library.cgiar.org/handle/10947/3865

CGIAR. 2015c. "Second Call for CGIAR Research Programs." https://www.cgiar.org/research/research-portfolio/second-call-for-cgiar-research-programs/

CGIAR. 2016a. "CGIAR System Framework." Approved by System's Funders and Centers June 17. http://library.cgiar.org/bitstream/handle/10947/4371/CGIAR%20System%20Framework%20-%20WEB.pdf

CGIAR. 2016b. "Final Report from the Mid-Term Review Panel of the CGIAR Reform." https://library.cgiar.org/bitstream/handle/10947/3390/Final%20Report%20from%20the%20MTR%20Panel%20of%20the%20CGIAR%20Reform,%20October%2028.pdf

CGIAR. 2016c. "2015 CGIAR Financial Report." June 2016, CGIAR Consortium Office and CGIAR Fund Office, Montpellier, France, and Washington, DC. https://library.cgiar.org/bitstream/handle/10947/4452/2015%20CGIAR%20Financial%20Report.pdf

CGIAR. 2017a. "Center Financial Result—2016." May 4, 2017. http://www.cgiar.org/wp-content/uploads/2017/05/Center-Financial-Result-2016-5-May-2017-for-SC.pdf

CGIAR. 2017b. "CGIAR System Annual Performance Report 2017." https://www.cgiar.org/wp/wp-content/uploads/2018/10/CGIAR-Annual-Performance-Report-2017.pdf

CGIAR. 2017c. "CGIAR System-Level Results Reporting: Progress and Plans." Agenda Item 5, Issued October 24 for 5th CGIAR System Council Meeting, Cali, Colombia, November 9–10.

CGIAR. 2017d. "Improving System Financing Modalities—A Scoping Note for the Further Development and Presentation to the System Council." Agenda Item 3, May 4, for the 4th System Council Meeting, The Netherlands, May 10–11. http://www.cgiar.org/wp-content/uploads/2017/04/SC4-03_Funding-Modalities-ScopingPaper_28April2017.pdf

CGIAR. 2017e. "Improving System Financing Modalities." Agenda Item 7 for Decision, October 24, CGIAR System Management Office. https://www.cgiar.org/wp/wp-content/uploads/2017/11/SC5-07_Financing-Modalities.pdf

CGIAR. 2017f. "Innovations for Global Food Security." CGIAR 2016 Annual Report. CGIAR, Montpellier.

CGIAR. 2017g. "SC5 Summary of Decisions: Chair's Summary of Highlights and Decisions 5th System Council Meeting, 9–10 November 2017." CGIAR. https://www.cgiar.org/wp-content/uploads/2017/11/SC5-11_Chairs-Summary_13Nov2017.pdf

CGIAR. 2017h. "2016 CGIAR Financial Report." July 2017, CGIAR System Management Office, Montpellier, France. https://cgspace.cgiar.org/bitstream/handle/10947/4666/2016-CGIAR-Financial-Report.pdf

CGIAR. 2017i. "2017 CGIAR Research Financing Plan." (2017 FINPLAN). Approved at System Management Board meeting, Rome, March 28–9. http://www.cgiar.org/wp-content/uploads/2017/05/FinPlan-2017-3-April-2017-post-SMB-approval-final.pdf

CGIAR. 2018a. "AfricaRice and IRRI Agree to a Step-Change in Partnership to Harness Synergies and Accelerate Their Impact in Africa on Rice-Based Food Systems." News and Events, March 21. https://www.cgiar.org/news-events/news/africarice-irri-agree-step-change-partnership-harness-synergies-accelerate-impact-africa-rice-based-food-systems/

CGIAR. 2018b. "Annual Performance Report 2018." CGIAR System Organization, Montpellier, France. https://cgspace.cgiar.org/bitstream/handle/10568/104045/CGIAR%20Performance%20Report%202018%20Web.pdf

CGIAR. 2018c. "CGIAR Financial Report for Year 2017." Prepared by the CGIAR System Management Office, Montpellier, France. https://cgspace.cgiar.org/bitstream/handle/10568/97418/2017-CGIAR-Financial-Report-Web.pdf?sequence=6

CGIAR. 2018d. "Terms of Reference of CGIAR's Independent Science for Development Council (ISDC)." Approved by the System Council with effect from October 4, 2018. https://www.cgiar.org/wp/wp-content/uploads/2018/10/TOR-ISDC_Appproved_04Oct2018.pdf

CGIAR 2019a. CGIAR Collaborative Platform for Gender Research, Gender Platform Brochure. https://pim.cgiar.org/files/2020/03/Gender-Platform-brochure-Dec2019.pdf

CGIAR. 2019b. "Charter of the CGIAR System Organization." CGIAR, Montpellier. https://cgspace.cgiar.org/bitstream/handle/10947/4370/Charter%20CGIAR%20Organization.pdf

CGIAR. 2019c. "Consent Agenda: System Management Board's ad hoc Working Group on Rules of Governance." Revision 2, ROG Working Group TOR, March 18. https://storage.googleapis.com/cgiarorg/2019/03/SMB13-12_WG_Rules-of-Governance.pdf

CGIAR. 2019d. 9th System Council Meeting. Chair's Summary, SC9. November 13–14, Chendu, P.R., China. https://storage.googleapis.com/cgiarorg/2019/11/SC9-Chairs-Summary.pdf

CGIAR. 2019e. "One CGIAR: A Bold Set of Recommendations to the System Council." SC9-02, CGIAR System Council Meeting, Chengdu, China, November 13–14. https://storage. googleapis.com/cgiarorg/2019/11/SC9-02_SRG-Recommendations-OneCGIAR.pdf

CGIAR. 2020a. "Action Plan for Gender, Diversity, and Inclusion in CGIAR's Workplaces: Principles, Key Objectives, Performance Benchmarks and Targets." https://cgspace.cgiar.org/handle/10568/108037

CGIAR. 2020b. "CGIAR System Annual Performance Report 2019: Summarized Report: Transforming the Globalized Food System." CGIAR System Organization, Montpellier, France. https://cgspace.cgiar.org/bitstream/handle/10568/109875/CGIAR%20Summarized%202019%20Performance%20Report.pdf

CGIAR 2020c. "Delivering as One CGIAR: Inaugural CGIAR Executive Management Team." News, posted June 8. https://www.cgiar.org/news-events/news/delivering-as-one-cgiar-inaugural-cgiar-executive-management-team-announced/

CGIAR. 2020d. "Framework for Gender, Diversity and Inclusion in CGIAR's Workplaces." https://hdl.handle.net/10568/108036

CGIAR. 2020e. "One CGIAR—Towards $2 Billion, Grow Back Better: Resource Mobilization, Communication, and Advocacy Strategy." Working Document, June 25.

CGIAR–IEA. 2016. "Evaluation of the 'Strengthening Impact Assessment in CGIAR' (SIAC) Project Phase 1, 2013–16." Independent Evaluation Arrangement (IEA) of CGIAR, Rome. https://cas.cgiar.org/sites/default/files/pdf/SIAC-final-report-2.pdf

CGIAR–IEA. 2017. "Evaluation of the Independent Science and Partnership Council (ISPC)." Independent Evaluation Arrangement (IEA) of CGIAR, Rome. https://www.cgiar.org/research/publication/evaluation-independent-science-partnership-council-ispc/

CGIAR Science Council. 2008. "Report of the First External Review of the Challenge Program on Water and Food (CPWF)." CGIAR Science Council Secretariat, Rome.

CIAT (International Center for Tropical Agriculture). 2018. "The International Center for Tropical Agriculture and Bioversity International name CEO." CIAT Blog, November 28. https://blog.ciat.cgiar.org/the-international-center-for-tropical-agriculture-and-bioversity-international-name-ceo/

CIFOR (Center for International Forestry Research). 2019. "CIFOR & ICRAF Directors General in Conversation: Merger, the Role of Staff & the Future." March 27. https://www.cifor.org/youtube/cifor-icraf-directors-general-in-conversation-merger-the-role-of-staff-the-future/

Compton, Julia, Diana McLean, Ben Emmons, and Mysbah Balagamwala. 2015. "Independent CRP-Commissioned External Evaluation of the CGIAR Research Program on Agriculture for Nutrition and Health (A4NH)." Evaluation commissioned by the CGIAR Research Program on A4NH. International Food Policy Research Institute, Washington, DC. http://a4nh.cgiar.org/files/2015/01/Volume-1-FINAL-REPORT-Evaluation-of-A4NH.pdf

Conway, Gordon. 2012. One Billion Hungry: Can We Feed the World? Ithaca, NY: Cornell University Press.

Doss, Cheryl, and Caitlin Kieran. 2013. "Standards for Collecting Sex-Disaggregated Data for Gender Analysis: A Guide for CGIAR Researchers." Paper presented at the Workshop on Methods and Standards for Research on Gender and Agriculture, Montpellier, June 19–21, organized by the CRP Policies, Institutions and Markets (PIM) and CGIAR Gender and Agriculture Research Network. https://cgspace.cgiar.org/bitstream/handle/10947/3072/Standards-for-Collecting-Sex-Disaggregated-Data-for-Gender-Analysis.pdf

Evenson, Robert E., and Douglas Gollin. 2003. "Assessing the Impact of the Green Revolution, 1960 to 2000." *Science* 300 (5620): 758–62.

FAO (Food and Agriculture Organization of the United Nations). 2007. "The Challenge of Renewal." Report of the Independent External Evaluation of the Food and Agriculture Organization of the United Nations (FAO), submitted to the Council Committee for the Independent External Evaluation of FAO (CC–IEE), September. ftp://ftp.fao.org/docrep/fao/meeting/012/k0827e02.pdf

FAO (Food and Agriculture Organization of the United Nations). 2011. *The State of Food and Agriculture 2010–11: Women in Agriculture—Closing the Gender Gap for Development.* Rome: FAO. http://www.fao.org/3/a-i2050e.pdf

FAO (Food and Agriculture Organization of the United Nations). 2019. *The State of the World's Biodiversity for Food and Agriculture,* edited by J. Bélanger and D. Pilling, FAO Commission on Genetic Resources for Food and Agriculture Assessments. Rome: FAO. http://www.fao.org/3/CA3129EN/CA3129EN.pdf

Fuglie, Keith. 2016. "The Growing Role of the Private Sector in Agricultural Research and Development World-Wide." *Global Food Security* 10: 29–38.

Fuglie, Keith, Nicole Ballenger, Kelly Day Rubenstein, Cassandra Klotz, Michael Ollinger, John Reilly, Utpal Vasavada, and Jet Yee. 1996. "Agricultural Research and Development: Public and Private Investments Under Alternative Markets and Institutions." Agricultural Economic Report No. (AER-735), Economic Research Service, United States Department of Agriculture, Washington, DC. https://www.ers.usda.gov/publications/pub-details/?pubid=40696

G20 (Group of 20). 2017. "G20 Leaders' Declaration: Shaping an Interconnected World." July 8, Hamburg. http://www.g20.utoronto.ca/2017/2017-G20-leaders-declaration.html

Garcia, Alberto. 2020. "The Environmental Impacts of Agricultural Intensification." GIAR Standing Panel on Impact Assessment Technical Note 9. Rome: CGIAR Advisory Services. https://cas.cgiar.org/spia/publications/environmental-impacts-agricultural-intensification

Garsd, Jasmine. 2018. "Uber's Online-Only Restaurants: The Future, Or The End Of Dining Out?" NPR, The Salt: What's on Your Plate, October 23. https://www.npr.org/sections/thesalt/2018/10/23/658436657/ubers-online-only-restaurants-the-future-or-the-end-of-dining-out

GFAR (Global Conference on Agricultural Research). 2012. "Leveling the Plowing Field: Reducing Persistent Malnutrition and Hunger." Global Conference on Women's Agriculture. http://www.gfar.net/events/global-conference-women-agriculture

GHI (Global Harvest Initiative). 2011. "Improving Agricultural Research Funding, Structure and Collaboration." Policy paper, April 20, GHI, http://www.globalharvestinitiative.org/Policy/Agricultural_Research_Hunger_FoodSecurity.pdf

GNR (Global Nutrition Report). 2020. "2020 Global Nutrition Report." https://globalnutritionreport.org/reports/2020-global-nutrition-report/

Government of India. 2016. Launching of "Feed the Future–India Triangular Training Program (FTF–ITT) on 25th July, 2016." Press Information Bureau, Ministry of Agriculture, Government of India, New Delhi, July 24. http://pib.nic.in/newsite/PrintRelease.aspx?relid=147597

Government of Norway. 2014. "Review of 29 Multilateral Organizations." Ministry of Foreign Affairs. https://www.regjeringen.no/en/topics/foreign-affairs/the-un/review-mulitilateral-org/id737780/

Hagstrom Report. 2015. "World Bank Continues CGIAR Funding Only After U.S. Push to Maintain It." The Hagstrom Report News Archive, August 19. http://www.hagstromreport.com/2015news_files/2015_0819_world-bank-continues-cgiar-funding.html

Hardin, Garrett. 1968. "The Tragedy of the Commons." *Science* 162 (1968): 1243–8.

HarvestPlus. 2020. "Nutrition." What We Do. http://www.harvestplus.org/what-we-do/nutrition

Hayami, Yujiro, Michael Lipton, and Harris Mule. 2003. "OED's Advisory Committee Report: The CGIAR at 31: An Independent Meta-Evaluation of the Consultative Group for International Agricultural Research." External Advisory Committee to CGIAR, Tokyo, Brighton, and Nairobi. http://ieg.worldbankgroup.org/sites/default/files/Data/reports/cgiar_ac_report.pdf

Hazell, Peter, and Roger Slade. 2016. "Taking Stock: Impacts of 40 Years of Policy Research at IFPRI." Independent Impact Assessment Report No. 42, International Food Policy Research Institute, Washington, DC.

Hurley, Terrance, Philip G. Pardey, Xudong Rao, and Robert S. Andrade. 2016. "Returns to Food and Agriculture R&D Investments Worldwide, 1958–2015." INSTEPP Brief, August, International Science and Technology Practice and Policy, University of Minnesota. https://ageconsearch.umn.edu/record/249356/files/InSTePPBriefAug2016.pdf

ICRISAT (International Crops Research Institute for the Semi-Arid Tropics). 2017. "Microsoft and ICRISAT's Intelligent Cloud Pilot for Agriculture in Andhra Pradesh Increase Crop Yield for Farmers." January 9. http://www.icrisat.org/microsoft-and-icrisats-intelligent-cloud-pilot-for-agriculture-in-andhra-pradesh-increase-crop-yield-for-farmers/

IDA (International Development Association). 2020. "IDA19: Ten Years to 2030: Growth, People, Resilience." Additions to IDA Resources: Nineteenth Replenishment. Report from the Executive Directors of the International Development Association to the Board of Governors, February 11. http://documents1.worldbank.org/curated/en/459531582153485508/pdf/Additions-to-IDA-Resources-Nineteenth-Replenishment-Ten-Years-to-2030-Growth-People-Resilience.pdf

IEG (Independent Evaluation Group). 2002. "The CGIAR at 31: An Independent Meta-Evaluation of the Consultative Group on International Agricultural Research (Volume 3: Annexes)." World Bank Group, Washington, DC. https://ieg.worldbankgroup.org/sites/default/files/Data/reports/cgiar_annexes.pdf

IEG (Independent Evaluation Group). 2010. "Cost-Benefit Analysis in World Bank Projects." World Bank, Washington, DC. https://openknowledge.worldbank.org/bitstream/handle/10986/2561/624700PUB0Cost00Box0361484B0PUBLIC0.pdf

IFPRI (International Food Policy Research Institute). 2016. *2016 Global Food Policy Report.* Washington, DC: IFPRI.

IPCC (Intergovernmental Panel on Climate Change). 2019. "Climate Change and Land." An IPCC special report on climate change, desertification, land degradation, sustainable land management, food security, and greenhouse gas fluxes in terrestrial ecosystems. https://www.ipcc.ch/report/srccl/

ISPC (Independent Science and Partnership Council of the CGIAR). 2012. "Strategic Overview of CGIAR Research Programs Part I. Theories of Change and Impact Pathways." December, ISPC, Rome. http://ispc.cgiar.org/sites/default/files/ISPC_WhitePaper_TOCsIPs.pdf?download=1

Jacobs, Andrew, and Matt Richtel. 2017. "A Nasty, Nafta-Related Surprise: Mexico's Soaring Obesity." *New York Times*, December 11. https://www.nytimes.com/2017/12/11/health/obesity-mexico-nafta.html

Jaruzelski, Barry, Volker Staack, and Tom Johnson. 2017. "The Role of Private-Sector R&D in Agricultural Innovation: Improving Yields, Equipment Productivity, and Sustainability." In *The Global Innovation Index 2017: Innovation Feeding the World*, 10th edition, edited by Soumitra Dutta, Bruno Lanvin, and Sacha Wunsch-Vincent, 89–95. WIPO, Ithaca, Fontainebleau, and Geneva: Cornell University, INSEAD, and the World Intellectual Property Organization.

Lele, Uma. 2020. "Growing Water Scarcities: Responses of India and China." Forthcoming, *Applied Economic Perspectives and Policy*.

Lele, Uma, and Balu Bumb. 1995. "The Food Crisis in South Asia: The Case of India." In *The Evolving Role of the World Bank: Helping Meet the Challenge of Development*, edited by K. Sarwar Lateef, 69–96. Washington, DC: World Bank.

Lele, Uma, and Arthur A. Goldsmith. 1989. "The Development of National Agricultural Research Capacity: India's Experience with the Rockefeller Foundation and Its Significance for Africa." *Economic Development and Cultural Change* 37 (2): 305–43.

Lele, Uma, and Sambuddha Goswami. 2017. "The Fourth Industrial Revolution, Agricultural and Rural Innovation, and Implications for Public Policy and Investments: A Case of India." *Agricultural Economics* 48 (S1): 87–100.

Lele, Uma, Jules Pretty, Eugene Terry, and Eduardo Trigo. 2010. "Transforming Agricultural Research for Development. The Global Forum for Agricultural Research (GFAR)." Report for the Global Conference on Agricultural Research (GCARD) 2010, Montpellier, France, March 28–31.

Lilja, Nina, and Jacqueline A. Ashby. 1999. "Types of Gender Analysis in Natural Resource Management and Plant Breeding." Working Document No. 8, CGIAR Systemwide Program on Participatory Research and Gender Analysis. CGIAR Participatory Research and Gender Analysis (PRGA), Cali, Colombia. http://ciat-library.ciat.cgiar.org/articulos_ciat/Working_Document_08.pdf

Lilja, Nina, Jacqueline A. Ashby, and Louise Sperling, eds., with the collaboration of Annie L. Jones. 2001. *Assessing the Impact of Participatory Research and Gender Analysis*. Cali, Colombia: CGIAR Program for Participatory Research and Gender Analysis (PRGA). https://idl-bnc-idrc.dspacedirect.org/bitstream/handle/10625/26891/117290.pdf

Malapit, Hazel, Agnes Quisumbing, Ruth Meinzen-Dick, Greg Seymour, Elena M. Martinez, Jessica Heckert, Deborah Rubin, Ana Vaz, Kathryn M. Yount, and the Gender Agriculture Assets Project Phase 2 (GAAP2) Study Team. 2019. "Development of the Project-level Women's Empowerment in Agriculture Index (pro-WEAI)." *World Development* 122: 675–92.

McCalla, Alex F. 2014. "CGIAR Reform—Why So Difficult?" Giannini Foundation of Agricultural Economics Working Paper No. 14–001, Department of Agricultural and Resource Economics, University of California, Davis.

McCalla, Alex F. 2017. "The Relevance of the CGIAR in a Modernizing World. Or Has It Been Reformed *ad infinitum* into Dysfunctionality?" In *Agriculture and Rural Development in a Globalizing World: Challenges and Opportunities*, edited by Prabhu Pingali and Gershon Feder, 353–69. London and New York: Routledge.

NASEM (National of Academies of Sciences, Engineering and Medicine). 2016. *Genetically Engineered Crops: Experiences and Prospects.* Washington, DC: National Academies Press.

NIFA (National Institute for Food and Agriculture). 2004. "A Proposal: Report of the Research, Education and Economics Task Force of the United States Department of Agriculture." July, NIFA, United States Department of Agriculture, Washington, DC.

Nwanze, Kanayo F. 2014. "Open Letter to African Heads of State." International Fund for Agricultural Development. https://www.ifad.org/en/event/tags/y2014/14219933

O'Kane, Mary, and Eija Pehu. 2017. "Evaluation of the Independent Science and Partnership Council (ISPC)." Final Report, October, Independent Evaluation Arrangement, CGIAR, Montpellier.

OECD (Organisation for Economic Co-operation and Development). 2016. "Definition and Minimum Recommended Criteria for the DAC Gender Equality Policy Marker." Development Assistance Committee (DAC), OECD–DAC Network on Gender Equality (Gendernet), December. https://www.oecd.org/dac/gender-development/Minimum-recommended-criteria-for-DAC-gender-marker.pdf

OED (Operations Evaluation Department). 2003. "The CGIAR at 31: An Independent Meta-Evaluation of the Consultative Group on International Agricultural Research." Revised Edition. OED, World Bank, Washington, DC. https://openknowledge.worldbank.org/bitstream/handle/10986/15041/281310PAPER0CGIAR0at0310see0also025926.pdf

Özgediz, Selçuk. 2012. *The CGIAR at 40: Institutional Evolution of the World's Premier Agricultural Research Network.* Washington, DC: CGIAR Fund Office. https://library.cgiar.org/handle/10947/2761

Pannell, David J., Julian M. Alston, Scott Jeffrey, Yvonne M. Buckley, Peter Vesk, Jonathan R. Rhodes, Eve McDonald-Madden, Simon Nally, Garry Goucher, and Tas Thamo. 2018. "Policy-oriented Environmental Research: What is it Worth?" *Environmental Science and Policy* 86: 64–71.

Pardey, Philip G. 2017. "Rethinking Realizing Value from Genetic Resources." Funding for the Genebanks, Side Meeting to the CGIAR System Council Meeting, Royal Tropical Institute, Amsterdam, May 9, 2017. https://www.cgiar.org/wp-content/uploads/2017/05/GBPres2-Pardey-2017-CG-Exec-9MAY2017v6.pdf

Pardey, Philip G., Julian M. Alston, and Roley R. Piggott. 2006. *Agricultural R&D in the Developing World: Too Little, Too Late?* Washington, DC: International Food Policy Research Institute.

Pardey, Philip G., Robert S. Andrade, Terrance M. Hurley, Xudong Rao, and Frikkie Liebenberg. 2016a. "Returns to Food and Agricultural R&D Investments in Sub-Saharan Africa, 1975–2014." *Food Policy* 65: 1–8.

Pardey, Philip G., and Nienke M. Beintema. 2001. "Slow Magic: Agricultural R&D a Century after Mendel." Agricultural Science and Technology Indicators (ASTI) Initiative, International Food Policy Research Institute, Washington, DC.

Pardey, Philip G., Connie Chan-Kang, Jason M. Beddow, and Steven P. Dehmer. 2016b. "Shifting Ground: Food and Agricultural R&D Spending Worldwide, 1960–2011." International Science & Technology Practice & Policy, University of Minnesota.

Pardey, Philip G., Connie Chan-Kang, Steven P. Dehmer, and Jason M. Beddow. 2016c. "Agricultural R&D is on the Move." *Nature* 537 (7620): 301–3. doi:10.1038/537301a

Pardey, Philip G., and Vincent H. Smith, eds. 2004. *What's Economics Worth? Valuing Policy Research.* Baltimore: Johns Hopkins University Press.

Quisumbing, Agnes, and Neha Kumar. 2014. "Land Rights, Knowledge and Conservation in Rural Ethiopia: Mind the Gender Gap." IFPRI Discussion Paper 1386, International Food Policy Research Institute, Washington, DC.

Quisumbing, Agnes R., Ruth Meinzen-Dick, and Jemimah Njuki, eds. 2019. *ReSAKSS 2019 Annual Trends and Outlook Report: Gender Equality in Rural Africa: From Commitments to Outcomes.* Washington, DC: International Food Policy Research Institute. https://www.ifpri.org/publica tion/2019-annual-trends-and-outlook-report-gender-equality-rural-africa-commitments-0

Quisumbing, Agnes R., Ruth Meinzen-Dick, Terri L. Raney, André Croppenstedt, Julia A. Behrman, and Amber Peterman, eds. 2014. *Gender in Agriculture: Closing the Knowledge Gap.* Dordrecht: Springer.

Reifschneider, Francisco José Becker, Luciano Lourenço Nass, Paulo de Camargo Duarte, and Rodrigo Montalvão Ferraz. 2016. *Agricultural Innovation Marketplace: South–South Cooperation Beyond Theory.* Brasilia: Agricultural Innovation MKTplace.

Renkow, Mitch. 2016. "Assessing the Impact of Policy-Oriented Research in the CGIAR: Methodological Challenges and Reasonable Expectations." Department of Agricultural and Resource Economics, North Carolina State University, Raleigh, NC.

Robinson, Maureen, Sophie Zimm, Alison King, and Urs Zollinger. 2014. "Review of CGIAR Research Programs' Governance and Management." Final Report, Independent Evaluation Arrangement (IEA) of CGIAR (CGIAR–IEA), Rome. https://ccafs.cgiar.org/publications/review-cgiar-research-programs-governance-and-management-final-report#.XM50jC-ZNE4

Seraj, Rachid, and Prabhu L. Pingali. 2018. *Agriculture & Food Systems: Global Trends, Challenges and Opportunities.* Hackensack, NJ: World Scientific Publishing.

Stevenson, J. R., and P. Vlek. 2018. "Assessing the Adoption and Diffusion of Natural Resource Management Practices: Synthesis of a New Set of Empirical Studies." Independent Science and Partnership Council (ISPC), CGIAR, Rome.

Theis, Sophie, Agnes Quisumbing, and Ruth Meinzen-Dick. 2015a. "Takeaways from Twenty Years of Gender and Rural Development Research at IFPRI: Closing Gender Gaps in Agriculture through Property rights and Governance." IFPRI Blog post, October 7. https://www.ifpri.org/blog/takeaways-twenty-years-gender-and-rural-development-research-ifpri-closing-gender-gaps

Theis, Sophie, Agnes Quisumbing, and Ruth Meinzen-Dick. 2015b. "Takeaways from Twenty Years of Gender and Rural Development Research at IFPRI: The Elements of Resilience." IFPRI Blog post, October 8. https://www.ifpri.org/blog/takeaways-twenty-years-gender-and-rural-development-research-ifpri-elements-resilience

Theis, Sophie, Agnes Quisumbing, and Ruth Meinzen-Dick. 2015c. "Takeaways from Twenty Years of Gender and Rural Development Research at IFPRI: Household Decision Making and Women's Control over Resources." IFPRI Blog post, October 6. https://www.ifpri.org/blog/takeaways-twenty-years-gender-and-rural-development-research-ifpri

Theis, Sophie, Agnes Quisumbing, and Ruth Meinzen-Dick. 2015d. "Takeaways from Twenty Years of Gender and Rural Development Research at IFPRI: Improving Measurements of Women's Empowerment and Data on Gender." IFPRI Blog post, October 9. https://www.ifpri.org/blog/takeaways-twenty-years-gender-and-rural-development-research-ifpri-improving-measurements

Traxler, Greg. 2004. "The Economic Impacts of Biotechnology-Based Technological Innovations." ESA Working Paper No. 04–08, May, Agricultural and Development Economics

Division, The Food and Agriculture Organization of the United Nations, Rome. http://www. fao.org/3/a-ae063t.pdf

UN (United Nations). 2019. "Population Trends." Department of Economic and Social Affairs, Population Division. http://www.un.org/en/development/desa/population/theme/trends/index.shtml

UN (United Nations). 2020a. "UN Food Systems Summit 2021." UN, New York.

UN (United Nations). 2020b. "United Nations Food Systems Summit 2020." UN, New York. https://www.un.org/sustainabledevelopment/food-systems-summit-2021/

Varinsky, Dana. 2018. "The $66 Billion Bayer–Monsanto Merger Just Got A Major Green Light—But Farmers Are Terrified." *Business Insider*, May 29. https://www.businessinsider. com/bayer-monsanto-merger-has-farmers-worried-2018-4

von Braun, Joachim, Hartwig de Haen, and Juergen Blanken. 1991. "Commercialization of Agriculture Under Population Pressure: Effects on Production, Consumption, and Nutrition in Rwanda." Research Report No. 85, January, International Food Policy Research Institute, Washington, DC.

von Braun, Joachim, David Hotchkiss, and Maarten Immink. 1989. "Nontraditional Export Crops in Guatemala: Effects on Production, Income, and Nutrition." Research Report No. 73, May, International Food Policy Research Institute, Washington, DC. https://ageconsearch. umn.edu/record/42169

von Braun, Joachim, and Eileen Kennedy, eds. 1994. *Agricultural Commercialization, Economic Development, and Nutrition*. Baltimore: Johns Hopkins University Press.

von Braun, Joachim, Detlev Puetz, and Patrick Webb. 1989. "Irrigation Technology and Commercialization of Rice in The Gambia: Effects on Income and Nutrition." Research Report No. 75, August, International Food Policy Research Institute (IFPRI), Washington, DC.

von Braun, Joachim, Tesfaye Teklu, and Patrick Webb. 1998. *Famine in Africa: Causes, Responses, and Prevention*. Baltimore: Johns Hopkins University Press. http://www.ifpri. org/sites/default/files/publications/famine_in_africa_causes_responses_and_prevention.pdf

von Braun, Joachim, and Patrick Webb. 1989. "The Impact of New Crop Technology on the Agricultural Division of Labor in a West African Setting." *Economic Development and Cultural Change* 37 (3): 513–34.

Wadsworth, Jonathan. 2016. "Brief History of the CGIAR Fund." Discussion Paper, April, CGIAR, Washington, DC. http://www.cgiar.org/wp-content/uploads/2016/03/Brief-history-of-the-CGIAR-Fund.pdf

WBG (World Bank Group). 2017. *Global Economic Prospects June 2017: A Fragile Recovery*. Washington, DC: World Bank. https://openknowledge.worldbank.org/bitstream/handle/10986/26800/9781464810244.pdf

Webb, Patrick, and Joachim von Braun. 1994. *Famine and Food Security in Ethiopia: Lessons for Africa*. Chichester, UK: John Wiley and Sons, for the International Food Policy Research Institute.

WEF (World Economic Forum). 2020. "Annual Report 2019–2020." WEF, Geneva. http://www3.weforum.org/docs/WEF_Annual_Report_2019_2020.pdf

White, Howard. 2014. "Building a Theory of Change: Using Evidence across the Causal Chain." International Initiative for Impact Evaluation, New Delhi. http://www.3ieimpact.org/media/filer_public/2014/09/16/1_building_a_theory_of_change_using_evidence_across_the_causal_chain.pdf

White, Howard, and David A. Raitzer. 2017. *Impact Evaluation of Development Interventions: A Practical Guide*. Manila: Asian Development Bank. https://www.adb.org/sites/default/files/publication/392376/impact-evaluation-development-interventions-guide.pdf

WHO (World Health Organization). 2020. Tropical Diseases. Health Topics. http://www.who.int/topics/tropical_diseases/en/

Willett, Walter, Johan Rockström, Brent Loken, Marco Springmann, Tim Lang, Sonja Vermeulen, Tara Garnett, David Tilman, Fabrice DeClerck, Amanda Wood, et al.; The Lancet Commission. 2019. "Food in the Anthropocene: The EAT-*Lancet* Commission on Healthy Diets from Sustainable Systems." *Lancet* 393 (10170): 447–92. https://www.thelancet.com/pdfs/journals/lancet/PIIS0140-6736(18)31788-4.pdf

Wong, Franz, Andrea Vos, Rhiannon Pyburn, and Julie Newton. 2019. "Implementing Gender Transformative Approaches in Agriculture." CGIAR Collaborative Platform for Gender Research. Discussion paper for the European Commission. https://gender.cgiar.org/wp-content/uploads/2019/06/Gender-Transformative-Approaches-in-Agriculture_Platform-Discussion-Paper-final-1.pdf

World Bank. 2016. "Annual Report 2016." World Bank, Washington, DC. http://documents.worldbank.org/curated/en/763601475489253430/pdf/108682-WBAR-v1-PUBLIC-English-PUBDATE-9-28-2016.pdf

World Bank. 2017. "An Overview of Links between Obesity and Food Systems: Implications for the Food and Agricultural Global Practice." June, Food and Agriculture Global Practice, World Bank, Washington, DC.

World Bank. 2020. "Povcalnet: An Online Analysis Tool for Global Poverty Monitoring." http://iresearch.worldbank.org/PovcalNet/home.aspx

Younta, Kathryn M., Yuk Fai Cheong, Lauren Maxwell, Jessica Heckert, Elena M. Martinez, and Gregory Seymour. 2019. "Measurement Properties of the Project-level Women's Empowerment in Agriculture Index." *World Development* 124: 104639.

11

The International Fund for Agricultural Development

Uma Lele and Brian C. Baldwin

Summary

The vision of the International Fund for Agricultural Development (IFAD) for the post-2015 rural world is one in which rural extreme poverty is eliminated through inclusive and sustainable agriculture and rural development, and in which poor rural people and communities, including those who live in remote areas, are empowered to build prosperous and sustainable livelihoods. IFAD's comparative advantage is focused on rural people at the bottom of the pyramid, women, and marginalized people. External evaluations have shown that IFAD, a small and agile organization, has been effective in addressing its declared mission. Its dilemma going forward is whether to assist poor people in only poor countries, or even in lower middle-income countries (LMICs) and middle-income countries (MICs), as it has done in the past. An assessment is needed of whether the current paradigms of average per capita country income are sufficiently robust to support IFAD's mandate, particularly in countries with acute per capita income inequality.

Demonstrating impacts beyond selected projects chosen for in-depth impact evaluations has been a challenge, but then IFAD is not alone in that regard. It has underway a vigorous program of impact assessments, but generalizing beyond findings of individual, costly, time-consuming impact evaluations has been a challenge at a time when the Eleventh Replenishment (IFAD11) may barely reach US$1.1 billion of the US$1.2 billion replenishment target over a three-year period. And, if the trend continues, the next replenishment, which starts in 2020, is likely to enter into the replenishment cycle of other institutions, including the Global Agriculture and Food Security Program (GAFSP) and GAVI (the Vaccine Alliance). The International Development Association (IDA) and the African Development Bank (AfDB) are also going through their replenishment processes, but in the case of IDA at a much higher level. The IDA18 replenishment was US$75 billion over three years.

If the stated aim of the Sustainable Development Goals (SDGs) to "leave no one behind" is to be achieved by 2030, IFAD's replenishment must be high on the donor agenda. There is a growing consensus that special measures are needed to address SDG2 (zero hunger and rural transformation), particularly SDG targets 2.3 and 2.4.[1] At the same time, the level of

---

[1] SDG Target 2.3: "By 2030, double the agricultural productivity and incomes of small-scale food producers, in particular women, indigenous peoples, family farmers, pastoralists and fishers, including through secure and equal access to land, other productive resources and inputs, knowledge, financial services, markets and opportunities for value addition and non-farm employment."

SDG Target 2.4: "By 2030, ensure sustainable food production systems and implement resilient agricultural practices that increase productivity and production, that help maintain ecosystems, that strengthen capacity for adaptation to climate change, extreme weather, drought, flooding and other disasters and that progressively improve land and soil quality."

See https://sustainabledevelopment.un.org/sdg2

Food for All: International Organizations and the Transformation of Agriculture. Uma Lele, Manmohan Agarwal, Brian C. Baldwin, and Sambuddha Goswami, Oxford University Press. © Uma Lele, Manmohan Agarwal, Brian C. Baldwin, and Sambuddha Goswami 2021.
DOI: 10.1093/oso/9780198755173.003.0012

indebtedness of some borrowing countries is real, and another process for Heavily Indebted Poor Countries (HIPC) is needed. As one of the founding and responsive institutions of the HIPC debt relief initiative (HIPC–DI), IFAD needs the financial support already provided to other HIPC–DI aligned institutions to ensure its continued involvement in addressing both debt relief and debt sustainability.

The challenges for IFAD, on the supply side, is whether it should continue with business as usual, which could be challenging, given stalling official development assistance (ODA) and implicit reduction in the program of loans and grants, or if it should turn to the market to leverage its replenishments against market forces. Responding to these developments will test IFAD's ingenuity, creativity, and capacity for innovation. On the demand side, there is a huge gap between needs and expectations and what can actually be delivered under the existing architecture and funding structure. ODA to agriculture represents only 5 percent of total ODA. Progress toward ending poverty and hunger has stalled while growing food insecurity, linked to fragility and climate change, threatens IFAD's ability to achieve the SDGs by 2030. IFAD is at a crossroads and, together with the development community and specifically, its Executive Board, it needs to choose among options. For IFAD to continue its declared mission of addressing rural poverty across and within *all* developing country member states, it will need both innovative financial and programmatic mechanisms, supported by the respective commitments and a broader range of partners.

Background

One of the major responses to the food crises in the early 1970s, and a significant outcome of the 1974 World Food Conference, was the establishment in 1977 of IFAD, the 13th specialized agency of the United Nations (UN).[2] The purpose in establishing IFAD was not only to increase investments in the poor, but also to recycle the petrodollars from the first oil shock for development purposes. The Organization of the Petroleum Exporting Countries (OPEC) played a significant role in the establishment of the Fund, including the provision of a portion of IFAD's initial funding, with the understanding that the Organisation for Economic Co-operation and Development (OECD) and other developing countries would also provide resources. This initial OPEC commitment led to an agreement that gave OPEC countries a role in the governance of IFAD, including equal voting power (on the basis of one country, one vote) among the three categories of members: OECD, OPEC, and developing countries (IFAD and the OPEC Fund 2005). However, as IFAD's funding base has evolved, so, too, has how the voting structure and voting rights are distributed, according to paid contributions. As of March 2017, the OECD category has 48.7 percent of votes; OPEC, 12.5 percent; and member countries, 38.8 percent. Except for two presidents, all of IFAD's presidents have come from OPEC countries, and Gilbert Fossoun Houngbo, former Prime Minister of Togo, took office as the sixth president of IFAD on April 1, 2017.

Structurally, the Governing Council has the highest decision-making authority (each member state is represented by one governor and an alternate), and the Executive Board is responsible for overseeing IFAD operations and approving its work program and budget. The Executive Board is composed of 18 members and up to 18 alternates, elected at the

---

[2] See IFAD: Governance: https://www.ifad.org/en/governance

annual session of the Governing Council, and is distributed as follows: List A has eight members and eight alternates (primarily countries in the OECD); List B has four members and four alternates (primarily countries in OPEC); and List C has six members and six alternates; two each in the three regional subdivisions of List C member states (developing countries). The president is appointed at the meeting of the Governing Council by a two-thirds majority of the total number of votes, for a four-year term and eligible for only one further term (IFAD 1976).

Article 2 of the agreement, which established IFAD, states:

> The objective of the Fund shall be to mobilize additional resources to be made available on concessional terms for agricultural development in developing Member States. In fulfilling this objective the Fund shall provide financing primarily for projects and programmes specifically designed to introduce, expand or improve food production systems and to strengthen related policies and institutions within the framework of national priorities and strategies, taking into consideration: the need to increase food production in the poorest food deficit countries; the potential for increasing food production in other developing countries; and the importance of improving the nutritional level of the poorest populations in developing countries and the conditions of their lives. (IFAD 1976, 4)

At the time of its founding, the emphasis was on increased production by the poor for the poor. It was further agreed that IFAD would focus on the provision of financing for agricultural development projects in poor rural areas. The agreement stated that IFAD would finance loans and grants on terms deemed appropriate by the Fund, based on a country's economic status and prospects in relation to the nature and requirements of the interventions needed. In 2007, alongside other international finance institutions, IFAD introduced the Debt Sustainability Framework (DSF) that allowed IFAD to provide development finance on grant terms to countries that the International Monetary Fund (IMF)/ World Bank had categorized as having unsustainable levels of debt. These terms were outlined in IFAD's "Policies and Criteria for IFAD Financing," updated several times over the years, the latest update being in September 2019. It states that its major target groups, regardless of a country's stage of economic development (an important perspective, bearing in mind the graduation of several members to MIC status), were to be small and landless farmers in the poorest countries and regions of the world. Attention would also be given to the promotion of the role of women in food production (IFAD 1978, latest revision 2013).

The future of smallholder agriculture and IFAD's niche, with its focus on serving the poorest people in rural areas of the developing world, has been a recurring theme in the agricultural economics profession and germane to the work of financial institutions. A policy brief for the Global Donor Platform for Rural Development (2008, 1) characterized challenges of service delivery in the context of the options that different types of small farmers face as, "Stepping up, stepping out, and hanging in," depending on their circumstances. The policy brief suggests the first option calls for increasing farm productivity, the second entails off-farm migration, and the third, mere survival, depending on the types of farms. In a separate paper, Poulton, Kydd, and Dorward (2006) also characterized small farms as staple crop producers making subsistence livings, cash crop producers, and supply chains of modern high-value producers (as opposed to traditional export commodity producers). They argued that a key issue is the difficulties that smallholders face in accessing coordinated services for more intensive production and market access, and the way that these differ between staple food crop production, traditional cash crop production, and export market production. The authors stressed the importance of coordination of service development and delivery, and depending on farmer needs, different forms of intermediary institutions needed to achieve such coordination. The challenge of organizing service delivery for small farmers has been perennial. Finding effective ways to reach them has not been easy. Donors-funded, integrated rural development projects in Africa in the 1970s were ineffective (Lele 1992).

Donors then pursued partial subsectoral approaches—such as extension and financial services, privatization of trade to substitute for marketing boards, and community-based organizations for extension and water management. *World Development Reports (WDRs)* in 2003 and 2004 were devoted to transforming institutions and making services work for the poor (World Bank 2003, 2004). *WDR* 2008 and the various World Bank agriculture and rural development strategies have addressed issues of service delivery (World Bank 2007). (See Chapter 8 on the World Bank.) New in recent literature is the avoidance of blueprints, an acknowledgment of the importance of domestic political commitment at the top, recognition of the need for political stability for the evolution of institutions through learning by doing, and substantial adaptive capacity of institutions and human capital in countries for innovation to materialize. As we document throughout this book, however, these concepts have been themes in development literature all along. Translating knowledge into policies and institutions over the long haul has been the harder challenge.

IFAD's Evolving Mission

In the 1980s, IFAD's niche status was unique among international financial institutions (IFIs) in its focus on the poorest rural groups (see "An Independent External Evaluation of the International Fund for Agricultural Development" [IFAD 2005]). IFAD's dual status as an IFI and a specialized UN agency distinguished it from its partner food and agriculture organizations in Rome—the Food and Agriculture Organization of the United Nations (FAO) and the World Food Programme (WFP).[3] It has always been predominantly a financing institution for programs and projects designed initially by member countries, using technical assistance provided by IFAD, and implemented by contracted cooperating institutions, usually IFIs.

In the 1990s, IFAD's mission evolved to encompass a broader agenda of rural development that included, alongside the infrastructure programs that were a feature of early IFAD funding, access to markets and financial services, and institutional strengthening. A statement of IFAD's vision in 1995 broadened the Fund's objectives to include "the design and implementation of innovative, cost-effective and replicable programmes" and asserted that IFAD "be the catalytic institution of a mutual enrichment process which mobilizes resources and knowledge in a strategic, complementary and dynamic coalition of clients...committed to the cause of the rural poor" (IFAD 1997, 5). Thus, IFAD began producing a comprehensive set of country strategic plans for investment opportunities, starting in 1985, and Country Strategic Opportunities Programmes (COSOPs) were introduced in 1998, through which it began identifying and designing its own projects. Evidence of a broadening mission is also visible in the late 1990s and 2000s, and in the report of its scorecard. *The Strategic Framework for 1998–2000* describes IFAD's core business as:

---

[3] See IFAD: United Nations Agencies: https://www.ifad.org/en/united-nations-agencies

...innovative pilot projects and programmes in rural and agricultural development (agricultural production, microcredit, rural infrastructure, self-help groups, land tenure); projects and programmes focusing on poverty eradication, household food security and new markets for marginal areas, and the formation of effective partnerships with other development institutions and organizations (at the international, national and subnational levels) to broaden development impact; and increasing public awareness of the situation and needs of the rural poor, while raising additional resources for them. (IFAD 1997, 12)

The Strategic Framework for 2002–6, *Enabling the Rural Poor to Overcome Their Poverty*, identified three strategic objectives: "strengthening the capacity of the rural poor and their organizations; improving equitable access to productive natural resources and technology; and increasing access of the poor to financial assets and markets" (IFAD 2001, 6).

IFAD's Strategic Framework for 2011–15 emphasized "enabling rural women and men to overcome poverty" (IFAD 2010e, 5) and its "overarching goal is: enabling poor rural people to improve their food security and nutrition, raise their incomes and strengthen their resilience" (IFAD 2010e, 7). The Framework called for better leverage of its comparative advantage: "working with poor rural people and with other partners to reduce poverty and improve food security" (2010e, 23), with a focus on achieving both a greater and more sustainable impact in its operations.

In 2014, as background to the 10th replenishment of its resources, IFAD announced its new "Strategic Vision for IFAD 2016–2025: Enabling Inclusive and Sustainable Rural Transformation" (Box 11.1). The new vision was needed, IFAD said:

The global context for smallholder agriculture and rural development has changed significantly in recent years and will undoubtedly continue to change in major ways in the post-2015 period. IFAD's operations and activities in the future will necessarily be affected by these changes and their development impact will depend on how well smallholder farmers, governments, and IFAD address key challenges, such as climate change, and how well they take advantage of emerging opportunities such as increasing demand for food resulting from higher incomes and rapid urbanization. (IFAD 2014h, 2)

The 2016–25 Strategic Framework is being operationalized through the 3-year Medium Term Plans (MTPs), aligned to the respective replenishment periods. As such, the MTP 2016–18 translates into action the strategic objectives set out in the IFAD Strategic Framework 2016–25: "It enables IFAD to achieve its stipulated outcomes, namely: (i) enabling policy and regulatory frameworks at national and international levels; (ii) increased levels of investment in the rural sector; and (iii) improved country-level capacity for rural policy and programme development, implementation and evaluation" (IFAD 2016f, iv). IFAD has increased its focus on value chains and markets, rural finance, natural resource management, climate change, and youth—recognizing that small farm development is critical in view of the nearly 500 million small farms globally. The challenge for IFAD will be to capture the knowledge that exists, identify the gaps, operationalize findings into a development strategy that delivers outcomes and impact at the country level, and at the same time, secure the financing and architecture to deliver these results with member countries across the spectrum of IFAD's global membership base.

IFAD adopted its first Nutrition Action Plan for 2016–18, subsequently revised to the Nutrition Action Plan 2019–25, with a framework to guide IFAD's actions in accelerating

Box 11.1 IFAD's Strategic Vision, 2016–2025: Enabling Inclusive and Sustainable Rural Transformation

In the global effort to realize [the Strategic] Vision:

- IFAD plays both a leadership and a catalytic role. It leads by forging partnerships with governments, rural communities, farmers' organizations, the Rome-based agencies (RBAs) and other development partners. Through such partnerships, it leverages its financial resources, expertise, and knowledge.
- IFAD is the partner of choice for governments, institutions, and smallholder farmers, and is recognized as the premier UN Agency and international financial institution (IFI) that has built a clear comparative advantage in smallholder agriculture and rural development.
- IFAD is the recognized global leader in investment in smallholder agriculture, rural people and rural communities achieved by mobilizing and leveraging resources and by developing innovative financing mechanisms and instruments.
- IFAD continues to develop and innovate in its areas of expertise and comparative advantage, adjusting its operational priorities in response to changes in smallholder agriculture and the rural economy. It recognizes the comparative advantage of its partners in other policy and development areas.
- In the IFAD10 period, IFAD consolidates and advances the work begun under IFAD9, paying particular attention to: mainstreaming gender equality and women's empowerment; mainstreaming climate-smart agriculture and the sustainable management of natural resources; promoting nutrition-sensitive agriculture; laying the foundations for stronger partnerships with the private sector; and promoting the social and economic empowerment of poor rural people and strengthening their resilience.
- IFAD mainstreams scaling up in all phases of its operations and gives greater emphasis to the sustainability of its programmes and projects, viewing scaling up as mission-critical.
- IFAD continues to diversify its knowledge and expertise and adopts a differentiated approach for its work in various country contexts-fragile states, low-income countries (LICs), and middle-income countries (MICs).
- IFAD develops its knowledge generation and sharing capacity, particularly in the area of impact evaluation studies, to learn from its experience, encourage innovation, support policy dialogue and improve the impact of its operations. IFAD encourages knowledge-sharing with members, with a particular focus on South-South and triangular cooperation.
- IFAD continues to enhance its effectiveness and efficiency by consolidating its reforms of the last 10 years in its business model, organizational structure, human resource management, and business processes. It ensures that its organization continues to be fit-for-purpose, demonstrating that investment in smallholder agriculture is good value for money. (IFAD 2014h, 1)

Source: "A Strategic Vision for IFAD 2016–2025" (IFAD 2014h).

the mainstreaming of nutrition into its investments. It has been developed in a highly participatory and consultative manner, involving IFAD staff (at headquarters and IFAD country offices/hubs), as well as with key partners and IFAD Executive Board representatives, with the objective of aligning it with the new IFAD11 target of mainstreaming nutrition into 50 percent of projects at design, capturing lessons learned to date in order to accelerate nutrition mainstreaming during IFAD11 and IFAD12, and building on opportunities created by IFAD's decentralization and restructuring (IFAD 2019b).

The 2019 Annual Report on the Results and Impact of Operations (ARRI) indicates that IFAD's project performance in the 2016–17 period has been flat, less well than the World Bank's but better than that of the Asian Development Bank (ADB) and AfDB (IFAD 2019h).

Diversification of Funding Sources

IFAD's original mandate to develop and provide funding for rural poverty alleviation has meant that IFAD has continually sought to seek additional financing outside the three-year replenishment process. Supplementary funding mechanisms, mainly bilateral, have provided resources that enable IFAD to make further allocations to member countries. A further example has been the Spanish Trust Fund, established in 2010–11, which was used to co-finance and scale up the country financing operations, especially in MICs (IFAD 2010c). This €300 million fund, for which IFAD was trustee, allowed IFAD to increase its external resources and to scale up projects that it funded, enabling a larger impact (IFAD 2010c). In addition, as another example, a framework agreement with the Islamic Development Bank would support co-financing rural development in 26 countries. Similarly, a partnership with the OPEC Fund for International Development promotes innovative financing mechanisms to attract private sector investment in agriculture (IFAD 2012b). In 2014, to supplement the 2013–15 financing program, IFAD secured a €400 million loan from KfW (KfW Bankengruppe), which has been used to on-lend to IFAD ordinary term borrowers, thereby securing lending targets to MICs, while also ensuring that IFAD replenishment sources resources are increasingly focused on the highly concessional (IDA) member countries (IFAD 2015b). This was followed, in 2016, with a similar arrangement with Agence Française de Développement, and, in the context of the IFAD11 replenishment discussions (2017), the possibility of accessing market funds, as practiced by other IFIs.

IFAD10 replenishment meetings concluded that IFAD's financial model was not sustainable for it to expand. The model of core replenishment contributions as the *sole* source of its external funding is unlikely to be adequate in the future, particularly if IFAD is to expand its operations to a level that reflects better the estimated demand for IFAD resources, yet is within the organization's capacity to deliver. IFAD would need to find alternative sources of financing besides replenishments options to expand the Programme of Loans and Grants (PoLG): sustained mobilization of core and unrestricted complementary contributions through replenishment cycles—borrowing to leverage IFAD's resources; borrowing from sovereign states and state-supported institutions in the short term; and exploring the scope for borrowing from the market in the long term. Market borrowing was not considered an option for IFAD10, however. Options also include expanding the programme of work (PoW) through supplementary funding and a more strategic and targeted approach to cofinancing.

IFAD11 was the first after the SDGs were adopted, and its deliberations related to IFAD's financing and operations for the period 2019–21. Meeting five times between February 2017 and February 2018 for the Consultation on the Eleventh Replenishment of IFAD's Resources, member states agreed to expand the Fund resources by US$100 million per year, to reach a total of US$3.5 billion for the three years of IFAD11. All combined, these changes and increased financing were made to enable IFAD to increase its outreach from almost 100 million poor rural people today, to 120 million by the end of 2021 and achieve greater impact across a range of the SDGs, with a focus on youth, the private sector, and poor rural areas and facilitating transformation. IFAD also undertook to examine how to leverage diversified sources of development finance to increase its PoLG.

The IFAD 11th Replenishment of its core financing for the 2019–21 period was concluded on February 12, 2018, prior to the session of IFAD's Governing Council, following a postponement of the final pledging session at the December 2017 replenishment meeting. The Governing Council (February 2019) subsequently reported that total pledges (as of January 31, 2019) amounted to US$934.4 million equivalent, corresponding to 78 percent of the IFAD11 target of US$1.2 billion, compared to US$1,030 million for IFAD10 (IFAD 2018c, 2019e, 2019f). Some countries, notably the United States, Spain, Denmark, and Belgium, did not pledge. Although unprecedented, these non-contributions (the United States' IFAD10 pledge was US$90 million) were partially offset by increased pledges from China (from US$60 million to US$81 million) and the Netherlands (from US$75 million to US$86 million).

The Replenishment target of US$1.2 billion is to provide for a lending and grant program of up to US$3.5 billion. IFAD will continue to use its Sovereign Borrowing Framework to borrow up to 50 percent of the replenishment target (from lenders such as KfW) and will consider concessional partner loan frameworks, similar to those introduced by IDA and the AfDB. Finally, IFAD has initiated discussions with member states to explore other possible market funding—for example, the Agri-Business Capital Fund and the Smallholder and Agri-SME Finance and Investment Network—but the amount and source of this funding are currently being assessed by management and would be subject to Governing Council authorization (IFAD 2019c).

Following changes to its allocation framework and as part of the IFAD11 Replenishment, IFAD will allocate 90 percent of its core finance to LICs and LMICs, with 10 percent going to upper middle-income countries (UMICs) (for example, China, Mexico, Brazil), which will mean a decrease in levels of funding to UMICs. In line with the Addis Ababa Financing for Development meeting, IFAD will try to further develop partnerships (and co-financing) with the private sector but has recognized that it remains a challenge (IFAD 2019c).

External Evaluations and Assessments of IFAD and IFAD's Responses

IFAD was subject to an independent external evaluation (IEE) in 2004–5. The evaluation, which reviewed IFAD's performance from 1994 to 2003, came to three strategic conclusions. First, IFAD needs to focus on improving its impact by increasing its efficiency, promoting innovations that can then be scaled up by others, and strengthening partnerships with other development actors. Second, to tackle challenges relating to the global demand to achieve the Millennium Development Goals (MDGs), despite the relative decline in ODA to the agriculture sector, IFAD would need to make significant changes to its operating model, including its management processes, and develop a new human resources policy. Third, IFAD would need to make changes to its governance, including a greater role for the Executive Board in overseeing the aid effectiveness of the Fund's activities (IFAD 2005). Following this evaluation, and in accordance with the findings, IFAD implemented rigorous reforms relating to targeting, decentralization, supervision, and country presence.

Furthermore, the IEE posed more strategic questions: namely, whether IFAD should consider "embrac[ing] a multi-sectoral approach to rural development and engage in new policy areas—including new aid modalities—related to rural poverty reduction, or focus [ing] on being an innovative, pro-risk institution that works specifically to support the agricultural productive potential of the poor, often in difficult and marginal areas" (IFAD 2005, 20). The evaluators believed this was an area where IFAD could exercise its specific expertise, but doing so would require a sharper operational approach to innovation and identification of groups to target.[4]

Another issue raised in the IEE is IFAD's comparative advantage. What makes IFAD different from the other IFIs? What value does it add? The answer could or should lie in IFAD's niche focus on the poorest of the poor in rural areas, and its mandate and experience within agricultural and rural development. No other UN agency or IFI claims to do so. It may also lie in its willingness to innovate, such as in its use of community empowerment approaches to rural poverty reduction, which enable governments to participate effectively in the process and can provide a basis for subsequent replication or expansion by governments and development agencies. Or it may lie in the relative weight of the Fund's contribution to agricultural and rural development, compared with overall ODA and the investments of IFIs. IFAD still has some way to go to fill this financing role in addressing rural poverty. Therefore, as the auspices for an increase in ODA are not bright, the role of IFAD as a mobilizer of funds for rural development would be both increasingly appropriate and in line with its founding charter (IFAD 2005). IFAD is now seeking to address this challenge with its evolving approach to borrowing funds (sovereign and, potentially, market based), particularly for lending to MICs.

In both 2010 and 2013, IFAD was assessed by the Multilateral Organisation Performance Assessment Network (MOPAN). Key findings were:

- "IFAD continues to be acknowledged for its clear and unique mandate and its commitment to instilling a results-oriented culture throughout the organisation" (MOPAN 2013, ix).
- "IFAD's country strategies systematically include objectives and results statements related to relevant cross-cutting priorities (gender, environment, and food security and nutrition)....In 2012 it launched an innovative Adaptation for Smallholder Agriculture Programme (ASAP), which provides financing to scale up and integrate climate change adaptation across IFAD's new investments" (MOPAN 2013, ix).
- IFAD "adopted a Country Presence Policy and Strategy [2014–15] in which it formally approved the establishment of up to 40 country offices..." (MOPAN 2013, 97).

---

[4] These same issues have come up periodically for the World Bank, and the Bank has gone back and forth between these choices. In Chapter 8 we argue that the World Bank, as the only multisectoral organization with larger resources, greater access to finance and planning ministries, and so forth, began looking at agriculture in the context of an overall structural transformation of economies, and assisting in addressing large infrastructure constraints (rural roads, power, water) and policy, and institutional challenges that keep people in poverty (Losch, Fréguin-Gresh, and White 2012).

"The 2013 corporate-level evaluation of IFAD's institutional efficiency noted that the limited substantive delegation of authority may conflict with the changing business needs associated with a decentralised institution" (MOPAN 2013, x).

- "IFAD has sound policies and practices in place for financial accountability,... has significantly improved its HR management policies and practices in recent years and remains committed to ambitious reforms in this area" (MOPAN 2013, x).
- "A review of IFAD's performance reports indicates that the organisation is delivering outputs in its thematic priority areas and reporting on these, but its reporting on higher level development results does not include sufficient data on its contributions to outcomes and impact" (MOPAN 2013, xii).
- "In the absence of a theory of change and data on outcomes and impact, it is difficult to appreciate the progress towards achieving the objectives outlined in IFAD's Strategic Framework 2011–2015" (MOPAN 2013, xii).

In response to these earlier MOPAN assessments, IFAD, as had other institutions assessed by MOPAN, highlighted the role of its own Executive Board-approved Results Framework and, additionally, the challenges of attribution of outcomes in a multi-stakeholder sector as diverse as agriculture.

The most recent MOPAN assessment 2017–18, noted that IFAD is "an agile, responsive and well-performing organisation. The Fund's strategy, organisational architecture and operating model are all very well geared to deliver IFAD's mandate and are sufficiently flexible to adapt to the changing global context and to member states' evolving needs and priorities" (MOPAN 2018, 7). In a similar vein to its earlier assessments, IFAD's 2017–18 MOPAN evaluation noted:

IFAD's results culture is strong and growing stronger, and the evaluation and accountability functions continue to be robust. The Fund has now established the basics of results-based budgeting. At the operations level, developments such as the Social, Environmental and Climate Assessment Procedures (SECAP) have further strengthened the intervention design process, including the mainstreaming of the cross-cutting issues such as gender and environment, although good governance and human rights remain a step back. Where outlooks could be stronger—notably on speed of disbursement—IFAD is making progress or is actively addressing the institutional shortcomings that have been linked with comparatively weaker performance. (MOPAN 2018, 7)

Although MOPAN notes that, "IFAD is better equipped to deal with a tighter financial environment," the assessment nevertheless indicates that with "the lack of growth in the value of member state core contributions" (MOPAN 2018, 8), a key "challenge for IFAD continues to be securing full funding for its programme of loans and grants" (MOPAN 2018, 19). In this regard, the move toward market borrowing, and the support of its members to do so, is key.

The World Bank, in its response to MOPAN's assessment of its performance, pointed out issues to MOPAN, which are also relevant to consider also in the context of MOPAN's assessment of IFAD. They include, the need to consider the organization's partnerships with other international organizations, as well as with all other stakeholders; to conduct MOPAN's assessment working with the development effectiveness scorecards of the organizations; and to consolidate reviews and evaluations being conducted by several different donors and organizations (UK's Department for International Development [DFID], the

Australian Agency for International Development [AusAID],[5] and MOPAN), rather than conducting them serially.[6] The assessments of IFAD by the DFID Multilateral Aid Review (MAR) and the Danish International Development Agency (DANIDA) are also cases in point of multiple assessments. In response to the World Bank's observations, the MOPAN 3.0 approach, initiated in 2016, puts an increased emphasis on assessing development effectiveness alongside organizational effectiveness (MOPAN n.d.). This issue of numerous, separate evaluations is also noted in the case of CGIAR (see Chapter 10). The reality is that bilateral donors still place great emphasis in decision-making of their own assessments, instead of trusting either the organizations or the evaluations carried out by other donors. In this regard, in 2017, DFID introduced a requirement at IFAD for a separate "Performance Report" (IFAD 2018a).

To the concern about multiple assessments, we would add the need to improve the statistics on which assessments are based, and the need to build country capacity and harmonized processes between donors and country statistical systems. The latter raises questions about looking at organizational and country performance on a project-by-project basis, as distinct from helping countries to put into place systems that will help them to achieve their stated development objectives on their own. The latter objective has received relatively little attention in ODA, despite being part of the Paris Declaration on Aid Effectiveness and the subsequent follow-up surveys and initiatives (OECD 2008).

In 2010–12, the Independent Office of Evaluation (IOE) evaluated IFAD's institutional efficiency and the efficiency of the operations it funded (IFAD 2013c). In line with OECD Development Assistance Committee (DAC) guidelines (OECD 2002), the evaluation defined efficiency as a measure of how economic resources (funds, expertise, and time) are converted into results. The efficiency evaluation, discussed with the Executive Board in early 2013, acknowledged that IFAD is "well recognized and valued as an institution dedicated to the eradication of rural poverty and improving food security in developing countries" (IFAD 2013c, 38), and confirmed that IFAD has introduced a number of "new operational processes and a new business and delivery model" (IFAD 2013c, 33). The evaluation's overarching message to IFAD was to "raise the bar" (IFAD 2013c, 7). The main findings are:

- IFAD has significantly increased its work program over the years, indicating progress toward its aim to be the leader in reducing global rural poverty.
- Partners and beneficiaries appreciate IFAD's focus on small and landless farmers, women, and other disadvantaged and marginalized groups.
- Performance is comparable to other multilateral development banks,[7] but IFAD's mandate and scale lead to higher costs relative to its outputs, and thus lower output efficiency than larger partners.
- To become a center of excellence, IFAD must catalyze scaling up and raise impact efficiency. The evaluation's view was that IFAD's value for money is compromised by too many projects across too many countries. Therefore, operations should be reduced, with larger programs focused on fewer countries.

---

[5] AusAID, however, considered IFAD's ratings on effectiveness as "strong" in relation to delivering results, aligning with Australia's priorities, strategic management and performance, cost and value consciousness, and transparency and accountability; and "satisfactory" in relation to contributing to the wider multilateral system and partnership behavior (Government of Australia 2012).

[6] The response was by Joachim von Amsberg, Vice President and Head of Network Operation Policy and Country Services, World Bank, to Gerry Cunningham, Chairman, MOPAN, Dublin, Ireland, January 17, 2003.

[7] The finding of comparable performance to other multilateral development banks is also supported by the "The 2012 Annual Report on Results and Impact of IFAD Operations," IOE of IFAD (IFAD 2012c).

- Improving efficiencies in the differences senses described will require greater prioritization and differentiation of operational services, with a stronger focus on results at
  country level.
- A stronger accountability framework, both within IFAD and its Executive Board, is
  fundamental for improving performance management (IFAD 2013c).

IFAD's Action Plan and Reform Agenda

In response to the 2004–5 evaluation, IFAD was to address the identified challenges through
an agreed Action Plan. These efforts were most visible in IFAD's operations and its
operating model. As part of these efforts, IFAD developed a number of new strategies
and policies, including a Targeting Policy (IFAD 2006c) and the results-driven 2007–10
Strategic Framework (IFAD 2006a), one of the key elements of its Action Plan. Within this
framework, IFAD's mission was further expanded, as evident in its overarching goal "that
rural women and men in developing countries are empowered to achieve higher incomes
and improved food security at the household level" (IFAD 2006a, v).

An independent, donor-sponsored review of the Action Plan was conducted in 2008.[8] Its
objectives were to assess the progress that IFAD had made in implementing reforms and the
potential effects of the reforms on development effectiveness. The review gave an overall
positive assessment of the Fund's progress in implementing the commitments, as outlined
in its Action Plan. It concluded that some meaningful steps had been taken to improve the
organization's development effectiveness (IFAD 2008a). For example, IFAD had produced
its first results measurement framework (IFAD 2007b), with a set of indicators for reporting
on progress achieved against the IFAD Strategic Framework 2007–10 (IFAD 2006a), which
included a new self-evaluation exercise. Innovation and knowledge management strategies
were developed, the Report on IFAD's Development Effectiveness (RIDE) was produced
(IFAD 2017c), and a new quality assurance system was implemented.

Following the IOE's 2010–12 evaluation of IFAD's institutional efficiency, IFAD's management (IFAD 2013g) and the Executive Board (IFAD 2013d) responded positively,
generally embracing these recommendations. The board also underlined the importance
of reconciling enhanced operational selectivity, which the evaluation recommended with
IFAD's mandate of operating in all regions to serve all borrowing member states, both LICs
and MICs. From a selectivity perspective, it is worth considering if IFAD needs to be in
high-middle-income countries, such as Brazil and China, where per capita gross domestic
product (GDP) is high. Nevertheless, along many non-income parameters, poverty is as
severe in some MICs as it is in LICs. A 2017 IFAD report, "Tailoring Operations to Country
Context—A Holistic Approach," noted that "countries experience the 'middle-income
trap'—a situation in which growth slows after reaching middle-income levels," which is
also compounded in rural areas with growing income inequality, as compared to urban
areas (IFAD 2017e, 6). This highlighted the need for South–South knowledge components
in IFAD projects, from which the poorer performers could learn some direct lessons on
strategy, policy, investment planning, and implementation of high quality. Moreover,
there is a case to consider that lending to high-income countries typically costs less in

---

[8] The independent assessment of the IFAD Action Plan, conducted in 2008, was commissioned by the
Governments of Canada, Norway, and the Netherlands; prepared by Ted Freeman, Goss Gilroy Inc. Management
Consultants (Canada), Stein Bie, and Noragric, The Norwegian University of Life Sciences, July 8, 2008.

preparation and larger project size is possible, with disbursements usually faster. This raises the question as to whether there is a trade-off between increasing efficiency and assisting the poorest in LICs.

However, such a trade-off would be somewhat in conflict with IFAD's mandate of operating in all regions to serve all borrowing member states. Although lending to high-income countries is typically for larger sized projects, it is not necessarily cheaper, and while disbursements may be faster, that is more likely a function of project type (for example, credit), than country type. Therefore, there is no substantive evidence of a trade-off of efficiency that should divert assistance away from the poorest in LICs.

IFAD management developed a Consolidated Action Plan to Enhance Operational and Institutional Efficiency. The plan, discussed in the IFAD Evaluation Committee and Executive Board in September 2013, covers each of the evaluation recommendations, addressing first the actions related to enhancing IFAD's operational effectiveness and efficiency and then the proposed actions to enhance institutional efficiency. The document also contains an annex listing each action, with its proposed timeframe and an indication of potential costs (IFAD 2013e). The Plan's progress is also assessed annually through the President's Report on the Implementation Status of Evaluation Recommendations and Management Actions (PRISMA), which reported that "almost all items are on track, and significant efforts and reforms have been initiated across departments" (IFAD 2015c, 8).

IFAD's Operating Model

As a result of IFAD's evolving strategy, and also, in response to the external evaluations and assessments, IFAD made several shifts in its operating model, performing its own supervision and increasing its country presence. This was accompanied by a sharper focus on targeting the poorest people in rural areas, which led to the development of the Results-Based Country Strategic Opportunities Programs (RB-COSOP) and a Targeting Policy (IFAD 2006c), both introduced in 2006. The RB-COSOP was to be aligned with national priorities. The documents emphasize synergies between lending and nonlending instruments, results and performance management, learning and accountability, partnership building and harmonization, and innovation and scaling up (IFAD 2013k).

Targeting

IFAD's Targeting Policy defines its overall target group as: "rural people who are living in poverty and experiencing food insecurity [in developing countries], and who are able to take advantage of the opportunities to be offered (sometimes referred to as the 'the productive poor' or 'active poor'") (IFAD 2006c, 12). Under the policy, a target group would be identified through gender-sensitive poverty and livelihood analysis, which incorporates the views of poor women, men, and their organizations. Attention is also to be paid to including marginalized minorities and indigenous peoples. Geographically, IFAD targets areas with high concentrations of poor people or with high poverty rates.

At the Governing Council session in February 2018, at the Consultation of the Eleventh Replenishment of IFAD's Resources, member states agreed on a Results Management Framework (RMF) for the Fund covering 2019–21 and including a range of indicators and associated targets. Those include targets for decentralization (3.6.1 [ratio of budgeted staff positions in IFAD country offices/regional hubs] and 3.6.3 [percentage of supervision/implementation support through IFAD country offices/regional hubs]) and institutional efficiency (3.7.1 [ratio of IFAD's administrative expenditure to PoLG], 3.7.2 [ratio of actual administrative expenditures to IFAD's PoW], 3.7.3 [ratio of IFAD's actual administrative expenditures to annual disbursements], and 3.7.4 [ratio of the administrative budget to the ongoing portfolio of loans and grants]. These targets in turn include six indicators related to decentralization and efficiency. IFAD targets were based on the updated information on decentralization, as well as informed by the revision of the delegation of the authority framework (IFAD 2018a).

Martin Ravallion, in his article, "How Relevant Is Targeting to the Success of an Antipoverty Program?" summarized his argument, based on a cash transfer program in China:

> Policy-oriented discussions often assume that "better targeting" implies larger impacts on poverty or more cost-effective interventions...standard measures of targeting performance are uninformative or even deceptive about impacts on poverty, and cost-effectiveness in reducing poverty....In program design and evaluation, it would be better to focus directly on the program's outcomes for poor people than to rely on prevailing measures of targeting. (Ravallion 2009, 205)

Other reports on targeting—for example, from the ADB, as discussed in Chapter 8 on the World Bank—suggest that based on a number of case studies of major Asian programs and a long history of targeting, there has very been limited impact of targeting on poverty reduction relative to macroeconomic policies.

Several evaluations conducted by IFAD's IOE have addressed geographic targeting and found that IFAD projects are implemented across a wide geographic area, spread too thinly across the country (which is especially a concern in larger countries), or cover non-adjoining states or provinces within countries.[9] The evaluations concluded that such geographic targeting has constrained effectiveness, efficiency, and sustainability, and therefore, merits attention in the design of future COSOPs and projects (IFAD 2013i).

Country Programme Evaluations (CPEs) confirm that IFAD's approach to targeting, in general, was appropriate in most countries and that thematic targeting in country (as opposed to geographic): that is, through value chains, has been more effective. The shift to strengthening the links between the rural poor and markets has enhanced relevance, although implementation has remained challenging. In Nigeria, Vietnam, and Zambia, the introduction of support for value chains has increased the relevance of IFAD support for vulnerable groups, such as landless laborers, farmers with very limited land, and unemployed youth. The use of local expertise and participation of local stakeholders in the design and implementation of IFAD-supported interventions have enhanced the relevance of IFAD support for some MICs, such as China. The poorer performance in other countries is attributable to weak institutional capacity in the areas where IFAD was working; greater difficulties in targeting the poor (Ecuador and Mexico); and weak government ownership

---

[9] Examples of IFAD Independent Office of Evaluations include: Country Programme Evaluations in Brazil (IFAD 2008b); Mali (IFAD 2007a); India (IFAD 2010d); and Indonesia (IFAD 2014c).

(Mexico). None of these were issues in China, where convergence with government programs generated significant government commitment (IFAD 2014b).

Nevertheless, IFAD's clear emphasis on the poor has helped to focus light on the poor in several MICs, and in doing so, emphasized the importance of rural poverty alleviation in countries with rapidly expanding national economies, highlighting the issues of political commitment, national ownership, and the importance of getting targeting right, if this is indeed the approach to pursue. Hence, IFAD's focus on Northeastern Brazil and areas of Southern Mexico where, within all projects, the specific component design usually has characteristics that focus on and respond to poorer households, reflects IFAD's predesign/ design household analysis.

Targeting remains of key concern to IFAD, and the ARRI of 2016 highlighted IFAD's targeting approach, central to its mandate of rural poverty reduction, noting, "Comprehensive targeting approaches enable operations to reach the poorest of the poor by combining solid livelihood and poverty analysis, based on context-specific circumstances, and dynamic participatory processes" (IFAD 2016a, 13). The report, however, noted, "The 2015 evaluations found that poverty analyses conducted at design do not sufficiently capture the differences among groups of poor rural people, [and] thus, more can be done to ensure that appropriate attention is devoted to IFAD's targeting strategies at design and that monitoring efforts are deployed during implementation" (IFAD 2016a, 13). In terms of strategies to address this approach, geographical targeting is an option, but can encounter other problems—lack of government commitment, working with minorities, remoteness, and lack of access to investments in rural infrastructure that could link poor farmers to markets—can all be very daunting, so that only where other supporting services exist or are developed can this work be beneficial. In China, benefits included savings in transport time and costs, and improved access to markets, services, and information. In Nigeria, by contrast, the CPE found that inadequate market linkages were a significant constraining factor, followed by deficiencies in roads and transport conditions, storage, access to credits, and market information (see, also, Nchuchuwe and Adejuwon 2012). In Ghana, flooded roads have been repaired and improved in one district, but the lack of production planning and marketing channel support has prevented local producers from taking full advantage of the improved infrastructure.

Attention to Africa

IFAD has also given a high priority to reducing poverty in Africa, committing 50 percent of its total resources. The deepest poverty and hunger are found in sub-Saharan Africa, with the largest number of fragile countries and countries with resource constraints, all providing special challenges. In July 2003, at the African Union summit in Maputo, Mozambique, leaders of the continent pledged to allocate at least 10 percent of their national budgets to agriculture and to achieve at least 6 percent annual agricultural growth. In the same year, they adopted the Comprehensive Africa Agriculture Development Programme (CAADP), pledging to develop national agriculture through defined investment plans. In 2006, African leaders committed to allocating 1 percent of agricultural GDP to agricultural research and development (R&D). IFAD noted in its report on Africa, "Fulfilling the Promise of African Agriculture":

In the decade since the Maputo Declaration, fewer than 20 per cent of countries have fulfilled either of their Maputo commitments; more than 30 have signed the CAADP compact with at least 19 countries launching detailed plans to accelerate agricultural development; and 8 countries have exceeded the R&D pledge.

With a view to scaling up investment in rural spaces, production systems, consumption markets, natural resources and environmental services, and influencing the post-2015 development agenda, IFAD supports the call for an "enhanced Maputo" agreement:[10]

- Increase investment and improve services to smallholder farmers, especially women, including concrete timetables for meeting their existing pledges.
- Prioritize and accelerate policies and investments that support smallholder farmers.
- Increase transparency and accountability in the implementation of an enhanced Maputo framework, while engaging smallholder farmers on accountability. (IFAD 2014a, 16)

The African Union declared 2014 the Year of Agriculture and Food Security with a spotlight on African agriculture. Against this background, IFAD asserted: "IFAD has delivered more, to more people, and delivered it better. At the end of 2013 there were 241 ongoing programmes and projects worldwide with an IFAD investment of US$5.4 billion, compared with US$3.9 billion for 217 programmes and projects at the end of 2009" (IFAD, 2014e, 1). Since its establishment, IFAD has invested US$15.6 billion in projects that have "reached" approximately 420 million people (IFAD 2014e, 6) and used the IFAD9 Replenishment discussion with member states to provide information on its Impact Evaluation Initiative, which covered household characteristics (assets).

Supervision

One step that IFAD took to increase its impact was the development of a Supervision and Implementation Support Policy in 2007. The agreement that established IFAD in 1977 did not allow for direct supervision, nor was IFAD expected to have a country presence or be involved in policy dialogue. The development of a Supervision and Implementation Support Policy was commended in an evaluation by the IOE, which noted that the policy provided IFAD the opportunity "to get 'closer to the ground' in borrowing countries and to understand the country context more fully" (IFAD 2012a, iii). The evaluation also said that the policy "facilitated more direct [and rapid] follow-up with implementing agencies to address bottlenecks that emerged during project implementation," and it allowed IFAD to better cultivate partnerships with multiple stakeholders (IFAD 2012a, iii). However, the evaluation concluded that implementation arrangements were inadequate, owing to lack of a basic supervision manual, insufficient training on implementation support, and absence of a coordinated approach to supervision across IFAD departments and regions. The evaluation recommended that IFAD consider "best practices from the different approaches to increase harmonization, efficiency and shared responsibilities [and accountability] across IFAD departments" (IFAD 2012a, iii).

[10] See the African Union's 2003 Maputo Declaration on Agriculture and Food Security: https://www.nepad.org/caadp/publication/au-2003-maputo-declaration-agriculture-and-food-security

Country Presence

Another significant reform of IFAD's operating model is the development of a permanent field presence. When the reform started in 2006, one country office was operational. By the end of 2010, 29 of the 30 authorized offices were operational, and by the end of 2016, 40 IFAD Country Offices (ICOs) were serving a total of 77 countries, covering approximately 80 percent of its total financing, with 58 percent of them in Africa. This initiative is being implemented through the Corporate Decentralization Plan, completed in 2016. It includes three models for ICOs: (1) subregional hubs; (2) country programme groups; and (3) single ICOs. This plan would enable IFAD to supervise its programs and projects more closely, reduce response times, and promote scaling up (IFAD 2016d). In its comments on the new Country Presence Policy (IFAD 2011a, 2011c), the evaluation office commended IFAD for its commitment to enhancing its development effectiveness, but suggested that portfolio performance and other criteria be considered when selecting countries in which to establish offices. The document also encouraged more clarity about the process for selecting the appropriate mode of presence. The evaluation office comments point out, for example, that hosting the IFAD presence in the country offices of a multilateral development banks would provide further opportunity for more focus on nonlending activities, such as policy dialogue, partnerships, and knowledge management, thought to be key components of the "mission critical" push to scale up IFAD operations (Hartmann et al. 2013, 1; IFAD 2013f). However, the majority of IFAD offices are linked to the United Nations Development Programme (UNDP), which has enabled bilateral agreements (and staffing and support services) to be more easily managed. Although the evolution of the overall process has emphasized a shift in emphasis from supervision by mission to a process of "continuous supervision," there is a concern that projects and programs, meant to be implemented by governments through loan or grant financing, could be perceived as IFAD initiatives implemented by IFAD with consequences for real government ownership and sustainability (IFAD 2013h, 59).

IFAD reports that its country presence has translated into cost savings, due to outposting of staff from headquarters and increased local hiring (IFAD 2010b). According to the Country Presence Strategy, the estimated cost of the 39 country offices (in 2013) was US $12.51 million, with US$8.65 million covering staff costs and US$3.86 million, non-staff costs (IFAD 2013f, 2). The 2017 work programme and budget has budgeted US$5.22 million for non-staff costs of the ICO program, but staff costs, including staff at IFAD permanently assigned to ICO management or staffing costs of IFAD Country Program Officers are not suballocated from existing departmental budgets (IFAD 2016f). IFAD country presence efforts have been complemented by progress in decentralizing its program, administrative, and financial operations to the field. Initial administrative procedures were issued in 2009, in a comprehensive *Country Presence Handbook*, outlining all administrative features of the set-up, and operation of country offices was developed in 2011 (IFAD 2011a, c). An updated "Country Presence Strategy (2014–2015)" was presented to the IFAD Executive Board in December 2013 (IFAD 2013f), followed in 2016 by the Corporate-level Evaluation of "IFAD's Decentralization Experience" (IFAD 2016d) and, as noted previously, the 2016 Corporate Decentralization Plan. The Plan indicated that there was a "consistent pattern of improvement in project efficiency and effectiveness due to decentralization, suggesting that more country presence is generally better" (IFAD 2016b, ii). The analysis, based on project status reports and project Completion

Reports, however, showed marginal improvements only, with only the Vietnam office given delegation of budget authority, an issue raised by MOPAN (2013).

IFAD Operations

Like many other development finance institutions, IFAD uses a performance-based alloca-tion system (PBAS) to allocate financing to member states. The IFAD PBAS allocates all of IFAD's Replenishment sourced to IFAD country lending/grant (DSF) programs. Resources are distributed to each respective country program, according to a formula approved by the Executive Board. The formula was initially based on rural population, per capita gross national income (GNI), and country performance. Other institutions that use a PBAS include the IDA of the World Bank (where the system was first developed), AfDB, ADB, the Inter-American Development Bank, the Caribbean Development Bank, and the Global Environment Facility (GEF). IFAD's PBAS follows similar approaches to the other institu-tions, with the exception that IFAD's approach included an annual Rural Sector Perfor-mance Assessment that emphasizes rural sector issues and has accordingly lessened the influence of the World Bank's Country Policy and Institutional Assessment (CPIA). The role of CPIA has been further reduced with modifications in IFAD's PBAS approach in 2016–17, following the evaluation,[11] and with the introduction of other variables, including climate vulnerability. However, for all the institutions utilizing a PBAS approach, such modifications are a zero-sum game, insofar as the total resources available for distribution among countries at any one time do not change. What can change is the allocation at country level, and in this regard IFAD faces, unlike other IFIs, a unique allocation man-agement problem, given the many eligible members (List C eligible borrowing countries currently total 139, compared to other IFIs, who have much fewer), but only limited annual resources to allocate. Although the number of borrowing countries usually averages 90 during a respective replenishment period, the total funds available are approximately only US$3.2 billion over the three-year period. The issue is compounded by the fact that only IFAD, of all the IFIs implementing a PBAS, includes ordinary term borrowing MICs in its PBAS to receive Replenishment-sourced financing. Other IFIs use market-based funds to finance ordinary term borrowers, and some member countries are concerned that their Replenishment contributions are going to MICs rather than least developed countries (LDCs).

Figure 11.1 shows the number of programs under implementation over time. Since starting operations in 1978, IFAD has financed low-interest loans and grants (about US$28 billion) for more than 900 projects and programs that have reached some 483

---

[11] According to "IFAD's Performance-based Allocation System Corporate-Level Evaluation" of April 2016 (IFAD 2016e), as summarized by the Evaluation Cooperation Group (ECG):

> Overall, the PBAS [has been] found to be relevant [MOPAN and bilateral assessments]. The formula should better factor in some key dimensions of IFAD's priorities, such as food security, nutrition and climate change. It also should improve the way it considers vulnerability issues as determinants of country needs. The evaluation finds the system's effectiveness to be on the whole moderately satisfactory. The rationale for including or excluding countries from the PBAS and the underlying mechanisms guiding the capping system should be made more explicit and institutionalized. Among the recommendations, the need to refine the PBAS design, by sharpening its objectives and strength-ening the rural poverty focus; streamline the process for better effectiveness; and enhance management and governance, by taking a more corporate approach to the PBAS in general. (ECG 2016)

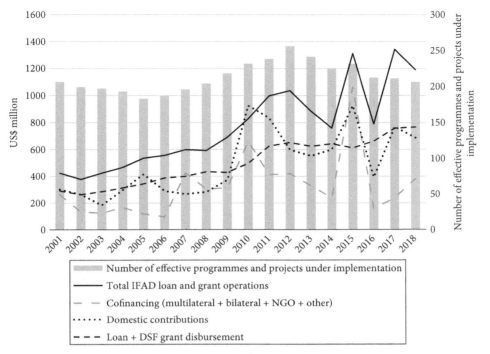

Figure 11.1 IFAD's operational summary, 2001–2018 (US$m)
Source: Based on IFAD Annual Reports.

million poor rural people.[12] Annual commitments rose to slightly over a billion in 2013 (about the same size as CGIAR's annual expenditures per year, although the two are not strictly comparable—IFAD creates investment projects, and CGIAR funds research projects). When leveraging co-financing by donors and governments is accounted for, however, IFAD's portfolio seems much larger. Including funds and external and domestic co-financing, total investments in agricultural development, poverty reduction, and improved food security between 2009 and 2013, leveraged by the annual commitments shown Figure 11.2, rose from US$7.9 billion to US$12.2 billion. In 2013, 72.8 percent of financing was for low-income, food-deficit countries (as classified by the FAO), and 52.6 percent was for the LDCs (as classified by the UN) (IFAD 2015a). As we showed in Chapter 8 on the World Bank, performance of LICs and LDCs has been consistently weaker than that of more advanced countries. This calls for special approaches to rural development strategies, as well as to project development and project implementation, such as the iterative processes being developed by the United States Agency for International Development (USAID). Figure 11.2 shows the total number of projects with IFAD and domestic financing.

---

[12] See "IFAD: About Us": https://www.ifad.org/en/about
 What it means to "reach" people is fraught with ambiguity. If they live near a road, it may mean access to markets, a very different matter than being reached by access to finance, seed, inputs, or knowledge. Moreover, the impacts of IFAD's projects and programs on incomes or welfare depend on another complex set of factors.

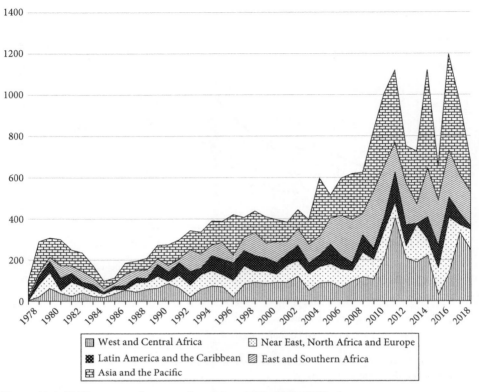

Figure 11.2 IFAD approved amount by region, 1978–2019 (US$m)
Source: https://www.ifad.org/en/web/operations/operations-dashboard

Scaling Up

In 2009, IFAD undertook an institutional scaling-up review, for which Brookings Institution conducted a desk analysis of IFAD's country and thematic operational approaches (Linn et al. 2010). The review also considered IFAD's corporate strategy, operational policies, processes, and instruments, as well as its budgetary and human resource management practices to determine whether they were supportive of a systematic scaling-up approach to development. In parallel, the IOE carried out a corporate evaluation of IFAD's approach to innovation and scaling up, which concluded that scaling up is critical for IFAD if it is to achieve its goal of reducing rural poverty. It also found that IFAD had effectively supported the scaling up of successful agricultural and rural development programs in a number of countries, but that this success has not always resulted from a systematic operational approach. It was often due to fortuitous circumstances. Therefore, IFAD's strategies, operational policies, processes, and instruments, as well as its budgeting and staff incentives, need to evolve to support a more proactive and systematic approach to scaling up (IFAD 2010a, 2012b; Thapa and Hessel 2016).

In 2010, IFAD commissioned another review of its approach to scaling up operations. The review, carried out by the Wolfensohn Center for Development at the Brookings Institution, concluded that "IFAD knows how to scale up and has done so successfully many times....But scaling up deserves greater and more explicit attention in IFAD's operational work than it has received to date" (Linn et al. 2010, 45). The assertion of successful scaling up seems to contradict IFAD's own assessment. It also concluded that scaling up will have to be a part of institutional change and a more systematic approach guided by a simple and focused strategy. The review warned against "creating a new 'mantra;' forgetting that scaling up is a means to an end, not the end itself; creating excessively burdensome processes; and spreading IFAD's human resources too thin" (Linn et al. 2010, 45).

The review's observations are perceptive, not simply because of what they state, but because the review was authored by former senior World Bank managers and is a commentary on aid, generally, if not at least on agriculture. Citing Hartmann and Linn (2008), the review notes that ambitious development goals have been set, but not yet met by the international community:

> The challenge is not just a matter of more, better coordinated and less volatile aid. A key constraint that needs to be overcome is that development interventions—projects, programs, policies—are all too often like small pebbles thrown into a big pond: they are limited in scale, short-lived, and therefore without lasting impact. This may explain why so many studies have found that external aid has had only a weak or no development impact in the aggregate at the global and at the country level, even though many individual interventions have been successful in terms of their project- or program-specific goals. (Linn et al. 2010, 2, citing Hartmann and Linn 2008, 2)

The review diagnosed a major challenge for IFAD. It is confronted the gap between its small size and the large scale of poverty in the rural areas it was mandated to address. Hartmann et al. (2013, 1) noted, "For many years, IFAD stressed innovation as the key to success, giving little attention to systematically replicating and building on successful innovations." Hartmann and Linn (2008, 8) defined what scaling up meant for IFAD, from a World Bank 2004 conference:[13] "expanding, adapting and sustaining successful policies, programs or projects in different places and over time to reach a greater number of people."

IFAD is devoting increased efforts to scaling up in recent years. In the Evaluation Synthesis Report on IFAD's Support to Scaling Up of Results, however, it was noted, "Almost all COSOPs since 2010 have made reference to scaling up, but few have articulated a strategy for it" (IFAD 2017b, vi). Only two countries (Liberia and Vietnam) included fully developed scaling-up strategies (IFAD 2017b). Other CPEs assessed scaling up as moderately satisfactory or in need of strengthening. Overall, scaling up is, typically, ad hoc, without sufficient consideration for linkages with knowledge management, policy dialogue, and partnership building. A more strategic and systematic effort might have ensured a wider replication and scaling up of successful innovations. Scaling up is particularly important in MICs, with their large number of rural poor. Promoting sustainability of benefits, as well as ensuring IFAD assistance, can have a wider impact on rural poverty at the national level. Partnerships with government, the private sector, and other donors are critical for scaling up, particularly, given IFAD's relatively limited resources. With regard to governments, this also requires IFAD to work with a range of national-level counterparts, both technically and nontechnically capable. This is, however, a challenge in some countries: for example, in China where only limited dialogue is possible between IFAD and the

[13] The World Bank conference, "Reducing Poverty, Sustaining Growth: Scaling Up Poverty Reduction. Case Study Summaries," A Global Learning Process and Conference, was held in Shanghai, May 25–7, 2004.

National Ministry of Agriculture. A strong partnership could possibly offer opportunities for scaling up successful innovations tested in IFAD-supported projects into national policy, with activities funded through domestic resources.

So, what does IFAD need to do? The Brookings review recommended several steps:

Step 1: Define the scale of the issue to be addressed and the appropriate scale of intervention up front along with a suitable time horizon.

Step 2: Define suitable pathways of scaling up by identifying the drivers and spaces for scaling up, including the costs of project implementation (or service delivery, etc.).

Step 3: Explore the institutional, organizational, and policy context that allows scaling up.

Step 4: Define the partners who can assist with or take over the scaling-up process and what needs to be done to bring them on board.

Step 5: Define the appropriate operational instruments (loans, grants, technical assistance, policy dialogue, etc.) for IFAD to support the scaling up process.

Step 6: Monitor and evaluate the pilot or experimental project as well as the scaling-up process in terms of the suitability of the pathway and impact on the rural poor. (Linn et al. 2010, 12)

According to the study, successful scaled-up innovations have been few and far between: "the River Blindness Program in West Africa, which largely helped to eradicate the widespread and deadly disease onchocerciasis; the Grameen Bank and BRAC [Building Resources Across Communities] programs of microcredit for poor people in Bangladesh; and the *Progresa-Opportunidades* program in Mexico and similar conditional cash transfer programs elsewhere in Latin America, which have helped tackle endemic poverty" (Linn et al. 2010, 3). The challenge lies in making sure that scaling up is appropriate. Therefore, the study suggests quite an elaborate approach to scaling up externally designed and funded projects. It does not point out, however, that some of the largest poverty programs in the developing world, including some of those cited by the Brookings study, were designed, championed, and implemented by national policymakers or social entrepreneurs. This applies, for example, to the Grameen Bank in Bangladesh, the Amul Dairy Schemes, the National Rural Employment Scheme in India, the cash transfer programs in Brazil and Mexico, and land reform in China. The probability of large impacts is much higher if indigenously conceived, planned, and implemented programs are supported by external aid, and their quality improved, rather than ideas always being introduced, designed, and financed externally. The latter often tend to experience too little domestic ownership.

And yet, the scope for improving public expenditures of developing countries remains vast. In a recent book on public works that have become popular interventions among developing country governments, Subbarao et al. (2013) noted:

While this combination of past and emerging experiences demonstrates the potential of public works programs as an important safety net for addressing the poor's vulnerability to shocks, the overall record of achievement is uneven. Public works programs are beset by myriad challenges involving transparency and leakage, including in India's nationwide flagship program MGNREGS [Mahatma Gandhi National Rural Employment Guarantee Scheme]. Issues of governance and corruption have arisen in many programs across the globe, and threaten to rob public works instruments of their credibility and repute in achieving their stated objectives. (Subbarao et al. 2013, 2)

The same is true of school feeding programs (see Chapter 12 on WFP). Looking to donors' pilot interventions to scale up, while overlooking the effectiveness of already existing government programs is a weakness of the Brookings proposal. *Progressa*, now called *Opportunidades* in Mexico, was a government intervention that has been responding to domestic evaluations. Indeed, demand for evaluation offices within governments has increased, as citizens are demanding more accountability of public funds. The challenge is to ensure evaluation findings have an impact on improving program interventions. Evaluations of many of the School Feeding Programs in India have had remarkably little impact on improving interventions.

The Consolidated Action Plan to Enhance Operational and Institutional Efficiency concluded:

> Scaled-up impact is the key to long-term efficiency, which in turn depends upon IFAD supporting high-quality projects and programmes with demonstrated impact...despite improvement in recent years, IFAD's performance is predominantly moderately satisfactory, which could limit opportunities for scaling up successful innovations promoted by IFAD-supported projects and programmes through partner resources. (IFAD 2013b, 1)

In commenting by the IOE on IFAD's Plan, their first recommendation was: "Scaling up of high-impact, innovative approaches emerging out of IFAD-supported projects and programmes should become the objective of IFAD's business model" (IFAD 2013b, 1).

Clearly, the challenge is to convince governments in the developing world and their cooperating donors to scale up those agricultural investments that are working and to introduce policies that create an enabling environment for innovation and scaling-up activities. An additional essential element to scaling up is the need to adhere to a long-term commitment rather than a one-off, three-to-five-year project, followed by a quick exit. IFAD's success in Peru, in which it supported the government in scaling up agricultural and rural development investments in poor areas of the Andes over a 20-year period, had two critical ingredients: government commitment to operating at scale and donor willingness to support governments in doing so (Cleaver 2013).

We concur with this assessment of the importance of domestic strategy and commitment from the outset to design sound programs that would have impacts and the need for long-term presence. While external actors can be critical to success, as they were for the River Blindness program or the Green Revolution, those conditions rarely exist in today's aid environment. So, as happened with Grameen, Amul, Mexico, or Brazil's conditional cash transfers, the desire to scale up must come first from domestic actors, from policymakers, civil society, or the private sector. They need a long enough presence, an ability to learn by doing, and exceptional domestic political and strategic savvy to succeed. Much of the writing on scaling up overlooks these important domestic commitments, which external actors can support. The Green Revolution and River Blindness programs were initiated and supported by outside agencies. In both cases, the World Bank, working with other partners, played a critical role. Yet, in both cases, the partners also had smart technological solutions, and they were willing to create institutions and to provide human capital and financial support long enough to nurture and sustain their growth. Those conditions often do not exist. Today's donors have a short-time horizon; they tend to be impatient for results, look for them mechanistically, and typically, are not interested in building long-term, domestic human or institutional capacity. Each of the large successful programs noted here have had a minimum of 10 to 15 years of a gestation period. While access to cell phone technology is, at a minimum, necessary, it is the institutions, policies, good practices, and their routine monitoring and independent evaluation that tend to take time to establish.

IFAD has made a significant effort to ensure that scaling up is mainstreamed into operational activities. It is explicitly incorporated as an institutional objective in the formulation of IFAD's Medium-Term Strategic Framework 2011–13 (IFAD 2011b). A scaling-up agenda under the program to be funded by the ninth replenishment of IFAD's resources during 2013–15 was approved by IFAD's Governing Council in February 2012, and IFAD's internal guidelines for formulation, implementation, and monitoring of country programs and projects have been adjusted to reflect the focus on scaling up. Replication and scaling up has also been added to the 2013–15 RMF with targets set for 2015. The IFAD Report on Development Effectiveness 2014 noted, "Performance with respect to replication and scaling up has strengthened considerably" (IFAD 2014f, 3). Nevertheless, scaling up can only happen when dialogue with clients is strong. IFAD is staffed with qualified, dedicated people in the field, who are respected by client countries; it is flexible in a variety of ways, and it carefully identifies national leaders who have the commitment and the demonstrated tenacity and potential to establish, monitor, and support scaled-up programs. In May 2019, IFAD announced new targets as part of its updated RMF for the 2019–21 period, as noted earlier in this chapter (IFAD 2019g). The six indicators on decentralization and institutional efficiency would be informed by IFAD's ongoing change and reform agenda, including co-financing targets and historical trends in mobilizing supplementary funds and other IFAD-managed resources. Decentralization targets include greater presence of field staff and greater country programming closer to the action, as well as targets for reduced operating costs.

IFAD's Approach to Rural Poverty in Middle-Income Countries

IFAD's evaluation of its engagement in MICs is full of rich insights relating to its strategy and raises strategic questions for IFAD, as well as for the development community committed to eradicating extreme poverty and promoting shared prosperity by 2030 (IFAD 2014b). Because the poorest of the poor are IFAD's declared focus, more so than other IFIs, the evaluation rightly stresses that MICs are highly diverse. The synthesis evaluation illustrates that there are many different ways of classifying MICs (Vázquez and Sumner 2012). The majority of the world's poor live in the MICs (including 75 percent below the poverty line). Half of the world's poor are in China and India alone; 67 percent are concentrated in only five MICs—India, China, Nigeria, Indonesia, and Pakistan— while 80 percent live in only 10 countries (IFAD 2014b). Given that IFAD resources may be spread across many countries, as many as 97 countries in 2013–15, the question arises whether it should concentrate its human and financial resources on fewer countries and achieve better results, particularly in light of other findings.

Second, by spreading IFAD's loans, grants, and staff over 97 countries, many countries receive as noted in the previous discussion on PBAS, very limited resources. The financial resources offered may be too little to make a significant difference—or even to be of interest—and the rationale for country presence will either be nonexistent or very limited. As the evaluation of "IFAD's Engagement in Middle-income Countries" pointed out, greater country selectivity would ensure that IFAD was able to deploy a minimum "critical mass" of resources wherever it worked (IFAD 2014b, 36). This is not the case at present.

IFAD is a global organization with a mandate to lend to all member states, and its membership may not agree to focus on only a few countries. Finally, as the evaluation notes, "a goal of maximizing the total impact on poverty...would suggest that resources should be allocated in line with the distribution of rural poverty, and in a way that maximizes the likely impact of those resources" (IFAD 2014b, 32). The PBAS partially does this, but the PBAS could be calibrated to further accentuate this goal by introducing indicators such as the UN Poverty Index.[14] Although some MICs have large numbers of poor people, many countries, such as Jordan and the Republic of Moldova, do not.[15] In 2013, 25 percent of the PBAS allocation went to "two largely MIC regions—LAC [Latin America and the Caribbean] and NEN [the Near East and North Africa], containing 1.7 percent to 2.3 percent of the rural people living in extreme poverty (US$1.25/day) or poverty (US$2/day) respectively" (IFAD 2014b, 32).

Distribution of resources is related to the issue of the internal graduation across financing terms and, eventually, to the possibility that countries "self-graduate by opting not to borrow or not to renew their membership" [and consider changing their List status] (IFAD 2014b, 33). Subject to "Policies and Criteria for IFAD Financing" (IFAD 2019d), replenishment resources are available to all List B and C members without respect to their income level: that is, to both MICs and LICs, and with lending terms calibrated to GNI per capita thresholds. This is different than the World Bank's IDA, "where replenishment resources are only available to a sub-set of IDA qualifying countries (currently those with GNI per capita up to US$1,205)" (IFAD 2014b, 33).[16] Once IDA countries graduate over the IDA cut-off rate, and through blend terms, countries become eligible to borrow from the International Bank for Reconstruction and Development (IBRD) at IBRD terms, sourced from market funds, not replenishment. Those same countries borrow at ordinary terms from IFAD, with the terms aligned to the London Interbank Offered Rate (LIBOR) benchmark rate, like IBRD.

As such, IFAD needs a strategic approach to both resource mobilization and program choice that either focuses on countries with the highest number of poor and excels in addressing their problems—or continues to spread itself too thin and raises far more resources to address those issues. ODA resources have become increasing scarce, however. IFAD has sought to address poverty through its engagement with MICs (IFAD 2011c), but also, in response to the evaluation of IFAD's middle-income strategy, the development of a country selectivity approach (IFAD 2014b), and developing an approach for sovereign borrowing (IFAD 2015d).

Finally, the evaluation synthesis for IFAD's engagement with MICs, reports:

There is no evidence from the project data that IFAD-supported projects perform better in MICs than in LICs, possibly because IFAD-supported projects in MICs tend to be located in poorer, remote and more difficult regions, where context is similar to that found in LICs, and in some cases, in fragile states. Moreover,...(i) the projects evaluated by the IOE in MICs were designed around a decade ago and would not have benefitted fully from important reforms introduced in recent years (e.g., wider country presence, direct

---

[14] The PBAS could be calibrated by increasing the −0.25 exponent on GNI/capita, for example.

[15] The international absolute poverty line US$1.90/day was updated from US$1.25/day in 2015, as the threshold for extreme poverty, but the World Bank has established two higher thresholds of US$3.20/day and US$5.50 per day in LMICs and UMICs, respectively (World Bank 2018).

[16] IDA eligibility was based on GNI per capita of US$1,175 in fiscal year 2020.

supervision, enhanced leadership of CPMs [Country Programme Managers] in project design processes, etc.); and (ii) the sample is relatively small and therefore more data and closer monitoring to validate and understand the differences in performance between upper UMICs and LMICs is needed. (IFAD 2014b, 15)

In many respects, IFAD programs face similar challenges in all types of countries, and of critical importance, programs in MICs are not necessarily different from those in LICs. Nevertheless, although previous evaluations reflect a range in performance across the world, the evaluation of IFAD projects in China notes that the latest round of four integrated rural development projects since 2009 has been very successful (IFAD 2014d). The IFAD evaluation of those projects further noted that projects are successful when they are well-designed and underlined that more resources must be allocated to enhancing no-lending activities (knowledge management, policy dialogue, and partnerships), as well as to South–South and triangular cooperation. IFAD has financed 27 agriculture and rural development projects and programs in China. IFAD's financial contribution of around US$775 million, since the approval of its first loan in 1981, corresponds to a total project cost of US$1.94 billion. China has been the second largest recipient of IFAD's assistance. IFAD's project results in China are very similar to those of the World Bank, discussed in Chapter 8. Interestingly, although the donor community rejected the idea of integration based on its experience of poor projects in sub-Saharan Africa in the 1970s, the integrated approach is alive and working well in China. Instead of completely abandoning it, the Chinese have made a religion of adaptation and learning from mistakes (IFAD 2014d).

Non-lending issues (policies, capacity, and partnerships) are particularly important in MICs (especially, UMICS) and are becoming more important as national incomes increase. "IFAD's non-lending activities will be more successful if they are supported and complemented by an adequate lending programme" (IFAD 2014b, 16). Non-lending activities have been the weakest area of IFAD's support, although there are signs of improvement after 2011. Knowledge management, policy dialogue, and partnerships are particularly important in MICs, and even more so in UMICs (IFAD 2014b).

IFAD's Performance in Measuring Development Effectiveness: The Use of Scorecards and Results Management Frameworks

IFAD, like FAO and the World Bank, measures its development effectiveness, not to be confused with impact assessment. In the case of IFAD, the World Bank, and other multilateral development banks, this has taken the form of RMFs, usually developed in parallel with respective replenishment processes that cover 3–4-year cycles (IFAD 2007b, 2009, 2011d, 2014g, 2017d, 2019f). Since 2005, IFAD has used a six-point ratings scale to assess performance on each evaluation criterion and report on operational performance in ARRI analyses. Ratings from 2002 onwards are recorded in an independent evaluation database, which is publicly available. Projects rated moderately satisfactory or better are in the "satisfactory" zone (4–6), while projects rated unsatisfactory or worse are in the "unsatisfactory" zone (1–3). These scorecards are used in the replenishment of resources, the processes of mobilizing resources, ensuring accountability for results, and enabling strategic dialogue with financiers and clients. These efforts continue to be improved, with considerable energy devoted to preparing RMFs/scorecards that tell us how lives of the poor are being transformed on the ground. This has led to both an elaboration of outcome indicators and separately of the development of impact evaluations. IFAD has come a long way in operationalizing these lessons and increased its effectiveness and efficiency. IFAD's performance, measured in terms of the ratings of its projects, reached an all-time low in 2003–5. After extensive reforms following the 2004–5 Independent External Evaluation, IFAD is now a more agile organization. The 2013–14 evaluation of institutional and programmatic efficiency has resulted in further reforms to achieve greater institutional efficiency in internal processes and procedures and in the efficiency of program outputs, outcomes, and impacts (IFAD 2013c). Despite the reforms, IFAD still faces challenges in the rapidly changing aid environment. Evaluations have called on it to "raise the bar" in the efficiency of its projects (IFAD 2013c, 7), in the measurement of its impacts, and on scaling up its operations. It has been urged to develop strategic collaboration with the other Rome-based food and agriculture agencies, specifically, streamlining administrative procedures, particularly disbursement, to reduce processing time and costs. Yet, each Rome-based agency has its own personality and identity, and despite many years of efforts, developing true, results-based partnerships has not been easy, as discussed in the Chapters 9 and 12 on FAO and WFP, respectively.

Like other IFIs, IFAD's overall structure of the RMF was conceived as a hierarchy in which an immediate lower level result (at the project level) underpins, explains, and contributes to higher level results (at the level of the portfolio, and then, the organization). The scope of the RMF has been expanded substantially over the years. It is also aligned with the reporting instruments of other IFIs, notably the World Bank, AfDB, and ADB.[17] Like the World Bank, the RMF is intrinsically an organizational scorecard linked to organizational efficiency and administrative budget allocation.

The RMF is tied to the replenishment period, a results and impact management system, a PBAS for transparent and predictable allocation of resources, and annual reporting on development effectiveness—the RIDE and ARRI, produced by the IOE.[18] In addition, IFAD, in the 2016 RIDE, has reported on impact-level indicators for the first time, assessed through the IFAD9 Impact Assessment Initiative (IAI) (IFAD 2016g). IFAD has noted that number of people that increased their incomes to above the poverty line is, on its own, inadequate to assess the impact on the well-being of IFAD's beneficiaries. IFAD argues in RIDE 2016 that rural poverty impact "is a composite of five impact domains: household income and assets, agriculture and food security, human empowerment and social capital, institutions and policies, and markets" (IFAD 2016f, 2). In parallel, IFAD has also produced a Development Effectiveness Framework for measuring results, including impact, underpinned by a theory of change (IFAD 2016c). A revised Results and Impact Management System (RIMS) consolidated RIMS indicators with the Core Indicators of the IFAD RMF: "For a subset of projects (approximately 15 percent of the portfolio), IFAD will conduct rigorous outcome and impact assessments on an 'attribution' basis, through its impact assessment programme" (IFAD 2017f, 5). Impact-level indicators, linked to SDG targets will include: the number of people experiencing economic mobility; the number of people with

[17] IFAD has chaired the Multilateral Development Bank Management for Development Results (MfDR) working group and coordinated the annual production of the Common Performance Assessment System (COMPAS) since 2012.

[18] IFAD has revised its RMF as part of the IFAD11 2019–21 replenishment process.

improved production; the number of people with improved market access; and the number of people with greater resilience. The 2016 RIDE reports that the IAI indicated:

> IFAD's investments in rural people generate results in a number of critical areas, including assets, resilience, livestock ownership, agricultural revenues, nutrition and women's empowerment. Projections indicate that some 44 million beneficiaries are enjoying substantial increases in agricultural revenues, and 28.8 million and 22.8 million beneficiaries have realized significant gains in poultry and livestock asset ownership, respectively. Moreover, impact estimates suggest that IFAD investments can reduce poverty by up to 9.9 per cent, corresponding to an aggregate result of 23.8 million people moved out of poverty in the 2010–2015 period. (IFAD 2016g, iv)

Although most IFIs use a 3- or 4-level RMF, IFAD uses a 5-level approach, with Level 1 reporting on global poverty, food security, and agricultural investment outcomes, including: the proportion of population below the international poverty line of US$1.90 a day; the prevalence of undernourishment in population; the prevalence of (moderate and severe) food insecurity; and the prevalence of stunting among children under five years of age. The second level, country-level development outcomes and impact delivered by IFAD-supported projects reports on the number of people experiencing economic mobility; the number of people with improved production, market access, and greater resilience, which link with FAO's Strategic Objectives and indicators (see Chapter 9).

Level 3 focuses on country-level development outputs delivered by IFAD-supported projects: for example, agricultural technologies, rural financial services, marketing, micro-enterprises, and climate change adaptation. Level 4 reports on operational effectiveness of IFAD-supported country programs and projects and examines issues such as portfolio management, while Level 5 assesses IFAD's institutional effectiveness and efficiency, including its administrative efficiency and human resources management. The analyses conducted as part of the RIDE by IFAD have indicated that "IFAD's systems are adequate for early identification of problem projects (including inefficiency and a lack of sustainability); and that the Fund has been able to improve performance of the majority of problem projects" (IFAD 2018b, 1–2).

The ARRI annually assesses IFAD's rural poverty impact, based on a sample of recent project evaluations, in terms of institutions and policies; natural resources, the environment, and climate change; food security and agricultural productivity; household income and assets; and human and social capital and empowerment.[19] Overall, the reported rural poverty impact of IFAD operations has improved over the past decade, and an upward trend is particularly visible in recent years, albeit from a slightly less than 60 percent of projects still rated as moderately satisfactory during the 2009–11 period (IFAD 2013a). This trend has continued with the 2016 ARRI noting "improved performance during IFAD9 on operational priorities such as rural poverty impact, human and social capital empowerment, innovation and scaling up, gender equality and women's empowerment" (IFAD 2016a).

The 2018 ARRI noted:[20]

---

[19] Rural poverty impact is defined as "the changes that have occurred or are expected to occur in the lives of the rural poor (whether positive or negative, direct or indirect, intended or unintended) as a result of development interventions" (IFAD 2017a, 6).

[20] The quantitative findings of the 2018 ARRI were drawn from a sample of 320 project evaluations, completed between 2002 and 2016, as well as 45 country strategy and programme evaluations, with a collection of 2,542

There is a lack of agreement within the Fund on the target group and strategies needed... [the] trend towards market-oriented projects as well as IFAD's increased focus on the need for greater attention in targeting to gender equality, indigenous peoples and youth calls attention to the possible need to re-examine and clarify IFAD's target group and strategies.

Effective targeting requires robust poverty analysis and well-informed targeting strategies to meet the needs of poor rural people. [IFAD's experience illustrates] the importance of developing targeting strategies and designing and implementing projects on a foundation of strong contextual understanding. There is also the need for realistic and flexible targeting to allow for modifications in a rapidly changing world, particularly in fragile or post-conflict contexts. (IFAD 2018d, 16)

The 2019 ARRI noted that, "Overall, the performance of IFAD operations shows flat or slightly declining trends. While 75 percent of all evaluation ratings were positive between 2007 and 2017, satisfactory and better ratings are diminishing. These trends are also reflected in Management's project completion report ratings for all criteria" (IFAD 2019h, 7). The Foreword to the ARRI by Oscar Garcia, Director, Independent Office of Evaluation of IFAD, further noted:

IFAD project performance continues to outperform that of the African Development Bank and Asian Development Bank in the agriculture sector in their respective regions. However, globally and in the regions of Latin American and the Caribbean as well as the Near East, North Africa and Europe, IFAD project performance is now lower than that of the World Bank, whose definition does not include sustainability of benefits. (IFAD 2019h, 7)

Impact Assessment

Generally, across major international institutions, there is a lack of impact indicators attributable to that institution. Only IFAD, CGIAR, GAFSP, and GEF have set at least one impact target generated by their own operations, whereas the others have reported only lower level outputs and outcomes. Moreover, only in the case of IFAD, and to some extent CGIAR, can one see an attributed impact target and an explanation for how it is to be produced and measured. In light of this, IFAD's approach of attempting to attribute an impact to the institution, rather than merely monitoring its contribution, remains unusual among IFIs. Winters and Garbero (2018) recounted the many challenges in doing impact assessment. They consider attribution of outcomes to a particular intervention and establishing a counterfactual by far to be the biggest challenge. There are also other challenges, including measuring costs and benefits, aggregating the impact of individual interventions/ projects to corporate-level impacts, issues of external validity—some of these are discussed in Chapter 8 on the World Bank. During the 9th Replenishment, which included the aspirational goal of raising 80 million people out of poverty, IFAD embarked on impact assessment as part of its RMF. It undertook to conduct impact assessments on 15 percent

---

ratings from their project reflect evaluations, which allows the Office of Evaluation of IFAD (IOE) to update and refine its statistical analyses (IFAD 2018d, 6).

of its portfolio to be able to report impacts on its corporate objectives (see, also, Gaarder and Brown 2019).

FAO has improved the data that countries collect routinely and which FAO reports (and which support the *State of Food Insecurity and Nutrition in the World* and the *State of Food and Agriculture* reports).[21] It is also supplementing these macro data with household surveys. It is no accident that there are few credible studies of donor or government interventions that relate outcomes to investments and influence policy.[22] Both FAO and IFAD are working closely with the World Bank on the 50 x 2030 initiative as a central theme to support better data management and results reporting at the country level. A key opportunity for both IFAD and FAO is the greater alignment of their results frameworks, consolidation of indicators, and further enhancement of their existing collaboration on SDG indicators (FAO 2018).

The 2018 ARRI concludes:

> Conducting benchmarking analysis, the 2018 ARRI finds that IFAD project performance continues to outperform the Asian Development Bank and African Development Bank in the agriculture sector in their respective regions. In Latin America and the Caribbean, IFAD project performance is on par with the World Bank, but falls behind in the Near East, North Africa and Europe region, as well as globally.... Overall, the performance of IFAD operations has been positive. Seventy-six percent of all evaluation ratings are moderately satisfactory or better in the period 2007–2016. Currently, 80 percent or more projects assessed against the criteria of relevance, innovation, scaling up, rural poverty impact and IFAD performance as a partner are rated moderately satisfactory or better. (IFAD 2018d, 6)

> When comparing performance between the periods 2007–2009 and 2014–2016, IFAD's performance as a partner shows good performance and improvement, while project performance has declined. Following a decline from 2009 to 2011, performance across the criteria improved up to the 2012–2014 period, after which rural poverty impact and government performance as a partner began to decline. In the period 2014–2016, only IFAD performance as a partner shows continuing improvement, having overtaken rural poverty impact as the strongest performing criterion since 2013–2015, while trends in overall project achievement and project performance are flat, and declining in rural poverty impact and government performance as a partner. (IFAD 2018d, 10–11)

> The 2018 ARRI highlights however that the portfolio performance trend is flat, with signs of deterioration. In the period 2014-2016, sustainability, efficiency, innovation, scaling up, gender equality and women's empowerment, government performance and rural poverty impact all declined slightly. Sustainability of benefits and efficiency remain long-standing

---

[21] See, for example, "Acting on Food Insecurity and Malnutrition, the Food Insecurity and Capacity Profile" (FAO 2014).

[22] Some notable exceptions are studies of Training and Visits extension, a Systematic Review of Farmer Field Schools. See Waddington and White (2014).

bottlenecks for project performance, with the lowest means in the entire period of 2007–2016. (IFAD 2018d, 6)

IFAD management has recognized these issues in the RIDE 2018, while recognizing the effect of using a 36-month rolling average and the impact of fragile state performance. Management has sought to address the concerns through decentralization; a programmatic approach; a streamlined design process to reduce time lags; and a facility for faster project start-up. Future ARRIs will need to specifically assess the effects of these initiatives as, in themselves, they have elements of commonality with similar approaches used by other IFIs.

Rural poverty impact showed an overall improvement from 2009–11 to 2012–14 for projects rated moderately satisfactory or better, declining to 81.4 percent in 2014–16. The 2018 ARRI noted: "Satisfactory ratings represent 32.2 percent of projects in 2014–2016, guaranteeing steady good performance. No highly satisfactory ratings have been reported in rural poverty impact" (Figure 11.3). Figure 11.4 depicts rural poverty impact by replenishment period (IFAD 2018d, 35).

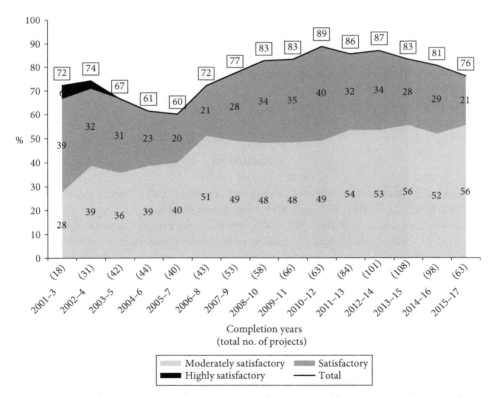

Figure 11.3 Rural poverty impact by project completion years (three-year moving period) (% of projects rated moderately satisfactory or better, all evaluation data series)

Source: Data provided by Jacqueline Souza, IFAD.

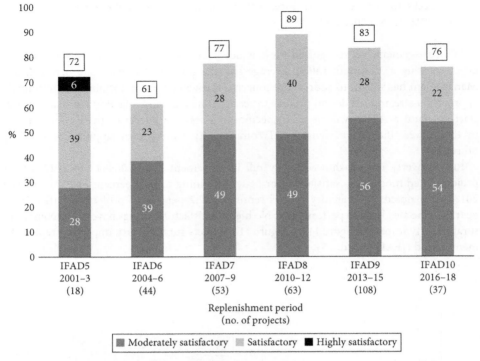

Figure 11.4 Rural poverty impact by replenishment period (% of projects rated moderately satisfactory or better, all evaluation series)

Source: Data provided by Jacqueline Souza, IFAD.

Conclusion

The 2019 *SOFI* report (*State of Food Security and Nutrition in the World*), jointly prepared by FAO, IFAD, UNICEF, WFP and WHO, has highlighted that 9.2 percent of the world population (or slightly more than 700 million people) were exposed to severe levels of food insecurity in 2018. An additional 17.2 percent of the world population, or 1.3 billion people, have experienced food insecurity at moderate levels, meaning they did not have regular access to nutritious and sufficient food. Moreover, overweight and obesity continue to increase in all regions, particularly among school-age children and adults. In 2018, an estimated 40 million children under five were overweight (FAO et al. 2019).

IFAD's vision in which rural extreme poverty is eliminated through inclusive and sustainable agriculture and rural development is of continued importance to address SDG2 (zero hunger and rural transformation), particularly SDG2.3 and SDG2.4. External evaluations have shown that IFAD, a small and agile organization, has been effective in addressing its declared mission, and therefore, remains a central tool for more investment through development programs. This investment needs to be made in rural areas in all member countries to strengthen resilience and adaptive capacity of food systems, people's livelihoods, and nutrition in response to climate variability and extremes. Moreover, IFAD's ability to develop partnerships with government, the private sector, domestic actors, policy-makers, civil society, and other donors supports SDG17 of the revitalization of global partnerships. This goal includes the targets both of promoting effective public, public–private, and civil society partnerships, and mobilizing additional financial resources for developing countries.

Addressing rural poverty across and within all IFAD's developing country member states will need both innovative financial and programmatic mechanisms, supported by the respective commitments and a broader range of partners. IFAD's mandate remains relevant, particularly in LMICs and MICs with acute per capita income inequality, but there is a huge gap between needs and expectations and what can actually be delivered under the existing architecture and funding structure. Responding to these developments and to the dilemma of whether only to assist poor people in poor countries (as defined by average per capita country income) will test IFAD's ingenuity, creativity, and capacity for innovation.

Going forward, however, IFAD faces several challenges going forward, which have been explored in the course of IFAD's 10th and 11th replenishment with no clear resolution yet. On the supply side, continuing with business as usual could be challenging, given stalling ODA and slow progress in increasing replenishments. ODA to agriculture has increased by 30 percent over the past five years, but it is still only 5 percent of total ODA. Implicit in the reliance on the traditional model of replenishments is the possibility of reduction in its program of loans and grants.

On the demand side, there is a huge gap between needs and expectations and what can actually be delivered under the existing architecture and funding structure. Progress toward ending poverty and hunger has stalled as growing food insecurity, linked to fragility and climate change, threatens IFAD's ability to contribute to achieving SDGs by 2030. IFAD is thus at a crossroads with several options on the supply and demand side, which we have discussed in this chapter.

Together with the development community, and specifically, its Executive Board, IFAD needs to choose among options. For IFAD to continue its declared mission of addressing rural poverty across and within *all* developing countries among its member states, IFAD will need both innovative financial and programmatic mechanisms, supported by commitments from a broader range of partners. IFAD is implementing recommendations of existing external evaluations and the IOE or the Officer of Audit and Oversight, but it should also carry out a further independent assessment in 2021.

The IFAD10 replenishment meetings concluded that IFAD's financial model, as the *sole* source of its external funding, is unlikely to be adequate in the future; particularly, if IFAD is to expand its operations to a level that better reflects the estimated demand for IFAD resources, and yet, is within the organization's capacity to deliver. IFAD would need to find alternative sources of financing beyond replenishments to expand its PoLG. This could mean sustained mobilization of core and unrestricted complementary contributions through replenishment cycles, and borrowing to leverage IFAD's resources in the short term from sovereign states and state-supported institutions and in the long term from the market. Options also include expanding the PoW through supplementary funding and a more strategic and targeted approach to co-financing. Market borrowing was not considered as an option for IFAD10.

The Eleventh Replenishment (IFAD11) was the first to occur after the SDGs were adopted, and its deliberations concerning IFAD's financing and operations were for the period 2019–21. Meeting five times between February 2017 and February 2018 for the Consultation on the Eleventh Replenishment of IFAD's Resources, member states agreed to expand the Fund resources by US$100 million per year to reach a total of US$3.5 billion for the three years of IFAD11. These changes, combined with increased financing, were effected to enable IFAD to increase its outreach from almost 100 million poor rural people today to 120 million by the end of 2021 and to achieve greater impact across a range of the SDGs, with a focus on youth, the private sector, and poor rural areas, facilitating transformation. IFAD also undertook to examine how to leverage diversified sources of development finance to increase its PoLG.

The drive by successive IFAD presidents to increase the PoLG has not come without consequences. Until the Ninth Replenishment, IFAD has traditionally relied on member state contributions to finance its PoLG (IFAD 2019a). Since the Ninth Replenishment of IFAD's resources, however, IFAD has gradually become more dependent on its capacity to generate internal resources (that is, reflows) and on borrowing. The use of advance commitment authority (ACA) was allowed with the regular IFAD9 contributions of US $1.17 billion, a Ninth Replenishment PoLG of US$2.4 billion (IFAD 2013j). The introduction of this approach was, as noted, "a major change with respect to the practice under previous replenishments" (IFAD 2013j, 1), and secured higher PoLGs, despite replenishment levels that had not shown substantial growth. IFAD has become, therefore, more dependent on its capacity to generate internal resources (reflows) and ensure that reflows match or exceed the rate of disbursements, in line with its Liquidity Policy (IFAD 2006b).

As the IFAD PoLG and loan commitments have increased, so, too, with a time lag, has the need to finance the increasing levels of disbursements required by the implementation of these approved loans. In addition, IFAD has also been disbursing for its approved grants, including those authorized under the DSF and making payments on the debt servicing of the sovereign borrowing as well (for example, Spain, Germany–KfW). This has put pressure clearly on IFAD's internal resources and the underlying assumptions, including the levels of investment income and loan reflows, in particular, from UMICs and LMICs (noting that some loans to MICs are entirely financed from sovereign borrowing), all of which have affected IFAD's liquidity levels. IFAD has recognized these issues, and as IFAD12 replenishment discussions proceed has, as of December 2019, approved a Capital Adequacy Policy and is finalizing a new Liquidity Policy, with the objectives of both securing a substantial replenishment and establishing the basis for IFAD to receive a AAA credit rating, as a basis for market borrowing.

Building on the resourcing strategies of partnerships is important for IFAD, particularly given IFAD's relatively limited resources and, as MOPAN 2017–18 notes "the lack of growth in the value of member state core contributions" (MOPAN 2018, 8) and the challenge in "securing full funding for its programme of loans and grants" (MOPAN 2018, 19). As IFAD11 barely reaches the US$1.1 billion of the US$1.2 billion replenishment targets, it places emphasis not only on the move toward market borrowing, and the support of its members to do so, but also on forging more profound partnerships with other financial institutions, including the World Bank Group, regional development banks, and other institutions such as GAFSP, whose partnership approaches to governance structures, civil society, and the private sector are lessons for IFAD.

IFAD's mandate remains relevant, including in LMICs and MICs with acute per capita income inequality, but there is a huge gap between needs and expectations and what can actually be delivered under the existing architecture and funding structure. As IFAD continues the IFAD12 Replenishment discussions, responding to these developments and the dilemma of whether only to assist poor people in poor countries (as defined by average per capita country income) will test IFAD's ingenuity, creativity, and capacity for partnership engagement, innovation, and financial management. IFAD will most certainly need and deserve more resources.

References

Cleaver, Kevin. 2013. "The Importance of Scaling Up for Agricultural and Rural Development. And a Success Story from Peru." IFAD Occasional Paper 4, IFAD, Rome. https://www.ifad.org/documents/10180/ae15c993-f5b7-4ab1-aaf8-800f1b59420a

ECG (Evaluation Cooperation Group). 2016. "Corporate-level Evaluation: IFAD's Performance-based Allocation System." https://www.ecgnet.org/document/corporate-level-evaluation-ifad%27s-performance-based-allocation-system

FAO (Food and Agriculture Organization of the United Nations). 2014. "Acting on Food Security and Malnutrition: Food Security Commitment and Capacity Profile." Methodology Paper, FAO, Rome. http://www.fao.org/3/a-i3998e.pdf

FAO (Food and Agriculture Organization of the United Nations). 2018. "Global Push to Stamp Out Hunger Hinges on Better Data." FAO News, September 25. http://www.fao.org/news/story/en/item/1154013/icode/

FAO (Food and Agriculture Organization of the United Nations), IFAD (International Fund for Agricultural Development), UNICEF (United Nations Children's Fund), WFP (World Food Programme), and WHO (World Health Organization). 2019. *The State of Food Security and Nutrition in the World 2019. Safeguarding against Economic Slowdowns and Downturns.* Rome: FAO. http://www.fao.org/publications/sofi/en/

Gaarder, Marie, and Liz Brown. 2019. "Sounds Good … But What Will It Cost? Making the Case for Rigorous Costing in Impact Evaluation Research." Evidence Matters blog, International Initiative for Impact Evaluation (3IE). https://www.3ieimpact.org/blogs/sounds-good-what-will-it-cost-making-case-rigorous-costing-impact-evaluation-research

Global Donor Platform for Rural Development. 2008. "The Future of Smallholder Agriculture." Platform Policy Brief No. 2, October. https://www.odi.org/sites/odi.org.uk/files/odi-assets/publications-opinion-files/3468.pdf

Government of Australia. 2012. "Assessment Summary: International Fund for Agricultural Development." In *Australian Multilateral Assessment*, 151–5. Canberra: Commonweath of Australia. https://dfat.gov.au/about-us/publications/Documents/ama-full-report-2.pdf

Hartmann, Arntraud, Homi Kharas, Richard Kohl, Johannes Lin, Barbara Massler, and Cheikh Sourang. 2013. "Scaling Up Programs for the Rural Poor: IFAD's Experience, Lessons, and Prospects (Phase 2)." Global Economy & Development Working Paper 54, January, Brookings Institution, Washington, DC. https://www.brookings.edu/wp-content/uploads/2016/06/ifad-rural-poor-kharas-linn-new.pdf

Hartmann, Arntraud, and Johannes Linn. 2008. "Scaling Up: A Framework and Lessons for Development Effectiveness from Literature and Practice." Wolfensohn Center for Development Working Paper No. 5, October, Brookings Institution, Washington, DC. https://www.brookings.edu/wp-content/uploads/2016/06/10_scaling_up_aid_linn.pdf

IFAD (International Fund for Agricultural Development). 1976. "Agreement Establishing the International Fund for Agricultural Development." Adopted by the United Nations Conference on the Establishment of an International Fund for Agricultural Development, Rome, June 13. https://www.ifad.org/documents/10180/3162024b-49d9-4961-a5de-8e2bbfabef9d

IFAD (International Fund for Agricultural Development). 1978. "Policies and Criteria for IFAD Financing." Adopted by the Governing Council at its Second Session, Rome, December 14. https://www.ifad.org/documents/10180/f1a1c976-ceec-4672-b1b0-c19c4237e5b1

IFAD (International Fund for Agricultural Development). 1997. "Meeting Challenges in a Changing World. IFAD's Strategic Framework for 1998–2000." IFAD, Rome.

IFAD (International Fund for Agricultural Development). 2001. "Enabling the Poor to Overcome Their Poverty. IFAD's Strategic Framework for 2002–2006." IFAD, Rome. https://www.ifad.org/documents/10180/fc169625-0f8e-4eab-8db4-198c3344bd94

IFAD (International Fund for Agricultural Development). 2005. "An Independent External Evaluation of the International Fund or Agricultural Development." September, Office of Evaluation, IFAD, Rome. http://www.sida.se/contentassets/00765cd8cefd47b4be1a095160890581/an-independent-external-evaluation-of-the-international-fund-or-agricultural-development_3140.pdf

IFAD (International Fund for Agricultural Development). 2006a. "IFAD Strategic Framework 2007–2010: Enabling the Rural poor to Overcome Poverty." IFAD, Rome. https://webapps.ifad.org/members/eb/89/docs/EB-2006-89-R-2-Rev-1.pdf

IFAD (International Fund for Agricultural Development). 2006b. "Liquidity Policy." EB 2006/89/R.40, November 14, Executive Board, 89th Session, IFAD, Rome. https://webapps.ifad.org/members/eb/89/docs/EB-2006-89-R-40.pdf

IFAD (International Fund for Agricultural Development). 2006c. "Targeting Policy: Reaching the Rural Poor." November, IFAD, Rome. https://www.ifad.org/documents/10180/dc9da3d9-b603-4a9a-ba67-e248b39cb34f

IFAD (International Fund for Agricultural Development). 2007a. "Mali Country Programme Evaluation." Independent Office of Evaluation, IFAD, Rome.

IFAD (International Fund for Agricultural Development). 2007b. "Results Measurement Framework for Reporting on Progress Achieved Against the IFAD Strategic Framework 2007–2010." IFAD, Rome.

IFAD (International Fund for Agricultural Development). 2008a. "Assessment of IFAD's Action Plan." Final Report. Prepared by Ted Freeman, Goss Gilroy, Inc. Management Consultants (Canada) and Stein Bie, Naragric, The Norwegian University of Life Sciences.

IFAD (International Fund for Agricultural Development). 2008b. "Brazil Country Programme Evaluation." Independent Office of Evaluation, IFAD, Rome.

IFAD (International Fund for Agricultural Development). 2009. "Results Measurement Framework for the Eighth Replenishment period (2010–2012)." August, IFAD, Rome. https://webapps.ifad.org/members/eb/97/docs/EB-2009-97-R-2.pdf

IFAD (International Fund for Agricultural Development). 2010a. "Corporate-Level Evaluation: IFAD's Capacity to Promote Innovation and Scaling Up." Report No. 2240, June, Office of Evaluation, IFAD, Rome. https://www.ifad.org/documents/10180/b39bba79-ad00-4911-ae1b-e0cce44c6ba3

IFAD (International Fund for Agricultural Development). 2010b. "Country Presence Brings IFAD Even More Closer to the People It Serves and Works with." (Anonymous post). IFAD Social Reporting Blog, November 11. http://ifad-un.blogspot.com/2010/11/country-presence-brings-ifad-even-more.html

IFAD (International Fund for Agricultural Development). 2010c. "Establishment of the Spanish Food Security Cofinancing Facility Trust Fund." IFAD, Rome. https://webapps.ifad.org/members/eb/100/docs/EB-2010-100-R-29-Rev-2.pdf

IFAD (International Fund for Agricultural Development). 2010d. "India Country Programme Evaluation." Independent Office of Evaluation, IFAD, Rome. https://www.ifad.org/en/web/ioe/evaluation/asset/39832000

IFAD (International Fund for Agricultural Development). 2010e. "IFAD Strategic Framework for 2011–2015. Enabling Poor Rural People to Improve Their Food Security, Raise Their

Incomes and Strengthen Their Resilience." EB 2010/101/R.12, November 24. IFAD, Rome. https://webapps.ifad.org/members/eb/101/docs/EB-2010-101-R-12.pdf

IFAD (International Fund for Agricultural Development). 2011a. "Comments of the Office of Evaluation on IFAD's Country Presence Policy and Strategy." April, IFAD, Rome. https://webapps.ifad.org/members/ec/67/docs/EC-2011-67-W-P-7-Add-1.pdf

IFAD (International Fund for Agricultural Development). 2011b. "IFAD Medium-term Plan 2011–2013." Document # EB 2011/102/R.32, May 9, 2011, IFAD, Rome. https://www.ifad.org/documents/38714170/39132730/strategic_e.pdf/97cfceb3-8b91-4c5f-9afa-0eb4d5729adf

IFAD (International Fund for Agricultural Development). 2011c. "IFAD's Engagement with Middle-Income Countries." May, IFAD, Rome. https://www.ifad.org/documents/10180/8794b336-34b6-467b-bff4-32f8c719f93a

IFAD (International Fund for Agricultural Development). 2011d. "Results Measurement Framework 2013–2015." Document # REPL.IX/3/R.4, September 29, IFAD, Rome. https://www.ifad.org/documents/10180/b7992d46-5a88-4814-a31d-c000fdd1ba27

IFAD (International Fund for Agricultural Development). 2012a. "IFAD's Direct Supervision and Implementation Support: Evaluation Synthesis." July, Report No. 2572, Independent Office of Evaluation, IFAD, Rome. https://www.ifad.org/documents/10180/60bb0f0a-2fd5-4595-aea2-d815337f3ae9

IFAD (International Fund for Agricultural Development). 2012b. "Transforming IFAD, Changing Lives." March, IFAD, Rome.

IFAD (International Fund for Agricultural Development). 2012c. "The 2012 Annual Report on Results and Impact of IFAD Operations (ARRI): Policy Dialogue." July, Independent Office of Evaluation, IFAD, Rome. https://www.ifad.org/documents/10180/f71ab140-4667-4318-95eb-fb95c04af94d

IFAD (International Fund for Agricultural Development). 2013a. "Annual Report on Results and Impact of IFAD Operations (ARRI): Understanding Exceptional Projects." Independent Office of Evaluation, IFAD, December, Rome. https://www.ifad.org/documents/10180/6c64194e-1b73-4328-9d51-94e371340264

IFAD (International Fund for Agricultural Development). 2013b. "Comments on the Independent Office of IFAD on the Consolidated Action Plan to Enhance Operational and Institutional Efficiency." EC 2013/78/W.P.5/Add.1, September, IFAD, Rome. https://webapps.ifad.org/members/ec/78/docs/EC-2013-78-W-P-5-Add-1.pdf

IFAD (International Fund for Agricultural Development). 2013c. "Corporate Level Evaluation of IFAD's Institutional Efficiency and Efficiency of IFAD-funded Operations." April, Independent Office of Evaluation, IFAD, IFAD, Rome. https://www.ifad.org/documents/10180/a781120f-3b52-493d-833a-e8d7fc1075ee

IFAD (International Fund for Agricultural Development). 2013d. "Decisions and Deliberations of the 108th Session of the Executive Board." May, IFAD, Rome.

IFAD (International Fund for Agricultural Development). 2013e. "IFAD Consolidated Action Plan to Enhance Operational and Institutional Efficiency." August, IFAD, Rome. https://webapps.ifad.org/members/ec/78/docs/EC-2013-78-W-P-5.pdf

IFAD (International Fund for Agricultural Development). 2013f. "IFAD Country Presence Strategy (2014–2015)." November, IFAD, Rome. https://webapps.ifad.org/members/eb/110/docs/EB-2013-110-R-5.pdf

IFAD (International Fund for Agricultural Development). 2013g. "IFAD Management Response to the Corporate Level Evaluation of IFAD's Institutional Efficiency and Efficiency of IFAD-funded Operations." March, IFAD, Rome.

IFAD (International Fund for Agricultural Development). 2013h. "IFAD's Supervision and Implementation Policy Support." Corporate-level Evaluation, Report No. 2846, Independent Office of Evaluation, IFAD, Rome. https://www.ifad.org/documents/38714182/39711115/supervision.pdf/0ff9d64d-a318-482a-b0f9-16dedc2a53c3

IFAD (International Fund for Agricultural Development). 2013i. "President's Report on the Implementation Status of Evaluation Recommendations and Management Actions (PRISMA)." EC 2013/77/W.P.8/Add. 2, June 20, Comments by the Independent Office of Evaluation, IFAD, Rome. https://webapps.ifad.org/members/ec/77/docs/EC-2013-77-W-P-8-Add-2.pdf

IFAD (International Fund for Agricultural Development). 2013j. "Resources Available for Commitment." EB 2013/108/R.7/Rev.1, April 10, Executive Board, 108th Session, IFAD, Rome. https://webapps.ifad.org/members/eb/108/docs/EB-2013-108-R-7-Rev-1.pdf

IFAD (International Fund for Agricultural Development). 2013k. "Results-Based Country Strategic Opportunities Programmes: Evaluation Synthesis." June, Report No. 2829, Independent Office of Evaluation, IFAD, Rome. https://www.ifad.org/documents/38714182/39720630/rb-cosop_report.pdf/37d6fc69-e79f-4e6f-aff5-d9ae7babb57c

IFAD (International Fund for Agricultural Development). 2014a. "Fulfilling the Promise of African Agriculture. IFAD in Africa." IFAD, Rome. https://www.ifad.org/documents/38714170/39148759/africa_agriculture_e.pdf/1b8a4bf7-8570-411a-9237-ecc8e3627cac

IFAD (International Fund for Agricultural Development). 2014b. "IFAD's Engagement in Middle-income Countries. Evaluation Synthesis." IFAD, Rome. https://www.ifad.org/evaluation/reports/evaluation_synthesis/tags/mics/y2014/9973915

IFAD (International Fund for Agricultural Development). 2014c. "Indonesia Country Programme Evaluation." Independent Office of Evaluation, IFAD, Rome.

IFAD (International Fund for Agricultural Development). 2014d. "People's Republic of China Country Programme Evaluation." November, Independent Office of Evaluation, IFAD, Rome. https://www.ecgnet.org/document/people%27s-republic-china-country-programme-evaluation

IFAD (International Fund for Agricultural Development). 2014e. "Reforming IFAD. Transforming Lives." IFAD, Rome. https://www.ifad.org/documents/38714170/39148759/reforming+ifad+en.pdf/2fce4b18-e317-4fa0-8fe0-f61963dabdc6

IFAD (International Fund for Agricultural Development). 2014f. "Report on IFAD's Development Effectiveness." December, IFAD, Rome. https://www.ifad.org/documents/38711624/40688275/Report+on+IFAD's+Development+Effectiveness+2014_e.pdf/adacc02b-ba9d-458f-9f4b-1a05a9e7066a

IFAD (International Fund for Agricultural Development). 2014g. "Results Measurement Framework (2016–2018)—IFAD10." Document #IFAD10/3/R.3, September 2, Consultation on the Tenth Replenishment of IFAD's Resources—Third Session, Rome, October 7–8. https://webapps.ifad.org/members/repl/10/3/docs/IFAD10-3-R-3.pdf

IFAD (International Fund for Agricultural Development). 2014h. "A Strategic Vision for IFAD 2016–2025: Enabling Inclusive and Sustainable Rural Transformation." Consultation on the Tenth Replenishment of IFAD's Resources—Second Session, Rome, June 9–10. https://webapps.ifad.org/members/repl/10/2/docs/IFAD10-2-R-2.pdf

IFAD (International Fund for Agricultural Development). 2015a. "Annual Report 2014." IFAD, Rome. https://www.ifad.org/en/web/knowledge/publication/asset/39218573

IFAD (International Fund for Agricultural Development). 2015b. "Emerging Trends in Mobilizing Concessional Resources for International Financial Institutions." Synthesis Report of the Roundtable Discussion, May 11–12, IFAD, Rome. https://www.ifad.org/es/web/latest/event/asset/39010500

IFAD (International Fund for Agricultural Development). 2015c. "President's Report on the Implementation Status of Evaluation Recommendations and Management Actions (PRISMA)." May, Comments by the Independent Office of Evaluation, IFAD, Rome. https://webapps.ifad.org/members/ec/88/docs/EC-2015-88-W-P-6.pdf

IFAD (International Fund for Agricultural Development). 2015d. "Sovereign Borrowing Framework: Borrowing from Sovereign States and State-Supported Institutions." EB2015/114/R.17/Rev. 1, April 23, IFAD, Rome. https://webapps.ifad.org/members/eb/114/docs/EB-2015-114-R-17-Rev-1.pdf

IFAD (International Fund for Agricultural Development). 2016a. "Annual Report on Results and Impact of IFAD Operations Evaluated in 2015." ARRI 2016, Independent Office of Evaluation, IFAD, Rome. https://www.ifad.org/documents/38714182/39709860/ARRI_2016_full.pdf/569bcea7-a84a-4d38-867f-89b3bb98e0e4

IFAD (International Fund for Agricultural Development). 2016b. "IFAD Corporate Decentralization Plan." EB 2016/119/R.11, November 9, IFAD, Rome. https://webapps.ifad.org/members/eb/119/docs/EB-2016-119-R-11.pdf

IFAD (International Fund for Agricultural Development) 2016c. "IFAD Development Effectiveness Framework." EB 2016/119/R.12, November 9, IFAD, Rome. https://webapps.ifad.org/members/eb/119/docs/EB-2016-119-R-12.pdf

IFAD (International Fund for Agricultural Development). 2016d. "IFAD's Decentralization Experience." Corporate-Level Evaluation, Independent Office of Evaluation, IFAD, Rome. https://www.ifad.org/documents/38714182/39711646/Decentralization+CLE+-+Full+Report+for+web.pdf/481d17e8-1ec9-4b73-a477-4d0e6204a7c6

IFAD (International Fund for Agricultural Development). 2016e. "IFAD's Performance-based Allocation System." Corporate-Level Evaluation, April, Independent Office of Evaluation, IFAD, Rome. https://www.ifad.org/documents/38714182/39711481/PBAS+CLE+-+Full+Report.pdf/15cb3af1-2e3f-43b2-a62d-8868734e23dd

IFAD (International Fund for Agricultural Development). 2016f. "IFAD's 2017 Results-based Programme of Work and Regular and Capital Budgets, the IOE Results-based Work Programme and Budget for 2017 and Indicative Plan for 2018–2019, and the HIPC and PBAS Progress Reports." EB 2016/119/R.2/Rev.1, December 14, Executive Board, 119th Session, Rome. https://webapps.ifad.org/members/eb/119/docs/EB-2016-119-R-2-Rev-1.pdf

IFAD (International Fund for Agricultural Development). 2016g. "Report on IFAD's Development Effectiveness (RIDE)." EB 2016/118/R.8, August 11, IFAD, Rome. https://www.ifad.org/documents/38711624/40688281/Report+on+IFAD's+Development+Effectiveness+2016_E.pdf/fe6170f0-0baa-4019-973d-ae242a0359f4

IFAD (International Fund for Agricultural Development). 2017a. "Agreement between IFAD Management and the Independent Office of Evaluation of IFAD on the Harmonization of IFAD's Independent Evaluation and Self-Evaluation Methods and Systems Part I: Evaluation Criteria." February, IFAD, Rome. https://webapps.ifad.org/members/eb/120/docs/EB-2017-120-INF-2.pdf

IFAD (International Fund for Agricultural Development). 2017b. "Evaluation Synthesis Report on IFAD's Support to Scaling Up of Results." EC 2017/96/W.P.6, February 16, IFAD, Rome. https://webapps.ifad.org/members/ec/96/docs/EC-2017-96-W-P-6.pdf

IFAD (International Fund for Agricultural Development). 2017c. "Report on IFAD's Development Effectiveness (RIDE)." https://www.ifad.org/documents/38711624/40688284/Report+on+IFAD's+Development+Effectiveness+2017.pdf/2c999836-b522-4f43-a8ac-ee17719f755c

IFAD (International Fund for Agricultural Development). 2017d. "Report on the IFAD11 Results Management Framework." IFAD/11/3/R.2, September 21, Consultation on the Eleventh Replenishment of IFAD's Resources, Third Session, Rome, October 19–20. https://webapps.ifad.org/members/repl/11/03/docs/IFAD11-3-R-2.pdf

IFAD (International Fund for Agricultural Development). 2017e. "Tailoring Operations to Country Context—A Holistic Approach." EB 2017/120/R.5, March 13, IFAD, Rome. https://webapps.ifad.org/members/eb/120/docs/EB-2017-120-R-5.pdf

IFAD (International Fund for Agricultural Development). 2017f. "Taking IFAD's Results and Impact Management System (RIMS) to the Next Level." EB 2017/120R/Rev. 1, April 10, IFAD, Rome. https://webapps.ifad.org/members/eb/120/docs/EB-2017-120-R-7-Rev-1.pdf

IFAD (International Fund for Agricultural Development). 2018a. "Report of the Consultation on the Eleventh Replenishment of IFAD's Resources. Leaving No One Behind: IFAD's Role in the 2030 Agenda." IFAD/11/5/INF.2, February 12, Rome. https://www.ifad.org/documents/38714174/40306705/Report+of+the+Consultation+on+the+Eleventh+Replenishment+of+IFAD%27s+Resources.pdf/3819f1bc-d975-45ce-9770-8f673e26caa0

IFAD (International Fund for Agricultural Development). 2018b. "Report on IFAD's Development Effectiveness (RIDE) for 2018." EC 2018/102/W.P.7, August, IFAD, Rome. https://www.ifad.org/documents/38711624/41001481/ride_2018_e.pdf/66d87970-03fd-726f-de08-d13e5618a2d3

IFAD (International Fund for Agricultural Development). 2018c. "Summary of the Status of Contributions to the Tenth Replenishment." June 30, IFAD, Rome. https://webapps.ifad.org/members/eb/124/docs/EB-2018-FFP7-AC-EB.pdf

IFAD (International Fund for Agricultural Development). 2018d. "2018 ARRI: 2018 Annual Report on Results and Impact of IFAD Operations 2018." Independent Office of Evaluation, IFAD, Rome. https://www.ifad.org/documents/38714182/40747488/ARRI2018_full+document.pdf/14274eca-9d92-4053-bce6-b7115ac42d0f

IFAD (International Fund for Agricultural Development). 2019a. "Approach to IFAD's New Liquidity Policy: Principles and Guidelines." EB 2019/128/R.47, November 6, IFAD, Rome. https://webapps.ifad.org/members/eb/128/docs/EB-2019-128-R-47.pdf

IFAD (International Fund for Agricultural Development). 2019b. "IFAD Action Plan: Nutrition 2019–2025. Mainstreaming Nutrition in IFAD." August, IFAD, Rome.

IFAD (International Fund for Agricultural Development). 2019c. "IFAD's 2019 Results-based Programme of Work and Regular and Capital Budgets, the IOE Results-based Work Programme and Budget for 2019 and Indicative Plan for 2020–2021, and the HIPC and PBAS Progress Reports." GC 42/L.6, January 18, Rome, IFAD. https://webapps.ifad.org/members/gc/42/docs/GC-42-L-6.pdf

IFAD (International Fund for Agricultural Development). 2019d. "Policies and Criteria for IFAD Financing." IFAD, Rome. https://www.ifad.org/en/document-detail/asset/39501039

IFAD (International Fund for Agricultural Development). 2019e. "Report on the Status of Contributions to the Eleventh Replenishment of IFAD's Resources." EB 2019/126/R.31, March 21, IFAD, Rome. https://webapps.ifad.org/members/eb/126/docs/EB-2019-126-R-31.pdf

IFAD (International Fund for Agricultural Development). 2019f. "Report on the Status of Replenishment of IFAD's Resources." GC 42/L.3, January 16, Governing Council, 42nd Session, Rome, February 14–15. https://webapps.ifad.org/members/gc/42/docs/GC-42-L-3.pdf

IFAD (International Fund for Agricultural Development). 2019g. "Setting Targets for the IFAD11 Results Management Framework: Institutional Efficiency and Decentralization." B 2019/126/R.5/Rev.1, May 2, IFAD, Rome. https://webapps.ifad.org/members/eb/126/docs/EB-2019-126-R-5-Rev-1.pdf

IFAD (International Fund for Agricultural Development). 2019h. "2019 Annual Report on Results and Impact of IFAD Operations (ARRI)." Independent Office of Evaluation, IFAD, Rome. https://www.ifad.org/en/web/ioe/evaluation/asset/41391061

IFAD (International Fund for Agricultural Development) and OPEC Fund. 2005. "A Partnership to Eradicate Rural Poverty." September, Rome.

Lele, Uma, ed. 1992. *Aid to African Agriculture: Lessons from Two Decades of Donors' Experience*. Baltimore: Johns Hopkins University Press for World Bank.

Linn, Johannes F., Arntraud Hartmann, Homi Kharas, Richard Kohl, and Barbara Massler. 2010. "Scaling Up the Fight Against Rural Poverty: An Institutional Review of IFAD's Approach." Global Working Paper No. 43, October, Global Economy and Development, Brookings Institution, Washington, DC.

Losch, Bruno, Sandrine Fréguin-Gresh, and Eric Thomas White. 2012. "Structural Transformation and Rural Change Revisited: Challenges for Late Developing Countries in a Globalizing World." Africa Development Forum, Agence Française de Développement and the World Bank, Washington, DC. http://documents.worldbank.org/curated/en/633201468003009411/pdf/Structural-transformation-and-rural-change-revisited-challenges-for-late-developing-countries-in-a-globalizing-world.pdf

MOPAN (Multilateral Organisation Performance Network). n.d. "MOPAN 3.0: A Reshaped Assessment Approach." http://www.mopanonline.org/ourwork/ourapproachmopan30/

MOPAN (Multilateral Organisation Performance Assessment Network). 2013. "Institutional Report, International Fund for Agricultural Development, 2013." http://www.mopanonline.org/assessments/ifad2013/index.htm

MOPAN (Multilateral Organisation Performance Assessment Network). 2018. "MOPAN 2017–18 Assessments: International Fund for Agricultural Development (IFAD)." http://www.mopanonline.org/assessments/ifad2017-18/IFAD%20Report.pdf

Nchuchuwe, Friday Francis, and Kehinde David Adejuwon. 2012. "The Challenges of Agriculture and Rural Development in Africa: The Case of Nigeria." *International Journal of Academic Research in Progressive Education and Development* 1 (3). http://www.hrmars.com/admin/pics/995.pdf

OECD (Organisation for Economic Co-operation and Development). 2002. "Glossary of Key Terms in Evaluation and Results Based Management." Development Assistance Committee (DAC), OECD, Paris. https://www.oecd.org/dac/evaluation/2754804.pdf

OECD (Organization for Economic Co-operation and Development). 2008. "Paris Declaration on Aid Effectiveness." In *Paris Declaration on Aid Effectiveness and the Accra Agenda for Action*, 1–13. Paris: OECD. https://www.oecd.org/dac/effectiveness/34428351.pdf

Poulton, Colin, Jonathan Kydd, and Andrew Dorward. 2006. "Overcoming Market Constraints on Pro-Poor Agricultural Growth in Sub-Saharan Africa." *Development Policy Review* 24 (3): 243–77.

Ravallion, Martin. 2009. "How Relevant is Targeting to the Success of an Antipoverty Program?" *World Bank Research Observer* 24 (2): 205–31.

Subbarao, Kalanidhi, Carlo del Ninno, Colin Andrews, and Claudia Rodríguez-Alas. 2013. *Public Works as a Safety Net Design, Evidence, and Implementation.* Washington, DC: World Bank.

Thapa, Ganesh, and Sarah Hessel. 2016. "IFAD's Experience in Scaling Up in Asia and the Pacific Region: Lessons Learned from Successful Projects and Way Forward." Occasional Paper 18: Knowledge for development effectiveness. IFAD, Rome. https://www.ifad.org/documents/38714170/40706338/OP18_web.pdf/230e1bc3-591e-4c2b-89d9-a3ce1d8322e6

Vázquez, Sergio Tezanos, and Andy Sumner. 2012. "Beyond Low and Middle Income Countries: What if There Were Five Clusters of Developing Countries?" *IDS Working Papers* 2012 (404): 1–40.

Waddington, Hugh, and Howard White. 2014. "Farmer Field Schools: From Agricultural Extension to Adult Education." Systematic Review Summary 1. International Initiative for Impact Evaluation (3ie), New Delhi. https://www.3ieimpact.org/evidence-hub/publications/systematic-review-summaries/farmer-field-schools-agricultural-extension

Winters, Paul, and Alessandra Garbero. 2018. "Approach to Attributing IFAD's Aggregrate Impact." In *Effective Rural Development: IFAD's Evidence-based Approach to Managing for Results,* 15–30, IFAD, Rome. https://www.ifad.org/en/web/knowledge/publication/asset/40704913

World Bank. 2003. *World Development Report 2003: Sustainable Development in a Dynamic World: Transforming Institutions, Growth, and Quality of Life.* Washington, DC: World Bank.

World Bank. 2004. *World Development Report 2004: Making Services Work for Poor People.* Washington, DC: World Bank.

World Bank. 2007. *World Development Report 2008: Agriculture for Development.* Washington, DC: World Bank. https://openknowledge.worldbank.org/handle/10986/5990

World Bank. 2018. *Piecing Together the Poverty Puzzle.* Washington, DC: World Bank. https://openknowledge.worldbank.org/bitstream/handle/10986/30418/978

12

The World Food Programme

Uma Lele and Sambuddha Goswami

Summary

The World Food Programme (WFP) is the world's largest humanitarian organization addressing hunger and promoting food security. The need for emergency food aid has increased. It is a result of a combination of several factors: climate change; the global economic crisis, prompted by the COVID-19 pandemic; and a growing population of involuntarily displaced people, resulting from conflicts throughout the world.

WFP started with an objective of internationalizing US food aid. President Eisenhower suggested initiating a pilot program in the Food and Agriculture Organization of the United Nations (FAO), reflecting the confidence that the United States held for FAO and the UN System, which it had helped to establish. Internationalizing food aid was intended, in part, to diffuse the controversy surrounding disposal of large US food surpluses—the outcome of US price policies—with the benefit of feeding food-deficit countries while also addressing the disincentive effects of food aid on domestic food production. Growing rapidly, international emergency assistance has gone through substantial evolution from aid in-kind to cash transfers, and from emergency aid to building capacity of developing countries to address emergencies. Most importantly, it has filled a void that would have existed had WFP not responded rapidly and innovatively to meet the growing needs of emergency assistance in serving the largest displaced human population in the world. For its achievements, WFP was awarded the 2020 Nobel Peace Prize. The award highlighted the need to address issues of peace and security, without which the needs for emergency food aid cannot be brought under control. The chapter shows how cooperation across international and bilateral organizations has evolved and where it needs to go in the future.

The World Food Programme at Its Establishment

When the United States desired a means to convert its bilateral food aid into a multilateral asset—a move that enjoyed strong support among US farmers and shipping companies—the idea behind WFP was born. US President Dwight Eisenhower first proposed such a food aid scheme, to be administered through the United Nations (UN) system in 1960. The scheme was formalized as a food aid "experiment" in 1961 by George McGovern, director of the US Food for Peace Program at the FAO. Seven months later, the UN General Assembly and FAO established WFP for a three-year trial period via parallel resolutions. In 1965, the UN General Assembly and FAO approved two additional resolutions to extend the organization for "as long as multilateral aid is found feasible and desirable," and WFP quickly solidified as part of the UN system (WFP 2020n). (See the chronology of events in the Appendix to this chapter.)

Food for All: International Organizations and the Transformation of Agriculture. Uma Lele, Manmohan Agarwal, Brian C. Baldwin, and Sambuddha Goswami, Oxford University Press. © Uma Lele, Manmohan Agarwal, Brian C. Baldwin, and Sambuddha Goswami 2021. DOI: 10.1093/oso/9780198755173.003.0013

When viewed from a contemporary state of international cooperation, the creation of WFP seems amazing. At the height of its economic and political power, the United States was willing to internationalize its food aid, and it turned to a UN agency to do the job, showing its trust in the multilateral system.

"In the 1960s, program food aid from donor harvests, provided in the case of the United States via concessional sales on easy credit terms, represented a substantial share of food aid" (Hoddinott, Cohen, and Barrett 2008, 295). The surplus aspect of food aid resulted in political tensions with some recipient nations, such as India.[1] The United States remains the largest contributor to WFP—in WFP's own words, a testament to WFP's comparative advantage as an operational, multilateral institution, and to its logistical and political efficiencies relative to bilateral aid (WFP 2020c). WFP's model has changed fundamentally since its establishment. The continued shift from food aid to food assistance for sustainable hunger solutions has positioned WFP well for the transformations called for by the 2030 Agenda. It has also led to the merging of emergency and development assistance, posing renewed challenges for the global development and humanitarian assistance architectures, as we pointed out in Chapter 8 on the World Bank. The World Bank has substantially increased its assistance to conflict countries, disaster assistance, and displaced people.

The World Food Programme's Strategic Planning Process

WFP's purpose, role, values, and principles have been calibrated under a series of strategic plans, beginning in 2004.[2] The 2004–7 Strategic Plan reflected, first, a new approach that linked WFP's priorities to the Millennium Development Goals (MDGs), outlined management priorities and business process mechanisms, stressed the need for partnerships, and introduced results-based management. The plan also added support for access to education, addressing gender disparity, and helping governments manage food assistance programs to WFP's strategic priorities (UN 2016b; WFP 2003).

WFP had not previously had a comparative advantage or a proven record of success in some of these areas. The subsequent 2006–9 Strategic Plan built on this foundation by providing a longer term perspective for WFP contributions to the MDGs and introducing a section on risk management (WFP 2005b). In this respect, WFP has been very good at using the strategic planning process to reframe and to demonstrate its continued relevance in a changing world.

According to the 2006–9 Strategic Plan, WFP's "core programme goal . . . is to contribute to meeting the Millennium Development Goals through food-assisted interventions targeting poor and hungry people" (WFP 2005b, 3). Though the plan does not represent a radical shift that would indicate a longer term approach, the five strategic objectives for the period were defined as contributing to global efforts to achieve the MDGs. The plan pointed out that the final report of the UN Millennium Project acknowledged food-based programs that contribute to the MDGs—among them school meals, deworming campaigns, nutrition support for pregnant and lactating women and children under five, and tree planting.

---

[1] US bilateral assistance was particularly large in India—10 million mt/years were imported from the United States during the food crisis in 1964–5 and 1965–6, raising issues about the use of counterpart funds that the Government of India generated through sale of the food to the public (Lele and Goldsmith 1989).

[2] The Final Report on the Governance Project states the strategic framework is supported by a Strategic Plan that provides the context for WFP's operations during a four-year period (WFP 2005a). These strategic plans included 2004–7 (WFP 2003); 2006–9 (WFP 2005b); and 2008–13 (WFP 2007).

The plan cited WFP assistance activities that align with these programs—food for education, mother and child health and nutrition, and food for work (WFP 2005b).

Going Forward: 2014–2017 Strategic Plan, Zero Hunger, and the 2030 Agenda

WFP's Strategic Plan 2014–17 framed its priorities around three "R's:" Respond, Reduce, and Rebuild (WFP 2013f). The plan called for pursuit of four Strategic Objectives based on MDGs:

- Save lives and protect livelihoods in emergencies;
- Support or restore food security and nutrition and establish or rebuild livelihoods in fragile settings and following emergencies;
- Reduce risk and enable people, communities, and countries to meet their own food and nutrition needs; and
- Reduce undernutrition and break the intergenerational cycle of hunger. (WFP 2013f, 3)

Further, the 2014–17 Strategic Plan articulated WFP's perceived role in achieving zero hunger, setting the stage for its resilience-building activities to reduce vulnerability of populations (WFP 2013f). WFP's operations are oriented toward fighting hunger and now are cast as responding to the UN Secretary-General's Zero Hunger Challenge. Thus, WFP's work in social protection, gender, disaster risk reduction, climate change adaptation, agricultural investment, and market strengthening has a place under an anti-hunger mandate, which is broader than its traditional and perceived humanitarian role.

Considerable internal planning has been underway to reorient WFP's work in the post-2015 humanitarian and development context, as defined through the 2015–16 Summit Season, and to increase the efficiency and effectiveness of WFP's delivery. Strategic priorities under the next revision of the Strategic Plan 2017–21 are based on achieving zero hunger and tied to Global Goal 2 (WFP 2016c).

Current World Food Programme Objectives and Strategies

The WFP Strategic Plan 2017–21 continues to provide the overall vision for achieving zero hunger and guides the organization within the context of the 2030 Agenda. WFP's five strategic objectives and eight strategic results are:

Strategic Objective 1: End hunger by protecting access to food
Strategic Result 1: Everyone has access to food
Strategic Objective 2: Improve nutrition
Strategic Result 2: No one suffers from malnutrition
Strategic Objective 3: Achieve food security
Strategic Result 3: Smallholders have improved food security and nutrition through improved productivity and incomes

Strategic Result 4: Food systems are sustainable

Strategic Objective 4: Support SDG [Sustainable Development Goal] implementation

Strategic Result 5: Developing countries have strengthened capacities to implement the SDGs

Strategic Result 6: Policies to support sustainable development are coherent

Strategic Objective 5: Partner for SDG results

Strategic Result 7: Developing countries access a range of financial resources for development investment

Strategic Result 8: Sharing of knowledge, expertise and technology, strengthen global partnership support to country efforts to achieve the SDGs (WFP 2017d, 4–5)

WFP's Annual Performance Report for 2019 noted:

> WFP achieved strong performance under **Strategic Objective 1**. . . . Activities for achieving Strategic Result 1 accounted for 68 percent of WFP's total direct expenditures in 2019 in 86 operations. WFP distributed 4 million mt of in-kind food and US$1.5 billion in cash-based transfers under this strategic result. Overall, 53 out of 69 countries with operations under Strategic Result 1 met their outcome targets. Unconditional food assistance enabled more than 80 percent of beneficiaries in nine countries to reach acceptable food consumption levels. However, many households in countries facing highly volatile situations and insufficient funding or access had poor food consumption patterns, leaving them exposed to critical health and nutrition challenges.
>
> Performance under **Strategic Objective 2**, improve nutrition, strengthened over 2018, driven largely by a combination of better performance and new reporting against Strategic Result 2, no one suffers from malnutrition. To combat high malnutrition rates, WFP and its partners implemented nutrition-specific treatment and prevention activities in 49 countries; in 2019, 47 percent of the 17.2 million beneficiaries of WFP nutrition activities were in countries experiencing Level 3 or Level 2 emergencies. Programmes for the treatment of moderate acute malnutrition achieved strong recovery rates of 90 percent among enrolled children during the year, while mortality rates were well below globally accepted levels. Overall, treatment programmes reached 60 percent of eligible children, women and girls. WFP also worked with governments to develop nutrition policies and programmes that, for example, provide nutritious school meals or food fortification. The scale-up of food fortification activities brought major successes in the Dominican Republic, Panama, and Peru, where 41 new commercial brands of fortified rice were launched on national markets.
>
> WFP partially achieved its targets under Strategic Objective 3, achieve food security, recording moderate progress under Strategic Result 3, smallholders have improved food security and nutrition, and satisfactory performance under Strategic Result 4, food systems are sustainable. Activities under these strategic results were carried out in 53 countries and were aimed at improving the productivity, sales and incomes of vulnerable people and smallholder farmers and addressing systemic problems in food systems. Under Strategic Result 3, although targets were met for smallholder sales made through WFP-supported aggregation systems, results against two other indicators related to food expenditures and the production of more nutritious crops deteriorated, compared with 2018. Under Strategic Result 4, a strong rating was achieved in 2019, with strong progress against targets on dietary diversity and smallholder sales and post-harvest losses, and

moderate progress on food consumption improvements. WFP's resilience work in 2019 included the Sahel integrated resilience programme (2019–2023), which assisted 1.3 million people in more than 1,400 villages through a package of activities including Food Assistance for Assets (FFA), school feeding, malnutrition treatment and prevention, and support for smallholder farmers.

Under Strategic Objective 4, on supporting SDG implementation, WFP performed well in 2019, as measured in terms of achievements against targets for Strategic Result 5, developing countries have strengthened capacities to implement the SDGs, and for Strategic Result 6, policies to support sustainable development are coherent. Available resources for Strategic Objective 4 amounted to US$143 million. Compared with 2018, there were substantial improvements in reporting. Of the 10 indicators used to track performance under Strategic Result 5, the targets for 7 were either achieved or on track to being achieved in 2019. Through country capacity strengthening activities in 44 countries, WFP enhanced food security and nutrition policies, programmes and systems while reaching or surpassing more than 75 percent of the targets for this area of work. In India, WFP supported the Government's Targeted Public Distribution System, the largest food safety net in the world, reaching 800 million vulnerable people each month. WFP also facilitated South–South and triangular cooperation through its centers of excellence in Brazil, China, and Côte d'Ivoire. The centers of excellence helped countries to design and implement 15 national anti-hunger policy documents and mobilized US$2.3 million for field-based projects.

Results under Strategic Result 6, which focuses on developing institutional reform and coherent policies to improve food security and nutrition, were positive in 2019. However, only four country offices included relevant indicators for this strategic result in their logical frameworks, limiting WFP's ability to provide an overall performance assessment. New capacity strengthening indicators were included in the revised corporate results framework to help resolve this issue in 2020.

WFP performed well under Strategic Objective 5, partner for SDG results, with nearly 100 percent of the 30 reporting countries meeting or exceeding 80 percent of their targets. In 2019, US$1.3 billion was available for work under this strategic objective. The good result demonstrates improvements made during the year to enhance the assessment of WFP performance by, for example, reporting results irrespective of the number of countries measuring the relevant indicator and introducing a new method for measuring outcome indicators. This strategic objective consists of Strategic Result 7, on ensuring developing countries have access to diverse resourcing, and Strategic Result 8, on enhancing global partnerships. (WFP 2020a, 12–13)

Evolving Mandate: Balance between Food Aid and Food Assistance

The 2008–13 Strategic Plan laid out a "historical [mandate] shift from WFP as a food aid agency to WFP as a food assistance agency, with a more nuanced and robust set of tools to respond to critical hunger needs" (WFP 2007, 1). It introduced a revised context for WFP's work and overarching approach to its activities that further defined WFP's role in food assistance and development, linking objectives, goals, and tools. Although the 2008–13 Strategic Plan formally framed this mandate shift, WFP's work had already been heading in this direction over the past two strategic plans (see Box 12.1) and continues in the form of

---

Box 12.1 Evolution of the World Food Programme's Mandate Shift through its Strategic Priorities

---

1994 *(Mission Statement): Save lives in refugee and other emergency situations*
  → 2004/2006 (Strategic Plans): Save lives in crisis situations.
  → 2008 (Strategic Plan): Save lives and protect livelihoods in emergencies.
1994: *To improve the nutrition and quality of life of the most vulnerable people at critical times in their lives; and*
  → 2004/2006: Support the improved nutrition and health status of children, mothers, and other vulnerable people.
  → 2008: Reduce chronic hunger and undernutrition.
1994: *To help build assets and promote the self-reliance of poor people and communities, particularly through labor-intensive programs*
  → 2004/2006: Protect livelihoods in crisis situations and enhance resilience to shocks.
  → 2008: Restore and rebuild lives and livelihoods in post-conflict, post-disaster, or transitional situations.
2004: *Help governments establish and manage national food assistance programs.*
  → 2006: Strengthen the capacities of countries and regions to establish and manage food assistance and hunger reduction programs.
  → 2008: Strengthen the capacities of countries to reduce hunger including through handover strategies and local purchase.
2004/2006: *Support access to education and reduce gender disparity in access to education and skills training.*
  → 2008: Taken out.
2008: Reduce acute hunger and invest in disaster preparedness and mitigation measures.
Source: WFP (2003, 2005b, 2007).

---

country strategies in the most recent period, as outlined later in the chapter. Language in this plan drew on WFP's historic mission and perceived comparative advantage within the global food and agriculture architecture to justify a new and broader development role for the organization; the 2014–17 Strategic Plan consolidated this evolution.

Beginning in 2016, WFP underwent a substantial *restructuring*. The process known as "Integrated Road Map" (IRM) aligned WFP to the SDGs and has moved the organization from project-based work to planning through Country Strategic Plans (CSPs) (WFP 2016b). This process has now been completed on a structural level, with all Country Offices having moved to a CSP (in November 2019, the last of the first-generation CSPs were approved). Operationally, WFP is still adapting as an organization to the massive increase of funding that it has experienced since 2015, and the overall UN reform process will also require WFP to adapt its planning processes (WFP 2018c). This restructuring, as well as factors such as climate change and the humanitarian–development–peace nexus, would certainly take on a stronger role in the next Strategic Plan.

WFP's strength lies in emergency response, especially in large-scale, sudden-onset disasters. The shift recognizes the specific contexts in which hunger occurs and provides resources and efforts to society's most vulnerable to alleviate those conditions. In terms of WFP's declared mission, this means not just short-term emergency interventions but also "multi-year support programmes designed to lift a whole nation's [food security and] nutritional indicators," balancing the urgency of eradicating hunger in the present with the long-term objective of ending hunger for all (WFP 2020j).

WFP classifies Emergency Response operations according to a three-level scale:

- Level 1 Response: Emergency operations within the response capabilities of the relevant WFP Country Office (CO), with routine support from Regional Bureaux (RB).
- Level 2 Response: Emergency Response operations requiring regional augmentation of country-level response capability.
- Level 3 Response: Emergency Response operations requiring mobilisation of WFP global response capabilities in support of the relevant CO(s) and/or RB, i.e., a Corporate Response. (WFP 2014g, 1)

The growing numbers of Level 3 emergencies and the frequency of their onslaught and intensity have "diverted attention from other protracted, chronic and lower-level emergencies" of less political importance and visibility (WFP 2017d, 14). In 2019, WFP responded to 18 Level 3 (six) and Level 2 (twelve) concurrent emergencies, the largest number that WFP had faced thus far at one time (WFP 2019g, 1–2). Two aspects stand out in this transition: first, from delivering food aid in-kind to providing food assistance, including cash-based transfers (CBTs), which is clearly discernible; and second, from food procured from traditional food surplus countries such as the United States to at least partially obtaining it from nearby emerging countries, thereby reducing costs with local procurement and delivery to beneficiaries (WFP 2017e). Of course, CBTs are not realistic in countries with shortages of food and high food prices: for example, in Syria and Yemen. So, WFP pursues a flexible policy.

Food aid still constitutes an important feature of WFP. It arose from a largely unidirectional, top-down vision: disposal of surplus food to hungry people. At least in theory, "food assistance, by contrast, involves a more complex appreciation of people's long-term nutritional needs and of the diverse approaches required to meet them. This conceptual shift has been at the core of WFP's transformation in recent years" (WFP 2020j). While WFP remains the world's leading humanitarian agency, it is aiming "to combine frontline action with the quest for durable solutions" (WFP 2020j).

WFP's funding has skyrocketed (US$8.0 billion in 2019), and so has its internal capacity (18,500 staff) (WFP 2020a). The organization has undergone restructuring to better link the emergency–development divide, making capacity building a strategic objective. One key consideration is what does a stronger role for WFP in development mean for its ability to uphold humanitarian principles. According to the United Nations Office for the Coordination of Humanitarian Assistance (OCHA), those principles are humanity, neutrality, impartiality, and independence. They provide the foundations for humanitarian action. In a time in which access is one of the main difficulties in emergency relief, this question is highly relevant today. Ultimately, as the Nobel Committee has emphasized, demands on WFP will diminish only when there is less conflict and more peace and security.

Food assistance has become part of a policy mix that advances social well-being in general. In line with the SDGs, and in particular with SDG2,[3] WFP has also shifted from

---

[3] SDG2: "End hunger, achieve food security and improved nutrition and promote sustainable agriculture." See https://sustainabledevelopment.un.org/sdg2

emphasis on the quantity and quality of food to one on the nutritious character and seasonality of food, with a roadmap to shift the focus of operations to the country level and to increase country capacity (see Table A.1.1 in Chapter 1 on the thematic framework of the SDGs). Crucially, WFP's food assistance attempts to enlist beneficiaries as actors— giving them a voice, and, wherever possible, a choice in what food they receive and how they receive it. This last principle has been steadily gaining prominence. And it helps explain why over the last decade, in-kind food assistance (the only type there was until the mid-2000s) has partly given way to CBTs. "Cash" for WFP means a range of instruments, in the form of physical bank notes, vouchers, or electronic funds, given to beneficiaries to spend directly. It is also more popular as a tool among most donors. "In fact, both cash and in-kind assistance are likely to co-exist for the foreseeable future, with WFP increasingly adept at using them singly, alternately or jointly, in any given setting" (WFP 2020j). Indeed, WFP is now the largest cash provider in the humanitarian community: for example, US$2.1 billion of CBTs and commodity vouchers were distributed to 27.9 million people in 2019, 38 percent of WFP's global assistance.

From 2011 to 2019, the increase in CBTs has been significant, a 866 percent growth in CTs, compared toa 17 percent growth in food transfers (in mt). WFP was expected to expand its delivery of CBTs to US$2.17 billion in 2019 (WFP 2019b).

We explore the reasoning behind this evolution later in the chapter.

Voluntary Funding Principally from Governments

The 1965 resolution language of "desirability" is reflected in WFP's mandate and govern-ance structure. Unlike FAO, WFP relies exclusively on voluntary contributions. Members are drawn from the UN system of state classifications, but the organization receives no dues or assessed contributions. Instead, donations of cash, food, and other in-kind contributions from governments, private actors, and individuals are the source of WFP's operations. Governments remain the principal source of WFP funding, with an average of 60 govern-ments underwriting projects on an entirely voluntary basis (WFP 2020l). The United States is the largest donor of food aid, giving about half of all food aid, but the European Commission (EC), Germany, Canada, Japan, Saudi Arabia, Sweden, and Australia are also major donors, along with Russia, China, and South Korea. The United Kingdom is the fourth largest donor (WFP 2020c). The World Bank contributes some resources, but those are not significant in the overall scheme of things.

International Framework for Food Assistance

WFP's evolution has occurred in the context of a rapidly evolving international framework for both humanitarian and development assistance. The Food Assistance Convention (FAC) was adopted by a number of key food aid donors in April 2012 in London. It replaced the previous food aid convention and deals with bilateral and multilateral food assistance. The idea behind the FAC, unlike in the past, is to address the food *and nutritional* needs of the most vulnerable people in the world. It is the only international legal agreement requiring signatories to provide a minimum amount of food aid (UN 2012). Ed Clay of the Overseas Development Institute (ODI) noted in his commentary, "What's the Use of the 2012 Food Assistance Convention?": "Symbolically, it implies a donor commitment to address world hunger." Following repeated renegotiations, FAC was drafted in December 2010 by "officials responsible for food aid from the United States (US), European Union (EU), Japan, Australia, Norway, Switzerland, and Argentina, and chaired by Canada" (Clay 2012).

According to Imogen Calderwood in her 2018 article, "76,000,000 Don't Have Enough Food. Here's How Food Helps Them" noted that the FAC enabled information sharing and guiding principles to 16 member countries providing food assistance, with countries' minimum annual requirements. She noted the United States was the largest donor and:

> ...made a minimum commitment of US$2.2 billion for 2018; the EU's commitment was 350 million euros; and Canada has committed CAD $250 million.

> There are many different ways that the funding committed by governments is distributed, with many governments also running their own projects overseas.

> But in general, governments assess the situation and work out who is best placed to deliver the necessary aid—whether that's through their own bilateral programmes, an NGO [nongovernmental organization], or a multilateral agency (which means funded by many different governments) like the [World Food Programme of the] United Nations. (Calderwood 2018)

Other international consultations and agreements which have helped international consensus and frame WFP assistance and its overarching strategy include:

1. The SDGs discussed extensively in the previous chapters, including, in particular, SDG2;
2. SDG17 on international partnerships. WFP has reformulated its strategy to be attuned to SDGs in much the same way as have FAO, the International Fund for Agricultural Development (IFAD), and CGIAR, as discussed in chapters concerning these organizations (UN 2020); and
3. The first humanitarian summit organized by UN Secretary-General in Istanbul in 2016, which was also a watershed in bringing member countries together around humanitarian issues and influencing WFP's strategy (Lattimer 2015).

Other major conferences and agreements, and their relevance to ending hunger include:

1. The World Conference on Disaster Risk Reduction (March 2015, Sendai, Japan): More than 80 percent of the world's food-insecure people live in countries that are prone to natural hazards and characterized by land and ecosystem degradation. Disasters affect all dimensions of food security: without protection from disaster risks, the most vulnerable people cannot begin to build their resilience (WFP 2015c). The Sendai Framework for Disaster Risk Reduction 2015−30, adopted at the World Conference, contributes to the 2030 Agenda and hunger reduction, especially by calling for investment in disaster risk reduction for resilience, including through social protection systems and enhanced disaster preparedness for effective response and to "Build Back Better" (UNISDR 2015, 21).
2. The International Conference on Financing for Development (July 2015, Addis Ababa, Ethiopia): The Addis Ababa Action Agenda is integrated into the 2030 Agenda

through SDG17. Despite progress reflected in the Addis Ababa Action Agenda, many issues remain unresolved (UN 2015).

3. The United Nations Framework Convention on Climate Change (Paris Agreement) (December 2015): Climate change has a disproportionately negative impact on food-insecure people and could increase the risk of hunger and malnutrition by up to 20 percent by 2050. Climate change will deepen vulnerability to disasters, especially in resource-scarce environments dominated by high prevalence of food insecurity and malnutrition (FAO 2017a; UNFCCC 2020).
4. The United Nations Summit for Refugees and Migrants (September 2016, New York): Large movements of people will continue or possibly increase as a result of violent conflict, poverty, inequality, climate change, disasters and environmental degradation (UN 2016a).
5. Third United Nations Conference on Housing and Sustainable Urban Development (HABITAT III) (October 2016): Hunger and malnutrition among the urban poor are recognized as a challenge to achievement of the 2030 Agenda (UN-Habitat 2020).
6. The first Global Refugee Forum organized by the United Nations High Commissioner for Refugees (UNHCR), December 16–18, 2019: Designed to be a platform to rally international financial and other support, including opportunities for refugee resettlement and to exchange good practices (Karasapan 2020).

In-Kind Food Distribution

WFP notes that providing food to people has been the "cornerstone" of their work (WFP 2020q). While WFP shifted from food aid to food assistance in the form of cash transfers—food in-kind has remained a fundamental part of WFP's work, often the best solution for fragile or crisis situations. WFP further states: "After a natural disaster, during lean seasons, or in conflict or displacement situations, when people are cut off from their normal sources of food and cannot access enough food to meet their needs, WFP's in-kind food assistance aims to fill the gap" (WFP 2020o).

Also, in situations of hyperinflation, as in Zimbabwe in December 2019, WFP was providing food for about 2 million people with an expected rapid scale-up aiming to support 4.1 million people.

Conflict as a Major Driver of Emergency Assistance

It is clear that WFP has become the frontline agency responding to emergencies caused by conflict, climate shocks, pandemics and other disasters, tackling ongoing emergencies in 15 countries or regions, but the majority are fueled by conflict. According to the WFP Management Plan 2020–2:

> In 2017, the global economic impact of violence was US$14.76 trillion in purchasing power parity, equivalent to 12.4 percent of global gross domestic product (GDP) and 45 percent of GDP in the ten countries most affected by conflict. The cost of armed conflict totalled US$1.02 trillion in 2017, driven by conflicts in the Middle East, North Africa and South Asia.

... About 74 million food-insecure people (or two-thirds of those facing acute hunger) are located in countries suffering conflict and insecurity. Sixty percent of hungry people and 75 percent of the world's 155 million stunted children live in conflict-affected countries. (WFP 2019h, 9–10)

UNHCR reported 79.5 million forcibly displaced people at the end of 2019, and as of mid-2020, at least 80 million people around the world, an all-time high, including refugees, internally displaced persons, and asylum seekers, who fled their homes to escape violence, conflict, human rights violations, and persecution (UNHCR 2019, 2021). Among them are nearly 26.9 million refugees, around half of whom are under the age of 18. There are millions of stateless people, who have been denied a nationality and lack access to basic rights, such as education, health care, employment, and freedom of movement.

The World Bank had reported a much lower number earlier. Omer Karasapan, Regional Knowledge and Learning Coordinator at the World Bank, in his commentary, "Sharing the Burden of the Global Refugee Crisis," noted that the "global forced displacement crisis continues unabated," with 71 million forcibly displaced people worldwide, and 37,000 new people fleeing their homes each day. Of the total, 25.9 million are living in foreign lands, and 41.3 are internally displaced (Karasapan 2020).

Two-thirds of WFP's work is in countries affected by conflict, where people are three times more likely to be undernourished as those living in countries without conflict. In addition, to emergency assistance, WFP's work focuses on relief and rehabilitation, development aid, and special operations (WFP 2020q).

Developing Countries Host Majority of Refugees

How widely known is it that developing countries face the bulk of the refugee problems? Developing countries have taken in 84 percent of the refugees (Karasapan 2020). Most of the refugees (57 percent) have fled Syria, Afghanistan, or South Sudan. Turkey, no longer a developing country, hosts the largest number (3.7 million) with Colombia hosting 1.8 million.

As a share of population, Lebanon and Jordan are first and second, with 156 and 72 refugees per 1,000 citizens, respectively. According to the WFP Management Plan 2020–2, "Most refugees do not want to leave their own homes. Nine out of ten migrants from Africa and eight out of ten from Asia prefer to stay on their own continent" (WFP 2019h, 10). And that explains why a large share of refugees reside in the regions of their origin, with huge burdens on conflict-affected regions.

Global Scale and Range of World Food Programme Activities

Food and cash transfers are the principal activities of WFP. In practice, however, WFP carries out a variety of activities and its fundraising strategies are closely aligned with its activities:

- Globally, WFP assisted 97.1 million people in 83 countries in 2019, 70 percent of those facing critical hunger levels (WFP 2020a). Women and girls comprise 52 percent of those receiving food assistance from WFP, while 1.3 million women take part in WFP's

FFA and Food for Training projects, which increase people's skills and resilience. In 2018, WFP had already provided direct assistance through its operations to 84.9 million people using cash-based and food transfers. The recipients included 14.7 million refugees—37 percent more than in 2017—and 3.4 million returnees and 13.1 million internally displaced persons. Children—26.8 million girls and 25.4 million boys—are the primary recipients of WFP assistance. They accounted for 62 percent of total beneficiaries (WFP 2019i, 2020a, 2020q).

- Food distributions remained the main response modality in 2019, increasing by 9 percent from US$3.2 billion in 2018 to US$3.5 billion. However, the largest growth rates were in the CBT modality, increasing by 22 percent since 2018, and capacity strengthening and service delivery activities, increasing by 31 percent.

- CBTs and associated costs accounted for 32 percent of total direct expenditures in 2019, compared with 30 percent in 2018, while the capacity strengthening and service delivery modality made up 9 percent of the total, compared with 7 percent in 2018. Continued investment in both areas is a central strategy for WFP in assisting beneficiaries, increasing their resilience and improving their livelihoods.

- An estimated 27.9 million people received CBTs in 2019. This included cash transfers, value vouchers, and commodity vouchers. Nearly half of the transfers were programmed in Syria and five other countries: Ethiopia, Kenya, Malawi, Somalia, and Yemen. The amount of transfers represents a significant increase from 2017 and 2016, in which 19.2 million beneficiaries and 14.3 million beneficiaries were assisted, respectively. Seventy-five percent of CBTs were made via digital payment mechanisms, such as cash accounts, e-vouchers, and mobile money transfers (WFP 2019a, 2020a). CBTs contribute to food security, also serving as a starting point or fostering financial inclusion and boosting markets and local financial sectors. Furthermore, CBTs have led to cost savings of US$0.9 million. WFP spent an average of 6.6 percent of the transfer value on transfer costs in 2019, which was less than in 2018 (WFP 2020b).

- In 2019, 4.2 million mt of food was distributed, 8 percent procured in developing countries (WFP 2020a). On any given day, according to WFP, it has 5,600 trucks, 20 ships, and 92 planes on the move, delivering food and other forms of assistance (WFP 2019i, 2019k, 2020q).

- WFP is also the largest provider of school feeding programs worldwide, providing school meals to more than 17.3 million children in 2019 (50 percent girls) in 59 countries, often in the hardest-to-reach areas, and improving both their nutrition and their access to potentially life-changing education (WFP 2020a). Its school feeding programs have been ongoing for 50 years, now partnering with governments in school feeding in 100 countries (WFP 2017b, 2017c, 2019a, 2020t).

- About 40 percent of total humanitarian spending is on food assistance. WFP's food assistance expenditures went up from 2009 to 2016, from US$2.2 billion to US$5.3 billion, more than doubling the spending. Food transfers went up by 17 percent from 2011 to 2019 (from 3.6 percent mt to 4.2 million mt). In 2019, 9.6 million people received WFP food assistance to cover immediate food shortfalls while they received training and constructed assets to build their resilience to shocks and strengthen their livelihoods. Since 1990, WFP has built the capacity of national governments, with 44 taking over school meal programs. Globally, 368 million children benefitted from daily school meals (WFP 2017e). While there has been major progress in this area, 73 million of the most vulnerable children worldwide still do not receive school meals (Partnership for Child Development 2018). In 2019, WFP invested in the future of more than 17 million girls and boys by partnering with governments to provide school meals, snacks, or take-home rations (WFP 2020a).

- WFP connects smallholder farmers to markets in 40 countries. In 2019, WFP procured US$37.2 million worth of food from smallholders in 29 countries (2 percent of the value of all food procured for 2019), who produce most of the world's food (WFP 2019c, 2020a, 2020u).
- Under WFP's FFA initiative, WFP has developed 134,000 hectares of land and non-farm land; 9,700 water points (ponds, shallow wells, reservoirs) used for agriculture, livestock, and/or fisheries were built or rehabilitated; and 8,800 km feeder roads were built or repaired (WFP 2020a).
- Six thousand, seven hundred bridges were restored, which improves people's long-term food security and resilience to climate change (WFP 2020a, 2020k).
- "WFP development projects focus on nutrition, especially for mothers and children, addressing malnutrition from the earliest stages through programmes targeting the first 1,000 days from conception to a child's second birthday, and later through school meals" (WFP 2019k). In 2019, 10.8 million children received special nutritional support; 6.4 million women received nutritional supplements; and 400,000 HIV-affected received food support, all together in 18 countries (WFP 2020a).
- "WFP also provides services to the humanitarian community, including passenger air transportation through the UN Humanitarian Air Service, which flies to more than 280 locations worldwide" (WFP 2020w).

WFP uses Forecast-based Financing in 10 countries to provide cash to vulnerable families, allowing them to buy food, reinforce their homes, and take other steps to build resilience ahead of climate disasters like droughts, storms or floods (FAO 2017b).

Types of World Food Programme Operations

The Annual Performance Report of 2019 for the World Food Programme reported: "WFP's direct assistance for beneficiaries in 2019 consisted of 4.2 million mt of food and US$2.1 billion in CBTs. This was in addition to the US$610 million invested in capacity strengthening and service delivery activities in support of the humanitarian and development community. Most of the food and CBTs were delivered through general food distributions, followed by nutrition, school feeding and food assistance for assets activities" (WFP 2019a, 39).

The majority of CBT activities in 2019 were in the Middle East, North Africa, Eastern Europe and Central Asia region, particularly in Yemen and for the Syrian regional refugee response. However, CBTs were used to some degree in two-thirds of all country offices in the region. In 2019, in Lebanon, when civil unrest contributed to the devaluation of the currency, WFP, in partnership with the Ministry of Social Affairs, responded with conditional and unconditional CBTs totaling US$285 million to support basic food needs for more than 1 million beneficiaries (WFP 2020a).

Level and Extent of Emergencies

The Annual Performance Report of 2019 for WFP also reported: "WFP was responding to seven Level 3 and 11 Level 2 emergencies in 20 countries at the end of 2019..."

WFP distributed 67 percent of its in-kind food, 78 percent of its cash-based assistance and 48 percent of its specialized nutritious foods (SNFs) to extremely food-insecure and malnourished people in some of the world's largest emergencies, which were in Yemen, the Democratic Republic of the Congo, the Syrian Arab Republic, South Sudan, Mozambique, three countries in central Sahel—Burkina Faso, Mali and the Niger—and Nigeria (WFP 2020a, 39–40).

Three other program areas of significance: school feeding, nutrition, and FFA, discussed previously, addressing immediate food needs through cash, voucher, or food transfers, while at the same time promoting the building or rehabilitation of assets that will improve long-term food security and resilience (WFP 2019a).

Trends in World Food Programme's Operations and Sources of Funding and Allocation

WFP has seen rapid growth in its activity in the new millennium (Figure 12.1). As discussed in Chapter 3, food aid needs temporarily spiked, starting in 2008, following the food and financial crises, but the recent rise in need for food aid is a result of conflict, leading to large involuntary displacement of human population, and climate change. In 2019, WFP raised a record US$8 billion, compared with US$7.2 billion in 2018, and yet, faced a funding gap of US$4.1 billion (WFP 2020a). WFP staff have had to make difficult decisions in the case of emergencies that are forgotten or overlooked by the international community, because they are of little political interest. Contributions to WFP, by October 3, 2020, reached US$8.5 billion in 2020, as of January 2021. The high cost of assisting people in long drawn-out conflicts needs more financial support than ever.

Sources of Funding
WFP's revenue increased by 10 percent to a record $US8 billion in 2019. The top five donors accounted for 76 percent of total contributions, and the top 10 donors accounted for 87

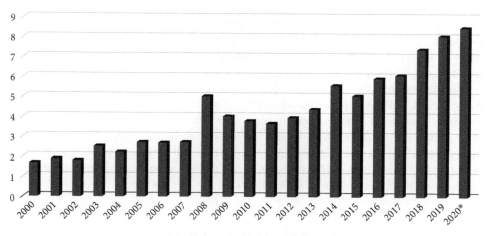

Figure 12.1 Total annual contributions to WFP, 2000–2020* (US$bn)

Note: *As of January 17, 2021.

Source: Based on data from https://www.wfp.org/funding

percent (that is, a 2 percent increased, compared with 2018), with the United States being WFP's top donor, with 36 percent designated for large-scale operations in South Sudan, the Syrian Arab Republic, and Yemen. The generous contributions were insufficient to cover identified needs of food insecure populations, with a funding gap of US$4.1 billion. Government donors provided 86 percent of 2019 funding, while the remainder came primarily from various UN funds, host governments, private donors, and the World Bank. In 2019, the largest increase was from the United States, which contributed US$910 million more than its 2018 contribution of at US$2.5 billion. Germany, the United Kingdom, the EC, and Saudi Arabia made up the remaining top five donors. All of the top five donors strengthened their commitments, except for the EC, from which overall funding decreased, compared to 2018. WFP's top 10 government donors (excluding UN pooled funds) in 2019 were the United States at US$3.4 billion (42 percent of all contributions), followed by Germany (US$887 million), the United Kingdom (US$698 million), the EC (US$686 million), Saudi Arabia (US$387 million), United Arab Emirates (US$272 million), Canada (US$190 million), Sweden (US$159 million), Japan (US$157 million), and Norway (US$89 million) (WFP 2020a, 2020c). And funding from nongovernmental partners, including private sector institutions, represented only 1.6 percent of the total (WFP 2020a, 2020d).

Similarly, 5 percent of WFP's funding, US$420 million in 2019, was unearmarked or softly earmarked. Known as flexible funding, it continued a worrisome trend of low levels of unearmarked contributions (Figure 12.2). The top 10 contributors of flexible funding in 2019 were Sweden, the United Kingdom, the Netherlands, Germany, Norway, Denmark, Australia, Canada, Ireland, and Belgium. Their combined contributions amounted to US$372 million, or 85 percent of total flexible funding (WFP 2020a).

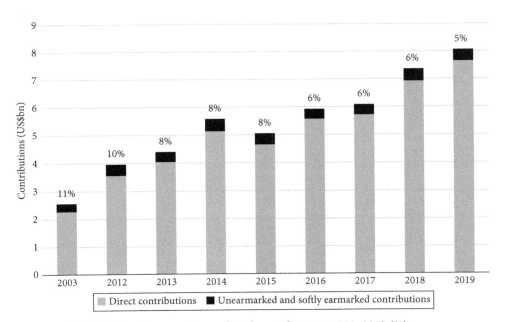

Figure 12.2 Flexible funding as a share of total contributions, 2003–2019 (%)

Source: Adapted from WFP (2019a, figure 3, 24); WFP (2020a, figure 4, 25).

When donors do not impose conditions, WFP can determine the country program or its activities in which "the contribution will be used and how it will be used" (WFP 2020h). They are crucial for WFP's responses to emergencies, protracted relief, and recovery efforts and allow WFP to respond with flexibility and predictability but also promptly to crises (WFP 2020h). At the activity level, however, some progress was made, with the percentage of earmarked funds decreasing from 80 percent in 2018 to 70 percent in 2019, mainly due to the increased flexibility of several of the top 10 donors—Canada, Germany, Japan, and Saudi Arabia elected to allocate funds to less restrictive levels of the "line of sight" from resources to results, including strategic outcomes, strategic results, and CSPs (WFP 2020a, 25). In 2019, the top 10 donors accounted for 87 percent of total contributions, a 2 percent increase compared with 2018, with the five top donors alone accounting for 76 percent. Government donors provided 86 percent of 2019 funding, while the remainder came primarily from various UN funds. To diversify its funding base and foster new partnerships, WFP adopted a five-year private sector partnership and fundraising strategy in 2019. The strategy covers the period from 2020 to 2025 and establishes ambitious targets for increasing contributions from individuals and businesses in the three pillars of the strategy: impact, income, and innovation.

Increasingly, recipient governments are also becoming donors although they provide small amounts. The top 10 in 2019 were: China, Honduras, Burkina Faso, Afghanistan, Pakistan, Benin, Burundi, Lesotho, Ghana, and South Sudan.[4] In statistical terms, the WFP story is one of successful multilateralization of bilateral food aid, termed food assistance, as food aid quantities have diminished, and donors have moved to cash transfers and other kinds of humanitarian aid are coming into vogue.[5]

Regional Allocation of World Food Programme Funding

Figure 12.3 illustrates the budget and funding received for operations in the six WFP regions.[6]

---

[4] See https://www.wfp.org/funding/2019

[5] In a study of alternative transfer options in Colombia and Ecuador by WFP and the International Food Policy Research Institute (IFPRI), Hidrobo et al. (2012) found that:

> The cash transfer incurs the lowest costs to participants in terms of waiting times and transportation costs. . . . The main complaints of voucher recipients are lack of food items and higher prices in supermarkets. The main complaint of food recipients is torn food packaging, and the main complaint of cash recipients is lack of understanding on how to use the debit cards. Across all three modalities, the transfers are reported to be mainly used for consumption of food items; however, voucher recipients in comparison to cash recipients spend a larger percentage on food. Almost none of the food transfer or voucher is sold to buy other items. Besides food consumption, food recipients tend to share their transfer with friends or family, or save their transfer for later use. Cash recipients also report saving a small share of their cash for later use and spending a small portion on nonfood items. (Hidrobo et al. 2012, xi)

Generally, these transfers seem to have positive effect on nutrition. How sustainable they are is unclear. Nutrition knowledge was found to increase from baseline to follow-up; largest knowledge gains occurred on food items rich in iron and vitamin A, and on infant feeding practices (Hidrobo et al. 2012).

[6] WFP's Annual Performance Report for 2019 noted:

> WFP's 2019 contribution revenue reached US$ 8 billion in 2019, 10 percent higher than in 2018 and 15 percent higher than 2017. Despite this historic level, the funding gap of US$4.1 billion was US$1.3 billion higher than the gap in 2018 as rising food insecurity outstripped contributions. While responses to Level 3 emergencies were generally well funded, operations in small and medium-sized countries suffered from lack of resources. Ten countries accounted for 65 percent of WFP's total direct expenditure in 2019, and 78 countries for the remaining 35 percent. The under-resourcing of many country operations led to reductions in numbers of people assisted and the sizes and duration of rations provided, helping to perpetuate inequalities and food insecurity. (WFP 2020a, 9)

The Annual Performance Report for 2019 also noted that with a funding gap of: " . . . US$ 4.1 billion, or 34 percent of identified needs, despite record contributions, . . . [and] could not reach the target of distributing 5.6 million mt of food . . . the 4.2 million mt distributed still represents the largest amount of in-kind distributions in WFP's history and 75-percent achievement of the yearly target" (WFP 2020a, 51).

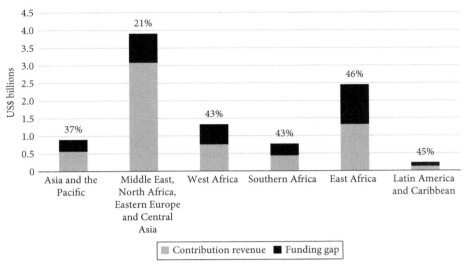

Figure 12.3 Funding gap by region, 2018 (US$bn)
Source: WFP (2019a, figure 6, 30).

According to WFP's Annual Performance Report for 2019:

> In 2019, WFP faced a funding gap of US$4.1 billion, or 34 percent of identified needs, despite record contributions [US$1.3 billion higher than the gap in 2018, as rising food insecurity outstripped contributions]. The organization could not therefore reach the target of distributing 5.6 million mt of food, but the 4.2 million mt distributed still represents the largest amount of in-kind distributions in WFP's history and 75-percent achievement of the yearly target... (WFP 2020a, 51)

According to WFP's Annual Performance Report for 2018:

> The Middle East, North Africa, Eastern Europe and Central Asia region is by far the largest by budget and contributions and encompasses some of WFP's largest operations, including those in Yemen, the Syrian Arab Republic and surrounding countries, the Sudan and Iraq. This region had the lowest funding gap in 2018, at 21 percent.... WFP's larger operations in all regions have generally been better funded.
>
> The Latin America and the Caribbean region had the second highest funding gap in 2018, at 45 percent. With the exception of Colombia, all countries in the region had needs-based plans with budgets less than US$50 million in 2018. The region as a whole has the smallest budget in WFP and includes relatively few direct deliveries, with efforts focused more on capacity strengthening... (WFP 2019a, 29)

WFP's Annual Performance Report for 2019 noted further:

> Aggregated expenditures of the regional bureaux show a similar trend as in previous years, with the Regional Bureau for the Middle East, North Africa, Eastern Europe and Central Asia accounting for 47 percent of total expenditures and the Regional Bureau for East Africa for 23 percent. These two regions contain nine of the ten countries with the greatest

expenditure, illustrating the extent to which WFP's efforts are concentrated in a small number of countries. The remaining regional bureaux received 11 percent for West Africa, 10 percent for Southern Africa, 7 percent for Asia and the Pacific and 3 percent for Latin America and the Caribbean. (WFP 2020a, 24)

Figures 12.4 and 12.5 illustrate the distribution of funds by region, as well as:

the ten recipient countries that accounted for 65 percent of WFP's total direct expenditures in 2019. The remaining 78 countries with active operations accounted for the outstanding 35 percent. All countries in the top ten received more in expenditures than in 2018, with the largest increases noted in Yemen (US$652 million), the Syrian Arab Republic (US$80 million) and Ethiopia (US$71 million). Expenditures increased in Mozambique by US$100 million in response to the devastation caused by Cyclone Idai, and in Zimbabwe by US$74 million as worsening drought increased needs. (WFP 2020a, 23)

The Importance of the Need for Regular and Increasing Contributions

FAO notes, "Since WFP has no independent source of funds, all donations either in cash or in-kind must be accompanied by the cash needed to move, manage, and monitor WFP food assistance" (WFP 2020l). (See Table 12.1.) After a spike in 2007–8, annual contributions to WFP resumed a downward trajectory of overall spending on food aid and agricultural development, and for official development assistance (ODA), the share of food and agriculture has dropped from 20 percent to the single digits since the 1970s (von Braun and Torero 2009; WFP 2017a).

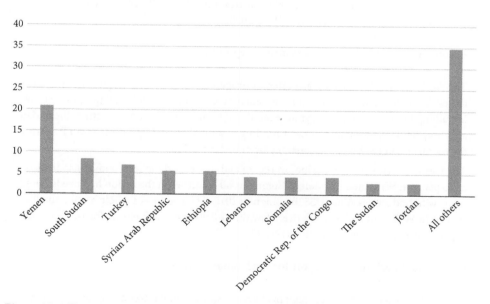

Figure 12.4 Top 10 recipient countries by direct expenditures, 2019 (%)

Note: Direct expenditure in 2019 was US$7.2 billion.

Source: WFP (2020a, figure 3, 24).

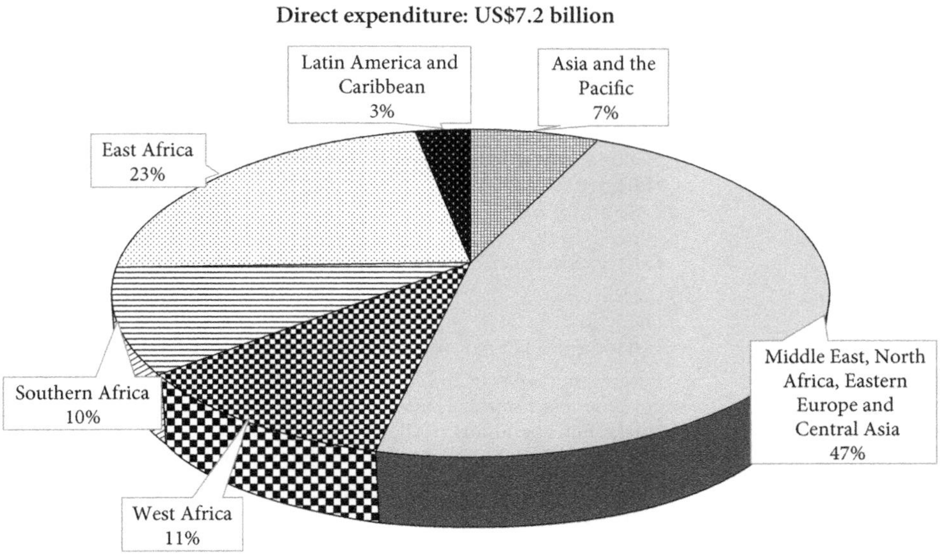

Direct expenditure: US$7.2 billion

Figure 12.5 Aggregated expenditures by the regional bureaux, 2019
Source: Adapted from WFP (2020a, 24).

Government contributors are relatively consistent—the top-ranked aggregate donors between 2015 and 2019 were the United States, Germany, EC, United Kingdom, Canada, Japan, Saudi Arabia, Sweden, United Arab Emirates, and Norway, in that order (WFP 2020c).[7] With the exception of Ethiopia and Pakistan, the top 20 government contributors to WFP were from upper-middle to high-income economies (WFP 2020c).

The 20 largest aggregate WFP donors between and 2015 and 2019 account for nearly 93 percent of total contributions, and 96 percent in 2019, much of which arrives with strings attached as tied donations and with earmarks, with limitations on activities (Ramachandran, Leo, and McCarthy 2010; WFP 2020c). This has been attributed both to donor preference for short-term, restricted commitments and to a "reactive and unpredictable revenue mobilization model," reliant on emergency appeals (Ramachandran, Leo, and McCarthy 2010, i).

Unrestricted contributions, the so-called direct or multilateral contributions, were around 5.4 percent of the total contribution in 2019; the largest providers traditionally have included Sweden, United Kingdom, the Netherlands, Germany, Norway, Denmark, Australia, and Canada (WFP 2019f, 2020h). In 2019, WFP received US$419.9 million in multilateral contributions, representing approximately 5.4 percent of total contributions received (WFP 2020a). However, flexible contributions (occasionally referred to as "multilateral" in WFP publications) remained at just 5 percent of WFP's total resources, well below a 20 percent mark in 2008 (Figure 12.6). The overall trend indicates that flexible donations to WFP are increasing (Figure 12.7), but not nearly what WFP should ideally have to reduce costs and increase flexibility in its own operations.

---

[7] Note: UN Central Emergency Response Fund (CERF) was the 8th top five-year aggregate donor, followed by Sweden (9), UN Other Funds and Agencies (excl. CERF) (10), United Arab Emirates (11), and Norway (12); private donors were number 13 in the 2019 list (WFP 2020c).

Table 12.1 World Food Programme contributions

Donors	Governments (traditional donors and host governments)* Organizations (corporations, nonprofit organizations) Individuals
Partners	National governments (donors, beneficiaries) Nongovernmental organizations (NGOs) FAO and IFAD Other UN agencies Corporate partners
Donation type	Cash Food In-kind (means to grow, store, cook, or transport food; fundraising)
Programme types	Programme types include the Country Portfolio Budget (CPB); development projects (DEV); Immediate Response Account (IRA); emergency operations (EMOP); protracted relief and recovery programs (PRRO); and flexible funding with no programme specified
Food aid category	Emergency (provided to victims of natural or man-made disasters on a short-term basis; freely distributed to targeted beneficiary groups and usually provided on a grant basis; channeled multilaterally, through NGOs, or sometimes bilaterally) Project (supports various types of projects such as agricultural, nutritional, and development; usually freely distributed to targeted beneficiary groups; can also be sold on the open market; provided on a grant basis and is channeled bilaterally, multilaterally or through NGOs) Program (provided on a government-to-government basis; not targeted at specific beneficiary groups; sold on the open market and can be provided either as a grant or a loan)
Delivery/purchase modes	Local Purchased, distributed, and used in recipient country Triangular Purchased in third country for use in recipient country Direct

Note: Note that "host government" refers to beneficiary countries. Although "national government" is sometimes the preferred term, as "host" can be perceived as patronizing, "host" is typically used to avoid confusion.

Source: Author's construction, based on http://www.wfp.org; WFP (2020e).

The top 10 multilateral contributors in 2019 were Sweden, United Kingdom, the Netherlands, Germany, Denmark, Norway, Australia, Canada, Ireland, and Belgium (WFP 2019f, 2020h).[8]

Over a five-year period, starting in 2008, WFP invested US$7.4 million in developing its capacity to mobilize private funds, yielding a US$549 million "return" that also contributed to operating costs and the Program Support and Administrative (PSA) budget. Of the total, US$283 million is considered sustainable, and US$266 million was received as "one-off" donations to specific projects or emergency appeals. The majority of private sector funding supported programs, such as school meals, health and nutrition, and emergency relief; approximately 10 percent was received in-kind.

---

[8] WFP classifies contributions as direct or multilateral, the latter indicating contributions with no usage restrictions.

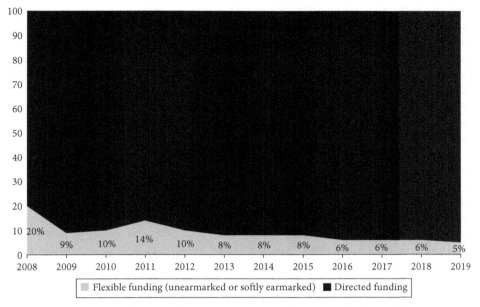

Figure 12.6 Share of flexible contributions in total contributions to the World Food Programme, 2008–2019 (%)
Source: Adapted from WFP (2019a, 2019f, 2020a, 2020h).

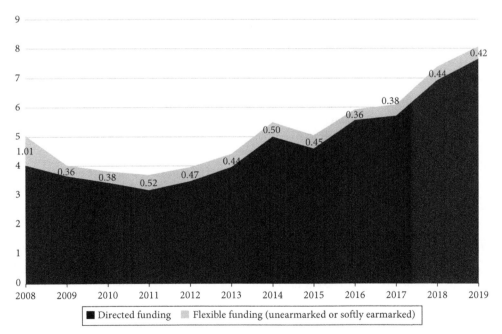

Figure 12.7 Directed (earmarked) and flexible contributions to the World Food Programme, 2008–2019 (US$bn)
Source: Adapted from WFP (2019a, 2019f, 2020h).

Private sector funding represented a small fraction of overall donations, and WFP has been actively working toward harnessing individual donors to the extent that the United Nations Children's Fund (UNICEF) and UNHCR, with their longer standing records are known for doing. The US$7.4 million was a loan from WFP to the private sector unit, and not an investment, as the WFP Executive Board asked that the new private sector function should be self-financing. Other UN agencies, like UNICEF and UNHCR, have had massive investments in their private sector functions (especially, on individual giving), which was not the case for WFP when this was written. So, the comparison needs to be interpreted with caution.

As an agency based on voluntary donor contributions, in many ways, WFP is only as good as the sum of its membership base—prone to least-common-denominator decision-making or open to the enterprise and innovation of its members. Beneficiary nations are likely disinclined to be assertive. However, forward-thinking countries stand to drive reform and innovation (Ramachandran, Leo, and McCarthy 2010). In addition, the graduation of countries from recipients to middle-income countries (MICs), attention to South–South cooperation, and aid funds being "passed through" beneficiary governments to fund WFP operations all stand to affect power dynamics and priorities. WFP is continuing shift to cash-based programming as an effective transfer modality, which provides beneficiaries with choices regarding how they utilize assistance to address multiple, cross-cutting needs.

World Food Programme Expenditures and the Focus on Fragile States

According to WFP's 2019 Annual Performance Report:

> WFP's continuing shift to cash-based programming as an effective transfer modality that provides beneficiaries with choices regarding how they utilize assistance to address multiple, cross-cutting needs.
>
> ...Food distributions remained the main response modality in 2019, increasing by 9 percent from USD 3.2 billion in 2018 to USD 3.5 billion. However, the largest growth rates were in the cash-based transfer (CBT) modality, increasing by 22 percent since 2018, and capacity strengthening and service delivery activities, increasing by 31 percent.
>
> CBTs and associated costs accounted for 32 percent of total direct expenditures, compared with 30 percent in 2018, while the capacity strengthening and service delivery modality made up 9 percent of the total, compared with 7 percent in 2018. Continued investment in both areas is a central strategy for WFP in assisting beneficiaries, increasing their resilience and improving their livelihoods. (WFP 2020a, 29)

According to WFP's 2019 Annual Performance Report, WFP spent US$7.2 billion in fiscal year 2019, compared with US$6.6 billion in 2018 (WFP 2020a). The 2019 APR further notes:

> The majority of CBT activities were in the Middle East, North Africa, Eastern Europe and Central Asia region, particularly in Yemen and for the Syrian regional refugee response. However, CBTs were used to some degree in two thirds of all country offices in the region. In 2019 in Lebanon, when civil unrest contributed to the devaluation of the currency, WFP in partnership with the Ministry of Social Affairs responded with conditional and

unconditional CBTs totalling USD 285 million to support basic food needs for more than 1 million beneficiaries [Figure 12.8]. (WFP 2020a, 30)

In 2019 expenses reached a record level for WFP, with an increase over 2018. The 2019 APR noted:

> WFP assisted 97 million people—the largest number since 2012—while operating in 88 countries. [It rapidly] responded to Level 3 and Level 2 emergencies in 20 countries—the highest annual total ever. These ranged from long-standing operations, such as in the Democratic Republic of the Congo, to the rapid scale-up of operations when Cyclone Idai hit Mozambique.
>
> ...[D]onors stepped up...and provided a record-breaking US$8 billion in confirmed contributions. [This unprecedented amount of funding] was a testament to donors' confidence in WFP's ability to save lives and change lives. [The funds were used to procure] food valued at more than US$2.3 billion,...including US$37 million-worth from smallholder farmers, for direct distribution. In addition, US$2.1 billion was provided as cash-based transfers.
>
> Roughly two-thirds of [WFP's life-saving] food assistance went to girls, boys, women and men facing severe food crises, overwhelmingly as a result of conflict. In South Sudan and Zimbabwe, WFP's ability to quickly ramp up humanitarian assistance helped to avoid famine. After the world's largest humanitarian crisis in Yemen deteriorated early in 2019, WFP nearly doubled its support in some areas despite huge security, access and supply constraints. In the Sudan, WFP became the first United Nations agency since 2011 to be given humanitarian access to Blue Nile State. (WFP 2020a, 4)

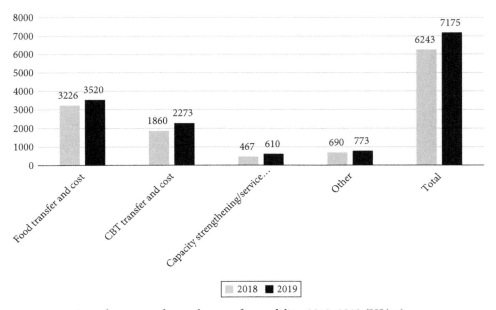

Figure 12.8 Growth in expenditures by transfer modality, 2018–2019 (US$m)

Note: "Other" includes implementation and direct support costs.

Source: Adapted from WFP (2020a, figure 8, 30).

The *State of Fragility 2018*, published by the Organisation for Economic Co-operation and Development (OECD) opens with an editorial, which asserts:

> Fragility poses a major global threat to the implementation of the 2030 Agenda for Sustainable Development. In 2016, more countries experienced some form of violent conflict than at any time in the past 30 years. Close to 26,000 people died from terrorist attacks and 560,000 people lost their lives because of violence. The number of displaced people in the world is the highest since the end of the Second World War. (OECD 2018, 7)

OECD classified 58 countries, with a total population of 1.8 billion persons, as fragile or living in conflict in 2016, but the number of persons affected by conflict is projected to grow to 2.3 billion by 2030 (28 percent) and 3.3 billion by 2050 (34 percent) (OECD 2018). "Poverty, too, is increasingly concentrated in fragile contexts" (OECD 2018, 17). Nearly 688 million people, or more than 80 percent of the world's poorest are chronically food insecure in 2019, according to FAO et al. (2020).

That means in 2019, almost 60 percent of the world's hungry people are living in areas affected by armed violence, conflict is the single greatest challenge to achieving zero hunger.[9] According to UNHCR (2021), at least 79.5 million people around the world have been forced to flee their homes. Among them are nearly 26 million refugees, around half of whom are under the age of 18. There are also millions of stateless people, who have been denied a nationality and lack access to basic rights, such as education, health care, employment, and freedom of movement. At a time when 1 percent of the world's population have fled their homes as a result of conflict or persecution, WFP's work is very important. Eighty percent of the stateless people face acute food insecurity. Most live in developing countries.

OECD (2020) noted that fragile contexts were home to 460 million people living in extreme poverty in 2020, or 76 percent of the worldwide total. Fragile contexts account for 23 percent of the world's population, but also 43 percent (26 million people) of those expected to fall into extreme poverty due to COVID-19 by the end of 2020. Even before the shock of COVID-19, the majority of fragile contexts were on track to meet just one SDG— SDG13 on climate action—and progress was particularly challenged on SDG2 (zero hunger), SDG 3 (health), and SDG 5 (gender equality).

Most of WFP's largest emergency operations take place in conflict areas, since 10 out of 13 of the world's main food crises are driven by conflict (WFP 2019e). A new dimension has recently been added: peace. The relevance of the humanitarian–development–peace nexus and its influence on policymakers has been underlined with the United Nations Security Council Resolution 2417, which condemned the starving of civilians as a method of warfare, as well as the unlawful denial of humanitarian access to civilian populations, in highlighting the link between peace and food security.[10] Food security is a key element of WFP Executive Director David Beasley's speeches, and WFP has begun to investigate its role in that nexus through a partnership with the Stockholm International Peace Research Institute (SIPRI).

---

[9] See "Food Assistance: A Step to Peace and Stability—Nobel Peace Prize 2020." https://www.wfp.org/conflict-and-hunger#:~:text=With%20almost%2060 %20percent%20of

[10] "Unanimously adopting resolution 2417 (2018), the Council drew attention to the link between armed conflict and conflict-induced food insecurity and the threat of famine." See https://www.un.org/press/en/2018/sc13354.doc.htm

For donors like Germany, operationalization of the nexus is a priority also with regard to WFP. Notably, food delivery is more costly in conflict-affected countries. When agriculture and trade are disrupted by conflict, "a simple plate of food can cost more than a day's wages. In South Sudan, for example, it could be the equivalent of a New Yorker having to pay US $348 for a modest lunch such as a plate of bean stew" (WFP 2019e). In 2019, this cost has increased to US$393.[11]

More than half of WFP's revenue was designated for WFP operations in South Sudan, the Syrian Arab Republic, and Yemen (WFP 2019a). WFP's 2019 Annual Performance Report noted:

> Nearly US$4.9 billion was spent on work under this strategic result [Strategic Objective 1: End hunger by protecting access to food]—a record amount accounting for 68 percent of total expenditures.
>
> A significant amount of work towards achieving Strategic Result 1 was carried out through emergency operations in Yemen, the Democratic Republic of the Congo, the Syrian Arab Republic, South Sudan, Mozambique, central Sahel and Nigeria.
>
> Unprecedented levels of funding allowed 86 operations to distribute 4 million mt of in-kind food and US$1.5 billion in CBTs and commodity vouchers, primarily through unconditional transfers to help meet immediate food needs. To address the underlying causes of malnutrition, 80 percent of WFP operations also incorporated nutrition-sensitive objectives into their programmes, while 34 countries integrated asset creation and livelihood activities into their emergency responses with the aim of fostering resilience to future shocks.
>
> In fragile settings, 67 operations supported schoolchildren with nutritious meals, snacks or take-home rations to provide an essential safety net for the children and their families and to help restore normality, reduce vulnerability to hunger and protect livelihoods. In more stable settings, WFP provided technical and capacity building support to governments for transition to and scale up of national school feeding programmes. (WFP 2020a, 55)

In many respects, 2019 Level 3 and Level 2 emergencies in 20 countries—the highest ever annual total—compares with seven Level 3 and nine Level 2 emergency responses by WFP in 2018, which were conflict or climate-related emergencies, presenting obstacles to humanitarian access. In 2018, WFP implemented its first-ever preemptive response, in the Sahel, to prevent "a lean season from becoming a large-scale crisis" (WFP 2019a, 8). While meeting these emergencies, WFP country offices continued to implement their CSPs, and the performance ratings of WFP's functional area (defined as a WFP division, department, or other unit that specializes in specific areas of WFP's work) were "medium" to "high." WFP is implementing all of its cross-cutting, using its policies and instruments to ensure that its operations account for key cross-cutting issues (WFP 2019a).

Factors Underlying Change in the Nature of Response

The reasons behind WFP's change in the response are several. First, key donors have moved from in-kind food aid to local and regional procurement. Cash transfers have increased, and there is greater interest in moving from short-term aid toward longer-term social

---

[11] See "The Cost of a Plate of Food 2020." https://cdn.wfp.org/2020/plate-of-food/

protection, safety nets, nutritional interventions, and school lunches. There is also growing evidence that traditional justification for US food aid, by far the largest food aid supplier, tied to US sources of food and shipments is wasteful. Strategically and politically, US food aid is less significant today than it was in the past.[12]

WFP argues that with these changes, the distinction between humanitarian assistance and development assistance has been blurred, as development assistance has begun to address food (in)security, and humanitarian assistance has begun to take on "resiliency," using food assistance to create livelihood security (WFP 2017d). This raises larger issues for the food security architecture. And yet, the share of development projects has declined relative to the various emergency responses, as shown later in the chapter.

Financially, humanitarian assistance comes from a different "pocket" in most donor countries than development assistance. Structurally, it raises issues about where food assistance belongs—whether with the larger food security architecture of FAO, the Committee on Food Security (CFS), the UN Secretary-General's High Level Task Force (HLTF) on Global Food and Nutrition Security initiative with Rome-based institutions, or with humanitarian and relief agencies of the UN and the NGO community. In the past, there have also been concerns about food aid displacing food trade and about issues related to the World Trade Organization. With declining food surpluses, trade displacement is less of a concern. On the other hand, with climate change, low and variable stocks, growing demand on food sources for biofuels, and growing food purchases coming from middle-income developing countries, there is also concern about whether cash and food would be readily available in periods of crisis, such as occurred with the rising food prices and low stocks in 2007–8.

The following analysis considers WFP's evolving mandate and governance in the larger context of global food aid and food assistance in a highly changed world of declining food surpluses and a declining justification for food aid in-kind[13]—and yet, with the continued, and indeed, growing need for emergency assistance, particularly in the context of urgent unexpected needs, including climate-related and other disasters, intrastate conflicts, and the threat of terrorism originating in and aided by failed states. Given the growing number of failed states, there is also an interest in establishing a more seamless transition in international assistance from emergencies to rehabilitation, reconstruction, and development—to ensure development gains are not reversed by humanitarian emergencies. This raises important questions about WFP's comparative advantage as the world's largest

---

[12] Stephanie Mercier, an independent agricultural policy consultant and a former chief economist for the Democratic staff of the Senate Committee on Agriculture, and Vincent Smith, director of the agricultural studies program at the American Enterprise Institute and a professor of agricultural economics at Montana State University, have argued that US food aid, which has not changed much since the 1950s, is in urgent need of reform. They call for "common sense reforms" to eliminate "wasteful mandates," protecting US shipping mercantile company interests, requiring almost 100 percent of all food aid be sourced in the United States and US ships to carry at least half of the US food aid. Food aid is less than 1 percent of US agricultural exports and a negligible proportion of all US agricultural production. Reforms that relax US sourcing and cargo preference requirements will save as much as US$400 million yearly, by reducing administrative and transportation costs. Such savings could enable the United States to help several million more people in need each year, literally saving the lives of tens of thousands of children. Citing Erin Lentz, Christopher Barrett, and Miguel Gomez (2013), the authors noted that a United States Department of Agriculture (USDA) pilot program in nine countries, authorized by the 2008 Farm Bill, allowed US food aid to be procured in or near the countries where help was needed. The study by Lentz, Barrett, and Gomez (2013) found that local and regional sourcing on average generated savings of 53 percent on grains and 25 percent on pulses and legumes, compared to US sourcing (Mercier and Smith 2018; see, also, Barrett [2017]).

[13] Of US$5.6 billion in confirmed donations in 2014, 73 percent, or US$4.2 billion, was in cash contributions—a record, and a 22 percent increase over 2013 (WFP 2015h).

humanitarian agency, par excellence, as it moves to provide development assistance, albeit with less of an advantage.

The 2030 Agenda for Sustainable Development and the SDGs, embodied in the WFP Strategic Plan 2017–21, remain the focus of WFP's work (UN 2020; WFP 2017d, 2019j). Global commitments in 2018 of relevance to WFP include those related to the reform of the UN development system and United Nations Security Council Resolution 2417, as discussed earlier (WFP 2017d, 2019d).

Large-Scale Emergency Funding

Large-scale emergency funding remained concentrated on a small number of operations, with more than 35 percent of the contribution revenue earmarked to Level 3 operations in South Sudan, the Syrian Arab Republic, and Yemen. Yemen was the largest operation, with an increase of 41 percent in directed contributions in 2019, compared to 2018, accounting for 20 percent of WFP's global portfolio (WFP 2020a, 23).

Funding for countries supporting refugees from the Syrian crisis saw a significant decrease in contributions: for example, for WFP operations in Turkey and Jordan. In Turkey, the level of contributions fell by nearly 50 percent, from US$792 million in 2018 to US$405 million in 2019, but beneficiary numbers also decreased significantly, owing to the closure of camps and continued devaluation of the Turkish lira (WFP 2020a, 23).

Governance and Recent Changes in Organizational Structure

A 36-member executive board oversees WFP's humanitarian and development food aid activities. This model is more akin to a shareholder model than the "one country, one vote" model of FAO. The composition of the Executive Board nevertheless ensures that developing nation members have a significant stake in decision-making. Board seats are determined by election and divided equally between the UN Economic and Social Council (ECOSOC) and FAO. Of the 36 seats in total, 21 are from developing countries, with the majority selected by FAO. Fifteen are from developed country donors, the majority selected by ECOSOC (WFP 2014c). In 2019, all but one of the developing countries on the board were contributing governments or had contributed in the preceding five-year period (the exception was Equatorial Guinea) (WFP 2020g).

The WFP Board, like the boards of other multilateral organizations, strives to make all decisions by consensus, and the Board President is expected to make every effort to achieve such consensus before a matter is put to a vote. The unique nature of WFP governance is unlike the other four international organizations we reviewed; WFP has two parent bodies (UN and FAO). The UN Secretary-General and FAO Director-General appoint the Executive Director in consultation with the board. The WFP Secretariat, led by the Executive Director, manages day-to-day operations and administration. Strategic direction is influenced by a confluence of external forces, as we demonstrated earlier, and its influence on the organizational architecture. While the board presidency has regularly rotated between northern and southern stakeholders, the Executive Director, apart from in an acting capacity, has usually been from a developed country. Since 1992, the Executive Director has been a US citizen—unique among UN agencies, and much like the World Bank, indicative of the top donor standing of the US government. The United States, through the Executive Director, has relatively greater potential political power to push for changes within the organization, while the Board has greater potential to influence the strategic direction of the organization with wider legitimacy and accountability (WFP 2020g, 2020m).

WFP has been an agile organization responding to rapidly changing external circumstances. WFP's governance, oversight and organizational reforms have been taking place at least since the beginning of the new millennium, but the most fundamental changes have been influenced by the shift of its mandate from food aid to food assistance and all that accompanies it. In November 2014, for example, "the High-Level Committee on Management endorsed the three lines of defense model promulgated by the Institute of Internal Auditors as a reference model on risk management, oversight and accountability for UN System organizations. WFP adopted the model as part of the update of its internal control framework in 2015," necessitated by its increasingly decentralized regional and country operations (WFP 2018e, 4). Figure 12.9 illustrates the model at WFP.[14]

In March 2019, WFP adopted a new organizational structure to increase the effectiveness of its response to the rapidly changing external environment. The new structure at headquarters "responds to the greater complexity of operations, including WFP's increasing recognition of the humanitarian, development and peace nexus and protracted crises" against a background of increasing resource levels, available to WFP, by more than 25 percent during 2017–19 (WFP 2019h, 12).

The new structure is underpinned by five interrelated pillars under the leadership of the Executive Director to provide a more accountable and coherent headquarters structure. The five pillars are: (1) resource management; (2) program and policy development; (3) operations management; (4) operations assistance; and (5) partnerships and advocacy. The regional directors who manage 85 percent of WFP's resources now have a direct reporting line to the Executive Director. Several other organizational changes include improved management of supply chains, the school feeding program, stronger treatment of gender issues, increase in monitoring and evaluation including decentralized monitoring in the field, and generally increased accountability of the organization (WFP 2019h).

WFP's overall governance and assurance architecture is presented in Figure 12.10; principal governing bodies and independent entities report to the Board.

As early as 1999, a Governance Project was initiated to make the Board more strategic and efficient; the exercise was driven by the Board and the then Executive Director Catherine Bertini's recognition of the shifting demands of global development challenges (WFP 2005a). The Governance Working Group called for new frameworks for strategy, policy, oversight, and accountability to serve as an action plan for the organization and future work. Under five headings, the group presented 23 recommendations, 22 of which were approved.[15] Tellingly, the one recommendation not approved regarded a redrafting of the mission statement; the Board feared such discussion might expose differences of opinion about WFP's role among members (WFP 2005a, 7). Reviewing current thinking, Harvey et al. (2010), captured this transition in a paper on food aid and food assistance in emergency and transitional contexts:

---

[14] The Ethics Office, which is part of the second line of defense at WFP, also carries out whistleblower protection activities, which are strictly independent of management.

[15] The five headings were roles of governance, functions of governance, processes of governance, annual programme of work, and structure of governance (WFP 2005a, 6).

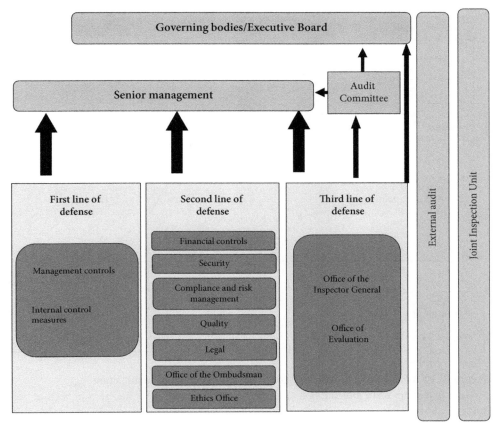

Figure 12.9 The three lines of defense at the World Food Programme
Source: WFP (2018e, figure 2, 5).

Food assistance instruments might include direct food-based transfers (such as general rations, food-for-work, supplementary feeding or vulnerable group feeding and school feeding), food subsidies, cash transfers and vouchers (including school or user fee waivers) and agricultural and livestock support. Food subsidies, fee waivers and livestock support are rarely considered to be part of food assistance, but do fit some definitions. Further ambiguity remains over when cash transfers should be counted as food assistance, and what forms of support to agricultural production (seed provision, fertiliser subsidies and extension services) and what aspects of nutritional interventions should count as food assistance. (Harvey et al. 2010, 3)

The paper identified five priority areas for action:

- developing a new food security architecture which incorporates food assistance;
- working towards greater clarity of terms and definitions;
- where appropriate, continuing to expand beyond food aid to the use of cash and a broader food assistance toolbox;
- linking food assistance more clearly to the expansion of social assistance within national social protection strategies; and

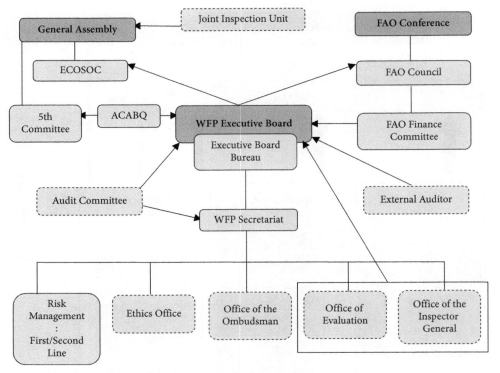

Figure 12.10 World Food Programme governance and assurance architecture
Source: Adapted from WFP (2018e, figure 1, 3).

- linking food assistance more clearly to overall nutrition strategies that address treatment as well as underlying causes. (Harvey et al. 2010, 4)

Harvey et al. (2010, 4) recommended, "These areas of action should be addressed in a number of contexts, from the highest levels of the UN to the G20/G8 to agencies implementing food assistance programmes on the ground." Taking these actions, the paper said, "will require serious thought and careful negotiations amongst stakeholders," and warned that:

The default policy option is to allow food aid to continue its decline into near irrelevance and put nothing else robust in its place. In a context where problems of food insecurity as a result of disasters are likely to increase as a result of climate change, and where large numbers of people experience protracted crisis, the need for a flexible, coherent and accountable system to meet the needs of food insecure and malnourished people should be an urgent priority for the international aid system. (Harvey et al. 2010, 4)

WFP's Hunger Map 2020 (Figure 12.11) depicts the prevalence of undernourishment in the population of each country in 2017–19; 8.9 percent of the world's population did not get enough to eat in 2019. If the current trends continue, the number of hungry people will reach 840 million by 2030. Using its Vulnerability Analysis and Mapping (VAM), WFP issues live maps that reflect the most recent state of food insecurity. VAM develops a range

Figure 12.11 Hunger Map, 2020

Source: © World Food Programme, 2020

https://www.wfp.org/publications/hunger-map-2020

of publicly available resources, such as live dashboards and the HungerMapLIVE, launched in 2020, that tracks food security in near real time in over 90 countries.[16]

Continuing trends since the late 1980s, emergency food aid delivery comprises a majority and increasing share of global food aid, with a decline in program aid.

Assistance Programs Have Increased

Although the majority of food aid continues to be in-kind transfers, the share of this type of aid fell from over 90 percent of food aid in 1991 to 62 percent in 2012 (WFP 2013e, 2020i). Figure 12.8 shows expenditures by transfer modality for 2018 and 2019: food transfers and costs makeup 49 percent of direct expenditures in 2019.

The proportion of food aid purchased both locally or triangularly decreased: that is, it declined by 26 percent for local purchases and by 21 percent for triangular purchases. The decline in physical delivery of food aid and an increased use of cash and voucher transfer modalities, which grew exponentially over the past decade, are reflective of WFP's shift to food assistance In the case of CBTs, WFP is the largest humanitarian agent of such transfers (WFP 2013d).

Using household data from Ethiopia's Productive Safety Net Programme, Hirvonen and Hoddinott (2020) examined recipients' preferences for cash or in-kind payments. Households that are closer to markets and financial services are more likely to prefer cash to food payments. However, when food prices rise, preferences are seen to shift to in-kind transfers. No more than 17 percent of surveyed households preferred only cash, and the median household preferred no more than 50 percent cash.

Financial Implications of the World Food Programme's Mandate: Shifting from Food Aid to Cash Transfers

WFP's ability to deliver both food aid and assistance, as well as on other development roles is dependent on both the volume and nature of voluntary contributions, as well as its financial framework.[17] Changes from donors would help WFP shore up its operations. Greater commitments of untied cash donations from the United States and other major donors can provide WFP significant operational flexibility to execute prudent financial management operations. Donor contributions to the proposed Food Security Trust Fund at the World Bank would further support WFP hedging operations.

A 2010 study by the Center for Global Development (CGD), noting that WFP has extremely limited ability to manage financial risk, stated:

> The WFP procures all its food through spot markets, which subjects it to substantial commodity and transport price risks and significant delays delivering food. Relying on

---

[16] See VAM: https://dataviz.vam.wfp.org/Reports_Explorer

[17] The financial framework refers to the general and financial regulations and rules, financial structures, policies, systems, and processes that support operations and provide financial oversight and accountability for stakeholders (WFP 2016a).

reactive emergency appeals and on donors that tend to earmark contributions and make commitments one year at a time only adds to operational inflexibility and uncertainty.

... The Programme should consider implementing a targeted hedging pilot strategy. (Ramachandran, Leo, and McCarthy, 2010, abstract)

The CDG report recommended that WFP adopt risk-management instruments, such as physical call options, forward contracts, and futures contracts. The plus side of the proposed strategy would be increased predictability and efficiency of WFP operations. The minus side would be that it would take away funds from long-term assistance, given that it has always been easier to raise funds for emergencies than for long-term development (Ramachandran, Leo, and McCarthy 2010).

WFP's current financial framework underwent a Financial Framework Review (FFR), completed in 2016, the goals of which were to: (1) increase predictability of resources; (2) increase flexibility; (3) enhance accountability; and (4) simplify resource management (WFP 2016a).

In a strategic planning document, in 2007, WFP described its work as an asset in bridging the "gap between crises, recovery and sustainable longer-term solutions" (WFP 2007, 3). That same theme continues in WFP's Strategic Plan 2017–21, albeit in a radically transformed world of SDGs and accelerated action needed to end poverty and hunger by 2030, in just ten years and in which multi-stakeholder engagement is crucial (WFP 2016c). Simultaneously, in its Strategic Plan 2017–21, WFP "responded to 13 major emergencies in 2014 and 12 major emergencies in 2015. Current trends in climate-, conflict- and health-related crises are increasing the number of people living in hunger and ... [point to the necessity] for WFP to ... focus on saving lives and livelihoods in emergencies, if it is to help countries achieve the 2030 Agenda" (WFP 2016c, 9). The Strategic Plan continued, "Climate change threatens to break down food systems by increasing frequency and severity of natural hazards, with a disproportionate impact on vulnerable food-insecure households. The global community cannot and should not keep saving the same lives every year" (WFP 2016c, 9).

The plan also noted that "protracted crises have become the new norm, while acute short-term crises are now the exception" (WFP 2016c, 10). Recognizing the impact of the crises on populations with food insecurity and undernutrition, CFS adopted the Framework for Action for Food Security and Nutrition in Protracted Crises (CFS–FFA) in 2015. "WFP has unique strengths and capacities for responding to affected populations in protracted crises, and for acting on the principles set out by the CFS-FFA" (WFP 2016c, 10). WFP has gained significant experience in both humanitarian and development contexts, so it is well suited "to help strengthen the resilience of affected people in protracted crises by also applying a development lens in its humanitarian response, and by aligning its recovery and development interventions accordingly" (WFP 2016c, 10).

Bridging Humanitarian and Development Functions: A Case for Safety Nets on Humanitarian and Productivity Grounds?

WFP frequently provides social protection, or safety-net types of assistance, in the case of emergencies to three types of countries: (1) countries which have no institutional infrastructure of safety nets; (2) countries with some but weak infrastructure; and (3) countries with relatively well established safety net infrastructure. Behavioral economics of poverty has suggested a strong need for institutions to better assist countries in bridging this gap between poverty and vulnerability. Together, such gaps often lead farmers to use technologies that may be less productive in good weather years, but more productive in bad weather years.[18] This may lock households into decision-making patterns that are less risky in the short term, but offer lower reward strategies for long-term development. The donor community increasingly sees food assistance and other social safety nets as freeing vulnerable populations to take risks to shift to more profitable forms of farming or other sources of income generation, rather than to continue to focus just on household survival. Building national systems—combined with a shift from short-run to more durable approaches—is increasingly becoming a unifying framework for assistance provided by different actors (WFP 2015f).

In a useful review of 12 case studies jointly undertaken by WFP and the World Bank on humanitarian assistance and social protection, it was noted:

> To some extent, however, a distinctive feature of humanitarian assistance revolves around the degree of involvement and engagement of national authorities (Konyndyk 2018; Stoddard 2017). For instance, ... out of the U$27.2 billion of international humanitarian assistance in 2017, only 2.5 percent was channeled through host governments. ... The rest was directed outside government structures, including via some 4,480 actors comprising international and national nongovernmental organizations, civil society, and others. Meanwhile, a number of national governments are, of course, also allocating domestic resources to address emergencies within their own borders... (Gentilini, Laughton, and O'Brien 2018, 2–3)

Gentilini, Laughton, and O'Brien (2018) identified several takeaway lessons from WFP and World Bank assistance, including possible challenges and trade-offs from practical experience. Small-scale, externally funded quality pilot programs of social safety nets can have demonstration effects at a national scale, as in the case of Mauritania, particularly for those countries supported by international organizations. Similarly, large-scale emergency responses can provide "proof of concept" for national social safety net programs, as in the case of Lebanon. Guinea's World Bank-funded and WFP-implemented school feeding pilot program in remote, Ebola-affected areas also offers promise of support for human capital. Sharing information, through common registries of humanitarian data, and building a bridge between humanitarian and development assistance has begun to take place, albeit on a small scale.

The spread of safety nets has its critics, not just among conservatives in donor countries but also among those who argue that excessive spread of safety nets creates dependency and adds to fiscal woes, particularly if the resources come at the cost of productive investments in agricultural research and development, physical infrastructure, or schooling. In any case, in low- to middle-income countries, such as Tanzania and Egypt, WFP provides new types of assistance, such as vouchers for use in markets to poor or marginalized communities. In less developed countries, WFP has partnered with FAO, IFAD, and the World Bank to help farmers broker transitions to more productive farming methods.[19] Even in a changed

---

[18] This might be because higher productivity technology may depend more on inputs purchased on credit, and crop failure in a bad year may result in a farmer becoming bankrupt, perhaps even losing his land. See Barrett and Lentz (2010); Banerjee and Duflo (2012).

[19] From the FAO/IFAD/WFP *Working Together* report:

environment, food and agriculture agencies can work together to help countries "graduate" from conflict, crisis, or emergency situations to rehabilitation, reconstruction, and development (WFP 2015f).

Beyond the household level, current trends—climate change, protracted conflict, displacement, and urbanization, discussed throughout this book—make a bigger case for bridging the gap, an argument articulated in WFP's corporate advocacy messages around the 2015 and 2016 global meetings. In making the case for "complementarity between humanitarian and development assistance," WFP emphasizes the imperative to protect development gains (WFP 2015i, 2). With shocks to be expected, humanitarian response, paired with emergency preparedness, are put forth as central to supporting the new Global Goals. WFP's advocacy promotes enhancing complementarity between humanitarian and development assistance.

Partners

WFP's long-standing mantra has been "we deliver better," but acknowledging that no single organization can address current complex food security and nutrition challenges alone, is shifting to "we deliver better together." WFP engages with governments, civil society, the private sector, other UN and international organizations, as well as with less traditional partners, such as academia, think tanks, and the media. A recently articulated Corporate Partnership Strategy 2014–17 (CPS) presented a typology of partners according to strategic contributions (WFP 2014f, 14–15):

- Resource partners who provide human, financial, and technical resources
- Knowledge partners who contribute information
- Policy/governance partners who work on both internal corporate and country- and regional-level hunger governance
- Advocacy partners who support global messaging around food security and nutrition
- Capability partners who support programs and operations

Next, this typology also helps to classify potential partners in Table 12.2.

In all cases, WFP applies three types of guiding principles for all types of WFP partnerships: (1) strategic principles—the framework within which all WFP partnerships must operate to further its goals; (2) precautionary principles to limit risk and exclude partnerships that may be detrimental to WFP's reputation, status, or operating efficiency; and (3) prescriptive principles to establish the rules of good practice for all partnership work; as a signatory to the 2007 Principles of Partnership in the UN Global Humanitarian Platform, it requires equality, transparency, a results-oriented approach, responsibility, and complementarity (WFP 2014f, 10–11).[20]

The CPS frames partnership strategically to promote improved outcomes for beneficiaries. Four levels of participation, which vary according to the situation, were identified as "key stages in a participatory process: (1) information sharing in a one-way flow; (2)

In Zambia, WFP is providing food rations to enable farmers to make the transition to 'conservation farming,' an agricultural system whose goal is to maintain and improve crop yields and resilience against drought and other hazards, while minimizing environmental degradation. At the same time, FAO provides seeds and implements to make the transition. (FAO, IFAD, and WFP 2003, 2)

[20] For more information about the 2007 Principles of Partnership, as defined in the UN Global Humanitarian Platform, see www.globalhumanitarianplatform.org

Table 12.2 Potential partners for humanitarian assistance

Typology	Illustrative types of partners (by no means exhaustive and sometimes overlapping)
1. Resource partners	Bilateral and multilateral partnersPhilanthropists, private sectorTraditional and nontraditional donors
2. Knowledge partners	Academia, research organizations, NGOs
3. Policy governance partners	Governments, think tanks
4. Advocacy partners	NGOs, communication experts
5. Capability partner	Knowledge, skills, and resources—universities, think tanks, research institutions

Notes: See, also, WFP (2004b), "New Partnerships to Expand the WFP Donor Base." Twinning "involves matching an in-kind contribution or service from a donor with a cash donation from another donor to meet the associated costs of a contribution" (WFP 2004a, 7). To assist donors, the following options are available: with another member state; a twinning fund; and twinning with private contributions. Contributions in cash or in-kind; debt swaps in return for funding, e.g., Italy's debt-swap agreement with Egypt, and South–South cooperation.
Source: WFP (2004a, 2004b, 2014f, 2020r).

consultation in at least a two-way flow of information; (3) collaboration with shared control over decision-making; and (4) empowerment with the transfer of control over decisions and resources" (WFP 2000, 5).

WFP works with a wide range of partnerships, from sharing information with potential partners to their involvement, and determination of who influences and/or shares control over food-assisted activities. Partners contribute to the design and or implementation of programs and provide feedback and advocacy. "Stability eventually allows participants to become empowered decision-makers, actively influencing the choice of activities and services, benefiting from higher returns and assuming greater risks. The challenge is to increase participation over time, with participants increasingly making decisions and controlling the use of resources" (WFP 2000, 5).

Partnerships with Civil Society

As a "major buyer of staple food—some 80 percent of which comes from developing countries—for a cash value of over US$1 billion a year," WFP's Purchase for Progress (P4P) program connects smallholder farmers to markets in 35 countries worldwide. WFP has pledged to source 10 percent of its food purchases from smallholder farmers and encourages national governments and the private sector to buy food also in ways that will benefit smallholders (WFP 2020s).

WFP describes the P4P further:

> On the supply side, P4P works with a variety of partners to promote smallholder farmers' entrepreneurship as a way to build resilience and address long-term nutrition needs. Working mainly with farmers' organizations and other partners, P4P provides training and assets to improve crop quality, facilitates access to finance and promotes marketing. Women, whose role in farming is often unpaid and labour-intensive, are particularly encouraged to take part in decision-making and benefit economically from their work. (WFP 2020s)

The Final Report for the P4P pilot (January 2009–December 2013) summarized these results:

> As of December 2013, P4P had engaged with over 830 FOs [farmers' organizations] over the duration of the pilot with 647 still being targeted in December 2013. These 647 FOs represent a total membership of over 1.5 million farmers. P4P capacity development has reached over 768,000 attendees since the first training sessions in 2009.... The number of training sessions delivered per year increased each year of the pilot, from just over 100 sessions delivered in 2009 to over 1,800 in 2013 alone. (WFP 2014c, 1)

Increasingly, WFP relies on NGO partnerships for its newer means of assistance, such as cash, vouchers, and P4P, but we simply do not know the precise numbers. Involvement fluctuates depending on the number of NGOs or projects at a given time in a given geography. WFP says it partners with more than 1,000 national and international NGOs (WFP 2020q).

The 2014–17 strategy, "We Deliver Better Together" (WFP 2014f), stated:

> Each year WFP works with 1,500 to 2,000 civil society organizations, the majority of which are local, community-based NGOs. Most of these relationships are quasi-contractual, where WFP is outsourcing local delivery to national or international NGOs. WFP's annual NGO Partnership consultations, held each year since 1995, have undergone a major transformation over the last two years. The meeting now takes place at Chief Executive Officer Level, with over 100 participating NGOs. This successful annual consultation will continue to be a key feature of WFP engagement with NGO partners. (WFP 2014f, 18)

WFP's 2019 Annual Evaluation Report (AER) noted that were 2,890 partnerships with national and international NGOs in program activities and 3,035 national and international NGO partnerships in services. The largest number of partnerships was in implementation, followed by monitoring (WFP 2020v).

Involvement fluctuates depending on the number of NGOs or projects at a given time in a given geography. NGOs are WFP's primary operational partners (see Box 12.2), providing food assistance distribution and helping to implement a variety of development activities, including education (especially in primary schools), health, and agricultural development (food-for-training), as well as its newer means of assistance such as cash, vouchers, and P4P.

Large international NGOs, such as World Vision International, Save the Children International, and CARE International, are the main NGO collaborators, though many

---

Box 12.2 Examples of Partnerships with Civil Society

- SARC, Aga Khan Foundation, and Action against Hunger—Syria
- World Vision—Myanmar
- Islamic Relief—Kenya
- Catholic Development Commission—Malawi
- Caritas Bolivia—Bolivia
- Christian Child Fund—Ghana

Source: "Partnerships in Action" (WFP 2020p).

smaller regional organizations work in five or more countries. There are pros and cons to reliance on international NGOs in terms of costs and long-term sustainability of operations, without continued reliance on external financing. Local NGOs have taken on increasing prominence where political, security, and cultural issues limit access by international NGOs and WFP itself, such as in conflict settings, though local capacity issues limit cooperation in some contexts.[21]

Private sector partners include corporations, local businesses, foundations, and private organizations (the Bill and Melinda Gates Foundation [BMGF] and the Alliance for a Green Revolution in Africa [AGRA], for example). As with US bilateral assistance, WFP increasingly seeks out public–private sector partnerships—not only for financial resources, but to tap specialized private sector expertise and personnel, particularly in nutrition, security, logistics, financial services, and business modeling,[22] not to mention employee giving, consumer campaigns, and public awareness.[23] In other instances, high-profile partnerships lend star power to fundraising campaigns and emergency appeals (WFP 2018a),[24]

WFP has traditionally collaborated on emergency relief, logistics, and operations. WFP's recognized expertise is formalized in its lead roles in the cluster system—including as lead agency of the global Logistics and Emergency Telecommunication clusters, providing UN-wide air transport and emergency information and communications technology (ICT) services, and co-lead of the Food Security cluster with FAO (OCHA 2020).

Collaborations with International Organizations

WFP collaborates within the UN and Bretton Woods systems with a view to developing quick and effective responses to crises. In its Annual Performance Report for 2018, in its efforts to achieve food security, WFP reports partnering with FAO, IFAD, the New Partnership for Africa's Development (NEPAD), the Global Child Nutrition Foundation, the Partnership for Child Development at Imperial College, London, and Brazil's Centre of Excellence against Hunger (WFP 2019a, 17). WFP works "side by side" with the United Nations Development Programme (UNDP) to provide "logistics support and expertise for the distribution of insecticide-treated mosquito nets" (WFP 2019a, 133). Also, in a collaboration on school feeding with a focus on girls' education, WFP has "successfully

---

[21] The Syrian crisis illustrates the near total reliance on local NGOs to reach populations effectively trapped by political and security access issues. Note that, in late 2015, the role of local NGOs and local capacity was at the heart of a series of IRIN News (now *The New Humanitarian*) interviews and articles and subsequent debate. See, for example, "What Refugees Really Think of Aid Agencies?" *The New Humanitarian*, March 5, 2015: http://www. thenewhumanitarian.org/analysis/2015/03/05/what-refugees-really-think-aid-agencies. The primacy of local ownership and capacity is a large issue not addressed in this chapter.

[22] Examples highlighted in WFP materials include: MasterCard providing technology and payment for e-card projects to allow beneficiaries to buy from markets, as well as marketing expertise, and PepsiCo Foundation providing supply chain and performance management assistance to improve logistics and operational efficiency. See https://www.wfp.org/news/mastercard-and-world-food-programme-announce-100-million-meals-commit ment and https://www.wfp.org/videos/teaming-pepsico-fight-child-malnutrition-0

[23] For example, in 2013, Michael Kors launched a WFP awareness campaign and promotional scheme, whereby a portion of watch purchases would be donated to WFP to "Stop Hunger" (see https://insight.wfp. org/sharethemeal-on-world-food-day-93337a59b31d). In cause-related marketing campaigning, companies encourage independent consumer giving, independent of product purchase.

[24] Examples of campaigns and celebrity involvement include: Christina Aguilera, Kate Hudson, the Malian group Amadou and Mariam (the first WFP Ambassadors Against Hunger for the EU, mobilizing donors among their fan base). See, for example, https://www.wfp.org/news/kate-hudson-named-goodwill-ambassador-united-nations-world-food-programme

operationalized approaches with partners such as the United Nations Children's Fund (UNICEF), the United Nations Population Fund [UNFPA] and the United Nations Entity for Gender Equality and the Empowerment of Women (UN-Women), to address... barriers through integrated platforms,... to be supported, scaled up and become a normal part of WFP school feeding programmes" (WFP 2019a, 53).

WFP has participated in "numerous critical initiatives to strengthen partnerships with fellow United Nations agencies and other partners" (WFP 2019a, 63). Some examples include: (1) WFP and the International Federation of the Red Cross and Red Crescent Societies implementing a pilot program for global national society capacity strengthening; (2) an addendum signed by WFP's Executive Director and UNHCR's High Commissioner on data sharing agreement of 2011; (3) WFP's strategic coloration as a member of the steering committees for the Scaling Up Nutrition (SUN) United Nations Network and the United Nations Standing Committee on Nutrition; and (4) WFP leadership in the Global Nutrition Cluster, and on the UN Inter-Agency Task Force on the Prevention and Control of Non-communicable Diseases (WFP 2019a).

The partnerships have taken on new dimensions in the changing humanitarian climate—as manifested in its close partnership with WHO throughout the Ebola response, and increasing work (if not competition) with UNHCR in serving refugee needs (WFP 2014b). The heads of WFP, UNHCR, and the UN Refugee Agency, signed an agreement in Geneva on May 15, 2017, which committed WFP and UNHCR to collaborate in providing cash-based assistance for refugees. Cash is a way to effectively assist refugees, with the participation of recipient communities, host governments, donors, and humanitarian agencies. Building on the strong long-standing partnership between the agencies, the agreement aims to improve the efficiency and effectiveness of cash-based aid through a predictable arrangement with the participation of all relevant stakeholders. The new agreement seeks to improve assistance to refugees while bringing benefits to local economies (UNHCR 2017).

The Rome-based agencies have "specific but complementary" mandates in the drive to reduce hunger, food insecurity, and rural poverty. Acknowledging respective missions and expertise, each organization states it has ensconced collaboration in its organization's strategic planning. In Chapters 9 and 11 on FAO and IFAD, respectively, we have shown the evolving nature of these organizations. Clearly, the pressure from the donors to collaborate has increased but fragmented, tied funding to each organization does not always enable them to play up to their comparative advantages.

In a simplified example of the division of labor, FAO provides agricultural development "inputs"—knowledge on policies, institutions, and technologies and materials—while WFP and its NGO partners can have on-the-ground community engagement "outputs" experience. In South Africa and Zambia, WFP and FAO paired immediate food relief with longer-term agricultural development assistance to enable farmers and communities to transition to sustainable and profitable farming systems. As early as 2003, these collaborations were underway (FAO, IFAD, and WFP 2003). WFP's agricultural livelihood work and recovery activities have been debated over time. Recovery and livelihoods require access to land that is often lost in emergencies, as well as seed and technical knowledge about what to grow and where. The expertise of FAO in providing development assistance—for example, on livelihoods and food policy—versus WFP's comparative advantage in the logistics of moving food aid has been a source of tension. WFP has more than 19,600 staff, of whom 87 percent are based in the field.[25]

---

[25] See "WFP at a Glance": https://www.wfp.org/stories/wfp-glance

Working with IFAD, WFP contributes to policy analysis, advocacy, and operational support. At a project level, WFP and IFAD combine international lending with works programs. In the broader architecture, FAO, IFAD, and WFP also officially collaborate via various international platforms (such as the World Food Summit), in developing coordinated approaches to international and regional initiatives (such as NEPAD), and in addressing development issues (such as HIV/AIDS and gender mainstreaming) (WFP 2019a).

Despite ongoing tensions regarding possible mission creep and overlap, as well as varying degrees of effectiveness of collaboration, the Rome-based agencies' recent policy and advocacy collaboration have resulted in the development and eventual acceptance of a stand-alone food security and of SDG2 for ending global hunger, which was widely heralded as a successful example of UN cooperation. FAO, IFAD, and WFP also issued joint messages, including, specifically, on social protection, in advance of the Addis Ababa Conference on Financing for Development referred to earlier.

Collaboration with the World Bank at the country level included the response to the Ebola epidemic, in which the Bank stepped outside of its normal development focus and supported WFP emergency efforts, including both logistics and food assistance (IEG 2013). Other examples include targeting in Lebanon to support social assistance through electronic vouchers;[26] as well as serving as an implementing partner to the Government of Chad to support refugees from the Central African Republic with relief and resilience activities under a Bank grant.[27]

WFP, UNICEF, and the World Bank worked together under the World Bank-funded Global Food Crisis Response Program (GFRP), described in Chapter 8, with WFP envisioned to lead the emergency response and the Bank providing assistance through transfers, workforce, and health and nutrition programs. In South Sudan, the World Bank, WFP, FAO, and UNICEF are participating in an Emergency Food and Nutrition Security Project, with US$50 million funding by the World Bank, for support and protection for 580,000 people (World Bank 2017).

WFP also contributed its expertise in school feeding (see Box 12.3), under GFRP, along with other social safety net activities, such as public works programs and transfers, as well as collaborating on needs assessments.[28] The reports from the World Bank on the crisis clearly suggest the World Bank was in the lead and that WFP played a key supportive role. Whereas WFP was using international NGOs, the cost of doing business was considerably higher, according to World Bank reports (see World Bank 2012).[29] In Chapters 9 and 10 on FAO

---

[26] For Lebanon, see http://documents.worldbank.org/curated/en/111451467996685776/pdf/94768-CAS-P151022-R2016-0126-OUO-9-Box396270B.pdf

[27] For Chad, see https://www.worldbank.org/en/news/press-release/2018/09/12/chad-a-60-million-world-bank-grant-to-support-refugees-and-host-communities

[28] According to "The World Bank Group and the Global Food Crisis: An Evaluation of the World Bank Group Response":
GFRP projects also financed the continuation or expansion of existing food-for-work programs—through community-driven development and social investment funds in projects financed by the Bank, other donors (such as WFP), or the government—designed to provide poor workers with an additional source of income even as they supported the creation, rehabilitation, and/or maintenance of public infrastructure. For public works programs to meet social safety net objectives, they need to have clear criteria for location, low wages to ensure self-selection of poorer workers, high labor intensity and use of unskilled labor, a portfolio of community-level investments, and sufficient duration to provide meaningful income transfers. These elements were not always present due to political economy considerations taking precedence. (IEG 2013, xvii)

[29] The Final Report of GFRP, "Progress and Lessons Learned," noted:
Strong coordination and partnerships with entities such as UN organizations and civil society organizations is important, however obligations should be clearly defined. For example, when partnering with UN organizations, such as the World Food Programme, collaboration on a common reporting standard should be clearly defined and meet the needs of both institutions. (World Bank 2012, 7)

Box 12.3 School Feeding Program

The World Food Programme's school feeding program has evolved considerably since its inception. The 2009 joint publication of the World Food Programme and the World Bank Group, "Rethinking School Feeding: Social Safety Nets, Child Development, and the Education Sector," provided "a new analysis of school feeding programs" (Bundy et al. 2009, x). It benefited "from combining the World Food Programme's practical experience in running school feeding programs with the World Bank Group's development policy dialogue and analysis" (Bundy et al. 2009, x). It explored "how food procurement may help local economies and . . . the centrality of the education sector in the policy dialogue on school feeding" (Bundy et al. 2009, x). Since that study, WFP has published reports to help governments, policymakers, donors, NGOs, and other partners to explore the costs and benefits of school feeding programs to help them design effective programs capable of responding quickly to today's crises, while maintaining fiscally sustainable investments in children's education and general human potential in the long term.

In the words of the then World Bank President Robert Zoellick and WFP Executive Director Josette Sheeran: "A key message from [the first and subsequent reports] . . . is that the transition to sustainable national programs depends on mainstreaming school feeding into national policies and plans, especially education sector plans" (Bundy et al. 2009, x). The international community appears to have gone "beyond the debate about whether school feeding makes sense as a way to reach the most vulnerable. . . . [to] focus on how school feeding programs can be designed and implemented in a cost-effective and sustainable way to benefit and protect those most in need of help today and in the future" (Bundy et al. 2009, x). Such reports are already becoming flagship products of WFP. According to the 2013 "State of School Feeding Worldwide" report, 368 million children received school meals, with up to US$75 billion invested each year. WFP advocattes school feeding as part of social protection systems to support the most vulnerable families and children and can be scaled up in response to crises. According to the report, at least 38 countries that WFP surveyed scaled up their programs in response to armed conflict, natural disasters, and food and financial crises. The program's performance, however, has been highly variable. In low-income countries, the programs are donor dependent and high in cost. The report noted that linking of school feeding to local agriculture was likely to make the program more sustainable but also urged greater aid coordination. Programs such as these emphasize the importance of linking WFP's work to the work of other international organizations, most notably IFAD's and the World Bank's development programs in agriculture and education to improve their chances of being more sustainable (WFP 2013d).

In its School Feeding Strategy 2020–30, "WFP lays out its vision of working with governments and partners" and gives many examples of countries with which it is working "to jointly ensure that all primary schoolchildren have access to good quality meals in school, accompanied by a broader integrated package of health and nutrition services" (WFP 2020x, 6). It has been particularly timely and relevant in the context of COVID-19.

Source: Bundy et al. (2009); WFP (2013d); WFP (2020x).

and CGIAR, respectively, we point out that bilateral donors present in the countries support CGIAR Centers or WFP; however, their staff at headquarters—who often represent the organizations on the boards of these organizations—do not necessarily address questions of the comparative advantage of the organizations and whether their assistance in the field may contribute to mission creep, rather than the organizations playing to their comparative advantages. Thus, for collaboration between international organizations to work sustainably on a longer-term basis, the WFP strategy would need to be reexamined on the grounds of effectiveness, efficiency, and sustainability. Since many of the same representatives serve on the boards of all Rome-based organizations, this should, in principle, be easily addressed.

Information Systems for Food Security

WFP's mandate requires effective food security monitoring for all program design, planning, and operations. Over the years, WFP has strengthened its Information Systems for Food Security (ISFS) initiatives, particularly through VAM, established in 1994 to improve monitoring of vulnerability to food insecurity. VAM supports "a comprehensive understanding of both structural and emergency factors causing food insecurity" (FAO 2010, 4; see, also, WFP 2007, 2015g).

Partner agencies draw on WFP's field experience and food security analysis functions, leveraging, in particular, WFP's deep field reach for its household and market monitoring.[30] Structural factors influencing food insecurity, it should be noted, have not been WFP's comparative advantage in the past, but as its emergency food aid activity has declined, it has been gradually carving out a niche for itself in this area. Although FAO houses regional and country-level knowledge and technical expertise, VAM has evolved to provide geospatial and economic analysis, food security monitoring and assessments, post-shock assessments, and thematic analysis. Additionally, VAM oversees WFP's near real-time food security monitoring capacity, with systems in place and tracking food security daily across 38 countries and counting.

WFP undertakes food security analysis in close collaboration with partners worldwide, including governments, UN agencies, local/international NGOs, regional bodies, and academic institutions. These partnerships ensure a shared understanding of food security problems and common priorities for action.

VAM has had particular expertise in and tools for analysis of household coping capacities and food access. And it has evolved into DataViz (DataViz.vam.wfp.org). Some contemporary products include:

- Market Functionality Index (MFI)
- Asset Impact Monitoring from Space (AIMS)
- Essential Needs Assessments
- The Minimum Expenditure Basket
- Emergency Food Security Assessment (EFSA)
- Comprehensive Food Security and Vulnerability Analysis (CFSVA)

---

[30] Including governments, Famine Early Warning Systems Network (FEWS NET), FAO, OCHA, UNHCR, WHO, the World Bank, research institutes, and local and international NGOs (WFP 2015g).

- Market Analysis and Monitoring, "The Market Monitor"
- Joint Assessment Missions (JAM), conducted with UNHCR
- Crop and Food Security Missions (CFSAM), conducted with FAO (WFP 2015g; see, also, WFP 2011a)

As part of an initiative on open data, WFP has made much of its data publicly available. The "VAM One Stop Shop" has now been replaced by DataViz (DataViz.vam.wfp.org), where all VAM resources can be accessed. In tandem with DataViz and as part of the efforts toward open data, WFP also launched the HungerMapLIVE (hungermap.wfp.org) in January 2020, a Global Hunger Monitoring System (and global public good) that tracks and predicts food security in near real time across over 90 countries.

In 2010, the governing bodies of WFP and FAO initiated an evaluation of the two agencies' support to IFIS, the first joint evaluation of its kind (FAO 2010). The evaluation concluded that the systems of WFP and FAO are increasingly built on partnership and consensus, although dimensions such as nutrition, gender, and urban issues were not sufficiently accounted for. In general, WFP provides critical household-level expertise on joint needs assessments in countries to which it provides food and other forms of assistance and increasingly, also engages in agricultural livelihood work and recovery activities, in addition to its more traditional distribution and logistics support.

The FAO and WFP Joint Thematic Evaluation describes FAO's contribution to food security analysis in this way:

> FAO develops, maintains and supports a wide range of global, regional and national ISFS initiatives including GIEWS [Global Information and Early Warning System], Food Insecurity and Vulnerability Information and Mapping Systems (FIVIMS), FAOSTAT [the statistics division of FAO], the *State of Food Insecurity* (SOFI), Food Outlook and market surveys, among others. An important part of FAO's ISFS support consists of capacity development at regional and national levels through initiatives such as the Food Security Information for Action programme. Many of these initiatives aim at enhancing national and local capacities to generate and manage food security information in support of policy analysis and decision-making. (FAO 2010, 4)

One joint initiative between FAO and WFP, that also included IFPRI, is the Food Security Information Network (FSIN), with 16 global and regional partners. Launched in October 2012, FSIN aims to strengthen ISFS and support decision-making. FSIN is intended to serve as a platform for standards and knowledge setting, with emphasis on linking country capacity needs with existing initiatives and expertise at the regional and global level—"a new vision for country-led information systems and networks for food and nutrition security" (FSIN n.d.). (See also WFP 2015f.)

WFP has sought to improve its program management and decision-making through the development of corporate ISFS to help meet its overall food assistance objective. And as we discuss below, the recent corporate strategies go substantially further to move action to the country level. The Joint Evaluation noted, "WFP is increasingly providing support to ISFS capacity development at national and regional levels. At the same time FAO's shrinking budget has led that agency to decrease its ISFS capacity development support" (FAO 2010, 4). As FAO's reforms are beginning to take hold, FAO is obtaining considerable support from donors for its resilience agenda at the field level (see Chapter 9).

Partners in Assistance

WFP follows a country ownership principle that, while not new, is particularly relevant to the changing context of humanitarian and development assistance (WFP 2007).[31] Collaboration with governments—both donors and beneficiaries—is built into the WFP partnership model. Ideally, WFP interventions are coherent with beneficiary government plans, such as the country strategy note, as in the US Millennium Challenge Corporation model.[32] Starting in 2009, WFP began piloting a country-level strategic and programmatic planning approach, the output of which would be the CSPs. This approach more closely tied activities to country priorities, defining WFP's role based on country needs and specifying government-determined targets (WFP 2015b).

Objective 5 of the 2008–13 strategy—to strengthen the capacities of countries to reduce hunger, including through hand-over strategies and local purchase—makes country ownership explicit (WFP 2007). The 2014–17 strategy more clearly emphasizes building countries' capacity to deal with emergencies as an objective, as shown earlier. If most WFP engagement is emergency assistance (and the current number of Level 3 emergencies shows no sign of abating), then it is unclear if WFP staff has the time, presence, and influence with governments on to affect important policy and strategic agendas. The 2014–17 Strategic Plan (discussed next in the section on the WFP mandate) also counts policy and programmatic advice as an important tool in meeting its strategic objectives. In asserting this quasi-technical assistance function, WFP language again notes its historic position in working closely with countries and communities and its expertise as relevant to an assistance role (WFP 2013f). However, in the past, that assistance was in the form of food aid, which has now diminished in importance.

World Food Programme's Comparative Advantage

Challenges to the global system, such as climate change and rising food prices, require new and more flexible tools to help the world's poor—a requirement that is increasingly acknowledged within the UN system and by changing bilateral approaches (Feed the Future and the Millennium Challenge Corporation). While WFP seeks a new role for itself, it also brings aspects of its past role to bear in meeting those changing demands. WFP considers itself the largest and most operational UN agency (WFP 2007), with considerable depth of field experience, logistics expertise, and staff resources. Credibility with local partners and governments, a "can-do" orientation demonstrated through staff motivation and commitment, and a problem-solving ethos are often-cited traits of the organization.[33] The WFP CPS includes an organizational "Unique Value Proposition," describing what partners have said they value and what they can expect to benefit from WFP (WFP 2014f, 13, 26):

---

[31] In its 2008–13 Strategic Plan, WFP subscribes to the "widely recognized principles of ownership, alignment, harmonization, management for results and mutual accountability" (WFP 2007, 8).

[32] According to the WFP mission statement, food aid should be integrated with country development plans and coordinated with other forms of assistance. The starting point is the country plan; the country strategy note is the framework. The 2008–13 Strategic Plan emphasized country ownership, stating: "In emergency contexts, when national capacities might be overwhelmed, WFP can help governments act... Governments should take the lead in disaster preparedness and response,... In longer-term development contexts, all WFP interventions must be coherent with and aligned with to governments' priorities and frameworks" (WFP 2007, 8).

[33] See the "Strategic Evaluations Synthesis" (WFP and GPPi 2015).

- Responsiveness and agility
- Expertise
- Accountability and transparency
- Delivery focus
- Scale of operations

WFP has unique experience working in poor security environments, a characteristic that is particularly valuable given recent security threats to development organization work around the world (as recently evidenced by WFP's presence in Syria).[34] Some of its capabilities are rooted in its multilateral nature—it can engage in environments where individual donor countries could not provide assistance, for either security or political reasons. Its deep-field reach can also be attributed to its network of NGO operational partners, on whom it relies for food delivery in many hard-to-reach areas.

These strengths are represented in its cluster system leadership—as lead for logistics and emergency telecommunication and co-lead on food security along with FAO. A 2015 headline in *The Guardian* asserted WFP to be one of the "best bits" of the UN:

> The reality is that WFP is still the best-placed, best-resourced global agency for distribut-ing food when disaster strikes. If it needs to build bridges and roads, it can. If it has to drop food out of planes, it will. Its staff have even used elephants, yaks and donkeys to fulfil what remains its core mission: to deliver food into the hands of the hungry poor. (Chonghaile 2015)

The same article goes on to acknowledge WFP's interest in moving beyond the image of food sacks. While in 2015, it appeared there would be no abating to the numbers left hungry by disaster, WFP was eager to highlight its development activities, under the resilience banner.

WFP's 2014 synthesis of evaluations of 2013 summarizes these strengths and challenges, noting that the institution's reputation for delivering large-scale humanitarian aid in difficult circumstances was confirmed by the evaluations, with commendations for its logistics capacity and food security analysis (WFP 2014a). WFP's programming has been aligned generally with governments and other external partners, and where possible, it has sought to move toward food assistance and long-term planning. And, yet, as stated in the AER for 2013:

> Funding was a significant and recurring challenge and one of the key factors influencing strategic choices. Dependencies on a single donor, and rigidities in donor support, particularly when in-kind donations were involved, often constrained programmatic choices and prevented adoption of long-term approaches. A further influence on strategic choice concerned country office access to appropriate human resources, particularly important for the shift from food aid to food assistance and for strengthening national capacities. (WFP 2014a, 8)

An important question for WFP is whether a short-term emergency assistance agency with uncertain clients and uncertain funding can realistically take on the challenges of long-term

---

[34] See Masood (2015): "Pakistan Warns Aid Groups to Follow Unspecified Rules."

development in areas in which it may not have had a comparative advantage? Or, should it just continue to focus on being the world's best emergency assistance agency, especially given that emergencies remain a growth industry, and work with others (FAO, IFAD, World Bank, regional banks) to address the transition from emergency to development?

Such thinking needs to be increasingly applied to organizations to establish them as centers of excellence, but given the current donor financing realities, it does not eliminate the unnecessary sense of competition and rivalry rather than a spirit of cooperation.

Development Activities

For WFP, development assistance involves increasing the capacity of nations to independently withstand and navigate crisis—effectively building in a sunset clause for food aid. Zero Hunger implies that there should no longer be a need for WFP's role as a food relief agency. At the same time, WFP's approach acknowledges that while the threat of hunger will always loom, given the rise in emergencies due to the effects of climate change and conflict and the attendant increase in displaced and refugee populations, nations can be better equipped to manage these causes.[35] WFP's new direction makes emergency relief paramount and incorporates nutrition, capacity building,[36] country ownership, support of and reliance on markets, and partnerships. WFP's development roles have evolved to be cast under a broad banner of a resilience agenda. WFP sees its new comparative advantage as a balance between its natural relief role (respond) and one of assisting nations to mitigate threats (reduce) and provide relief themselves (respond, rebuild).

Consistent among WFP's priorities throughout the evolution of its mandate are saving lives and supporting livelihoods. Newer development activities are generally supportive of these overarching strategic objectives. How WFP contributes to saving lives is apparent in the tools it uses for its emergency food relief work: targeted food and nutrition assistance, work-for-food programs, cash or voucher-based social safety net programs that facilitate food access and support markets, and activities to rebuild infrastructure following crises.[37]

In 2019, WFP gave assistance through a combination of food, cash-based assistance, and vouchers to 97.1 million people, compared to 84.9 million in 2018, and 88.9 million in 2017. This included 23 million men, 15,7 million women, 29.5 million girls, and 28.9 million boys. Also included were 10.6 million refugees, 2.9 million returnees, 15.5 million internally displaced persons (IDPs) and 68.1 million residents. This entailed 3.9 million tons of food and cash-based assistance and vouchers to 27.9 million people, as well as conditional cash transfers to 60 million people, with 17.3 million school children receiving school meals and take-home food (WFP 2020a).

Despite this orientation, the majority of WFP assistance is still emergency relief, largely to countries that are not able to take care of their own relief (WFP 2012c). If this trend continues, WFP will find it difficult to claim to be knowledgeable about food security in countries where poverty and hunger are most prevalent—most of these are MICs, such as

---

[35] Observers are also redefining humanitarian response vis-à-vis "traditional" development activities, acknowledging a broad array of longer-term engagements and multidimensional approaches needed "to save lives, alleviate suffering and maintain and protect human dignity before, during, and after man-made crises and natural disasters" (GHA 2016, 2).

[36] WFP's country capacity strengthening (CCS) is provided, in response to stakeholders' request, for support of national food security and nutrition systems, enhancing the autonomy and resilience of nations. See WFP (2018d).

[37] WFP Strategic Plan 2008–13, Strategic Objectives One and Three (WFP 2007).

India, though some of the least developed states also have high poverty incidence. The countries with the greatest prevalence of undernourishment in 2019 were Haiti, Democratic People's Republic of Korea, Madagascar, Chad, Liberia, Rwanda, Mozambique, Lesotho. Countries with the worst food crises in 2019 were Yemen, Democratic Republic of the Congo, Afghanistan, Ethiopia, South Sudan, Syrian Arab Republic, The Sudan, and Nigeria. Furthermore, it will be challenged to have the internal capacity to do enough to help countries prepare for their own emergency assistance, with a view to getting itself out of that business.

Resilience

WFP's policy on resilience describes its perceived comparative advantages in food security and nutrition, explicitly articulating a dual humanitarian and development mandate.[38] Within the policy, WFP defines a new resilience-building approach to programming—the way activities are conceived and designed, as well as aligned with governments and partners' plans and actions: "A resilience-building approach to programming helps to mitigate the damaging effects of shocks and stressors before, during and after crises, thereby minimizing human suffering and economic losses" (WFP 2015d, 2).

This language deftly and explicitly bridges the humanitarian and development divide, and the policy seeks to connect its proven expertise in responding to emergencies to the development context, asserting: "WFP's long experience in humanitarian and development contexts has established areas of comparative advantage in building resilience for food security and nutrition" (WFP 2015d, 8). However, WFP's role will be seen through its ability to deliver on this approach and in the political dialogue around the World Humanitarian Summit and implementation plans for SDGs 2 and 17. Indeed, resilience is the area where organization's relative comparative advantages will likely manifest most visibly. FAO, IFAD and WFP have engaged to frame their collaboration and partnership around strengthening resilience and food security (FAO, IFAD and WFP 2015).

WFP's guiding principle is to permanently change people's lives for the better by bridging the divide between humanitarian and development activities. In the five countries of the central Sahel region, where vast humanitarian, development, and peace challenges collide, WFP implemented an integrated five-year resilience programme designed to build resilience and ultimately reduce the need for emergency support. This combined effort by the Rome-based agencies; international, regional, and national partners; government institutions; and universities enabled 1.3 million people to receive a package of support, ranging from school meals to community asset creation, in the first year of the operation. WFP's cost–benefit analysis indicates that investing in resilience programmes in the Niger alone can generate a nearly fourfold return over a 20-year period for every dollar spent.

This approach helps break the cycle of intergenerational poverty by connecting people— particularly the schoolchildren, women, and smallholder farmers who are furthest behind in educational and economic opportunities.

Alongside conflict, the other major driver of global hunger is the impact of a changing climate on agricultural production, which requires multi-year investments in resilience

---

[38] Note that definitions of the resilience concept differ according to various development actors. WFP focuses on the abilities to absorb, adapt, and transform, ensuring "that shocks and stressors do not have long-lasting adverse development consequences" (WFP 2015d, 3).

Earlier, we mentioned WFP investments in the future of more than 17 million girls and boys by partnering with governments to provide school meals, snacks, or take-home rations.

Disaster Risk Reduction

WFP's ability to respond to crisis is contingent on early warning and preparedness systems. It is in the area of disaster risk reduction where WFP has perhaps the clearest comparative advantage to lend to development contexts, frequently expressed as the means to safeguard development and prevent losses of development gains from shocks and stresses, and a prerequisite for eliminating hunger. Disaster risk reduction activities include: the Platform for Real-time Impact and Situation Monitoring (PRISM),[39] early warning systems, asset creation activities aimed at preserving resources and infrastructure, VAM (discussed earlier), supply chain management, logistics, and emergency communications. WFP seeks to support governments in development capacity in these areas, including through new finance and risk-transfer tools. Examples include weather risk insurance and climate-related risk capacities.

Climate Change

WFP's engagement around climate change is underpinned by the reality of the majority of the world's hungry living in environments especially prone to climate change—over the past decade, nearly half of WFP's emergency and recovery operations responded to climate-related disasters (WFP 2014e). WFP's asset creation programs are intended to help protect the livelihoods of vulnerable households from extreme weather shocks. In 2019, these activities paved the way for rural transformation through the rehabilitation and reforestation of an area of land roughly twice the size of Singapore, and increased access to markets and natural resources through the construction or repair of roads, bridges, and wells. FAO et al. (2018) noted that 51 low- and middle-income countries experienced early or delayed onset of seasons; the number of extreme weather events has doubled since the early 1990s (WFP 2018f).

WFP draws on disaster risk reduction mechanisms and analysis capacity, described earlier, to support communities in: climate change adaptation, climate and food security analysis, climate services, and safe energy for cooking (WFP 2018b).[40] Between 2010 and 2015, 40 percent of its operations included climate adaptation activities.

With the assets created by this project, smallholder farmers were able to concentrate on agricultural commercialization. Activities included helping households to diversify their livelihoods, improve community assets, generate income from fruit and vegetable production, beekeeping and fishponds, and create micro-irrigation schemes and water harvesting systems to ensure access to water for agriculture. As part of an integrated package of interventions, climate services were provided to targeted people and work started on the development of microinsurance products.

[39] See https://innovation.wfp.org/project/prism?
[40] See "Climate Services": https://www.wfp.org/climate-services; and "Climate Action": https://www.wfp.org/climate-action

Social Protection

Social protection is defined as the policies and programs designed to protect people from shocks and stresses throughout their lives. Social protection for food security and nutrition promote activities that transfer income and food to participants as a safety net, and promote livelihoods.[41] WFP cites 40 years of experience in the implementation of safety net and asset-building programs (WFP 2014e). From the 2012 Safety Nets Policy Update: "WFP plays several core roles in supporting national safety nets…defined in line with WFP's comparative advantages" (WFP 2012d, 3), as related to food assistance for food and nutrition security. The nexus of WFP's comparative advantage with the broader field of social protection is through safety nets for food security and nutrition. Activities include community asset creation projects, engagement to promote mother and child health, school feeding, cash-for-work programs, as well as through cash or voucher-based transfer modalities for food assistance. As noted earlier, WFP is focusing more on extending technical advice to support national social protection schemes. Two of the more well-known elements of WFP's engagement in social projection are FAA and School Meals.

FAA provides vulnerable households with food, cash, or vouchers to cover food gaps and allow resource allocation to livelihood or human capital, in return for their participation in asset creation and protection (WFP 2015f). Based on a 2005 internal review of its development policy and upon the recommendation of the FAO director-general, WFP committed to expand the FAA program under the Resilience Unit to support agricultural livelihoods (WFP 2005b, 2007). From 2014 to 2019:

- 78,909 km of roads were built or repaired
- 53,748 ponds, wells, and reservoirs were built or rehabilitated
- 1,545,755 hectares of land were rehabilitated (the definition of rehabilitated land has varied across reporting years, with some including forests planted).[42]

The program provides food in exchange for a resource that vulnerable communities have in abundant supply—labor. Work is tied to complementary development projects, such as infrastructure (irrigation, schools, roads), environment (forest recovery), or small business development.

School Feeding is a safety net provided to ensure every child's access to education, health, and nutrition, including in-school meals, take-home rations, and homegrown school feeding programs to support local agriculture.[43] WFP has long been engaged in school feeding, which uses food as incentives to promote multifaceted development goals—nutrition, school enrollment, girls' participation, and in the instance of local procurement, agricultural development and markets. School Feeding is one of the more visible WFP social protection programs, particularly popular with its donors. In 2019, WFP invested in the future of more than 17 million girls and boys by partnering with governments to provide school meals, snacks, or take-home rations. It is a powerful incentive for poorer families to send their sons and—especially, their daughters to school and keep them there. WFP also provided technical and capacity-building support to governments of MICs to enable them to scale up their own national school feeding programs. However, WFP acknowledges that it needs

---

[41] See "Social Protection and Safety Nets": https://www.wfp.org/social-protection-and-safety-nets
[42] Based on WFP Annual Performance Reports.
[43] See "School Meals": https://www.wfp.org/school-meals and WFP (2014d, 2017c).

to be even more ambitious. So, in 2019, WFP developed the School Feeding Strategy for 2020–30, which sets out how WFP will work with partners to ensure that children living in extreme poverty benefit from school meals (WFP 2020x).

These activities reflect WFP's efforts to build a niche in technical assistance and capacity development. WFP engages increasingly in policy dialogue and supporting knowledge exchange between countries.

Nutrition

WFP's nutrition programs serve its vision of assured access to the right foods at the right time to ensure an active and healthy life. WFP took on a new approach in 2009, which included mother and child health and nutrition (MCHN), school feeding, care and support for people living with disease, and management of pandemics (WFP is the lead agency for dietary and nutrition support under the UNAIDS division of labor and supported 2.3 million people in 28 countries in 2011, and provided policy and programmatic advice through its HIV and TB programs).[44] Nutrition is seen as cutting across all operations and programs, including emergency-related food distribution. As such, a key WFP nutritional input is determining and advising about appropriate food baskets for people facing hunger and malnutrition.

WFP implemented a variety of nutrition programs in 74 countries in 2019. Nutrition-specific programs for preventing and treating acute malnutrition, preventing stunting and micronutrient deficiencies, and treating malnourished clients undergoing HIV and tuberculosis treatment reached 10.8 million children and 6.4 million women and girls. WFP worked with governments to develop nutrition policies and programs for the provision of nutritious school meals and for food fortification. In 2019, more than 287,000 mt of SNFs were distributed in 50 countries to complement WFP's general food and cash-based assistance. Social and behavior change communication activities in 44 countries fostered improved attitudes and behavior regarding health, nutrition, and child feeding practices among vulnerable people (WFP 2020a).

In 2019, 10.8 million children received special nutritional support, 6.4 million women received additional nutritional support, 400,000 people affected by AIDs received food assistance, and 18 of the 35 countries affected by HIVAIDS were to receive food assistance (WFP 2020a). Specific WFP interventions range from developing micronutrient powders,[45] support for locally produced brands of foods and supplements to prevent or treat malnutrition, and dietary education in communities.

As previously discussed, WFP asserts an advantage to addressing malnutrition attributed to its deep field presence, which allows it to tailor responses to meet specific nutritional needs. Despite its many activities, however, it faces ongoing challenges to articulate its value added, vis-à-vis traditional development agencies, particularly with governments. Perhaps necessarily, nutrition activities illustrate WFP's global advocacy efforts and its diverse partnerships in managing the crowded development landscape. The 2012 Nutrition Policy

---

[44] WFP implements HIV programs in 50 countries. See "UNAIDS/Co-sponsors/World Food Programme": https://www.unaids.org/en/aboutunaids/unaidscosponsors/wfp and WFP (2013a).

[45] Special nutritional products include: Fortified Blended Foods, Ready-Use Foods, and High Energy Biscuits. See "Specialized Nutritious Foods": https://documents.wfp.org/stellent/groups/public/documents/communications/wfp255508.pdf

set out its work with UN partners, civil society, academia, and the private sector (WFP 2012e). WFP's efforts are coordinated with UNICEF, FAO, and WHO, all subscribing to the Scaling Up Nutrition (SUN) roadmap of actions to address malnutrition. As such, each commits to exploit its comparative advantage in advocacy, technical assistance, and enhancement of national capacities (WFP 2012e). WFP's focus is on treatment of moderate acute malnutrition, prevention of moderate acute malnutrition (wasting), prevention of chronic malnutrition (stunting) and micronutrient deficiencies, and nutrition-sensitive programming. Under an agreement with UNICEF, WFP addresses moderate acute malnutrition and UNICEF handles severe acute malnutrition.

WFP is a leader in the Global Alliance for Improved Nutrition (GAIN). GAIN and WFP co-convene the SUN Business Network, which facilitates business engagement with nutrition interventions in the movement's 33 member countries. In June 2013, WFP along with the FAO, IFAD, UNICEF, and WHO signed a joint Commitment Letter and Work Plan that outlined a harmonized framework for UN support of the SUN Movement, including a platform for interagency cooperation. At the same time (June 8, 2013), WFP Executive Director Ertharin Cousin announced new collaborations with SUN, including an expanding partnership with UNFPA and private sector initiatives. She announced that WFP would join the "Every Woman, Every Child," Health 4+, and Adolescent Girls Initiatives, under which WFP would expand support to more than 50 UNFPA program countries, starting with pilot countries Burkina Faso, Niger, Sierra Leone, and Zambia. Further, she announced that the Sun Business Network co-chairs, WFP and GAIN, had launched a Business and Innovation Program to provide technical support to governments to assist them in involving local private sectors in national SUN activities (WFP 2013b). SUN has evolved substantially.

Capacity Building

Capacity building has become a crosscutting theme for WFP, ensconced in its strategic objectives at least since 2004, and based on its experience and long-standing field presence, working closely with beneficiaries.[46] As an illustration, WFP undertakes support for small-scale farming, training, works programs, and policy and programmatic advice, all areas in which WFP had no previous record or comparative advantage. To this end, WFP increasingly seeks to leverage external expertise.[47]

Purchase for Progress

As the world's leading humanitarian agency, WFP is a major buyer of staple food, some 80 percent of which comes from developing countries, for a cash value of over US$1 billion per year.[48] By adopting smallholder-friendly procurement, WFP contributes to the strengthening of local economies and supports the increased resilience and productivity of rural communities—one of the pillars of its hunger eradication strategy.

---

[46] See "The Year in Review, 2011" (WFP 2011c).
[47] Three modalities are cited in WFP's discussion of its Country Strategic Planning Process: (1) Centres of Excellence, (2) a Technical Experts Network, and (3) South–South and triangular cooperation (WFP 2015b).
[48] For the latest information, see "Purchase for Progress": https://www.wfp.org/purchase-for-progress

Through the P4P program, WFP, which has pledged to source 10 percent of its food purchases from smallholder farmers, encourages national governments and the private sector to buy food in ways that benefit smallholders.

On the supply side, P4P works with a variety of partners to promote smallholder farmers' entrepreneurship as a way to build resilience and address long-term nutrition needs. Working mainly with farmers' organizations and other partners, P4P provides training and assets to improve crop quality, facilitates access to finance and promotes marketing. Women, whose role in farming is often unpaid and labor-intensive, are particularly encouraged to take part in decision-making and benefit economically from their work.

Over the years, P4P has expanded to some 35 countries, and helped transform the way more than one million smallholder farmers in Africa, Latin America, and, to a lesser extent, Asia interact with markets.

WFP cites several examples of how P4P is changing people's lives abound. Zambian farmer Harriet Chabala increased her production of beans by 50 percent over two years. In recognition of her entrepreneurial skills and consistent supply to WFP for three consecutive marketing seasons, she received an equipment loan from her local cooperative for a tricycle. The tricycle can navigate poor quality roads, enabling Harriet to provide transport services to move crops and people to and from towns and markets. She is planning to repay her loan in just one year, instead of over the three years as she had agreed. The benefits of P4P are clearly visible in her village: farmers have replaced grass roofing with metal sheeting, and today, there are three cars and more than 10 motorbikes where previously there were none.

P4P's experience demonstrates the roles that demand-driven, pro-smallholder procurement can play in addressing nutritional and other developmental challenges; building stronger markets; lifting rural communities out of poverty; and contributing to SDG2 (eradication of hunger) and SDG15 (responsible consumption and production).

On the other hand, there are examples, such as in Kenya, where a combination of droughts and lack of cash by local governments have posed challenges for the sustainability of the school feeding program.

P4P was launched in September 2008, at the onset of the transformative strategic plan period and was underway in 19 pilot countries a year later (WFP 2012b). The pilot program (through 2013) aimed to increase incomes of small farmers through purchase of local food commodities, providing supply-side technical expertise and access to credit. In 2014, WFP reported 370,000 mt of food were purchased under the project, putting U$148 million in the hands of local farmers (WFP 2015j). P4P provided over 10,000 farmers and 80 farmers' organizations with new skills in management and farming techniques (another example of mission creep) (WFP 2011b). US advocates for bilateral Local and Regional Purchase (LRP) have singled out P4P as an example of a well-tested, highly accountable process (Borgen Project 2013). Over 50 government, UN, organizational, and private sector partners collaborate on the program.

The evaluation of the pilot initiative highlights the benefits for the organization in elevating host-government perceptions of it as a viable development partner. At the same time, it shows that the amount of capacity-building improvement of farmer organizations was less and took longer to achieve than envisioned as an outcome of the project (WFP 2015e).

Although P4P materials credit the project with combining WFP demand with partners' capacity development efforts (WFP 2015e), the evaluation recommends for future programming that WFP "concentrate on its areas of comparative advantage," focusing on the demand side (procurement) and leaving the supply-side capability to other players—that is, its development partners (WFP 2015e, 3). Again, P4P materials described the pilot as "a neat intersection for the mandates of the three [Rome-based] agencies" (WFP 2015e, 22). Both FAO and IFAD have partnered to some degree—with FAO providing supply-side support, technical assistance, and investment analysis, and IFAD linking smallholders to credit and P4P to IFAD-funded programs, though the evaluation observes that a lack of definition of roles resulted in "friction" (WFP 2015e, 7).

The latest data on the P4P program indicate 300,000 women participate, three times the number in 2008, and 1 million farmers have changed the way they engage with markets. Six hundred thousand metric tons of food have been purchased directly from smallholder farmers through P4P.

Support for Markets

The key objectives of WFP have been:

- Improve effectiveness of food assistance by improving cost-effectiveness and improving timeliness;
- Increase the capacity of suppliers and school meals procurement committees to effectively and efficiently procure local commodities for school's meals, promoting sustainability of school feeding;
- Strengthen local and regional food market systems, improving access to culturally acceptable commodities and connecting them to Government of Kenya Home Grown School Meals Program; and
- Improve nutrition of students by increasing access to and use of various high-quality, nutritious and culturally appropriate foods in school's meals.

Some of its work has entailed:

1. Assessment of local food systems,
2. Capacity building for national and county institutions,
3. Capacity strengthening for local traders and FOs,
4. Develop school meal menus using local and nutritious produce, and
5. Procure locally produced, drought-tolerant crops.

Emerging Lessons Based on Evaluations: World Food Programme's Emergency vs. Development Mandate

An estimated 80 percent of global humanitarian needs are in areas facing violent conflict. The Development Assistance Committee (DAC) Recommendation on the Humanitarian–Development–Peace Nexus3 adopted by the DAC of OECD, provides a framework for guiding Member States and UN entities in enhancing effective collaboration across humanitarian, development, and peace strategies in relevant settings. WFP is committed to adhering to this framework.

In 2019, WFP performed very well in governance and independent oversight functions. The organization was ranked first among more than 1,000 organizations in the Aid

Transparency Index, scoring 99 percent. It reduced the number of outstanding high-risk audit recommendations from 68 to 62 and carried out 87 percent of actions requested at Executive Board sessions by agreed deadlines. This was slightly below the target of 95 percent because of the record number of documents submitted to the Board—the highest in WFP's history, which increased the total number of requested actions by nearly 50 percent.

WFP evaluations and an earlier examination by CGD also pointed out the need for new funding systems to support assistance activities, particularly as the majority of contributions and food delivery continues to be for emergency relief. In its consideration of new modalities for food aid and assistance, the CGD found that donor earmarks hinder WFP's ability to use new tools (in this case, LRP). The authors of the CGD report (who did not address the broader WFP mandate shift, but appear to have taken it for granted) called for financial hedging and increased untied contributions from its primary donor members. Development activities require more predictable, multi-year funding streams to support long-term objectives (Ramachandran, Leo, and McCarthy 2010). Current numbers suggest donor support has not yet caught up with WFP's new model and vision.

The lessons learned and conclusions of the post-2008 internal evaluations indicate that the primary constraints to implementing WFP's new vision are internal and systemic. The four evaluations generated 24 recommendations with 6 common courses of action:

a) Adapt and strengthen systems for management support to the change process.

b) Clarify conceptual ambiguities and programme priorities and sharpen WFP's strategic positioning, building on existing strengths.

c) As part of (B), enhance communication and understanding with partners.

d) Adapt WFP's internal systems and procedures to support and enable the changes required (or accelerate where already in hand). These include strengthening monitoring and evaluation to provide the evidence base to demonstrate effectiveness.

e) Developing a funding system that better assures predictable, long-term funding to support the type of activities undertaken in the food assistance approach.

f) Assertively adapt human resource development plans and/or partnering strategies to ensure the technical expertise and skill sets needed for the new or expanding fields of endeavour. (WFP 2012a, 9)

The World Food Programme's Nobel Peace Prize

The Norwegian Nobel Committee awarded the Nobel Peace Prize for 2020 to WFP "for its efforts to combat hunger, for its contribution to bettering conditions for peace in conflict-affected areas and for acting as a driving force in efforts to prevent the use of hunger as a weapon of war and conflict" (NobelPrize.org 2020).

According to the press release from the Nobel Committee, WFP "is the world's largest humanitarian organization addressing hunger and promoting food security. In 2019, WFP provided assistance to close to 100 million people in 88 countries who are victims of acute food insecurity and hunger" (NobelPrize.org 2020). As the UN's primary instrument for eradicating hunger, SDG2, demands on WFP have increased. In 2019, 135 million people suffered from acute hunger, the highest number in many years. Most of the increase was caused by war and armed conflict.

The Nobel Committee noted:

> The coronavirus pandemic has contributed to a strong upsurge in the number of victims of hunger in the world. In countries such as Yemen, the Democratic Republic of Congo, Nigeria, South Sudan and Burkina Faso, the combination of violent conflict and the pandemic has led to a dramatic rise in the number of people living on the brink of starvation. In the face of the pandemic, the World Food Programme has demonstrated an impressive ability to intensify its efforts. As the organisation itself has stated, "Until the day we have a medical vaccine, food is the best vaccine against chaos." (NobelPrize.org 2020)

And the awarding of Nobel prize was also a call to the international community to continue to support WFP and in support of multilateral cooperation. The Nobel Committee wanted to stress the importance of international cooperation to tackle complex problems and the need for WFP to receive the financial support it has requested. It noted:

> The link between hunger and armed conflict is a vicious circle: war and conflict can cause food insecurity and hunger, just as hunger and food insecurity can cause latent conflicts to flare up and trigger the use of violence. We will never achieve the goal of zero hunger unless we also put an end to war and armed conflict. (NobelPrize.org 2020)

The Nobel Committee emphasized:

> Providing assistance to increase food security not only prevents hunger, but can also help to improve prospects for stability and peace. The World Food Programme has taken the lead in combining humanitarian work with peace efforts through pioneering projects in South America, Africa and Asia.
>
> The World Food Programme was an active participant in the diplomatic process that culminated in May 2018 in the UN Security Council's unanimous adoption of Resolution 2417, which for the first time explicitly addressed the link between conflict and hunger. The Security Council also underscored UN Member States' obligation to help ensure that food assistance reaches those in need, and condemned the use of starvation as a method of warfare.
>
> With this year's award, the Norwegian Nobel Committee wishes to turn the eyes of the world towards the millions of people who suffer from or face the threat of hunger. The World Food Programme also plays a key role in multilateral cooperation on making food security an instrument of peace, and has made a strong contribution towards mobilising UN Member States to combat the use of hunger as a weapon of war and conflict. As the UN's largest specialised agency, the World Food Programme is a modern version of the peace congresses that the Nobel Peace Prize is intended to promote. The work of the World Food Programme to the benefit of humankind is an endeavour that all the nations of the world should be able to endorse and support. (NobelPrize.org 2020)

In response to the announcement of the Nobel Peace Prize on October 9, 2020, the Executive Director of WFP, David Beasley, former Republican governor of South Carolina, spoke characteristically with passion from Niger in a PBS interview. He noted that with the COVID-19 pandemic, 270 million are expected to be hungry, compared to 135 million in

2020. WFP will need addition US$5 billion dollars. He appealed to the world's 200 billionaires, as he has in the past, to contribute more funds to WFP as soon as possible. Or, he said the consequence would be massive famines, mass migration, and destabilization due to war and conflicts (*PBS News Hour* 2020).

Developments in 2020

The WFP Executive Director noted that 2020 would be the worst year for humanitarian crises since the Second World War, affected by the unending wars in the Syrian Arab Republic and Yemen, the deepening crises in hotspots such as South Sudan and the central Sahel region of Africa, the increasingly frequent natural disasters and changing weather patterns, and the economic crisis in Lebanon affecting millions of Syrian refugees (Lederer 2020). An estimated 135 million people suffered acute hunger in 55 countries in 2019; this number was predicted to double in 2020, as COVID-19 became a new driver of food insecurity. The world was already facing a "perfect storm." The COVID-19 pandemic is the worst health and socioeconomic disaster in more than a century, overwhelming the global humanitarian system. It has swept through the developed world, as well as threatened hunger crises in the poorest countries where the majority of WFP's beneficiaries live (WFP 2020f).

WFP's revenue to a record US$8 billion in 2019, an increase of 10 percent. The top five donors to WFP contributed 76 percent of funding, designating 36 percent for large-scale operations in South Sudan, the Syrian Arab Republic, and Yemen. Despite the generous contributions, they were insufficient, with a funding gap of US$4.1 billion, to cover identified needs of food insecure populations (WFP 2020a, 8).

In 2019, WFP responded to an unprecedented number of Level 3 and Level 2 emergencies in 20 countries (see Box 12.4). Across 88 countries, it provided assistance to 68.1 million local residents—27 percent higher number than in 2018, in addition to 10.6 million refugees, 2.9 million returnees, and 15.5 internally displaced persons—18 percent more than in 2018 (WFP 2020a, 4, 36).

School meals or take-home rations were provided to 17.3 million children, and 17.2 million in nutrition programs in 2019, of which 10.8 million children and 6.4 million women received support (WFP 2020a, 114).

Through food assistance for assets programs, nearly 134,000 ha of land and forest were rehabilitated or replanted, and more than 50,000 community assets, such as community infrastructure, roads, and water points, were built, rehabilitated, or developed in 2019. Also, WFP distributed a record US$2.1 billion in CBTs. WFP's overall performance in functional areas was rated "medium" to "high," as in 2018, with work in 90 percent of these areas rated as meeting, or on track to meet, WFP's targets. The year 2019 marked the first that performance reporting was fully aligned with the aims of CSPs (WFP 2020a, 8).

So, the difference in 2019, over previous years, was the growing number of emergencies, their complexity, intensity, and long duration, as well as WFP's ability to fundraise and respond to 7 Level 3 and 11 Level 2 emergencies in 20 countries.

Violent conflicts were the primary drivers of the emergencies. Level 3 emergency responses were also established in the central Sahel and Mozambique, and continued support was provided for existing Level 3 responses in the Democratic Republic of the Congo, Nigeria, South Sudan, the Syrian Arab Republic, and Yemen (WFP 2020a, 9).

Box 12.4 Growing Role of Emergencies in Food Assistance

WFP classifies Emergency Response operations according to a three-level scale:

- Level 1 Response: Emergency operations within the response capabilities of the relevant WFP Country Office (CO), with routine support from Regional Bureaux (RB).
- Level 2 Response: Emergency Response operations requiring regional augmentation of country-level response capability.
- Level 3 Response: Emergency Response operations requiring mobilisation of WFP global response capabilities in support of the relevant CO(s) and/or RB, i.e. a Corporate Response. (WFP 2014g, 1)

The growing numbers of Level 3 emergencies and the frequency of their onslaught and intensity have "diverted attention from other protracted, chronic and lower-level emergencies" of less political importance and visibility (WFP 2017d, 14). In 2019, WFP responded to 18 Level 3 (six) and Level 2 (twelve) concurrent emergencies, the largest number that WFP had faced thus far at one time (WFP 2019g, 1–2). Two aspects stand out in this transition: first, from delivering food aid in-kind to providing food assistance, including CBTs and second, from food procured from traditional food surplus countries such as the United States to at least partially obtaining it from nearby emerging countries, thereby reducing costs with local procurement and delivery to beneficiaries (WFP 2017e).

Food aid still constitutes an important feature of WFP. It arose from a largely unidirectional, top-down vision: disposal of surplus food to hungry people. At least in theory, "food assistance, by contrast, involves a more complex appreciation of people's long-term nutritional needs and of the diverse approaches required to meet them. This conceptual shift has been at the core of WFP's transformation in recent years" (WFP 2020j). While WFP remains the world's leading humanitarian agency, it is aiming "to combine frontline action with the quest for durable solutions" (WFP 2020j).

Emergencies affected more people than in any of the previous 20 years, with protracted conflicts in several countries, including Afghanistan, the Democratic Republic of the Congo, Somalia, the Syrian Arab Republic, and Yemen, as well as the adverse impacts of climate change on agricultural production and food security. Among the top five global hazards identified in 2019 were environmental risks such as extreme weather events. While infectious disease outbreaks have increased in frequency, many countries were unprepared to respond to a pandemic (WFP 2020a, 8–9).

Donors gave a record-breaking US$8 billion in confirmed contributions in 2019. Funds were used by WFP to procure food, valued at more than US$2.3 billion, including US$37 million worth from smallholder farmers, for direct distribution. An additional US$2.1 billion in CBTs was provided (WFP 2020a, 4).

Among the steps that WFP took was the establishment of the Global Surge Unit early in the year, which ensured that experienced staff are available for immediate deployment during emergencies. This unit enabled staff deployment within the first hours following a crisis in countries, including Burkina Faso, Cameroon, and Mozambique. Overall, in 2019,

WFP provided 4.2 million tons of food, 2.1 billion of cash transfers and vouchers, and trained 620,000 people (WFP 2020a, 9).

Strategic Result 1 of the WFP Strategic Plan 2017–21 that everyone has access to food (discussed later in the chapter) accounted for 78 percent of the 2019 earmarked funds. Earmarked funding increased by 23 times, whereas completely flexible funding remained flat. In 2019, only 5 percent of WFP's total contribution revenue was fully flexible, a lower percentage than in the previous three years. The top 10 donors accounted for 87 percent of total contributions, which was an increase of 2 percent over 2018; the top five donors accounted for 76 percent of total contributions. Government donors provided 86 percent of 2019 funding (WFP 2020a, 9).

Earmarked funding is tied in two ways: the destination for which is it used, and within the destination the purposes for which it is used. Thus, not only do the top 5 or top 10 countries get most of the emergency funding but also within it, Strategic Result 1, which accounted for 78 percent of 2019 earmarked funds (WFP 2020a, 9). In contrast, Strategic Result 2, that no one suffers from malnutrition, received only 6 percent of earmarked funds, and WFP had minimal activity in terms of Strategic Result 6 (policies to support sustainable development are coherent) and Result 7 (developing countries have access to a range of financial resources for development investment) (WFP 2020a, 25). These data offer substantial insight into donor support as distinct from general rhetoric. Similarly, high-profile emergencies are well funded in terms of share of needs funded, compared to less visible needs.

The United States contributed US$3.4 billion, accounting for 42 percent of all contributions in 2019. The next biggest donor countries were Germany (11 percent), the United Kingdom (9 percent), and Saudi Arabia (5 percent). The EC contributed 9 percent of 2019 funds (WFP 2020a, 22). To diversify funding and reduce the risk of reliance on a single donor, WFP adopted, in 2019, a five-year, private sector partnership and fundraising strategy (2020–5) that is focused on three pillars—impact, income, and innovation—for a private sector funding facility (WFP 2020a, 9).

Ending Poverty and Hunger—Questions for Future Sustainability

WFP has been an emergency assistance agency par excellence and takes pride in that distinction. Humanitarian assistance has been the fastest growing segment of development. WFP's non-bureaucratic procedures have enabled it to respond to emergencies quickly, although FAO's emergency assistance also has been increasing and its procedures have improved considerably. WFP has been reinventing itself in development assistance, while also having established its position as the humanitarian response agency of choice. This view of a new role is still not broadly shared within the agency, but many now recognize that food aid in tonnage cannot remain the sole focus of WFP in the future, if it is to remain in business. Even experts in logistics and procurement, therefore, are accepting this new reality and recognize that to survive and grow, the organization must change with the times and be innovative. It is a major cultural shift, however, for WFP to move from the "getting things done"/logistics focus to one that is based on innovation, policy and programs, and building the capacity of vulnerable countries to help themselves. Moreover, it is not clear if WFP is cost-effective in undertaking some of these activities.

WFP is betting that it can bank on its humanitarian expertise as its comparative advantage while moving into a new and expanded role. It recognizes that it cannot and should not take on certain development roles and must work with UN partners. There is clearly a learning curve. How steep it is and how it will play out remains to be seen.

Emergency assistance will remain an important part of international assistance. With climate change, extreme droughts and floods, continued internal strife, accelerated globalization leading to rapid cross-border spread of communicable diseases from birds and animals to humans and across national borders, WFP will continue to have business. And regardless of investments in national policies and systems to prepare for and respond to crises made or developed by international actors and increasingly by countries themselves, the humanitarian community will continue to have a role where national resources are absent or insufficient. These conditions do not appear to be abating—to the contrary, are on the rise—and the costs of providing for beneficiaries are higher.

WFP also has established a niche in school feeding and public works—areas in which it used food aid in the past. Most of the growth of safety nets in low-income countries, particularly in Africa, has been financed through short-term donor assistance, whereas MICs are increasingly using their own resources to provide such safety net programs. Many of these country programs entail substantial fiscal commitments and major policy and institutional issues. The World Bank decidedly has had a comparative advantage in addressing them. Whether WFP can go beyond piloting small-scale experiments and help to embed them at scale in countries' own strategies, with respect to safety nets, is as yet unclear.

WFP could develop capacity in developing countries for emergency assistance, but it faces a number of obstacles. Field staff view it as a development activity rather than a humanitarian endeavor. As in other international organizations, field staff tends to be skeptical of "policy" and "strategy" involved in capacity building. WFP has seen itself as operational, rather than policy-focused or academically focused (which is WFP's perception of FAO or IFAD). The challenge lies in bridging the divide and translating the idea of capacity to WFP's in-country work and convincing donors that this is worthwhile to fund. Also, capacity development tends to be a crosscutting theme, rather than a strategic objective in and of itself, under the 2014–17 Strategic Plan (WFP 2013f). How should we interpret this? Capacity development should either be emphasized across the board, or if it is indeed seen internally as less important, then it should be removed as a strategic objective and slowly phased out. The evaluations noted a need for "adequate human and financial resources for the longer-term and predictable engagement this [capacity development] requires," in contrast to WFP's short-term, rapid emergency response expertise (WFP 2015a, 3).

The world is moving to local procurement, South–South cooperation, and twinning arrangements (pairing cash with developing world donations of food to developing world partners to cover transportation costs). WFP's comparative advantage in long-term development assistance needs to be demonstrated and documented. Lack of evidence is not lack of advantage. It may be too soon to tell in terms of its activities in certain areas, though cash transfers and vouchers are proving promising. WFP is innovative but may not be good at knowledge management. WFP's cost effectiveness also could be better documented. Some activities in local procurement, cash transfers, and vouchers also demonstrate that these mechanisms get food to people faster than food aid did; this needs to be documented. It is not clear what happens to the movement to develop capacity of civil society to provide development assistance in developing countries when international institutions like WFP expand their roles, together with international NGOs, often at the cost of building the capacity of the domestic civil society—a criticism figuring largely in the debate in the 2015–16 summit season. International NGOs are sometimes vilified, because they thrive on emergencies in developing countries and donor governments support them—sometimes at the cost of building national capacity. Haiti is a classic example of the NGO "hives" obstructing the development of domestic capacity, even if inadvertently. On the other side of the spectrum, Syria is an example of the essential role of national capacity and national organizations needed to access populations.

There is evidence that, typically, multilateral aid tends to be delivered, more cost effectively than bilateral aid; food-related development assistance would benefit from an independent evaluation to assess its efficiency and explore how it could be linked more effectively to long-term development assistance provided by FAO, IFAD, and the World Bank to achieve sustainable food security. At the same time, we believe emergency assistance will continue to remain an important dimension of international assistance, and WFP, having excelled in this area, should not abandon that critical mission, including through the building of capacity in developing countries to help themselves in emergencies.

Finally, the changed global environment means that not only the governing boards of the individual organizations but also the G7 and G20 need to assess the implications of increasing emergencies and populations living in conflict areas, to better address the transition from emergency aid to rehabilitation, reconstruction, and development in a holistic global architecture for food and agriculture. To begin with, the governing members of collaborating organizations need to clearly identify the comparative advantages and disadvantages of each organization. Representation on the governing boards across WFP, FAO, and IFAD is common for several member countries. Yet, it is unclear if they address the larger issues of the long-term comparative advantages of the three Rome-based organizations and their implications for reforms from a strategic perspective. Such a look needs to take account of each organization's performance on the ground, which is increasingly available through their independent evaluations, and now WFP's Nobel Peace Prize, and consider how developed and developing countries alike can strengthen the international organizations to achieve excellence rather than promote mission creep. Furthermore, since 2008, the international financial institutions, like World Bank and IFAD, have geared up to address food and financial crises and unexpected pandemonium, individually and collectively, through global partnerships (see Chapter 8 on the World Bank and its treatment of the food crisis). IFAD similarly undertook an evaluation of its operations in fragile countries. The radical changes in the world call for a Bretton Woods-type examination of the need for a new architecture, building on the one inherited 70 years ago.

Appendix: Chronology

1960s

1960   US President Dwight D. Eisenhower proposed a food aid "scheme" to the UN General Assembly.

1961   George McGovern, director of the US Food for Peace Program proposed establishment of a multilateral food aid program with a fund of US$100 million in commodities and cash, as a three-year experiment. WFP officially established November 24, 1961, with UN General Assembly resolution.

1962   WFP's first Executive Director, Addeke Henrik Boerma was appointed, serving from May 1962 to December 1967. WFP's first emergency operation was in response to an earthquake in Iran in September that resulted in 12,000 deaths. WFP sends survivors 1,500 mt of wheat, 270 tons of sugar and 27 tons of tea.

1963   WFP's first development program was launched for the Nubians in Sudan, after the construction of the Aswan High Dam on the Nile River in southern Egypt led to the resettlement of 50,000 indigenous Nubian people thousands of kilometers to the south of their homeland. Over four years, WFP provided food aid, as Nubians developed their new lands.WFP's first school meals project in Togo was approved. Five thousand school children were provided nourishment in the pilot project that also aimed to increase school attendance.

1970s

1973   WFP responded to famine after six years of drought in Africa's western Sahel in seven countries, home to 25 million people, with 30 cargo aircraft from 12 national air forces, in a relief effort that lasted three years.

1975   WFP's cash shortages, arising from a global food shortage in 1972 and an energy crisis resulting from a war in the Middle East, were alleviated with a series of cash donations from Saudi Arabia's King Faisal, beginning with a US$50 million grant in 1975, the largest donation to date from a single country after the United States.

1980s

1980   WFP led a multinational inter-agency relief effort for the first time, to assist 370,000 Cambodian refugees, who fled violence in Thailand.

1984   WFP delivered 2 million tons of food aid in response to Ethiopian famine. Media images of the famine's devastating effects prompted "Band Aid" and "Live Aid" fundraising efforts. WFP led 87 separate relief operations.

1989   WFP worked amid chaos in the "failed state" of Somalia, run by war lords in the absence of centralized authority.

1989   Operation Lifeline Sudan was launched. Leading a consortium of UN agencies and 40 NGOs, WFP airdrops 1.5 million tons of food, in a dawn-to-dusk operation with 20 cargo aircraft, above what is now South Sudan, to save hundreds of thousands of lives threatened by civil war.

1990s

The balance between development programs and emergency interventions shifted back and forth.

1992   WFP's first large-scale relief operation in Europe was prompted by the disintegration of Yugoslavia, involving thousands of people in worst humanitarian crisis since the Second World War.

1992   Catherine Bertini became WFP's first woman to serve as Executive Director of WFP. Also the first woman to head a UN organization, Ms. Bertini was the 9th executive director, service from April 1992 to April 2002.

1994   The Rwandan genocide led to massive displacements of the population, with 3 million people fleeing into the then eastern Zaire, Tanzania, Uganda, and Burundi. WFP responded to the crisis with food aid and later played a key role in rebuilding the ravaged country.

1997   The Kyoto Protocol was signed, acknowledging the impact of climate change. WFP develops longer term aid projects, with more partnerships.

1998   WFP delivered more than 330,000 tons of wheat and rice to feed 19 million people affective by flooding in Bangladesh.

1999   During the Kosovo armed conflict, WFP established a network of mobile bakeries when conflict led to Europe's largest refugee crisis since 1945. WFP provided relief to hundreds of thousands of Kosovar refugees in Albania and Macedonia. Eight mobile bakeries supplied flour to local bakeries to produce bread for more than 200,000 people on a daily basis.

2000s

The Millennium Development Goals established shared, measurable objectives to reduce hunger and poverty. Food aid was increasingly replaced by food assistance, with cash and vouchers emerging as a complement to in-kind food distributions.

2000   WFP established the first UN humanitarian response facility located in Brindisi, Italy, for strategic pre-positioning of emergency relief supplies for international organizations, NGOs, and other UN agencies.

2002	WFP was certified by the Guinness World Records as the largest humanitarian agency with 14,500 staff members, about 90 percent, working in the field rather than at headquarters in Rome.
2002	WFP partnered with the private sector for the first time with a collaboration with an international logistics company TNT.
2003	WFP established and manages the UN Humanitarian Air Service (UNHAS), which moves thousands of people in and out of conflict and disaster zones each year.
2004	WFP led an emergency relief effort for victims of the Indian Ocean earthquake and tsunami, which affected 14 countries—Bangladesh, India, Indonesia, Kenya, Madagascar, Malaysia, the Maldives, Myanmar, the Seychelles, Somalia, South Africa, Sri Lanka, Tanzania, and Thailand.
2005	WFP responded to UN, assuming leadership for all humanitarian logistics for all UN agencies and NGOs to ensure coordination of work.
2005	WFP innovated its relief operations with a pilot program that provided cash-based assistance for the first time, assisting victims of a Sri Lankan tsunami, allowing recipients to select and buy their own food in local markets.
2010	WFP, for the first time, provided cash assistance through mobile phones in a pilot project in Kenya.An earthquake in Haiti presented another emergent need for humanitarian assistance, and WFP helped 4.5 million victims at the peak of operation, and reached more than two-thirds of the population in the affected areas.
2010s	
2011	WFP scaled up its emergency response in Syria from 2011, providing food and assistance to millions in Syria and war refugees from the Syrian conflict in Turkey, Lebanon, Jordan, Iraq, and Egypt.
2013	Making deliveries by truck, boat, and airdrops, WFP responded to emergency in South Sudan when 2 million were forced from their homes by conflict.
2014	Ebola virus outbreak in West Africa brought the humanitarian community together in a unified response, with Logistics Cluster, managed by WFP. WFP provided food for the more than 3 million people affected by the outbreak and helped 22,000 survivors.
2015	WFP responded to two Nepali earthquake survivors in remote mountainous communities.
2016	Increased incidence of conflict. WFP adopted "Integrated Road Map" (IRM), aligning WFP to the SDGs, and moved the organization from project-based work to planning through CSPs.
2019	WFP responded to 18 Level 3 (six) and Level 2 (twelve) concurrent emergencies, the largest number that WFP had faced thus far at one time.
2020	Nobel Peace Prize

Source: The chronology of WFP is based on WFP (2016b, 2019g, 2020n).

References

Banerjee, Abhijit, and Esther Duflo. 2012. *Poor Economics: A Radical Rethinking of the Way to Fight Global Poverty*. New York: PublicAffairs.

Barrett, Christopher B. 2017. Testimony before the United States Senate Committee on Foreign Relations Hearing on "Modernizing the Food for Peace Program." Room 419, Dirksen Senate Office Building, October 19. https://www.foreign.senate.gov/imo/media/doc/101917_Barrett_Testimony.pdf

Barrett, Christopher B., and Erin C. Lentz. 2010. "Food Insecurity." In *The International Studies Encyclopedia*, edited by Robert A. Denemark and Renée Marlin-Bennett, 2291–311. Malden, MA: Wiley-Blackwell.

Borgen Project. 2013. "5 Key Facts on U.S. Food Reform." Revised July 2. http://borgenproject.org/wp-content/uploads/5-Facts-on-Food-Aid-Reform.pdf

Bundy, Donald, Carmen Burbano, Margaret E. Grosh, Aulo Gelli, Matthew Juke, and Drake Lesley. 2009. "Rethinking School Feeding: Social Safety Nets, Child Development, and the Education Sector." Directions in Development, Human Development, World Bank and World Food Programme, Washington, DC.

Calderwood, Imogen. 2018. "76,000,000 Don't Have Enough Food. Here's How Food Aid Helps Them." Global Citizen. https://www.globalcitizen.org/en/content/follow-the-food-aid-how-it-works/

Chonghaile, Clár Ní. 2015. "What's the Best Bit of the UN? No. 3: The World Food Programme." *The Guardian*, September 8. https://www.theguardian.com/world/2015/sep/08/best-bit-un-united-nations-wfp-world-food-programme

Clay, Edward. 2012. "What's the Use of the 2012 Food Assistance Convention?" Comment, June 25, Overseas Development Institute (ODI), London. https://www.odi.org/blogs/6656-what-s-use-2012-food-assistance-convention

FAO (Food and Agriculture Organization of the United Nations) 2010. "Joint Thematic Evaluation of FAO and WFP Support to Information Systems for Food Security." Summary Report, February 2010, PC 103/8, Programme Committee, 103rd Session, Rome, April 12–16. http://www.fao.org/docrep/meeting/018/k7296e.pdf

FAO (Food and Agriculture Organization of the United Nations). 2017a. "Climate Change Puts Millions of People in Vicious Cycle of Food Insecurity, Malnutrition and Poverty." November 14, FAO, Rome. http://www.fao.org/news/story/en/item/1062612/icode/

FAO (Food and Agriculture Organization of the United Nations). 2017b. "WFP Management Plan (2018–2020)." 168th Session, Finance Committee, Rome, November 2–3. http://www.fao.org/3/a-mu593e.pdf.

FAO (Food and Agriculture Organization of the United Nations), IFAD (International Fund for Agricultural Development), UNICEF (United Nations Children's Fund), WFP (World Food Programme), and WHO (World Health Organization). 2018. *The State of Food Security and Nutrition in the World 2018. Building Climate Resilience for Food Security and Nutrition.* Rome: FAO. http://www.fao.org/3/I9553EN/i9553en.pdf

FAO (Food and Agriculture Organization of the United Nations), IFAD (International Fund for Agricultural Development), UNICEF (United Nations Children's Fund), WFP (World Food Programme), and WHO (World Health Organization). 2020. *The State of Food Security and Nutrition in the World 2020: Transforming Food Systems for Affordable Healthy Diets.* Rome: FAO. http://www.fao.org/3/ca9692en/CA9692EN.pdf

FAO (Food and Agriculture Organization of the United Nations), IFAD (International Fund for Agricultural Development), and WFP (World Food Programme). 2003. "Working Together." Issue 5, February 2003, FAO, Rome. https://www.ifad.org/documents/10180/494385c3-5572-4bc3-a24b-4a2bac2d7a46

FAO (Food and Agriculture Organization of the United Nations), IFAD (International Fund for Agricultural Development), and WFP (World Food Programme). 2015. "Strengthening Resilience for Food Security and Nutrition." |A Conceptual Framework for Collaboration and Partnership among the Rome-based Agencies, April 2015. https://www.wfp.org/rba-joint-resilience-framework

FSIN (Food Security Information Network). n.d. FSIN Brochure. http://www.fsincop.net/fileadmin/user_upload/fsin/docs/FSIN-brochure-EN.pdf

Gentilini, Ugo, Sarah Laughton, and Clare O'Brien. 2018. "Human(itarian) Capital? Lessons on Better Connecting Humanitarian Assistance and Social Protection." Social Protection and

Jobs Discussion Paper No. 1802. World Food Programme, Rome, and World Bank Group, Washington, DC. https://www.wfp.org/publications/humanitarian-capital-lessons-better-connecting-humanitarian-assistance-and-social-protection

GHA (Global Humanitarian Assistance). 2016. "Think Piece: Humanitarian Funding." Development Initiatives Paper prepared for the World Humanitarian Summit, Rome, 2016. http://www.globalhumanitarianassistance.org/wp-content/uploads/2015/03/Final_Financing_Think-Piece_20140116.pdf

Harvey, Paul, Karen Proudlock, Edward Clay, Barry Riley, and Susanne Jaspars. 2010. "Food Aid and Food Assistance in Emergency and Transitional Contexts: A Review of Current Thinking." Synthesis Paper, June, Humanitarian Policy Group, Overseas Development Institute, London. https://www.odi.org/sites/odi.org.uk/files/odi-assets/publications-opinion-files/6036.pdf

Hidrobo, Melissa, John Hoddinott, Amy Margolies, Vanessa Moreira, and Amber Peterman. 2012. "Impact Evaluation of Cash, Food Vouchers, and Food Transfers among Colombian Refugees and Poor Ecuadorians in Carchi and Sucumbíos." WFP/IFPRI Final Report, International Food Policy Research Institute, Poverty, Health, and Nutrition Division, Washington, DC. http://documents.wfp.org/stellent/groups/public/documents/resources/wfp257675.pdf

Hirvonen, Kalie, and John Hoddinott. 2020. "Beneficiary Views on Cash and In-Kind Payments: Evidence from Ethiopia's Productive Safety Net Programme." Policy Research Working Paper No. 9125, Knowledge and Strategy Team, Development Economics, World Bank Group, Washington, DC. http://documents.worldbank.org/curated/en/568961580228524626/pdf/Beneficiary-Views-on-Cash-and-In-Kind-Payments-Evidence-from-Ethiopias-Productive-Safety.pdf

Hoddinott, John, Marc J. Cohen, and Christopher B. Barrett. 2008. "Renegotiating the Food Aid Convention: Background, Context, and Issues." *Global Governance* 14 (3): 283–304.

IEG (Independent Evaluation Group). 2013. "The World Bank Group and the Global Food Crisis: An Evaluation of the World Bank Group Response." IEG, World Bank Group, Washington, DC. http://documents.worldbank.org/curated/en/543311468323944900/pdf/The-World-Bank-Group-and-the-global-food-crisis-an-evaluation-of-the-World-Bank-Group-response.pdf

Karasapan, Omer. 2020. "Sharing the Burden of the Global Refugee Crisis." Future Development, January 27, Brookings Institution, Washington, DC. https://www.brookings.edu/blog/future-development/2020/01/27/sharing-the-burden-of-the-global-refugee-crisis

Konyndyk, Jeremy. 2018. "Rethinking the Humanitarian Business Model." CGD Brief, Center for Global Development, Washington, DC.

Lattimer, Charlotte. 2015. "Making Financing Work for Crisis-Affected People." Position paper for The World Humanitarian Summit (WHS), Istanbul, May 2016. http://devinit.org/wp-content/uploads/2015/07/The-World-Humanitarian-Summit-making-financing-work-for-crisis-affected-people.pdf

Lederer, Edith M. 2020. "WFP Chief Seeks Million From Donors, Billionaires for Food." Associated Press, October 20. https://abcnews.go.com/US/wireStory/wfp-chief-seeks-million-donors-billionaires-food-73533419

Lele, Uma, and Arthur A. Goldsmith. 1989. "The Development of National Agricultural Research Capacity: India's Experience with the Rockefeller Foundation and Its Significance for Africa." *Economic Development and Cultural Change* 37 (2): 305–43.

Lentz, Erin C., Christopher B. Barrett, and Miguel I. Gómez. 2013. "Tradeoffs or Synergies? Assessing Local and Regional Food Aid Procurement through Case Studies in Burkina Faso and Guatemala." *World Development* 49 (9): 44–57.

Masood, Salman. 2015. "Pakistan Warns Aid Groups to Follow Unspecified Rules." *New York Times*, June 12. https://www.nytimes.com/2015/06/13/world/asia/pakistan-warns-aid-groups-to-follow-unspecified-rules.html

Mercier, Stephanie, and Vincent Smith. 2018. "The Time for Food Aid Reform is Now." *The Hill*, May 1. https://thehill.com/opinion/international/385622-the-time-for-food-aid-reform-is-now

NobelPrize.org. 2020. The Nobel Peace Prize for 2020. Announcement, Oslo, October 9. https://www.nobelprize.org/prizes/peace/2020/press-release/

OCHA (United Nations Office for the Coordination of Humanitarian Affairs). 2020. "Humanitarian Response: Logistics." https://www.humanitarianresponse.info/en/coordination/clusters/logistics

OECD (Organisation for Economic Co-operation and Development). 2018. *States of Fragility*. Paris: OECD Publishing. https://www.oecd.org/dac/states-of-fragility-2018-9789264302075-en.htm

OECD (Organisation for Economic Co-operation and Development). 2020. *States of Fragility*. Paris: OECD Publishing. http://www.oecd.org/dac/states-of-fragility-fa5a6770-en.htm

Partnership for Child Development. 2018. "Memo: Global Figures for Children in Need of School Feeding." Imperial College, London.

PBS News Hour. 2020. "Leader of Nobel Peace Prize-winning World Food Programme on Global Starvation Crisis." Interview with David Beasley, October 9. https://www.pbs.org/newshour/show/leader-of-nobel-peace-prize-winning-world-food-programme-on-global-starvation-crisis#transcript

Ramachandran, Vijaya, Benjamin Leo, and Owen McCarthy. 2010. "Financing Food Assistance: Options for the World Food Programme to Save Lives and Dollars." Working Paper 209, April, Center for Global Development, Washington, DC. https://www.cgdev.org/publication/financing-food-assistance-options-world-food-programme-save-lives-and-dollars-working

Stoddard, Abby. 2017. "Humanitarian Funding to Sub-Saharan Africa: Tracking Flows Through and Outside Government Structures." Background paper produced for the World Bank, Washington, DC.

UN (United Nations). 2012. "Food Assistance Convention." May 8, UN, New York. https://treaties.un.org/doc/source/signature/2012/CTC_XIX-48.pdf

UN (United Nations). 2015. "Addis Ababa Action Agenda of the Third International Conference on Financing for Development." Department of Economic and Social Affairs, Financing for Development Office, New York. http://www.un.org/esa/ffd/wp-content/uploads/2015/08/AAAA_Outcome.pdf

UN (United Nations). 2016a. "UN Summit for Refugees and Migrants." September 16, UN, New York. https://refugeesmigrants.un.org/summit

UN (United Nations). 2016b. We Can End Poverty. Millennium Development Goals and Beyond 2015. http://www.un.org/millenniumgoals/

UN (United Nations). 2020. The 17 Goals: Sustainable Development. Department of Economic and Social Affairs. https://sdgs.un.org/goals

UN-Habitat (United Nations Human Settlements Programme). 2020. "Habitat III." UN Conference on Housing and Sustainable Urban Development, Quito, Ecuador, October 17–20. https://unhabitat.org/habitat-iii

UNFCCC (United Framework Convention on Climate Change). 2020. The Paris Agreement. https://unfccc.int/process-and-meetings/the-paris-agreement/the-paris-agreement

UNHCR (UN Refugee Agency). 2017. "UNHCR, WFP Agreement Creates Combined Efficiencies to Benefit Refugees." Press Release, May 15. https://www.unhcr.org/en-us/news/press/2017/5/592467934/unhcr-wfp-agreement-creates-combined-efficiencies-benefit-refugees.html

UNHCR (UN Refugee Agency). 2019. "Global Trends: Forced Displacement in 2019." UNCR Global Data Service, Copenhagen. https://www.unhcr.org/globaltrends2019/

UNHCR (UN Refugee Agency). 2021. Figures at a Glance. https://www.unhcr.org/figures-at-a-glance.html

UNISDR (United Nations Office for Disaster Risk Reduction). 2015. "Sendai Framework for Disaster Risk Reduction 2015–2030." UNISDR, Geneva. https://www.preventionweb.net/files/43291_sendaiframeworkfordrren.pdf

von Braun, Joachim, and Maximo Torero. 2009. "Exploring the Price Spike." *Choices* (AAEA) 24 (1): 16–21. https://pdfs.semanticscholar.org/f0ff/272626326bf8d97bf6ff4c276e68b1ff2a90.pdf

WFP (World Food Programme). 2000. "Participatory Approaches." WFP/EB.3/2000/3-D, Policy Issues, Executive Board, Third Regular Session, Rome, October 23–6.

WFP (World Food Programme). 2003. "WFP Strategic Plan 2004–2007." WFP/EB.3/2003/4-A/1, October 13, 2003, WFP, Rome. https://www.wfp.org/content/wfp-strategic-plan-2004-2007

WFP (World Food Programme). 2004a. "Annual Report for 2003." WFP, Rome. https://www.wfp.org/publications/wfp-annual-report-2003

WFP (World Food Programme). 2004b. "New Partnerships to Meet Rising Needs—Expanding the WFP Donor Base." WFP/EB.3/2004/4-C, Executive Board, Third Regular Session, Rome, October 11–14. http://www.fao.org/tempref/UNFAO/BODIES/FC/fc121/7879e.pdf (Annex II)

WFP (World Food Programme). 2005a. "Final Report on the Governance Project." WFP/EB.2/2005/4-C/Rev.1, November 9, WFP, Rome. http://one.wfp.org/eb/docs/2005/wfp076984~2.pdf

WFP (World Food Programme). 2005b. "WFP Strategic Plan 2006–2009." WFP/EB.A/2005/5-A/Rev.1, June 9, WFP, Rome. http://one.wfp.org/eb/docs/2005/wfp050757~2.pdf

WFP (World Food Programme). 2007. "WFP Strategic Plan 2008–2013." WFP, Rome. https://www.wfp.org/publications/wfp-strategic-plan-2008-2013

WFP (World Food Programme). 2011a. "FAO–WFP Joint Strategy on Information Systems for Food and Nutrition Security." Strategy Timeframe: 2012–2017. WFP/EB.2/2011/12-B, WFP, November 14–17, Rome.

WFP (World Food Programme). 2011b. "Fighting Hunger Worldwide." Annual Report 2010, WFP, Rome.

WFP (World Food Programme). 2011c. "The Year in Review, 2011." WFP, Rome.

WFP (World Food Programme). 2012a. "Four Strategic Evaluations on the Transition from Food Aid to Food Assistance: A Synthesis." Report number: OE/2012/S002, Commissioned by the Office of Evaluation, Prepared by the Konterra Group: Terrence Jantzi and Everett Ressler, May 2012, WFP, Rome.

WFP (World Food Programme). 2012b. "Summary P4P Procurement Report: September 2008–March 2012." Updated May 2012, WFP, Rome.

WFP (World Food Programme). 2012c. "2011 Food Aid Flows." International Food Aid Information System, August, WFP, Rome.

WFP (World Food Programme). 2012d. "Update of WFP's Safety Net Policy: The Role of Food Assistance in Social Protection." June, WFP, Rome.

WFP (World Food Programme). 2012e. "WFP Nutrition Policy." WFP/EB.1/2012/5-A, January 17, 2012, WFP, Rome.

WFP (World Food Programme). 2013a. "HIV, AIDS, TB, and Nutrition." November, WFP, Rome.

WFP (World Food Programme). 2013b. "Remarks by Ertharin Cousin at the Nutrition for Growth High Level Event, London." https://www.huffingtonpost.co.uk/ertharin-cousin/world-food-programme-malnutrition_b_3403736.html

WFP (World Food Programme). 2013c. "State of School Feeding Worldwide 2013." WFP, Rome. https://www.wfp.org/content/state-school-feeding-worldwide-2013

WFP (World Food Programme). 2013d. "2012 Food Aid Flows." December 2013, WFP, Rome.

WFP (World Food Programme). 2013e "WFP Private-Sector Partnerships and Fundraising Strategy 2013–2017." WFP/EB.A/2013/5-B, May 9, 2013, WFP, Rome.

WFP (World Food Programme). 2013f. "WFP Strategic Plan (2014–2017)." WFP/EB.A/2013/5-A/1, May 8, 2013, WFP, Rome. http://documents.wfp.org/stellent/groups/public/documents/eb/wfpdoc062522.pdf

WFP (World Food Programme). 2014a. "Annual Evaluation Report for 2013." May, Office of Evaluation, WFP, Rome.

WFP (World Food Programme). 2014b. "Annual Performance Report for 2013." May 21, WFP, Rome.

WFP (World Food Programme). 2014c. "Purchase for Progress. Final Consolidated Farmers' Organizations and Capacity Development Report (January 2009–December 2013)." WFP, Rome. https://www.wfp.org/publications/p4p-farmers-organizations-and-capacity-development-final-consolidated-report

WFP (World Food Programme). 2014d. "School Meals." WFP, Rome.

WFP (World Food Programme). 2014e. "Two Minutes on Climate Change and Hunger: A Zero Hunger World Needs Climate Resilience." November, Climate Resilience for Food Security Unit (OSZIR), Policy, Programme and Innovations Division, WFP, Rome.

WFP (World Food Programme). 2014f. "WFP Corporate Partnership Strategy 2014–2017: We Deliver Better Together." July, WFP, Rome. https://www.wfp.org/publications/wfp-corporate-partnership-strategy-2014–2017

WFP (World Food Programme). 2014g. "WFP Emergency Response Classifications." May 8, WFP, Rome. https://reliefweb.int/sites/reliefweb.int/files/resources/wfp262867.pdf

WFP (World Food Programme). 2015a. "Annual Evaluation Report for 2014." Office of Evaluation, May, WFP, Rome. https://www.wfp.org/publications/annual-evaluation-report-2014

WFP (World Food Programme). 2015b. "Background Paper: Country Strategic Plans." Informal Consultation, September 21, WFP, Rome.

WFP (World Food Programme). 2015c. "Disaster Risk Reduction Crucial for Meeting Future Hunger Challenges." March 11, WFP, Rome. https://www.wfp.org/news/disaster-risk-reduction-crucial-meeting-future-hunger-challenges

WFP (World Food Programme). 2015d. "Draft Paper on Building Resilience for Food Security and Nutrition." Informal Consultation, April 8, WFP, Rome.

WFP (World Food Programme). 2015e. "P4P Purchase for Progress: The Story. Connecting Farmers to Markets." February, WFP, Rome. https://www.wfp.org/publications/p4p-story-connecting-farmers-markets

WFP (World Food Programme). 2015f. "Two Minutes on Social Protection: Ending Hunger and Improving Nutrition." September, Safety Nets and Protection Unit (OSZIS), Policy and Programme Division, WFP, Rome. https://www.wfp.org/content/2015-two-minutes-social-protection

WFP (World Food Programme). 2015g. "Vulnerability Analysis and Mapping At a Glance." Food Security Analysis, WFP, Rome.

WFP (World Food Programme). 2015h. "WFP Funding in 2014." Issue No. 1, September. WFP, Rome.

WFP (World Food Programme). 2015i. "WFP Position Paper." World Humanitarian Summit, August, WFP, Rome. https://reliefweb.int/report/world/world-humanitarian-summit-wfp-position-paper

WFP (World Food Programme). 2015j. "The World Food Programme in 2014: Facts and Figures." WFP, Rome.

WFP (World Food Programme). 2016a. "Draft Update on the Financial Framework Review." Informal Consultation, April 1, WFP, Rome.

WFP (World Food Programme). 2016b. "Integrated Road Map: Positioning WFP for a Changing World." WFP, Rome.

WFP (World Food Programme). 2016c. "WFP Strategic Plan (2017–2021)." November 14, WFP/EB.2/2016/4-A/1/Rev.2, WFP, Rome. https://www.wfp.org/content/wfp-strategic-plan-2017-2021

WFP (World Food Programme). 2017a. "Contributions to WFP in 2016." Funding. Contributions by Year. https://www.wfp.org/funding/2016

WFP (World Food Programme). 2017b. "Counting the Beans—The True Cost of a Plate of Food Around the World." October 12, WFP, Rome. https://www.wfp.org/publications/2017-counting-beans-true-cost-plate-food-around-world

WFP (World Food Programme). 2017c. "Two Minutes to Learn about: School Meals." May, WFP, Rome. https://www.wfp.org/publications/2017-two-minutes-learn-about-school-meals

WFP (World Food Programme). 2017d. "WFP Strategic Plan (2017–2021)." July, WFP, Rome. https://www.wfp.org/publications/wfp-strategic-plan-2017-2021

WFP (World Food Programme). 2017e. "World Food Assistance 2017: Taking Stock and Looking Ahead." July 18, WFP, Rome. https://www.wfp.org/publications/2017-world-food-assistance-taking-stock-and-looking-ahead

WFP (World Food Programme). 2018a. "Private Sector Partnerships and Fundraising Strategy (2018–2021)." Second informal consultation, April 26, WFP, Rome. https://docs.wfp.org/api/documents/WFP-0000069587/download/

WFP (World Food Programme). 2018b. "Two Minutes on Climate Change and Hunger: A Zero Hunger World Needs Climate Resilience." November, Climate Resilience for Food Security Unit (OSZIR), WFP, Rome. https://docs.wfp.org/api/documents/WFP-0000009143/download/

WFP (World Food Programme). 2018c. "Update on the Integrated Road Map." WFP/EB.2/2018/5-A/1, Executive Board, Second Regular Session, Rome, November 26–9. https://docs.wfp.org/api/documents/WFP-0000099355/download/

WFP (World Food Programme). 2018d. "WFP Capacity Strengthening Supports Nations to End Hunger." Beyond the Annual Performance Report 2018 Series, November, WFP, Rome. https://docs.wfp.org/api/documents/WFP-0000110346/download/

WFP (World Food Programme). 2018e. "WFP Oversight Framework." Executive Summary: Vision and Framework for Oversight at WFP. Executive Board, Annual Session, Rome, June 18–22. https://docs.wfp.org/api/documents/0f2b776a0fd347259260dc10e2193ad7/download/

WFP (World Food Programme). 2018f. "What a 2°C and 4°C Warmer World Could Mean for Global Food Insecurity." https://docs.wfp.org/api/documents/WFP-0000072935/download/?_ga=2.93530077.1503022692.1614143510–1477752500.1613452108

WFP (World Food Programme). 2019a. "Annual Performance Report for 2018." June 7, WFP/ EB.A/2019/4-A/Rev.2, WFP Rome. https://docs.wfp.org/api/documents/WFP-0000104617/ download/

WFP (World Food Programme). 2019b. "Cash-based Transfers: January 2019 Update." https:// docs.wfp.org/api/documents/0d767a801449440286ab50684b5b5aea/download

WFP (World Food Programme). 2019c. "Changing Lives for Smallholder Farmers." Beyond the Annual Performance Report 2018 Series, November, WFP, Rome. https://docs.wfp.org/api/ documents/WFP-0000110345/download/

WFP (World Food Programme). 2019d. "Conflict-driven Hunger Worsens." January 28. https://www.wfp.org/news/conflict-driven-hunger-worsens

WFP (World Food Programme). 2019e. "Fact Sheet: Hunger & Conflict." June, WFP, Rome. https://docs.wfp.org/api/documents/WFP-0000105972/download/

WFP (World Food Programme) 2019f. "Flexible Historical Funding." June 19. https://www.wfp. org/publications/flexible-historical-funding

WFP (World Food Programme). 2019g. "For the Displaced and the Forgotten: The World Food Programme's Use of Flexible and Immediate Response Account Funding in 2018." World Food Programme Insight, May 31, WFP, Rome. https://insight.wfp.org/the-world-food-programme-wfp-s-use-of-flexible-and-ira-funding-in-2018-246cf88663d6

WFP (World Food Programme). 2019h. "WFP Management Plan (2020–2022)." Executive Board, Second regular session, Rome, November 18–21. http://www.fao.org/3/na714en/ na714en.pdf

WFP (World Food Programme). 2019i. "WFP—Year in Review 2018." WFP, Rome. https:// www.wfp.org/publications/wfp-year-review-2018

WFP (World Food Programme). 2019j. "World Food Programme: Humanitarian Development." https://docs.wfp.org/api/documents/WFP-0000110373/download/

WFP (World Food Programme). 2019k. "The World Food Programme: Saving Lives, Changing Lives." World Food Programme Insight, November 11, WFP, Rome. https://insight.wfp.org/ overview-1211270a8b06

WFP (World Food Programme). 2020a. "Annual Performance Report for 2019." WFP/EB.A/ 2020/4-A*, June 19. https://docs.wfp.org/ai/documents/WFP-0000115522/download

WFP (World Food Programme). 2020b. "Cash Transfers." https://www.wfp.org/cash-transfers

WFP (World Food Programme). 2020c. "Contributions to WFP: Comparative Figures and Five-Year Aggregate Ranking." As of November 15. https://docs.wfp.org/api/documents/ 3f66543adf5c482a95810d57a2b1518b/download

WFP (World Food Programme). 2020d. "Contributions to WFP: Comparative Figures by Donor Type." As of November 15. http://documents.wfp.org/stellent/groups/public/documents/ research/wfp245536.pdf

WFP (World Food Programme). 2020e. "Contributions to WFP by Programme Category." As of November 15. http://documents.wfp.org/stellent/groups/public/documents/research/wfp 216778.pdf

WFP (World Food Programme). 2020f. "COVID-19 Will Double Number of People Facing Food Crises Unless Swift Action is Taken." WFP, Rome, April 20. https://www.wfp.org/news/ covid-19-will-double-number-people-facing-food-crises-unless-swift-action-taken

WFP (World Food Programme). 2020g "Executive Board." https://executiveboard.wfp.or g/members-board

WFP (World Food Programme). 2020h. "Flexible Funding." https://www.wfp.org/flexible-funding

WFP (World Food Programme). 2020i. Food Aid Information System (FAIS). Database. http://www.wfp.org/fais/

WFP (World Food Programme). 2020j. "Food Assistance: Cash and In-Kind." https://www.wfp.org/food-assistance

WFP (World Food Programme). 2020k. "Food Assistance for Assets." https://www.wfp.org/food-assistance-for-assets

WFP (World Food Programme). 2020l. "Funding and Donors." http://www1.wfp.org/funding-and-donors

WFP (World Food Programme). 2020m. "Governance and Leadership." https://www.wfp.org/governance-and-leadership

WFP (World Food Programme). 2020n. "History." World Food Programme. Who We Are. https://www.wfp.org/history

WFP (World Food Programme). 2020o. "In-Kind Food Distribution." https://www.wfp.org/in-kind-food-distribution

WFP (World Food Programme). 2020p. "Non-governmental Organizations" https://www.wfp.org/non-governmental-organizations

WFP (World Food Programme). 2020q. "Overview." https://www.wfp.org/overview

WFP (World Food Programme). 2020r. "Partnering with WFP for NGOs." https://www.wfp.org/partnering-with-wfp-for-ngos

WFP (World Food Programme). 2020s. "Purchase for Progress." https://www.wfp.org/purchase-for-progress

WFP (World Food Programme). 2020t. "School Feeding." https://www.wfp.org/school-meals

WFP (World Food Programme). 2020u. "Smallholder Market Support." https://www.wfp.org/smallholder-market-support

WFP (World Food Programme). 2020v. 2019 in Review. Annual Evaluation Report. https://docs.wfp.org/api/documents/WFP-0000115255/download

WFP (World Food Programme). 2020w. "UN Humanitarian Air Service." https://www.wfp.org/unhas

WFP (World Food Programme). 2020x. "World Food Programme Feeding Strategy 2020–2030: A Chance for Every Schoolchild—Partnering to Scale Up School Health and Nutrition for Human Capital." January, WFP, Rome. https://docs.wfp.org/api/documents/WFP-0000112101/download/?_ga=2.52468712.1197888911.1613684103–1477752500.1613452108

WFP (World Food Programme) and GPPi (Global Public Policy Institute). 2015. "Strategic Evaluations Synthesis." Synthesis Report of the Evaluation Series of WFP's Emergency Preparedness and Response (2012–2015). Report No. OEV/2015/0210, Prepared by GPPi: Julia Steets and Andras Derzsi-Horvath. Commissioned by the WFP of Evaluation. https://documents.wfp.org/stellent/groups/public/documents/reports/wfp278692.pdf?_ga=1.158718963.875795177.1419468489

World Bank. 2012. "Global Food Crisis Response Program (GRFP): Progress and Lessons Learned." Board Report #74147, November 30, 2012, World Bank, Washington, DC. http://documents.worldbank.org/curated/en/960011468337870506/pdf/NonAsciiFileName0.pdf

World Bank. 2017. "Fact Sheet: The World Bank Group's Response to the Famine Crisis." Brief, last updated November 28. https://www.worldbank.org/en/topic/fragilityconflictviolence/brief/fact-sheet-the-world-bank-groups-response-to-the-famine-crisis

13

Perspectives Moving Forward

*Uma Lele, Manmohan Agarwal, Brian C. Baldwin,
and Sambuddha Goswami*

> The test of our progress is not whether we add more to the abundance of those who have much; it is whether we provide enough for those who have too little...
>
> Franklin D. Roosevelt, Inaugural Address, January 20, 1937[1]

Summary: Why and When of the Study

This study had been underway for several years and was completed just before COVID-19 crisis gripped the world. Several factors prompted the study. First, was a recognition that differentiation among developing countries was increasing, while seemingly a consensus about convergence was emerging in the literature. Not only sub-Saharan Africa (SSA), but also South Asia (SA) was falling behind in structural transformation: that is, in the decline in the share of agriculture and increase in productive employment in nonagriculture, particularly in manufacturing. Again, considerable differences were noticeable within and among regions: for example, in SA, Bangladesh was surging ahead while India's growth was beginning to slow, and similarly, Vietnam was surging ahead in Southeast Asia. Relatedly, the growing complexity of the development process and the consequent increasing specialization in the economics profession meant that agricultural economists were largely focused on specific determinants of smallholder productivity levels and growth in developing countries, and often within it, on component parts, such as research and extension or fertilizer subsidies. General economists, on the other hand, have focused on industrialization and there has been relatively little interaction between these sectoral specializations, in contrast to the early days of development economics. Second, external aid, particularly, from international organizations (IOs)—such as the World Bank, the Food and Agriculture Organization of the United Nations (FAO), CGIAR, the International Fund for Agricultural Development (IFAD), and the World Food Programme (WFP)—had played an active role in the areas of agricultural and rural development and food security until the end of the 1980s, but their roles had diminished, as developing countries had come into their own. We wanted to explore the reasons behind the change in the level and type of external support and the phenomenon of emerging countries.

All five IOs that we have focused on were established in the post-Second World War period. If anything, their relevance has increased, with growing demographic pressures, urbanization, climate change, and a humanitarian crisis of unprecedented proportion with

---

[1] See https://www.loc.gov/item/today-in-history/january-20/

Food for All: International Organizations and the Transformation of Agriculture. Uma Lele, Manmohan Agarwal, Brian C. Baldwin, and Sambuddha Goswami, Oxford University Press. © Uma Lele, Manmohan Agarwal, Brian C. Baldwin, and Sambuddha Goswami 2021.
DOI: 10.1093/oso/9780198755173.003.0014

the largest involuntary displacement of people since the Second World War. Most IOs, perhaps with the exception of the World Bank, however, are now strapped for resources. Furthermore, bringing the humanitarian crisis under control would require exceptional leadership from the superpowers that have contributed to the conflict and involuntary displacement, causing untold misery to millions of innocent households. Third, China's emergence as a superpower has changed the balance of power globally with its growing role in trade, aid, and foreign direct investment (FDI). In November 2020, China entered into the largest trade agreement with its neighbors, following the withdrawal of the United States, after Trump's election in 2016, from the Trans-Pacific Partnership. The previous Obama administration had helped to put the agreement together, after years of negotiations. At the time of the completion of this manuscript, neither the United States nor India had joined the Regional Comprehensive Economic Partnership agreement (RCEP), comprising the Association of Southeast Asian Nations (ASEAN), Australia, China, Japan, Korea, and New Zealand.

Also, the global architecture meticulously built on a liberal world order in the post-Second World War period under the United States' leadership has developed cracks. Donald Trump's election in 2016 made those cracks highly visible, reminding the world that US presidential elections have global consequences. Yet, those cracks already had been faintly visible during the Obama presidency. For outside observers, Obama's election was a tribute to the American democracy of unity in diversity, when after a 400-year history of slavery, the first Black man was voted into the White House. However, by Obama's own blunt admission in his new book, *A Promised Land*, his election, signifying the political power of the Black and Brown voters, rattled the white middle class (Obama 2020). They had already suffered from globalization with the loss of factory jobs, following China's entry into the global economy in the 1980s, paradoxically engineered by a Republican US president (Nixon), leading to China's entry into the World Trade Organization (WTO). China then became the world's largest supplier of manufactured goods. The Biden–Harris victory has assured the United States' multilateral reengagement, but it has also stressed the fragility of the international system, based on US election results. The continued sense of insecurity among the white middle class in the United States is reflected in the denial of the election results among a large portion of the 72 million Americans who voted for Trump in the 2020 election. It limits the degree of freedom of the Biden–Harris administration in foreign policy. In short, although Trump has lost the election, Trumpism has not ended and may well make it difficult for the new US administration to pursue bold pro-multilateral strategies in the areas of trade, aid, and climate change. The realignment of the balance of global economic power from North–South to East–West further complicates matters, if not making the return to the old-style multilateralism difficult.

The COVID-19 pandemic and the global economic slowdown have accelerated digitalization. That, in turn, has further exposed the inequities in global economic growth and the lack of access to health care and job security for millions in the working class, a result of growing within-country income inequalities, which are more acute in the United States than in Europe. Six individuals own half the stock in the stock market. Additionally, environmental challenges of climate change, soil degradation, water shortages, forest fires, and deforestation have been knocking on a few doors, and they are not confined to developing countries. California is a hotspot for water shortages, and California and Australia for forest fires, with the largest loss of biodiversity in Australia (Give2Asia 2020).

At the end of this inquiry, the global tragedy of COVID-19 arrived. It hit the poorest and the working class the most, but also highlighted the triumph of the rapidly emerging science in the discovery of vaccines in record time. It dispelled many of the myths created in four years of the Trump administration. The frequently assailed "deep state" played a positive role in establishing public–private partnerships, which led to the manufacturing of vaccines—although with the right leadership at the top, it could have done much more to promote health messages based on science. Immigrant entrepreneurs from Lebanon and Turkey played key roles in the discovery of the Pfizer and Moderna vaccines. Global supply chains expedited vaccine production and delivery. With differential performance on COVID-19 control, even among G20 countries, rapid access of the world's population to the vaccines has now reached urgency both on humanitarian grounds and as the only way to achieve global economic recovery.

On the downside, the rapid spread of COVID-19 has been accompanied by the rapid spread of hunger including in the United States, the richest country and one of the most productive in agriculture. Social media have played a key role in spreading misinformation, leading to large-scale rejection of common-sense solutions, such as the use of masks, social distancing, and other precautions needed to contain COVID-19. Social media's counterproductive role in the spread of misinformation has undermined science, facts, and evidence. It has implications for the containment of the current and future pandemics, as well as the realization of Sustainable Development Goals (SDGs), and more broadly, about the role of regulation of private platforms to achieve public good.

In response to these challenges, or perhaps because of them, the global community has been setting high goals in the form of SDGs, the Paris Climate Change Accord, and the United Nations Secretary-General's Food Systems Summit in 2021. The latter calls for a total transformation of the global food system to achieve environmentally sustainable food production, and nutritious, equitable, healthy food consumption, broadly defined as a sustainable food system, within the planetary limits of growth. The Summit aims to accelerate achievement of Sustainable Development Goal 2 (SDG2) and other related SDGs, which are currently off track, to reach the stated goals by 2030 (UN 2020e).

Against this background, in this study, we have explored the progress to date on food and nutrition security. What does it tell us about how the challenges of hunger and food insecurity have been addressed over the decades? How has the state of knowledge influenced what decisions were made? Were the emerging opportunities fully exploited to tackle the challenges? How were lessons of experience used to modify strategies to help transform the food system? And, equally important, what do we need to do differently than in the past to achieve the new high goals?

In the preceding chapters, we have documented that the Green Revolution was both necessary and timely to address the recurring food shortages in developing countries, particularly in Asia in the 1960s and 1970s. The focus was on productivity growth and calorie needs for human consumption. How did "movements" affect analysis? The environmental costs of land use changes (deforestation and biodiversity loss) were not counted in productivity measures, even though the environmental movement had taken hold prior to the United Nations Conference on Environment and Development (UNCED) in 1992. Land conversion to oil palm in Indonesia, and livestock and soybean production in the Amazon, are part of the quarter of greenhouse gas (GHG) emissions which now come from agriculture. Focus shifted from agricultural productivity growth to improved nutrition around 2007–8, due to the advocacy of the international nutrition community (a nutrition movement?), starting with a series of articles in *Lancet*. A more balanced diet is now considered desirable, consisting largely of plant-based foods—for example, in the EAT-*Lancet* Commission report (Willett et al. 2019)—including pulses, livestock, fruit, vegetables, and dairy. What is clear from the evidence, however, is that higher income has not necessarily translated into better nutrition. On the contrary, evidence is mounting that often higher income is associated with decline in diet quality, leading to obesity and increased incidence of disease. Furthermore, higher production does not ensure the poor have access to food. These various knowledge gaps between aspirations and reality in the spheres of productivity growth and GHG emissions, between income and nutrition, and between production and nutrition need to be closed. Yet, our knowledge on how to close these gaps is limited.[2] Also, translation of existing knowledge into practice is often well behind the state of knowledge, which means there is huge scope to improve outcomes.

Reforms have occurred differentially across developing countries, including in achieving diversified food production and linking it to the quantity and quality of nutritious food consumption, particularly among poor populations. Such an outcome is complexly related to the process of structural transformation: that is, whether productive employment is created in the agricultural or the nonagricultural sector, and if it generates enough income for households to afford access to nutritious foods through the food system. Structural transformation has lagged in many countries, but even where transformation has occurred, as in the now advanced countries, environmental management has been inadequate and nutritious healthy food is not always consumed. This situation suggests that the past notion of structural transformation is in need of refinement to account for new concerns based on accumulated evidence. In the rest of this chapter, we bring these pieces of the puzzle together and indicate gaps in our knowledge and gaps in the application of the existing knowledge to achieve sustainable food systems for all.

FAO and the World Health Organization (WHO) have defined a healthy diet as a dietary pattern that meets a person's nutritional needs (macronutrients and micronutrients), ensures optimal growth and development, and promotes health across the lifespan, specific to their gender, age, physical activity level, and physiological state. It must supply adequate calories for energy balance and include a wide variety of high-quality and safe foods across a diversity of food groups to provide the various macronutrients, micronutrients, and other food components needed to lead an active and healthy and enjoyable life. Healthy diets should include: at least 400 g of fruit and vegetables per day (excluding starchy roots); legumes, nuts, and whole grains; energy intake balanced with expenditure (on average 2,000–2,500 kcal per person), with less than 10 percent of total energy intake from free sugars (FAO 2004; FAO and WHO 2019; WHO 2020a).

The concept of "food systems" is relatively recent. FAO introduced the concept in its *State of the Food and Agriculture (SOFA)* report in 2013 (FAO 2013). The Second Nutrition Conference in 2014 and subsequent reports of the High Level Panel of Experts (HLPE) on Food Security and Nutrition elaborated on the concepts—for example, the HLPE reports on "Food Losses and Waste in the Context of Sustainable Food Systems" and "Nutrition and Food Systems," and the various *Global Nutrition Reports (GNRs)* have refined these ideas

---

[2] Alston, MacEwan, and Okrent argued:

> Well-directed taxes on calories, sugar, or fat might be economically efficient ways of reducing obesity, as might regulation of television advertising, food labeling policies, or other nutrition education programs. Policies that induce the food industry to redesign foods may be more effective than policies that rely on inducing response by consumers. Farm subsidies and nutrition policies are largely irrelevant to the issue and modifying agricultural R&D [research and development] policy is not an economical way to curb obesity. However, preventive approaches directed at children show some promise. (Alston, MacEwan, and Okrent 2016, 443)

(FAO 2013; HLPE 2014, 2017; IFPRI 2014, 2015; 2016; Development Initiatives 2017, 2018; GNR 2020). The food systems concept broadly includes all actors, ranging from producers to consumers, and their interactions influencing food security and nutrition outcomes. It considers the increased role of supermarkets, multinationals, and FDI at one end of the spectrum and traditional small-scale, informal food systems at the other end. Among these, the HLPE (2017) Framework has been, by far, the most widely referred to by IOs, and FAO introduced a dashboard in June 2020 based on the HLPE recommendation (https:// foodsystemsdashboard.org).

In a paper on food systems, Brouwer, McDermott, and Ruben (2020) noted that 32 international reports were produced in a period of less than a decade that use different concepts of food systems. They discussed how the concept of food system has evolved, distinguishing different pathways for food system transformation. They outlined the analytical underpinnings, implications for multi-stakeholder governance, and how those concepts deal with critical trade-offs between multiple food system objectives—namely, nutrition and health, environmental sustainability, and resilience—and social inclusion, among others. So, the objective function has become increasingly complex. And yet, the human capital and the institutional capacity, including regulatory systems to address the complexity, have not kept pace with the challenges in developing countries, particularly in low-income countries (LICs) and low-middle-income countries (LMICs) with the greatest incidence of poverty and hunger. Furthermore, the extent to which these concepts have been embraced by developing country members of the UN System, as a holistic policy-making device, or by their citizens as practice to be applied to their daily diets, remains to be seen, and it is impetus for the UN Secretary General's 2021 Food Summit (UN 2020d). The idea is to prompt a bottom-up demand.

The definition of food security was first introduced at the 1974 World Food Conference (UN 1975). Its four pillars of availability, access, utilization, and stability have taken years to be widely debated and understood, with the focus in most LICs and LMICs still being largely on production and, perhaps, some on access. The latter came into currency as Sen's work on entitlements influenced the UN System and Right to Food movements through nongovernmental organizations (NGOs) (see Sen [1981]), and in response to the excessive stringencies of the structural adjustment period of the 1980s. So, institutional infrastructure for safety nets was established and/or strengthened as part of the public infrastructure. However, safety nets are still weak. Where the fiscal base is weak, countries are dependent on foreign aid, and even in large developing countries like Brazil, India, and Indonesia, there is scope for better targeting, for avoiding leakages, and for increasing efficiency.

The concept of sustainability of food systems is even more recent, although the idea of sustainability has been around at least since the Brundtland Report, and perhaps, much earlier in Hicks' *Value and Capital*; for example, income is what can be consumed sustainably, with many conceptual interpretations, such as intergenerational sustainability, sustainability, and equity, and many challenges for measurement and operationalization of the concept (Hicks 1939; WCED 1987). An excellent recent paper by Béné et al. noted that the concept of sustainability, "although widely used by all the different communities of practice, remains poorly defined, and applied in different ways and usually based on a relatively narrow interpretation" (Béné et al. 2019, 116). In so doing, the authors argued—and we concur—that attempts "to equate or subsume healthy diets within sustainability in the context of food system may be misleading and need to be challenged. . . . [T]rade-offs between different dimensions of food system sustainability are unavoidable and need to be navigated in an explicit manner when developing or implementing sustainable food system initiatives" (Béné et al. 2019, 116).

Agricultural economics literature has extensively discussed the growth of value chains, starting with the supermarket revolution (Reardon et al. 2003; Reardon, Timmer, and Minten 2012), but the literature exploring impacts is generally new for supermarkets and other value chain-related revolutions on (1) dietary transition; (2) equity in terms of changes in rural and urban employment (for example, impacts of scale economies); (3) environment (from increased processing, packaging, transportation, refrigeration); and (4) energy use, and thus, more generally, on "sustainable" food systems (Reardon et al. 2012). Additionally, in the context of the COVID-19 pandemic, there is much reevaluation of the benefits of the emerging food systems in terms of sustainability, as illustrated by the recent World Bank paper, which stressed the benefits of *deconcentration of marketed surpluses*, traceability, and a more transparent market information system, owing to digitalization, whereas in the past, scale economies were considered inevitable and efficient (Lampietti, Elabed, and Schroeder 2020). In short, we will need a universally understood, easily accepted, and monitorable concept of a sustainable food system that reflects the diversity of circumstances. Developing countries will have to embrace these ideas and make them their own, and they will have to explore the full implications of sustainability, including trade-offs. Thus, much work remains to be done to meet the ambition of the proposed Food System Summit 2021, given the gap between past efforts and future ambition.

Outline of the Chapter

In the first section, we report some **early known impacts of the COVID-19 pandemic tragedy** on the poverty–food security–nutrition–health nexus and its implications for action.

In the second section on outcome indicators, we summarize **what the various indicators suggest the world had achieved prior to the pandemic** in reducing poverty; increasing food security and nutrition; reducing infant and child mortality, stunting, wasting, anemia; and improving gender empowerment since progress on the Millennium Development Goals (MDGs) began to be monitored. Already visible was differing state capacity to address agricultural productivity growth and achieving food security and nutrition, one of the important subgoals of SDG2 (see Box 4.4). To learn lessons, our retrospective review dates back 75 years to when President Roosevelt led the establishment of liberal world order. In 1941, by co-signing the Atlantic Charter with Churchill, he created the framework of the liberal world order. He took the initiative with the Hot Springs Conference in 1943, for the creation of FAO and the UN. The Bretton Woods Conference was held during July 1–22, 1944. The Bretton Woods institutions were established in October 1945, after Roosevelt's death in April 1945. President Truman followed up on many of these initiatives and more. The General Agreement on Tariffs and Trade (GATT) was established in 1947, with a legal agreement between many countries, and had the purpose of promoting international trade by reducing or eliminating trade barriers, such as tariffs or quotas. Its purpose was the "substantial reduction of tariffs and other trade barriers and the elimination of discriminatory treatment in international commerce . . . on a reciprocal and advantageous basis" (GATT 1947, 2, 22).

In the third section on agricultural productivity growth, **we report how agricultural total factor productivity (TFP) growth, albeit without the measurement of environmental**

losses or gains, has performed across regions and countries over time, using various measures. Productivity growth is vital to food security and nutrition and to structural transformation. There are huge differences in aggregate productivity growth performance across regions and countries, and by and large, countries that have done poorly in agricultural productivity growth have also lagged behind in structural transformation. As we have pointed out, however, structural transformation has not assured transformational change in food systems for the better.

Furthermore, the proposition that small farms perform better than large farms in productivity has been dispelled. How productivity is measured has also changed over time from partial to total productivity. Recent evidence suggests that all sizes of farms can achieve productivity growth and success, but for smallholders to be productive requires the functioning of the factor and product markets, as well as strong public policy where markets do not function or where small farmers have limited access to information, knowledge, inputs, and markets. Productivity growth measures have not included changes in the quality or quantity of natural resources (Fuglie et al. 2020). This is beginning to change, but this analysis is in the early stages of development and not yet a useful guide for moving toward sustainability.

Finally, we present extensive evidence of **premature deindustrialization** in developing countries: that is, their share of the industrial sector in gross domestic productivity (GDP) peaks at earlier levels of per capita GDP than is true for industrialized countries.

In the fourth section, we describe the **overall financial flows** to developing countries and, specifically, to food and agriculture, and the current woefully low levels of investment and low share of official development assistance (ODA) in these flows, and why ODA needs to be used strategically to leverage greater public and private investments in food and agriculture and related sectors. We summarize the contribution of the five major IOs—the World Bank, FAO, WFP, CGIAR, and IFAD—to food security, productivity growth, structural transformation, and global governance. Together, they commit about US$21.3 billion annually in the form of financial flows and technical assistance, of which nearly US$8 billion was in the form of emergency assistance in 2018–19. A recent study, titled "Growing Better: Ten Critical Transitions to Transform Food and Land Use," estimated needed resources of US$300–50 billion annually for the transformation of food and land use systems to 2030 or a total of US$2 trillion. The study envisages support from multilateral banks, bilateral donors, philanthropic contributions, and the private sector, among others (FOLU 2019). Researchers working on the Ceres2030 project, on the other hand, suggest a much more modest amount of needed resources: "donor governments must spend an additional US$14 billion a year on average until 2030 to end hunger, double the incomes of 545 million small-scale farmers, and limit agricultural emissions in line with the Paris climate agreement" (Ceres2030 2020). This means roughly doubling the amount of aid given for food security and nutrition each year, and must also be accompanied by an additional US$19 billion a year from the budgets of LICs and middle-income countries (MICs).

These estimates are not comparable. They have different stated objectives and different models of underlying estimates, but each suggests substantially larger than current resource flows to developing countries of total annual ODA of US$150 billion to all sectors.

With climate change, growing environmental pressures, the need for healthy consumption for all, and the range of new technologies that have come on stream, which we list in Chapter 2, substantial investments are needed in human and institutional capital and physical infrastructure to realize the potential of technical change, even taking into account other private financial resources and national investments to achieve sustainable production.

In the fifth section on global governance of food and agriculture, we discuss **the role of the G20 in the global architecture for food and agriculture.** Whereas they started with a promising start at the beginning of the 2008 financial crisis, as a collective, their contribution has not increased relative to their potential. We explain why.

Finally, in the sixth section, **we outline the role of a grouping of 54 industrial and emerging countries** for which the Organisation for Economic Co-operation and Development (OECD) monitors agricultural policies, to show that changes in their policies would offer scope for improvement in the overall policy environment and investment climate at the global level of between US$500 billion and US$700 billion annually. The World Bank, in collaboration with FAO, OECD, and developing countries, has initiated a project to repurpose subsidies to achieve a triple win of increased efficiency, more targeted benefits, and better environmental outcomes (personal communication, Madhur Gautam, World Bank Lead Economist with Agriculture Global Practice, with Uma Lele, December 21, 2020).

Experience of the last five decades shows our understanding of the growing complexity of achieving food security and nutrition, with the multiplicity of systemic risks presenting a need for us to adopt a system's view, which enables horizontal and vertical integration. On the other hand, there has been an increased tendency to simplify solutions in bits and pieces to strip away complexity, interactions, externalities, and spillovers. With reforms at the country level, resources could be released and reallocated for greater, more equitable, and hopefully, more sustainable global outcomes enshrined in the SDGs—goals to be achieved by 2030. SDG2 is presented in Box 4.4.

COVID-19: An Extraordinary Tragedy and the Imperative to Build Better

International Monetary Fund (IMF) Managing Director Kristalina Georgieva noted in her plenary speech on October 15, 2020,[3] "an economic calamity that will make the world economy 4.4% smaller this year and strip an estimated $11 trillion of output by next year." She also noted "untold human desperation in the face of huge disruption and rising poverty for the first time in decades." She continued, "We face...a *Long Ascent for the global economy*: a climb that will be difficult, uneven, uncertain—and prone to setbacks," but suggested, "we will have a chance to address some persistent problems—low productivity, slow growth, high inequalities, a looming climate crisis. We can do better than build back the pre-pandemic world—we can *build forward* to a world that is more resilient, sustainable, and inclusive."

IMF's World Economic Outlook (WEO) report in October 2020 noted "global growth is projected to be –4.4 percent in 2020," an upward revision of 0.8 percentage points, compared to the June update, as there were signs of a stronger recovery in the third quarter, offset partly by downgrades in some emerging and developing economies. In 2021, growth is projected to rebound to 5.2 percent, 0.2 percentage points below the June projection, but

---

[3] See "A New Bretton Woods Moment by Kristalina Georgieva, IMF Managing Director, Washington, DC": https://www.imf.org/en/News/Articles/2020/10/15/sp101520-a-new-bretton-woods-moment

with a decline in GDP per capita in emerging countries, except for China, more than in industrial countries (IMF 2020d, xv).

IMF estimated the cumulative COVID-19-related output loss over 2020 and 2021 could be around US$9 trillion, the greatest downturn since the Great Depression of 1929 (Gopinath 2020). IMF's WEO update of June 2020 estimated the Latin America and Caribbean (LAC) region will shrink by 9.4 percent in 2020, nearly four percentage points worse than the April projection. SSA's projected GDP trade, expected to decline by 3.2 percent in 2020, is double the contraction predicted in April of 1.6 percent. On average, per capita incomes across the region will fall by 5.5 percent in 2020, to levels last seen nearly a decade ago. This will likely lead to more poverty and widen income inequality, as lockdowns disproportionately affect informal sector workers and small- and medium-sized companies in the services sectors. Asia's economic output in 2022 is expected to be about 5 percent lower than the level predicted before the crisis, and this estimated gap is much larger, if we exclude China, where economic activity has already started to rebound (IMF 2020b). Furthermore, IMF notes that "support from all development partners is essential to address the sizable financing needs, including debt relief for the most vulnerable countries," including particularly those in Africa (IMF 2020a, v).

China is the only developing country that has achieved a positive GDP growth (CGTN 2020). Since then, IMF's April 2021 forecast suggested global prospects are looking better one year into the pandemic, albeit highly uncertain. The latest WEO places growth at 6 percent for 2021, compared to 2020's unprecedented contraction of –3.3 percent. Recovery is, by and large, dependent on vaccination globally, and the lack of access to vaccines is making recovery hard to imagine for some countries, while others are making good progress. Dr. Malhar Nabar, Division Chief of the World Economic Studies Division in IMF's Research Department, in a podcast, described these divergent recoveries as a big concern. Two important messages from this section are, first, the growing differentiation between China and the rest of the developing world, and second, the vulnerability of the working class—those who do not have the luxury of working from home—to pandemics. And this phenomenon prevails throughout the world, a result of growing structural inequalities, weak social protection, and different degrees of political will and state capacity to address these issues.

Economists from the International Food Policy Research Institute (IFPRI) have argued that key elements are impacts on labor supply; effects of social distancing; shifts in demand from services involving close contact; increases in the cost of logistics in food and other supply chains; and reductions in savings and investment (Laborde, Martin, and Vos 2020). The fastest, most effective responses have come from countries in East Asia, in addition to China: that is, South Korea, Taiwan, Singapore, and in Oceania, New Zealand. The wealthiest nation has not been the most effective in protecting its working class from COVID-19. Going forward, a well-functioning public health system and adequate social protection are critical—and the reasons for and consequences of not acting expeditiously need to be well understood.

Historian Ramachandra Guha (2020) has called COVID-19 a sixfold tragedy that is still unfolding: a medical crisis, an economic crisis, a humanitarian crisis (part of a broader social crisis), a psychological crisis, governance crises, and a crisis in democracy itself. The multiplicity of crises raises more fundamental questions about development strategy than did the 2006–7 financial crisis.

The big tension since the Reagan–Thatcher period, over the last 40 years, has been about whether incentives to the rich, as "job creators," will achieve broad-based growth, or whether distribution of benefits directly to the needy is necessary. In the post-structural adjustment period, there has been a growing international consensus, including, particularly, among Bretton Woods institutions that were at the forefront of the Washington Consensus, about the need to balance incentives to the rich to create jobs with direct distribution to the poor by actively promoting social safety nets (World Bank 2012). Social safety nets are now widely accepted and promoted. Yet, the already acute income inequality has worsened in the COVID-19 pandemic. More than 50 percent of the stock value on Wall Street was owned by only six individuals at the end of 2020. The COVID-19 pandemic has exposed many of the weaknesses in the existing pattern of growth.

Poorest people throughout the world are affected more by COVID-19 than the well-off. The stimulus packages and financial policies of low interest rates and easy money, which industrial countries have provided, are based on important lessons that policymakers learned from the 2008 financial crisis: act quickly and decisively. At the same time, there has been disjuncture between the real economies and the stock market. COVID-19 has also highlighted that universal health services are needed, including an agile, responsive, evidence-based public health system essential to delivering, including to the poor and the most vulnerable, rapidly and effectively—particularly when spillovers of communicable disease are substantial, knowledge about the disease evolves with the spread of the disease, and the spread needs to be contained speedily. In addition to China, relatively more democratic East Asian countries, including Taiwan, South Korea, and New Zealand in Oceania, have shown this effectively, as have countries such as Germany and Italy—and in the latter case, even after a substantial initial setback. The United States, the richest country in the world with a sophisticated medical infrastructure, has lacked a public health system, as have developing countries like India.

The COVID-19 pandemic has also brought home the universal nature of the health and economic crises. No country is spared. Yet, economies in SSA are the hardest hit, being affected not only by the health and social distancing impacts, but also by lower commodity prices and declines in remittances, as noted by Laborde, Martin, and Vos (2020). They also estimate that, globally, almost 150 million people are projected to fall into extreme poverty and food insecurity. Other estimates differ from theirs, which Laborde, Martin, and Vos (2020) argued are a result of less refined analysis than theirs.

Millions of poor people worldwide have lost their jobs; 25 million in the United States, of whom 6 million had regained their jobs by mid-July 2020. An estimated 288 million migrants of the 600 to 700 million rural residents in China (Wang et al. 2020), and an estimated 56 million migrants in India had to return home (Lele, Bansal, and Meenakshi 2020). With the exception of some industrial countries, such as Canada, Germany, and Denmark, with strong social safety nets, they have operated well below their capacity. In much of the rest of the world, the poor have very limited or no social safety nets, no unemployment insurance, no furloughs or emergency payments. Almost all are paid on a per day or per month basis (so, no work means no income).

As poor households depend mainly on their labor for income, they face the tightest income constraint, and a trade-off between hunger and risk of exposure to the virus, stressing the urgent need for social safety nets (Ravallion 2020). Even before the COVID-19 pandemic, our research presented in earlier chapters showed that SDG indicators on poverty reduction and decline in hunger show little relationship. In 2010, the World Bank declared a goal to end poverty (MDG Targets 1.1: "To halve the proportion of people whose daily income is less than $1.25" and 1.3: "To halve the proportion of individuals suffering from hunger in the period between 1990 and 2015").[4] Whereas poverty declined by two-thirds, mostly in Asia, incidence of hunger, measured mainly as a calorie gap, declined by only 256 million using FAO's Prevalence of Undernourished (PoU) and, indeed, the downward trend in hunger turned in an upward direction in 2015, with a reported 821 million hungry, even before COVID-19 was detected. How firm are the hunger numbers? FAO substantially revised its hunger estimates in 2020, but not for the first time. The revisions were in two respects: based on new survey data going back 10 years, FAO revised China's estimate downward, as having reached less than 2 percent of the hungry population, meaning, technically, China reported no more hunger (FAO et al. 2020, 5–6). FAO, on the other hand, revised African hunger upward, so that by 2030, it was estimated that 412 million would be undernourished, compared to 204 million undernourished by 2030 in SA (FAO et al. 2020, 11, table 2). The revisions, described subsequently, do not incorporate the effects of the COVID-19 pandemic, but they highlight the lack of affordability of nutritious diets for a large majority of the population.

Fanzo et al. (2020) have advocated a dashboard approach, and FAO formally adopted this approach in June 2020. Yet, major data gaps exist on actual food consumption. The incidence of hunger has increased since the COVID-19 pandemic, with extensive losses of jobs associated with adherence to social distancing measures and other containment measures that countries have adopted.[5] Social distancing is next to impossible in crowded slums of LICs, but also in low-income neighborhoods in New York or New Jersey. The poor have limited savings and little or no access to institutional finance (Baye 2020; Jones, Egger, and Santos 2020). Lack of access of small businesses to finance is a phenomenon throughout the developing world. With their limited access to the health care infrastructure and the type of jobs they hold, which requires them to work in the field rather than at a desk, the so-called essential workers are more exposed to infections, particularly as deadly as COVID-19 (Lele, Bansal, and Meenakshi 2020). So, in the short run, there is a huge trade-off in protecting health and earning a living.

Studies in China show zero income for migrant wage earners in the month of February, with substantial declines in spending on food (56 percent), children's education, and health. The specter of undernourished men, women, and children walking scores of miles across states to reach their homes in India has been difficult to watch. The situation for labor in India is worse than in China, because with three decades of strong growth, China had already met all MDGs by 2010, whereas India still bears a third of the global burden of hunger and malnutrition, a higher than average level of the world's stunted children, and a growing incidence of noncommunicable diseases (NCDs), particularly, diabetes and cancers, increasing the population's vulnerability to COVID-19.

Agricultural production, and indeed, agricultural trade, as a whole, has held up better during the COVID-19 pandemic than it did during the food crisis in 2007, as discussed in

---

[4] See MDG Monitor for targets, https://www.mdgmonitor.org/mdg-1-eradicate-poverty-hunger/.

The World Bank's Millennium Development Goals website declared for MDG1: "The world achieved Goal 1 five years ahead of schedule. In 2010, an estimated 21% of people in the developing world lived at or below $1.25 a day—down from 43% in 1990."

The site further indicates that only "54% of developing countries have met or are on track to meet the goal of cutting extreme poverty in half" (https://www5.worldbank.org/mdgs/poverty_hunger.html)

[5] The Alliance for a Green Revolution in Africa (AGRA) reported multiple shocks (the COVID-19 pandemic and containment measures, armed conflict, and insecurity) in many parts of the African continent, causing severe disruptions to agricultural farming systems with devastating impacts on affected populations. These shocks have severely affected the functioning of food markets, among other impacts, disrupting the movement of food from surplus to deficit areas (AGRA 2020).

Chapter 3, in part because the pandemic has been largely a demand shock, with occasional disruptions in supply chains, whereas the 2007 crisis, which continued until 2012, was primarily a supply shock. Global trade increased threefold from 2000 to 2016, and most countries are more dependent on agricultural imports today than 20 years ago (Schmidhuber and Qiao 2020). So, observers worry that disruptions caused by COVID-19 could trigger a repeat of the food crisis of 2007–8, when a sharp rise in prices was exacerbated by panicking governments imposing export bans. In contrast, supplies on the global markets in 2020 have been abundant. There are many more exporters and importers, so competition is stiff and international shipping costs have diminished (Schmidhuber and Qiao 2020). Torero (2020) confirms this observation. Also, in 2020, fewer countries have imposed export bans, as compared to 2007–12 (like Vietnam did on rice). The message to keep supplies flowing that was learned in the 2007–8 crisis sees echoes throughout the world. Thus, although there is less cause for worry on the trade front, with climate change, the global food situation can turn around quickly if there are successive droughts in major commodity-exporting countries, as happened during the 2007–12 crisis (Torero 2020). And, except for the Agricultural Market Information System (AMIS), an initiative started in 2010 to improve market information, and the small Global Agriculture and Food Security Program (GAFSP) to meet the investment deficit, established following the food crisis, not much has changed for the better. These initiatives, while limited in scope, show that, with the collective political will exercised by the G20, which we discuss later, much more can be accomplished going forward.

"Remittance flows into low-income and fragile states represent a lifeline that supports households as well as provides much-needed tax revenue" (Sayeh and Chami 2020, 16). Remittance flows in 2018 to LICs and fragile countries reached US$350 billion, exceeding FDI, portfolio investment, and foreign aid as the single most important source of income from abroad. According to the World Bank, remittance flows are expected to drop 20 percent, a fall of about US$100 billion in 2020 over 2019 (Sayeh and Chami 2020, 17). For small countries most dependent on migration, the drop has been as high as 40 percent (Emont 2020). Such a drop "is likely to heighten economic, fiscal, and social pressures on governments of these countries already struggling to cope even in normal times" (Sayeh and Chami 2020, 16).

Evolution of trade has been more complex. According to a 2019 McKinsey Global Institute report:

Goods-producing value chains have become less trade-intensive...Between 2007 and 2017, exports declined from 28.1 to 22.5 percent of gross output in goods-producing value chains.

Cross-border services are growing more than 60 percent faster than trade in goods, and they generate far more economic value than traditional trade statistics capture...[There are at least] three uncounted aspects [of service trade] made (the value-added services contribute to exported goods, the intangibles companies send to foreign affiliates, and free digital services made available to global users). National statistics attribute 23 percent of all trade to services. (Lund et al. 2019)

Yet, with declining commodity prices, commodity exporters have faced growing trade deficits and increased indebtedness. Also, in Africa, rapid population growth has cut into the per capita growth in agricultural productivity and GDP. Additionally, conflict and climate change have been aggravating the problem of increased incidence of hunger around the world, since 2015, with a growing demand for humanitarian assistance, even without considering the effect of the pandemic, according to joint publications of FAO, IFAD, the United Nations Children's Fund (UNICEF), WFP, and WHO (FAO et al. 2018, 2019).

Impacts of Pandemic Could Have Been Minimized

Some form of a pandemic was fully anticipated and could have been contained by investing a small fraction of the lost GDP in preparation, with a high return on investment and avoidance of much human suffering.[6] Experts are already predicting future pandemics, due to growing population densities, forest clearing, urbanization, and growing interaction between wildlife and human population. There is a lesson for preparedness to deal with those coming down the pike—among other things, the need for much stronger health systems with universal access to health, if not on ethical grounds, then because of the infectious nature of COVID-19 (and other viruses), which hit the least protected the greatest.

How Is COVID-19 Different than Other Pandemics?

Like the 1918 influenza pandemic, but unlike the more recent 2014–16 Ebola virus or the 2009 H1N1 "swine flu" outbreaks that became regional pandemics, COVID-19 is a world-wide phenomenon. Unlike severe acute respiratory syndrome (SARS), recognized in 2003, it is more infectious, with yet unknown effects on the human body (WHO 2020d). Rapid globalization and increased travel and communication have helped COVID spread more quickly. Unlike the past food or financial crisis, there is also huge uncertainty about both the response to policy actions, such as the success in "bending the curve," and the emergence of second and third waves. China and Singapore are experiencing second waves, and there have been small recurrences in New Zealand. Therefore, the importance of vigilance, trust in government, broad knowledge in the population, and a scientific approach to the control of COVID-19 involving all stakeholders—the scientific community, government at all levels, citizens, and the private sector—that has involved shutting down entire cities, countries, and sectors; staying at home; movement restrictions; contact tracing; testing;

---

[6] In 2005, President George W. Bush unveiled an ambitious US$7.1 billion plan to ready the United States for a possible pandemic. It called for early detection, international cooperation, stockpiling of vaccines and medical equipment, and public education about pandemic prevention (Charatan 2005). The Bank approved a Global Program on Avian Influenza Control and Human Pandemic Preparedness and Response (GPAI) in January 2006, a horizontal Adaptable Program Loan (APL) that allowed for use of up to US$500 million (extended to US$1 billion in June 2009) to finance national avian influenza control and human pandemic preparedness projects. The Independent Evaluation Group (IEG) report on "Responding to Global Public Bads" demonstrated the tremendous convening power of the Bank to mobilize support, but also how the World Bank struggles to continue to support important global agendas. "Following the example of the Bank's successful shift in approach to natural disasters, moving from a responsive approach using emergency instruments to one that favors preemptive risk reduction and risk management through regular country programs and operations" may be the way to achieve success (IEG 2013, viii). In 2015, Bill Gates gave a TED Talk on pandemics and the Obama administration briefed the incoming Trump administration through convening US expert panels just before its departure (Gates 2015; *PBS News Hour* 2020). The IEG report recognized the high convening capacity of the Bank but also noted that "once the spotlight has moved on, particularly for issues that do not fit neatly into existing institutional structures and strategies," the Bank is unable to sustain this interest on a long-term basis (IEG 2013, 47).

diagnosis; and treatment are of paramount importance to gain time and devise more specific strategies. Full economic activity cannot realistically resume until and unless the virus is under control, and business, labor, and consumers have confidence that returning to work and spending their hard-earned income is safe again (Taylor 2020).

A related and quite unanticipated tragedy highlighted by the pandemic is the growing hostility of some key advanced industrial countries' leaders, including in the United States and the United Kingdom, toward science and evidence, and an unwillingness to learn from other more successful countries in their crisis mitigation. Thus, they could no longer be seen as role models, as in the past. *The Economist* describes the United Kingdom's response as a "bad response, badly handled" (*Economist* 2020b). The Biden victory in the United States will almost certainly change the state of affairs there, but with two-thirds of the 70+ million voters questioning even the 2020 presidential election outcome, the road ahead for evidence-based policy, including vigorous action on climate change mitigation, will not be easy in the United States. The disjuncture between the scientific approach and politics is strident in the United States, whether it relates to the response to the pandemic at home, contributions to the WHO, or withdrawal from the Paris Climate Change Accord and multilateral trade agreements. It is symptomatic of the current malaise of global cooperation, while global challenges requiring global cooperation are accumulating (see, for example, Friedman and Plumer 2020; Joseph 2020).

Notwithstanding the deprivation, there are also scores of inspiring stories of human spirit—a 15-year-old girl in India bicycling over 700 miles to bring her sick father home, riding on the back of her bicycle (Gettleman and Raj 2020), and scores of health workers and other "essential workers," including migrants, serving their own or adopted societies at substantial risk to their health and the health of their families.

Who would have imagined that not just China, but small countries in the East Asia and Pacific region (EAP), like Taiwan, South Korea, Singapore, and New Zealand, having quickly implemented "test, trace, and treat," would be able to contain the disease while it proliferated in highly developed countries, exposing the countries' long-standing structural weaknesses of income and wealth disparities, and exercise of individual freedom over social responsibility?

Important questions about trust in leaders and public institutions, and relatedly, political leadership, reliable information versus opinion and rumors (often propagated via social media), not to mention state capacity—issues which were already under threat before the pandemic got underway—have been laid bare by it. COVID-19 has exposed deep-seated weaknesses in the past growth patterns, including growing societal apathy toward acute and increasing income and wealth inequalities; neglect of the environment; lack of universal access to sick leave, health, and education; and inadequate social security systems in rich and poor countries alike for the laboring class whose crucial roles in the service economy are only now universally being recognized as "essential service" providers (Tomer and Kane 2020).

The pandemic has stressed the imperative to "build a better," environmentally resilient, socially more humane world—away from business as usual. While there are positive signs in the growth of movements like Black Lives Matter, which have spread rapidly from the United States to Europe, it is unclear how robust or long lasting they are likely to be in transforming hearts and minds of societies from the vestiges of slavery, Jim Crow laws, and plain old colonial views of Blacks and other nonwhite races. Will arms sales to countries in the Middle East and Africa, which are fueling conflict and creating refugees and thereby increasing demands on WFP, be curtailed with an active focus on peacemaking? How the West responds matters as a good or a bad example to developing countries.

Elsewhere, we have argued that addressing complex challenges requires strong, thoughtful leadership and state capacity. While some countries have shown state capacity, there is chaos in global governance at the regional and global levels. *The Economist* noted in its June 2020 issue on "The New World Disorder" that 75 years after the creation of the United Nations:

> The UN is struggling, as are many of the structures, like the World Trade Organization (WTO) and the Nuclear Non-Proliferation Treaty (NPT), designed to help create order out of chaos. This system, with the UN at its apex, is beset by internal problems, by the global struggle to cope with the rise of China, and most of all by the neglect—antipathy even—of the country that was its chief architect and sponsor, the United States.

> The threat to the global order weighs on everyone, including America. But if the United States pulls back, then everyone must step forward... (*The Economist* 2020a, 8)

If other countries do not step up, the world risks "a great unravelling, much like the nightmare in the 1920s and 1930s that first impelled the allies to create the UN and its siblings" (*The Economist* 2020a, 8). The Biden administration has introduced a sense of normality into the global world order but has not yet begun to tackle the key global challenges: income and power, inequalities, climate change, future threats of pandemics, human rights, and an arms race.

An important need of developing countries, lagging in development, is for their future growth strategies to be more holistic, effective, humane, and equitable, with their leadership and their states having the political will to deliver on these goals, and with the involvement of civil society, the private sector, religious groups, and all other actors.

Outcome Indicators: What Did We Achieve before the Pandemic?

In the previous chapters, we demonstrated that prior to COVID-19, the world had witnessed extraordinary progress in human development, particularly since 1990. Nearly 1.2 billion people had been lifted out of poverty since 1990, after the international community adopted eight MDGs (including 21 targets and 60 indicators) in 2000 and started monitoring their progress until 2015, the end of the MDG period (UN 2016).

The number of people living in extreme poverty fell from 1.9 billion in 1990 to 836 million in 2015. Most progress occurred in the new millennium. By 2011, all developing regions, with the exception of SSA, had achieved the target of halving the number of people living in extreme poverty. The most populous countries in the world—China and India—played a major role in the worldwide reduction of poverty. China's remarkable progress reduced extreme poverty in EAP from 54 percent to 2.1 percent between 1990 and 2015. SA's progress has also been impressive, with a decline from 52 to 12.4 percent in the same time period, but with accelerated reduction since 2008. In contrast, the poverty level in SSA did not change between 1990 and 2002. The rate of poverty decline has accelerated since, though about 43 percent of sub-Saharan population continued to live in extreme poverty in 2015 (UN DESA 2016).

Another measure of poverty is the Oxford Poverty and Human Development Initiative at the University of Oxford and the Human Development Report Office of the United Nations Development Programme (UNDP), a measure that we described in Chapter 4. Key findings of the report of the Global Multidimensional Poverty Index 2020, "Charting Pathways out of Multidimensional Poverty: Achieving the SDGs" include:

- Across 107 developing countries, 1.3 billion people—22 percent—live in multidimensional poverty.

- Children show higher rates of multidimensional poverty: half of multidimensionally poor people (644 million) are children under age 18. One in three children is poor compared with one in six adults.

- About 84.3 percent of multidimensionally poor people live in Sub-Saharan Africa (558 million) and South Asia (530 million).

- 67 percent of multidimensionally poor people are in middle-income countries, where the incidence of multidimensional poverty ranges from 0 percent to 57 percent nationally and from 0 percent to 91 percent subnationally.

- Every multidimensionally poor person is being left behind in a critical mass of indicators. For example, 803 million multidimensionally poor people live in a household where someone is undernourished, 476 million have an out-of-school child at home, 1.2 billion lack access to clean cooking fuel, 687 million lack electricity and 1.03 billion have substandard housing materials.

- 65 countries reduced their global Multidimensional Poverty Index (MPI) value significantly in absolute terms. Those countries are home to 96 percent of the population of the 75 countries studied for poverty trends. The fastest, Sierra Leone (2013–2017), did so during the Ebola epidemic.

- Four countries halved their MPI value. India (2005/2006–2015/2016) did so nationally and among children and had the biggest reduction in the number of multidimensionally poor people (273 million). Ten countries, including China, came close to halving their MPI value. (OPHI and UNDP 2020, 3)

Macro-level estimates suggest that there has been faster progress on reducing income poverty, as estimated by the World Bank, over recent decades than in reducing hunger, a puzzle that we explored in Chapter 4. In the *State of Food Security and Nutrition (SOFI)* 2020, FAO has revised the hunger estimates again, both retroactively and prospectively, so the overall hunger level in 2020 is 690 million, compared to the earlier estimate of 821 million, and yet, incidence of hunger has increased by about 60 million people since 2014, with a substantially higher incidence of hunger in Africa forecast by 2030 (FAO et al. 2020, viii).[7] This comparative picture is presented in Figures 13.1 and 13.2.

Thus, although there was a decline in the numbers of undernourished in developing countries, FAO estimated that, until 2015, this decline was smaller than the huge decline in the number of poor that the World Bank estimated. In 1990, 1.01 billion people were undernourished, compared to 785 million in 2015, a. drop in undernourished of only 226

---

[7] The drastic acceleration of food insecurity to 2030 in *SOFI* 2020, compared to the projections of the previous year's *SOFI*, appears to be mainly due to revisions in population estimates. Indeed, the report asks readers, who tend to be consummate readers of FAO's food insecurity estimates, not to compare the old and new estimates. Furthermore, the changes appeared to be based on adjustments in just a few countries (FAO et al. 2020).

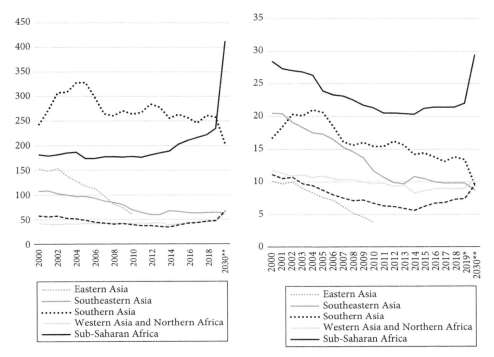

Figure 13.1 FAO's latest (2020) estimates of hunger and projections show slower decline in hunger than World Bank estimates and projections of poverty: Performance and projections by region, 1990–2030

Note: *Projected values. **The projections up to 2030 do not reflect the potential impact of the COVID-19 pandemic; and Eastern Asia's data not reported after 2010, as the prevalence of undernourishment is less than 2.5 percent.

Source: Based on data from FAO et al. (2020).

million (FAO et al. 2019, table 2, 9). The proportion of undernourished people (PoU) in the developing regions has fallen by almost half since 1990, from 23.3 percent in 1990–2 to 12.9 percent in 2014–16; this is close to the MDG hunger target, which was to halve the proportion of undernourished (UN DESA 2016, 5). Between 2005 and 2015, greater progress was made. Nearly twice as many people escaped chronic undernutrition during the latter decade compared to 1990–2005. The faster decrease in poverty was partly due to faster economic growth during this period. The rate of hunger reduction varied widely by region: East Asia, Latin America, Southeast Asia, and the Caucasus and Central Asia achieved the MDG target. China alone accounted for almost two-thirds of the total reduction in the number of undernourished people in the developing regions since 1990. Northern Africa attained an overall level below 5 percent. In contrast, the pace of reduction in SA and SSA, where there are still high concentrations of undernourished people, had been too slow to achieve the target. In SSA, for 2014–16, the rate of undernourishment was almost 23 percent. Although the hunger rate has fallen, since 1990 the number of under-nourished people has increased by 44 million, indicative of the high population growth. There is wide variation across the subregions. Northern, Southern, and Western Africa have already achieved or are close to meeting the target. In Central Africa, however, progress has been hampered by rapid population growth, environmental fragility, and economic and

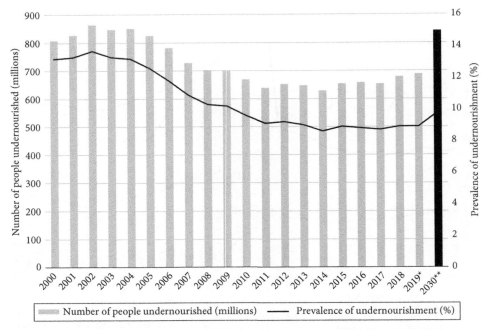

Figure 13.2 World: Number of people undernourished (millions) and prevalence of undernourishment (%)—projections to 2030

Note: *Projected values. **The projections up to 2030 do not reflect the potential impact of the COVID-19 pandemic.

Source: Based on data from FAO et al. (2020).

political upheaval, with the number of undernourished doubling between 1990 and 2015 (UN DESA 2016, 21). According to the latest World Bank estimates of poverty, the only remaining incidence of poverty will be in Africa in 2030, if we consider the $1.90 (2011 PPP) per day poverty line. Only 53 percent of the world's population, about 3.9 billion of the 7.3 billion, earned at least income of US$5.5 per day (2011 PPP) in 2015, enough to afford a nutritious diet, and nearly three-quarters earned at least US$3.2 per day (2011 PPP) (Figure 13.3). Similarly, projections of hunger show increases mostly in Africa. Under the old projections, the number of hungry by 2030 was estimated to be 216 million in SSA and the prevalence (percentage of population) was 7.4 percent. According to new estimates, the number of undernourished people was estimated to be 235 million in 2019, and will be 412 million by 2030, with a prevalence of 29.4 (FAO et al. 2020, 9, table 1, 11; table 2). FAO's most conservative estimate is that more than 3 billion people in the world cannot afford healthy diets. The cost of a healthy diet is five times the cost of basic minimum diet, making it unaffordable for the poor. The cost also exceeds average food expenditures in most countries in the Global South: 57 percent or more of the population cannot afford a healthy diet throughout SSA and SA (FAO et al. 2020, 66). This number is like the World Bank's estimate of the population earning more than US$5.50 per day (2011 PPP) year (Figure 13.3).

The development community then adopted the more ambitious 17 SDGs in 2015 with 169 targets and 231 unique indicators (UN 2020c).

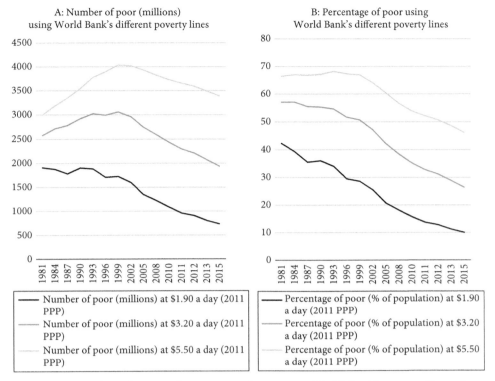

A: Number of poor (millions)
using World Bank's different poverty lines

B: Percentage of poor using
World Bank's different poverty lines

—— Number of poor (millions) at $1.90 a day (2011 PPP)
—— Number of poor (millions) at $3.20 a day (2011 PPP)
—— Number of poor (millions) at $5.50 a day (2011 PPP)

—— Percentage of poor (% of population) at $1.90 a day (2011 PPP)
—— Percentage of poor (% of population) at $3.20 a day (2011 PPP)
—— Percentage of poor (% of population) at $5.50 a day (2011 PPP)

Figure 13.3 Number of poor and percentage of poor using World Bank's poverty lines of US$1.9, US$3.2, and US$5.5 per day, 1981–2015 (using 2011 PPP)

Source: Based on data from the World Development Indicators (World Bank 2020b), http://data.worldbank.org/data-catalog/world-development-indicators

In 2015, 736 million people lived in extreme poverty, and this was reduced to about 650 million in 2018.[8] Extreme poverty dropped just 1.4 percentage points in the three years between 2015 and 2018 (Sánchez-Páramo 2020). Uneven progress across regions as well as in countries is very significant.

According to Carolina Sánchez-Páramo, Global Director of the Poverty and Equity Global Practice (GP) at the World Bank:

The two regions with the poorest people in 1990 were East Asia and Pacific and South Asia, accounting for 80 percent of the extreme poor. With China's rapid reduction of poverty, the concentration of the global poor shifted from East Asia in 1990s to South Asia in 2002, and then to sub-Saharan Africa in 2010.... [H]alf of the world's poor live in just five countries—India, Nigeria, Democratic Republic of Congo, Ethiopia, and Bangladesh. The top two countries—Nigeria and India—are showing diverging trends [even before COVID-19]. Nigeria may have already overtaken India as the country with the most extreme poor while India has been rapidly reducing extreme poverty and estimates forecast that the country can achieve the extreme poverty goal. (Sánchez-Páramo 2020)

[8] The World Bank estimated that the share of people in extreme poverty declined to 8.6 percent of the world population in 2018 (World Bank 2018).

The decline of global extreme poverty continued, but was slowing before the COVID-19 pandemic, in part because of the decline in growth. The deceleration indicated that the world was not on track to achieve the "zero hunger" (SDG1) target, even before the pandemic. "The share of the world population living in extreme poverty declined to 10 per cent in 2015, down from 16 percent in 2010 and 36 percent in 1990" (UN Statistics Division 2020). However, the pace of poverty reduction was already decelerating, estimated to be 8.6 percent in 2018. Moreover, baseline projections suggested that 6 percent of the world population would still be living in extreme poverty in 2030, missing the target of ending poverty. Thus, if growth slows, poverty reduction will also decline.

Hunger reduction has not occurred as rapidly as poverty reduction. After decades of steady decline, the trend in world hunger—as measured by the prevalence of undernourishment—reversed course in 2014. The new estimates of 690 million hungry amount to 8.9 percent of the world population, but it is still up by 10 million people in one year and by nearly 60 million over five years from 2014 to 2019, confirming the trend reported in past editions, even as the number has changed from that published in recent reports (FAO et al. 2020, 5–6). The new estimates underscore "the immense challenge of achieving the Zero Hunger target by 2030" (SDG2) (UN 2020a). FAO attributes the rise to the increasing incidence of conflict-affected countries (often a leading cause of famine), compounded by climate-related factors, such as the El Niño phenomenon, inflicting both drought and flood conditions (FAO et al. 2018). The global PoU also suggests a reversal of the downward trend that was sustained over recent decades (FAO et al. 2018). *SOFI* 2020 reported:

> The reasons for the observed increase of the last few years are multiple. Much of the recent increase in food insecurity can be attributed to the greater number of conflicts, often exacerbated by climate-related shocks. Even in some peaceful settings, food security has deteriorated as a result of economic slowdowns threatening access to food for the poor.

> The evidence also reveals that the world is not on track to achieve the SDG 2.1 Zero Hunger target by 2030. Combined projections of recent trends in the size and composition of the population, in the total food availability, and in the degree of inequality in food access point to an increase of the PoU by almost 1 percentage point. As a result, the global *number* of undernourished people in 2030 would exceed 840 million.

> The PoU in Africa was 19.1 percent of the population in 2019, or more than 250 million undernourished people, up from 17.6 percent in 2014. This prevalence is more than twice the world average (8.9 percent) and is the highest among all regions. [Africa's per capita agricultural output had increased slightly in 2016 from the peak reached in the early 1970s, but after a precipitous drop from the mid 1970s to 1983, from which it recovered by 2005 with a sharp V and since increased slightly.]

> Asia is home to more than half of the total undernourished people in the world—an estimated 381 million people in 2019. Yet, the PoU in the population for the region is 8.3 percent, below the world average (8.9 percent), and less than half of that of Africa. Asia has shown progress in reducing the number of hungry people in recent years, down by 8 million since 2015.

> In Latin America and the Caribbean, the PoU was 7.4 percent in 2019, below the world prevalence of 8.9 percent, which still translates into almost 48 million undernourished people. The region has seen a rise in hunger in the past few years, with the number of undernourished people increasing by 9 million between 2015 and 2019.

In terms of the outlook for 2030, Africa is significantly off track to achieve the Zero Hunger target in 2030. If recent rates of increase persist, its PoU will rise from 19.1 to 25.7 percent. Latin America and the Caribbean is also off track, although to a much lower degree. Mostly due to deterioration in recent years, its PoU is expected to increase from 7.4 percent in 2019 to 9.5 in 2030. Asia, while making progress, will also not achieve the 2030 target based on recent trends.

Overall, and without considering the effects of COVID-19, projected trends in under-nourishment would change the geographic distribution of world hunger dramatically. While Asia would still be home to almost 330 million hungry people in 2030, its share of the world's hunger would shrink substantially. Africa would overtake Asia to become the region with the highest number of undernourished people (433 million), accounting for 51.5 percent of the total. (FAO et al. 2020, xviii–xix)

Other forms of malnutrition include more than 2 billion people with micronutrient deficiencies and 600 million obese, data monitored by WHO (2020b, 2020c).[9] One in seven newborns suffered from low birthweight in 2015; no progress has been made in reducing low birthweight since 2012 (UNICEF 2019).

Stunting has been decreasing in nearly every region since 2000. Globally, stunting declined from one in three to just over one in five between 2000 and 2019. UNICEF noted:

In 2019, 21.3 per cent [144 million],[10] or more than one in five children under age 5 worldwide had stunted growth. That said, overall trends are positive. Between 2000 and 2019, stunting prevalence globally declined from 32.4 per cent to 21.3 per cent, and the number of children affected fell from 199.5 million to 144.0 million. In 2019, nearly two

---

[9] *SOFI* 2020's reported on food insecurity in the world:

While the 746 million people facing severe food insecurity are of utmost concern, an additional 16 percent of the world population, or more than 1.25 billion people, have experienced food insecurity at moderate levels....

The prevalence of both moderate and severe levels of food insecurity (SDG Indicator 2.1.2) is estimated to be 25.9 percent in 2019 for the world as a whole. This translates into a total of 2 billion people.... Total food insecurity (moderate or severe) has consistently increased at the global level since 2014, mostly because of the increase in moderate food insecurity. (FAO et al. 2020, xix)

The report further noted that "out of the 2 billion people suffering from food insecurity, 1.03 billion are in Asia, 675 million in Africa, 205 million in Latin America and the Caribbean, 88 million in Northern America and Europe and 5.9 million in Oceania" (FAO et al. 2020, 23).

SOFI 2020 also noted how the pandemic will affect its estimates: "The global crisis induced by the COVID-19 pandemic will certainly bring these figures to much higher levels, even in regions of the world like Northern America and Europe, which have traditionally been more food secure" (FAO et al. 2020, 23).

With respect to obesity, *SOFI* 2020 noted:

Adult obesity continues to rise, from 11.8 percent in 2012 to 13.1 percent in 2016 and is not on track to reach the global target to halt the rise in adult obesity by 2025. If the prevalence continues to increase by 2.6 percent per year, adult obesity will increase by 40 percent by 2025, compared to the 2012 level. (FAO et al. 2020, xx)

[10] *SOFI* 2020, observing some progress in reducing stunting, noted:

Rates of stunting reduction are far below what is needed to reach the World Health Assembly (WHA) target for 2025 and the SDG target for 2030. If recent trends continue, these targets will only be achieved in 2035 and 2043, respectively.

...Most regions have made some progress in reducing stunting between 2012 and 2019 but not at the rate needed to achieve the 2025 and 2030 targets. Globally, stunting estimates vary by wealth. Children from the poorest wealth quintile had a stunting prevalence that was more than double that of children from the richest quintile. (FAO et al. 2020, xx)

out of five stunted children lived in South Asia while another two out of five lived in sub-Saharan Africa [representing 40 percent and 54 percent of all stunted children in the world, respectively].... [N]umbers have increased at an alarming rate in West and Central Africa—from 22.4 million to 29.0 million.

In 2019 globally, 47 million children under five were wasted of which 14.3 million were severely wasted. This translates into a prevalence of 6.9 per cent and 2.1 per cent, respectively [significantly above the 2025 target (5 percent) and the 2030 target (3 percent for this indicator)]. In 2019, more than half of all wasted children lived in South Asia and one quarter in sub-Saharan Africa, with similar proportions for severely wasted children. At 14.8 percent, South Asia's wasting prevalence represents a situation requiring a serious need for intervention with appropriate treatment programmes. Under-five wasting and severe wasting are highly sensitive to change.

Middle East and North Africa had the highest overweight prevalence in 2019 with 11.0 percent affected, followed by Eastern Europe and Central Asia at 10.8 per cent and North America at 8.9 per cent. The lowest overweight prevalence in 2019 was seen in South Asia at 2.5 per cent followed by West and Central Africa at 2.6 percent. East Asia and the Pacific had the highest number of overweight children in 2019 with 10.4 million affected, followed by Middle East and North Africa with an estimated 5.4 million overweight. Overall, the two Asian regions (East Asia and the Pacific and South Asia) account for nearly two out of every five overweight children in the world. North America is the only region that has seen a statistically significant increase in the number of overweight children between 2000 and 2019. (UNICEF 2020a)

The global prevalence of overweight children under 5 years of age has not improved, going from 5.3 percent in 2012 to 5.6 percent, or 38.3 million children, in 2019 (FAO et al. 2020). The number of overweight children worldwide has remained stagnant for more than a decade.[11]

SOFI 2019 reported that overweight and obesity "continue to increase in all regions, particularly among school-age children and adults" (FAO et al. 2019, viii). "In 2018, an estimated 40 million children under five were overweight. In 2016, 131 million children 5–9 years old, 207 million adolescents and 2 billion adults were overweight. About a third of overweight adolescents and adults, and 44 percent of overweight children aged 5–9 were obese" (FAO et al. 2019, xiv).

Both the under-5 mortality rate and the number of under-5 deaths have fallen by more than half since 1990 but less than the targeted amount.

---

[11] According to *SOFI* 2020:

Worldwide, 14.6 percent of infants were born with low birthweight (less than 2,500 g) in 2015. The trends for this indicator at global and regional levels show that some progress has been made in recent years, but not enough to achieve the target of a 30 percent reduction in low birthweight by 2025 or even by 2030.

Globally, as of 2019, it is estimated that 44 percent of infants aged less than six months were exclusively breastfed. Currently, the world is on track to achieve the 2025 target of at least 50 percent of babies younger than six months being exclusively breastfed. If additional efforts are not made, however, the global target for 2030 of at least 70 percent will not be achieved before 2038. Most subregions are making at least some progress, except Eastern Asia and the Caribbean. If the Eastern Africa, Central Asia and Southern Asia subregions maintain their current rates of progress, they will reach the targets set for both 2025 and 2030. (FAO et al. 2020, xx)

As UNICEF noted:

The world made remarkable progress in child survival in the past few decades, and millions of children have better survival chances than in 1990–5, 1 in 26 children died before reaching age five in 2018, compared to 1 in 11 in 1990. Moreover, progress in reducing child mortality . . . accelerated in the 2000–2018 period compared with the 1990s, with the annual rate of reduction in the global under-five mortality rate increasing from 2.0 per cent in 1990–2000 to 3.8 per cent in 2000–2018. Despite the global progress in reducing child mortality over the past few decades, an estimated 5.3 million children under age five died in 2018roughly half of those deaths occurred in sub-Saharan Africa. The global under-five mortality rate declined by 59 per cent, from 93 deaths per 1,000 live births in 1990 to 39 in 2018. Despite this considerable progress, improving child survival remains a matter of urgent concern. In 2018 alone, roughly 15,000 under-five deaths occurred every day, an intolerably high number of largely preventable child deaths. (UNICEF 2020b)

Nearly half of all deaths in children under 5 are attributable to undernutrition; under-nutrition puts children at greater risk of dying from common infections, increases the frequency and severity of such infections, and delays recovery.

COVID-19 may have just wiped out recent years of progress on global poverty reduction. For the first time since 1990, there has been an increase in estimated global poverty, with the poorest regions (SA and SSA) the hardest hit. Kharas and Hamel's (2020) revised estimate of the number of poor people in the world as a result of the pandemic shows that about 690 million people are likely to be in poor households in 2020, compared to their previous estimate of 640 million people. Their post-COVID-19 estimate of extreme poverty is that the world will see a rise this year of about 50 million people compared to their original 2020 estimate and by 40 million people compared to their 2019 forecast. Kharas and Hamel noted further that "the number is, however, far smaller than the estimates put forward in one scenario by Sumner and co-authors [Sumner, Hoy, and Ortiz-Juarez 2020], who suggested that poverty could rise by 420 million to 580 million people, a figure that has been picked up by the media and advocacy organizations as 'half a billion'" (Kharas and Hamel 2020). The IMF scenario for 2020 suggests that all the progress in reducing poverty since the launch of the SDGs in September 2015 has been lost, and that 2020 will be the first time in this century that the number of poor people will rise, a fact which can be seen in real time as the World Poverty Clock ticks "backward" (IMF 2020c). This setback comes after a period of poverty reduction, averaging almost 100 million people per year between 2008 and 2013 (Kharas and Hamel 2020). The authors have tried to identify the most seriously affected countries of the COVID-19 crisis, and show 12 countries likely to experience an increase in poverty of over 1 million people in 2020 as a result of the pandemic. They are located mainly in Asia and Africa, with the exception being Brazil. India and Nigeria are likely to add 10 million and 8 million to the poverty rolls in 2020. The COVID-19 pandemic has underscored the vulnerability of people who have only recently been able to escape poverty. See, also, Lele, Bansal, and Meenakshi (2020).

Analysis done by Schmidhuber and Qiao (2020) of FAO shows that most countries are more dependent on imports today than they were 20 years ago. This has made observers worry that disruptions caused by the COVID-19 pandemic could trigger a repeat of the food crisis of 2007–8, when a sharp rise in prices was exacerbated by panicking governments. (See, also, Schmidhuber, Pound, and Qiao [2020].)

Agricultural Productivity Growth across Regions and Countries Using Various Measures and Relationship to Structural Transformation

Changes in poverty and hunger need to be seen in the context of structural transformation, movement of population out of agriculture to higher productivity manufacturing, and its relationship to the farm structure, which has been changing, too, with growing differentiation in farm sizes across countries and substantial differences among countries and over time in their agricultural productivity growth. This performance, in turn, influences progress on structural transformation, but it is unclear if a reduction in rural population through urban migration increases average labor productivity, or whether an increase in labor productivity results in a reduction in the share of labor in agriculture through rural–urban migration. Differing rates of demographic transition add to the complexity. Demographic transition was very rapid in East Asia but is the slowest in SSA with SA in the middle.

Our analysis of structural transformation evolved from a two-sector to a three-sector analysis, providing new insights. It started with a transformation of the economies from agriculture to the nonagricultural sector using data on 127 countries, covering a 34-year period (1980–2013) (Lele, Agarwal, and Goswami 2013, 2014, 2018). The data generated by FAO provided estimates of economically active populations in the agricultural and nonagricultural sectors and was an input into the World Bank's study of "Accelerating Agricultural Productivity Growth" in India (World Bank 2014). Our work essentially followed Timmer's approach to structural transformation. It showed that:

1. India had fallen behind in structural transformation relative to China and Indonesia, by several different criteria: that is, decline in the share of population in agriculture at the beginning and the end of the period, share of manufacturing sector in the economy over time, and demographic transition, even though the three countries started with similar initial conditions in the early 1960s of small farm-dominated agriculture. Indonesia developed a thriving plantation sector, producing rubber, palm oil, and other cash crops, albeit at the cost of rapid deforestation, typically not measured either in the work on transformation, or in Fuglie's TFP estimates. Productivity, measured as value-added per worker, increased in all three countries in both the agricultural and the nonagricultural sector, a unique achievement compared to other developing regions.
2. The productivity in the nonagricultural sector was faster than in agriculture in all three countries, more so in China than in India. Indonesia's growth stumbled during the 1997 financial crisis and resumed after a lag.
3. Internal terms of trade between agriculture and nonagriculture moved in favor of the nonagricultural sector in all three countries: that is, relative prices moved against agriculture.

The next stage of our analysis (Lele, Goswami, and Nico 2017) used panel data on a three-way sectoral breakdown of employment in agriculture, manufacturing, and service sectors for 139 (104 developing + 35 developed) countries over the 1991–2014 period, from International Labour Organization (ILO)–Global Employment Trend (GET). ILO's breakdown of employment in the agriculture, manufacturing, and service sectors is based on household labor force surveys and employment surveys, and therefore, likely measures labor input in sectors, including in agriculture, more accurately than FAO's earlier estimates of the economically active population in agriculture without the actual input. It is an important breakthrough in understanding the process of structural transformation. Where does labor move when it leaves agriculture—to the manufacturing or the service sector? And what are the labor productivity differences in these sectors? A difference in the ILO and FAO data used earlier, apart from the intersectoral breakdown of employment, is in the estimation of labor input.[12] With a few notable exceptions, ILO estimates of labor in agriculture, which measures labor input more directly than FAO, as the population dependent on agriculture, are lower than FAO estimates of labor in agriculture: for example, in Brazil. There are also some differences in trends in the labor inputs in agriculture between the FAO and ILO data. This data set helped us to explore differences in employment generated and changes in productivity of labor in the agriculture, industry, and service sectors over time. The analysis covered the period of rapid economic growth in developing countries—that is, from the 1990s—and the slowdown since the 2007–8 crisis.

Difference in the shares in GDP and employment is at the heart of structural transformation, and the difference is much larger in developing countries at early stages of development, reflecting the large backlog of labor in the traditional sector. This difference narrows (approaches to near zero) rapidly, as per capita income increases and labor moves out of agriculture to other sectors. In developed countries the shares of value-added and employment are very close and reach near zero as income increases.

The share of value-added in the industrial sector in total GDP increases with the increase in per capita income, first in both developing and developed countries, but then the share of value-added in the industrial sector starts to decline in developing countries, exhibiting the phenomenon of premature deindustrialization (Rodrik 2016). Furthermore premature deindustrialization occurs at earlier income levels in developing countries. The inverted U-shaped trend in the share of industrial value-added with changes in per capita income means that as countries mature in their economic growth process, industry's share in GDP declines. Regional analysis shows different results: African countries are by far the most diverse in patterns of structural transformation.

Thinking has evolved not only on what numbers tell us about poverty and hunger, but what measures to use to assess farm productivity and changes in it, and how it is related to farm structure: that is, to the distribution of farm sizes and changes in them over time. Considerable consensus existed for nearly half a century, perhaps when markets were less dynamic, that small farms are more productive than medium and large farms, and productivity was often measured in terms of yields per unit of land. The international development community has supported small farm development based on that consensus. Over the past decade, however, there has been more extensive use of TFP as a measure, replacing partial productivity; the former is done using panel data across time periods to determine changes, and improved econometric methods have helped in this measurement (Foster and Rozensweig 2017; Gautam and Ahmed 2018; Rada and Fuglie 2019). Since land is the scarce factor in Asia with little scope for land expansion, this may be an appropriate

---

[12] FAO's data on the economically active population refer to the number of employed and unemployed persons, including those seeking work for the first time, and cover employers; self-employed workers; salaried employees; wage earners; unpaid workers assisting in a family, farm, or business operation; members of producers' cooperatives; and members of the armed forces. The economically active population is also called the labor force. ILO's data on employment refer to all persons above a specified age, who were, during a specified brief period— either one week or one day—in the following categories: paid employment (whether at work or with a job but not at work) and self-employment (whether at work or with an enterprise but not at work). For the purposes of the aggregate sectors (agriculture, industry, and services), definitions of the International Standard Industrial Classification (ISIC) System were used.

measure there and not necessarily in LAC and SSA. Nevertheless, the consensus on efficacy of small farm development has broken down, with growing recognition of the importance of factor markets in agriculture and access to inputs in determining farm factor productivity, including in LAC and SSA.

Several key areas of economies of scale: include (1) skills and technology; (2) finance and access to capital; and (3) the organization and logistics of trading, marketing, and storage. (See, for example, Collier and Dercon [2014]; Dercon and Gollin [2014].) Related reasons for questioning traditional thinking—namely, that small farms are more productive than medium and large farms—include:

1. Questions about the historical, theoretical, and empirical validity of the body of literature on the leading role of agriculture in transformation;
2. The changing comparative advantage of small and large farms under globalization and its consequences, from the growing injection of external capital into agriculture or FDI, also often described as "land grab" in SSA;
3. More importantly, investments by the African urban elite in farming (Jayne et al. 2014), with communal land increasingly being converted to private ownership in collaboration with officials. This latter is understandably less controversial than land acquired through FDI;
4. Inability of small farmers to compete, in responding to the new opportunities provided by the growth of value chains and supermarkets; and
5. Returns to investment in agriculture, relative to other sectors. With improved access to inputs, in Bangladesh, even the tiniest farms can use fertilizer, high-yielding crop varieties, and increasingly are able to rent mechanization services, with consequent positive effects on farm productivity.

A recent nuanced consensus has emerged that productivity exhibits a U-shaped distribution with respect to farm size, across a broad range of countries with quite different levels of per capita income and farm size (Rada and Fuglie 2019: for example, in Bangladesh and India. At one end of the spectrum with a predominance of small farms are countries like China and Tanzania, and at the other end, in Brazil, even the smallest farms are often multiple times the size of the large farms in Bangladesh and China. Overall mid-size farms may lose the labor advantage of small farms without the advantage of access to better factor and output markets of large farms. Access to capital to substitute machines for labor and output markets are clearly important incentives to increasing productivity on medium-sized farms. A variety of institutional innovations have emerged to use mechanical equipment: for example, through the emergence of rental markets. Characteristics such as soil quality, thought to be better on small farms, seem not to have held up when tested empirically (Bevis and Barrett 2020). At the same time, measurement error and heterogeneity together account for as much as 70 percent of the dispersion in measured productivity. Yet, another revisionist view in recent years is that the potential for efficiency gains through reallocation of land across farms and farmers may be relatively modest (Gollin and Udry 2019; Rada and Fuglie 2019).

The reason for the U-shaped curve, with respect to farm size, seems to be that the smallest farms are able to cultivate their land intensively mostly using their own labor, but as farm size increases, the ability to mobilize additional resources does not increase commensurately until the farms reach a significant size, when they are able to deploy machinery and have access to capital. Institutional changes within countries, such as secure rental contracts in China, which Bangladesh still lacks, and access to small-scale machinery in Bangladesh, which liberalization of imports has enabled, make a difference in outcomes. By reporting the measurement of technical efficiency by farm size, Gautam and Ahmed (2018) argued that further policy reforms, such as more secure land tenure in Bangladesh, will also encourage less efficient, larger farms to rent their land to smaller farmers who are more efficient, with the farm sector as a whole moving closer to the technical efficiency frontier, as these large farms seem to encounter greater technical inefficiency problems than small farms.

Although evidence has accumulated on how TFP can be increased by reducing techno-logical inefficiency and by improving policy, infrastructure, and institutions (Fuglie 2012), there is now extensive evidence, also, which we presented in earlier chapters, that there has been substantial difference in TFP growth among regions, and between low-, middle- and high-income countries. East Asian countries have experienced the most rapid growth, followed by West Asia, and Latin America.

Despite a leg-up, starting with the Green Revolution, TFP in SA has not maintained high growth. Africa's productivity growth is the slowest. Productivity growth by income levels of countries also shows that higher income countries perform better, while LICs perform the least well. Hence, country-specific strategies are needed to improve markets of particular importance to particular countries.

The cause and effect of this is unclear, but our research does show that high-income countries invest much more in agriculture, when measured as the share of GDP invested in agriculture, than do LICs. This phenomenon is related in part to the low savings and investment rates of LICs, as we documented in Chapter 2, and low investment in human and institutional capital, for which we offer reasons later.

How does TFP growth relate to structural transformation of countries? In a closed economy, rapid productivity growth in agriculture assures increased supply of "wages goods"—that is, food, fiber, and other raw materials—as well as labor supply to a burgeon-ing urban/manufacturing sector, increased savings and investments for growth of the manufacturing sector, and rural markets for good and services in the manufacturing sector. W. Arthur Lewis (1954) and Johnston and Mellor (1961) articulated these intersectoral linkages, and Timmer (2009) formalized these relationships. How has this played out in reality? Writings of Lewis and early scholars of transformation did not devote much attention to the issues of how markets develop and evolve and how they operate in absence of regulation. They assumed that intersectoral transfers of food, labor, and capital occur automatically in the course of transformation.

Recent analysts have devoted considerable energy to developing literature on value chains; most notable among them is Thomas Reardon. He acknowledged in a paper coauthored with Barry Popkin, whose work has focused on dietary transition, that the literature on value chains has lacked integration of different strands, particularly relating to deteriorating diet quality, a process Popkin and Reardon (2018) described in their work on supermarkets and changing food habits in Latin America. The phenomenon, they noted, is also accompanying development of supermarkets and subsequent phases of value chains in Asia and Africa. "The Latin America and Caribbean (LAC) region faces a major diet-related health problem," with enormous economic and social costs, which they argued is a result of profound shifts:

> Major shifts in intake of less-healthful low-nutrient-density foods and sugary beverages, changes in away-from-home eating and snacking and rapid shifts towards very high levels of overweight and obesity among all ages along with, in some countries, high burdens of

stunting. Diet changes have occurred in parallel to, and in two-way causality with, changes in the broad food system—the set of supply chains from farms, through midstream segments of processing, wholesale and logistics, to downstream segments of retail and food service (restaurants and fast food chains). (Popkin and Reardon 2018, 1028)

They "marry and integrate the nutrition transition literature with the literature on the economics of food system transformation," thus far largely unconnected, a phenomenon they called "two ships passing in the night" (Popkin and Reardon 2018, 1028).

Documenting the "rapid growth and transformation of that broad food system in LAC, with the rapid rise of supermarkets, large processors, fast food chains and food logistics firms" is a "double-edged sword" (Popkin and Reardon 2018, 1028). With respect to negative dietary trends, they noted the "the rise of consumption of fast food and highly processed food . . . in parallel to various positive trends, e.g. the reduction of the cost of food, de-seasonalization, increase of convenience of food preparation reducing women's time associated with that, and increase of availability of some nutritious foods like meat and dairy" (Popkin and Reardon 2018, 1028).

The authors noted further:

> One striking aspect of the conditioners of food system transformation in LAC is that the central influential policy was dismantling of government control of the food system— liberalization of FDI, elimination of food price controls and subsidies, privatization of the government systems of food and farm input distribution—that was largely not accompanied by regulations that managed the rapid development of the private food system, with the exception of some public food safety and phytosanitary standards. The latter were regulations encouraged by global food companies. However, the social consequences of the food system transformation, e.g. the impacts on health . . . were not part of the public debate. There was also little or no regulatory attention to curbing bad health effects (e.g. taxes on sodas and required caloric labelling). Debates on them have only recently begun in LAC. (Popkin and Reardon 2018, 1040)

Regulatory systems need to be further developed. Popkin and Reardon (2018, 1057) argued that "when consumers demand healthier foods and beverages, we will begin to see these changes for an array of fiscal and regulatory reasons." Chile, Mexico, and Brazil have begun to adopt such actions. It is unclear if such regulation is a result of stronger consumer demand for healthy food, or improved technical knowledge among policymakers on the role of nutrition for health. It could also be a result of international advocacy. Future research should better understand the origins of policies. Computational power and data multiply every two years, but the road ahead is long and success will not be easy. Asia and Africa are behind Latin America in urbanization, but the challenges of unhealthy food systems and weak regulation remain equally daunting.

As the *SOFI* 2020 report indicates: "many lower-income countries, where populations already suffer nutrient deficiencies, may need to increase their carbon footprint in order to first meet recommended dietary needs and meet nutrition targets, including those on undernutrition" (FAO et al. 2020, xxiv). We can expect, therefore, to see these themes further explored in the lead-up to, and including, the Food Systems Summit in 2021 and three of the specific objectives that will focus on "shifting to sustainable consumption patterns"; "nature-positive production at sufficient scale" and "advancing equitable livelihoods and value distribution" (UN 2020d).

Stalling of structural transformation in India and SSA, relative to East and Southeast Asian countries, is in part because agricultural productivity growth has been slower, population growth higher, and investment in R&D and physical and human capital lower than in the countries in East and Southeast Asia. Even Bangladesh, which was well behind India, has made more rapid progress, especially since 1996, by adopting a variety of reforms and moving toward transformation (Gautam and Ahmed 2018). (See Lele [2019] for a comparison of growth in India, China, and Bangladesh.)

Yet, in India, unlike in SSA, overall supply of food has not been a challenge. More significant is uneven performance across regions in the absence of a national food market, thwarted by the policy of Agricultural Produce Marketing Committee Act until 2020, and the lack of an effective demand for food.[13]

Agri-food supply chains, including processors; wholesalers and retailers; traditional, small-scale operations; family operated stores; and modern processors and supermarkets now constitute 70 to 80 percent of the value-added that consumers pay outside the farming sector—that is, in the service sector—which creates nonfarm employment. Farmers with market access and larger farms have an edge over small farmers with poor links to markets. Kshirsagar and Gautam (2013) documented this well in the case of India.

Not all the evidence related to transformation enables the telling of a consistent story: for example, about industrialization. Martin and Mitra (2001) provided evidence that agricultural productivity growth was higher than industrial productivity growth in 49 countries for which they analyzed data during the 1967–92 period. Considerable recent evidence presented in the preceding chapters, however, shows no convergence in the rates of agricultural productivity among regions, and the levels are the lowest in SSA. The lack of convergence seems to be related to the limited transferability of biological agricultural technology, as technology is often more location-specific than we assume, due to highly divergent ecological conditions. In the case of hybrid sorghum and millet varieties delivered by the International Crops Research Institute for the Semi-Arid Tropics (ICRISAT), they have spread more rapidly in India than in Africa due to the presence of a more active private sector in India (K. Shalinder, personal communication, June 22, 2020).[14] Thus, location-specific research and technology development is needed, and often this has been lacking.

---

[13] India's Agricultural Produce Marketing Act (APMA) is a relic of the colonial period. It was intended to regulate market fees that producers pay to middlemen by individual states enacting laws—given agriculture is a state subject. APMAs were meant to avoid farmer exploitation by middlemen, first initiated with regard to cotton marketing and exports in the 1930s. In the 1960s a number of states passed APMAs and appointed Agricultural Produce Marketing Committees, but over time, the committees became a vested interest, more interested in collecting fees than reforming market infrastructures. They limited the freedom of farmers to sell produce to outsiders in or outside the states, as technology enabled digital information and online sales, thereby reducing options of and returns to farmers. In May 2020, the central government announced it would formulate a central policy that will allow interstate sale of commodities, including online sales. It will have to garner support from state governments, some of which are opposed to reforms.

[14] The Indian seed industry has grown rapidly and is quite robust now. Policy reforms have played a significant role. (See Singh and Chand 2010; Chauhan et al. 2016.) Where open pollinated varieties (OPVs) are used, such as in pulses and most of rice, farmers can use their own seed for 3–4 years. Hence, the profit margin for the private sector is not attractive in OPVs (they are also bulky and another entity can produce OPVs by using the same seed and sell in the market). With the lack of private sector interest in OPVs, these are mostly made available through government seed corporations.

ICRISAT India exchanges parent material with SSA countries to be used to develop hybrid lines in that environment. They have to do crossing and multi-location trials using different parent materials in India and SSA. Normally, it is not possible simply to transfer the same seed to SSA. They need to do the crossing in those locations and then, following local policy, they announce the hybrid developed. This is being done currently and, hopefully, the private sector is likely to emerge in the near future there.

In the case of machinery, however, although technology is transferable in principle, it may be indivisible, if the machines are not of the size that can fit small farms, as noted by Foster and Rozensweig (2017) in India.

Furthermore, we provide considerable evidence of premature deindustrialization in many countries with rapid growth of the service sector. Some of this evidence may be explained, in part, by the nature of the data. Services reported earlier as manufacturing have been separated now and are reported as belonging to the service sector. There is more to the slow progress on industrialization in India, compared to China. See Lele and Goswami (2020).

While there is growing attention to sustainability issues, defining sustainability has been a challenge. In addition, there are many different interpretations of sustainability, rather than actual empirical evidence of sustainability (Echeverría 2020). Sustainability is not incorporated in the measurement of productivity growth in agriculture across countries, as we reported earlier. The TFP measurement for Southeast Asian countries, which we discussed in Chapter 2, includes the value of oil palm production, but does not include the loss of forests and carbon emissions caused by it. Several countries (OECD and emerging countries) have adopted targets, plans, and policies to mitigate GHGs or to facilitate adaptation to climate change, but only New Zealand and Ireland have clear legally binding targets (OECD 2020). World Bank projects' measurement of carbon emissions or reduction in them is ad hoc.

Several projects address issues of water savings, but unlike in China, where an integrated approach to water savings is pursued, there is little systematic measurement of water savings (Lele 2021, forthcoming). We provide some examples of quantitative measurement—for example, studies that explore the environmental dimensions quantitatively, such as the growth of area under minimum tillage in Brazil, leading to increased sustainability of land use, or the economics and environmental impacts of land conversion of forests to oil palm in Malaysia and Indonesia, and why without sizeable payments for environmental services, land conversion is difficult to contain in light of dynamic demand for palm oil in Asia. Yet, overall, notwithstanding the massive literature, environmental sustainability has not received the attention it deserves (Bhattacharyya et al. 2015; Noel et al. 2015; Nkonya, Mirzabaev, and von Braun 2016). Much of the work is fragmented, such as on water, forestry, soils, or climate change, rather than with an integrated view of sustainability.

Role of Small, Medium, and Large Farms

Issues of productivity by farm size and its determinants, as we discussed earlier, are fundamental to poverty reduction, food and nutrition security, and environmental sustainability. We discuss here the sheer magnitude of the small farmer challenge globally and suggest that farms of all sizes have an important role, either directly or indirectly, in poverty alleviation and structural transformation from agriculture to nonagriculture, including industrial development. FAO estimates are by far the most comprehensive and documented, as we described in Chapter 2. While not perfect, they are based on national agricultural censuses carried out in more than 100 countries, using standard concepts, albeit conducted at different times. Other estimates are based on household surveys, which, typically, have attracted much attention from researchers, but are not representative and focus only on small farms. Globally, as much as 84 percent of farms are smaller than 2 ha, and they operate only about 12 percent of farmland; they have been at the center of external assistance for more than half a century, particularly the assistance of IOs. In countries at lower levels of income, smaller farms operate a far larger share of farmland than do smaller farms in higher income countries. In low- and lower middle-income countries, as well as in countries of EAP (excluding China), SA, and SSA, 70–80 percent of farms are smaller than 2 ha and operate about 30 to 40 percent of the land (Lowder, Skoet, and Raney 2016). Globally, Lowder, Skoet, and Raney (2016, 24) estimate that more than 410 million farms are less than 1 ha in size, and more than 475 million farms are less than 2 ha in size, supporting claims that there are about 500 million small farms worldwide (those with less than 2 ha). Further analysis by FAO has underscored "the importance of not referring to family farms and small farms (i.e., those of less than 2 ha) interchangeably: the latter account for 84 percent of all farms worldwide, but operate only around 12 percent of all agricultural land, and produce roughly 36 percent of the world's food" (Lowder, Sánchez, and Bertini 2019, v).

Clearly, small farms alone are not feeding the world, as is sometimes mistakenly asserted and as we documented in Chapter 2. And indeed, most of the world's exports, except for rice, come from North and South America. Yet, 400 to 500 million small farms involve at least 2 billion people, assuming a family size of four, and they have the potential to make rural areas, where there is the most food insecurity and poverty, more food secure. Hence, the SDGs' focus on smallholder agriculture, which is the focus of IOs and assistance as well.

In Chapter 2, we documented that small farms are getting smaller (in Asia, and increasingly, in Africa), and large farms are getting larger, mostly in the Americas. There appears to be little land consolidation in developing countries of Asia, outside of China, in part because progress on land titling has been slow, although technological progress on land registration has been considerable.

Emergence of medium-sized farms seems to be an important trend in Africa. How real is this trend? Jayne and Muyanga (2018) described it and defined medium-scale farms as ranging from 5 ha. to 100 ha. Using demographic household survey data over time, they showed that the share of these farms in total cultivated land in Africa is growing relative to the customary land cultivated by small farmers, a result of the larger role of urban, middle-class Africans investing in agriculture. "The rapid rise of medium-scale holdings in most cases reflects increased interest in land by urban-based professionals or influential rural people. About half of these farmers obtained their land later in life, financed by nonfarm income" (Jayne et al. 2016, 197). Many medium-scale farms, owned by influential rural and urban people, purchase land in customary areas and convert it to leasehold or freehold titled land.

Jayne and Muyanga (2018) observed that with rapid population growth, small farms are getting smaller in Africa, and food surplus is coming from a small number of these medium-scale farms with few growth linkages to the rest of the rural areas. It is the kind of phenomenon that Lele and Mellor (1981) described in their paper, "Technological Change, Distributive Bias and Labour Transfers in a Two Sector Economy." Depending on the nature of technological bias, whether capital- or labor-intensive, farm sizes and technologies tend to have very different implications for rural employment and the nature of direct and indirect growth linkages, depending on the size of marketed surpluses and rural employment that farms generate. Marketed surpluses also affect home consumption and food prices, given the differing income elasticities of food for different farm households.

Relatedly, Jayne, Chamberlin, and Benfica (2018) noted nearly three decades later:

New private actors are investing heavily in areas of agricultural commercialisation. Sitko, Burke, and Jayne (2018) document the rapid investment by large-scale traders in regions where medium-scale farms (and hence marketed farm surpluses) are growing rapidly. The sheer volume of food needed to support Africa's rapidly growing cities is creating major new opportunities for not only farmers, but for small- and medium-scale trading and processing enterprises within food value chains (Reardon 2015). (Jayne, Chamberlin, and Benfica 2018, 782)

This literature illustrates the role of medium-sized farms in agricultural development as new production techniques, digitalization, and marketing are being used. As these new farms produce for urban markets, the need for imports of food staples (for example, rice) could decline if urban households switch to more indigenous crops. The purchasing power of "influential rural and urban people" will continue, however, increasingly supplemented by local, institutional capital, attracted to such enterprises as they see the business risks being reduced.

The IOs reviewed in this book have consistently embraced a small farm strategy for more than half a century. There has been a growing literature in the last decade questioning the focus on the small farm only, and raising the trade-offs between production, employment, rural poverty alleviation, and urban food requirements. Some economists have supported development of medium-scale and large farms, arguing that the burgeoning urban demand for food in Africa can only be met by supporting larger farmers (Collier and Dercon 2014; Dercon and Gollin 2014). Africa's food import dependence has increased, and therefore, it is imperative to support larger farmers. Furthermore, if more labor is pulled out of agriculture, labor productivity, and presumably TFP, increases in both sectors. Next, we explore how those productivities evolve by farm size based on evidence.

To understand these various strands of argument, we first empirically examined the process of structural transformation, now quite different than that envisaged by W. Arthur Lewis (1954) and Simon Kuznets (1955, 1966).

Using ILO data for 139 (104 developing + 35 developed) countries over 1991 to 2014 for three sectors—the agriculture, industry, and service sectors—we tested these ideas. In earlier analysis, we had done so using two sectors starting in 1980 (Lele, Agarwal, and Goswami 2018). Three-sector analysis of this more recent period showed that whereas developed and developing countries as a group follow the behavior that Lewis (1954) and Kuznets (1955, 1966) described, there are considerable differences across regions and within countries in this pattern. Concern about premature deindustrialization is strongly confirmed from the data, with those developing countries generally lagging in SDGs, such as in SA and Africa, also lagging in structural transformation. Their share of agriculture in GDP has declined rapidly, but their share of employment in agriculture has not declined rapidly enough. As a result, a large share of poverty remains in rural areas. Their demographic transition has been slower, too. Unlike in East Asia, birth rates have declined less slowly than death rates. Land, labor, and total factor productivity in agriculture has grown, but more slowly than countries where irrigated wheat and rice or plantation crops have accelerated transformation. Much of the employment growth has occurred in the service sector rather than in manufacturing. Even when labor has migrated to urban areas, it has led to the creation of more slums, rather than a labor force finding employment in manufacturing in large numbers.

Regression analysis showed that the share of employment in agriculture to total employment declines in developing countries and labor productivity in agriculture increases rapidly, but this growth in productivity tapers off as per capita income grows, whereas in developed countries agricultural worker productivity growth accelerates, as we showed in Chapter 2. This is, perhaps, because FAO data on the Agriculture Orientation Index (AOI) of government expenditures continue to increase in industrial countries—that is, the countries continue to invest in agriculture—whereas developing countries, other than China, have failed to do so. The AOI measures the central government's contribution to the agriculture sector, compared to the sector's contribution to GDP.

In developing countries, agricultural value-added per worker increases at an increasing rate, unlike in developing countries, perhaps because of the continued higher investment in agriculture. The inverted U-curve trend in the share of industrial value-added, with changes in per capita income, reveals the phenomenon of premature deindustrialization—as countries mature in their economic growth process, industry's share in GDP declines. Value-added per worker in industry rises faster in developed countries than developing countries, and in the service sector it increases at the same rate in the two groups of countries, as per capita income grows. The results for all 139 countries (38 developed and 101 developing) suggest that the elasticity of labor productivity, with respect to changes in per capita income, is highest in agriculture, followed by the industry and service sectors in developing economies. In developed economies, however, the elasticity of labor productivity is highest in industry, followed by the service and agriculture sectors, as we showed in Chapter 2. This outcome in the developing economies could be a result of increased investment in agriculture, but it could also be explained by the rapid withdrawal of labor from agriculture to the industrial or the service sector. The difference in patterns of structural transformation across regions is characterized by where the displaced labor goes. In LAC, labor productivity in nonagriculture is lower than in agriculture, supporting the findings of Martin and Mitra (2001) (as we discuss later), so that the process of growth slows down. Labor productivity in other regions is higher in industry than in services. Where labor moves predominantly to the service sector, the process of growth is slower. As per capita income increases, the difference between the share of value-added in agriculture and the share of employment in agriculture approaches zero (as labor moves out of agriculture), as poverty in agriculture declines and productivity differences between agriculture and nonagricultural sectors close. Countries exporting food, agricultural raw materials, and manufactures show these tendencies, but the rest of the SSA subgroups (such as exporters of fuels and exporters of ores and metals) do not. All subgroups, except food-exporting countries, show signs of premature deindustrialization at different per capita GDP thresholds.

There also continues to be a debate on the role of agriculture vs. industry in terms of economic growth. Industry has traditionally been considered to be the escalator of growth, first articulated by Kaldor (1966) and later by Page (2015), Rodrik (2016), and others, noting that elasticity of demand for industrial products tends to be higher than for agriculture or the service sector until the economy matures. In addition, technological change is faster, and the scope for productivity growth greater, in the industrial sector than in agriculture. Therefore, the faster the growth of manufacturing, the faster the growth of overall GDP. Indeed, today's industrialized countries experienced more rapid growth of manufacturing than GDP growth from the 1950s until 1973, after which their manufacturing growth decelerated and even became negative, and the service sector came into the ascendancy, which was explained largely in terms of higher income elasticity of demand for services than manufacturing in mature economies.

Dasgupta and Singh (2006, 16), like several others we reviewed, noted "pathological deindustrialization" in several Latin American and African countries in the 1980s and 1990s. Per capita income fell for almost a quarter of a century after 1982 in SSA. They explained the triple phenomenon of premature deindustrialization, jobless growth of manufacturing in the formal sector, and faster growth of services than of manufacturing.

They used the Kaldorian framework and generalizations derived by Kaldor about the relationship between the growth of output and employment in different sectors of the economy. The service sector, consisting of information and communications technology (ICT), telecommunications, business services, and finance, is replacing or complementing manufacturing as a new or as an additional engine of economic growth in emerging countries, in much the same way that we documented the case of the changing structure of trade in goods and services in the Introduction.

Page (2015) explained failure to industrialize in SSA by a combination of factors related to trade, agglomeration, and skills. He argued Africa and India no longer have the option of labor-intensive exports, which East Asia experienced earlier. Technology has been changing rapidly, and it calls for complex networked interactions.

The new narrative of global supply chains, however, has stressed the close complementarity of industry and service sectors during globalization, with a less clear distinction of the "desirability" of manufacturing as the escalator of growth. Bangladesh and Vietnam have done well on manufacturing. So, it is likely that some countries will do better than others. In the meantime, the global supply chains, which were given credit in the literature as sources of growth, focusing particularly on East Asia as the hub, had already slowed by 2018 (IMF, World Bank, and WTO 2018). The IMF and other analysts attributed the slowing of the global trade to the China–US trade dispute. The global COVID-19 crisis, with growing evidence of dependence on China for supply chains of medical equipment, has reinforced concerns about undue dependence on trade.

Developing countries spend a lower share of total expenditures on agriculture than their industrial counterparts, and they spend much of that support in the form of input subsidies. Despite those subsidies, some like Argentina and India implicitly tax their agriculture, as the OECD's Agricultural Policy Monitoring and Evaluation 2020 report noted (OECD 2020). Only one-eighth of total support goes to agricultural innovation systems, inspection and control systems, and rural infrastructure. If those are excluded, then their support for public goods, particularly for research, extension education, and transportation that would link farms to markets, is limited indeed (UNCTAD 2019). These findings are significant, given other evidence that:

1. Traditional sources of OECD ODA are shrinking relative to other sources (for example, private finance, remittances, philanthropy, and South–South cooperation);
2. Competition from other sectors, in need of large-scale capital and promising quick disbursements, is crowding out investment in agriculture, with the result that public goods in agriculture have been—and continue to be—underfunded by donors and governments alike;
3. Rapid growth in the domestic revenues of developing countries has not necessarily resulted in more resources to agricultural development;
4. There are substantial increases in private sector funding, South–South cooperation, and remittances, but information is limited on their extent, or how they benefit agriculture;
5. Innovative sources of financing, such as taxes on transactions, airlines, and auctions, have not been explored much in areas for climate change mitigation, biodiversity conservation, and water management; and
6. Governments could provide targeted payments to produce environmental public goods; however, only a handful of countries have adopted these policies, and they represent a small share of total support for agriculture.

Overall Financial Flows to Developing Countries and the Role of International Organizations

In Chapter 7, we outlined the financing picture. The "Big Five" organizations together spent or committed about US$21.4 billion annually on food and agriculture (of which about one-third is humanitarian or emergency assistance assistance) in 2018–19. Their role should be seen in the context of the overall financial flows, including remittances to developing countries (OECD 2019b). Those flows reached US$1 trillion in 2010, 3.6 times greater than 2002, and peaked in 2016 at US$1.5 trillion (in 2016 constant prices) (see Figure 7.1) (OECD 2018, 2019c).

Over recent years, growth has been driven particularly by rapid increases in remittances, growing almost 4.4 times since 2002, and in private resource flows, predominantly FDI. Over the past two decades, developing countries have steadily increased their share of global FDI receipts. FDI has represented one of the largest sources of developing countries' external financing, although FDI to developing countries dropped by about a third over 2016–17, following a 12 percent drop in overall external finance from 2013 to 2016, as well as project finance down 30 percent in the first quarter of 2018. External finance to poor countries is declining, despite a promise by the international community three years ago to increase development finance flows, through private investment. The latter have remained in decline in recent years, as we discuss below (OECD 2018).

ODA from advanced economies is below target and has fallen as a share of total resources received by many developing countries, while other flows such as remittances and philanthropy are increasing but comparatively small in recent years (OECD 2019c). In overall financial flows (US$1.3 trillion in 2017), over 46 percent was from private flows, nearly one-third as personal remittances, only 15 percent from ODA, and the remaining 6 percent was other official flows (OOF), including export credits in 2017. In 2018, net ODA flows from Development Assistance Committee (DAC) member countries amounted to US$150.4 billion (constant 2017 US dollars) in the form of grants, official aid loans, or contributions to multilateral institutions, and this amount had fallen by 2.7 percent from 2017, with a declining share going to the neediest countries (OECD 2019a, 2021).

Total ODA commitments to Agriculture, Forestry and Fishing (AFF) amounted to only US$11.2 billion (constant 2017 US dollars) (see Chapter 7, Figure 7.8).

By 2020, of all the different kinds of financial flows, only ODA flows had slightly increased to US$161.2 billion, or 0.32 percent of the combined gross national income (GNI) of OECD member countries, compared to 3 percent in earlier years (USAID 2019a, 2021). According to the World Bank, remittances and private capital flows had collapsed. Global remittances were projected to decline sharply by about 20 percent in 2020 due to the COVID-19 pandemic and shutdown, the sharpest decline in recent history. UNCTAD noted that global foreign direct investment fell by 42 percent in 2020, and outlook remained weakin 2021 (UNCTAD 2021). (See Chapter 7, Figure 7.1.)

Remittance inflows totaled US$706.6 billion in 2019, of which US$550.5 billion was going to LMICs (an increase of about 4.7 percent over the previous year), and these flows were projected to reach US$574 billion in 2020 and US$597 billion by 2021, involving some 272 million migrants (Ratha et al. 2019). FDI flows to developed economies had already fallen sharply to an estimated US$643 billion in 2019, from their revised US$683 billion in 2018 (UNCTAD 2020).

FDI inflows to AFF increased from US$0.33 billion in 1991 to US$1.8 billion in 2017, with significant year-to-year volatility. FDI inflows to AFF peaked in 2007, when they reached a record high of US$11.6 billion (in constant 2010 US dollars) (FAO 2020a).

Role of International Organizations

In these unprecedented times of global pandemic and the post-pandemic challenges, the world needs extraordinary leadership at the global and national levels of the kind President Roosevelt provided when he established the United Nations and the Bretton Woods institutions at the zenith of US economic and military power, when the United States could have been less magnanimous and less full of forethought. The G20 discussed later in this chapter has largely accepted and advocated for this world order, although Trump systematically undermined the multilateral system. FDR coined the term "United Nations," first used in the "Declaration by United Nations" of January 1, 1942, during the Second World War. Representatives of 26 nations pledged their governments to continue fighting together against the Axis Powers (UN 2020b). The invisible COVID-19 pandemic and the deep global recession are different, but equally complex challenges to overcome as were the Axis Powers. COVID-19 respects no borders and quickly became a global epidemic.

The World Bank in Food and Agriculture

Our history of the World Bank is longer than that of other organizations because it has had the longest and biggest financial presence in the largest number of countries, wrestling with the evolution of development thought, and particularly, the role of agriculture. Starting in 1944 until the time of this writing in 2020, and covering activities of 14 World Bank presidents, has allowed us to look at how the rapidly changing external and internal environment influenced Bank operations. We use periodization as an approach. In 1973, in a speech by President McNamara in Nairobi at that year's Annual Meetings in Kenya, McNamara made the case that the Bank's mission should be to alleviate "absolute poverty," which he described as "a condition of life so degrading as to insult human dignity," yet, "so common as to be the lot of some 40% of the peoples of the developing countries" (McNamara 1973). Since then, poverty alleviation of the lowest income groups has been the Bank's central mission, transforming the Bank from a staid infrastructure funding organization into a premier development organization, although World Bank presidents prior to McNamara laid a strong foundation for the Bank as well as for agriculture. In 2013, the Bank added to this mission the need to achieve shared prosperity (World Bank 2018, xi). Although we have discussed several indicators of performance, including decline in poverty and hunger, infant and child mortality, nutritional status, stunting and wasting, and total productivity growth, which are central to the missions of poverty eradication and shared prosperity, it is not possible to relate these outcomes directly to Bank inventions. However, there are number of other qualitative ways in which we can determine the World Bank contribution, and we do so here.

Several key conclusions specific to agriculture contained in Chapter 8 on the World Bank are highlighted here. First, developing countries' active voice in the Bretton Woods Conference in 1944, particularly the Mexican representation, forever defined the scope of the

World Bank, making it an institution addressing reconstruction as well as development. Second, early presidents, in the 1950 and 1960s, laid important foundations for the Bank's role in agriculture. The Green Revolution preceded the McNamara presidency. The Bank's contribution and the contribution of US bilateral aid and private foundations to the Green Revolution has been much deeper and wider, despite the controversy that surrounds it—more enduring than the Bank's role in integrated rural development in Africa under McNamara, although a number of environmental challenges including soil degradation, water shortages, loss of biodiversity, and GHG emissions have ensued following the Green Revolution, and regrettably, they have not been addressed as effectively and rapidly as they should have been. Without the Green Revolution, there would have been no food security or political stability throughout Asia. Issues currently being debated between developed and developing countries, including the developing country shares in the Bank's subscribed capital and the debt burden, have been perennial since the Bretton Woods Conference, where 44 delegations met and thrashed out the articles of agreement, and have yet to the tackled (Lowrey 2012).

Establishment of the International Financial Corporation (IFC) and the Economic Development Institute (EDI) (now called World Bank Institute) were important to advancing the Bank's mission in agriculture. EDI offered training on project appraisals for developing country nationals. EDI was established in 1956 and played a pivotal role in helping developing countries to prepare projects. Project lending became an innovative instrument for discreet investments, which the Bank could use to persuade skeptical Wall Street investors to invest in the Bank, minimizing defaults on loans—an important factor in the Bank's ability to mobilize commercial capital on the open market with the backing of callable capital provided by governments. With its transformation into the World Bank Institute (WBI), the scope of WBI expanded to develop individual, institutional, and organizational capacity through knowledge exchange, but it has never achieved the greatness of a university within the World Bank (Youker 2003; WBG 2009). IFC remains a very active player with its lending to agriculture larger than that of the International Bank for Reconstruction and Development (IBRD) and the International Development Association (IDA), but IFC's project-by-project (more appropriately described as "deal-by-deal") approach has had limitations in helping developing countries create an overarching environment favorable to private investment—which IFC is in the process of shedding in favor of a more strategic transformative approach (IFC 2019).

Then, in 1960, the Bank established the IDA to provide concessional assistance, starting with India's balance of payments crisis in 1958, extending assistance to all LICs, using a strict GDP per capita income criterion. IDA was instrumental in turning the Bank into the development institution that it is today. The Bank's approaches to financing practices have been adopted by other financial institutions, such as the Asian and African Development Banks and IFAD. IDA helped turned the Bank into a premier development leader in the global community (IDA 2007). The latest IDA19 replenishment contains an historic US$82 billion financing package for IDA-eligible countries for fiscal years 2021–3. It is a 3 percent increase in real terms, compared to IDA18 (IDA 2020), the largest pledge of assistance in a three-year period by any single organization. And, it is a testament to the confidence that donors, and increasingly, developing countries have in the Bank as an institution, particularly those that contribute to IDA. We argue, however, that it is time for the Bank to increase the voice of its shareholders from emerging and developing countries in its governance and in defining the Bank's strategic directions. According to convention, the United States appoints the Bank president, and Europe appoints IMF's managing directors.

All Bank presidents have been American males, with only one woman as an interim acting president for two months from February to April 2019. And, even with increased voting shares, developing and transition countries' shares amount to 46.6 percent (see Chapter 6, Figure 6.1).

IDA19 builds on the strong momentum of IDA18 to accelerate progress toward the World Bank Group twin goals of reducing poverty and achieving shared prosperity and the SDGs. Under the overarching appealing theme of "Ten Years to 2030: Growth, People, and Resilience," IDA19 supports the world's poorest and most vulnerable countries to implement *country-driven solutions* that are people-centered, boost economic growth, and *bolster resilience to climate shocks and natural disasters*. IDA19 focuses on five special themes: (1) climate change; (2) fragility, conflict, and violence; (3) gender; (4) governance and institutions; and (5) jobs and economic transformation. IDA19 also incorporates four crosscutting issues: debt, disability, human capital, and technology. Together with the IBRD capital increase, the Bank is the largest lender for development assistance, and particularly, to food and agriculture, even without considering lending of the entire Bank Group of five IOs, including IFC (founded in 1956) and the Multilateral Investment Guarantee Agency (MIGA, established in 1988) (MIGA 2015; IFC 2019). The Bank's role in financial transfers to developing countries towers over contributions of other international institutions.

Concessional assistance has been critical to minimizing indebtedness, but shares of agriculture in Bank lending and shares of World Bank lending in total capital flows to developing countries had declined over time since 1988—yet, the needs of developing countries have increased, even before the pandemic. It is hard to measure the Bank's role in crowding in private capital into developing economies and into agriculture, but it has been largely limited to helping make transformative policy and institutional changes in developing countries. An agreement with FAO to create the FAO–CP (cooperative program) in 1964 also expanded the Bank's capacity to lend to softer sectors like food and agriculture.

With IDA support, the Green Revolution ushered in a *package approach* of new technology consisting of hybrid seed, fertilizer, agricultural extension, credit, irrigation, and market access to farmers, demonstrating that complexity can be addressed in Bank lending. The IDA support injected energy in the stalled community development program. Working with the Rockefeller Foundation and the United States Agency for International Development (USAID), each of which promoted investment in training of scientists through training abroad and the establishment of land grant universities, the Bank promoted the package approach throughout Asia (see Heisey and Fuglie 2013).[15] The approach was nonideological and recognized market failures, creating a public sector delivery system in extension, seed production and distribution, fertilizer supply, credit, and a government food procurement program, established as part of the US conditionality of aid in the 1960s. Some have questioned if the private sector could have played this role then—was government involvement necessary on such a scale? Our research has led us to conclude that without

---

[15] The publication, *USAID Higher Education: A Retrospective 1960–2020* notes that since the Office of American Schools and Hospitals Abroad (ASHA) was incorporated into USAID in 1961, USAID/ASHA has provided assistance "to approximately 300 institutions globally" and aided "in the development of innovative and state-of-the-art schools, libraries, and medical centers in more than 80 countries," including in Africa: Cameroon, Ethiopia, Republic of Congo, Liberia, Nigeria, Sierra Leone, Tunisia, Zambia, Uganda, Kenya, Tanzania, and Malawi (McMaster et al. 2019). Had the rates of return to higher education not been wrongly estimated in an influential World Bank report in the 1980s, compared to returns on basic education, more investment would have been made in the much needed higher education, particularly in Africa (Tan, Jimenez, and Psacharopoulos 1986).

government's role, the Green Revolution would not have occurred on the scale it did. One of the weaknesses, we point out in Chapter 8, however, was that with the exceptions of China and Brazil, developing countries have not encouraged the private sector's role in seed and fertilizer as rapidly as they could have with better, more predictable policies and enough public investment in public goods—that is, higher education, research, infrastructure, and communications—to create a more robust green revolution, as discussed in Chapters 8 and 10 on the World Bank and CGIAR, respectively.

Africa faces far more daunting challenges in developing its agriculture: for example, limited human, physical, and institutional capital, and more complex ecologies. The *integrated rural development approach to agriculture*, which the Bank promoted during McNamara's time in the 1970s, and which was supported by donors, worked less well than in Asia, except for some recent examples of success, such as in Ethiopia. It should be recalled, however, that the Bank has been present in Africa's rural development since the early 1970s. Lele's early studies of rural development in the 1970s included case studies of World Bank and the Swedish Assistance to rural development in Ethiopia and other countries. Yet, few had memories of those projects when Lele visited Africa 20 or 30 years later. Little of what donors invested remained on the ground, unlike in Asia. Much time was wasted in agriculture and rural development due to political instability (Lele 1975, 1992). Several indicators of performance offer evidence: the Bank's own ratings of project performance for well over 2,000 projects in agriculture it has financed over 40 years, presented in Chapter 8, show ratings of African projects have been poorer than in the rest of the regions, even when African performance has improved. Given the nature of political systems, weak internal capacity has been a challenge, even when countries, such as Nigeria and Ghana, started with well-trained nationals in early years.

A report prepared by the Association of Public and Land-Grant Universities (APLU) for USAID noted:

> Higher education had been relatively neglected for some time by the international development community, stemming from the belief that it yielded lower social returns relative to other investments, especially primary and secondary education, and therefore should receive fewer public resources. Even more importantly, investments in higher education have often been considered regressive, reproducing existing social and economic inequalities. A 1986 World Bank study estimated that social rates of return for higher education in developing countries were on average 13 per cent lower than the returns from basic education [Tan, Jimenez, and Psacharopoulos 1986].

> These rates of return, however, were calculated using a narrow definition of benefits that typically considered only worker earnings (including income taxes). Analyses measuring the larger, broader and well-recognized social benefits lead to substantially different measures. Re-evaluations of data suggest that traditional estimates of social returns to higher education do not accurately reflect positive public "externalities," as metrics have tended to be based on the private returns measured by wage differentials and the social costs associated with education.

> A [recent] ... study by Claudio Montenegro and Harry Patrinos [2014] on rates of return to schooling around the world, which used data from 545 households in 131 economies from 1970–2011, shows that private rates of return to schooling are significantly higher in sub-Saharan Africa than in other world regions. ... This study also found that returns are highest globally at the tertiary level with a world average of 16.8 percent, while primary

and secondary returns are at 10.3 percent and 6.9 percent, respectively. Tertiary rates of return were also highest in sub-Saharan Africa at 21.9 percent. (APLU 2014, iii–v)

Given the state of education in Africa, more donor-funded projects are externally prepared and are less well vetted internally in Africa. Unfavorable external environments, such as commodity price declines, have also affected Africa more than most regions.

Neglect of Investment in Research and Education
Investment in R&D similarly has had huge returns, as the Green Revolution and CGIAR research shows. The World Bank's vigorous support to large public extension systems, through the Training and Visit (T&V) system, however, turned out to be a fad, leading to incentive problems among staff and managers of extension, as well as within the Bank itself for those who took exception to it (Anderson, Feder, and Ganguly 2006). Issues of scale, inadequate interaction with the national agricultural research systems (NARS), inability to attribute benefits, weak accountability, lack of political support, and limited budgetary resources all posed problems. Domestic stakeholders and external donor agencies also had different perspectives, posing other challenges. The main cause of the T&V system's disappearance was the incompatibility of its high recurrent costs with the limited budgets available domestically, leading to fiscal unsustainability.

In a study, "Hard Work and Hazard: Young People and Agricultural Commercialisation in Africa," Yeboah et al. (2020) examined whether rural transformation will provide farm and nonfarm employment opportunities for young people in Africa and how youth engage with the rural economy:

> The research was organized around two questions: (1) in commercialisation hotspots, what pathways do young people use to get themselves started in economic activities? and, (2) how are the pathways available and outcomes experienced influenced by factors of social difference, including gender? [The authors identified] three commercialization hot spots...Techiman North District in Brong Ahafo, Ghana; Dumila Ward in Morogoro, Tanzania; and Mvurwi farming area, Mazowe District, Mashonaland Central Province, Zimbabwe. Together they represent some of the historical and agro-ecological diversity within which agricultural commercialization is intensifying. (Yeboah et al. 2020, 144)

The study's results "challenges the assumption in policy discourse that migration to urban areas is the default option for rural young people": the authors do not find clear evidence that "additional training or skills would make a material difference to the lives of young people" and yet, "without much better basic education, including but not limited to literacy and numeracy skills, it is hard to see how the pathways and outcomes of young people will change for the better" (Yeboah et al. 2020, 150).

Performance of Africa
African projects were too large and complex, relative to Africa's absorptive capacity, initially a result of McNamara's push to meet lending targets he had established for agriculture and rural development, and did not invest enough resources to build African institutional and technological capacity (USAID 2013). Unlike in India and other parts of Asia, after an initial spurt in the 1970s, the Bank and donors such as USAID did not invest in capacity building in land grant universities globally, as they had in the past, and to the extent that they continued educational institutions and regional research organizations, did not achieve the

same effectiveness as in other regions. That USAID approach had been the gold standard (USAID 2013).

The APLU report on higher education in Africa noted:

> A growing body of literature suggests that the conventional estimates of the returns to investments in higher education do not accurately reflect the social value added by higher education, including job creation, good economic and political governance, increased entrepreneurship, and increased intergenerational mobility.
>
> Enrollment in tertiary education in SSA grew by 8.6 percent annually over the past 40 years, compared to 4.8 percent annually on average for the rest of the world. In 1970, there were approximately 200,000 higher education students in SSA. That number had increased to 4.5 million in 2008 and to 6.3 million in 2011.
>
> Even with this rapid growth in enrollment in higher education institutions in SSA, the Gross Enrollment Ratio [GER] for higher education is the lowest in the world, at 7.6 percent in 2011 . . . far lower than the global average of 30.1 percent. Therefore, with a very low GER and a large cohort of 17–20 years olds coming along, the potential for rapid increases in demand for higher education is quite great.
>
> Despite these dramatic increases in numbers of students, public funding for higher education increased at only 6 percent annually in SSA from 1970–2008. (APLU 2014, iv, v–vi)

Africa's reliance on rainfed agriculture and limited physical infrastructure have been additional challenges. Furthermore, while food shortages in Asia led to a strong political commitment to food self-sufficiency, African countries lacked the same political commitment as India, China, or Bangladesh, perhaps because African food deficits were not as dire. The self-sufficiency imperative was a major driver in Asia, and capacity building by the United States and private foundations were key to this effort in India and throughout Asia (Lele and Goldsmith 1986; Lele and Bumb 1994; Lele and Goswami 2020). In contrast to India, the Chinese investment in human capital has been much more internally driven.

The World Bank's approach to these challenges changed from one decade to the next. From the 1970s to the start of the early 1980s, when commodity prices deteriorated and debt mounted, in Ravi Kanbur's words, the situation changed from a dogma "where the state could do no wrong to one where the state could do no right" (Kanbur 2005, 12–13). The era of structural adjustment was followed more vigorously in the more aid-dependent Africa than in Asia. Although privatization proceeded, it has not led to a measurable improvement in performance and produced mixed results, for the reasons Dercon and Gollin (2014) outlined. Unlike in Latin America, Asian and African countries did not develop a thriving private sector service delivery. Pursuit of privatization by the Bank in the 1980s was followed by *participatory management* in the 1990s. Following the monumental internal Wapenhans (a senior manager in the Bank) inquiry in the early 1990s, undertaken by the Bank during the presidency of Lewis Preston, which examined the poor performance of the Bank lending portfolio and excesses of the structural adjustment period, the Bank shifted from the top-down approach to lending it had followed to a bottom-up approach. The principal messages of the Wapenhans report were threefold: (1) the need to improve quality of lending; (2) the need to improve country ownership; and (3) the need to shift from being a supply-driven to a demand-driven institution, with greater focus on the countries' input into country assistance strategies (World Bank 1992). Community-driven development

(CDD) was one of the outcomes. It is being practiced widely and has worked better in social areas than in agriculture. For example, India has the world's largest numbers of women's self-help groups which, while based on India's own initiative, were helped considerably by the Bank's livelihood projects. Participatory irrigation management, however, introduced when governments were strapped for resources, and agricultural extension have worked less well—except in China where the idea of participation was embraced and made into its own—than building community-demanded rural infrastructure, such as access to village-to-market roads. Mansuri and Rao were highly critical of the CDD approach in the early 2000s (Mansuri and Rao 2004, 2013). Perhaps, both the Bank's CDD approach and its evaluators' views have evolved over time. In Asian countries, like Indonesia and India, CDD projects, called by different local names (for example, in Indonesia, the Kecamatan Development Program [Pollock and Kendrick 2015]; in India, Self-Help Groups [Brody et al. 2015]), are embedded in countries' own strategies.

In terms of learning by the Bank's clients, China has demonstrated ability to discriminatingly take on new ideas and make them its own, when Chinese policymakers are convinced they make sense for China. The Chinese have also been effective implementers of Bank projects. Among other countries, Vietnam's agricultural portfolio, albeit smaller than China's or India's, has performed the best, followed by that of China.[16] India received the maximum amount of IDA and the maximum number of IDA projects, and its performance has been less stellar than that of China or Vietnam. These differences in performance among countries and over time have huge lessons for developing countries.

Demand for agricultural lending has been lukewarm since the Bank shifted to using country demand and country ownership as an approach. This is an important issue which future research needs to investigate. Governments have found agricultural projects to be small and slow in disbursing relative to sectors, such as infrastructure and education.

The Bank's "Vision to Action" report in 1997 and its "Reaching the Rural Poor" report in 2003 on food and agriculture were ineffective in increasing lending to agriculture (Ayres and McCalla 1997; World Bank 2003). They had emphasized research and extension through NGOs; sector policy lending in support of policy reforms that governments had undertaken; and sector investment lending, which in some cases helped consolidate donor projects into public expenditure support programs.

Rural development, as distinct from agriculture, involved NGOs and community-driven development—for example, the transfer of responsibilities for irrigation and drainage in most regions (as in northeast Brazil) to communities, at risk of reliance on overcentralized bureaucracies; rural finance focused on increased savings; and increased use of microfinance,

---

[16] The World Bank described Vietnam's development over the last 30 years as "remarkable." The Bank reported:

> Economic and political reforms under Đổi Mới, launched in 1986, have spurred rapid economic growth, transforming what was then one of the world's poorest nations into a lower middle-income country. Between 2002 and 2018, GDP per capita increased by 2.7 times, reaching over US$2,700 in 2019, and more than 45 million people were lifted out of poverty. Poverty rates declined sharply from over 70 percent to below 6 percent (US$3.2/day PPP). The vast majority of Vietnam's remaining poor—86 percent—are ethnic minorities.

In 2019, Vietnam's economy continued to show fundamental strength and resilience, supported by robust domestic demand and export-oriented manufacturing. Preliminary data indicate that real GDP grew by about 7 percent in 2019, close to the rate reported in 2018, and one of the fastest growth rates in the region. (World Bank 2020a)

less use of subsidies and promotion of increased competition, and land reform through market-assisted policies (Ayres and McCalla 1997).

The Bank-funded pilot land reform project in Brazil was successful, but it is unclear how much impact it has had on public policy at large. China's land reform was internally driven. Overall, it is unclear how much progress has occurred in countries on issues of land titling at scale.

The growing criticism of the "Washington Consensus" led President Wolfensohn during his 10-year tenure (1995–2005) to achieve debt rescheduling in 1996, greater focus on social safety nets, and increased aid to health and education. Lending to agriculture, however, did not increase. Poverty reduction was back on the agenda with the rise of CDD and the adoption of the Comprehensive Development Framework.

The *World Development Report (WDR) 2008: Agriculture for Development* was a reexamination of where the Bank and past assistance had gone wrong and what the direction for the future should be (World Bank 2007). *WDR*'s conceptual framework of three worlds in which it classified countries as predominantly agricultural, transitioning, and urbanized caught on in the international literature, as a useful device along with its implications for strategy. The *WDR* made a strong case for greater investment in smallholder agriculture and created an international buzz. It happened to coincide with a major food and financial crisis in 2007–8, and there was a temporary rise in investment, but it is unclear if it was due to the *WDR* or the food crisis. Overall, we have argued that much of the advocacy on agriculture by the international community has fallen flat in terms of developing countries investing more of their own resources, with some notable exceptions, such as China, which has shown spectacular results.

President Zoellick (2007–12) came to the Bank at the time of the food and financial crises. Despite many consultations following the crises, as we showed in Chapter 3, the donors' response to the crises was weak. A notable exception was the Bank's important Rapid Response through the Global Food Crisis, amounting to over US$1.6 billion that reached 66 million vulnerable people in 49 countries, mostly in Africa. It set a precedent for rapid response, which has become good practice in the complex world of COVID-19 and beyond.

Another signature achievement of Zoellick was the open data system, which has thrown sunshine on Bank operations and made standardized global data widely available, as well as provided a boost to the development research industry.

The World Bank's Response to Resilience, Natural Resource Management, and Climate Change

The Bank's response to building resilience in the 1960s and 1970s was largely through investment in surface irrigation for which there has been large potential in Asia and the Middle East, and through forestry projects. Investment in surface irrigation was also an important way to keep lending programs to agriculture up, but performance of irrigation projects has been mixed. Groundwater overdraft and soil degradation have been growing challenges, which were overlooked in irrigation lending. Over time, the Bank has shifted from large-scale irrigation to promotion of micro-irrigation and farmer-led irrigation, as well as investments in forestry projects that have promoted social and community forestry, sustainable management of tropical forests, poverty reduction, and payment for environmental services, disaster risk management, and more recently, digital agriculture (Dewees, Kishor, and Ivers 2020). However, on the whole, attention to resilience building has been relatively small beyond popular approaches, such as highly subsidized crop insurance, small-scale farmer-led irrigation, and international trade. On healthy food consumption the Bank has been promoting nutrition programs for women and children and food safety standards, but it has not tackled the more difficult issue of dietary transition, which involves working with the private sector, consumer education, and regulation.

Going Forward for the World Bank

In the preceding discussion, we explored the areas in which the Bank's lending could be more focused and prioritize investments in essential public goods, particularly research, education (capacity building) and extension, and community participation than it has done so far. It could do more to make factor and commodity markets work better by helping to improve the overarching policies of governments toward the private sector rather than financing projects. A study from the World Resources Institute by Searchinger et al. (2018) is one of the few that takes an integrated view of sustainable development and proposes a 22-item menu of options that could allow the world to achieve a sustainable food future. It does so by providing a conceptual framework that simultaneously meets growing demands for food and avoids deforestation, and reforests or restores abandoned and unproductive land—and in ways that help stabilize the climate, promote economic development, and reduce poverty, while closing three gaps: the food gap, the land gap and the GHG mitigation gap. Each country needs to develop such comprehensive approaches, which are currently lacking. The Bank/IDA can help them in achieving this objective. These options and approach can well support the forthcoming Food Systems Summit and the need, as stated by the Secretary General, that "transforming food systems is crucial for delivering all the SDGS" (UN 2020e).

Food and Agriculture Organization of the United Nations

FAO is a unique organization among the Big Five organizations. It is not a "development" organization like the other four we review here, which are focused on developing countries. FAO was conceived as a membership organization of equal partners, 45 member states when it was established in 1945, and now with 194 member states, 1 member organization (the European Union [EU]), and two associate members (Faroe Islands and Tokelau). Understandably, after the Second World War, with widespread incidence of hunger, nutrition was at the center stage of FAO's mission. In the 1970s and 1980s, with one of the sharpest rises in food and energy prices, the sale of US grains to the Soviet Union and the erosion of US food surpluses in 1972, attention of the international community shifted to food security, with a focus on meeting the calorie gap. Nutrition has returned to the center stage since the beginning of the 1990s, with combined efforts with UNICEF on child nutrition and WHO on health and nutrition (FAO 2015).

FAO was intended to be and continues today as a global platform for discussion of issues that confront all member countries, in order to reach international agreements on issues, such as food safety standards, control of cross-border pests and diseases, information and knowledge on all matters pertaining to food and agriculture—broadly defined to include forestry, fisheries, livestock, and the management of natural resources. There is much literature on safety standards too large to summarize here. (See, for example, Unnevehr and Ronchi [2014]; Jaffee et al. [2019].)

FAO is the only organization among the five with the legitimacy to provide global public goods with regard to food and agriculture, but over the years it has also been expected to provide technical assistance to member countries in support of these objectives.

In Chapter 4 on food security, we document the shifts in FAO's focus over time from developing an international consensus on food security, to its downstream work on food security at the country level, which received much criticism. At the end of the 1990s, FAO played a critical role in getting "reducing hunger" by half, as part of the twin MDG1 goals (reducing poverty and hunger), and then retaining and broadening that focus when the UN adopted the SDGs in 2015. From 2012 to 2013, FAO repositioned itself to monitor progress on SDG2 ("no hunger"), and over time, it has faced tension concerning its global public goods (GPGs) function. The reality is, of course, more complex and is related, in part, to FAO's financing.

FAO is also unique in the way it has been financed since its establishment. Its financing has come from assessed contributions of member countries. As these contributions have not increased in monetary terms and have declined in real terms, FAO has increasingly relied on voluntary contributions as its agenda has expanded. FAO allocates its assessed contributions in support of its GPG functions, and voluntary contributions provided by donor countries steer work accordingly. So, land tenure gets voluntary funding from member states (for example, from funding from Switzerland and Germany), which may include bilateral technical assistance. Norway finances antimicrobial resistance (AMR) or locust control, but again, that is its choice, reflecting the broad development agenda of member states and support to FAO.

Thus, a matrix to analyze sources of funding and types of programs can be instructive on what gets funded. If FAO has the assurance of the scale, delivery, and timeliness of payment delivery of assessed contributions, combined with multilateral governance and strategic direction funded by assured voluntary support, a stronger FAO could emerge. Yet, as the US withdrawal from WHO reveals, member countries have not been of one mind.

Out of the biannual budget of about US$2.6 billion (US$1.3 annually), FAO allocates a portion of its assessed contribution in support of its GPG functions, and voluntary contributions now provide 61 percent of the total budget (FAO 2020b). It is not surprising, therefore, that perhaps even inadvertently, donors drive the agenda.

The data FAO collects from countries are a global public good. The data are used extensively, and the world relies on timely quality data for analysis of the global, regional, and national food security situation. Its 50X2030: Data-Smart Agriculture initiative is meant to close the Agricultural Data Gap through a multipartner effort that seeks to bridge the global agricultural data gap by transforming country data systems across 50 countries in Africa, Asia, the Middle East, and Latin America by 2030. This unprecedented initiative focuses on improving country-level data by building strong nationally representative survey programs—building upon the experiences of the FAO Agricultural Integrated Survey (AGRISurvey) Programme and the World Bank's Living Standards Measurement Study–Integrated Surveys on Agriculture (LSMS–ISA)—that produce high-quality and timely agricultural data and make evidence-based decision-making in agriculture the norm.

The locusts in East Africa, the fall armyworm (FAW) in Latin America and Asia, together with the global pandemic of COVID-19, with diseases spread from plants and animals to humans, have stressed the importance of both the GPG functions and the country-level technical programs that FAO can deliver. These capabilities will also provide important knowledge and direction for at least some of the specific objectives of the forthcoming Food Systems Summit 2021, including "ensuring access to safe and nutritious food for all"; "shifting to sustainable consumption patterns"; and "nature-positive production at sufficient scale" (UN 2020d, 2). FAO management, staff, and member states have already been actively involved in the initial preparations for the Summit.

FAO played a key role in containing the H1N1 pandemic, working jointly with WHO and the Organisation for Animal Health (OIE) in containing cross-border spread of H1N1, which has become endemic in Asia (IEG 2013).

The key issue is the need for funding of FAO on a predictable, sustainable basis, beyond its current assessed contribution.

CGIAR

CGIAR has made extraordinary contributions to productivity growth since its founding, mostly through its plant breeding programs and a few key innovations, such as the control of the cassava mealybug. As yield growth slowed and pressure on natural resources has increased, the scope of CGIAR's research has increased and become more complex. Donor demand on CGIAR to show results on the ground has also increased the shift of research to applied and adaptive research, which ideally should be carried out by strong and capable NARS, with CGIAR generating global and regional public goods that require long-term, complex scientific inputs that are too big for most countries to provide. CGIAR has been in an almost perpetual state of reform from the start of the new millennium:

- 2001 to 2007: First steps to formalization of governance and management; movement toward a centralized model
- 2008 to 2015 (June): Transformational change in governance and management
- 2015 (June) to 2016 (July) to present: Further changes to governance and management
- 2019 (November–December): One CGIAR—a unified governance and management through a reconstituted System Management Board and new Executive Management Team.

CGIAR's challenges have been many. First, it has worked to develop an integrated System-level research program across the System's 15 independent research centers, with different research mandates. Second, it seeks to promote research innovations that transform food, land, and water systems, in the context of climate change, to ensure a scientifically sound program. Third, demonstrating its contribution to the realization of SDG2, CGIAR works to reduce hunger and foster diet diversification by addressing issues of micronutrient deficiencies. CGIAR must carry out an increasingly complex research agenda under conditions of fragmented and uncertain financial resources tied to numerous small projects. Finally, the excessive reliance for food security of the poor on basic staple crops and livestock (wheat, rice, maize, beans and root crops), which has been at the center of CGIAR's research, must be curtailed to incorporate biodiversity into the farming systems to increase resilience to climate change and resource pressures and promote dietary diversity.

In the light of these strategic imperatives, CGIAR has responded to its funding and management challenges creatively. The 9th Systems Council (November 2019) approved yet one more institutional innovation of a unified and integrated "One CGIAR," to adapt to the rapidly changing global conditions, while also making the CGIAR System more relevant and effective. The process of moving to One CGIAR, as agreed to at the Extraordinary General Assembly of the Centers (Rome, December 2019) includes a unified governance and management through a reconstituted System Management Board and new Executive Management Team. An established unifying mission of "Ending hunger by 2030—through science to transform food, land, and water systems in a climate crisis," focused on five impact areas: nutrition, poverty, gender, climate, and environment in support of the SDGs to support a more unified and integrated CGIAR as the "One CGIAR" (CGIAR 2019, 2020).

The 2018 CGIAR Annual Performance Report noted that 105 policies, legal instruments, and investments were modified in their design or implementation, informed by CGIAR research which involved 1,003 partnerships (CGIAR 2018, 10). The new management structure of the "one CGIAR" is now in place, with three able managing directors. An important lesson of the CGIAR experience is that the actual impact of CGIAR derives from the contribution of its research results and outcomes to complementary policies and investments at the national level in developing countries, as occurred during the first Green Revolution. In the successive reforms of CGIAR, the need for substantial complementary investments in R&D and human and institutional development in developing countries to foster effective partnerships, with support from the World Bank, bilateral donors, and national governments, have somehow not received the attention they deserve.

These developments should be seen in the context of the substantial decline in the funding for public sector research in developed countries, which was the backbone of supply of upstream technologies that CGIAR could draw upon. CGIAR research, in turn, benefited both developing as well as developed countries. Rapid technological change in a variety of fields has led to substantial increase in private sector research filling the void created by slowdown in public sector research. Relatedly, there has also been a growing concentration of research in the hands of few multinational companies; issues of intellectual property have become more complex with growing role of the private sector. And finally, civil society's resistance to new genetically modified technologies remains strong, even to gene editing; thus, even where technologies are available, they are not being introduced. This is a big difference between the Green Revolution period and 2020. Barrett attributes a decline in public sector research to a more difficult "regulatory" environment and the post-2000 EU Cartagena precautionary principle,[17] increasingly complex intellectual property, and weak anti-trust enforcement, with only large, well-funded private institutions able to take on these challenges (Barrett 2020). On the other hand, the need for new technologies to the growing environmental constraints to make agriculture more resistant is greater than ever.

CGIAR's outputs to deliver the needed impact upon revitalized and connected food systems requires that the CGIAR reforms be complemented by creative, new funding instruments: for example, impact investments, results-based investments, investments in digital agriculture and physical and human capital at the national, and where appropriate, regional levels. We make a case for investment of IDA and IBRD resources in CGIAR.

The International Fund for Agricultural Development

IFAD came into being because of the 1974 World Food Conference's focus on the need to increase investment in food production and the less documented issue of the levels of international capital generated by high oil prices and production. Three years after the

---

[17] The Cartagena Protocol on Biosafety to the Convention on Biological Diversity is an international agreement adopted on January 29, 2000, and entering into force on September 11, 2003, which seeks to ensure the safe handling, transport, and use of living modified organisms (LMOs), derived from biotechnology, that could have adverse effects on biological diversity or present risks to human health. See the "Convention on Biological Diversity": https://bch.cbd.int/protocol/

Rome Conference in 1974, IFAD was set up in 1977, as a specialized agency of the United Nations, to finance agricultural development projects (with loans on concessional terms together with some grants) primarily for food production in the developing countries (IFAD 1976). As an international financial institution (IFI), IFAD's basic documents (for example, Lending Policies and Criteria adopted by the Governing Council in 1978 [IFAD 1978]) broadly followed the procedures and processes of the World Bank's IDA and the Funds of both the Asian and African Development Banks (ADB and AfDB). Projects and programs to "introduce, expand or improve food production systems and to strengthen related policies and institutions within the framework of national priorities and strategies" were intended to be developed by member state governments, appraised by other IFIs, funded by IFAD, and then and implemented/supervised by other IFIs, as formally designated "Cooperating Institutions" (IFAD 2016, 23).

IFAD's financial modalities were established to follow the standard IFI replenishment processes, consisting of a three-year cycle with contributions coming from member states, with equal voting rights.[18] IFAD further subdivided its members into three categories, I, II and III, or Lists A, B and C, as they have become more commonly known. These three categories, reflected in the IFAD logo itself, represented the founding financial principle of IFAD, that the financial contributions of List A (OECD countries) would be matched by equal contributions (*grosso modo*) by List B (Organization of the Petroleum Exporting Countries [OPEC] countries), with developing states (List C) also invited to contribute. This was reflected in the initial contributions (IFAD1) at the time of IFAD's establishment of SDR 496m, SDR 381m and SDR 7.8m.[19] President Al-Sudeary, from Saudi Arabia, was elected in 1977, as the first IFAD President, to be followed by presidents who, with the exception of President Båge (Sweden), have all been from OPEC member states.

The unique OPEC/OECD/member financial proposition that underpins IFAD was put under immediate stress by the Iranian Revolution in 1977–9, with the consequence that Iran's initial pledge of US$124.75 million has, to date, not yet been fully received. Nevertheless, List A contributions remained consistent from 1980 to 2010 with regular, strong contributions from the United States (with the IFAD funding decisions moving into Treasury from the State Department), Italy, the United Kingdom, Germany, and the Nordic countries.

With competition for funds and donor earmarking a constant characteristic of multilateral aid, the need to demonstrate relevance and results has become a key parameter, as well as maintaining the assessments (Multilateral Organisation Performance Assessment Network [MOPAN], Multilateral aid review [MAR]) of its efficiency and effectiveness. This was initially led by President Idriss Jazairy (1984–92), who focused on IFAD's strategy, resources, and operations on targeting the rural poor and the marginalized, including women, both creating a specific role for IFAD and differentiating itself from the broader agricultural sector investments of the World Bank and other multilateral development banks.[20]

Despite the validation of IFAD's role,[21] and the evidence of on the ground performance, the contributions of member states' replenishment commitments (1997–2012) only covered about a third of IFAD's loans and grants program. IFAD's internal resources covered the

---

[18] IFAD Replenishment https://www.ifad.org/en/replenishment, and Consultation on the Replenishment of IFAD's Resources: https://webapps.ifad.org/members/repl

[19] Initial pledges in Special Drawing Rights (SDR) and freely convertible national currencies (IFAD 1976)

[20] In 1992, IFAD organized the Summit on the Economic Advancement of Rural Women in Geneva.

[21] The World Bank's *World Development Report 2008: Agriculture for Development* was a key output at this juncture (World Bank 2007).

remaining two-thirds, the highest such ratio among IFIs (IFAD 2011). For IFAD7 and IFAD8 (2007–12), these internally generated resources included some pre-commitments of predicted future loan repayments, the Advanced Commitment Authority (ACA). For IFAD9 onward (2013), the ACA was replaced with a sustainable cash flow approach, whereby financial obligations are projected and matched by a sequence of forecasted cash inflows over the disbursement period (IFAD 2012).

The fragility of the IFAD financial model was highlighted during the IFAD9 replenishment (2013–15).

While List A's total contributions more than doubled over the three replenishment periods, an important proportion of List A's IFAD9 pledges were complementary contributions for the Adaptation for Smallholder Agriculture Programme (ASAP).[22] The 2014 Corporate-level Evaluation: "IFAD's Replenishments" noted:

> The United Kingdom, Sweden, Belgium, and Canada pledged a portion of their replenishment contributions for the ASAP—a total of US$312 million. Setting aside the funds pledged for ASAP, List A's IFAD9 contributions were only three percent higher than their IFAD8 commitments of US$859 million. Without ASAP, List A's contributions—and indeed the entire replenishment—would have been significantly lower. (IFAD 2014, 49)

As ASAP was a grant program, effectively, it did qualify as "regular resources," as it did not generate any loan reflows into IFAD's financial model. Additionally, while total replenishments grew, fewer countries participated in IFAD9 than in IFAD7 and IFAD8. This has continued with, in IFAD11, no participation from the United States, Spain, Denmark or Belgium (the latter being the originator and financier of the Belgium Survival Fund). These concerns were well recognized in 2014 by IFAD's own evaluation: "In a scenario of low growth from traditional donors in List A there is however not sufficient evidence to determine if new and returning members' replenishment pledges will grow fast enough to keep up with the increasing demand for IFAD's assistance" (IFAD 2014, 56). In this regard, the Evaluation also noted, "the classification of members into three categories (the "List system"), which is unique to IFAD and not applied in any other international organization, seems under some pressure" (IFAD 2014, v). And, while "valid when IFAD was established, has not kept up with global economic development" (IFAD 2014, vi).

Seeking to diversify funding, IFAD established the EUR300 million Spanish Food Security Co-financing Facility Trust Fund to augment the resources allocated to IFAD-funded projects in September 2010, with IFAD administering the trust fund as Trustee. As the repaid loan funds are returned to Spain, there are no reflows entering IFAD's financial model for subsequent on-lending (unlike IFAD loans funded by replenishment or other contributions). Similar additional resources have been mobilized from KfW Development Bank (Germany) and France, Agence Française de Développement (AFD), though as the Evaluation notes "any associate risks will have to be carefully addressed upfront" (IFAD 2014, 56).

As IFAD embarks on the IFAD12 replenishment process, in the face of the continued pressure on IFAD's finances, cash flow, and liquidity, the ambition to access market resources for funding would, perhaps, have been concomitantly strengthened by addressing some of the evaluation lessons clearly identified in 2014. This requires strong and clear

---

[22] ASAP provides climate and environmental finance to smallholder farmers. See https://www.ifad.org/documents/38714170/40213192/asap.pdf

leadership both by IFAD and by its members. The competition for multilateral resources remains high, as does the need, and while IFAD's effectiveness and efficiency have been well documented, a greater openness to innovative partnerships with entities such as GAFSP would send a stronger signal of IFAD's ability to fundamentally adapt.

This IFAD "specificity" should allow it to make a tangible contribution in the preparations for, and at, the Food Systems Summit, and in particular, the specific Summit objective #4 for "advancing equitable livelihoods and value distribution (raising incomes, distributing risk, expanding inclusion, and promoting full and productive employment and decent work for all)" (UN 2020d, 2). These are all areas where IFAD has credible, ground-level experience.

The World Food Programme

WFP won the 2020 Nobel Peace Prize, well deserved for its achievements against many odds. It is hard to discuss "Food for All" without mentioning geopolitics behind the man-made crises arising out of power politics. The UN System and its individual agencies are operating with one hand tied behind their collective back. The Middle East has been the hotspot for conflicts. WFP, the world's largest humanitarian agency, faces many other conflicts in the world, which go unnoticed or are overshadowed by larger ones. Half of WFP's emergency assistance went to the Middle East and North Africa in 2018. As preparations for the Food Systems Summit in 2021 continue, the experience of WFP should bring needed knowledge and experience to one of the Summit's specific objectives: "building resilience to vulnerabilities, shocks and stresses (ensuring the continued functionality of healthy and sustainable food systems)" (UN 2020d, 2).

As this chapter was being finalized, 1 million people from the Idlib Province in Syria were on the move. On *Amanpour & Co.* broadcast on *PBS* on July 6, 2020, correspondent Arwa Damon showed babies who had frozen to death in the middle of the night, as freezing temperatures in Idlib were displacing families, lacking food and clothing, on the move. WFP Executive Director, David Beasley, former Governor of South Carolina (1995–9) and Republican Party politician, was making a passionate yet rational argument to the donors in Geneva to ensure food and cash were flowing to these deprived children, women, and men.

Yemen, another hotspot, suffers from internecine conflicts between Shias and Sunnis, supported by regional powers, Saudi Arabia and United Arab Emirates versus Iran-backed Houthi, with superpowers, the United States, United Kingdom, and France, allied with Saudis, and Russia allied with Iran. According to the charity Save the Children, an estimated 85,000 children with severe acute malnutrition may have died between April 2015 and October 2018 (Save the Children 2018). About 80 percent of the population, or 24 million people, need humanitarian assistance and protection. Some 20 million people need help securing food, according to the UN. Almost 10 million people are considered to be "one step away from famine" (UN News 2019).

David Miliband, CEO of the International Rescue Committee, argued that an immediate ceasefire and resumption of peace talks, with assured food and financial assistance, is the only solution to this suffering, in which the United States has a major peacemaking role, which it is not exercising.

The COVID-19 pandemic temporarily suspended the war in Yemen. The Saudi-led coalition fighting in the country implemented a unilateral, two-week ceasefire, hoping to support a political solution to the conflict and help prevent the spread of COVID-19. While United Nations Secretary General António Guterres welcomed the decision, a Houthi opposition official described the move as "just another ploy" (BBC News 2020b). Rejecting the ceasefire, the Houthis demanded lifting of air and sea blockades. The UN has warned that the death toll from the COVID-19 virus could "exceed the combined toll of war, disease, and hunger over the last five years" and warns that Yemen is "on the brink of the world's worst famine in 100 years if the war continues" (BBC News 2020a).

Similar heartbreaking stories of the children separated from their families on the United States' southern border made one wonder when international leadership and governance would address these issues. President-Elect Biden has vowed to reunite nearly 500 children with their parents. Since June, increasing numbers of COVID-19 cases have been reported at detention facilities because of the viral outbreaks. A federal judge ruled that the US Department of Homeland security must release children at the facilities, but the court did not make an argument for the parents of the children to be released. This followed the order of another district in Los Angeles who ordered US Immigration and Customs Enforcement (ICE) on June 26 to release children from three family residential centers, writing that the centers were "on fire and there is no more time for half measures" (Hsu 2020).

President Eisenhower approached the United Nations to establish a world food program in 1961, to dispose of US food surpluses, created by US agricultural policies. It also displayed the degree of confidence the United States had in the UN System at the height of its economic power. First established within FAO, it soon became clear that WFP's emergency response function was incompatible with FAO's more deliberative, bureaucratic approach to addressing issues of global agreements. WFP became an independent entity. Its Executive Director is still appointed jointly by the UN Secretary-General and the Director-General of FAO. Like CGIAR, WFP's funding is entirely based on voluntary contributions with 42.2 percent of the contributions coming from the United States in 2019. WFP's operations have also seen considerable growth, with total assistance increasing from US$1.7 billion in 2000 to US$8 billion in 2019.[23] Globally, WFP assisted 86.7 million people in 83 countries in 2018, 70 percent of those facing critical hunger levels (WFP 2020h).

WFP has undergone several transitions: first, from delivering food aid in-kind to providing food assistance, including cash-based transfers (CBTs). This means the traditional development activities of its public works program have contracted, but WFP still remains the largest provider of school feeding programs to well over 16 million children. Food aid was a top-down, one-way process, whereas food assistance, into which it has morphed, involves more complex appreciation of people's long-term development needs and the diverse approaches needed to achieve them. WFP distributes food in areas where it is scarce. In places where food is available, but unaffordable, WFP provides vulnerable people cash or vouchers to buy nutritious foods. These CBTs give people more choice, protect them from financial exploitation, and support the local economy (WFP 2020c, 2020d, 2020e), but such distribution programs that increase access can also create distortions.

Second, and related, is the transition from procuring food from traditional food surplus countries such as the United States to at least partially obtaining it from nearby emerging countries, thereby reducing procurement costs and speeding up delivery to beneficiaries (WFP 2017). Third, while remaining the world's leading humanitarian agency, it is aiming

---

[23] See "Contributions by Year," https://www.wfp.org/funding

to straddle humanitarian aid with development goals, to "combine frontline action with the quest for durable solutions" (WFP 2020c).

WFP's CBTs include a range of instruments, ranging from physical bank notes, vouchers, or electronic funds, given to beneficiaries to spend directly, "empowering people to feed themselves," as "a long-haul process: as of early 2016, cash still only represented just over a quarter of all WFP assistance. But with its benefits of flexibility, efficiency and beneficiary choice, cash is growing rapidly within [WFP's] hunger-fighting portfolio" (WFP 2020c).

Growth in the WFP operations is a result of emergencies caused by a combination of conflict, climate shocks, pandemics, and other disasters. Among the ongoing emergencies in 15 countries or regions, the majority are fueled by conflicts in the Middle East, North Africa, and Myanmar in SA, with 68.5 million forced to flee their homes. Of this total, more than 40 million are internally displaced, and nearly 25.4 million are refugees (WFP 2019a).

At the same time, the importance of linking emergency/humanitarian aid to long-term development assistance is greater than ever to build capacity in the countries to address long-term needs of development, agriculture, schooling, safety nets—areas in which WFP has a lot to contribute.

WFP uses state-of-the-art technology to help forecast emergencies and direct assistance to where it is most needed. Through its global networks, WFP develops quality emergency programs that help WFP plan, pre-position supplies, and minimize the time needed to deliver life-saving food assistance. A recent WFP news release reported that the COVID-19 pandemic "could almost double the number of people suffering acute hunger, pushing it to more than a quarter billion by the end of 2020" (WFP 2020b).

Specific Roles of the World Food Programme

WFP leads the Logistics and Emergency Telecommunications clusters and co-leads the Food Security cluster. WFP also provides the United Nations Humanitarian Air Service for all concerned humanitarian agencies and the United Nations Humanitarian Response Depots for use by the humanitarian community (WFP 2019a, 2019b, 2020g).

Country Capacity Strengthening

National governments are increasingly taking the lead in the fight against hunger. WFP offers a wide range of capacity development and technical assistance services to facilitate the design and delivery of sustainable national solutions to combat hunger and malnutrition (WFP 2018, 2020a).

South–South Cooperation

The WFP supports governments of developing countries in their efforts to achieve Zero Hunger by facilitating the transfer of knowledge, skills, resources, and technical know-how, as well as through policy, advocacy, and regional collective action, to strengthen national capacities. WFP's Centers of Excellence in Brazil and China are among WFP's key mechanisms for South–South cooperation.

As WFP explains these mechanisms:

> Driven by rising country demand, we have stepped up support to governments through South–South and triangular cooperation. The expression covers the direct exchange of knowledge, experiences, skills, resources and technical know-how among developing countries, often assisted by a donor or multilateral organization, such as WFP. This

"triangular" facilitation may take the form of funding, training, management, technological systems, or other types of support. (WFP 2020f)

In describing its country/capacity strengthening, WFP notes:

> The World Food Programme (WFP) offers nationally tailored technical assistance and capacity development to strengthen individual government capacities in all these fields. We respond to capacity gaps identified through an assessment process that is led by the partner government, facilitated by ourselves, and supported by other partners.
>
> This process helps identify national demand for capacity strengthening along five critical pathways, as relevant to achieving national food security and nutrition objectives:
>
> • Policies and legislation
> • Institutional accountability
> • Strategic planning and financing
> • National programme design and delivery
> • Engagement and participation of non-state actors
>
> These areas also guide WFP's offer of technical assistance and capacity strengthening. Demand for WFP assistance must be articulated around national development priorities, critical needs, and available resources. Appropriate sustainable food security and nutrition solutions are jointly decided by the national government and all development partners, including ourselves. These solutions may entail enhancing capacity for emergency preparedness and response, logistics, and supply chain management; strengthening risk reduction capabilities through social safety nets; and bolstering climate risk management, adaptation, and resilience. Frequently included in country programmes is support to local market development and capacity building in crosscutting areas such as nutrition and HIV/AIDS programmes.
>
> Both technical assistance and capacity strengthening may be provided through WFP's own staff and as part of its programme activities, or through the deployment of external experts. WFP may...facilitate the transfer of knowledge by third parties, for example through South–South or Triangular Cooperation models, which promote peer-to-peer sharing of best practices between developing nations. (WFP 2020a)

Global Governance of Food and Agriculture

Global governance should be seen in the context of the rising challenges of pandemics; climate change; the growing ideological divide between the right and left philosophies; the increased number of actors at the global level, including bilateral and multilateral donors, philanthropic and civil society organizations, and the private sector; and the chaos it has led to in global governance, particularly as the United States abandoned its pivotal role in the liberal world order, which it had founded. The agreements included the withdrawal from the Paris Accord, the Trans-Pacific Partnership and support for WHO at the critical time of the pandemic, when the need for cooperation is greater than ever. The Biden–Harris administration has rejoined almost all of those efforts, but delivering results will be challenging for the United States, given that Trump won 72 million votes despite his abominable performance on many fronts. Further, with the Democrats holding only

48 seats in the Senate (with 2 Independents caucusing with them and Vice-President Harris casting tie-breaking votes), Biden needs to generate support from all members in his party and some Republicans to pursue a multilateral agenda.

For these and other reasons, the Big Five organizations need to work together more by playing to their comparative advantages and partnering more actively to mobilize public and private funds. Even if they work together more effectively than they have to date, however, the available resources are too small relative to the investment needs of LICs.

The G20 has shown the capacity to provide the critical bridge between IOs and the larger UN System. In its latest communiqué, the G20 provided strong support for the work of WHO on COVID-19, but it also has a large potential for playing a significant role in emerging challenges—such as efforts toward the achievement of universal access to vaccines for COVID-19 and other future pandemics—in the same way that it responded to the financial crisis.

Role of the G20 in Global Architecture

The G20 countries account for nearly two-thirds of the world's population, about 85 percent of global GDP, almost 80 percent of global trade in food and agricultural commodities, and around 60 percent of the world's agricultural land.[24] Together, they hold an enormous potential to be the interface between the world's richest countries that have led the liberal world order since the Second World War, and the United Nations' family of 196 countries and islands. Their potential to provide a collective leadership role has surely emerged over the last decade, but it is yet to be fully realized with many roadblocks, which will have to be overcome.

The G20 was established at the level of finance ministers and central bank governors after the Asian financial crisis in 1997, but had a marginal role in global affairs. It was upgraded to leader's level at the instigation of President Bush after the global financial crisis of 2008, when the credibility of the G7 was low, given that the crisis had originated in New York and London. At the Third Summit in Pittsburgh, Pennsylvania, in September 2009, the G20 was designated as the premier forum for discussing, planning, and monitoring international economic cooperation. Its objective was to provide strong, sustainable, and balanced growth (SSB) with wide ownership (OECD 2009; G20 Information Centre 2015). The G20 successfully acted as a coordinating agency to tackle the 2008 financial crisis and some G20 members also contributed their savings through the IMF to alleviate the financial crises in several countries. The G20 thus transformed itself over time as an agent for change, nudging other IOs in desired directions (Cooper 2019). Yet, it has also been criticized for mission creep, as each rotating presidency has sought to introduce new issues. Nevertheless, with a few exceptions, most notably the development agenda introduced by the Republic of (South) Korea in 2010, the G20 has not succeeded in doing so with any sustained impact (Cooper, 2019). Some analysts have described the G20 and its role in international economic governance more as an interregnum rather than a regime (Helleiner 2010). Yet, by now the G20 has embedded itself into the system of international governance

---

[24] The G20 is made up of 19 countries and the EU. The 19 countries are Argentina, Australia, Brazil, Canada, China, Germany, France, India, Indonesia, Italy, Japan, Mexico, the Russian Federation, Saudi Arabia, South Africa, South Korea, Turkey, the United Kingdom, and the United States.

(Cooper 2019). It is the only body that can deal with issues spanning IOs, ministries, and countries and is thus critical for successfully addressing many of the international challenges, such as climate change, environmental degradation, global pandemic, financial instability, trade, food insecurity, and growing displacement of refugees.

The G20 successfully engineered a recovery from the 2008 crisis through coordinated expansionary policies. It has failed to deliver, however, on its promise at the Pittsburgh Summit to promote strong, sustainable, and balanced growth. Also, although the Seoul Summit successfully put development on the international agenda, so far, there has not been noticeable progress in this area. Recent IMF estimates suggest a significant decline in GDP in LAC and SSA.

From the beginning, questions have been raised about the legitimacy of the G20, seen either as a self-appointed body or one formed by US President Bush. Delivery on development is critical for raising its legitimacy among developing countries and particularly, for the legitimacy of the developing country members of the G20 (Agarwal and Whalley 2013).

In the area of development, the G20 has focused on agriculture and infrastructure. G20 agriculture ministers first met for in Paris on June 22–3, 2011, in response to the global food crisis. A dramatic spike in food prices occurred, as a result of the perfect storm described in Chapter 3. With food riots breaking out by January 2009 in more than 30 cities, as an aftermath of food price spikes, and growing concerns about political instability, G20 leaders convened their agriculture ministers to manage the crisis. This first meeting, in Paris in 2011, produced the Action Plan on Food Price Volatility and Agriculture, with several recommendations on productivity growth. The interagency policy report by key IOs (FAO, IFAD, IMF, OECD, UNCTAD, WFP, the World Bank, WTO, IFPRI and the UN HLTF) also made 10 recommendations and several sub-recommendations (G20 2011, 2012). The G20 leaders endorsed these recommendations at Cannes a few months later in November 2011. One of these recommendations is AMIS, housed in FAO and funded by donors. They also led to the financing of GAFSP. These decisions show the power of what the G20 countries can do if they put their mind to it. Other key recommendations they should implement include greater investment in agriculture, less protection of agriculture, and generally, the creation of a level playing field for all countries.

The ideas emerging in Paris were reinforced in the meeting of the agriculture vice ministers in Mexico City in May 2012, and by the G20 leaders at the 2012 Los Cabos Summit that followed in June. Several other countries had imposed bans on exports of wheat and rice before the agriculture ministers met. As global food prices declined in 2013 and 2014, a consensus emerged that export bans should be avoided to minimize collateral damage on importing countries. That consensus has lasted through the COVID-19 crisis, as reported earlier.

The Ebola virus and the Russian annexation of the Crimea diverted attention in subsequent meetings until Istanbul on May 7–8, 2015, when G20 agriculture ministers met for a second time and made several commitments, followed by the G20 leaders' 2015 summit in Antalya.

They have repeatedly called for a halt to any increase in trade protection and for completion of the Doha Round, but protection levels have gone up broadly. Global Trade Alert tracks state interventions taken since November 2008 to date, which are likely to affect foreign commerce—trade in goods and services, foreign investment, and labor migration. From 2008, 17,928 protectionist interventions were undertaken by G20 countries, compared to 7,271 liberalizing interventions, and there has been a precipitous drop in both liberalizing and protectionist interventions since 2019, when the COVID-19 pandemic started (GTA 2020).

Yearly, interventions were rising until 2017 for liberalizing actions and until 2018 for protectionist actions. Since then, annual interventions have decreased for both kinds of interventions, but protectionist interventions remain greater than liberalizing ones (GTA 2020).

The G20 has not been effective in pushing for a successful conclusion to the Doha Round of the WTO membership, in which the G20 countries are major stakeholders. The G20 declaration of the G20 Extraordinary Agriculture Ministers Meeting in 2020 reaffirmed the importance of "continued flow of food, products, and inputs essential for agricultural and food production across borders," and acknowledged the challenges of "minimizing the risk of COVID-19 while keeping food supply chains functioning" and ensuring "the health, safety, welfare, and mobility of workers in agriculture and throughout the food supply chain." They also stressed the important role of AMIS and the need for financial support of it. They agreed "not to impose export restrictions or extraordinary taxes on food and agricultural products purchased for non-commercial humanitarian purposes by the World Food Programme (WFP) and other humanitarian agencies." They called on "other members to continue providing timely and reliable information on global food market fundamentals to help markets, countries, and consumers make informed choices" (G20 Information Centre 2020).

"Acknowledging the critical role of the private sector in food systems," the ministers called for "enhanced public and private partnership to help mobilize rapid and innovative responses to the impacts of this pandemic on the agriculture and food sectors." Given the current challenging circumstances, they further urged the avoidance of "food losses and waste caused by disruptions throughout food supply chains." The ministers further urged that, "in line with the One Health approach," there was a need to strengthen "mechanisms for monitoring, early warning, preparedness, prevention, detection, response, and control of zoonotic diseases, and for developing science-based international guidelines on stricter safety and hygienic measures for zoonosis control" (G20 Information Centre 2020).

The ministers expressed gratitude to the farmers, workers, and "small, medium, and large scale agri-food businesses for their continuous efforts to ensure our food supply." The ministers stated that they would intensify efforts, "in line with WTO rules and the 2030 Agenda for Sustainable Development, to support them to sustain their activities and livelihoods during the crisis and to assist their recovery afterwards" (G20 Information Centre 2020).

The G20 ministers declared their intention to continue their:

> ... cooperation with relevant international organizations and within their mandates to work to: reinforce international cooperation; identify additional actions to alleviate the impacts of COVID-19 on food security and nutrition; share best practices and lessons learned, such as addressing barriers to supply chains; promote evidence and science-based information and combat misinformation; provide capacity building and technical assistance; and promote research, responsible investments, innovations and reforms that will improve the sustainability and resilience of agriculture and food systems.

> This work could build on the Food and Agriculture Organization's (FAO's) evolving response to COVID-19, the International Fund for Agricultural Development's (IFAD's) evolving efforts to support a strong recovery from the effects of COVID-19, policy monitoring and analysis by the OECD, and other relevant initiatives, such as the preparation for the 2021 UN Food Systems Summit. (G20 Information Centre 2020)

To summarize, G20 has rhetorically adopted a huge agenda. With slowing economic growth in OECD countries, however, even before the COVID-19 pandemic and the economic crisis that the pandemic has caused, combined with aid weariness, the prospect of generating more aid does not seem promising. Hence, the need to shift from billions to trillions has largely entailed a call for either more private sector investment or public–private partnerships. To realize the G20 declarations, some countries have provided support to IOs to tackle issues: for example, in addition to support to AMIS, the German government has provided support to FAO to work on water security and water quality. G20 does not have its own secretariat. Central monitoring to follow up on compliance of these declarations is ad hoc, except for worthy programs like at the University of Toronto or the Global Trade Alert. More fundamentally, growing tensions among G20 members, such as the Sino-American tensions, the growing tension between the United States and EU members, and the China–India border dispute and the proxy war between Saudi Arabia and Iran, which is playing out in Yemen, have the potential to reduce the effectiveness of the G20. Differential performance among G20 countries with respect to the COVID-19 pandemic has highlighted some key issues such as the importance of national leadership—well illustrated by the changed outcomes concerning COVID-19 infection in the United States, following the change of leadership after the 2020 presidential election. Also, there is the urgent need to learn cross-country lessons on best practices with regard to the containment of COVID-19 within G20 countries: for example, from the experiences—besides in China—of the successful South Korea. Trade and intellectual property issues affecting vaccine know-how, given the case that most of the developing world lacks access to vaccines, have been raised by several southern members of G20, including Brazil, South Africa, and India. Along with these issues, there are, of course, the thorny issues of human rights.

In addition to Trump's exit, the G20 is losing some of its highly respected leaders such as Angela Merkel. It needs to fill the leadership vacuum to credibly address the vacuum that currently exists at the level of global governance and begin to address some of the key issues of climate change, pandemics, health, food security, and trade aid.

Role of 54 Industrial and Emerging Countries Going Forward

In this book, we reviewed history of thought and action on food and nutrition security, covering a 75-year period. Success in achieving broad-based food and nutrition security contributed in a positive way to the pace and pattern of structural transformation of some countries. Global and national governance and international assistance have played a key role in that process. The share of emerging countries in global GDP has increased dramatically since the 1990s.

Yet, food security for all has not been realized. Where success has been achieved, it has required broad-based investment in the population and in education. Those investments have helped achieve rapid demographic transition among the Asian Tigers, and later, in China and Southeast Asia. Investment in infrastructure and in R&D helps to accelerate transformation. In these Asian countries, where small farmers dominate, even the smallest farms have been highly productive.

In Asia, external assistance played a demonstrably positive role. East Asian and Southeast Asian countries have done well, not only in food and nutrition security, but in structural transformation and industrialization. Their higher domestic savings and investments and generally open economies have helped.

SA and Africa have done less well. The countries still face many challenges, including persistent poverty, widespread chronic and transitory food and nutrition insecurity, increasing income inequality, large gender gaps, environmental degradation, climate change (seriously affecting the Pacific Island countries), and continuing inadequate access to health and education, electricity, and safe drinking water. There is no room for complacency.

Most of these countries have been relatively peaceful, although several African countries (Ethiopia, Côte d'Ivoire, for example) have experienced considerable internal conflict that has affected their development.

Peace and stability set the groundwork for Asia's economic success.

There are overarching policy issues at the global and regional level, which influence incentives for agricultural production in developing countries. We list below the 11 recommendations of the OECD report, *Agricultural Policy Monitoring and Evaluation 2020*, of 54 countries which support agriculture at levels between US$500 billion and US$700 billion *annually*, depending on how they are measured. This compares with the enhanced IDA of US$85 billion over *three years*. Reforms in these policies would not only release substantial resources to assist developing countries but also improve incentives for production and trade by creating a level playing field, as well as improving environmental management. The recommendations are:

1. *Dismantle, in a gradual but consistent process, all policies identified as particularly detrimental to market efficiency and the sector's environmental performance.* The priority reform should be the sectors where high support is provided via the most distorting measures. Such reforms would reduce intra-sectoral distortions and allow markets to function better, while simultaneously reducing environmental pressures that derive from incentives to intensify production in unsustainable ways.

2. *Phase out distorting budgetary support.* This would liberate funds for more targeted policies, as well as for investments to make agriculture more productive, environmentally sustainable, and resilient. Such funds could be allocated to wider societal priorities including climate adaptation and mitigation.

3. *Remove, as quickly as possible, trade restrictions imposed in the context of the COVID-19 pandemic.* This would allow the market to perform its distributing and signalling role.

4. *Ideally, anchor reductions in distorting support and associated trade protection through the multilateral process.* If that cannot be achieved, the trend towards broader and deeper regional trade agreements can offer a way forward.

5. *Improve the efficiency of support to individual producers* by targeting well-defined, quantifiable outcomes of public interest. Payments for non-commodity outputs (such as the landscape) are means to create markets for public goods, while providing agricultural producers with additional income opportunities.

6. *Strengthen the efficiency of agri-environmental policies* by successively raising baseline requirements for agricultural practices, including by making cross-compliance mandatory where relevant. More ambitious public good and environmental outcomes can be delivered through targeted support.

7. *Integrate farm households into social security systems* to reduce the need for spending on agriculture-specific income support. Governments should improve their understanding of the financial situation of farm households and target any market failures that lead to persistent low incomes within the agriculture sector.

8. *Focus public efforts in risk management* on catastrophic and systemic risks for which private solutions cannot be developed. Care should be taken that public support does not crowd out on-farm and market-based risk-management tools. Governments should prioritise investments that build farmers' capacity to both manage current risks and to adapt to an evolving risk environment, especially under climate change.

9. Collect lessons from the ongoing COVID-19 pandemic, notably regarding the effectiveness of different forms of government interventions in responding to shocks and developing preparedness.

10. Increasingly prioritise the provision of key public services to the sector by investing in agricultural innovation systems, in relevant hard and soft infrastructure, and appropriate biosecurity systems protecting human, animal and plant health. Explore opportunities to improve the delivery of such services via digital technologies.

11. Improve the coherence and transparency of policy packages by avoiding the provision of conflicting incentives to market participants, and by integrating agricultural policies into economy-wide programmes, such as those related to labor markets and social security, the environment, transportation and communication, trade and other infrastructure. (OECD 2020, 20–1)

Healthy food systems similarly call for improved information to consumers and smart government regulation, implementation, and monitoring. These are not areas in which conventional aid projects have been active. To date, food systems that extend beyond the farm have almost exclusively been in the private sector. Whereas there has been a great deal of analytical work on the growth of value chains, economists have not wrestled with the impact of these value chains on accelerating dietary transition, which would require active involvement of both the private sector and consumers. A food systems approach links food and agricultural production to human health, planetary health, and economic health. The food value chain, as the COVID-19 pandemic has shown, influences what is produced, where it is produced and consumed, lost or wasted, processed and traded locally, regionally, and internationally. As we document in Chapter 4, countries would need more political commitment to healthy food systems; the development of coherent cross-sectoral policies, combined with more investment in institutional capacity at all levels; engagement with both national and international food processors; and value chains to develop the right initiatives for production (for all farm scales); and marketing, including at consumer level to support the right choices being made by those both purchasing and preparing food. This political commitment should come from the forthcoming Food Systems Summit and the leadership of the Secretary-General António Guterres in recognizing that "Transforming food systems is crucial for delivering all the Sustainable Development Goals," together with the specific objectives of the Summit (UN 2020d, 1):

1. Ensuring access to safe and nutritious food for all (enabling all people to be nourished and healthy, progressive realization of the right to food);

2. Shifting to sustainable consumption patterns (promoting and creating demand for healthy and sustainable diets, reducing waste);

3. Boosting nature-positive production at sufficient scale (acting on climate change, reducing emissions and increasing carbon capture, regenerating and protecting critical ecosystems and reducing food loss and energy usage, without undermining health or nutritious diets);

4. Advancing equitable livelihoods and value distribution (raising incomes, distributing risk, expanding inclusion, promote full and productive employment and decent work for all); and

5. Building resilience to vulnerabilities, shocks and stresses (ensuring the continued functionality of healthy and sustainable food systems). (UN 2020d, 2)

These recommendations entail addressing national, regional, and global reforms that need to be undertaken collectively. The broad range of stakeholders involved in the process offers a singular opportunity to address the need for environmentally sustainable food production and nutritious, healthy food. Repurposing Agricultural Policies and Support for Sustainable Food Systems is an ambitious program of work that the World Bank has developed jointly with FAO and OECD and developing countries to achieve the necessary adjustments in policies, which will achieve the triple win in equity, efficiency, and environmental sustainability (personal exchange, Madhur Gautam, December 21, 2020)

In these and other efforts, Africa will need special attention—more political commitment, more investment in human capital and institutions, and more transfer of international public funds over a predictable, consistent, nonideological basis and on a long-term basis—to achieve results. Africans will have to drive the development agenda.

References

Agarwal, Manmohan, and John Whalley. 2013. "China and India: Reforms and the Response: How Differently Have the Economies Behaved." NBER Working Paper 19006, National Bureau of Economic Research, Cambridge, MA. http://www.nber.org/papers/w19006.pdf

AGRA (Alliance for a Green Revolution in Africa). 2020. "Multiple Shocks Are Disrupting Agricultural Farming Systems in Sub-Saharan Africa." In *Food Security Monitor: Africa Food Trade and Resilience Initiative*, Edition #4, June. Nairobi: AGRA. https://agra.org/news/agras-june-food-security-monitor-finds-that-multiple-shocks-are-causing-severe-disruptions-to-agricultural-farming-systems-in-sub-saharan-africa/

Alston, Julian, Joanna P. MacEwan, and Abigail Okrent. 2016. "The Economics of Obesity and Related Policy." *Annual Review of Resource Economics* 8 (1): 443–65.

Anderson, Jock R., Gershon Feder, and Sushma Ganguly. 2006. "The Rise and Fall of Training and Visit Extension: An Asian Mini-drama with an African Epilogue." Working Paper Policy Research Working Paper No. 3928, May, and Rural Development Department, World Bank, Washington, DC. http://documents.worldbank.org/curated/en/190121468140386154/pdf/wps3928.pdf

APLU (Association of Public and Land-Grant Universities). 2014. "African Higher Education: Opportunities for Transformative Change for Sustainable Development." Prepared for review by the United States Agency for International Development (USAID). APLU Knowledge Center on Higher Education for African Development, Washington, DC. https://www.aplu.org/library/african-higher-education-opportunities-for-transformative-change-for-sustainable-development/file

Ayres, Wendy Schreiber, and Alexander F. McCalla. 1997. "Rural Development: From Vision to Action." Environmental and Socially Sustainable Development Studies (ESSD) and Monograph Series No. 12. Washington DC, World Bank. http://documents.worldbank.org/curated/en/445541468326432599/Rural-development-from-vision-to-action

Barrett, Christopher. 2020. "Overcoming Global Food Security Challenges through Science and Solidarity." Fellows Address, August 11. Agricultural & Applied Economics Association (AAEA) Annual Meetings, *American Journal of Agricultural Economics*. https://doi.org/10.1111/ajae.12160

Baye, Kaleab. 2020. "COVID-19 Prevention Measures in Ethiopia: Current Realities and Prospects." ESSP Working Paper 142, Ethiopia Strategy Support Program International Food Policy Research Institute (IFPRI), Washington, DC, and Federal Democratic Republic of Ethiopia Policy Studies Institute, Addis Ababa. https://www.ifpri.org/publication/covid-19-prevention-measures-ethiopia-current-realities-and-prospects

BBC News. 2020a. "Yemen Crisis: Why is There a War?" June 19. https://www.bbc.com/news/world-middle-east-29319423

BBC News. 2020b. "Yemen War: Coalition Ceasefire to Help Combat Coronavirus Begins." April 9. https://www.bbc.com/news/world-middle-east-52224358

Béné, Christophe, Peter Oosterveer, Lea Lamotte, Inge D. Brouwer, Stef de Haan, and Steve D. Prager. 2019. "When Food Systems Meet Sustainability—Current Narratives and Implications for Actions." *World Development* 113: 116–30.

Bevis, Leah E. M., and Christopher B. Barrett. 2020. "Close to the Edge: High Productivity at Plot Peripheries and the Inverse Size-Productivity Relationship." *Journal of Development Economics* 143: 102377 (March).

Bhattacharyya, Ranjan, Birendra Nath Ghosh, Prasanta Kumar Mishra, Biswapati Mandal, Cherukumalli Srinivasa Rao, Dibyendu Sarkar, Krishnendu Das, Kokkuvayil Sankaranarayanan Anil, Manickam Lalitha, Kuntal Mouli Hati, and Alan Joseph Franzluebbers. 2015. "Soil Degradation in India: Challenges and Potential Solutions." *Sustainability* 7 (4): 3528–7. https://www.mdpi.com/2071-1050/7/4/3528

Brody, Carinne, Thomas de Hoop, Martina Vojtkova, Ruby Warnock, Meghan Dunbar, Padmini Murthy, and Shari L. Dworkin. 2015. "Economic Self-Help Group Programs for Improving Women's Empowerment: A Systematic Review." *Campbell Systematic Reviews* 11 (1): 1–182. https://onlinelibrary.wiley.com/doi/full/10.4073/csr.2015.19

Brouwer, Inge D., John McDermott, and Ruerd Ruben. 2020. "Food Systems Everywhere: Improving Relevance in Practice." *Global Food Security* 26: 100398.

Ceres2030. 2020. "Donors Must Double Aid to End Hunger—And Spend It Wisely." https://ceres2030.org/shorthand_story/donors-must-double-aid-to-end-hunger-and-spend-it-wisely/

CGIAR. 2018. "CGIAR System Annual Performance Report 2018." CGIAR System Organization, Montpellier, France. https://storage.googleapis.com/cgiarorg/2019/09/7657b19f-pr-2018-executive-summary.pdf

CGIAR. 2019. "One CGIAR: A Bold Set of Recommendations to the System Council." SC9-02, CGIAR System Council Meeting, Chengdu, China, November 13–14. https://storage.googleapis.com/cgiarorg/2019/11/SC9-02_SRG-Recommendations-OneCGIAR.pdf

CGIAR. 2020. "What's Next for CGIAR?" News, February 2. https://www.cgiar.org/news-events/news/whats-next-for-cgiar/

CGTN. 2020. "China to Be the Only Economy with Positive Growth in 2020, Says IMF Report." October 19, Beijing. https://www.cgtn.com

Charatan, Fred. 2005. "Bush Announces US Plan for Flu Pandemic." *BMJ* 331 (7525): 1103.

Chauhan, Jitendra M. S., S. Rajendra Prasad, Satinder Pal, Pranab Ranjan Choudhury, and K. Udaya Bhaskar. 2016. "Seed Production of Field Crops in India: Quality Assurance, Status, Impact and Way Forward." *Indian Journal of Agricultural Sciences* 86 (5): 563–79.

Collier, Paul, and Stefan Dercon. 2014. "African Agriculture in 50 Years: Smallholders in a Rapidly Changing World." *World Development* 63: 92–101.

Cooper, Andrew F. 2019. "The G20 Is Dead as a Crisis or Steering Committee: Long Live the G20 as Hybrid Focal Point." *South African Journal of International Affairs* 26 (4): 505–20.

Dasgupta, Sukti, and Ajit Singh. 2006. "Manufacturing, Services and Premature Deindustrialization in Developing Countries: A Kaldorian Analysis." UNU–WIDER Research Paper No. 2006/49, May, United Nations University–World Institute for Development, Helsinki.

Dercon, Stefan, and Douglas Gollin. 2014. "Agriculture in African Development: A Review of Theories and Strategies." CSAE Working Paper WPS/2014–22, Centre for the Study of African Economies, University of Oxford, Oxford. http://www.csae.ox.ac.uk/materials/papers/csae-wps-2014-22.pdf

Development Initiatives. 2017. *Global Nutrition Report 2017: Nourishing the SDGs*. Bristol, UK: Development Initiatives. https://globalnutritionreport.org/reports/2017-global-nutrition-report/

Development Initiatives. 2018. *2018 Global Nutrition Report: Shining a Light to Spur Action on Nutrition*. Bristol, UK: Development Initiatives. https://globalnutritionreport.org/reports/global-nutrition-report-2018/

Dewees, P. A., N. Kishor, and L. Ivers. 2020. "John Spears, A Life in Forestry: An Introduction to the Special Issue." *International Forestry Review* 22 (S1): 1–8.

Echeverría, Ruben. 2020. "Fixing the Global Food System after Coronavirus." IFPRI Blog, May 15, International Food Policy Research Institute, Washington, DC. https://www.ifpri.org/blog/fixing-global-food-system-after-coronavirus

Economist, The. 2020a. "The New World Disorder." Leaders, June 18. https://www.economist.com/leaders/2020/06/18/the-new-world-disorder

Economist, The. 2020b. "Why Britain Has So Many COVID-19 Deaths." April 18. https://www.economist.com/britain/2020/04/18/why-britain-has-so-many-covid-19-deaths

Emont, Jon. 2020. "Developing World Loses Billions in Money from Migrant Workers." *Wall Street Journal*, July 5.

Fanzo, Jessica, Lawrence Haddad, Rebecca McLaren, Quinn Marshall, Claire Davis, Anna Herforth, Andrew Jones, Ty Beal, David Tschrley, Alexandra Bellows, Lais Miachon, Yuxuan Gu, Martin Bloem, and Arun Kapuria. 2020. "The Food Systems Dashboard is A New Tool to Inform Better Food Policy." *Nature Food* 1: 243–6.

FAO (Food and Agriculture Organization of the United Nations). 2004. "Human Energy Requirements." Report of a Joint FAO/WHO/UNU Expert Consultation, Rome, October 17–24, 2001, FAO Food and Nutrition Technical Report Series No. 1. http://www.fao.org/3/a-y5686e.pdf

FAO (Food and Agriculture Organization of the United Nations). 2013. *The State of Food and Agriculture: Food Systems for Better Nutrition*. Rome: FAO. http://www.fao.org/3/i3300e/i3300e00.htm

FAO (Food and Agriculture Organization of the United Nations). 2015. *70 Years of FAO (1945–2015)*. Rome: FAO. http://www.fao.org/3/i5142e/I5142E.pdf

FAO (Food and Agriculture Organization of the United Nations). 2020a. Statistics. Foreign Direct Investment to Agriculture, Forestry and Fishery. http://www.fao.org/economic/ess/investment/fdi/en/

FAO (Food and Agriculture Organization of the United Nations). 2020b. "Strategic Planning." About FAO. http://www.fao.org/about/strategic-planning/en/

FAO (Food and Agriculture Organization of the United Nations), IFAD (International Fund for Agricultural Development), UNICEF (United Nations Children's Fund), WFP (World Food Programme), and WHO (World Health Organization). 2018. *The State of Food Security and Nutrition in the World 2018: Building Climate Resilience for Food Security and Nutrition.* Rome: FAO. http://www.fao.org/3/I9553EN/i9553en.pdf

FAO (Food and Agriculture Organization of the United Nations), IFAD (International Fund for Agricultural Development), UNICEF (United Nations Children's Fund), WFP (World Food Programme), and WHO (World Health Organization). 2019. *The State of Food Security and Nutrition in the World 2019. Safeguarding against Economic Slowdowns and Downturns.* Rome: FAO. http://www.fao.org/publications/sofi/en/india/cid/1775032

FAO (Food and Agriculture Organization of the United Nations), IFAD (International Fund for Agricultural Development), UNICEF (United Nations Children's Fund), WFP (World Food Programme), and WHO (World Health Organization). 2020. *The State of Food Security and Nutrition in the World 2020: Transforming Food Systems for Affordable Healthy Diets.* Rome: FAO. http://www.fao.org/3/ca9692en/online/ca9692en.html

FAO (Food and Agriculture Organization of the United Nations), and WHO (World Health Organization). 2019. "Sustainable Healthy Diets—Guiding Principles." Rome. http://www.fao.org/3/ca6640en/ca6640en.pdf

FOLU (Food and Land Use Coalition). 2019. "Growing Better: Ten Critical Transitions to Transform Food and Land Use." The Global Consultation Report of the Food and Land Use Coalition, September. https://www.foodandlandusecoalition.org/wp-content/uploads/2019/09/FOLU-GrowingBetter-GlobalReport.pdf

Foster, Andrew D., and Mark R. Rosenzweig. 2017. "Are There Too Many Farms in the World? Labor-Market Transaction Costs, Machine Capacities and Optimal Farm Size." NBER Working Paper No. 23909, National Bureau of Economic Research, Cambridge, MA. https://www.nber.org/papers/w23909.pdf

Friedman, Lisa, and Brad Plumer. 2020. "Trump's Response to Virus Reflects a Long Disregard for Science." *New York Times*, April 28. https://www.nytimes.com/2020/04/28/climate/trump-coronavirus-climate-science.html

Fuglie, Keith O. 2012 "Productivity Growth and Technology Capital in the Global Agricultural Economy." In *Productivity Growth in Agriculture: An International Perspective*, edited by Keith O. Fuglie, V. Eldon Ball, and Sun Ling Wang, 335–68. Wallingford: CABI.

Fuglie, Keith, Boubaker Dhehibi, Ali Ahmed Ibrahim El Shahat, and Aden Aw-Hassan. 2020. "Water, Policy, and Productivity in Egyptian Agriculture." *American Journal of Agricultural Economics* (early online version). https://doi.org/10.1111/ajae.12148

G20 (Group of 20). 2011. "Price Volatility in Food and Agricultural Markets: Policy Responses." G20 Interagency report with contributions from FAO (Food and Agriculture Organization of the United Nations), IFAD (International Fund for Agricultural Development), IMF (International Monetary Fund), OECD (Organisation of for Economic Co-operation and Development), UNCTAD (United Nations Conference on Trade and Development), WFP (World Food Programme), the World Bank, the WTO (World Trade Organization), IFPRI (International Food Policy Research Institute), and the UN HLTF (High Level Task Force on Global Food and Nutrition Security), June 2. http://www.foodsecurityportal.org/sites/default/files/g20_interagency_report_food_price_volatility.pdf

G20 (Group of 20). 2012. "Sustainable Agricultural Productivity Growth and Bridging the Gap for Small Family Farms." Interagency Report to the Mexican G20 Presidency with contributions by Diversity, CGIAR Consortium, FAO (Food and Agriculture Organization of the United Nations), IFAD (International Fund for Agricultural Development), IFPRI (International Food Policy Research Institute), IICA (Inter-American Institute for Cooperation on Agriculture), OECD (Organization of for Economic Co-operation and Development), UNCTAD (United Nations Conference on Trade and Development), UN High Level Task Force on the Food Security Crisis, WFP (World Food Program), World Bank, and WTO (World Trade Organization), April 5. http://www.sagarpa.gob.mx/G20/Documents%20G20/G20%20agricultural%20productivity%20draft%20report_5%20April%202012.pdf

G20 Information Centre. 2015. "G20 Summit Commitments by Issue: 2008 to 2015." Munk School of Global Affairs & Public Policy, Trinity College, University of Toronto. http://www.g20.utoronto.ca/compliance/commitments.html

G20 Information Centre. 2020. "Ministerial Statement on COVID-19 Virtual Meeting." G20 Extraordinary Agriculture Ministers Meeting, April 21. Munk School of Global Affairs & Public Policy, Trinity College, University of Toronto. http://www.g20.utoronto.ca/2020/G20_Agriculture_Ministers_Meeting_Statement_EN.pdf

Gates, Bill. 2015. "The Next Outbreak? We're Not Ready." TEDTalk, March. https://www.ted.com/talks/bill_gates_the_next_outbreak_we_re_not_ready?language=en

GATT (General Agreement on Tariffs and Trade). 1947. World Trade Organization, Geneva.

Gautam, Madhur, and Mansur Ahmed. 2018. "Too Small to Be Beautiful? The Farm Size and Productivity Relationship in Bangladesh." Policy Research Working Paper 8387, Agriculture Global Practice, World Bank Group, Washington, DC.

Gettleman, Jeffrey, and Suhasini Raj. 2020. "'Lionhearted' Girl Bikes Dad Across India, Inspiring a Nation." New York Times, New Delhi, May 22. https://www.nytimes.com/2020/05/22/world/asia/india-bicycle-girl-migrants.html

Give2Asia. 2020. "2020 Australian Bushfire Crisis." January 14, Give2Asia, Oakland, CA. https://give2asia.org/australian-bushfire-crisis-2019-2020/

GNR (Global Nutrition Report). 2020. 2020 Global Nutrition Report. https://globalnutritionreport.org

Gollin, Douglas, and Christopher Udry. 2019. "Heterogeneity, Measurement Error, and Misallocation: Evidence from African Agriculture." Global Poverty Research Lab Working Paper No. 18–108, December. Global Poverty Research Lab, Northwestern University, Evanston, IL.

Gopinath, Gita. 2020. "The Great Lockdown: 20 Worst Economic Downtown Since the Great Depression." IMF Blog, April 14. https://blogs.imf.org/2020/04/14/the-great-lockdown-worst-economic-downturn-since-the-great-depression/

GTA (Global Trade Alert). 2020. Global Dynamics. A Centre for Economic Policy Research (CEPR) Initiative. https://www.globaltradealert.org/global_dynamics

Guha, Ramachandra. 2020. "The Darkest Hour: Politics and Play: A Six-fold Crisis Confronts India." The Telegraph, May 22. https://www.telegraphindia.com/opinion/coronavirus-a-six-fold-crisis-confronts-

Heisey, Paul, and Keith Fuglie. 2013. "The United States Experience." Technical Session II—Agricultural Research, Education and Extension Integration for Development: Status, Elements of Successes, Issues, Challenges and Prospects, for "Agricultural Education—Shaping India's Future," XI Agricultural Science Congress 2013, Indian Council of Agricultural Research (ICAR), Bhubaneswar, India, February 7–9.

Helleiner, Eric. 2010. "A Bretton Woods Moment? The 2007–2008 Crisis and the Future of Global Finance." *International Affairs* 86 (3): 619–36.

Hicks, John R. 1939. *Value and Capital.* Oxford: Clarendon Press.

HLPE (High Level Panel of Experts on Food Security and Nutrition). 2014. "Food Losses and Waste in the Context of Sustainable Food Systems." HLPE Report 8, June, Committee on World Food Security, Rome. http://www.fao.org/fileadmin/user_upload/hlpe/hlpe_documents/HLPE_Reports/HLPE-Report-8_EN.pdf

HLPE (High Level Panel of Experts on Food Security and Nutrition). 2017. "Nutrition and Food Systems." HLPE Report 12, September, Committee on World Food Security, Rome. http://www.fao.org/3/a-i7846e.pdf

Hsu, Spencer S. 2020. "U.S. Might Separate Families after Federal Judge Orders ICE To Free Migrant Children." *Washington Post*, July 7. https://www.washingtonpost.com/local/legal-issues/us-may-separate-families-after-federal-judge-orders-ice-to-free-migrant-children/2020/07/07/a1758ad6-c067-11ea-b178-bb7b05b94af1_story.html

IDA (International Development Association). 2007. "The Role of IDA in the Global Aid Architecture: Supporting the Country-Based Development Model." Resource Mobilization Department, IDA, Washington, DC.

IDA (International Development Association). 2020. Replenishments. IDA, World Bank Group. http://ida.worldbank.org/replenishments

IEG (Independent Evaluation Group). 2013. "Responding to Global Public Bads: Learning from Evaluation of the World Bank Experience with Avian Influenza 2006–13." IEG, World Bank Group, Washington, DC. https://ieg.worldbankgroup.org/sites/default/files/Data/reports/avian_flu1.pdf

IFAD (International Fund for Agricultural Development). 1976. "Agreement Establishing the International Fund for Agricultural Development." Adopted by the United Nations Conference on the Establishment of an International Fund for Agricultural Development, Rome, June 13. https://www.ifad.org/documents/10180/3162024b-49d9-4961-a5de-8e2bbfabef9d

IFAD (International Fund for Agricultural Development). 1978. "Policies and Criteria for IFAD Financing." Adopted by the Governing Council at its Second Session, Rome, December 14. https://www.ifad.org/documents/10180/f1a1c976-ceec-4672-b1b0-c19c4237e5b1

IFAD (International Fund for Agricultural Development). 2011. "Financing Requirements and Modalities for IFAD9." REPL. IX/2/R.5. 24, May, IFAD, Rome.

IFAD (International Fund for Agricultural Development). 2012. "Report on the Consultation on the Ninth Replenishment of IFAD's Resources." GC 35/L.4, January 25, IFAD, Rome. https://webapps.ifad.org/members/gc/35/docs/GC-35-L-4.pdf

IFAD (International Fund for Agricultural Development). 2014. "IFAD Replenishments." Corporate-level Evaluation, May, Report No. 3377, Independent Office of Evaluation, IFAD, Rome. https://www.ecgnet.org/sites/default/files/IFAD_replenishments_June2014.pdf

IFAD (International Fund for Agricultural Development). 2016. "Annual Report on Results and Impact of IFAD Operations Evaluated in 2015." ARRI 2016, Independent Office of Evaluation, IFAD, Rome. https://www.ifad.org/documents/38714182/39709860/ARRI_2016_full.pdf/569bcea7-a84a-4d38-867f-89b3bb98e0e4

IFC (International Finance Corporation). 2019. "Creating Impact: The Promise of Impact Investing." April, IFC, World Bank Group, Washington, DC. https://www.ifc.org/wps/wcm/connect/66e30dce-0cdd-4490-93e4-d5f895c5e3fc/The-Promise-of-Impact-Investing.pdf?MOD=AJPERES&CVID=mHZTSds

IFPRI (International Food Policy Research Institute). 2014. *Global Nutrition Report 2014: Actions and Accountability to Accelerate the World's Progress on Nutrition.* Washington, DC: IFPRI. https://globalnutritionreport.org/reports/2014-global-nutrition-report/

IFPRI (International Food Policy Research Institute). 2015. *Global Nutrition Report 2015: Actions and Accountability to Advance Nutrition and Sustainable Development.* Washington, DC: IFPRI. https://globalnutritionreport.org/reports/2015-global-nutrition-report/

IFPRI (International Food Policy Research Institute). 2016. *Global Nutrition Report 2016: From Promise to Impact: Ending Malnutrition by 2030.* Washington, DC: IFPRI. https://global nutritionreport.org/reports/2016-global-nutrition-report/

IMF (International Monetary Fund). 2020a. "COVID-19: An Unprecedented Threat to Development." Regional Economic Outlook: Sub-Saharan Africa, April, IMF, Washington, DC. https://www.imf.org/en/Publications/REO/SSA/Issues/2020/04/01/sreo0420

IMF (International Monetary Fund). 2020b. "A Crisis Like No Other, An Uncertain Recovery." World Economic Outlook Update, June, IMF, Washington, DC. https://www.imf.org/en/Publications/WEO/Issues/2020/06/24/WEOUpdateJune2020

IMF (International Monetary Fund). 2020c. "World Economic Outlook: The Great Lockdown." April, IMF, Washington, DC. https://www.imf.org/en/Publications/WEO/Issues/2020/04/14/World-Economic-Outlook-April-2020-The-Great-Lockdown-49306

IMF (International Monetary Fund). 2020d. "World Economic Outlook: A Long and Difficult Ascent." October, IMF, Washington, DC. https://www.imf.org/en/Publications/WEO/Issues/2020/09/30/world-economic-outlook-october-2020

IMF (International Monetary Fund), World Bank, and WTO (World Trade Organization). 2018. "Reinvigorating Trade and Inclusive Growth." https://www.wto.org/english/news_e/news18_e/igo_30sep18_e.pdf

Jaffee, Steven, Spencer Henson, Laurian Unnevehr, Delia Grace, and Emilie Cassou. 2019. *The Safe Food Imperative: Accelerating Progress in Low- and Middle-Income Countries.* Agriculture and Food Series. Washington, DC: World Bank Publications.

Jayne, Thomas S., Jordan Chamberlin, and Rui Benfica. 2018. "Africa's Unfolding Economic Transformation." *Journal of Development Studies* 54 (5): 777–87.

Jayne, Thomas S., Jordan Chamberlin, Lulama Traub, Nicholas Sitko, Milu Muyanga, Felix K. Yeboah, Ward Anseeuw, Antony Chapoto, Ayala Wineman, Chewe Nkonde, and Richard Kachule. 2016. "Africa's Changing Farm Size Distribution Patterns: The Rise of Medium-Scale Farms." *Agricultural Economics* 47 (S1): 197–214.

Jayne, Thomas S., Antony Chapoto, Nicholas Sitko, Chewe Nkonde, Milu Muyanga, and Jordan Chamberlin. 2014. "Is the Scramble for Land in Africa Foreclosing a Smallholder Agricultural Expansion Strategy?" *Journal of International Affairs* 67 (2): 35–53.

Jayne, Thomas, and Milu Muyanga. 2018. "Are Medium-Scale Farms Driving Agricultural Transformation in Africa?" Agrilinks blog, June 21, Feed the Future. https://www.agrilinks.org/post/are-medium-scale-farms-driving-agricultural-transformation-africa

Johnston, Bruce F., and John W. Mellor. 1961. "The Role of Agriculture in Economic Development." *American Economic Review* 51 (4): 566–93.

Jones, Sam, Eva-Maria Egger, and Ricardo Santos. 2020. "Is Mozambique Prepared for a Lockdown during the COVID-19 Pandemic?" UNU–WIDER Blog, April, United Nations University–World Institute for Development Economics Research, Helsinki. https://www.wider.unu.edu/publication/mozambique-prepared-lockdown-during-COVID-19-pandemic

Joseph, Andrew. 2020. "Rising COVID-19 Cases And Hospitalizations Underscore the Long Road Ahead." *Nature*, STAT, June 17. https://www.statnews.com/2020/06/17/rising-covid-19-cases-hospitalization-long-road

Kaldor, Nicholas. 1966. *Causes of the Slow Rate of Economic Growth of the United Kingdom: An Inaugural Lecture.* London: Cambridge University Press.

Kanbur, Ravi. 2005. "The Development of Development Thinking." Lecture delivered at the Institute for Social and Economic Change, Bangalore, June 10, 2004. https://pdfs.sem anticscholar.org/236e/f782775392e455d181e8936dd64d0687426a.pdf

Kharas, Homi, and Kristofer Hamel. 2020. "Turning Back the Poverty Clock: How Will COVID-19 Impact the World's Poorest People?" Future Development blog, May 6. Brookings Institution, Washington, DC. https://www.brookings.edu/blog/future-development/2020/05/06/turning-back-the-poverty-clock-how-will-covid-19-impact-the-worlds-poorest-people

Kshirsagar, V., and M. Gautam. 2013. "Agriculture Productivity Trends in India: A District Level Analysis." Background paper of the World Bank Report *Republic of India: Accelerating Agricultural Productivity Growth*, 2014.

Kuznets, Simon. 1955. "Economic Growth and Income Inequality." *American Economic Review* 45 (1): 1–28.

Kuznets, Simon. 1966. *Modern Economic Growth: A Rate, Structure, and Spread.* New Haven, CT: Yale University Press.

Laborde, David, Will Martin, and Rob Vos. 2020. "Impacts of COVID-19 on Global Poverty, Food Security and Diets." July 24, International Food Policy Research Institute, Washington, DC.

Lampietti, Julian, Ghada Elabed, and Kateryna Schroeder. 2020. "Beyond the Pandemic: Harnessing the Digital Revolution to Set Food Systems on a Better Course." News, August 6, World Bank, Washington, DC. https://www.worldbank.org/en/news/immersive-story/2020/08/06/beyond-the-pandemic-harnessing-the-digital-revolution-to-set-food-systems-on-a-better-course

Lele, Uma. 1975. *The Design of Rural Development: Lessons from Africa.* Baltimore, MD: Johns Hopkins University Press for the World Bank.

Lele, Uma, ed. 1992. A*id to African Agriculture: Lessons from Two Decades of Donors' Experience.* Baltimore: Johns Hopkins University Press for World Bank.

Lele, Uma. 2019. "Special Lecture in Honor of Dr. Samar Ranjan Sen." 79th Annual Conference of the Indian Society of Agricultural Economics, Indira Gandhi Krishi Vishwavidyalaya (IGKV), Raipur, November 22.

Lele, Uma. 2021, forthcoming. "Growing Water Scarcities: Responses of India and China." *Applied Economic Perspectives and Policy.* First published online: February 2, 2021. https://doi.org/10.1002/aepp.13146

Lele, Uma, Manmohan Agarwal, and Sambuddha Goswami. 2013. "Lessons of the Global Structural Transformation Experience for the East African Community." International Symposium and Exhibition on Agriculture, organized by Kilimo Trust, Kampala, Uganda, November.

Lele, Uma, Manmohan Agarwal, and Sambuddha Goswami. 2014. Presentation at the Conference on "Innovation in Indian Agriculture: Ways Forward." Institute of Economic Growth and International Food Policy Research Institute, New Delhi, December 4–5.

Lele, Uma, Manmohan Agarwal, and Sambuddha Goswami. 2018. *Patterns of Structural Transformation and Agricultural Productivity Growth (with Special Focus on Brazil, China, Indonesia and India)*. Pune, India: Gokhale Institute of Politics and Economics.

Lele, Uma, Sangeeta Bansal, and J. V. Meenakshi. 2020. "Health and Nutrition of India's Labour Force and COVID-19 Challenges." *Economic & Political Weekly* 55 (21), May 23.

Lele, Uma, and Balu Bumb. 1994. *South Asia's Food Crisis: The Case of India*. Washington, DC: Banco Mundial.

Lele, Uma, and Arthur A. Goldsmith. 1986. "Building Agricultural Research Capacity: India's Experience with the Rockefeller Foundation and Its Significance for Africa." Development Research Department discussion paper no. DRD 2013, World Bank, Washington, DC. https://documents.worldbank.org/en/publication/documents-reports/documentdetail/625031468267011221/building-agricultural-research-capacity-indias-experience-with-the-rockefeller-foundation-and-its-significance-for-africa

Lele, Uma, and Sambuddha Goswami. 2020. "Agricultural Policy Reforms: Roles of Markets and States in China and India." *Global Food Security* 26: 100371.

Lele, Uma, Sambuddha Goswami, and Gianluigi Nico. 2017. "Structural Transformation and the Transition from Concessional Assistance to Commercial Flows: The Past and Possible Future Contributions of the World Bank." In *Agriculture and Rural Development in a Globalizing World: Challenges and Opportunities*, edited by Prabhu Pingali and Gershon Feder, 325–52. London and New York: Routledge.

Lele, Uma, and John W. Mellor. 1981. "Technological Change, Distribution Bias and Labour Transfer in a Two Sector Economy." *Oxford Economic Papers* 33 (3): 426–41.

Lewis, W. Arthur. 1954. "Economic Development with Unlimited Supplies of Labour." *The Manchester School* 22 (2): 139–91.

Lowder, Sarah K. Marco V. Sánchez and Raffaele Bertini. 2019. "Farms, Family Farms, Farmland Distribution and Farm Labour: What Do We Know Today?" FAO Agricultural Development Economics Working Paper 19–08, FAO, Rome.

Lowder, Sarah K., Jacob Skoet, and Terri Raney. 2016. "The Number, Size, and Distribution of Farms, Smallholder Farms, and Family Farms Worldwide." *World Development* 87: 16–29.

Lowrey, Annie. 2012. "Transcript of 1944 Bretton Woods Conference Found at Treasury." *New York Times*, October 25. https://www.nytimes.com/2012/10/26/business/transcript-of-1944-bretton-woods-meeting-found-at-treasury.html

Lund, Susan, James Manyika, Jonathan Woetzel, Jacques Bughin, Mekala Krishnan, Jeongmin Seong, and Mac Muir. 2019. "Globalization in Transition: The Future of Trade and Value Chains." McKinsey Global Institute, McKinsey & Company Report, January. https://www.mckinsey.com/featured-insights/innovation-and-growth/globalization-in-transition-the-future-of-trade-and-value-chains

Mansuri, Ghazala, and Vijayendra Rao. 2004. "Community-Based and -Driven Development: A Critical Review." Working Paper #3209, February, World Bank, Washington, DC. http://documents1.worldbank.org/curated/zh/399341468761669595/pdf/wps3209community.pdf

Mansuri, Ghazala, and Vijayendra Rao. 2013. "Localizing Development: Does Participation Work?" Policy Research Report, World Bank, Washington, DC. http://documents.worldbank.org/curated/en/461701468150309553/pdf/NonAsciiFileName0.pdf

Martin, Will, and Devashish Mitra. 2001. "Productivity Growth and Convergence in Agriculture versus Manufacturing." *Economic Development and Cultural Change* 49 (20): 403–22.

McMaster, Morgan, Alejandra Guevara, Lacey Roberts, and Samantha Alvis. 2019. *USAID Higher Education: A Retrospective 1960–2020*. Washington, DC: United States Agency for International Development (USAID).

McNamara, Robert S. 1973. "The Nairobi Speech: Address to the Board of Governors," World Bank Group, Nairobi, September 24. http://www.juerg-buergi.ch/Archiv/ EntwicklungspolitikA/EntwicklungspolitikA/assets/McNamara_Nairobi_speech.pdf

MIGA (Multilateral Investment Guarantee Agency). 2015. "MIGA: Cultivating Agribusiness Growth." Agribusiness MIGABRIEF, July, World Bank Group, Washington, DC. https:// www.miga.org/sites/default/files/2018-06/agribusinessbrief.pdf

Montenegro, Claudio E., and Harry Anthony Patrinos. 2014. "Comparable Estimates of Returns to Schooling Around the World." Policy Research Working Paper 7020, World Bank, Washington, DC.

Nkonya, Ephraim, Alisher Mirzabaev, and Joachim von Braun, eds. 2016. *Economics of Land Degradation and Improvement: A Global Assessment for Sustainable Development*. Cham, Switzerland, Springer International Publishing. https://link.springer.com/book/10.1007/978-3-319-19168-3

Noel, Stacey, Friederike Mikulcak, Naomi Stewart, and Hannes Etter. 2015. "Report for Policy and Decision Makers: Reaping Economic and Environmental Benefits from Sustainable Land Management." September, Economics of Land Degradation (ELD) Initiative, Bonn. https:// www.eld-initiative.org/fileadmin/pdf/ELD-pm-report_05_web_300dpi.pdf

Obama, Barack. 2020. *A Promised Land*. New York: Random House.

OECD (Organisation for Economic Co-Operation and Development). 2009. "G20 Summit. Pittsburgh, United States, 2009." https://www.oecd.org/g20/summits/pittsburgh/

OECD (Organisation for Economic Co-operation and Development). 2018. *Global Outlook on Financing for Sustainable Development 2019: Time to Face the Challenge*. Paris: OECD Publishing. https://www.oecd-ilibrary.org/docserver/9789264307995-en.pdf

OECD (Organisation for Economic Co-operation and Development). 2019a. "Development Aid Drops in 2018, Especially to Neediest Countries. OECD Adopts New Methodology for Counting Loans in Official Aid Data." April 10, OECD, Paris. https://www.oecd.org/ dac/financing-sustainable-development/development-finance-data/ODA-2018-detailed-summary.pdf

OECD (Organisation for Economic-Co-operation and Development). 2019b. "The High Level Fora on Aid Effectiveness: A History." OECD/Development Co-operation Directorate (DCD–DAC)/Effective Development Co-operation. http://www.oecd.org/dac/effectiveness/ thehighlevelforaonaideffectivenessahistory.htm

OECD (Organisation for Economic Co-operation and Development). 2019c. Official Development Assistance (ODA). https://www.oecd.org/dac/financing-sustainable-development/development-finance-standards/official-development-assistance.htm

OECD (Organisation for Economic Co-operation and Development). 2020. *Agricultural Policy Monitoring and Evaluation 2020*. Paris: OECD Publishing. https://www.oecd.org/agriculture/ topics/agricultural-policy-monitoring-and-evaluation/

OECD (Organisation for Economic Co-operation and Development). 2021. "COVID-19 Spending Helped to Lift Foreign Aid to an All-Time High in 2020." Detailed Note, Paris, OECD, April 13. https://www.oecd.org/dac/financing-sustainable-development/development-finance-data/ODA-2020-detailed-summary.pdf

OECD.Stat. 2020. Organisation for Economic Co-operation and Development. Statistics. Total Flows by Donor (ODA + OOF + Private) [DAC1]. http://stats.oecd.org/viewhtml.aspx? datasetcode=TABLE1&lang=en

OPHI (Oxford Poverty & Human Development Initiative) and UNDP (United Nations Development Programme). 2020. "Charting Pathways Out of Multidimensional Poverty: Achieving the SDGs." Global Multidimensional Poverty Index 2020. http://hdr.undp.org/sites/default/files/2020_mpi_report_en.pdf

Page, John. 2015. "Made in Africa: Some New Thinking for Africa Industrialization Day." Africa in Focus blog, November 19, The Brookings Institution, Washington, DC. https://www.brookings.edu/blog/africa-in-focus/2015/11/19/made-in-africa-some-new-thinking-for-africa-industrialization-day/

PBS News Hour. 2020. "Obama Team Left Pandemic Playbook for Trump Administration, Officials Confirm." PBS, May 15. https://www.pbs.org/newshour/nation/obama-team-left-pandemic-playbook-for-trump-administration-officials-confirm

Pollock, Ian, and Anita Kendrick. 2015. "15 Years of Indonesia's National Community-Driven Development Programs: The Kecamatan Development Program (KDP); The National Program for Community Empowerment (PNPM)." The World Bank, PNPM Support Facility, Jakarta, Indonesia. http://documents1.worldbank.org/curated/en/988141467998234335/pdf/101951-WP-PUBLIC-Box394819B.pdf

Popkin, Barry M., and Thomas Reardon. 2018. "Obesity and the Food System Transformation in Latin America." Obesity Reviews 19 (8): 1028–64. https://doi.org/10.1111/obr.12694

Rada, Nicholas E., and Keith O. Fuglie. 2019. "New Perspectives on Farm Size and Productivity." Food Policy 84: 147–52.

Ratha, Dilip, Supriyo De, Eung Ju Kim, Sonia Plaza, Ganesh Seshan, and Nadege Desiree Yameogo. 2019. "Data Release: Remittances to Low- and Middle-Income Countries on Track to Reach $551 Billion in 2019 and $597 Billion by 2021." World Bank blog, October 16. https://blogs.worldbank.org/peoplemove/data-release-remittances-low-and-middle-income-countries-track-reach-551-billion-2019

Ravallion, Martin. 2020. "Could Pandemic Lead to Famine?" Project Syndicate, April 15. https://www.project-syndicate.org/commentary/covid19-lockdowns-threaten-famine-in-poor-countries-by-martin-ravallion-2020-04

Reardon, Thomas. 2015. "The Hidden Middle: The Quiet Revolution in the Midstream of Agrifood Value Chains in Developing Countries." Oxford Review of Economic Policy 31 (1): 45–63.

Reardon, Thomas, C. Peter Timmer, Christopher B. Barrett, and Julio Berdegué. 2003. "The Rise of Supermarkets in Africa, Asia, and Latin America." American Journal of Agricultural Economics 85 (5): 1140–6.

Reardon, Thomas, C. Peter Timmer, and Bart Minten. 2012. "Supermarket Revolution in Asia and Emerging Development Strategies to Include Small Farmers." PNAS 109 (31): 12332–7.

Rodrik, Dani. 2016. "Premature Deindustrialization." Journal of Economic Growth 21 (1): 1–33.

Sánchez-Páramo, Carolina. 2020. "Countdown to 2030: A Race against Time to End Extreme Poverty." Voices: Perspectives on Development, World Bank blog, January 7. https://blogs.worldbank.org/voices/countdown-2030-race-against-time-end-extreme-poverty

Save the Children. 2018. "Yemen: 85,000 Children May Have Died from Starvation Since Start of War." News Release, November 20, Fairfield CT. https://www.savethechildren.org/us/about-us/media-and-news/2018-press-releases/yemen-85000-children-may-have-died-from-starvation

Sayeh, Antoinette, and Ralph Chami. 2020. "Lifelines in Danger." *Finance and Development* (IMF) 57 (2): 16–19. https://www.imf.org/external/pubs/ft/fandd/2020/06/pdf/COVID19-pandemic-impact-on-remittance-flows-sayeh.pdf

Schmidhuber, Josef, Jonathan Pound, and Bing Qiao. 2020. "COVID-19: Channels of Transmission to Food and Agriculture." Trade and Market Division Economic and Social Development Department, FAO, Rome. https://doi.org/10.4060/ca8430en

Schmidhuber, Josef, and Bing Qiao. 2020. "Comparing Crises: 'Great Lockdown' vs 'Great Recession.'" Trade and Market Division Economic and Social Development Department, FAO, Rome. https://doi.org/10.4060/ca8833en

Searchinger, Tim, Richard Waite, Craig Hanson, Janet Ranganthan, Patrice Dumas, and Emily Matthews. 2018. "Creating a Sustainable Food Future: A Menu of Solutions to Feed Nearly 10 Billion People by 2050." World Resources Report, Synthesis Report, December. World Resources Institute, Washington, DC. https://files.wri.org/s3fs-public/creating-sustainable-food-future_2.pdf

Sen, Amartya. 1981. *Poverty and Famines: An Essay on Entitlement and Deprivation.* Oxford: Clarendon Press.

Singh, Harbir, and Ramesh Chand. 2010. "The Seeds Bill, 2010—A Critical Appraisal." Policy Brief 33, Indian Council of Agricultural Research (ICAR), National Centre for Agricultural Economics and Policy Research, New Delhi. http://www.niap.res.in/upload_files/policy_brief/pb33.pdf

Sitko, Nicholas J., William J. Burke, T. S. Jayne. 2018. "The Quiet Rise of Large-Scale Trading Firms in East and Southern Africa." *Journal of Development Studies* 54 (4): 895–914.

Sumner, Andy, Chris Hoy, and Eduardo Ortiz-Juarez. 2020. "Estimates of the Impact of COVID-19 on Global Poverty." WIDER Working Paper 2020/43, United Nations University–World Institute for Development Economics Research (UNU–WIDER), Helsinki. https://www.wider.unu.edu/sites/default/files/Publications/Working-paper/PDF/wp2020-43.pdf

Tan, Jee-Peng, Emmanuel Jimenez, and George Psacharopoulos, George. 1986. *Financing Education in Developing Countries: An Exploration of Policy Options.* Washington, DC: World Bank Group. http://documents.worldbank.org/curated/en/409491468763761554/Financing-education-in-developing-countries-an-exploration-of-policy-options

Taylor, Adam. 2020. "Beijing's New Coronavirus Outbreak Carries an Urgent Message for the World." *Washington Post*, June 17. https://www.washingtonpost.com/world/2020/06/18/beijing-coronavirus-outbreak-meaning/

Timmer, C. Peter. 2009. *A World without Agriculture: The Structural Transformation in Historical Perspective.* Washington, DC: American Enterprise Institute Press.

Tomer, Adie, and Joseph W. Kane. 2020. "How to Protect Essential Workers during COVID-19." Report, March 31, Brookings Institution, Washington, DC. https://www.brookings.edu/research/how-to-protect-essential-workers-during-covid-19/

Torero, Maximo. 2020. "Prepare Food Systems for a Long-Haul Fight against COVID-19." July 2, IFPRI Blog, International Food Policy Research Institute, Washington, DC. https://www.ifpri.org/blog/prepare-food-systems-long-haul-fight-against-covid-19

UN (United Nations). 1975. "Report of the World Food Conference." Rome, November 5–16 1974. UN, New York. https://digitallibrary.un.org/record/701143?ln=en

UN (United Nations). 2016. We Can End Poverty. Millennium Development Goals and Beyond 2015. http://www.un.org/millenniumgoals/

UN (United Nations). 2020a. "Global Issues: Food." https://www.un.org/en/sections/issues-depth/food/index.html

UN (United Nations). 2020b. "History of the United Nations." About the UN. https://www.un.org/en/sections/history/history-united-nations/index.html

UN (United Nations). 2020c. The 17 Goals: Sustainable Development. Department of Economic and Social Affairs. https://sdgs.un.org/goals

UN (United Nations). 2020d. "UN Food Systems Summit 2021." Press Release, UN, New York.

UN (United Nations). 2020e. United Nations Food Systems Summit 2020. https://www.un.org/sustainabledevelopment/food-systems-summit-2021/

UN DESA (United Nations Department of Economic and Social Affairs). 2016. *The Millennium Development Goals Report 2015.* New York: United Nations. https://www.un.org/millenniumgoals/2015_MDG_Report/pdf/MDG%202015%20rev%20(July%201).pdf

UN News. 2019. "With 10 Million Yemenis "One Step Away from Famine," Donors Pledge US $2.6 Million." February 26, Humanitarian Aid, UN, New York. https://news.un.org/en/story/2019/02/1033582

UN Statistics Division. 2020. "SDG Goals. 1-No Poverty: End Poverty in All Its Forms Everywhere." Report, Department of Economic and Social Affairs, United Nations, New York. https://unstats.un.org/sdgs/report/2019/goal-01/

UNCTAD (United Nations Conference on Trade and Development). 2019. *World Investment Report 2019. Special Economic Zones.* New York and Geneva: UN. https://unctad.org/en/PublicationsLibrary/wir2019_en.pdf

UNCTAD (United Nations Conference on Trade and Development). 2020. "Investment Trends Monitor." Issue 33, January. United Nations. https://unctad.org/en/PublicationsLibrary/diaeiainf2020d1_en.pdf

UNCTAD (United Nations Conference on Trade and Development). 2021. "Investment Trends Monitor." Issue 38, January. United Nations. https://unctad.org/webflyer/global-investment-trend-monitor-no-38

UNICEF (United Nations Children's Fund). 2019. "1 in 7 Babies Worldwide Born with a Low Birthweight—The Lancet Global Health, UNICEF, WHO." Press Release, May 15, New York/London/Geneva, UNICEF. https://www.unicef.org/press-releases/1-7-babies-worldwide-born-low-birthweight-lancet-global-health-unicef-who

UNICEF (United Nations Children's Fund). 2020a. "Malnutrition." March 2020. Data by Topic and Country. https://data.unicef.org/topic/nutrition/malnutrition/

UNICEF (United Nations Children's Fund). 2020b. "Under-five Mortality." Data by Topic and Country. https://data.unicef.org/topic/child-survival/under-five-mortality/

Unnevehr, Laurian, and Loraine Ronchi. 2014. "Food Safety Standards: Economic and Market Impacts in Developing Countries." Viewpoint—Public Policy for the Private Sector, July. Trade and Competitiveness Global Practice, World Bank Group. http://documents1.worldbank.org/curated/en/681851471859603213/pdf/107910-VIEWPOINT-PUBLIC-TAG-TOPIC-investment-climate.pdf

USAID (United States Agency for International Development). 2013. "USAID's Legacy in Agricultural Development: 50 Years of Progress." November, USAID, Washington, DC. http://www.aiard.org/uploads/1/6/9/4/16941550/usaid_legacy_ag_development_report_nov2013.pdf

Wang, Huan, Markus Zhang, Robin Li, Oliver Zhong, Hannah Johnstone, Huan Zhou, Hao Xue, Sean Sylvia, Matthew Boswell, Prashant Loyalka, and Scott Rozelle. 2020. "Tracking the

Impact of COVID-19 in Rural China Over Time." Rural Education Action Program Working Paper, Stanford University, Palo Alto, CA.

WBG (World Bank Group). 2009. "About the World Bank Institute." https://web.worldbank.org/archive/website01006/WEB/0__CON-2.HTM

WCED (World Commission on Environment and Development). 1987. *Our Common Future.* Brundtland Commission. Oxford and New York: Oxford University Press.

WFP (World Food Programme). 2017. "World Food Assistance 2017: Taking Stock and Looking Ahead." July 18, WFP, Rome. https://www.wfp.org/publications/2017-world-food-assistance-taking-stock-and-looking-ahead

WFP (World Food Programme). 2018. "WFP Capacity Strengthening Supports Nations to End Hunger." Beyond the Annual Performance Report 2018 Series, November, WFP, Rome. https://docs.wfp.org/api/documents/WFP-0000110346/download/

WFP (World Food Programme). 2019a. "World Food Programme: Humanitarian Development." https://docs.wfp.org/api/documents/WFP-0000110373/download/

WFP (World Food Programme). 2019b. "The World Food Programme: Saving Lives, Changing Lives." World Food Programme Insight, November 11, WFP, Rome. https://insight.wfp.org/overview-1211270a8b06

WFP (World Food Programme). 2020a. "Country Capacity Strengthening." https://www.wfp.org/country-capacity-strengthening

WFP (World Food Programme). 2020b. "COVID-19 Will Double Number of People Facing Food Crises Unless Swift Action Is Taken." News Release, Rome, April 21. https://www.wfp.org/news/covid-19-will-double-number-people-facing-food-crises-unless-swift-action-taken

WFP (World Food Programme). 2020c. "Food Assistance: Cash and In-Kind." https://www.wfp.org/food-assistance

WFP (World Food Programme). 2020d. "In-Kind Food Distribution." https://www.wfp.org/in-kind-food-distribution

WFP (World Food Programme). 2020e. "School Feeding." https://www.wfp.org/school-meals

WFP (World Food Programme). 2020f. "South–South Cooperation." https://www.wfp.org/south-south-cooperation

WFP (World Food Programme). 2020g. "UN Humanitarian Air Service." https://www.wfp.org/unhas

WFP (World Food Programme). 2020h. "WFP At a Glance." World Food Programme Insight, February 7. https://insight.wfp.org/wfp-at-a-glance-75c0a78be56c

WHO (World Health Organization). 2020a. "Healthy Diet." April 20 Fact sheet, https://www.who.int/news-room/fact-sheets/detail/healthy-diet

WHO (World Health Organization). 2020b. "Micronutrient Deficiencies." Nutrition. https://www.who.int/nutrition/topics/ida/en/

WHO (World Health Organization). 2020c. Obesity and Overweight. Fact Sheet, April 1, 2020. http://www.who.int/mediacentre/factsheets/fs311/en/

WHO (World Health Organization). 2020d. "Past Pandemics." Health Topics. https://www.euro.who.int/en/health-topics/communicable-diseases/influenza/pandemic-influenza/past-pandemics

Willett, Walter, Johan Rockström, Brent Loken, Marco Springmann, Tim Lang, Sonja Vermeulen, Tara Garnett, David Tilman, Fabrice DeClerck, Amanda Wood, et al.; The *Lancet* Commission. 2019. "Food in the Anthropocene: The EAT-*Lancet* Commission on Healthy

Diets from Sustainable Systems." *Lancet* 393 (10170): 447–92. https://www.thelancet.com/pdfs/journals/lancet/PIIS0140-6736(18)31788-4.pdf

World Bank. 1992. *Effective Implementation: Key to Development Impact* (Wapenhans Report). Washington, DC: World Bank. http://documents.worldbank.org/curated/en/596521467145356248/pdf/multi0page.pdf

World Bank. 2003. "Reaching the Rural Poor: A Renewed Strategy for Rural Development." World Bank, Washington, DC. https://openknowledge.worldbank.org/bitstream/handle/10986/14084/267630REACHING0THE0RURAL0POOR0.pdf

World Bank. 2007. *World Development Report 2008: Agriculture for Development.* Washington, DC: World Bank. https://openknowledge.worldbank.org/handle/10986/5990

World Bank. 2012. "Resilience, Equity, and Opportunity: The World Bank's Social Protection and Labor Strategy 2012–2022." World Bank, Washington, DC. http://documents1.worldbank.org/curated/en/443791468157506768/pdf/732350BR0CODE200doc0version0REVISED.pdf

World Bank. 2014. *Republic of India: Accelerating Agricultural Productivity Growth.* Washington, DC: World Bank Group. http://documents.worldbank.org/curated/en/587471468035437545/pdf/880930REVISED00ivity0Growth00PUBLIC.pdf

World Bank. 2018. *Poverty and Shared Prosperity 2018: Piecing Together the Poverty Puzzle.* Washington, DC: World Bank. https://openknowledge.worldbank.org/bitstream/handle/10986/30418/9781464813306.pdf

World Bank. 2020a. "The World Bank in Vietnam." Overview. https://www.worldbank.org/en/country/vietnam/overview

World Bank. 2020b. World Development Indicators (database). http://data.worldbank.org/data-catalog/world-development-indicators

Yeboah, Thomas, Easther Chigumira, Innocensia John, Nana Akua Anyidoho, Victor Manyong, Justin Flynn, and James Sunberg. 2020. "Hard Work and Hazard: Young People and Agricultural Commercialisation in Africa." *Journal of Rural Studies* 76: 142–51.

Youker, Robert. 2003. "A Brief History of World Bank Institute (WBI) or Economic Development Institute (EDI)." Working Paper, World Bank, Washington, DC. http://documents1.worldbank.org/curated/en/372291468129005130/pdf/936580WP0EDI0h0Box385399B00PUBLIC00.pdf

Index